PHILIP'S
EASYREAD
Europe

▲Warsaw Old Town *hp_photo / iStockphoto.com*

Legend to route planning maps pages 2–23

●——	Motorway with selected junctions
▪▫▫▫▫▫ ▪ ▪ ▪ ▪	tunnel, under construction
———	Toll motorway
———	Pre-pay motorway
———	Main through route
———	Other major road
———	Other road
25	European road number
56	Motorway number
55	National road number
⚬ 56 ⚬	Distances – in kilometres
———	International boundary
– – – –	National boundary
— — 🚢 —	Car ferry and destination *LE HAVRE*
⤬	Mountain pass
✈	International airport
1089 ▲	Height in metres
	National park

Town – population

MOSKVA ▣	5 million +	Gävle ⊙	50000–100000
BERLIN ◎	2–5 million	Nybro ○	20000–50000
MINSK ▢	1–2 million	Ikast ○	10000–20000
Oslo ◉	500000–1million	Skjern ○	5000–10000
Århus ⊙	200000-500000	Lillesand ○	0–5000
Turku ◎	100000-200000		

Legend to road maps pages 26–200

⑦——⑧	**Motorway with junctions** – full, restricted access
◇	services
⊢▪▪▪▪▪—	tunnel
▪▪▪▪▪▪▪	under construction
———	**Toll Motorway**
——— Ⓐ ⒸⒽ ⒸⱫ Ⓗ ⓈⓀ	**Pre-pay motorway** – 'Vignette' must be purchased before travel, see pages V–VIII
———	**Principal trunk highway** – single / dual carriageway
⊢▪▪▪▪▪▪—⊣	tunnel
▪▪▪▪▪▪▪▪▪	under construction
———	**Other main highway** – single / dual carriageway
———	**Other important road**
———	**Other road**
E25	European road number
A49	Motorway number
135	National road number
▼ Col Bayard 1248 ▲	Mountain pass
◀	Scenic route, gradient – arrow points uphill
⚬ 143 ⚬	**Distances** – in kilometres, major
⚬ 28 ⚬	minor
———	**Principal railway**
⟩▪▪▪▪⟨	tunnel
Nápoli 15:30	**Ferry route with journey time** – hours : minutes
▪▪▪▪▪▪▪	**Short ferry route**
–▪–▪–▪–	International boundary
– – – –	National boundary
	National park
	Natural park
HEATHROW ✈	Airport
KNOSSOS 🏛	Ancient monument
⤨	Beach
SCHLOSS LAHNECK 🏰	Castle or house
GROTTE DE HAN-SUR-LESSE ⌂	Cave
PARQUE JURASSICO ✦	Other place of interest
GIVERNY ✿	Park or garden
SANTA CRUZ ✝	Religious building
⛷	Ski resort
DISNEYLAND PARIS 🎡	Theme park
POMPEI ◈	World Heritage site
1754 ▲	Spot height
Sevilla	World Heritage town
Verona	Town of tourist interest

Scale

Pages 2–23

1:3200000 1cm = 32km 1 in = 50.51 miles

0	20	40	60	80 miles

| 0 | 20 | 40 | 60 | 80 | 100 | 120 | 140 km |

Pages 26–181

1:753800 1cm = 7.5km 1 inch = 12 miles

| 0 | 5 | 10 | 15 | 20 miles |

| 0 | 5 | 10 | 15 | 20 | 25 | 30 | 35 km |

Pages 182–200

1:1507600 • 1cm = 15km, 1 inch = 24 miles

| 0 | 10 | 20 | 30 | 40 miles |

| 0 | 10 | 20 | 30 | 40 | 50 | 60 | 70 km |

Contents

II Travel information

II	European driving – cut through the confusion
V	Driving regulations
VIII	Ski resorts
XI	Sights of Europe
XXV	European politics and economics

1 Route planning maps

1	Key map

24 Road maps

24	Key map · Distance table

201 City plans

201	Legends to city plans and approach maps

Alicante C	201	**London** UC	212/213
Amsterdam C	202	**Luxembourg** C	211
Antwerp Antwerpen C	201	**Lyon** CU	213
Athens Athina CU	202	**Madrid** CU	214
Barcelona CU	203	**Marseilles** Marseille C	214
Berlin CU	204	**Milan** Milano CU	215
Bordeaux CU	205	**Munich** München CU	216
Brussels Bruxelles C	203	**Naples** Nápoli CU	216
Budapest C	205	**Oslo** CU	217
Cologne Köln C	211	**Paris** UC	218/219
Copenhagen København CU	210	**Prague** Praha CU	219
Dublin C	205	**Rome** Roma CU	220
Düsseldorf UC	206/207	**Seville** Sevilla C	222
Edinburgh C	207	**Stockholm** CU	221
Florence Firenze C	207	**Strasbourg** CU	222
Frankfurt C	207	**Stuttgart** C	222
Geneva Genève C	208	**Turin** Torino CU	223
Gothenburg Göteborg C	208	**Vienna** Wien CU	224
Hamburg CU	208	**Warsaw** Warszawa C	223
Helsinki CU	209	**Zürich** C	224
Istanbul U	210	C = City street plan	
Lisbon Lisboa CU	211	U = Urban area map	

225 Index to road maps

www.philips-maps.co.uk

First published in 2007 by
Philip's, a division of Octopus Publishing Group Ltd
www.octopusbooks.co.uk
2–4 Heron Quays, London E14 4JP
An Hachette Livre UK Company
www.hachettelivre.co.uk

Second edition 2008
First impression 2008

Ordnance Survey® This product includes mapping data licensed from Ordnance Survey®, with the permission of the Controller of Her Majesty's Stationery Office © Crown copyright 2008. All rights reserved. Licence number 100011710.

This product includes mapping data licensed from Ordnance Survey of Northern Ireland® reproduced by permission of the Chief Executive, acting on behalf of the Controller of Her Majesty's Stationery Office. © Crown Copyright 2008 Permit No 80104

The mapping on page 212 and the town plans of Edinburgh and London are based on mapping data licenced from Ordnance Survey with the permission of the Controller of Her Majesty's Stationery Office, © Crown Copyright 2008. All rights reserved. Licence number 100011710.

The maps of Ireland on pages 26 to 30 and the town plan of Dublin are based on Ordnance Survey Ireland by permission of the Government Permit Number 8408 © Ordnance Survey Ireland and Government of Ireland, and Ordnance Survey Northern Ireland on behalf of the Controller of Her Majesty's Stationery Office © Crown Copyright 2008 Permit Number 80104

Cartography by Philip's
Copyright © Philip's 2008

Photographic acknowledgements
page II, left *Bjorn Barton-Pye /iStockphoto.com;*
right *sarent /iStockphoto.com*
page III, left *Edward Shaw / iStockphoto.com;*
right *Mario Hornik / iStockphoto.com*

page IV left *Ralph Loesche /iStockphoto.com*
right *Michael Jay / iStockphoto.com;*
below right *pixonaut / iStockphoto.com*

Printed in China

European driving – cut through the confusion

Around eight million of us drive abroad while on holiday each year, yet according to recent research we don't appear very good at preparing for journeys, planning routes or ensuring we carry the right documents and equipment.

It's not easy getting to grips with the finer points of driving in other countries, however experienced you may be as a motorist. Whether you have notched up thousands of miles of European driving or are preparing to make your first journey, the chances are you will always manage to find some road sign or legal requirement that will cause confusion.

What's more, 'driving in Europe' covers such a huge area. There are twenty-seven countries in the European Union alone, each with its own line-up of road traffic laws and motoring customs. Driving in Europe can mean a spectacular and sunny coastal road that's within sight of Africa, or a snowy track and biting cold north of the Arctic Circle, where the only others on the road are reindeer. Add to this some of the world's most congested cities, dense clusters of motorways (many with confusing numbers!) and an alarming variation in safety standards and attitudes to risk. No wonder we so often get lost, take wrong turnings or perhaps stop where we shouldn't!

Forewarned is forearmed, and it certainly pays to do a bit of research before you go, just to ensure you and your vehicle are up to the journey, your documents are in order and you're carrying the correct levels of equipment to keep the law enforcers happy.

Are you confused about European driving laws?

Do you need advice about equipment requirements and which documents to take?

Are you new to driving on the right hand side?

How will you know what speed limits apply?

Who do you call if you have an accident or break down?

Stay safe with GEM Motoring Assist

Frequently asked questions

Do I need to use dipped headlights all the time? It is currently mandatory to use dipped headlights for daytime journeys in fourteen of the twenty-seven EU countries.

If I hire a car in one country, am I allowed to take it into another country? The issue is most likely to be with insurance, so check with the hiring company before setting off. Ask to see something in writing so you are sure that you are getting the right information. Often, when hiring, you will find you have only the minimum cover required for driving in the country where you hired the car. If you plan to take it into other countries, then make sure your insurance will cover you and purchase a top-up policy if necessary.

Do German motorways still not have speed limits? In fact, speed limits apply to around 30% of German motorways. A further 10% of motorway in Germany is subject to variable speed limits, determined by motorway control rooms. Across other stretches there is a recommended speed limit of 130km/h. It is worth remembering that whereas exceeding this limit is not an offence, the penalties for a high-speed driver being involved in an accident are much higher.

Why do European motorways all seem to have two numbers on the map and the road signs? This is because the roads form the international network of 'E-roads'. In most countries maps and signs will have the European road number (shown in white on a green background) alongside the appropriate national road number. However, in Sweden and Belgium only the E-road number will be shown.

Before you go

Some sensible planning will help make sure your European journey is enjoyable and – we hope – stress-free. So take some time before departure to ensure everything is in good shape: and that includes you, your travelling companions and your vehicle.

For starters, try to become familiar with the driving laws of your holiday destination, including the local speed limits and which side of the road to drive on! You will be subject to these laws when driving abroad and if you are stopped by the police it is not an excuse to say that you were unaware of them. The Foreign and Commonwealth Office (**www.fco.gov.uk/travel**) gives country-specific travel advice and information on driving.

For the vehicle

Service
It makes sense to get your car serviced before you travel. As a minimum, ensure the tyres have plenty of tread left and that water and oil levels are checked and topped up if required. Check them regularly during your time away.

Vehicle Registration Document
Police in many countries can demand that you prove you have the right to be driving your car. That means you need to show the registration document, or a suitable letter of authorisation if the registration document is not in your name. Remember you should never leave the registration document in the car.

Nationality plate
Your vehicle must display a nationality plate of an approved pattern, design and size.

MOT
If your car is more than three years old, make sure you take its current MOT test certificate with you.

Insurance
If you are planning a trip to Europe, you should find that your car insurance policy provides you with the minimum amount of cover you need. But it's important to contact your insurer before you go, to confirm exactly what level of cover you have and for how many days it will be valid.

Mechanical adjustments
Check the adjustments required for your headlights before you go. Beam deflectors are a legal requirement if you drive in Europe. They are generally sold at the ports, on ferries and in the Folkestone Eurotunnel terminal, but be warned – the instructions can be a little confusing! The alternative is to ask a local garage to do the job for you before you go. If you choose this, then make sure you shop around as prices for undertaking this very simple task vary enormously.

For you and your fellow travellers

Passports
Check everyone's passport to make sure they are all valid. Don't wait for your passport to expire. Unused time, rounded up to whole months (minimum one month, maximum nine months), will usually be added to your new passport.

New passports usually take two weeks to arrive. The Passport Office (0871 521 0410, **www.ips.gov.uk**) offers a faster service if you need a replacement passport urgently, but you'll have to pay a lot more.

Driving Licence
The new style photocard driving licence is valid in all European Union countries. However, you must ensure you carry both parts: the credit card-size photocard and the paper licence. The previously used pink EU format UK licence is also valid, though it may not be recognised in some areas. So if you haven't already done so, now is the time to update your old licence. For more information, contact the DVLA (0870 240 0009, **www.dvla.gov.uk**).

Travel Insurance
Travel insurance is vital as it covers you against medical emergencies, accidents, thefts and cancellations, and repatriation. Ask for details before buying any travel insurance policy. Find out what it covers you for, and to what value. More important, check what's not covered. One of the key benefits of GEM membership is the excellent discount you can get on travel insurance. For more details, please visit our website: **www.motoringassist.com/philipsmaps**.

European Breakdown Cover
Don't risk letting a breakdown ruin your European trip. Ensure you purchase a policy that will cover you for roadside assistance, emergency repair and recovery of your vehicle to the UK, wherever in Europe you may be heading. Once again, GEM members enjoy a specially discounted rate. You'll find the details at **www.motoringassist.com/philipsmaps**

EHIC
The E111 medical treatment form is no longer valid. Instead, you need an EHIC card for everyone travelling. These are free and cover you for any medical treatment you may need during a trip to another EU country or Switzerland. However, do check at the time of requiring assistance that your EHIC will be accepted. Apply online (**www.dh.gov.uk**), by telephone (0845 606 2030) or complete an application form, available from a Post Office. Allow up to fourteen days for the cards to arrive.

Equipment checklist
This checklist represents GEM's suggestions for what you should take with you in the car. Different countries have different rules about what's compulsory and these rules change from time to time. So it's important to check carefully before you set out. For country-by-country guidance see pages V–VIII of this atlas.
- Fire extinguisher
- First aid kit
- High-visibility jacket – one for each occupant
- Two warning triangles
- Replacement bulbs and fuses
- Spare spectacles (if worn) for each driver
- Snow chains for winter journeys into the mountains
- Disposable camera and notebook. Keep in your glove compartment and record any collisions or damage for insurance purposes (if it is safe).

Contact details
Make sure you have all relevant emergency helpline numbers with you, including emergency services, breakdown assistance, the local British consulate and your insurance company. There are links to embassies and consulates around the world from the Foreign Office website (**www.fco.gov.uk**). For information, the European emergency telephone number (our equivalent of 999) is 112 (see below).

Collisions abroad occur not just because of poor driving conditions locally, but also because we do not always take the same safety precautions as we might expect to take at home, for example by not wearing a seatbelt or by drinking and driving.

1 Plan your route before you go. That includes the journey you make to reach your destination (with sufficient breaks built in) and any excursions or local journeys you make while you're there.

2 Remember that, wherever you drive, you will be subject to the same laws as local drivers. Claiming ignorance of these laws will not be accepted as an excuse.

3 Take extra care at junctions when you re driving on the right hand side of the road. If driving in a family group, involve every member in a quick 'junction safety check' to help reduce the risk of a collision. Having everybody in the car call out a catchphrase such as "DriLL DriLL DriLL" (Driver Look Left) on the approach to junctions and roundabouts is a small but potentially life-saving habit.

4 Take fatigue seriously. The excellent European motorway network means you can cover big distances with ease. But you must also make time for proper breaks (experts recommend a break of at least fifteen minutes after every two hours of driving). If possible, share the driving and set strict daily limits to the number of driving hours.

5 Be aware that drink-driving limits across Europe are almost universally lower than those in the UK, in some cases zero. Bear this in mind if you're flying to a holiday or business destination and plan to have a drink on the plane, as the combination of unfamiliar roads and alcohol in your bloodstream is not a safe one. It's also worth remembering that drivers who cause collisions because they were drinking are likely to find their insurance policy will not cover them.

6 Expect the unexpected. Styles of driving in your destination country are likely to be very different from those you know in the UK. Drive defensively and certainly don't get involved in any altercations on the road.

7 Don't overload your car while away, however tempting the local bargains may appear. Also, make sure you have good all-round visibility by ensuring you don't pile up items on the parcel shelf or boot, and keep your windscreen clear of dirt and dust.

8 Always wear a seatbelt and ensure everyone else on board wears one. Check specific regulations regarding the carriage of children: in some countries children under the age of twelve are not permitted to travel in the front of the car.

9 Don't use your mobile phone while driving. Even though laws on phone use while driving differ from country to country, the practice is just as dangerous wherever you are.

10 When you're exploring on foot, be wise to road safety as a pedestrian. You may get into trouble for 'jay-walking', so don't just wander across a road. Use a proper crossing, but remember that drivers may not stop for you! And don't forget that traffic closest to you approaches from the LEFT.

Dial 112 for emergency services in Austria, Belgium, Croatia, Cyprus, Czech Republic, Denmark, Estonia, Finland, France, Germany, Greece, Hungary, Iceland, Ireland, Italy, Latvia, Liechtenstein, Lithuania, Luxembourg, Republic of Macedonia, Malta, Netherlands, Norway, Poland, Portugal, Romania, Russia, Serbia, Slovak Republic, Slovenia, Spain, Sweden, Switzerland, Ukraine and the United Kingdom

	Ambulance	Fire	Police
Albania	17	18	19
Andorra	118	118	110
Belarus	03	01	02
Bosnia Herzegovina	94	93/94	92
Bulgaria	150	160	166
Channel Islands	999	999	999
Gibraltar	999	999	999
Italy (Carabinieri 112)	118	115	113
Moldova	903	902	902
Montenegro	94	93	92
Turkey	112	110	155

Motorway vignettes

Some countries require you to purchase (and in some cases display) a vignette before using motorways.

In Austria you will need to purchase and display a vignette on the inside of your windscreen. Vignettes are available for purchase at border crossings and petrol stations. More details from **www.austria.info**.

In the Czech Republic you can buy a vignette at the border and at petrol stations. Be sure to write your vehicle registration number on the vignette before displaying it. Roads without toll are indicated by a traffic sign saying "Bez poplatku". More details from **www.ceskedalnice.cz**.

In Hungary a new e-vignette system was introduced at the beginning of 2008. It is therefore no longer necessary to display the vignette, though you should make doubly sure the information you give on your vehicle is accurate. Vignettes are sold at petrol stations throughout the country. Buy online at **www.autopalyamatrica.hu**.

In Slovakia a vignette is also required before using the motorways. This is sold in two kinds at the Slovak border and petrol stations. You will need to write your vehicle registration plate on the vignette before displaying it. More details from **www.slovensko.com**.

In Switzerland you will need to purchase and display a 'vignette' before you drive on the motorway. Bear in mind you will need a separate vignette if you are towing a caravan. Purchase the Swiss vignette in advance from **www.stc.co.uk**.

Stop and give way

Who has priority?

Make sure you keep a watchful eye on signs telling you who has priority on the road. Look for a yellow diamond sign, which tells you that traffic already on the road has priority. If you see the yellow diamond sign crossed out, then you must give way to traffic joining the road.

Priorité a droite

Despite the use of the yellow diamond signs, be aware that on some French roads (especially roundabouts in Paris), the traditional 'priorité a droite' practice is followed, even though it may no longer be legal. In theory these days, the rule no longer applies unless it is clearly signed. In practice, though, it makes sense to anticipate a driver pulling out in front of you, even though the priority may be yours.

Stop means stop!

If you come to a solid white line with an octagonal 'STOP' sign, then you must come to a complete stop. In other words your wheels must stop turning. Adherence to the 'STOP' sign is generally much more rigorously enforced in European countries than you may be used to here.

Headlight flash

Bear in mind that the practice of flashing headlights at a junction in France does not mean the same thing as it might in the UK. If another motorist flashes his headlights at you, he's telling you that he has priority and will be coming through in front of you.

Low Emission Zones

More than seventy cities and towns in eight countries across Europe have, or are preparing, 'Low Emission Zones' (LEZs), or 'Environment Zones', to help meet health-based air quality standards (Austria has an LEZ along the A12 motorway between Innsbruck and Kufstein). These include cities such as Amsterdam, Berlin, London and Stockholm. LEZs are areas where the most polluting vehicles are regulated. This means that vehicles may be banned, or in some cases charged if they enter the LEZ when their emissions are over a set level.

Before entering an LEZ in Germany, Sweden or Denmark you will need to purchase a windscreen sticker, while in London your vehicle needs to be registered. Remember that although all LEZs affect heavy good vehicles, there are different local rules for other vehicles. For example, Italian LEZs affect all vehicles including motorcycles. For more information please visit **www.lowemissionzones.eu**.

GEM Motoring Assist

Since its foundation in 1932, GEM Motoring Assist has been at the forefront of road safety in the UK. Now one of the largest member-led road safety organisations, GEM provides a wide range of discounts and benefits for its 60,000+ members, including the UK's best-value range of breakdown recovery insurance products for motorists, motorcyclists and caravanners. GEM members also benefit from discounts on European breakdown cover and travel insurance, as well as enjoying free access to GEM's Accident Management Service, which provides free-of-charge legal help following any road traffic collision. Members receive Good Motoring, a free quarterly magazine and access to an excellent line-up of road safety leaflets and web-based advice.

Why not make GEM Motoring Assist your one-stop shop for trouble-free motoring! Visit **www.motoringassist.com/philipsmaps** today.

Other laws to be aware of

Belgium You will have to pay to use most public toilets – including those at motorway service stations. You are not permitted to use cruise control on motorways when traffic is heavy.

Denmark Cars towing caravans and trailers are prohibited from overtaking on motorways at certain times of day.

Finland If you hit an elk or deer, you must report the collision to the police. Speeding fines are worked out according to your income.

France If you're caught driving well above the speed limit, you might find yourself stranded on the spot. Police have the power to confiscate your driving licence and impound your vehicle.

Germany Check your fuel contents regularly as it's an offence to run out of fuel on a German motorway. If you do, then you face an on-the-spot fine. It is also an offence to make rude signs to other road users.

Greece Greece has Europe's highest accident rate in terms of the number of crashes per vehicle. Pay particular attention at traffic light junctions, as red lights are frequently ignored. Carrying a petrol can in a vehicle is forbidden.

Ireland Beware of rural three-lane roads, where the middle overtaking lane is used by traffic travelling in both directions. On wider rural roads it's the accepted practice for slower vehicles to pull over to let faster traffic through.

Italy Police can impound your vehicle if you cannot present the relevant ownership documents when requested. You will need a red and white warning sign if you plan to use any rear-mounted luggage rack such as a bike rack.

Portugal If you are towing a caravan, you must have a current inventory of the caravan's contents to show a police officer if requested.

Spain If you need glasses for driving, then the law requires you to carry a spare pair with you in the car. It is compulsory to carry two warning triangles, spare bulbs and reflective jackets.

Turkey Take great caution if you're driving at dusk. Many local drivers put off using their lights until it's properly dark, so you may find oncoming traffic very hard to spot. During the time of Ramadan, many people will fast between the hours of sunrise and sunset. This can seriously reduce levels of alertness, especially among people driving buses, trucks and taxis.

Driving regulations

A national vehicle identification plate is always required when taking a vehicle abroad. It is important for your own safety and that of other drivers to fit headlamp converters or beam deflectors when taking a right-hand drive car to a country where driving is on the right (every country in Europe except the UK and Ireland). When the headlamps are dipped on a right-hand drive car, the lenses of the headlamps cause the beam to shine upwards to the left – and so, when driving on the right, into the eyes of oncoming motorists.

All countries require that you carry a driving licence, green card/insurance documentation, registration document or hire certificate, and passport.

The penalties for infringements of regulations vary considerably from one country to another. In many countries the police have the right to impose on-the-spot fines (you should always request a receipt for any fine paid). Penalties can be severe for serious infringements, particularly for drinking when driving which in some countries can lead to immediate imprisonment. Insurance is important, and you may be forced to take out cover at the frontier if you cannot produce acceptable proof that you are insured.

Please note that driving regulations often change.

Symbols

Symbol	Meaning
🚗	Motorway
⚠	Dual carriageway
⚠	Single carriageway
🚙	Surfaced road
🚙	Unsurfaced / gravel road
🏙	Urban area
🕐	Speed limit in kilometres per hour (kph)
🔖	Seat belts
👶	Children
🍷	Blood alcohol level
△	Warning triangle
🧰	First aid kit
💡	Spare bulb kit
🔥	Fire extinguisher
🪖	Motorcycle helmet
⊖	Minimum driving age
📄	Additional documents required
📱	Mobile phones
★	Other information

The publishers have made every effort to ensure that the information given here was correct at the time of going to press. No responsibility can be accepted for any errors or their consequences.

Andorra (AND)

🚗	⚠	⚠	🏙
n/a	90	60/90	50

- 🔖 Compulsory in front seats
- 👶 Over 10 only allowed in front seats if over 150cm
- 🍷 0.05%
- △ Compulsory
- 🧰 Recommended
- 💡 Compulsory
- 🔥 Recommended
- 🪖 Compulsory for all riders
- ⊖ 18 (16-18 accompanied)
- 📱 Use not permitted whilst driving

Austria (A)

🚗	⚠	⚠	🏙
130	100	100	50

If towing trailer under 750kg

🚗	⚠	⚠	🏙
100	100	100	50

If towing trailer over 750kg

🚗	⚠	⚠	🏙
100	100	80	50

- 🔖 Compulsory in front and rear seats
- 👶 Under 12 and under 150cm cannot travel as a front or rear passenger unless they use a suitable child restraint; under 12 over 150cm must wear adult seat belt
- 🍷 0.05%
- △ Compulsory
- 🧰 Compulsory
- 💡 Recommended
- 🔥 Recommended
- 🪖 Compulsory for all riders
- ⊖ 18 (16 for mopeds)
- 📄 Third party insurance
- 📱 Only allowed with hands-free kit
- ★ If you intend to drive on motorways or expressways, a motorway vignette must be purchased at the border. These are available for 10 days, 2 months or 1 year.
- ★ Dipped headlights must be used at all times on motorbikes.
- ★ Visibility vest compulsory

Belarus (BY)

🚗	⚠	⚠	🏙
110	90	90	60

If towing trailer under 750kg

🚗	⚠	⚠	🏙
90	70	70	

- Vehicle towing another vehicle 50 kph limit • If full driving licence held for less than two years, must not exceed 70 kph
- 🔖 Compulsory in front seats, and rear seats if fitted
- 👶 Under 12 in front seats only in child safety seat
- 🍷 0.00%
- △ Compulsory
- 🧰 Compulsory
- 💡 Recommended
- 🔥 Compulsory
- 🪖 Compulsory for all riders
- ⊖ 18 (16 for motorbikes)
- 📄 Third party insurance; visa (ensure it's specific to driving); vehicle technical check stamp; international driving permit
- 📱 Only with a hands-free kit
- ★ Belarus insurance and temporary vehicle import certificate must be purchased on entry, and driver must be registered
- ★ Dipped headlights compulsory at all times from November to March
- ★ Fees payable for driving on highways

Belgium (B)

🚗	⚠	⚠	🏙
120*	120*	90	50

*Minimum speed of 70kph may be applied in certain conditions on motorways and some dual carriageways

If towing trailer

🚗	⚠	⚠	🏙
90	90	60	50

- 🔖 Compulsory in front and rear seats
- 👶 Children under 12 must use an appropriate child restraint front and rear
- 🍷 0.05%
- △ Compulsory
- 🧰 Compulsory
- 💡 Recommended
- 🔥 Compulsory
- 🪖 Compulsory for all riders
- ⊖ 18 (16 for mopeds)
- 📄 Third party insurance
- 📱 Only with a hands-free kit
- ★ Dipped headlight compulsory for motorcycles during day and other vehicles during poor daytime visibility
- ★ Visibility vest compulsory

Bulgaria (BG)

🚗	⚠	⚠	🏙
130	90	90	50

If towing trailer

🚗	⚠	⚠	🏙
100	70	70	50

- 🔖 Compulsory in front and rear seats
- 👶 Under 10 not allowed in front seats
- 🍷 0.05%
- △ Compulsory
- 🧰 Compulsory
- 💡 Recommended
- 🔥 Compulsory
- 🪖 Compulsory for all riders
- ⊖ 18 (16 for mopeds)
- 📄 Driving licence with translation or international driving permit, third party insurance
- 📱 Only with a hands-free kit
- ★ Fee at border
- ★ Vignette system in operation, can be purchased from all border-crossing points and available annually, monthly and weekly.

Croatia (HR)

🚗	⚠	⚠	🏙
130	110	90	50

If towing

🚗	⚠	⚠	🏙
110	80	80	50

- 🔖 Compulsory if fitted
- 👶 Under 12 not allowed in front seats
- 🍷 0.05%
- △ Compulsory
- 🧰 Compulsory
- 💡 Compulsory
- 🪖 Compulsory for all riders
- ⊖ 18
- 📱 Only allowed with hands-free kit
- ★ Dipped headlights compulsory for all vehicles
- ★ Visibility vests compulsory

Cyprus (CY)

🚗	⚠	⚠	🏙
100	100	80/50	50

If towing

🚗	⚠	⚠	🏙
100	100	80/50	50

- 🔖 Compulsory for front and rear seat passengers (for vehicles manufactured after 01/01/1988)
- 👶 Children under 12 years old or less than 150cm height must be fastened with appropiate safety belts
- 🍷 0.05% blood, 0.02% breath
- △ Compulsory
- 🧰 Compulsory for public vehicles, recommended for the rest
- 💡 N/A
- 🔥 Compulsory for public vehicles, recommended for the rest
- 🪖 Compulsory for all riders
- ⊖ 18 (17 for mopeds)
- 📱 Only with a hands-free kit
- ★ Speed restriction for trucks: 80 kph on motorways and dual carriageways
- ★ No tolls apply but a circulation licence is paid according to engine capacity. Trucks pay the circulation licence according to the type of suspension and number of axies.

Czech Republic (CZ)

🚗	⚠	⚠	🏙
130	130	90	50

If towing

🚗	⚠	⚠	🏙
80	80	80	50

- 🔖 Compulsory in front seats and, if fitted, in rear
- 👶 Under 12 or under 150cm not allowed in front seats
- 🍷 0.00%
- △ Compulsory
- 🧰 Compulsory
- 💡 Compulsory
- 🪖 Compulsory for all riders
- ⊖ 18 (16 for motorcycles under 125 cc)
- 📄 International driving permit
- 📱 Only with a hands-free kit
- ★ Vignette needed for motorway driving, available for 1 year, 60 days, 15 days. Toll specific to lorries introduced 2006.

Denmark (DK)

🛣	🛤	▲	🏭
130	80	80	50

If towing

🛣	🛤	▲	🏭
80	70	70	50

- Compulsory in front seats and, if fitted, in rear
- Children under 12 must use an appropriate child restraint front and rear
- 0.05%
- △ Compulsory
- Recommended
- Recommended
- Recommended
- Compulsory for all riders
- 18
- Third party insurance
- Only with a hands-free kit
- ★ Dipped headlights must be used at all times

Estonia (EST)

🛣	🛤	▲	🏭
n/a	90*	70	50

*In summer, the speed limit on some dual carriageways may be raised to 100/110 kph

- Compulsory in front seats and if fitted in rear seats
- Under 12 not allowed in front seats; under 7 must have child safety seat in rear
- 0.00%
- △ Compulsory
- Compulsory
- Recommended
- Compulsory
- Compulsory for all riders
- 18 (16 for motorcycles, 14 for mopeds)
- International driving permit recommended
- Only with a hands-free kit

Finland (FIN)

🛣	🛤	▲	🏭
120	100	80*	30-60

*100 in summer

If towing

🛣	🛤	▲	🏭
80	80	80	30-60

If towing a vehicle by rope, cable or rod, max speed limit 60 kph. •Maximum of 80 kph for vans and lorries •Speed limits are often lowered in winter

- Compulsory in front and rear
- Children use a safety belt or special child's seat
- 0.05%
- △ Compulsory
- Recommended
- Recommended
- Recommended
- Compulsory for all riders
- 18
- Third party insurance

- Only allowed with hands-free kit
- ★ Dipped headlights must be used at all times

France (F)

🛣	🛤	▲	🏭
130	110	90	50

On wet roads or if full driving licence held for less than 2 years

🛣	🛤	▲	🏭
110	90	80	50

If towing

🛣	🛤	▲	🏭
110	100	50	50

50kph on all roads if fog reduces visibility to less than 50m. Licence will be lost and driver fined for exceeding speed limit by over 40kph

- Compulsory in front seats and, if fitted, in rear
- Under 10 not allowed in front seats; in rear, if 4 or under, must have a child safety seat (rear facing if up to 9 months); if 5 to 10 must use an appropriate restraint system
- 0.05%
- △ Compulsory unless hazard warning lights are fitted; compulsory for vehicles over 3,500kg or towing a trailer
- Recommended
- Recommended
- Compulsory for all riders
- 18 (14 for mopeds; 16 for light motorbikes,)
- Use not permitted whilst driving
- ★ Tolls on motorways

Germany (D)

🛣	🛤	▲	🏭
*	*	100	50

If towing

🛣	🛤	▲	🏭
80	80	80	50

*no limit, 130 kph recommended

- Compulsory
- Children under 12 and under 150cm must have a child safety seat, in front and rear
- 0.05%
- △ Compulsory
- Compulsory
- Recommended
- Recommended
- Compulsory for all riders
- 18 (motorbikes: 16 if not more than 125cc and limited to 11 kW)
- Third party insurance
- Use permitted only with hands-free kit – also applies to drivers of motorbikes and bicycles

Greece (GR)

🛣	🛤	▲	🏭
120	110	110	50

If towing

🛣	🛤	▲	🏭
90	70	70	40

- Compulsory in front seats and, if fitted, in rear
- Under 12 not allowed in front seats except with suitable safety seat; under 10 not allowed in front seats
- 0.025%
- △ Compulsory
- Compulsory
- Recommended
- Compulsory
- Compulsory for all riders
- 18 (16 for low cc motorcycles)
- Third party insurance
- Only with a hands-free kit

Hungary (H)

🛣	🛤	▲	🏭
130	110	90	50

If towing

🛣	🛤	▲	🏭
80	70	70	50

- Compulsory in front seats and if fitted in rear seats
- Under 12 or under 140cm not allowed in front seats
- 0.00%
- △ Compulsory
- Compulsory
- Compulsory
- Recommended
- Compulsory for all riders
- 18
- Third party insurance
- Only with a hands-free kit
- ★ All motorways are toll and operate the vignette system, tickets are available for 4 days, 10 days, 1 month, 1 year; motorcyclists must use electronic payment system
- ★ Dipped headlights are compulsory during daylight hours (cars exempt in built-up areas)

Iceland (IS)

🛣	🚗	🚗	🏭
n/a	90	80	50

- Compulsory in front and rear seats
- Under 12 or under 140cm not allowed in front seats
- 0.00%
- △ Compulsory
- Compulsory
- Compulsory
- Compulsory for all riders

- ★ Motorcyclists must use dipped headlights at all times; other vehicles must use dipped headlights during poor daytime visibility.

Greece —

- 18
- Third party insurance
- Only with a hands-free kit
- ★ Headlights are compulsory at all times
- ★ Highland roads are not suitable for ordinary cars
- ★ Driving off marked roads is forbidden

Ireland (IRL)

🛣	🛤	▲	🏭
120	100	80	50

If towing

🛣	🛤	▲	🏭
80	80	80	50

- Compulsory where fitted. Driver responsible for ensuring passengers under 17 comply
- Under 3 must use appropriate child restraint when travelling in cars fitted with seatbelts
- 0.08%
- △ Recommended
- Recommended
- Recommended
- Recommended
- Compulsory for all riders
- 17 (16 for motorbikes up to 125cc; 18 for over 125cc; 18 for lorries; 21 bus/minibus)
- Third party insurance; international driving permit for non-EU drivers
- Only with a hands-free kit
- ★ Dipped headlights are compulsory during daylight hours
- ★ Driving is on the left
- ★ Tolls are being introduced on some motorways

Italy (I)

🛣	🛤	▲	🏭
130	110	90	50

If towing

🛣	🛤	▲	🏭
80	70	70	50

Some motorways with emergency lanes have speed limit of 150 kph

- Compulsory in front seats and, if fitted, in rear
- Under 12 not allowed in front seats except in child safety seat; children under 3 must have special seat in the back
- 0.08%
- △ Compulsory
- Recommended
- Compulsory
- Recommended
- Compulsory for all motorcylists
- 18 (14 for mopeds, 16 for up to 125cc, 20 for up to 350cc)
- International Driving Licence unless you have photocard licence

- Only allowed with hands-free kit
- ★ Visibility vest compulsory
- ★ Dipped headlights compulsory for motorcycles at all times, and ither vehicles in poor daytime visibility and tunnels, and on motorways
- ★ Tolls on motorways

Latvia (LV)

🛣	🛤	▲	🏭
90/100	90	90	50

If towing

🛣	🛤	▲	🏭
90/100	90	90	50

In residential areas limit is 20kph • If full driving licence held for less than two years, must not exceed 80 kph

- Compulsory in front seats and if fitted in rear
- If under 12 years and 150cm must use child restraint in front and rear seats
- 0.05%
- △ Compulsory
- Compulsory
- Recommended
- Compulsory
- Compulsory for all riders
- 18 (14 for mopeds, 16 for up to 125cc, 21 for up to 350cc)
- International driving permit if licence is not in accordance with Vienna Convention
- Only allowed with hands-free kit
- ★ Dipped headlights must be used at all times all year round
- ★ Cars and minibuses under 3.5 tonnes must have winter tyres from 1 Dec-1 Mar

Lithuania (LT)

🛣	🛤	▲	🏭
130	110	90	50

If towing

🛣	🛤	▲	🏭
n/a	70	70	50

- Compulsory in front seats and if fitted in rear seats
- Under 12 not allowed in front seats unless in a child safety seat
- 0.04%
- △ Compulsory
- Compulsory
- Recommended
- Compulsory
- Compulsory for all riders
- 18 (14 for mopeds)
- Visa for some non-EU citizens
- Only with a hands-free kit
- ★ Dipped headlights must be used at all times

Luxembourg (L)

130/110	90	90	50
If towing			
90	75	75	50

If full driving licence held for less than two years, must not exceed 75 kph

- Compulsory
- Under 12 or 150cm not allowed in front seats unless in a child restraint system; under 3 must have child safety seat in rear seats; 3-11 must have child restraint system if under 150cm
- 0.08%
- Compulsory
- Compulsory (buses)
- Compulsory
- Compulsory (buses, transport of dangerous goods)
- Compulsory for all riders
- 18 (16 for mopeds)
- Third party insurance
- Use permitted only with hands-free kit
- Motorcyclists must use dipped headlights at all times.

Macedonia (MK)

120	100	60	60
If towing			
80	70	50	50

- Compulsory in front seats; compulsory if fitted in rear seats
- Under 12 not allowed in front seats
- 0.05%
- Compulsory
- Compulsory
- Compulsory
- Recommended
- Compulsory for all riders
- 18 (mopeds 16)
- International driving permit; visa
- Use not permitted whilst driving
- Headlights must be used at all times

Moldova (MD)

90	90	90	50
If towing or if licence held under 1 year			
70	70	70	60

- Compulsory in front seats and, if fitted, in rear seats
- Under 12 not allowed in front seats
- 0.00%
- Compulsory
- Compulsory
- Recommended
- Compulsory

- Compulsory for all riders
- 18 (mopeds / motorbikes, 16; vehicles with more than eight passenger places, taxis or towing heavy vehicles, 21)
- International driving permit (preferred), third party insurance, visa
- Only allowed with hands-free kit
- Motorcyclists must use dipped headlights at all times
- Winter tyres recommended from November to February

Montenegro (MNE)

n/a	100	80	60

80kph speed limit if towing a caravan

- Compulsory in front and rear seats
- Under 12 not allowed in front seats
- 0.05%
- Compulsory
- Compulsory
- Recommended
- Compulsory
- Compulsory
- 18 (16 for motorbikes less than 125cc; 14 for mopeds)
- International driving permit; visa
- No legislation
- Tolls on some primary roads
- All types of fuel available at petrol stations

Netherlands (NL)

120	80	80	50

- Compulsory in front seats and, if fitted, rear
- Under 12 not allowed in front seats except in child restraint; in rear, 0-3 child safety restraint, 4-12 child restraint or seat belt
- 0.05%
- Recommended
- Recommended
- Recommended
- Recommended
- Compulsory for all riders
- 18 (16 for mopeds)
- Third party insurance
- Only with a hands-free kit
- dipped headlights compulsory for motorcycles

Norway (N)

90/100	80	80	30/50
If towing braked trailer			
80	80	80	50

If towing trailer without brakes

60	60	60	50

- Compulsory in front seats and, if fitted, in rear
- Children less than 150cm tall must use appropriate child restraint where available. Children under 4 must use child safety seat or safety restraint (cot)
- 0.02%
- Compulsory
- Recommended
- Recommended
- Recommended
- Compulsory for all riders
- 18 (16 mopeds, heavy vehicles 18/21)
- Only with a hands-free kit
- Dipped headlights must be used at all times
- Visibility vest compulsory
- In winter, winter or all-year tyres are compulsory
- Tolls apply on some bridges, tunnels and access roads into major cities

Poland (PL)

Motor vehicle only roads[1]

Vehicles under 3.5 tonnes

130[2]	110	100	n/a

Vehicles 3.5 tonnes or over

80[2]	80	80	n/a

If towing

n/a	80	80	n/a

Other roads

Vehicles under 3.5 tonnes

n/a	100	90	50/60[3]

Vehicles 3.5 tonnes or over

n/a	80	70	50/60[3]

If towing

n/a	60	60	30

[1]Indicated by signs with white car on blue background. [2]Minimum speed 40 kph. [3]50 kph 05.00–23.00; 60 kph 23.00–05.00; 20 kph in marked residential areas

- Compulsory in front seats and, if fitted, in rear
- Under 12 not allowed in front seats unless in a child safety seat; in rear seats children under 12 and less than 150 cm must use child safety seat
- 0.02%
- Compulsory
- Recommended
- Recommended
- Compulsory
- Compulsory for all riders

- 18 (mopeds and motorbikes – 16)
- International permit (recommended)
- Only with a hands-free kit
- Dipped headlights compulsory at all times

Portugal (P)

120*	100	90	50
If towing			
100*	90	80	50

*40kph minimum; 90kph maximum if licence held under 1 year

- Compulsory in front seats; compulsory if fitted in rear seats
- Under 3 not allowed in front seats unless in a child seat; 3–12 not allowed in front seats except in approved restraint system
- 0.05%. Imprisonment for 0.12% or more
- Compulsory
- Recommended
- Recommended
- Recommended
- Compulsory for all riders
- 18 (motorcycles under 50cc 16)
- Only allowed with hands-free kit
- Spectacles-wearers must carry a spare pair in their vehicle at all times
- Dipped headlights compulsory for motorcycles, and for other vehicles in poor daytime visibility
- Tolls on motorways

Romania (RO)

Cars and motorcycles			
120/130	100	90	50
Vans			
110	90	80	50

For motor vehicles with trailers or if full driving licence has been held for less than one year, speed limits are 20kph lower than those listed above. Jeep-like vehicles: 70kph outside built-up areas but 60kph in all areas if diesel

- Compulsory in front seats and, if fitted, in rear
- Under 12 not allowed in front seats
- 0.00%
- Recommended
- Compulsory
- Recommended
- Recommended
- Compulsory for all riders
- 18 (16 for mopeds)

- Registration certificate (only if stay over 90 days for EU citizens); third party insurance
- Only allowed with hands-free kit
- Compulsary vignette (rovinieta) valid for variety of periods available at customs points, petrol stations; price depends on emissions category

Russia (RUS)

110	90	90	60

- Compulsory in front seats
- Under 12 not allowed in front seats
- 0.03%
- Compulsory
- Compulsory
- Recommended
- Compulsory
- Compulsory
- 18
- International driving licence with Russian translation; visa
- Only with a hands-free kit

Serbia (SRB)

120	100	80	60

- Compulsory in front and rear seats
- Under 12 not allowed in front seats
- 0.05%
- Compulsory
- Compulsory
- Compulsory
- Compulsory
- Compulsory
- 18 (16 for motorbikes less than 125cc; 14 for mopeds)
- International driving permit
- No legislation
- Tolls on motorways and some primary roads
- All types of fuel available at petrol stations
- 80km/h speed limit if towing a caravan

Slovak Republic (SK)

130	90	90	60

- Compulsory in front seats and, if fitted, in rear
- Under 12 not allowed in front seats unless in a child safety seat
- 0.0
- Compulsory
- Compulsory
- Compulsory
- Recommended
- Compulsory for motorcyclists

- ⊖ 18 (15 for mopeds)
- International driving permit
- Only with a hands-free kit
- ★ Tow rope recommended
- ★ Vignette required for motorways, car valid for 1 year, 30 days, 7 days; lorry vignettes carry a higher charge.

Slovenia (SLO)

🛣	🛤	🛤	🏙
130	100*	90*	50
If towing			
80	80*	80*	50

*70kph in urban areas

- Compulsory in front seats and, if fitted, in rear
- Under 12 only allowed in the front seats with special seat; babies must use child safety seat
- 0.05%
- Compulsory
- Compulsory
- Compulsory
- Recommended
- Compulsory for all riders
- ⊖ 18 (motorbikes up to 125cc – 16, up to 350cc – 18)
- Only allowed with hands-free kit
- ★ Dipped headlights must be used at all times

Spain (E)

🛣	🛤	🛤	🏙
120	100	90	50
If towing			
80	80	70	50

- Compulsory in front seats and if fitted in rear seats
- Under 12 not allowed in front seats except in a child safety seat; in rear children under 135cm must use child restraint system
- 0.05% (0.03% if vehicle over 3,500 kgs or carries more than 9 passengers, and in first two years of driving licence)
- Two compulsory (one for in front, one for behind)
- Recommended
- Compulsory in adverse weather conditions
- Recommended
- Compulsory for all riders
- ⊖ 18 (18/21 heavy vehicles; 18 for motorbikes over 125cc; 16 for motorbikes up to 125cc; 14 for mopeds up to 75cc)
- Third party insurance
- Only allowed with hands-free kit
- ★ Visibility vest compulsory
- ★ Spectacles-wearers must carry a spare pair in their vehicle at all times

- ★ Tolls on motorways

Sweden (S)

🛣	🛤	🛤	🏙
110	90	70	50
If towing trailer with brakes			
80	80	70	50

- Compulsory in front and rear seats
- Under 7 must have safety seat or other suitable restraint
- 0.02%
- Compulsory
- Recommended
- Recommended
- Recommended
- Compulsory for all riders
- ⊖ 18
- Third party insurance
- No legislation
- ★ Dipped headlights must be used at all times
- ★ New, more variable and often lower, speed limits to be introduced during 2009

Switzerland (CH)

🛣	🛤	🛤	🏙
120	100	80	50/30
If towing up to 1 tonne			
80	80	80	50/30
If towing over 1 tonne			
80	80	60	50/30

- Compulsory in front and, if fitted, in rear
- Under 7 not allowed in front seats unless in child restraint; between 7 and 12 must use child restraint or seatbelt
- 0.05%
- Compulsory
- Recommended
- Recommended
- Recommended
- Compulsory for all riders
- ⊖ 18 (mopeds up to 50cc – 16)
- Third party insurance
- Only with a hands-free kit
- ★ Motorways are all toll and a vignette must be purchased at the border. Can also be purchased online at www.stc.co.uk, by phone on 020 7420 4934 or freephone 00800 10020030. The vignette costs £21.50 (CHF40) and is valid for one calendar year.

Turkey (TR)

🛣	🛤	🛤	🏙
120	90	90	50
If towing			
70	70	70	40

- Compulsory in front seats
- Under 10 not allowed in front seats

- 0.05%
- Two compulsory (one in front, one behind)
- Compulsory
- Compulsory
- Compulsory
- Compulsory for all riders
- ⊖ 18
- International driving permit advised; note that Turkey is in both Europe and Asia
- Only allowed with hands-free kit
- ★ Tow rope and tool kit must be carried

Ukraine (UA)

🛣	🛤	🛤	🏙
130	90	90	60
If towing			
80	80	80	60

Speed limit in pedestrian zone 20 kph

- Compulsory in front and rear seats
- Under 12 not allowed in front seats
- 0.0%
- Compulsory
- Compulsory
- Optional
- Compulsory
- Compulsory for all riders
- ⊖ 18 cars; 16 motorbikes
- International driving permit; visa
- No legislation
- ★ Tow rope and tool kit recommended

United Kingdom (GB)

🛣	🛤	🛤	🏙
112	112	96	48
If towing			
96	96	80	48

- Compulsory in front seats and if fitted in rear seats
- Under 3 not allowed in front seats except with appropriate restraint, and in rear must use child restraint if available; 3–12 and under 150cm must use appropriate restraint or seat belt in front seats, and in rear if available
- 0.08%
- Recommended
- Recommended
- Recommended
- Recommended
- Compulsory for all riders
- ⊖ 17 (16 for mopeds)
- Only allowed with hands-free kit
- ★ Driving is on the left
- ★ Smoking is banned in all commercial vehicles

Ski resorts

The resorts listed are popular ski centres, therefore road access to most is normally good and supported by road clearing during snow falls. However, mountain driving is never predictable and drivers should make sure they take suitable snow chains as well as emergency provisions and clothing. Listed for each resort are: the atlas page and grid square; the altitude; the number of lifts; the season start and end dates; the nearest town (with its distance in km) and the telephone number of the local tourist information centre ('00' prefix required for calls from the UK).

Andorra

Pyrenees

Pas de la Casa / Grau Roig 146 B2 2640m 67 lifts Dec–Apr •Andorra La Vella (30km) ☎+376 801060 ✉http://pas_grau.andorramania.com *Access via Envalira Pass (2407m), highest in Pyrenees, snow chains essential.*

Austria

Alps

A 24-hour driving conditions information line is provided by the Tourist Office of Austria www.austria.info +43 1 588 660

Bad Gastein 109 B4 1002m 51 lifts Dec–Mar •Bad Hofgastein (6km) ☎+43 6432 85044 ✉www.skigastein.at *Snow report: +43 6432 64555.*

Bad Hofgastein 109 B4 860m 51 lifts Dec–Apr •Salzburg (90km) ☎+43 6432 3393260 ✉www.badhofgastein.com

Bad Kleinkirchheim 109 C4 1100m 26 lifts Dec–Mar •Villach (35km) ☎+43 4240 8212 ✉www.badkleinkirchheim.at *Snowfone:+43 4240 8222. Near Ebene Reichenau.*

Ehrwald 108 B1 1000m 22 lifts Dec–Mar •Imst (30km) ✉www.tiscover.at/ehrwald ☎+43 5673 20000208 *Weather report: +43 5673 3329*

Innsbruck 108 B2 574m 75 lifts Dec–Apr •Innsbruck ☎+43 5125 9850 ✉www.ski-innsbruck.at *Motorway normally clear. The motorway through to Italy and through the Arlberg Tunnel West to Austria are both toll roads.*

Ischgl 107 B5 1400m 40 lifts Dec–May •Landeck (25km) ✉www.ischgl.com ☎+43 50990 100 *Car entry to resort prohibited between 2200hrs and 0600hrs.*

Kaprun 109 B3 885m, 25 lifts Jan–Dec •Zell am See (10km) ✉www.zellamsee-kaprun.com ☎+43 6542 7700 *Snowfone:+43 6547 73684.*

Kirchberg in Tyrol 109 B3 860m 55 lifts Dec–Apr •Kitzbühel (6km) ✉www.kirchberg.at ☎+43 5357 2300 *Easily reached from Munich International Airport (120 km)*

Kitzbühel 109 B3 800m 56 lifts Dec–Apr •Wörgl (40km) ☎+43 5356 777 ✉www.kitzbuehel.com

Lech/Oberlech 107 B5 1450m 83 lifts Dec–Apr •Bludenz (50km) ✉www.lech-zuers.at ☎+43 5583 21610 *Roads normally cleared but keep chains accessible because of altitude. Road conditions report tel +43 5583 1515.*

Mayrhofen 108 B2 630m 48 lifts Dec–Apr •Jenbach (35km) ☎+43 5285 6760 ✉www.mayrhofen.at *Chains rarely required.*

Obertauern 109 B4 1740m 28 lifts Nov–Apr •Radstadt (20km) ✉www.obertauern.com ☎+43 6456 7252 *Roads normally cleared but chains accessibility recommended. Camper vans and caravans not allowed; park these in Radstadt*

Saalbach Hinterglemm 109 B3 1003m 52 lifts Nov–Apr •Zell am See (19km) ☎+43 6541 6800 68 ✉www.saalbach.com *Both village centres are pedestrianised and there is a good ski bus service during the daytime*

St Anton am Arlberg 107 B5 1304m 41 lifts Dec–Apr •Innsbruck (104km) ☎+43 5446 22690 ✉www.stantonamarlberg.com *Snow report tel +43 5446 2565*

Schladming 109 B4 2708m 84 lifts Dec–Mar •Schladming ☎+43 3687 22777 ✉www.schladming.com

Serfaus 108 B1 1427m 53 lifts Dec–Apr •Landeck (30km)

🖥 www.serfaus-fiss-ladis.at
☎ +43 5476 62390 *Cars banned from village, use world's only 'hover'-powered underground railway.*

Sölden 108 C2 1377m, 34 lifts all year •Imst (50km) ☎ +43 572 000 200 🖥 www.soelden.com *Roads normally cleared but snow chains recommended because of altitude. The route from Italy and the south over the Timmelsjoch via Obergurgl is closed in the winter and anyone arriving from the south should use the Brenner Pass motorway. Snow information tel +43 5254 2666.*

Zell am See 109 B3 758m 27 lifts Dec–Mar •Zell am See 🖥 www.zellamsee-kaprun.com ☎ +43 6542 7700 *Snowfone +43 6542 73694 Low altitude, so good access and no mountain passes to cross.*

Zell im Zillertal (Zell am Ziller) 109 B3 580m 22 lifts Dec–Apr •Jenbach (25km) ☎ +43 5282 2281 🖥 www.zell.at *Snowfone +43 5282 716526.*

Zürs 107 B5 1720m 83 lifts Dec–May •Bludenz (30km) 🖥 www.lech-zuers.at ☎ +43 5583 2245 *Roads normally cleared but keep chains accessible because of altitude. Village has garage with 24-hour self-service gas/petrol, breakdown service and wheel chains supply.*

France

Alps

Alpe d'Huez 118 B3 1860m 87 lifts Dec–Apr •Grenoble (63km) 🖥 www.alpedhuez.com ☎ +33 4 76 11 44 44 *Snow chains may be required on access road to resort. Road report tel +33 4 76 11 44 50.*

Avoriaz 118 A3 2277m 36 lifts Dec–May •Morzine (14km) 🖥 www.avoriaz.com ☎ +33 4 50 74 02 11 *Chains may be required for access road from Morzine. Car*

free resort, park on edge of village. Horse-drawn sleigh service available.

Chamonix-Mont-Blanc 119 B3 1035m 49 lifts Nov–May •Martigny (38km) ☎ +33 4 50 53 00 24 🖥 www.chamonix.com

Chamrousse 118 B2 1700m 26 lifts Dec–Apr •Grenoble (30km) ☎ +33 4 76 89 92 65 🖥 www.chamrousse.com *Roads normally cleared, keep chains accessible because of altitude.*

Châtel 119 A3 2200m 54 lifts Dec–Apr •Thonon Les Bains (35km) ☎ +33 4 50 73 22 44 🖥 www.chatel.com

Courchevel 118 B3 1850m 67 lifts Dec–Apr •Moûtiers (23km) ☎ +33 4 79 08 00 29 🖥 www.courchevel.com *Roads normally cleared but keep chains accessible. Traffic 'discouraged' within the four resort bases. Traffic info: +33 4 79 37 73 37.*

Flaine 118 A3 1800m 28 lifts Dec–Apr •Cluses (25km) 🖥 www.flaine.com ☎ +33 4 50 90 40 00 *Keep chains accessible for D6 from Cluses to Flaine. Car access for depositing luggage and passengers only. 1500-space car park outside resort. Road conditions report tel +33 4 50 25 20 50. Near Sixt-Fer-á-Cheval.*

La Clusaz 118 B3 1100m 4 lifts Dec–Apr •Annecy (32km) 🖥 www.laclusaz.com ☎ +33 4 50 32 65 00 *Roads normally clear but keep chains accessible for final road from Annecy.*

La Plagne 118 B3 2100m 141 lifts Dec–Apr Moûtiers (32km) 🖥 www.la-plagne.com ☎ +33 4 79 09 79 79 *Ten different centres up to 2100m altitude. Road access via Bozel, Landry or Aime normally cleared.*

Les Arcs 119 B3 2600m 141 lifts Dec–May •Bourg-St-Maurice (15km) ☎ +33 4 79 07 12 57 🖥 www.lesarcs.com *Three base areas up to 2000 metres; keep chains accessible. Pay parking at edge of each base resort.*

Les Carroz d'Araches 118 A3 1140m 80 lifts Dec–Apr •Cluses (13km) ☎ +33 450 90 07 00 🖥 www.lescarroz.com

Les Deux-Alpes 118 C3 1650m 51 lifts Dec–Apr •Grenoble (75km) ☎ +33 4 76 79 22 00 🖥 www.les2alpes.com *Roads normally cleared, however snow chains recommended for D213 up from valley road (D1091).*

Les Gets 118 A3 1172m 52 lifts Dec–Apr •Cluses (18km) ☎ +33 4 50 75 80 80 🖥 www.lesgets.com

Les Ménuires 118 B3 1815m 35 lifts Dec–Apr •Moûtiers (27km) 🖥 www.lesmenuires.com ☎ +33 4 79 00 73 00 *Keep chains accessible for D117 from Moûtiers.*

Les Sept Laux 118 B3 1350m, 24 lifts Dec–Apr •Grenoble (38km) ☎ +33 4 76 08 17 86 🖥 www.les7laux.com *Roads normally cleared, however keep chains accessible for mountain road up from the A41 motorway. Near St Sorlin d'Arves.*

Megève 118 B3 2350m 81 lifts Dec–Apr •Sallanches (12km) 🖥 www.megeve.com ☎ +33 4 50 21 29 52 *Horse-drawn sleigh rides available.*

Méribel 118 B3 1400m 57 lifts Dec–May •Moûtiers (18km) 🖥 www.meribel.net ☎ +33 4 79 08 60 01 *Keep chains accessible for 18km to resort on D90 from Moûtiers.*

Morzine 118 A3 1000m 42 lifts, Dec–Apr •Thonon-Les-Bains (30km) ☎ +33 4 50 74 72 72 🖥 www.morzine.com

Pra Loup 132 A2 1600m 53 lifts Dec–Apr •Barcelonnette (10km) 🖥 www.praloup.com ☎ +33 4 92 84 10 04 *Roads normally cleared but chains accessibility recommended.*

Risoul 118 C3 1850m 57 lifts Dec–Apr •Briançon (40km) 🖥 www.risoul.com ☎ +33 4 92 46 02 60 *Keep chains accessible. Near Guillestre.*

St Gervais 118 B3 850m 125 lifts Dec–Apr •Sallanches (10km) 🖥 www.st-gervais.com ☎ +33 4 50 47 76 08

Serre-Chevalier 118 C3 1350m 68 lifts Dec–Apr •Briançon (10km) ☎ +33 4 92 24 98 98 🖥 www.serre-chevalier.com *Made up of 13 small villages along the valley road, which is normally cleared.*

Tignes 119 B3 2100m 43 lifts Jan–Dec •Bourg St Maurice (26km) ☎ +33 4 79 40 04 40 🖥 www.tignes.net *Keep chains accessible because of altitude. Parking information tel +33 4 79 06 39 45.*

Val d'Isère 119 B3 1850m 46 lifts Nov–May •Bourg-St-Maurice (30km) ☎ +33 4 79 06 06 60 🖥 www.valdisere.com *Roads normally cleared but keep chains accessible.*

Val Thorens 118 B3 2300m 29 lifts Dec–Apr •Moûtiers (37km) 🖥 www.valthorens.com ☎ +33 4 79 00 08 08 *Chains essential – highest ski resort in Europe. Obligatory paid parking on edge of resort.*

Valloire 118 B3 1430m 19 lifts Dec–Apr •Modane (20km) 🖥 www.valloire.net ☎ +33 4 79 59 03 96 *Road normally clear up to the Col du Galbier, to the south of the resort, which is closed from 1st November to 1st June.*

Valmeinier 118 B3 2600m 33 lifts Dec–Apr •St Michel de Maurienne (47km) 🖥 www.valmeinier.com ☎ +33 4 79 59 53 69 *Access from north on D1006 / D902. Col du Galbier, to the south of the resort closed from 1st November to 1st June. Near Valloire.*

Valmorel 118 B3 1400m 49 lifts Dec–Apr •Moûtiers (15km) 🖥 www.valmorel.com ☎ +33 4 79 09 85 55 *Near St Jean-de-Belleville.*

Vars Les Claux 118 C3 1850m 51 lifts Dec–Apr •Briançon (40km) ☎ +33 4 92 46 51 31 🖥 www.vars-ski.com *Four base resorts up to 1850 metres. Keep chains accessible. Road and weather information tel +33 4 36 68 02 05 and +33 4 91 78 78 78. Snowfone +33 492 46 51 04*

Villard-de-Lans 118 B2 1050m 28 lifts Dec–Apr •Grenoble (32km) ☎ +33 4 76 95 10 38 🖥 www.villard-de-lans.com

Pyrenees

Font-Romeu 146 B3 1800m 21 lifts Nov–Apr •Perpignan (87km) ☎ +33 4 68 30 68 30 🖥 www.font-romeu.fr *Roads normally cleared but keep chains accessible.*

St Lary-Soulan 145 B4 830m 32 lifts Dec–Mar •Tarbes (75km) 🖥 www.saintlary.com ☎ +33 5 62 39 50 81 *Access roads constantly cleared of snow.*

Vosges

La Bresse-Hohneck 106 A1 900m 33 lifts Dec–Mar •Cornimont (6km) 🖥 www.labresse-remy.com ☎ +33 3 29 25 41 29

Germany

Alps

Garmisch-Partenkirchen 108 B2 702m 38 lifts Dec–Apr •Munich (95km) 🖥 www.garmisch-partenkirchen.de ☎ +49 8821 180 700 *Roads usually clear, chains rarely needed.*

Oberaudorf 108 B3 483m 25 lifts Dec–Apr •Kufstein (15km) 🖥 www.oberaudorf.de ☎ +49 8033 301 20 *Motorway normally kept clear. Near Bayrischzell.*

Oberstdorf 107 B5 815m 26 lifts Dec–Apr •Sonthofen (15km) 🖥 www.oberstdorf.de ☎ +49 8322 7000 *Snow information on tel +49 8322 3035 or 1095 or 5757.*

Rothaargebirge

Winterberg 81 A4 700m 22 lifts Dec–Mar •Brilon (30km) 🖥 www.winterberg.de ☎ +49 2981 925 00 *Roads usually cleared, chains rarely required.*

Greece

Central Greece

Mountain Parnassos: Kelaria-Fterolakka 182 E4 1750–1950m 13 lifts Dec–Apr •Amfiklia

☎Kelaria +30 22340 22694, Fterolakka 22340 22373
🖥www.parnassos-ski.gr

Mountain Parnassos: Gerondovrahos 182 E4
1800–2390m 3 lifts Dec–Apr •Amfiklia ☎+30 29444 70371

Ipiros

Mountain Pindos: Karakoli 182 D3 1350–1700m 1 lift Dec–Mar •Metsovo
☎+30 26560 41333

Mountain Pindos: Profitis Ilias 182 D3 1500–1700m 3 lifts Dec–Mar •Metsovo
☎+30 26560 41095

Peloponnisos

Mountain Helmos: Kalavrita Ski Centre 184 A3
1650–2340m 7 lifts Dec–Mar •Kalavrita 🖥www.kalavrita-ski.gr/en/default.asp
☎+30 26920 24451/24452

Mountain Menalo: Ostrakina 184 B3 1600m 4 lifts Dec–Mar •Tripoli ☎+30 210 578 1880

Macedonia

Mountain Falakro: Agio Pneuma 183 B6 1720m 3 lifts Dec–Apr •Drama ☎+30 25210 62224 🖥www.falakro.gr

Mountain Vasilitsa: Vasilitsa 182 C3 1750m 2 lifts Dec–Mar •Konitsa ☎+30 24620 84100 🖥www.vasilitsa.com

Mountain Vermio: Seli 182 C4 1500m 9 lifts Dec–Mar •Kozani ☎+30 23310 26237 🖥www.seli-ski.gr (Greek only)

Mountain Vermio: Tria-Pente Pigadia 182 C3 1420–2005m 4 lifts Dec–Mar •Ptolemaida 🖥www.3-5pigadia.gr (Greek only) ☎+30 23320 44944

Mountain Verno: Vigla 182 C3 1650–1900m 5 lifts Dec–Mar •Florina ☎+30 23850 45928 🖥www.vigla-ski.gr (Greek only)

Mountain Vrondous: Lailias 183 B5 1847m 3 lifts Dec–Mar •Serres ☎+30 23210 62400

Thessalia

Mountain Pilio: Agriolefkes 183 D5 1500m 3 lifts Dec–Mar •Volos ☎+30 24280 73719 🖥www.skipilio.gr (Greek only)

Italy

Alps

Bardonecchia 118 B3 1312m 21 lifts Dec–Apr •Bardonecchia ☎+39 122 99137 🖥www.bardonecchiaski.com Snowfone +39 122 907778 *Resort reached through the 11km Frejus tunnel from France, roads normally cleared.*

Bórmio 107 C5 1225m 24 lifts Dec–Apr •Tirano (40km) 🖥www.bormio.com ☎+39 342

902424 *Tolls payable in Ponte del Gallo Tunnel, open 0800hrs–2000hrs.*

Breuil-Cervinia 119 B4 2050m 73 lifts Jan–Dec •Aosta (54km) ☎+39 166 949136 🖥www.breuil-cervinia.it *Snow chains strongly recommended. Bus from Milan airport.*

Courmayeur 119 B3 1224m 16 lifts Dec–Apr •Aosta (40km) ☎+39 165 842060 🖥www.turismo.courmayeur.ao.it *Access through the Mont Blanc tunnel from France. Roads constantly cleared.*

Limone Piemonte 133 A3 1050m 29 lifts Dec–Apr •Cuneo (27km) ☎+39 171 925280 🖥www.limonepiemonte.it *Roads normally cleared, chains rarely required. Snow report tel +39 171 926254.*

Livigno 107 C5 1816m 33 lifts Nov–May •Zernez (CH) (27km) ☎+39 342 052200 🖥www.livigno.com *Keep chains accessible. La Drosa Tunnel from Zernez, Switzerland, is open only from 0800hrs to 2000hrs.*

Sestrière 119 C3 2035m 92 lifts Dec–Apr •Oulx (22km) ☎+39 122 755444 🖥www.sestriere.it *One of Europe's highest resorts; although roads are normally cleared keep chains accessible.*

Appennines

Roccaraso – Aremogna 169 B4 1285m 24 lifts Dec–Apr •Castel di Sangro (7km) ☎+39 864 62210 🖥www.roccaraso.net

Dolomites

Andalo – Fai della Paganella 121 A3 1042m 22 lifts Dec–Apr •Trento (40km) ☎+39 461 585588 🖥www.paganella.net

Arabba 108 C2 2500m 29 lifts Dec–Mar •Brunico (45km) 🖥www.arabba.it ☎+39 436 780019 *Roads normally cleared but keep chains accessible.*

Cortina d'Ampezzo 108 C3 1224m 47 lifts Dec–Apr •Belluno (72km) 🖥www.cortinadampezzo.it *Access from north on route 51 over the Cimabanche Pass may require chains.*

Corvara (Alta Badia) 108 C2 1568m 52 lifts Dec–Apr •Brunico (38km) ☎+39 471 836176 🖥www.altabadia.it *Roads normally clear but keep chains accessible.*

Madonna di Campiglio 121 A3 1550m 19 lifts Dec–Apr •Trento (60km) ☎+39 465 447501 🖥www.campiglio.net *Roads normally cleared but keep chains accessible.*

Moena di Fassa (Sorte/Ronchi) 108 C2 1184m 8 lifts Dec–Apr •Bolzano (40km) ☎+39 462 609500 🖥www.fassa.com

Selva di Val Gardena/Wolkenstein Groden 108 C2 1563m 84 lifts Dec–Apr •Bolzano (40km) ☎+39 471 792277 🖥www.valgardena.it *Roads normally cleared but keep chains accessible.*

Norway

Hemsedal 47 B5 650m 14 lifts Nov–May •Honefoss (150km) ☎+47 32 055030 🖥www.skistar.com/english *Be prepared for extreme weather conditions.*

Trysil (Trysilfjellet) 49 A4 465m 32 lifts Nov–Apr •Elverum (100km) ☎+47 62 451000 🖥www.skistar.com/english *Be prepared for extreme weather conditions.*

Slovak Republic

Chopok 99 C3 2024m 48 lifts Dec–Apr •Jasna ☎+421 48 5591505 🖥www.jasna.sk

Donovaly 99 C3 1360m 17 lifts Nov–Apr •Ruzomberok ☎+421 48 4199900 🖥www.parksnow.sk

Martinske Hole 98 B2 1456m 7 lifts Nov–May •Zilina ☎+421 43 430 6000 🖥www.martinskehole.sk

Plejsy 99 C4 912m 9 lifts Dec–Mar •Krompachy ☎+421 53 4297 994 🖥www.plejsy.com

Strbske Pleso 99 B4 1915m 5 lifts Dec–Mar •Poprad ☎+421 52 449 2343 🖥www.parksnow.sk

Rohace 99 B3 1450m 4 lifts Dec–Apr •Liptovsky Mikulas ☎+421 43 5320777 🖥www.zuberec.sk

Slovenia

Julijske Alpe

Kanin 122 A2 2289m 4 lifts Dec–Apr •Bovec ☎+386 5 3841 919 🖥www.bovec.si

Kobla 122 A2 1480m 6 lifts Dec–Mar •Bohinjska Bistrica ☎+386 4 5747 100 🖥www.bohinj.si/kobla

Kranjska Gora 122 A2 1620m 17 lifts Dec–Mar •Kranjska Gora ☎+386 4 5809 440 🖥www.kranjska-gora.si

Vogel 122 A2 1800m 7 lifts Dec–Apr •Bohinjska Bistrica ☎+386 4 5729 712 🖥www.vogel.si

Kawiniske Savinjske Alpe

Krvavec 122 A3 1970m 10 lifts Dec–Apr •Kranj ☎+386 4 2525 930 🖥www.rtc-krvavec.si

Pohorje

Rogla 123 A4 1517m 13 lifts

Dec–Apr •Slovenska Bistrica ☎+386 3 7576 154 🖥www.rogla.si

Spain

Pyrenees

Baqueira-Beret/Bonaigua 145 B4 1500m 33 lifts Dec–Apr •Vielha (15km) ☎+34 973 639010 🖥www.baqueira.es *Roads normally clear but keep chains accessible. Snowfone tel +34 973 639025. Near Salardú.*

Sistema Penibetico

Sierra Nevada 163 A4 2102m 22 lifts Dec–May •Granada (32km) ☎+34 958 249100 🖥www.sierranevadaski.com *Access road designed to be avalanche safe and is snow cleared. Snowfone +34 958 249119.*

Sweden

Idre Fjäll 199 D9 710m 33 lifts Nov–Apr •Mora (140km) ☎+46 253 41000 🖥www.idrefjall.se *Be prepared for extreme weather conditions.*

Sälen 49 A5 360m 85 lifts Nov–Apr •Malung (70km) 🖥www.skistar.com/english ☎+46 771 840000 *Be prepared for extreme weather conditions.*

Switzerland

Alps

Adelboden 106 C2 1353m 56 lifts Dec–Apr •Frutigen (15km) ☎+41 33 673 80 80 🖥www.adelboden.ch

Arosa 107 C4 1800m 16 lifts Dec–Apr •Chur (30km) ☎+41 81 378 70 20 🖥www.arosa.ch *Roads cleared but keep chains accessible because of high altitude (1800m).*

Crans Montana 119 A4 1500m 30 lifts Dec–Apr, Jul–Oct •Sierre (15km) ☎+41 27 485 04 04 🖥www.crans-montana.ch *Roads normally cleared, however keep chains accessible for ascent from Sierre.*

Davos 107 C4 1560m 54 lifts Nov–Apr •Davos ☎+41 81 415 21 21 🖥www.davos.ch

Engelberg 106 C3 1000m 26 lifts Nov–May •Luzern (39km) ☎+41 41 639 77 77 🖥www.engelberg.ch *Straight access road normally cleared.*

Flums (Flumserberg) 107 B4 1400m 16 lifts Dec–Apr •Buchs (25km) ☎+41 81 720 18 18 🖥www.flumserberg.ch *Roads normally cleared, but 1000-metre vertical ascent; keep chains accessible.*

Grindelwald 106 C3 1034m 40 lifts Dec–Apr •Interlaken (20km) ☎+41 33 854 12 12 🖥www.grindelwald.ch

Gstaad – Saanenland 106 C2 1050m 62 lifts Dec–Apr •Gstaad ☎+41 33 748 81 81 🖥www.gstaad.ch

Klosters 107 C4 1191m 52 lifts Dec–Apr •Davos (10km) 🖥www.klosters.ch ☎+41 81 410 20 20 *Roads normally clear but keep chains accessible*

Leysin 119 A4 1263m 14 lifts Dec–Apr •Aigle (6km) ☎+41 24 493 33 00 🖥www.leysin.ch

Mürren 106 C2 1650m 40 lifts Dec–Apr •Interlaken (18km) ☎+41 33 856 86 86 🖥www.wengen-muerren.ch *No road access. Park in Strechelberg (1500 free places) and take the two-stage cable car.*

Nendaz 119 A4 1365m 92 lifts Nov–Apr •Sion (16km) ☎+41 27 289 55 89 🖥www.nendaz.ch *Roads normally cleared, however keep chains accessible for ascent from Sion. Near Vex.*

Saas-Fee 119 A4 1800m 23 lifts Jan–Dec •Brig (35km) ☎+41 27 958 18 58 🖥www.saas-fee.ch *Roads normally cleared but keep chains accessible because of altitude.*

St Moritz 107 C4 1856m 56 lifts Nov–May •Chur (89km) ☎+41 81 837 33 33 🖥www.stmoritz.ch *Roads normally cleared but keep chains accessible because of altitude.*

Samnaun 107 C5 1846m 42 lifts Dec–May •Scuol (30km) ☎+41 81 868 58 58 🖥www.samnaun.ch *Roads normally cleared but keep chains accessible.*

Verbier 119 A4 1500m 34 lifts Nov–Apr, Jun–Jul •Martigny (27km) ☎+41 27 775 38 88 🖥www.verbier.ch *Roads normally cleared.*

Villars 119 A4 1253m 36 lifts Dec–Apr, Jun–Jul •Montreux (35km) ☎+41 24 495 32 32 🖥www.villars.ch *Roads normally cleared but keep chains accessible for ascent from N9. Near Bex.*

Wengen 106 C2 1270m 40 lifts Dec–Apr •Interlaken (12km) 🖥www.wengen-muerren.ch ☎+41 33 855 14 14 *No road access. Park at Lauterbrunnen and take mountain railway.*

Zermatt 119 A4 1620m 71 lifts all year •Brig (42km) ☎+41 27 966 81 00 🖥www.zermatt.ch *Cars not permitted in resort, park in Täsch (3km) and take shuttle train.*

Turkey

North Anatolian Mountains

Uludag 186 B4 2543m 14 lifts Dec–March •Bursa (36km) ☎+90 224 254 22 74

300 greatest sights of Europe

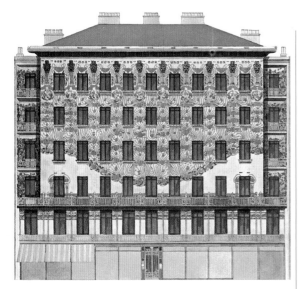

Maholicahaus, Vienna, Austria

Albania Shqipëria

www.albanian.com

Berat
Fascinating old town with picturesque Ottoman Empire buildings and traditional Balkan domestic architecture. **182 C1**

Tirana Tiranë
Capital of Albania. Skanderbeg Square has main historic buildings. Also: 18c Haxhi Ethem Bey Mosque; Art Gallery (Albanian); National Museum of History. Nearby: medieval Krujë; Roman monuments. **182 B1**

Austria Österreich

www.austria-tourism.at

Bregenz
Lakeside town bordering Germany, Liechtenstein, Switzerland. Locals, known as Vorarlbergers, have their own dialect. St Martinsturm 17th century tower, 17th century town hall, Kunsthaus Bregenz gallery of modern art, Vorarlberger Landesmuseum, Festspielhaus www.bregenz.ws **107 B4**

Graz
University town, seat of imperial court to 1619. Historic centre around Hauptplatz. Imperial monuments: Burg; mausoleum of Ferdinand II; towers of 16c schloss; 17c Schloss Eggenburg. Also: 16c Town Hall; Zeughaus; 15c cathedral. Museums: Old Gallery (Gothic, Flemish); New Gallery (good 19–20c). www.graztourismus.at **110 B2**

Innsbruck
Old town is reached by Maria-Theresien-Strasse with famous views. Buildings: Goldenes Dachl (1490s); 18c cathedral; remains of Hofburg imperial residence; 16c Hofkirche (tomb of Maximilian I). www.innsbruck.info **108 B2**

Krems
On a hill above the Danube, medieval quarter has Renaissance mansions. Also: Gothic Piaristenkirche; Wienstadt Museum. www.krems.at **97 C3**

Linz
Port on the Danube. Historic buildings are concentrated on Hauptplatz below the imperial 15c schloss. Notable: Baroque Old Cathedral; 16c Town Hall; New Gallery. www.linz.at **96 C2**

Melk
Set on a rocky hill above the Danube, the fortified abbey is the greatest Baroque achievement in Austria – particularly the Grand Library and abbey church. www.stiftmelk.at **110 A2**

Salzburg
Set in subalpine scenery, the town was associated with powerful 16-17c prince-archbishops. The 17c cathedral has a complex of archiepiscopal buildings: the Residence and its gallery (excellent 16–19c); the 13c Franciscan Church (notable altar). Other sights: Mozart's birthplace; the Hohensalzburg fortress; the Collegiate Church of St Peter (cemetery, catacombs); scenic views from Mönchsberg and Hettwer Bastei. The Grosse Festspielhaus runs the Salzburg festival. www2.salzburg.info **109 B4**

Salzkammergut
Natural beauty with 76 lakes (Wolfgangersee, Altersee, Gosausee, Traunsee, Grundlsee) in mountain scenery. Attractive villages (St Wolfgang) and towns (Bad Ischl, Gmunden) include Hallstatt, famous for Celtic remains. www.salzkammergut.at **109 B4**

Vienna Wien
Capital of Austria. The historic centre lies within the Ring. Churches: Gothic St Stephen's Cathedral; 17c Imperial Vault; 14c Augustine Church; 14c Church of the Teutonic Order (treasure); 18c Baroque churches (Jesuit Church, Franciscan Church, St Peter, St Charles). Imperial residences: Hofburg; Schönbrunn. Architecture of Historicism on Ringstrasse (from 1857). Art Nouveau: Station Pavilions, Postsparkasse, Looshaus, Majolicahaus. Exceptional museums: Art History Museum (antiquities, old masters); Cathedral and Diocesan Museum (15c); Academy of Fine Arts (Flemish); Belvedere (Gothic, Baroque, 19–20c). www.wien.gv.at **111 A3**

Belgium Belgique

www.visitbelgium.com

Antwerp Antwerpen
City with many tall gabled Flemish houses on the river. Heart of the city is Great Market with 16–17c guildhouses and Town Hall. 14–16c Gothic cathedral has Rubens paintings. Rubens also at the Rubens House and his burial place in St Jacob's Church. Excellent museums: Mayer van den Berg Museum (applied arts); Koninklijk Museum of Fine Arts (Flemish, Belgian). www.visitantwerp.be **79 A4**

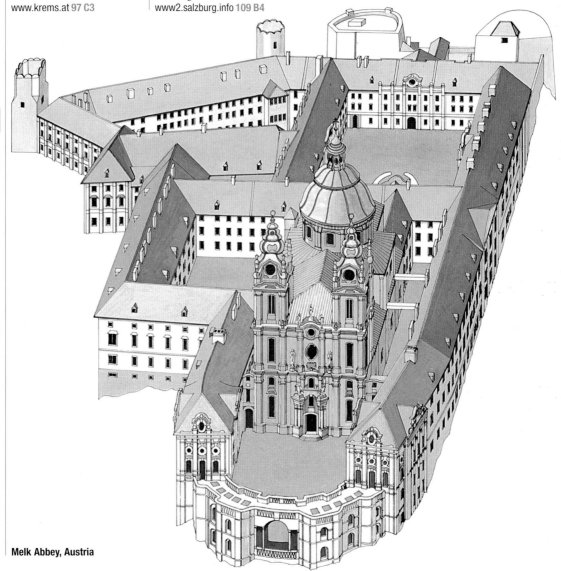

Melk Abbey, Austria

Town Hall, Antwerp, Belgium

Bruges Brugge

Well-preserved medieval town with narrow streets and canals. Main squares: the Market with 13c Belfort and covered market; the Burg with Basilica of the Holy Blood and Town Hall. The Groeninge Museum and Memling museum in St Jans Hospital show 15c Flemish masters. The Onze Lieve Vrouwekerk has a famous *Madonna and Child* by Michelangelo www.brugge.be **78 A3**

Brussels Bruxelles

Capital of Belgium. The Lower Town is centred on the enormous Grand Place with Hôtel de Ville and rebuilt guildhouses. Symbols of the city include the 'Manneken Pis' and Atomium (giant model of a molecule). The 13c Notre Dame de la Chapelle is the oldest church. The Upper Town contains: Gothic cathedral; Neoclassical Place Royale; 18c King's Palace; Royal Museums of Fine Arts (old and modern masters). Also: much Art Nouveau (Victor Horta Museum, Hôtel Tassel, Hôtel Solvay); Place du Petit Sablon and Place du Grand Sablon; 19c Palais de Justice. www.brusselsinternational.be **79 B4**

Ghent Gent

Medieval town built on islands surrounded by canals and rivers. Views from Pont St-Michel. The Graslei and Koornlei quays have Flemish guild houses. The Gothic cathedral has famous Van Eyck altarpiece. Also: Belfort; Cloth Market; Gothic Town Hall; Gravensteen. Museums: Bijloke Museum in beautiful abbey (provincial and applied art); Museum of Fine Arts (old masters). www.gent.be **79 A3**

Namur

Reconstructed medieval citadel is the major sight of Namur, which also has a cathedral and provincial museums. www.namur.be **79 B4**

Tournai

The Romanesque-Gothic cathedral is Belgium's finest (much excellent art). Fine Arts Museum has a good collection (15–20c). www.tournai.be **78 B3**

Bulgaria Bulgariya

www.bulgariatravel.org

Black Sea Coast

Beautiful unspoiled beaches (Zlatni Pyasŭtsi). The delightful resort Varna is popular. Nesebŭr is famous for Byzantine churches. Also: Danube Delta in Hungary. **17 D7**

Koprivshtitsa

Beautiful village known both for its half-timbered houses and links with the April Rising of 1876. Six house museums amongst which the Lyutov House and the Oslekov House, plus the birthplaces of Georgi Benkovski, Dimcho Debelyanov, Todor Kableshkov, and Lyuben Karavelov.

Plovdiv

City set spectacularly on three hills. The old town has buildings from many periods: 2c Roman stadium and amphitheatre; 14c Dzumaiya Mosque; 19c Koyumdjioglu House and Museum (traditional objects). Nearby: Bačkovo Monastery (frescoes). www.plovdiv.org **183 A6**

Rila

Bulgaria's finest monastery, set in the most beautiful scenery of the Rila mountains. The church is richly decorated with frescoes.

Sofia Sofiya

Capital of Bulgaria. Sights: exceptional neo-Byzantine cathedral; Church of St Sofia; 4c rotunda of St George (frescoes); Byzantine Boyana Church (frescoes) on panoramic Mount Vitoša. Museums: National Historical Museum (particularly for Thracian artefacts); National Art Gallery (icons, Bulgarian art). www.sofia.bg/en **17 D5**

Veliko Tŭrnovo

Medieval capital with narrow streets. Notable buildings: House of the Little Monkey; Hadji Nicoli Inn; ruins of medieval citadel; Baudouin Tower; churches of the Forty Martyrs and of SS Peter and Paul (frescoes); 14c Monastery of the Transfiguration. www.veliko-tarnovo.net **17 D6**

Croatia Hrvatska

www.croatia.hr

Dalmatia Dalmacija

Exceptionally beautiful coast along the Adriatic. Among its 1185 islands, those of the Kornati Archipelago and Brijuni Islands are perhaps the most spectacular. Along the coast are several attractive medieval and Renaissance towns, most notably Dubrovnik, Split, Šibenik, Trogir, Zadar. www.dalmacija.net **138 B2**

Dubrovnik

Surrounded by medieval and Renaissance walls, the city's architecture dates principally from 15–16c. Sights: many churches and monasteries including Church of St Vlah and Dominican monastery (art collection); promenade street of Stradun, Dubrovnik Museums; Renaissance Rector's Palace; Onofrio's fountain; Sponza Palace. The surrounding area has some 80 16c noblemen's summer villas. www.dubrovnik-online.com **139 C4**

Islands of Croatia

There are over 1,000 islands off the coast of Croatia among which there is Brač, known for its white marble and the beautiful beaches of Bol (www.bol.hr); Hvar (www.hvar.hr) is beautifully green with fields of lavender, marjoram, rosemary, sage and thyme; Vis (www.tz-vis.hr) has the beautiful towns of Komiža and Vis Town, with the Blue Cave on nearby Biševo. **123 & 137–138**

Istria Istra

Peninsula with a number of ancient coastal towns (Rovinj, Poreč, Pula, Piran in Slovene Istria) and medieval hill-top towns (Motovun). Pula has Roman monuments (exceptional 1c amphitheatre). Poreč has narrow old streets; the mosaics in 6c Byzantine basilica of St Euphrasius are exceptional. See also Slovenia. www.istra.com **122 B2**

Plitvička Jezera

Outstandingly beautiful world of water and woodlands with 16 lakes and 92 waterfalls interwoven by canyons. www.np-plitvicka-jezera.hr **123 C4**

Split

Most notable for the exceptional 4c palace of Roman Emperor Diocletian, elements of which are incorporated into the streets and buildings of the town itself. The town also has a cathedral (11c baptistry) and a Franciscan monastery. www.split.hr **138 B2**

Trogir

The 13–15c town centre is surrounded by medieval city walls. Romanesque-Gothic cathedral includes the chapel of Ivan the Blessed. Dominican and Benedictine monasteries house art collections. www.trogir-online.com **138 B2**

Zagreb

Capital city of Croatia with cathedral and Archbishop's Palace in Kaptol and to the west Gradec with Baroque palaces. Donji Grad is home to the Archaological Museum, Art Pavilion, Museum of Arts and Crafts, Ethnographic Museum, Mimara Museum and National Theatre. www.zagreb-touristinfo.hr **124 B1**

Czech Republic Česka Republica

www.czech.cz

Brno

Capital of Moravia. Sights: Vegetable Market and Old Town Hall; Capuchin crypt decorated with bones of dead monks; hill of St Peter with Gothic cathedral; Mies van der Rohe's buildings (Bata, Avion Hotel, Togendhat House). Museums: UPM (modern applied arts); Pražáků Palace (19c Czech art). www.brno.cz **97 B4**

České Budějovice

Famous for Budvar beer, the medieval town is centred on náměsti Přemysla Otokara II. The Black Tower gives fine views. Nearby: medieval Český Krumlov. www.c-budejovice.cz **96 C2**

Kutná Hora

A town with strong silver mining heritage shown in the magnificent Cathedral of sv Barbara which was built by the miners. See also the ossuary with 40,000 complete sets of bones moulded into sculptures and decorations. www.kutnohorsko.cz **97 B3**

Olomouc

Well-preserved medieval university town of squares and fountains. The Upper Square has the Town Hall. Also: 18c Holy Trinity; Baroque Church of St Michael. www.olomoucko.cz **98 B1**

Plzeň

Best known for Plzeňský Prazdroj (Pilsener Urquell), beer has been brewed here since 1295. An industrial town with eclectic architecture shown in the railway stations and the namesti Republiky (main square). www.zcu.cz/plzen **96 B1**

Prague Praha

Capital of Czech Republic and Bohemia. The Castle Quarter has a complex of buildings behind the walls (Royal Castle; Royal Palace; cathedral). The Basilica of St George has a fine Romanesque interior. The Belvedere is the best example of Renaissance architecture. Hradčani Square has aristocratic palaces and the National Gallery. The Little Quarter has many Renaissance (Wallenstein Palace) and Baroque mansions and the Baroque Church of St Nicholas. The Old Town has its centre at the Old Town Square with the Old Town

Hall (astronomical clock), Art Nouveau Jan Hus monument and Gothic Týn church. The Jewish quarter has 14c Staranova Synagogue and Old Jewish Cemetery. The Charles Bridge is famous. The medieval New Town has many Art Nouveau buildings and is centred on Wenceslas Square. www.prague.cz **84 B2**

Spas of Bohemia

Spa towns of Karlovy Vary (Carlsbad), Márianske Lázně (Marienbad) and Frantiskovy Lázně (Franzenbad). **83 B4**

Denmark Danmark

www.visitdenmark.com

Århus

Second largest city in Denmark with a mixture of old and new architecture that blends well, Århus has been dubbed the culture capital of Denmark with the Gothic Domkirke; Latin Quarter; 13th Century Vor Frue Kirke; Den Gamle By, open air museum of traditional Danish life; ARoS, Århus Art Museum. www.visitaarhus.com **59 B3**

Copenhagen
København

Capital of Denmark. Old centre has fine early 20c Town Hall. Latin Quarter has 19c cathedral. 18c Kastellet has statue of the Little Mermaid nearby. The 17c Rosenborg Castle was a royal residence, as was the Christianborg (now government offices). Other popular sights: Nyhavn canal; Tivoli Gardens. Excellent art collections: Ny Carlsberg Glypotek; State Art Museum; National Museum. www.visitcopenhagen.dk **61 D2**

Hillerød

Frederiksborg is a fine red-brick Renaissance castle set among three lakes. **61 D2**

Roskilde

Ancient capital of Denmark. The marvellous cathedral is a burial place of the Danish monarchy. The Viking Ship Museum houses the remains of five 11c Viking ships excavated in the 1960s. www.visitroskilde.com **61 D2**

Estonia Eesti

www.visitestonia.com

Kuressaare

Main town on the island of Saaremaa with the 14c Kuressaare Kindlus. www.kuressaare.ee **8 C3**

Pärnu

Sea resort with an old town centre. Sights: 15c Red Tower; neoclassical Town Hall; St Catherine's Church. www.parnu.ee **8 C4**

Tallinn

Capital of Estonia. The old town is centred on the Town Hall Square. Sights: 15c Town Hall; Toompea Castle; Three Sisters houses. Churches: Gothic St Nicholas; 14c Church of the Holy Spirit; St Olaf's Church. www.tallinn.ee **8 C4**

Tartu

Historic town with 19c university. The Town Hall Square is surrounded by neoclassical buildings. Also: remains of 13c cathedral; Estonian National Museum. www.tartu.ee **8 C5**

Finland Suomi

http://virtual.finland.fi

Finnish Lakes

Area of outstanding natural beauty covering about one third of the country with thousands of lakes, of which Päijänne and Saimaa are the most important. Tampere, industrial centre of the region, has numerous museums, including the Sara Hildén Art Museum (modern). Savonlinna has the medieval Olavinlinna Castle. Kuopio has the Orthodox and Regional Museums. **8 A5**

Helsinki

Capital of Finland. The 19c neoclassical town planning between the Esplanade and Senate Square includes the Lutheran cathedral. There is also a Russian Orthodox cathedral. The Constructivist Stockmann Department Store is the largest in Europe. The main railway station is Art Nouveau. Gracious 20c buildings in Mannerheimintie avenue include Finlandiatalo by Alvar Aalto. Many good museums: Art Museum of the Ateneum (19–20c); National Museum; Museum of Applied Arts; Helsinki City Art Museum (modern Finnish); Open Air Museum (vernacular architecture); 18c fortress of Suomenlinna has several museums. www.hel.fi **8 B4**

Lappland (Finnish)

Vast unspoiled rural area. Lappland is home to thousands of nomadic Sámi living in a traditional way. The capital, Rovaniemi, was rebuilt after WWII; museums show Sámi history and culture. Nearby is the Arctic Circle with the famous Santa Claus Village. Inari is a centre of Sámi culture. See also Norway and Sweden. www.laplandfinland.com **192–193**

France

www.franceguide.com

Albi

Old town with rosy brick architecture. The vast Cathédrale Ste-Cécile (begun 13c) holds some good art. The Berbie Palace houses the Toulouse-Lautrec museum. www.mairie-albi.fr **130 B1**

Alps

Grenoble, capital of the French Alps, has a good 20c collection in the Museum of Painting and Sculpture. The Vanoise Massif has the greatest number of resorts (Val d'Isère, Courchevel). Chamonix has spectacular views on Mont Blanc, France's and Europe's highest peak. www.thealps.com **118 B2**

Amiens

France's largest Gothic cathedral has beautiful decoration. The Museum of Picardy has unique 16c panel paintings. www.amiens.fr **90 B2**

Arles

Ancient, picturesque town with Roman relics (1c amphitheatre), 11c cathedral, Archaeological Museum (Roman art). www.tourisme.ville-arles.fr **131 B3**

Avignon

Medieval papal capital (1309–77) with 14c walls and many ecclesiastical buildings. Vast Palace of the Popes has stunning frescoes. The Little Palace has fine Italian Renaissance painting. The 12–13c Bridge of St Bénézet is famous. www.ot-avignon.fr **131 B3**

Bourges

The Gothic Cathedral of St Etienne, one of the finest in France, has a superb sculptured choir. Also notable is the House of Jacques Coeur. www.bourgestourisme.com **103 B4**

Burgundy Bourgogne

Rural wine region with a rich Romanesque, Gothic and Renaissance heritage. The 12c cathedral in Autun and 12c basilica in Vézelay have fine Romanesque sculpture. Monasteries include 11c L'Abbaye de Cluny (ruins) and L'Abbaye de Fontenay. Beaune

Abbaye aux Hommes, Caen, France

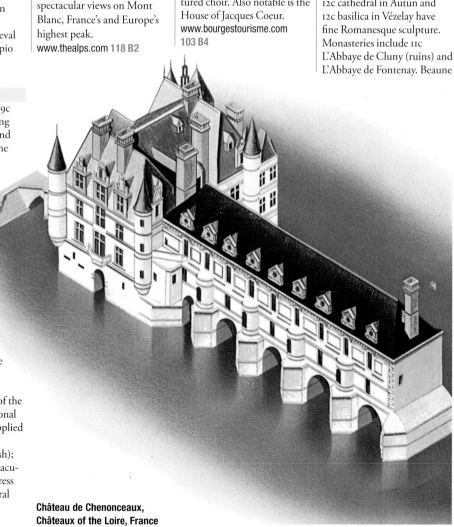

Château de Chenonceaux, Châteaux of the Loire, France

has beautiful Gothic Hôtel-Dieu and 15c Nicolas Rolin hospices. www.burgundy-tourism.com **104 B3**

Brittany Bretagne

Brittany is famous for cliffs, sandy beaches and wild landscape. It is also renowned for megalithic monuments (Carnac) and Celtic culture. Its capital, Rennes, has the Palais de Justice and good collections in the Museum of Brittany (history) and Museum of Fine Arts. Also: Nantes; St-Malo. **100–101** www.brittany-bretagne.com

Caen

City with two beautiful Romanesque buildings: Abbaye aux Hommes; Abbaye aux Dames. The château has two museums (15–20c painting; history). The *Bayeux Tapestry* is displayed in nearby Bayeux. www.ville-caen.fr **89 A3**

Carcassonne

Unusual double-walled fortified town of narrow streets with an inner fortress. The fine Romanesque Church of St Nazaire has superb stained glass. www.carcassonne.org **130 B1**

Chartres

The 12–13c cathedral is an exceptionally fine example of Gothic architecture (Royal Doorway, stained glass, choir screen). The Fine Arts Museum has a good collection. www.chartres.com **90 C1**

Loire Valley

The Loire Valley has many 15–16c châteaux built amid beautiful scenery by French monarchs and members of their courts. Among the most splendid are Azay-le-Rideau, Chenonceaux and Loches. Also: Abbaye de Fontévraud. www.lvo.com **102 B2**

Clermont-Ferrand

The old centre contains the cathedral built out of lava and Romanesque basilica. The Puy de Dôme and Puy de Sancy give spectacular views over some 60 extinct volcanic peaks (*puys*). www.ville-clermont-ferrand.fr **116 B3**

Colmar

Town characterised by Alsatian half-timbered houses. The Unterlinden Museum has excellent German religious art including the famous Isenheim altarpiece. The Dominican church also has a fine altarpiece. www.ot-colmar.fr **106 A2**

Corsica Corse

Corsica has a beautiful rocky coast and mountainous interior. Napoleon's birthplace of Ajaccio has: Fesch Museum with Imperial Chapel and a large collection of Italian art; Maison Bonaparte; cathedral. Bonifacio, a medieval town, is spectacularly set on a rock over the sea. www.visit-corsica.com **180**

Côte d'Azur

The French Riviera is best known for its coastline and glamorous resorts. There are many relics of artists who worked here: St-Tropez has Musée de l'Annonciade; Antibes has 12c Château Grimaldi with the Picasso Museum; Cagnes has the Renoir House and Mediterranean Museum of Modern Art; St-Paul-de-Vence has the excellent Maeght Foundation and Matisse's Chapelle du Rosaire. Cannes is famous for its film festival. Also: Marseille, Monaco, Nice. www.cote.azur.fr **133 B3**

Dijon

Great 15c cultural centre. The Palais des Ducs et des Etats is the most notable monument and contains the Museum of Fine Arts. Also: the Charterhouse of Champmol. www.dijon-tourism.com **105 B4**

Disneyland Paris

Europe's largest theme park follows in the footsteps of its famous predecessors in the United States. www.disneylandparis.com **90 C2**

Le Puy-en-Velay

Medieval town bizarrely set on the peaks of dead volcanoes. It is dominated by the Romanesque cathedral (cloisters). The Romanesque chapel of St-Michel is dramatically situated on the highest rock. www.ot-lepuyenvelay.fr **117 B3**

Lyon

France's third largest city has an old centre and many museums including the Museum of the History of Textiles and the Museum of Fine Arts (old masters). www.lyon-france.com **117 B4**

Marseilles Marseille

Second largest city in France. Spectacular views from the 19c Notre-Dame-de-la-Garde. The Old Port has 11–12c Basilique St Victor (crypt, catacombs). Cantini Museum has major collection of 20c French art. Château d'If was the setting for Dumas' *The Count of Monte Cristo*. www.marseille-tourisme.com **131 B4**

Mont-St-Michel

Gothic pilgrim abbey (11–12c) set dramatically on a steep rock island rising from mud flats and connected to the land by a road covered by the tide. The abbey is made up of a complex of buildings. www.e-mont-saint-michel.com **101 A4**

Nancy

A centre of Art Nouveau. The 18c Place Stanislas was constructed by dethroned Polish king Stanislas. Museums: School of Nancy Museum (Art Nouveau furniture); Fine Arts Museum. www.ot-nancy.fr **92 C2**

Nantes

Former capital of Brittany, with the 15c Château des ducs de Bretagne. The cathedral has a striking interior. www.nantes-tourisme.com **101 B4**

Nice

Capital of the Côte d'Azur, the old town is centred on the old castle on the hill. The seafront includes the famous 19c Promenade des Anglais. The aristocratic quarter of the Cimiez Hill has the Marc Chagall Museum and the Matisse Museum. Also: Museum of Modern and Contemporary Art (especially neo-Realism and Pop Art). www.nicetourism.com **133 B3**

Paris

Capital of France, one of Europe's most interesting cities. The Île de la Cité area, an island in the River Seine has the 12–13c Gothic Notre Dame (wonderful stained glass) and La Sainte-Chapelle (1240–48), one of the jewels of Gothic art. The Left Bank area: Latin Quarter with the famous Sorbonne university; Museum of Cluny housing medieval art; the Panthéon; Luxembourg Palace and Gardens; Montparnasse, interwar artistic and literary centre; Eiffel Tower; Hôtel des Invalides with Napoleon's tomb. Right Bank: the great boulevards (Avenue des Champs-Élysées joining the Arc de Triomphe and Place de la Concorde); 19c Opéra Quarter; Marais, former aristocratic quarter of elegant mansions (Place des Vosges); Bois de Boulogne, the largest park in Paris; Montmartre, centre of 19c bohemianism, with the Basilique

Sacré-Coeur. The Church of St Denis is the first gothic church and the mausoleum of the French monarchy. Paris has three of the world's greatest art collections: The Louvre (to 19c, *Mona Lisa*), Musée d'Orsay (19–20c) and National Modern Art Museum in the Pompidou Centre. Other major museums include: Orangery Museum; Paris Museum of Modern Art; Rodin Museum; Picasso Museum. Notable cemeteries with graves of the famous: Père-Lachaise, Montmartre, Montparnasse. Near Paris are the royal residences of Fontainebleau and Versailles. www.paris.fr **90 C2**

Pyrenees

Beautiful unspoiled mountain range. Towns include: delightful sea resorts of St-Jean-de-Luz and Biarritz; Pau, with access to the Pyrenees National Park; pilgrimage centre Lourdes. **144–145** www.pyrenees-online.fr

Reims

Together with nearby Epernay, the centre of champagne production. The 13c Gothic cathedral is one of the greatest architectural achievements in France (stained glass by Chagall). Other sights: Palais du Tau with cathedral sculpture, 11c Basilica of St Rémi; cellars on Place St-Niçaise and Place des Droits-des-Hommes. www.reims-tourisme.com **91 B4**

Rouen

Old centre with many half-timbered houses and 12–13c Gothic cathedral and the Gothic Church of St Maclou with its fascinating remains of a dance macabre on the former cemetery of Aître St-Maclou. The Fine Arts Museum has a good collection. www.mairie-rouen.fr **89 A5**

St-Malo

Fortified town (much rebuilt) in a fine coastal setting. There is a magnificent boat trip along the river Rance to Dinan, a splendid well-preserved medieval town. www.saint-malo.fr **101 A3**

Strasbourg

Town whose historic centre includes a well-preserved quarter of medieval half-timbered Alsatian houses, many of them set on the canal. The cathedral is one of the best in France. The Palais Rohan contains several museums. www.strasbourg.fr **93 C3**

Toulouse

Medieval university town characterised by flat pink brick (Hôtel Assézat). The Basilique St Sernin, the largest Romanesque church in France, has many art treasures. Marvellous Church of the Jacobins holds the body of St Thomas Aquinas. www.ot-toulouse.fr **129 C4**

Tours

Historic town centred on Place Plumereau. Good collections in the Guilds Museum and Fine Arts Museum. www.tours.fr **102 B2**

Versailles

Vast royal palace built for Louis XIV, primarily by Mansart, set in large formal gardens with magnificent fountains. The extensive and much-imitated state apartments include the famous Hall of Mirrors and the exceptional Baroque chapel. www.chateauversailles.fr **90 C2**

Vézère Valley Caves

A number of prehistoric sites, most notably the cave paintings of Lascaux (some 17,000 years old), now only seen in a duplicate cave, and the cave of Font de Gaume. The National Museum of Prehistory is in Les Eyzies. www.leseyzies.com **129 B4**

Germany Deutschland

www.germany-tourism.de

Northern Germany

Aachen

Once capital of the Holy Roman Empire. Old town around the Münsterplatz with magnificent cathedral. An exceptionally rich treasure is in the Schatzkammer. The Town Hall is on the medieval Market. www.aachen.de **80 B2**

Berlin

Capital of Germany. Sights include: the Kurfürstendamm avenue; Brandenburg Gate, former symbol of the division between East and West Germany; Tiergarten; Unter den Linden; 19c Reichstag. Berlin has many excellent art and history collections. Museum Island includes: Pergamon Museum (classical antiquity, Near and Far East, Islam); Bode Museum (Egyptian, Early Christian, Byzantine and European); Old National Gallery (19–20c German). Dahlem Museums: Picture Gallery (13–18c); Sculpture Collection (13–19c); Prints

and Drawings Collection; Die Brücke Museum (German Expressionism). Tiergarten Museums: New National Gallery (19–20c); Decorative Arts Museum; Bauhaus Archive. In the Kreuzberg area: Berlin Museum; Grupius Building with Jewish Museum and Berlin Gallery; remains of Berlin Wall and Checkpoint Charlie House. Schloss Charlottenburg houses a number of collections including the National Gallery's Romantic Gallery; the Egyptian Museum is nearby. www.berlin-tourist-information. de **74 B2**

Cologne Köln
Ancient city with 13–19c cathedral (rich display of art). In the old town are the Town Hall and many Romanesque churches (Gross St Martin, St Maria im Kapitol, St Maria im Lyskirchen, St Ursula, St Georg, St Severin, St Pantaleon, St Apostolen). Museums: Diocesan Museum (religious art); Roman-German Museum (ancient history); Wallraf-Richartz/ Ludwig Museum (14–20c art). www.koeln.de **80 B2**

Dresden
Historic centre with a rich display of Baroque architecture. Major buildings: Castle of the Electors of Saxony; 18c Hofkirche; Zwinger Palace with fountains and pavilions (excellent old masters); Albertinum with excellent Gallery of New Masters; treasury of Grünes Gewölbe. The Baroque-planned New Town contains the Japanese Palace and Schloss Pillnitz. www.dresden.de **84 A1**

Frankfurt
Financial capital of Germany. The historic centre around the Römerberg Square has 13–15c cathedral, 15c Town Hall, Gothic St Nicholas Church, Saalhof (12c chapel). Museums: Museum of Modern Art (post-war); State Art Institute. www.frankfurt.de **81 B4**

Hamburg
Port city with many parks, lakes and canals. The Kunsthalle has Old Masters and 19–20c German art. Buildings: 19c Town Hall; Baroque St Michael's Church. www.hamburg-tourismus.de **72 A3**

Hildesheim
City of Romanesque architecture (much destroyed). Principal sights: St Michael's Church; cathedral (11c interior, sculptured doors, St Anne's Chapel); superb 15c Tempelhaus on the Market Place. www.hildesheim.de **72 B2**

Lübeck
Beautiful old town built on an island and characterised by Gothic brick architecture. Sights: 15c Holsten Gate; Market with the Town Hall and Gothic brick St Mary's Church; 12–13c cathedral; St Ann Museum. www.luebeck-tourism.de **65 C3**

Mainz
The Electoral Palatinate schloss and Market fountain are Renaissance. Churches: 12c Romanesque cathedral; Gothic St Steven's (with stained glass by Marc Chagall). www.mainz.de **93 A4**

Marburg
Medieval university town with the Market Place and Town Hall, St Elizabeth's Church (frescoes, statues, 13c shrine), 15–16c schloss. www.marburg.de **81 B4**

Münster
Historic city with well-preserved Gothic and Renaissance buildings: 14c Town Hall; Romanesque-Gothic cathedral. The Westphalian Museum holds regional art. www.munster.de **71 C4**

Potsdam
Beautiful Sanssouci Park contains several 18–19c buildings including: Schloss Sanssouci; Gallery (European masters); Orangery; New Palace; Chinese Teahouse. www.potsdam.de **74 B2**

Rhein Valley Rheintal
Beautiful 80km gorge of the Rhein Valley between Mainz and Koblenz with rocks (Loreley), vineyards (Bacharach, Rüdesheim), white medieval towns (Rhens, Oberwesel) and castles. Some castles are medieval (Marksburg, Rheinfels, island fortress Pfalzgrafenstein) others were built or rebuilt in the 19c (Stolzenfles, Rheinstein). www.rheintal.de **80 B3**

Weimar
The Neoclassical schloss, once an important seat of government, now houses a good art collection. Church of SS Peter and Paul has a Cranach masterpiece. Houses of famous people: Goethe, Schiller, Liszt. The famous Bauhaus was founded at the School of Architecture and Engineering. www.weimar.de **82 B3**

Southern Germany

Alpine Road
Deutsche Alpenstrasse
German Alpine Road in the Bavarian Alps, from Lindau on Bodensee to Berchtesgaden. The setting for 19c fairy-tale follies of Ludwig II of Bavaria (Linderhof, Hohenschwangau, Neuschwanstein), charming old villages (Oberammergau) and Baroque churches (Weiss, Ottobeuren). Garmisch-Partenkirchen has views on Germany's highest peak, the Zugspitze. www.deutsche-alpenstrasse.de **108 B2**

Augsburg
Attractive old city. The Town Hall is one of Germany's finest Renaissance buildings. Maximilianstrasse has several Renaissance houses and Rococo Schaezler Palace (good art collection). Churches:

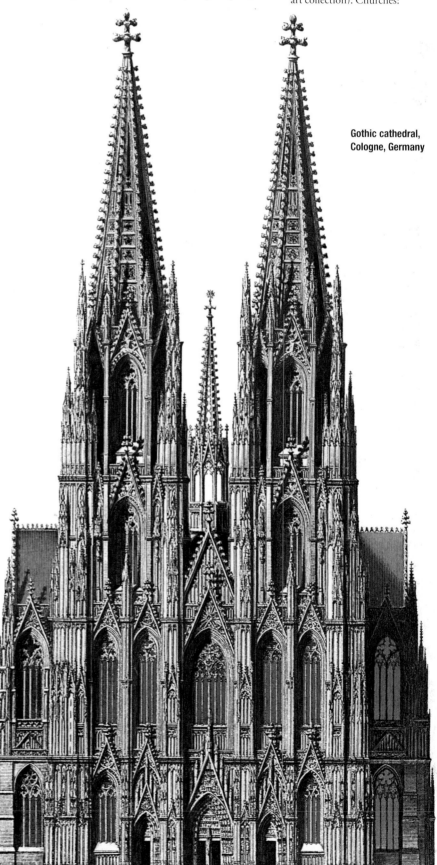

Gothic cathedral, Cologne, Germany

Romanesque-Gothic cathedral; Renaissance St Anne's Church. The Fuggerei, founded 1519 as an estate for the poor, is still in use. www.augsburg.de **94 C2**

Bamberg

Well-preserved medieval town. The island, connected by two bridges, has the Town Hall and views of Klein Venedig. Romanesque-Gothic cathedral (good art) is on an exceptional square of Gothic, Renaissance and Baroque buildings – Alte Hofhalttung; Neue Residenz with State Gallery (German masters); Ratstube. www.bamberg.info **94 B2**

Black Forest
Schwarzwald

Hilly region between Basel and Karlsruhe, the largest and most picturesque woodland in Germany, with the highest summit, Feldberg, lake resorts (Titisee), health resorts (Baden-Baden) and clock craft (Triberg). Freiburg is regional capital. www.schwarzwald.de **93 C4**

Freiburg

Old university town with system of streams running through the streets. The Gothic Minster is surrounded by the town's finest buildings. Two towers remain of the medieval walls. The Augustine Museum has a good collection. www.freiburg.de **106 B2**

Heidelberg

Germany's oldest university town, majestically set on the banks of the river and romantically dominated by the ruined schloss. The Gothic Church of the Holy Spirit is on the Market Place with the Baroque Town Hall. Other sights include the 16c Knight's House and the Baroque Morass Palace with a museum of Gothic art. www.heidelberg.de **93 B4**

Lake Constance
Bodensee

Lake Constance, with many pleasant lake resorts. Lindau, on an island, has numerous gabled houses. Birnau has an 18c Rococo church. Konstanz (Swiss side) has the Minster set above the Old Town. www.bodensee.de **107 B4**

Munich München

Old town centred on the Marienplatz with 15c Old Town Hall and 19c New Town Hall. Many richly decorated churches: St Peter's (14c tower); Gothic red-brick

cathedral; Renaissance St Michael's (royal portraits on the façade); Rococo St Asam's. The Residenz palace consists of seven splendid buildings holding many art objects. Schloss Nymphenburg has a palace, park, botanical gardens and four beautiful pavilions. Superb museums: Old Gallery (old masters), New Gallery (18–19c), Lenbachhaus (modern German). Many famous beer gardens. www.muenchen.de **108 A2**

Nuremberg Nürnberg

Beautiful medieval walled city dominated by the 12c Kaiserburg. Romanesque-Gothic St Sebaldus Church and Gothic St Laurence Church are rich in art. On Hauptmarkt is the famous 14c Schöner Brunnen. Also notable is 15c Dürer House. The German National Museum has excellent German medieval and Renaissance art. www.nuernberg.de **94 B3**

Regensburg

Medieval city set majestically on the Danube. Views from 12c Steinerne Brücke. Churches: Gothic cathedral; Romanesque St Jacob's; Gothic St Blaisius; Baroque St Emmeram. Other sights: Old Town Hall (museum); Haidplatz; Schloss Thurn und Taxis; State Museum. www.regensburg.de **95 B4**

Romantic Road
Romantische Strasse

Romantic route between Aschaffenburg and Füssen, leading through picturesque towns and villages of medieval Germany. The most popular section is the section between Würzburg and Augsburg, centred on Rothenburg ob der Tauber. Also notable are Nördlingen, Harburg Castle, Dinkelsbühl, Creglingen. www.romantischestrasse.de **94 B2**

Rothenburg ob der Tauber

Attractive medieval walled town with tall gabled and half-timbered houses on narrow cobbled streets. The Market Place has Gothic-Renaissance Town Hall, Rattrinke-stubbe and Gothic St Jacob's Church (altarpiece). www.rothenburg.de **94 B2**

Speyer

The 11c cathedral is one of the largest and best Romanesque buildings in Germany. 12c Jewish Baths are well-preserved. www.speyer.de **93 B4**

Stuttgart

Largely modern city with old centre around the Old Schloss, Renaissance Alte Kanzlei, 15c Collegiate Church and Baroque New Schloss. Museums: Regional Museum; post-modern State Gallery (old masters, 20c German). The 1930s Weissenhofsiedlung is by several famous architects. www.stuttgart.de **94 C1**

Trier

Superb Roman monuments: Porta Nigra; Aula Palatina (now a church); Imperial Baths; amphitheatre. The Regional Museum has Roman artefacts. Also, Gothic Church of Our Lady; Romanesque cathedral. www.trier.de **92 B2**

Ulm

Old town with half-timbered gabled houses set on a canal. Gothic 14–19c minster has tallest spire in the world (161m). www.tourismus.ulm.de **94 C1**

Würzburg

Set among vineyard hills, the medieval town is centred on the Market Place with the Rococo House of the Falcon. The 18c episcopal princes' residence (frescoes) is magnificent. The cathedral is rich in art. Work of the great local Gothic sculptor, Riemenschneider, is in Gothic St Mary's Chapel, Baroque New Minster, and the Mainfränkisches Museum. www.wuerzburg.de **94 B1**

Great Britain

www.visitbritain.com

England

Bath

Elegant spa town with notable 18c architecture: Circus, Royal Crescent, Pulteney Bridge, Assembly Rooms; Pump Room. Also: well-preserved Roman baths; superb Perpendicular Gothic Bath Abbey. Nearby: Elizabethan Longleat House; exceptional 18c landscaped gardens at Stourhead. www.visitbath.co.uk **43 A4**

Brighton

Resort with a sea-front of Georgian, Regency and Victorian buildings with the Palace Pier, and an old town of narrow lanes. The main sight is the 19c Royal Pavilion in Oriental styles. www.brighton.co.uk **44 C3**

Bristol

Old port city with the fascinating Floating Harbour.

Major sights include Gothic 13–14c Church of St Mary Redcliffe and 19c Clifton Suspension Bridge. www.visitbristol.co.uk **43 A4**

Cambridge

City with university founded in the early 13c. Peterhouse (1284) is the oldest college. Most famous colleges were founded in 14–16c: Queen's, King's (with the superb Perpendicular Gothic 15–16c King's College Chapel), St John's (with famous 19c Bridge of Sighs), Trinity, Clare, Gonville and Caius, Magdalene. Museums: excellent Fitzwilliam Museum (classical, medieval, old masters). Kettle's Yard (20c British). www.visitcambridge.org **45 A4**

Canterbury

Medieval city and old centre of Christianity. The Norman-Gothic cathedral has many sights and was a major medieval pilgrimage site (as related in Chaucer's *Canterbury Tales*). St Augustine, sent to convert the English in 597, founded St Augustine's Abbey, now in ruins. www.canterbury.co.uk **45 B5**

Chatsworth

One of the richest aristocratic country houses in England (largely 17c) set in a large landscaped park. The palatial interior has some 175 richly furnished rooms and a major art collection. www.chatsworth-house.co.uk **40 B2**

Chester

Charming medieval city with complete walls. The Norman-Gothic cathedral has several abbey buildings. www.visitchester.co.uk **38 A4**

Cornish Coast

Scenic landscape of cliffs and sandy beaches (the north coast being a popular surfing destination) with picturesque villages (Fowey, Mevagissey). St Ives has the Tate Gallery with work of the St Ives Group. The island of St Michael's Mount holds a priory. www.cornwalltouristboard.co.uk **42 B1**

Dartmoor

Beautiful wilderness area in Devon with tors and its own breed of wild pony as well as free-ranging cattle and sheep. www.dartmoor-npa.gov.uk **42 B3**

Durham

Historic city with England's finest Norman cathedral and a

castle, both placed majestically on a rock above the river. www.durham.gov.uk **37 B5**

Eden Project

Centre showing the diversity of plant life on the planet, built in a disused clay pit. Two biomes, one with Mediterranean and Southern African focus and the larger featuring a waterfall, river and tropical trees plants and flowers. Outdoors also features plantations including bamboo and tea. www.edenproject.com **42 B2**

Hadrian's Wall

Built to protect the northernmost border of the Roman Empire in the 2c AD, the walls originally extended some 120km with castles every mile and 16 forts. Best-preserved walls around Hexam; forts at Housesteads and Chesters. www.hadrians-wall.org **37 A4**

Lake District

Beautiful landscape of lakes (Windermere, Coniston) and England's high peaks (Scafell Pike, Skiddaw, Old Man), famous for its poets, particularly Wordsworth. www.lake-district.gov.uk **36 B3**

Leeds Castle

One of the oldest and most romantic English castles, standing in the middle of a lake. Most of the present appearance dates from 19c. www.leeds-castle.com **45 B4**

Lincoln

Old city perched on a hill with narrow streets, majestically dominated by the Norman-Gothic cathedral and castle. www.visitlincolnshire.com **40 B3**

Liverpool

City on site of port founded in 1207 and focused around 1846 Albert Dock, now a heritage attraction. Croxteth Hall and Country Park; Speke Hall; Sudley House; Royal Liver Building; Liverpool Cathedral; Walker Art Gallery; University of Liverpool Art Gallery. www.visitliverpool.com **38 A4**

London

Capital of UK and Europe's largest city. To the east of the medieval heart of the city – now the largely modern financial district and known as the City of London – is the Tower of London (11c White Tower, Crown Jewels) and 1880s Tower Bridge. The popular heart of the city and its entertainment is the West End, around Piccadilly

Circus, Leicester Square and Trafalgar Square (Nelson's Column). Many sights of political and royal power: Whitehall (Banqueting House, 10 Downing Street, Horse Guards); Neo-Gothic Palace of Westminster (Houses of Parliament) with Big Ben; The Mall leading to Buckingham Palace (royal residence, famous ceremony of the Changing of the Guard). Numerous churches include: 13–16c Gothic Westminster Abbey (many tombs, Henry VII's Chapel); Wren's Baroque St Paul's Cathedral, St Mary-le-Bow, spire of St Bride's, St Stephen Walbrook. Museums of world fame: British Museum (prehistory, oriental and classical antiquity, medieval); Victoria and Albert Museum (decorative arts); National Gallery (old masters to 19c); National Portrait Gallery (historic and current British portraiture); Tate – Britain and Modern; Science Museum; Natural History Museum. Madame Tussaud's waxworks museum is hugely popular. Other sights include: London Eye, Kensington Palace; Greenwich with Old Royal Observatory (Greenwich meridian), Baroque Royal Naval College, Palladian Queen's House; Tudor Hampton Court Palace; Syon House. Nearby: Windsor Castle (art collection, St George's Chapel). www.visitlondon.com **44 B3**

Longleat
One of the earliest and finest Elizabethan palaces in England. The palace is richly decorated. Some of the grounds have been turned into a pleasure park, with the Safari Park, the first of its kind outside Africa. www.longleat.co.uk **43 A4**

Manchester
Founded on a Roman settlement of 79AD and a main player in the Industrial Revolution. Victorian Gothic Town Hall; Royal Exchange;

Cathedral. Many museums including Imperial War Museum North, Lowry Centre and Manchester Art Gallery. www.visitmanchester.com **40 B1**

Newcastle
A key player in the Industrial Revolution with 12th century cathedral and many museums as well as strong railway heritage. www.visitnewcastle.co.uk **37 B5**

Norwich
Medieval quarter has half-timbered houses. 15c castle keep houses a museum and gallery. Many medieval churches include the Norman-Gothic cathedral. www.visitnorwich.co.uk **41 C5**

Oxford
Old university city. Earliest colleges date from 13c: University College; Balliol; Merton. 14–16c colleges include: New College; Magdalen; Christ Church (perhaps the finest). Other buildings: Bodleian Library; Radcliffe Camera; Sheldonian Theatre; cathedral. Good museums: Ashmolean Museum (antiquity to 20c); Museum of Modern Art; Christ Church Picture Gallery (14–17c). Nearby: outstanding 18c Blenheim Palace. www.visitoxford.org **44 B2**

Petworth
House (17c) with one of the finest country-house art collections (old masters), set in a huge landscaped park. www.nationaltrust.org.uk **44 C3**

Salisbury
Pleasant old city with a magnificent 13c cathedral built in an unusually unified Gothic style. Nearby: Wilton House. www.visitsalisburyuk.com **44 B2**

Stonehenge
Some 4000 years old, one of the most famous and haunting Neolithic monuments in Europe. Many other Neolithic sites are nearby. **44 B2** www.english-heritage.org.uk

Stourhead
Early 18c palace famous for its grounds, one of the finest examples of neoclassical landscaped gardening, consisting of a lake surrounded by numerous temples. www.nationaltrust.org.uk **43 A4**

Stratford-upon-Avon
Old town of Tudor and Jacobean half-timbered houses, famed as the birth and burial place of William Shakespeare. Nearby: Warwick Castle. www.shakespeare-country.co.uk **44 A2**

Wells
Charming city with beautiful 12–16c cathedral (west facade, scissor arches, chapter house, medieval clock). Also Bishop's Palace; Vicar's Close. **43 A4**

Winchester
Historic city with 11–16c cathedral (tombs of early English kings). Also: 13c Great Hall; Winchester College; St Cross almshouses. www.visitwinchester. co.uk **44 B2**

York
Attractive medieval city surrounded by well-preserved walls with magnificent Gothic 13–15c Minster. Museums: York City Art Gallery (14–19c); Jorvik Viking Centre. Nearby: Castle Howard. www.york-tourism.co.uk **40 B2**

Scotland

Edinburgh
Capital of Scotland, built on volcanic hills. The medieval Old Town is dominated by the castle set high on a volcanic rock (Norman St Margaret's Chapel, state apartments, Crown Room). Holyrood House (15c and 17c) has lavishly decorated state apartments and the ruins of Holyrood Abbey (remains of Scottish monarchs). The 15c cathedral has the Crown Spire and Thistle Chapel. The New Town has good Georgian architecture (Charlotte Square, Georgian House). Excellent museums: Scottish National Portrait Gallery, National Gallery of Scotland; Scottish National Gallery of Modern Art. www.edinburgh.org **35 C4**

Glamis Castle
In beautiful, almost flat landscaped grounds, 14c fortress, rebuilt 17c, gives a fairy-tale impression. www.glamis-castle.co.uk **35 B5**

Glasgow
Scotland's largest city, with centre around George Square and 13–15c Gothic cathedral. The Glasgow School of Art is the masterpiece of Charles Rennie Mackintosh. Fine art collections: Glasgow Museum and Art Gallery; Hunterian Gallery; Burrell Collection. www.seeglasgow.com **35 C3**

Loch Ness
In the heart of the Highlands, the lake forms part of the scenic Great Glen running from Inverness to Fort William. Famous as home of the fabled Loch Ness Monster (exhibition at Drumnadrochit). Nearby: ruins of 14–16c Urquhart Castle. **32 D2** www.loch-ness-scotland.com

Wales

Caernarfon
Town dominated by a magnificent 13c castle, one of a series built by Edward I in Wales (others include Harlech, Conwy, Beaumaris, Caerphilly). www.visitcaernafon.com **38 A2**

Cardiff
Capital of Wales, most famous for its medieval castle, restored 19c in Greek, Gothic and Oriental styles. Also: National Museum and Gallery. www.visitcardiff.info **39 C3**

Greece Ellas
www.gnto.gr

Athens Athina
Capital of Greece. The Acropolis, with 5c BC sanctuary complex (Parthenon, Propylaia, Erechtheion, Temple of Athena Nike), is the greatest architectural achievement of antiquity in Europe. The Agora was a public meeting place in ancient Athens. Plaka has narrow streets and small Byzantine churches (Kapnikarea). The Olympeum was the larg-

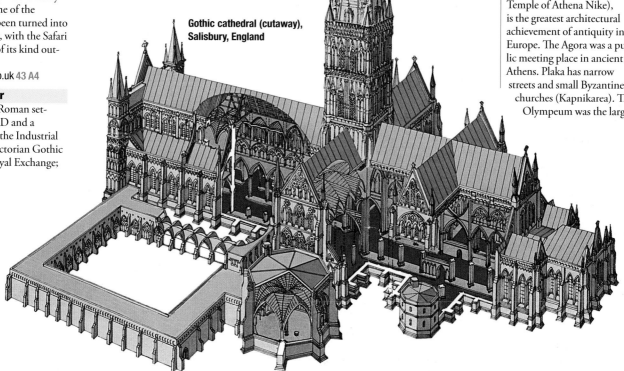

Gothic cathedral (cutaway), Salisbury, England

Radcliffe Camera
(cutaway),
Oxford, England

est temple in Greece. Also: Olympic Stadium; excellent collections of ancient artefacts (Museum of Cycladic and Ancient Greek Art; Acropolis Museum; National Archeological Museum; Benaki Museum). www.athens.gr **185 B4**

Corinth Korinthos
Ancient Corinth (ruins), with 5c BC Temple of Apollo, was in 44 BC made capital of Roman Greece by Julius Caesar. Set above the city, the Greek-built acropolis hill of Acrocorinth became the Roman and Byzantine citadel (ruins). **184 B3**

Crete Kriti
Largest Greek island, Crete was home to the great Minoan civilization (2800–1100 BC). The main relics are the ruined Palace of Knossos and Malia. Gortys was capital of the Roman province. Picturesque Rethimno has narrow medieval streets, a Venetian fortress and a former Turkish mosque. Matala has beautiful beaches and famous caves cut into cliffs. Iraklio (Heraklion), the capital, has a good Archeological Museum. **185 D6**

Delphi
At the foot of the Mount Parnassos, Delphi was the seat of the Delphic Oracle of Apollo, the most important oracle in Ancient Greece. Delphi was also a political meeting place and the site of the Pythian Games. The Sanctuary of Apollo consists of: Temple of Apollo, led to by the Sacred Way; Theatre; Stadium. The museum has a display of objects from the site (5c BC Charioteer). www.delphi.gr **182 E4**

Epidavros
Formerly a spa and religious centre focused on the Sanctuary of Asclepius (ruins). The enormous 4c BC theatre is probably the finest of all ancient theatres. www.ancientepidavros.org **184 B4**

Greek Islands
Popular islands with some of the most beautiful and spectacular beaches in Europe. The many islands are divided into various groups and individual islands: The major groups are the Kiklades and Dodekanisa in the Aegean Sea, the largest islands are Kerkyra (Corfu) in the Ionian Sea and Kriti. **182–185 & 188**

Meteora
The tops of bizarre vertical cylinders of rock and towering cliffs are the setting for 14c Cenobitic monasteries, until recently only accessible by baskets or removable ladders. Mega Meteoro is the grandest and set on the highest point. Roussánou has the most extraordinary site. Varlaám is one of the oldest and most beautiful, with the Ascent Tower and 16c church with frescoes. Aghiou Nikolaou also has good frescoes. **182 D3**

Mistras
Set in a beautiful landscape, Mistras is the site of a Byzantine city, now in ruins, with palaces, frescoed churches, monasteries and houses. **184 B3**

Mount Olympus
Oros Olymbos
Mount Olympus, mythical seat of the Greek gods, is the highest, most dramatic peak in Greece. **182 C4**

Mycenae Mikines
The citadel of Mycenae prospered between 1950 BC and 1100 BC and consists of the royal complex of Agamemnon: Lion Gate, royal burial site, Royal Palace, South House, Great Court. **184 B3**

Olympia
In a stunning setting, the Panhellenic Games were held here for a millennium. Ruins of the sanctuary of Olympia consist of the Doric temples of Zeus and Hera and the vast Stadium. There is also a museum (4c BC figure of Hermes). **184 B2**

Rhodes
One of the most attractive islands with wonderful sandy beaches. The city of Rhodes has a well-preserved medieval centre with the Palace of the Grand Masters and the Turkish Süleymaniye Mosque. **188 C2**

Salonica Thessaloniki
Largely modern city with Byzantine walls and many fine churches: 8c Aghia Sofia; 11c Panaghia Halkeo; 14c Dodeka Apostoli; 14c Aghios Nikolaos Orfanos; 5c Aghios Dimitrios (largest in Greece, 7c Mosaics). www.thessalonikicity.gr **183 C5**

Hungary Magyarország

www.hungarytourism.hu

Balaton
The 'Hungarian sea', famous for its holiday resorts: Balatonfüred, Tihany, Badasconytomaj, Keszthely. www.balaton.hu **111 C4**

Budapest
Capital of Hungary on River Danube, with historic area centring on the Castle Hill of Buda district. Sights include: Matthias church; Pest district with late 19c architecture, centred on Ferenciek tere; neo-Gothic Parliament Building on river; Millennium Monument. The Royal Castle houses a number of museums: Hungarian National Gallery, Budapest History Museum; Ludwig Collection. Other museums: National Museum of Fine Arts (excellent Old and Modern masters); Hungarian National Museum (Hungarian history). Famous for public thermal baths: Király and Rudas baths, both made under Turkish rule; Gellért baths, the most visited. www.budapestinfo.hu **112 B3**

Esztergom
Medieval capital of Hungary set in scenic landscape. Sights: Hungary's largest basilica (completed 1856); royal palace ruins. www.esztergom.hu **112 B2**

Pécs
Attractive old town with Europe's fifth oldest university (founded 1367). Famous for Turkish architecture (Mosque of Gazi Kasim Pasha, Jakovali Hassan Mosque). www.pecs.hu **125 A4**

Sopron
Beautiful walled town with many Gothic and Renaissance houses. Nearby: Fertöd with the marvellous Eszergázy Palace. www.sopron.hu **111 B3**

Ireland

www.discoverireland.com

Northern Ireland

Antrim Coast
Spectacular coast with diverse scenery of glens (Glenarm, Glenariff), cliffs (Murlough Bay) and the famous Giant's Causeway, consisting of some 40,000 basalt columns. Carrickefergus Castle is the largest and best-preserved Norman castle in Ireland. www.northantrim.com **27 A4**

Belfast
Capital of Northern Ireland. Sights: Donegall Square with 18c Town Hall; neo-Romanesque Protestant cathedral; University Square; Ulster Museum (European painting). www.gotobelfast.com **27 B5**

Giant's Causeway
Spectacular and unique rock formations in the North Antrim coast, formed by volcanic activity 50–60 million years ago. World Heritage Site. www.northantrim.com **27 A4**

Republic of Ireland

Aran Islands
Islands with spectacular cliffs and notable pre-Christian and Christian sights, especially on Inishmore. www.visitaranislands.com **26 B2**

Cashel
Town dominated by the Rock of Cashel (61m) topped by ecclesiastical ruins including 13c cathedral; 15c Halls of the Vicars; beautiful Romanesque 12c Cormac's Chapel (fine carvings). www.connemar-tourism.org **29 B4**

Connemara
Beautiful wild landscape of mountains, lakes, peninsulas and beaches. Clifden is the capital. www.connemar-tourism.org **28 A1**

Cork
Pleasant city with its centre along St Patrick's Street and Grand Parade lined with fine 18c buildings. Churches: Georgian St Anne's Shandon (bell tower); 19c cathedral. www.corkcorp.ie **29 C3**

County Donegal
Rich scenic landscape of mystical lakes and glens and seascape of cliffs (Slieve League cliffs are the highest in Europe). The town of Donegal has a finely preserved Jacobean castle. www.donegaldirect.ie **26 B2**

Dublin
Capital of Ireland. City of elegant 18c neoclassical and Georgian architecture with gardens and parks (St Stephen's Green, Merrion Square with Leinster House – now seat of Irish parliament). City's main landmark, Trinity College (founded 1591), houses in its Old Library fine Irish manuscripts (7c Book of Durrow, 8c Book of Kells). Two Norman cathedrals: Christ Church; St Patrick's. Other buildings: originally medieval Dublin Castle with State Apartments; James Gandon's masterpieces: Custom House; Four Courts. Museums: National Museum (Irish history); National Gallery (old masters,

Impressionists, Irish painting); Guinness Brewery Museum; Dublin Writers' Museum (Joyce, Wilde, Yeats and others). www.visitdublin.com **30 A2**

Glendalough
Impressive ruins of an important early Celtic (6c) monastery with 9c cathedral, 12c St Kevin's Cross, oratory of St Kevin's Church. www.wicklow.com/glendalough **30 A2**

Kilkenny
Charming medieval town, with narrow streets dominated by 12c castle (restored 19c). The 13c Gothic cathedral has notable tomb monuments. www.kilkenny.ie **30 B1**

Newgrange
One of the best passage graves in Europe, the massive 4500-year-old tomb has stones richly decorated with patterns. www.knowth.com/newgrange **30 A2**

Ring of Kerry
Route around the Iveragh peninsula with beautiful lakes (Lough Leane), peaks overlooking the coastline and islands (Valencia Island, Skelling). Also: Killarney; ruins of 15c Muckross Abbey. www.ringofkerrytourism.com **29 B2**

Italy Italia
www.enit.it

Northern Italy

Alps
Wonderful stretch of the Alps running from the Swiss and French borders to Austria. The region of Valle d'Aosta is one of the most popular ski regions, bordered by the highest peaks of the Alps. www.thealps.com **108–109 & 119–120**

Arezzo
Beautiful old town set on a hill dominated by 13c cathedral. Piazza Grande is surrounded by medieval and Renaissance palaces. Main sight: Piero della Francesca's frescoes in the choir of San Francesco. www.arezzocitta.com **135 B4**

Assisi
Hill-top town that attracts crowds of pilgrims to the shrine of St Francis of Assisi at the Basilica di San Francesco, consisting of two churches, Lower and Upper, with superb frescoes (particularly Giotto's in the Upper). www.assisi.com **136 B1**

Bologna
Elegant city with oldest university in Italy. Historical centre around Piazza Maggiore and Piazza del Nettuno with the Town Hall, Palazzo del Podestà, Basilica di San Petronio. Other churches: San Domenico; San Giacomo Maggiore. The two towers (one incomplete) are symbols of the city. Good collec-

tion in the National Gallery (Bolognese). www.commune.bologna.it/bolognaturismo **135 A4**

Dolomites Dolomiti
Part of the Alps, this mountain range spreads over the region of Trentino-Alto Adige, with the most picturesque scenery between Bolzano and Cortina d'Ampezzo. www.dolomiti.it **121 A4**

Ferrara
Old town centre around Romanesque-Gothic cathedral and Palazzo Communale. Also: Castello Estense; Palazzo Schifanoia (frescoes); Palazzo dei Diamanti housing Pinacoteca Nazionale. www.ferraraturismo.it **121 C4**

Florence Firenze
City with exceptionally rich medieval and Renaissance heritage. Piazza del Duomo has:13–15c cathedral (first dome since antiquity); 14c campanile; 11c baptistry (bronze doors). Piazza della Signoria has: 14c Palazzo Vecchio (frescoes); Loggia della Signoria (sculpture); 16c Uffizi Gallery with one of the world's greatest collections (13–18c). Other great paintings: Museo di San Marco; Palatine Gallery in 15–16c

Pitti Palace surrounded by Boboli Gardens. Sculpture: Cathedral Works Museum; Bargello Museum; Academy Gallery (Michelangelo's *David*). Among many other Renaissance palaces: Medici-Riccardi; Rucellai; Strozzi. The 15c church of San Lorenzo has Michelangelo's tombs of the

Medici. Many churches have richly frescoed chapels: Santa Maria Novella, Santa Croce, Santa Maria del Carmine. The 13c Ponte Vecchio is one of the most famous sights. www.firenzeturismo.it **135 B4**

Italian Lakes
Beautiful district at the foot of the Alps, most of the lakes with holiday resorts. Many lakes are surrounded by aristocratic villas (Maggiore, Como, Garda). **120–121**

Il Redentore (cutaway), Venice, Italy

Mantua Mántova
Attractive city surrounded by three lakes. Two exceptional palaces: Palazzo Ducale (Sala del Pisanello; Camera degli Sposi, Castello San Giorgio); luxurious Palazzo Tè (brilliant frescoes). Also: 15c Church of Sant'Andrea; 13c law courts. www.mantova.com **121 B3**

Milan Milano
Modern city, Italy's fashion and design capital (Corso and

Galleria Vittoro Emmanuelle II). Churches include: Gothic cathedral (1386–1813), the world's largest (4c baptistry); Romanesque St Ambrose; 15c San Satiro; Santa Maria delle Grazie with Leonardo da Vinci's *Last Supper* in the convent refectory. Great art collections, Brera Gallery, Ambrosian Library, Museum of Contemporary Art. Castello Sforzesco (15c, 19c) also has a gallery. The famous La Scala theatre opened in 1778. Nearby: monastery at Pavia. www.milaninfotourist.com **120 B2**

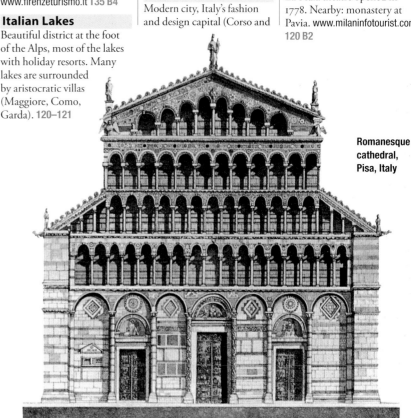

Romanesque cathedral, Pisa, Italy

Padua Pádova

Pleasant old town with arcaded streets. Basilica del Santo is a place of pilgrimage to the tomb of St Anthony. Giotto's frescoes in the Scrovegni chapel are exceptional. Also: Piazza dei Signori with Palazzo del Capitano; vast Palazzo della Ragione; church of the Eremitani (frescoes). www.turismopadova.it **121 B4**

Parma

Attractive city centre, famous for Correggio's frescoes in the Romanesque cathedral and church of St John the Evangelist, and Parmigianino's frescoes in the church of Madonna della Steccata. Their works are also in the National Gallery. www.commune.parma.it **120 C3**

Perúgia

Hill-top town centred around Piazza Quattro Novembre with the cathedral, Fontana Maggiore and Palazzo dei Priori. Also: Collegio di Cambio (frescoes); National Gallery of Umbria; many churches. www.perugiaonline.com **136 B1**

Pisa

Medieval town centred on the Piazza dei Miracoli. Sights: famous Romanesque Leaning Tower, Romanesque cathedral (excellent façade, Gothic pulpit); 12–13c Baptistry; 13c Camposanto cloistered cemetery (fascinating 14c frescoes). www.commune.pisa.it **134 B3**

Ravenna

Ancient town with exceptionally well-preserved Byzantine mosaics. The finest are in 5c Mausoleo di Galla Placidia and 6c Basilica di San Vitale. Good mosaics also in the basilicas of Sant'Apollinare in Classe and Sant'Apollinare Nuovo. www.turismo.ravenna.it **135 A5**

Siena

Outstanding 13–14c medieval town centred on beautiful Piazza del Campo with Gothic Palazzo Publico (frescoes of secular life). Delightful Romanesque-Gothic Duomo (Libreria Piccolomini, baptistry, art works). Many other richly decorated churches. Fine Sienese painting in Pinacoteca Nazionale and Museo dell'Opera del Duomo. www.terresiena.it **135 B4**

Turin Torino

City centre has 17-18c Baroque layout dominated by twin Baroque churches. Also:

15c cathedral (holds Turin Shroud); Palazzo Reale; 18c Superga Basilica; Academy of Science with two museums (Egyptian antiquities; European painting). www.commune.torino.it **119 B4**

Urbino

Set in beautiful hilly landscape, Urbino's heritage is mainly due to the 15c court of Federico da Montefeltro at the magnificent Ducal Palace (notable Studiolo), now also a gallery. www.turismo. pesaurbino.it **136 B1**

Venice Venezia

Stunning old city built on islands in a lagoon, with some 150 canals. The Grand Canal is crossed by the famous 16c Rialto Bridge and is lined with elegant palaces (Gothic Ca'd'Oro and Ca'Foscari, Renaissance Palazzo Grimani, Baroque Rezzonico). The district of San Marco has the core of the best known sights and is centred on Piazza San Marco with 11c Basilica di San Marco (bronze horses, 13c mosaics); Campanile (exceptional views) and Ducal Palace (connected with the prison by the famous Bridge of Sighs). Many churches (Santa Maria Gloriosa dei Frari, Santa Maria della Salute, Redentore, San Giorgio Maggiore, San Giovanni e Paolo) and scuole (Scuola di San Rocco, Scuola di San Giorgio degli Schiavoni) have excellent works of art. The Gallery of the Academy houses superb 14–18c Venetian art. The Guggenheim Museum holds 20c art. http://english.comune. venezia.it **122 B1**

Verona

Old town with remains of 1c Roman Arena and medieval sights including the Palazzo degli Scaligeri; Arche Scaligere; Romanesque Santa Maria Antica; Castelvecchio; Ponte Scaliger. The famous 14c House of Juliet has associations with *Romeo and Juliet*. Many churches with fine art works (cathedral; Sant'Anastasia; basilica di San Zeno Maggiore). www.tourism.verona.it **121 B4**

Vicenza

Beautiful town, famous for the architecture of Palladio, including the Olympic Theatre (extraordinary stage), Corso Palladio with many of his palaces, and Palazzo Chiericati. Nearby: Villa Rotonda, the most influential of all Palladian buildings.

www.vicenzae.org **121 B4**

Southern Italy

Naples Napoli

Historical centre around Gothic cathedral (crypt). Spaccanapoli area has numerous churches (bizarre Cappella Sansevero, Gesù Nuovo, Gothic Santa Chiara with fabulous tombs). Buildings: 13c Castello Nuovo; 13c Castel dell'Ovo; 15c Palazzo Cuomo. Museums: National Archeological Museum (artefacts from Pompeii and Herculaneum); National Museum of Capodimonte (Renaissance painting). Nearby: spectacular coast around Amalfi; Pompeii; Herculaneum. www.inaples.it **170 C2**

Orvieto

Medieval hill-top town with a number of monuments including the Romanesque-Gothic cathedral (façade, frescoes). www.commune.orvieto.tr.it **168 A2**

Rome Roma

Capital of Italy, exceptionally rich in sights from many eras. Ancient sights: Colosseum; Arch of Constantine; Trajan's Column; Roman and Imperial

fora; hills of Palatino and Campidoglio (Capitoline Museum shows antiquities); Pantheon; Castel Sant' Angelo; Baths of Caracalla). Early Christian sights: catacombs (San Calisto, San Sebastiano, Domitilla); basilicas (San Giovanni in Laterano, Santa Maria Maggiore, San Paolo Fuori le Mura). Rome is known for richly decorated Baroque churches: il Gesù, Sant'Ignazio, Santa Maria della Vittoria, Chiesa Nuova. Other churches, often with art

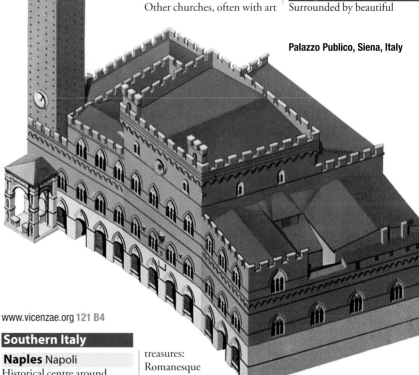

Palazzo Publico, Siena, Italy

treasures: Romanesque Santa Maria in Cosmedin, Gothic Santa Maria Sopra Minerva, Renaissance Santa Maria del Popolo, San Pietro in Vincoli. Several Renaissance and Baroque palaces and villas house superb art collections (Palazzo Barberini, Palazzo Doria Pamphilj, Palazzo Spada, Palazzo Corsini, Villa Giulia, Galleria Borghese) and are beautifully frescoed (Villa Farnesina). Fine Baroque public spaces with fountains: Piazza Navona; Piazza di Spagna with the Spanish Steps; also Trevi Fountain. Nearby: Tivoli; Villa Adriana. Rome also contains the Vatican City (Città del Vaticano). www.romaturismo.com **168 B2**

Volcanic Region

Region from Naples to Sicily. Mount Etna is one of the most famous European volcanoes. Vesuvius dominates the Bay of Naples and has at its foot two of Italy's finest Roman sites, Pompeii and Herculaneum, both destroyed by its eruption

in 79ad. Stromboli is one of the beautiful Aeolian Islands.

Sardinia Sardegna

Sardinia has some of the most beautiful beaches in Italy (Alghero). Unique are the nuraghi, some 7000 stone constructions (Su Nuraxi, Serra Orios), the remains of an old civilization (1500–400 BC). Old towns include Cagliari and Sássari. www.sardi.it **178–179**

Sicily Sicilia

Surrounded by beautiful beaches and full of monuments of many periods, Sicily is the largest island in the Mediterranean. Taormina with its Greek theatre has one of the most spectacular beaches, lying under the mildly active volcano Mount Etna. Also: Agrigento; Palermo, Siracusa. www. regione.sicilia.it/turismo/web_ turismo **176–177**

Agrigento

Set on a hill above the sea and famed for the Valley of the Temples. The nine originally 5c BC Doric temples are Sicily's best-preserved Greek remains. www.agrigento-sicilia.it **176 B2**

Palermo

City with Moorish, Norman and Baroque architecture, especially around the main squares (Quattro Canti, Piazza Pretoria, Piazza Bellini). Sights: remains of Norman palace (12c Palatine Chapel); Norman cathedral; Regional Gallery (medieval); some 8000 preserved bodies in the

catacombs of the Cappuchin Convent. Nearby: 12c Norman Duomo di Monreale. www.commune.palermo.it **176 A2**

Syracuse Siracusa

Built on an island connected to the mainland by a bridge, the old town has a 7c cathedral, ruins of the Temple of Apollo; Fountain of Arethusa; archaeological museum. On the mainland: 5c BC Greek theatre with seats cut out of rock; Greek fortress of Euralus; 2c Roman amphitheatre; 5–6c Catacombs of St John. www.apt-siracusa.it **177 B4**

Latvia Latvija

www.lv

Riga

Well-preserved medieval town centre around the cathedral. Sights: Riga Castle; medieval Hanseatic houses; Great Guild Hall; Gothic Church of St Peter; Art Nouveau buildings in the New Town. Nearby: Baroque Rundale Castle. www.riga.lv **8 D4**

Lithuania Lietuva

www.tourism.lt

Vilnius

Baroque old town with fine architecture including: cathedral; Gediminas Tower; university complex; Archbishop's Palace; Church of St Anne. Also: remains of Jewish life; Vilnius Picture Gallery (16–19c regional); Lithuanian National Museum. www.vilnius.lt **13 A6**

Luxembourg

www.ont.lu

Luxembourg

Capital of Luxembourg, built on a rock with fine views. Old town is around the Place d'Armes. Buildings: Grand Ducal Palace; fortifications of Rocher du Bock; cathedral. Museum of History and Art holds an excellent regional collection. www.ont.lu **92 B2**

Macedonia Makedonija

www.macedonia.org

Skopje

Historic town with Turkish citadel, fine 15c mosques, oriental bazaar, ancient bridge. Superb Byzantine churches nearby. **182 A3** www.skopjeonline.com.mk

Ohrid

Old town, beautifully set by a lake, with houses of wood and brick, remains of a Turkish citadel, many churches (two cathedrals; St Naum south of the lake). www.ohrid.org.mk **182 B2**

Malta

www.visitmalta.com

Valletta

Capital of Malta. Historic walled city, founded in 16c by the Maltese Knights, with 16c Grand Master's Palace and a richly decorated cathedral. **175 C3**

Monaco

www.visitmonaco.com

Monaco

Major resort area in a beautiful location. Sights include: Monte Carlo casino, Prince's Palace at Monaco-Ville; 19c cathedral; oceanographic museum. www.visitmonaco.com **133 B3**

The Netherlands Nederland

www.visitholland.com

Amsterdam

Capital of the Netherlands. Old centre has picturesque canals lined with distinctive elegant 17–18c merchants' houses. Dam Square has 15c New Church and Royal Palace. Other churches include Westerkerk. The Museumplein has three world-famous museums: Rijksmuseum (several art collections including 15–17c painting); Van Gogh

Westerkerk, Amsterdam, Netherlands

Museum; Municipal Museum (art from 1850 on). Other museums: Anne Frank House; Jewish Historical Museum; Rembrandt House. www.visitamsterdam.nl **70 B1**

Delft

Well-preserved old Dutch town with gabled red-roofed houses along canals. Gothic churches: New Church; Old Church. Famous for Delftware (two museums). www.delft.nl **70 B1**

The Hague Den Haag

Seat of Government and of the royal house of the Netherlands. The 17c Mauritshuis houses the Royal Picture Gallery (excellent 15–18c Flemish and Dutch). Other good collections: Prince William V Gallery; Hesdag Museum; Municipal Museum www.denhaag.nl **70 B1**

Haarlem

Many medieval gabled houses centred on the Great Market with 14c Town Hall and 15c Church of St Bavon. Museums: Frans Hals Museum; Teylers Museum. www.haarlem.nl **70 B1**

Het Loo

Former royal palace and gardens set in a vast landscape (commissioned by future Queen of England, Mary Stuart). www.paleishetloo.nl **70 B2**

Keukenhof

Landscaped gardens, planted with bulbs of many varieties, are the largest flower gardens in the world. www.keukenhof.nl **70 B1**

Leiden

University town of beautiful gabled houses set along canals. The Rijksmuseum Van Oudheden is Holland's most important home to archaeological artefacts from the Antiquity. The 16c Hortus Botanicus is one of the oldest botanical gardens in Europe. The Cloth Hall with van Leyden's *Last Judgement*. www.leidenpromotie.nl **70 B1**

Rotterdam

The largest port in the world. The Boymans-van Beuningen Museum has a huge and excellent decorative and fine art collection (old and modern). Nearby: 18c Kinderdijk with 19 windmills. www.rotterdam.nl **79 A4**

Utrecht

Delightful old town centre along canals with the Netherlands' oldest university and Gothic cathedral. Good art collections: Central Museum; National Museum. www.utrecht.nl **70 B2**

Norway Norge

www.norway.no

Bergen

Norway's second city in a scenic setting. The Quay has many painted wooden medieval buildings. Sights: 12c Romanesque St Mary's Church; Bergenhus fortress with 13c Haakon's Hall; Rosenkrantztårnet; Grieghallen; Rasmus Meyer Collection (Norwegian art); Bryggens Museum. www.visitbergen.com **46 B2**

Lappland (Norwegian)

Vast land of Finnmark is home to the Sámi. Nordkapp is the northern point of Europe. Also Finland, Sweden. www.lappland.no **192–193**

Norwegian Fjords

Beautiful and majestic landscape of deep glacial valleys filled by the sea. The most thrilling fjords are between Bergen and Ålesund. www.fjords.com **46 & 198**

Oslo

Capital of Norway with a modern centre. Buildings: 17c cathedral; 19c city hall, 19c royal palace; 19c Stortinget (housing parliament); 19c University; 13c Akershus (castle); 12c Akerskirke (church). Museums: National Gallery; Munch Museum; Viking Ship Museum; Folk Museum (reconstructed buildings). www.visitoslo.com **48 C2**

Stavkirker

Wooden medieval stave churches of bizarre pyramidal structure, carved with images from Nordic mythology. Best preserved in southern Norway.

Tromsø

Main arctic city of Norway with a university and two cathedrals. www.destinasjontromso.no **192 C3**

Trondheim

Set on the edge of a fjord, a modern city with the superb Nidaros cathedral (rebuilt 19c). Also: Stiftsgaard (royal

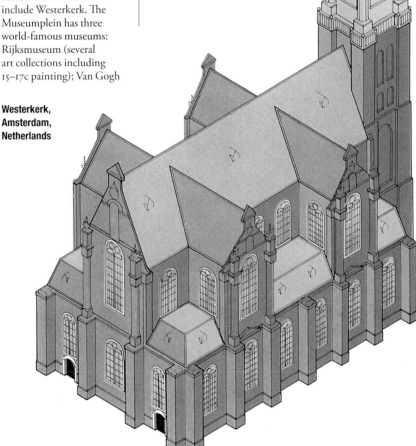

residence); Applied Arts Museum. www.trondheim.com **199 B7**

Poland Polska

www.poland.pl

Częstochowa

Centre of Polish Catholicism, with the 14c monastery of Jasna Góra a pilgrimage site to the icon of the Black Madonna for six centuries. **86 B3**

Gdańsk

Medieval centre with: 14c Town Hall (state rooms); Gothic brick St Mary's Church, Poland's largest; Long Market has fine buildings (Artus Court); National Art Museum. www.gdansk.pl **69 A3**

Kraków

Old university city, rich in architecture, centred on superb 16c Marketplace with Gothic-Renaissance Cloth Hall containing the Art Gallery (19c Polish), Clock Tower, Gothic red-brick St Mary's Church (altarpiece). Czartoryski Palace has city's finest art collection. Wawel Hill has the Gothic cathedral and splendid Renaissance Royal Palace. The former Jewish ghetto in Kazimierz district has 16c Old Synagogue, now a museum. www.krakow.pl **99 A3**

Poznań

Town centred on the Old Square with Renaissance Town Hall and Baroque mansions. Also: medieval castle; Gothic cathedral; National Museum (European masters). www.plot.poznan.pl **76 B1**

Tatry

One of Europe's most delightful mountain ranges with many beautiful ski resorts (Zakopane). Also in Slovakia. **99 B3**

Warsaw Warszawa

Capital of Poland, with many historic monuments in the Old Town with the Royal Castle (museum) and Old Town Square surrounded by reconstructed 17–18c merchants' houses. Several churches including: Gothic cathedral; Baroque Church of the Nuns of Visitation. Richly decorated royal palaces and gardens: Neoclassical Łazienki Palace; Baroque palace in Wilanów. The National Museum has Polish and European art. www.warsawtour.pl **77 C6**

Wrocław

Historic town centred on the Market Square with 15c Town Hall and mansions. Churches: Baroque cathedral; St Elizabeth; St Adalbert. National Museum displays fine art. Vast painting of Battle of Racławice is specially housed. www.wroclaw.pl **85 A5**

Portugal

www.visitportugal.pt

Alcobaça

Monastery of Santa Maria, one of the best examples of a Cistercian abbey, founded in 1147 (exterior 17–18c). The church is Portugal's largest (14c tombs). **154 A1**

Algarve

Modern seaside resorts among picturesque sandy beaches and rocky coves (Praia da Rocha). Old towns: Lagos; Faro. www.rtalgarve.pt **160 B1**

Batalha

Abbey is one of the masterpieces of French Gothic and Manueline architecture (tombs, English Perpendicular chapel, unfinished pantheon). **154 A2**

Braga

Historic town with cathedral and large Archbishop's Palace. www.cm-braga.com.pt **148 A1**

Coimbra

Old town with narrow streets set on a hill. The Romanesque cathedral is particularly fine (portal). The university (founded 1290) has a fascinating Baroque library. Also: Museum of Machado de Castro; many monasteries and convents. **148 B1**

Évora

Centre of the town, surrounded by walls, has narrow streets of Moorish character and medieval and Renaissance architecture. Churches: 12–13c Gothic cathedral; São Francisco with a chapel decorated with bones of some 5000 monks; 15c Convent of Dos Lóis. The Jesuit university was founded in 1559. Museum of Évora holds fine art (particularly Flemish and Portugese). **154 B3**

Guimarães

Old town with a castle with seven towers on a vast keep. Churches: Romanesque chapel of São Miguel; São Francisco. Alberto Sampaio Museum and Martins Sarmento Museum are excellent. **148 A1**

Lisbon Lisboa

Capital of Portugal. Baixa is the Neoclassical heart of Lisbon with the Praça do Comércio and Rossío squares. São Jorge castle (Visigothic, Moorish, Romanesque) is surrounded by the medieval quarters. Bairro Alto is famous for *fado* (songs). Monastery of Jerónimos is exceptional. Churches: 12c cathedral; São Vicente de Fora; São Roque (tiled chapels); Torre de Belém; Convento da Madre de Deus. Museums: Gulbenkian Museum (ancient, oriental, European), National Museum of Antique Art (old masters), Modern Art Centre; Azulejo Museum (decorative tiles). Nearby: palatial monastic complex Mafra; royal resort Sintra. www.cm-lisboa.pt **154 B1**

Porto

Historic centre with narrow streets. Views from Clérigos Tower. Churches: São Francisco; cathedral. Soares dos Reis Museum holds fine and decorative arts (18–19c). The suburb of Vila Nova de Gaia is the centre for port wine. www.portoturismo.pt **148 A1**

Tomar

Attractive town with the Convento de Cristo, founded in 1162 as the headquarters of the Knights Templar (Charola temple, chapter house, Renaissance cloisters). **154 A2**

Romania

www.turism.ro

Bucovina

Beautiful region in northern Romanian Moldova renowned for a number of 15–16c monasteries and their fresco cycles. Of particular note are Moldovita, Voroneţ and Suceviţa. **17 B6**

Bucharest Bucureşti

Capital of Romania with the majority of sites along the Calea Victoriei and centring on Piaţa Revoluţiei with 19c Romanian Athenaeum and 1930s Royal Palace housing the National Art Gallery. The infamous 1980s Civic Centre with People's Palace is a symbol of dictatorial aggrandisement. www.bucuresti.ro **17 C7**

Carpathian Mountains Carpaţii

The beautiful Carpathian Mountains have several ski resorts (Sinaia) and peaks noted for first-rate mountaineering (Făgă raşuiui, Rodnei).

Danube Delta Europe's largest marshland, a spectacular nature reserve. Travel in the area is by boat, with Tulcea the starting point for visitors. The Romanian Black Sea Coast has a stretch of resorts (Mamaia, Eforie) between Constantaţ and the border, and well-preserved Roman remains in Histria. **17 B6**

Transylvania Transilvania

Beautiful and fascinating scenic region of medieval citadels (Timişoara, Sibiu) provides a setting for the haunting image of the legendary Dracula (Sighişoara, Braşov, Bran Castle). Cluj-Napoca is the main town. **17 B5**

Russia Rossiya

www.russia.com

Moscow Moskva

Capital of Russia, with many monuments. Within the Kremlin's red walls are: 15c Cathedral of the Dormition; 16c Cathedral of the Archangel; Cathedral of the Annunciation (icons), Armour Palace. Outside the walls, Red Square has the Lenin Mausoleum and 16c St Basil's Cathedral. There are a number of monasteries (16c Novodevichi). Two superb museums: Tretiakov Art Gallery (Russian); Pushkin Museum of Fine Art (European). Kolomenskoe, once a royal summer retreat, has the Church of the Ascension. The VDNKh is a symbol of the Stalinist era. www.moscow-guide.ru **9 E10**

Novgorod

One of Russia's oldest towns, centred on 15c Kremlin with St Sophia Cathedral (iconostasis, west door). Two other cathedrals: St Nicholas; St George. Museum of History, Architecture and Art has notable icons and other artefacts. www.novgorod.ru **9 C7**

Petrodvorets

Grand palace with numerous pavilions (Monplaisir) set in beautiful parkland interwoven by a system of fountains, cascades and waterways connected to the sea. www.petrodvorets.ru **9 C6**

Pushkin

(Tsarskoye Selo) Birthplace of Alexander Pushkin, with the vast Baroque Catherine Palace – splendid state apartments, beautiful gardens and lakes. www.pushkin-town.net **9 C7**

Saint Petersburg Sankt Peterburg

Founded in 1703 with the SS Peter and Paul Fortress and its cathedral by Peter the Great, and functioning as seat of court and government until 1918. Many of the most famous sights are around elegant Nevski Prospekt. The Hermitage, one of the world's largest and finest art collections, is housed in five buildings including the Baroque Winter and Summer palaces. The Mikhailovsky Palace houses the Russian Museum (Russian art). Other sights: neoclassical Admiralty; 19c St Isaac's Cathedral and St Kazan Cathedral; Vasilievsky Island with 18c Menshikov Palace; Alexander Nevsky Monastery; 18c Smolny Convent. www.spb.ru **9 C7**

Sergiev Posad

(Zagorsk) Trinity St Sergius monastery with 15c cathedral. www.musobl.divo.ru **9 D11**

Serbia Srbija

www.serbia-tourism.org

Belgrade Beograd

Capital of Serbia. The largely modern city is set between the Danube and Sava rivers. The National Museum holds European art. To the south there are numerous fascinating medieval monasteries, richly embellished with frescoes. www.belgradetourism.org.yu **127 C2**

Spain España

www.spaintour.com

Ávila

Medieval town with 2km-long 11c walls. Pilgrimage site to shrines to St Teresa of Ávila (Convent of Santa Teresa, Convent of the Incarnation). www.avila.world-guides.com **150 B3**

Barcelona

Showcase of Gothic ('Barri Gòtic': cathedral; Santa María del Mar; mansions on Carrer de Montcada) and *modernista* architecture ('Eixample' area with Manzana de la Discòrdia; Sagrada Familia, Güell Park, La Pedrera). Many elegant boulevards (La Rambla, Passeig de Gràcia). Museums: Modern Catalan Art; Picasso Museum, Miró Museum; Tàpies Museum. Nearby: monastery of Montserrat (Madonna); Figueres (Dali Museum). www.barcelonaturisme.com **147 C3**

Burgos
Medieval town with Gothic cathedral, Moorish-Gothic Royal Monastery and Charterhouse of Miraflores. www.burgos.es **143 B3**

Cáceres
Medieval town surrounded by originally Moorish walls and with several aristocratic palaces with solars. www.caceres.es **155 A4**

Córdoba
Capital of Moorish Spain with a labyrinth of streets and houses with tile-decorated patios. The 8–10c Mezquita is the finest mosque in Spain. A 16c cathedral was added at the centre of the building and a 17c tower replaced the minaret. The old Jewish quarter has 14c synagogue www.cordoba.es **156 C3**

El Escorial
Immense Renaissance complex of palatial and monastic buildings and mausoleum of the Spanish monarchs. www.patrimonionacional.es/escorial/escorial.htm **151 B3**

Granada
The Alhambra was hill-top palace-fortress of the rulers of the last Moorish kingdom and is the most splendid example of Moorish art and architecture in Spain. The complex has three principal parts: Alcazaba fortress (11c); Casa Real palace (14c, with later Palace of Carlos V); Generalife gardens. Also: Moorish quarter; gypsy quarter; Royal Chapel with good art in the sacristy. www.granadatur.com **163 A4**

León
Gothic cathedral has notable stained glass. Royal Pantheon commemorates early kings of Castile and León. **142 B1**

Madrid
Capital of Spain, a mainly modern city with 17–19c architecture at its centre around Plaza Mayor. Sights: Royal Palace with lavish apartments; Descalzas Reales Convent (tapestries and other works); Royal Armoury museum. Spain's three leading galleries: Prado (15–18c); Queen Sofia Centre (20c Spanish, Picasso's *Guernica*); Thyssen-Bornemisza Museum (medieval to modern). www.munimadrid.es **151 B4**

Oviedo
Gothic cathedral with 12c sanctuary. Three Visigoth (9c) churches: Santullano, Santa María del Naranco, San

El Escorial (cutaway), Spain

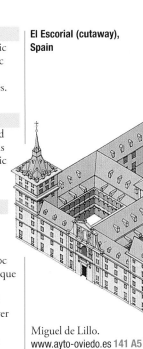

Miguel de Lillo. www.ayto-oviedo.es **141 A5**

Palma
Situated on Mallorca, the largest and most beautiful of the Balearic islands, with an impressive Gothic cathedral. www.a-palma.es **166 B2**

Picos de Europa
Mountain range with river gorges and peaks topped by Visigothic and Romanesque churches. **142 A2**

Pyrenees
Unspoiled mountain range with beautiful landscape and villages full of Romanesque architecture (cathedral of Jaca). The Ordesa National Park has many waterfalls and canyons. **144–145**

Salamanca
Delightful old city with some uniquely Spanish architecture: Renaissance Plateresque is famously seen on 16c portal of the university (founded 1215); Baroque Churrigueresque on 18c Plaza Mayo; both styles at the Convent of San Estaban. Also: Romanesque Old Cathedral; Gothic-Plateresque New Cathedral; House of Shells. www.salamanca.com **150 B2**

Santiago di Compostela
Medieval city with many churches and religious institutions. The famous pilgrimage to the shrine of St James the Apostle ends here in the magnificent cathedral, originally Romanesque with many later elements (18c Baroque façade). www.santiagoturismo.com **140 B2**

Segovia
Old town set on a rock with a 1c Roman aqueduct. Also: 16c Gothic cathedral; Alcázar (14–15c, rebuilt 19c); 12-sided 13c Templar church of Vera Cruz. www.viasegovia.com **151 B3**

Seville Sevilla
City noted for festivals and flamenco. The world's largest Gothic cathedral (15c) retains the Orange Court and minaret of a mosque. The Alcazar is a fine example of Moorish architecture. The massive 18c tobacco factory, now part of the university, was the setting for Bizet's *Carmen*. Barrio de Santa Cruz is the old Jewish quarter with narrow streets and white houses. Casa de Pilatos (15–16c) has a fine domestic patio. Hospital de la Caridad has good Spanish painting. Nearby: Roman Italica with amphitheatre. www.sevilla.org **162 A2**

Tarragona
The city and its surroundings have some of the best-preserved Roman heritage in Spain. Also: Gothic cathedral (cloister); Archaeological Museum. www.tarragona.es **147 C2**

Toledo
Historic city with Moorish, Jewish and Christian sights. The small 11c mosque of El Cristo de la Luz is one of the earliest in Spain. Two synagogues have been preserved: Santa María la Blanca; El Tránsito. Churches: San Juan de los Reyes; Gothic cathedral (good artworks). El Greco's *Burial of the Count of Orgaz* is in the Church of Santo Tomé. More of his works are in the El Greco house and, with other art, in Hospital de Santa Cruz. www.toledo.es **151 C3**

Valencia
The old town has houses and palaces with elaborate façades. Also: Gothic cathedral and Lonja de la Seda church. www.comunitatvalenciana.com **159 B3**

Zaragoza
Town notable for Moorish architecture (11c Aljafería Palace). The Basilica de Nuestra Señora del Pilar, one of two cathedrals, is highly venerated. www.zaragoza-ciudad.com **153 A3**

Slovenia Slovenija
www.slovenia-tourism.si

Istria Istra
Two town centres, Koper and Piran, with medieval and Renaissance squares and Baroque palaces. See also Croatia. www.slo-istra.com **122 B2**

Julian Alps Julijske Alpe
Wonderfully scenic section of the Alps with lakes (Bled, Bohinj), deep valleys (Planica, Vrata) and ski resorts (Kranjska Gora, Bohinjska Bistrica). **122 A2**

Karst Caves
Numerous caves with huge galleries, extraordinary stalactites and stalagmites, and underground rivers. The most spectacular are Postojna (the most famous, with Predjamski Castle nearby) and Škocjan. www.postojnska-jama.si **123 B3**

Ljubljana
Capital of Slovenia. The old town, dominated by the castle (good views), is principally between Prešeren Square and Town Hall (15c, 18c), with the Three Bridges and colonnaded market. Many Baroque churches (cathedral, St Jacob, St Francis, Ursuline) and palaces (Bishop's Palace, Seminary, Gruber Palace). Also: 17c Križanke church and monastery complex; National Gallery and Modern Gallery show Slovene art. www.ljubljana.si **123 A3**

Slovakia Slovenska Republika
www.slovenska-republika.com

Bratislava
Capital of Slovakia, dominated by the castle (Slovak National Museum, good views). Old Town centred on the Main Square with Old Town Hall and Jesuit Church. Many 18–19c palaces (Mirbach Palace, Pálffy Palace, Primate's Palace), churches (Gothic cathedral, Corpus Christi Chapel) and museums (Slovak National Gallery). www.bratislava.sk **111 A4**

Košice
Charming old town with many Baroque and neoclassical buildings and Gothic cathedral. www.kosice.sk **12 D4**

Spišské Podhradie

Region, east of the Tatry, full of picturesque medieval towns (Levoča, Kežmarok, Prešov) and architectural monuments (Spišský Castle). **99 B4**

Tatry

Beautiful mountain region. Poprad is an old town with 19c villas. Starý Smokovec is a popular ski resort. See also Poland. www.tatry.sk **99 B3**

Sweden Sverige

www.sweden.se

Abisko

Popular resort in the Swedish part of Lapland set in an inspiring landscape of lakes and mountains.
www.abisko.nu **194 B9**

Gothenburg Göteborg

Largest port in Sweden, the historic centre has 17–18c Dutch architectural character (Kronhuset). The Art Museum has interesting Swedish works.
www.goteborg.com **60 B1**

Gotland

Island with Sweden's most popular beach resorts (Ljugarn) and unspoiled countryside with churches in Baltic Gothic style (Dahlem, Bunge). Visby is a pleasant walled medieval town.
www.gotland.se **57 C4**

Lappland (Swedish)

Swedish part of Lappland with 18c Arvidsjaur the oldest preserved Sámi village. Jokkmokk is a Sámi cultural centre, Abisko a popular resort in fine scenery. Also Finland, Norway. www.lappland.se **192–193**

Lund

Charming university city with medieval centre and a fine 12c Romanesque cathedral (14c astronomical clock, carved tombs). www.lund.se **61 D3**

Malmö

Old town centre set among canals and parks dominated by a red-brick castle (museums) and a vast market square with Town Hall and Gothic Church of St Peter.
www.malmo.se **61 D3**

Mora

Delightful village on the shores of Siljan Lake in the heart of the Dalarna region, home to folklore and traditional crafts.
www.mora.se **50 A1**

Stockholm

Capital of Sweden built on a number of islands. The Old Town is largely on three islands with 17–18c houses, Baroque Royal Castle (apartments and museums), Gothic cathedral, parliament. Riddarholms church has tombs of the monarchy. Museums include: Modern Gallery (one of world's best modern collections); Nordiska Museet (cultural history); open-air Skansen (Swedish houses). Baroque Drottningholm Castle is the residence of the monarchy.
www.stockholm.se
57 A4

Swedish Lakes

Beautiful region around the Vättern and Vänern Lakes. Siljan Lake is in the Dalarna region where folklore and crafts are preserved (Leksand, Mora, Rättvik).
55 B4

Uppsala

Appealing university town with a medieval centre around the massive Gothic cathedral.
www.uppsala.se **51 C4**

Switzerland Schweiz

www.myswitzerland.com

Alps

The most popular Alpine region is the Berner Oberland with the town of Interlaken a starting point for exploring the large number of picturesque peaks (Jungfrau). The valleys of the Graubünden have famous ski resorts (Davos, St Moritz). Zermatt lies below the highest and most recognizable Swiss peak, the Matterhorn.
www.thealps.com **119 A4**

Basle Basel

Medieval university town with Romanesque-Gothic cathedral (tomb of Erasmus). Superb collections: Art Museum; Museum of Contemporary Art. www.baseltourismus.ch
106 B2

Bern

Capital of Switzerland. Medieval centre has fountains, characteristic streets (Spitalgasse) and tower-gates. The Bärengraben is famed for its bears. Also: Gothic cathedral; good Fine Arts Museum. www.berne.ch
106 C2

Geneva Genève

Wonderfully situated on the lake with the world's highest fountain. The historic area is centred on the Romanesque cathedral and Place du Bourg du Four. Excellent collections: Art and History Museum;

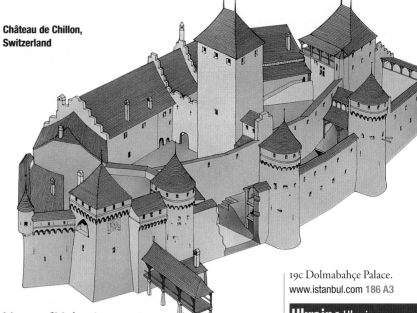

Château de Chillon, Switzerland

Museum of Modern Art in 19c Petit Palais. On the lake shore: splendid medieval Château de Chillon.
www.geneva-tourism.ch **118 A3**

Interlaken

Starting point for excursions to the most delightful part of the Swiss Alps, the Bernese Oberland, with Grindelwald and Lauterbrunnen – one of the most thrilling valleys leading up to the ski resort of Wengen with views on the Jungfrau.
www.interlakentourism.ch
106 C2

Lucerne Luzern

On the beautiful shores of Vierwaldstättersee, a charming medieval town of white houses on narrow streets and of wooden bridges (Kapellbrücke, Spreuerbrücke). It is centred on the Kornmarkt with the Renaissance Old Town Hall and Am Rhyn-Haus (Picasso collection). www.luzern.org
106 C1

Zürich

Set on Zürichsee, the old quarter is around Niederdorf with 15c cathedral. Gothic Fraumünster has stained glass by Chagall. Museums: Swiss National Museum (history); Art Museum (old and modern masters); Bührle Foundation (Impressionists, Post-impressionists). www.zuerich.com
107 B3

Turkey Türkiye

www.tourismturkey.org

Istanbul

Divided by the spectcular Bosphorus, the stretch of water that separates Europe from Asia, the historic district is surrounded by the Golden Horn, Sea of Marmara and the 5c wall of Theodosius. Major sights: 6c Byzantine church of St Sophia (converted first to a mosque in 1453 and then a museum in 1934); 15c Topkapi Palace; treasury and Archaeological Museum; 17c Blue Mosque; 19c Bazaar; 16c Süleymaniye Mosque; 12c Kariye Camii; European district with Galata Tower and 19c Dolmabahçe Palace.
www.istanbul.com **186 A3**

Ukraine Ukraina

www.ukraine.com

Kiev Kyïv

Capital of Ukraine, known for its cathedral (11c, 17c) with Byzantine frescoes and mosaics. The Monastery of the Caves has churches, monastic buildings and catacombs.
www.uazone.net/kiev **13 C9**

Vatican City
Città del Vaticano

www.vatican.va

Vatican City
Città del Vaticano

Independent state within Rome. On Piazza San Pietro is the 15–16c Renaissance-Baroque Basilica San Pietro (Michelangelo's dome and *Pietà*), the world's most important Roman Catholic church. The Vatican Palace contains the Vatican Museums with many fine art treasures including Michelangelo's frescoes in the Sistine Chapel.
www.vatican.va **168 B2**

The facade of Basilica San Pietro, Vatican City

European politics and economics

EUROPEAN UNION MEMBERSHIP

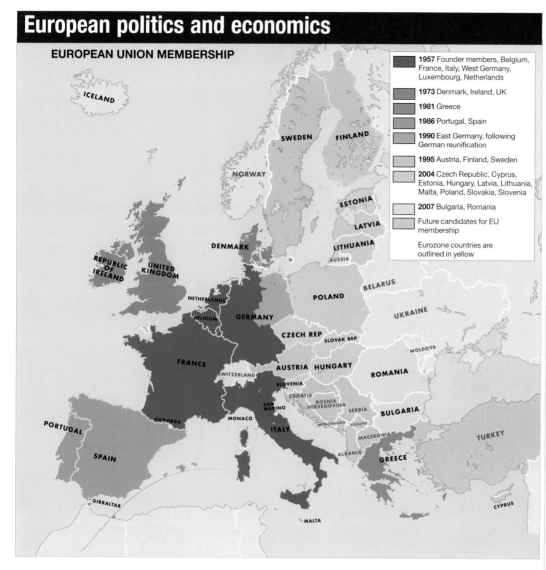

1957	Founder members, Belgium, France, Italy, West Germany, Luxembourg, Netherlands
1973	Denmark, Ireland, UK
1981	Greece
1986	Portugal, Spain
1990	East Germany, following German reunification
1995	Austria, Finland, Sweden
2004	Czech Republic, Cyprus, Estonia, Hungary, Latvia, Lithuania, Malta, Poland, Slovakia, Slovenia
2007	Bulgaria, Romania
	Future candidates for EU membership
	Eurozone countries are outlined in yellow

Democrats and the Greens. In July 2004 President Fischer's predecessor Thomas Klestil died of a heart attack one day before Heinz Fischer was due to take his place. After parliamentary elections in October 2006, a coalition between the Social Democrats and the People's Party was inaugurated in January 2007, sparking protests from students, trades unionists and members of the Social Democrats.

Economy Has a well-developed market economy and high standard of living. Per capita GDP rose sharply in 2007. The leading economic activity is the manufacture of metals and tourism. Dairy and livestock farming are the principal agricultural activities. To meet increased competition from both EU and Central European countries, particularly the new EU members, Austria will need to continue restructuring, emphasising knowledge-based sectors of the economy and encouraging greater labour flexibility

Belarus

Area 207,600 sq km (80,154 sq miles)
Population 9,724,723
Capital Minsk (1,754,000)
Languages Belarusian, Russian (both official)
GDP 2007 US$1,200
Currency Belarussian ruble = 100 kopek
Government Republic
Head of state President Alexander Lukashenko, 1994
Head of government Prime Minister Sergei Sidorsky, 2003
Website www.mfa.gov.by/eng
Events Belarus attained its independence in 1991. As a result of a referendum in 1996 the president increased his power at the expense of parliament. In 1997, Belarus signed a Union Treaty committing it to political and economic integration with Russia. Since his election in July 1994 as the country's first president, Alexander Lukashenko, has steadily consolidated his power through authoritarian means. Government restrictions on freedom of speech, the press and religion continue and in early 2005, the US listed Belarus as an outpost of tyranny. Alexander Lukashenko was declared to have won a third term as president in March 2006, although observers said the elections were flawed and protests continued in 2007.
Economy Belarus has faced problems in the transition to a free-market economy and there is little private enterprise. In 1995 an agreement with Russia enabled Belarus to receive subsidised fuel, but in 2006-2007 rows with Moscow over prices and unpaid debts led to threats to cut off gas supplies, a temporary shut-down of the oil pipeline and restrictions on supplies. Belarus' economy posted impressive growth in 2007. Agriculture, especially meat and dairy farming, is important

Albania Shqipëria

Area 28,748 sq km (11,100 sq miles)
Population 3,600,523
Capital Tirana / Tiranë (380,400)
Languages Albanian (official), Greek, Vlach, Romani and Slavic
GDP 2007 US$5,500
Currency Lek = 100 Quindars
Government multiparty republic
Head of state President Bamir Topi, 2007
Head of government Prime Minister Sali Berisha, Democratic Party, 2005
Website www.keshilliministrave.al/english
Events In the 2005 general elections, the Democratic Party and its allies won a decisive victory on pledges of reducing crime and corruption, promoting economic growth and decreasing the size of government. The election, and particularly the orderly transition of power, was considered an important step forward. After three years of talks, a Stabilisation and Association Agreement was signed with the EU in June 2006, and the country is still working towards becoming a member. In April 2008 NATO leaders invited Albania to join the organisation.

Economy Economic growth has stalled and Albania is still one of the poorest countries in Europe. 56% of the workforce are engaged in agriculture. Private ownership of land has been encouraged since 1991.

Andorra Principat d'Andorra

Area 468 sq km (181 sq miles)
Population 71,822
Capital Andorra la Vella (20,300)
Languages Catalan (official), French, Castilian and Portuguese
GDP 2007 US$38,800
Currency Euro = 100 cents
Government independent state and co-principality
Head of state co-princes: Joan Enric Vives i Sicilia, Bishop of Urgell, 2003 and Nicholas Sarkozy (see France), 2007
Head of government Chief Executive Albert Pintat, Liberal Party, 2005
Website www.andorra.ad
Events In 1993 a new democratic constitution was adopted that reduced the roles of the President of France and the Bishop of Urgell to purely constitutional figureheads.
Economy Tourism accounts for more than 80% of GDP with an estimated 11.6 million visiting annually, attracted by duty-free status and its sum-

mer and winter resorts. Agricultural production is limited (2% of the land is arable) and most food has to be imported. The principal livestock activity is sheep raising. Manufacturing output consists mainly of cigarettes, cigars, and furniture. Per capita GDP remained static in 2007.

Austria Österreich

Area 83,859 sq km (32,377 sq miles)
Population 8,199,783
Capital Vienna / Wien (1,807,000)
Languages German (official)
GDP 2007 US$39,00
Currency Euro = 100 cents
Government federal republic
Head of state President Heinz Fischer, Social Democrats, 2004
Head of government Federal Chancellor Alfred Gusenbauer, Social Democratic Party, 2007
Website www.austria.gv.at
Events In general elections in 1999, the extreme right Freedom Party, under Jörg Haider, made gains at the expense of the Social Democrats. He subsequently resigned as leader. People's Party electoral win in 2002 wasn't sufficient to form a government so a new government coalition was formed with the Freedom Party after failure of talks with the Social

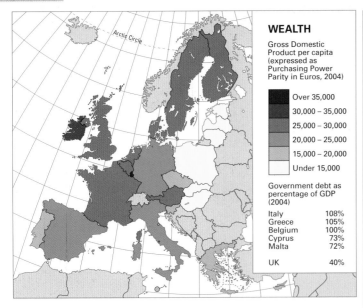

WEALTH

Gross Domestic Product per capita (expressed as Purchasing Power Parity in Euros, 2004)

	Over 35,000
	30,000 – 35,000
	25,000 – 30,000
	20,000 – 25,000
	15,000 – 20,000
	Under 15,000

Government debt as percentage of GDP (2004)

Italy	108%
Greece	105%
Belgium	100%
Cyprus	73%
Malta	72%
UK	40%

Belgium Belgique

Area 30,528 sq km (11,786 sq miles)
Population 10,392,226
Capital Brussels/Bruxelles (1,040,000)
Languages Dutch, French, German (all official)
GDP 2007 US$36,500
Currency Euro = 100 cents
Government federal constitutional monarchy
Head of state King Albert II, 1993
Head of government Prime Minister Yves Leterne, Christian Democrats, 2008
Website www.belgium.be
Events In 1993 Belgium adopted a federal system of government, each of the regions having its own parliament. Each main party is split into two – half for the Flemish and half for the Walloons. Elections in June 2007 led to the Christian Democrats gaining almost 30% of the vote in Flanders. A five-party coalition was eventually formed in March 2008, but negotiations for constitutional reform stalled in July. King Albert rejected Leterne's resignation and set-up a three-man commission to look at how to restart talks.
Economy Belgium is a major trading nation with a modern, private-enterprise economy, which experience strong growth in 2007. The leading activity is manufacturing i.e. steel and chemicals. With few natural resources, it imports substantial quantities of raw materials and export a large volume of manufactures. Belgium began circulating the Euro in January 2002.

Bosnia-Herzegovina
Bosna i Hercegovina

Area 51,197 sq km (19,767 sq miles)
Population 4,552,198
Capital Sarajevo (737,350)
Languages Bosnian/Croatian/Serbian
GDP 2007 US$6,600
Currency Convertible Marka = 100 convertible pfenniga

Government federal republic
Head of state Chairman of the Presidency Željko Komšić, Social Democratic Party, 2007
Head of government Chairman of the Council of Ministers Nikola Špirić, Alliance of Independent Social Democrats, 2007
Website www.bhtourism.ba
Events In 1992 a referendum approved independence from the Yugoslav federation. The Bosnian Serb population was against independence and in the resulting war occupied over two-thirds of the land. Croat forces seized other parts of the country. The 1995 Dayton Peace Accord ended the war and set up the Bosnian Muslim/Croat Federation and the Bosnian Serb Republic, each with their own president, government, parliament, military and police. There is also a central Bosnian government and rotating presidency the other members of which are Nebojša Radmanović (Alliance of Independent Social Democrats) and Dr Haris Silajdžiš (Party for Bosnia and Herzegovina). The office of High Representative has the power to impose decisions where the authorities are unable to agree or where political or economic interests are affected: the current incumbent, Miroslav Lajčák took over the role from Christian Schwarz-Schilling in June 2007. The Marka is pegged to the Euro. Eufor troops took over from the NATO-led force as peacekeepers in 2004. In late 2005, agreement was reached to set up a state-wide police defence and security forces, a state court and state taxation system and the EU gave the go-ahead for talks on a Stabilisation and Association Agreement. In December 2006 Bosnia joined NATO's Partnership for Peace programme.
Economy Excluding Macedonia, Bosnia was the least developed of the former republics of Yugoslavia. Currently receiving substantial aid, though this will be reduced. The economy grew slightly in 2007.

Bulgaria Bulgariya

Area 110,912 sq km (42,822 sq miles)
Population 7,322,858
Capital Sofia (1,126,000)
Languages Bulgarian (official), Turkish
GDP 2007 US$11,800
Currency Lev = 100 stotinki
Government multiparty republic
Head of state President Georgi Parvanov, Bulgarian Socialist Party, 2002
Head of government Prime Minister Sergei Stanishev, Bulgarian Socialist Party, 2005
Website www.president.bg/en/index.php
Events In 1990 the first non-communist president for 40 years, Zhelyu Zhelev, was elected. A new constitution in 1991 saw the adoption of free-market reforms. The Lev has been pegged to the Euro since 2002. Bulgaria joined NATO in 2004. Elections in June 2005 were inconclusive. Sergei Stanishev's Socialist Party is the major player in a three-party coalition with the Movement for Rights and Freedoms and the National Movement Simeon II. The president was re-elected in 2006. Bulgaria joined the EU in January 2007, but lack of progress in tackling corruption has led to decisions to withhold some EU funds.
Economy Bulgaria has experienced macroeconomic stability and strong growth since 1996 when a major economic downturn led to the fall of the then socialist government. Bulgaria averaged 4% growth since 2000, and per capita GDP rose by 13% in 2007. The economy has begun to attract significant amounts of foreign direct investment. Manufacturing is the leading economic activity but has outdated technology. The main products are chemicals, metals, machinery and textiles. The valleys of the Maritsa are ideal for winemaking, plums and tobacco. Tourism is increasing rapidly.

Croatia Hrvatska

Area 56,538 sq km (21,829 sq miles)
Population 4,453,500 (est)
Capital Zagreb (est 785,000)
Languages Croatian
GDP 2007 US$15,500
Currency Kuna = 100 lipa
Government multiparty republic
Head of state President Stjepan Mesic, 2000
Head of government Prime Minister Ivo Sanader, Croatian Democratic Union, 2003
Website www.croatia.hr
Events A 1991 referendum voted overwhelmingly in favour of independence from Yugoslavia. Serb-dominated areas took up arms to remain in the federation. Serbia armed Croatian Serbs, war broke out between Serbia and Croatia, and Croatia lost much territory. In 1992 United Nations peacekeeping troops were deployed. Following the Dayton Peace Accord of 1995, Croatia and Yugoslavia established diplomatic relations. An agreement between the Croatian government and Croatian Serbs provided for the eventual reintegration of Krajina into Croatia in 1998. PM Sanader leads a minority government with the support of many smaller parties. Croatia applied for EU membership in 2003. The green light was given for talks to proceed in 2005, but slowed in 2006 because of concerns about corruption and intolerance of ethnic minorities and the earliest date for accession is 2012. In April 2008 NATO leaders invited Croatia to join the organisation.
Economy The wars have badly disrupted Croatia's relatively prosperous economy but it emerged from a mild recession in 2000 with tourism, banking, and public investments leading the way and growth continued in although growth stalled 2007. Unemployment remains high, with structural factors slowing its decline. Croatia has a wide range of manufacturing industries, such as steel, chemicals, oil refining, and wood products. Agriculture is the principal employer. Crops include maize, soya beans, sugar beet and wheat.

Czech Republic Česka Republica

Area 78,864 sq km (30,449 sq miles)
Population 10,228,744
Capital Prague/Praha (1,181,000)
Languages Czech (official), Moravian
GDP 2007 US$24,400
Currency Czech Koruna = 100 haler
Government multiparty republic
Head of state President Václav Klaus, 2003
Head of government Prime Minister Mirek Topolanek, Civic Democratics, 2007
Website www.czech.cz
Events In 1992 the government agreed to the secession of the Slovak Republic, and on 1 January 1993 the Czech Republic was created. The Czech Republic was granted full membership of NATO in 1999 and joined the EU in May 2004. An election to the Chamber of Deputies took place in June 2006, and after months of deadlock Mirek Topolanek's three-party, centre-right coalition gained a vote of confidence in January 2007 and formed a new government. In July 2008 the government signed a treaty to allow components of a US missile shield on Czech land, prompting protests and angering the Russian government.
Economy The country has deposits of coal, uranium, iron ore, tin and zinc. Industries include chemicals, beer, iron and steel. Private ownership of land is gradually being restored. Agriculture employs 12% of the workforce. Inflation is under control. Intensified restructuring among large enterprises, improvements in the financial sector, and effective use of available EU funds should strengthen output

growth. Prague is now a major tourist destination.

Denmark Danmark

Area 43,094 sq km
(16,638 sq miles)
Population 5,468,120
Capital Copenhagen / København
(1,083,000)
Languages Danish (official)
GDP 2007 US$37,400
Currency Krone = 100 øre
Government
parliamentary monarchy
Head of state
Queen Margrethe II, 1972
Head of government Prime Minister
Anders Fogh Rasmussen, Venstre
(Left) Party, 2001
Website www.denmark.dk
Events In 1992 Denmark rejected
the Maastricht Treaty, but reversed
the decision in a 1993 referendum.
In 1998 the Amsterdam Treaty was
ratified by a further referendum. The
Krone is pegged to the Euro, but still
independent. The government is a
coalition formed with the Conservative Party. Anti-immigration policies
are backed by the well-supported
far-right Danish People's Party. Early
elections in November 2007 gave
Rasmussen's Venstre Party a third term
in power.
Economy Danes enjoy a high
standard of living with a thoroughly
modern market economy featuring
high-tech agriculture, up-to-date
small-scale and corporate industry,
comfortable living standards and a
stable currency. Economic growth
gained momentum in 2004, but after
several years of strong growth, this
slowed in 2007. Denmark is self-suf-
ficient in oil and natural gas. Services,
including tourism, form the largest
sector (63% of GDP). Farming employs
only 4% of the workforce but is highly
productive. Fishing is also important.

Estonia Eesti

Area 45,100 sq km
(17,413 sq miles)
Population 1,315,912
Capital Tallinn (395,000)
Languages Estonian (official), Russian
GDP 2007 US$21,800
Currency Kroon = 100 sents
Government multiparty republic
Head of state
President Toomas Hendrik Ilves,
Social Democratic Party, 2006
Head of government Prime Minister
Andrus Ansip, Reform Party 2005
Website www.riik.ee/en
Events In 1992 Estonia adopted a new
constitution and multiparty elections
were held. Estonia joined NATO in
March 2004 and the EU in May 2004.
In June 2004 the value of the Kroon
was fixed against the Euro with a view
to joining in 2007, although this has
been deferred to 2011. In 2005 a treaty
defining the border with Russia was
signed, but Russia refused to ratify it
after Estonia introduced a reference to
the Russian occupation of Estonia. Par-

liamentary elections in 2007 resulted
in Andrus Ansip retaining his position
at the head of a coalition. Further tensions with Russia rose when a memo-
rial to the Red Army was removed
from a square in Tallinn.
Economy Privatisation and free-trade
reforms have increased foreign investment and trade with the EU. Chief natural resources are oil shale and forests.
The economy benefits from strong
electronics and telecommunications
sectors. The state budget is essentially
in balance and public debt is low.
Manufactures include petrochemicals,
fertilisers and textiles.

Finland Suomi

Area 338,145 sq km
(130,557 sq miles)
Population 5,238,460
Capital Helsinki (568,000)
Languages Finnish, Swedish
(both official)
GDP 2007 US$35,500
Currency Euro = 100 cents
Government multiparty republic
Head of state President Tarja Kaarina
Halonen, 2000
Head of government Prime Minister
Matti Vanhanen, Centre Party, 2003
Website www.government.fi
Events In 1986 Finland became a
member of EFTA, and in 1995 joined
the EU. A new constitution was estab-
lished in March 2000. The Finnish
Parliament voted for the EU constitution in 2006. A coalition was set up
between the Centre Party, National
Coalition, Greens and Swedish Peoples' Party after close parliamentary
election results in 2007.
Economy Forests are Finland's most
valuable resource, with wood and
paper products accounting for 35%
of exports. Engineering, shipbuilding
and textile industries have grown.
Finland excels in high-tech exports
and is a leading light in the telecoms
industry. Farming employs 9% of the
workforce. High unemployment is
a persistent problem, and the Prime
Minister made tackling this a major
election pledge.

France

Area 551,500 sq km
(212,934 sq miles)
Population 60,875,136
Capital Paris (city 2,178,000; urban
9,630,000)
Languages French (official),
Breton, Occitan
GDP 2007 US$33,800
Currency Euro = 100 cents
Government multiparty republic
Head of state President Nicholas
Sarkozy, Union pour un Mouvement
Populaire, 2007
Head of government Prime Minister
François Fillon, Union pour un Mouve-
ment Populaire, 2007
Website www.elysee.fr
Events Nicholas Sarkozy beat the
left-wing candidate, Ségolène Royale,
in the 2007 presidential elections.
Policies include interventionist eco-

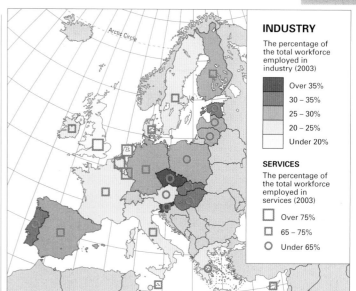

INDUSTRY
The percentage of
the total workforce
employed in
industry (2003)

Over 35%
30 – 35%
25 – 30%
20 – 25%
Under 20%

SERVICES
The percentage of
the total workforce
employed in
services (2003)

Over 75%
65 – 75%
Under 65%

nomic and monetary policies, tougher
rules on immigration and reform of
France's vast civil service. His vision of
European free-trade does not include
reform of the Common Agricultural
Policy and his clashes with the EU
Trade Commissioner, Peter Mandel-
son, over free-market reforms and
external tariffs marked the first weeks
of France's EU presidency.
Economy France is a leading industrial nation. It is the world's fourth-larg-
est manufacturer of cars. Industries
include chemicals and steel. It is the
leading producer of farm products
in western Europe. Livestock and
dairy farming are vital sectors. It is the
world's second largest producer of
cheese and wine. Tourism is a major
industry.

Germany Deutschland

Area 357,022 sq km
(137,846 sq miles)
Population 82,400,996
Capital Berlin (3,441,991)
Languages German (official)
GDP 2007 US$34,400
Currency Euro = 100 cents
Government
federal multiparty republic
Head of state
President Horst Köehler,
Christian Democratic Union, 2004
Head of government Chancellor
Angela Merkel Christian Democratic
Union, 2005
Website www.deutschland.de
Events Germany is a major supporter
of the European Union, and former
chancellor Helmut Köhl was the driv-
ing force behind the creation of the
Euro. As a result of their opposition
to the 2003 war in Iraq, Germany and
France have forged closer ties. In July
2005, Chancellor Gerhard Schröder
triggered early general elections,
which took place in September 2005.
The opposition Christian Democratic
Union (CDU) and its sister party, the
Christian Social Union (CSU), sig-
nificantly lost momentum during the
campaign and ultimately won only 1%
more votes. Exit polls showed clearly

that neither coalition group had won a
majority of seats. On October 10, 2005,
officials indicated that negotiations
had concluded successfully and that
the CDU and CSU would form a Grand
Coalition with the Social Democrats,
with Angela Merkel as Chancellor. During Germany's presidency of the EU,
Merkel was instrumental in incorpo-
rating many of the reforms intended
for the EU constitution into the EU
treaty.
Economy Germany is one of the
world's greatest economic powers.
Services form the largest economic
sector. Machinery and transport
equipment account for 50% of
exports. It is the world's third-largest
car producer. Other major products:
ships, iron, steel, petroleum, tyres. It
has the world's second-largest lignite
mining industry. Other minerals: copper, potash, lead, salt, zinc, aluminium.
Germany is the world's second-largest producer of hops and beer, and
fifth-largest of wine. Other products:
cheese and milk, barley, rye, pork.

Greece Ellas

Area 131,957 sq km
(50,948 sq miles)
Population 10,706,290
Capital Athens / Athina
(city 752,000; metropolitan 3,116,000)
Languages Greek (official)
GDP 2007 US$30,500
Currency Euro = 100 cents
Government multiparty republic
Head of state President Karolos
Papoulias, Panhellenic Socialist
Movement (PASOK), 2005
Head of government
Prime Minister Costas Karamanlis,
New Democracy Party, 2004
Website www.primeminister.gr
Events In 1981 Greece joined the EU
and Andreas Papandreou became
Greece's first socialist prime minister,
1981-89 and 1993-96. PM Costas Kara-
manlis is the nephew of former Greek
president Constantine Karamanlis.
The issue of Cyprus is still contentious
in Greece's relations with Turkey,
although Greece does support Tur-

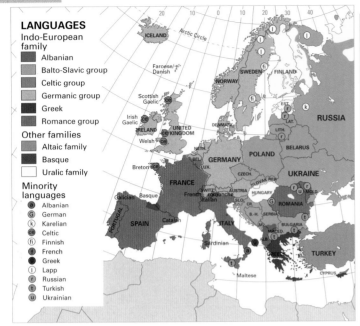

LANGUAGES
Indo-European family
Albanian
Balto-Slavic group
Celtic group
Germanic group
Greek
Romance group
Other families
Altaic family
Basque
Uralic family
Minority languages
ⓑ Albanian
ⓖ German
ⓚ Karelian
ⓒ Celtic
ⓕ Finnish
ⓕ French
ⓗ Greek
ⓘ Lapp
ⓡ Russian
ⓣ Turkish
ⓤ Ukrainian

key's admission to the EU. Snap elections resulted in a narrow win for the New Democracy Party in September 2007 despite unrest because of high unemployment, rising inflation and planned pension and labour reforms.
Economy Greece is one of the poorest members of the European Union, although per capita GDP grew strongly in 2007. Manufacturing is important. Products: textiles, cement, chemicals, metallurgy. Minerals: lignite, bauxite, chromite. Farmland covers 33% of Greece, grazing land 40%. Major crops: tobacco, olives, grapes, cotton, wheat. Livestock are raised. Tourism provides 15% of GDP.

Hungary Magyarorszàg

Area 93,032 sq km (35,919 sq miles)
Population 9,956,108
Capital Budapest (1,667,000)
Languages Hungarian (official)
GDP 2007 US$19,500
Currency Forint = 100 filler
Government multiparty republic
Head of state President Laszlo Solyom, 2005
Head of government Prime Minister Ferenc Gyurcsany, Socialist Party, 2004
Website www.magyarorszag.hu/english
Events In 1990 multiparty elections were won by the conservative Democratic Forum. In 1999 Hungary joined NATO and in 2004 acceded to the European Union. Ferenc Gyurcsany became PM in late 2004, and his coalition with the Free Democrats retained control in 2006, although the latter withdrew from the coalition in April 2008. Afterwards, Gyurcsany revealed plans to cut public sector jobs, raise taxes and reduce the budget deficit. Unrest followed revelations that the government had lied to the electorate before the elections over the state economy. Adoption of the [euro h]as been deferred until at least

2012. Hungary still has problems with discrimination against the Roma community.
Economy Since the early 1990s, Hungary has adopted market reforms and privatisation programmes. Inflation has fallen from a high of 14% in 1998, while per capita GDP rose by more than 12% in 2007. Germany is by far Hungary's largest economic partner. The manufacture of machinery and transport is the most valuable sector. Hungary's resources include bauxite, coal and natural gas. Major crops include grapes for wine-making, maize, potatoes, sugar beet and wheat. Tourism is a growing sector.

Iceland Ísland

Area 103,000 sq km (39,768 sq miles)
Population 299,388
Capital Reykjavik (114,500)
Languages Icelandic
GDP 2007 US$39,400
Currency Krona = 100 aurar
Government multiparty republic
Head of state President Olafur Ragnar Grimsson, 1996
Head of government Prime Minister Geir Haarde, Independence Party, 2006
Website http://government.is
Events In 1944, a referendum decisively voted to sever links with Denmark, and Iceland became a fully independent republic. In 1946 it joined NATO. In 1970 Iceland joined the European Free Trade Association. The last post-war US military personnel left in September 2006. Geir Haarde took over as PM from Halldor Asgrimsson of coalition partner the Progressive Party in 2006 and in the ensuing general election the coalition held on by one seat, but the Progressive Party withdrew and a new coalition was formed with the Social Democratic Alliance. In 2006, the government voted to resume commercial whaling

and there are also concerns about the environmental impact of major new industrial complexes powered by Iceland's abundant thermal energy.
Economy The economy remains sensitive to declining fish stocks as well as to fluctuations in world prices for its main exports: fish and fish products, aluminum, and ferrosilicon. There is low unemployment, and remarkably even distribution of income. Investing in overseas companies is an increasingly important part of economic activity.

Ireland, Republic of Eire

Area 70,273 sq km (27,132 sq miles)
Population 4,109,086
Capital Dublin (1,058,000)
Languages Irish, English (both official)
GDP 2007 US$45,600
Currency Euro = 100 cents
Government multiparty republic
Head of state President Mary McAleese, 1997
Head of government Taoiseach Brian Cowen, Fianna Fáil, 2008
Website www.irlgov.ie
Events In 1948 Ireland withdrew from the British Commonwealth and joined the European Community in 1973. The Anglo-Irish Agreement (1985) gave Ireland a consultative role in the affairs of Northern Ireland. Following a 1995 referendum, divorce was legalised. Abortion remains a contentious political issue. In the Good Friday Agreement of 1998 the Irish Republic gave up its constitutional claim to Northern Ireland and a North-South Ministerial Council was established. Sinn Fein got its first seats in the European elections of June 2004. In 2008, long-standing PM Bertie Ahern stood down and Brian Cowen now leads a coalition with the Green Party, several independents and the Progressive Democrats. The Irish referendum rejection of the new EU treaty caused fury in Brussels and Paris.
Economy Ireland has benefited greatly from its membership of the European Union. It joined in circulating the Euro in 2002. Grants have enabled the modernisation of farming, which employs 14% of the workforce. Major products include cereals, cattle and dairy products, sheep, sugar beet and potatoes. Fishing is important. Traditional sectors, such as brewing, distilling and textiles, have been supplemented by high-tech industries, such as electronics. Tourism is the most important component of the service industry. The economy has also benefited from a rise in consumer spending, construction and business investment, but growth slowed in 2007.

Italy Italia

Area 301,318 sq km (116,338 sq miles)
Population 58,147,733
Capital Rome / Roma (2,512,523)
Languages Italian (official)
GDP 2007 US$31,000
Currency Euro = 100 cents
Government social democracy
Head of state President Giorgio Napolitano, 2006
Head of government Silvio Berlusconi, Forza Italia, 2008
Website www.enit.it
Events In the 2006 general election, Romano Prodi, leader of the centre-left L'Unione had gained power, but after almost two years of instability, he was forced out by a vote of no confidence and long-standing PM Berlusconi regained control. Among new measures the new government has brought in is the compulsary finger-printing of the entire Roma ethnic minority. The apparent influx of economic migrants from eastern European countries is also a major concern.
Economy Italy's main industrial region is the north-western triangle of Milan, Turin and Genoa. It is the world's eighth-largest car and steel producer. Machinery and transport equipment account for 37% of exports. Agricultural production is important. Italy is the world's largest producer of wine. Tourism is a vital economic sector. Per capita GDP rose by 4% in 2007, but unemployment remains at a high level.

Latvia Latvija

Area 64,589 sq km (24,942 sq miles)
Population 2,259,810
Capital Riga (717,000)
Languages Latvian (official), Russian
GDP 2007 US$17,700
Currency Lats = 100 santims
Government multiparty republic
Head of state President Valdis Zatlers, 2007
Head of government Prime Minister Ivars Godmanis, People's Party, 2007
Website www.lv
Events Latvia became a member of NATO and the EU in spring 2004. People applying for citizenship are now required to pass a Latvian language test, which has caused much upset amongst the one third of the population who are Russian speakers. As a result many are without citizenship. After the resignation of the ruling minority coalition in October 2004 following rejection of Indulis Emsis' budget for 2005, a new 4-party coalition was approved by parliament in December and reelected in 2006, but forced to resign in December 2007 although the new cabinet was very little changed from its predecessor. Latvia currently aims to adopt the Euro in 2012 at the earliest.

Economy Latvia is a lower-middle-income country. The country has to import many of the materials needed for manufacturing. Latvia produces only 10% of the electricity it needs, and the rest has to be imported from Belarus, Russia and Ukraine. Manufactures include electronic goods, farm machinery and fertiliser. Farm exports include beef, dairy products and pork. The majority of companies, banks, and real estate have been privatised.

Liechtenstein

Area 157 sq km
(61 sq miles)
Population 34,247
Capital Vaduz (5,200)
Languages German (official)
GDP 2007 US$25,000
Currency Swiss franc = 100 centimes
Government
independent principality
Head of state
Prince Hans Adam, 1989
Head of government
Prime Minister Ottmar Hasler,
Progressive Citizens Party, 2001
Website www.liechtenstein.li/en
Events Women finally got the vote in 1984. The principality joined the UN in 1990. In 2003 the people voted in a referendum to give Prince Hans Adam II new political powers, rendering the country Europe's only absolute monarchy with the prince having power of veto over the government. Its status as a tax haven has been criticised as it has been alleged that many billions are laundered there each year. The law has been reformed to ensure that anonymity is no longer permitted when opening a bank account. In August 2004 Prince Hans Adam II transferred the day-to-day running of the country to his son Prince Alois, though he did not abdicate and remains titular head of state. Following elections in 2005, the government is made up of 3 ministers from the Progressive Citizens Party and 2 from the People's Union. In the same year, legislation allowing abortion was approved by referendum.
Economy Liechtenstein is the fourth-smallest country in the world and one of the richest per capita. Since 1945 it has rapidly developed a specialised manufacturing base. It imports more than 90% of its energy requirements. The economy is widely diversified with a large number of small businesses. Tourism is increasingly important.

Lithuania Lietuva

Area 65,200 sq km
(25,173 sq miles)
Population 3,575,489
Capital Vilnius (543,000)
Languages Lithuanian (official),
Russian, Polish
GDP 2006 US$16,700
Currency Litas = 100 centai
Government multiparty republic
Head of state
President Valdas Adamkus, 2004

Head of government Premier Gediminas Kirkilas, Social Democratic Party, 2006
Website www.lrvk.lt/main_en.php
Events The Soviet Union recognised Lithuania as independent in September 1991. Lithuania joined NATO in March 2004 and the EU in May 2004. In June 2004 Lithuania fixed the value of the Litas against the Euro with a view to joining in 2007, but entry is now planned for 2010. The Labour party pulled out of the ruling coalition in July 2006, leading to Algirdas Brazauskas' resignation as premier and Gediminas Kirkilas leads a minority coalition.
Economy Lithuania is dependent on Russian raw materials. Manufacturing is the most valuable export sector and major products include chemicals, electronic goods and machine tools. Dairy and meat farming and fishing are also important activities. More than 80% of enterprises have been privatised.

Luxembourg

Area 2,586 sq km
(998 sq miles)
Population 480,222
Capital Luxembourg (76,300)
Languages Luxembourgian /
Letzeburgish (official), French, German
GDP 2007 US$80,800
Currency Euro = 100 cents
Government constitutional
monarchy (or grand duchy)
Head of state
Grand Duke Henri, 2000
Head of government
Prime Minister Jean-Claude Juncker,
Christian Social People's Party, 1995
Website www.gouvernement.lu/en
Events Following 1994 elections, the Christian Social People's Party (CD) and the Luxembourg Socialist Workers' Party (SOC) formed a coalition government, which lasted until 1999 and was followed by a 5-year coalition with the Democratic Party. Grand Duke Jean abdicated in favour of his son Henri in October 2000. In general elections in 2004, the CD held on to power, again in coalition with the SOC.
Economy It has a stable, high-income economy, benefiting from its proximity to France, Germany and Belgium. Per capita GDP rose by more than 17% in 2007. The city of Luxembourg is a major centre of European administration and finance. Its strict laws on secrecy in banking have meant that tax evasion and fraud are prevalent. There are rich deposits of iron ore, and is a major producer of iron and steel. Other industries include chemicals, textiles, tourism, banking and electronics.

Macedonia Makedonija

Area 25,713 sq km
(9,927 sq miles)
Population 2,055,915
Capital Skopje (478,125)
Languages
Macedonian (official), Albanian

GDP 2007 US$8,400
Currency Denar = 100 deni
Government multiparty republic
Head of state President Branko Crvenkovski, Social Democrat Union, 2004
Head of government Nikola Gruevski, VMRO-DPMNE, 2006
Website www.vlada.mk/english/index_en.htm
Events In 1993 the UN accepted the new republic as a member. It retains the FYR prefix because of Greek fears that the name implies territorial ambitions towards the Greek region named Macedonia. President Branko Crvenovski was elected in April 2004 as a result of the death in a plane crash of Boris Trajkovski. He aims to continue the improvement of the country with EU membership as the goal. In August 2004, proposed expansion of rights and local autonomy for Albanians provoked riots by Macedonian nationalists, but the measures went through. In December 2005, EU leaders agreed that Macedonia should become a candidate for membership, if corruption was, but in February 2007 expressed alarm at political developments during 2006 and continuing problems about rights for ethnic Albanians. In November 2006, NATO leaders announced that Macedonia could expect to be invited to join at its next summit in 2008, but Greece vetoed this in March 2008 because of the issue of the country's name. Elections in the wake of this decision were won by the leading coalition, but observers declared them unsatisfactory because of problems in ethnic Albanian areas.
Economy Macedonia is a developing country. The poorest of the six former republics of Yugoslavia, its economy was devastated by UN trade damaged by sanctions against Yugoslavia and by the Greek embargo. Per capita GDP rose slightly in 2007. Manufactures, especially metals, dominate exports. Agriculture employs 17% of the work-

force. Major crops include cotton, fruits, maize, tobacco and wheat.

Malta

Area 316 sq km
(122 sq miles)
Population 401,890
Capital Valetta (6,700)
Languages Maltese,
English (both official)
GDP 2006 US$23,200
Currency Euro = 100 cents
Government multiparty republic
Head of state President Edward Fenech Adami, Christian Democratic Nationalist Party, 2004
Head of government Prime Minister Lawrence Gonzi, Christian Democratic Nationalist Party, 2004
Website www.gov.mt
Events In 1990 Malta applied to join the EU. In 1997 the newly elected Malta Labour Party pledged to rescind the application. The Christian Democratic Nationalist Party, led by the pro-European Edward Fenech Adami, regained power in 1998 elections and won again by a narrow margin in March 2008. Malta joined the EU in May 2004 and adopted the Euro on 1 January 2008. Malta has suffered increasing problems with large numbers of asylum seekers and has been criticised by the UN for its policy of keeping them in detention for 18 months.
Economy Malta produces only about 20% of its food needs, has limited fresh water supplies and has few domestic energy sources. Machinery and transport equipment account for more than 50% of exports. Malta's historic naval dockyards are now used for commercial shipbuilding and repair. Manufactures include chemicals, electronic equipment and textiles. The largest sector is services, especially tourism. Privatisation of state-controlled companies and liberalisation of markets is still a contentious issue.

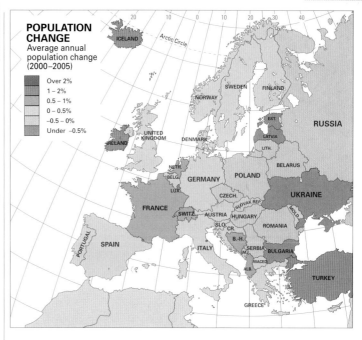

POPULATION CHANGE
Average annual population change (2000–2005)

Over 2%
1 – 2%
0.5 – 1%
0 – 0.5%
–0.5 – 0%
Under –0.5%

Moldova

Area 33,851 sq km
(13,069 sq miles)
Population 4,320,490
Capital Chisinau (596,355)
Languages
Moldovan / Romanian (official)
GDP 2007 US$2,200
Currency Leu = 100 bani
Government multiparty republic
Head of state President Vladimir
Voronin, Communist Party, 2001
Head of government
Prime Minister Zinaida Greceanii,
Communist Party, 2008
Website
www.parliament.md/en.html
Events In 1994 a referendum rejected
reunification with Romania and Par-
liament voted to join the CIS. A new
constitution established a presidential parliamentary republic. In 2001
Vladimir Voronin was elected president - the first Communist elected as
president in a former Soviet state - and
was re-elected in 2005. The Transnistria region mainly inhabited by Russian and Ukrainian speakers declared
independence from Moldova in 1990
fearing the impact of closer ties with
Romania. This independence has
never been recognised and a regional
referendum in Transnistria in 2006
that supported eventual union of the
region with Russia is similarly being
ignored. Relations between Chisinau
and Moscow worsened in early 2006
when the Russian giant Gazprom
cut off gas supplies when Moldova
refused to double the price paid. New
prices were agreed in July and raised
again in 2007. President Voronin is
actively seeking ties with the west
and met the leader of Transnistria, Igor
Smirnov, in April 2008, resulting in the
agreement that peace talks should
resume.
Economy There is a favourable cli-
mate and good farmland but no major
mineral deposits. Agriculture is important and major products include fruits
and grapes for wine-making. Farmers
also raise livestock, including dairy
cattle and pigs. Moldova has to import
materials and fuels for its industries.
Exports include food, wine, tobacco
and textiles. The economy remains
vulnerable to high fuel prices and
poor agricultural weather. Per capita
GDP rose slightly in 2007.

Monaco

Area 1.5 sq km (0.6 sq miles)
Population 32,671
Capital Monaco-Ville (970)
Languages French (official), Italian,
Monegasque
GDP 2007 US$30,000
Currency Euro = 100 cents
Government principality
Head of state Prince Albert II, 2005
Head of government Minister of
State Jean-Paul Proust, 2005
...te www.monaco.gouv.mc
Monaco has been ruled by the
...amily since the end of the

13th century and been under the pro-
tection of France since 1860.
Economy The chief source of income
is tourism. The state retains monopo-
lies in tobacco, the telephone network
and the postal service. There is some
light industry, including printing,
textiles and postage stamps. Also a
major banking centre, residents live
tax free. Prince Albert wishes to attract
high-tech industries and to prove that
Monaco is not a haven for money-
launderers.

Montenegro Crna Gora

Area 13,812 sq km
(5,333 sq miles)
Population 684,736
Capital Podgorica (160,100)
Languages Serbian
(of the Ijekavian dialect)
GDP 2007 US$3,800
Currency Euro = 100 cents
Government federal republic
Head of state
President of Montenegro Filip
Vujanovic, 2003
Head of government Prime Minister
Milo Djukanovic Zeljko Sturanovic,
Democratic Party of Socialists, 2008
Website www.vlada.cg.yu/eng.yu
Events In 1992 Montenegro went into
federation with Serbia, first as Federal
Republic of Yugoslavia, then as a
looser State Union of Serbia and Mon-
tenegro. Montenegro formed its own
economic policy and adopted the
Deutschmark as its currency in 1999.
It currently uses the Euro, though it is
not formally part of the Eurozone. In
2002, Serbia and Montenegro came
to a new agreement regarding continued cooperation. On 21 May 2006,
the status of the union was decided as
55.54% of voters voted for independence of Montenegro, narrowly passing
the 55% threshold needed to validate
the referendum under rules set by the
EU. On 3 June 2006 the Parliament of
Montenegro declared independence.
Montenegro was rapidly admitted to
the UN, the World Bank and the IMF,
joined NATO's Partnership for Peace
programme and in 2007 initiated a
Stability and Association Agreement
with the EU.
Economy A rapid period of urbanisa-
tion and industrialisation was created
within the communism era of Montenegro. During 1993, two thirds of the
Montenegrin population lived below
the poverty line. Financial losses
under the effects of the UN sanctions
on the economy of Montenegro are
estimated to be $6.39 billion. Today
there is faster and more efficient privatisation, introduction of VAT and usage
of the Euro.

The Netherlands Nederland

Area 41,526 sq km
(16,033 sq miles)
Population 16,570,613
Capital Amsterdam (city 750,000;
urban 1,105,000); administrative
capital 's-Gravenhage (The Hague)
(474,000)

Languages Dutch (official), Frisian
GDP 2007 US$38,600
Currency Euro = 100 cents
Government
constitutional monarchy
Head of state Queen Beatrix, 1980
Head of government
Prime Minister Jan Peter Balkenende,
Christian Democrats, 2002
Website www.holland.com
Events A founding member of NATO
and the EU. Jan Peter Balkenende's
coalition cabinet with the Democrats-
66 and VVD (Peoples' Party for Freedom and Democracy) collapsed in
June 2006 in a row over immigration
policy and after general elections in
November, he formed a new coalition
with the Labour Party and the Christian Union in February 2007.
Economy The Netherlands has prospered through its close European ties.
Private enterprise has successfully
combined with progressive social policies. It is highly industrialised. Products include aircraft, chemicals, electronics and machinery. Agriculture is
intensive and mechanised, employing
only 5% of the workforce. Dairy farming is the leading agricultural activity.
It continues to be one of the leading
European nations for attracting foreign direct investment.

Norway Norge

Area 323,877 sq km
(125,049 sq miles)
Population 4,627,926
Capital Oslo (852,000)
Languages Norwegian (official),
Lappish, Finnish
GDP 2007 US$55,600
Currency Krone = 100 øre
Government
constitutional monarchy
Head of state King Harald V, 1991
Head of government Prime Minister
Jens Stoltenberg, Labour, 2005
Website www.norge.no
Events In referenda in 1972 and 1994
Norway rejected joining the EU. A cen-
tre-left coalition, the Labour-led 'Red-
Green Alliance' won closely contested
elections in September 2005.
Economy Norway has one of the
world's highest standards of living.
Discovery of oil and gas in adjacent
waters in the late 1960s boosted its
economic fortunes, with its chief
exports now oil and natural gas.
Per capita, it is the world's largest
producer of hydroelectricity. It is possible oil and gas will begin to run out
in Norway in the next two decades
but it has been saving its oil budget
surpluses and is invested abroad in a
fund, now valued at more than $250
billion. Major manufactures include
petroleum products, chemicals, aluminium, wood pulp and paper. The
chief farming activities are dairy and
meat production, but Norway has to
import food.

Poland Polska

Area 323,250 sq km
(124,807 sq miles)
Population 39,518,241
Capital Warsaw / Warszawa
(1,706,000)
Languages Polish (official)
GDP 2007 US$16,200
Currency Zloty = 100 groszy
Government multiparty republic
Head of state
President Lech Kaczynski, Law and
Justice (PiS), 2005
Head of government Prime Minister
Donald Tusk, Civic Platform, 2007
Website www.poland.gov.pl
Events In 1996 Poland joined the
Organisation for Economic Coopera-
tion and Development. Poland joined
NATO in 1999 and the EU in May 2004.
The 2005 elections brought in Presi-
dent Kaczynski of the right-wing Law
and Justice party. The coalition led by
the president's brother collapsed in
2007, and Civic Platform now rules in
coalition with the Peasants Party, leading in a change in attitudes to both
the EU and Russia. In February 2008,
the government agreed in principle
to host part of the new US missile
defence system, which has angered
Russia.
Economy Of the workforce, 27% is
employed in agriculture and 37% in
industry. Poland is the world's fifth-
largest producer of lignite and ships.
Copper ore is also a vital resource.
Manufacturing accounts for 24% of
exports. Agriculture remains important. Major crops include barley, potatoes and wheat. Economic growth is
continuing to improve.

Portugal

Area 88,797 sq km
(34,284 sq miles)
Population 10,642,836
Capital Lisbon / Lisboa (491,888
municipality; urban 3,861,000)
Languages Portuguese (official)
GDP 2007 US$21,800
Currency Euro = 100 cents
Government multiparty republic
Head of state
President Anibal Cavaco Silva,
Social Democratic Party, 2006
Head of government Jose Socrates,
Socialist Party, 2005
Website www.portugal.gov.pt
Events In 1986 Portugal joined the
EU. In 2002 the Social Democrat Party
won the election and formed a coali-
tion government with the Popular
Party. The opposition Socialist Party
were clear victors in European elec-
tions of June 2004, a result attributed
in part to the ruling party's support for
the war in Iraq. In the general election
in February 2005, the Socialists won
an outright majority under their leader
Jose Socrates, who has cut public
spending sharply in order to revive the
economy.
Economy Portugal's commitment to
the EU has seen the economy emerge
from recession, but a poor educa-

tional system, in particular, has been an obstacle to greater productivity and growth. Manufacturing accounts for 33% of exports. Textiles, footwear and clothing are major exports. Portugal is the world's fifth-largest producer of tungsten and eighth-largest producer of wine. Olives, potatoes and wheat are also grown. Tourism is very important.

Romania

Area 238,391 sq km (92,042 sq miles)
Population 22,276,056
Capital Bucharest / Bucuresti (1,921,000)
Languages Romanian (official), Hungarian
GDP 2007 U$11,100
Currency Romanian leu = 100 bani
Government multiparty republic
Head of state President Traian Basescu, 2004
Head of government Calin Popescu-Tariceanu, 2004
Website www.gov.ro/engleza
Events A new constitution was introduced in 1991. Ion Iliescu, a former communist official, was re-elected in 2000, but barred from standing again in 2004, when he was replaced by Traian Basescu. Tariceanu's government is a centrist coalition, which was re-elected in 2007. Romania joined NATO in March 2004 and signed its EU accession treaty in April 2005 and joined the latter in January 2007 after making progress towards tackling corruption, although this is still an issue. Currently, it aims to adopt the Euro no earlier than 2012. Clashes between the President and PM over reforms led to MPs trying to impeach the former but this was rejected in a national referendum. The Romany minority still suffers from discrimination.
Economy In 2005, confidence in the economic process was emphasised when the government re-valued its currency, making 10,000 'old' Lei equal to 1 'new' Lei and the economy grew slightly in 2006.

Russia Rossiya

Area 17,075,000 sq km (6,592,800 sq miles)
Population 141,377,752
Capital Moscow / Moskva (10,224,000)
Languages Russian (official), and many others
GDP 2007 US$14,600
Currency Russian ruble = 100 kopeks
Government federal multiparty republic
Head of state President Dmitry Medvedev, 2008
Head of government Premier Vladimir Putin, 2008
Website www.gov.ru
Events In 1992 the Russian Federation became a co-founder of the CIS (Commonwealth of Independent States). A new Federal Treaty was signed between the central government and the autonomous republics within the

Russian Federation, Chechnya refused to sign and declared independence. In December 1993 a new democratic constitution was adopted. From 1994 to 1996, Russia fought a civil war in Chechnya which flared up again in 1999. Putin's chosen successor, Medvedev, was elected by a landslide in elections that were criticised by outside observers for biased media coverage. Central control over the regions was assumed in the wake of the of the 2004 school siege in Chechnya. Relationships with the West have been coloured by the war in Iraq, the question of sanctions against Iran, the cancellation of major contracts with western businesses, the deaths of dissidents both within Russia and in other countries, and the arrests of 'oligarchs' - tycoons who have made billions from the privatisation of state industries, the perceived use of gas and oil supplies to Europe as a diplomatic weapon and the US proposal to site its missile defence shield near Russia's western border.
Economy In 1993 mass privatisation began. By 1996, 80% of the Russian economy was in private hands. A major problem remains the size of Russia's foreign debt. It is reliant on world oil prices to keep its economy from crashing. Industry employs 46% of the workforce and contributes 48% of GDP. Mining is the most valuable activity. Russia is the world's leading producer of natural gas and nickel, the second largest producer of aluminium and phosphates. and the third-largest of crude oil, lignite and brown coal. Most farmland is still government-owned or run as collectives, with important products barley, oats, rye, potatoes, beef and veal. In 2006, the ruble became a convertable currency.

San Marino

Area 61 sq km (24 sq miles)
Population 29,615
Capital San Marino (4,600)
Languages Italian (official)
GDP 2007 US$34,100
Currency Euro = 100 cents
Government multiparty republic
Head of state co-Chiefs of State: Captain Regent Federico Pedini Amati and Captain Regent Rosa Zafferani
Head of government Secretary of State for Foreign and Political Affairs Fiorenzo Stolfi, 2006
Website www.omniway.sm
Events World's smallest republic and perhaps Europe's oldest state, San Marino's links with Italy led to the adoption of the Euro. Its 60-member Great and General Council is elected every five years and headed by two captains-regent, who are elected by the council every six months.
Economy The economy is largely agricultural. Tourism is vital to the state's income, contributing over 50% of GDP. Also a tax haven used by many non-residents. Per capita GDP remained stable in 2007

Serbia Srbija

Area 88,412 sq km (34,137 sq miles), including Kosovo
Population 10,150,245, including Kosovo
Capital Belgrade / Beograd (1,104,240)
Languages Serbian
GDP 2007 US$7,700
Currency Dinar = 100 paras
Government federal republic
Head of state President of Serbia Boris Tadic, Democratic Party of Serbia, 2004
Head of government Prime Minister Mirko Cvetkovic, Democratic Party of Servia, 2008
Website www.srbija.sr.gov.yu
Events Serbian attempts to dominate the Yugoslav federation led to the secession of Slovenia and Croatia in 1991 and to Bosnia-Herzegovina's declaration of independence in 1992 and the three-year war that ended only with the signing of the Dayton Peace Accord. Slobodan Milosovic became president of Yugoslavia in 1997. Kostunica won the elections of September 2000: Milosevic refused to hand over power, but was ousted after a week. From 2003 to 2006, Serbia was part of the State Union of Serbia and Montenegro, After a referendum in May 2006, the Parliament of Montenegro declared Montenegro independent. Serbia became the successor to the State Union and assumed the State Union's UN membership. Despite misgivings on the part of both organisations because Serbia had still not located three indicted war criminals wanted by the International Court in the Hague for atrocities committed during the Bosnian War, in December 2006 Serbia joined the NATO Partnership for Peace programme and in April 2008 signed a Stability and Association Agreement with the EU, and within weeks had elected a more pro-western government. The most-wanted of the war criminals, Radavan Karadzic, was arrested by Serb forces 5 days after the new PM's order to find him. In 2007 the UN envoy detailed a draft Settlement plan for the de facto UN protectorate of Kosovo, which was rejected by the Serbian government and Kosovo's independence is not recognised everywhere.
Economy The lower-middle income economy was devastated by war and economic sanctions. Industrial production collapsed. Natural resources include bauxite, coal and copper. There is some oil and natural gas. Manufacturing includes aluminium, cars, machinery, plastics, steel and textiles. Agriculture is important.

Slovak Republic
Slovenska Republika

Area 49,012 sq km (18,923 sq miles)
Population 5,447,502
Capital Bratislava (424,000)

Languages Slovak (official), Hungarian
GDP 2006 US$19,800
Currency Koruna = 100 halierov
Government multiparty republic
Head of state President Ivan Gasparovic, 2004
Head of government Prime Minister Robert Fico, Smer Party, 2006
Website www.prezident.sk/introduction
Events In 1993 the Slovak Republic became a sovereign state, breaking peaceably from the Czech Republic, with whom it maintains close relations. In 1996 the Slovak Republic and Hungary ratified a treaty confirming their borders and stipulating basic rights for the 560,000 Hungarians in the country. The Slovak Republic joined NATO in March 2004 and the EU in May 2004. There is still a problem with the Romany population. Parliamentary elections in 2006 led to a coalition between the Smer Party, Movement for a Democratic Slovakia and the Slovak National Party. The country looks on course to for adoption of the Euro in January 2009.
Economy The transition from communism to private ownership was initially painful with industrial output falling, unemployment and inflation rising, but the economy has become more stable and per capita GDP grew by more than 11% in 2007. Manufacturing employs 33% of the workforce. Bratislava and Košice are the chief industrial cities. Major products include ceramics, machinery and steel. Farming employs 12% of the workforce. Crops include barley and grapes. Tourism is growing.

Slovenia Slovenija

Area 20,256 sq km (7,820 sq miles)
Population 2,009,245
Capital Ljubljana (254,100)
Languages Slovene
GDP 2006 US$27,300
Currency Euro = 100 cents
Government multiparty republic
Head of state President Danilo Türk, 2008
Head of government Prime Minister Janez Jansa, Slovenian Democratic Party, 2004
Website www.gov.si
Events In 1990 Slovenia declared itself independent, which led to brief fighting between Slovenes and the federal army. In 1992 the EU recognised Slovenia's independence. Janez Drnovsek was elected president in December 2002 and immediately stepped down as prime minister. Slovenia joined NATO in March 2004 and the EU in May 2004. In June 2004 the value of the Tolar was fixed against the Euro, which it joined in 2007. The 2004 general election resulted in a coalition government of the Slovenian Democratic Party, New Slovenia, the People's Party and the Democratic Party of Pensioners.
Economy The transformation of a

centrally planned economy and the fighting in other parts of former Yugoslavia caused problems for Slovenia but the economy is now experiencing strong growth in per capita GDP. Manufacturing is the leading activity. Major manufactures include chemicals, machinery, transport equipment, metal goods and textiles. Major crops include maize, fruit, potatoes and wheat.

Spain España

Area 497,548 sq km (192,103 sq miles)
Population 40,448,191
Capital Madrid (3,108,000)
Languages Castilian Spanish (official), Catalan, Galician, Basque
GDP 2006 US$33,700
Currency Euro = 100 cents
Government constitutional monarchy
Head of state King Juan Carlos I, 1975
Head of government Prime Minister Jose Luis Rodriguez Zapatero, Socialist Party, 2004
Website www.la-moncloa.es/IDIOMAS/en-GB
Events From 1959 the militant Basque organisation ETA waged a campaign of terror but announced a ceasefire in 1998. In March 2004 Al qaeda bombers killed 191 people in Madrid. The government initially claimed this as the work of ETA but in the elections three days later was voted out, largely because people blamed government support of the US in Iraq, and the sending of Spanish troops, for bombing. The new PM subsequently withdrew all troops from Iraq. In 2008 elections, the Socialists increased their numbers in Parliament, but do not have a majority. In 2006, a Catalan referendum resulted in greater autonomy for the region. ETA declared a ceasefire in March 2006, but broke this with a bomb attack on Madrid airport at the end of the year, and said that in June 2007 that the ceasefire was over.
Economy Spain has rapidly transformed from a largely poor, agrarian society into a prosperous industrial nation with strong economic growth. Agriculture now employs only 10% of the workforce and the sector is shrinking further because of recurrent droughts. Spain is the world's third-largest wine producer. Other crops include citrus fruits, tomatoes and olives. Industries: cars, ships, chemicals, electronics, metal goods, steel, textiles.

Sweden Sverige

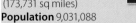

Area 449,964 sq km (173,731 sq miles)
Population 9,031,088
Capital Stockholm (1,266,000)
Languages Swedish (official), Finnish
GDP 2006 US$36,900
Currency Swedish krona = 100 ore
Government constitutional monarchy
Head of state King Carl XVI Gustaf, 1973

Head of government Prime Minister Fredrik Reinfeldt, Moderate Party, 2006
Website www.sweden.gov.se
Events In 1995 Sweden joined the European Union. The cost of maintaining Sweden's extensive welfare services has become a major political issue. In 2003 Sweden rejected adoption of the Euro. The elections of 2006 resulted in the Alliance for Sweden, a multi-party centre-right coalition led by the Moderate Party, which supports NATO entry.
Economy Sweden is a highly developed industrial country. It has rich iron ore deposits. Privately owned firms account for about 90% of industrial output. Steel is a major product, used to manufacture aircraft, cars, machinery and ships. Forestry and fishing are important. Agriculture accounts for only 2% of GDP and of jobs. The Swedish central bank focuses on price stability with its inflation target of 2%.

Switzerland Schweiz

Area 41,284 sq km (15,939 sq miles)
Population 7,554,661
Capital Bern (120,500)
Languages French, German, Italian, Romansch (all official)
GDP 2007 US$39,800
Currency Swiss Franc = 100 centimes
Government federal republic
Head of state President Pascal Cachepin, 2008
Website www.gov.ch
Events Priding themselves on their neutrality, Swiss voters rejected membership of the UN in 1986 and the EU in 1992 and 2001. However, Switzerland finally became a partner country of NATO in 1997 and joined the organisation in 2002. The federal council is made up of seven federal ministers from whom the president is chosen on an annual basis. A 2005 referendum backed membership of EU Schengen and Dublin agreements, bringing Switzerland into the European passport-free zone and increasing co-operation on crime and asylum seekers. Immigration is becoming an increasingly divisive issue.
Economy Switzerland is wealthy and a stable modern market economy with low unemployment, although per capita GDP did shrink slightly in 2006. Manufactures include chemicals, electrical equipment, machinery, precision instruments, watches and textiles. Livestock raising, notably dairy farming, is the chief agricultural activity. Tourism is important, and Swiss banks remain a safehaven for investors.

Turkey Türkiye

Area 774,815 sq km (299,156 sq miles)
Population 75,158,647
Capital Ankara (3,203,000)
Languages Turkish (official), Kurdish
GDP 2007 US$9,400
Currency New Turkish lira = 100 kurus
Government multiparty republic

Head of state President Abdullah Gül, Justice and Development Party (AK), 2007
Head of government Prime Minister Recep Tayyip Erdogan, Justice and Development Party (AK), Party, 2003
Website www.cankaya.tr
Events The Kurdistan Workers Party (PKK) carried out terrorist activities throughout the 1980s and 1990s, but declared a ceasefire in 1999, changed their name to Congress for Freedom and Democracy in Kurdistan (KADEK) and said they wanted to campaign peacefully for Kurdish rights. In September 2003 they ended a 4-year ceasefire, but declared another in 2006, although this did not hold. In October 2005, the EU opened accession negotiations with Ankara. Membership of the EU is an aim but human rights, the Cyprus issue and the hostility of successive French governments are barriers. The PM and President are both former Islamists, although they say they are committed to secularism. Retaliatory strikes have been launched against KADEK bases in Iraq. Escalating tensions between secularists and the government, epitomised by the debate on whether the Islamic headscarf may be worn in universities, have led to attempts to have the AK banned and the arrests of several ex-generals, accused of plotting another military coup.
Economy Turkey is a lower-middle income developing country. Agriculture employs 47% of the workforce. Turkey is a leading producer of citrus fruits, barley, cotton, wheat, tobacco and tea. It is a major producer of chromium and phosphate fertilisers. Tourism is a vital source of foreign exchange. In January 2005, the New Turkish lira was introduced at a rate of 1 to 1,000,000 old Turkish lira. Privatisation sales are currently approaching $21 billion.

Ukraine Ukraina

Area 603,700 sq km (233,088 sq miles)
Population 46,299,872
Capital Kiev / Kyviv (2,546,000)
Languages Ukrainian (official), Russian
GDP 2007 US$6,900
Currency Hryvnia = 100 kopiykas
Government multiparty republic
Head of state President Viktor Yushchenko, 2005
Head of government Prime Minister Viktor Yulia Tymoshenko, All Ukrainian Union "Fatherland", 2007
Website www.president.gov.ua/en
Events The Chernobyl disaster of 1986 contaminated large areas of Ukraine. Final independence was achieved in 1991 with the dissolution of the USSR. Leonid Kuchma was elected president in 1994. He continued the policy of establishing closer ties with the West and sped up the pace of privatisation. Ukraine is pushing for membership of NATO though reforms are required before this can happen. The Presiden-

tial election of November 2004 was thrown into turmoil after opposition candidate Yushchenko was poisoned and victory declared for former PM Viktor Yanukovich leading to accusations of electoral fraud, and widespread demonstrations. The Supreme Court declared the vote invalid and the elections were re-run, resulting in victory for the pro-west Yushchenko. In September 2005, Yushchenko sacked the entire cabinete. After elections in March 2006 and months of wrangling, Yanukovic became Prime Minister, leading a broad coalition, but was defeated by the coalition led by former PM Yulia Tymoshenko. Russia cut off gas supplies in early 2006 because of rows over prices: these doubled and then rose again in 2007.
Economy Ukraine is a lower-middle-income economy. Agriculture is important. It is the world's leading producer of sugar beet, the second-largest producer of barley, and a major producer of wheat. Ukraine has extensive raw materials, including coal (though many mines are exhausted), iron ore and manganese ore. Ukraine is reliant on oil and natural gas imports. Per capita GDP dropped in 2007.

United Kingdom

Area 241,857 sq km (93,381 sq miles)
Population 60,776,238
Capital London (7,622,000)
Languages English (official), Welsh (also official in Wales), Gaelic
GDP 2007 US$35,300
Currency Sterling (pound) = 100 pence
Government constitutional monarchy
Head of state Queen Elizabeth II, 1952
Head of government Prime Minister Gordon Brown, Labour Party, 2007
Website www.parliament.uk
Events The United Kingdom of Great Britain and Northern Ireland is a union of four countries – England, Northern Ireland, Scotland and Wales. In 1997 referenda on devolution saw Scotland and Wales gain their own legislative assemblies. The Scottish assembly was given tax-varying power. The Good Friday Agreement of 1998 offered the best chance of peace in Northern Ireland for a generation. In 2005 the IRA announced a permanent cessation of hostilities and the Northern Ireland Assembly was finally reinstated in early 2007. The war in Iraq remains a contentious issue. Regional elections led to the Scottish Nationalists taking power in Edinburgh. Immigration, particularly from Eastern Europe, religious fundamentalism and terrorism remain key issues.
Economy The UK is a major industrial and trading nation. A producer of oil, petroleum products, natural gas, potash, salt and lead. Financial services and tourism are the leading service industries.

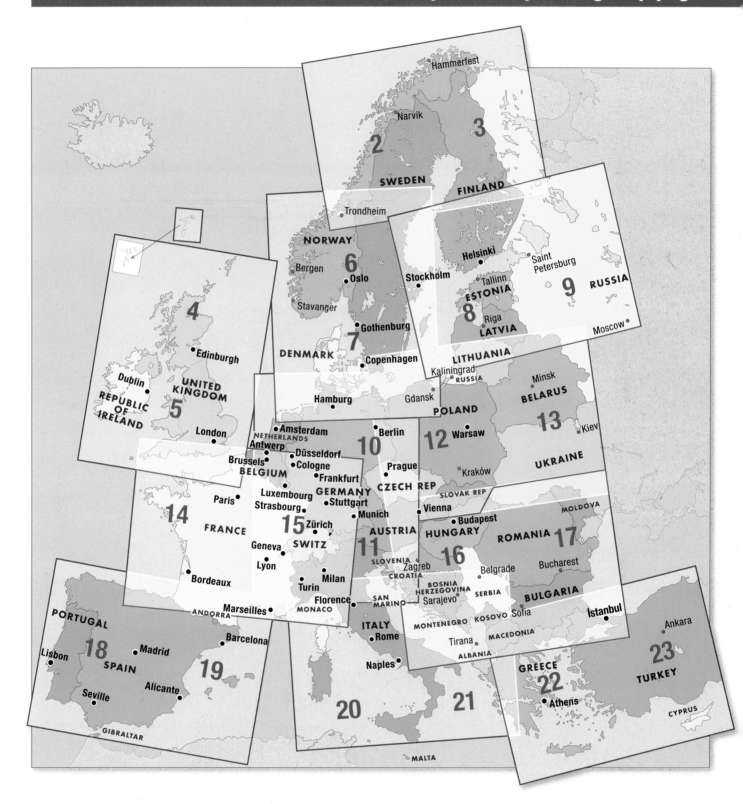

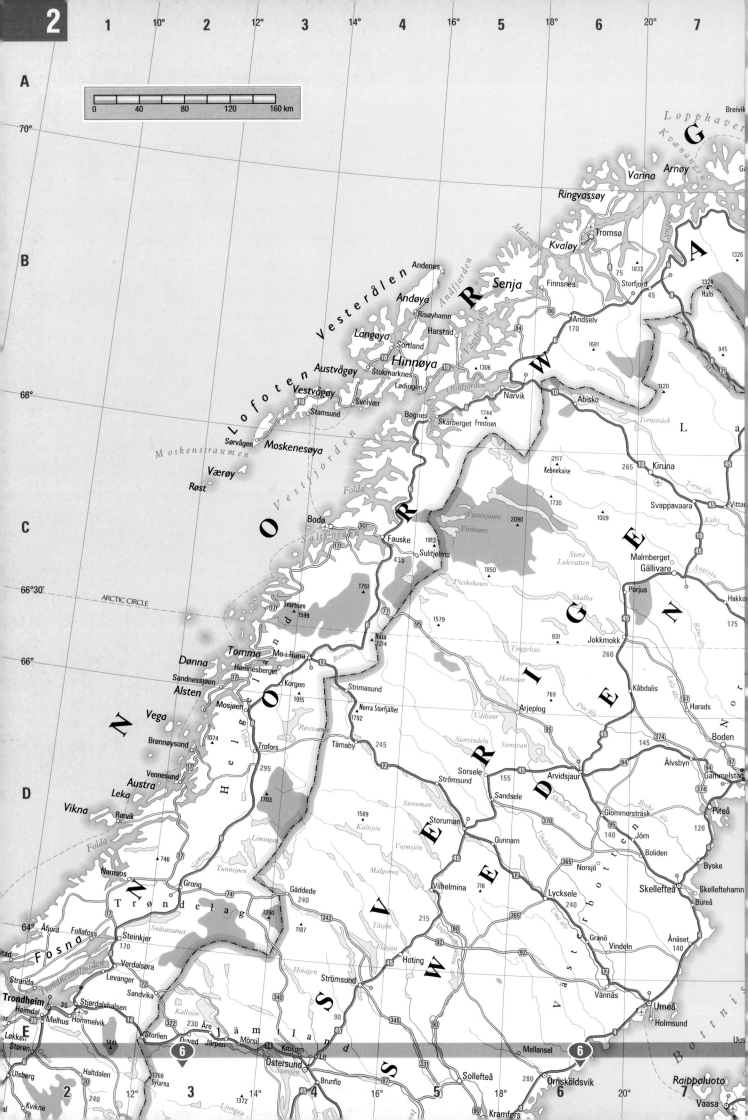

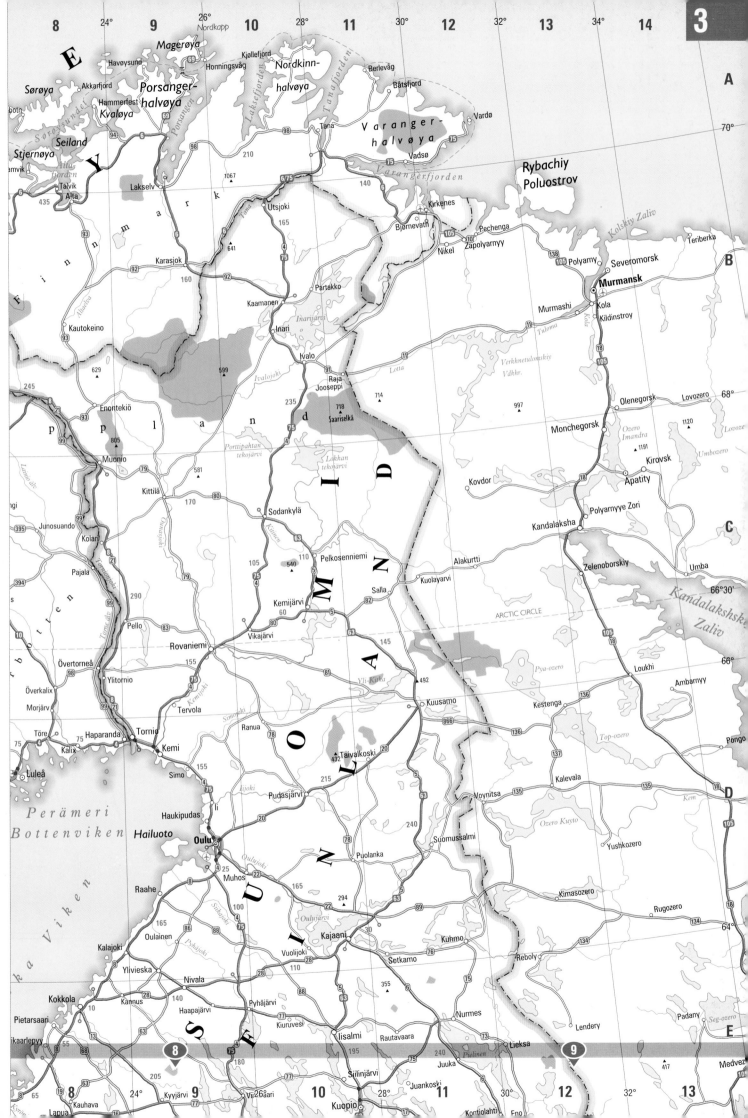

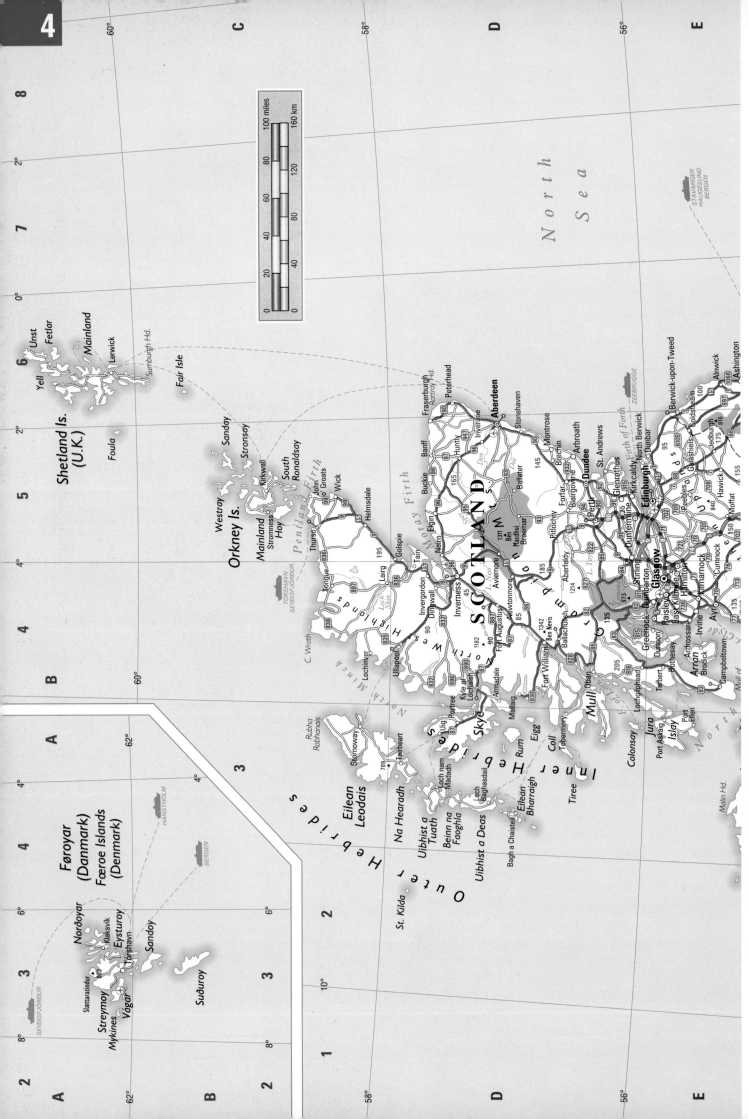

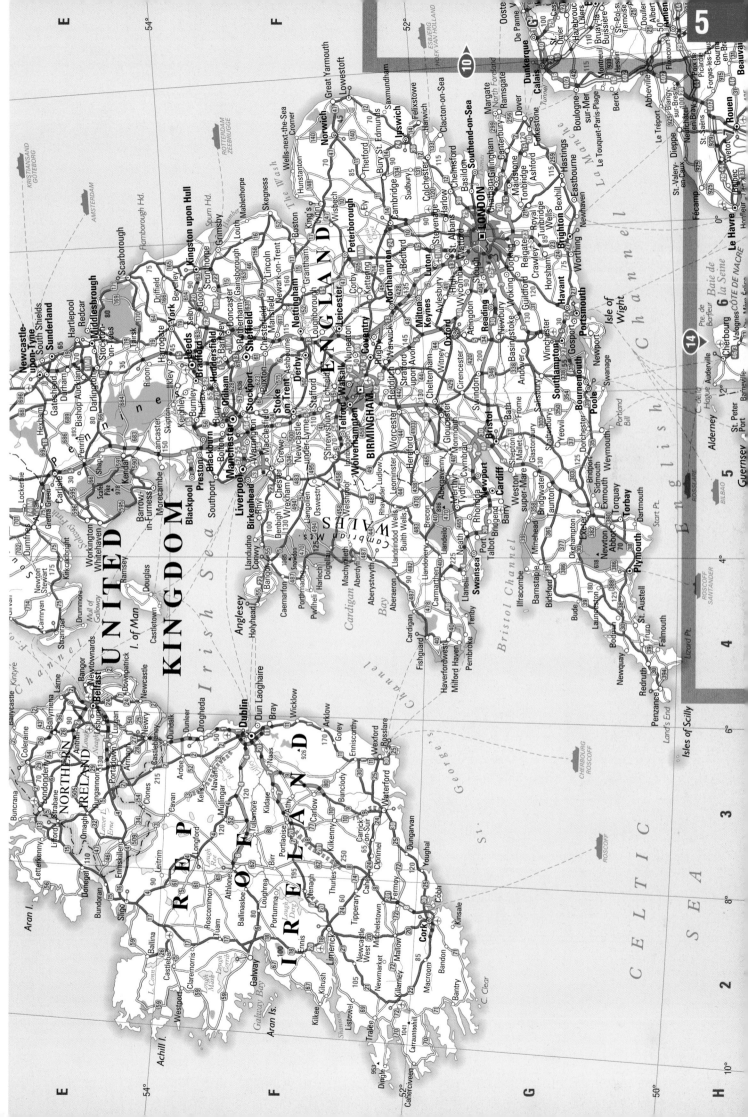

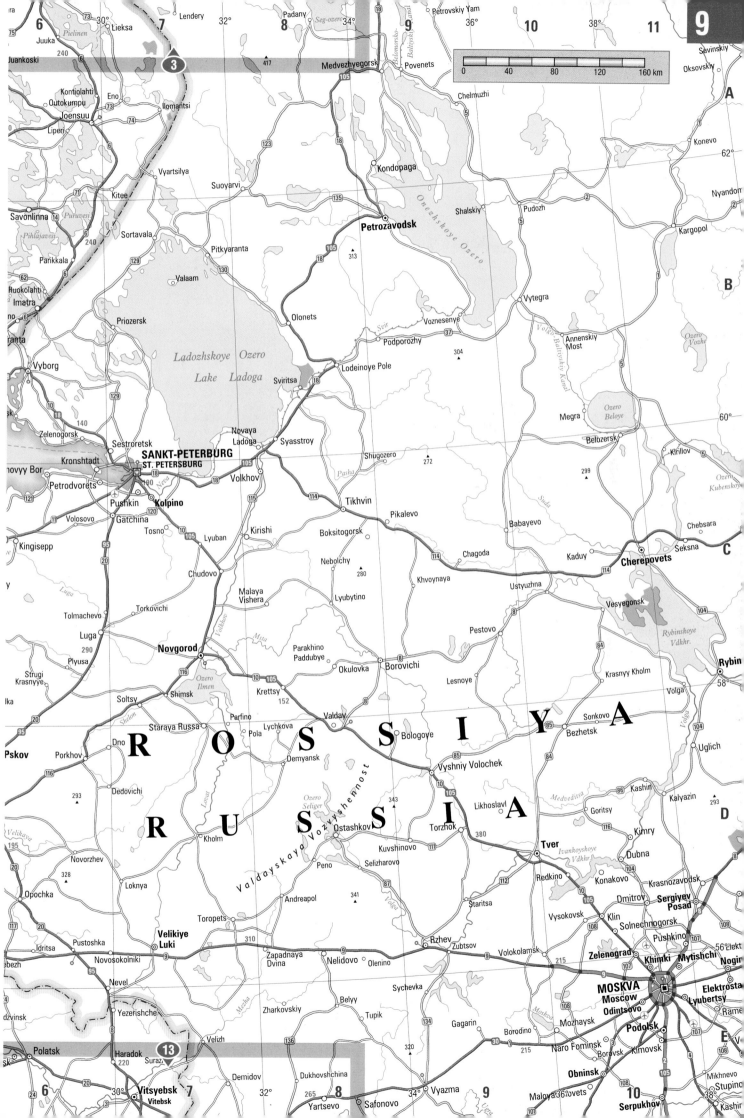

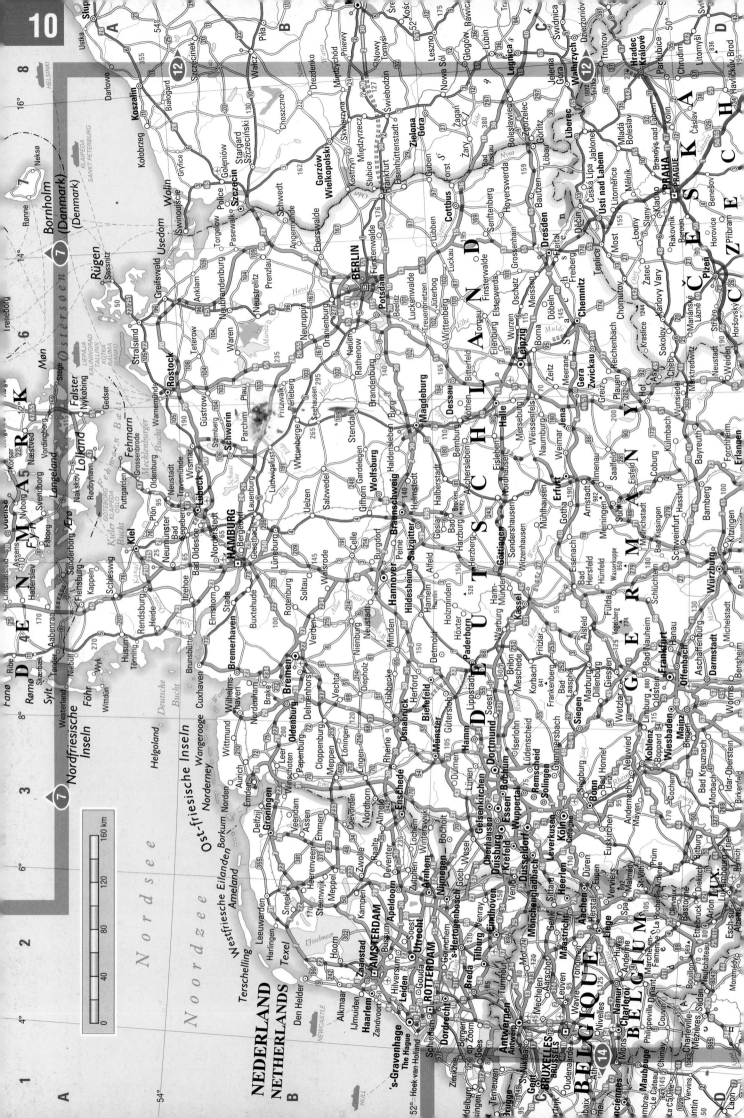

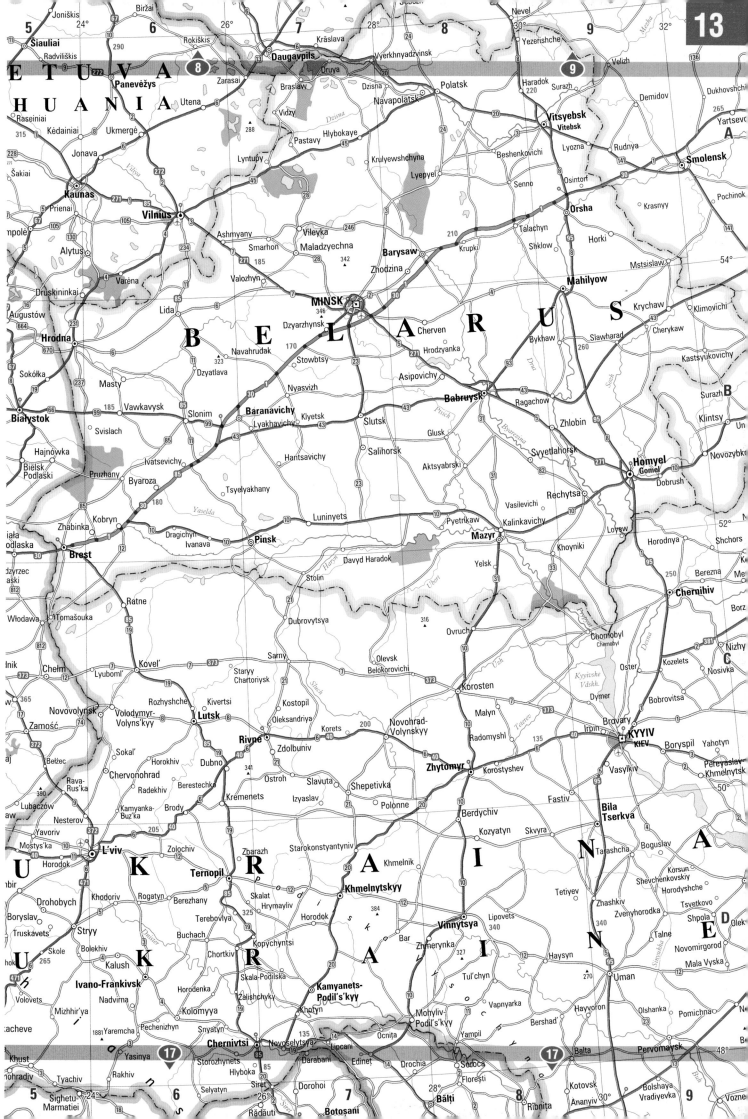

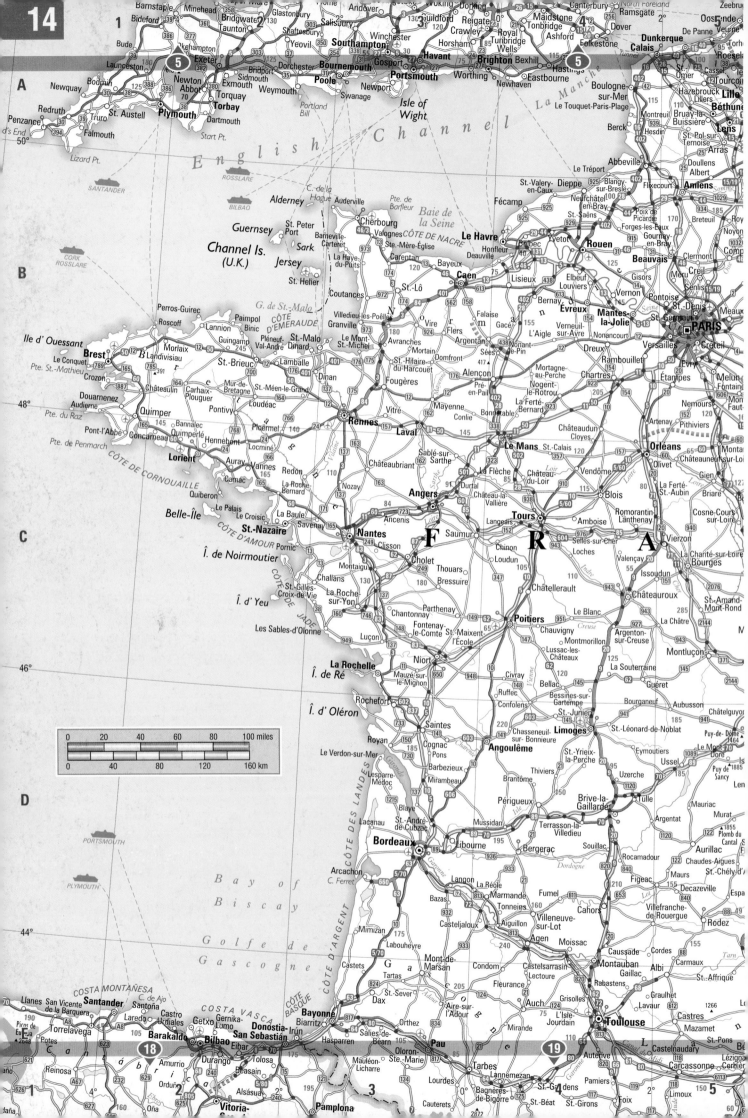

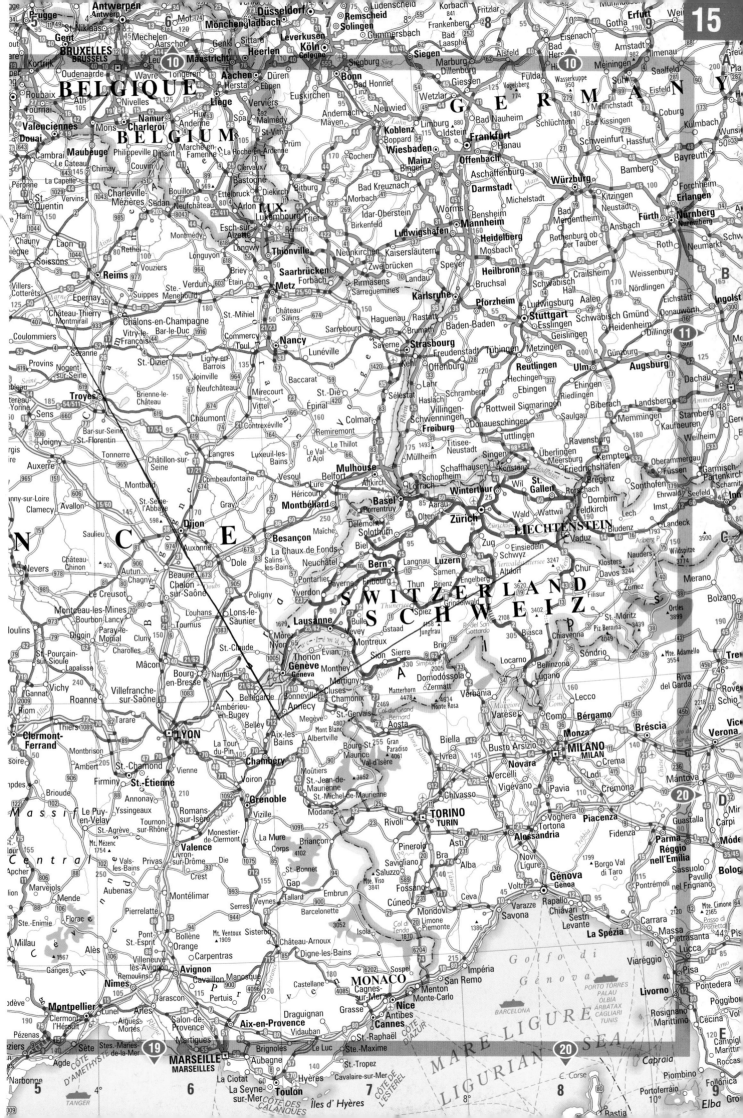

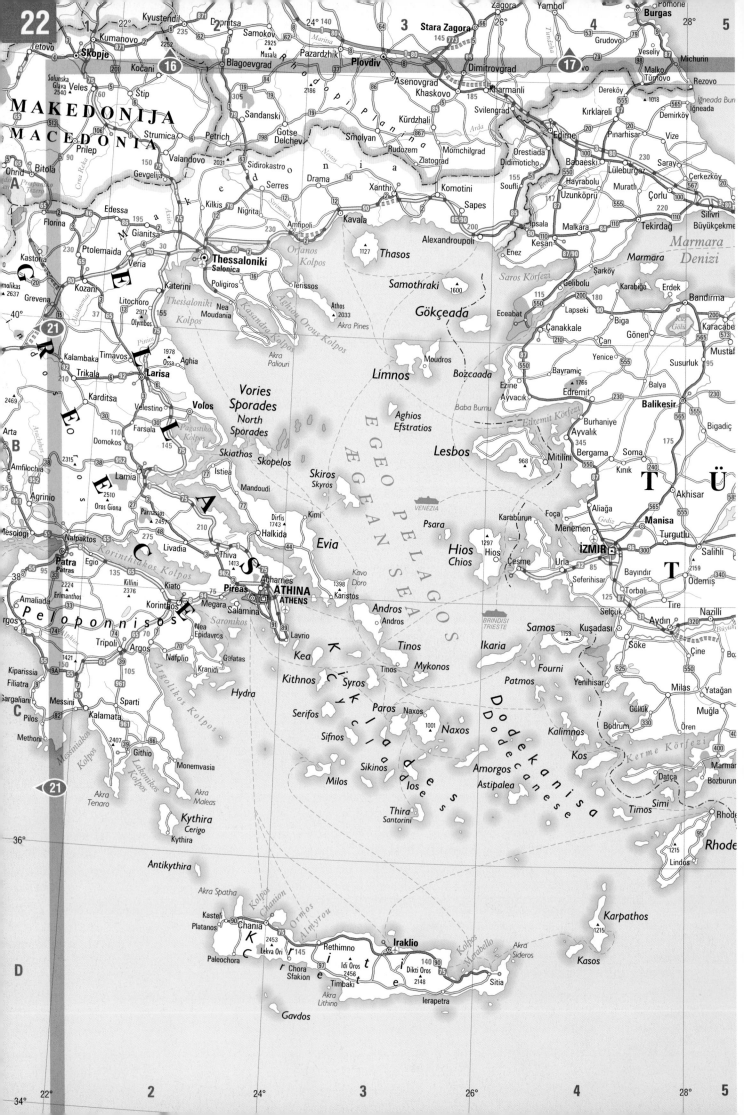

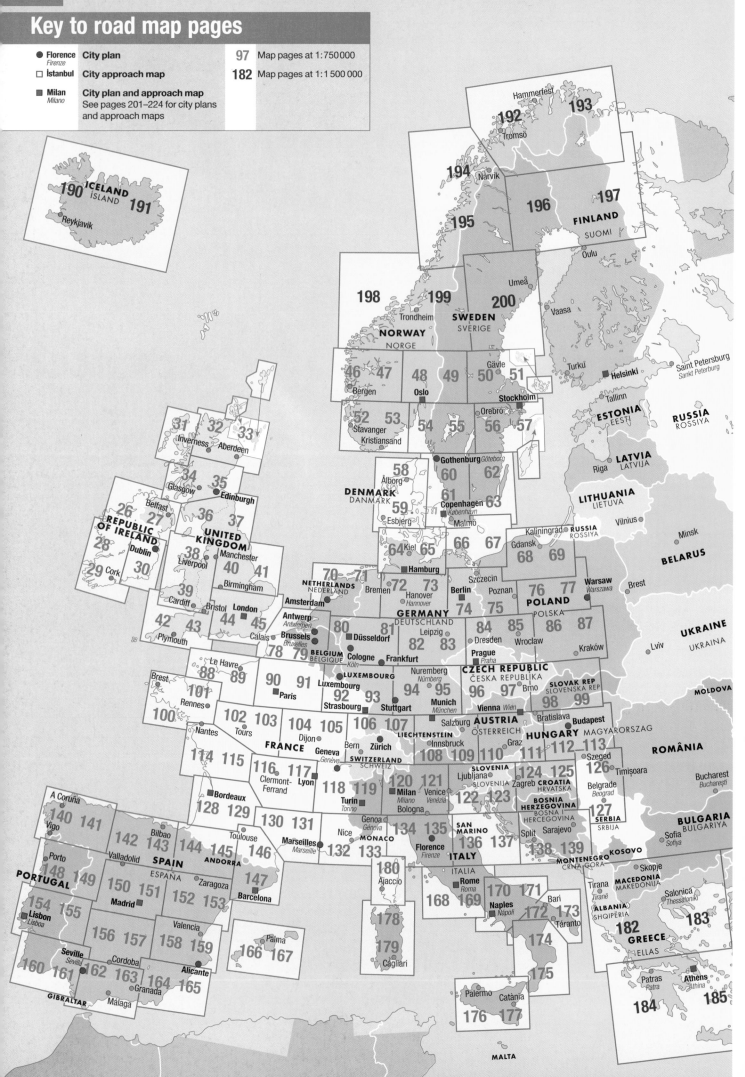

Key to road map pages

- ● Florence *Firenze* — **City plan**
- □ İstanbul — **City approach map**
- ■ Milan *Milano* — **City plan and approach map**
  See pages 201–224 for city plans and approach maps

97 Map pages at 1:750 000
182 Map pages at 1:1 500 000

190 191 ICELAND ÍSLAND
Reykjavik

192 193
Hammerfest
Tromsö
194
Narvik
195 196 197
FINLAND SUOMI
Oulu

198 199 200
SWEDEN SVERIGE
Trondheim
NORWAY NORGE
Umeå
Vaasa
Turku
Saint Petersburg *Sankt Peterburg*

46 47 48 49 50 51
Bergen Oslo
Gävle
Stockholm
Helsinki
Tallinn
ESTONIA EESTI
RUSSIA ROSSIYA

52 53 54 55 56 57
Stavanger
Kristiansand
Orebro
Riga
LATVIA LATVIJA

58 60 62
DENMARK DANMARK
Ålborg
Gothenburg *Göteborg*
LITHUANIA LIETUVA

61 63
Copenhagen *København*
Esbjerg
Malmö
Minsk

59
64 65 66 67
Kiel
Kaliningrad RUSSIA ROSSIYA
Gdansk
BELARUS

68 69

70 71 72 73 74 75 76 77
NETHERLANDS NEDERLAND
Amsterdam
Bremen Hamburg
Hanover *Hannover*
Berlin
Szczecin
Poznan
Warsaw *Warszawa*
POLAND POLSKA
Brest

31 32 33
Inverness Aberdeen

34 35
Glasgow Edinburgh
Belfast

26 27 36 37
REPUBLIC OF IRELAND
UNITED KINGDOM

28 38 40 41
Dublin Manchester
Liverpool
Birmingham

29 30 39
Cork
Cardiff
Bristol London

42 43 44 45
Plymouth Calais

80 81 82 83 84 85 86 87
Düsseldorf
GERMANY DEUTSCHLAND
Leipzig
Dresden
Wroclaw
Kraków
UKRAINE UKRAINA
Lviv

Antwerp *Antwerpen*
78 79
Brussels *Bruxelles*
BELGIUM BELGIQUE
Cologne *Köln*
Frankfurt

88 89 90 91 92 93 94 95 96 97
Le Havre
Brest
LUXEMBOURG
Luxembourg
Nuremberg *Nürnberg*
Prague *Praha*
CZECH REPUBLIC ČESKÁ REPUBLIKA
Brno
MOLDOVA

101 100 102 103 104 105 106 107 108 109 110
Rennes
Paris
Strasbourg Stuttgart
Munich *München*
Salzburg
AUSTRIA ÖSTERREICH
Vienna *Wien*
SLOVAK REP SLOVENSKÁ REP
98 99
Bratislava
Budapest
HUNGARY MAGYARORSZAG

Nantes Tours Dijon
FRANCE
Geneva *Genève*
Bern Zürich
SWITZERLAND SCHWEIZ
LIECHTENSTEIN
Innsbruck
Graz
111 112 113
Szeged
Timişoara
ROMÂNIA

114 115 116 117 118 119 120 121
Clermont-Ferrand
Lyon
Turin *Torino*
Milan *Milano*
Venice *Venézia*
SLOVENIA SLOVENIJA
Ljubljana
Zagreb CROATIA HRVATSKA
124 125 126
Belgrade *Beograd*
Bucharest *Bucureşti*
BULGARIA BULGARIYA

128 129 130 131
Bordeaux
Toulouse
Marseilles *Marseille*
132 133 134 135
Genoa *Génova*
Nice MONACO
Bologna
SAN MARINO
136 137
Florence *Firenze*
ITALY ITALIA
122 123
BOSNIA HERZEGOVINA BOSNA I HERCEGOVINA
Split Sarajevo
138 139
SERBIA SRBIJA
127
MONTENEGRO CRNA GORA
KOSOVO
Skopje
MACEDONIA MAKEDONIJA
Sofia *Sofiya*

140 141 142 143 144 145 146 147
A Coruña
Vigo
Porto
Bilbao
Valladolid
SPAIN ESPAÑA
ANDORRA
Zaragoza
Barcelona

148 149 150 151 152 153
PORTUGAL
Madrid
Valencia

154 155 156 157 158 159
Lisbon *Lisboa*

160 161 162 163 164 165
Seville *Sevilla*
Cordoba
Granada
Alicante
GIBRALTAR
Málaga

166 167
Palma

180 178 179
Ajaccio
Cágliari

168 169 170 171 172 173 174 175
Rome *Roma*
Naples *Nápoli*
Bari
Táranto
ITALY ITALIA

176 177
Palermo
Catània
MALTA

182 183
Tirana *Tiranë*
ALBANIA SHQIPËRIA
GREECE ELLAS
Salonica *Thessaloníki*

184 185
Patras *Patra*
Athens *Athína*

Distance table

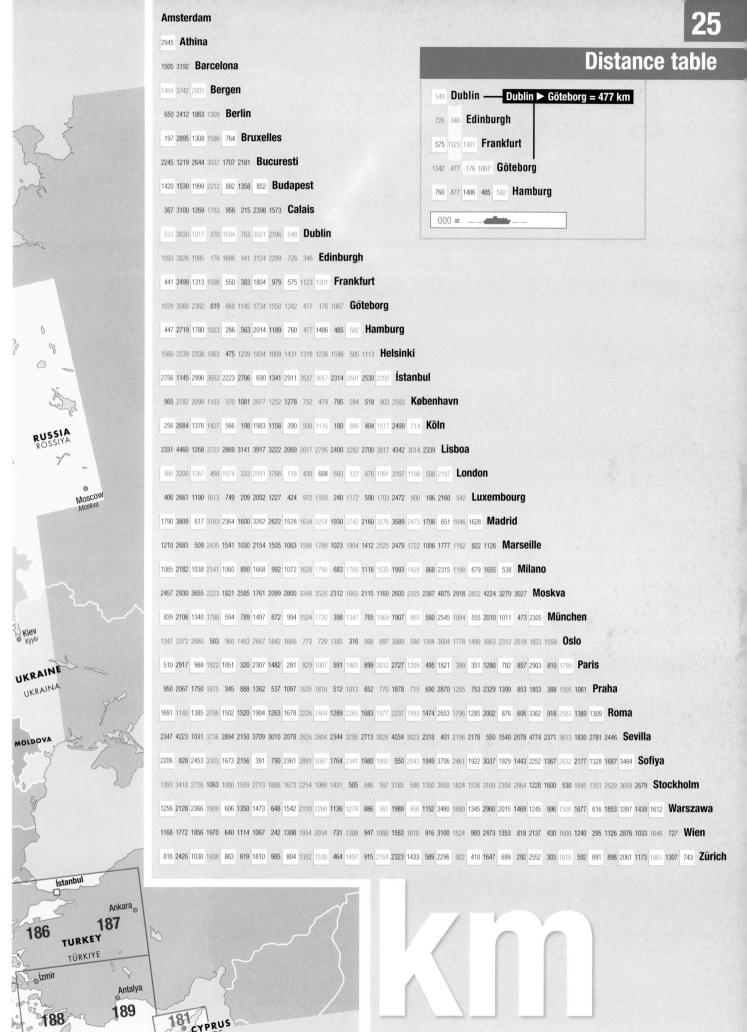

Legend:

548	Dublin	Dublin ▶ Göteborg = 477 km
726 346	Edinburgh	
575 1123 1301	Frankfurt	
1342 477 176 1067	Göteborg	
760 477 1486 485 582	Hamburg	

000 = (ferry)

	Amsterdam	Athina	Barcelona	Bergen	Berlin	Bruxelles	Bucuresti	Budapest	Calais	Dublin	Edinburgh	Frankfurt	Göteborg	Hamburg	Helsinki	İstanbul	København	Köln	Lisboa	London	Luxembourg	Madrid	Marseille	Milano	Moskva	München	Oslo	Paris	Praha	Roma	Sevilla	Sofiya	Stockholm	Warszawa	Wien
Athina	2945																																		
Barcelona	1505	3192																																	
Bergen	1484	3742	2803																																
Berlin	650	2412	1863	1309																															
Bruxelles	197	2895	1308	1586	764																														
Bucuresti	2245	1219	2644	3037	1707	2181																													
Budapest	1420	1530	1999	2212	882	1358	852																												
Calais	367	3100	1269	1783	956	215	2398	1573																											
Dublin	533	3630	1817	270	1504	763	3021	2196	548																										
Edinburgh	1093	3826	1995	176	1696	941	3124	2299	726	346																									
Frankfurt	441	2499	1313	1508	550	383	1804	979	575	1123	1301																								
Göteborg	1029	3080	2362	819	668	1145	1734	1550	1342	477	176	1067																							
Hamburg	447	2719	1780	1023	286	563	2014	1189	760	477	1486	485	582																						
Helsinki	1560	2539	2338	1063	475	1239	1834	1009	1431	1318	1236	1598	505	1113																					
İstanbul	2756	1145	2990	3653	2223	2706	690	1341	2911	3537	3657	2314	2891	2530	2350																				
København	965	2782	2090	1103	370	1081	2077	1252	1278	752	479	795	284	518	803	2593																			
Köln	256	2684	1376	1427	566	198	1983	1158	390	938	1116	180	986	404	1517	2499	714																		
Lisboa	2331	4460	1268	3723	2869	3141	3917	3222	2069	2617	2795	2400	3282	2700	3817	4342	3014	2339																	
London	480	3200	1387	458	1074	333	2591	1766	118	430	608	693	122	878	1991	3107	1188	508	2187																
Luxembourg	406	2661	1190	1613	749	209	2052	1227	424	972	1150	240	1172	590	1703	2472	900	186	2160	542															
Madrid	1790	3809	617	3183	2364	1600	3262	2622	1528	1634	2254	1930	2742	2160	3276	3589	2473	1798	651	1646	1628														
Marseille	1210	2683	509	2435	1541	1030	2154	1505	1063	1588	1789	1023	1994	1412	2525	2479	1722	1006	1777	1182	822	1126													
Milano	1085	2182	1038	2141	1060	890	1668	992	1072	1620	1798	683	1700	1118	1535	1993	1428	868	2315	1190	679	1655	538												
Moskva	2457	2930	3655	2223	1821	2585	1761	2099	2800	3348	3526	2312	1665	2115	1160	2605	2325	2387	4875	2918	2852	4224	3270	3027											
München	839	2106	1340	1788	594	789	1497	672	994	1524	1720	398	1347	765	1069	1907	969	580	2545	1094	555	2010	1011	473	2305										
Oslo	1347	3372	2680	503	960	1463	2667	1842	1660	773	729	1385	316	900	697	3089	590	1304	3604	1778	1490	3063	2312	2018	1823	1559									
Paris	510	2917	988	1922	1051	320	2307	1482	281	829	1007	591	1481	899	2012	2727	1209	495	1821	399	351	1280	782	857	2903	810	1799								
Praha	950	2067	1750	1675	345	888	1362	537	1097	1635	1816	512	1013	652	770	1878	715	690	2870	1205	753	2329	1399	853	1853	388	1305	1061							
Roma	1691	1140	1385	2706	1502	1520	1904	1263	1678	2226	2404	1289	2265	1683	1977	2237	1993	1474	2653	1796	1285	2002	876	606	3362	918	2583	1389	1309						
Sevilla	2347	4223	1031	3736	2894	2150	3709	3010	2078	2626	2804	2344	3295	2713	3826	4034	3023	2318	401	2196	2178	550	1540	2078	4774	2371	3613	1830	2781	2446					
Sofiya	2206	828	2453	3103	1673	2156	391	790	2361	2891	3087	1764	2341	1980	1800	550	2043	1949	3706	2461	1922	3037	1929	1443	2252	1367	2632	2177	1328	1687	3484				
Stockholm	1393	3418	2726	1063	1006	1509	2713	1888	1673	2254	1069	1431	505	946	167	3185	590	1350	3650	1834	1536	3109	2358	2064	1228	1600	530	1845	1351	2629	3659	2679			
Warszawa	1256	2128	2366	1909	606	1350	1473	648	1542	2110	2268	1136	1274	886	361	1989	956	1152	3480	1680	1345	2960	2015	1469	1245	996	1506	1677	616	1853	3397	1439	1612		
Wien	1168	1772	1856	1970	640	1114	1067	242	1308	1954	2034	731	1308	947	1088	1583	1010	916	3100	1524	993	2473	1353	818	2137	430	1600	1240	295	1126	2876	1033	1646	727	
Zürich	816	2426	1030	1938	863	619	1810	985	804	1352	1530	464	1497	915	2164	2323	1433	589	2296	922	410	1647	699	292	2552	303	1815	592	691	898	2061	1173	1861	1307	743

km

RUSSIA ROSSIYA

Moscow Moskva

Kiev Kyyiv

UKRAINE UKRAINA

MOLDOVA

İstanbul

Ankara

186 **187**

TURKEY TÜRKIYE

İzmir

Antalya

188 **189**

181 CYPRUS KYPROS
Nicosia

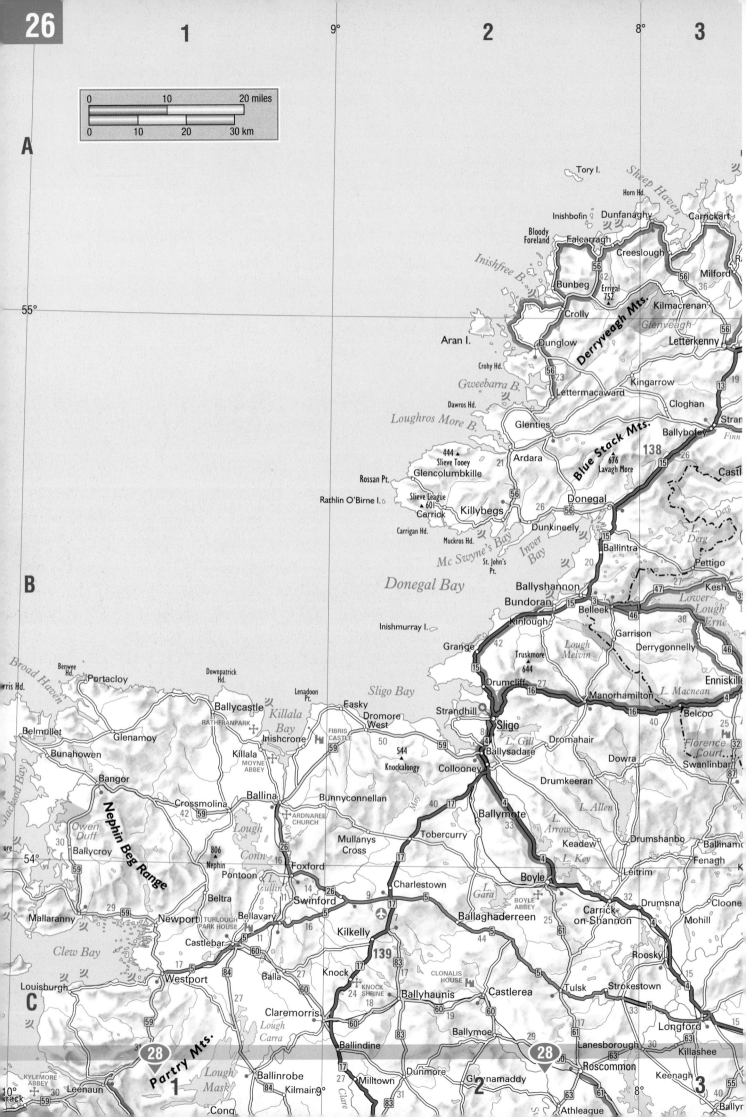

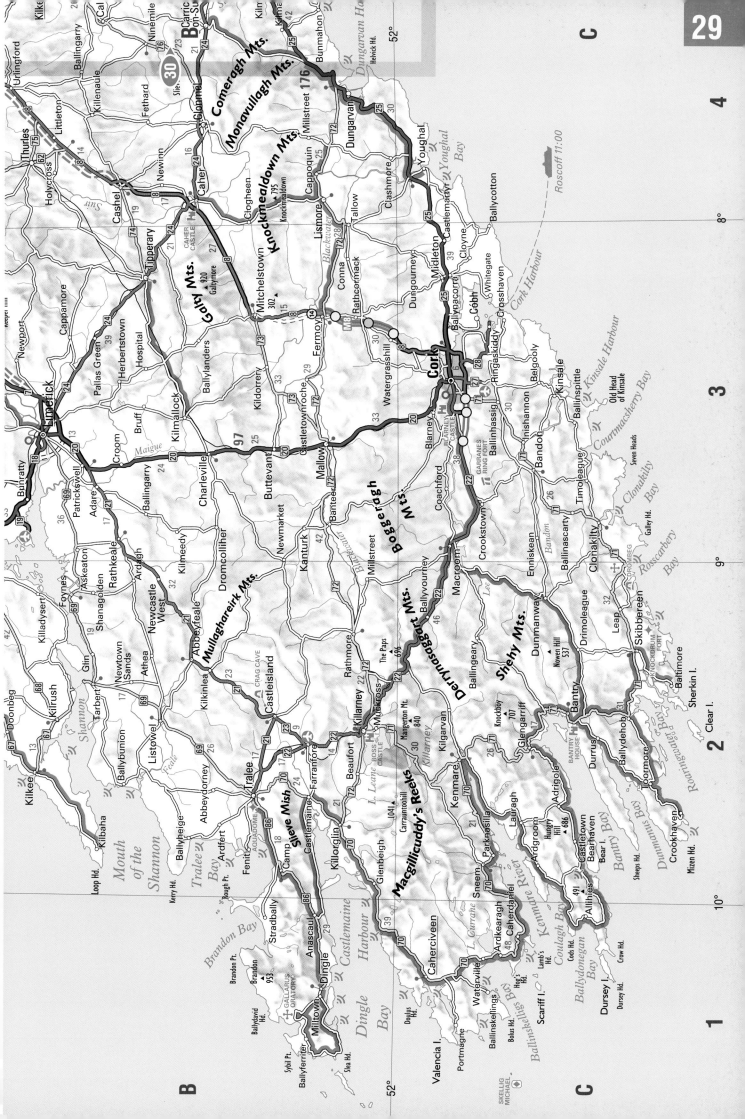

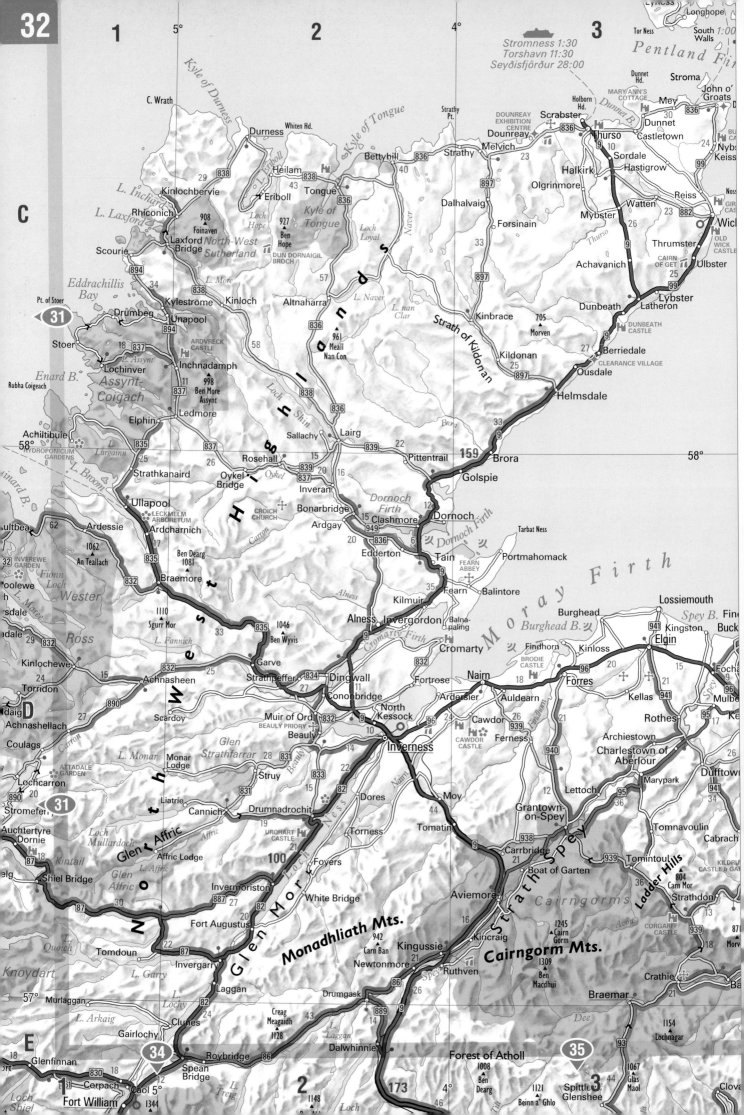

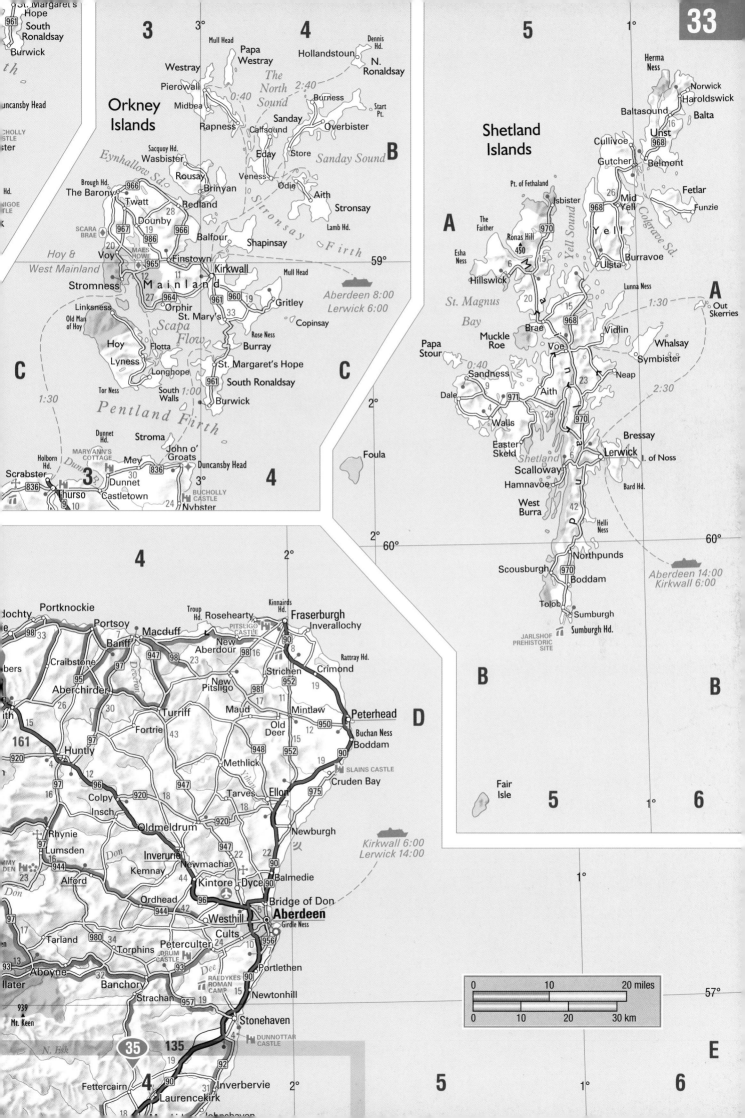

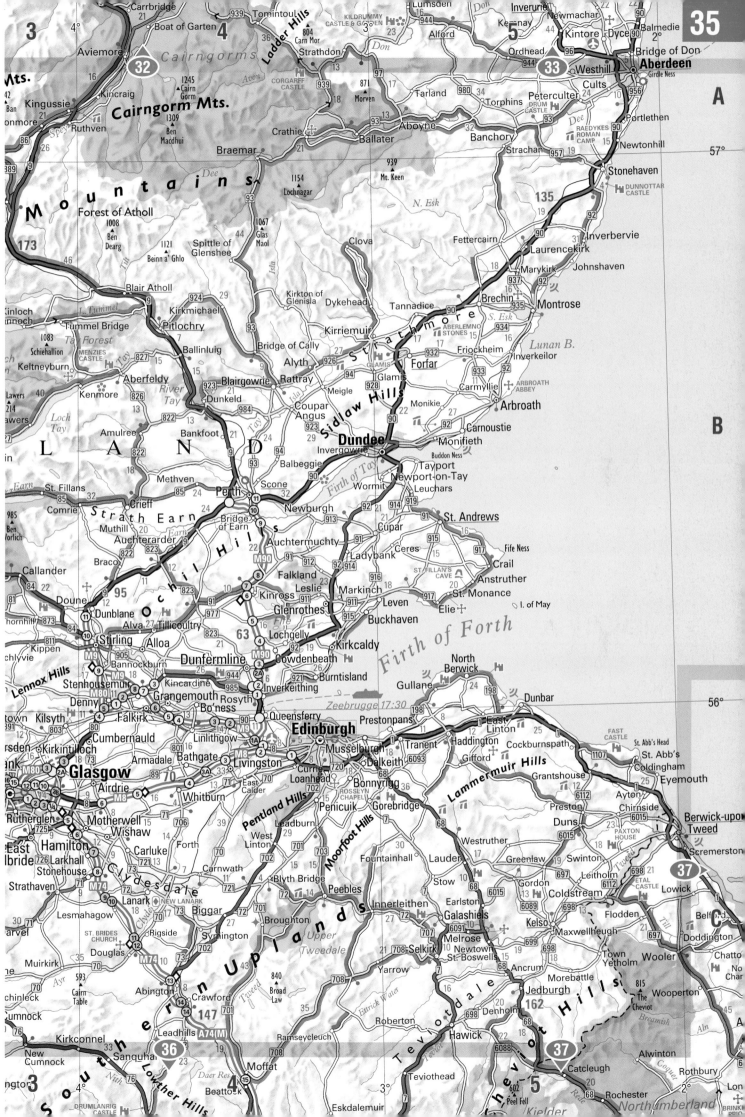

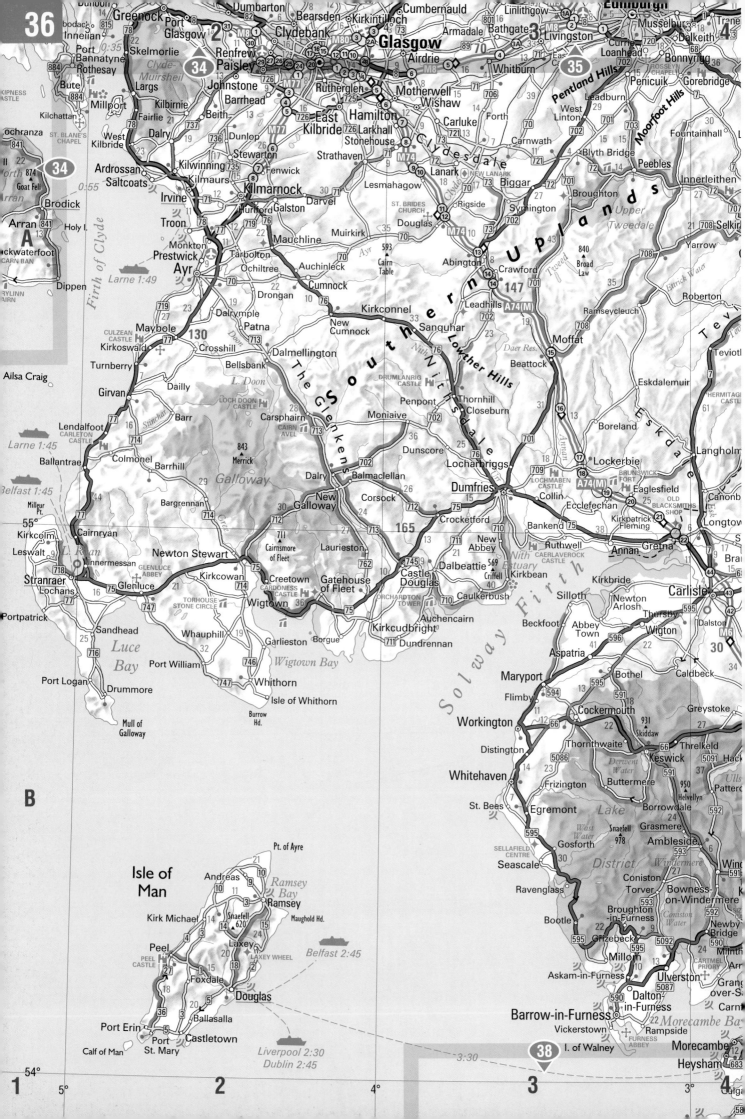

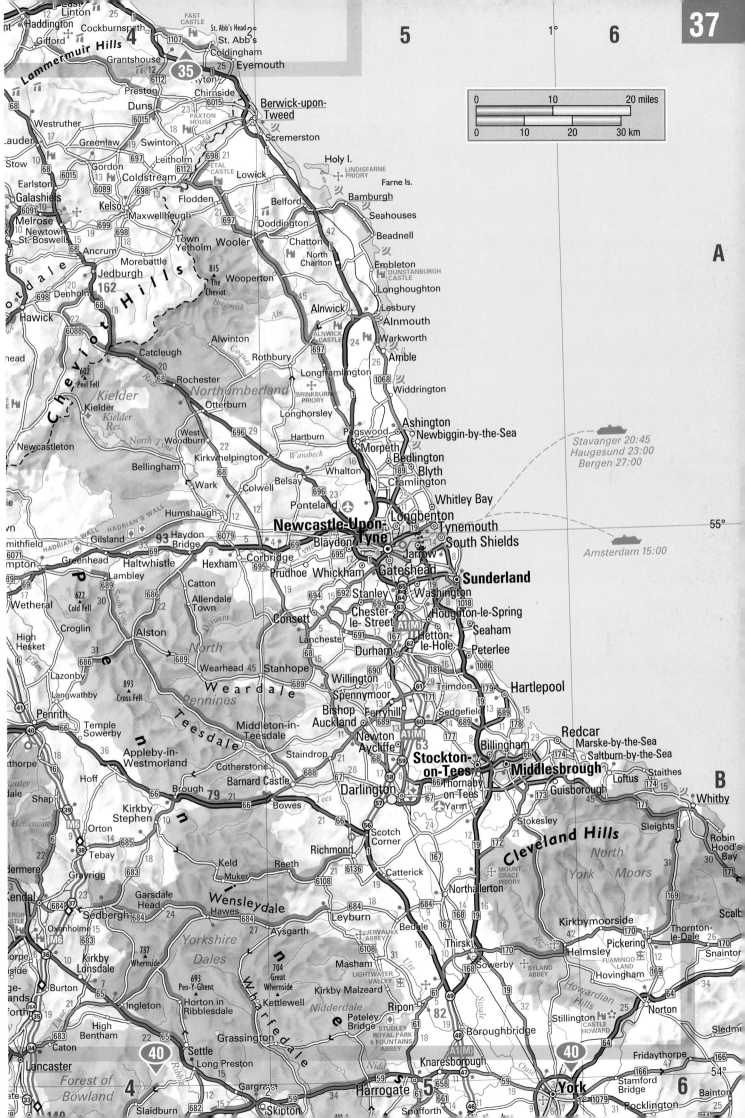

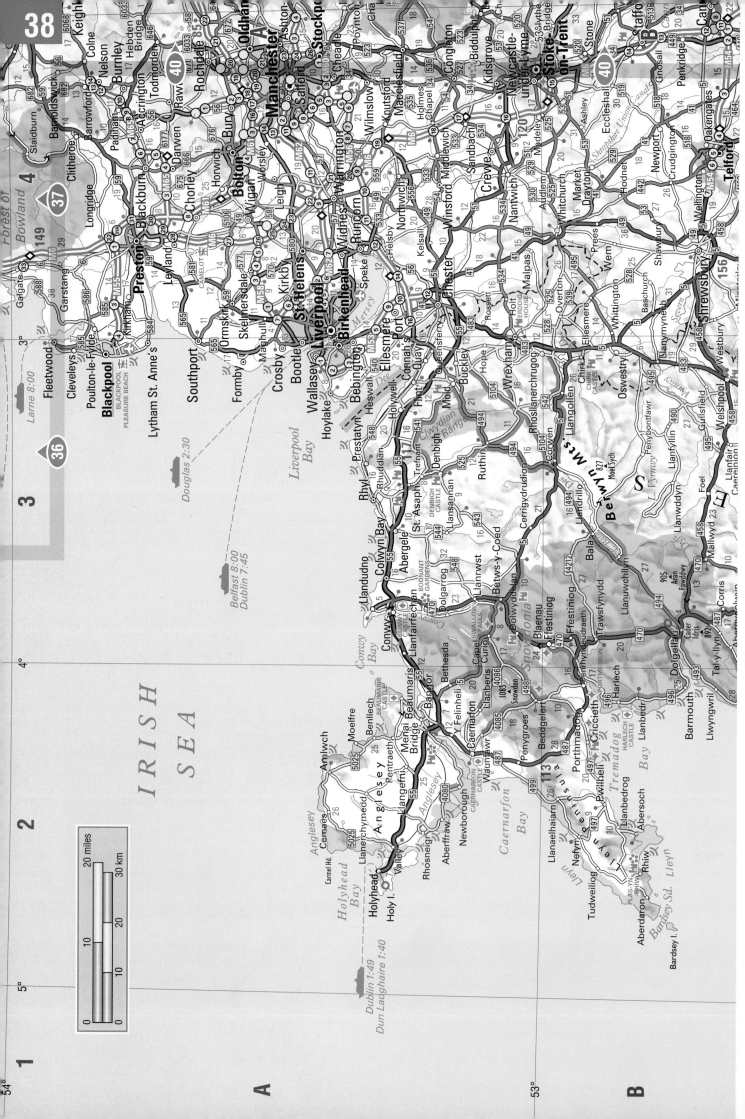

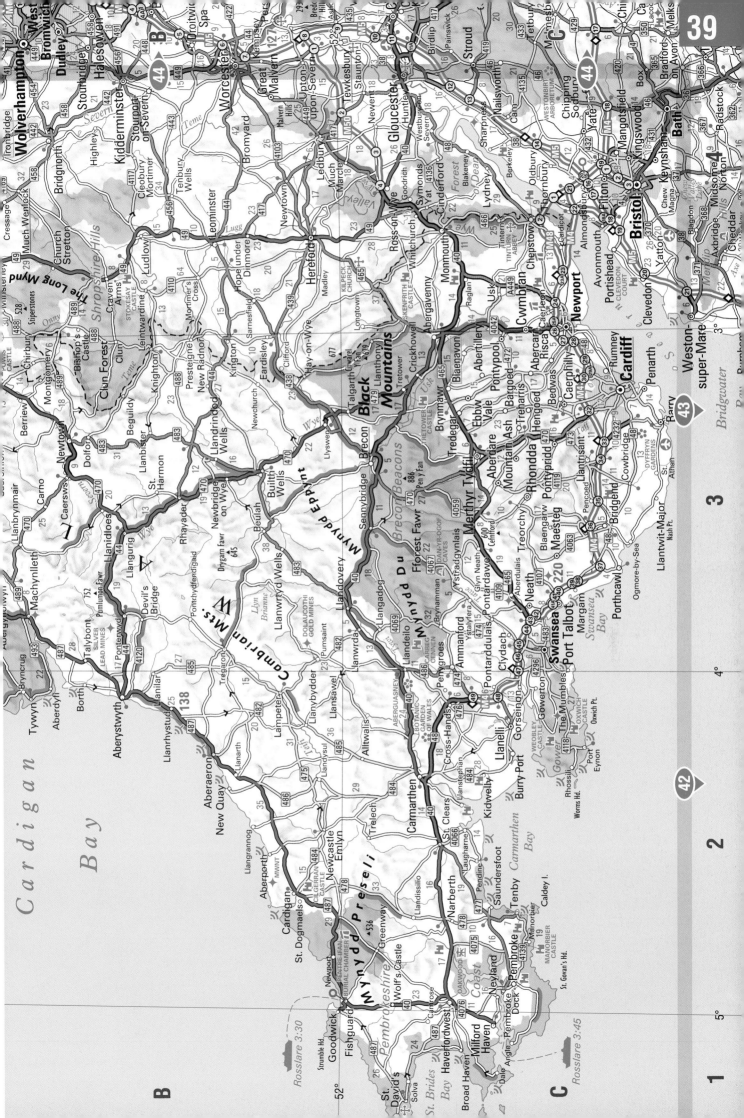

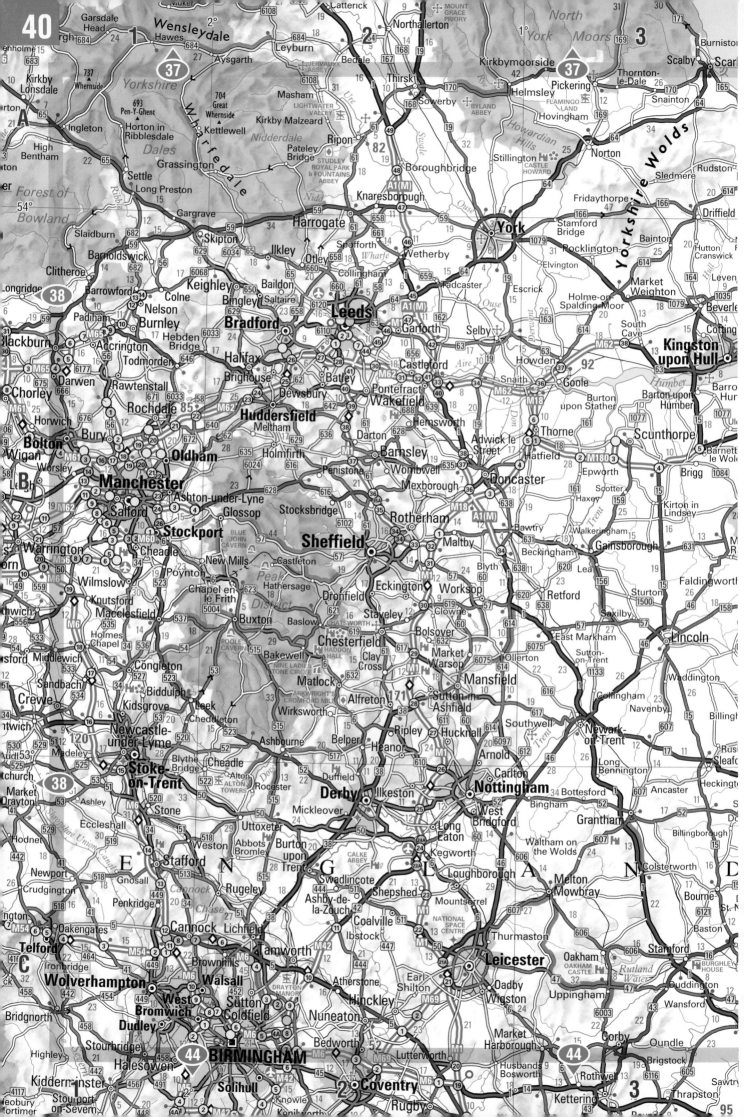

3 0° **4** 1° **5** A

NORTH SEA

Filey

165

Flamborough

Bridlington
Burton Agnes

Bridlington Bay

54°

165

Skipsea

North Frodingham

25

Hornsea

165

Aldbrough

ham 19

Sproatley

Hedon

1033

Withernsea

Keyingham

w upon nber 31

1033

Patrington

Easington

160

Immingham

ceby

24
18

Grimsby

Spurn Hd.

180

Cleethorpes

Laceby

Humberston

Rotterdam 12:30
Zeebrugge 12:45

B

1173

18

Caistor

1031

North Somercotes

North Thoresby

Saltfleet

46

16

Market asen 27

Binbrook

631

41

ST. JAMES CHURCH

1031

Louth

135

157

22

Wragby

135

21

Withern

157

Mablethorpe

Sutton-on-Sea

16

23

Scamblesby

1104

Huttoft

157

158

20

1111

Bardney

16

1028

Alford 26

Horncastle

52

Woodhall Spa

16

Partney

158

Burgh le Marsh

135

Mareham le Fen

Spilsby

16

Skegness

33

155

Coningsby

16

Wainfleet All Saints

hay

135

29

34

52

The Wash

kington ord

Sibsey

Wrangle

Norfolk Coast

53°

on

17

12

1121

Benington

Brancaster

Wells-next-the-Sea

Cley

Sheringham

52

Boston

16

149

Burnham Market

31

149

Cromer

neshead

12

Kirton

25

HOLKHAM HALL

148

onington

8

Hunstanton

Heacham

Docking

Little Walsingham

34

Holt

Mundesley

Gosberton

11

18

Dersingham

148

140

Saxthorpe

Pinchbeck

9

Long Sutton

SANDRINGHAM

149

Fakenham

BICKLING HALL

149

North Walsham

Spalding

151

Holbeach

27

1067

Reepham

34

Aylsham

36

Stalham

51

17

20

King's Lynn

148

26

39

DINOSAUR ADVENTURE PARK

140

Coltishall

151

149

29

Martham

Deeping Nicholas

16

1101

14

Gayton

1065

Litcham

1067

Drayton

19

Wroxham

1064

Caister-on-Sea

22

1073

20

CASTLE ACRE PRIORY

25

Dereham

16

47

Norwich

47

Acle

47

Great Yarmouth

Market Deeping

Crowland

Wisbech

15

13

Swaffham

1075

New Costessey

BURGH CASTLE

The Broads

Gorleston-on-sea

15

16

47

Downham Market

1122

Fincham OXBURGH HALL

47

20

11

18

26

143

12

Eye

Nene

Outwell

4

1065

Stoke Ferry

Watton

Wymondham

146

Oulton

Corton

Peterborough

141

March

Hilgay

Methwold

Attleborough

45

21

Oulton Broad

Lowestoft

16

Yaxley

20

134

37

11

31

9

16

A1(M)

F e n s

Breckland

Bu

45

Beccles

146

15

Ramsey

142

Chatteris

45

Littleport

GRIMES GRAVES

10

1075

140

23

27

14

141

Somersham

20

Lakenheath

Brandon

Thetford

31

69

Harleston

22

145

Wrentham

Ely

1065

Diss

Scole

12

3 **4** 1° **5**

0 10 20 miles
0 10 20 30 km

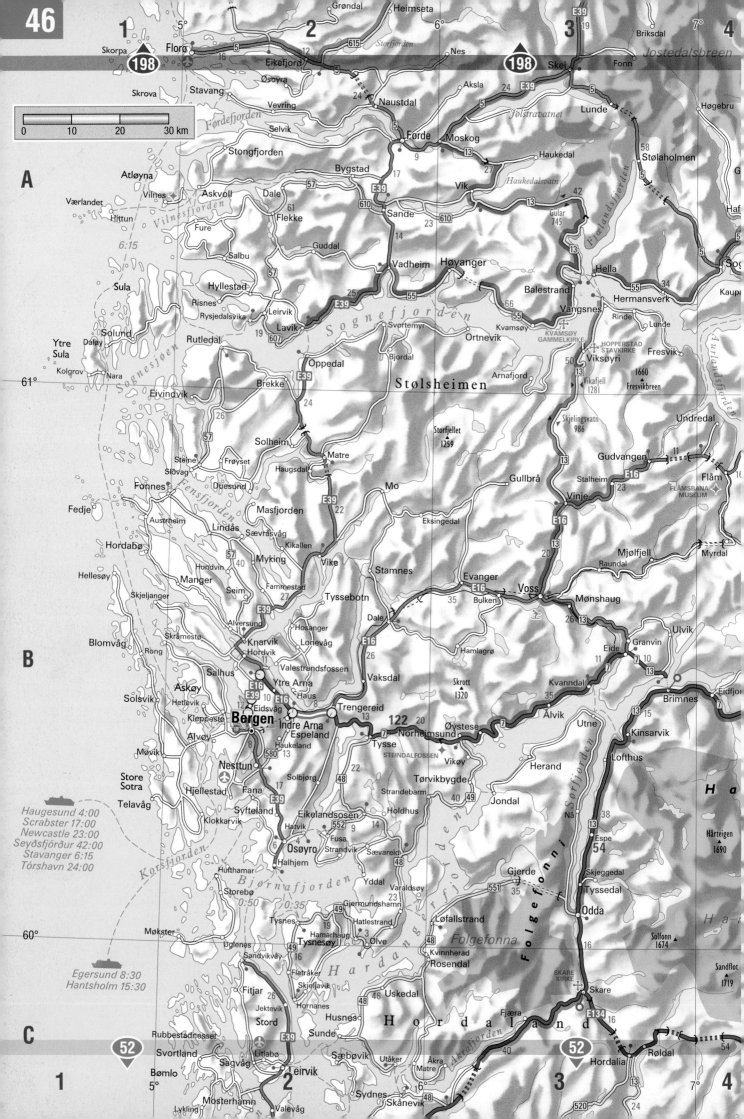

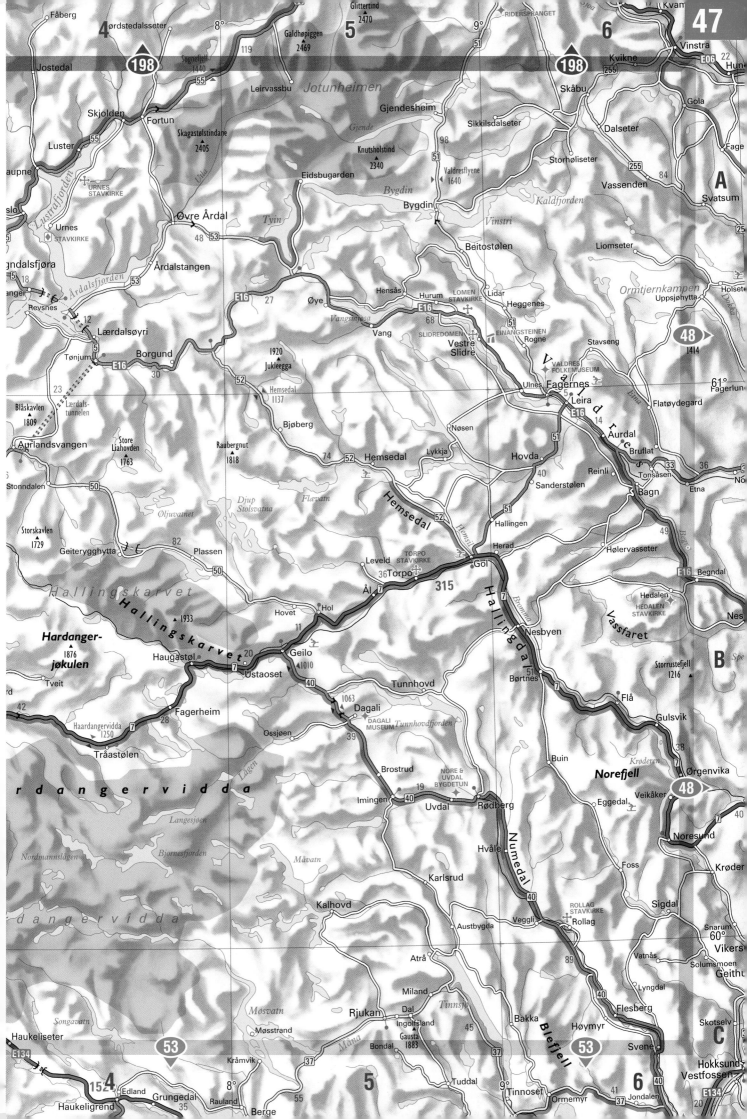

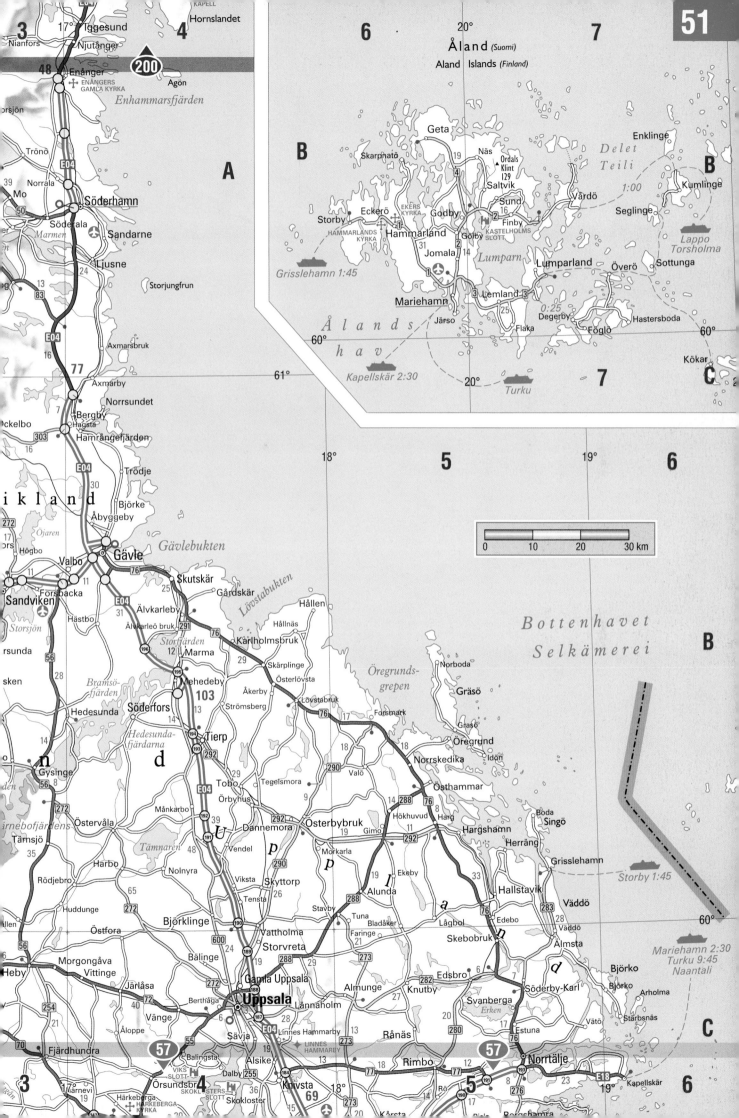

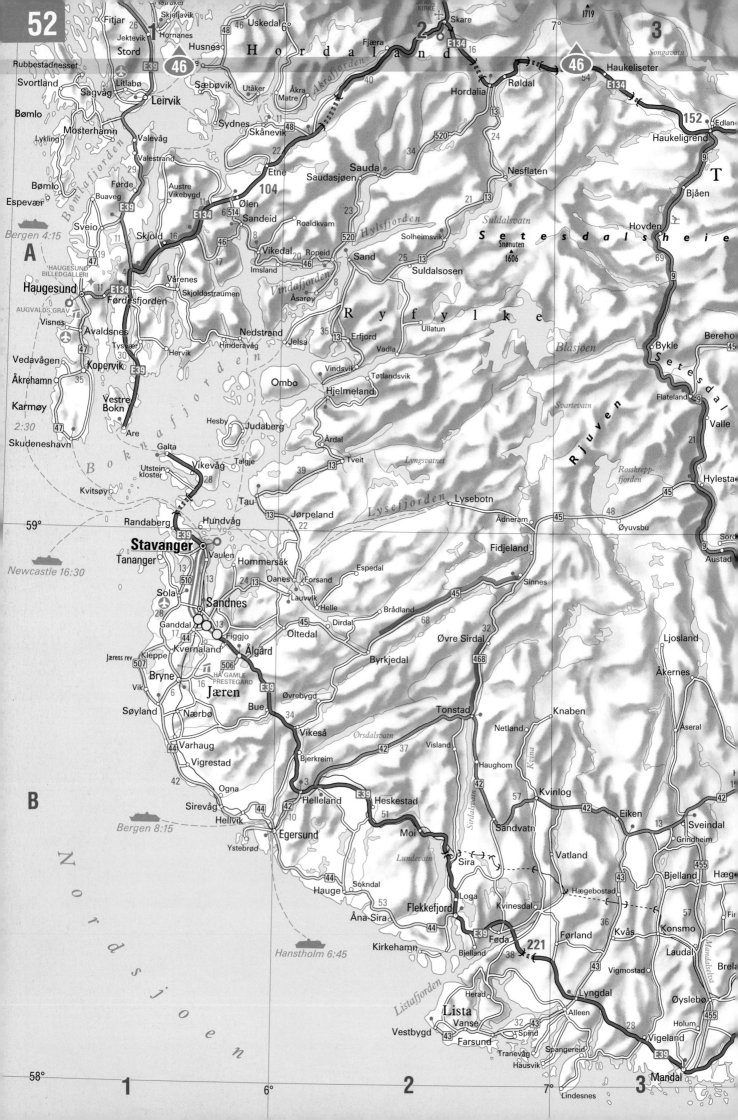

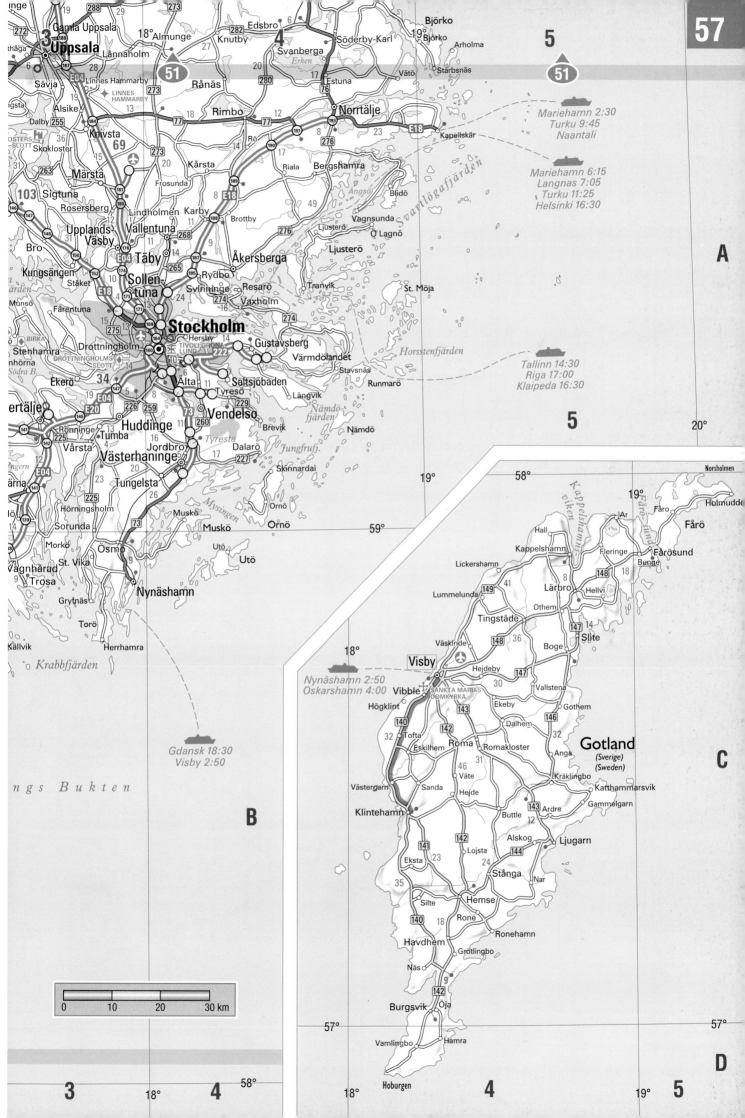

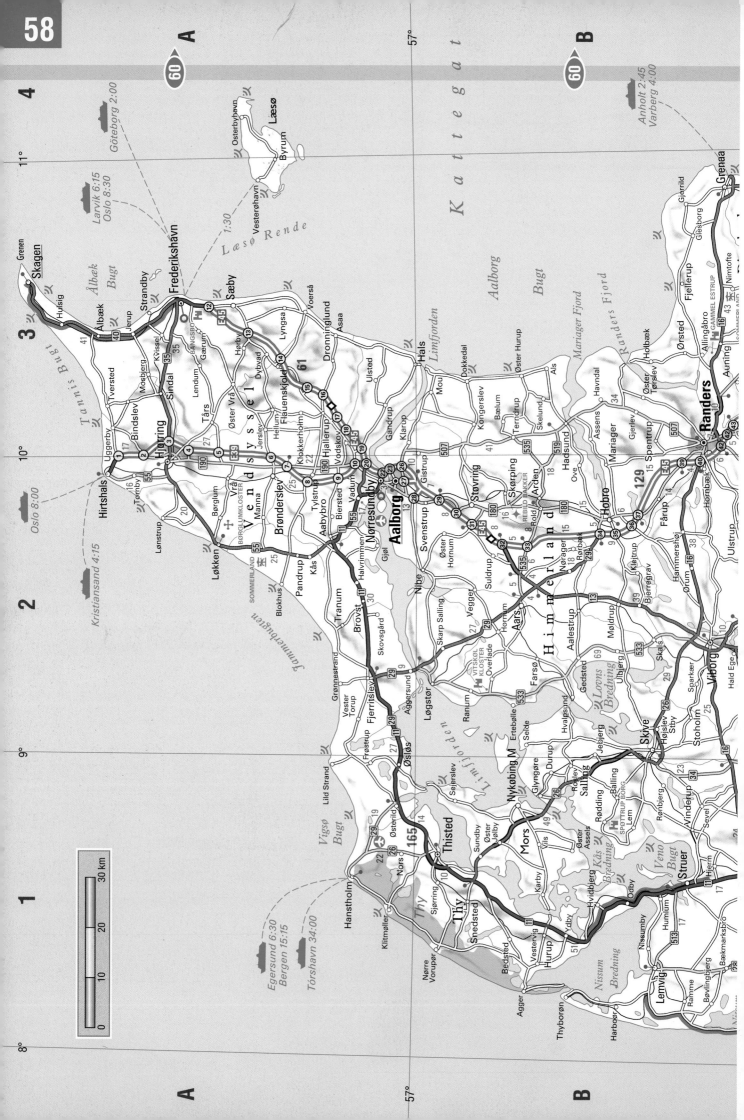

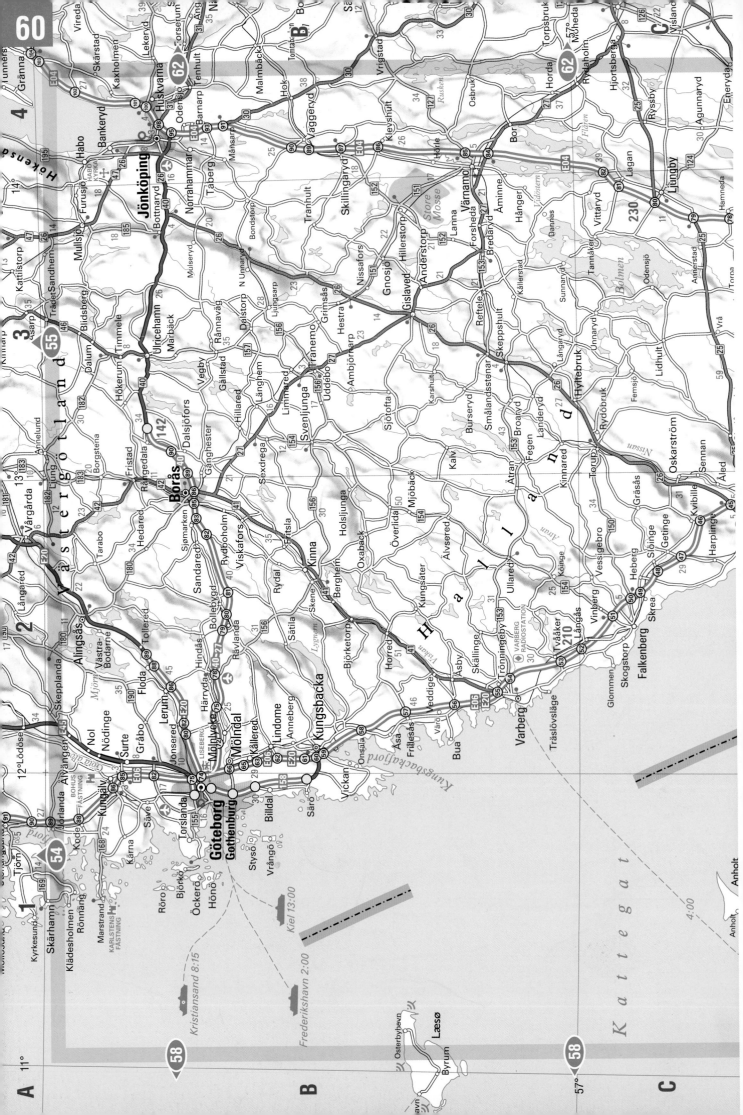

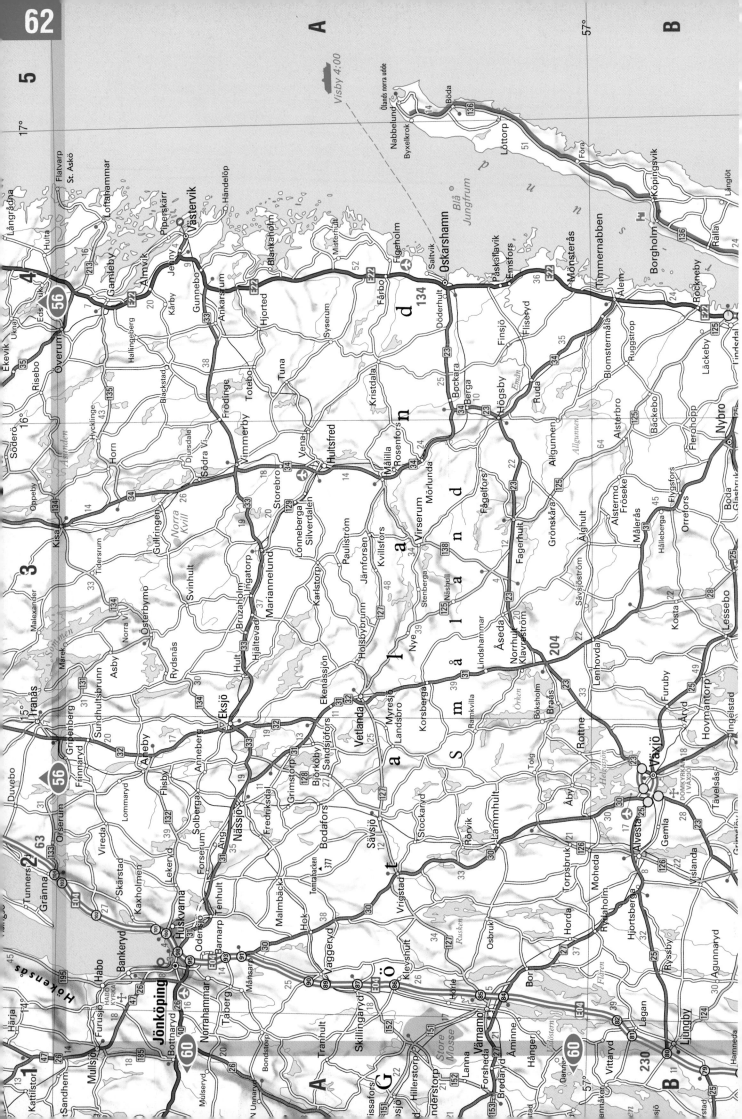

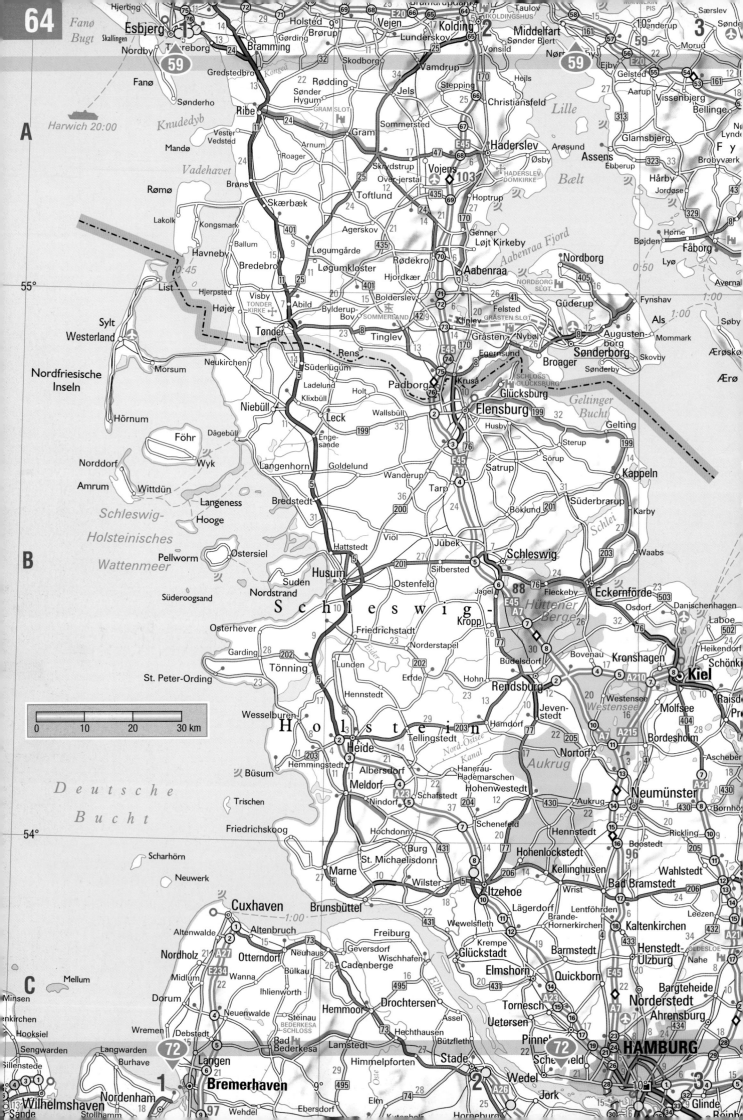

Stenshuvud **3** 15° **4** 16° **5**

0 10 20 30 km

A

Vik

Simrishamn

s

MMINGEHUS

Skillinge

ren

holmsgattet

Ertholmene

Hammeren

HAMMARSHUS Sandvig-Allinge

Tejn

Bornholm Rø Gudhjem

(Danmark) Hasle Klemensker

(Denmark) Nyker Svaneke

Øster-

marie

København 6:00 Rønne Nylars 38 Åkirkeby Neksø

28

Pedersker Snogebæk

55°

5:15

Jaroslawiec

B

J. Kopań

203 64 *Wieprza*

Darłowo Stary
Jaroslaw

Dąbki MUZEUM
DARŁOWO Sławn

København 9:00 **68**

Malmö 9:00 Łazy *J.* E28 32

Ystad 6:30 203 *Bukowo* 6 Ostrowi

Mielno *J. Jamno* Lejkowo

Jamno

Ustronie Sarbinowo Sianów

Morskie 42 11 6 206 35 Nacław

Mrzeżyno 11 Koszalin Bonin

Dobrzyca ZAMEK W. Manowo

Dygowo Wrzosowo KOSZALINIE

27 26 Biesiekierz Mostowo

Niechorze 102 163 Bieśiekierz Rosnowo 37 11 *R*

Rewal Trzebiatów 21 Niedalino 31 167

Pobierowo 102 31 Gościno 166 Białogard Dargiń 54°

Dziwnów 103 Cerkwica 18 19 Karlino 19 25 Bobolice

Międzywodzie 23 109 Gorawino E28 t6 163 12 169 171

Kamień Swierzno 17 6 Rymań Sławoborze 167 Tychowo

Wolinski 102 32 Kolczewo 105 Rzesznikowo 219 Tychówka 29

Pomorski Mechowo 33 Rabino 167 Grzmiąca C

Międzyzdroje 107 13 Gryfice 6 Zabrowo 23 162 23 Białowąs **5**

ujscie 3 21 15 18 108 Słowa 75 Polczyn- 172 18

Lubin Gołczewo 20 Płoty E28 Resko Rusinowo Zdrój 163

Wolin E65 **75** 152 35 Świdwin 24 172

r Haff 106 Stragard ZAMEK W. Barwice **5**

Zalew Przybiernów Żabowo 18 Brzeźno POŁCZYNIE 171 Ostropole

Szczeciński **3** 15° **4** 151 16°

Nowe Warpno Radowo *Drawski* 27

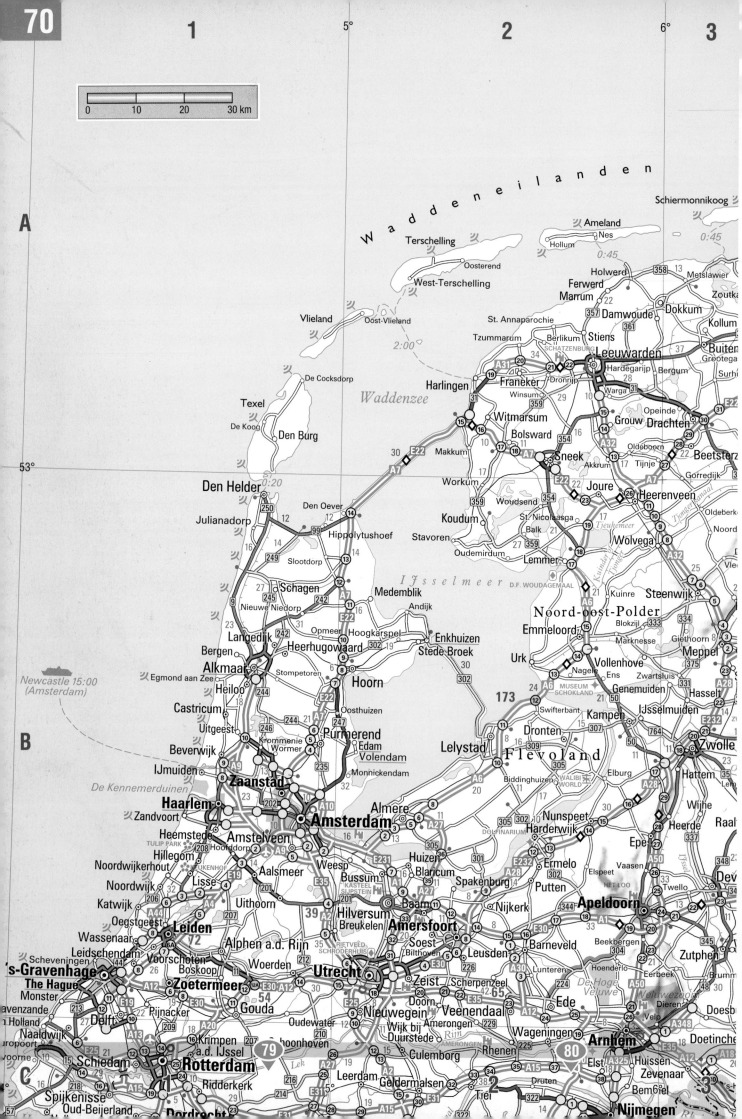

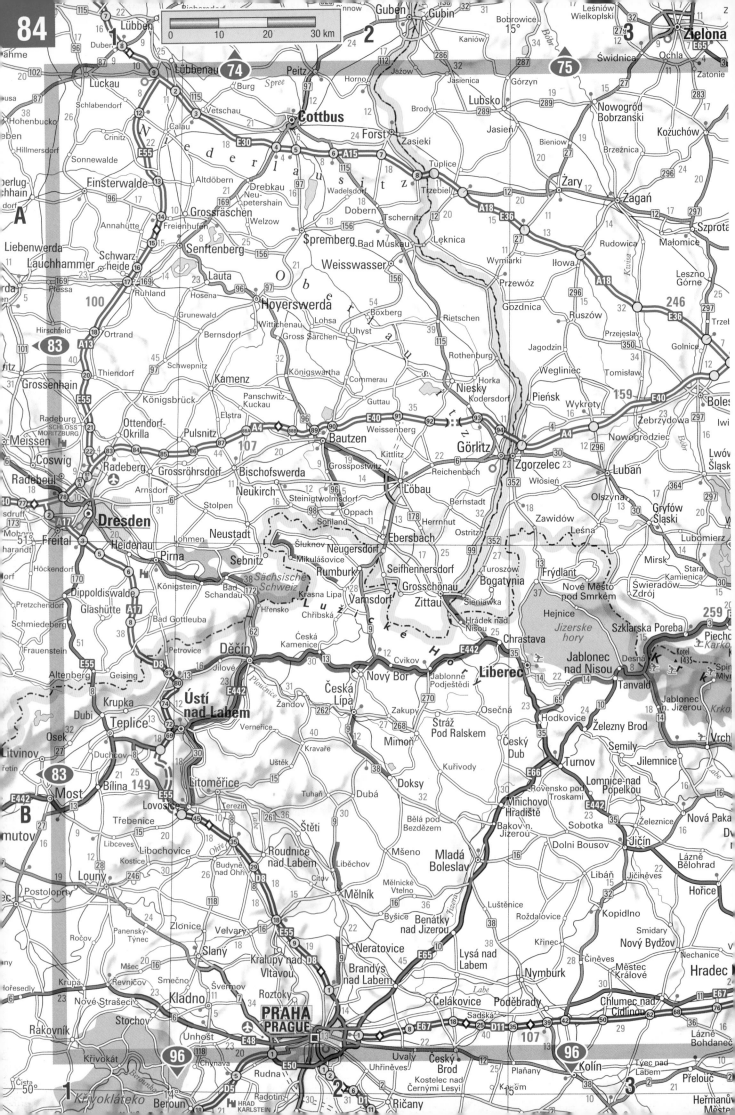

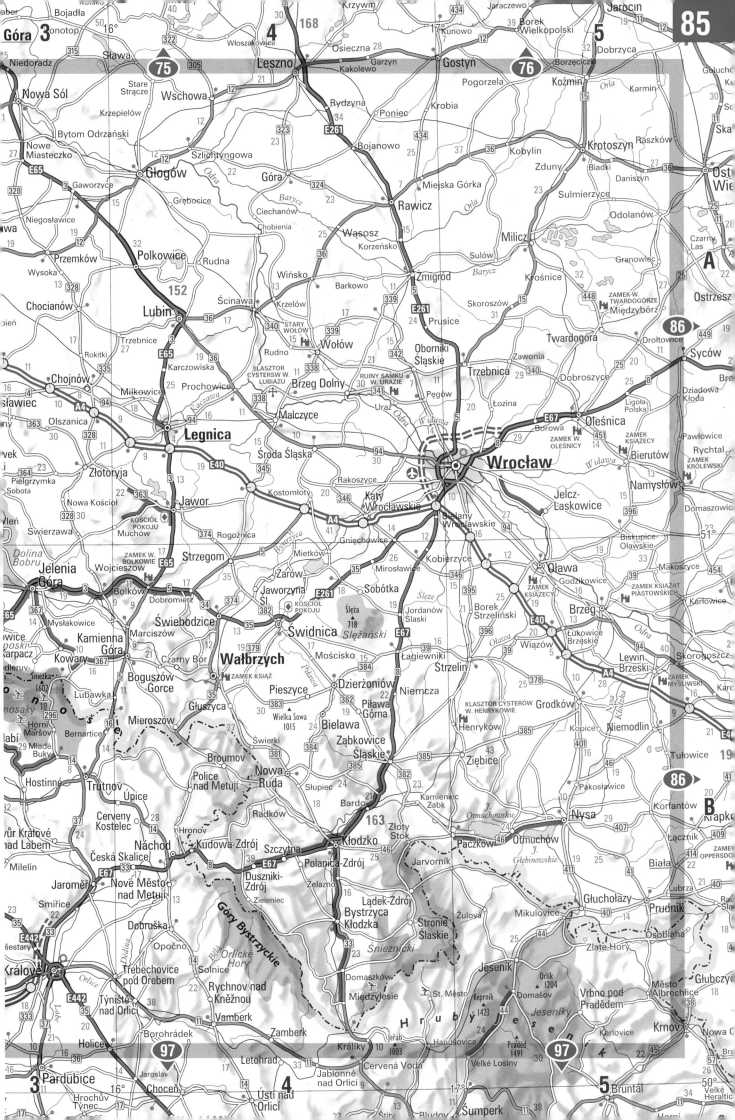

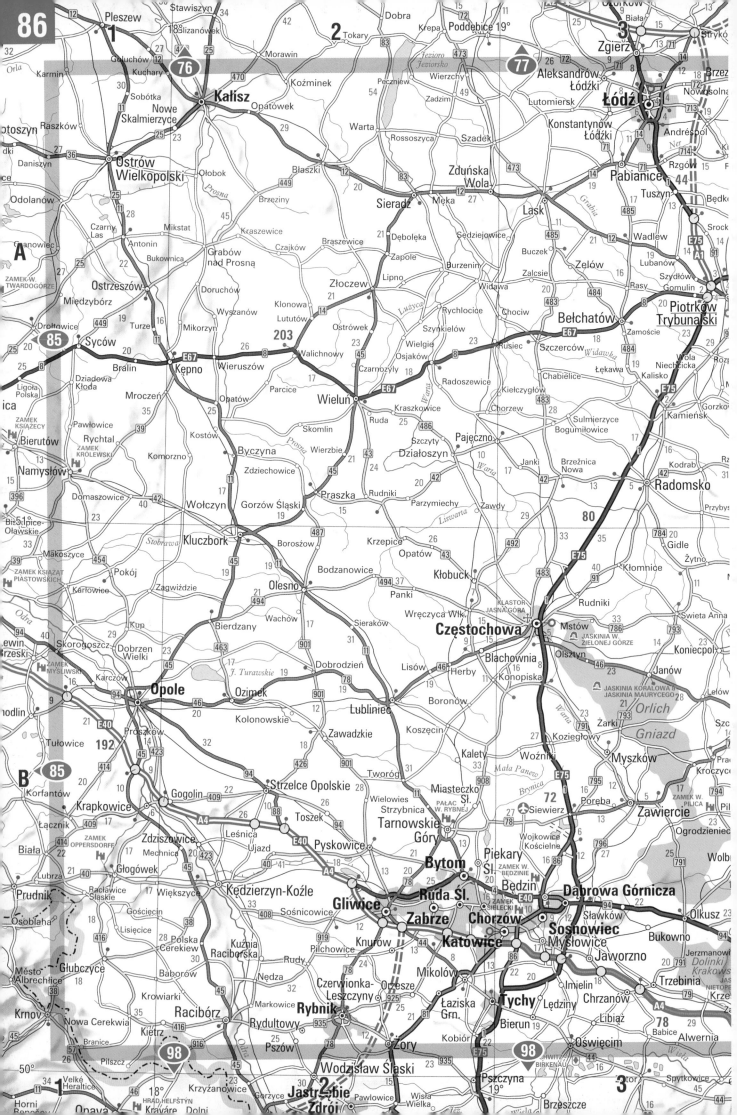

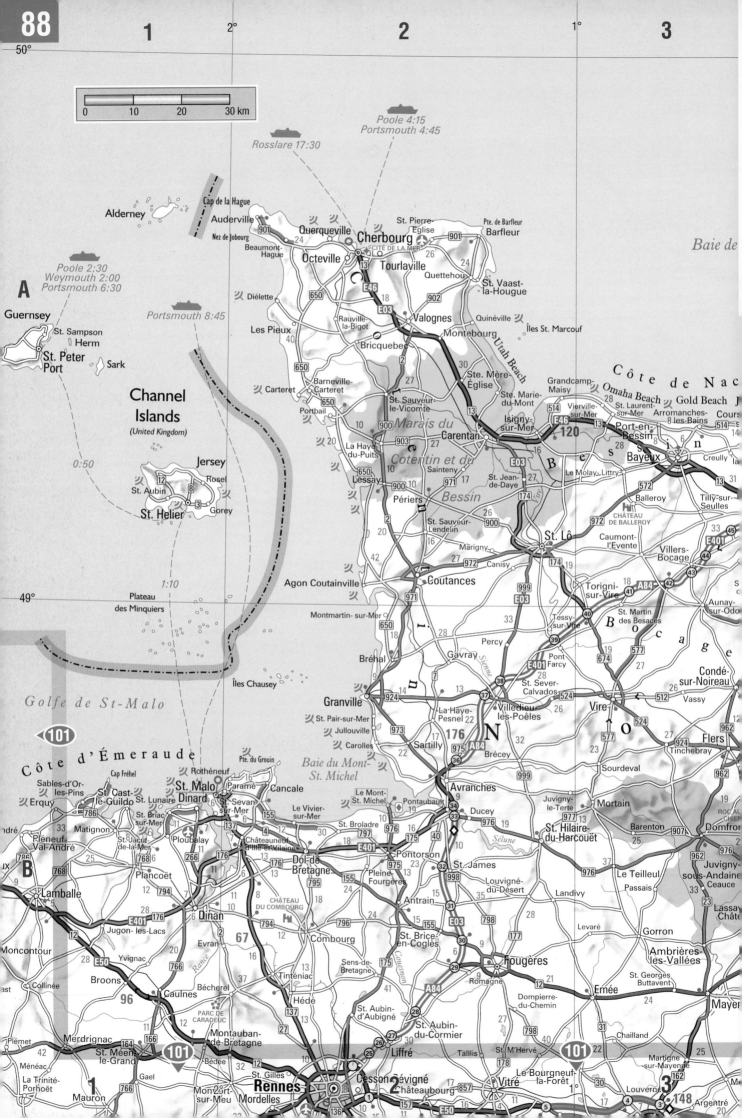

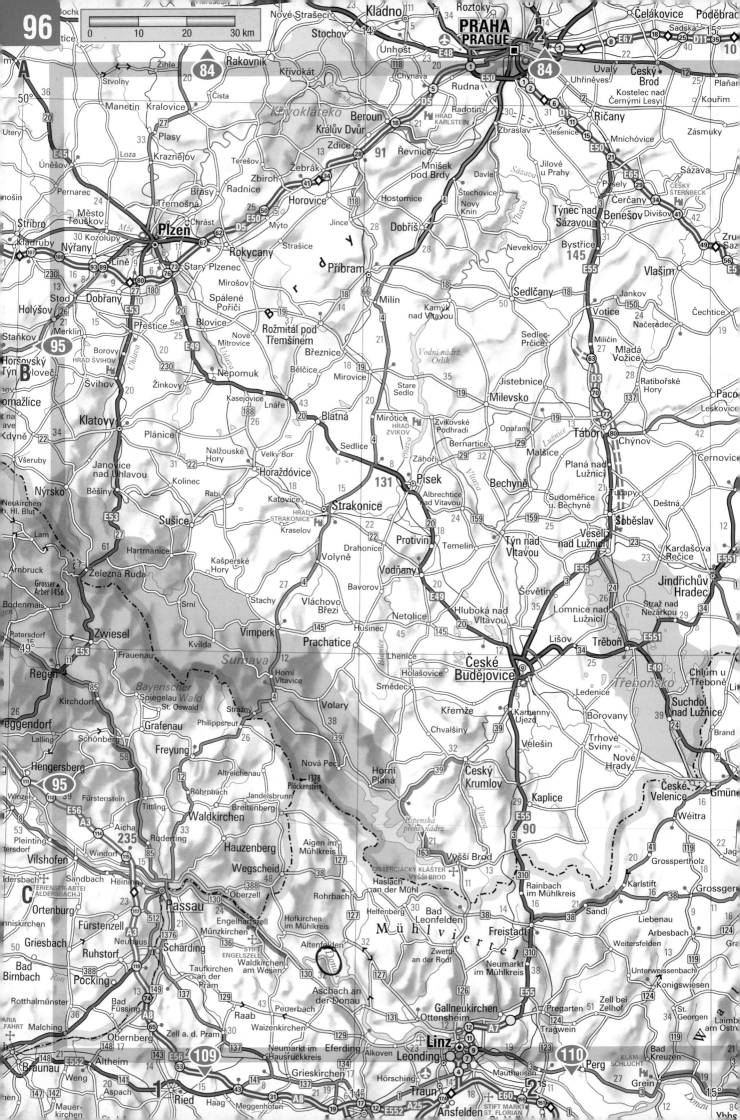

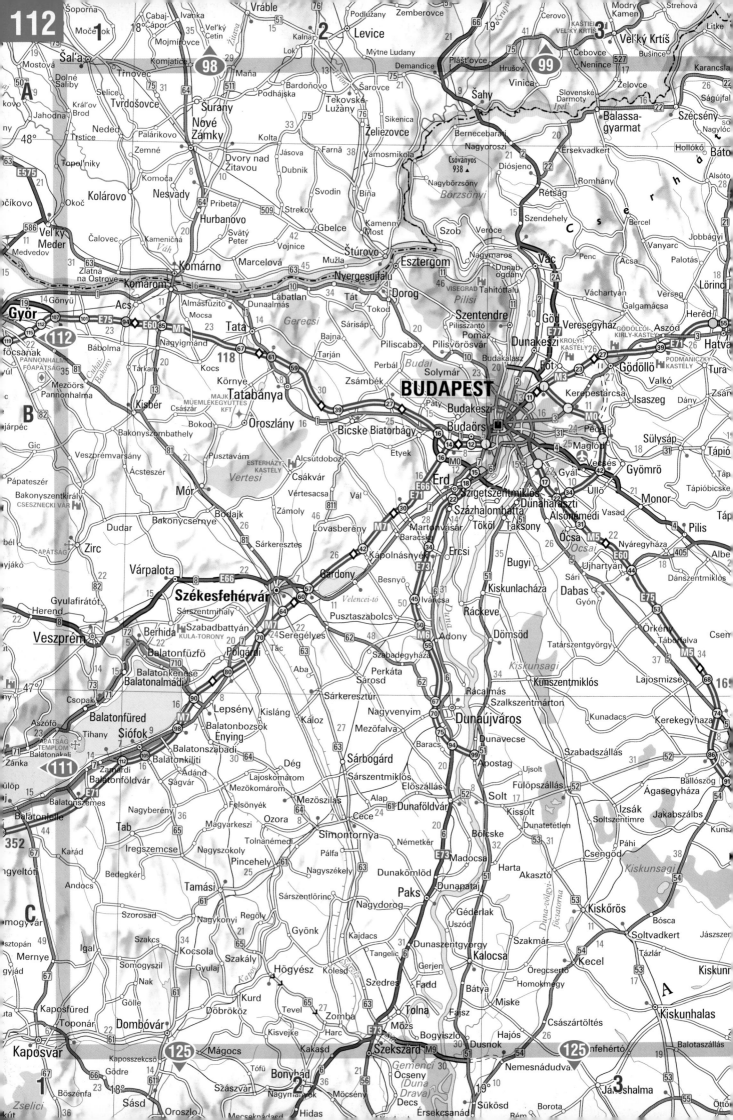

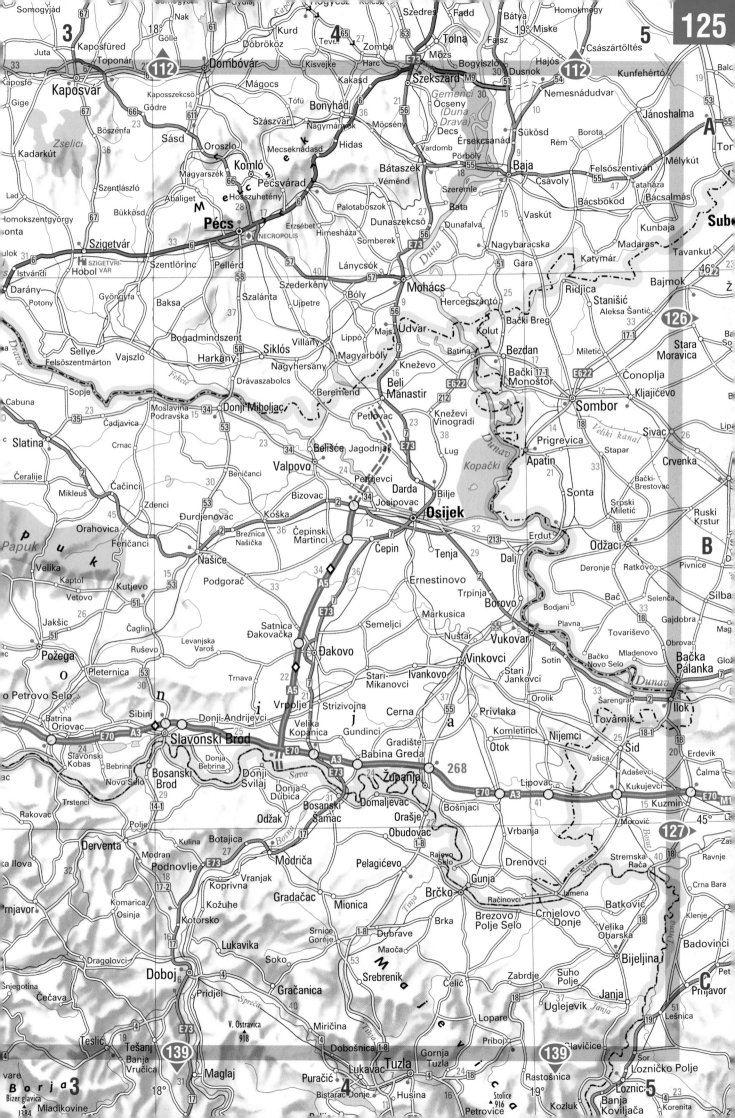

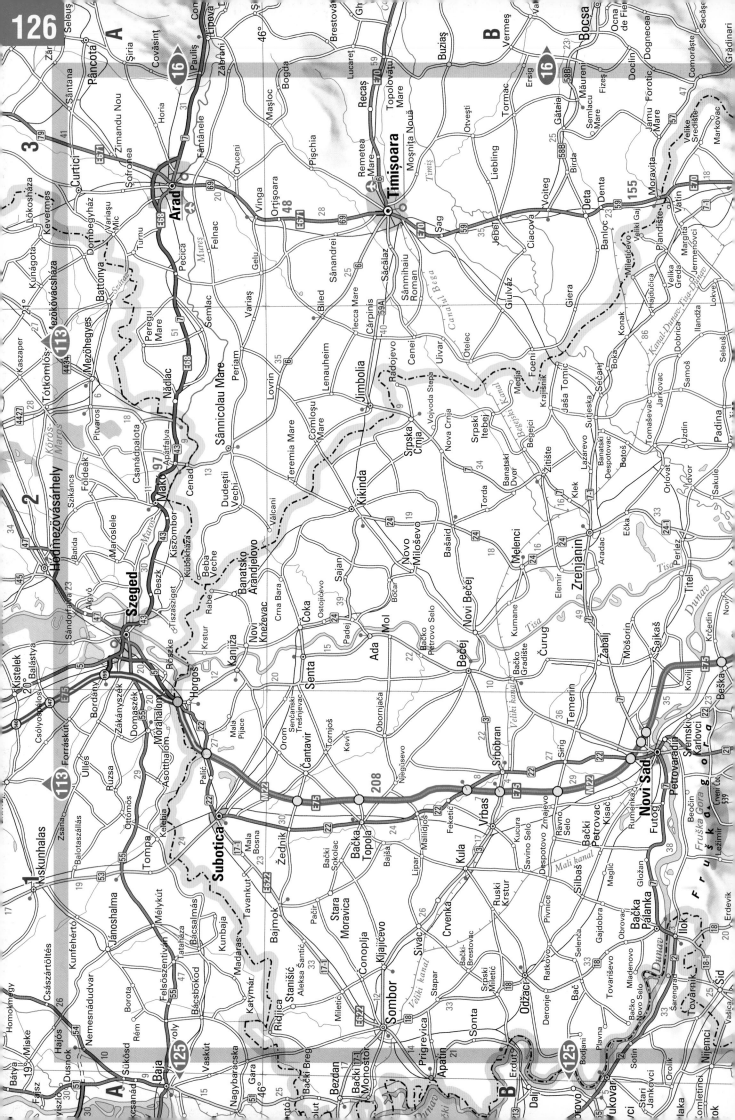

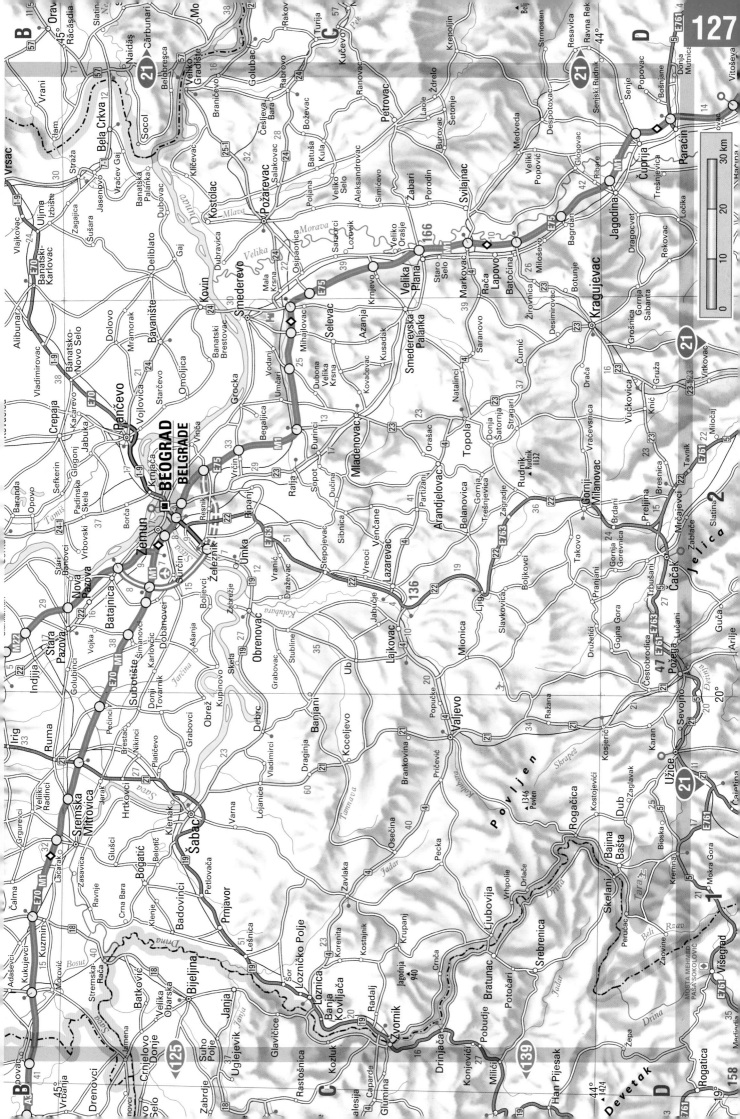

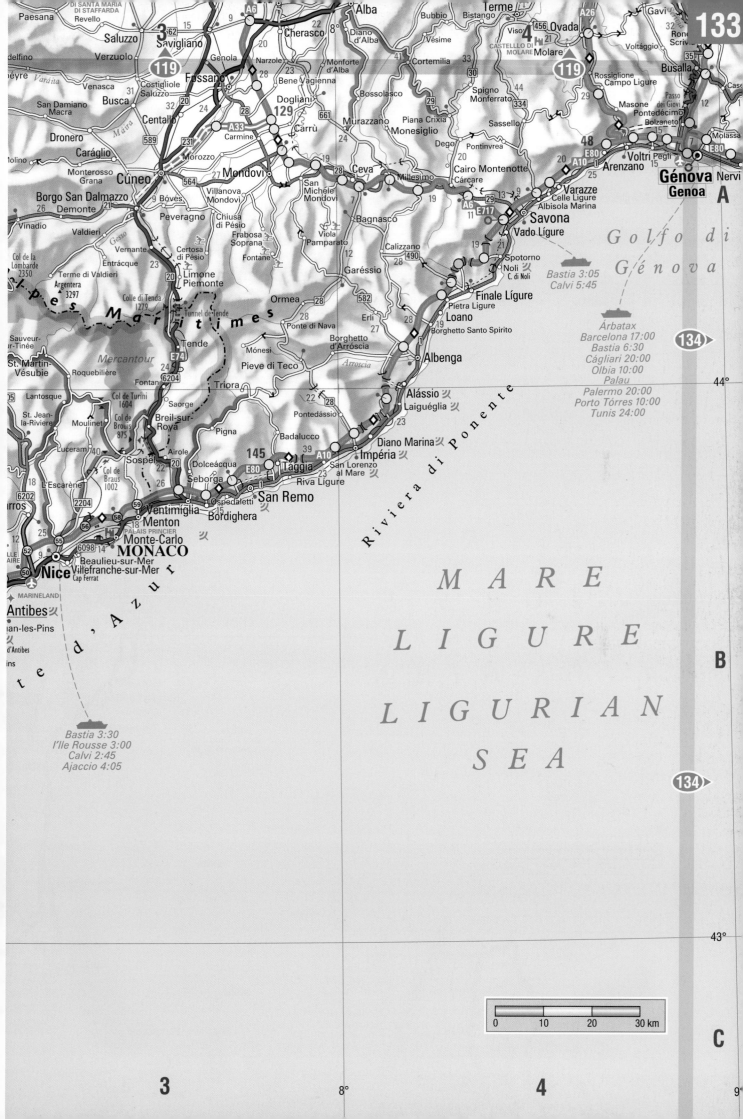

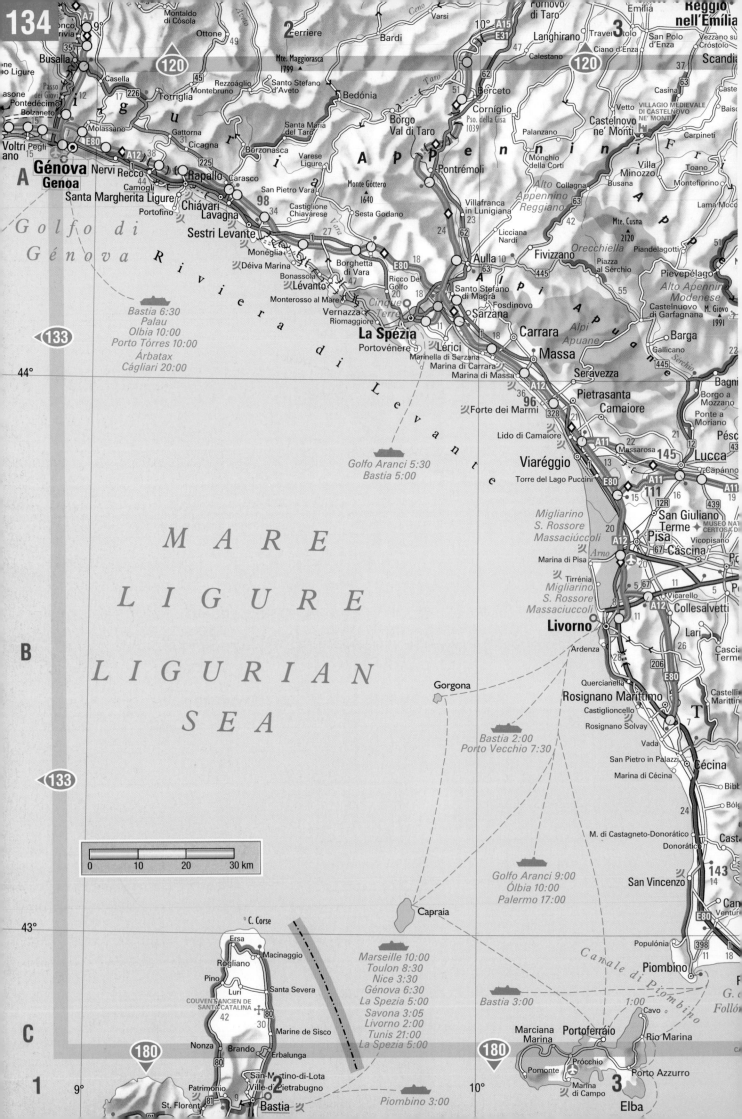

Unije
Nerezine
Čunski
3
Pula 3:00
Mali Lošinj
Veli Lošinj
Susak
123
1:30
Silba
Premuda
Ist
Molat
2:15
Virsko more
Sestrunj
Petrčane
1:20
Božava
Ancona 6:00
Ugljan
Preko
TVRĐAVA SV.
MIHOVILA
Brbinj
Kali
Kukljica
Dugi Otok
Zaglav
Pašman
Sali
Pašman
Telašćica
Žut
Split 5:15
Kornati
Kornat
Murter
Tisno

A D R I A T I C   S E A

Zadar 6:00

Šibenik 8:30
Split 4:30
Starigrad 9:30
Vis 8:00
Hvar 5:00
Vela Luka 6:20
Ubli 7:30
Bar 32:00
Durrës 18:00

Jabucka

Svetac

43°

el Tronto

3
15°
4

degli Abruzzi

Prizna
15°
Stara
Novalja
Cesarica
Novalja
Karlobag
E65 928
Pag
Metajna
25
Pag
Gorica
Lukovo
Šugorje
29
Vir
Povljana
Vir
Privlaka
Vrsi
AENONA
Nin

Klanac
Lički
Osik
Gospić
Brušane
Bilaj
28
Medak
Vaganski
vrh
1757
Barič Draga
Tribanj
Kruščica
Starigrad-
Paklenica
Ražanac
12
Jasenice
Poličnik
Posedarje
E65
Murvica
Novigrad
Zadar
Zemunik Donji
Bibinje
Sukošan
Miranje
Turanj
Biograd na Moru
Pakoštane
Stankovci
Vransko
Jezero
Pirovac
Vodice
KATEDRALA
SV JAKOVA
Žablaće
Ančona 8:30
Žirje
Krapanj
Primošten
Rogoznica

Odlapača
Jošan
Donj
4
389
Vrebac
Udbina
123
Gornja
Ploča
1591
Kremen
Bruvno
Maz
Radučl
Sveti Rok
Velebit
Gračac
Obrovac
Medvide
Ervenik
Kaštel
Žegarski
Zrmanja
Benkovac
ASSERIA
138
BURNUM
44°
Krka
Đevrske
MANASTIR
KRKA
Skradin
33
Proskljansko
Jezero
Šibeni
149

138

B

C

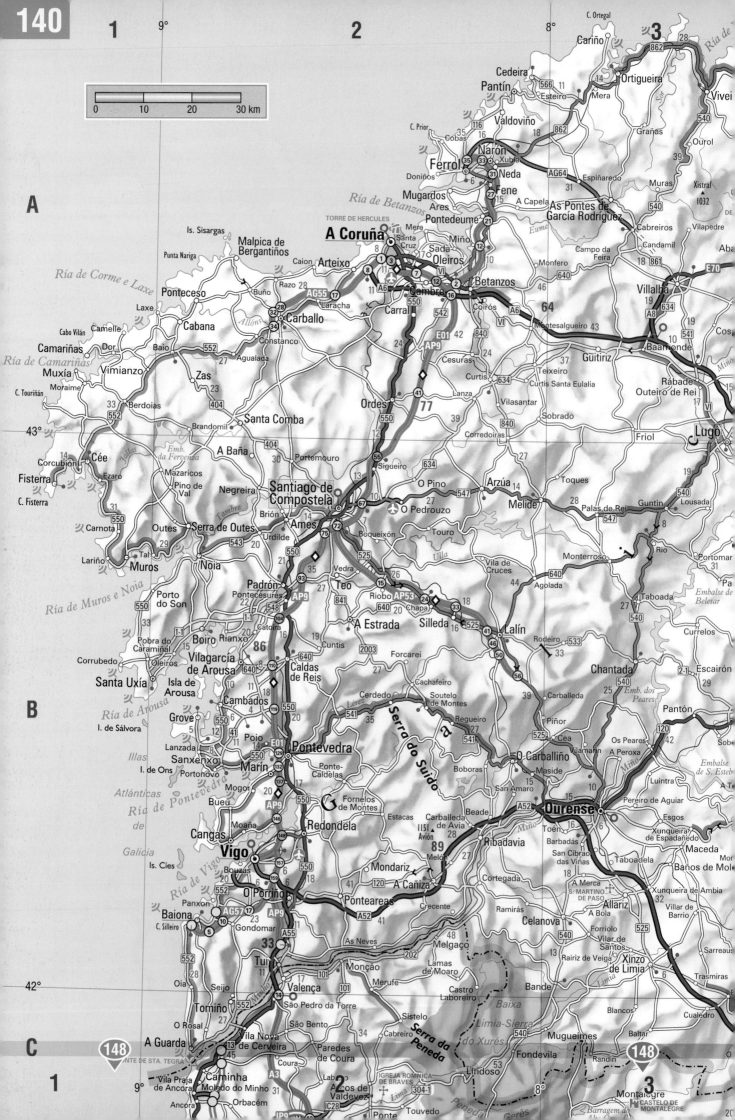

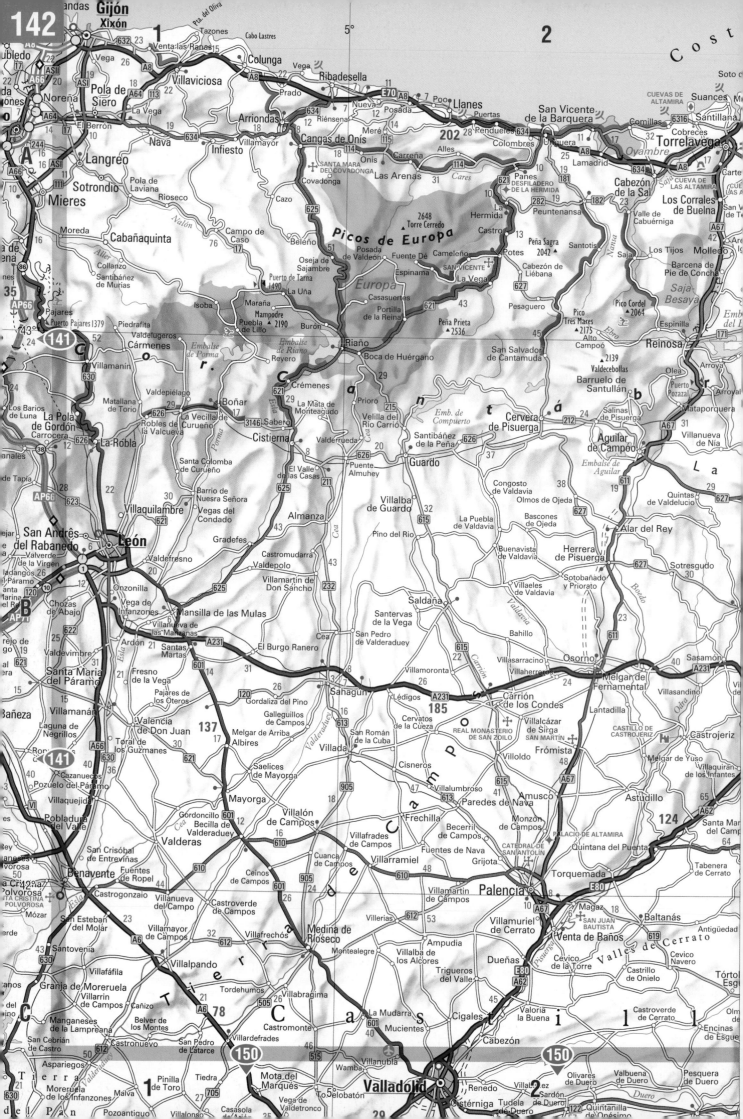

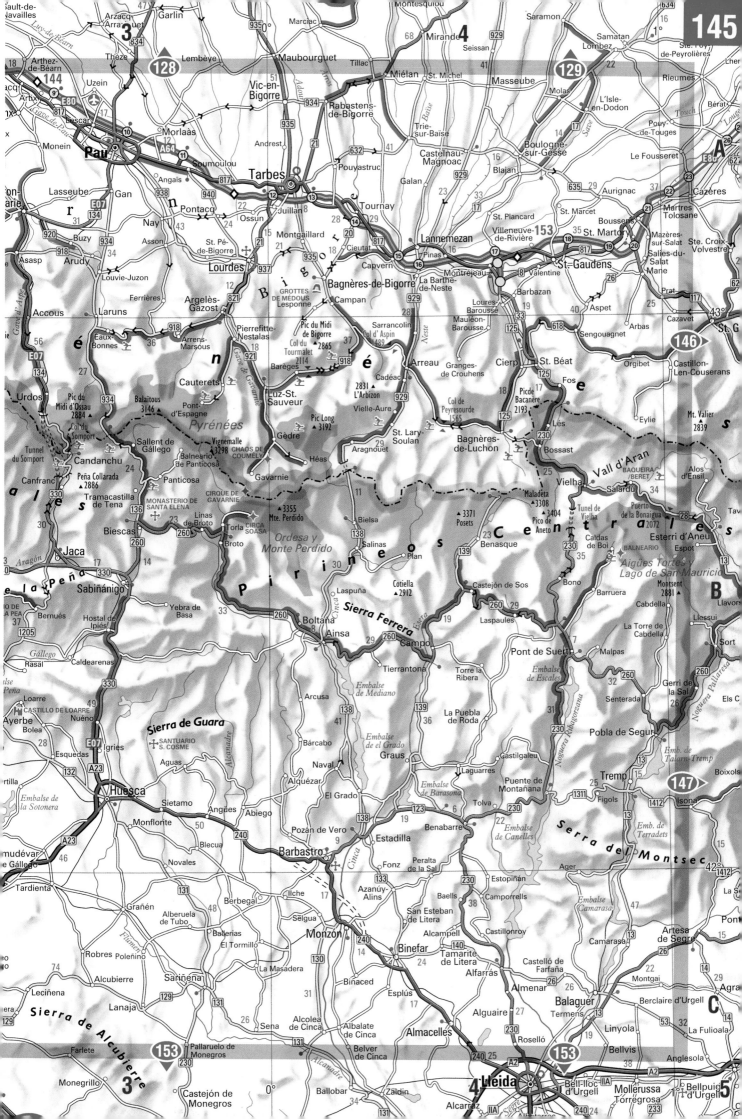

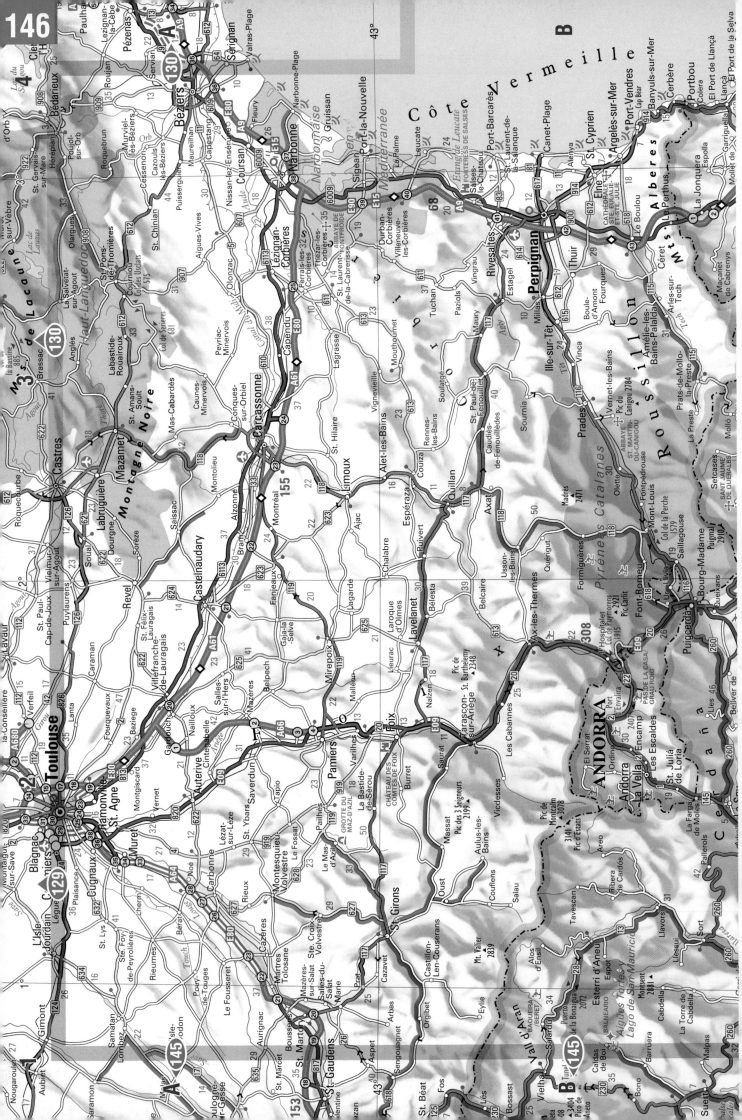

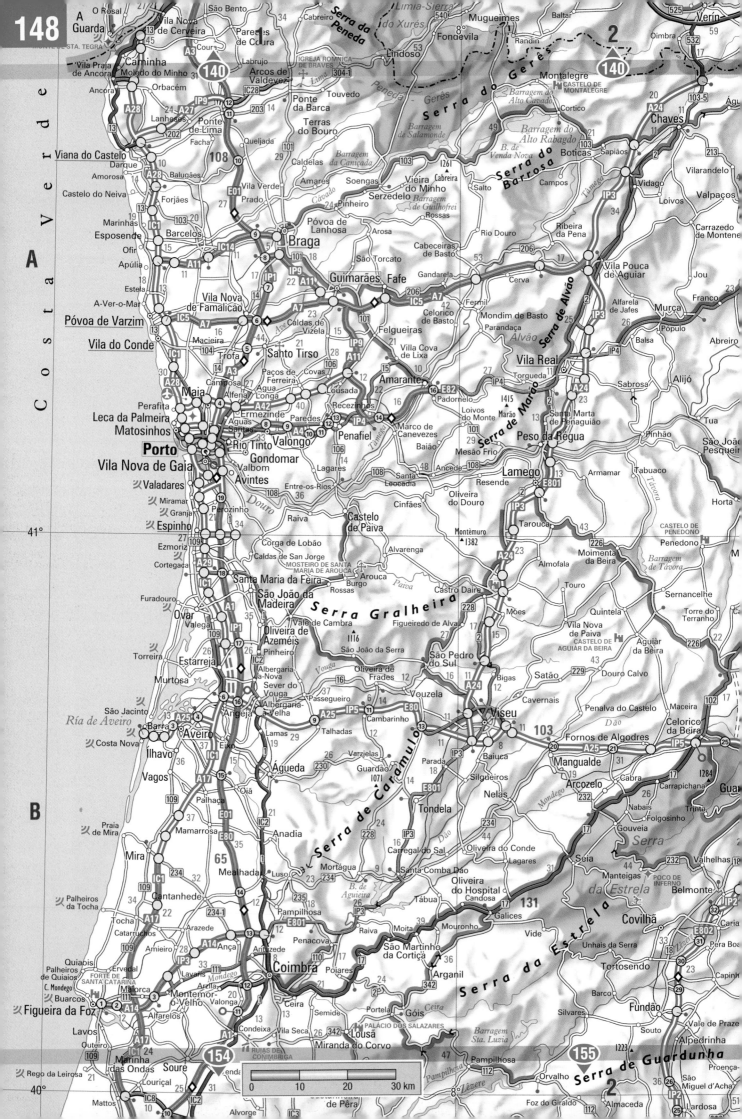

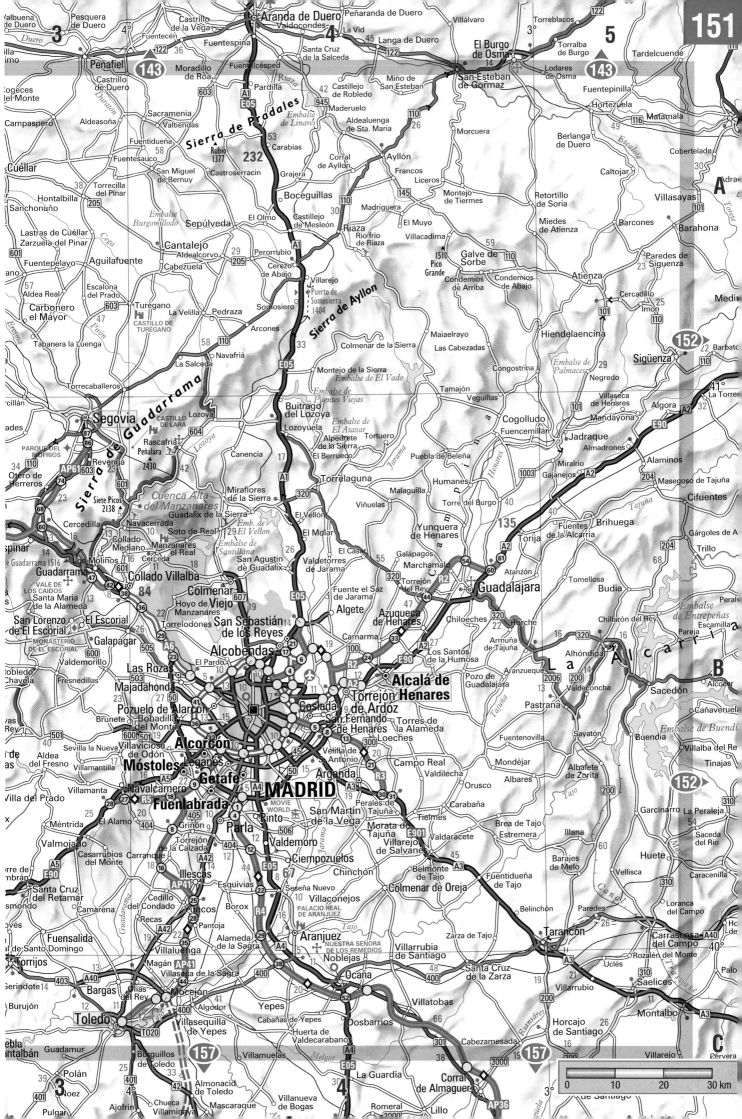

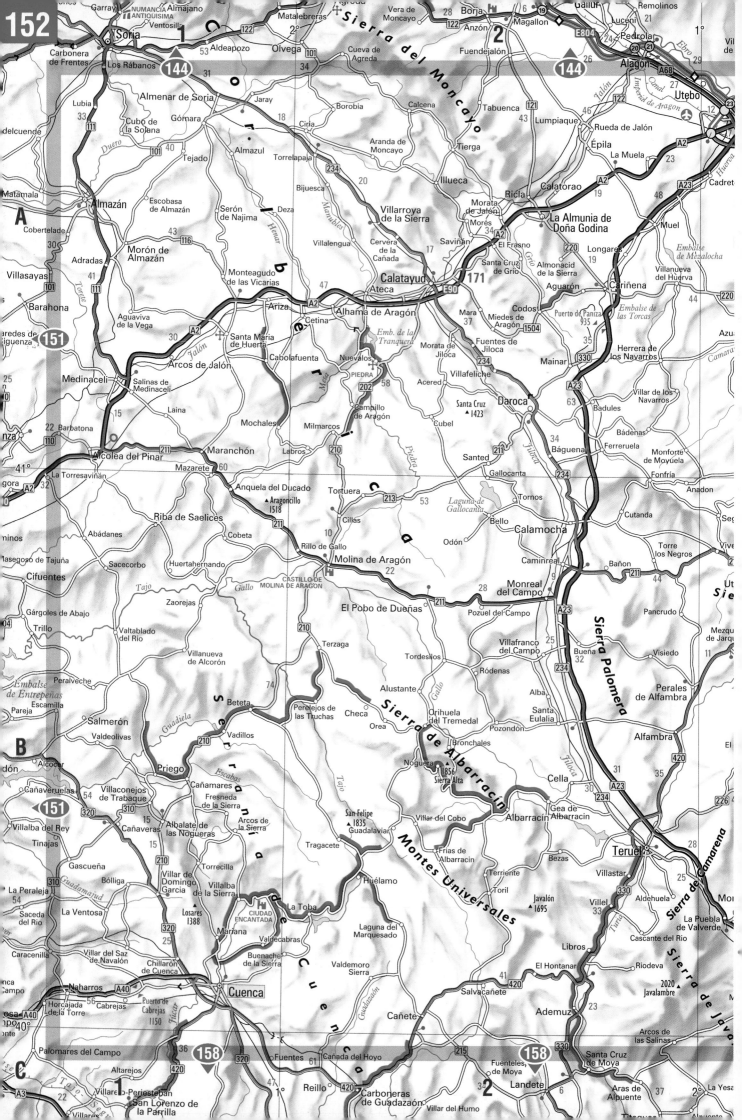

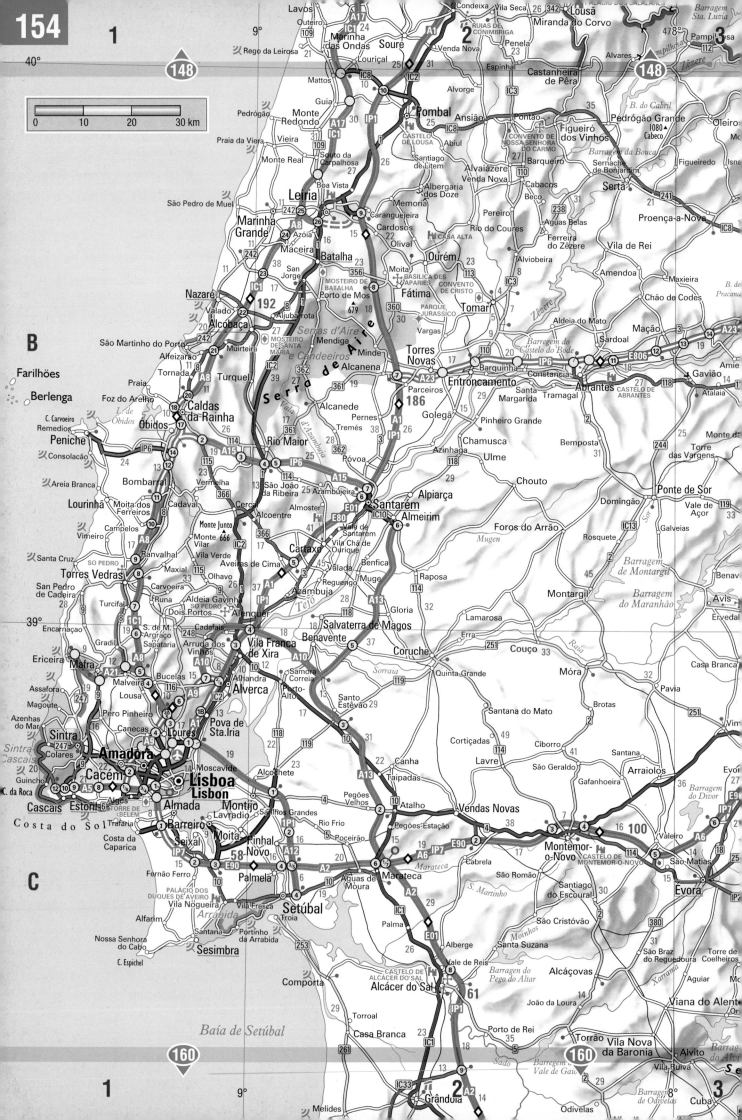

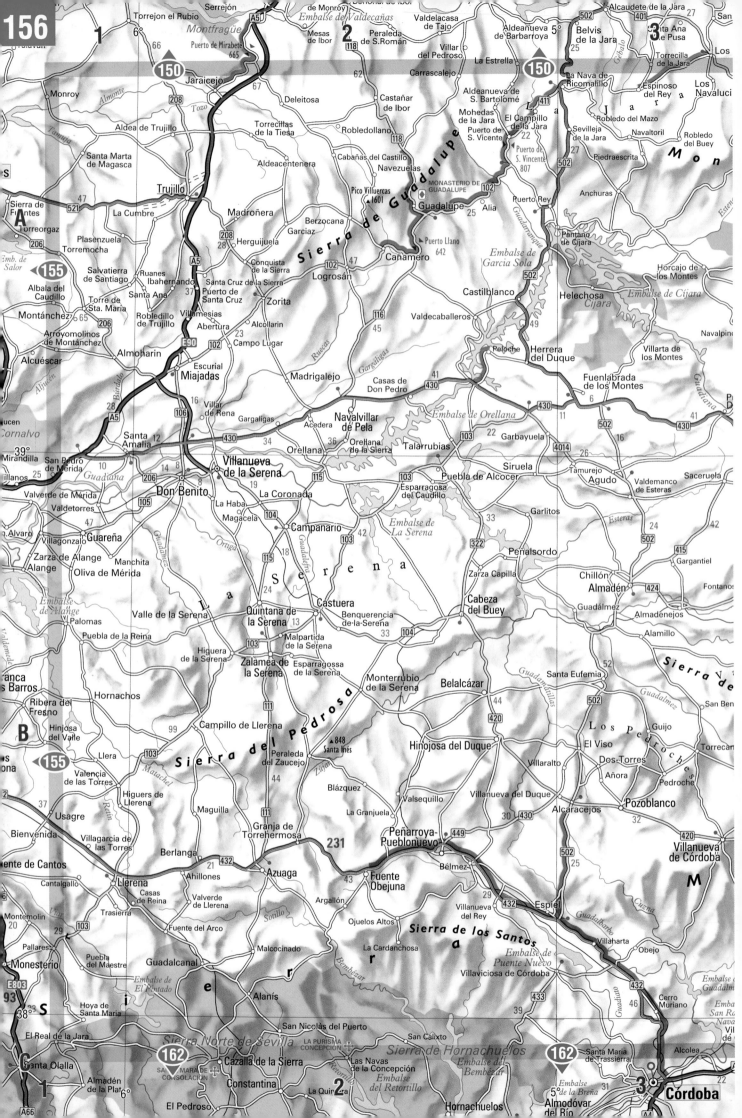

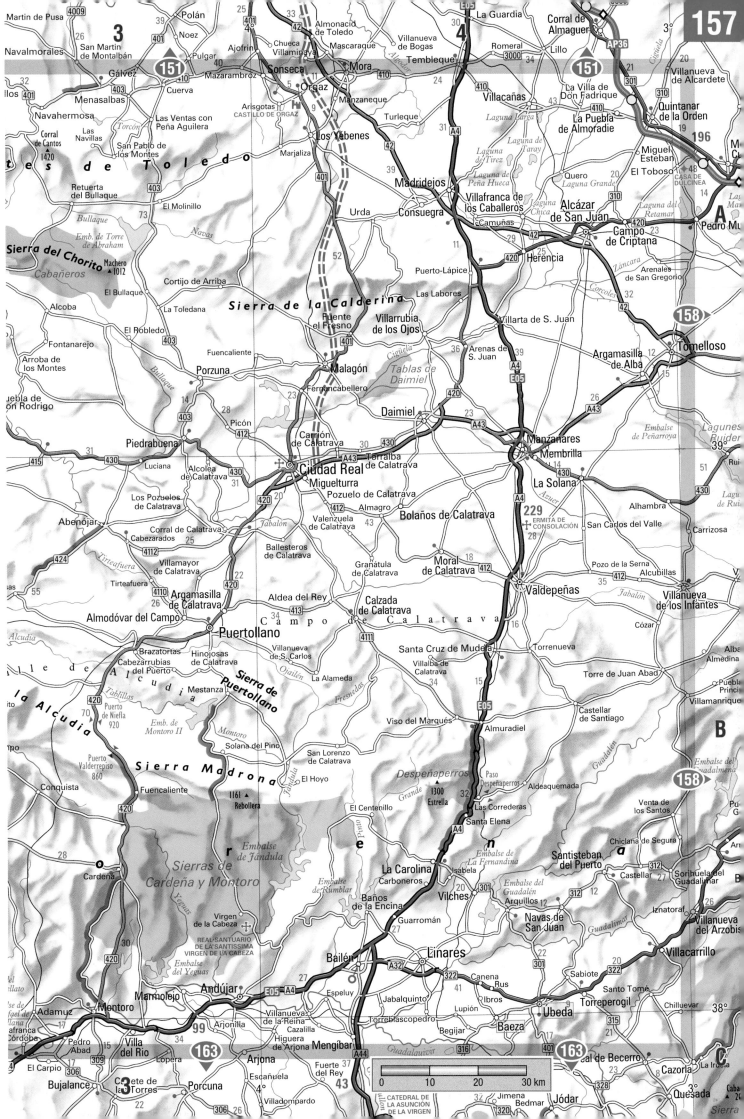

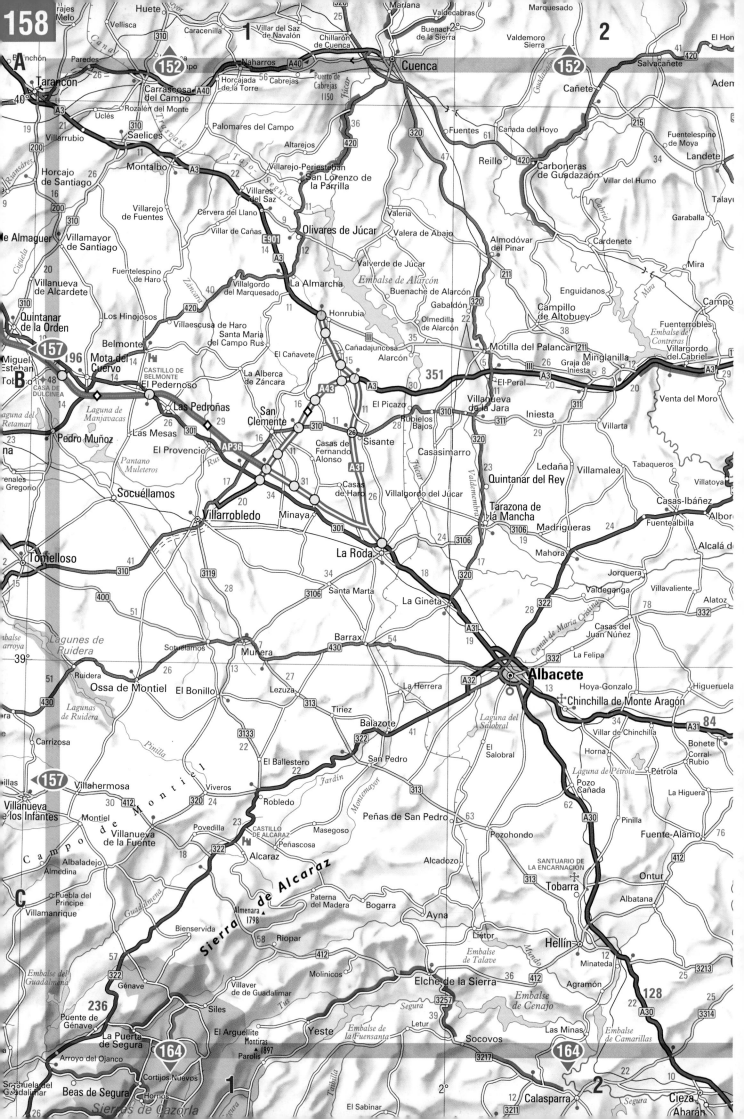

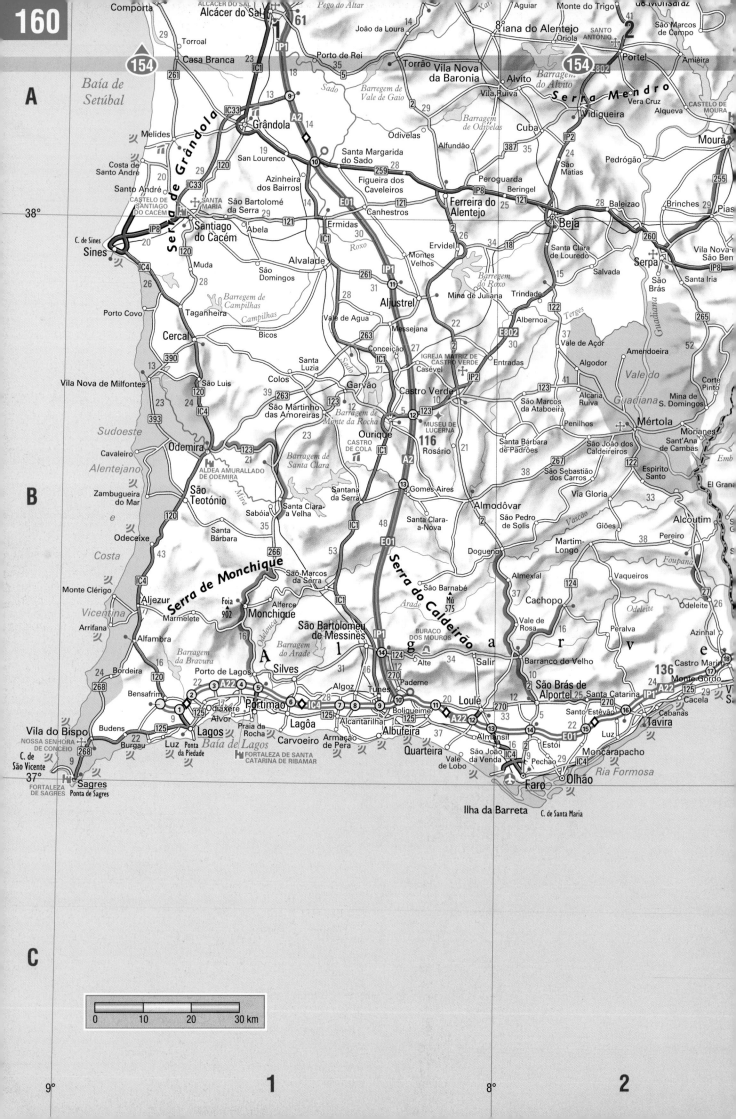

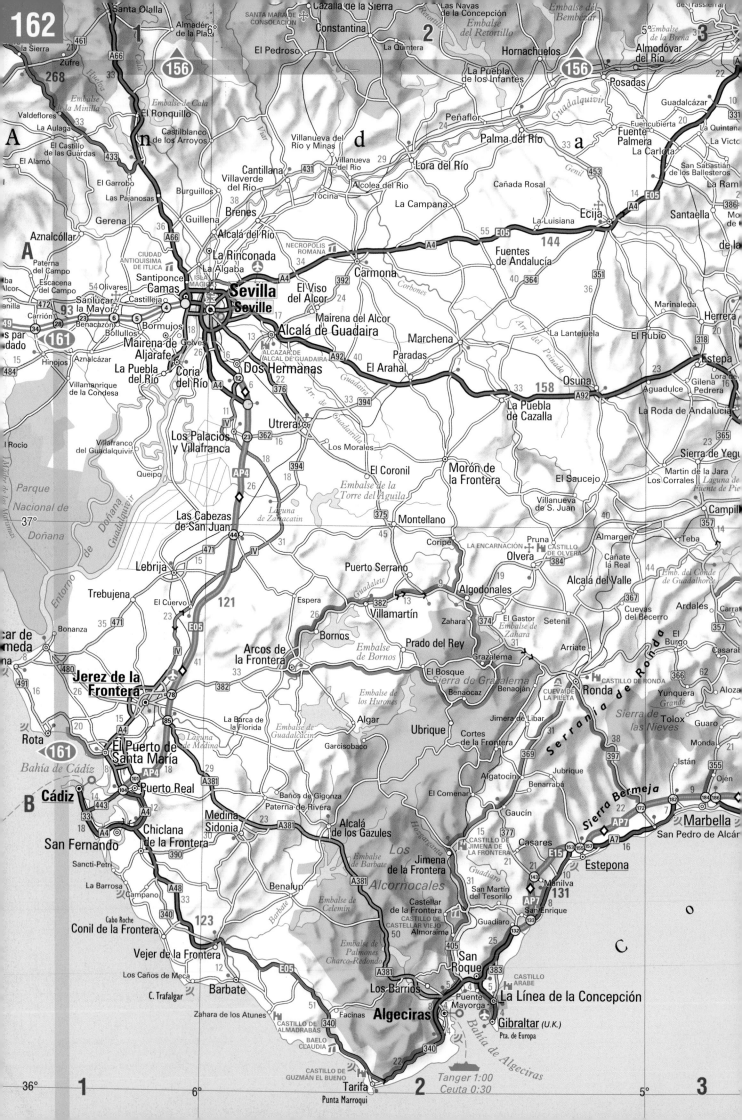

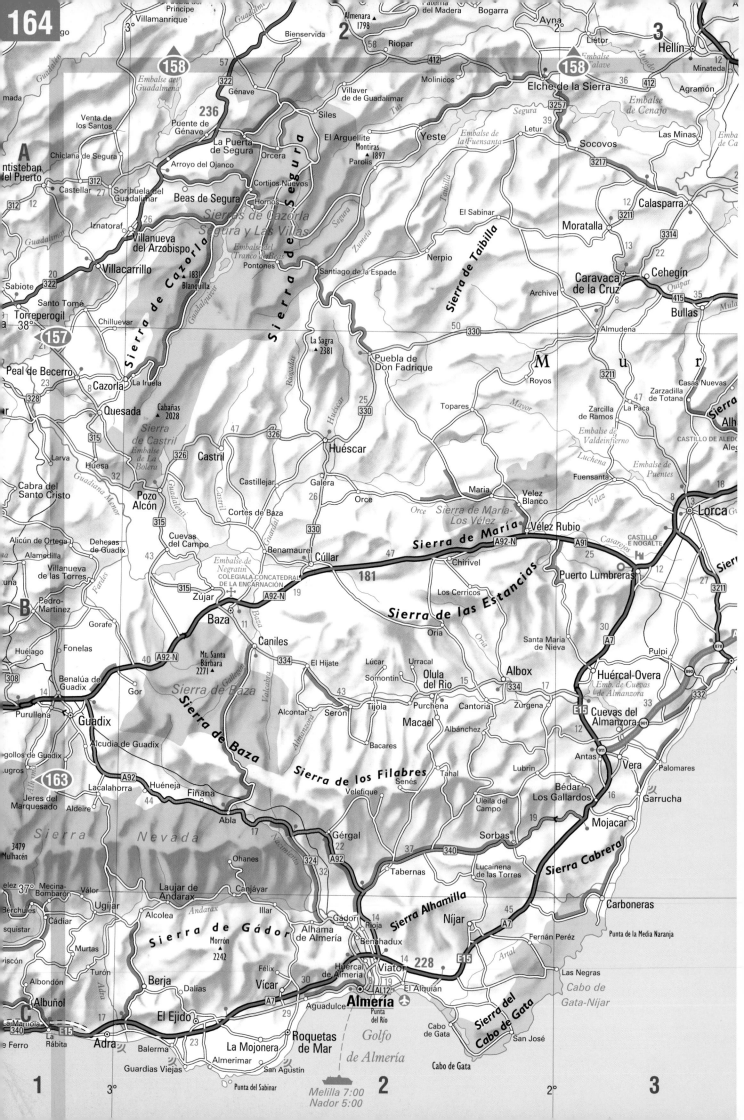

Ibatana
26
344
3
Jumilla
159
3223
3213
30

128
25 3213
A30 22
Casas del Puerto
25
3314
Pinoso
83
21 3213
344
29

Ise marillas
A30
10
Pila ▲ 1265
3223
46
3223

Cieza
Abarán
Blanca
14
Fortuna
Abanilla
Segura

Archena
Lorquí
Molina de Segura
E15
340
Ceutí

Mula
Alguazas
415
Pliego
38
9 8
Alcantarilla
36

Sangonera la Verde
E15
30
a
Murcia
El Valle
17
Librilla
Puerto de la Cadena
372
Corvera

de Espuña
3315
Sierra de Espuña
26
12
3
Totana
84
15
602
Fuente-Álamo de Murciá
48

A7
27
48
La Pinilla
36

Guadalentín
36
602

ra de la Almenara
AP7
332

845
Mazarrón
Campico López
▲ 879
Talayón
332
867

P7
866
33
Puntas de Calnegre

Cope
Cabo Cope

Aguilas

Castalla
14
17
Sax
A31
9
89
Elda
Petrer
Monóvar
24
Salinas
Laguna de Salinas

Novelda
Aspe
Monforte del Cid
27

Hondón de los Frailes
29
325
84
Crevillente
82

Albatera
730
724
Catral
9
19
733
Dolores
Callosa de Segura
A7
11
18
737
Orihuela
340
14
Almoradí
740
Benejúzar
743
Bigastro
745
Santomera
Monteagudo
95
24
751 14
90
Rojales

Emb. de la Pedrera
754
759
San Miguel de Salinas
11
10
332
768
Sucina
14
770
Pilar de la Horadada
774
San Javier
AP7
780
San Pedro del Pinatar
782
Santiago de la Ribera
786
Lo Pagán
790
Los Alcázares
18
794
810
805
797
Albujón
20
812
800
El Algar
829
Los Nietos
3319
Torre-Pacheco
Aljorra
812
Los Dolores
815
Cartagena
332
10
La Unión
312

Puerto de Mazarrón
Cabo Tiñoso
Escombreras
Portman

Golfo de Mazarrón

Jijona
340
4
38
Tibi
Aguas de Busot
Busot
32
A7
24
AP7
15
67
Campello
San Juan de Alicante
SAN VICENTE DEL RASPEIG
San Vincente del Raspeig
10
A31
8
Alicante
340
21
16
865
Elche
13
332
17
917
Santa Pola
Cabo de Santo Pola
Nueva Tabarca

Guardamar del Segura
Salinas de la Mata
13
Salinas de Torrevieja
Torrevieja
108
15

Orchete
41
E15
AP7
42
159

Relleu
Benidorm
TERRA MITICA
Villajoyosa
65
332

AQU & MU

Marseille

Oran

Costa Blanca

Mar Menor
Cabo de Palos
Cabo de Palos

A
38°
B
37°
C

km
0   10   20   30 km

3
1°
4

A

1   2°   2

40°

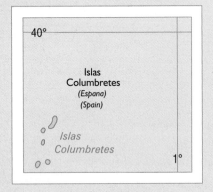

Islas
Columbretes
(Espana)
(Spain)

*Islas
Columbretes*

40°

1°

B

ISLAS
BALEARES

BALEARIC
ISLANDS

Port de Sóller   Fo
Deià   Sóller
Valldemossa   Tunel de Sóller
Banyalbufar   Alar
Estellencs   Esporles   Bunyo
Puigpunyent   Marratxi
Sa Dragonera   **Palma de Mallorca**
Andratx   12
Port d'Andratx   Calvià   6
Peguera   15   Palma   10
Barcelona 3:00   13   Nova   Can Pastilla
Santa Ponça   Magaluf   S'Arenal
Cap Enderrocat
Cap de Cala Figuera   *Bahía de Palma*
Maó 6:30
Valencia 6:00   **Mallorca**
Majorca
Eivissa 2:15
Denia 9:00

39°

Eivissa
Ibiza
Portinatx
Sant Miquel   Sant Joan Baptista
Santa Agnès   Pta. Grossa
Sant Carlos
Sant Antoni   733   Tagomago
Abat   Es Caná
16   23   Santa Eulàlia des Riu
Sant Rafel   731
Cala Llonga
Sant Josep   8
Eivissa
801   Ibiza
Sant Francesc   Palma de Mallorca 2:15
Es Vedrà   de ses Salines   Barcelona 9:30
Cap
Llentrisca   Punta Portás
S'Espardell
Denia 4:00   S'Espalmador
Valencia 3:15   0:25
Formentera
Sa Savina   Es Pujols
Sant Ferran
Sant Francesc de   Nuestra Señora
Formentera   Sa Verge des Pilar
C. de Barbària   Pta. Rotja

C

1   2°   2

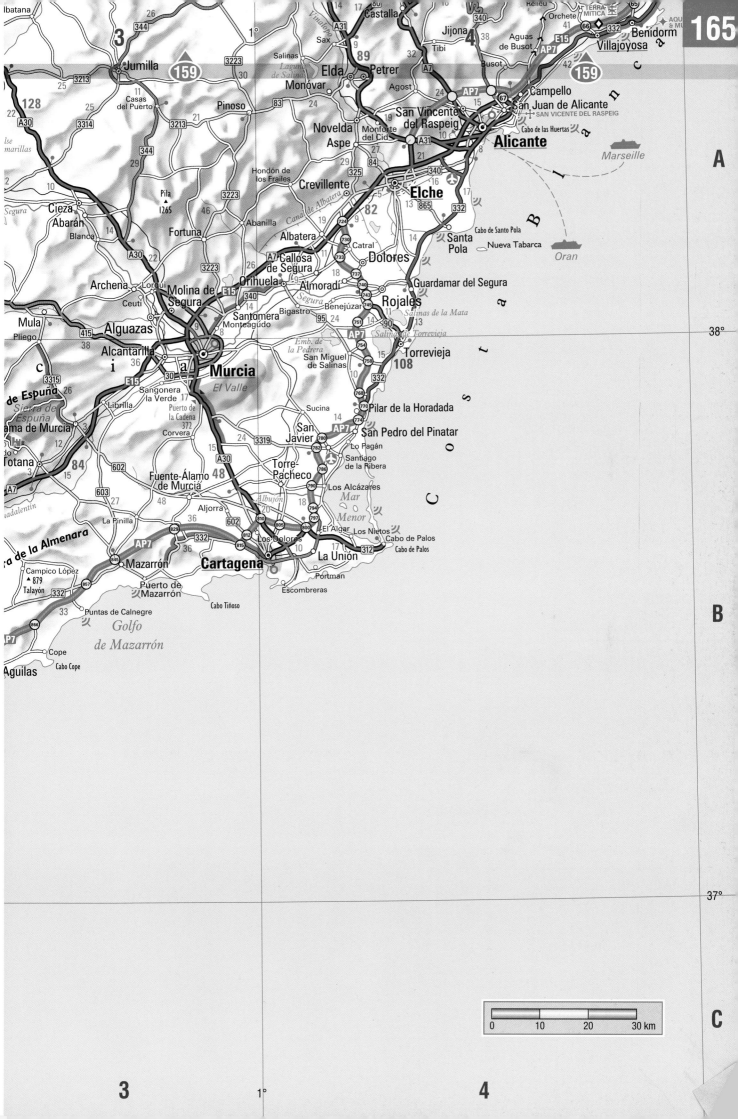

40°

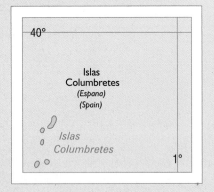

Islas
Columbretes
(España)
(Spain)

*Islas
Columbretes*

40°

1°

B

ISLAS
BALEARES

BALEARIC
ISLANDS

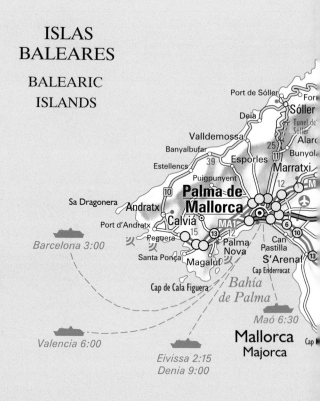

Port de Sóller
For
Sóller
Deià
Tunel de
Sóller
Valldemossa
Alar
25
Banyalbufar
Esporles
11
Bunyol
Estellencs
39
Marratxi
Puigpunyent
10
M
Sa Dragonera
**Palma de
Mallorca**
12
Andratx
Calvià
MA1
6
Port d'Andratx
13
10
Barcelona 3:00
15
12
Can
Pastilla
Peguera
Palma
Nova
S'Arenal
Santa Ponça
Magaluf
13
Cap Enderrocat
Cap de Cala Figuera
*Bahía
de Palma*
Maó 6:30
Valencia 6:00
Mallorca
Majorca
Eivissa 2:15
Cap
Denia 9:00

39°

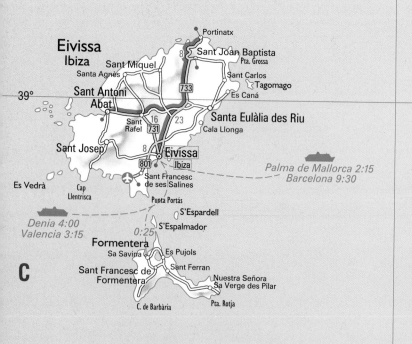

Portinatx
Eivissa
Ibiza
Sant Joan Baptista
Sant Miquel
Pta. Grossa
Santa Agnès
8
Sant Carlos
Tagomago
Sant Antoni
733
Es Caná
Abat
Sant
16
23
Santa Eulàlia des Riu
Rafel
731
Cala Llonga
Sant Josep
8
Eivissa
801
Ibiza
Es Vedrà
Sant Francesc
Cap
de ses Salines
Palma de Mallorca 2:15
Llentrisca
Barcelona 9:30
Punta Portás
S'Espardell
Denia 4:00
S'Espalmador
Valencia 3:15
0:25
Formentera
Sa Savina
Es Pujols
Sant Francesc de
Sant Ferran
Formentera
Nuestra Señora
Sa Verge des Pilar
C. de Barbària
Pta. Rotja

C

2 3° 3 4° 4

A

Barcelona 9:00

Capo de Cavalleria
Punta Nati Cala Morell Fornells
7
15
9
23 Es
Ciudadela Mercadal Cap de Faváritx 40°
de Menorca Ferreries 358
Toro
Cala Alaior 1
Galdana Es Migjorn 20
C. de Artrutx Gran Maó
Son Bou
Menorca Sant Pta. de s'Esperó
Minorca Climent Es Castell
Sant Luis
Punta Prima
I. de l'Aire

Palma de Mallorca 7:00
Valencia 16:00

Cap de Formentor
Punta Beca Port de Pollença B. de Pollença
Pollença 14 Cap des Pinar
10 2220 Alcúdia
12 10 Es Port d'Alcúdia
39 2200
Puig Major 13 B. d'Alcúdia
nalutx 1445 12 Sa Pobla C'an Picafort Cap Ferrutx
Selva MA13 12 562 Cap des Freu
Lloseta 33 Morey
Inca Muro Santa Artà 9 Cala Ratjada
13A Margalida 15 Capdepera
Sta. Maria Cap des Pinar
del Camí Sencelles Sineu Sant Llorenç CUEVAS DE ARTA
A13 20 des Carctassar 20 Son Servera
Petra Cala Millor
Montuïri Punta de n'Amer
35 15 Manacor
Algaida 18 14 Porto Cristo
MONASTERIO 27 CUEVAS DEL DRACH
DE CORA
L 29 Porreres
Llucmajor Cales de Mallorca
MA19 SAN SALVADOR
19 27 (MONASTERIO)
Campos del Port Porto Colom
Cala d'Or
Blanc Ses Salines Porto Petro
Colònia de Santanyí
Sant Jordi

Cap de ses Salines

B

I. des Conills
Parque Nacional
de Cabrera
Cabrera

39°

C

0 10 20 30 km

2 3° 3 4° 4

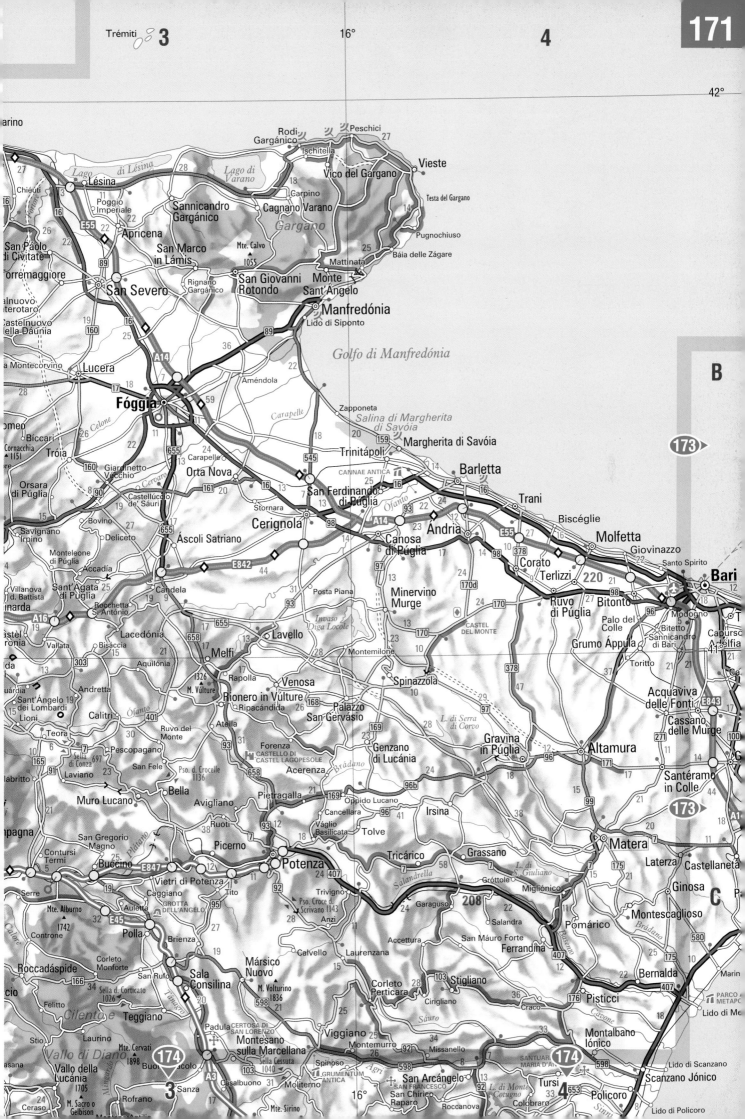

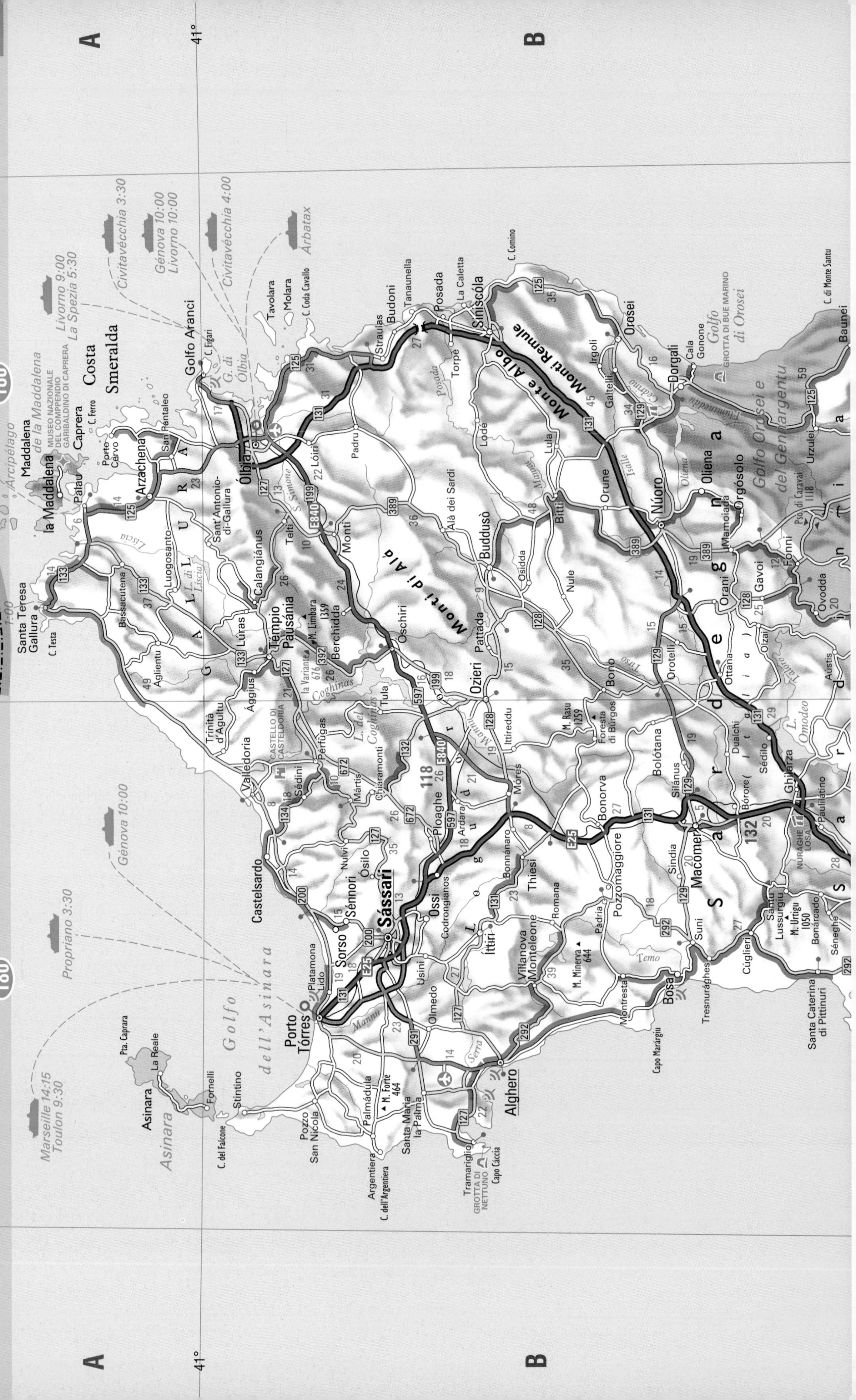

A B · 4 3 2 1 · A B

41° · 10° · 9° · 8° · 41°

Bonifacio
C. Pertusato
île de Cavallo
Pta. Caprara
La Reale
Asinara
C. del Falcone
Fornelli
Stintino
Pozzo San Nicola
Argentiera
C. dell'Argentiera
Palmádula
Santa Maria la Palma
M. Forte 464
Tramariglio
GROTTA DI NETTUNO
Capo Cáccia
Alghero

Bouches de Bonifacio
Golfo dell'Asinara
Asinara
Golfo dell'Asinara

Marseille 14:15 Toulon 9:30
Génova 10:00
Propriano 3:30
Génova Porto-Vecchio
Arcipélago
Génova Livorno 10:00 10:00
Génova Livorno 9:00 La Spezia 5:30
Civitavecchia 3:30
Civitavecchia 4:00
Árbatax

Santa Teresa Gallura
C. Testa
la Maddalena
Maddalena de la Maddalena
MUSEO NAZIONALE DEL COMPENDIO GARIBALDINO DI CAPRERA
Caprera
Pálau
Porto Cervo
Costa Smeralda
Golfo Aranci
C. Fígari
G. di Olbia
Tavolara
Molara
C. Coda Cavallo

Arzachena
Sant'Antonio di Gallura
San Pántaleo
Olbia
Lóiri
Padru
Loídu
Tanaunella
Budoni
Posada
La Caletta
Siniscola
C. Comino
Orosei
Golfo di Orosei
GROTTA DI BUE MARINO
Gonone
Cala
Dorgali
C. di Monte Santu
Báunei

GALLURA
Luogosanto
Bessacutena
Áglientu
Trinità d'Agultu
Aggius
Luras
Calangiánus
Tempio Pausánia
M. Limbara 1359
la Variante 676
Berchidda
Monti
Telti
Calangiánus

Costa Smeralda

Monte Albo
Monti Remule
Gaitelli
Irgoli
Lula
Lodè
Torpè
Straulas

Valledoria
Castelsardo
CASTELLO DI CASTELDÓRIA
Sédini
Pérfugas
Chiaramonti
Mártis
Núlvi
Ósilo
Sorso
Sénnori
Sássari
Ossi
Códrongiános
Ploaghe
Ardara
Mores
Ittíri
Usini
Olmedo
Villanova Monteleone
Romana
Pádria
Thiesi
Bonnánaro
Bonnánaro
Tula
Oschiri
Ozieri
Pattada
Budusò
Alà dei Sardi
Osidda
Bitti
Orune
Nule
M. Rasu 1259
Foresta di Búrgos
Ittireddu
Bono
Bolótana
Silánus
Sindia
Pozzomaggiore
Cúglieri
Suni
Tresnuraghes
Montresta
Bosa
Bonárcado
M. Urtigu 1050
M. Minerva 644
Temo
Santu Lussurgiu
Séneghe
Santa Caterina di Pittinuri
Capo Marargiu

Porto Tórres
Platamona Lido
Mannu

Oruen
Oliena
Nuoro
Oliena
Orósolo
Olzai
Urzulei
Piulitaínu
Baronie
Fonni
Gavoi
Ovodda
Austis
Orani
Ottana
Oroteli
Sédilo
Ghilarza
NURAGHE LOSA
Paulilatino
Borore
Dualchi
Macomer
Santa
LAGO Omodeo

Sárdegna

E25
118
131
132
133
125
127
129
389
199
392
597
672
200
292

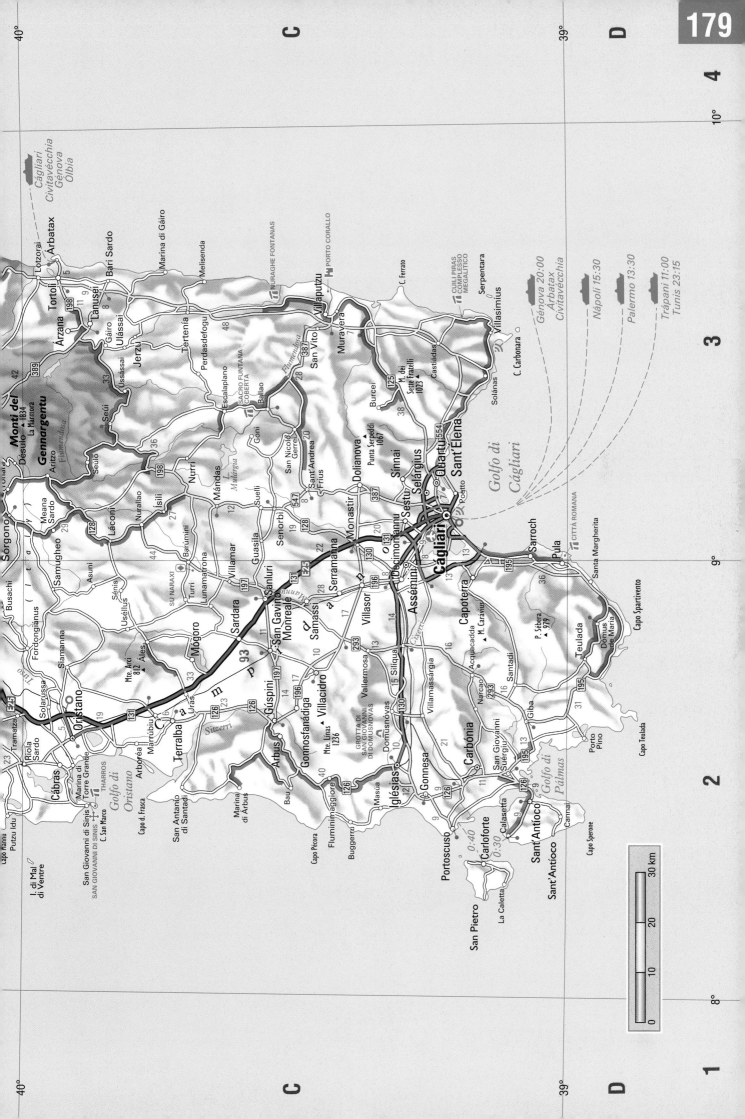

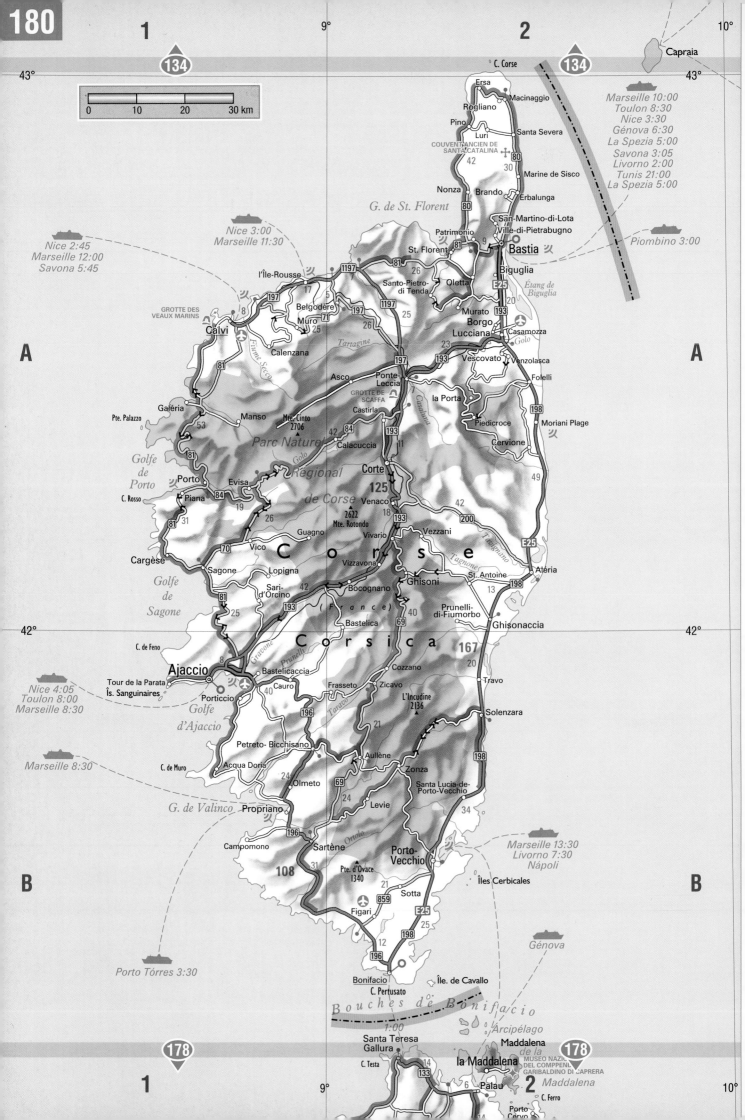

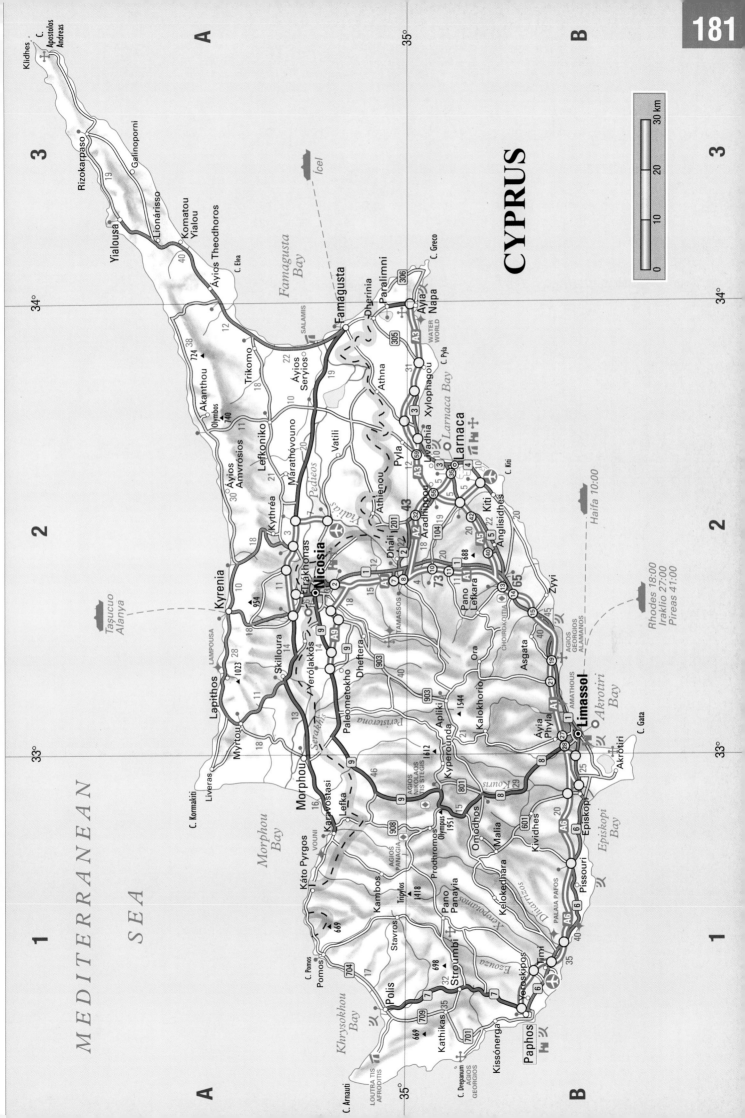

CYPRUS

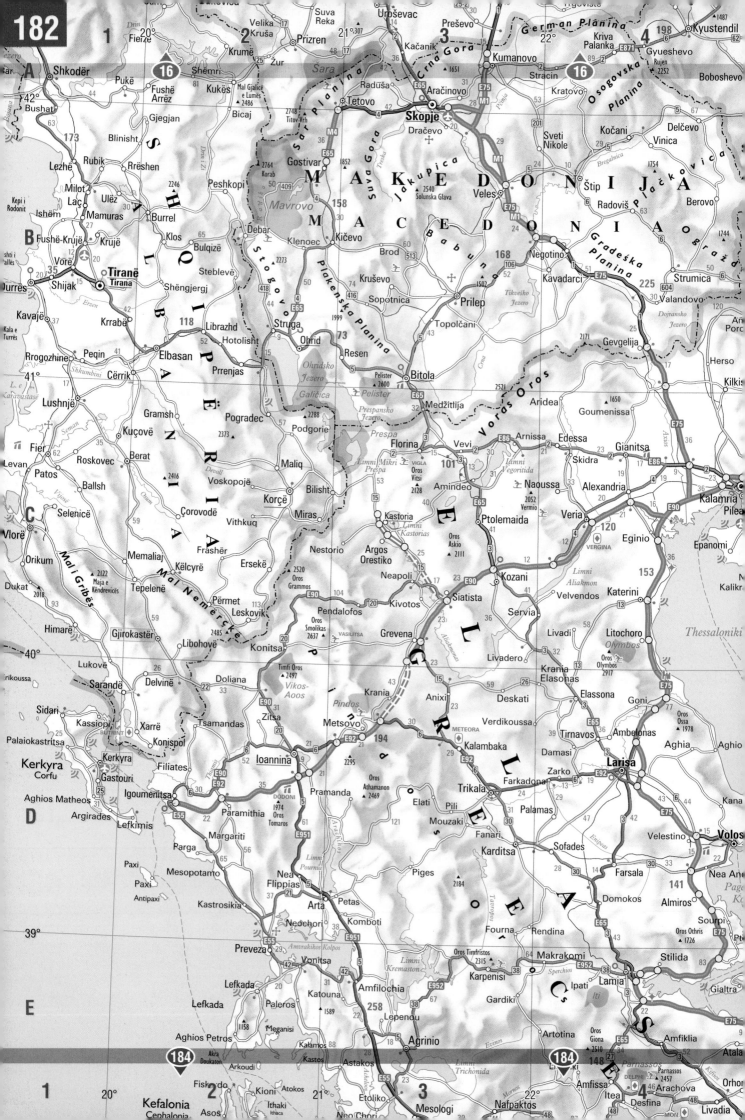

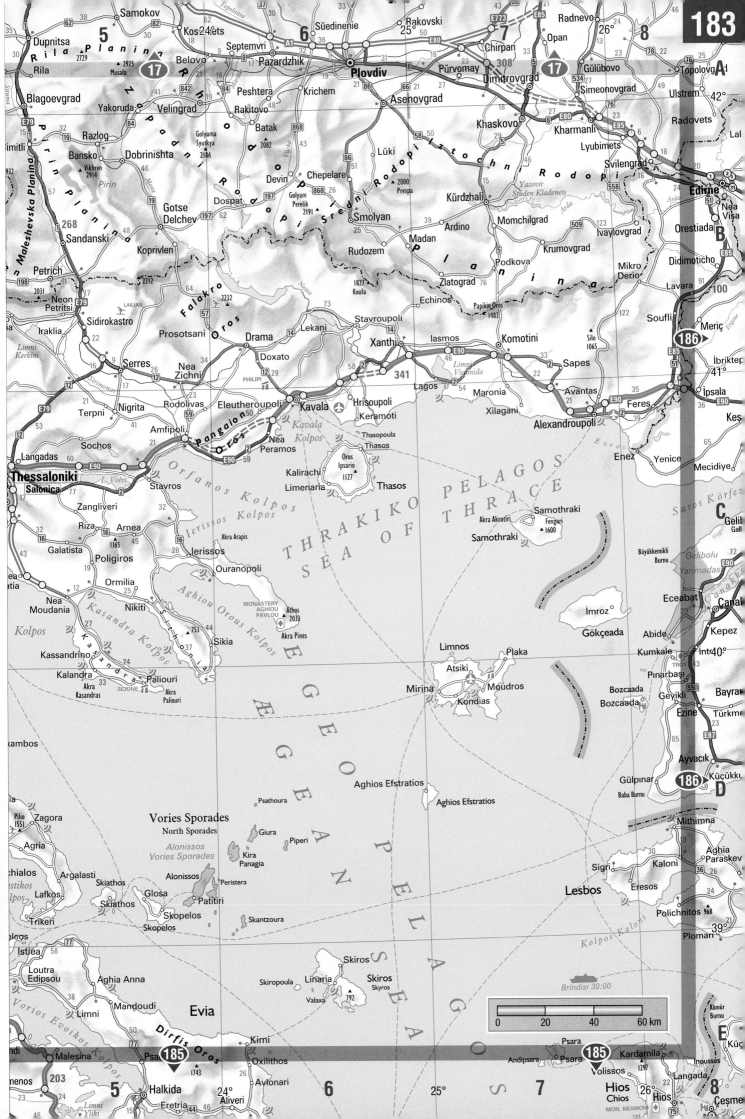

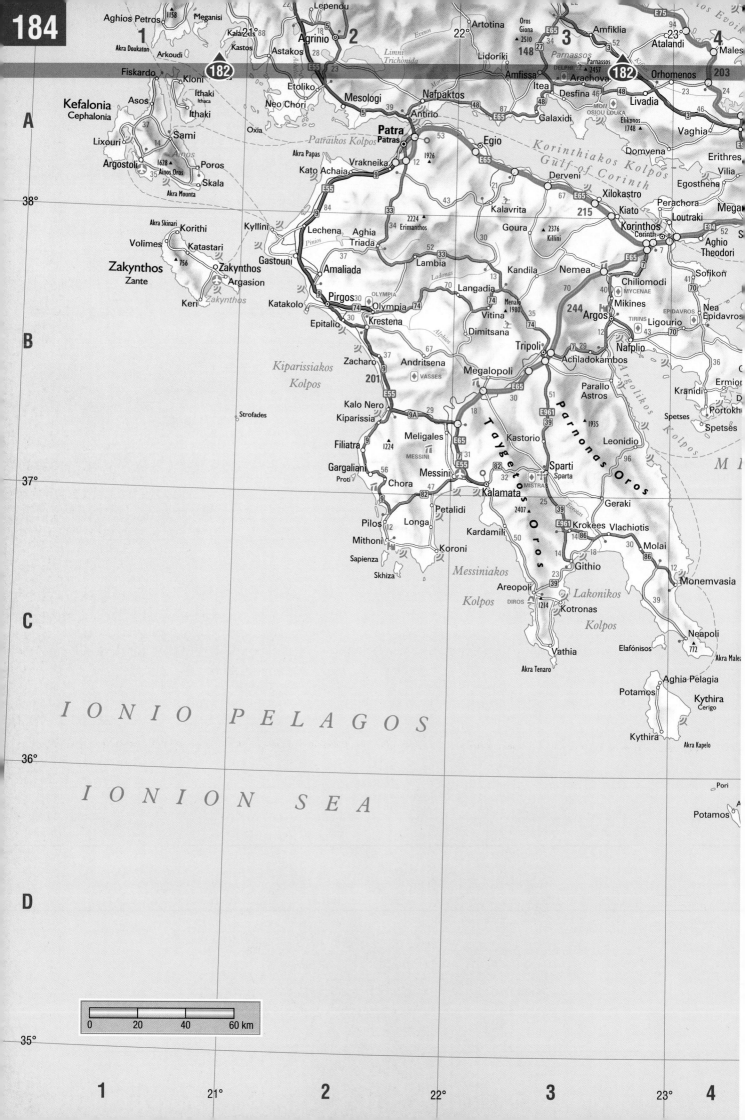

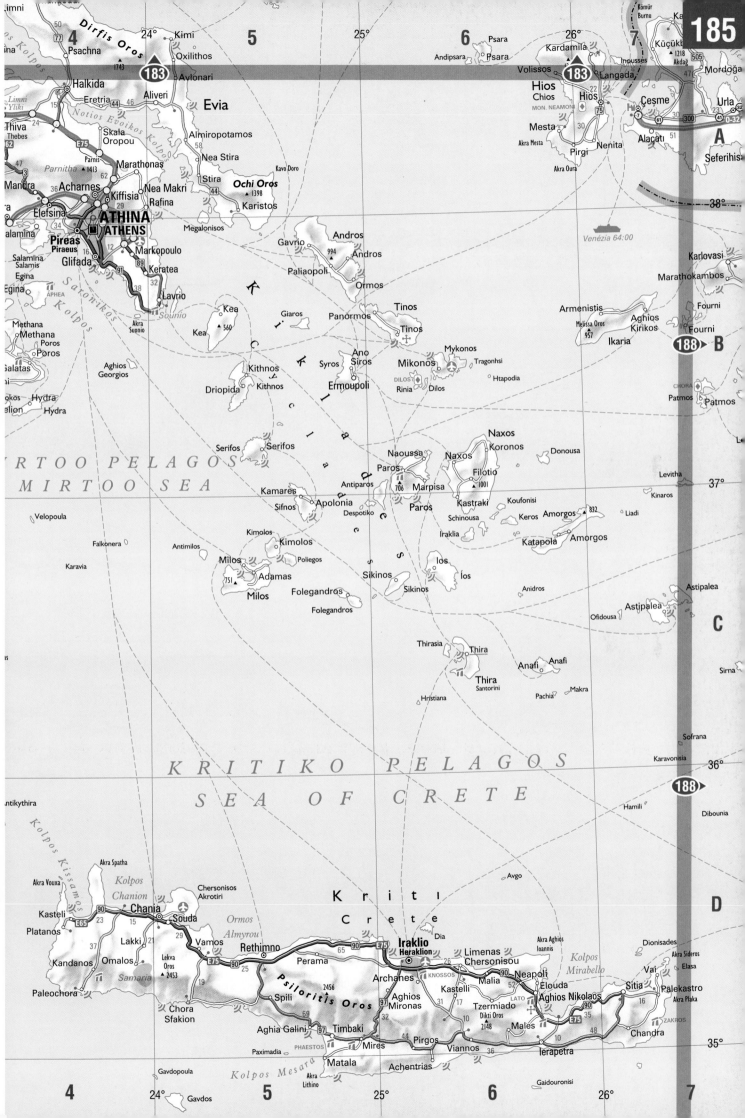

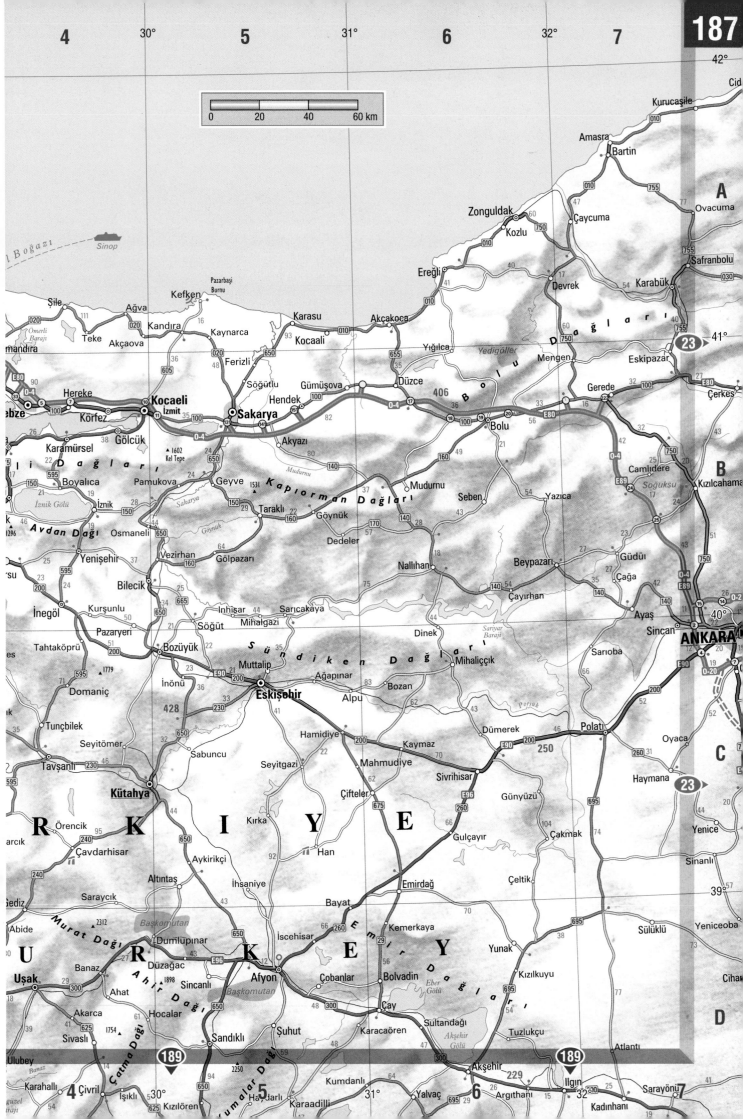

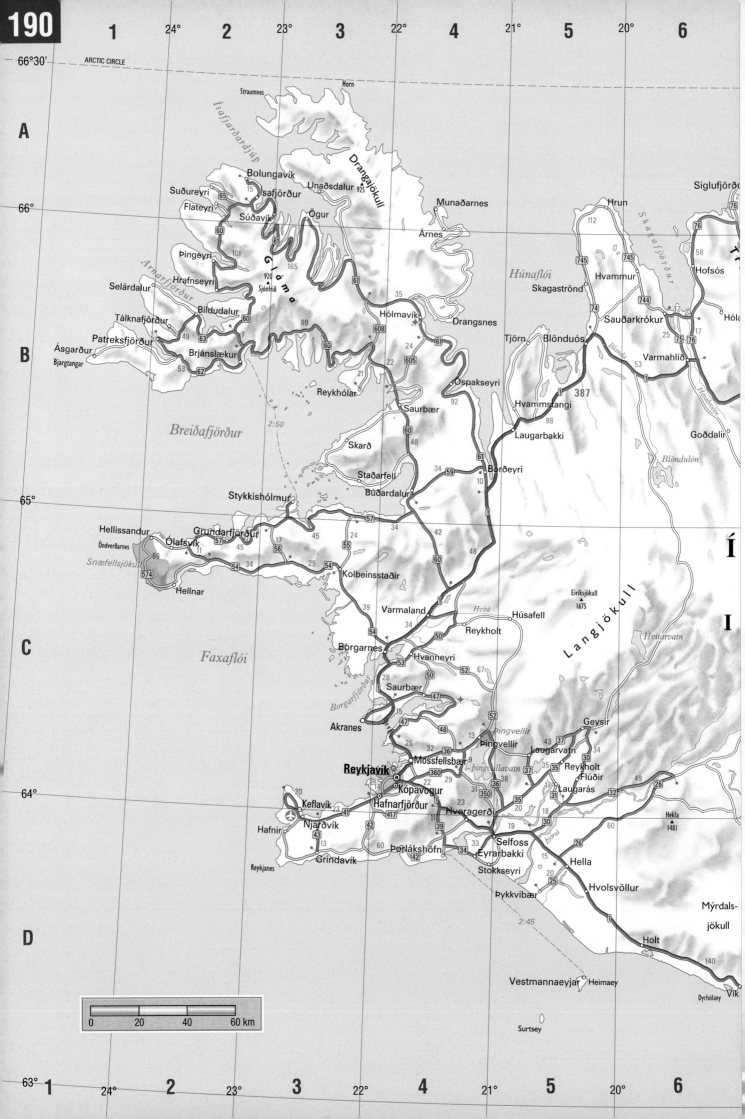

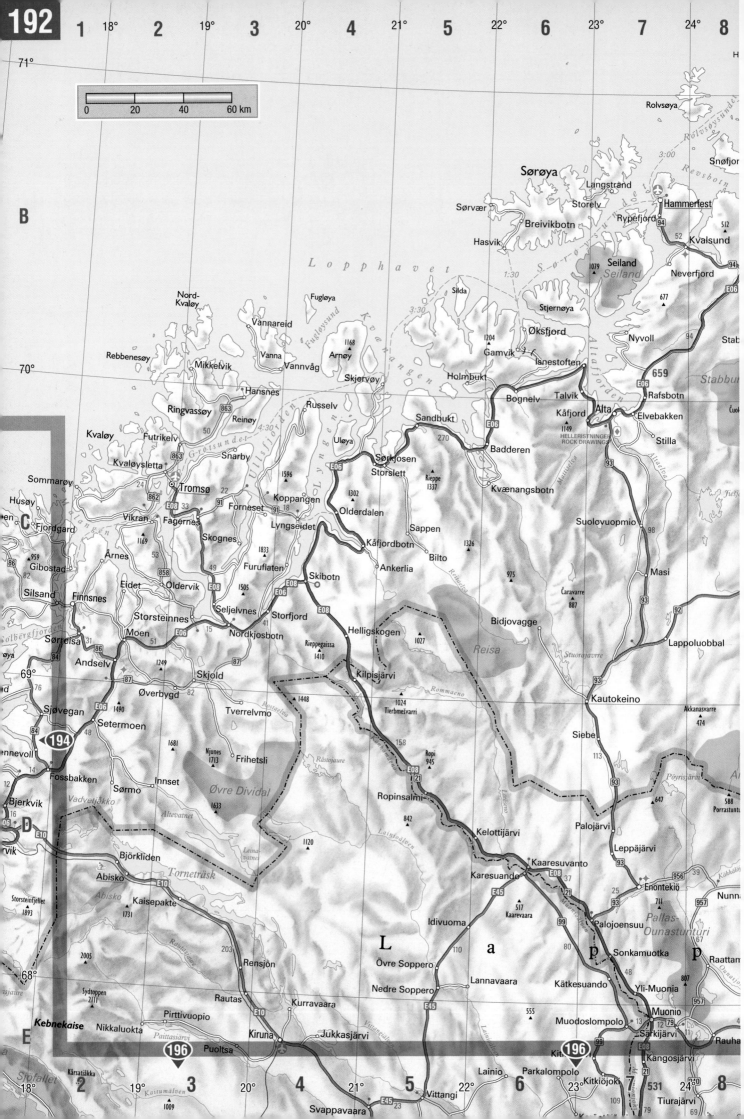

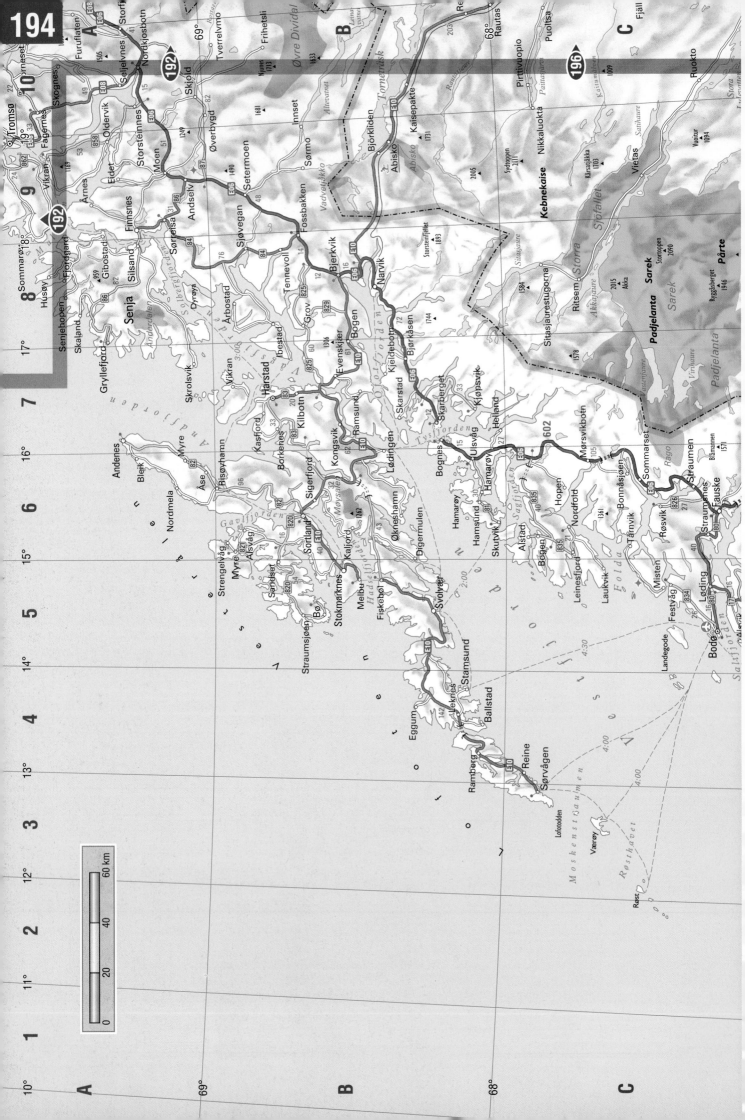

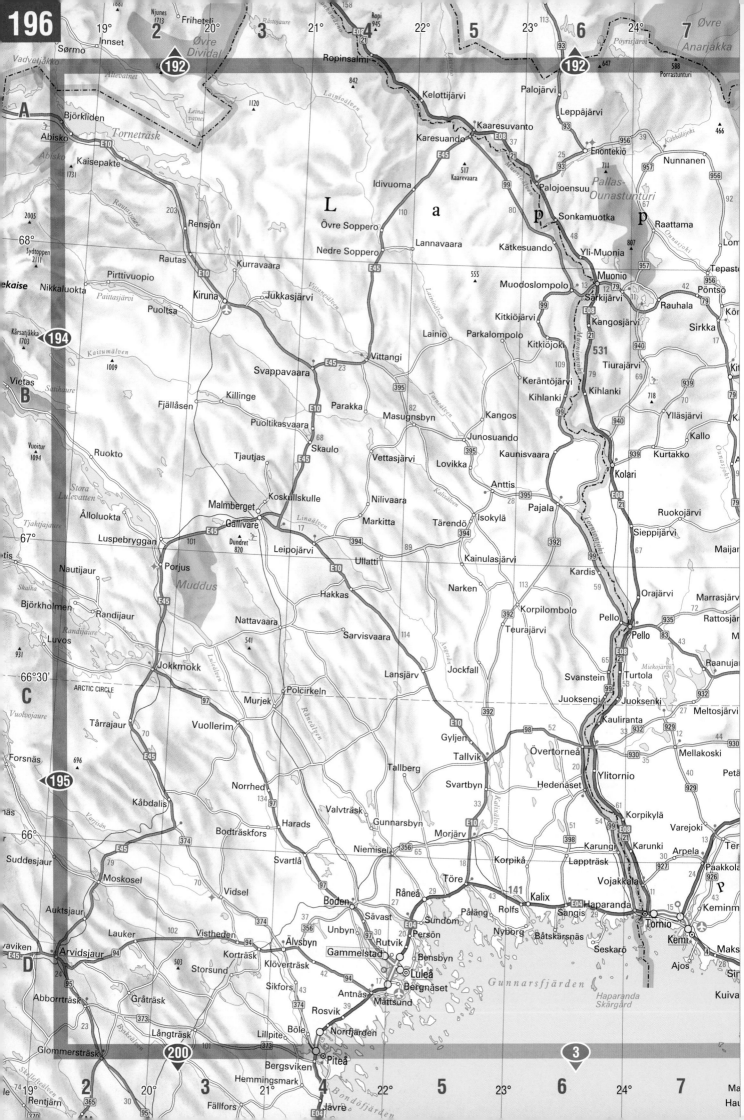

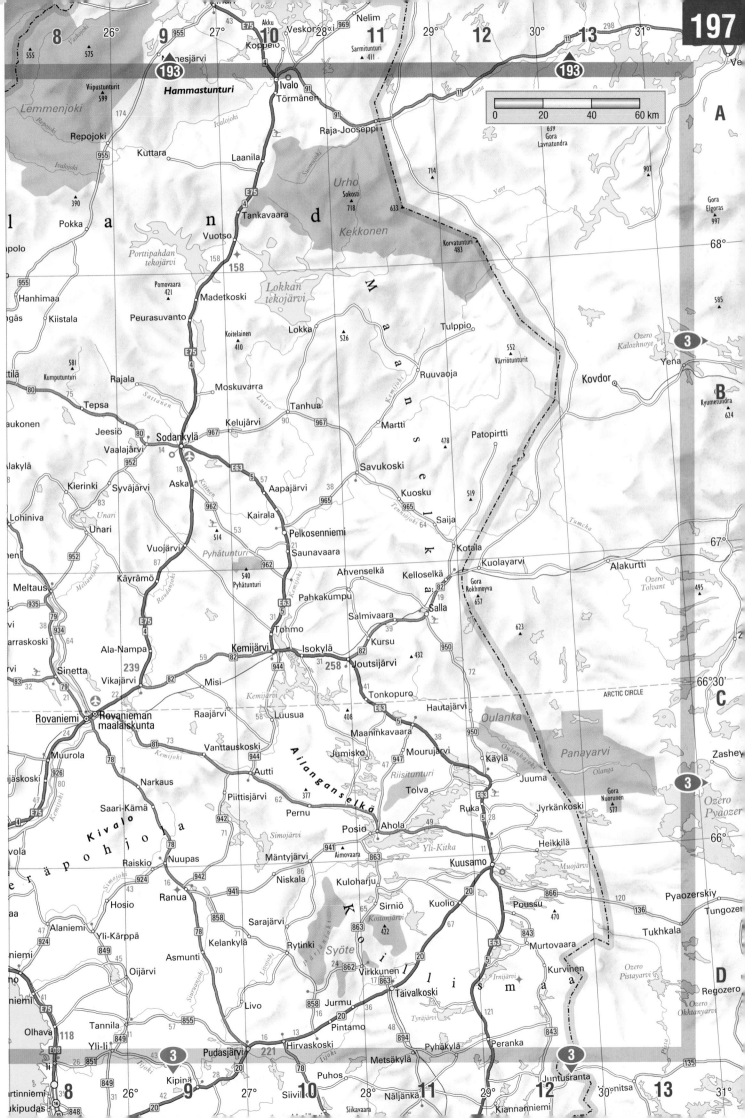

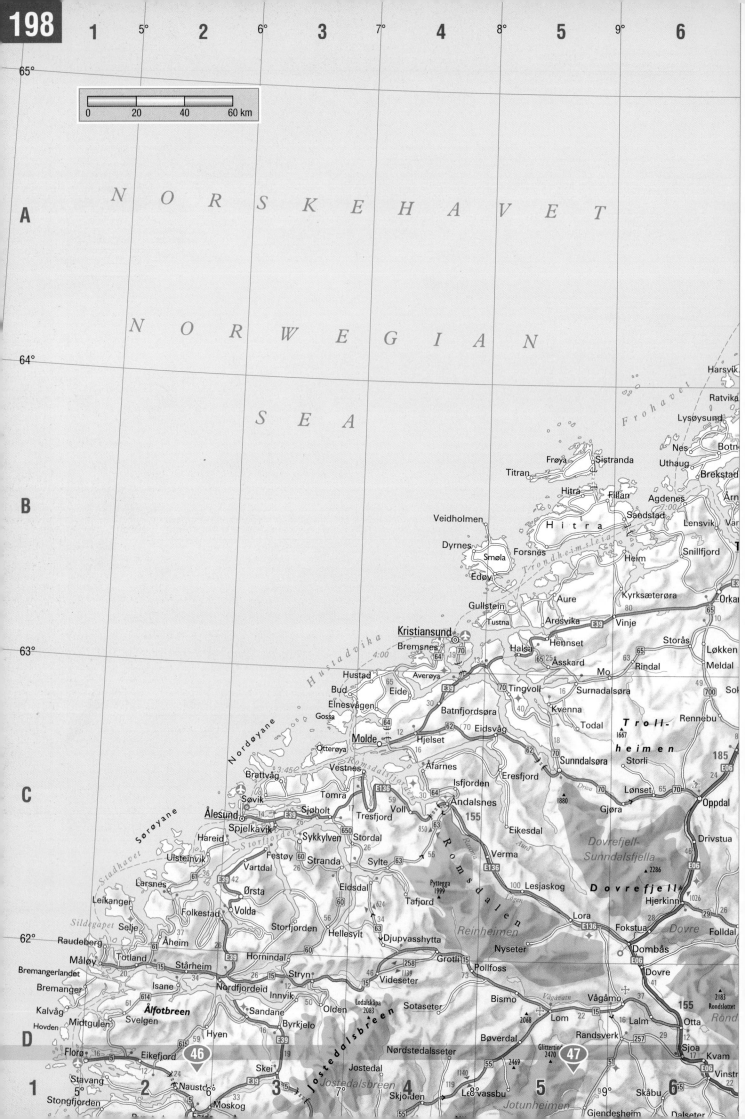

1   5°   2   6°   3   7°   4   8°   5   9°   6

65°

A

N O R S K E H A V E T

N O R W E G I A N

64°

S E A

Frohavet

Harsvik

Ratvika

Lysøysund

Nes   Botn

Uthaug

Titran   Frøya   Sistranda   Brekstad

Hitra   Fillan   Agdenes   Arn

B

Veidholmen   Sandstad   H i t r a   Lensvik   Va

Dyrnes   Forsnes   Trondheimsleia

Smøla   Helm   Snillfjord   T

Edøy

Gullstein   Aure   Kyrksæterøra

Tustna   Aresvika   E39   Vinje   Orkan

Kristiansund   80   65

63°   65

Bremsnes   64   19 70   Hennset   Storås

Hustadvika 4:00   13   Halsa   Åsskard   63 65   Løkken

Hustad   Averøya   E39   65 25   Mo   Rindal   Meldal

Bud   Eide   70 Tingvoll   49   700   So

Elnesvågen   30   16   Surnadalsøra

Gossa   Batnfjordsøra   40   Kvenna

Nordøyane   64   62 70 Eidsvåg   18   Todal   T r o l l -

Molde   12   Hjelset   62   70 Sunndalsøra   h e i m e n   1667

Otterøya   16   Storli

Romsdalsfjorden   Åfarnes   Eresfjord   Driva   Lønset   65 70   185

Brattvåg   3:45   Isfjorden   1880   Gjøra   Oppdal   E06

Søvik   Vestnes   Tomra   64   30   Andalsnes   155

C   Ålesund   14   Sjøholt   59   Voll   Eikesdal   Drivstua

Spjelkavik   E39   26   Tresfjord   17   Verma   Dovrefjell- 2286

Hareid   Storfjorden   Sykkylven   Stordal   850   63 55   Sunndalsfjella   D o v r e f j e l l   1026

Ulsteinvik   Festøy   60   Stranda   26   Sylte   63   55   E136   46   Hjerkinn

Larsnes   61   36   Vartdal   Eidsdal   624   Lesjaskog   100   29

Leikanger   E39   42   Ørsta   60   34   Tafjord   Pyttegga   Lora   E136   Fokstua   28   Folldal

Folkestad   Volda   56   63   1999   Reinheimen   Dombås

Sildegapet   Selje   37   Storfjorden   60   Hellesylt   Djupvasshytta   Nyseter   E06   Dovre

62° Raudeberg   Åheim   26   Hornindal   258   Grotli   15   Pollfoss   41   155

Måløy   Totland   15   Stårheim   46 1139   Videseter   73   Bismo   Vågåmo   37   Rondslottet

Bremangerlandet   20   Isane   Stryn   Sotaseter   22   15   16   Lalm   257   Otta

Bremanger   614   Nordfjordeid   Innvik   50   Olden   Lodalskåpa   Lom   Randsverk   29   Sjoa

Kalvåg   Ålfotbreen   Sandane   Byrkjelo   2083   Bøverdal   2068   Glittertin   47   155

Hovden   Midtgulen   Svelgen   Hyen   16   16   Nørdstedalsseter   2470   51   Kvam

D   Florø   615   46   Jostedalsbreen   1140   55   2469   E06

Stavang   5   Eikefjord   19   Skei   E39   Lé vassbu   99   Skåbu   Vinstr

Stongfjorden   24   Naustc   Moskog   Jostedal   Skjolden   119   Jotunheimen

1   5°   2   6°   3   7°   4   8°   5   9°   6

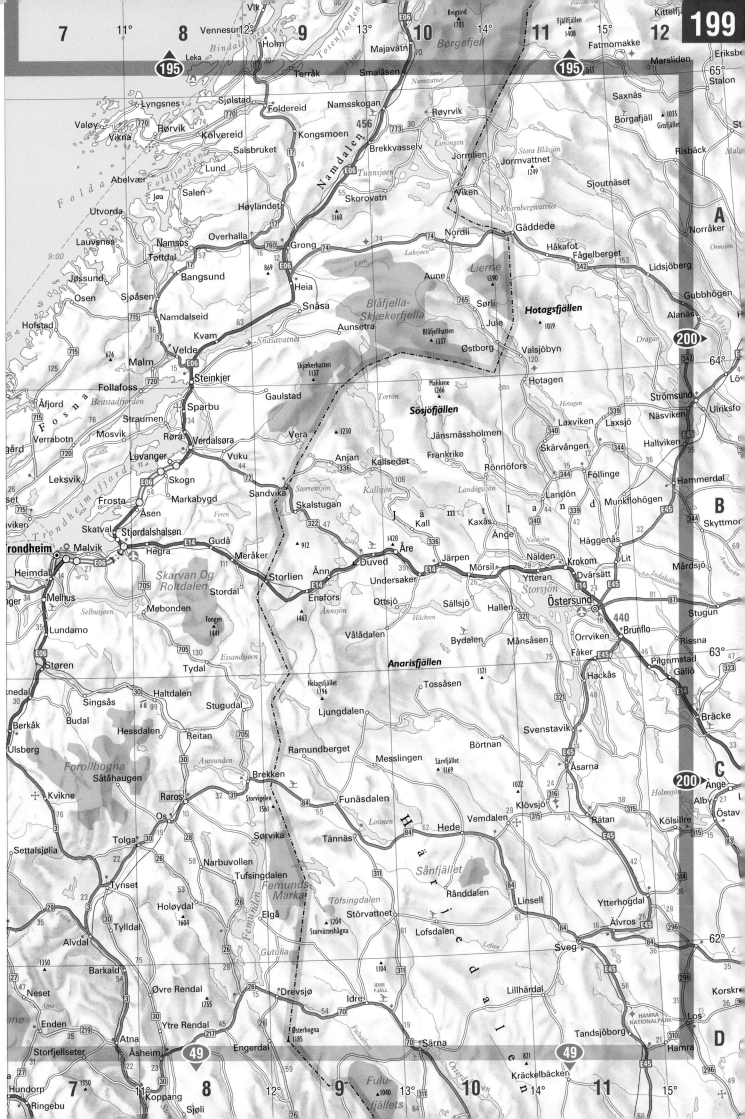

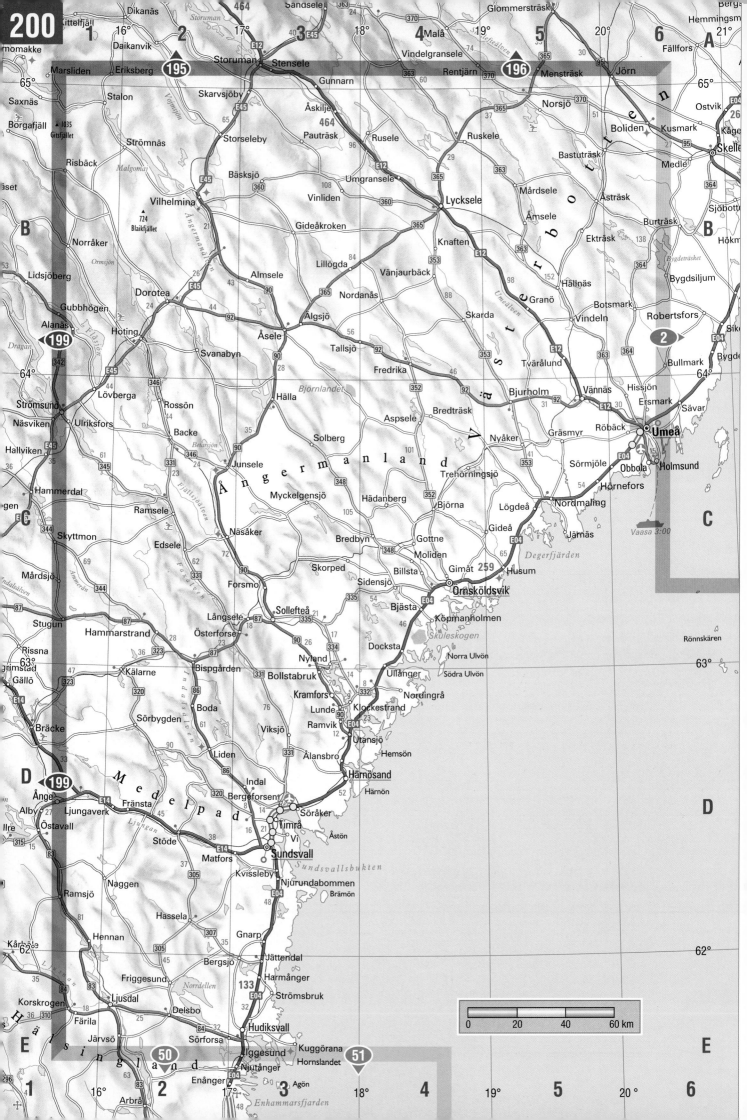

City plans • Plans de villes
Stadtpläne • Piante di città

Motorway	Autoroute	Autobahn		Autostrada
Major through route	Route principale majeur	Hauptstrecke		Strada di grande comunicazione
Through route	Route principale	Schnellstrasse		Strada d'importanza regionale
Secondary road	Route secondaire	Nebenstrasse		Strada d'interesse locale
Dual carriageway	Chaussées séparées			
Other road	Autre route	Zweispurig Schnellstrasse		Strada a carreggiate doppie
Tunnel	Tunnel	Nebenstrecke		Altra strada
Limited access / pedestrian road	Rue réglementée / rue piétonne	Tunnel		Galleria stradale
One-way street	Sens unique	Beschränkter Zugang / Fussgängerzone		Strada pedonale / a accesso limitato
Parking	Parc de stationnement	Einbahnstrasse		Senso unico
Motorway number	A7 Numéro d'autoroute	Parkplatz	P	Parcheggio
National road number	447 Numéro de route nationale	Autobahnnummer	A7	Numero di autostrada
European road number	E45 Numéro de route européenne	Nationalstrassen-nummer	447	Numero di strada nazionale
Destination	GENT Destination	Europäische Strassennummer	E45	Numero di strada europea
Car ferry	Bac passant les autos	Ziel	GENT	Destinazione
Railway	Chemin de fer	Autofähre		Traghetto automobili
Rail/bus station	Gare / gare routière	Eisenbahn		Ferrovia
Underground, metro station	Station de métro	Bahnhof / Busstation		Stazione ferrovia / pullman
Cable car	Téléférique	U-Bahnstation		Metropolitano
Abbey, cathedral	Abbaye, cathédrale	Drahtseilbahn		Funivia
Church of interest	Église intéressante	Abtei, Kloster, Kathedrale		Abbazia, duomo
Synagogue	Synagogue	Interessante Kirche		Chiesa da vedere
Hospital	Hôpital	Synagoge		Sinagoga
Police station	Police	Krankenhaus		Ospedale
Post office	Bureau de poste	Polizeiwache	POL	Polizia
Tourist information	Office de tourisme	Postamt		Ufficio postale
Place of interest	Theatre Autre curiosité	Informationsbüro		Ufficio informazioni turistiche
		Sonstige Sehenswürdigkeit	Theatre	Luogo da vedere

Approach maps • Agglomérations
Carte régionale • Regionalkarte

Toll motorway – with motorway number	A10 Autoroute à péage – avec numéro d'autoroute	Gebührenpflichtige Autobahn – mit Autobahnnummer	A10	Autostrada a pedaggio – con numero
Toll-free motorway – with European road number	E51 Autoroute – avec numéro de route européenne	Gebührenfreie Autobahn – Europäische Strassennummer	E51	Autostrada – con numero di strada europea
Pre-pay motorway – vignette required	Autoroute – 'vignette'	Autobahn – 'vignette'		Autostrada – 'vignette'
Motorway services	Aire de service	Autobahnservice		Area di servizio autostradale
Motorway junction – full/restricted	Échangeur d'autoroute – accès libre/ accès reglémenté	Autobahnkreuz – voller/begrenzter Zugang		Raccordi autostradali – completo/parziali
Under construction	En construction	Im Bau		In construzione
Tunnel	Tunnel	Tunnel		Galleria stradale
Major route dual carriageway single carriageway	14 chausées séparées 14 chaussée sans séparation	Hauptstrecke		Strada di grande communicazione
Secondary route dual carriageway single carriageway	96 chaussées séparées 96 chausée sans séparation	zweispurige Schnellstrasse	14 14	carreggiata doppia carreggiata unica
Other road	Autre route	Nebenstrasse		Strada d'interesse locale
Car ferry	Bac passant les autos	zweispurige Schnellstrasse	96 96	carreggiata doppia carreggiata unica
Destination	GIRONA Destination	Nebenstrecke		Altra strada
Railway	Chemin de fer	Autofähre		Traghetto automobili
Railway station	Estación Central Gare	Ziel	GIRONA	Destinazione
Height above sea level – in metres	234 Altitude – en mètres	Eisenbahn		Ferrovia
Airport	Aéroport principal	Hauptbahnhof	Estación Central	Stazione ferrovia
Airfield	Autre aéroport	Höhe über dem Meeresspiegel	234	Altezza in metri
City plan coverage area	Région de plan de ville	Flughafen		Aeroporto
		Flugplatz		Aerodromo/campo d'aviazione
		Vom Stadtplan abgedecktes Gebiet		Area della pianta della città

Alicante
0 km 0.5

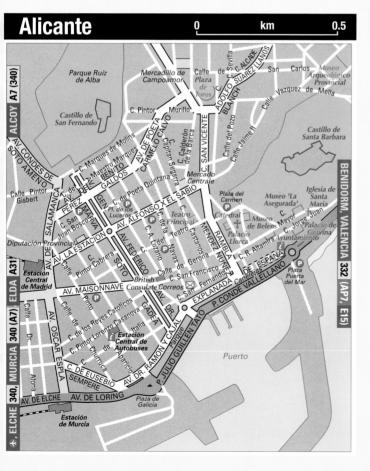

Antwerpen Antwerp
0 km 1

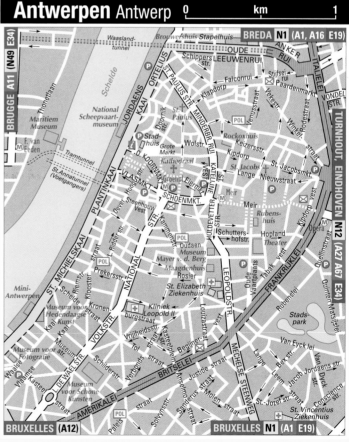

Amsterdam

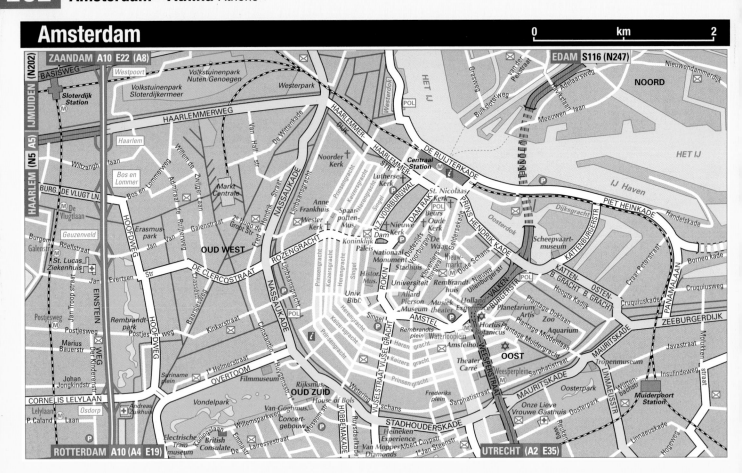

Athina Athens

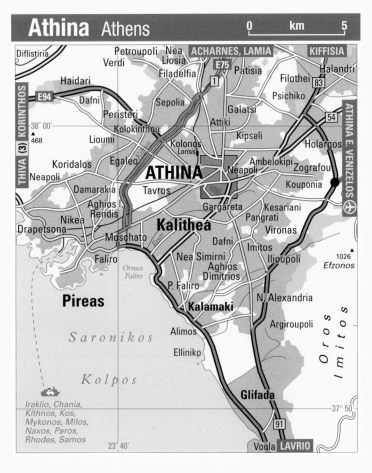

Athina Athens

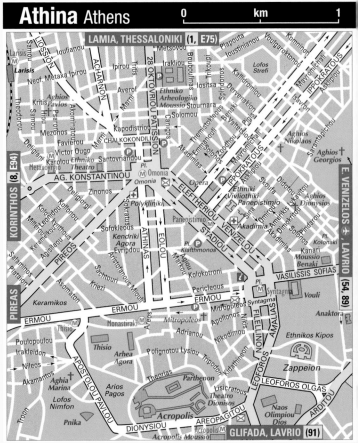

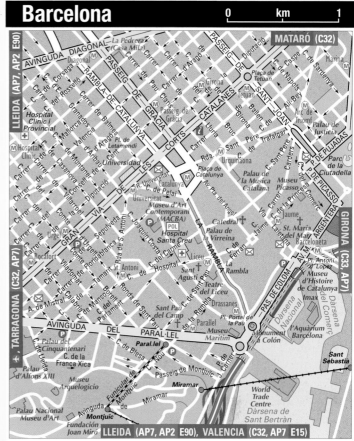

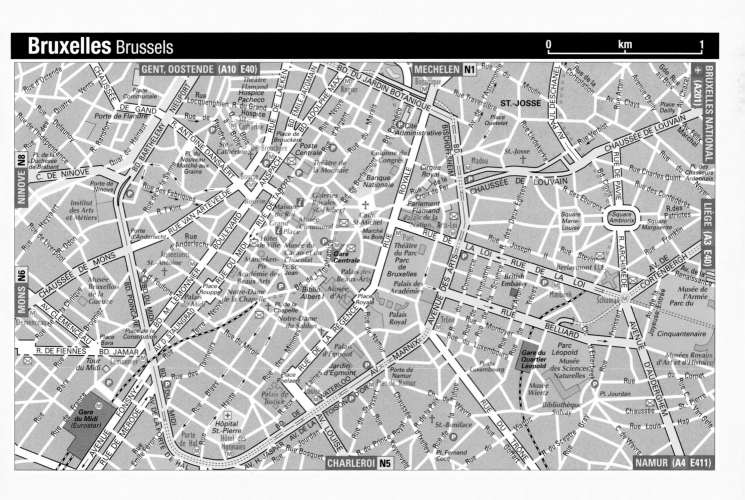

Berlin

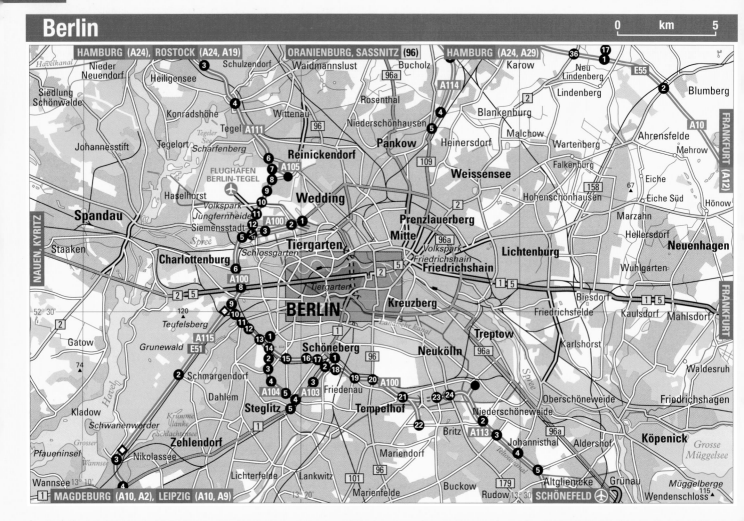

Berlin

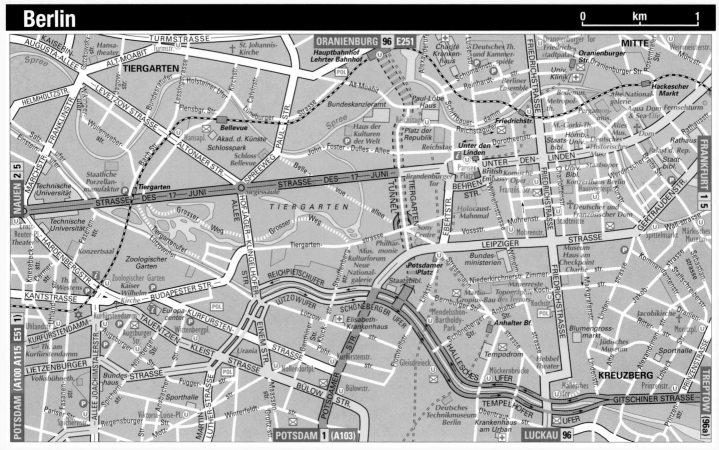

Bordeaux

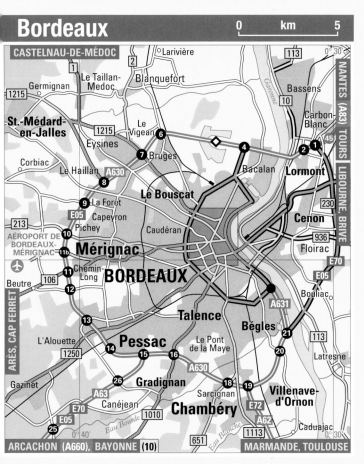

Bordeaux

Budapest

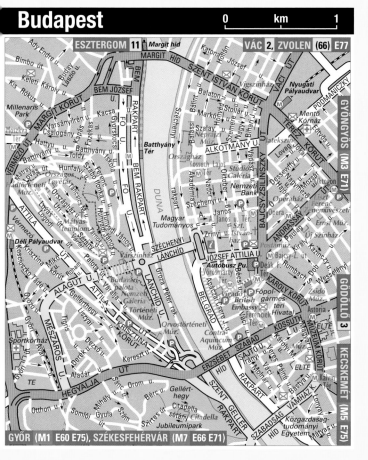

Dublin

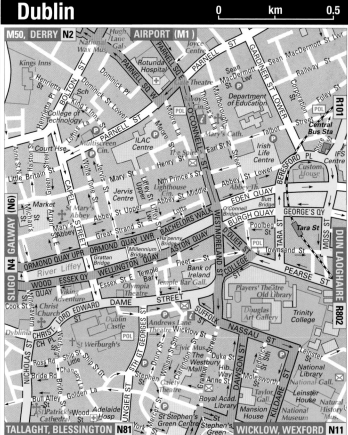

For **Cologne** see page 211
For **Copenhagen** see page 210

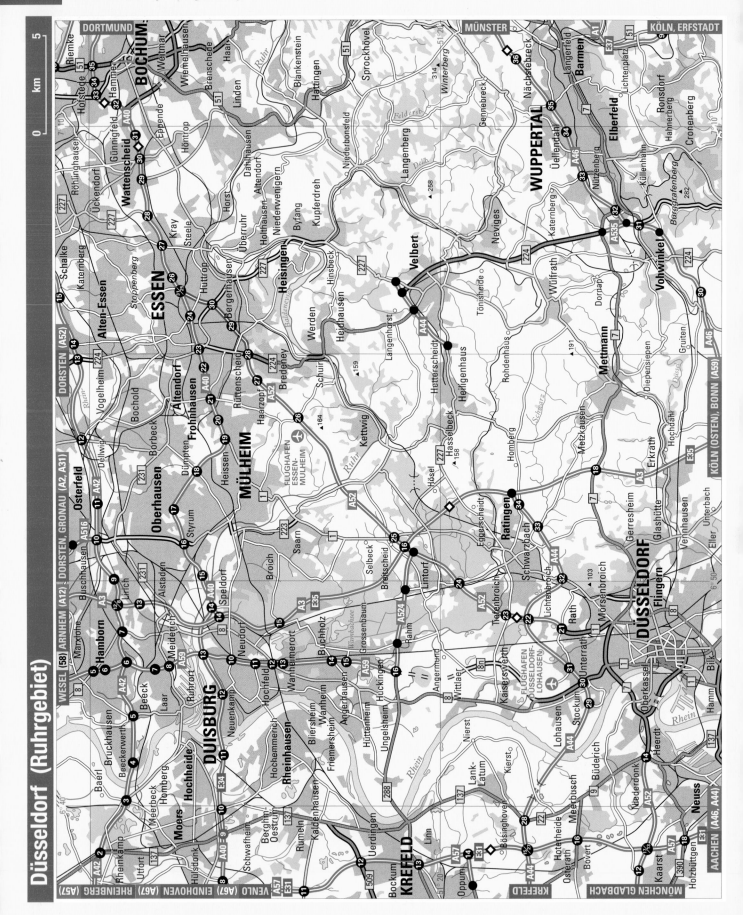

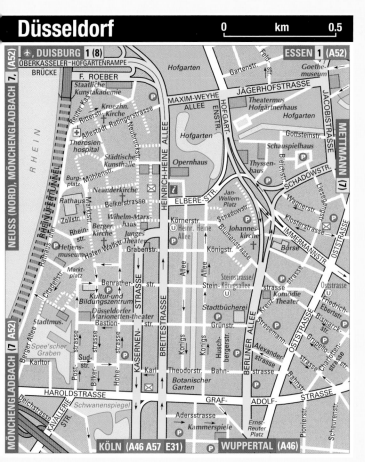

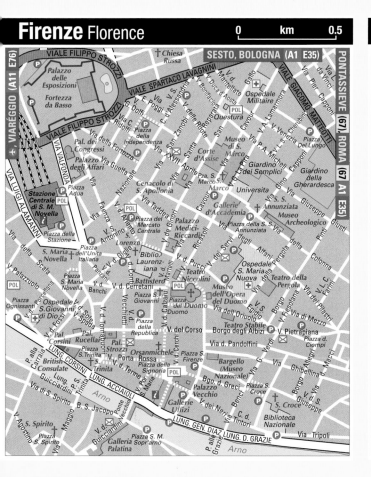

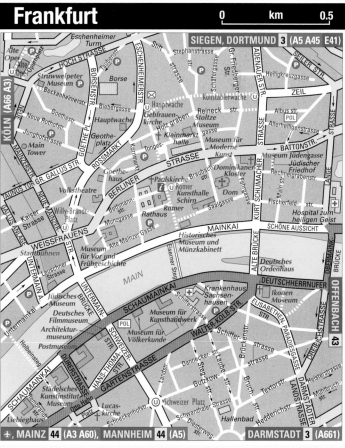

Genève Geneva

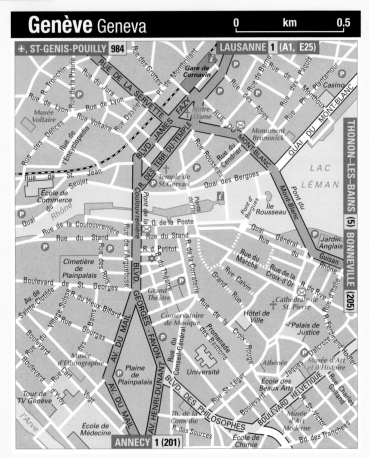

Göteborg Gothenburg

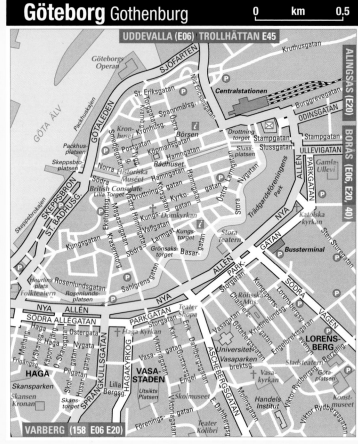

Hamburg

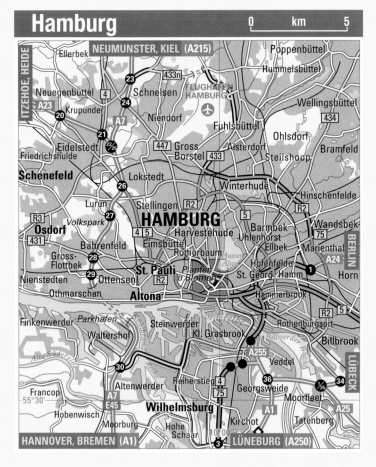

Hamburg

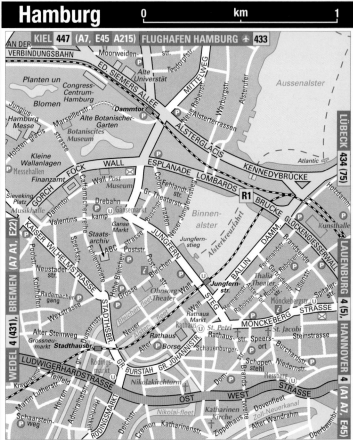

Helsinki

0 km 10

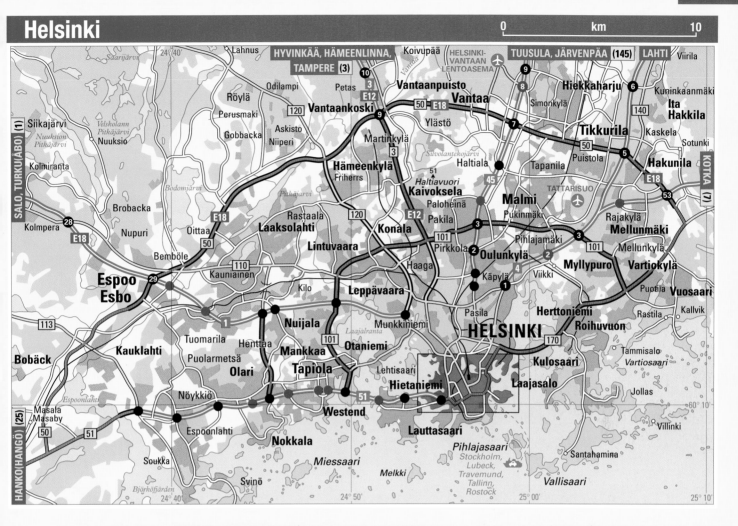

Säärijärvi · 24° 40' · Lahnus · Koivupää · **HYVINKÄÄ, HÄMEENLINNA,** · HELSINKI-VANTAAN LENTOASEMA · **TUUSULA, JÄRVENPÄÄ** (145) · **LAHTI** · Viirila

SALO, TURKU(ÅBO) (1)

Siikajärvi · Röylä · Odilampi · Petas · **TAMPERE** (3) · **10** · **Vantaanpuisto** · **9** · **8** · **Hiekkaharju** · **6** · Kuninkaanmäki
Velskolann Pitkäjärvi · Nuuksion Pitkäjärvi · Nuuksio · Perusmaki · 3 · Vantaa · Simonkylä · **Ita Hakkila**
Kolmiranta · Gobbacka · Askisto · E12 · **Vantaankoski** · 9 · **Vantaa** · Ylästö · 7 · **Tikkurila** · Kaskela · 140
Brobacka · Nupuri · 120 · Niiperi · Martinkylä · 50 · E18 · 50 · 50 · Sotunki
28 · Oittaa · 3 · **Hämeenkylä** · Friherrs · Silvolantekojärvi · 45 · Puistola · 5 · **Hakunila**
Kolmpera · E18 · 50 · **Laaksolahti** · Rastaala · 120 · E12 · Haltiala · Tapanila · E18
E18 · Bemböle · 110 · **Lintuvaara** · Konala · 101 · **Kaivoksela** · Paloheinä · TATTARISUO · 53
Espoo Esbo · 29 · Kauniainen · Kilo · **Leppävaara** · Haaga · Pakila · **Malmi** · Pukinmäki · 3 · Rajakylä · **Mellunmäki**
113 · 1 · Tuomarila · **Nuijala** · Munkkiniemi · Pirkkola · 3 · 2 · **Oulunkylä** · Pihlajamäki · 3 · Mellunkylä · 101
Bobäck · **Kauklahti** · Henttaa · **Mankkaa** · **Otaniemi** · Laajalranta · 101 · Käpylä · 1 · 4 · Viikki · 2 · **Myllypuro** · **Vartiokylä**
Puolarmetsä · **Olari** · **Tapiola** · Lehtisaari · Pasila · **HELSINKI** · 170 · Puotila · **Vuosaari**
Masala Masaby · Nöykkiö · 51 · **Hietaniemi** · **Herttoniemi** · **Roihuvuori** · Rastila · Kallvik
25 · 50 · 51 · Espoonlahti · **Westend** · **Kulosaari** · Tammisalo · Vartiosaari
HANKO(HANGÖ) · Soukka · **Nokkala** · **Lauttasaari** · **Laajasalo** · Jollas
Svinö · Björköfjärden · 24° 40' · Miessaari · Melkki · **Pihlajasaari** · Stockholm, Lubeck, Travemund, Tallinn, Rostock · Vallisaari · Santahamina · Villinki · 60° 10'
24° 50' · 25° 00' · 25° 10'

Helsinki

0 km 1

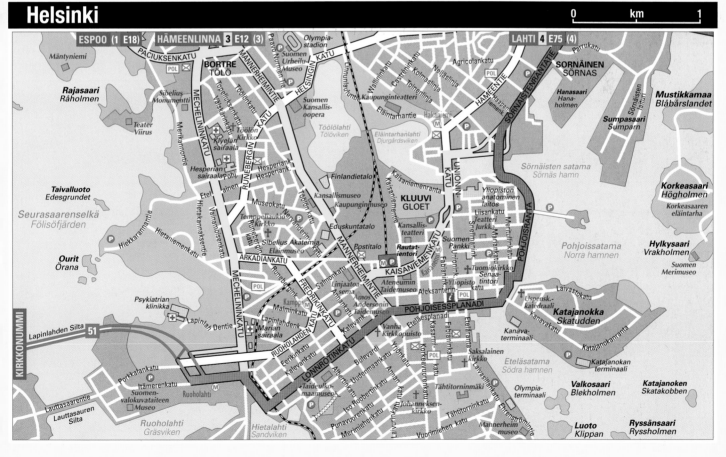

ESPOO (1 E18) · **HÄMEENLINNA** 3 E12 (3) · Olympia-stadion · **LAHTI** 4 E75 (4) · Parrukatu

Mäntyniemi · PACIUKSENKATU · Suomen Urheilu-Museo · Agricolankatu · POL · SÖRNÄINEN SÖRNÄS
Rajasaari Råholmen · Sibelius Monumentti · BORTRE TÖLÖ · Suomen Kansallis-oopera · Kaupunginteatteri · Hakaniemi · HÄMEENTIE · Hanasaari Hanaholmen · **Mustikkamaa Blåbärslandet**
Teater Viirus · Töölön Kirkko · Töölölahti Tölöviken · Eläintarhantie · Sumpasaari Sumparn
Taivalluoto Edesgrundet · Kivelän sairaala · Hesperian sairaalaPohj. · Hesperiank. · Finlandietalo · Eläintarhanlahti Djurgårdsviken · Sörnäisten satama Sörnäs hamn · **Korkeasaari Högholmen**
Seurasaarenselkä Fölisöfjärden · Meritakannasentie · Museokatu · Kansallismuseo · KLUUVI GLOET · Yliopiston anatominen laitos · Pohjoissatama Norra hamnen · Korkeasaaren eläintarha
Ourit Örana · Hietakannaksentie · Temppeliaukio Kirkko · Eduskuntatalo · Kansallis-teatteri · Liisankatu · Teatteri Jurkka · **Hylkysaari Vrakholmen**
Psykiatrian klinikka · Sibelius Akatemia Eläinmuseo · Postitalo · Rautatientori · ARKADIANKATU · Suomen Pankki · Tuomiokirkko Senaa-tintori · Suomen Merimuseo
KIRKKONUMMI · Lapinlahden Silta · 51 · POL · Linjatonasema · Ateneumin Taidemuseo · Kaisaniemenkatu · Yliopisto · Senaatin katu · POL · Uspensk-katedraali · **Katajanokka Skatudden**
Hiekkarannantie · Lapinlahdenk · Marian sairaala · Amos Andersonin Taidemuseo · POHJOISESPLANADI · Saksalainen kirkko · Katajanokan terminaali
Porkkalankatu · Eerikink Kalevankatu · ANNANKATU · Vanha Kirkkopuisto · Etelä-ranta · **Valkosaari Blekholmen** · **Katajanoken Skatakobben**
Itämerenkatu · Ruoholahti · Taideollu-maamuseo · Johanneksen-kirkko · Tähtitorninmäki · Olympia-terminaali · Mannerheim museo · **Luoto Klippan** · **Ryssänsaari Ryssholmen**
Lauttasaarentie · Lauttasaaren Silta · **Ruoholahti Gräsviken** · Hietalahti Sandviken · Vuorimiehen katu · Eläsatama Södra hamnen

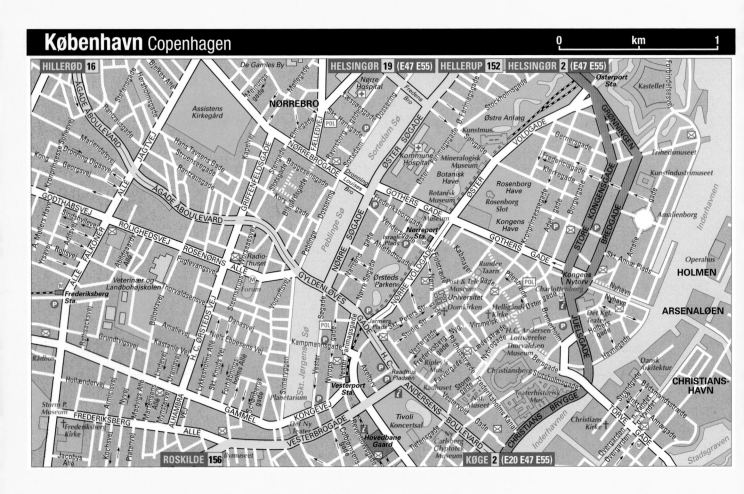

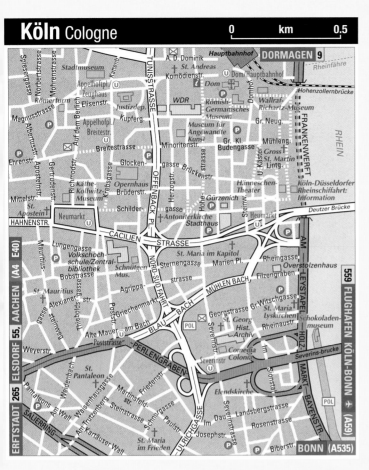

Köln Cologne

0 — km — 0.5

Luxembourg

0 — km — 0.5

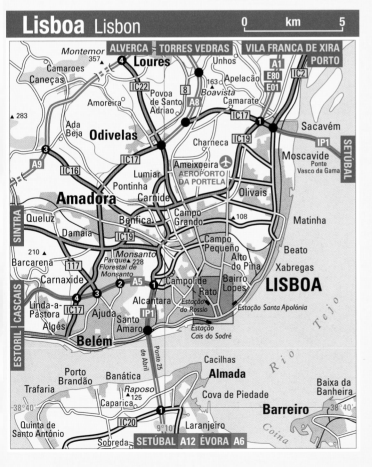

Lisboa Lisbon

0 — km — 5

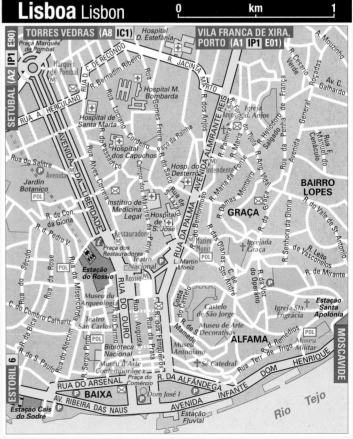

Lisboa Lisbon

0 — km — 1

London

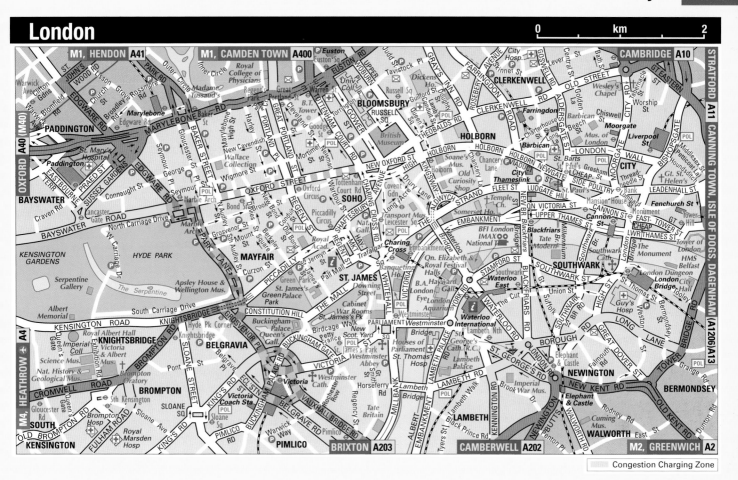

London

0 km 2

M1, HENDON A41 | M1, CAMDEN TOWN A400 | CAMBRIDGE A10

STRATFORD A11 CANNING TOWN, ISLE OF DOGS, DAGENHAM A1206/A13

OXFORD A40 (M40)

PADDINGTON

BAYSWATER

M4, HEATHROW A4

KNIGHTSBRIDGE

BROMPTON

SOUTH KENSINGTON

HYDE PARK

KENSINGTON GARDENS

MAYFAIR

BELGRAVIA

PIMLICO

BLOOMSBURY

SOHO

ST. JAMES

CLERKENWELL

HOLBORN

CITY

SOUTHWARK

NEWINGTON

BERMONDSEY

LAMBETH

WALWORTH

BRIXTON A203 | CAMBERWELL A202 | M2, GREENWICH A2

Congestion Charging Zone

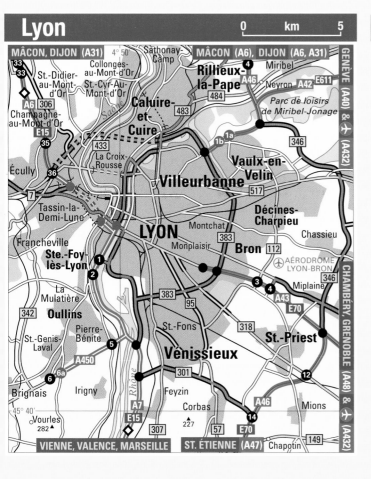

Lyon

0 km 5

MÂCON, DIJON (A31) | MÂCON (A6), DIJON (A6, A31)

GENÈVE (A40) & ✈ (A432)

CHAMBÉRY, GRENOBLE (A48) & ✈ (A432)

VIENNE, VALENCE, MARSEILLE | ST. ÉTIENNE (A47)

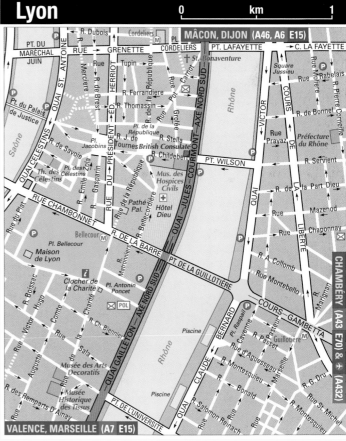

Lyon

0 km 1

MÂCON, DIJON (A46, A6 E15)

CHAMBÉRY (A43 E70) & ✈ (A432)

VALENCE, MARSEILLE (A7 E15)

Madrid

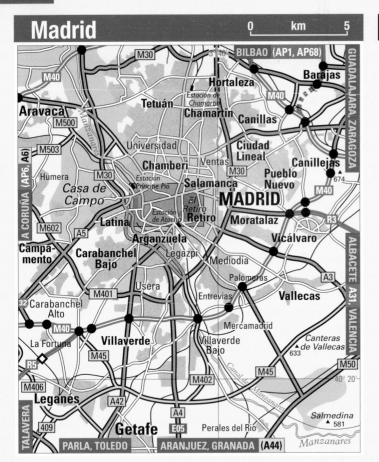

Marseille Marseilles

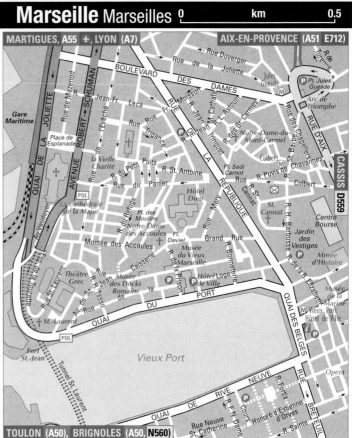

Madrid

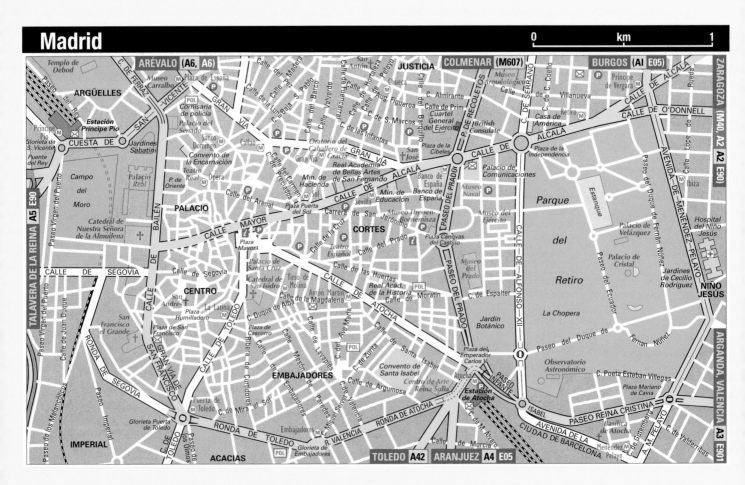

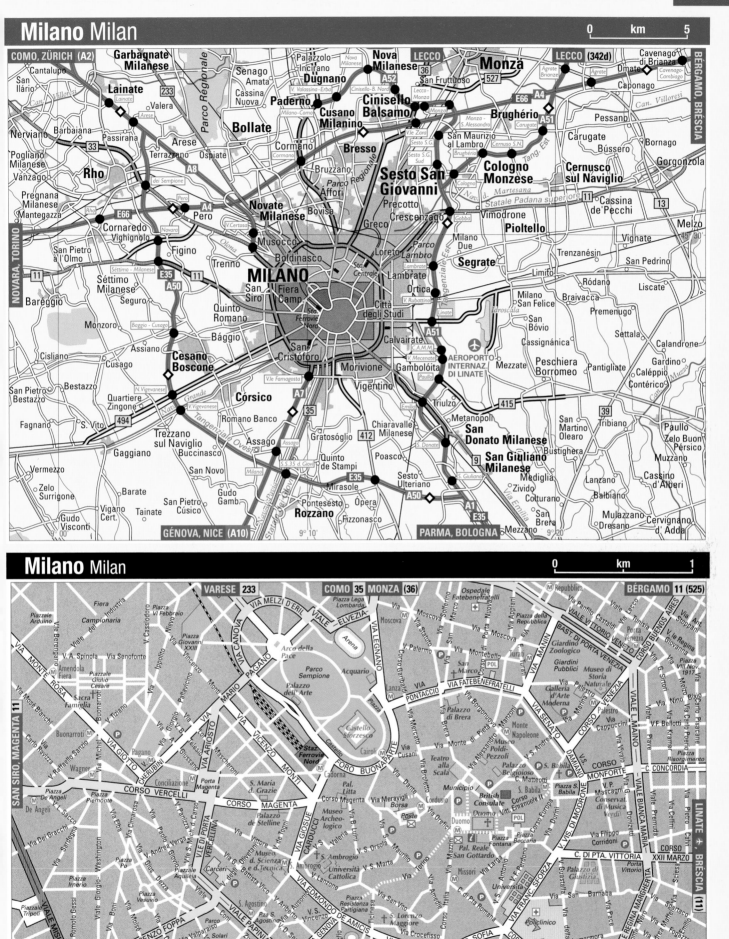

München Munich

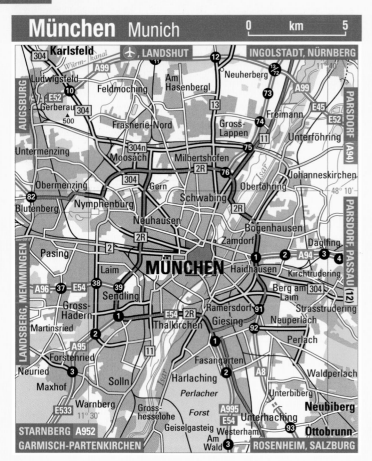

München Munich

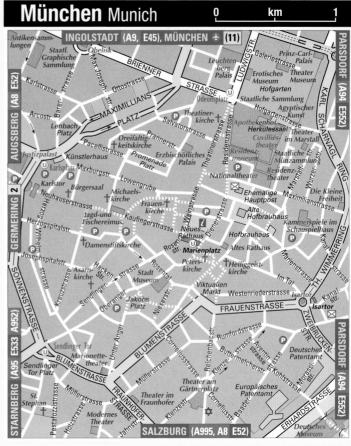

Nápoli Naples

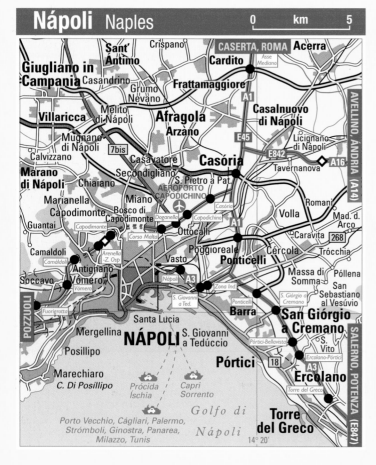

Nápoli Naples

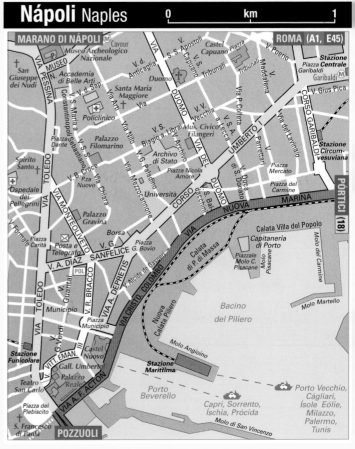

Oslo

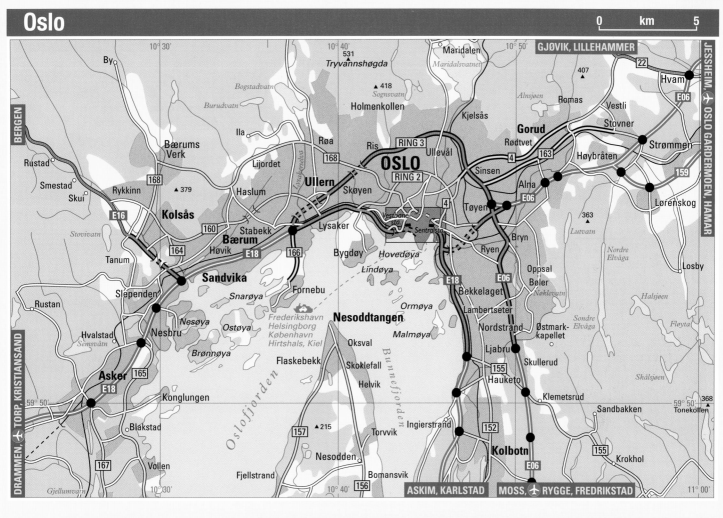

0 km 5

GJØVIK, LILLEHAMMER

JESSHEIM, ✈ OSLO GARDERMOEN, HAMAR

BERGEN

DRAMMEN, ✈ TORP, KRISTIANSAND

ASKIM, KARLSTAD   MOSS, ✈ RYGGE, FREDRIKSTAD

By · 10°30′ · 531 Tryvannshøgda · 10°40′ · Maridalen · Maridalsvatnet · 10°50′ · 22 · Hvam · E06

Bogstadvatn · Burudvatn · ▲418 Sognsvatn · Holmenkollen · Kjelsås · Alnsjøen · Romas · Vestli · Stovner · 407 · Strømmen

Rustad · Bærums Verk · Ila · Røa · Ris · RING 3 · Ulleval · Gorud · Rødtvet · 4 · 163 · Høybråten · 159 · Lørenskog

Smestad · Skui · Rykkinn · 168 · Lijordet · Skøyen · OSLO · RING 2 · Sinsen · Alna · E06 · 363 · Lutvatn · Losby · Nordre Elvåga

E16 · Kolsås · 160 · Stabekk · Haslum · Ullern · Tøyen · Bryn · Oppsal · Bøler · Østmark-kapellet · Halsjøen · Fløyta

Tanum · 164 · Høvik · Bærum · E18 · Lysaker · 166 · Bygdøy · Hovedøya · E18 · E06 · Ryen · Bekkelaget · Lambertseter · Nordstrand · Sondre Elvåga · Skålsjøen

Sandvika · Slependen · Snarøya · Fornebu · Lindøya · Nesoddtangen · Ormøya · Malmøya · Nøklevatn · Ljabru · 155 · Skullerud

Rustan · Hvalstad · Nesøya · Ostøya · Frederikshavn Helsingborg København Hirtshals, Kiel · Oksval · Hauketo · Klemetsrud · Sandbakken · 368 Tonekollen

Asker · 165 · Nesbru · Brønnøya · Flaskebekk · Skoklefall · Helvik · 59°50′ Ingierstrand · 152 · Kolbotn · 155 · Krokhol · 11°00′

E18 · Konglungen · ▲215 · Torvvik · E06 · 59°50′

167 · Blakstad · Vollen · Nesodden · Fjellstrand · Bomansvik · 156

Oslofjorden · Bunnefjorden · Gjellumvatn

Oslo

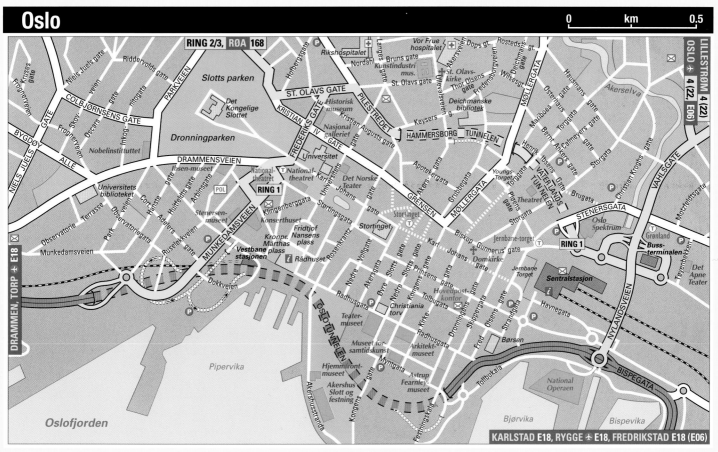

0 km 0.5

LILLESTRØM 4 (22)

OSLO ✈ 4 (22, E06)

DRAMMEN, TORP ✈ E18

KARLSTAD E18, RYGGE ✈ E18, FREDRIKSTAD E18 (E06)

RING 2/3, RØA 168 · Vor Frue hospitalet · Rostedsh gt. · ⊠

Riddervolds gate · Rikshospitalet · Nordahl · Kunstindustri mus. · Bruns gate · St. Olavs kirke · Thor Olsens gate · Deichmanske bibliotek · Akerselva

Niels Juels gate · Frognerveien · Parkveien · ST. OLAVS GATE · St. Olavs gate · Ullevalsveien · Hausmanns gate · Osterhaus gate

COLBJØRNSENS GATE · Slotts parken · Det Kongelige Slottet · Historisk museum · Kristian Augusts gate · Keysers g. · HAMMERSBORG TUNNELEN · Maridboes gate · Calmeyers gate · Storgata

BYGDØY · Oscars gate · Frognerveien · Dronningparken · Nasjonal galleriet · Apotekergata · Henrik Ibsens gate · Brugata

Nobelinstituttet · DRAMMENSVEIEN · Universitet · Det Norske Teater · Youngs-Torget · Christian Krohgs gate

NIELS JUELS ALLE · Universitets biblioteket · Ibsen-museet · National-theatret · Johans gate · GRENSEN · MØLLERGATA · Theatret · Oslo Spektrum

Observatorie Terrasse · Stenersen-museet · POL · RING 1 · Stortingsgata · Stortinget · Biskop Gunnerus gate · STENERSGATA · RING 1 · Grønland · Buss-terminalen

Park · Konserthuset · Kronpr. Märthas plass · Fridtjof Nansens plass · Karl Johans gate · Domkirke gate · Jernbane-torget · Sentralstasjon · Det Apne Teater

Munkedamsveien · MUNKEDAMSVEIEN · Vestbane stasjonen · Rådhuset · Rosenkrantz · Stortinget · Nedre Slotts gate · Hovedpost kontor · Havnegata · NYLANDSVEIEN

Dokkveien · Christiania torv · Kirke · Radhusgata · Fred Olsens gate · Børsen · BISPEGATA

OSLO TUNNELEN · Teater-museet · Myntgata · Astrup Fearnley-museet · National Operaen

Piervika · Hjemmefront-museet · Museet for samtidskunst · Arkitekt-museet · Bjørvika · Bispevika

Akershus Slott og festning · Festningsstranda · Kongens gate

Oslofjorden

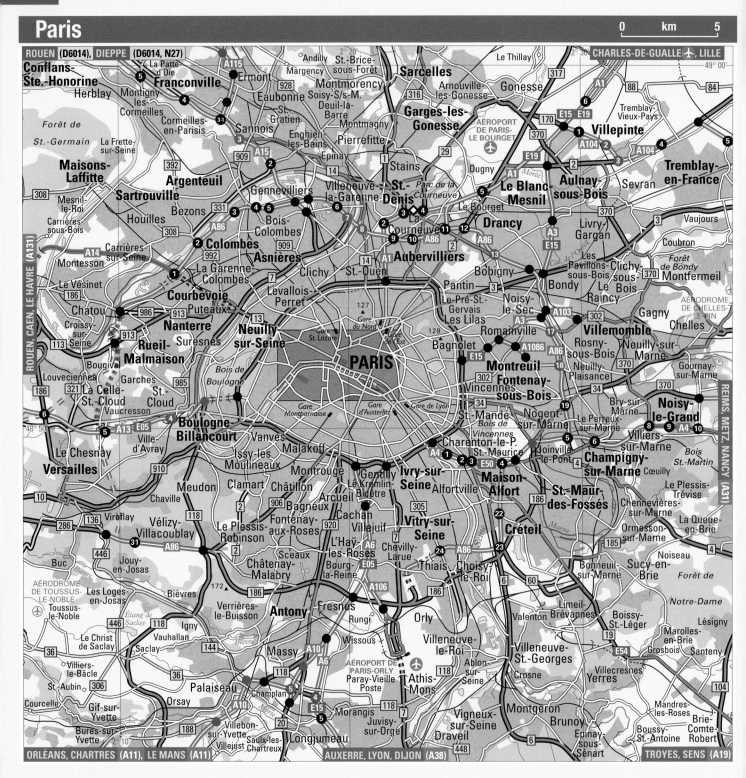

Paris

0 km 5

ROUEN (D6014), DIEPPE (D6014, N27)

CHARLES-DE-GUALLE, LILLE

ROUEN, CAEN, LE HAVRE (A131)

REIMS, METZ, NANCY (A31)

ORLÉANS, CHARTRES (A11), LE MANS (A11)

AUXERRE, LYON, DIJON (A38)

TROYES, SENS (A19)

Paris

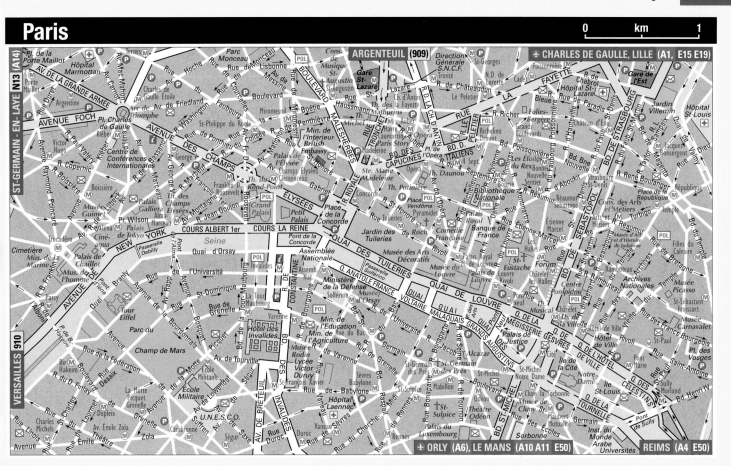

Praha Prague

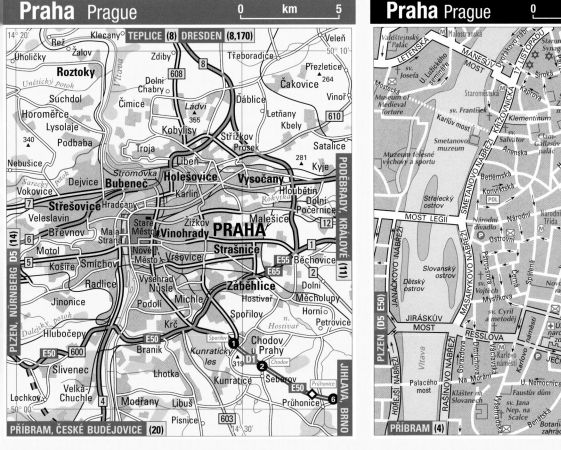

Praha Prague

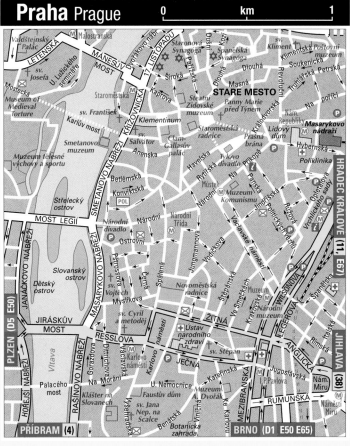

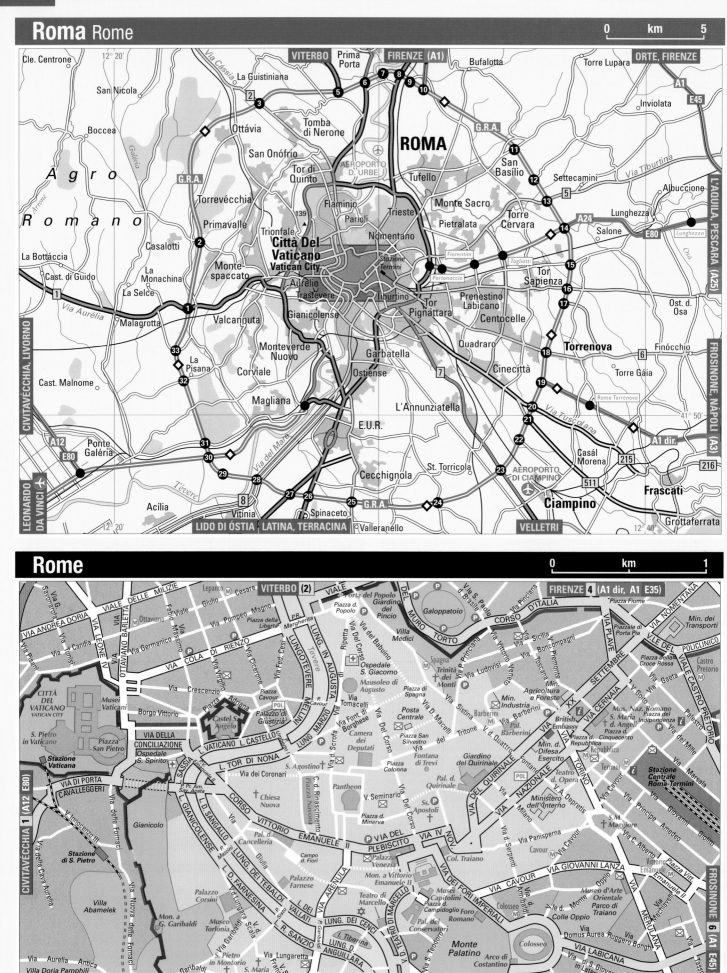

Roma Rome

0 ——— km ——— 5

VITERBO · Prima Porta · FIRENZE (A1) · Bufalotta · ORTE, FIRENZE

Cle. Centrone · 12° 20' · La Guistiniana · 7 · 8 · 9 · Torre Lupàra · A1 · E45

San Nicola · 2 · 6 · 10 · Inviolata

Boccea · 3 · Ottávia · Tomba di Nerone · ROMA · G.R.A.

G.R.A. · San Onófrio · Aeroporto d'Urbe · Tufello · San Basílio · 11 · Via Tiburtina

Agro · Torrevécchia · Tor di Quinto · Flaminio · Monte Sacro · 12 · Settecamini · Albuccione

Primavalle · 139 · Trionfale · Pietralata · Torre Cervara · 13 · 5 · L'AQUILA, PESCARA (A25)

Romano · Trionfale · Città Del Vaticano · Parioli · Trieste · A24 · 14 · Salone · Lunghezza · E80 · Lunghezza

La Bottáccia · 2 · Casalotti · Vatican City · Nomentano · Stazione Termini · Fiorentini · 15 · Osa

Cast. di Guido · Monte-spaccato · La Monachina · Aurélio · Portonaccio · Togliatti · Tor Sapienza · Ost. d. Osa

La Selce · Trastevere · Tiburtino · 16

1 · Via Aurélia · Valcannuta · Gianicolense · Tor Pignàttara · Prenestino Labicano · 17 · FROSINONE, NÁPOLI (A3)

Malagrotta · Centocelle · Quadraro · 18 · Torrenova · 6 · Finócchio

33 · Monteverde Nuovo · Garbatella · Cinecittà · Torre Gáia · Roma Torrenova

La Pisana · Corviale · Ostiense · 7 · 19 · A1 dir.

32 · 20 · Via Tuscolana · 215 · 216

Cast. Malnome · Magliana · L'Annunziatella · 21 · Casàl Morena · 511

A12 · E.U.R. · 22 · AEROPORTO DI CIAMPINO · Frascati

Ponte Galéria · E80 · 31 · Via del Mare · St. Torricola · 23 · 511 · Ciampino · Grottaferrata

30 · Cecchignola ·

LEONARDO DA VINCI · 29 · 28 · 24

Acília · 27 · 26 · 25 · G.R.A. · VELLETRI · 12° 40'

8 · Vitínia · Spinaceto · Vallerancllo

12° 20' · LIDO DI ÓSTIA · LATINA, TERRACINA

Rome

0 ——— km ——— 1

VITERBO (2) · FIRENZE 4 (A1 dir, A1 E35)

(street map of central Rome)

Restricted Zones (ZTL)

CIVITAVECCHIA 1 (A12 E80) · 'LEONARDO DA VINCI' (A12) · LATINA 148 · FROSINONE 6 (A1 E45)

Stockholm

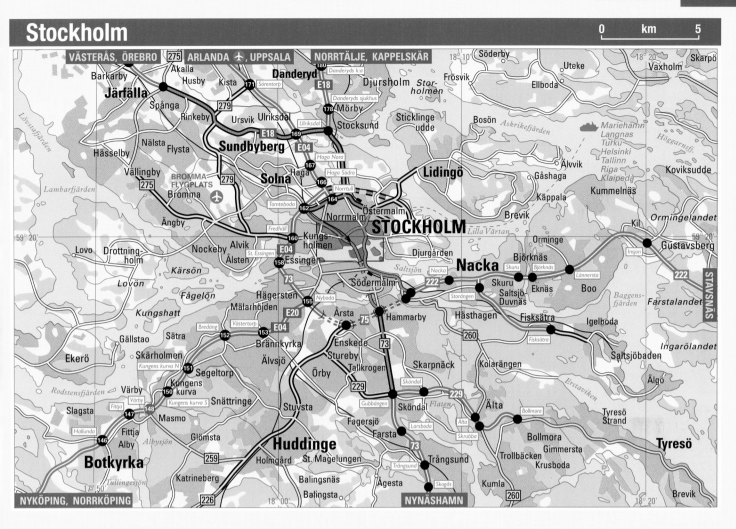

0 km 5

VÄSTERÅS, ÖREBRO 275 ARLANDA ✈, UPPSALA NORRTÄLJE, KAPPELSKÄR

Barkarby
Akalla
Husby
Kista
171 Sörentorp
Danderyd
Danderyds k:a
E18
Djursholm
Storholmen
Frösvik
Söderby
Uteke
Skarpö
Vaxholm

Järfälla
Spånga
Rinkeby
279
Ursvik Ulriksdal
Ulriksdal
178 Mörby
Danderyds sjukhus
Stocksund
Sticklinge udde
Bosön
Askrikefjärden
Mariehamn
Langnas
Turku
Helsinki
Tallinn
Riga
Klaipeda
Höggarnsfj.
Koviksudde

Hässelby
Nälsta
Flysta
Sundbyberg
E18
169
E04
Haga Nora
Haga Södra
167
Solna
Haga
166
Lidingö
Älvvik
Gåshaga
Käppala
Kummelnäs
Brevik

Vällingby
BROMMA FLYGPLATS
279
Bromma
Ängby
Tomteboda
162
164
Norrtull
Norrmalm
Östermalm
STOCKHOLM
Lilla Värtan
Kil
Orminge
Insjön
Ormingelandet
Gustavsberg
222
STAVSNÄS

59° 20'
Lovo
Drottningholm
Nockeby
Alvik
Ålsten
St. Essingen
160 Kungsholmen
158 Essingen
73
Djurgården
Saltsjön
Nacka
222
Skuru
Björknäs
Lännersta
Boo
Baggensfjärden
Färstalandet

Lambarfjärden
Lovön
Kärsön
Fågelön
Kungshatt
Hägersten
Mälarhöjden
Nyboda
155
E20
Årsta
75
Hammarby
Nyboda
Södermalm
Storängen
Skuru
Saltsjö Duvnäs
Eknäs
Fisksätra
Igelboda
Ingarölandet

Gällstao
Sätra
Skärholmen
Bredäng
Västertorp
E04
152
153
Brännkyrka
Enskede
Stureby
Tallkrogen
73
260
Fisksätra
Saltsjöbaden
Älgö

Ekerö
Värby
Kungens kurva N
151
Segeltorp
Kungens kurva
Örby
Skarpnäck
Skondal
229
Kolarängen

Rodstensfjärden
150
Kungens kurva S
Snättringe
Stuvsta
229
Flaten
Älta
Bollmora
Tyresö Strand

Slagsta
Fittja
148
Masmo
Glömsta
Fagersjö
Farsta
Gubbängen
Sköndal
Skrubba
Bollmora
Gimmersta
Krusboda
Tyresö

146
Fittja
Alby
Huddinge
Holmgård
St. Magelungen
Larsboda
73
Trångsund
Trollbäcken
Brevik

Botkyrka
259
Katrineberg
Balingsnäs
Balingsta
Ågesta
Trångsund
Skogås
Kumla
260

NYKÖPING, NORRKÖPING
226
NYNÄSHAMN

Stockholm

0 km 1

UPPSALA (E04), NORRTÄLJE E04, (E18)   LIDINGO E20 227

VÄSTERÅS (E04, E18)
SÖDERTÄLJE 275 (E4, E20)

NORRMALM
KUNGSHOLMEN
ÖSTERMALM
SKEPPSHOLMEN
RIDDARHOLMEN
GAMLA STAN

Riddarfjärden
Strömmen

NYNÄSHAMN 73 (73) GUSTAVSBERG 222 (222)

Strasbourg

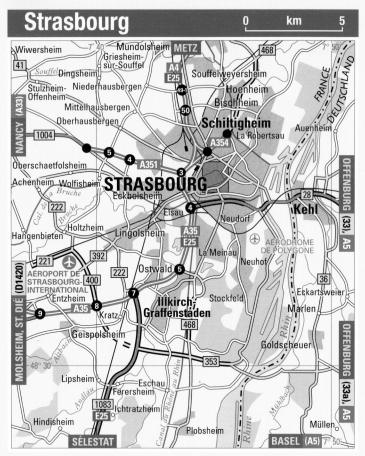

Strasbourg

Sevilla Seville

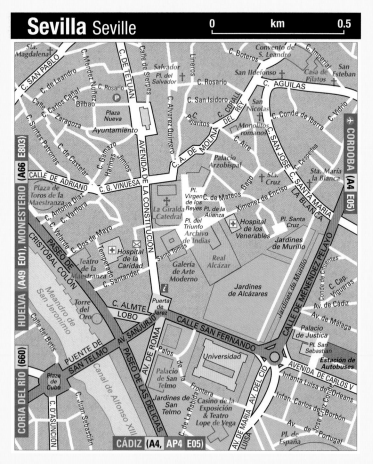

Stuttgart

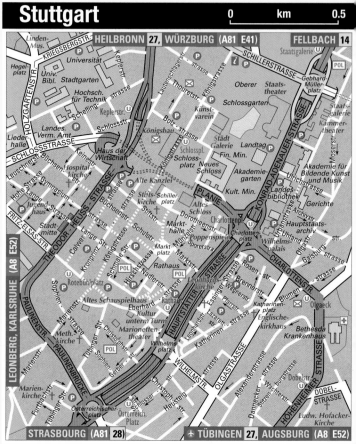

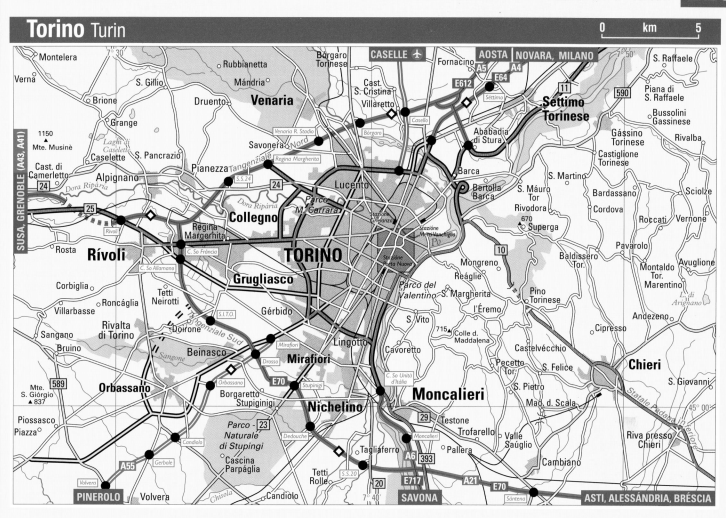

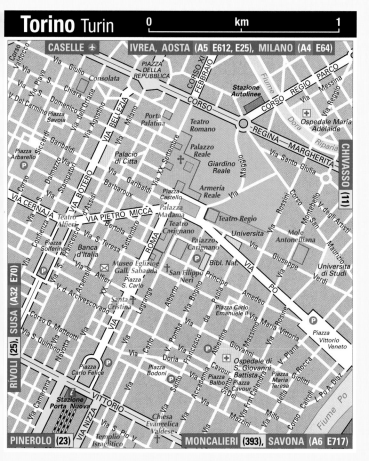

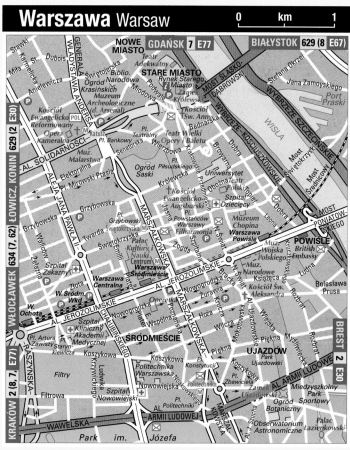

For **Vienna** see page 224

Wien Vienna

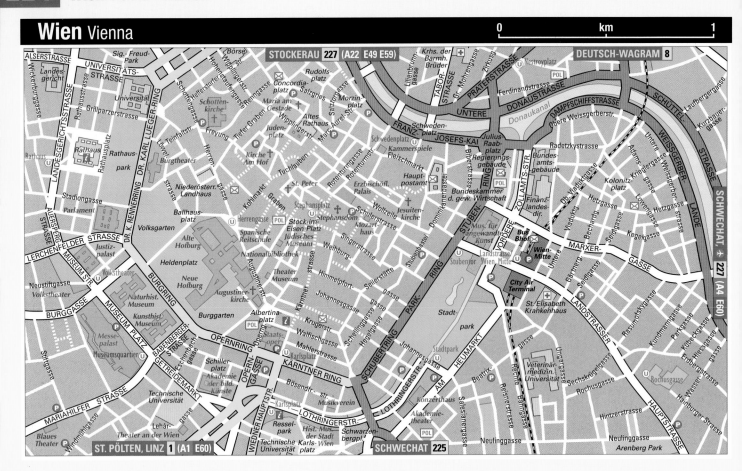

Wien Vienna

Zürich

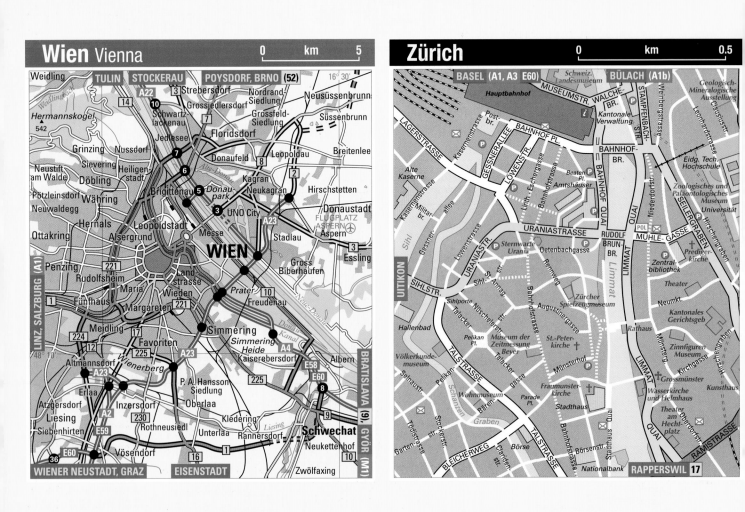

	GB	F	D	I
A	Austria	Autriche	Österreich	Austria
AL	Albania	Albanie	Albanien	Albania
AND	Andorra	Andorre	Andorra	Andorra
B	Belgium	Belgique	Belgien	Belgio
BG	Bulgaria	Bulgarie	Bulgarien	Bulgaria
BIH	Bosnia-Herzegovin	Bosnia-Herzegovine	Bosnien-Herzegowina	Bosnia-Herzogovina
BY	Belarus	Belarus	Weissrussland	Bielorussia
CH	Switzerland	Suisse	Schweiz	Svizzera
CY	Cyprus	Chypre	Zypern	Cipro
CZ	Czech Republic	République Tchèque	Tschechische Republik	Repubblica Ceca
D	Germany	Allemagne	Deutschland	Germania
DK	Denmark	Danemark	Dänemark	Danimarca
E	Spain	Espagne	Spanien	Spagna
EST	Estonia	Estonie	Estland	Estonia
F	France	France	Frankreich	Francia
FIN	Finland	Finlande	Finnland	Finlandia
FL	Liechtenstein	Liechtenstein	Liechtenstein	Liechtenstein
FO	Faeroe Islands	Îles Féroé	Färöer-Inseln	Isole Faroe
GB	United Kingdom	Royaume Uni	Grossbritannien und Nordirland	Regno Unito
GBZ	Gibraltar	Gibraltar	Gibraltar	Gibilterra
GR	Greece	Grèce	Greichenland	Grecia
H	Hungary	Hongrie	Ungarn	Ungheria
HR	Croatia	Croatie	Kroatien	Croazia
I	Italy	Italie	Italien	Italia
IRL	Ireland	Irlande	Irland	Irlanda
IS	Iceland	Islande	Island	Islanda
KOS	Kosovo	Kosovo	Kosovo	Kosovo
L	Luxembourg	Luxembourg	Luxemburg	Lussemburgo
LT	Lithuania	Lituanie	Litauen	Lituania
LV	Latvia	Lettonie	Lettland	Lettonia
M	Malta	Malte	Malta	Malta
MC	Monaco	Monaco	Monaco	Monaco
MD	Moldova	Moldavie	Moldawien	Moldavia
MK	Macedonia	Macédoine	Makedonien	Macedonia
MNE	Montenegro	Monténégro	Montenegro	Montenegro
N	Norway	Norvège	Norwegen	Norvegia
NL	Netherlands	Pays-Bas	Niederlande	Paesi Bassi
P	Portugal	Portugal	Portugal	Portogallo
PL	Poland	Pologne	Polen	Polonia
RO	Romania	Roumanie	Rumanien	Romania
RSM	San Marino	Saint-Marin	San Marino	San Marino
RUS	Russia	Russie	Russland	Russia
S	Sweden	Suède	Schweden	Svezia
SK	Slovak Republic	République Slovaque	Slowak Republik	Repubblica Slovacca
SLO	Slovenia	Slovénie	Slowenien	Slovenia
SRB	Serbia	Serbie	Serbien	Serbia
TR	Turkey	Turquie	Türkei	Turchia
UA	Ukraine	Ukraine	Ukraine	Ucraina

A

A Baña E 140 B2
A Bola E 140 B3
A Cañiza E 140 A2
A Capela E 140 A2
A Coruña E 140 A2
A Estrada E 140 B2
A Fonsagrada E 141 A3
A Guarda E 140 C2
A Gudiña E 141 B3
A Merca E 140 B3
A Peroxa E 140 B3
A Pontenova E 141 A3
A Rúa E 141 B3
A Teixeira E 141 B3
A Veiga E 141 B3
A-Ver-o-Mar P 148 A1
Aabenraa DK 64 A2
Aabybro DK 58 A2
Aach D 107 B4
Aachen D 80 B2
Aalborg DK 58 A2
Aalen D 94 C2
Aalestrup DK 58 B2
Aalsmeer NL 70 B1
Aalst B 79 B4
Aalten NL 71 C3
Aalter B 79 A3
Äänekoski FIN 8 A4
Aapajärvi FIN 197 B10
Aarau CH 106 B3
Aarberg CH 106 B2
Aarburg CH 106 B2
Aardenburg NL 79 A3
Aars DK 58 B2
Aarschot B 79 B4
Aarup DK 59 C3
Aba H 112 B2
Abádanes E 152 B1
Abades E 151 B3
Abadin E 141 A3
Abádszalók H 113 B4
Abaliget H 125 A4
Abana TR 23 A8
Abanilla E 165 A3
Abano Terme I 121 B4
Abarán E 165 A3
Abasár H 113 B4
Abbadia San Salvatore I 135 C4
Abbaue D 74 A2
Abbehausen D 72 A1
Abbekås S 66 A2
Abbeville F 90 A1
Abbey IRL 28 A3
Abbey Town GB 36 B3
Abbeydorney IRL 29 B2
Abbeyfeale IRL 29 B2
Abbeyleix IRL 30 B1
Abbiategrasso I 120 B1
Abborrträsk S 196 D2
Abbots Bromley GB 40 C2
Abbotsbury GB 43 B4
Abda H 111 B4
Abejar E 143 C4
Abela P 160 B1
Abelvær N 199 A8
Abenberg D 94 B2
Abenójar E 157 B3
Abensberg D 95 C3
Aberaeron GB 39 B2
Abercarn GB 39 C3
Aberchirder GB 33 D4
Aberdare GB 39 C3
Aberdaron GB 38 B2
Aberdeen GB 33 D4

Aberdulais GB 39 C3
Aberdyfi GB 39 B2
Aberfeldy GB 35 B4
Aberffraw GB 38 A2
Aberfoyle GB 34 B3
Abergavenny GB 39 C3
Abergele GB 38 A3
Abergynolwyn GB 38 B3
Aberporth GB 39 B2
Abersoch GB 38 B2
Abertillery GB 39 C3
Abertura E 156 A2
Aberystwyth GB 39 B2
Abetone I 135 A3
Abfaltersbach A 109 C3
Abide, Çanakkale TR 186 B1
Abide, Kütahya TR 187 D4
Abiego E 145 B3
Abild DK 64 B1
Abingdon GB 44 B2
Abington GB 36 A3
Abisko S 194 B9
Abiul P 154 B2
Abla E 164 B2
Ablis F 90 C1
Abondance F 118 A3
Abony H 113 B4
Aboyne GB 33 D4
Abrantes P 154 B2
Abreiro P 148 A2
Abreschviller F 92 C3
Abrest F 117 A3
Abriès F 119 C3
Abrud RO 17 B5
Absdorf A 97 C3
Abtenau A 109 B4
Abtsgmünd D 94 C1
Abusejo E 149 B3
Åby, Kronoberg S 62 A2
Åby, Östergötland S 56 B2
Åbyggeby S 51 B4
Åbytorp S 55 A6
Acate I 177 B3
Accadía I 171 B3
Accéglio I 132 A2
Accettura I 172 B2
Acciaroli I 170 C3
Accous F 145 A3
Accrington GB 40 B1
Accúmoli I 169 A3
Acedera E 156 A2
Acehúche E 155 B4
Acered E 152 A2
Acerenza I 172 B1
Acerno I 170 C3
Acerra I 170 C2
Aceuchal E 155 C4
Acharacle GB 34 B2
Acharnes GR 185 A4
Achavanich GB 32 C3
Achene B 79 B5
Achenkirch A 108 B2
Achensee A 108 B2
Achenthal A 108 B2
Achentrias GR 185 E6
Achern D 93 C4
Acheux-en-Amiénois F 90 A2
Achiltibuie GB 32 C1
Achim D 72 A2
Achladokambos GR 184 B3
Achnasheen GB 32 D1
Achnashellach GB 32 D1
Achosnich GB 34 B1
Aci Castello I 177 B4

Aci Catena I 177 B4
Acilia I 168 B2
Acıpayam TR 189 B4
Acireale I 177 B4
Acle GB 41 C5
Acqua Doria F 180 B1
Acquacadda I 179 C2
Acquanegra sul Chiese I 121 B3
Acquapendente I 168 A1
Acquasanta Terme I 136 C2
Acquasparta I 168 A2
Acquaviva I 135 B4
Acquaviva delle Fonti I 171 C4
Acquaviva Picena I 136 C2
Ácqui Terme I 119 C5
Acquigny F 89 A5
Acri I 174 B2
Acs H 112 B2
Acsa H 112 B3
Ácsteszér H 112 B1
Acy-en-Multien F 90 B2
Ada SRB 126 B2
Adak S 195 E9
Ádalsbruk N 48 B3
Adamas GR 185 C5
Adamsfjord N 193 B10
Adamuz E 157 B3
Adana TR 23 C8
Ádánd H 112 C2
Adanero E 150 B3
Adare IRL 29 B3
Adaševci SRB 125 B5
Adeanueva de Ebro E 144 B2
Adelboden CH 106 C2
Adelebsen D 82 A1
Adélfia I 173 A2
Adelmannsfelden D 94 C2
Adelsheim D 94 B1
Adelsö S 57 A3
Ademuz E 152 B2
Adenau D 80 B2
Adendorf D 72 A3
Adinkerke B 78 A2
Adjud RO 17 B7
Adliswil CH 107 B3
Admont A 110 B1
Adneram N 52 A2
Adolfsström S 195 D7
Adony H 112 B2
Adorf, Hessen D 81 A4
Adorf, Sachsen D 83 B4
Adra E 164 C1
Adradas E 152 A1
Adrall E 147 B2
Adrano I 177 B3
Adria I 121 B5
Adrigole IRL 29 C2
Adwick le Street GB 40 B2
Adzaneta E 153 B3
Ærøskøbing DK 65 B3
Áfandou GR 188 C3
Åfarnes N 198 C4
Affing D 94 C2
Affoltern CH 106 B3
Åfjord N 199 B7
Aflenz Kurort A 110 B2
Afragóla I 170 C2
Afritz A 109 C4
Afyon TR 187 D5

Ağapınar TR 187 C5
Ágasegyháza H 112 C3
Agay F 132 B2
Agazzano I 120 C2
Agde F 130 B2
Agdenes N 198 B6
Agen F 129 B3
Ager E 145 C4
Agerbæk DK 59 C1
Agerskov DK 64 A2
Agger DK 58 B1
Aggersund DK 58 A2
Ághia I 178 B3
Aggsbach Dorf A 97 C3
Aggsbach Markt A 97 C3
Aggtelek H 99 C4
Aghalee GB 27 B4
Aghia GR 182 D4
Aghia Anna GR 183 E5
Aghia Marina, Dodekanisa GR 188 D1
Aghia Marina, Dodekanisa GR 188 B1
Aghia Paraskevi GR 186 C1
Aghia Pelagia GR 184 C3
Aghia Triada GR 184 B2
Aghio Theodori GR 184 B4
Aghiokambos GR 182 D4
Aghios Efstratios GR 183 D6
Aghios Kirikos GR 185 B7
Aghios Matheos GR 182 D1
Aghios Mironas GR 185 D6
Aghios Nikolaos GR 185 D6
Aghios Petros GR 182 E2
Agiči BIH 124 C2
Agira I 177 B3
Ağlasun TR 189 B5
Aglientu I 178 A3
Agna I 121 B5
Agnières F 118 C2
Agno CH 120 B1
Agnone I 170 B2
Agolada E 140 B2
Agon Coutainville F 88 A2
Ágordo I 121 A5
Agost E 165 A4
Agramón E 158 C2
Agramunt E 147 C2
Agreda E 144 C2
Agria GR 183 D5
Agrigento I 176 B2
Agrinio GR 182 E3
Agrón E 163 A4
Agrópoli I 170 C2
Agua Longa P 148 A1
Aguadulce, Almería E 164 C2
Aguadulce, Sevilla E 162 A3
Agualada E 140 A2
Aguarón E 152 A2
Aguas E 145 B3
Aguas Belas P 154 B2
Aguas de Busot E 159 C3
Aguas de Moura P 154 C2
Águas Frias P 148 A2
Aguas Santas P 148 A1
Aguaviva E 153 B3
Aguaviva de la Vega E 152 A1
Agudo E 156 B3
Agueda P 148 B1
Aguessac F 130 A2
Agugliano I 136 B2
Aguiar P 154 C2
Aguiàr da Beira P 148 B2

Aguilafuente E 151 A3
Aguilar de Campóo E 142 B2
Aguilar de la Frontera E 163 A3
Agunnaryd S 60 C4
Ağva TR 187 A4
Ahat TR 187 D4
Ahaus D 71 B3
Åheim N 198 C2
Ahigal E 149 B3
Ahigal de Villarino E 149 A3
Ahillones E 156 B2
Ahlbeck, Mecklenburg-Vorpommern D 66 C3
Ahlbeck, Mecklenburg-Vorpommern D 74 A3
Ahlen D 81 A3
Ahlhorn D 71 B5
Ahmetbey TR 186 A2
Ahmetler TR 188 A4
Ahmetli TR 188 A2
Ahoghill GB 27 B4
Ahola FIN 197 C11
Ahrensbök D 65 B3
Ahrensburg D 72 A3
Ahrenshoop D 66 B1
Ahun F 116 A2
Åhus S 63 C2
Ahvenselkä FIN 197 C11
Aibar E 144 B2
Aich D 95 C4
Aicha D 96 C1
Aichach D 94 C3
Aidone I 177 B3
Aielo de Malferit I 175 B2
Aiello Cálabro I 175 B2
Aigen im Mühlkreis A 96 C1
Aigle CH 119 A3
Aignan F 128 C3
Aignay-le-Duc F 104 B3
Aigre F 115 C4
Aigrefeuille-d'Aunis F 114 B3
Aigrefeuille-sur-Maine F 101 B4
Aiguablava E 147 C4
Aiguebelette F 118 B2
Aiguebelle F 118 B3
Aigueperse F 116 A3
Aigues-Mortes F 131 B3
Aigues-Vives F 130 B1
Aiguilles F 119 C3
Aiguillon F 129 B3
Aigurande F 103 C3
Ailefroide F 118 C3
Aillant-sur-Tholon F 104 B2
Ailly-sur-Noye F 90 B2
Ailly-sur-Somme F 90 B2
Aimargues F 131 B3
Ainaži LV 8 D4
Ainet A 109 C3
Ainhoa F 144 A2
Ainsa E 145 B4
Airaines F 90 B1
Aird GB 34 B2
Aird Asaig Tairbeart GB 31 B2
Airdrie GB 35 C4
Aire-sur-la-Lys F 78 B2
Aire-sur-l'Adour F 128 C2
Airole I 133 B3

Airolo CH 107 C3
Airvault F 102 C1
Aisey-sur-Seine F 104 B3
Aïssey F 105 B5
Aisy-sur-Armançon F 104 B3
Aiterhofen D 95 C4
Aith, Orkney GB 33 B4
Aith, Shetland GB 33 A5
Aitona E 153 A4
Aitrach D 107 B5
Aiud RO 17 B5
Aix-en-Othe F 104 A2
Aix-en-Provence F 131 B4
Aix-les-Bains F 118 B2
Aixe-sur-Vienne F 115 C5
Aizenay F 114 B2
Aizkraukle LV 8 D4
Aizpute LV 8 D2
Ajac F 146 A3
Ajaccio F 180 B1
Ajain F 116 A1
Ajaureforsen S 195 E6
Ajdovščina SLO 122 B2
Ajka H 111 B4
Ajo E 143 A3
Ajofrin E 157 A4
Ajos FIN 196 D7
Ajuda P 155 C3
Akanthou CY 181 A2
Akarca TR 189 A4
Akasztó H 112 C3
Akçakoca TR 187 A6
Akçaova TR 187 A4
Akçay TR 189 C4
Aken D 83 A4
Åkerby S 51 B4
Åkernes N 52 B3
Åkers styckebruk S 56 A3
Åkersberga S 57 A4
Åkervik N 195 E4
Akhisar TR 186 D2
Åkirkeby DK 67 A3
Akköy TR 188 B2
Akkrum NL 70 A2
Akören TR 189 B7
Åkra N 52 A2
Akranes IS 190 C3
Åkrehamn N 52 A1
Akrotiri CY 181 B1
Aksaray TR 23 B8
Akşehir TR 189 A6
Akseki TR 189 B6
Aksla N 46 A3
Aksu TR 189 C5
Aktsyabrski BY 13 B8
Akureyri IS 191 B7
Åkvåg N 53 B5
Akyazı TR 187 B5
Ål N 47 B5
Ala I 121 B4
Alà dei Sardi I 178 B3
Ala di Stura I 119 B4
Ala-Nampa FIN 197 C9
Alacaatlı TR 23 A8
Alaçam TR 23 A8
Alaçatı TR 188 A1
Alaejos E 150 A2
Alagna Valsésia I 119 B4
Alagón E 144 C2
Alaior E 167 B4
Alájar E 161 B3
Alakurtti RUS 197 C13
Alakylä FIN 196 B7
Alameda E 163 A3

Name		Page	Grid
Alameda de la Sagra	E	151	B4
Alamedilla	E	163	A4
Alamillo	E	156	B3
Alaminos	E	151	B5
Alanäs	S	199	A12
Alandroal	P	155	C3
Alange	E	156	B1
Alaniemi	FIN	197	D8
Alanís	E	156	B2
Alanno	I	169	A3
Ålansbro	S	200	D3
Alanya	TR	189	C7
Alap	H	112	C2
Alaquáso	E	159	B3
Alar del Rey	E	142	B2
Alaraz	E	150	B2
Alarcón	E	158	B1
Alaró	E	167	B3
Alaşehir	TR	188	A3
Alássio	I	133	A4
Alatoz	E	158	B2
Alatri	I	169	B3
Alavus	FIN	8	A3
Alba	E	152	B2
Alba	I	119	C5
Alba Adriática	I	136	C2
Alba de Tormes	E	150	B2
Alba de Yeltes	E	149	B3
Alba-Iulia	RO	17	B3
Ålbæk	DK	58	A3
Albaida	E	159	C3
Albala del Caudillo	E	156	A1
Albaladejo	E	158	C1
Albalat	E	159	B3
Albalate de Cinca	E	145	C4
Albalate de las Nogueras	E	152	B1
Albalate del Arzobispo	E	153	A3
Albalete de Zorita	E	151	B5
Alban	F	130	B1
Albánchez	E	164	B2
Albánchez de Ubeda	E	163	A4
Albano Laziale	I	168	B2
Albanyà	E	147	B3
Albaredo d'Adige	I	121	B4
Albares	E	151	B4
Albarracín	E	152	B2
Albatana	E	158	C2
Albatarrec	E	153	A4
Albatera	E	165	A4
Albbruck	D	106	B3
Albedin	E	163	A3
Albelda de Iregua	E	143	B4
Albenga	I	133	A4
Albens	F	118	B2
Ålberga, Södermanland	S	56	B2
Ålberga, Södermanland	S	56	A2
Albergaria-a-Nova	P	148	B1
Albergaria-a-Velha	P	148	B1
Albergaria dos Doze	P	154	B2
Alberge	E	154	C2
Alberic	E	159	B3
Albernoa	P	160	B2
Alberobello	I	173	B3
Alberoni	I	122	B1
Albersdorf	D	64	B2
Albersloh	D	81	A3
Albert	F	90	A2
Albertirsa	H	112	B3
Albertville	F	118	B3
Alberuela de Tubo	E	145	C3
Albi	F	130	B1
Albidona	I	174	B2
Albínia	I	168	A1
Albino	I	120	B2
Albinshof	D	66	C2
Albires	E	142	B1
Albisola Marina	I	133	A4
Albocácer	E	153	B4
Albolote	E	163	A4
Albondón	E	164	C1
Alborea	E	158	B2
Albox	E	164	B2
Albrechtice nad Vltavou	CZ	96	B2
Albstadt	D	107	A4
Albufeira	P	160	B1
Albuñol	E	164	C1
Albuñuelas	E	163	B4
Alburquerque	E	155	B3
Alby, Öland	S	63	B4
Alby, Västernorrland	S	200	D1
Alcácer do Sal	P	154	C2
Alcáçovas	P	154	C2
Alcadozo	E	158	C2
Alcafoces	P	155	B3
Alcains	P	155	B3
Alcalá de Guadaira	E	162	A2
Alcalá de Gurrea	E	144	B3
Alcalá de Henares	E	151	B4
Alcalá de la Selva	E	153	B3
Alcalá de los Gazules	E	162	B2
Alcalá de Xivert	E	153	B4
Alcalá del Júcar	E	158	B2
Alcalá del Río	E	162	A2
Alcalá del Valle	E	162	B2
Alcalá la Real	E	163	A4
Álcamo	I	176	B1
Alcampell	E	145	C4
Alcanadre	E	144	B1
Alcanar	E	153	B4
Alcanede	P	154	B2
Alcanena	P	154	B2
Alcañices	E	149	A3
Alcántara	E	155	B4
Alcantarilha	P	160	B1
Alcantarilla	E	165	B3
Alcañiz	E	153	A3
Alcara il Fusi	I	177	A3
Alcaracejos	E	156	B3
Alcaraz	E	158	C1
Alcaria Ruiva	P	160	B2
Alcarraz	E	153	A4
Alcaudete	E	163	A3
Alcaudete de la Jara	E	150	C3
Alcázar de San Juan	E	157	A4
Alcazarén	E	150	A3
Alcoba	E	157	A3
Alcobaça	P	154	B1
Alcobendas	E	151	B4
Alcocer	E	151	B5
Alcochete	P	154	C2
Alcoentre	P	154	B2
Alcolea, Almería	E	164	C2
Alcolea, Córdoba	E	156	C3
Alcolea de Calatrava	E	157	B3
Alcolea de Cinca	E	145	C4
Alcolea de Tajo	E	150	C2
Alcolea del Pinar	E	152	A1
Alcolea del Rio	E	162	A2
Alcollarin	E	156	A2
Alconchel	E	155	C3
Alconera	E	155	C4
Alcontar	E	164	B2
Alcora	E	153	B3
Alcorcón	E	151	B4
Alcorisa	E	153	B3
Alcossebre	E	153	B4
Alcoutim	P	160	B2
Alcover	E	147	C2
Alcoy	E	159	C3
Alcsútdoboz	H	112	B2
Alcubierre	E	145	C3
Alcubilla de Avellaneda	E	143	C3
Alcubilla de Nogales	E	141	B5
Alcubillas	E	157	B4
Alcublas	E	159	B3
Alcúdia de Guadix	E	164	B1
Alcuéscar	E	155	A4
Aldbrough	GB	41	B3
Aldea de Trujillo	E	156	A2
Aldea del Cano	E	155	A4
Aldea del Fresno	E	151	B3
Aldea del Obispo	E	149	B3
Aldea del Rey	E	157	B4
Aldea Real	E	151	A3
Aldeacentenera	E	156	A2
Aldeadávila de la Ribera	E	149	A3
Aldealcorvo	E	151	A4
Aldealuenga de Santa Maria	E	151	A4
Aldeamayor de San Martin	E	150	A3
Aldeanueva de Barbarroya	E	150	C2
Aldeanueva de San Bartolomé	E	156	A2
Aldeanueva del Camino	E	149	B4
Aldeanueva del Codonal	E	150	A3
Aldeapozo	E	144	C1
Aldeaquemada	E	157	B4
Aldeaseca de la Frontera	E	150	B2
Aldeasoña	E	151	A3
Aldeatejada	E	150	B2
Aldeavieja	E	150	B3
Aldeburgh	GB	45	A5
Aldehuela	E	152	B2
Aldehuela de Calatañazor	E	143	C4
Aldeia da Serra	P	155	C3
Aldeia do Bispo	P	149	B3
Aldeia do Mato	P	154	B2
Aldeia Gavinha	P	154	B1
Aldeire	E	164	B1
Aldenhoven	D	80	B2
Aldersbach	D	95	C5
Aldershot	GB	44	B3
Aldudes	F	144	A2
Åled	S	60	C2
Aledo	E	165	B3
Alegria	E	143	B4
Aleksa Šantić	SRB	126	B1
Aleksandrovac	SRB	127	C3
Aleksandrów Kujawski	PL	76	B3
Aleksandrów Łódźki	PL	86	A3
Ålem	S	62	B4
Alençon	F	89	B4
Alenquer	P	154	B1
Alenya	F	146	B3
Aléria	F	180	A2
Alès	F	131	A3
Áles	I	179	C2
Alessándria	I	120	C1
Alessándria della Rocca	I	176	B2
Alessano	I	173	C4
Ålesund	N	198	C3
Alet-les-Bains	F	146	B3
Alexandria	GB	34	B3
Alexandria	GR	182	C4
Alexandria	RO	17	D6
Alexandroupoli	GR	183	C7
Aleyrac	F	131	A3
Alézio	I	173	B4
Alfacar	E	163	A4
Alfaiates	P	149	B3
Alfajarin	E	153	A3
Alfambra	E	152	B2
Alfambra	P	160	B1
Alfândega da Fé	P	149	A3
Alfarela de Jafes	P	148	A2
Alfarelos	P	148	B1
Alfarim	P	154	C1
Alfarnate	E	163	B3
Alfaro	E	144	B2
Alfarrás	E	145	C4
Alfaz del Pi	E	159	C3
Alfedena	I	169	B4
Alfeizerão	P	154	B1
Alfeld, Bayern	D	95	B3
Alfeld, Niedersachsen	D	72	C2
Alfena	P	148	A1
Alferce	P	160	B1
Alfhausen	D	71	B4
Alfonsine	I	135	A5
Alford, Aberdeenshire	GB	33	D4
Alford, Lincolnshire	GB	41	B4
Alforja	E	147	C1
Alfoz	E	141	A3
Alfreton	GB	40	B2
Alfta	S	50	A3
Alfundão	P	160	A1
Algaida	E	167	B2
Algar	E	162	B2
Ålgaräs	S	55	B5
Ålgård	N	52	B1
Algarinejo	E	163	A3
Algarrobo	E	163	B3
Algatocin	E	162	B2
Algeciras	E	162	B2
Algemesí	E	159	B3
Algés	P	154	C1
Algete	E	151	B4
Alghero	I	178	B2
Älghult	S	62	A3
Alginet	E	159	B3
Algodonales	E	162	B2
Algodor	E	151	C4
Algodor	P	160	B2
Algora	E	151	B5
Algoso	P	149	A3
Algoz	P	160	B1
Ålgsjö	S	200	B3
Alguaire	E	145	C4
Alguazas	E	165	A3
Algutsrum	S	63	B4
Algyö	H	126	A2
Alhama de Almería	E	164	C2
Alhama de Aragón	E	152	A2
Alhama de Granada	E	163	B4
Alhama de Murcia	E	165	B3
Alhambra	E	157	B4
Alhandra	P	154	C1
Alhaurin de la Torre	E	163	B3
Alhaurín el Grande	E	163	B3
Alhendin	E	163	A4
Alhóndiga	E	151	B5
Ali Terme	I	177	A4
Ália	I	176	B2
Aliaga	E	153	B3
Aliağa	TR	186	D1
Alibunar	SRB	127	B3
Alicante	E	165	A4
Alicún de Ortega	E	164	B1
Alife	I	170	B2
Alija del Infantado	E	141	B5
Alijó	P	148	A2
Alimena	I	177	B3
Alingsås	S	60	B2
Alinyà	E	147	B2
Aliseda	E	155	B4
Aliveri	GR	185	A5
Alixan	F	117	C5
Aljaraque	E	161	B2
Aljezur	P	160	B1
Aljorra	E	165	B3
Aljubarrota	P	154	B2
Aljucen	E	155	B4
Aljustrel	P	160	B1
Alken	B	79	B5
Alkmaar	NL	70	B1
Alkoven	A	96	C2
Allaines	F	103	A3
Allaire	F	101	B3
Allanche	F	116	B2
Alland	A	111	A3
Allariz	E	140	B3
Allassac	F	129	A4
Allauch	F	131	B4
Alleen	N	52	B3
Allègre	F	117	B3
Allemont	F	118	B3
Allendale Town	GB	37	B4
Allendorf	D	81	B4
Allentsteig	A	97	C3
Allepuz	E	153	B3
Allersberg	D	95	B3
Allershausen	D	95	C3
Alles	E	142	A2
Allevard	F	118	B3
Allgunnen	S	62	A3
Allihies	IRL	29	C1
Allingåbro	DK	58	B3
Allmannsdorf	D	107	B4
Allo	E	144	B1
Alloa	GB	35	B4
Allogny	F	103	B4
Alloluokta	S	196	B2
Allones, Eure et Loire	F	90	C1
Allones, Maine-et-Loire	F	102	B2
Allonnes	F	102	B2
Allons	F	128	B2
Allos	F	132	A2
Allstedt	D	82	A3
Alltwalis	GB	39	C2
Allumiere	I	168	A1
Almaceda	P	155	B3
Almacelles	E	145	C4
Almachar	E	163	B3
Almada	P	154	C1
Almadén	E	156	B3
Almadén de la Plata	E	161	B3
Almadenejos	E	156	B3
Almadrones	E	151	B5
Almagro	E	157	B4
Almajano	E	144	C1
Almansa	E	159	C2
Almanza	E	142	B1
Almaraz	E	150	C2
Almargen	E	162	B2
Almarza	E	143	C4
Almásfüzitö	H	112	B2
Almassora	E	159	B3
Almazán	E	152	A1
Almazul	E	152	A2
Alme	D	81	A4
Almedina	E	158	C1
Almedinilla	E	163	A3
Almeida	E	149	B3
Almeida	P	149	B3
Almeirim	P	154	B2
Almelo	NL	71	B3
Almenar	E	145	C4
Almenar de Soria	E	152	A1
Almenara	E	159	B3
Almendra	P	149	B2
Almendral	E	155	C4
Almendral de la Cañada	E	150	B3
Almendralejo	E	155	C4
Almenno San Bartolomeo	I	120	B2
Almere	NL	70	B2
Almería	E	164	C2
Almerimar	E	164	C2
Almese	I	119	B4
Almexial	P	160	B2
Älmhult	S	63	B2
Almiropotamos	GR	185	A5
Almirós	GR	182	D4
Almodôvar	P	160	B1
Almodóvar del Campo	E	157	B3
Almodóvar del Pinar	E	158	B2
Almodóvar del Río	E	162	A2
Almofala	P	148	B2
Almogia	E	163	B3
Almoharin	E	156	A1
Almonacid de la Sierra	E	152	A2
Almonacid de Toledo	E	157	A4
Almonaster la Real	E	161	B3
Almonte	E	161	B3
Almoradí	E	165	A4
Almoraima	E	162	B2
Almorox	E	150	B3
Almoster	P	154	B2
Almsele	S	200	B3
Älmsta	S	51	C5
Almudena	E	164	A3
Almudévar	E	145	B3
Almuñécar	E	163	B4
Almunge	S	51	C5
Almuradiel	E	157	B4
Almussafes	E	159	B3
Almvik	S	62	A4
Alness	GB	32	D2
Alnmouth	GB	37	A5
Alnwick	GB	37	A5
Aloppe	S	51	C4
Álora	E	163	B3
Alos d'Ensil	E	146	B2
Alosno	E	161	B2
Alozaina	E	162	B3
Alpbach	A	108	B2
Alpedrete de la Sierra	E	151	B4
Alpedrinha	P	148	B2
Alpen	D	80	A2
Alpera	E	159	C2
Alphen aan de Rijn	NL	70	B1
Alpiarça	P	154	B2
Alpignano	I	119	B4
Alpirsbach	D	93	C4
Alpu	TR	187	C5
Alpuente	E	159	B2
Alquézar	E	145	B4
Als	DK	58	B3
Alsasua	E	144	B1
Alsdorf	D	80	B2
Alselv	DK	59	C1
Alsfeld	D	81	B5
Alsike	S	57	B3
Alsleben	D	83	A3
Alsónémedi	H	112	B3
Alsótold	H	112	B3
Alsóújlak	H	111	B3
Alstad	N	194	C6
Alstätte	D	71	B3
Alsterbro	S	62	B3
Alstermo	S	62	B3
Alston	GB	37	B4
Alsvåg	N	194	B6
Alsvik	N	194	C5
Alt Ruppin	D	74	B1
Alta	N	192	C7
Älta	S	57	A4
Altamura	I	172	B2
Altarejos	E	158	B1
Altaussee	A	109	B4
Altavilla Irpina	I	170	B2
Altavilla Silentina	I	170	C3
Altdöbern	D	84	A2
Altdorf	CH	107	C3
Altdorf	D	95	C4
Altdorf bei Nürnberg	D	95	B3
Alte	P	160	B1
Altea	E	159	C3
Altedo	I	121	C4
Altena	D	81	A3
Altenau	D	82	A2
Altenberg	D	84	B1
Altenberge	D	71	B4
Altenbruch	D	64	C1
Altenburg	D	83	B4
Altenfelden	A	96	C1
Altengronau	D	82	B1
Altenheim	D	93	C3
Altenhundem	D	81	A4
Altenkirchen, Mecklenburg-Vorpommern	D	66	B2
Altenkirchen, Radom	D	81	B3
Altenkunstadt	D	82	B3
Altenmarkt	D	109	B3
Altenmarkt im Pongall	A	109	B4
Altensteig	D	93	C4
Altentreptow	D	74	A2
Altenwalde	D	64	C1
Alter do Chão	P	155	B3
Altfraunhofen	D	95	C4
Altheim	A	109	A4
Altheim	D	94	B1
Althofen	A	110	C1
Altınoluk	TR	186	C1
Altınova	TR	186	C1
Altıntaş	TR	187	C5
Altınyaka	TR	189	C5
Altınyayla	TR	189	B4
Altkirch	F	106	B2
Altlandsberg	D	74	B2
Altlewin	D	74	B3
Altmannstein	D	95	C3
Altmorschen	D	82	A1
Altmunster	A	109	B4
Altnaharra	GB	32	C2
Alto Campoó	E	142	A2
Altofonte	I	176	A2
Altomonte	I	174	B2
Alton, Hampshire	GB	44	B3
Alton, Staffordshire	GB	40	C2
Altopáscio	I	135	B3
Altötting	D	109	A3
Altreichenau	D	96	C1
Altshausen	D	107	B4
Altstätten	CH	107	B4
Altura	E	159	B3
Altusried	D	107	B5
Alūksne	LV	8	D5
Alunda	S	51	B5
Alustante	E	152	B2
Alva	GB	35	B4
Alvaiázere	P	154	B2
Alvalade	P	160	B1
Älvängen	S	60	B2
Alvarenga	P	148	B1
Alvares	P	154	A2
Alvdal	N	199	C7
Älvdalen	S	49	A6
Alverca	P	154	C1
Alversund	N	46	B2
Alvesta	S	62	B2
Alvignac	F	129	B4
Alvignano	I	170	B2
Ålvik	N	46	B3
Alvik	S	50	B1
Alvimare	F	89	A4
Alviobeira	P	154	B2
Alvito	P	160	A2
Älvkarleby	S	51	B4
Älvkarleö bruk	S	51	B4
Alvor	P	160	B1
Alvorge	P	154	B2
Alvøy	N	46	B2
Älvros	S	199	C11
Alvsbacka	S	55	A4
Älvsbyn	S	196	D4
Älvsered	S	60	B2
Alwernia	PL	86	B3
Alwinton	GB	37	A4
Alyth	GB	35	B4
Alytus	LT	13	A6
Alzénau	D	93	A5
Alzey	D	93	B4
Alzira	E	159	B3
Alzonne	F	146	A3
Amadora	P	154	C1
Åmål	S	55	A3
Amalfi	I	170	C2
Amaliada	GR	184	B2
Amance	F	105	B5
Amancey	F	105	B5
Amándola	I	136	C2
Amantea	I	175	B2
Amarante	P	148	A1
Amareleja	P	161	A2
Amares	P	148	A1
Amaseno	I	169	B3
Amasra	TR	187	A7
Amatrice	I	169	A3
Amay	B	79	B5
Ambarnyy	RUS	3	D13
Ambazac	F	115	C5
Ambelonas	GR	182	D4
Amberg	D	95	B3
Ambérieu-en-Bugey	F	118	B2
Ambérieux-en-Dombes	F	117	A4
Ambert	F	117	B3
Ambés	F	128	A2
Ambjörby	S	49	B5
Ambjörnarp	S	60	B3
Amble	GB	37	A5
Ambleside	GB	36	B4
Ambleteuse	F	78	B1
Amboise	F	102	B2
Ambrières-les-Vallées	F	88	B3
Amden	CH	107	B4
Amel	B	80	B2
Amélia	I	168	A2
Amélie-les-Bains-Palalda	F	146	B3
Amelinghausen	D	72	A3
Amendoa	P	154	B2
Amendoeira	P	160	B2
Améndola	I	171	B3
Amendolara	I	174	B2
Amer	E	147	B3
Amerongen	NL	70	B2
Amersfoort	NL	70	B2
Amersham	GB	44	B3
Ames	E	140	B2
Amesbury	GB	44	B2
Amfíklia	GR	182	E4
Amfilochia	GR	182	E3
Amfipoli	GR	183	C5
Amfissa	GR	184	A3
Amièira, Évora	P	155	C3
Amieira, Portalegre	P	154	B2
Amiens	F	90	B2
Amindeo	GR	182	C3
Åminne	S	60	B3
Åmli	N	53	B4
Åmlwch	GB	38	A2
Ammanford	GB	39	C3
Ammarnäs	S	195	E7
Åmmeberg	S	55	B5
Amorbach	D	94	B1
Amorebieta	E	143	A4
Amorgos	GR	185	C6
Amorosa	P	148	A1
Amoroto	E	143	A4
Åmot, Buskerud	N	48	C1
Åmot, Telemark	N	53	A3
Åmot	S	50	B3
Åmotfors	S	54	A3
Åmotsdal	N	53	A4
Amou	F	128	C2
Ampezzo	I	122	A1

Ampfing D 95 C4
Ampflwang A 109 A4
Amplepuis F 117 B4
Amposta E 153 B4
Ampthill GB 44 A3
Ampudia E 142 C2
Ampuero E 143 A3
Amriswil CH 107 B4
Åmsele S 200 B5
Amstelveen NL 70 B1
Amsterdam NL 70 B1
Amstetten A 110 A1
Amtzell D 107 B4
Amulree GB 35 B4
Amurrio E 143 A4
Amusco E 142 B2
An t-Ob GB 31 B1
Åna-Sira N 52 B2
Anacapri I 170 C2
Anadia P 148 B1
Anadon E 152 B2
Anafi GR 185 C6
Anagni I 169 B3
Anamur TR 23 C7
Ananyiv UA 17 B8
Anascaul IRL 29 B1
Ånäset S 2 D7
Anastaźewo PL 76 B3
Anaya de Alba E 150 B2
Ança P 148 B1
Ancaster GB 40 C3
Ancede P 148 A1
Ancenis F 101 B4
Ancerville F 91 C5
Anchuras E 156 A3
Ancona I 136 B2
Ancora P 148 A1
Ancrum GB 35 C5
Ancy-le-Franc F 104 B3
Andalo I 121 A3
Åndalsnes N 198 C4
Andance F 117 B4
Andau A 111 B4
Andebu N 53 A6
Andeer CH 107 C4
Andelfingen CH 107 B3
Andelot F 105 A4
Andelot-en-Montagne F 105 C4
Andenes N 194 A7
Andenne B 79 B5
Anderlues B 79 B4
Andermatt CH 107 C3
Andernach D 80 B3
Andernos-les-Bains F 128 B1
Anderslöv S 66 A2
Anderstorp S 60 B3
Andijk NL 70 B2
Andoain E 144 A1
Andocs H 112 C1
Andolsheim F 106 A2
Andorra E 153 B3
Andorra La Vella AND 146 B2
Andosilla E 144 B2
Andover GB 44 B2
Andratx E 166 B2
Andreapol RUS 9 D8
Andreas GB 36 B2
Andréspol PL 86 A3
Andrest F 145 A4
Andretta I 172 B1
Andrezieux-Bouthéon F 117 B4
Ándria I 171 B4
Andrijevica MNE 16 D3
Andritsena GR 184 B2
Andros GR 185 B5
Andrychów PL 99 B3
Andselv N 194 A9
Andújar E 157 B3
Anduze F 131 A2
Åneby N 48 B2
Aneby S 62 A2
Añes E 143 A3
Anet F 90 C1
Anfo I 121 B3
Ang S 62 A2
Anga S 57 C4
Angaïs F 145 A3
Ånge, Jämtland S 199 B11
Ånge, Västernorrland S 200 D1
Angeja P 148 B1
Ängelholm S 61 C2
Angeli FIN 193 D9
Ängelsberg S 50 C3
Anger A 110 B2
Angera I 120 B1
Angermünde D 74 A3
Angern A 97 C4
Angers F 102 B1
Angerville F 90 C2
Anghiari I 135 B5
Angle GB 39 C1
Anglès E 147 C3
Anglés, Tarn F 130 B1
Angles, Vendée F 114 B2
Angles sur l'Anglin F 115 B4
Anglesola E 147 C2
Anglet F 128 C1
Anglisidhes CY 181 B2
Anglure F 91 C3
Angoulême F 115 C4
Angoulins F 114 B2
Angsö S 56 A2

Angueira P 149 A3
Angües E 145 B3
Anguiano E 143 B4
Anguillara Sabazia I 168 A2
Anguillara Véneta I 121 B4
Anhée B 79 B4
Anholt DK 60 C1
Aniane F 130 B2
Aniche F 78 B3
Anina RO 16 C4
Anixi GR 182 D3
Anizy-le-Château F 91 B3
Anjalankoski FIN 8 B5
Anjan S 199 B9
Ankara TR 187 C7
Ankaran SLO 122 B2
Ankarsrum S 62 A4
Ankerlia N 192 C4
Anklam D 66 C2
Ankum D 71 B4
Anlauftal A 109 B4
Anlezy F 104 C2
Ånn S 199 B9
Annaberg A 110 B2
Annaberg-Buchholz D 83 B5
Annaberg im Lammertal A 109 B4
Annaburg D 83 A5
Annahütte D 84 A1
Annalong GB 27 B5
Annan GB 36 B3
Anndalsvågen N 195 E3
Anneberg, Halland S 60 B2
Anneberg, Jönköping S 62 A2
Annecy F 118 B3
Annelund S 60 B3
Annemasse F 118 B3
Annenskiy Most RUS 9 B10
Annerstad S 60 C3
Annestown IRL 30 B1
Annevoie-Rouillon B 79 B4
Annonay F 117 B4
Annot F 132 B2
Annweiler D 93 B3
Ano Poroia GR 183 B5
Ano Siros GR 185 B5
Añora E 156 B3
Anould F 106 A1
Anquela del Ducado E 152 B1
Anröchte D 81 A4
Ans DK 59 B2
Ansager DK 59 C1
Ansbach D 94 B2
Anse F 117 B4
Anserœul B 79 B3
Ansfelden A 110 A1
Ansião P 154 B2
Ansó E 144 B3
Ansoain E 144 B2
Anstruther GB 35 B5
Antalya TR 189 C5
Antas E 164 B3
Antegnate I 120 B2
Antequera E 163 A3
Anterselva di Mezzo I 108 C3
Antibes F 132 B3
Antigüedad E 142 C2
Antillo I 177 B4
Antirio GR 184 A2
Antnäs S 196 D5
Antoing B 79 B3
Antonin PL 86 A1
Antrain F 88 B2
Antrim GB 27 B4
Antrodoco I 169 A3
Antronapiana I 119 A5
Anttis S 196 B5
Antuzede P 148 B1
Antwerp = Antwerpen B 79 A4
Antwerpen = Antwerp B 79 A4
Anversa d'Abruzzi I 169 B3
Anvin F 78 B2
Ánzio I 168 B2
Anzola d'Emilia I 135 A4
Anzón E 144 C2
Aoiz E 144 B2
Aosta I 119 B4
Apalhão P 155 B3
Apátfalva H 126 A2
Apatin SRB 125 B5
Apatity RUS 3 C13
Apc H 112 B3
Apécchio I 136 B1
Apeldoorn NL 70 B2
Apen D 71 A4
Apenburg D 73 B4
Apensen D 72 A2
Apiro I 136 B2
Apliki CY 181 B2
Apolda D 82 A3
Apolonia GR 185 C5
Apostag H 112 C2

Äppelbo S 49 B6
Appennino I 136 C2
Appenzell CH 107 B4
Appiano I 108 C2
Appingedam NL 71 A3
Appleby-in-Westmorland GB 37 B4
Applecross GB 31 B3
Appledore GB 42 A2
Appoigny F 104 B2
Apremont-la-Forêt F 92 C1
Aprica I 120 A3
Apricena I 171 B3
Aprigliano I 174 B2
Aprília I 168 B2
Apt F 131 B4
Apúlia P 148 A1
Aquiléia I 122 B2
Aquilónia I 172 B1
Aquino I 169 B3
Ar S 57 C4
Arabayona E 150 A2
Arabba I 108 C2
Araç TR 23 A7
Aracena E 161 B3
Arachova GR 184 A3
Aračinovo MK 182 A3
Arad RO 126 A3
Aradac SRB 126 B2
Aradhippou CY 181 B2
Aragnouet F 145 B4
Aragona I 176 B2
Aramits F 144 A3
Aramon F 131 B3
Aranda de Duero E 143 C3
Aranda de Moncayo E 152 A2
Arandjelovac SRB 127 C2
Aranjuez E 151 B4
Arantzazu E 143 B4
Aranzueque E 151 B4
Aras de Alpuente E 159 B2
Arauzo de Miel E 143 C3
Arazede P 148 B1
Arbas F 145 B4
Árbatax I 179 C3
Arbeca E 147 C1
Arberg D 94 B2
Arbesbach A 96 C2
Arboga S 56 A1
Arbois F 105 C4
Arbon CH 107 B4
Arborea I 179 C2
Arbório I 119 B5
Årbostad N 194 B8
Arbrå S 50 A3
Arbroath GB 35 B5
Arbúcies E 147 C3
Arbuniel E 163 A4
Arbus I 179 C2
Arc-en-Barrois F 105 B3
Arc-et-Senans F 105 B4
Arc-lès-Gray F 105 B4
Arc-sur-Tille F 105 B4
Arcachon F 128 B1
Arce I 169 B3
Arcen NL 80 A2
Arces-Dilo F 104 A2
Arcévia I 136 B1
Arcey F 106 B1
Archanes GR 185 D6
Archangelos GR 188 C3
Archena E 165 A3
Archez E 163 B4
Archiac F 115 C3
Archidona E 163 A3
Archiestown GB 32 D3
Archivel E 164 A3
Arcidosso I 135 C4
Arcille I 135 C4
Arcis-sur-Aube F 91 C4
Arco I 121 B3
Arcones E 151 A4
Arcos E 143 B3
Arcos de Jalón E 152 A1
Arcos de la Frontera E 162 B2
Arcos de la Sierra E 152 B1
Arcos de las Salinas E 159 B2
Arcos de Valdevez P 148 A1
Arcozelo P 148 B2
Arcusa E 145 B4
Arcy-sur-Cure F 104 B2
Ardagh IRL 29 B2
Årdal N 52 A2
Ardala S 55 B4
Ardales E 162 B3
Ardalstangen N 47 A4
Ardara I 178 B2
Ardara IRL 26 B2
Ardarroch GB 31 B3
Ardbeg GB 34 C1
Ardcharnich GB 32 D1
Ardchyle GB 34 B3
Ardee IRL 27 C4
Arden DK 58 B2
Ardentes F 103 C3
Ardenza I 134 B3
Ardersier GB 32 D2
Ardes F 116 B3
Ardez CH 107 C5
Ardfert IRL 29 B2

Ardgay GB 32 D2
Ardglass GB 27 B5
Ardgroom IRL 29 C2
Ardhasig GB 31 B2
Ardino BG 183 B7
Ardisa E 144 B3
Ardkearagh IRL 29 C1
Ardlui GB 34 B3
Ardlussa GB 34 B2
Ardón E 142 B1
Ardooie B 78 B3
Ardore I 175 C2
Ardre S 57 C4
Ardres F 78 B1
Ardrishaig GB 34 B2
Ardrossan GB 34 C3
Åre N 52 A1
Areia Branca P 154 B1
Aremark N 54 A2
Arenales de San Gregorio E 157 A4
Arenas E 163 B3
Arenas de Iguña E 142 A2
Arenas de San Juan E 157 A4
Arenas de San Pedro E 150 B2
Arenas del Rey E 163 B4
Arendal N 53 B4
Arendonk B 79 A5
Arengosse F 128 B2
Arentorp S 55 B3
Arenzano I 133 A4
Areo E 146 B2
Areopoli GR 184 C3
Ares E 140 A2
Arès F 128 B1
Ares del Maestrat E 153 B3
Aresvika N 198 B5
Arette F 144 A3
Aretxabaleta E 143 A4
Arevalillo E 150 B2
Arévalo E 150 A3
Arez P 155 B3
Arezzo I 135 B4
Arfeuilles F 117 A3
Argalasti GR 183 D5
Argallón E 156 B2
Argamasilla de Alba E 157 A4
Argamasilla de Calatrava E 157 B3
Arganda E 151 B4
Arganil P 148 B1
Argasion GR 184 B1
Argegno I 120 B2
Argelès-Gazost F 145 A3
Argelès-sur-Mer F 146 B4
Argent-sur-Sauldre F 103 B4
Argenta I 121 C4
Argentan F 89 B3
Argentat F 116 B1
Argentera I 132 A2
Argenteuil F 90 C2
Argenthal D 93 B3
Argentiera I 178 B2
Argenton-Château F 102 C1
Argenton-sur-Creuse F 103 C3
Argentona E 147 C3
Argentré F 102 A1
Argentré-du-Plessis F 101 A4
Argirades GR 182 D1
Argithani TR 189 A6
Argos GR 184 B3
Argos Orestiko GR 182 C3
Argostoli GR 184 A1
Argote E 143 B4
Arguedas E 144 B2
Argueil F 90 B1
Arguis E 145 B3
Arholma S 51 C6
Århus DK 59 B3
Ariano Irpino I 170 B3
Ariano nel Polésine I 121 C5
Aribe E 144 B2
Aridea GR 182 C4
Arienzo I 170 B2
Arild S 61 C2
Arileod GB 34 B1
Arinagour GB 34 B1
Ariño E 153 A3
Arinthod F 118 A2
Arisaig GB 34 B2
Arisgotas E 157 A3
Aritzo I 179 C3
Ariza E 152 A1
Årjäng S 54 A3
Arjeplog S 195 D8
Arjona E 157 C3
Arjonilla E 157 C3
Arkasa GR 188 D2
Arkelstorp S 63 B2
Arklow IRL 30 B2
Arkösund S 56 B2
Ärla S 56 A2
Arlanc F 117 B3
Arlanzón E 143 B3
Arlebosc F 117 B4
Arlena di Castro I 168 A1

Arles F 131 B3
Arles-sur-Tech F 146 B3
Arló H 113 A4
Arlon B 92 B1
Armação de Pera P 160 B1
Armadale, Highland GB 31 B3
Armadale, West Lothian GB 35 C4
Armagh GB 27 B4
Armamar P 148 A2
Armenistis GR 185 B7
Armeno I 119 B5
Armentières F 78 B2
Armilla E 163 A4
Armiñón E 143 B4
Armoy GB 27 A4
Armuña de Tajuña E 151 B4
Armutlu, Bursa TR 186 B3
Armutlu, İzmir TR 188 A2
Arnac-Pompadour F 115 C5
Arnafjord N 46 A3
Arnage F 102 B2
Arnas F 117 A4
Årnäs S 55 B4
Arnay-le-Duc F 104 B3
Arnborg DK 59 B2
Arnbruck D 95 B4
Arnea GR 183 C5
Arneberg, Hedmark N 49 B4
Arneberg, Hedmark N 48 A2
Arneburg D 73 B5
Arnedillo E 144 B1
Arnedo E 144 B1
Arneguy F 144 A2
Arnés E 153 B4
Årnes, Akershus N 48 B3
Årnes, Troms N 194 A9
Arnfels A 110 C2
Arnhem NL 70 C2
Arnissa GR 182 C3
Arno S 56 B3
Arnold GB 40 B2
Arnoldstein A 109 C4
Arnsberg D 81 A4
Arnschwang D 95 B4
Arnsdorf D 84 A1
Årnset N 198 B6
Arnside GB 37 B4
Arnstadt D 82 B2
Arnstein D 94 B1
Arnstorf D 95 C4
Arnum DK 59 C1
Aroche E 161 B3
Árokttö H 113 A4
Arolla CH 119 A4
Arolsen D 81 A5
Arona I 119 B5
Äros N 54 A1
Arosa CH 107 C4
Arosa E 140 B2
Arøsund DK 59 C2
Arouca P 148 B1
Arousa E 140 B2
Arpajon F 90 C2
Arpajon-sur-Cère F 116 C2
Arpela FIN 196 C7
Arpino I 169 B3
Arquata del Tronto I 136 C2
Arques F 78 B2
Arques-la-Bataille F 89 A5
Arquillos E 157 B4
Arraia-Maeztu E 143 B4
Arraiolos P 154 C2
Arrancourt F 92 C2
Arras F 78 B2
Arrasate E 143 B4
Arreau F 145 B4
Arredondo E 143 A3
Arrens-Marsous F 145 B3
Arriate E 162 B2
Arrifana P 160 B1
Arrigorriaga E 143 A4
Arriondas E 142 A1
Arroba de los Montes E 157 A3
Arrochar GB 34 B3
Arromanches-les-Bains F 88 A3
Arronches P 155 B3
Arroniz E 144 B1
Arrou F 103 A3
Arroya de Cuéllar E 150 A3
Arroyal E 142 B2
Arroyo de la Luz E 155 B4
Arroyo de San Servan E 155 C4
Arroyo del Ojanco E 164 A2
Arroyomolinos de León E 161 A3
Arroyomolinos de Montánchez E 156 A1

Arruda dos Vinhos P 154 C1
Ars-en-Ré F 114 B2
Ars-sur-Moselle F 92 B2
Arsac F 128 B2
Arsiè I 121 B4
Arsiero I 121 B4
Årslev DK 59 C3
Ársoli I 169 A3
Årsunda S 50 B3
Artà E 167 B3
Arta GR 182 D3
Artajona E 144 B2
Arteixo E 140 A2
Artegna I 122 A2
Artemare F 118 B2
Arten I 121 B4
Artena I 169 B2
Artenay F 103 A3
Artern D 82 A3
Artés E 147 C2
Artesa de Segre E 147 C2
Arth CH 107 B3
Arthez-de-Béarn F 145 A3
Arthon-en-Retz F 101 B4
Arthurstown IRL 30 B2
Artieda E 144 B3
Artix F 145 A3
Artotina GR 182 E4
Artsyz UA 17 B8
Arudy F 145 A3
Arundel GB 44 C3
Arveyres F 128 B2
Arvidsjaur S 196 D2
Arvieux F 118 C3
Arvika S 54 A3
Åryd, Blekinge S 63 B3
Åryd, Kronoberg S 62 B2
Arzachena I 178 A3
Arzacq-Arraziguet F 128 C2
Árzana I 179 C3
Arzano F 100 B2
Aržano HR 138 B2
Arzberg D 95 A4
Arzignano I 121 B4
Arzila P 148 B1
Arzl im Pitztal A 108 B1
Arzúa E 140 B2
As B 80 A1
Aš CZ 83 B4
Ås N 54 A1
As Neves E 140 B2
As Nogaís E 141 B3
As Pontes de García Rodríguez E 140 A3
Åsa S 60 B2
Asaa DK 58 A3
Aşağıçiğil TR 189 A6
Ašanja SRB 127 C2
Åsarna S 199 C11
Åsarp S 55 B4
Asasp F 145 A3
Åsbro S 55 A6
Åsby, Halland S 60 B2
Asby, Östergötland S 62 A3
Åsbygri IS 191 A9
Ascain F 144 A2
Ascea I 172 B1
Ascha D 95 B4
Aschach an der Donau A 96 C2
Aschaffenburg D 93 B5
Aschbach Markt A 110 A1
Ascheberg, Nordrhein-Westfalen D 81 A3
Ascheberg, Schleswig-Holstein D 65 B3
Aschendorf D 71 A4
Aschersleben D 82 A3
Asciano I 135 B4
Ascó E 153 A4
Asco F 180 A2
Áscoli Piceno I 136 C2
Áscoli Satriano I 171 B3
Ascona CH 120 A1
Ascot GB 44 B3
Ascoux F 103 A4
Åse N 194 A6
Åseda S 62 A3
Åsele S 200 B3
Åsen N 199 B8
Åsen S 49 A5
Asendorf D 72 B2
Asenovgrad BG 183 A6
Asensbruk S 54 B3
Åseral N 52 B3
Asfeld F 91 B4
Ásgarður IS 190 B1
Åsgårdstrand N 54 A1
Asgate CY 181 B2
Ash, Kent GB 45 B5
Ash, Surrey GB 44 B3
Åshammar S 50 B3
Ashbourne GB 40 B2
Ashbourne IRL 30 A2
Ashburton GB 43 B3
Ashby-de-la-Zouch GB 40 C2
Ashchurch GB 44 B1
Åsheim N 199 D8

Ashford GB 45 B4
Ashington GB 37 A5
Ashley GB 38 B4
Ashmyany BY 13 A6
Ashton Under Lyne GB 40 B1
Ashwell GB 44 A3
Asiago I 121 B4
Asipovichy BY 13 B8
Aska FIN 197 B9
Askam-in-Furness GB 36 B3
Askeaton IRL 29 B3
Asker N 48 C2
Askersund S 55 B5
Åskilje S 200 B3
Askim N 54 A2
Askland N 53 B4
Äsköping S 56 A2
Askvoll N 46 A2
Åsljunga S 61 C3
Asmunti FIN 197 D9
Asnæs DK 61 D1
Ásola I 120 B3
Asolo I 121 B4
Asos GR 184 A1
Asotthalom H 126 A1
Aspach A 109 A4
Aspang Markt A 111 B3
Aspariegos E 149 A4
Asparn an der Zaya A 97 C4
Aspatria GB 36 B3
Aspberg S 55 A4
Aspe E 165 A4
Aspet F 145 A4
Äspö S 63 B3
Aspres-sur-Buëch F 132 A1
Aspsele S 200 C4
Assafora P 154 C1
Asse B 79 B4
Assebakte N 193 C9
Assel D 72 A2
Asselborn L 92 A1
Assémini I 179 C2
Assen NL 71 B3
Assenede B 79 A3
Assens, *Aarhus Amt.* DK 58 B3
Assens, *Fyns Amt.* DK 59 C2
Assesse B 79 B5
Assisi I 136 B1
Åsskard N 198 B5
Assling D 108 B3
Asso I 120 B2
Asson F 145 A3
Ássoro I 177 B3
Assumar P 155 B3
Åsta N 48 A3
Astaffort F 129 B3
Astakos GR 184 A2
Asten NL 80 A1
Asti I 119 C5
Astipalea GR 188 C1
Astorga E 141 B4
Åstorp S 61 C2
Åsträsk S 200 B5
Astudillo E 142 B2
Asuni I 179 C2
Asványráró H 111 B4
Aszód H 112 B3
Aszófő H 111 C4
Atabey TR 189 B5
Atalaia P 154 B3
Atalandi GR 182 E4
Atalho P 154 C2
Átány H 113 B4
Atanzón E 151 B4
Ataquines E 150 A3
Atarfe E 163 A4
Atça TR 188 B3
Ateca E 152 A2
Atella I 172 B1
Atessa I 169 A4
Ath B 79 B3
Athboy IRL 30 A2
Athea IRL 29 B2
Athenry IRL 28 A3
Athens = Athina GR 185 B4
Atherstone GB 40 C2
Athienou CY 181 A2
Athies F 90 B2
Athies-sous-Laon F 91 B3
Athina = Athens GR 185 B4
Athleague IRL 28 A3
Athlone IRL 28 A4
Athna CY 181 A2
Athy IRL 30 B2
Atienza E 151 A5
Atina I 169 B3
Atkár H 113 B3
Atlantı TR 189 A7
Atna N 199 D7
Åtorp S 55 A5
Atrå N 47 C5
Åtran S 60 B2
Atri I 169 A3
Atripalda I 170 C2
Atsiki GR 183 D7
Attendorn D 81 A3
Attichy F 90 B3
Attigliano I 168 A2
Attigny F 91 B4
Attleborough GB 41 C5
Åtvidaberg S 56 B1
Atzendorf D 73 C4
Au, *Steiermark* A 110 B2
Au, *Vorarlberg* A 107 B4
Au, *Bayern* D 108 B2
Au, *Bayern* D 95 C3
Aub D 94 B2
Aubagne F 132 B1
Aubange B 92 B1
Aubel B 80 B1
Aubenas F 117 C4
Aubenton F 91 B4
Auberive F 105 B4
Aubeterre-sur-Dronne F 128 A3
Aubiet F 129 C3
Aubigné F 115 B3
Aubigny F 114 B2
Aubigny-au-Bac F 78 B3
Aubigny-en-Artois F 78 B2
Aubigny-sur-Nère F 103 B4
Aubin F 130 A1
Aubonne CH 105 C5
Aubrac F 116 C2
Aubusson F 116 B2
Auch F 129 C3
Auchencairn GB 36 B3
Auchinleck GB 36 A2
Auchterarder GB 35 B4
Auchtermuchty GB 35 B4
Auchtertyre GB 31 B3
Auchy-au-Bois F 78 B2
Audenge F 128 B1
Auderville F 88 A2
Audierne F 100 A1
Audincourt F 106 B1
Audlem GB 38 B4
Audruicq F 78 B2
Audun-le-Roman F 92 B1
Audun-le-Tiche F 92 B1
Aue, *Nordrhein-Westfalen* D 81 A4
Aue, *Sachsen* D 83 B4
Auerbach, *Bayern* D 95 B3
Auerbach, *Sachsen* D 83 B4
Auffach A 108 B3
Augher GB 27 B3
Aughnacloy GB 27 B4
Aughrim IRL 30 B2
Augignac F 115 C4
Augsburg D 94 C2
Augusta I 177 B4
Augusten-borg DK 64 B2
Augustfehn D 71 A4
Augustów PL 12 B5
Aukrug D 64 B2
Auktsjaur S 196 D2
Auldearn GB 32 D3
Aulendorf D 107 B4
Auletta I 172 B1
Aulla I 134 A2
Aullène F 180 B2
Aulnay F 115 B3
Aulnoye-Aymeries F 79 B3
Ault F 90 A1
Aultbea GB 31 B3
Aulum DK 59 B1
Aulus-les-Bains F 146 B2
Auma D 83 B3
Aumale F 90 B1
Aumetz F 92 B1
Aumont-Aubrac F 116 C3
Aunay-en-Bazois F 104 B2
Aunay-sur-Odon F 88 A3
Aune N 199 A10
Auneau F 90 C1
Auneuil F 90 B1
Auning DK 58 B3
Aunsetra N 199 A9
Aups F 132 B2
Aura D 82 B1
Auray F 100 B3
Aurdal N 47 B6
Aure N 198 B5
Aurich D 71 A4
Aurignac F 145 A4
Aurillac F 116 C2
Auriol F 132 B1
Auritz-Burguette E 144 B2
Aurlandsvangen N 47 B4
Auronzo di Cadore I 109 C3
Auros F 128 B2
Auroux F 117 C3
Aurskog N 48 C3
Aursmoen N 48 C3
Ausónia I 169 B3
Ausservillgraton A 109 C3
Austad N 52 B3
Austbygda N 47 B5
Aústis I 178 B3
Austmarka N 49 B4
Austre Moland N 53 B4
Austre Vikebygd N 52 A1
Austrheim N 46 B1
Auterive F 146 A2
Autheuil-Authouillet F 89 A5
Authon F 132 A2
Authon-du-Perche F 102 A2
Autol E 144 B2
Autreville F 92 C1
Autrey-lès-Gray F 105 B4
Autti FIN 197 C10
Autun F 104 C3
Auty-le-Châtel F 103 B4
Auvelais B 79 B4
Auvillar F 129 B3
Auxerre F 104 B2
Auxi-le-Château F 78 B2
Auxon F 104 A2
Auxonne F 105 B4
Auxy F 104 C3
Auzances F 116 A2
Auzon F 117 B3
Availles-Limouzine F 115 B4
Avaldsnes N 52 A1
Avallon F 104 B2
Avantas GR 183 C7
Avaviken S 195 E9
Avebury GB 44 B2
Aveiras de Cima P 154 B2
Aveiro P 148 B1
Avelgem B 79 B3
Avellino I 170 C2
Avenches CH 106 C2
Aversa I 170 C2
Avesnes-le-Comte F 78 B2
Avesnes-sur-Helpe F 91 A3
Avesta S 50 B3
Avetrana I 173 B3
Avezzano I 169 A3
Avià E 147 B2
Aviano I 122 A1
Aviemore GB 32 D3
Avigliana I 119 B4
Avigliano I 172 B1
Avignon F 131 B3
Ávila E 150 B3
Avilés E 141 A5
Avilley F 105 B5
Avintes P 148 A1
Avinyo E 147 C2
Àvio I 121 B3
Avioth F 92 B1
Avis P 154 B3
Avize F 91 C4
Avlonari GR 185 A5
Ávola I 177 C4
Avon F 90 C2
Avonmouth GB 43 A4
Avord F 103 B4
Avranches F 88 B2
Avril F 92 B1
Avrillé F 102 B1
Avtovac BIH 139 B4
Awans B 79 B5
Ax-les-Thermes F 146 B2
Axams A 108 B2
Axat F 146 B3
Axbridge GB 43 A4
Axel NL 79 A3
Axmarby S 51 B4
Axmarsbruk S 51 A4
Axminster GB 43 B3
Axvall S 55 B4
Ay F 91 B4
Aya E 144 A1
Ayamonte E 161 B2
Ayancık TR 23 A8
Ayaş TR 187 B7
Aydın TR 188 B2
Ayelo de Malferit E 159 C3
Ayer CH 119 A4
Ayerbe E 144 B3
Ayette F 78 B2
Ayia Napa CY 181 B2
Áyia Phyla CY 181 B2
Áyios Amvrósios CY 181 A2
Áyios Seryios CY 181 A2
Áyios Theodhoros CY 181 A3
Aykirikçi TR 187 C5
Aylesbury GB 44 B3
Ayllón E 151 A4
Aylsham GB 41 C5
Ayna E 158 C1
Ayódar E 159 B3
Ayora E 159 B2
Ayr GB 36 A2
Ayrancı TR 23 C7
Ayrancılar TR 188 A2
Ayron F 115 B4
Aysgarth GB 37 B4
Ayton GB 35 C5
Aytos BG 17 D7
Ayvacık TR 186 C1
Ayvalık TR 186 C1
Aywaille B 80 B1
Azaila E 153 A3
Azambuja P 154 B2
Azambujeira P 154 B2
Azanja SRB 127 C2
Azannes-et-Soumazannes F 92 B1
Azanúy-Alins E 145 C4
Azaruja P 155 C3
Azay-le-Ferron F 115 B5
Azay-le-Rideau F 102 B2
Azcoitia E 143 A4
Azé F 117 A4
Azeiteiros P 155 B3
Azenhas do Mar P 154 C1
Azinhaga P 154 B2
Azinhal P 160 B2
Azinheira dos Bairros P 160 A1
Aznalcázar E 161 B3
Aznalcóllar E 161 B3
Azóia P 154 B2
Azpeitia E 144 A1
Azuaga E 156 B2
Azuara E 153 A3
Azuqueca de Henares E 151 B4
Azur F 128 C1
Azzano Décimo I 122 B1

B

Baad A 107 B5
Baamonde E 140 A3
Baar CH 107 B3
Baarle-Nassau B 79 A4
Baarn NL 70 B2
Babadag RO 17 C8
Babadağ TR 188 B3
Babaeski TR 186 A2
Babayevo RUS 9 C9
Babenhausen, *Bayern* D 107 A5
Babenhausen, *Hessen* D 93 B4
Babiak PL 76 B3
Babice PL 86 B3
Babigoszcz PL 75 A3
Babimost PL 75 B4
Babina Greda HR 125 B4
Babócsa H 124 A3
Bábolma H 112 B1
Baborów PL 86 B1
Baboszewo PL 77 B5
Babót H 111 B4
Babruysk BY 13 B8
Babsk PL 87 A4
Bac GB 31 A2
Bač SRB 125 B5
Bacares E 164 B2
Bacău RO 17 B7
Baccarat F 92 C2
Bacharach D 93 A3
Backa S 50 B2
Bačka Palanka SRB 126 B1
Bačka Topola SRB 126 B1
Backaryd S 63 B3
Backe S 200 C2
Bäckebo S 62 B4
Bäckefors S 54 B3
Bäckhammar S 55 A5
Bački Breg SRB 125 B4
Bački-Brestovac SRB 126 B1
Bački Monoštor SRB 125 B4
Bački Petrovac SRB 126 B1
Bački Sokolac SRB 126 B1
Backnang D 94 C1
Bačko Gradište SRB 126 B2
Bačko Novo Selo SRB 125 B5
Bačko Petrovo Selo SRB 126 B2
Bácoli I 170 C2
Bacqueville-en-Caux F 89 A5
Bácsalmás H 126 A1
Bácsbokod H 125 A5
Bad Abbach D 95 C4
Bad Aibling D 108 B3
Bad Aussee A 109 B4
Bad Bederkesa D 72 A1
Bad Bentheim D 71 B4
Bad Bergzabern D 93 B3
Bad Berka D 82 B3
Bad Berleburg D 81 A4
Bad Berneck D 95 A3
Bad Bevensen D 73 A3
Bad Bibra D 82 A3
Bad Birnbach D 95 C5
Bad Blankenburg D 82 B3
Bad Bleiberg A 109 C4
Bad Brambach D 83 B4
Bad Bramstedt D 64 C2
Bad Breisig D 80 B3
Bad Brückenau D 82 B1
Bad Buchau D 107 A4
Bad Camberg D 81 B4
Bad Doberan D 65 B4
Bad Driburg D 81 A5
Bad Düben D 83 A4
Bad Dürkheim D 93 B4
Bad Dürrenberg D 83 A4
Bad Dürrheim D 107 A3
Bad Elster D 83 B4
Bad Ems D 81 B3
Bad Endorf D 109 B3
Bad Essen D 71 B5
Bad Fischau A 111 B3
Bad Frankenhausen D 82 A3
Bad Freienwalde D 74 B3
Bad Friedrichshall D 93 B5
Bad Füssing D 96 C1
Bad Gandersheim D 82 A2
Bad Gastein A 109 B4
Bad Gleichenberg A 110 C2
Bad Goisern A 109 B4
Bad Gottleuba D 84 B1
Bad Grund D 82 A2
Bad Hall A 110 A1
Bad Harzburg D 82 A2
Bad Herrenalb D 93 C4
Bad Hersfeld D 82 B1
Bad Hofgastein A 109 B4
Bad Homburg D 81 B4
Bad Honnef D 80 B3
Bad Hönningen D 80 B3
Bad Iburg D 71 B5
Bad Inner-laterns A 107 B4
Bad Ischl A 109 B4
Bad Karlshafen D 81 A5
Bad Kemmeriboden CH 106 C2
Bad Kissingen D 82 B2
Bad Kleinen D 65 C4
Bad Kohlgrub D 108 B2
Bad König D 93 B5
Bad Königshofen D 82 B2
Bad Köstritz D 83 B4
Bad Kreuzen A 110 A1
Bad Kreuznach D 93 B3
Bad Krozingen D 106 B2
Bad Laasphe D 81 B4
Bad Langensalza D 82 A2
Bad Lauchstädt D 83 A3
Bad Lausick D 83 A4
Bad Lauterberg D 82 A2
Bad Leonfelden A 96 C2
Bad Liebenwerda D 83 A5
Bad Liebenzell D 93 C4
Bad Lippspringe D 81 A4
Bad Meinberg D 81 A4
Bad Mergentheim D 94 B1
Bad Mitterndorf A 109 B4
Bad Münder D 72 B2
Bad Münstereifel D 80 B2
Bad Muskau D 84 A2
Bad Nauheim D 81 B4
Bad Nenndorf D 72 B2
Bad Neuenahr-Ahrweiler D 80 B3
Bad Neustadt D 82 B2
Bad Oeynhausen D 72 B1
Bad Oldesloe D 65 C3
Bad Orb D 81 B5
Bad Peterstal D 93 C4
Bad Pyrmont D 72 C2
Bad Radkersburg A 110 C2
Bad Ragaz CH 107 C4
Bad Rappenau D 93 B5
Bad Reichenhall D 109 B3
Bad Saarow-Pieskow D 74 B3
Bad Sachsa D 82 A2
Bad Säckingen D 106 B2
Bad Salzdetfurth D 72 B3
Bad Salzig D 81 B3
Bad Salzuflen D 72 B1
Bad Salzungen D 82 B2
Bad Sankt Leonhard A 110 C1
Bad Sassendorf D 81 A4
Bad Schandau D 84 B2
Bad Schmiedeberg D 83 A4
Bad Schönborn D 93 B4
Bad Schussenried D 107 A4
Bad Schwalbach D 81 B4
Bad Schwartau D 65 C3
Bad Segeberg D 64 C3
Bad Soden D 81 B4
Bad Soden-Salmünster D 81 B5
Bad Sooden-Allendorf D 82 A1
Bad Sulza D 83 A3
Bad Sülze D 66 B1
Bad Tatzmannsdorf A 111 B3
Bad Tennstedt D 82 A2
Bad Tölz D 108 B2
Bad Urach D 94 C1
Bad Vellach A 110 C1
Bad Vilbel D 81 B4
Bad Vöslau A 111 B3
Bad Waldsee D 107 B4
Bad Wiessee D 108 B2
Bad Wildungen D 81 A5
Bad Wilsnack D 73 B4
Bad Windsheim D 94 B2
Bad Wörishafen D 108 A1
Bad Wurzach D 107 B4
Bad Zwesten D 81 A5
Bad Zwischenahn D 71 A5
Badacsonytomaj H 111 C4
Badajoz E 155 C4
Badalona E 147 C3
Badalucco I 133 B3
Badderen N 192 C6
Baden A 111 A3
Baden CH 106 B3
Baden-Baden D 93 C4
Bádenas E 152 A2
Badenweiler D 106 B2
Baderna HR 122 B2
Badia Calavena I 121 B4
Badia Polésine I 121 B4
Badia Pratáglia I 135 B4
Badia Tedalda I 135 B5
Bądki PL 69 B3
Badkowo PL 76 B3
Badljevina HR 124 B3
Badolato I 175 C2
Badolatosa E 163 A3
Badonviller F 92 C2
Badovinci SRB 127 C1
Badules E 152 A2
Bække DK 59 C2
Bækmarksbro DK 58 B1
Baells E 145 C4
Bælum DK 58 B3
Baena E 163 A3
Baesweiler D 80 B2
Baeza E 157 C4
Baflo NL 71 A3
Baga E 147 B2
Bagaladi I 175 C1
Bağarasi TR 188 B2
Bagenkop DK 65 B3
Baggetorp S 56 A2
Bagh a Chaisteil GB 31 C1
Bagheria I 176 A2
Bagn N 47 B6
Bagnacavallo I 135 A4
Bagnáia I 168 A2
Bagnara Cálabra I 175 C1
Bagnasco I 133 A4
Bagnères-de-Bigorre F 145 A4
Bagnères-de-Luchon F 145 B4
Bagni del Másino I 120 A2
Bagni di Lucca I 134 A3
Bagni di Rabbi I 121 A3
Bagni di Tivoli I 168 B2
Bagno di Romagna I 135 B4
Bagnoles-de-l'Orne F 89 B3
Bagnoli dei Trigno I 170 B2
Bagnoli di Sopra I 121 B4
Bagnoli Irpino I 170 C3
Bagnolo Mella I 120 B3
Bagnols-en-Forêt F 132 B2
Bagnols-sur-Cèze F 131 A3
Bagnorégio I 168 A2
Bagolino I 121 B3
Bagrationovsk RUS 12 A4
Bagrdan SRB 127 C3
Báguena E 152 A2
Bahabón de Esgueva E 143 C3
Bahillo E 142 B2
Báia delle Zágare I 171 B4
Báia Domizia I 169 B3
Baia Mare RO 17 B5
Baiano I 170 C2
Baião P 148 A1
Baiersbronn D 93 C4
Baiersdorf D 94 B3
Baignes-Ste. Radegonde F 115 C3
Baigneux-les-Juifs F 104 B3
Baildon GB 40 B2
Bailén E 157 B4
Băileşti RO 17 C5
Baileux B 91 A4
Bailieborough IRL 27 C4
Bailleul F 78 B2
Baillonville B 79 B5
Bailó E 144 B3
Bain-de-Bretagne F 101 B4
Bains F 117 B3
Bains-les-Bains F 105 A5
Bainton GB 40 B3
Baio E 140 A2
Baiona E 140 B2
Bais F 89 B3
Baiso I 134 A3
Baiuca P 148 B2
Baja H 125 A4
Bajánsenye H 111 C3
Bajina Bašta SRB 127 D1
Bajmok SRB 126 B1
Bajna H 112 B2
Bajovo Polje MNE 139 B4
Bajša SRB 126 B1
Bak H 111 C3
Bakar HR 123 B3
Bakewell GB 40 B2
Bakio E 143 A4
Bakka N 47 C6
Bakkafjörður IS 191 A11
Bakkagerði IS 191 B12
Bakken N 48 B3
Baklan TR 189 B4
Bakonybél H 111 B4
Bakonycsernye H 112 B2
Bakonyjákó H 111 B4
Bakonyszentkirály H 111 B4
Bakonyszombathely H 112 B1

Bakov nad Jizerou CZ 84 B2
Bąkowiec PL 87 A5
Baks H 113 C4
Baksa H 125 B4
Bakum D 71 B5
Bala GB 38 B3
Bâlâ TR 23 B7
Balaguer E 145 C4
Balassagyarmat H 112 A3
Balástya H 113 C4
Balatonakali H 111 C4
Balatonalmádi H 112 B2
Balatonboglár H 111 C4
Balatonbozsok H 112 C2
Balatonederics H 111 C4
Balatonfenyves H 111 C4
Balatonföldvár H 112 C1
Balatonfüred H 112 C1
Balatonfüzfö H 112 B2
Balatonkenese H 112 B2
Balatonkiliti H 112 C2
Balatonlelle H 111 C4
Balatonszabadi H 112 C2
Balatonszemes H 111 C4
Balatonszentgyörgy H 111 C4
Balazote E 158 C1
Balbeggie GB 35 B4
Balbigny F 117 B4
Balboa E 141 B4
Balbriggan IRL 30 A2
Balchik BG 17 D8
Balçova TR 188 A2
Baldock GB 44 B3
Bale HR 122 B2
Baleira E 141 A3
Baleizao P 160 A2
Balen B 79 A5
Balerma E 164 C2
Balestrand N 46 A3
Balestrate I 176 A2
Balfour GB 33 B4
Bälganet S 63 B3
Balıkesir TR 186 C2
Balıklıçeşme TR 186 B2
Bälinge S 51 C4
Balingen D 107 A3
Balingsta S 56 A3
Balintore GB 32 D3
Balizac F 128 B2
Balk NL 70 B2
Balkbrug NL 71 B3
Balla IRL 28 A2
Ballachulish GB 34 B2
Ballaghaderreen IRL 26 C2
Ballancourt-sur-Essonne F 90 C2
Ballantrae GB 36 A2
Ballao I 179 C3
Ballasalla GB 36 B2
Ballater GB 32 D3
Ballen DK 59 C3
Ballenstedt D 82 A3
Ballerias E 145 C3
Balleroy F 88 A3
Ballerup DK 61 D2
Ballesteros de Calatrava E 157 B4
Ballı TR 186 B2
Ballina IRL 26 B1
Ballinalack IRL 30 A1
Ballinamore IRL 26 B3
Ballinascarty IRL 29 C3
Ballinasloe IRL 28 A3
Ballindine IRL 28 A3
Balling DK 58 B1
Ballingarry, *Limerick* IRL 29 B3
Ballingarry, *Tipperary* IRL 30 B1
Ballingeary IRL 29 C2
Ballinhassig IRL 29 C3
Ballinluig GB 35 B4
Ballino I 121 B3
Ballinrobe IRL 28 A2
Ballinskellings IRL 29 C1
Ballinspittle IRL 29 C3
Ballintra IRL 26 B2
Ballivor IRL 30 A2
Ballobar E 153 A4
Ballon F 102 A2
Ballon IRL 30 B2
Ballószög H 112 C3
Ballsh AL 182 C1
Ballstad N 194 B4
Ballum DK 64 A1
Ballybay IRL 27 B4
Ballybofey IRL 26 B3
Ballybunion IRL 29 B2
Ballycanew IRL 30 B2
Ballycarry GB 27 B5
Ballycastle GB 27 A4
Ballycastle IRL 26 B1
Ballyclare GB 27 B5
Ballyconneely IRL 28 A1
Ballycotton IRL 29 C3
Ballycroy IRL 26 B1
Ballydehob IRL 29 C2
Ballyferriter IRL 29 B1
Ballygawley GB 27 B3
Ballygowan GB 27 B5
Ballyhaunis IRL 28 A3
Ballyheige IRL 29 B2
Ballyjamesduff IRL 27 C3
Ballylanders IRL 29 B3
Ballylynan IRL 30 B1
Ballymahon IRL 28 A4
Ballymena GB 27 B4
Ballymoe IRL 28 A3
Ballymoney GB 27 A4
Ballymore IRL 28 A4
Ballymote IRL 26 B2
Ballynacorra IRL 29 C3
Ballynagore IRL 30 A1
Ballynahinch GB 27 B5
Ballynure GB 27 B5
Ballyragget IRL 30 B1
Ballysadare IRL 26 B2
Ballyshannon IRL 26 B2
Ballyvaghan IRL 28 A2
Ballyvourney IRL 29 C2
Ballywalter GB 27 B5
Balmaclellan GB 36 A2
Balmaseda E 143 A3
Balmazújváros H 113 B5
Balme I 119 B4
Balmedie GB 33 D4
Balmuccia I 119 B5
Balna-paling GB 32 D2
Balneario de Panticosa E 145 B3
Balotaszállás H 126 A1
Balsa P 148 A2
Balsareny E 147 C2
Balsorano-Nuovo I 169 B3
Bålsta S 57 A3
Balsthal CH 106 B2
Balta UA 17 A8
Baltanás E 142 C2
Baltar E 140 C3
Baltasound GB 33 A6
Bălţi MD 17 B7
Baltimore IRL 29 C2
Baltinglass IRL 30 B2
Baltiysk RUS 69 A4
Baltów PL 87 A5
Balugães P 148 A1
Balve D 81 A3
Balvi LV 8 D5
Balvicar GB 34 B2
Balya TR 186 C2
Balzo I 136 C2
Bamberg D 94 B2
Bamburgh GB 37 A5
Banatska Palanka SRB 127 C3
Banatski Brestovac SRB 127 C2
Banatski Despotovac SRB 126 B2
Banatski Dvor SRB 126 B2
Banatski-Karlovac SRB 127 B3
Banatsko Arandjelovo SRB 126 A2
Banatsko-Novo Selo SRB 127 C2
Banaz TR 187 D4
Banbridge GB 27 B4
Banbury GB 44 A2
Banchory GB 33 D4
Bande B 79 B5
Bande E 140 B3
Bandholm DK 65 B4
Bandırma TR 186 B2
Bandol F 132 B1
Bandon IRL 29 C3
Bañeres E 159 C3
Banff GB 33 D4
Bangor F 100 B2
Bangor, *Down* GB 27 B5
Bangor, *Gwynedd* GB 38 A2
Bangor IRL 26 B1
Bangsund N 199 A8
Banie PL 74 A3
Banja Koviljača SRB 127 C1
Banja Luka BIH 124 C3
Banja Vručica BIH 125 C3
Banjaloka SLO 123 B3
Banjani SRB 127 C1
Banka SK 98 C1
Bankekind S 56 B1
Bankend GB 36 A3
Bankeryd S 62 A2
Bankfoot GB 35 B4
Banloc RO 126 B3
Bannalec F 100 B2
Bannes F 91 C3
Bannockburn GB 35 B4
Bañobárez E 149 B3
Bañon E 152 B2
Banon F 132 A1
Baños E 149 B4
Baños de Gigonza E 162 B2
Baños de la Encina E 157 B4
Baños de Molgas E 140 B3
Baños de Rio Tobia E 143 B4
Baños de Valdearados E 143 C3
Bánov CZ 98 C1
Banova Jaruga HR 124 B2
Bánovce nad Bebravou SK 98 C2
Banovići BIH 139 A4
Banovići Selo BIH 139 A4
Bánréve H 99 C4
Bansin D 66 C3
Banská Belá SK 98 C2
Banská Bystrica SK 99 C3
Banská Štiavnica SK 98 C2
Bansko BG 183 B5
Banstead GB 44 B3
Banteer IRL 29 B3
Bantheville F 91 B5
Bantry IRL 29 C2
Bantzenheim F 106 B2
Banyalbufar E 166 B2
Banyoles E 147 B3
Banyuls-sur-Mer F 146 B4
Bapaume F 90 A2
Bar MNE 16 D3
Bar UA 13 D7
Bar-le-Duc F 91 C5
Bar-sur-Aube F 104 A3
Bar-sur-Seine F 104 A3
Barabhas GB 31 A2
Barači BIH 138 A2
Baracs H 112 C2
Baracska H 112 B2
Barahona E 151 A5
Barajes de Melo E 151 B5
Barakaldo E 143 A4
Baralla E 141 B3
Barañain E 144 B2
Baranavichy BY 13 B7
Báránd H 113 B5
Baranda SRB 127 B2
Baranello I 170 B2
Baranów Sandomierski PL 87 B5
Baraqueville F 130 A1
Barasoain E 144 B2
Barbacena P 155 C3
Barbadás E 140 B3
Barbadillo E 149 B4
Barbadillo de Herreros E 143 B3
Barbadillo del Mercado E 143 B3
Barbadillo del Pez E 143 B3
Barban HR 123 B3
Barbarano Vicento I 121 B4
Barbariga HR 122 C2
Barbaros TR 186 B2
Barbastro E 145 B4
Barbate E 162 B2
Barbatona E 152 A1
Barbâtre F 114 B1
Barbazan F 145 A4
Barbeitos E 141 A3
Barbentane F 131 B3
Barberino di Mugello I 135 A4
Barbezieux-St. Hilaire F 115 C3
Barbonne-Fayel F 91 C3
Barbotan-les-Thermes F 128 C2
Barby D 73 C4
Barca de Alva P 149 A3
Bárcabo E 145 B4
Barcarrota E 155 C4
Barcellona-Pozzo di Gotto I 177 A4
Barcelona E 147 C3
Barcelonette F 132 A2
Barcelos P 148 A1
Barcena de Pie de Concha E 142 A2
Bárcena del Monasterio E 141 A4
Barchfeld D 82 B2
Barcin PL 76 B2
Barcino PL 68 A1
Bárcis I 122 A1
Barco P 148 B2
Barcones E 151 A5
Barcs H 124 B3
Barcus F 144 A3
Bardejov SK 12 D4
Bårdesø DK 59 C3
Bardi I 120 C2
Bardney GB 40 B3
Bardo PL 85 B4
Bardolino I 121 B3
Bardonécchia I 118 B3
Bardoňovo SK 112 A2
Barèges F 145 B4
Barenstein D 83 B5
Barentin F 89 A4
Barenton F 88 B3
Barevo BIH 138 A3
Barfleur F 88 A2
Barga I 134 A3
Bargas E 151 C3
Barge I 119 C4
Bargemon F 132 B2
Barghe I 120 B3
Bargoed GB 39 C3
Bargrennan GB 36 A2
Bargteheide D 64 C3
Barham GB 45 B5
Bari I 173 A2
Bari Sardo I 179 C3
Barič Draga HR 137 A4
Barilović HR 123 B4
Barisciano I 169 A3
Barjac F 131 A3
Barjols F 132 B1
Barjon F 105 B3
Bårkåker N 54 A1
Barkald N 199 D7
Barkowo, *Dolnośląskie* PL 85 A4
Barkowo, *Pomorskie* PL 68 B2
Bârlad RO 17 B7
Barles F 132 A2
Barletta I 171 B4
Barlinek PL 75 B4
Barmouth GB 38 B2
Barmstedt D 64 C2
Barnard Castle GB 37 B5
Barnarp S 62 A2
Bärnau D 95 B4
Bärnbach A 110 B2
Barneberg D 73 B4
Barnenitz D 74 B1
Barnet GB 44 B3
Barnetby le Wold GB 40 B3
Barneveld NL 70 B2
Barneville-Carteret F 88 A2
Barnoldswick GB 40 B1
Barnowko PL 75 B3
Barnsley GB 40 B2
Barnstädt D 83 A3
Barnstaple GB 42 A2
Barnstorf D 72 B1
Barntrup D 72 C2
Baron F 90 B2
Baronissi I 170 C2
Barqueiro P 154 B2
Barquinha P 154 B2
Barr F 93 C3
Barr GB 36 A2
Barra P 148 B1
Barracas E 159 A3
Barraco E 150 B3
Barrado E 150 B2
Barrafranca I 177 B3
Barranco do Velho P 160 B2
Barrancos P 161 A3
Barrax E 158 B1
Barrbaar D 94 C2
Barre-des-Cevennes F 130 A2
Barreiro P 154 C1
Barreiros E 141 A3
Barrême F 132 B2
Barret-le-Bas F 132 A1
Barrhead GB 34 C3
Barrhill GB 36 A2
Barrio de Nuesra Señora E 142 B1
Barrow-in-Furness GB 36 B3
Barrow upon Humber GB 40 B3
Barrowford GB 40 B1
Barruecopardo E 149 A3
Barruelo de Santullán E 142 B2
Barruera E 145 B4
Barry GB 39 C3
Bårse DK 65 A4
Barsinghausen D 72 B2
Barssel D 71 A4
Barth D 66 B1
Bartholomä D 94 C1
Bartin TR 187 A7
Barton upon Humber GB 40 B3
Barúmini I 179 C2
Baruth D 74 B2
Barvaux B 80 B1
Barver D 72 B1
Barwatd PL 99 B3
Barwice PL 68 B1
Barysaw BY 13 A8
Barzana E 141 A5
Bârzava RO 16 B4
Bárzio I 120 B2
Bas E 147 B3
Bašaid SRB 126 B2
Basaluzzo I 120 C1
Basarabeasca MD 17 B8
Basauri E 143 A4
Baschi I 168 A2
Baschurch GB 38 B4
Basconcillos del Tozo E 143 B3
Bascones de Ojeda E 142 B2
Basécles B 79 B3
Basel CH 106 B2
Basélice I 170 B2
Basildon GB 45 B4
Basingstoke GB 44 B2
Baška CZ 98 B2
Baška HR 123 C3
Baška Voda HR 138 B2
Bäsksjö S 200 B3
Baslow GB 40 B2
Başmakçı TR 189 B5
Basovizza I 122 B2
Bassacutena I 178 A3
Bassano del Grappa I 121 B4
Bassano Romano I 168 A2
Bassecourt CH 106 B2
Bassella E 147 B2
Bassevuovdde N 193 D9
Bassou F 104 B2
Bassoues F 128 C3
Bassum D 72 B1
Båstad S 61 C2
Bastardo I 136 C1
Bastelica F 180 A2
Bastelicaccia F 180 B1
Bastia F 180 A2
Bastia I 136 B1
Bastogne B 92 A1
Baston GB 40 C3
Bastuträsk S 200 B6
Bata H 125 A4
Batajnica SRB 127 C2
Batak BG 183 B6
Batalha P 154 B2
Bátaszék H 125 A4
Batea E 153 A4
Batelov CZ 97 B3
Bath GB 43 A4
Bathgate GB 35 C4
Batida H 126 A2
Batignano I 135 C4
Batina HR 125 B4
Bátka SK 99 C4
Batković BIH 125 C5
Batley GB 40 B2
Batnfjordsøra N 198 C4
Batočina SRB 127 C3
Bátonyterenye H 113 B3
Batrina HR 125 B3
Båtsfjord N 193 B13
Båtskärsnäs S 196 D6
Battaglia Terme I 121 B4
Bätterkinden CH 106 B2
Battice B 80 B1
Battipáglia I 170 C2
Battle GB 45 C4
Battonya H 126 A3
Batuša SRB 127 C3
Bátya H 112 C2
Bau I 179 C2
Baud F 100 B2
Baudour B 79 B3
Baugé F 102 B1
Baugy F 103 B4
Bauma CH 107 B3
Baume-les-Dames F 105 B5
Baumholder D 93 B3
Baunatal D 81 A5
Baunei I 178 B3
Bauska LV 8 D4
Bautzen D 84 A2
Bavanište SRB 127 C2
Bavay F 79 B3
Bavilliers F 106 B1
Bavorov CZ 96 B2
Bawdsey GB 45 A5
Bawinkel D 71 B4
Bawtry GB 40 B2
Bayat TR 187 D5
Bayel F 105 A3
Bayeux F 88 A3
Bayındır TR 188 A2
Bayon F 92 C2
Bayonne F 128 C1
Bayons F 132 A2
Bayramiç TR 186 C1
Bayreuth D 95 B3
Bayrischzell D 108 B3
Baza E 164 B2
Bazas F 128 B2
Baziege F 146 A2
Bazoches-les-Gallerandes F 103 A4
Bazoches-sur-Hoëne F 89 B4
Bazzano I 135 A4
Beaconsfield GB 44 B3
Beade E 140 B2
Beadnell GB 37 A5
Beaminster GB 43 B4
Bearsden GB 34 C3
Beas E 161 B3
Beas de Segura E 164 A2
Beasain E 144 A1
Beattock GB 36 A3
Beaubery F 117 A4
Beaucaire F 131 B3
Beaufort F 118 B3
Beaufort IRL 29 B2
Beaufort-en Vallée F 102 B1
Beaugency F 103 B3
Beaujeu, *Alpes-de-Haute-Provence* F 132 A2
Beaujeu, *Rhône* F 117 A4
Beaulac F 128 B2
Beaulieu F 103 B4
Beaulieu GB 44 C2
Beaulieu-sous-la-Roche F 114 B2
Beaulieu-sur-Dordogne F 129 B4
Beaulieu-sur-Mer F 133 B3
Beaulon F 104 C2
Beauly GB 32 D2
Beaumaris GB 38 A2
Beaumesnil F 89 A4
Beaumetz-lès-Loges F 78 B2
Beaumont B 79 B4
Beaumont F 129 B3
Beaumont-de-Lomagne F 129 C3
Beaumont-du-Gâtinais F 103 A4
Beaumont-en-Argonne F 91 B5
Beaumont-Hague F 88 A2
Beaumont-la-Ronce F 102 B2
Beaumont-le-Roger F 89 A4
Beaumont-sur-Oise F 90 B2
Beaumont-sur-Sarthe F 102 A2
Beaune F 105 B3
Beaune-la-Rolande F 103 A4
Beaupréau F 101 B5
Beauraing B 91 A4
Beaurepaire F 117 B5
Beaurepaire-en-Bresse F 105 C4
Beaurières F 132 A1
Beauvais F 90 B2
Beauval F 90 A2
Beauville F 129 B3
Beauvoir-sur-Mer F 114 B1
Beauvoir-sur-Niort F 114 B3
Beba Veche RO 126 A2
Bebertal D 73 B4
Bebington GB 38 A3
Bebra D 82 B1
Bebrina HR 125 B3
Beccles GB 45 A5
Becedas E 150 B2
Beceite E 153 B4
Bečej SRB 126 B2
Becerreá E 141 B3
Becerril de Campos E 142 B2
Bécherel F 101 A4
Bechhofen D 94 B2
Bechyně CZ 96 B2
Becilla de Valderaduey E 142 B1
Beckfoot GB 36 B3
Beckingham GB 40 B3
Beckum D 81 A4
Beco P 154 B2
Bécon-les-Granits F 102 B1
Bečov nad Teplou CZ 83 B4
Becsehely H 111 C3
Bedale GB 37 B5
Bedames E 143 A3
Bédar E 164 B3
Bédarieux F 130 B2
Bédarrides F 131 A3
Bedburg D 80 B2
Beddgelert GB 38 A2
Beddingestrand S 66 A2
Bédée F 101 A4
Bedegkér H 112 C2
Beden TR 189 C7
Bedford GB 44 A3
Będków PL 87 A3
Bedlington GB 37 A5
Bedlno PL 77 B4
Bedmar E 163 A4
Bédoin F 131 A4
Bedónia I 134 A2
Bedretto CH 107 C3
Bedsted DK 58 B1
Bedum NL 71 A3
Bedwas GB 39 C3
Bedworth GB 40 C2
Będzin PL 86 B3
Beek en Donk NL 80 A1
Beekbergen NL 70 B2
Beelen D 71 C5
Beelitz D 74 B1
Beer GB 43 B3
Beerfelde D 74 B3
Beerfelden D 93 B4
Beernem B 78 A3
Beeskow D 74 B3
Beetsterzwaag NL 70 A3
Beetzendorf D 73 B4
Beflelay CH 106 B2
Begaljica SRB 127 C2
Bégard F 100 A2
Begejci SRB 126 B2
Begijar E 157 C4
Begijnendijk B 79 A4
Begndal N 48 B1
Begues E 147 C2
Beguildy GB 39 B3
Begur E 147 C4
Beho B 80 B1
Behringen D 82 A2
Beilen NL 71 B3
Beilngries D 95 B3
Beine-Nauroy F 91 B4
Beinwil CH 106 B3
Beiseförth D 82 A1
Beith GB 34 C3
Beitostølen N 47 A5
Beiuş RO 16 B5
Beja P 160 A2
Béjar E 149 B4
Bekçiler TR 189 C4
Békés H 113 C5
Békéscsaba H 113 C5
Bekilli TR 189 A4

Name		Page	Grid
Bekkarfjord	N	193	B11
Bela	SK	98	B2
Bela Crkva	SRB	127	C3
Belá nad Radbuzou	CZ	95	B4
Bělá pod Bezdězem	CZ	84	B2
Bélábre	F	115	B5
Belalcázar	E	156	A3
Belanovica	SRB	127	C2
Bélapátfalva	H	113	A4
Belcaire	F	146	B2
Bełchatów	PL	86	A3
Belchite	E	153	A4
Belcoo	GB	26	B3
Belecke	D	81	A4
Beled	H	111	B4
Belej	HR	123	C3
Beleño	E	142	A1
Bélesta	F	146	B2
Belevi	TR	188	A2
Belfast	GB	27	B5
Belford	GB	37	A5
Belfort	F	106	B1
Belgentier	F	132	B1
Belgern	D	83	A5
Belgioioso	I	120	B2
Belgodère	F	180	A2
Belgooly	IRL	29	C3
Belgrade = Beograd	SRB	127	C2
Belhade	F	128	B2
Beli Manastir	HR	125	B4
Belica	HR	124	A2
Belin-Bèliet	F	128	B2
Belinchón	E	151	B4
Belišče	HR	125	B4
Bělkovice-Lašt'any	CZ	98	B1
Bell-lloc d'Urgell	E	153	A4
Bella	I	172	B1
Bellac	F	115	B5
Bellágio	I	120	B2
Bellananagh	IRL	27	C3
Bellano	I	120	A2
Bellária	I	136	A1
Bellavary	IRL	26	C1
Belle-Isle-en-Terre	F	100	A2
Belleau	F	90	B3
Belleek	GB	26	B2
Bellegarde, Gard	F	131	B3
Bellegarde, Loiret	F	103	B4
Bellegarde-en-Diois	F	132	A1
Bellegarde-en-Marche	F	116	B2
Bellegarde-sur-Valserine	F	118	A2
Bellême	F	89	B4
Bellenaves	F	116	A3
Bellentre	F	118	B3
Bellevaux	F	118	A3
Bellevesvre	F	105	C4
Belleville	F	117	A4
Belleville-sur-Vie	F	114	B2
Bellevue-la-Montagne	F	117	B3
Belley	F	118	B2
Bellheim	D	93	B4
Bellinge	DK	59	C3
Bellingham	GB	37	A4
Bellinzago Novarese	I	120	B1
Bellinzona	CH	120	A2
Bello	E	152	B2
Bellpuig d'Urgell	E	147	C2
Bellreguart	E	159	C3
Bellsbank	GB	36	A3
Belltall	E	147	C2
Belluno	I	121	A5
Bellver de Cerdanya	E	146	B2
Bellvis	E	147	C1
Bélmez	E	156	B2
Belmez de la Moraleda	E	163	A4
Belmont	GB	33	A6
Belmont-de-la-Loire	F	117	A4
Belmont-sur-Rance	F	130	B1
Belmonte, Asturias	E	141	A4
Belmonte, Cuenca	E	158	B1
Belmonte	P	148	B2
Belmonte de San José	E	153	B3
Belmonte de Tajo	E	151	B4
Belmullet	IRL	26	B1
Belobreşca	RO	127	C3
Beloeil	B	79	B3
Belogradchik	BG	16	D5
Belokorovichi	UA	13	C8
Belorado	E	143	B3
Belotič	SRB	127	C1
Bělotín	CZ	98	B1
Belovo	BG	183	A6
Belozërsk	RUS	9	C10
Belp	CH	106	C2
Belpasso	I	177	B3
Belpech	F	146	A2
Belper	GB	40	B2
Belsay	GB	37	A5
Belsk Duzy	PL	87	A4
Beltinci	SLO	111	C3
Beltra	IRL	26	C1
Belturbet	IRL	27	B3
Beluša	SK	98	B2
Belvedere Marittimo	I	174	B1
Belver de Cinca	E	153	A4
Belver de los Montes	E	142	C1
Belvès	F	129	B3
Belvezet	F	130	A2
Belvis de la Jara	E	150	C3
Belvis de Monroy	E	150	C2
Belyy	RUS	9	E8
Belz	F	100	B2
Bełżec	PL	13	C5
Belzig	D	73	B5
Bembibre	E	141	B4
Bembridge	GB	44	C2
Bemmel	NL	80	A1
Bemposta, Bragança	P	149	A3
Bemposta, Santarém	P	154	B2
Benabarre	E	145	B4
Benacazón	E	161	B3
Benaguacil	E	159	B3
Benahadux	E	164	C2
Benalmádena	E	163	B3
Benalúa de Guadix	E	164	B1
Benalúa de las Villas	E	163	A4
Benalup	E	162	B2
Benamargosa	E	163	B3
Benamaurel	E	164	B2
Benameji	E	163	A3
Benamocarra	E	163	B3
Benaocaz	E	162	B2
Benaoján	E	162	B2
Benarrabá	E	162	B2
Benasque	E	145	B4
Benátky nad Jizerou	CZ	84	B2
Benavente	E	142	B1
Benavente	P	154	C2
Benavides de Órbigo	E	141	B5
Benavila	P	154	B3
Bendorf	D	81	B3
Bene Vagienna	I	133	A3
Benedikt	SLO	110	C2
Benejama	E	159	C3
Benejúzar	E	165	A4
Benešov	CZ	96	B2
Bénestroff	F	92	C2
Benet	F	114	B3
Bénévent-l'Abbaye	F	116	A1
Benevento	I	170	B2
Benfeld	F	93	C3
Benfica	P	154	B2
Bengtsfors	S	54	A3
Bengtsheden	S	50	B2
Beničanci	HR	125	B4
Benicarló	E	153	B4
Benicàssim	E	153	B4
Benidorm	E	159	C3
Benifaió	E	159	B3
Beniganim	E	159	C3
Benington	GB	41	B4
Benisa	E	159	C4
Benkovac	HR	137	A4
Benllech	GB	38	A2
Benneckenstein	D	82	A2
Bénodet	F	100	B1
Benquerencia de la Serena	E	156	B2
Bensafrim	P	160	B1
Bensbyn	S	196	D5
Bensdorf	D	73	B5
Benshausen	D	82	B2
Bensheim	D	93	B4
Bentley	GB	44	B3
Bentwisch	D	65	B5
Beočin	SRB	126	B1
Beograd = Belgrade	SRB	127	C2
Beragh	GB	27	B3
Beranga	E	143	A3
Berat	AL	182	C1
Bérat	F	146	A2
Beratzhausen	D	95	B3
Bérbaltavár	H	111	B3
Berbegal	E	145	C3
Berbenno di Valtellina	I	120	A2
Berberana	E	143	B3
Bercel	H	112	B3
Bercenay-le-Hayer	F	91	C3
Berceto	I	134	A3
Berchem	B	79	B3
Berchidda	I	178	B3
Berching	D	95	B3
Berchtesgaden	D	109	B4
Bérchules	E	163	B4
Bercianos de Aliste	E	149	A3
Berck	F	78	B1
Berclaire d'Urgell	E	147	C1
Berdoias	E	140	A1
Berducedo	E	141	A4
Berdún	E	144	B3
Berdychiv	UA	13	D8
Bere Alston	GB	42	B2
Bere Regis	GB	43	B4
Bereguardo	I	120	B2
Berehommen	N	53	A3
Berehove	UA	16	A5
Berek	BIH	124	B3
Beremend	H	125	B4
Berestechko	UA	13	C6
Berettyóújfalu	H	113	B5
Berezhany	UA	13	D6
Berezivka	UA	17	B9
Berezna	UA	13	C9
Berg	E	95	B3
Berg	N	195	E3
Berg	S	56	B2
Berg im Gau	D	95	C3
Berga, Sachsen-Anhalt	D	82	A3
Berga, Thüringen	D	83	B4
Berga	E	147	B2
Berga	S	62	A4
Bergama	TR	186	C2
Bérgamo	I	120	B2
Bergara	E	143	A4
Bergby	S	51	B4
Berge, Brandenburg	D	74	B1
Berge, Niedersachsen	D	71	B4
Berge, Telemark	N	53	A4
Berge, Telemark	N	53	A4
Bergeforsen	S	200	D3
Bergen, Mecklenburg-Vorpommern	D	66	B2
Bergen, Niedersachsen	D	72	B2
Bergen, Niedersachsen	D	73	B3
Bergen	N	46	B2
Bergen	NL	70	B1
Bergen op Zoom	NL	79	A4
Bergerac	F	129	B3
Bergères-lés-Vertus	F	91	C4
Bergeyk	NL	79	A5
Berghausen	D	93	C4
Bergheim	D	80	B2
Berghem	S	60	B2
Bergisch Gladbach	D	80	B3
Bergkamen	D	81	A3
Bergkvara	S	63	B4
Berglern	D	95	C3
Bergnäset	S	196	D5
Bergneustadt	D	81	A3
Bergs slussar	S	56	B1
Bergsäng	S	49	B5
Bergshamra	S	57	A4
Bergsjö	S	200	E3
Bergsviken	S	196	D4
Bergtheim	D	94	B2
Bergues	F	78	B2
Bergum	NL	70	A2
Bergün Bravuogn	CH	107	C4
Bergwitz	D	83	A4
Berhida	H	112	B2
Beringel	P	160	A2
Beringen	B	79	A5
Berja	E	164	C2
Berkåk	N	199	C7
Berkeley	GB	43	A4
Berkenthin	D	65	C3
Berkhamsted	GB	44	B3
Berkheim	D	107	A5
Berkhof	D	72	B2
Berkovići	BIH	139	B4
Berkovitsa	BG	17	D5
Berlanga	E	156	B2
Berlanga de Duero	E	151	A5
Berlevåg	N	193	B13
Berlikum	NL	70	A2
Berlin	D	74	B2
Berlstedt	D	82	A3
Bermeo	E	143	A4
Bermillo de Sayago	E	149	A3
Bern	CH	106	C2
Bernalda	I	174	A2
Bernardos	E	150	A3
Bernartice, Jihočeský	CZ	96	B2
Bernartice, Vychodočeský	CZ	85	B3
Bernau, Baden-Württemberg	D	106	B2
Bernau, Bayern	D	109	B3
Bernau, Brandenburg	D	74	B2
Bernaville	F	90	A2
Bernay	F	89	A4
Bernburg	D	83	A3
Berndorf	A	111	B3
Berne	D	72	A1
Bernecebaráti	H	112	A2
Bernhardsthal	A	97	C4
Bernkastel-Kues	D	92	B3
Bernolakovo	SK	111	A4
Bernsdorf	D	84	A2
Bernstadt	D	84	A2
Bernstein	A	111	B3
Bernués	E	145	B3
Beromünster	CH	106	B3
Beroun	CZ	96	B2
Berovo	MK	182	B4
Berre-l'Etang	F	131	B4
Berriedale	GB	32	C3
Berriew	GB	39	B3
Berrocal	E	161	B3
Bersenbrück	D	71	B4
Bershad'	UA	13	D8
Berthåga	S	51	C4
Berthelming	F	92	C2
Bertincourt	F	90	A2
Bertinoro	I	135	A5
Bertogne	B	92	A1
Bertrix	B	91	B5
Berufjörður	IS	191	C11
Berville-sur-Mer	F	89	A4
Berwick-upon-Tweed	GB	37	A4
Berzasca	RO	16	C4
Berzence	H	124	A3
Berzocana	E	156	A2
Besalú	E	147	B3
Besançon	F	105	B5
Besenfeld	D	93	C4
Besenyötelek	H	113	B4
Besenyszög	H	113	B4
Beshenkovichi	BY	13	A8
Besigheim	D	93	C5
Běšiny	CZ	96	B1
Beška	SRB	126	B2
Beşkonak	TR	189	B6
Besle	F	101	B4
Besnyö	H	112	B2
Bessais-le-Fromental	F	103	C4
Bessan	F	130	B2
Besse-en-Chandesse	F	116	B2
Bessé-sur-Braye	F	102	B2
Bessèges	F	131	A3
Bessines-sur-Gartempe	F	115	B5
Best	NL	79	A5
Bestorp	S	56	B1
Betanzos	E	140	A2
Betelu	E	144	A2
Bétera	E	159	B3
Beteta	E	152	B1
Béthenville	F	91	B4
Bethesda	GB	38	A2
Béthune	F	78	B2
Beton-Bazoches	F	90	C3
Bettembourg	L	92	B2
Betterdorf	L	92	B2
Bettna	S	56	B2
Béttola	I	120	C2
Bettona	I	136	B1
Bettyhill	GB	32	C2
Betws-y-Coed	GB	38	A3
Betxi	E	159	B3
Betz	F	90	B2
Betzdorf	D	81	B3
Beuil	F	132	A2
Beulah	GB	39	B3
Beuzeville	F	89	A4
Bevagna	I	136	C1
Bevens-bruk	S	56	A1
Beveren	B	79	A4
Beverley	GB	40	B3
Bevern	D	81	A5
Beverstedt	D	72	A1
Beverungen	D	81	A5
Beverwijk	NL	70	B1
Bex	CH	119	A4
Bexhill	GB	45	C4
Beyazköy	TR	186	A2
Beychevelle	F	128	A2
Beydağ	TR	188	A3
Beyeğaç	TR	188	B3
Beykoz	TR	186	A4
Beynat	F	129	A4
Beyoğlu	TR	186	A4
Beypazarı	TR	187	B6
Beyşehir	TR	189	B6
Bezas	E	152	B2
Bezau	A	107	B4
Bezdan	SRB	125	B4
Bèze	F	105	B4
Bezenet	F	116	A2
Bezhetsk	RUS	9	D10
Béziers	F	130	B2
Bezzecca	I	121	B3
Biadki	PL	85	A5
Biała, Łódzkie	PL	77	C4
Biała, Opolskie	PL	85	B5
Biała Podlaska	PL	13	B5
Biała Rawska	PL	87	A4
Białaczów	PL	87	A4
Biale Błota	PL	76	A2
Białobrzegi	PL	87	A4
Białogard	PL	67	C4
Białośliwie	PL	76	A2
Białowąs	PL	68	B1
Biały Bór	PL	68	B1
Białystok	PL	13	B5
Biancavilla	I	177	B3
Bianco	I	175	C2
Biandrate	I	119	B5
Biar	E	159	C3
Biarritz	F	144	A2
Bias	F	128	B1
Biasca	CH	120	A1
Biatorbágy	H	112	B2
Bibbiena	I	135	B4
Bibbona	I	134	B3
Biberach, Baden-Württemberg	D	107	A4
Biberach, Baden-Württemberg	D	93	C4
Bibinje	HR	137	A4
Bibione	I	122	B3
Biblis	D	93	B4
Bibury	GB	44	B2
Bicaj	AL	182	B2
Bíccari	I	171	B3
Bicester	GB	44	B2
Bichl	D	108	B2
Bichlbach	A	108	B1
Bicorp	E	159	B3
Bicos	P	160	B1
Bicske	H	112	B2
Bidache	F	128	C1
Bidart	F	144	A2
Biddinghuizen	NL	70	B2
Biddulph	GB	40	B1
Bideford	GB	42	A2
Bidford-on-Avon	GB	44	A2
Bidjovagge	N	192	C6
Bie	S	56	A2
Bieber	D	81	B5
Biebersdorf	D	74	C2
Biedenkopf	D	81	B4
Biel	CH	106	B2
Biel	E	144	B3
Bielany Wroclawskie	PL	85	A4
Bielawa	PL	85	B4
Bielawy	PL	77	B4
Bielefeld	D	72	B1
Biella	I	119	B5
Bielsa	E	145	B4
Bielsk	PL	77	B4
Bielsk Podlaski	PL	13	B5
Bielsko-Biała	PL	99	B3
Bienenbuttel	D	72	A3
Bieniow	PL	84	A3
Bienservida	E	158	C1
Bienvenida	E	156	B1
Bierdzany	PL	86	B2
Bierné	F	102	B1
Biersted	DK	58	A2
Bierun	PL	86	B3
Bierutów	PL	85	A5
Bierwart	B	79	B5
Bierzwina	PL	75	A4
Bierzwnik	PL	75	A4
Biescas	E	145	B3
Biesenthal	D	74	B2
Biesiekierz	PL	67	B5
Bietigheim-Bissingen	D	93	C5
Bièvre	B	91	B5
Bieżuń	PL	77	B4
Biga	TR	186	B2
Bigadiç	TR	186	C3
Biganos	F	128	B2
Bigas	P	148	B2
Bigastro	E	165	A4
Bigbury	GB	42	B3
Biggar	GB	36	A3
Biggin Hill	GB	45	B4
Biggleswade	GB	44	A3
Bignasco	CH	119	A5
Biguglia	F	180	A2
Bihać	BIH	124	C1
Biharnagybajom	H	113	B5
Bijeljani	BIH	139	B4
Bijeljina	BIH	125	C5
Bijuesca	E	152	A2
Bila Tserkva	UA	13	D9
Bilaj	HR	137	A4
Bilbao	E	143	A4
Bilcza	PL	87	B4
Bíldudalur	IS	190	B2
Bileća	BIH	139	C4
Bilecik	TR	187	B4
Biled	RO	126	B2
Biłgoraj	PL	12	C5
Bilhorod-Dnistrovskyy	UA	17	B9
Bílina	CZ	84	B1
Bilisht	AL	182	C2
Billdal	S	60	B1
Billerbeck	D	71	C4
Billericay	GB	45	B4
Billesholm	S	61	C2
Billingborough	GB	40	C3
Billinge	S	61	D3
Billingham	GB	37	B5
Billinghay	GB	41	B3
Billingsfors	S	54	B3
Billingshurst	GB	44	B3
Billom	F	116	B3
Billsta	S	200	C4
Billund	DK	59	C2
Bílovec	CZ	98	B2
Bilstein	D	81	A4
Bilthoven	NL	70	B2
Bilto	N	192	C5
Bilzen	B	80	B1
Biña	SK	112	B2
Binaced	E	145	C4
Binasco	I	120	B2
Binbrook	GB	41	B3
Binche	B	79	B4
Bindlach	D	95	B3
Bindslev	DK	58	A3
Binefar	E	145	C4
Bingen	D	93	B3
Bingham	GB	40	C3
Bingley	GB	40	B2
Bingsjö	S	50	A2
Binic	F	100	A3
Binz	D	66	B2
Biograd na Moru	HR	137	B4
Bionaz	I	119	B4
Bioska	SRB	127	D1
Birda	RO	126	B3
Birdlip	GB	44	B1
Biri	N	48	B2
Birkeland	N	53	B4
Birkenfeld, Baden-Württemberg	D	93	C4
Birkenfeld, Rheinland-Pfalz	D	92	B3
Birkenhead	GB	38	A3
Birkerød	DK	61	D2
Birkfeld	A	110	B2
Birkirkara	M	175	C3
Birmingham	GB	40	C2
Birr	IRL	28	A4
Birresborn	D	80	B2
Birstein	D	81	B5
Biržai	LT	8	D4
Birzebbuga	M	175	C3
Bisáccia	I	172	A1
Bisacquino	I	176	B2
Bisbal de Falset	E	153	A4
Biscarrosse	F	128	B1
Biscarrosse Plage	F	128	B1
Biscarrués	E	144	B3
Biscéglie	I	171	B4
Bischberg	D	94	B2
Bischofsheim	D	82	B1
Bischofshofen	A	109	B4
Bischofswerda	D	84	A2
Bischofswiesen	D	109	B3
Bischofszell	CH	107	B4
Bischwiller	F	93	C3
Bisenti	I	169	A3
Bishop Auckland	GB	37	B5
Bishop's Castle	GB	39	B4
Bishops Lydeard	GB	43	A3
Bishop's Stortford	GB	45	B4
Bishop's Waltham	GB	44	C2
Bisignano	I	174	B2
Bisingen	D	93	C4
Biskupice-Oławskie	PL	85	A5
Biskupiec	PL	69	B4
Bismark	D	73	B4
Bismo	N	198	D5
Bispgården	S	200	C2
Bispingen	D	72	A2
Bissen	L	92	B2
Bissendorf	D	71	B5
Bisserup	DK	65	A4
Bistango	I	119	C5
Bistarac Donje	BIH	139	A4
Bistrica	BIH	124	C3
Bistrica ob Sotli	SLO	123	A4
Bistriţa	RO	17	B6
Bitburg	D	92	B2
Bitche	F	93	B3
Bitetto	I	171	B4
Bitola	MK	182	B3
Bitonto	I	171	B4
Bitschwiller	F	106	B2
Bitterfeld	D	83	A4
Bitti	I	178	B3
Biville-sur-Mer	F	89	A5
Bivona	I	176	B2
Biwer	L	92	B2
Bizeljsko	SLO	123	A4
Bizovac	HR	125	B4
Bjåen	N	52	A3
Bjärnum	S	61	C3
Bjärred	S	61	D3
Bjästa	S	200	C4
Bjelland, Vest-Agder	N	52	B3
Bjelland, Vest-Agder	N	52	B2
Bjelovar	HR	124	B2
Bjerkreim	N	52	B2
Bjerkvik	N	194	B8
Bjerreby	DK	65	B3
Bjerregrav	DK	58	B2
Bjerringbro	DK	59	B2
Bjøberg	N	47	B5
Bjøllånes	N	195	D5
Björbo	S	50	B1
Bjordal	N	46	A2
Björg	IS	191	B8
Bjørkåsen	N	194	B7
Björke, Gävleborg	S	51	B4
Björke, Östergötland	S	56	B1
Bjørkelangen	N	48	C3
Björketorp	S	60	B2
Björkholmen	S	196	C2
Björklinge	S	51	B4
Björko, Stockholm	S	57	C6
Björkö, Västra Götaland	S	60	B1
Björköby	S	62	A2
Bjørkvik	N	56	B2

Name	Country	Page	Grid
Bjørn	N	195	D3
Björna	S	200	C4
Björneborg	S	55	A5
Björnerod	S	54	A2
Bjørnevatn	N	193	C13
Björnlunda	S	56	A3
Bjørnstad	N	193	C14
Björsäter	S	56	B2
Bjurberget	S	49	B4
Bjurholm	S	200	C5
Bjursås	S	50	B2
Bjurtjärn	S	55	A5
Bjuv	S	61	C2
Blachownia	PL	86	B2
Blackburn	GB	38	A4
Blackpool	GB	38	A3
Blackstad	S	62	A4
Blackwater	IRL	30	B2
Blackwaterfoot	GB	34	C2
Blacy	F	91	C4
Bladåker	S	51	B5
Blaenau Ffestiniog	GB	38	B3
Blaenavon	GB	39	C3
Blaengarw	GB	39	C3
Blagaj	BIH	139	B3
Blagaj	BIH	124	B2
Blagdon	GB	43	A4
Blagnac	F	129	C4
Blagoevgrad	BG	183	A5
Blaichach	D	107	B5
Blain	F	101	B4
Blainville-sur-l'Eau	F	92	C2
Blair Atholl	GB	35	B4
Blairgowrie	GB	35	B4
Blajan	F	145	A4
Blakeney	GB	39	C4
Blakstad	N	53	B4
Blâmont	F	92	C2
Blanca	E	165	A3
Blancos	E	140	C3
Blandford Forum	GB	43	B4
Blanes	E	147	C3
Blangy-sur-Bresle	F	90	B1
Blankaholm	S	62	A4
Blankenberge	B	78	A3
Blankenburg	D	82	A2
Blankenfelde	D	74	B2
Blankenhain	D	82	B3
Blankenheim	D	80	B2
Blanquefort	F	128	B2
Blansko	CZ	97	B4
Blanzac	F	115	C4
Blanzy	F	104	C3
Blaricum	NL	70	B2
Blarney	IRL	29	C3
Blascomillán	E	150	B2
Blascosancho	E	150	B3
Błaszki	PL	86	A2
Blatná	CZ	96	B1
Blatné	SK	111	A4
Blatnice	CZ	98	C1
Blatnika	BIH	139	A3
Blato	HR	138	C2
Blato na Cetini	HR	138	B2
Blatten	CH	119	A4
Blattnicksele	S	195	E8
Blatzheim	D	80	B2
Blaubeuren	D	94	C1
Blaufelden	D	94	B1
Blaustein	D	94	C1
Blaydon	GB	37	B5
Blaye	F	128	A2
Blaye-les-Mines	F	130	A1
Blázquez	E	156	B2
Bleckede	D	73	A3
Blecua	E	145	B3
Bled	SLO	123	A3
Bleiburg	A	110	C1
Bleichenbach	D	81	B5
Bleicherode	D	82	A2
Bleik	N	194	A6
Bleikvassli	N	195	E4
Bléneau	F	104	B1
Blentarp	S	61	D3
Blera	I	168	A2
Blérancourt	F	90	B3
Bléré	F	102	B2
Blesle	F	116	B3
Blessington	IRL	30	A2
Blet	F	103	C4
Bletchley	GB	44	B3
Bletterans	F	105	C4
Blidö	S	57	A4
Blidsberg	S	60	B3
Blieskastel	D	92	B3
Bligny-sur-Ouche	F	104	B3
Blikstorp	S	55	B4
Blinisht	AL	182	B1
Blinja	HR	124	B2
Blizanówek	PL	76	C3
Bliżyn	PL	87	A4
Blois	F	103	B3
Blokhus	DK	58	A2
Blokzijl	NL	70	B2
Blombacka	S	55	A4
Blomberg	D	72	C2
Blomskog	S	54	A3
Blomstermåla	S	62	B4
Blomvåg	N	46	B1
Blönduós	IS	190	B5
Błonie	PL	77	B5
Blonville-sur-Mer	F	89	A4
Blötberget	S	50	B2
Blovice	CZ	96	B1
Bloxham	GB	44	A2
Blšany	CZ	83	B5
Bludenz	A	107	B4
Bludov	CZ	97	B4
Blumberg	D	107	B4
Blyberg	S	49	A6
Blyth, Northumberland	GB	37	A5
Blyth, Nottinghamshire	GB	40	B2
Blyth Bridge	GB	35	C4
Blythburgh	GB	45	A5
Blythe Bridge	GB	40	C1
Bø, Nordland	N	194	B5
Bø, Telemark	N	53	A5
Boa Vista	P	154	B2
Boal	E	141	A4
Boan	MNE	139	C5
Boario Terme	I	120	B3
Boat of Garten	GB	32	D3
Boba	H	111	B4
Bobadilla, Logroño	E	143	B4
Bobadilla, Málaga	E	163	A3
Bobadilla del Campo	E	150	A2
Bobadilla del Monte	E	151	B4
Bóbbio	I	120	C2
Bóbbio Pellice	I	119	C4
Bobigny	F	90	C2
Bobingen	D	94	C2
Böblingen	D	93	C5
Bobolice	PL	68	B1
Boboras	E	140	B2
Boboshevo	BG	182	A4
Bobowa	PL	99	B4
Bobrová	CZ	97	B4
Bobrovitsa	UA	13	C9
Bobrowice	PL	75	C4
Bobrówko	PL	75	B5
Boca de Huérgano	E	142	B2
Bocairent	E	159	C3
Bočar	SRB	126	B2
Bocchigliero	I	174	B2
Boceguillas	E	151	A4
Bochnia	PL	99	B4
Bocholt	B	80	A1
Bocholt	D	80	A2
Bochov	CZ	83	B5
Bochum	D	80	A3
Bockara	S	62	A4
Bockenem	D	72	B3
Bockfliess	A	97	C4
Bockhorn	D	71	A5
Bočna	SLO	123	A3
Bocognano	F	180	A2
Boconád	H	113	B4
Bőcs	H	113	A4
Boczów	PL	75	B3
Boda, Dalarnas	S	50	A2
Böda, Öland	S	62	A5
Boda, Stockholm	S	51	B5
Boda, Värmland	S	55	A4
Boda, Västernorrland	S	200	D2
Boda Glasbruk	S	63	B3
Bodafors	S	62	A2
Bodajk	H	112	B2
Boddam, Aberdeenshire	GB	33	D5
Boddam, Shetland	GB	33	B5
Boddin	D	73	A4
Bödefeld-Freiheit	D	81	A4
Boden	S	196	D4
Bodenmais	D	95	B5
Bodenteich	D	73	B3
Bodenwerder	D	72	C2
Bodiam	GB	45	B4
Bodinnick	GB	42	B2
Bodio	CH	120	A1
Bodjani	SRB	125	B5
Bodmin	GB	42	B2
Bodø	N	194	C5
Bodonal de la Sierra	E	161	A3
Bodrum	TR	188	B2
Bodstedt	D	66	B1
Bodträskfors	S	196	C3
Bodzanów	PL	77	B5
Bodzanowice	PL	86	B2
Bodzechów	PL	87	B5
Bodzentyn	PL	87	B4
Boecillo	E	150	A3
Boëge	F	118	A3
Boën	F	117	B3
Bogács	H	113	B4
Bogadmindszent	H	125	B4
Bogajo	E	149	B3
Bogarra	E	158	C1
Bogarre	E	163	A4
Bogatić	SRB	127	C1
Bogatynia	PL	84	B2
Boğazkale	TR	23	A8
Boğazlıyan	TR	23	B8
Bogda	RO	126	B3
Bogdaniec	PL	75	B4
Boge	S	57	C4
Bogen	D	95	C4
Bogen, Nordland	N	194	C6
Bogen, Nordland	N	194	B7
Bogen	N	49	B4
Bogense	DK	59	C3
Bognanco Fonti	I	119	A5
Bognelv	N	192	B6
Bognes	N	194	B7
Bogno	CH	120	A2
Bognor Regis	GB	44	C3
Bogoria	PL	87	B5
Bograngen	S	49	B4
Boguchwały	PL	69	B5
Bogumiłowice	PL	86	A3
Boguslav	UA	13	D9
Boguszów-Gorce	PL	85	B4
Bogyiszló	H	112	C2
Bohain-en-Vermandois	F	91	B3
Böheimkirchen	A	110	A2
Bohinjska Bistrica	SLO	122	A2
Böhlen	D	83	A4
Böhmenkirch	D	94	C1
Bohmte	D	71	B5
Bohonal de Ibor	E	150	C2
Böhönye	H	124	A3
Bohumín	CZ	98	B2
Boiro	E	140	B2
Bois-d'Amont	F	105	C5
Boisseron	F	131	B3
Boitzenburg	D	74	A2
Boixols	E	147	B2
Boizenburg	D	73	A3
Bojadła	PL	75	C4
Bojano	I	170	B2
Bojanowo	PL	85	A4
Bojderup	DK	64	A3
Bojkovice	CZ	98	B1
Bojná	SK	98	C2
Bojnice	SK	98	C2
Boka	SRB	126	B2
Böklund	D	64	B2
Bokod	H	112	B2
Böksholm	S	62	A2
Boksitogorsk	RUS	9	C8
Bol	HR	138	B2
Bolaños de Calatrava	E	157	B4
Bolayır	TR	186	B1
Bolbec	F	89	A4
Bölcske	H	112	C2
Bolderslev	DK	64	B2
Boldog	H	112	B3
Boldva	H	113	A4
Böle	S	196	D4
Bolea	E	145	B3
Bolekhiv	UA	13	D5
Bolesławiec	PL	84	A3
Boleszkowice	PL	74	B3
Bolewice	PL	75	B5
Bólgheri	I	134	B3
Bolhrad	UA	17	C8
Boliden	S	200	B6
Bolimów	PL	77	B5
Boliqueime	P	160	B1
Boljevci	SRB	127	C2
Boljkovci	SRB	127	C2
Bolków	PL	85	B4
Bollebygd	S	60	B2
Bollène	F	131	A3
Bólliga	E	152	B1
Bollnäs	S	50	A3
Bollstabruk	S	200	D3
Bollullos	E	161	B3
Bollullos par del Condado	E	161	B3
Bologna	I	135	A4
Bologne	F	105	A4
Bolognetta	I	176	B2
Bolognola	I	136	C2
Bologoye	RUS	9	D9
Bolótana	I	178	B2
Bolsena	I	168	A1
Bolshaya Vradiyevka	UA	17	B9
Bolsover	GB	40	B2
Bolstad	S	54	B3
Bolsward	NL	70	A2
Boltaña	E	145	B4
Boltenhagen	D	65	C4
Bolton	GB	38	A4
Bolu	TR	187	B6
Bolungavík	IS	190	A2
Bolvadin	TR	187	D6
Bóly	H	125	B4
Bolzaneto	I	133	A4
Bolzano	I	108	C2
Bomba	I	169	A4
Bombarral	P	154	B1
Bömenzien	D	73	B4
Bomlitz	D	72	B2
Bømlo	N	52	A1
Bon-Encontre	F	129	B3
Bonaduz	CH	107	C4
Bonanza	E	161	C3
Boñar	E	142	B1
Bonarbridge	GB	32	D2
Bonárcado	I	178	B2
Bonares	E	161	B3
Bonäs	S	50	A1
Bonassola	I	134	A2
Bonawe	GB	34	B2
Bondal	N	53	A4
Bondeno	I	121	C4
Bondorf	D	93	C4
Bondstorp	S	60	B3
Bo'ness	GB	35	B4
Bonete	E	158	C2
Bonifacio	F	180	B2
Bonigen	CH	106	C2
Bonin	PL	67	B5
Bonn	D	80	B3
Bonnánaro	I	178	B2
Bonnåsjøen	N	194	C6
Bonnat	F	116	A1
Bonndorf	D	106	B3
Bonnétable	F	102	A2
Bonnétage	F	106	B1
Bonneuil-les-Eaux	F	90	B2
Bonneuil-Matours	F	115	B4
Bonneval	F	103	A3
Bonneval-sur-Arc	F	119	B4
Bonneville	F	118	A3
Bonnières-sur-Seine	F	90	B1
Bonnieux	F	131	B4
Bönnigheim	D	93	B5
Bonny-sur-Loire	F	103	B4
Bonnyrigg	GB	35	C4
Bono	E	145	B4
Bono	I	178	B3
Bonorva	I	178	B2
Bønsnes	N	48	B2
Bonyhád	H	125	A4
Boom	B	79	A4
Boos	F	89	A5
Boostedt	D	64	B3
Bootle, Cumbria	GB	36	B3
Bootle, Merseyside	GB	38	A3
Bopfingen	D	94	C2
Boppard	D	81	B3
Boqueixón	E	140	B2
Bor	CZ	95	B4
Bor	S	62	A2
Bor	SRB	16	C5
Bor	TR	23	C8
Boran-sur-Oise	F	90	B2
Borås	S	60	B2
Borba	P	155	C3
Borbona	I	169	A3
Borča	SRB	127	C2
Borci	BIH	139	B4
Borculo	NL	71	B3
Bordány	H	126	A1
Bordeaux	F	128	B2
Bordeira	P	160	B1
Bordesholm	D	64	B3
Borðeyri	IS	190	B4
Bordighera	I	133	B3
Bording	DK	59	B2
Bordón	E	153	B3
Bore	I	120	C2
Borehamwood	GB	44	B3
Borek Strzeliński	PL	85	B5
Borek Wielkopolski	PL	76	C2
Boreland	GB	36	A3
Borello	I	135	A5
Borensberg	S	56	B1
Borgafjäll	S	199	A12
Borgarnes	IS	190	C4
Borgentreich	D	81	A5
Börger	D	71	B4
Borger	NL	71	B3
Borggård	S	56	B1
Borghamn	S	55	B5
Borghetto di Vara	I	134	A2
Borghetto d'Arróscia	I	133	A3
Borghetto Santo Spirito	I	133	A4
Borgholm	S	62	B4
Borghorst	D	71	B4
Bórgia	I	175	C2
Borgloon	B	79	B5
Børglum	DK	58	A2
Borgo	F	180	A2
Borgo a Mozzano	I	134	B3
Borgo alla Collina	I	135	B4
Borgo Pace	I	135	B5
Borgo San Dalmazzo	I	133	A3
Borgo San Lorenzo	I	135	B4
Borgo Val di Taro	I	134	A2
Borgo Valsugana	I	121	A4
Borgomanero	I	119	B5
Borgomasino	I	119	B4
Borgonovo Val Tidone	I	120	B2
Borgorose	I	169	A3
Borgosésia	I	119	B5
Borgstena	S	60	B3
Borgue	GB	36	B3
Borgund	N	47	A4
Borgvik	S	55	A3
Borja	E	144	C2
Bork	D	80	A3
Borken	D	80	A2
Borkenes	N	194	B7
Borkowice	PL	87	A4
Borkowo	PL	77	B5
Borkum	D	71	A4
Borlänge	S	50	B2
Borlu	TR	186	D3
Bormes-les-Mimosas	F	132	B2
Bórmio	I	107	C5
Bormujos	E	161	B3
Borna	D	83	A4
Borne	NL	71	B3
Borne Sulinowo	PL	68	B1
Bornes	P	149	A2
Bornheim	D	80	B2
Bornhöved	D	64	B3
Börnicke	D	74	B1
Bornos	E	162	B2
Borobia	E	152	A2
Borodino	RUS	9	E9
Borohrádek	CZ	85	B4
Boronów	PL	86	B2
Bórore	I	178	B2
Boroszów	PL	86	B2
Borota	H	126	A1
Boroughbridge	GB	40	A2
Borovany	CZ	96	C2
Borovichi	RUS	9	C8
Borovnica	SLO	123	B3
Borovo	HR	125	B4
Borovsk	RUS	9	E10
Borovy	CZ	96	B1
Borowa	PL	85	A5
Borox	E	151	B4
Borrby	S	66	A3
Borre	DK	65	B5
Borre	N	54	A1
Borredá	E	147	B2
Borrenes	E	141	B4
Borriol	E	159	A3
Borris	DK	59	C1
Borris	IRL	30	B2
Borris-in-Ossory	IRL	28	B4
Borrisokane	IRL	28	B3
Borrisoleigh	IRL	28	B4
Borrowdale	GB	36	B3
Børrud	N	49	C4
Borşa	RO	17	B6
Borsdorf	D	83	A4
Børselv	N	193	B9
Borsfa	H	111	C3
Borský Mikuláš	SK	98	C1
Borsodivánka	H	113	B4
Borsodnádasd	H	113	A4
Bort-les-Orgues	F	116	B2
Börte	N	53	A4
Börtnan	S	199	C10
Børtnes	N	47	B6
Boruja Kościelne	PL	75	B5
Borup	DK	61	D1
Boryslav	UA	13	D5
Boryspil	UA	13	C9
Boryszyn	PL	75	B4
Borzęciczki	PL	85	A5
Borzęcin	PL	77	B5
Borzonasca	I	134	A2
Borzyszkowy	PL	68	A2
Borzytuchom	PL	68	A2
Bosa	I	178	B2
Bosáca	SK	98	C1
Bosanci	HR	123	B4
Bosanska Dubica	BIH	124	B2
Bosanska Gradiška	BIH	124	B3
Bosanska Kostajnica	BIH	124	B2
Bosanska Krupa	BIH	124	C2
Bosanski Brod	BIH	125	B3
Bosanski Novi	BIH	124	B2
Bosanski Petrovac	BIH	124	C2
Bosanski Šamac	BIH	125	B4
Bosansko Grahovo	BIH	138	A2
Bošány	SK	98	C2
Bosárkány	H	111	B4
Bosau	D	65	B3
Bósca	H	112	C3
Boscastle	GB	42	B2
Bosco	I	120	C1
Bosco Chiesanuova	I	121	B4
Bösdorf	D	65	B3
Bösel	D	71	A4
Bosham	GB	44	C3
Bösingfeld	D	72	B2
Bosjön	S	49	C5
Boskoop	NL	70	B1
Boskovice	CZ	97	B4
Bošnjaci	HR	125	B4
Bošnjane	SRB	127	C2
Bossast	E	145	B4
Bossolasco	I	133	A4
Boštanj	SLO	123	A4
Bostrak	N	53	B4
Böszénfa	H	125	A3
Bot	E	153	A4
Botajica	BIH	125	C4
Bőte By	DK	65	B4
Bothel	GB	36	B3
Boticas	P	148	A2
Botilsäter	S	55	A4
Botngård	N	198	B6
Botoš	SRB	126	B2
Botoşani	RO	17	B7
Botricello	I	175	C2
Botsmark	S	200	B6
Bottendorf	D	81	A4
Bottesford	GB	40	C3
Bottnaryd	S	60	B3
Bottrop	D	80	A2
Botunje	SRB	127	C3
Bötzingen	D	106	A2
Bouaye	F	101	B4
Bouça	P	149	A2
Boucau	F	128	C1
Bouchain	F	78	B3
Bouchoir	F	90	B2
Boudreville	F	105	B3
Boudry	CH	106	C1
Bouesse	F	103	C3
Bouguenais	F	101	B4
Bouhy	F	104	B2
Bouillargues	F	131	B3
Bouillon	B	91	B5
Bouilly	F	104	A2
Bouin	F	114	B2
Boulay-Moselle	F	92	B2
Boulazac	F	129	A3
Boule-d'Amont	F	146	B3
Bouligny	F	92	B1
Boulogne-sur-Gesse	F	145	A4
Boulogne-sur-Mer	F	78	B1
Bouloire	F	102	B2
Bouquemaison	F	78	B2
Bourbon-Lancy	F	104	C2
Bourbon-l'Archambault	F	104	C2
Bourbonne-les-Bains	F	105	B4
Bourbourg	F	78	B2
Bourbriac	F	100	A2
Bourcefranc-le-Chapus	F	114	C2
Bourdeaux	F	131	A4
Bouresse	F	115	B4
Bourg	F	128	A2
Bourg-Achard	F	89	A4
Bourg-Argental	F	117	B4
Bourg-de-Péage	F	117	B5
Bourg-de-Thizy	F	117	A4
Bourg-de-Visa	F	129	B3
Bourg-en-Bresse	F	118	A2
Bourg-et-Comin	F	91	B3
Bourg-Lastic	F	116	B2
Bourg-Madame	F	146	B2
Bourg-St. Andéol	F	131	A3
Bourg-St. Maurice	F	119	B3
Bourganeuf	F	116	B1
Bourges	F	103	B4
Bourgneuf-en-Retz	F	114	A2
Bourgogne	F	91	B4
Bourgoin-Jallieu	F	118	B2
Bourgtheroulde	F	89	A4
Bourgueil	F	102	B2
Bourmont	F	105	A4
Bourne	GB	40	C3
Bournemouth	GB	43	B5
Bourneville	F	89	A4
Bournezeau	F	114	B2
Bourran	F	129	B3
Bourret	F	129	C4
Bourron-Marlotte	F	90	C2
Bourton-on-The-Water	GB	44	B2
Boussac	F	116	A2
Boussens	F	145	A4
Boutersem	F	79	B4
Bouttencourt	F	90	B1
Bouvières	F	131	A4
Bouvron	F	101	B4
Bouxwiller	F	93	C3
Bouzas	E	140	B2
Bouzonville	F	92	B2
Bova	I	175	D1
Bova Marina	I	175	D1
Bovalino Marina	I	175	C2
Bovallstrand	S	54	B2
Bóveda	E	141	B3
Bovegno	I	120	B3
Bovenau	D	64	B2
Bøverdal	N	198	D5
Bóves	F	133	A3
Bovey Tracey	GB	43	B3
Bovino	I	171	B3
Bøvlingbjerg	DK	58	B1
Bovolenta	I	121	B4
Bovolone	I	121	B4
Bowes	GB	37	B5
Bowmore	GB	34	C1
Bowness-on-Windermere	GB	36	B4
Box	GB	43	A4
Boxberg, Baden-Württemberg	D	94	B1
Boxberg, Sachsen	D	84	A2
Boxholm	S	55	B6
Boxmeer	NL	80	A1
Boxtel	NL	79	A5

232

Name	Ctry	Pg	Grid
Boyabat	TR	23	A8
Boyalıca	TR	187	B4
Boyle	IRL	26	C2
Bozan	TR	187	C6
Božava	HR	137	A3
Bozburun	TR	188	C3
Bozcaada	TR	186	C1
Bozdoğan	TR	188	B3
Bożepole Wielkie	PL	68	A2
Boževac	SRB	127	C2
Boži Dar	CZ	83	B4
Božice	CZ	97	C4
Bozkır	TR	189	B7
Bozouls	F	130	A1
Bozova	TR	189	B5
Bozüyük	TR	187	C5
Bózzolo	I	121	B4
Bra	I	119	C4
Braås	S	62	A3
Brabrand	DK	59	B3
Bracadale	GB	31	B2
Bracciano	I	168	A2
Bracieux	F	103	B3
Bräcke	S	199	C12
Brackenheim	D	93	B5
Brackley	GB	44	A2
Bracklin	IRL	27	C4
Bracknell	GB	44	B3
Brackwede	D	72	C1
Braco	GB	35	B4
Brad	RO	16	B5
Bradford	GB	40	B2
Bradford on Avon	GB	43	A4
Bradina	BIH	139	B4
Brådland	N	52	B2
Brae	GB	33	A5
Brædstrup	DK	59	C2
Braemar	GB	32	D3
Braemore	GB	32	D1
Braga	P	148	A1
Bragança	P	149	A3
Brăila	RO	17	C7
Braine	F	91	B3
Braine-le-Comte	B	79	B4
Braintree	GB	45	B4
Braives	B	79	B5
Brake	D	72	A1
Brakel	B	79	B3
Brakel	D	81	A5
Bräkne-Hoby	S	63	B3
Brålanda	S	54	B3
Bralin	PL	86	A1
Brallo di Pregola	I	120	C2
Bram	F	146	A3
Bramafan	F	132	B2
Bramberg am Wildkogel	A	109	B3
Bramdrupdam	DK	59	C2
Bramming	DK	59	C1
Brampton	GB	37	B4
Bramsche	D	71	B4
Branca	I	136	B1
Brancaleone Marina	I	175	D2
Brancaster	GB	41	C4
Brand, Nieder Österreich	A	96	C3
Brand, Vorarlberg	A	107	B4
Brand-Erbisdorf	D	83	B5
Brandbu	N	48	B2
Brande	DK	59	C2
Brande-Hornerkirchen	D	64	C2
Brandenberg	A	108	B2
Brandenburg	D	73	B5
Brandis	D	83	A4
Brando	F	180	A2
Brandomil	E	140	A2
Brandon	GB	45	B4
Brandshagen	D	66	B2
Brandval	N	49	B4
Brandýs nad Labem	CZ	84	B2
Branice	PL	98	A1
Braničevo	SRB	127	C2
Braniewo	PL	69	A4
Branik	SLO	122	B2
Brankovina	SRB	127	C1
Branky	CZ	98	B1
Branne	F	128	B2
Brannenburg-Degerndorf	D	108	B3
Brantôme	F	115	C4
Branzi	I	120	A2
Bras d'Asse	F	132	B2
Braskereidfoss	N	48	B3
Braslaw	BY	13	A7
Brașov	RO	17	C6
Brasparts	F	100	A2
Brassac, Charente	F	115	C3
Brassac, Tarn	F	130	B1
Brassac-les-Mines	F	116	B3
Brasschaat	B	79	A4
Brastad	S	54	B2
Břasy	CZ	96	B1
Brąszewice	PL	86	A2
Bratislava	SK	111	A4
Brattfors	S	55	A5
Brattvåg	N	198	C3
Bratunac	BIH	127	C1
Braubach	D	81	B3
Braunau	A	95	C4
Braunfels	D	81	B4
Braunlage	D	82	A2
Braunsbedra	D	83	A3
Braunschweig	D	73	B3
Bray	IRL	30	A2
Bray Dunes	F	78	A2
Bray-sur-Seine	F	90	C3
Bray-sur-Somme	F	90	B2
Brazatortas	E	157	B3
Brazey-en-Plaine	F	105	B4
Brbinj	HR	137	A4
Brčko	BIH	125	C4
Brdani	SRB	127	D2
Brdów	PL	76	B3
Brea de Tajo	E	151	B4
Brécey	F	88	B2
Brechen	D	81	B4
Brechin	GB	35	B5
Brecht	B	79	A4
Brecketfeld	D	80	A3
Břeclav	CZ	97	C4
Brecon	GB	39	C3
Brécy	F	103	B4
Breda	E	147	C3
Breda	NL	79	A4
Bredaryd	S	60	B3
Bredbyn	S	200	C4
Breddin	D	73	B5
Bredebro	DK	64	A1
Bredelar	D	81	A4
Bredenfelde	D	74	A2
Bredsjö	S	50	C1
Bredstedt	D	64	B1
Bredsten	DK	59	C2
Bredträsk	S	200	C4
Bredviken	S	195	D5
Bree	B	80	A1
Bregana	HR	123	B4
Breganze	I	121	B4
Bregenz	A	107	B4
Bréhal	F	88	B2
Brehna	D	83	A4
Breidenbach	F	93	B3
Breiðdalsvík	IS	191	C11
Breil-sur-Roya	F	133	B3
Breisach	D	106	A2
Breitenbach	CH	106	B2
Breitenbach	D	81	B5
Breitenberg	D	96	C1
Breitenfelde	D	73	A3
Breitengussbach	D	94	B2
Breivikbotn	N	192	B6
Brejning	DK	59	C2
Brekke	N	46	A2
Brekken	N	199	C8
Brekkestø	N	53	B4
Brekkvasselv	N	199	A10
Brekstad	N	198	B6
Breland	N	53	B2
Brem-sur-Mer	F	114	B2
Bremanger	N	198	D1
Bremen	D	72	A1
Bremerhaven	D	72	A1
Bremervörde	D	72	A2
Bremgarten	CH	106	B3
Bremnes	N	198	B4
Bremsnes	N	198	B4
Brenderup	DK	59	C2
Brenes	E	162	A2
Brengova	SLO	110	C2
Brenna	PL	98	B2
Breno	I	120	B3
Brénod	F	118	A2
Brensbach	D	93	B4
Brentwood	GB	45	B4
Brescello	I	121	C3
Bréscia	I	120	B3
Breskens	NL	79	A3
Bresles	F	90	B2
Bresnica	SRB	127	D2
Bressana	I	120	B2
Bressanone	I	108	C2
Bressuire	F	102	C1
Brest	BY	13	B5
Brest	F	100	A1
Brest	HR	122	B2
Brestač	SRB	127	C1
Brestanica	SLO	123	A4
Brestova	HR	123	B3
Brestovac	HR	125	B3
Bretenoux	F	129	B4
Breteuil, Eure	F	89	B4
Breteuil, Oise	F	90	B2
Brétigny-sur-Orge	F	90	C2
Bretten	D	93	B4
Bretteville-sur-Laize	F	89	A3
Brettheim	D	94	B2
Breuil-Cervínia	I	119	B4
Breukelen	NL	70	B2
Brevik	N	53	A5
Brevik, Stockholm	S	57	A4
Brevik, Västra Götaland	S	55	B5
Breza	BIH	139	A4
Brežice	SLO	123	B4
Bréziers	F	132	A2
Breznica	HR	124	A2
Breznica Našička	HR	125	B4
Březnice	CZ	96	B1
Brezno	SK	99	C3
Březová nad Svitavou	CZ	97	B4
Brezová pod Bradlom	SK	98	C1
Brezovica	SK	99	B4
Brezovica	SLO	123	A3
Brezovo Polje Selo	BIH	125	C4
Briançon	F	118	C3
Brianconnet	F	132	B2
Briare	F	103	B4
Briatexte	F	129	C4
Briático	I	175	C2
Briaucourt	F	105	A4
Bribir	HR	123	B3
Bricquebec	F	88	A2
Bridge of Cally	GB	35	B4
Bridge of Don	GB	33	D4
Bridge of Earn	GB	35	B4
Bridge of Orchy	GB	34	B3
Bridgend, Argyll & Bute	GB	34	C1
Bridgend, Bridgend	GB	39	C3
Bridgnorth	GB	39	B4
Bridgwater	GB	43	A4
Břidličná	CZ	98	B1
Bridlington	GB	41	A3
Bridport	GB	43	B4
Brie-Comte-Robert	F	90	C2
Briec	F	100	A1
Brienne-le-Château	F	91	C4
Brienon-sur-Armançon	F	104	B2
Brienz	CH	106	C3
Brienza	I	172	B1
Briesen	D	74	B3
Brieskow Finkenheerd	D	74	B3
Brietlingen	D	72	A3
Brieva de Cameros	E	143	B4
Briey	F	92	B1
Brig	CH	119	A5
Brigg	GB	40	B3
Brighouse	GB	40	B2
Brightlingsea	GB	45	B5
Brighton	GB	44	C3
Brignogan-Plage	F	100	A1
Brignoles	F	132	B2
Brigstock	GB	40	C3
Brihuega	E	151	B5
Brijuni	HR	122	C2
Brillon-en-Barrois	F	91	C5
Brilon	D	81	A4
Brimnes	N	46	B3
Brinches	P	160	A2
Bríndisi	I	173	B3
Brinje	HR	123	B4
Brinon-sur-Beuvron	F	104	B2
Brinon-sur-Sauldre	F	103	B4
Brinyan	GB	33	B3
Brión	E	140	B2
Briones	E	143	B4
Brionne	F	89	A4
Brioude	F	117	B3
Brioux-sur-Boutonne	F	115	B3
Briouze	F	89	B3
Briscous	F	144	A2
Brisighella	I	135	A4
Brissac-Quincé	F	102	B1
Brissago	CH	120	A1
Bristol	GB	43	A4
Brive-la-Gaillarde	F	129	A4
Briviesca	E	143	B3
Brixham	GB	43	B3
Brixlegg	A	108	B2
Brjánslækur	IS	190	B2
Brka	BIH	125	C4
Brnaze	HR	138	B2
Brněnec	CZ	97	B4
Brno	CZ	97	B4
Bro	S	57	A3
Broad Haven	GB	39	C1
Broadclyst	GB	43	B3
Broadford	GB	31	B3
Broadford	IRL	28	B3
Broadstairs	GB	45	B5
Broadstone	GB	43	B4
Broadway	GB	44	A2
Broager	DK	64	B2
Broaryd	S	60	B3
Broby	S	61	C3
Brobyværk	DK	59	C3
Bročanac	BIH	138	B3
Brocas	F	128	B2
Brock	D	71	B4
Brockel	D	72	A2
Brockenhurst	GB	44	C2
Broczyno	PL	75	A5
Brod	MK	182	B3
Brod na Kupi	HR	123	B3
Brodalen	S	54	B2
Broddbo	S	50	B3
Brodek u Přerova	CZ	98	B1
Broden-bach	D	80	B3
Brodick	GB	34	C2
Brodnica	PL	69	B4
Brodnica Graniczna	PL	68	A3
Brodowe Łąki	PL	77	A6
Brody, Lubuskie	PL	84	A2
Brody, Lubuskie	PL	75	B4
Brody, Mazowieckie	PL	77	B5
Brody	UA	13	C6
Broglie	F	89	B4
Brójce	PL	75	B4
Brokind	S	56	B1
Brolo	I	177	A3
Brome	D	73	B3
Bromley	GB	45	B4
Bromölla	S	63	B2
Bromont-Lamothe	F	116	B2
Brömsebro	S	63	B3
Bromsgrove	GB	44	A1
Bromyard	GB	39	B4
Bronchales	E	152	B2
Bronco	E	149	B3
Brønderslev	DK	58	A2
Broni	I	120	B2
Brønnøysund	N	195	E3
Brøns	DK	59	C1
Bronte	I	177	B3
Bronzani Mejdan	BIH	124	C2
Bronzolo	I	121	A4
Broons	F	101	A3
Broquies	F	130	A1
Brora	GB	32	C3
Brørup	DK	59	C2
Brösarp	S	63	C2
Brostrud	N	47	B5
Brotas	P	154	C2
Brötjärna	S	50	B2
Broto	E	145	B3
Brottby	S	57	A4
Brøttum	N	48	A2
Brou	F	103	A3
Brouage	F	114	C2
Brough	GB	37	B4
Broughshane	GB	27	B4
Broughton	GB	35	C4
Broughton-in-Furness	GB	36	B3
Broumov	CZ	85	B4
Broût-Vernet	F	116	A3
Brouvelieures	F	106	A1
Brouwershaven	NL	79	A3
Brovary	UA	13	C9
Brovst	DK	58	A2
Brownhills	GB	40	C2
Brozas	E	155	B4
Brozzo	I	120	B3
Brtnice	CZ	97	B3
Brtonigla	HR	122	B2
Bruay-la-Buissière	F	78	B2
Bruchhausen-Vilsen	D	72	B2
Bruchsal	D	93	B4
Bruck, Bayern	D	95	B4
Brück, Brandenburg	D	74	B2
Bruck an der Grossglocknerstrasse	A	109	B3
Bruck an der Leitha	A	111	A3
Bruck an der Mur	A	110	B2
Brückl	A	110	C1
Bruckmühl	D	108	B2
Brue-Auriac	F	132	B1
Brüel	D	65	C4
Bruen	CH	107	C3
Bruère-Allichamps	F	103	C4
Bruff	IRL	29	B3
Bruflat	N	47	B6
Brugg	CH	106	B3
Brugge	B	78	A3
Brüggen	D	80	A2
Brühl	D	80	B2
Bruinisse	NL	79	A4
Brûlon	F	102	B1
Brumano	I	120	B1
Brumath	F	93	C3
Brummen	NL	70	B3
Brumov-Bylnice	CZ	98	B2
Brumunddal	N	48	B2
Brunau	D	73	B4
Brunehamel	F	91	B4
Brünen	D	80	A2
Brunete	E	151	B3
Brunflo	S	199	B11
Brunico	I	108	C2
Brunkeberg	N	53	A4
Brunn	D	74	A2
Brunnen	CH	107	C3
Brunsbüttel	D	64	C2
Brunssum	NL	80	B1
Bruntál	CZ	98	B1
Brušane	HR	137	A4
Brusasco	I	119	B5
Brusio	CH	120	A5
Brusno	SK	99	C3
Brusque	F	130	B1
Brussel = Brussels	B	79	B4
Brüssow	D	74	A3
Brusy	PL	68	B2
Bruton	GB	43	A4
Bruvno	HR	138	A1
Bruvoll	N	48	B3
Bruxelles = Brussels	B	79	B4
Bruyères	F	106	A1
Bruz	F	101	A4
Bruzaholm	S	62	A3
Brwinów	PL	77	B5
Brynamman	GB	39	C3
Bryncrug	GB	39	B2
Bryne	N	52	B1
Brynmawr	GB	39	C3
Bryrup	DK	59	B2
Brzeg	PL	85	B5
Brzeg Dolny	PL	85	A4
Brześć Kujawski	PL	76	B3
Brzesko	PL	99	B4
Brzeszcze	PL	99	B3
Brzezie	PL	68	B1
Brzeziny, Łódzkie	PL	87	A3
Brzeziny, Wielkopolskie	PL	86	A2
Brzeźnica	PL	84	A3
Brzeźnica Nowa	PL	86	A3
Brzeźno	PL	75	A4
Brzotin	SK	99	C4
Brzozie Lubawskie	PL	69	B4
Bua	S	60	B2
Buarcos	P	148	B1
Buaveg	N	52	A1
Bubbio	I	119	C5
Bubry	F	100	B2
Buca	TR	188	A2
Bucak	TR	189	B5
Bučany	SK	98	C1
Buccheri	I	177	B3
Buccino	I	172	B1
Bucelas	P	154	C1
Buch, Bayern	D	94	C2
Buch, Bayern	D	95	C4
Buchach	UA	13	D6
Bucharest = Bucureşti	RO	17	C7
Buchbach	D	95	C4
Buchboden	A	107	B4
Buchen, Baden-Württemberg	D	94	B1
Büchen, Schleswig-Holstein	D	73	A3
Buchenberg	D	107	B5
Buchères	F	104	B3
Buchholz	D	72	A2
Buchloe	D	108	A1
Buchlovice	CZ	98	B1
Buchlyvie	GB	34	B3
Bucholz	D	73	A5
Buchs	CH	107	B4
Buchy	F	89	A5
Bückeburg	D	72	B2
Buckfastleigh	GB	42	B3
Buckhaven	GB	35	B4
Buckie	GB	33	D4
Buckingham	GB	44	A3
Buckley	GB	38	A3
Bučovice	CZ	97	B5
Bucsa	H	113	B5
Bucureşti = Bucharest	RO	17	C7
Bucy-lés-Pierreport	F	91	B3
Buczek	PL	86	A3
Bud	N	198	C3
Budakalasz	H	112	B3
Budakeszi	H	112	B2
Budal	N	199	C7
Budaörs	H	112	B2
Budapest	H	112	B3
Búðardalur	IS	190	B4
Budča	SK	99	C3
Buddusò	I	178	B3
Bude	GB	42	B2
Budeč	CZ	97	B3
Büdelsdorf	D	64	B2
Budens	P	160	B1
Büderich	D	80	A2
Budia	E	151	B5
Budimlić-Japra	BIH	124	C2
Büdingen	D	81	B5
Budinšćina	HR	124	A2
Budišov	CZ	98	B1
Budleigh Salterton	GB	43	B3
Budmerice	SK	98	C1
Budoni	I	178	B3
Búdrio	I	135	A4
Budva	MNE	16	D3
Budyně nad Ohří	CZ	84	B2
Budziszewice	PL	87	A3
Budzyń	PL	76	B1
Bue	S	52	B1
Bueña	E	152	B2
Buenache de Alarcón	E	158	B1
Buenache de la Sierra	E	152	B2
Buenaventura	E	150	B3
Buenavista de Valdavia	E	142	B2
Buendia	E	151	B5
Bueu	E	140	B2
Bugac	H	112	B3
Bugarra	E	159	B3
Bugeat	F	116	B2
Buggerru	I	179	C2
Bugojno	BIH	138	A3
Bugøyfjord	N	193	C13
Bugøynes	N	193	C13
Bugyi	H	112	B3
Buharkent	TR	188	B3
Bühl, Baden-Württemberg	D	93	C4
Bühl, Bayern	D	107	B5
Bühlertal	D	93	C4
Bühlertann	D	94	B1
Buia	I	122	A2
Builth Wells	GB	39	B3
Buk	N	47	B6
Buis-les-Baronnies	F	131	A4
Buitenpost	NL	70	A3
Buitrago del Lozoya	E	151	B4
Bujalance	E	157	A3
Bujaraloz	E	153	A3
Buje	HR	122	B2
Bujedo	E	143	B3
Bük	H	111	B3
Buk	PL	75	B5
Bükkösd	H	125	A3
Bükkzsérc	H	113	B4
Bukovci	SLO	124	A1
Bukowiec	PL	75	B5
Bukowina Tatrzańska	PL	99	B4
Bukownica	PL	86	A2
Bukowno	PL	86	B3
Bülach	CH	107	B3
Búland	IS	191	D7
Buldan	TR	188	A3
Bulgnéville	F	105	A4
Bulgurca	TR	188	A2
Bülkau	D	64	C1
Bulken	N	46	B3
Bulkowo	PL	77	B5
Bullas	E	164	A3
Bulle	CH	106	C2
Büllingen	B	80	B2
Bullmark	S	200	B6
Bulqizë	AL	182	B2
Buna	BIH	139	B3
Bunahowen	IRL	26	B1
Bunbeg	IRL	26	A2
Bunclody	IRL	30	B2
Buncrana	IRL	27	A3
Bunde, Niedersachsen	D	71	A4
Bünde, Nordrhein-Westfalen	D	72	B1
Bundoran	IRL	26	B2
Bunessan	GB	34	B1
Bungay	GB	45	A5
Bunge	S	57	C5
Bunić	HR	123	C4
Bunmahon	IRL	30	B1
Bunnyconnellan	IRL	26	B1
Buño	E	140	A2
Buñol	E	159	B3
Bunratty	IRL	29	B3
Bunsbeek	B	79	B4
Buñuel	E	144	C2
Bunyola	E	166	B2
Buonabitácolo	I	172	B1
Buonalbergo	I	170	B2
Buonconvento	I	135	B4
Buonvicino	I	174	B1
Burano	I	122	B1
Burbach	D	81	B4
Burcei	I	179	C3
Burdons-sur-Rognon	F	105	A4
Burdur	TR	189	B5
Bureå	S	2	D7
Burela	E	141	A3
Büren	D	81	A4
Büren an der Aare	CH	106	B2
Burford	GB	44	B2
Burg, Cottbus	D	84	A2
Burg, Magdeburg	D	73	B4
Burg, Schleswig-Holstein	D	64	C2
Burg auf Fehmarn	D	65	B4
Burg Stargard	D	74	A2
Burgas	BG	17	D7
Burgau	A	111	B3
Burgau	D	94	C2
Burgau	P	160	B1
Burgbernheim	D	94	B2
Burgdorf	CH	106	B2
Burgdorf	D	72	B3
Burgebrach	D	94	B2
Bürgel	D	83	B3
Burgess Hill	GB	44	C3
Burghaslach	D	94	B2
Burghausen	D	109	A3
Burghead	GB	32	D3
Burgheim	D	94	C3
Búrgio	I	176	B2
Burgkirchen	A	109	A3
Burgkunstadt	D	82	B3
Burglengenfeld	D	95	B4
Burgo	P	148	B1
Burgoberbach	D	94	B2
Burgohondo	E	150	B3
Burgos	E	143	B3
Burgsinn	D	82	B1
Burgstädt	D	83	B4
Burgstall	D	73	B4
Burgsvik	S	57	C4
Burgui	E	144	B3

Name		Page	Grid
Burguillos	E	162	A2
Burguillos de Toledo	E	151	C4
Burguillos del Cerro	E	155	C4
Burhaniye	TR	186	C1
Burhave	D	71	A5
Burie	F	114	C3
Burjassot	E	159	B3
Burk	D	94	B2
Burkhardtsdorf	D	83	B4
Burlada	E	144	B2
Burladingen	D	107	A4
Burlage	D	71	A4
Burness	GB	33	B4
Burnham	GB	44	B3
Burnham Market	GB	41	C4
Burnham-on-Crouch	GB	45	B4
Burnham-on-Sea	GB	43	A4
Burniston	GB	40	A3
Burnley	GB	40	B1
Burntisland	GB	35	B4
Burón	E	142	A1
Buronzo	I	119	B5
Burovac	SRB	127	C3
Burow	D	74	A2
Burravoe	GB	33	A5
Burrel	AL	182	B2
Burret	F	146	B2
Burriana	E	159	B3
Burry Port	GB	39	C2
Bürs	A	107	B4
Bursa	TR	186	B4
Burseryd	S	60	B3
Bürstadt	D	93	B4
Burton	GB	37	B4
Burton Agnes	GB	41	A4
Burton Bradstock	GB	43	B4
Burton Latimer	GB	44	A3
Burton upon Stather	GB	40	B3
Burton upon Trent	GB	40	C2
Burträsk	S	200	B6
Burujón	E	151	C3
Burwell	GB	45	A4
Burwick	GB	33	C4
Bury	GB	40	B1
Bury St. Edmunds	GB	45	A4
Burzenin	PL	86	A2
Busachi	I	179	B2
Busalla	I	134	A1
Busana	I	134	A3
Busano	I	119	B4
Busca	I	133	A3
Busch	D	73	B4
Buševec	HR	124	B2
Bushat	AL	182	B1
Bushey	GB	44	B3
Bushmills	GB	27	A4
Bušince	SK	112	A3
Buskhyttan	S	56	B2
Busko-Zdrój	PL	87	B4
Busot	E	159	C3
Busovača	BIH	139	A3
Busquistar	E	163	B4
Bussang	F	106	B1
Busseto	I	120	C3
Bussière-Badil	F	115	C4
Bussière-Poitevine	F	115	B4
Bussolengo	I	121	B3
Bussoleno	I	119	B4
Bussum	NL	70	B2
Busto Arsízio	I	120	B1
Büsum	D	64	B1
Butera	I	177	B3
Butgenbach	B	80	B2
Butler's Bridge	IRL	27	B3
Butryny	PL	77	A5
Bütschwil	CH	107	B4
Buttermere	GB	36	B3
Buttevant	IRL	29	B3
Buttle	S	57	C4
Buttstädt	D	82	A3
Butzbach	D	81	B4
Bützfleth	D	72	A2
Bützow	D	65	C4
Buxières-les-Mines	F	104	C1
Buxtehude	D	72	A2
Buxton	GB	40	B2
Buxy	F	104	C3
Büyükçekmece	TR	186	A3
Büyükkarıştıran	TR	186	A2
Büyükorhan	TR	186	C3
Buzancais	F	103	C3
Buzancy	F	91	B4
Buzău	RO	17	C7
Buzet	HR	122	B2
Buziaş	RO	126	B3
Buzsák	H	111	C4
Buzy	F	145	A3
By	S	50	B3
Byala	BG	17	D6
Byaroza	BY	13	B6
Byczyna	PL	86	A2
Bydalen	S	199	B10
Bydgoszcz	PL	76	A3
Bygdin	N	47	A5
Bygdsiljum	S	200	B6
Bygland	N	53	B3
Byglandsfjord	N	53	B3
Bygstad	N	46	A2
Bykhaw	BY	13	B9
Bykle	N	52	A3
Bylderup-Bov	DK	64	B2
Byrkjedal	N	52	B2
Byrkjelo	N	198	D3
Byrum	DK	58	A3
Byšice	CZ	84	B2
Byske	S	2	D7
Býškovice	CZ	98	B1
Bysław	PL	76	A2
Bystré	CZ	97	B4
Bystřice, *Středočeský*	CZ	98	B2
Bystřice, *Středočeský*	CZ	96	B2
Bystřice nad Pernštejnem	CZ	97	B4
Bystřice pod Hostýnem	CZ	98	B1
Bystrzyca Kłodzka	PL	85	B4
Bytča	SK	98	B2
Bytnica	PL	75	B4
Bytom	PL	86	B2
Bytom Odrzański	PL	85	A3
Bytów	PL	68	A2
Byxelkrok	S	62	A5
Bzenec	CZ	98	C1
Bzince	SK	98	C1

C

Name		Page	Grid
Cabacos	P	154	B2
Cabaj-Čápor	SK	98	C2
Cabana	E	140	A2
Cabanac-et-Villagrains	F	128	B2
Cabañaquinta	E	142	A1
Cabanas	P	160	B2
Cabañas de Yepes	E	151	C4
Cabañas del Castillo	E	156	A2
Cabanelles	E	147	B3
Cabanes	E	153	B4
Cabanillas	E	144	B2
Čabar	HR	123	B3
Cabasse	F	132	B2
Cabdella	E	146	B2
Cabeceiras de Basto	P	148	A1
Cabeço de Vide	P	155	B3
Cabella Ligure	I	120	C2
Cabeza del Buey	E	156	B2
Cabeza la Vaca	E	161	A3
Cabezamesada	E	151	C4
Cabezarados	E	157	B3
Cabezarrubias del Puerto	E	157	B3
Cabezas del Villar	E	150	B2
Cabezas Rubias	E	161	B2
Cabezón	E	142	C2
Cabezón de la Sal	E	142	A2
Cabezón de Liébana	E	142	A2
Cabezuela	E	151	A4
Cabezuela del Valle	E	149	B4
Cabo de Gata	E	164	C2
Cabo de Palos	E	165	B4
Cabolafuente	E	152	A1
Cabourg	F	89	A3
Cabra	E	163	A3
Cabra del Santo Cristo	E	163	A4
Cabrach	GB	32	D3
Cábras	I	179	C2
Cabreiro	P	140	C2
Cabreiros	E	140	A3
Cabrejas	E	152	B1
Cabrela	P	154	C2
Cabrillas	E	149	B3
Cabuna	HR	125	B3
Čačak	SRB	127	D2
Cáccamo	I	176	B2
Caccuri	I	174	B2
Cacela	P	160	B2
Cacém	P	154	C1
Cáceres	E	155	B4
Cachafeiro	E	140	B2
Cachopo	P	160	B2
Cacin	E	163	A4
Čačinci	HR	125	B3
Cadafais	P	154	C1
Cadalen	F	129	C5
Cadalso	E	149	B3
Cadaqués	E	147	B4
Cadaval	P	154	B1
Cadavedo	E	141	A4
Čadavica	BIH	138	A2
Čadca	SK	98	B2
Cadeac	F	145	B4
Cadelbosco di Sopra	I	121	C3
Cadenazzo	CH	120	A1
Cadenberge	D	64	C2
Cadeuil	F	114	C3
Cádiar	E	164	C1
Cadillac	F	128	B2
Cádiz	E	162	B1
Čadjavica	HR	125	B3
Cadouin	F	129	B3
Cadours	F	129	C4
Cadrete	E	152	A3
Caen	F	89	A3
Caerleon	GB	39	C4
Caernarfon	GB	38	A2
Caerphilly	GB	39	C3
Caersws	GB	39	B3
Cafede	P	155	B3
Çağa	TR	187	B7
Caggiano	I	172	B1
Cagli	I	136	B1
Cágliari	I	179	C3
Čaglin	HR	125	B3
Cagnano Varano	I	171	B3
Cagnes-sur-Mer	F	132	B3
Caher	IRL	29	B4
Caherciveen	IRL	29	C1
Caherdaniel	IRL	29	C1
Cahors	F	129	B4
Cahul	MD	17	C8
Caiazzo	I	170	B2
Caion	E	140	A2
Cairndow	GB	34	B3
Cairnryan	GB	36	B1
Cairo Montenotte	I	133	A4
Caister-on-Sea	GB	41	C5
Caistor	GB	41	B3
Caivano	I	170	C2
Cajarc	F	129	B4
Čajniče	BIH	139	B5
Çakırlar	TR	189	C5
Çakmak	TR	187	C6
Čakovec	HR	124	A2
Çal	TR	189	A4
Cala	E	161	B3
Cala d'Or	E	167	B3
Cala Galdana	E	167	B3
Cala Gonone	I	178	B3
Cala Llonga	E	166	C1
Cala Millor	E	167	B3
Cala Morell	E	167	A3
Cala Ratjada	E	167	B3
Calabritto	I	172	B1
Calaceite	E	153	B4
Calacuccia	F	180	A2
Calaf	E	147	C2
Calafat	RO	17	C5
Calafell	E	147	C2
Calahonda, *Granada*	E	163	B4
Calahonda, *Málaga*	E	163	B3
Calahorra	E	144	B2
Calais	F	78	B1
Calalzo di Cadore	I	109	C3
Calamocha	E	152	B2
Calamonte	E	155	C4
Calanais	GB	31	A2
Calañas	E	161	B3
Calanda	E	153	B3
Calangiánus	I	178	B3
Călărași	RO	17	C7
Calascibetta	I	177	B3
Calasetta	I	179	C2
Calasparra	E	164	A3
Calatafimi	I	176	B1
Calatañazor	E	143	C4
Calatayud	E	152	A2
Calatorao	E	152	A2
Calau	D	84	A1
Calbe	D	73	C4
Calcena	E	152	A2
Calcinelli	I	136	B1
Calco	I	120	B2
Caldaro sulla strada del Vino	I	121	A4
Caldarola	I	136	B2
Caldas da Rainha	P	154	B1
Caldas de Boì	E	145	B4
Caldas de Malavella	E	147	C3
Caldas de Reis	E	140	B2
Caldas de San Jorge	P	148	B1
Caldas de Vizela	P	148	A1
Caldaso de los Vidrios	E	150	B3
Caldbeck	GB	36	B3
Caldearenas	E	145	B3
Caldelas	P	148	A1
Calders	E	147	C2
Caldes de Montbui	E	147	C3
Caldicot	GB	39	C4
Caldirola	I	120	C2
Caledon	GB	27	B4
Calella, *Barcelona*	E	147	C3
Calella, *Girona*	E	147	C4
Calenzana	F	180	A1
Calera de León	E	161	A3
Calera y Chozas	E	150	C3
Caleruega	E	143	C3
Caleruela	E	150	C2
Cales de Mallorca	E	167	B3
Calestano	I	134	A3
Calfsound	GB	33	B4
Calgary	GB	34	B1
Calimera	I	173	B4
Calitri	I	172	B1
Calizzano	I	133	A4
Callac	F	100	A2
Callan	IRL	30	B1
Callander	GB	35	B3
Callas	F	132	B2
Calliano, *Piemonte*	I	119	B5
Calliano, *Trentino Alto Adige*	I	121	B4
Callington	GB	42	B2
Callosa de Ensarriá	E	159	C3
Callosa de Segura	E	165	A4
Callús	E	147	C2
Čalma	SRB	127	B1
Calmbach	D	93	C4
Calne	GB	43	A5
Calolziocorte	I	120	B2
Calonge	E	147	C4
Čalovec	SK	112	B1
Calpe	E	159	C4
Caltabellotta	I	176	B2
Caltagirone	I	177	B3
Caltanissetta	I	177	B3
Caltavuturo	I	176	B2
Çaltılıbük	TR	186	C3
Caltojar	E	151	A5
Caluire-et-Cuire	F	117	B4
Caluso	I	119	B4
Calvello	I	172	B1
Calvi	F	180	A1
Calviá	E	166	B2
Calvinet	F	116	C2
Calvisson	F	131	B3
Calvörde	D	73	B4
Calw	D	93	C4
Calzada de Calatrava	E	157	B4
Calzada de Valdunciel	E	150	A2
Calzadilla de los Barros	E	155	C4
Cam	GB	43	A4
Camaiore	I	134	B3
Camarasa	E	145	C4
Camarena	E	151	B3
Camarès	F	130	B1
Camaret-sur-Aigues	F	131	A3
Camaret-sur-Mer	F	100	A1
Camarillas	E	153	B3
Camariñas	E	140	A1
Camarma	E	151	B4
Camarzana de Tera	E	141	B4
Camas	E	162	A1
Camastra	I	176	B2
Cambados	E	140	B2
Cambarinho	P	148	B1
Camberley	GB	44	B3
Cambil	E	163	A4
Cambligeu	F	78	B2
Cambo-les-Bains	F	144	A2
Camborne	GB	42	B1
Cambrai	F	78	B3
Cambre	E	140	A2
Cambridge	GB	45	A4
Cambrils	E	147	C2
Cambs	D	65	C4
Camburg	D	83	A3
Camden	GB	44	B3
Cameleño	E	142	A2
Camelford	GB	42	B2
Çameli	TR	189	B4
Camelle	E	140	A1
Camerano	I	136	B2
Camerino	I	136	B2
Camerota	I	172	B1
Camigliatello Silano	I	174	B2
Caminha	P	148	A1
Caminomorisco	E	149	B3
Caminreal	E	152	B2
Camisano Vicentino	I	121	B4
Camlıdere	TR	187	B7
Cammarata	I	176	B2
Camogli	I	134	A2
Camors	F	100	B3
Camp	IRL	29	B2
Campagna	I	172	B1
Campagnano di Roma	I	168	A2
Campagnático	I	135	C4
Campan	F	145	A4
Campana	I	174	B2
Campanario	E	156	B2
Campanillas	E	163	B3
Campano	E	162	B1
Campaspero	E	151	A3
Campbeltown	GB	34	C2
Campello	E	159	C4
Campelos	P	154	B1
Campi Bisénzio	I	135	B4
Campi Salentina	I	173	B4
Campico López	E	165	B3
Campíglia Maríttima	I	134	B3
Campillo de Altobuey	E	158	B2
Campillo de Aragón	E	152	A2
Campillo de Arenas	E	163	A4
Campillo de Llerena	E	156	B2
Campillos	E	162	A3
Câmpina	RO	17	C6
Campli	I	136	C2
Campo	E	145	B4
Campo da Feira	E	140	A3
Campo de Bacerros	E	141	B3
Campo de Caso	E	142	A1
Campo de Criptana	E	157	A4
Campo Ligure	I	133	A4
Campo Lugar	E	156	A2
Campo Maior	P	155	B3
Campo Molino	I	133	A3
Campo Real	E	151	B4
Campo Túres	I	108	C2
Campobasso	I	170	B2
Campobello di Licata	I	176	B2
Campobello di Mazara	I	176	B1
Campodársego	I	121	B4
Campodolcino	I	120	A2
Campofelice di Roccella	I	176	B2
Campofiorito	I	176	B2
Campofórmido	I	122	A2
Campofranco	I	176	B2
Campofrio	E	161	B3
Campogalliano	I	121	C3
Campolongo	I	109	C3
Campomanes	E	141	A5
Campomarino	I	170	B3
Camporeale	I	176	B2
Camporeggiano	I	136	B1
Camporrells	E	145	C4
Camporrobles	E	158	B2
Campos	E	148	A2
Campos del Port	E	167	B3
Camposa	P	148	A1
Camposampiero	I	121	B4
Camposines	E	153	A4
Campotéjar	E	163	A4
Campotosto	I	169	A3
Camprodón	E	147	B3
Campsegret	F	129	B3
Camrose	GB	39	C1
Camuñas	E	157	A4
Çamyolu	TR	189	C7
Çan	TR	186	B2
Can Pastilla	E	166	B2
C'an Picafort	E	167	B3
Cana	I	135	C4
Cañada del Hoyo	E	158	B2
Cañada Rosal	E	162	A2
Cañadajuncosa	E	158	B1
Čanak	HR	123	C4
Çanakkale	TR	186	B1
Canal San Bovo	I	121	A4
Canale	I	119	C4
Canales, *Asturias*	E	141	B5
Canales, *Castellón de la Plana*	E	159	B3
Canals	E	159	C3
Cañamares	E	152	B1
Cañamero	E	156	A2
Cañar	E	163	B4
Cañate la Real	E	162	B2
Cañaveral	E	155	B4
Cañaveral de León	E	161	A3
Cañaveras	E	152	B1
Cañaveruelas	E	151	B5
Canazei	I	108	C2
Cancale	F	88	B2
Cancellara	I	172	B1
Cancello ed Arnone	I	170	B2
Cancon	F	129	B3
Canda	E	141	B4
Candamil	E	140	A3
Candanchu	E	145	B3
Çandarlı	TR	186	D1
Candas	E	141	A5
Candasnos	E	153	A4
Candé	F	101	B4
Candela	I	172	A1
Candelario	E	150	B2
Candeleda	E	150	B2
Cándia Lomellina	I	120	B1
Candide Casamazzagno	I	109	C3
Candin	E	141	B4
Candosa	P	148	B2
Canecas	P	154	C1
Canelli	I	119	C5
Canena	E	157	B4
Canencia	E	151	B4
Canero	E	141	A4
Canet de Mar	E	147	C3
Canet d'en Berenguer	E	159	B3
Canet-Plage	F	146	B4
Cañete	E	158	A2
Cañete de las Torres	E	163	A3
Canfranc	E	145	B3
Cangas, *Lugo*	E	141	A3
Cangas, *Pontevedra*	E	140	B2
Cangas de Narcea	E	141	A4
Cangas de Onís	E	142	A1
Canha	P	154	C2
Canhestros	E	160	A1
Canicatti	I	176	B2
Canicattini Bagni	I	177	B4
Canicosa de la Sierra	E	143	C3
Caniles	E	164	B2
Canillas de Aceituno	E	163	B3
Canino	I	168	A1
Canisy	F	88	A2
Cañizal	E	150	A2
Cañizo	E	142	C1
Canjáyar	E	164	C2
Çankırı	TR	23	A7
Cannai	I	179	C2
Cannara	I	136	B1
Cánnero Riviera	I	120	A1
Cannes	F	132	B3
Canneto, *Sicilia*	I	177	A3
Canneto, *Toscana*	I	135	B3
Canneto sull'Oglio	I	120	B3
Cannich	GB	32	D2
Cannóbio	I	120	A1
Cannock	GB	40	C1
Canonbie	GB	36	A4
Canosa di Púglia	I	171	B4
Cantalapiedra	E	150	A2
Cantalejo	E	151	A4
Cantalgallo	E	161	A3
Cantalice	I	169	A2
Cantalpino	E	150	A2
Cantalupo in Sabina	I	168	A2
Cantanhede	P	148	B1
Cantavieja	E	153	B3
Čantavir	SRB	126	B1
Canterbury	GB	45	B5
Cantiano	I	136	B1
Cantillana	E	162	A2
Cantiveros	E	150	B3
Cantoria	E	164	B2
Cantù	I	120	B2
Canvey	GB	45	B4
Cany-Barville	F	89	A4
Canyet de Mar	E	147	C3
Caol	GB	34	B2
Cáorle	I	122	B1
Caorso	I	120	B2
Cap-de-Pin	F	128	B2
Cap Ferret	F	128	B1
Capáccio	I	172	B1
Capaci	I	176	A2
Capálbio	I	168	A1
Capánnori	I	134	B3
Caparde	BIH	139	A4
Caparroso	E	144	B2
Capbreton	F	128	C1
Capdenac-Gare	F	116	C2
Capdepera	E	167	B3
Capel Curig	GB	38	A3
Capellades	E	147	C2
Capena	I	168	A2
Capendu	F	146	A3
Capestang	F	130	B2
Capestrano	I	169	A3
Capileira	E	163	B4
Capinha	P	148	B2
Ca'Pisani	I	122	C1
Capistrello	I	169	B3
Capizzi	I	177	B3
Čaplje	BIH	124	C2
Čapljina	BIH	139	B3
Capo di Ponte	I	120	A3
Caposile	I	122	B1
Capoterra	I	179	C2
Cappamore	IRL	29	B3
Cappeln	D	71	B5
Cappoquin	IRL	29	B4
Capracotta	I	169	B4
Capránica	I	168	A2
Caprarola	I	168	A2
Capretta	I	135	C5
Capri	I	170	C2
Capriati a Volturno	I	170	B2
Caprino Veronese	I	121	B3
Captieux	F	128	B2
Cápua	I	170	B2
Capurso	I	173	A2
Capvern	F	145	A4
Carabaña	E	151	B4
Carabias	E	151	A4
Caracal	RO	17	C6
Caracenilla	E	152	B1
Carágio	P	133	A3
Caraman	F	146	A2
Caramánico Terme	I	169	A4
Caranga	E	141	A4
Caranguejeira	P	154	B2
Caransebeş	RO	16	C5
Carantec	F	100	A2
Carapelle	I	171	B3
Carasco	I	134	A2

Name		Page	Grid
Carate Brianza	I	120	B2
Caravaca de la Cruz	E	164	A3
Caravággio	I	120	B2
Carbajal	E	163	B3
Carbajo	E	155	B3
Carballeda	E	140	B3
Carballeda de Avia	E	140	B3
Carballo	E	140	A2
Carbis Bay	GB	42	B1
Carbon-Blanc	F	128	B2
Carbonera de Frentes	E	143	C4
Carboneras	E	164	C3
Carboneras de Guadazaón	E	158	B2
Carbonero el Mayor	E	151	A3
Carboneros	E	157	B4
Carbónia	I	179	C2
Carbonin	I	108	C3
Carbonne	F	146	A2
Carbost, Highland	GB	31	B2
Carbost, Highland	GB	31	B2
Carcaboso	E	149	B3
Carcabuey	E	163	A3
Carcaixent	E	159	B3
Carcans	F	128	A1
Carcans-Plage	F	128	A1
Carção	P	149	A3
Carcar	E	144	B2
Cárcare	I	133	A4
Carcassonne	F	146	A3
Carcastillo	E	144	B2
Carcedo de Burgos	E	143	B3
Carcelén	E	159	B2
Carcès	F	132	B2
Carchelejo	E	163	A4
Çardak, Çanakkale	TR	186	B1
Çardak, Denizli	TR	189	B4
Cardedeu	E	147	C3
Cardeña	E	157	B3
Cardenete	E	158	B2
Cardeñosa	E	150	B3
Cardeto	I	175	C1
Cardiff	GB	39	C3
Cardigan	GB	39	B2
Cardona	E	147	C2
Cardosos	E	154	B2
Carei	RO	16	B5
Carentan	F	88	A2
Carentoir	F	101	B3
Careri	I	175	C2
Carevdar	HR	124	A2
Cargèse	F	180	A1
Carhaix-Plouguer	F	100	A2
Caria	P	148	B2
Cariati	I	174	B2
Carignan	F	91	B5
Carignano	I	119	C4
Cariñena	E	152	A2
Carini	I	176	A2
Cariño	E	140	A3
Carínola	I	170	B1
Carisbrooke	GB	44	C1
Carlabhagh	GB	31	A2
Carlepont	F	90	B3
Carlet	E	159	B3
Carlingford	IRL	27	B4
Carlisle	GB	36	B4
Carloforte	I	179	C2
Carlópoli	I	175	B2
Carlow	D	65	C3
Carlow	IRL	30	B2
Carlton	GB	40	C2
Carluke	GB	35	C4
Carmagnola	I	119	C4
Carmarthen	GB	39	C2
Carmaux	F	130	A1
Carmena	E	150	C3
Cármenes	E	142	B1
Carmine	I	133	A4
Carmona	E	162	A2
Carmonita	E	155	B4
Carmyllie	GB	35	B5
Carnac	F	100	B2
Carndonagh	IRL	27	A3
Carnew	IRL	30	B2
Carnforth	GB	37	B4
Cárnia	I	122	A2
Carnlough	GB	27	B5
Carno	GB	39	B3
Carnon Plage	F	131	B2
Carnota	E	140	B1
Carnoustie	GB	35	B5
Carnwath	GB	35	C4
Carolei	I	174	B2
Carolinensiel	D	71	A4
Carolles	F	88	B2
Carona	I	120	A2
Caronía	I	177	A3
Carovigno	I	173	B3
Carovilli	I	170	B2
Carpaneto Piacentino	I	120	C2
Carpegna	I	135	B5
Carpenédolo	I	121	B3
Carpentras	F	131	A4
Carpi	I	121	C3
Carpignano Sésia	I	119	B5
Carpineti	I	134	A3
Carpineto Romano	I	169	B3
Cărpinis	RO	126	B2
Carpino	I	171	B3
Carpinone	I	170	B2
Carpio	E	150	A2
Carquefou	F	101	B4
Carqueiranne	F	132	B2
Carral	E	140	A2
Carranque	E	151	B3
Carrapichana	P	148	B2
Carrara	I	134	A3
Carraroe	IRL	28	A2
Carrascalejo	E	156	A2
Carrascosa del Campo	E	151	B5
Carratraca	E	162	B3
Carrazeda de Ansiães	P	148	A2
Carrazedo de Montenegro	P	148	A2
Carrbridge	GB	32	D3
Carregal do Sal	P	148	B1
Carreña	E	142	A2
Carrick	IRL	26	B2
Carrick-on-Shannon	IRL	26	C2
Carrick-on-Suir	IRL	30	B1
Carrickart	IRL	26	A3
Carrickfergus	GB	27	B5
Carrickmacross	IRL	27	C4
Carrigallen	IRL	27	C3
Carrión de Calatrava	E	157	A4
Carrión de los Condes	E	142	B2
Carrizo de la Ribera	E	141	B5
Carrizosa	E	157	B5
Carro	F	131	B4
Carrocera	E	142	B1
Carros	F	133	B3
Carrouge	CH	106	C1
Carrouges	F	89	B3
Carrù	I	133	A4
Carry-le-Rouet	F	131	B4
Carryduff	GB	27	B5
Carsóli	I	169	A3
Carsphairn	GB	36	A2
Cartagena	E	165	B4
Cártama	E	163	B3
Cartaxo	P	154	B2
Cartaya	E	161	B2
Carteret	F	88	A2
Cartes	E	142	A2
Carúnchio	I	170	B2
Carviças	P	149	A3
Carvin	F	78	B2
Carvoeira	P	154	B1
Carvoeiro	P	160	B1
Casa Branca, Portalegre	P	154	C3
Casa Branca, Setúbal	P	154	C2
Casa Castalda	I	136	B1
Casa l'Abate	I	173	B4
Casabermeja	E	163	B3
Casacalenda	I	170	B2
Casaio	E	141	B4
Casàl di Principe	I	170	B1
Casalarreina	E	143	B4
Casalbordino	I	169	A4
Casalborgone	I	119	B4
Casalbuono	I	174	A1
Casalbuttano ed Uniti	I	120	B2
Casale Monferrato	I	119	B5
Casalécchio di Reno	I	135	A4
Casalina	I	136	C1
Casalmaggiore	I	121	C3
Casalnuovo Monterotaro	I	170	B3
Casaloldo	I	121	B3
Casalpusterlengo	I	120	B2
Casamássima	I	173	B2
Casamicciola Terme	I	170	C1
Casamozza	F	180	A2
Casar de Cáceres	E	155	B4
Casar de Palomero	E	149	B3
Casarabonela	E	162	B3
Casarano	I	173	B4
Casarejos	E	143	C3
Casares	E	162	B2
Casares de las Hurdes	E	149	B3
Casariche	E	163	A3
Casarrubios del Monte	E	151	B3
Casas de Don Pedro	E	156	A2
Casas de Fernando Alonso	E	158	B1
Casas de Haro	E	158	B1
Casas de Juan Gil	E	159	B2
Casas de Millán	E	155	B4
Casas de Reina	E	156	B2
Casas de Ves	E	159	B2
Casas del Juan Núñez	E	158	B2
Casas del Puerto	E	159	C2
Casas del Rio	E	159	B2
Casas-Ibáñez	E	158	B2
Casas Nuevas	E	164	B3
Casasimarro	E	158	B1
Casasola	E	150	B3
Casasola de Arión	E	150	A2
Casasuertes	E	142	A2
Casatejada	E	150	C2
Casavieja	E	150	B3
Casazza	I	120	B2
Cascais	P	154	C1
Cascante	E	144	C2
Cascante del Rio	E	152	B2
Cáscia	I	169	A3
Casciana Terme	I	134	B3
Cáscina	I	134	B3
Cáseda	E	144	B2
Casekow	D	74	A3
Casella	I	134	A2
Caselle Torinese	I	119	B4
Casemurate	I	135	A5
Casenove	I	136	C1
Caseres	E	153	A4
Caserío Benali	E	159	B3
Caserta	I	170	B2
Casével	P	160	B1
Cashel	IRL	29	B4
Casillas	E	150	B3
Casillas de Coria	E	155	B4
Casina	I	134	A3
Casinos	E	159	B3
Čáslav	CZ	97	B3
Cásola Valsénio	I	135	A4
Cásole d'Elsa	I	135	B4
Cásoli	I	169	A4
Casória	I	170	C2
Caspe	E	153	A4
Cassà de la Selva	I	147	C3
Cassagnas	F	130	A2
Cassagnes-Bégonhès	F	130	A1
Cassano allo Iónio	I	174	B2
Cassano d'Adda	I	120	B2
Cassano delle Murge	I	171	C4
Cassano Magnago	I	120	B1
Cassano Spinola	I	120	C1
Cassel	F	78	B2
Cassíbile	I	177	C4
Cassine	I	119	C5
Cassino	I	169	B3
Cassis	F	132	B1
Cassolnovo	I	120	B1
Cassuéjouls	F	116	C2
Častá	SK	98	C1
Castagnaro	I	121	B4
Castagneto Carducci	I	134	B3
Castagnola	CH	120	A1
Castalla	E	159	C3
Castañar de Ibor	E	156	A2
Castanheira de Pêra	P	154	A2
Cástano Primo	I	120	B1
Castasegna	CH	120	A2
Castéggio	I	120	B2
Casteição	P	148	B2
Castejón	E	144	B2
Castejón de Monegros	E	153	A3
Castejón de Sos	E	145	B4
Castejón de Valdejasa	E	144	C3
Castèl Baronia	I	172	A1
Castel Bolognese	I	135	A4
Castel d'Aiano	I	135	A3
Castel d'Ario	I	121	B3
Castel de Cabra	E	153	B3
Castèl del Monte	I	169	A3
Castel del Piano	I	135	C4
Castèl di Iúdica	I	177	B3
Castèl di Rio	I	135	A4
Castèl di Sangro	I	169	B4
Castèl di Tora	I	169	A2
Castèl Frentano	I	169	A4
Castel San Gimignano	I	135	B4
Castèl San Giovanni	I	120	B2
Castèl San Pietro Terme	I	135	A4
Castél Sant'Elia	I	168	A2
Castèl Volturno	I	170	B1
Castelbuono	I	177	B3
Casteldáccia	I	176	A2
Casteldelfino	I	132	A3
Castelfidardo	I	136	B2
Castelfiorentino	I	135	B4
Castelforte	I	169	B3
Castelfranco Emília	I	121	C4
Castelfranco in Miscano	I	170	B3
Castelfranco Véneto	I	121	B4
Casteljaloux	F	128	B2
Castell Arquato	I	120	C2
Castell de Cabres	E	153	B4
Castell de Castells	E	159	C3
Castell de Ferro	E	163	B4
Castellabate	I	170	C2
Castellammare del Golfo	I	176	A1
Castellammare di Stábia	I	170	C2
Castellamonte	I	119	B4
Castellana Grotte	I	173	B3
Castellane	F	132	B2
Castellaneta	I	173	B2
Castellaneta Marina	I	173	B2
Castellar	I	157	B4
Castellar de la Frontera	E	162	B2
Castellar de la Ribera	E	147	B2
Castellar de Santiago	E	157	B4
Castellar del Vallès	E	147	C3
Castellarano	I	135	A3
Castell'Azzara	I	135	C4
Castellbell i Villar	E	147	C2
Castelldans	E	153	A4
Castelldefels	E	147	C2
Castelleone	I	120	B2
Castellet	I	147	C2
Castelletto di Brenzone	I	121	B3
Castellfollit de la Roca	E	147	B3
Castellfollit de Riubregos	E	147	C2
Castellfort	E	153	B3
Castellina in Chianti	I	135	B4
Castellina Marittima	I	134	B3
Castello de Farfaña	E	145	C4
Castelló de la Plana	E	159	B3
Castello d'Empúries	E	147	B4
Castello di Fiemme	I	121	A4
Castello Tesino	I	121	A4
Castelloli	I	147	C2
Castellón de Rugat	E	159	C3
Castellote	E	153	B3
Castellterçol	E	147	C3
Castelluccio Inferiore	I	174	B1
Castelmassa	I	121	B4
Castelmáuro	I	170	B2
Castelmoron-sur-Lot	F	129	B3
Castelnau-de-Médoc	F	128	A2
Castelnau-de-Montmirail	F	129	C4
Castelnau-Magnoac	F	145	A4
Castelnau-Montratier	F	129	B4
Castelnaudary	F	146	A2
Castelnou	E	153	A3
Castelnovo ne'Monti	I	134	A3
Castelnuovo Berardenga	I	135	B4
Castelnuovo della Dáunia	I	170	B3
Castelnuovo di Garfagnana	I	134	A3
Castelnuovo di Val di Cécina	I	135	B3
Castelnuovo Don Bosco	I	119	B4
Castelnuovo Scrivia	I	120	C1
Castelo Branco, Bragança	P	149	A3
Castelo Branco, Castelo Branco	P	155	B3
Castelo de Paiva	P	148	A1
Castelo de Vide	P	155	B3
Castelo do Neiva	P	148	A1
Castelo Mendo	P	149	B3
Castelraimondo	I	136	B2
Castelsantángelo	I	136	C2
Castelsaraceno	I	174	A1
Castelsardo	I	178	B2
Castelsarrasin	F	129	B4
Castelserás	E	153	B3
Casteltérmini	I	176	B2
Castelvecchio Subéquo	I	169	A3
Castelvetrano	I	176	B1
Castenédolo	I	120	B3
Castets	F	128	C1
Castiádas	I	179	C3
Castiglion Fibocchi	I	135	B4
Castiglion Fiorentino	I	135	B4
Castiglioncello	I	134	B3
Castiglione	I	169	A3
Castiglione Chiavarese	I	134	A2
Castiglione d'Adda	I	120	B2
Castiglione dei Pepoli	I	135	A4
Castiglione del Lago	I	135	B5
Castiglione della Pescáia	I	135	C3
Castiglione delle Stiviere	I	121	B3
Castiglione di Sicília	I	177	B4
Castiglione d'Órcia	I	135	B5
Castiglione Messer Marino	I	170	B2
Castiglione Messer Raimondo	I	169	A3
Castil de Peones	E	143	B3
Castilblanco	E	156	A2
Castilblanco de los Arroyos	E	161	B4
Castilfrio de la Sierra	E	144	C1
Castilgaleu	E	145	B4
Castilisar	E	144	B2
Castilleja	E	161	B3
Castillejar	E	164	B2
Castillejo de Martin Viejo	E	149	B3
Castillejo de Mesleón	E	151	A4
Castillejo de Robledo	E	151	A4
Castillo de Bayuela	E	150	B3
Castillo de Locubín	E	163	A4
Castillon-la-Bataille	F	128	B2
Castillon-Len-Couserans	F	146	B2
Castillonès	F	129	B3
Castillonroy	E	145	C4
Castilruiz	E	144	C1
Castione	CH	120	A2
Castions di Strada	I	122	B2
Castirla	F	180	A2
Castle Cary	GB	43	A4
Castle Douglas	GB	36	B3
Castlebar	IRL	28	A2
Castlebellingham	IRL	27	C4
Castleblaney	IRL	27	B4
Castlebridge	IRL	30	B2
Castlecomer	IRL	30	B1
Castlederg	GB	27	B3
Castledermot	IRL	30	B2
Castleford	GB	40	B2
Castleisland	IRL	29	B2
Castlemaine	IRL	29	B2
Castlemartyr	IRL	29	C3
Castlepollard	IRL	30	A1
Castlerea	IRL	28	A3
Castleton	GB	40	B2
Castletown, Highland	GB	32	C3
Castletown, Isle of Man	GB	36	B2
Castletown Bearhaven	IRL	29	C2
Castletownroche	IRL	29	B3
Castlewellan	GB	27	B5
Casto	I	120	B3
Castrejón	E	150	A2
Castrelo del Valle	E	141	B3
Castres	F	130	B1
Castricum	NL	70	B1
Castries	F	131	B2
Castrignano del Capo	I	173	C4
Castril	E	164	B2
Castrillo de Duero	E	151	A4
Castrillo de la Vega	E	143	C3
Castrillo de Onielo	E	142	C2
Castro	E	142	A2
Castro	I	173	B4
Castro-Caldelas	E	141	B3
Castro Daire	P	148	B2
Castro del Rey	E	141	A3
Castro dei Volsci	I	169	B3
Castro del Río	E	163	A3
Castro Laboreiro	P	140	B2
Castro Marim	P	160	B2
Castro-Urdiales	E	143	A3
Castro Verde	P	160	B1
Castrocabón	E	141	B5
Castrocaro Terme	I	135	A4
Castrocontrigo	E	141	B4
Castrofilippo	I	176	B2
Castrogonzaio	E	142	B1
Castrojeriz	E	142	B2
Castromonte	E	142	C1
Castromudarra	E	142	B1
Castronuevo	E	142	C1
Castronuño	E	150	A2
Castropol	E	141	A3
Castroreale	I	177	A4
Castroserracin	E	151	A4
Castroverde	E	141	A3
Castroverde de Campos	E	142	C1
Castroverde de Cerrato	E	142	C2
Castrovillari	I	174	B2
Castuera	E	156	B2
Catadau	E	159	B3
Cataéggio	I	120	A2
Çatalca	TR	186	A3
Catallar	TR	189	C5
Çatalzeytin	TR	23	A8
Catánia	I	177	B4
Catanzaro	I	175	C2
Catanzaro Marina	I	175	C2
Catarroja	E	159	B3
Catarruchos	P	148	B1
Catcleugh	GB	37	A4
Catenanuova	I	177	B3
Caterham	GB	44	B3
Cati	E	153	B4
Čatići	BIH	139	A4
Catignano	I	169	A3
Catillon	F	91	A3
Catoira	E	140	B2
Caton	GB	37	B4
Catral	E	165	A4
Catterick	GB	37	B5
Cáttolica	I	136	B1
Cáttolica Eraclea	I	176	B2
Catton	GB	37	B4
Caudebec-en-Caux	F	89	A4
Caudete	E	159	C3
Caudete de las Fuentes	E	159	B2
Caudiel	E	159	B3
Caudiès-de-Fenouillèdes	F	146	B3
Caudry	F	91	A3
Caulkerbush	GB	36	B3
Caulnes	F	101	A3
Caulónia	I	175	C2
Caumont-l'Evente	F	88	A3
Caunes-Minervois	F	146	A3
Cauro	F	180	B1
Caussade	F	129	B4
Causse-de-la-Selle	F	130	B2
Cauterets	F	145	B3
Cava de Tirreni	I	170	C2
Cavaglia	I	119	B5
Cavaillon	F	131	B4
Cavalaire-sur-Mer	F	132	B2
Cavaleiro	P	160	B1
Cavalese	I	121	A4
Cavallermaggiore	I	119	C4
Cavallino	I	122	B1
Cavan	IRL	27	C3
Cavárzere	I	121	B5
Çavdarhisar	TR	187	B4
Çavdır	TR	189	B4
Cavernais	P	148	B2
Cavezzo	I	121	C4
Cavignac	F	128	A2
Čavle	HR	123	B3
Cavo	I	134	C3
Cavour	I	119	C4
Cawdor	GB	32	D3
Çay	TR	187	D6
Çaycuma	TR	187	A7
Cayeux-sur-Mer	F	78	B1
Çayıralan	TR	23	B8
Çayırhan	TR	187	B6
Caylus	F	129	B4
Cayres	F	117	C3
Cazalilla	E	157	C4
Cazalla de la Sierra	E	156	C2
Cazals	F	129	B4
Cazanuecos	E	142	B1
Cazaubon	F	128	C2
Cazaux	F	128	B1
Cazavet	F	146	A2
Cazères	F	146	A2
Cazin	BIH	124	C1
Cazis	CH	107	C4
Čazma	HR	124	B2
Cazo	E	142	A1
Cazorla	E	164	B2
Cazouls-lès-Béziers	F	130	B2
Cea, León	E	142	B1
Cea, Orense	E	140	B3
Ceánuri	E	143	A4
Ceauce	F	88	B3
Cebolla	E	150	C3
Cebreros	E	150	B3
Čečava	BIH	125	C3
Ceccano	I	169	B3
Cece	H	112	C2
Cecenowo	PL	68	A2
Čechtice	CZ	96	B3
Čechtín	CZ	97	B3
Cécina	I	134	B3
Ceclavín	E	155	B4
Cedégolo	I	120	A3
Cedeira	E	140	A2
Cedillo	E	155	B3

Cedillo del Condado E 151 B4
Cedrillas E 153 B3
Cedynia PL 74 B3
Cée E 140 B1
Cefalù I 177 A3
Céggia I 122 B1
Cegléd H 113 B3
Ceglédbercel H 112 B3
Céglie Messápica I 173 B3
Cehegín E 164 A3
Ceilhes-et-Rocozels F 130 B2
Ceinos de Campos E 142 B1
Ceira P 148 B1
Čejč CZ 97 C4
Cekcyn PL 76 A3
Cela BIH 124 C2
Čelákovice CZ 84 B2
Celano I 169 A3
Celanova E 140 B3
Celbridge IRL 30 A2
Čelebič BIH 138 B2
Celenza Valfortore I 170 B2
Čelić BIH 125 C4
Čelinac BIH 124 C3
Celje SLO 123 A4
Cella E 152 B2
Celldömölk H 111 B4
Celle D 72 B3
Celle Ligure I 133 A4
Celles B 79 B4
Celles-sur-Belle F 115 B3
Cellino San Marco I 173 B3
Celorico da Beira P 148 B2
Celorico de Basto P 148 A1
Çeltik TR 187 C6
Çeltikçi TR 189 B5
Cemaes GB 38 A2
Cembra I 121 A4
Čemerno BIH 139 B4
Cenad RO 126 A2
Cencenighe Agordino I 121 A4
Cenei RO 126 B2
Ceneselli I 121 B4
Cenicero E 143 B4
Cenicientos E 150 B3
Censeau F 105 C5
Čenta SRB 126 B2
Centallo I 133 A3
Centelles E 147 C3
Cento I 121 C4
Centúripe I 177 B3
Cepeda la Mora E 150 B2
Cépet F 129 C4
Čepin HR 125 B4
Čepinski Martinci HR 125 B4
Cepovan SLO 122 A2
Ceprano I 169 B3
Čeralije HR 125 B3
Cerami I 177 B3
Cerano I 120 B1
Cérans Foulletourte F 102 B2
Ceraso I 172 B1
Cerbaia I 135 B4
Cerbère F 146 B4
Cercadillo E 151 A5
Cercal, *Lisboa* P 154 B1
Cercal, *Setúbal* P 160 B1
Čerčany CZ 96 B2
Cerceda E 151 B4
Cercedilla E 151 B3
Cercemaggiore I 170 B2
Cercs E 147 B2
Cercy-la-Tour F 104 C2
Cerda I 176 B2
Cerdedo E 140 B2
Cerdeira P 149 B2
Cerdon F 103 B4
Cerea I 121 B4
Ceres GB 35 B5
Ceres I 119 B4
Cerese I 121 B3
Ceresole-Reale I 119 B4
Cereste F 132 B1
Céret F 146 B3
Cerezo de Abajo E 151 A4
Cerezo de Riotirón E 143 B3
Cerfontaine B 79 B4
Cergy F 90 B2
Cerignola I 171 B3
Cérilly F 103 C4
Cerisiers F 104 A2
Cerizay F 114 B3
Çerkeş TR 23 A7
Çerkezköy TR 186 A3
Cerkije SLO 123 A3
Cerknica SLO 123 B3
Cerkno SLO 122 A2
Cerkwica PL 67 B4
Cerna HR 125 B4
Černá Hora CZ 97 B4
Cernavodă RO 17 C8
Cernay F 106 B2
Cerne Abbas GB 43 B4
Cernégula E 143 B3
Cernik HR 124 B3
Cernóbbio I 120 B2
Černošin CZ 95 B4
Cernovice CZ 96 B2
Cérons F 128 B2
Cerovlje HR 123 B3
Cerovo SK 99 C3
Cerqueto I 135 C5
Cerralbo E 149 B3
Cerreto d'Esi I 136 B1
Cerreto Sannita I 170 B2
Cerrigydrudion GB 38 A3
Cërrik AL 182 B1
Cerro Muriano E 156 B3
Certaldo I 135 B4
Certosa di Pésio I 133 A3
Cerva P 148 A2
Cervaro I 169 B3
Cervatos de la Cueza E 142 B2
Červena Řečice CZ 97 B3
Červená-Skala SK 99 C4
Cervená Voda CZ 97 A4
Cerveny Kostelec CZ 85 B4
Cervera E 147 C2
Cervera de la Cañada E 152 A2
Cervera de Pisuerga E 142 B2
Cervera del Llano E 158 B1
Cervera del Río Alhama E 144 B2
Cervéteri I 168 B2
Cérvia I 135 A5
Cerviá de les Garriques E 147 C1
Cervignano del Friuli I 122 B2
Cervinara I 170 B2
Cervione F 180 A2
Cervo E 141 A3
Cervon F 104 B2
Cesana Torinese I 119 C3
Cesarica HR 137 A4
Cesarò I 177 B3
Cesena I 135 A5
Cesenático I 135 A5
Cēsis LV 8 D4
Česká Belá CZ 97 B3
Česká Kamenice CZ 84 B2
Česká Lípa CZ 84 B2
Česká Skalice CZ 85 B4
Česká Třebová CZ 97 B4
České Budějovice CZ 96 C2
České Velenice CZ 96 C2
Český Brod CZ 96 A2
Český Dub CZ 84 B2
Český Krumlov CZ 96 C2
Český Těšin CZ 98 B2
Češljeva Bara SRB 127 C3
Çeşme TR 188 A1
Cessenon F 130 B2
Cesson-Sévigné F 101 A4
Cestas F 128 B2
Čestobrodica SRB 127 D2
Cesuras E 140 A2
Cetin Grad HR 123 B4
Cetina E 152 A2
Cetinje MNE 16 D3
Cetraro I 174 B1
Ceuti E 165 A3
Ceva I 133 A4
Cevico de la Torre E 142 C2
Cevico Navero E 142 C2
Cevins F 118 B3
Cévio CH 119 A5
Cevizli TR 189 B6
Cewice PL 68 A2
Ceylan TR 189 C3
Ceyrat F 116 B3
Ceyzériat F 118 A2
Chaam NL 79 A4
Chabanais F 115 C4
Chabeuil F 117 C5
Chabielice PL 86 A3
Chablis F 104 B2
Châbons F 118 B2
Chabówka PL 99 B3
Chabreloche F 117 B3
Chabris F 103 B3
Chagford GB 42 B3
Chagny F 105 C3
Chagoda RUS 9 C9
Chaherrero E 150 B3
Chailland F 88 B3
Chaillé-les-Marais F 114 B2
Chailles F 103 B3
Chailley F 104 A2
Chalabre F 146 B3
Chalais F 128 A3
Chalamont F 118 B2
Châlette-sur-Loing F 103 A4
Chalindrey F 105 B4
Challacombe GB 42 A3
Challans F 114 B2
Challes-les-Eaux F 118 B2
Chalmazel F 117 B3
Chalmoux F 104 C2
Chalon-sur-Saône F 105 C3
Chalonnes-sur-Loire F 102 B1
Châlons-en-Champagne F 91 C4
Chalupy PL 69 A3
Châlus F 115 C4
Cham CH 106 B3
Cham D 95 B4
Chamberet F 116 B1
Chambéry F 118 B2
Chambilly F 117 A4
Chambley F 92 B1
Chambly F 90 B2
Chambois F 89 B4
Chambon-sur-Lac F 116 B2
Chambon-sur-Voueize F 116 A2
Chambord F 103 B3
Chamborigaud F 131 A2
Chamboulive F 116 B1
Chamerau D 95 B4
Chamonix-Mont Blanc F 119 B3
Chamoux-sur-Gelon F 118 B3
Champagnac-le-Vieux F 117 B3
Champagney F 106 B1
Champagnole F 105 C4
Champagny-Mouton F 115 B4
Champaubert F 91 C3
Champdeniers-St. Denis F 114 B3
Champdieu F 117 B4
Champdôtre F 105 B4
Champeix F 116 B3
Champéry CH 119 A3
Champigne F 102 B1
Champignelles F 104 B2
Champigny-sur-Veude F 102 B2
Champlitte-et-le-Prelot F 105 B4
Champoluc I 119 B4
Champoly F 117 B3
Champorcher I 119 B4
Champrond-en-Gâtine F 89 B5
Champs-sur-Tarentaine F 116 B2
Champs-sur-Yonne F 104 B2
Champtoceaux F 101 B4
Chamrousse F 118 B2
Chamusca P 154 B2
Chanac F 130 A2
Chanaleilles F 117 C3
Chandler's Ford GB 44 C2
Chandra GR 185 D7
Chandrexa de Queixa E 141 B3
Chañe E 150 A3
Changy F 117 A3
Chania GR 185 D5
Channes F 104 B3
Chantada E 140 B3
Chantelle F 116 A3
Chantenay-St. Imbert F 104 C2
Chanteuges F 117 B3
Chantilly F 90 B2
Chantonnay F 114 B2
Chão de Codes P 154 B2
Chaource F 104 A3
Chapa E 140 B2
Chapareillan F 118 B2
Chapel en le Frith GB 40 B2
Chapelle Royale F 103 A3
Chapelle-St. Laurent F 102 C1
Charbonnat F 104 C3
Chard GB 43 B4
Charenton-du-Cher F 103 C4
Charlbury GB 44 B2
Charleroi B 79 B4
Charlestown GB 42 B2
Charlestown IRL 26 C2
Charlestown of Aberlour GB 32 D3
Charleville IRL 29 B3
Charleville-Mézières F 91 B4
Charlieu F 117 A4
Charlottenberg S 49 C4
Charlton Kings GB 44 B1
Charly F 90 C3
Charmes F 92 C2
Charmes-sur-Rhône F 117 C4
Charmey CH 106 C2
Charminster GB 43 B4
Charmont-en-Beauce F 103 A4
Charny F 104 B2
Charolles F 117 A4
Chârost F 103 C4
Charquemont F 106 B1
Charrin F 104 C2
Charroux F 115 B4
Chartres F 90 C1
Charzykow PL 68 B2
Chasseneuil-sur-Bonnieure F 115 C4
Chassigny F 105 B4
Château-Arnoux F 132 A2
Château-Chinon F 104 B2
Château-d'Oex CH 106 C2
Château-d'Olonne F 114 B2
Château-du-Loir F 102 B2
Château-Gontier F 102 B1
Château-la-Vallière F 102 B2
Château-Landon F 103 A4
Château-l'Evêque F 129 A3
Château-Porcien F 91 B4
Château-Renault F 102 B2
Château-Salins F 92 C2
Château-Thierry F 91 B3
Châteaubernard F 115 C3
Châteaubourg F 101 A4
Châteaubriant F 101 B4
Châteaudun F 103 A3
Châteaugiron F 101 A4
Châteaulin F 100 A1
Châteaumeillant F 103 C4
Châteauneuf, *Nièvre* F 104 B2
Châteauneuf, *Saône-et-Loire* F 117 A4
Châteauneuf-de-Randon F 117 C3
Châteauneuf-d'Ille-et-Vilaine F 88 B2
Châteauneuf-du-Faou F 100 A2
Châteauneuf-du-Pape F 131 A3
Châteauneuf-en-Thymerais F 89 B5
Châteauneuf la-Forêt F 116 B1
Châteauneuf-le-Rouge F 132 B1
Châteauneuf-sur-Charente F 115 C3
Châteauneuf-sur-Cher F 103 C4
Châteauneuf-sur-Loire F 103 B4
Châteauneuf-sur-Sarthe F 102 B1
Châteauponsac F 115 B5
Châteauredon F 132 A2
Châteaurenard, *Bouches du Rhône* F 131 B3
Châteaurenard, *Loiret* F 104 B1
Châteauroux F 103 C3
Châteauroux-les-Alpes F 118 C3
Châteauvillain F 105 A3
Châtel F 119 A3
Châtel-Censoir F 104 B2
Châtel-de-Neuvre F 116 A3
Châtel-Montagne F 117 A3
Châtel-St. Denis CH 106 C1
Châtel-sur-Moselle F 92 C2
Châtelaillon-Plage F 114 B2
Châtelaudren F 100 A3
Châtelet B 79 B4
Châtelguyon F 116 B3
Châtellerault F 115 B4
Châtelus-Malvaleix F 116 A2
Châtenois F 105 A4
Châtenois-les-Forges F 106 B1
Chatham GB 45 B4
Châtillon I 119 B4
Châtillon-Coligny F 103 B4
Châtillon-en-Bazois F 104 B2
Châtillon-en-Diois F 118 C2
Châtillon-sur Chalaronne F 117 A4
Châtillon-sur-Indre F 103 C3
Châtillon-sur-Loire F 103 B4
Châtillon-sur-Marne F 91 B3
Châtillon-sur-Seine F 104 B3
Châtres F 91 C3
Chatteris GB 45 A4
Chatton GB 37 A5
Chauchina E 163 A4
Chaudes-Aigues F 116 C3
Chaudrey F 91 C4
Chauffailles F 117 A4
Chaulnes F 90 B2
Chaument Gistoux B 79 B4
Chaumergy F 105 C4
Chaumont F 105 A4
Chaumont-en-Vexin F 90 B1
Chaumont-Porcien F 91 B4
Chaumont-sur-Aire F 91 C5
Chaumont-sur-Loire F 103 B3
Chaunay F 115 B4
Chauny F 90 B3
Chaussin F 105 C4
Chauvigny F 115 B4
Chavagnes-en-Paillers F 114 B2
Chavanges F 91 C4
Chaves P 148 A2
Chavignon F 91 B3
Chazelles-sur-Lyon F 117 B4
Chazey-Bons F 118 B2
Cheadle, *Greater Manchester* GB 40 B1
Cheadle, *Staffordshire* GB 40 C2
Cheb CZ 83 B4
Chebsara RUS 9 C11
Checa E 152 B2
Chęciny PL 87 B4
Cheddar GB 43 A4
Cheddleton GB 40 B1
Chef-Boutonne F 115 B3
Cheles E 155 C3
Chella E 159 B3
Chelles F 90 C2
Chełm PL 13 C5
Chełmno, *Kujawsko-Pomorskie* PL 76 A3
Chełmno, *Wielkopolskie* PL 76 B3
Chelmsford GB 45 B4
Chelmuzhi RUS 9 A9
Chełmża PL 76 A3
Cheltenham GB 44 B1
Chelva E 159 B2
Chémery F 103 B3
Chemery-sur-Bar F 91 B4
Chemillé F 102 B1
Chemin F 105 C4
Chemnitz D 83 B4
Chénerailles F 116 A2
Cheniménil F 105 A5
Chenonceaux F 103 B3
Chenôve F 105 B3
Chepelare BG 183 B6
Chepstow GB 39 C4
Chera E 159 B3
Cherasco I 119 C4
Cherbonnières F 115 C3
Cherbourg F 88 A2
Cherchiara di Calábria I 174 B2
Cherepovets RUS 9 C10
Chernihiv UA 13 C9
Chernivtsi UA 17 A6
Chernobyl = Chornobyl UA 13 C9
Chernyakhovsk RUS 12 A4
Chéroy F 104 A1
Cherven BY 13 B8
Chervonohrad UA 13 C6
Cherykaw BY 13 B9
Chesham GB 44 B3
Cheshunt GB 44 B3
Chessy-lès-Pres F 104 A2
Cheste E 159 B3
Chester GB 38 A4
Chester-le-Street GB 37 B5
Chesterfield GB 40 B2
Chevagnes F 104 C2
Chevanceaux F 115 C3
Chevillon F 91 C5
Chevilly F 103 A3
Chew Magna GB 43 A4
Chézery-Forens F 118 A2
Chialamberto I 119 B4
Chiampo I 121 B4
Chianale I 119 C4
Chianciano Terme I 135 B4
Chiaramonte Gulfi I 177 B3
Chiaramonti I 178 B2
Chiaravalle I 136 B2
Chiaravalle Centrale I 175 C2
Chiaréggio I 120 A2
Chiari I 120 B2
Chiaromonte I 174 A2
Chiasso CH 120 B2
Chiávari I 134 A2
Chiavenna I 120 A2
Chiché F 102 C1
Chichester GB 44 C3
Chiclana de la Frontera E 162 B1
Chiclana de Segura E 164 A1
Chiddingfold GB 44 B3
Chieri I 119 B4
Chiesa in Valmalenco I 120 A2
Chieti I 169 A4
Chieti Scalo I 169 A4
Chiéuti I 171 B3
Chigwell GB 45 B4
Chiliomodi GR 184 B3
Chillarón de Cuenca E 152 B1
Chillarón del Rey E 151 B5
Chilleurs-aux-Bois F 103 A4
Chillón E 156 B3
Chilluevar E 164 B1
Chiloeches E 151 B4
Chimay B 91 A4
Chimeneas E 163 A4
Chinchilla de Monte Aragón E 158 C2
Chinchón E 151 B4
Chingford GB 45 B4
Chinon F 102 B2
Chióggia I 122 B1
Chiomonte I 119 B3
Chipiona E 161 C3
Chippenham GB 43 A4
Chipping Campden GB 44 A2
Chipping Norton GB 44 B2
Chipping Ongar GB 45 B4
Chipping Sodbury GB 43 A4
Chirac F 130 A2
Chirbury GB 39 B3
Chirens F 118 B2
Chirivel E 164 B2
Chirk GB 38 B3
Chirnside GB 35 C5
Chişinău = Khisinev MD 17 B8
Chişineu Criş RO 113 C5
Chissey-en-Morvan F 104 B3
Chiusa I 108 C2
Chiusa di Pésio I 133 A3
Chiusa Scláfani I 176 B2
Chiusaforte I 122 A2
Chiusi I 135 B4
Chiva E 159 B3
Chivasso I 119 B4
Chlewiska PL 87 A4
Chludowo PL 75 B5
Chlum u Třeboně CZ 96 C2
Chlumec nad Cidlinou CZ 84 B3
Chmielnik PL 87 B4
Chobienia PL 85 A4
Chobienice PL 75 B4
Choceň CZ 97 A4
Choceń PL 77 B4
Chochołow PL 99 B3
Chocianów PL 85 A3
Chociw PL 86 A3
Chociwel PL 75 A4
Choczewo PL 68 A2
Chodaków PL 77 B5
Chodecz PL 77 B4
Chodov CZ 83 B4
Chodzież PL 75 B5
Chojna PL 74 B3
Chojnice PL 68 B2
Chojno, *Kujawsko-Pomorskie* PL 77 B4
Chojno, *Wielkopolskie* PL 75 B5
Chojnów PL 85 A3
Cholet F 114 A3
Chomérac F 117 C4
Chomutov CZ 83 B5
Chop UA 12 D5
Chora GR 184 B2
Chora Sfakion GR 185 D5
Chorges F 132 A2
Chorley GB 38 A4
Chornobyl = Chernobyl UA 13 C9
Chortkiv UA 13 D6
Chorzele PL 77 A5
Chorzew PL 86 A2
Chorzów PL 86 B2
Choszczno PL 75 A4
Chotěboř CZ 97 B3
Chouilly F 91 B4
Chouto P 154 B2
Chouzy-sur-Cisse F 103 B3
Chozas de Abajo E 142 B1
Chrast, *Vychodočeský* CZ 97 B3
Chrást, *Západočeský* CZ 96 B1
Chrastava CZ 84 B2
Chřibská CZ 84 B2
Christchurch GB 44 C2
Christiansfeld DK 59 C2
Chroberz PL 87 B4
Chropyně CZ 98 B1
Chrudim CZ 97 B3
Chrzanów PL 86 B3
Chtelnica SK 98 C1
Chudovo RUS 9 C7
Chueca E 157 A4
Chulmleigh GB 42 B3
Chur CH 107 C4
Church Stretton GB 39 B4
Churriana E 163 B3
Churwalden CH 107 C4
Chvalšiny CZ 96 C2
Chwaszczyno PL 69 A3
Chynava CZ 96 A2
Chýnov CZ 96 B2
Ciacova RO 126 B3
Ciadîr-Lunga MD 17 B8
Ciadoncha E 143 B3
Cianciana I 176 B2

Name		Page	Grid
Ciano d'Enza	I	134	A3
Ciążen	PL	76	B2
Cibakhaza	H	113	C4
Ciborro	P	154	C2
Cicagna	I	134	A2
Cicciano	I	170	A4
Ciciliano	I	169	B2
Cicognolo	I	120	B3
Cidadelhe	P	149	A2
Cide	TR	23	A7
Cidones	E	143	C4
Ciechanów, Dolnośląskie	PL	85	A4
Ciechanów, Mazowieckie	PL	77	B5
Ciechocinek	PL	76	B3
Cielądz	PL	87	A4
Ciemnik	PL	75	A4
Ciempozuelos	E	151	B4
Ciepielów	PL	87	A5
Čierny Balog	SK	99	C3
Cierp	F	145	B4
Cierpice	PL	76	B3
Ciervana	E	143	A3
Cierznie	PL	68	B2
Cieslé	PL	77	B5
Cieszyn	PL	98	B2
Cieutat	F	145	A4
Cieza	E	165	A3
Cifer	SK	98	C1
Cifuentes	E	151	B5
Cigales	E	142	C2
Cigliano	I	119	B5
Cihanbeyli	TR	23	B7
Cillas	E	152	B2
Cilleros	E	149	B3
Cilleruelo de Arriba	E	143	C3
Cilleruelo de Bezana	E	143	B3
Cimalmotto	CH	119	A5
Cimanes del Tejar	E	141	B5
Ciminna	I	176	B2
Cimişlia	MD	17	B8
Cimoláis	I	122	A1
Cîmpulung	RO	17	C6
Çınarcık	TR	186	B4
Cinctorres	E	153	B3
Cinderford	GB	39	C4
Çine	TR	188	B3
Ciněves	CZ	84	B3
Ciney	B	79	B5
Cinfães	P	148	A1
Cingia de Botti	I	120	B3
Cíngoli	I	136	B2
Cinigiano	I	135	C4
Cinobaňa	SK	99	C3
Cinq-Mars-la-Pile	F	102	B2
Cinquefrondi	I	175	C2
Cintegabelle	F	146	A2
Cintruénigo	E	144	B2
Ciółkowo	PL	77	B4
Ciperez	E	149	B3
Cirat	E	153	B3
Cirella	I	174	B1
Cirencester	GB	44	B2
Cirey-sur-Vezouze	F	92	C2
Ciria	E	152	A2
Ciriè	I	119	B4
Cirigliano	I	174	A2
Cirò	I	174	B3
Cirò Marina	I	174	B3
Ciry-le-Noble	F	104	C3
Cislău	RO	17	C7
Cismon del Grappa	I	121	B4
Cisneros	E	142	B2
Cissac-Médoc	F	128	A2
Čista	CZ	96	A1
Cisterna di Latina	I	169	B2
Cistérniga	E	150	A3
Cisternino	I	173	B3
Cistierna	E	142	B1
Čitluk	BIH	139	B3
Cítov	CZ	84	B2
Città del Vaticano = Vatican City	I	168	B2
Città della Pieve	I	135	C5
Città di Castello	I	135	B5
Città Sant'Angelo	I	169	A4
Cittadella	I	121	B4
Cittaducale	I	169	A2
Cittanova	I	175	C2
Ciudad Real	E	157	B4
Ciudad Rodrigo	E	149	B3
Ciudadela de Menorca	E	167	B3
Cividale del Friuli	I	122	A2
Cívita	I	169	A3
Cívita Castellana	I	168	A2
Civitanova Alta	I	136	B2
Civitanova Marche	I	136	B2
Civitavécchia	I	168	A1
Civitella di Romagna	I	135	A4
Civitella di Tronto	I	136	C2
Civitella Roveto	I	169	B3
Civray	F	115	B4
Çivril	TR	189	A4
Cizur Mayor	E	144	B2
Cjutadilla	E	147	C2
Clabhach	GB	34	B1
Clachan	GB	31	B2
Clachan na Luib	GB	31	B1
Clacton-on-Sea	GB	45	B5
Cladich	GB	34	B2
Claggan	GB	34	B2
Clairvaux-les-Lacs	F	105	C4
Clamecy	F	104	B2
Claonaig	GB	34	C2
Clarecastle	IRL	28	B3
Claregalway	IRL	28	A3
Claremorris	IRL	28	A2
Clarinbridge	IRL	28	A3
Clashmore	GB	32	D2
Clashmore	IRL	29	B4
Claudy	GB	27	B3
Clausthal-Zellerfeld	D	82	A2
Cláut	I	122	A1
Clay Cross	GB	40	B2
Claye-Souilly	F	90	C2
Cléder	F	100	A1
Cleethorpes	GB	41	B3
Clefmont	F	105	A4
Cléguérec	F	100	A2
Clelles	F	118	C2
Clenze	D	73	B3
Cleobury Mortimer	GB	39	B4
Cléon-d'Andran	F	117	C4
Cléré-les-Pins	F	102	B2
Clères	F	89	A5
Clermont	F	90	B2
Clermont-en-Argonne	F	91	B5
Clermont-Ferrand	F	116	B3
Clermont-l'Hérault	F	130	B2
Clerval	F	105	B5
Clervaux	L	92	A2
Clèry-St. André	F	103	B3
Cles	I	121	A4
Clevedon	GB	43	B4
Cleveleys	GB	38	A3
Cley	GB	41	C5
Clifden	IRL	28	A1
Clifford	GB	39	B3
Clisson	F	101	B4
Clitheroe	GB	40	B1
Clogh	IRL	30	B1
Cloghan, Donegal	IRL	26	B3
Cloghan, Offaly	IRL	28	A4
Clogheen	IRL	29	B4
Clogher	GB	27	B3
Cloghjordan	IRL	28	B3
Clohars-Carnoët	F	100	B2
Clonakilty	IRL	29	C3
Clonaslee	IRL	30	A1
Clondalkin	IRL	30	A2
Clones	IRL	27	B3
Clonmany	IRL	27	A3
Clonmel	IRL	29	B4
Clonmellon	IRL	30	A1
Clonord	IRL	30	A1
Clonroche	IRL	30	B2
Cloone	IRL	26	C3
Cloppenburg	D	71	B5
Closeburn	GB	36	A3
Clough	GB	27	B5
Clova	GB	35	B4
Clovelly	GB	42	B2
Clowne	GB	40	B2
Cloyes-sur-le-Loir	F	103	B3
Cloyne	IRL	29	C3
Cluis	F	103	C3
Cluj-Napoca	RO	17	B5
Clun	GB	39	B3
Clunes	GB	34	B3
Cluny	F	117	A4
Cluses	F	118	A3
Clusone	I	120	B2
Clydach	GB	39	C3
Clydebank	GB	34	C3
Coachford	IRL	29	C3
Coagh	GB	27	B4
Coalisland	GB	27	B4
Coalville	GB	40	C2
Coaña	E	141	A4
Çobanlar	TR	187	D5
Cobas	E	140	A2
Cobertelade	E	151	A5
Cobeta	E	152	B1
Cóbh	IRL	29	C3
Cobreces	E	142	A2
Coburg	D	82	B2
Coca	E	150	A3
Cocentaina	E	159	C3
Cochem	D	80	B3
Cockburnspath	GB	35	C5
Cockermouth	GB	36	B3
Codigoro	I	121	C5
Codogno	I	120	B2
Codos	E	152	A2
Codróipo	I	122	B1
Codrongianos	I	178	B2
Coelhoso	P	149	A3
Coesfeld	D	71	C4
Coevorden	NL	71	B3
Cofrentes	E	159	B2
Cogeces del Monte	E	150	A3
Coggeshall	GB	45	B4
Cognac	F	115	C3
Cogne	I	119	B4
Cognin	F	118	B2
Cogolin	F	132	B2
Cogollos de Guadix	E	164	B1
Cogollos-Vega	E	163	A4
Cogolludo	E	151	B4
Coimbra	P	148	B1
Coín	E	163	B3
Coirós	E	140	A2
Čoka	SRB	126	B2
Col	SLO	123	B3
Colares	E	154	C1
Cölbe	D	81	B4
Colbitz	D	73	B4
Colchester	GB	45	B4
Coldingham	GB	35	C5
Colditz	D	83	A4
Coldstream	GB	35	C5
Colebrooke	GB	43	B3
Colera	E	146	B4
Coleraine	GB	27	A4
Colfiorito	I	136	B1
Cólico	I	120	A2
Coligny	F	118	A2
Colindres	E	143	A3
Coll de Nargó	E	147	B2
Collado-Mediano	E	151	B3
Collado Villalba	E	151	B4
Collagna	I	134	A3
Collanzo	E	142	A1
Collat	F	117	B3
Colle di Val d'Elsa	I	135	B4
Colle Isarco	I	108	C2
Colle Sannita	I	170	B2
Collécchio	I	120	C3
Colledimezzo	I	169	B4
Colleferro	I	169	B3
Collelongo	I	169	B3
Collepasso	I	173	B4
Collepepe	I	136	C1
Collesalvetti	I	134	B3
Collesano	I	176	B2
Colli a Volturno	I	169	B4
Collin	GB	36	A3
Collinée	F	101	A3
Collingham, Nottinghamshire	GB	40	B2
Collingham, West Yorkshire	GB	40	B2
Collinghorst	D	71	A4
Cóllio	I	120	B3
Collobrières	F	132	B2
Collon	IRL	27	C4
Collooney	IRL	26	B2
Colmar	F	106	A2
Colmars	F	132	A2
Colmenar	E	163	B3
Colmenar de la Sierra	E	151	A4
Colmenar de Oreja	E	151	B4
Colmenar Viejo	E	151	B4
Colmonel	GB	36	A2
Colne	GB	40	B1
Colobraro	I	174	A2
Cologna Véneta	I	121	B4
Cologne = Köln	D	80	B2
Cologne	F	129	C3
Cologne al Serio	I	120	B2
Colombey-les-Belles	F	92	C1
Colombey-les-deux-Églises	F	105	A3
Colombres	E	142	A2
Colomera	E	163	A4
Colomers	E	147	B3
Colomiers	F	129	C4
Colònia de Sant Jordi	E	167	B3
Colorno	I	120	C3
Colos	P	160	B1
Cölpin	D	74	A2
Colpy	GB	33	D4
Colsterworth	GB	40	C3
Coltishall	GB	41	C5
Colunga	E	142	A1
Colwell	GB	37	A4
Colwyn Bay	GB	38	A3
Colyford	GB	43	B3
Colyton	GB	43	B3
Coma-ruga	E	147	C2
Comácchio	I	121	C5
Combarros	E	141	B4
Combeaufontaine	F	105	B4
Comber	GB	27	B5
Comblain-au-Pont	B	80	B1
Combloux	F	118	B3
Combourg	F	88	B2
Combronde	F	116	B3
Comeglians	I	109	C3
Comillas	E	142	A2
Comines	F	78	B3
Cómiso	I	177	C3
Comloşu Mare	RO	126	B2
Commensacq	F	128	B2
Commentry	F	116	A2
Commerau	D	84	A2
Commercy	F	92	C1
Como	I	120	B2
Cómpeta	E	163	B4
Compiègne	F	90	B2
Comporta	P	154	C2
Comps-sur-Artuby	F	132	B2
Comrat	MD	17	B8
Comrie	GB	35	B4
Comunanza	I	136	C2
Cona, Emilia Romagna	I	121	C4
Cona, Veneto	I	121	B5
Concarneau	F	100	B2
Conceição	P	160	B1
Conches-en-Ouche	F	89	B4
Concordia Sagittária	I	122	B1
Concordia sulla Sécchia	I	121	C3
Concots	F	129	B4
Condat	F	116	B2
Condé-en-Brie	F	91	C3
Condé-sur-l'Escaut	F	79	B3
Condé-sur-Marne	F	91	B4
Condé-sur-Noireau	F	88	B3
Condeixa	P	148	B1
Condemios de Abajo	E	151	A4
Condemios de Arriba	E	151	A4
Condino	I	121	B3
Condom	F	129	C3
Condove	I	119	B4
Condrieu	F	117	B4
Conegliano	I	122	B1
Conflans-sur-Lanterne	F	105	B5
Confolens	F	115	B4
Conforto	E	141	A3
Cong	IRL	28	A2
Congleton	GB	40	B1
Congosto	E	141	B4
Congosto de Valdavia	E	142	B2
Congostrina	E	151	A4
Conil de la Frontera	E	162	B1
Coningsby	GB	41	B3
Coniston	GB	36	B3
Conlie	F	102	A1
Conliège	F	105	C4
Conna	IRL	29	B3
Connah's Quay	GB	38	A3
Connantre	F	91	C3
Connaugh	IRL	28	B3
Connaux	F	131	A3
Connel	GB	34	B2
Connerré	F	102	A2
Connonbridge	GB	32	D2
Conoplja	SRB	126	B1
Conques	F	116	C2
Conques-sur-Orbiel	F	146	A3
Conquista	E	157	B3
Conquista de la Sierra	E	156	A2
Consándolo	I	121	C4
Consélice	I	135	A4
Conselve	I	121	B4
Consenvoye	F	91	B5
Consett	GB	37	B5
Consolacão	P	154	B1
Constancia	P	154	B2
Constanco	E	140	A2
Constanţa	RO	17	C8
Constanti	E	147	C2
Constantina	E	162	A2
Consuegra	E	157	A4
Consuma	I	135	B4
Contarina	I	122	B1
Contay	F	90	B2
Conthey	CH	119	A4
Contigliano	I	168	A2
Contis-Plage	F	128	B1
Contrada	I	170	C2
Contres	F	103	B3
Contrexéville	F	105	A4
Controne	I	172	B1
Contursi Termi	I	172	B1
Conty	F	90	B2
Conversano	I	173	B3
Conwy	GB	38	A3
Cookstown	GB	27	B4
Coole	F	91	C4
Coolgreany	IRL	30	B2
Cooneen	GB	27	B3
Cootehill	IRL	27	B3
Cope	E	165	B3
Copenhagen = København	DK	61	D2
Copertino	I	173	B4
Copparo	I	121	C4
Coppenbrugge	D	72	B2
Corabia	RO	17	D6
Córaci	I	175	B2
Coralići	BIH	124	C1
Corato	I	171	B4
Coray	F	100	A2
Corbeil-Essonnes	F	90	C2
Corbeny	F	91	B3
Corbera	E	159	B3
Corbie	F	90	B2
Corbigny	F	104	B2
Corbion	B	91	B4
Corbridge	GB	37	B4
Corby	GB	40	C3
Corconte	E	143	A3
Corcubión	E	140	B1
Corcumello	I	169	A3
Cordenòns	I	122	B1
Cordes-sur-Ciel	F	129	B4
Córdoba	E	156	C3
Cordobilla de Lácara	E	155	B4
Cordovado	I	122	B1
Corella	E	144	B2
Coreses	E	150	A2
Corfe Castle	GB	43	B4
Corga de Lobão	P	148	B1
Cori	I	169	B2
Coria	E	155	B3
Coria del Río	E	162	A1
Corigliano Cálabro	I	174	B2
Corinaldo	I	136	B1
Corinth = Korinthos	GR	184	B3
Cório	I	119	B4
Coripe	E	162	B2
Cork	IRL	29	C3
Corlay	F	100	A2
Corleone	I	176	B2
Corleto Monforte	I	172	B1
Corleto Perticara	I	174	A2
Çorlu	TR	186	A2
Cormainville	F	103	A3
Cormatin	F	104	C3
Cormeilles	F	89	A4
Cormery	F	102	B2
Cormòns	I	122	B2
Cormoz	F	118	A2
Cornago	E	144	B1
Cornberg	D	82	A1
Cornellana	E	141	A4
Cornești	MD	17	B8
Corníglio	I	134	A3
Cornimont	F	106	B1
Corniolo	I	135	B4
Cornuda	I	121	B5
Cornudella de Montsant	E	147	C1
Cornudilla	E	143	B3
Cornus	F	130	B2
Corpach	GB	34	B2
Corps	F	118	C2
Corps Nuds	F	101	B4
Corral de Almaguer	E	157	A4
Corral de Ayllón	E	151	A4
Corral de Calatrava	E	157	B3
Corral-Rubio	E	158	C2
Corrales	E	149	A4
Corran	GB	34	B2
Corredoiras	E	140	A2
Corréggio	I	121	C3
Corrèze	F	116	B1
Corridónia	I	136	B2
Corris	GB	38	B3
Corrubedo	E	140	B1
Córsico	I	120	B2
Corsock	GB	36	A3
Corte	F	180	A2
Corte de Peleas	E	155	C4
Corte Pinto	P	160	B2
Corteconceptión	E	161	B3
Cortegaca	P	148	B1
Cortegada	E	140	B2
Cortegana	E	161	B3
Cortemaggiore	I	120	B2
Cortemilia	I	133	A4
Cortes	E	144	C2
Cortes de Aragón	E	153	B3
Cortes de Arenoso	E	153	B3
Cortes de Baza	E	164	B2
Cortes de la Frontera	E	162	B2
Cortes de Pallás	E	159	B3
Cortiçadas	P	154	C2
Cortico	P	148	A2
Cortijo de Arriba	E	157	A3
Cortijos Nuevos	E	164	A2
Cortina d'Ampezzo	I	108	C3
Corton	GB	41	C5
Cortona	I	135	B4
Coruche	P	154	C2
Corullón	E	141	B4
Çorum	TR	23	A8
Corvara in Badia	I	108	C2
Corvera	E	165	B3
Corwen	GB	38	B3
Cosenza	I	174	B2
Cosham	GB	44	C2
Coslada	E	151	B4
Cosne-Cours-sur-Loire	F	104	B1
Cosne d'Allier	F	103	C4
Cospeito	E	140	A3
Cossato	I	119	B5
Cossaye	F	104	C2
Cossé-le-Vivien	F	101	B5
Cossonay	CH	105	C5
Costa da Caparica	P	154	C1
Costa de Santo André	P	160	A1
Costa Nova	P	148	B1
Costalpino	I	135	B4
Costaros	F	117	C3
Costeşti	RO	17	C6
Costigliole d'Asti	I	119	C5
Costigliole Saluzzo	I	133	A3
Coswig, Sachsen-Anhalt	D	83	A4
Coswig, Sachsen	D	83	A5
Cotherstone	GB	37	B5
Cotronei	I	175	B2
Cottbus	D	84	A2
Cottenham	GB	45	A4
Cottingham	GB	40	B3
Coublanc	F	105	B4
Couches	F	104	C3
Couço	P	154	C2
Coucouron	F	117	C3
Coucy-le-Château-Auffrique	F	90	B3
Couëron	F	101	B4
Couflens	F	146	B2
Couhé	F	115	B4
Couiza	F	146	B3
Coulags	GB	31	B3
Coulanges	F	104	C2
Coulanges-la-Vineuse	F	104	B2
Coulanges-sur-Yonne	F	104	B2
Couleuvre	F	104	C1
Coulmier-le-Sec	F	104	B3
Coulommiers	F	90	C3
Coulonges-sur-l'Autize	F	114	B3
Coulounieix-Chamiers	F	129	A3
Coulport	GB	34	B3
Coupar Angus	GB	35	B4
Coupéville	F	91	C4
Couptrain	F	89	B3
Cour-Cheverny	F	103	B3
Cour-et-Buis	F	117	B4
Coura	F	140	C2
Courcelles	B	79	B4
Courcelles-Chaussy	F	92	B2
Courchevel	F	118	B3
Courcôme	F	115	C4
Courçon	F	114	B3
Courgenay	CH	106	B2
Courmayeur	I	119	B3
Courniou	F	130	B1
Cournon-d'Auvergne	F	116	B3
Cournonterral	F	130	B2
Courpière	F	117	B3
Cours-la-Ville	F	117	A4
Coursan	F	130	B2
Courseulles-sur-Mer	F	89	A3
Courson-les-Carrières	F	104	B2
Courtalain	F	103	A3
Courtenay	F	104	A2
Courtomer	F	89	B4
Courville, Eure-et-Loire	F	89	B5
Courville, Marne	F	91	B3
Coussac-Bonneval	F	115	C5
Coutances	F	88	A2
Couterne	F	89	B3
Coutras	F	128	A2
Couvet	CH	106	C1
Couvin	B	91	A4
Couzon	F	104	C2
Covadonga	E	142	A1
Covaleda	E	143	C4
Covarrubias	E	143	B3
Covas	P	148	A1
Cove	GB	31	B3
Coventry	GB	44	A2
Coverack	GB	42	B1
Covigliáio	I	135	A4
Covilhã	P	148	B2
Cowbridge	GB	39	C3
Cowdenbeath	GB	35	B4
Cowes	GB	44	C2
Cox	F	129	C4
Cózar	E	157	B4
Cozes	F	114	C3
Cozzano	F	180	B2
Craco	I	174	A2
Cracow = Kraków	PL	99	A3
Craibstone	GB	33	D4
Craighouse	GB	34	C2
Craignure	GB	34	B2
Crail	GB	35	B5
Crailsheim	D	94	B2
Craiova	RO	17	C5
Cramlington	GB	37	A5
Cranleigh	GB	44	B3
Craon	F	101	B5
Craonne	F	91	B3
Craponne-sur-Arzon	F	117	B3
Crathie	GB	32	D3
Crato	P	155	B3

Name		Page	Grid
Craughwell	IRL	28	A3
Craven Arms	GB	39	B4
Crawford	GB	36	A3
Crawinkel	D	82	B2
Crawley	GB	44	B4
Creag Ghoraidh	GB	31	B1
Crecente	E	140	B2
Crèches-sur-Saône	F	117	A4
Crécy-en-Ponthieu	F	78	B1
Crécy-la-Chapelle	F	90	C2
Crécy-sur-Serre	F	91	B3
Crediton	GB	43	B3
Creeslough	IRL	26	A3
Creetown	GB	36	B2
Creeve	GB	27	B4
Creglingen	D	94	B2
Creil	F	90	B2
Creissels	F	130	A2
Crema	I	120	B2
Cremeaux	F	117	B3
Crémenes	E	142	B1
Crémieu	F	118	B2
Cremlingen	D	73	B3
Cremona	I	120	B3
Creney	F	91	C4
Črenšovci	SLO	111	C3
Créon	F	128	B2
Crepaja	SRB	127	B2
Crépey	F	92	C1
Crépy	F	91	B3
Crépy-en-Valois	F	90	B2
Cres	HR	123	C3
Crescentino	I	119	B5
Crespino	I	121	C4
Crespos	E	150	B3
Cressage	GB	39	B4
Cressensac	F	129	A4
Cressia	F	105	C4
Crest	F	117	C5
Cresta	CH	107	C4
Créteil	F	90	C2
Creully	F	88	A3
Creussen	D	95	B3
Creutzwald	F	92	B2
Creuzburg	D	82	A2
Crevalcore	I	121	C4
Crèvecœur-le-Grand	F	90	B2
Crevillente	E	165	A4
Crévola d'Ossola	I	119	A5
Crewe	GB	38	A4
Crewkerne	GB	43	B4
Criales	E	143	B3
Crianlarich	GB	34	B3
Criccieth	GB	38	C2
Crickhowell	GB	39	C3
Cricklade	GB	44	B2
Crieff	GB	35	B4
Criel-sur-Mer	F	90	A1
Crikvenica	HR	123	B3
Crillon	F	90	B1
Crimmitschau	D	83	B4
Crimond	GB	33	D5
Crinitz	D	84	A1
Cripán	E	143	B4
Criquetot-l'Esneval	F	89	A4
Crispiano	I	173	B3
Crissolo	I	119	C4
Cristóbal	E	149	B4
Crivitz	D	73	A4
Črna	SLO	110	C1
Crna Bara, *Srbija*	SRB	127	C1
Crna Bara, *Vojvodina*	SRB	126	B2
Crnac	HR	125	B3
Crnča	SRB	127	C1
Crni Lug	BIH	138	A2
Crni Lug	HR	123	B3
Črni Vrh	SLO	123	B3
Crnjelovo Donje	BIH	125	C5
Črnomelj	SLO	123	B4
Crocketford	GB	36	A3
Crocq	F	116	B2
Crodo	I	119	A5
Croglin	GB	37	B4
Crolly	IRL	26	A2
Cromarty	GB	32	D2
Cromer	GB	41	C5
Cronat	F	104	C2
Crookhaven	IRL	29	C2
Crookstown	IRL	29	C3
Croom	IRL	29	B3
Cropalati	I	174	B2
Crópani	I	175	C2
Crosbost	GB	31	A2
Crosby	GB	38	A3
Crosía	I	174	B2
Cross-Hands	GB	39	C2
Crossakiel	IRL	27	C3
Crosshaven	IRL	29	C3
Crosshill	GB	36	A2
Crossmolina	IRL	26	B1
Crotone	I	175	B3
Crottendorf	D	83	B4
Crouy	F	90	B3
Crowborough	GB	45	B4
Crowland	GB	41	C3
Crowthorne	GB	44	B3
Croyde	GB	42	A2
Croydon	GB	44	B3
Crozon	F	100	A1
Cruas	F	117	C4
Cruceni	RO	126	A3
Crúcoli	I	174	B3
Cruden Bay	GB	33	D5
Crudgington	GB	38	B4
Cruis	F	132	A2
Crumlin	GB	27	B4
Crusheen	IRL	28	B3
Cruz de Incio	E	141	B3
Crvenka	SRB	126	B1
Červený Kamen	SK	98	B2
Csabacsúd	H	113	C4
Csabrendek	H	111	B4
Csákánydoroszló	H	111	C3
Csákvár	H	112	B2
Csanádapáca	H	113	C4
Csanádpalota	H	126	A2
Csány	H	113	B3
Csanytelek	H	113	C4
Csapod	H	111	B3
Császár	H	112	B2
Császártöltés	H	112	C3
Csávoly	H	125	A5
Csemő	H	113	B3
Csengöd	H	112	C3
Csépa	H	113	C4
Csepreg	H	111	B3
Cserkeszölö	H	113	C4
Csernely	H	113	A4
Csesztreg	H	111	C3
Csökmö	H	113	B5
Csököly	H	124	A3
Csokonyavisonta	H	124	A3
Csólyospálos	H	113	C3
Csongrád	H	113	C4
Csopak	H	112	C1
Csorna	H	111	B4
Csorvás	H	113	C4
Csurgo	H	124	A3
Cuacos de Yuste	E	150	B2
Cualedro	E	140	C3
Cuanca de Campos	E	142	B1
Cuba	P	160	A2
Cubel	E	152	A2
Cubelles	E	147	C2
Cubillos	E	143	C4
Cubillos del Sil	E	141	B4
Cubjac	F	129	A3
Cubo de la Solana	E	152	A1
Çubuk	TR	23	A7
Cuckfield	GB	44	B3
Cucuron	F	131	B4
Cudillero	E	141	A4
Cuéllar	E	151	A3
Cuenca	E	152	B1
Cuers	F	132	B2
Cuerva	E	157	A3
Cueva de Agreda	E	144	C2
Cuevas Bajas	E	163	A3
Cuevas de San Clemente	E	143	B3
Cuevas de San Marcos	E	163	A3
Cuevas del Almanzora	E	164	B3
Cuevas del Becerro	E	162	B2
Cuevas del Campo	E	164	B2
Cuevas del Valle	E	150	B2
Cuges-les-Pins	F	132	B1
Cúglieri	I	178	B2
Cugnaux	F	129	C4
Cuijk	NL	80	A1
Cuinzier	F	117	A4
Cuiseaux	F	105	C4
Cuisery	F	105	C4
Culan	F	103	C4
Culemborg	NL	79	A5
Cúllar	E	164	B2
Cullaville	GB	27	B4
Cullera	E	159	B3
Cullivoe	GB	33	A5
Cullompton	GB	43	B3
Cully	CH	106	C1
Culoz	F	118	B2
Cults	GB	33	D4
Cumbernauld	GB	35	C4
Cumbres de San Bartolomé	E	161	A3
Cumbres Mayores	E	161	A3
Cumiana	I	119	C4
Čumić	SRB	127	C2
Cumnock	GB	36	A2
Çumra	TR	23	C7
Cúneo	I	133	A3
Cunlhat	F	117	B3
Čunski	HR	123	C3
Cuntis	E	140	B2
Cuorgnè	I	119	B4
Cupar	GB	35	B4
Cupello	I	170	B2
Cupra Maríttima	I	136	B2
Cupramontana	I	136	B2
Čuprija	SRB	127	D3
Curinga	I	175	C2
Currelos	E	140	B3
Currie	GB	35	C4
Curtea de Argeş	RO	17	C6
Curtici	RO	126	A3
Curtis	E	140	A2
Curtis Santa Eulalia	E	140	A2
Čurug	SRB	126	B2
Cusano Mutri	I	170	B2
Cushendall	GB	27	A4
Cusset	F	117	A3
Cussy-les-Forges	F	104	B3
Custines	F	92	C2
Cutanda	E	152	B2
Cutro	I	175	B2
Cutrofiano	I	173	B4
Cuts	F	90	B3
Cuvilly	F	90	B2
Cuxhaven	D	64	C1
Cvikov	CZ	84	B2
Cwmbran	GB	39	C3
Cybinka	PL	75	B3
Czacz	PL	75	B5
Czajków	PL	86	A2
Czaplinek	PL	75	A5
Czarlin	PL	69	A3
Czarna-Dąbrówka	PL	68	A2
Czarna Woda	PL	68	B3
Czarnca	PL	87	B3
Czarne	PL	68	B1
Czarnków	PL	75	B5
Czarnowo	PL	76	A3
Czarnozyly	PL	86	A2
Czarny Bór	PL	85	B4
Czarny-Dunajec	PL	99	B3
Czarny Las	PL	86	A1
Czchow	PL	99	B4
Czechowice-Dziedzice	PL	98	B2
Czempiń	PL	75	B5
Czermno	PL	87	A4
Czernichow	PL	99	B3
Czerniejewo	PL	76	B2
Czernikowo	PL	76	B3
Czersk	PL	68	B2
Czerwieńsk	PL	75	B4
Czerwionka-Leszczyny	PL	86	B2
Częstochowa	PL	86	B3
Czeszewo	PL	76	B2
Człopa	PL	75	A5
Człuchów	PL	68	B2
Czołpino	PL	68	A2

D

Name		Page	Grid
Daaden	D	81	B3
Dabas	H	112	B3
Dąbie	PL	76	B3
Dąbki	PL	67	B5
Dabo	F	92	C3
Dabrowa	PL	76	B2
Dąbrowa Górnicza	PL	86	B3
Dąbrowa Tarnowska	PL	87	B4
Dąbrowice	PL	77	B4
Dabrowno	PL	77	A5
Dachau	D	108	A2
Dačice	CZ	97	B3
Daday	TR	23	A7
Dağ	TR	189	B5
Dagali	N	47	B5
Dägebüll	D	64	B1
Dagmersellen	CH	106	B2
Dahlen	D	83	A4
Dahlenburg	D	73	A3
Dahme	D	83	A5
Dahn	D	93	B3
Dähre	D	73	B3
Daikanvik	S	195	E7
Dail bho Dheas	GB	31	A2
Dailly	GB	36	A2
Daimiel	E	157	A4
Daingean	IRL	30	A1
Đakovica	KOS	16	D4
Đakovo	HR	125	B4
Dal, *Akershus*	N	48	B3
Dal, *Telemark*	N	47	C5
Dala-Floda	S	50	B1
Dala-Husby	S	50	B2
Dala-Järna	S	50	B1
Dalaas	A	107	B5
Dalabrog	GB	31	B1
Dalaman	TR	188	C3
Dalarö	S	57	A4
Dalbeattie	GB	36	B3
Dalby	DK	59	C3
Dalby, *Skåne*	S	61	D3
Dalby, *Uppsala*	S	57	A3
Dalby, *Värmland*	S	49	B4
Dale, *Pembrokeshire*	GB	39	C1
Dale, *Shetland*	GB	33	A5
Dale, *Hordaland*	N	46	B2
Dale, *Sogn og Fjordane*	N	46	A2
Dalen, *Akershus*	N	48	C3
Dalen, *Telemark*	N	53	A4
Daleszyce	PL	87	B4
Dalhalvaig	GB	32	C3
Dalheim	L	92	B2
Dalhem	S	57	C4
Dalías	E	164	C2
Dalj	HR	125	B4
Dalkeith	GB	35	C4
Dalkey	IRL	30	A2
Dalmally	GB	34	B3
Dalmellington	GB	36	A2
Dalmose	DK	65	A4
Daløy	N	46	A1
Dalry, *Dumfries & Galloway*	GB	34	C3
Dalry, *North Ayrshire*	GB	36	A2
Dalrymple	GB	36	A2
Dals Långed	S	54	B3
Dals Rostock	S	54	B3
Dalseter	N	47	A6
Dalsjöfors	S	60	B3
Dalskog	S	54	B3
Dalston	GB	36	B4
Dalstorp	S	60	B3
Dalton-in-Furness	GB	36	B3
Daluis	F	132	A2
Dalum	D	71	B4
Dalum	S	60	B3
Dalvík	IS	191	B7
Dalwhinnie	GB	32	E2
Dalyan	TR	188	C3
Damasi	GR	182	D4
Damasławek	PL	76	B2
Damazan	F	129	B3
Dammartin-en-Goële	F	90	B2
Damme	D	71	B5
Damnica	PL	68	A2
Dampierre	F	105	B4
Dampierre-sur-Salon	F	105	B4
Damüls	A	107	B4
Damville	F	89	B5
Damvillers	F	92	B1
Damwoude	NL	70	A2
Danasjö	S	195	E7
Danbury	GB	45	B4
Dangé-St. Romain	F	102	C2
Dångebo	S	63	B3
Dangers	F	89	B5
Dangeul	F	89	B4
Danilovgrad	MNE	16	D3
Danischenhagen	D	64	B3
Daniszyn	PL	85	A5
Danjoutin	F	106	B1
Dannas	S	60	B3
Dannemarie	F	106	B2
Dannemora	S	51	B4
Dannenberg	D	73	A4
Dánszentmiklós	H	112	B3
Dány	H	112	B3
Daoulas	F	100	A1
Darabani	RO	17	A7
Darány	H	125	B3
Darda	HR	125	B4
Dardesheim	D	73	C3
Darfeld	D	71	B4
Darfo	I	120	B3
Dargiń	PL	68	A1
Dargun	D	66	C1
Darlington	GB	37	B5
Darłowo	PL	68	A1
Darmstadt	D	93	B4
Darney	F	105	A5
Daroca	E	152	A2
Darque	P	148	A1
Darragh	IRL	28	B2
Dartford	GB	45	B4
Dartington	GB	43	B3
Dartmouth	GB	43	B3
Darton	GB	40	B2
Daruvar	HR	124	B3
Darvas	H	113	B5
Darvel	GB	36	A2
Darwen	GB	38	A4
Dassel	D	82	A1
Dassow	D	65	C3
Datça	TR	188	C2
Datteln	D	80	A3
Dattenfeld	D	81	B3
Daugard	DK	59	C2
Daugavpils	LV	8	E5
Daumeray	F	102	B1
Daun	D	80	B2
Davle	CZ	96	B2
Davor	HR	124	B3
Davos	CH	107	C4
Davutlar	TR	188	B2
Davyd Haradok	BY	13	B7
Dawlish	GB	43	B3
Dazkırı	TR	189	B4
De Cocksdorp	NL	70	A1
De Haan	B	78	A3
De Koog	NL	70	A1
De Panne	B	78	A2
De Wijk	NL	71	B3
Deal	GB	45	B5
Deauville	F	89	A4
Deba	E	143	A4
Debar	MK	182	B2
Dębe	PL	77	B5
Dębica	PL	87	B5
Dęblin	PL	87	A5
Dębno	PL	74	B3
Dębolęka	PL	86	A2
Dębowa Łąka	PL	69	B4
Debrc	SRB	127	C1
Debrecen	H	113	B5
Debrznica	PL	75	B4
Debrzno	PL	68	B2
Debstedt	D	72	A1
Decazeville	F	130	A1
Dechtice	SK	98	C1
Decima	I	168	B2
Decimomannu	I	179	C2
Děčín	CZ	84	B2
Decize	F	104	C2
Decollatura	I	175	B2
Decs	H	125	A4
Deddington	GB	44	B2
Dedeler	TR	187	B5
Dedelow	D	74	A2
Dedemli	TR	189	B7
Dedemsvaart	NL	71	B3
Dédestapolcsány	H	113	A4
Dedovichi	RUS	9	D6
Deeping St. Nicholas	GB	41	C3
Dég	H	112	C2
Degaña	E	141	B4
Degeberga	S	61	D4
Degerby	FIN	51	B7
Degerfors	S	55	A5
Degerhamn	S	63	B4
Degernes	N	54	A2
Deggendorf	D	95	C4
Deggingen	D	94	C1
Dego	I	133	A4
Degolados	P	155	B3
Dehesas de Guadix	E	164	B1
Dehesas Viejas	E	163	A4
Deia	E	166	B2
Deining	D	95	B3
Deinze	B	79	B3
Déiva Marina	I	134	A2
Dej	RO	17	B5
Deje	S	55	A4
Delabole	GB	42	B2
Delary	S	61	C3
Delbrück	D	81	A4
Delčevo	MK	182	B4
Delden	NL	71	B3
Deleitosa	E	156	A2
Delekovec	HR	124	A2
Delémont	CH	106	B2
Delft	NL	70	B1
Delfzijl	NL	71	A3
Délia	I	176	B2
Delianuova	I	175	C1
Deliblato	SRB	127	C3
Delice	TR	23	B7
Deliceto	I	171	B3
Delitzsch	D	83	A4
Dellach	A	109	C4
Delle	F	106	B2
Delme	F	92	C2
Delmen-horst	D	72	A1
Delnice	HR	123	B3
Delsbo	S	200	E2
Delvin	IRL	30	A1
Delvinë	AL	182	D2
Demandice	SK	112	A2
Demen	D	73	A4
Demidov	RUS	13	A9
Demigny	F	105	C3
Demirci	TR	186	C3
Demirköy	TR	186	A2
Demirtaş	TR	186	B4
Demmin	D	66	C2
Demonte	I	133	A3
Demyansk	RUS	9	D8
Den Burg	NL	70	A1
Den Ham	NL	71	B3
Den Helder	NL	70	B1
Den Oever	NL	70	B2
Denain	F	78	B3
Denbigh	GB	38	A3
Dender-monde	B	79	A4
Denekamp	NL	71	B4
Denholm	GB	35	C5
Denia	E	159	C4
Denizli	TR	188	B4
Denkendorf	D	95	C3
Denklingen	D	81	B3
Denny	GB	35	B4
Denta	RO	126	B3
Déols	F	103	C3
Derby	GB	40	C2
Derecske	H	113	B5
Dereköy	TR	186	A2
Derenberg	D	82	A2
Derinkuyu	TR	23	B8
Dermbach	D	82	B2
Dermulo	I	121	A4
Deronje	SRB	125	B5
Derrygonnelly	GB	26	B3
Derrylin	GB	27	B3
Derry/Londonderry	GB	27	B3
Dersingham	GB	41	C4
Deruta	I	136	C1
Dervaig	GB	34	B1
Derval	F	101	B4
Derveni	GR	184	A3
Derventa	BIH	125	C3
Dervock	GB	27	A4
Desana	I	119	B5
Descartes	F	102	C2
Desenzano del Garda	I	121	B3
Deset	N	48	A3
Deševa	BIH	139	B4
Desfina	GR	184	A3
Desimirovac	SRB	127	C2
Désio	I	120	B2
Deskati	GR	182	D3
Deskle	SLO	122	A2
Desná	CZ	84	B3
Dešov	CZ	97	C3
Despotovac	SRB	127	C3
Despotovo	SRB	126	B1
Dessau	D	83	A4
Deštná	CZ	96	B2
Destriana	E	141	B4
Désulo	I	179	B3
Desvres	F	78	B1
Deszk	H	126	A2
Deta	RO	126	B3
Detmold	D	72	C1
Dětřichov	CZ	98	B1
Dettelbach	D	94	B2
Dettingen, *Baden-Württemberg*	D	94	C1
Dettingen, *Baden-Württemberg*	D	107	B4
Dettwiller	F	93	C3
Detva	SK	99	C3
Deurne	NL	80	A1
Deutsch Wagram	A	111	A3
Deutschkreutz	A	111	B3
Deutschlandsberg	A	110	C2
Deva	RO	16	C5
Dévaványa	H	113	B4
Devecikonağı	TR	186	C3
Devecser	H	111	B4
Develi	TR	23	B8
Devil's Bridge	GB	39	B3
Devin	BG	183	B6
Devinska Nova Ves	SK	111	A3
Devizes	GB	43	A5
Devonport	GB	42	B2
Devrek	TR	187	A6
Devrekâni	TR	23	A7
Đevrske	HR	137	B4
Dewsbury	GB	40	B2
Deza	E	152	A1
Dežanovac	HR	124	B3
Dezzo	I	120	B3
Dhali	CY	181	A2
Dheftera	CY	181	A2
Dherinia	CY	181	A2
Diamante	I	174	B1
Dianalund	DK	61	D1
Diano d'Alba	I	119	C5
Diano Marina	I	133	B4
Dicomano	I	135	B4
Didcot	GB	44	B2
Didimoticho	GR	186	A1
Die	F	118	C2
Diebling	F	92	B2
Dieburg	D	93	B4
Diego del Carpio	E	150	B2
Diekirch	L	92	B2
Diélette	F	88	A2
Diémoz	F	118	B2
Diepenbeck	B	79	B5
Diepholz	D	71	B5
Dieppe	F	89	A5
Dierberg	D	74	A1
Dierdorf	D	81	B3
Dieren	NL	70	B3
Dierhagen	D	66	B1
Diesdorf	D	73	B3
Diessen	D	108	B2
Diest	B	79	B5
Dietenheim	D	94	C2
Dietfurt	D	95	B3
Dietikon	CH	106	B3
Dietzenbach	D	93	A4
Dieue-sur-Meuse	F	92	B1
Dieulefit	F	131	A4
Dieulouard	F	92	C2
Dieuze	F	92	C2
Diever	NL	71	B3
Diez	D	81	B4
Diezma	E	163	A4
Differdange	L	92	B1
Digermulen	N	194	B6
Dignac	F	115	C4
Dignano	I	122	A1
Digne-les-Bains	F	132	A2
Digny	F	89	B5
Digoin	F	104	C2
Dijon	F	105	B4
Dikanäs	S	195	E7
Dikili	TR	186	C1
Diksmuide	B	78	A2
Dilar	E	163	A4
Dillenburg	D	81	B4
Dillingen, *Bayern*	D	94	C2
Dillingen, *Saarland*	D	92	B2
Dilsen	B	80	A1
Dimaro	I	121	A4
Dimitrovgrad	BG	183	A7
Dimitsana	GR	184	B3
Dinami	I	175	C2
Dinan	F	101	A3
Dinant	B	79	B4
Dinar	TR	189	A5
Dinard	F	101	A3
Dinek	TR	187	C6

Place	Country	Page	Grid
Dingden	D	80	A2
Dingelstädt	D	82	A3
Dingle	IRL	29	B1
Dingle	S	54	B2
Dingolfing	D	95	C4
Dingwall	GB	32	D2
Dinkelsbühl	D	94	B2
Dinkelscherben	D	94	C4
Dinklage	D	71	B5
Dinslaken	D	80	A2
Dinxperlo	NL	80	A2
Diö	S	63	B2
Diósgyör	H	113	A4
Diósjeno	H	112	B3
Diou	F	104	C2
Dippen	GB	34	C2
Dipperz	D	82	B1
Dippoldiswalde	D	84	B1
Dirdal	N	52	B2
Dirksland	NL	79	A4
Dirlewang	D	108	B1
Dischingen	D	94	C2
Disentis	CH	107	C3
Diso	I	173	B4
Diss	GB	45	A5
Dissen	D	71	B5
Distington	GB	36	B3
Ditzingen	D	93	C5
Ditzum	D	71	A4
Divača	SLO	122	B2
Dives-sur-Mer	F	89	A3
Divín	SK	99	C3
Divion	F	78	B2
Divišov	CZ	96	B2
Divonne les Bains	F	118	A3
Dixmont	F	104	A2
Dizy-le-Gros	F	91	B4
Djúpivogur	IS	191	C11
Djupvasshytta	N	198	C4
Djura	S	50	B1
Djurås	S	50	B2
Djurmo	S	50	B2
Djursdala	S	62	A3
Dlouhá Loucka	CZ	98	B1
Długowola	PL	87	A5
Dmitrov	RUS	9	D10
Dno	RUS	9	D6
Doade	E	141	B3
Dobanovci	SRB	127	C2
Dobbertin	D	73	A4
Dobbiaco	I	108	C3
Dobczyce	PL	99	B4
Dobele	LV	8	D3
Döbeln	D	83	A5
Doberlug-Kirchhain	D	83	A5
Dobern	D	84	A2
Dobersberg	A	97	C3
Dobiegniew	PL	75	B4
Dobieszyn	PL	87	A5
Doboj	BIH	125	C4
Dobošnica	BIH	125	C4
Doboz	H	113	C5
Dobrá	CZ	98	B2
Dobra, Wielkopolskie	PL	76	C3
Dobra, Zachodnio-Pomorskie	PL	75	A4
Dobra, Zachodnio-Pomorskie	PL	74	A3
Dobrá Niva	SK	99	C3
Dobřany	CZ	96	B1
Dobre	PL	76	B3
Dobre Miasto	PL	69	B5
Dobreta-Turnu-Severin	RO	16	C5
Dobri	H	111	C3
Dobrica	SRB	126	B2
Dobrich	BG	17	D7
Dobrinishta	BG	183	B5
Dobříš	CZ	96	B2
Dobro	E	143	B3
Dobrodzień	PL	86	B2
Döbrököz	H	112	C2
Dobromierz	PL	85	B4
Dobrosołowo	PL	76	B3
Dobroszyce	PL	85	A5
Dobrovnik	SLO	111	C3
Dobrush	BY	13	B9
Dobruška	CZ	85	B4
Dobrzany	PL	75	A4
Dobrzen Wielki	PL	86	B1
Dobrzyca, Wielkopolskie	PL	75	A5
Dobrzyca, Wielkopolskie	PL	85	A5
Dobrzyca, Zachodnio-Pomorskie	PL	67	B4
Dobrzyń nad Wisłą	PL	77	B4
Dobšiná	SK	99	C4
Dobwalls	GB	42	B2
Dochamps	B	80	B1
Docking	GB	41	C4
Docksta	S	200	C4
Doddington	GB	37	B4
Döderhult	S	62	A4
Doesburg	NL	70	B3
Doetinchem	NL	71	B3
Doğanhisar	TR	189	A6
Dogliani	I	133	A4
Dogueno	P	160	B2
Dois Portos	P	154	B1
Doische	B	91	A4
Dojč	SK	98	C1
Dokka	N	48	B2
Dokkedal	DK	58	B3
Dokkum	NL	70	A2
Dokležovje	SLO	111	C3
Doksy	CZ	84	B2
Dokuz	TR	189	A7
Dol-de-Bretagne	F	88	B2
Dolancourt	F	104	A3
Dolceácqua	I	133	B3
Dole	F	105	B4
Dølemo	N	53	B4
Dolenja vas	SLO	123	B3
Dolenjske Toplice	SLO	123	B4
Dolfor	GB	39	B3
Dolgarrog	GB	38	A3
Dolgellau	GB	38	B3
Doliana	GR	182	D2
Dolianova	I	179	C3
Dolice	PL	75	A4
Doljani	I	138	A2
Döllach im Mölltal	A	109	C3
Dolle	D	73	B4
Dollnstein	D	94	C3
Dollot	F	104	A2
Döllstadt	D	82	A2
Dolný Kubín	SK	99	B3
Dolo	I	121	B5
Dolores	E	165	A4
Dolovo	SRB	127	C2
Dölsach	A	109	C3
Dolsk	PL	76	B2
Dolwyddelan	GB	38	A3
Domaljevac	BIH	125	B4
Domaniç	TR	187	C4
Domaniža	SK	98	B2
Domanovići	BIH	139	B3
Domašov	CZ	85	B5
Domaszék	H	126	A1
Domaszków	PL	85	B4
Domaszowice	PL	86	A1
Domat-Ems	CH	107	C4
Domažlice	CZ	95	B4
Dombås	N	198	C6
Dombasle-sur-Meurthe	F	92	C2
Dombegyház	H	126	A3
Dombóvár	H	112	C2
Domène	F	118	B2
Domérat	F	116	A2
Domfessel	F	92	C3
Domfront	F	88	B3
Domfront-en-Champagne	F	102	A2
Domingão	P	154	B2
Domingo Pérez, Granada	E	163	A4
Domingo Pérez, Toledo	E	150	C3
Dömitz	D	73	A4
Dommartin	F	91	C4
Dommartin-le-Franc	F	91	C4
Domme	F	129	B4
Dommitzsch	D	83	A4
Domodóssola	I	119	A5
Domokos	GR	182	D4
Domoszló	H	113	A4
Dompaire	F	105	A5
Dompierre-du-Chemin	F	88	B2
Dompierre-sur-Besbre	F	104	C2
Dompierre-sur-Mer	F	114	B2
Domrémy-la-Pucelle	F	92	C1
Dömsöd	H	112	B3
Domsure	F	118	A2
Dómus de Maria	I	179	D2
Domusnóvas	I	179	C2
Domvena	GR	184	A3
Domžale	SLO	123	A3
Don Alvaro	E	155	C4
Don Benito	E	156	B2
Doña Mencía	E	163	A3
Donado	E	141	B4
Donaghadee	GB	27	B5
Donaueschingen	D	106	B3
Donauwörth	D	94	C2
Doncaster	GB	40	B2
Donegal	IRL	26	B2
Donestebe-Santesteban	E	144	A2
Dongen	NL	79	A5
Donges	F	101	B3
Dongo	I	120	A2
Donington	GB	41	C3
Doniños	E	140	A2
Donja Bebrina	HR	125	B4
Donja Brela	HR	138	B2
Donja Dubica	BIH	125	B4
Donja Dubrava	HR	124	A2
Donja Kupčina	HR	123	B4
Donja Šatornja	SRB	127	C2
Donja Stubica	HR	124	B1
Donje Brišnik	BIH	138	B3
Donje Stative	HR	123	B4
Donji-Andrijevci	HR	125	B4
Donji Kazanci	BIH	138	B2
Donji Koričáni	BIH	138	A3
Donji Lapac	HR	124	C1
Donji Malovan	BIH	138	B3
Donji Miholjac	HR	125	B4
Donji Mosti	HR	124	A2
Donji Poloj	HR	123	B4
Donji-Rujani	BIH	138	B2
Donji Srb	HR	138	A2
Donji Svilaj	BIH	125	B4
Donji Tovarnik	SRB	127	C1
Donji Vakuf	BIH	138	A3
Donnalucata	I	177	C3
Donnemarie-Dontilly	F	90	C3
Donnersbach	A	110	B1
Donnersbachwald	A	109	B5
Donnerskirchen	A	111	B3
Donorático	I	134	B3
Donostia-San Sebastián	E	144	A2
Donovaly	SK	99	C3
Donzenac	F	129	A4
Donzère	F	131	A3
Donzy	F	104	B2
Doonbeg	IRL	29	B2
Doorn	NL	70	B2
Dor	TR	140	A1
Dorchester	GB	43	B4
Dørdal	N	53	B5
Dordrecht	NL	79	A4
Dörenthe	D	71	B4
Dores	GB	32	D2
Dorf Mecklenburg	D	65	C4
Dorfen	D	95	C4
Dorfgastein	A	109	B4
Dorfmark	D	72	B2
Dorgali	I	178	B3
Dorking	GB	44	B3
Dormagen	D	80	A2
Dormánd	H	113	B4
Dormans	F	91	B3
Dornava	SLO	124	A1
Dornbirn	A	107	B4
Dornburg	D	83	A3
Dorndorf	D	82	B2
Dornecy	F	104	B2
Dornes	F	104	C2
Dornhan	D	93	C4
Dornie	GB	31	B3
Dornoch	GB	32	D2
Dornum	D	71	A4
Dorog	H	112	B2
Dorohoi	RO	17	B7
Dorotea	S	200	B3
Dorotowo	PL	69	B5
Dörpen	D	71	B4
Dorsten	D	80	A2
Dortan	F	118	A2
Dortmund	D	80	A3
Doruchów	PL	86	A2
Dorum	D	64	C1
Dörverden	D	72	B2
Dörzbach	D	94	B1
Dos Aguas	E	159	B3
Dos Hermanas	E	162	A2
Dos-Torres	E	156	B3
Dosbarrios	E	151	C4
Döşemealtı	TR	189	B5
Dospat	BG	183	B6
Dötlingen	D	72	B1
Dottignies	B	78	B3
Döttingen	CH	106	B3
Douai	F	78	B3
Douarnenez	F	100	A1
Douchy	F	104	B2
Douchy-les-Mines	F	78	B3
Doucier	F	105	C4
Doudeville	F	89	A4
Doué-la-Fontaine	F	102	B1
Douglas, Isle of Man	GB	36	B2
Douglas, South Lanarkshire	GB	36	A3
Doulaincourt	F	91	C5
Doulevant-le-Château	F	91	C4
Doullens	F	90	A2
Dounby	GB	33	B3
Doune	GB	35	B3
Dounreay	GB	32	C3
Dour	B	79	B3
Dourdan	F	90	C2
Dourgne	F	146	A3
Douro Calvo	P	148	B2
Douvaine	F	118	A3
Douvres-la-Délivrande	F	89	A3
Douzy	F	91	B5
Dover	GB	45	B5
Dovje	SLO	109	C4
Dovre	N	198	D6
Downham Market	GB	41	C4
Downhill	GB	27	A4
Downpatrick	GB	27	B5
Doxato	GR	183	B6
Doyet	F	116	A2
Dozule	F	89	A3
Drača	SRB	127	C2
Dračevo	BIH	139	C4
Dračevo	MK	182	B3
Drachten	NL	70	A3
Draga	SLO	123	B3
Drăgăşani	RO	17	C6
Dragatuš	SLO	123	B4
Dragichyn	BY	13	B6
Draginja	SRB	127	C1
Dragocvet	SRB	127	C3
Dragolovci	BIH	125	C3
Dragoni	I	170	B2
Dragør	DK	61	D2
Dragotina	HR	124	B2
Dragotinja	BIH	124	B2
Dragozetići	HR	123	B3
Draguignan	F	132	B2
Drahnsdorf	D	74	C2
Drahonice	CZ	96	B2
Drahovce	SK	98	C1
Drama	GR	183	B6
Drammen	N	54	A1
Drangedal	N	53	A5
Drangsnes	IS	190	B4
Dransfeld	D	82	A1
Dranske	D	66	B2
Draperstown	GB	27	B4
Drassburg	A	111	B3
Dravaszabolcs	H	125	B4
Dravograd	SLO	110	C2
Drawno	PL	75	A4
Drawsko Pomorskie	PL	75	A4
Drayton	GB	41	C5
Draždžewo	PL	77	A6
Draženov	CZ	95	B4
Draževac	SRB	127	C2
Dražice	HR	123	B3
Drebkau	D	84	A2
Dreieich	D	93	A4
Dreisen	D	93	B4
Drenovci	HR	125	C4
Drensteinfurt	D	81	A3
Dresden	D	84	A1
Dretyń	PL	68	A1
Dreux	F	89	B5
Dřevohostice	CZ	98	B1
Drevsjø	N	199	D9
Drewitz	D	73	B5
Drezdenko	PL	75	B4
Drežnica	HR	123	B4
Drežnik-Grad	HR	123	C4
Drietona	SK	98	C1
Driffield	GB	40	A3
Drimnin	GB	34	B2
Drimoleague	IRL	29	C2
Dringenberg	D	81	A5
Drinić	BIH	138	A2
Drinjača	BIH	139	A5
Drinovci	BIH	138	B3
Driopida	GR	185	B5
Drivstua	N	198	C6
Drlače	SRB	127	C1
Drnholec	CZ	97	C4
Drniš	HR	138	B2
Drnje	HR	124	A2
Drnovice	CZ	97	B4
Dro	I	121	B3
Drøbak	N	54	A1
Drobin	PL	77	B5
Drochia	MD	17	A7
Drochtersen	D	64	C2
Drogheda	IRL	30	A2
Drohobych	UA	13	D5
Droitwich Spa	GB	44	A1
Drołtowice	PL	85	A5
Dromahair	IRL	26	B2
Dromcolliher	IRL	29	B3
Dromore, Down	GB	27	B4
Dromore, Tyrone	GB	27	B3
Dromore West	IRL	26	B2
Dronero	I	133	A3
Dronfield	GB	40	B2
Drongan	GB	36	A2
Dronninglund	DK	58	A3
Dronrijp	NL	70	A2
Dronten	NL	70	B2
Drosendorf	A	97	C3
Drösing	A	97	C4
Drottningholm	S	57	A3
Droué	F	103	A3
Drulingen	F	92	C3
Drumbeg	GB	32	C1
Drumcliff	IRL	26	B2
Drumgask	GB	32	D2
Drumkeeran	IRL	26	B2
Drummore	GB	36	B2
Drumnadrochit	GB	32	D2
Drumquin	GB	27	B3
Drumshanbo	IRL	26	B2
Drumsna	IRL	26	C2
Drunen	NL	79	A5
Druskininkai	LT	13	A5
Druten	NL	80	A1
Druya	BY	13	A7
Družetići	SRB	127	C2
Drvar	BIH	138	A2
Drvenik	HR	138	B3
Drwalew	PL	77	C6
Drymen	GB	34	B3
Drynoch	GB	31	B2
Drzewce	PL	76	B2
Drzewiany	PL	68	B1
Dub	SRB	127	D1
Dubá	CZ	84	B2
Dubăsari	MD	17	B8
Duben	D	74	C2
Dübendorf	CH	107	B3
Dubi	CZ	84	B1
Dubica	HR	124	B2
Dubna	RUS	9	D10
Dubňany	CZ	98	C1
Dubnica nad Váhom	SK	98	C2
Dubno	UA	13	C6
Dubodiel	SK	98	C2
Dubona	SRB	127	C3
Dubovac	SRB	127	C3
Dubovic	BIH	124	C2
Dubranec	HR	124	B1
Dubrava	HR	124	B2
Dubrava	BIH	125	C4
Dubravica	HR	123	B4
Dubravica	SRB	127	C3
Dubrovnik	HR	139	C4
Dubrovytsya	UA	13	C7
Ducey	F	88	B2
Duchcov	CZ	84	B1
Ducherow	D	74	A2
Dučina	SRB	127	C2
Duclair	F	89	A4
Dudar	H	112	B1
Duddington	GB	40	C3
Duderstadt	D	82	A2
Dudeştii Vechi	RO	126	A2
Dudley	GB	40	C1
Dueñas	E	142	C2
Duesund	N	46	B2
Dueville	I	121	B4
Duffel	B	79	A4
Duffield	GB	40	C2
Dufftown	GB	32	D3
Duga Resa	HR	123	B4
Dugi Rat	HR	138	B2
Dugny-sur-Meuse	F	92	B1
Dugo Selo	HR	124	B2
Dugopolje	HR	138	B2
Duino	I	122	B2
Duisburg	D	80	A2
Dukat	AL	182	C1
Dukovany	CZ	97	B4
Duleek	IRL	30	A2
Dülken	D	80	A2
Dülmen	D	80	A3
Dulovo	BG	17	D7
Dulpetorpet	N	49	B4
Dulverton	GB	43	A3
Dumbarton	GB	34	C3
Dümerek	TR	187	C6
Dumfries	GB	36	A3
Dumlupınar	TR	187	D4
Dümpelfeld	D	80	B2
Dun Laoghaire	IRL	30	A2
Dun-le-Palestel	F	116	A1
Dun-les-Places	F	104	B3
Dun-sur-Auron	F	103	C4
Dun-sur-Meuse	F	91	B5
Dunaalmás	H	112	B2
Dunabogdány	H	112	B3
Dunafalva	H	125	A4
Dunaföldvár	H	112	C2
Dunaharaszti	H	112	B3
Dunajská Streda	SK	111	B4
Dunakeszi	H	112	B3
Dunakiliti	H	111	B4
Dunakömlöd	H	112	C2
Dunapataj	H	112	C2
Dunaszekcsö	H	125	A4
Dunaszentgyorgy	H	112	C2
Dunatetétlen	H	112	C3
Dunaújváros	H	112	C2
Dunavecse	H	112	C2
Dunbar	GB	35	B5
Dunbeath	GB	32	C3
Dunblane	GB	35	B4
Dunboyne	IRL	30	A2
Dundalk	IRL	27	B4
Dundee	GB	35	B5
Dundrennan	GB	36	B3
Dundrum	GB	27	B5
Dunfanaghy	IRL	26	A3
Dunfermline	GB	35	B4
Dungannon	GB	27	B4
Dungarvan	IRL	29	B4
Dungiven	GB	27	B4
Dunglow	IRL	26	B2
Dungourney	IRL	29	C3
Duninowo	PL	68	A1
Dunkeld	GB	35	B4
Dunker	S	56	A2
Dunkerque = Dunkirk	F	78	A2
Dunkineely	IRL	26	B2
Dunkirk = Dunkerque	F	78	A2
Dunlavin	IRL	30	A2
Dunleer	IRL	27	C4
Dunlop	GB	36	A2
Dunmanway	IRL	29	C2
Dunmore	IRL	28	A3
Dunmore East	IRL	30	B2
Dunmurry	GB	27	B4
Dunnet	GB	32	C3
Dunningen	D	107	A3
Dunoon	GB	34	C3
Duns	GB	35	C5
Dunscore	GB	36	A3
Dunsford	GB	43	B3
Dunshaughlin	IRL	30	A2
Dunstable	GB	44	B3
Dunster	GB	43	A3
Dunvegan	GB	31	B2
Duplek	SLO	110	C2
Dupnitsa	BG	17	D5
Durach	D	107	B5
Durağan	TR	23	A8
Durak	TR	186	C3
Durana	E	143	B4
Durance	F	128	B3
Durango	E	143	A4
Durankulak	BG	17	D8
Duras	F	128	B3
Durban-Corbières	F	146	B3
Dürbheim	D	107	A3
Durbuy	B	79	B5
Dúrcal	E	163	B4
Đurdjenovac	HR	125	B4
Đurdjevac	HR	124	A3
Đurdjevik	BIH	139	A4
Düren	D	80	B2
Durham	GB	37	B5
Đurinci	SRB	127	C2
Durlach	D	93	C4
Đurmanec	HR	124	A1
Durness	GB	32	C2
Dürnkrut	A	97	C4
Dürrboden	CH	107	C4
Dürrenboden	CH	107	C3
Durrës	AL	182	B1
Durrow	IRL	30	B1
Durrus	IRL	29	C2
Dursunbey	TR	186	C3
Durtal	F	102	B1
Durup	DK	58	B1
Durusu	TR	186	A3
Dusina	BIH	139	B3
Dusnok	H	112	C2
Dusocin	PL	69	B3
Düsseldorf	D	80	A2
Dusslingen	D	93	C5
Duszniki	PL	75	B5
Duszniki-Zdrój	PL	85	B4
Dutovlje	SLO	122	B2
Duvebo	S	55	B5
Duved	S	199	B9
Düzağac	TR	187	D5
Düzce	TR	187	B6
Dvärsätt	S	199	B11
Dvor	HR	124	B2
Dvorce	CZ	98	B1
Dvorníky	SK	98	C1
Dvory nad Žitavou	SK	112	B2
Dvůr Králové nad Labem	CZ	85	B3
Dybvad	DK	58	A3
Dyce	GB	33	D4
Dygowo	PL	67	B4
Dykehead	GB	35	B4
Dymchurch	GB	45	B5
Dymer	UA	13	C9
Dyrnes	N	198	B4
Dywity	PL	69	B5
Dżanići	BIH	139	B3
Dziadowa Kłoda	PL	86	A1
Działdowo	PL	77	A5
Działoszyce	PL	87	B4
Działoszyn	PL	86	A2
Dziemiany	PL	68	A2
Dzierzążnia	PL	77	B5
Dzierzgoń	PL	69	B4
Dzierzgowo	PL	77	A5
Dzierżoniów	PL	85	B4
Dzisna	BY	13	A8
Dziwnów	PL	67	B3
Dźwierzuty	PL	77	A5
Dzyarzhynsk	BY	13	B7
Dzyatlava	BY	13	B6

E

Place	Country	Page	Grid
Ea	E	143	A4
Eaglesfield	GB	36	A3
Ealing	GB	44	B3
Eardisley	GB	39	B3
Earl Shilton	GB	40	C2
Earls Barton	GB	44	A3
Earlston	GB	35	C5
Easington	GB	41	B4
Easky	IRL	26	B2
East Calder	GB	35	C4
East Dereham	GB	41	C4
East Grinstead	GB	44	B3
East Ilsley	GB	44	B2
East Kilbride	GB	36	A2
East Linton	GB	35	C5
East Markham	GB	40	B3
East Wittering	GB	44	C3
Eastbourne	GB	45	C4
Easter Skeld	GB	33	A5
Eastleigh	GB	44	C2
Easton	GB	43	B4
Eaton Socon	GB	44	A3
Eaux-Bonnes	F	145	B3
Eauze	F	128	C3
Ebberup	DK	59	C2
Ebbs	A	108	B3
Ebbw Vale	GB	39	C3
Ebeleben	D	82	A2
Ebeltoft	DK	59	B3

Name		Page	Grid
Eben im Pongau	A	109	B4
Ebene Reichenau	A	109	C4
Ebensee	A	109	B4
Ebensfeld	D	94	A2
Eberbach	D	93	B4
Ebergötzen	D	82	A2
Ebermann-Stadt	D	94	B3
Ebern	D	82	B2
Eberndorf	A	110	C1
Ebersbach	D	84	A4
Ebersberg	D	108	A2
Ebersdorf, *Bayern*	D	82	B3
Ebersdorf, *Niedersachsen*	D	72	A2
Eberstein	A	110	C1
Eberswalde	D	74	B2
Ebnat-Kappel	CH	107	B4
Éboli	I	170	C3
Ebrach	D	94	B2
Ebreichsdorf	A	111	B3
Ebreuil	F	116	A3
Ebstorf	D	72	A3
Ecclefechan	GB	36	A3
Eccleshall	GB	40	C1
Eceabat	TR	186	B1
Echallens	CH	106	C1
Echauri	E	144	B2
Echinos	GR	183	B7
Echiré	F	114	B3
Échirolles	F	118	B2
Echourgnac	F	128	A3
Echt	NL	80	A1
Echte	D	82	A2
Echternach	L	92	B2
Ecija	E	162	A2
Ečka	SRB	126	B2
Eckartsberga	D	82	A3
Eckelshausen	D	81	B4
Eckental	D	94	B3
Eckernförde	D	64	B2
Eckerö	FIN	51	B6
Eckington	GB	40	B2
Éclaron	F	91	C4
Écommoy	F	102	B2
Écouché	F	89	B3
Écouis	F	90	B1
Ecséd	H	113	B3
Ecsegfalva	H	113	B4
Écueillé	F	103	B3
Ed	S	54	B2
Eda	S	49	C4
Eda glasbruk	S	49	C4
Edam	NL	70	B2
Edane	S	55	A3
Edderton	GB	32	D2
Ede	NL	70	B2
Edebäck	S	49	B5
Edebo	S	51	B5
Edelény	H	99	C4
Edelschrott	A	110	B2
Edemissen	D	72	B3
Edenbridge	GB	45	B4
Edenderry	IRL	30	A1
Edenkoben	D	93	B4
Edesheim	D	93	B4
Edessa	GR	182	C4
Edewecht	D	71	A4
Edgeworthstown	IRL	30	A1
Edinburgh	GB	35	C4
Edineţ	MD	17	A7
Edirne	TR	186	A1
Edland	N	52	A3
Edolo	I	120	A3
Edøy	N	198	B5
Edremit	TR	186	C2
Eds bruk	S	56	B2
Edsbro	S	51	C5
Edsbyn	S	50	A2
Edsele	S	200	C2
Edsvalla	S	55	A4
Eekloo	B	79	A3
Eemshaven	NL	71	A3
Eerbeek	NL	70	B3
Eersel	NL	79	A4
Eferding	A	96	C2
Effiat	F	116	A3
Efteløt	N	53	A5
Egeln	D	73	C4
Eger	H	113	B4
Egerbakta	H	113	B4
Egernsund	DK	64	B2
Egersund	N	52	B2
Egerszólát	H	113	B4
Egervár	H	111	C3
Egg	A	107	B4
Egg	D	107	A5
Eggby	S	55	B4
Eggedal	N	47	B6
Eggenburg	A	97	C3
Eggenfelden	D	95	C4
Eggesin	D	74	A3
Eggum	N	194	B5
Egham	GB	44	B3
Éghezée	B	79	B4
Egiertowo	PL	68	A3
Egilsstaðir	IS	191	B11
Egina	GR	185	B4
Eginio	GR	182	C4
Egio	GR	184	A3
Égletons	F	116	B2
Egling	D	108	B2
Eglinton	GB	27	A3
Eglisau	CH	107	B3
Égliseneuve-d'Entraigues	F	116	B2
Eglofs	D	107	B4
Egmond aan Zee	NL	70	B1
Egna	I	121	A4
Egosthena	GR	184	A4
Egremont	GB	36	B3
Eğridir	TR	189	B5
Egtved	DK	59	C2
Eguilles	F	131	B4
Eguilly-sous-Bois	F	104	A3
Éguzon-Chantôme	F	103	C3
Egyek	H	113	B4
Egyházasrádóc	H	111	B3
Ehekirchen	D	94	C3
Ehingen	D	94	C1
Ehra-Lessien	D	73	B3
Ehrang	D	92	B2
Ehrenfriedersdorf	D	83	B4
Ehrenhain	D	83	B4
Ehrenhausen	A	110	C2
Ehringshausen	D	81	B4
Ehrwald	A	108	B1
Eibar	E	143	A4
Eibelstadt	D	94	B2
Eibenstock	D	83	B4
Eibergen	NL	71	B3
Eibiswald	A	110	C2
Eichenbarleben	D	73	B4
Eichendorf	D	95	C4
Eichstätt	D	95	C3
Eickelborn	D	81	A4
Eide, *Hordaland*	N	46	B3
Eide, *Møre og Romsdal*	N	198	C4
Eidet	N	194	A9
Eidfjord	N	46	B4
Eidsberg	N	54	A2
Eidsbugarden	N	47	A5
Eidsdal	N	198	C4
Eidsfoss	N	53	A6
Eidskog	N	49	B4
Eidsvåg, *Hordaland*	N	46	B2
Eidsvåg, *Møre og Romsdal*	N	198	C5
Eidsvoll	N	48	B3
Eikefjord	N	46	A2
Eikelandsosen	N	46	B2
Eiken	N	52	B3
Eikesdal	N	198	C5
Eikstrand	N	53	A5
Eilenburg	D	83	A4
Eilsleben	D	73	B4
Eina	N	48	B2
Einbeck	D	82	A1
Eindhoven	NL	79	A5
Einsiedeln	CH	107	B3
Einville-au-Jard	F	92	C2
Eisenach	D	82	B2
Eisenberg, *Rheinland-Pfalz*	D	93	B4
Eisenberg, *Thüringen*	D	83	B3
Eisenerz	A	110	B1
Eisenhüttenstadt	D	74	B3
Eisenkappel	A	110	C1
Eisenstadt	A	111	B3
Eisentratten	A	109	C4
Eisfeld	D	82	B2
Eisleben	D	82	A3
Eislingen	D	94	C1
Eitensheim	D	95	C3
Eiterfeld	D	82	B1
Eitorf	D	80	B3
Eivindvik	N	46	A2
Eivissa = Ibiza	E	166	C1
Eixo	P	148	B1
Ejby	DK	59	C2
Ejea de los Caballeros	E	144	B2
Ejstrupholm	DK	59	C2
Ejulve	E	153	B3
Eke	B	79	B3
Ekeby, *Gotland*	S	57	C4
Ekeby, *Skåne*	S	61	D2
Ekeby, *Uppsala*	S	51	B5
Ekeby-Almby	S	56	A1
Ekenäs	S	55	B4
Ekenässjön	S	62	A3
Ekerö	S	57	A3
Eket	S	61	C3
Eketorp	S	63	B4
Ekevik	S	56	B2
Ekkerøy	N	193	B14
Ekshärad	S	49	B5
Eksingedal	N	46	B2
Eksjö	S	62	A2
Eksta	S	57	C4
Ekträsk	S	200	B5
El Alamo, *Madrid*	E	151	B4
El Alamo, *Sevilla*	E	161	B3
El Algar	E	165	B4
El Almendro	E	161	B2
El Alquián	E	164	C2
El Arahal	E	162	A2
El Arenal	E	150	B3
El Arguellite	E	164	A2
El Astillero	E	143	A3
El Ballestero	E	158	C1
El Barco de Ávila	E	150	B2
El Berrón	E	142	A1
El Berrueco	E	151	B4
El Bodón	E	149	B3
El Bonillo	E	158	C1
El Bosque	E	162	B2
El Bullaque	E	157	A3
El Burgo	E	162	B3
El Burgo de Ebro	E	153	A3
El Burgo de Osma	E	151	A4
El Burgo Ranero	E	142	B1
El Buste	E	144	C2
El Cabaco	E	149	B3
El Callejo	E	143	A3
El Campillo	E	161	B3
El Campillo de la Jara	E	156	A2
El Cañavete	E	158	B1
El Carpio	E	157	C3
El Carpio de Tajo	E	150	C3
El Casar	E	151	B4
El Casar de Escalona	E	150	B3
El Castillo de las Guardas	E	161	B3
El Centenillo	E	157	B4
El Cerro	E	149	B4
El Cerro de Andévalo	E	161	B3
El Comenar	E	162	B2
El Coronil	E	162	A2
El Crucero	E	141	A4
El Cubo de Tierra del Vino	E	149	A4
El Cuervo	E	162	B1
El Ejido	E	164	C2
El Escorial	E	151	B3
El Espinar	E	151	B3
El Frago	E	144	B3
El Franco	E	141	A4
El Frasno	E	152	A2
El Garrobo	E	161	B3
El Gastor	E	162	B2
El Gordo	E	150	C2
El Grado	E	145	B4
El Granado	E	161	B2
El Grao de Castelló	E	159	B4
El Grau	E	159	C3
El Higuera	E	163	A3
El Hijate	E	164	B2
El Hontanar	E	152	B2
El Hoyo	E	157	B4
El Madroño	E	161	B3
El Maillo	E	149	B3
El Masnou	E	147	C3
El Mirón	E	150	B2
El Molar	E	151	B4
El Molinillo	E	157	A3
El Morell	E	147	C2
El Muyo	E	151	A4
El Olmo	E	151	A4
El Palo	E	163	B3
El Pardo	E	151	B4
El Payo	E	149	B3
El Pedernoso	E	158	B1
El Pedroso	E	162	A2
El Peral	E	158	B2
El Perelló, *Tarragona*	E	153	B4
El Perelló, *Valencia*	E	159	B3
El Picazo	E	158	B1
El Pinell de Bray	E	153	A4
El Piñero	E	150	A2
El Pla de Santa Maria	E	147	C2
El Pobo	E	153	B3
El Pobo de Dueñas	E	152	B2
El Pont d'Armentera	E	147	C2
El Port de la Selva	E	147	B4
El Port de Llançà	E	146	B4
El Port de Sagunt	E	159	B3
El Prat de Llobregat	E	147	C3
El Provencio	E	158	B1
El Puente	E	143	A3
El Puente del Arzobispo	E	150	C2
El Puerto	E	141	A4
El Puerto de Santa María	E	162	B1
El Real de la Jara	E	161	B3
El Real de San Vincente	E	150	B3
El Robledo	E	157	A3
El Rocio	E	161	B3
El Rompido	E	161	B2
El Ronquillo	E	161	B3
El Royo	E	143	C4
El Rubio	E	162	A3
El Sabinar	E	164	A2
El Saler	E	159	B3
El Salobral	E	158	C2
El Saucejo	E	162	A2
El Serrat	AND	146	B2
El Temple	E	144	C3
El Tiemblo	E	150	B3
El Toboso	E	157	A5
El Tormillo	E	145	C3
El Torno	E	149	B4
El Valle de las Casas	E	142	B1
El Vellón	E	151	B4
El Vendrell	E	147	C2
El Villar de Arnedo	E	144	B1
El Viso	E	156	B3
El Viso del Alcor	E	162	A2
Élancourt	F	90	C1
Elassona	GR	182	D3
Elati	GR	182	D3
Elbasan	AL	182	B2
Elbeuf	F	89	A4
Elbingerode	D	82	A2
Elbląg	PL	69	A4
Elburg	NL	70	B2
Elche	E	165	A4
Elche de la Sierra	E	158	C1
Elchingen	D	94	C2
Elda	E	159	C3
Eldena	D	73	A4
Eldingen	D	72	B3
Elefsina	GR	185	A4
Elek	H	113	C5
Elemir	SRB	126	B2
Eleutheroupoli	GR	183	C6
Elgå	N	199	C8
Elgin	GB	32	D3
Elgoibar	E	143	A4
Elgol	GB	31	B2
Elgshøa	N	49	A4
Elie	GB	35	B5
Elizondo	E	144	A2
Ełk	PL	12	B5
Elkhovo	BG	17	D7
Ellenberg	D	94	B2
Ellesmere	GB	38	B4
Ellesmere Port	GB	38	A4
Ellezelles	B	79	B3
Ellingen	D	94	B2
Ellmau	A	109	B3
Ellon	GB	33	D4
Ellös	S	54	B2
Ellrich	D	82	A2
Ellwangen	D	94	C2
Elm	CH	107	C4
Elm	D	72	A2
Elmadağ	TR	23	B7
Elmalı	TR	189	C4
Elmshorn	D	64	C2
Elmstein	D	93	B3
Elne	F	146	B3
Elnesvågen	N	198	C4
Elorrio	E	143	A4
Előszállás	H	112	C2
Elouda	GR	185	D6
Éloyes	F	105	A5
Elphin	GB	32	C1
Els Castells	E	147	B2
Elsdorf	D	80	B2
Elsenfeld	D	93	B5
Elsfleth	D	72	A1
Elspeet	NL	70	B2
Elst	NL	70	C2
Elstead	GB	44	B3
Elster	D	83	A4
Elsterberg	D	83	B4
Elsterwerda	D	83	A5
Elstra	D	84	A2
Eltmann	D	94	B2
Eltville	D	93	A4
Elvas	P	155	C3
Elvebakken	N	192	C7
Elven	F	101	B3
Elverum	N	48	B3
Elvington	GB	40	B3
Elxleben	D	82	A2
Ely	GB	45	A4
Elzach	D	106	A3
Elze	D	72	B2
Emådalen	S	50	A1
Embleton	GB	37	A5
Embonas	GR	188	C2
Embrun	F	132	A2
Embún	E	144	B3
Emden	D	71	A4
Emecik	TR	188	C2
Emet	TR	186	C4
Emirdağ	TR	187	C6
Emlichheim	D	71	B3
Emmaboda	S	63	B3
Emmaljunga	S	61	C3
Emmeloord	NL	70	B2
Emmen	CH	106	B3
Emmen	NL	71	B3
Emmendingen	D	106	A2
Emmer-Compascuum	NL	71	B4
Emmerich	D	80	A2
Emmern	D	72	B2
Emöd	H	113	B4
Émpoli	I	135	B3
Emsbüren	D	71	B4
Emsdetten	D	71	B4
Emsfors	S	62	A4
Emskirchen	D	94	B2
Emstek	D	71	B5
Emsworth	GB	44	C3
Emyvale	IRL	27	B4
Enafors	S	199	B9
Enånger	S	51	A4
Encamp	AND	146	B2
Encarnaçao	P	154	C1
Encinas de Abajo	E	150	B2
Encinas de Esgueva	E	142	C2
Encinas Reales	E	163	A3
Encinasola	E	161	A3
Encio	E	143	B3
Enciso	E	144	B1
Enden	N	199	D7
Endingen	D	106	A2
Endrinal	E	149	B4
Endröd	H	113	C4
Enebakk	N	54	A2
Eneryda	S	63	B2
Enese	H	111	B4
Enez	TR	183	C8
Enfield	IRL	30	A2
Eng	A	108	B2
Enge-sande	D	64	B1
Engelberg	CH	106	C3
Engelhartszell	A	96	C1
Engelskirchen	D	80	B3
Engen	D	107	B3
Enger	N	48	B2
Engerdal	N	199	D8
Engerneset	N	49	A4
Engesvang	DK	59	B2
Enghien	B	79	B4
Engstingen	D	94	C1
Engter	D	71	B5
Enguera	E	159	C3
Enguidanos	E	158	B2
Enkenbach	D	93	B3
Enkhuizen	NL	70	B2
Enklinge	FIN	51	B7
Enköping	S	56	A3
Enna	I	177	B3
Ennezat	F	116	B3
Ennigerloh	D	81	A4
Enningdal	N	54	B2
Ennis	IRL	28	B3
Enniscorthy	IRL	30	B2
Enniskean	IRL	29	C3
Enniskillen	GB	27	B3
Ennistimon	IRL	28	B2
Enns	A	110	A1
Eno	FIN	9	A7
Enontekiö	FIN	196	A6
Ens	NL	70	B2
Enschede	NL	71	B3
Ensdorf	D	95	B3
Ensisheim	F	106	B2
Enstaberga	S	56	B2
Enstone	GB	44	B2
Entlebuch	CH	106	B3
Entrácque	I	133	A3
Entradas	P	160	B1
Entrains-sur-Nohain	F	104	B2
Entrambasaguas	E	143	A3
Entrambasmestas	E	143	A3
Entraygues-sur-Truyère	F	116	C2
Entre-os-Rios	P	148	A1
Entrevaux	F	132	B2
Entrin Bajo	E	155	C4
Entroncamento	P	154	B2
Entzheim	F	93	C3
Envermeu	F	89	A5
Enviken	S	50	B2
Enying	H	112	C2
Enzingerboden	A	109	B3
Enzklösterle	D	93	C4
Épagny	F	90	B3
Épalinges	CH	106	C1
Épannes	F	114	B3
Epanomi	GR	182	C4
Epe	D	71	B4
Epe	NL	70	B2
Épernay	F	91	B3
Épernon	F	90	C1
Epfig	F	93	C3
Épierre	F	118	B3
Épila	E	152	A2
Épinac	F	104	C3
Épinal	F	105	A5
Episcopia	I	174	A2
Episkopi	CY	181	B1
Epitalio	GR	184	B2
Epoisses	F	104	B3
Eppenbrunn	D	93	B3
Eppendorf	D	83	B5
Epping	GB	45	B4
Eppingen	D	93	B4
Epsom	GB	44	B3
Epworth	GB	40	B3
Eraclea	I	122	B1
Eraclea Mare	I	122	B1
Erba	I	120	B2
Erbach, *Baden-Württemberg*	D	94	C1
Erbach, *Hessen*	D	93	B4
Erbalunga	F	180	A2
Erbendorf	D	95	B4
Érchie	I	173	B3
Ercolano	I	170	C2
Ercsi	H	112	B2
Érd	H	112	B2
Erdek	TR	186	B2
Erdemli	TR	23	C8
Erdevik	SRB	126	B1
Erding	D	95	C3
Erdötelek	H	113	B4
Erdut	HR	125	B5
Erdweg	D	95	C3
Eregli, *Konya*	TR	23	C8
Eregli, *Zonguldak*	TR	187	A6
Erenkaya	TR	189	B7
Eresfjord	N	198	C5
Eresos	GR	183	D7
Eretria	GR	185	A4
Erfde	D	64	B2
Erfjord	N	52	A2
Erfstadt	D	80	B2
Erfurt	D	82	B3
Érgli	LV	8	D4
Ergoldsbach	D	95	C4
Eriboll	GB	32	C2
Érice	I	176	A1
Ericeira	P	154	C1
Eriksberg	S	195	E6
Eriksmåla	S	62	B3
Eringsboda	S	63	B3
Eriswil	CH	106	B2
Erithres	GR	185	A4
Erkelenz	D	80	A2
Erkner	D	74	B2
Erkrath	D	80	A2
Erla	E	144	B3
Erlangen	D	94	B3
Erli	I	133	A4
Erlsbach	A	109	C3
Ermelo	NL	70	B2
Ermenak	TR	23	C7
Ermenonville	F	90	B2
Ermezinde	P	148	A1
Ermidas	P	160	A1
Ermioni	GR	184	B4
Ermoupoli	GR	185	B5
Ermsleben	D	82	A3
Erndtebrück	D	81	B4
Ernée	F	88	B3
Ernestinovo	HR	125	B4
Ernstbrunn	A	97	C4
Erolzheim	D	107	A5
Erquy	F	101	A3
Erra	P	154	C2
Erratzu	E	144	A2
Errindlev	DK	65	B4
Erro	E	144	B2
Ersa	F	180	A2
Érsekcsanád	H	125	A4
Ersekë	AL	182	C2
Érsekvadkert	H	112	B3
Ersmark	S	200	C6
Erstein	F	93	C3
Erstfeld	CH	107	C3
Ertebølle	DK	58	B2
Ertingen	D	107	A4
Ervedal, *Coimbra*	P	148	B1
Ervedal, *Portalegre*	P	154	B3
Ervenik	HR	138	A1
Ervidel	P	160	B1
Ervy-le-Châtel	F	104	A2
Erwitte	D	81	A4
Erxleben	D	73	B4
Erzsébet	H	125	A4
Es Caná	E	166	B1
Es Castell	E	167	B4
Es Mercadal	E	167	B4
Es Migjorn Gran	E	167	B4
Es Port d'Alcúdia	E	167	B3
Es Pujols	E	166	C1
Es Soleràs	E	153	A4
Esbjerg	DK	59	C1
Esbly	F	90	C2
Escacena del Campo	E	161	B3
Escairón	E	140	B3
Escalada	E	143	B3
Escalante	E	143	A3
Escalaplano	I	179	C3
Escalona	E	150	B3
Escalona del Prado	E	151	A3
Escalonilla	E	150	C3
Escalos de Baixo	P	155	B3
Escalos de Cima	P	155	B3
Escamilla	E	152	B1
Escañuela	E	157	C3
Escatrón	E	153	A3
Esch-sur-Alzette	L	92	B1
Esch-sur-Sûre	L	92	B1
Eschach	D	107	B4
Eschau	D	94	B1
Eschede	D	72	B3
Eschenau	D	95	B3
Eschenbach	D	95	B3
Eschenz	CH	107	B3
Eschershausen	D	72	C2
Eschwege	D	82	A2
Eschweiler	D	80	B2
Escobasa de Almazán	E	152	A1
Escoeuilles	F	78	B1
Escombreras	E	165	B4
Escos	F	144	A2
Escource	F	128	B1
Escragnolles	F	132	B2
Escrick	GB	40	B2
Escúrial	E	156	A2
Escurial de la Sierra	E	149	B4
Esgos	E	140	B3
Esher	GB	44	B3
Eskdalemuir	GB	36	A3
Eskifjörður	IS	191	B12
Eskilhem	S	57	C4
Eskilsäter	S	55	B4
Eskilstrup	DK	65	B4
Eskilstuna	S	56	A2

Eskipazar TR 187 B7
Eskişehir TR 187 C5
Eslarn D 95 B4
Eslava E 144 B2
Eslida E 159 B3
Eslohe D 81 A4
Eslöv S 61 D3
Eşme TR 188 A3
Espa N 48 B3
Espalion F 130 A1
Esparragalejo E 155 C4
Esparragosa del Caudillo E 156 B2
Esparragosa de la Serena E 156 B2
Esparreguera E 147 C2
Esparron F 132 B1
Espe N 46 B3
Espedal N 52 B2
Espejo, *Alava* E 143 B3
Espejo, *Córdoba* E 163 A3
Espeland N 46 B2
Espelkamp D 72 B1
Espeluche F 131 A3
Espeluy E 157 B4
Espera E 162 B2
Esperança P 155 B3
Espéraza F 146 B3
Espéria I 169 B3
Espevær N 52 A1
Espiel E 156 B2
Espinama E 142 A2
Espiñaredo E 140 A3
Espinasses F 132 A2
Espinelves E 147 C3
Espinhal P 154 A2
Espinho P 148 A1
Espinilla E 142 A2
Espinosa de Cerrato E 143 C3
Espinosa de los Monteros E 143 A3
Espinoso del Rey E 156 A3
Espirito Santo P 160 B2
Espluga de Francolí E 147 C2
Esplús E 145 C4
Espolla E 146 B3
Espoo FIN 8 B4
Esporles E 166 B2
Esposende P 148 A1
Espot E 146 B2
Esquedas E 145 B3
Esquivias E 151 B4
Essay F 89 B4
Essen B 79 A4
Essen, *Niedersachsen* D 71 B4
Essen, *Nordrhein-Westfalen* D 80 A3
Essenbach D 95 C4
Essertaux F 90 B2
Essingen D 94 C2
Esslingen D 94 C1
Essoyes F 104 A3
Estacas E 140 B2
Estadilla E 145 B4
Estagel F 146 B3
Estaires F 78 B2
Estang F 128 C2
Estarreja P 148 B1
Estartit E 147 B4
Estavayer-le-Lac CH 106 C1
Este I 121 B4
Esteiro E 140 A2
Estela P 148 A1
Estella E 144 B1
Estellencs E 166 B2
Estepa E 162 A3
Estépar E 143 B3
Estepona E 162 B2
Esternay F 91 C3
Esterri d'Aneu E 146 B2
Esterwegen D 71 B4
Estissac F 104 A2
Estivadas E 140 B3
Estivareilles F 116 A2
Estivella E 159 B3
Estói P 160 B2
Estopiñán E 145 C4
Estoril P 154 C1
Estoublon F 132 B2
Estrée-Blanche F 78 B2
Estrées-St. Denis F 90 B2
Estrela P 155 C3
Estremera E 151 B4
Estremoz P 155 C3
Estuna S 51 C5
Esyres F 102 B2
Esztergom H 112 B2
Etables-sur-Mer F 100 A3
Étain F 92 B1
Étalans F 105 B5
Etalle B 92 B1
Étampes F 90 C2
Etang-sur-Arroux F 104 C3
Étaples F 78 B1
Etauliers F 128 A2
Etili TR 186 C1
Etna N 48 B1
Etne N 52 A1
Etoges F 91 C3
Etoliko GR 184 A2
Eton GB 44 B3
Etréaupont F 91 B3
Étréchy F 90 C2
Étrépagny F 90 B1
Étretat F 89 A4
Étrœungt F 91 A3
Étroubles I 119 B4
Ettal D 108 B2
Ettelbruck L 92 B2
Etten NL 79 A4
Ettenheim D 106 A2
Ettington GB 44 A2
Ettlingen D 93 C4
Ettringen D 108 A1
Etuz F 105 B4
Etxarri-Aranatz E 144 B1
Etyek H 112 B2
Eu F 90 A1
Euerdorf D 82 B2
Eulate E 144 B1
Eupen B 80 B2
Europoort NL 79 A4
Euskirchen D 80 B2
Eutin D 65 B3
Evanger N 46 B3
Évaux-les-Bains F 116 A2
Evciler, *Afyon* TR 189 A4
Evciler, *Çanakkale* TR 186 C1
Evenskjær N 194 B7
Evenstad N 48 A3
Evercreech GB 43 A4
Evergem B 79 A3
Everöd S 61 D4
Eversberg D 81 A4
Everswinkel D 71 C4
Evertsberg S 49 A5
Evesham GB 44 A2
Évian-les-Bains F 118 A3
Evisa F 180 A1
Evje N 53 B3
Evolène CH 119 A4
Évora P 154 C3
Evoramonte P 155 C3
Evran F 101 A4
Evrecy F 89 A3
Évreux F 89 A5
Évron F 102 A1
Évry F 90 C2
Ewell GB 44 B3
Ewersbach D 81 B4
Excideuil F 115 C5
Exeter GB 43 B3
Exmes F 89 B4
Exminster GB 43 B3
Exmouth GB 43 B3
Eydehamn N 53 B4
Eye, *Peterborough* GB 41 C3
Eye, *Suffolk* GB 45 A5
Eyemouth GB 35 C5
Eyguians F 132 A1
Eyguières F 131 B4
Eygurande F 116 B2
Eylie F 145 B4
Eymet F 129 B3
Eymoutiers F 116 B1
Eynsham GB 44 B2
Eyrarbakki IS 190 D4
Eystrup D 72 B2
Ezaro E 140 B1
Ezcaray E 143 B4
Ezcároz E 144 B2
Ezine TR 186 C1
Ezmoriz P 148 B1

F

Fabara E 153 A4
Fábbrico I 121 C3
Fåberg N 48 A2
Fabero E 141 B4
Fábiánsebestyén H 113 C4
Fåborg DK 64 A3
Fabrègues F 130 B2
Fabriano I 136 B1
Fabrizia I 175 C2
Facha P 148 A1
Facinas E 162 B2
Fačkov SK 98 B2
Fadagosa P 155 B3
Fadd H 112 C2
Faédis I 122 A2
Faenza I 135 A4
Fafe P 148 A1
Fagagna I 122 A2
Făgăraş RO 17 C6
Fågelberget S 199 A11
Fågelfors S 62 A3
Fågelmara S 63 B3
Fågelsta S 55 B6
Fågerås S 55 A4
Fagerheim N 47 B4
Fagerhøy N 48 A1
Fagerhult S 62 A3
Fagerlund N 48 B2
Fagernes, *Oppland* N 47 B6
Fagernes, *Troms* N 192 C3
Fagersanna S 55 B5
Fagersta S 50 B2
Fåglavik S 55 B4
Fagnano Castello I 174 B2
Fagnières F 91 C4
Faido CH 107 C3
Fains F 91 C5
Fairford GB 44 B2
Fairlie GB 34 C3
Fajsz H 112 C2
Fakenham GB 41 C4
Fåker S 199 B11
Fakse DK 65 A5
Fakse Ladeplads DK 65 A5
Falaise F 89 B3
Falcade I 121 A4
Falcarragh IRL 26 A2
Falces E 144 B2
Fălciu RO 17 B8
Falconara I 177 B3
Falconara Maríttima I 136 B2
Falcone I 177 A4
Faldingworth GB 40 B3
Falerum S 56 B2
Fălești MD 17 B7
Falkenberg, *Bayern* D 95 B4
Falkenberg, *Bayern* D 95 C4
Falkenberg, *Brandenburg* D 83 A5
Falkenberg S 60 C2
Falkensee D 74 B2
Falkenstein, *Bayern* D 95 B4
Falkenstein, *Sachsen* D 83 B4
Falkenthal D 74 B2
Falkirk GB 35 B4
Falkland GB 35 B4
Falköping S 55 B4
Fall D 108 B2
Falla S 56 B1
Fallingbostel D 72 B2
Falmouth GB 42 B1
Falset E 147 C1
Fălticeni RO 17 B7
Falun S 50 B2
Famagusta CY 181 A2
Fammestad N 46 B2
Fana N 46 B2
Fanano I 135 A3
Fanari GR 182 D3
Fanjeaux F 146 A3
Fano I 136 B2
Fântânele RO 126 A3
Fara in Sabina I 168 A2
Fara Novarese I 119 B5
Faramontanos de Tábara E 149 A4
Farasdues E 144 B2
Fårbo S 62 A4
Fareham GB 44 C2
Färentuna S 57 A3
Färgelanda S 54 B2
Färila S 200 E1
Faringdon GB 44 B2
Faringe S 51 C5
Farini I 120 C2
Fariza E 149 A3
Färjestaden S 63 B4
Farkadona GR 182 D4
Farkasfa H 111 C3
Farlete E 153 A3
Färlöv S 61 C4
Farmos H 113 B3
Farnă SK 112 B2
Färnäs S 50 B1
Farnborough GB 44 B3
Farnese I 168 A1
Farnham GB 44 B3
Farnroda D 82 B2
Faro P 160 B2
Fåro S 57 C5
Fårösund S 57 C5
Farra d'Alpago I 122 A1
Farranfore IRL 29 B2
Farre DK 59 B2
Farsala GR 182 D4
Farsø DK 58 B2
Farsund N 52 B2
Farum DK 61 D2
Fårup DK 58 B2
Fasana I 172 B1
Fasano I 173 B3
Fáskrúðsfjörður IS 191 C11
Fassberg D 72 B3
Fastiv UA 13 C8
Fastnäs S 49 B5
Fátima P 154 B2
Fatmomakke S 195 E6
Fättjaur S 195 E6
Faucogney-et-la-Mer F 105 B5
Fauguerolles F 128 B3
Faulenrost D 74 A1
Faulquemont F 92 B2
Fauquembergues F 78 B2
Fauske N 194 C6
Fauville-en-Caux F 89 A4
Fauvillers B 92 B1
Fåvang N 48 A2
Favara E 159 B3
Favara I 176 B2
Faverges F 118 B3
Faverney F 105 B5
Faversham GB 45 B4
Favignana I 176 B1
Fawley GB 44 C2
Fay-aux-Loges F 103 B4
Fayence F 132 B2
Fayet F 130 B1
Fayl-Billot F 105 B4
Fayón E 153 A4
Fearn GB 32 D3
Fécamp F 89 A4
Feda N 52 B2
Fedje N 46 B1
Feeny GB 27 B3
Fegen S 60 B3
Fegyvernek H 113 B4
Fehrbellin D 74 B1
Fehring A 111 C3
Feichten A 108 B1
Feiring N 48 B3
Feistritz im Rosental A 110 C1
Feketić SRB 126 B1
Felanitx E 167 B3
Feld am See A 109 C4
Feldbach A 110 C2
Feldberg D 74 A2
Feldkirch A 107 B4
Feldkirchen in Kärnten A 109 C5
Feldkirchen-Westerham D 108 B2
Felgueiras P 148 A1
Felitto I 172 B1
Félix E 164 C2
Felixstowe GB 45 B5
Felizzano I 119 C5
Felletin F 116 B2
Fellingsbro S 56 A1
Felnac RO 126 A3
Felnémet H 113 B4
Felpéc H 111 B4
Fels am Wagram A 97 C3
Felsberg D 81 A5
Felsönyék H 112 C2
Felsöszentiván H 126 A1
Felsöszentmárton H 125 B3
Felsözsolca H 113 A4
Felsted DK 64 B2
Feltre I 121 A4
Femsjö S 60 C3
Fenagh IRL 26 B3
Fene E 140 A2
Fenestrelle I 119 B4
Fénétrange F 92 C3
Feneu F 102 B1
Fengersfors S 54 B3
Fenit IRL 29 B2
Fensmark DK 65 A4
Fenwick GB 36 A2
Feolin Ferry GB 34 C1
Ferbane IRL 28 A4
Ferdinandovac HR 124 A3
Ferdinandshof D 74 A2
Fère-Champenoise F 91 C3
Fère-en-Tardenois F 91 B3
Ferentillo I 168 A2
Ferentino I 169 B3
Feres GR 183 C8
Feria E 155 C4
Feričanci HR 125 B3
Ferizli TR 187 B5
Ferla I 177 B3
Ferlach A 110 C1
Ferleiten A 109 B3
Fermil P 148 A2
Fermo I 136 B2
Fermoselle E 149 A3
Fermoy IRL 29 B3
Fernán Nuñéz E 163 A3
Fernán Peréz E 164 C2
Fernancabellero E 157 A4
Fernão Ferro P 154 C1
Fernay-Voltaire F 118 A3
Ferndown GB 43 B5
Ferness GB 32 D3
Fernhurst GB 44 B3
Ferns IRL 30 B2
Ferpècle CH 119 A4
Ferrals-les-Corbières F 146 A3
Ferrandina I 172 B2
Ferrara I 121 C4
Ferrara di Monte Baldo I 121 B3
Ferreira E 141 A3
Ferreira do Alentejo P 160 A1
Ferreira do Zêzere P 154 B2
Ferreras de Abajo E 141 C4
Ferreras de Arriba E 141 C4
Ferreries E 167 B4
Ferreruela E 152 A2
Ferreruela de Tabara E 149 A3
Ferret CH 119 B4
Ferrette F 106 B2
Ferriere I 120 C2
Ferrière-la-Grande F 79 B3
Ferrières, *Hautes-Pyrénées* F 145 A3
Ferrières, *Loiret* F 103 A4
Ferrières, *Oise* F 90 B2
Ferrières-sur-Sichon F 117 A3
Ferrol E 140 A2
Ferryhill GB 37 B5
Fertörakos H 111 B3
Fertöszentmiklós H 111 B3
Ferwerd NL 70 A2
Festieux F 91 B3
Festøy N 198 C3
Festvåg N 194 C5
Fetești RO 17 C7
Fethard, *Tipperary* IRL 29 B4
Fethard, *Wexford* IRL 30 B2
Fethiye TR 188 C4
Fetsund N 48 C3
Fettercairn GB 35 B5
Feucht D 95 B3
Feuchtwangen D 94 B2
Feudingen D 81 B4
Feuges F 91 C4
Feuquières F 90 B1
Feurs F 117 B4
Fevik N 53 B4
Ffestiniog GB 38 B3
Fiamignano I 169 A3
Fiano I 119 B4
Ficarazzi I 176 A2
Ficarolo I 121 C4
Fichtelberg D 95 A3
Ficulle I 135 C5
Fidenza I 120 C3
Fidjeland N 52 B2
Fieberbrunn A 109 B3
Fier AL 182 C1
Fiera di Primiero I 121 A4
Fiesch CH 119 A5
Fiesso Umbertiano I 121 C4
Figari F 180 B2
Figeac F 116 C2
Figeholm S 62 A4
Figgjo N 52 B1
Figline Valdarno I 135 B4
Figols E 145 B4
Figueira da Foz P 148 B1
Figueira de Castelo Rodrigo P 149 B3
Figueira dos Caveleiros P 160 A1
Figueiredo P 154 B3
Figueiredo de Alva P 148 B2
Figueiró dos Vinhos P 154 B2
Figueres E 147 B3
Figueroles E 153 B3
Figueruela de Arriba E 141 C4
Filadélfia I 175 C2
Fil'akovo SK 99 C3
Filderstadt D 94 C1
Filey GB 41 A3
Filiași RO 17 C5
Filiates GR 182 D2
Filiatra GR 184 B2
Filipstad S 55 A5
Filisur CH 107 C4
Fillan N 198 B5
Filotio GR 185 B6
Filottrano I 136 B2
Filskov DK 59 C2
Filton GB 43 A4
Filtvet N 54 A1
Filzmoos A 109 B4
Finale Emília I 121 C4
Finale Ligure I 133 A4
Fiñana E 164 B2
Finby FIN 51 B7
Fincham GB 41 C4
Finchingfield GB 45 B4
Findhorn GB 32 D3
Findochty GB 33 D4
Finike TR 189 C5
Finkenberg A 108 B2
Finnea IRL 27 C3
Finneidfjord N 195 D4
Finnerödja S 55 B5
Finnskog N 49 B4
Finnsnes N 194 A9
Finntorp S 54 A3
Finócchio I 168 B2
Finsjö S 62 A4
Finsland N 52 B3
Finspång S 56 B1
Finsterwalde D 84 A1
Finsterwolde NL 71 A4
Finstown GB 33 B3
Fintona GB 27 B3
Fionnphort GB 34 B1
Fiorenzuola d'Arda I 120 C2
Firenze = Florence I 135 B4
Firenzuola I 135 A4
Firmi F 130 A1
Firminy F 117 B4
Firmo I 174 B2
Fischamend Markt A 111 A3
Fischbach A 110 B2
Fischbach D 93 B3
Fischbeck D 73 B5
Fischen D 107 B5
Fishbourne GB 44 C2
Fishguard GB 39 C2
Fiskardo GR 184 A1
Fiskebäckskil S 54 B2
Fiskebøl N 194 B5
Fismes F 91 B3
Fisterra E 140 B1
Fitero E 144 B2
Fitjar N 46 C2
Fiuggi I 169 B3
Fiumata I 169 A3
Fiumefreddo Brúzio I 174 B2
Fiumefreddo di Sicília I 177 B4
Fiumicino I 168 B2
Fivemiletown GB 27 B3
Fivizzano I 134 A3
Fjæra N 46 C3
Fjälkinge S 63 B2
Fjällåsen S 196 B3
Fjällbacka S 54 B2
Fjärdhundra S 56 A2
Fjellerup DK 58 B3
Fjerritslev DK 58 A2
Fjordgard N 194 A8
Fjugesta S 55 A5
Flå N 47 B6
Flåbygd N 53 A4
Flaça E 147 B3
Flace F 117 A4
Fladungen D 82 B2
Flaine F 118 A3
Flaka FIN 51 B7
Flåm N 46 B4
Flamatt CH 106 C2
Flamborough GB 41 A3
Flammersfeld D 81 B3
Flassans-sur-Issole F 132 B2
Flatdal N 53 A4
Flateby N 48 C3
Flateland N 52 A3
Flateyri IS 190 A2
Flatøydegard N 47 B6
Flatråker N 46 C2
Flattach A 109 C4
Flatvarp S 62 A4
Flauenskjold DK 58 A3
Flavigny-sur-Moselle F 92 C2
Flavy-le-Martel F 90 B3
Flawil CH 107 B4
Flayosc F 132 B2
Flechtingen D 73 B4
Fleckeby D 64 B2
Fleet GB 44 B3
Fleetmark D 73 B4
Fleetwood GB 38 A3
Flehingen D 93 B4
Flekke N 46 A2
Flekkefjord N 52 B2
Flen S 56 A2
Flensburg D 64 B2
Fleringe S 57 C4
Flerohopp S 62 B3
Flers F 88 B3
Flesberg N 47 C6
Fleurance F 129 C3
Fleuré F 115 B4
Fleurier CH 105 C5
Fleurus B 79 B4
Fleury, *Hérault* F 130 B2
Fleury, *Yonne* F 104 B2
Fleury-les-Aubrais F 103 B3
Fleury-sur-Andelle F 89 A5
Fleury-sur-Orne F 89 A3
Flieden D 81 B5
Flimby GB 36 B3
Flims CH 107 C4
Flines-lèz-Raches F 78 B3
Flint GB 38 A3
Flirey F 92 C1
Flirsch A 108 B1
Flisa N 49 B4
Flisby S 62 A2
Fliseryd S 62 A4
Flix E 153 A4
Flixecourt F 90 A2
Flize F 91 B4
Flobecq B 79 B3
Floby S 55 B4
Floda S 60 B2
Flodden GB 37 A4
Flogny-la-Chapelle F 104 B2
Flöha D 83 B5
Flonheim D 93 B4
Florac F 130 A2
Floreffe B 79 B4
Florence = Firenze I 135 B4
Florennes B 79 B4
Florensac F 130 B2
Florentin F 129 C5
Florenville B 91 B5
Flores de Avila E 150 B2
Floresta I 177 B3
Florești MD 17 B8
Florídia I 177 B4
Florina GR 182 C3
Florø N 46 A2
Flörsheim D 93 A4
Floss D 95 B4
Fluberg N 48 B2
Flúðir IS 190 C5
Flühli CH 106 C3
Flumet F 118 B3
Fluminimaggiore I 179 C2

Name		Page	Grid
Flums	CH	107	B4
Flyeryd	S	63	B3
Flygsfors	S	62	B3
Foča	BIH	139	B4
Foça	TR	186	A1
Fochabers	GB	32	D3
Focşani	RO	17	C7
Foel	GB	38	B3
Foeni	RO	126	B2
Fogdö	S	56	A2
Fóggia	I	171	B3
Foglianise	I	170	B2
Föglö	FIN	51	B7
Fohnsdorf	A	110	B2
Foiano della Chiana	I	135	B4
Foix	F	146	B2
Fojnica	BIH	139	B3
Fojnica	BIH	139	B3
Fokstua	N	198	C6
Földeák	H	126	A2
Foldereid	N	199	A9
Földes	H	113	B5
Folegandros	GR	185	C5
Folelli	F	180	A2
Folgaria	I	121	B4
Folgosinho	P	148	B2
Folgoso de la Ribera	E	141	B4
Folgoso do Courel	E	141	B3
Foligno	I	136	C1
Folkärna	S	50	B3
Folkestad	N	198	C3
Folkestone	GB	45	B5
Follafoss	N	199	B8
Folldal	N	198	C6
Follebu	N	48	A2
Follina	I	121	B5
Fölinge	S	199	B11
Follónica	I	135	C3
Fölsbyn	S	54	A3
Foncebadón	E	141	B4
Foncine-le-Bas	F	105	C5
Fondevila	E	140	C2
Fondi	I	169	B3
Fondo	I	121	A4
Fonelas	E	164	B1
Fonfría, *Teruel*	E	152	A2
Fonfría, *Zamora*	E	149	A3
Fonn	N	46	A3
Fonnes	N	46	B1
Fonni	I	178	B3
Font-Romeu	F	146	B3
Fontaine	F	91	C4
Fontaine de Vaucluse	F	131	B4
Fontaine-Française	F	105	B4
Fontaine-le-Dun	F	89	A4
Fontainebleau	F	90	C2
Fontan	F	133	A3
Fontanarejo	E	157	A3
Fontane	I	133	A3
Fontanélice	I	135	A4
Fontanières	F	116	A2
Fontanosas	E	157	A3
Fonteblanda	I	168	A1
Fontenay-le-Comte	F	114	B3
Fontenay-Trésigny	F	90	C2
Fontevrault-l'Abbaye	F	102	B2
Fontiveros	E	150	B3
Fontoy	F	92	B1
Fontpédrouse	F	146	B3
Fontstown	IRL	30	A2
Fonyód	H	111	C4
Fonz	E	145	B4
Fonzaso	I	121	A4
Fóppolo	I	120	A2
Föra	S	62	A4
Forbach	D	93	C4
Forbach	F	92	B2
Forcall	E	153	B3
Forcalquier	F	132	B1
Forcarei	E	140	B2
Forchheim	D	94	B3
Forchtenau	A	111	B3
Forchtenberg	D	94	B1
Ford	GB	34	B2
Førde, *Hordaland*	N	52	A1
Førde, *Sogn og Fjordane*	N	46	A2
Förderstedt	D	83	A3
Førdesfjorden	N	52	A1
Fordham	GB	45	A4
Fordingbridge	GB	44	C2
Fordon	PL	76	A3
Fordongiánus	I	179	C2
Forenza	I	172	B1
Foresta di Búrgos	I	178	B2
Forfar	GB	35	B5
Forges-les-Eaux	F	90	B1
Foria	I	172	B1
Forío	I	170	C1
Forjães	P	148	A1
Førland	N	52	B3
Forlì	I	135	A5
Forlimpopoli	I	135	A5
Formazza	I	119	A5
Formby	GB	38	A3
Formerie	F	90	B1
Fórmia	I	169	B3
Formígine	I	135	A3
Formigliana	I	119	B5
Formiguères	F	146	B3
Fornalutx	E	166	B2
Fornåsa	S	56	B1
Fornelli	I	178	B2
Fornells	E	167	A4
Fornelos de Montes	E	140	B2
Fornes	E	163	B4
Forneset	N	192	C3
Forni Avoltri	I	109	C3
Forni di Sopra	I	122	A1
Forni di Sotto	I	122	A1
Forno, *Piemonte*	I	119	B5
Forno, *Piemonte*	I	119	B4
Forno Alpi-Gráie	I	119	B4
Forno di Zoldo	I	121	A5
Fornos de Algodres	P	148	B2
Fornovo di Taro	I	120	C3
Foros do Arrão	P	154	B2
Forráskút	H	126	A1
Forres	GB	32	D3
Forriolo	E	140	B3
Fors	N	50	B3
Forsand	N	52	B1
Forsbacka	S	51	B3
Forserum	S	62	A2
Forshaga	S	55	A4
Forsheda	S	60	B3
Forsinain	GB	32	C3
Førslev	DK	65	A4
Förslöv	S	61	C2
Forsmark, *Uppsala*	S	51	B5
Forsmark, *Västerbotten*	S	195	E6
Forsmo	S	200	C3
Forsnäs	S	195	D9
Forsnes	N	198	B5
Forssa	FIN	8	B3
Forssjöbruk	S	56	B2
Forst	D	84	A2
Forsvik	S	55	B5
Fort Augustus	GB	32	D2
Fort-Mahon-Plage	F	78	B1
Fort William	GB	34	B2
Fortanete	E	153	B3
Forte dei Marmi	I	134	B3
Fortezza	I	108	C2
Forth	GB	35	C4
Fortrie	GB	33	D4
Fortrose	GB	32	D2
Fortun	N	47	A4
Fortuna	E	165	A3
Fortuneswell	GB	43	B4
Forvik	N	195	E3
Fos	F	145	B4
Fos-sur-Mer	F	131	B3
Fosdinovo	I	134	A3
Foss	N	47	B6
Fossacésia	I	169	A4
Fossano	I	133	A3
Fossato di Vico	I	136	B1
Fossbakken	N	194	B8
Fosse-la-Ville	B	79	B4
Fossombrone	I	136	B1
Fot	H	112	B3
Fouchères	F	104	A3
Fouesnant	F	100	B1
Foug	F	92	C1
Fougères	F	88	B2
Fougerolles	F	105	B5
Foulain	F	105	B4
Fountainhall	GB	35	C5
Fouras	F	114	C2
Fourchambault	F	104	B2
Fourmies	F	91	A4
Fourna	GR	182	D3
Fournels	F	116	C3
Fourni	GR	188	B1
Fournols	F	117	B3
Fourques	F	146	B3
Fourquevaux	F	146	A2
Fours	F	104	C2
Fowey	GB	42	B2
Foxdale	GB	36	B1
Foxford	IRL	26	C1
Foyers	GB	32	D2
Foynes	IRL	29	B2
Foz	E	141	A3
Foz do Arelho	P	154	B1
Foz do Giraldo	P	155	B3
Foza	I	121	B4
Frabosa Soprana	I	133	A3
Frades de la Sierra	E	149	B4
Fraga	E	153	A4
Fragagnano	I	173	B3
Frailes	E	163	A4
Fraire	B	79	B4
Fraize	F	106	A1
Framlingham	GB	45	A5
Frammersbach	D	94	A1
Framnes	N	54	A1
Franca	F	141	C4
Francaltroff	F	92	C2
Francavilla al Mare	I	169	A4
Francavilla di Sicília	I	177	B4
Francavilla Fontana	I	173	B3
Francavilla in Sinni	I	174	A2
Francescas	F	129	B3
Franco	P	148	A2
Francofonte	I	177	B3
Francos	E	151	A4
Frändefors	S	54	B3
Franeker	NL	70	A2
Frangy	F	118	A2
Frankenau	D	81	A4
Frankenberg, *Hessen*	D	81	A4
Frankenberg, *Sachsen*	D	83	B5
Frankenburg	A	109	A4
Frankenfels	A	110	B2
Frankenmarkt	A	109	B4
Frankenthal	D	93	B4
Frankfurt, *Brandenburg*	D	74	B3
Frankfurt, *Hessen*	D	81	B4
Frankrike	S	199	B10
Fränsta	S	200	D2
Františkovy Lázně	CZ	83	B4
Franzburg	D	66	B1
Frascati	I	168	B2
Frasdorf	D	109	B3
Fraserburgh	GB	33	D4
Frashër	AL	182	C2
Frasne	F	105	C5
Frasnes-lez-Anvaing	B	79	B3
Frasseto	F	180	B2
Frastanz	A	107	B4
Fratel	P	155	B3
Fratta Todina	I	135	C5
Frauenau	D	96	C1
Frauenfeld	CH	107	B3
Frauenkirchen	A	111	B3
Frauenstein	D	83	B5
Frauental	A	110	C2
Frayssinet	F	129	B4
Frayssinet-le-Gélat	F	129	B4
Frechas	P	149	A2
Frechen	D	80	B2
Frechilla	E	142	B2
Freckenhorst	D	71	C4
Fredeburg	D	81	A4
Fredelsloh	D	82	A1
Fredeng	N	48	B2
Fredensborg	DK	61	D2
Fredericia	DK	59	C2
Frederiks	DK	59	B2
Frederikshavn	DK	58	A3
Frederikssund	DK	61	D2
Frederiksværk	DK	61	D2
Fredrika	S	200	B4
Fredriksberg	S	50	B1
Fredriksdal	S	62	A2
Fredrikstad	S	54	A1
Fregenal de la Sierra	E	161	A3
Fregene	I	168	B2
Freiberg	D	83	B5
Freiburg, *Baden-Württemberg*	D	106	B2
Freiburg, *Niedersachsen*	D	64	C2
Freienhagen	D	81	A5
Freienhufen	D	84	A1
Freiensteinau	D	81	B5
Freihung	D	95	B3
Freilassing	D	109	B3
Freisen	D	92	B3
Freising	D	95	C3
Freistadt	A	96	C2
Freital	D	84	A1
Freixedas	P	149	B2
Freixo de Espada à Cinta	P	149	A3
Fréjus	F	132	B2
Fremdingen	D	94	C2
Frenštát pod Radhoštěm	CZ	98	B2
Freren	D	71	B4
Freshford	IRL	30	B1
Freshwater	GB	44	C2
Fresnay-sur-Sarthe	F	89	B4
Fresne-St.-Mamès	F	105	B4
Fresneda de la Sierra	E	152	B1
Fresneda de la Sierra Tiron	E	143	B3
Fresnedillas	E	151	B3
Fresnes-en-Woevre	F	92	B1
Fresno Alhandiga	E	150	B2
Fresno de la Ribera	E	150	A2
Fresno de la Vega	E	142	B1
Fresno de Sayago	E	149	A3
Fresnoy-Folny	F	90	B1
Fresnoy-le-Grand	F	91	B3
Fressenville	F	90	A1
Fresvik	N	46	A3
Fréteval	F	103	B3
Fretigney	F	105	B4
Freudenberg, *Baden-Württemberg*	D	94	B1
Freudenberg, *Nordrhein-Westfalen*	D	81	B3
Freudenstadt	D	93	C4
Freux	B	92	B1
Frévent	F	78	B2
Freyburg	D	83	A3
Freyenstein	D	73	A5
Freyming-Merlebach	F	92	B2
Freystadt	D	95	B3
Freyung	D	96	C1
Frias de Albarracin	E	152	B2
Fribourg	CH	106	C2
Frick	CH	106	B3
Fridafors	S	63	B2
Fridaythorpe	GB	40	A3
Friedberg, *Bayern*	D	94	C2
Friedberg, *Hessen*	D	81	B4
Friedeburg	D	71	A4
Friedewald	D	82	B1
Friedland, *Brandenburg*	D	74	B3
Friedland, *Mecklenburg-Vorpommern*	D	74	A2
Friedland, *Niedersachsen*	D	82	A1
Friedrichroda	D	82	B2
Friedrichsdorf	D	81	B4
Friedrichshafen	D	107	B4
Friedrichskoog	D	64	B1
Friedrichstadt	D	64	B2
Friedrichswalde	D	74	A2
Friesach	A	110	C1
Friesack	D	73	B5
Friesenheim	D	93	C3
Friesoythe	D	71	A4
Friggesund	S	200	E2
Frigiliana	E	163	B4
Frihetsli	N	192	D3
Frillesås	S	60	B2
Frinnaryd	S	62	A2
Frinton-on-Sea	GB	45	B5
Friockheim	GB	35	B5
Friol	E	140	A3
Fristad	S	60	B2
Fritsla	S	60	B2
Fritzlar	D	81	A5
Frizington	GB	36	B3
Frödinge	S	62	A4
Froges	F	118	B2
Frohburg	D	83	A4
Frohnhausen	D	81	B4
Frohnleiten	A	110	B2
Froissy	F	90	B2
Frombork	PL	69	A4
Frome	GB	43	A4
Frómista	E	142	B2
Fröndenberg	D	81	A3
Fronsac	F	128	B2
Front	I	119	B4
Fronteira	P	155	B3
Frontenay-Rohan-Rohan	F	114	B3
Frontenhausen	D	95	C4
Frontignan	F	130	B2
Fronton	F	129	C4
Fröseke	S	62	B3
Frosinone	I	169	B3
Frosolone	I	170	B2
Frosta	N	199	B7
Frøstrup	DK	58	A1
Frosunda	S	57	A4
Frouard	F	92	C2
Frövi	S	56	A1
Frøyset	N	46	B2
Fruges	F	78	B2
Frutigen	CH	106	C2
Frýdek-Místek	CZ	98	B2
Frýdlant	CZ	84	B1
Frýdlant nad Ostravicí	CZ	98	B2
Frygnowo	PL	77	A5
Fryšták	CZ	98	B1
Fucécchio	I	135	B3
Fuencaliente, *Ciudad Real*	E	157	B3
Fuencaliente, *Ciudad Real*	E	157	A4
Fuencemillán	E	151	B4
Fuendejalón	E	144	C2
Fuengirola	E	163	B3
Fuenlabrada	E	151	B4
Fuenlabrada de los Montes	E	156	A3
Fuensalida	E	151	B3
Fuensanta	E	164	B2
Fuensanta de Martos	E	163	A4
Fuente al Olmo de Iscar	E	150	A3
Fuente-Álamo	E	158	C2
Fuente-Álamo de Murcia	E	165	B3
Fuente Dé	E	142	A2
Fuente de Cantos	E	155	C4
Fuente de Santa Cruz	E	150	A3
Fuente del Arco	E	156	B2
Fuente del Conde	E	163	A3
Fuente del Maestre	E	155	C4
Fuente el Fresno	E	157	A4
Fuente el Saz de Jarama	E	151	B4
Fuente el Sol	E	150	A3
Fuente Obejuna	E	156	B2
Fuente Palmera	E	162	A2
Fuente-Tójar	E	163	A3
Fuente Vaqueros	E	163	A4
Fuentealbilla	E	158	B2
Fuentecén	E	151	A4
Fuenteguinaldo	E	149	B3
Fuentelapeña	E	150	A2
Fuentelcésped	E	151	A4
Fuentenovilla	E	151	B4
Fuentepelayo	E	151	A3
Fuentepinilla	E	151	A4
Fuenterroble de Salvatierra	E	150	B2
Fuenterrobles	E	158	B2
Fuentes	E	158	B1
Fuentes de Andalucía	E	162	A2
Fuentes de Ebro	E	153	A3
Fuentes de Jiloca	E	152	A2
Fuentes de la Alcarria	E	151	B5
Fuentes de León	E	161	A3
Fuentes de Nava	E	142	B2
Fuentes de Oñoro	E	149	B3
Fuentes de Ropel	E	142	B1
Fuentesauco, *Segovia*	E	151	A3
Fuentesaúco, *Zamora*	E	150	A2
Fuentespalda	E	153	B4
Fuentespina	E	151	A4
Fuentidueña	E	151	A4
Fuentidueña de Tajo	E	151	B4
Fuerte del Rey	E	157	C4
Fügen	A	108	B2
Fuglebjerg	DK	65	A4
Fuglevik	N	54	A1
Fuhrberg	D	72	B2
Fulda	D	82	B1
Fulgatore	I	176	B1
Fully	CH	119	A4
Fulnek	CZ	98	B1
Fülöpszállás	H	112	C3
Fulpmes	A	108	B2
Fulunäs	S	49	A5
Fumay	F	91	B4
Fumel	F	129	B3
Funäsdalen	S	199	C9
Fundão	P	148	B2
Funzie	GB	33	A6
Furadouro	P	148	B1
Fure	N	46	A2
Fürstenau, *Niedersachsen*	D	71	B4
Furstenau, *Nordrhein-Westfalen*	D	81	A5
Fürstenberg	D	74	A2
Fürstenfeld	A	111	B3
Fürstenfeldbruck	D	108	A2
Fürstenstein	D	96	C1
Fürstenwalde	D	74	B3
Fürstenwerder	D	74	A2
Fürstenzell	D	96	C1
Furta	H	113	B5
Fürth, *Bayern*	D	94	B2
Fürth, *Hessen*	D	93	B4
Furth im Wald	D	95	B4
Furtwangen	D	106	A3
Furuby	S	62	B3
Furudal	S	50	A2
Furuflaten	N	192	C4
Furulund	S	61	D3
Furusjö	S	60	B3
Fusa	N	46	B2
Fuscaldo	I	174	B2
Fusch an der Grossglocknerstrasse	A	109	B3
Fushë Arrëz	AL	182	B2
Fushë-Krujë	AL	182	B1
Fusina	I	122	B1
Fusio	CH	107	C3
Füssen	D	108	B1
Fustiñana	E	144	B2
Futog	SRB	126	B1
Futrikelv	N	192	C3
Füzesabony	H	113	B4
Füzesgyarmat	H	113	B5
Fužine	HR	123	B3
Fyllinge	S	61	C2
Fynshav	DK	64	B2
Fyresdal	N	53	A4

G

Name		Page	Grid
Gaaldorf	A	110	B1
Gabaldón	E	158	B1
Gabarret	F	128	C2
Gabčíkovo	SK	111	B4
Gabin	PL	77	B4
Gabriac	F	130	A1
Gabrovo	BG	17	D6
Gaby	I	119	B4
Gacé	F	89	B4
Gacko	BIH	139	B4
Gäddede	S	199	A11
Gadebusch	D	65	C4
Gadmen	CH	106	C3
Gádor	E	164	C2
Gádoros	H	113	C4
Gael	F	101	A3
Gærum	DK	58	A3
Găești	RO	17	C6
Gaeta	I	169	B3
Gafanhoeira	P	154	C2
Gaflenz	A	110	B1
Gagarin	RUS	9	E9
Gaggenau	D	93	C4
Gagliano Castelferrato	I	177	B3
Gagliano del Capo	I	173	C4
Gagnet	S	50	B2
Gaibanella	I	121	C4
Gaildorf	D	94	B1
Gaillac	F	129	C4
Gaillefontaine	F	90	B1
Gaillon	F	89	A5
Gainsborough	GB	40	B3
Gairloch	GB	31	B3
Gairlochy	GB	34	B3
Gáiro	I	179	C3
Gaj	HR	124	B3
Gaj	SRB	127	C3
Gaja-la-Selve	F	146	A2
Gajanejos	E	151	B5
Gajary	SK	97	C4
Gajdobra	SRB	126	B1
Galan	F	145	A4
Galanta	SK	111	A4
Galapagar	E	151	B3
Galápagos	E	151	B4
Galaroza	E	161	B3
Galashiels	GB	35	C5
Galatas	GR	185	B4
Galați	RO	17	C8
Galatina	I	173	B4
Galatista	GR	183	C5
Galátone	I	173	B4
Galaxidi	GR	184	A3
Galdakao	E	143	A4
Galeata	I	135	B4
Galende	E	141	B4
Galera	E	164	B2
Galéria	F	180	A1
Galgamácsa	H	112	B3
Galgate	GB	38	A4
Galgon	F	128	B2
Galices	P	148	B2
Galinduste	E	150	B2
Galinoporni	CY	181	A3
Galisteo	E	155	B4
Galków	PL	87	A3
Gallardon	F	90	C1
Gallardos	E	164	B2
Gallegos de Argañán	E	149	B3
Gallegos del Solmirón	E	150	B2
Galleguillos de Campos	E	142	B1
Galleno	I	135	B3
Galliate	I	120	B1
Gallicano	I	134	A3
Gállio	I	121	B4
Gallípoli	I	173	B3
Gallípoli = Gelibolu	TR	186	B1
Gällivare	S	196	B3
Gallizien	A	110	C1
Gallneukirchen	A	96	C2
Gällö	S	199	C12
Gallocanta	E	152	B2
Gällstad	S	60	B3
Gallur	E	144	C2
Galmisdale	GB	31	C2
Galmpton	GB	43	B3
Galston	GB	36	A2
Galta	N	52	A1
Galtelli	I	178	B3
Galten	DK	59	B2
Galtür	A	107	C5
Galve de Sorbe	E	151	A4
Galveias	P	154	B2
Gálvez	E	157	A3
Galway	IRL	28	A2
Gamaches	F	90	B1
Gámbara	I	120	B3
Gambárie	I	175	C1
Gambassi Terme	I	135	B3
Gambatesa	I	170	B2
Gambolò	I	120	B1
Gaming	A	110	B2
Gamla Uppsala	S	51	C4
Gamleby	S	62	A4
Gamlingay	GB	44	A3
Gammelgarn	S	57	C4
Gammelstaden	S	196	D5
Gammertingen	D	107	A4
Gams	CH	107	B4
Gamvik, *Finnmark*	N	192	B6
Gamvik, *Finnmark*	N	193	A12
Gan	F	145	A3
Gáname	E	149	A3
Ganda di Martello	I	108	C1

Gandarela P 148 A1
Ganddal N 52 B1
Ganderkesee D 72 A1
Gandesa E 153 A4
Gandía E 159 C3
Gandino I 120 B2
Gandrup DK 58 A3
Ganges F 130 B2
Gånghester S 60 B3
Gangi I 177 B3
Gangkofen D 95 C4
Gannat F 116 A3
Gannay-sur-Loire F 104 C2
Gänserdorf A 97 C4
Ganzlin D 73 A5
Gap F 132 A2
Gara H 125 A5
Garaballa E 158 B2
Garaguso I 172 B2
Garbayuela E 156 A2
Garbhallt GB 34 B2
Garbsen D 72 B2
Garching D 109 A3
Garciaz E 156 A2
Garcihernández E 150 B2
Garcillán E 151 B3
Garcinarro E 151 B5
Garcisobaco E 162 B2
Garda I 121 B3
Gardanne F 131 B4
Gärdås S 49 B5
Gårdby S 63 B4
Gardeja PL 69 B3
Gardelegen D 73 B4
Gardermoen N 48 B3
Gardiki GR 182 E3
Garding D 64 B1
Gardone Riviera I 121 B3
Gardone Val Trómpia I 120 B3
Gárdony H 112 B2
Gardouch F 146 A2
Gards Köpinge S 63 C2
Gårdsjö S 55 B5
Gårdskär S 51 B4
Garein F 128 B2
Garelochhead GB 34 B3
Garéoult F 132 B2
Garešnica HR 124 B2
Garéssio I 133 A4
Garforth GB 40 B2
Gargaliani GR 184 B2
Gargaligas E 156 A2
Gargallo E 153 B3
Garganta la Olla E 150 B2
Gargantiel E 156 B3
Gargellen A 107 C4
Gargilesse-Dampierre F 103 C3
Gargnano I 121 B3
Gargnäs S 195 E8
Gárgoles de Abajo E 152 B1
Gargrave GB 40 B1
Garitz D 73 C5
Garlasco I 120 B1
Garlieston GB 36 B2
Garlin F 128 C2
Garlitos E 156 B2
Garmisch-Partenkirchen D 108 B2
Garnat-sur-Engièvre F 104 C2
Garpenberg S 50 B3
Garphyttan S 55 A5
Garray E 143 C4
Garrel D 71 B5
Garriguella E 146 B4
Garrison GB 26 B2
Garrovillas E 155 B4
Garrucha E 164 B3
Gars-am-Kamp A 97 C3
Garsås S 50 B1
Garsdale Head GB 37 B4
Gärsnäs S 63 C2
Garstang GB 38 A4
Gartow D 73 A4
Gartz D 74 A3
Garvagh GB 27 B4
Garvão P 160 B1
Garve GB 32 D2
Garwolin PL 12 C4
Garz D 66 B2
Garzyn PL 85 A4
Gąsawa PL 76 B2
Gåsborn S 49 C6
Gaschurn A 107 C5
Gascueña E 152 B1
Gasny F 90 B1
Gąsocin PL 77 B5
Gastes F 128 B1
Gastouni GR 184 B2
Gastouri GR 182 D1
Gata E 149 B3
Gata HR 138 B2
Gata de Gorgos E 159 C4
Gătaia RO 126 B3
Gatchina RUS 9 C7
Gatehouse of Fleet GB 36 B2
Gátér H 113 C3
Gateshead GB 37 B5
Gátova E 159 B3
Gattendorf A 111 A3
Gatteo a Mare I 136 A1
Gattinara I 119 B5
Gattorna I 134 A2
Gaucín E 162 B2
Gaulstad N 199 B9
Gaupne N 47 A4
Gautefall N 53 A4
Gauting D 108 A2
Gauto S 195 D7
Gava E 147 C3
Gavardo I 121 B3
Gavarnie F 145 B3
Gávavencsello H 113 A5
Gavi I 120 C1
Gavião P 154 B3
Gavirate I 120 B1
Gävle S 51 B4
Gavoi I 178 B3
Gavorrano I 135 C3
Gavray F 88 B2
Gavrio GR 185 B5
Gävunda S 49 B6
Gaweinstal A 97 C4
Gaworzyce PL 85 A3
Gawroniec PL 75 A5
Gaydon GB 44 A2
Gayton GB 41 C4
Gazipaşa TR 189 C7
Gazoldo degli Ippoliti I 121 B3
Gazzuolo I 121 B3
Gbelce SK 112 B2
Gdańsk PL 69 A3
Gdinj HR 138 B2
Gdov RUS 8 C5
Gdów PL 99 B4
Gdynia PL 69 A3
Gea de Albarracin E 152 B2
Geary GB 31 B2
Géaudot F 91 C4
Geaune F 128 C2
Gebesee D 82 A2
Gebiz TR 189 B5
Gebze TR 187 B4
Géderlak H 112 C2
Gedern D 81 B5
Gedinne B 91 B4
Gediz TR 187 D4
Gèdre F 145 B4
Gedser DK 65 B4
Gedsted DK 58 B2
Geel B 79 A4
Geesthacht D 72 A3
Geetbets B 79 B5
Gefell D 83 B3
Gehrden D 72 B2
Gehren D 82 B3
Geilenkirchen D 80 B2
Geilo N 47 B5
Geinsheim D 93 B4
Geisa D 82 B1
Geiselhöring D 95 C4
Geiselwind D 94 B2
Geisenfeld D 95 C3
Geisenhausen D 95 C4
Geisenheim D 93 B4
Geising D 84 B1
Geisingen D 107 B3
Geislingen D 94 C1
Geistthal A 110 B2
Geiterygghytta N 47 B4
Geithain D 83 A4
Geithus N 48 C1
Gela I 177 B3
Geldermalsen NL 79 A5
Geldern D 80 A2
Geldrop NL 80 A1
Geleen NL 80 B1
Gelembe TR 186 C2
Gelendost TR 189 A6
Gelibolu = Gallipoli TR 186 B1
Gelida E 147 C2
Gelnhausen D 81 B5
Gelnica SK 99 C4
Gelsa E 153 A3
Gelse H 111 C3
Gelsenkirchen D 80 A3
Gelsted DK 59 C2
Geltendorf D 108 A2
Gelterkinden CH 106 B2
Gelting D 64 B2
Gelu RO 126 A3
Gelves E 162 A1
Gembloux B 79 B4
Gemeaux F 105 B4
Gémenos F 132 B1
Gemerská Poloma SK 99 C4
Gemerská Ves SK 99 C4
Gemert NL 80 A1
Gemla S 62 B2
Gemlik TR 186 B4
Gemmenich B 80 B1
Gemona del Friuli I 122 A2
Gémozac F 114 C3
Gemund D 80 B2
Gemünden, *Bayern* D 94 A1
Gemünden, *Hessen* D 81 B4
Gemünden, *Rheinland-Pfalz* D 93 B3
Genappe B 79 B4
Génave E 164 A2
Genazzano I 169 B2
Gençay F 115 B4
Gencsapáti H 111 B3
Gendringen NL 80 A2
Genelard F 104 C3
Genemuiden NL 70 B3
Generalski Stol HR 123 B4
Geneva = Genève CH 118 A3
Genevad S 61 C3
Genève = Geneva CH 118 A3
Genevriéres F 105 B4
Gengenbach D 93 C4
Genillé F 103 B3
Genk B 80 B1
Genlis F 105 B4
Gennep NL 80 A1
Genner DK 64 A2
Gennes F 102 B1
Genoa = Génova I 134 A1
Genola I 133 A3
Génova = Genoa I 134 A1
Genowefa PL 76 B3
Gensingen D 93 B3
Gent = Ghent B 79 A3
Genthin D 73 B5
Gentioux F 116 B1
Genzano di Lucánia I 172 B2
Genzano di Roma I 168 B2
Georgenthal D 82 B2
Georgsmarienhütte D 71 B5
Gera D 83 B4
Geraards-bergen B 79 B3
Gerace I 175 C2
Geraci Sículo I 177 B3
Geraki GR 184 C3
Gérardmer F 106 A1
Geras A 97 C3
Gerbéviller F 92 C2
Gerbini I 177 B3
Gerbstedt D 83 A3
Gerði IS 191 C9
Gerede TR 187 B7
Gerena E 161 B3
Geretsried D 108 B2
Gérgal E 164 B2
Gergy F 105 C3
Gerindote E 150 C3
Gerjen H 112 C2
Gerlos A 108 B3
Germay F 92 C1
Germencik TR 188 B2
Germering D 108 A2
Germersheim D 93 B4
Gernika-Lumo E 143 A4
Gernrode D 82 A3
Gernsbach D 93 C4
Gernsheim D 93 B4
Geroda D 82 B1
Gerola Alta I 120 A2
Geroldsgrun D 83 B3
Gerolsbach D 95 C3
Gerolstein D 80 B2
Gerolzhofen D 94 B2
Gerovo HR 123 B3
Gerpinnes B 79 B4
Gerrards Cross GB 44 B3
Gerri de la Sal E 147 B2
Gersfeld D 82 B1
Gerstetten D 94 C2
Gersthofen D 94 C2
Gerstungen D 82 B2
Gerswalde D 74 A2
Gerzat F 116 B3
Gerze TR 23 A8
Gerzen D 95 C4
Gescher D 71 C4
Geseke D 81 A4
Geslau D 94 B2
Gespunsart F 91 B4
Gesté F 101 B4
Gestorf D 72 B2
Gesualda I 170 C3
Gesunda S 50 B1
Gesztely H 113 A4
Geta FIN 51 B6
Getafe E 151 B4
Getinge S 60 C2
Getxo E 143 A4
Geversdorf D 64 C2
Gevgelija MK 182 B4
Gevora del Caudillo E 155 C4
Gevrey-Chambertin F 105 B3
Gex F 118 A3
Gey D 80 B2
Geyikli TR 186 C1
Geysir IS 190 C5
Geyve TR 187 B5
Gföhl A 97 C3
Ghedi I 120 B3
Ghent = Gent B 79 A3
Gheorgheni RO 17 B6
Ghigo I 119 C4
Ghilarza I 178 B2
Ghisonaccia F 180 A2
Ghisoni F 180 A2
Gialtra GR 182 E4
Gianitsa GR 182 C4
Giardinetto Vécchio I 171 B3
Giardini Naxos I 177 B4
Giarratana I 177 B3
Giarre I 177 B4
Giat F 116 B2
Giaveno I 119 B4
Giazza I 121 B4
Giba I 179 C2
Gibellina Nuova I 176 B1
Gibostad N 194 A9
Gibraleón E 161 B3
Gibraltar GBZ 162 B2
Gic H 111 B4
Gideå S 200 C5
Gideåkroken S 200 B3
Gidle PL 86 B3
Giebelstadt D 94 B1
Gieboldehausen D 82 A2
Gielniów PL 87 A4
Gielow D 74 A1
Gien F 103 B4
Giengen D 94 C2
Giens F 132 B2
Giera RO 126 B2
Gieselwerder D 81 A5
Giessen D 81 B4
Gieten NL 71 A3
Giethoorn NL 70 B3
Giffaumont-Champaubert F 91 C4
Gifford GB 35 C5
Gifhorn D 73 B3
Gige H 125 A3
Gignac F 130 B2
Gijón = Xixón E 142 A1
Gilena E 162 A3
Gilford GB 27 B4
Gillberga S 55 A3
Gilleleje DK 61 C2
Gilley F 105 B5
Gilley-sur-Loire F 104 C2
Gillingham, *Dorset* GB 43 A4
Gillingham, *Medway* GB 45 B4
Gilocourt F 90 B2
Gilserberg D 81 B5
Gilsland GB 37 B4
Gilze NL 79 A4
Gimåt S 200 C4
Gimo S 51 B5
Gimont F 129 C3
Ginasservis F 132 B1
Gingelom B 79 B5
Gingst D 66 B2
Ginosa I 171 C4
Ginzling A 108 B2
Giões P 160 B2
Gióia dei Marsi I 169 B3
Gióia del Colle I 173 B2
Gióia Sannitica I 170 B2
Gióia Táuro I 175 C1
Gioiosa Iónica I 175 C2
Gioiosa Marea I 177 A3
Giosla GB 31 A2
Giovinazzo I 171 B4
Girifalco I 175 C2
Giromagny F 106 B1
Girona E 147 C3
Gironcourt-sur-Vraine F 92 C1
Gironella E 147 B2
Gironville-sous-les-Côtes F 92 C1
Girvan GB 36 A2
Gislaved S 60 B3
Gislev DK 59 C3
Gisors F 90 B1
Gissi I 170 A2
Gistad S 56 B1
Gistel B 78 A2
Gistrup DK 58 B3
Giswil CH 106 C3
Githio GR 184 C3
Giugliano in Campania I 170 C2
Giulianova I 136 C2
Giulvăz RO 126 B2
Giurgiu RO 17 D6
Give DK 59 C2
Givet F 91 A4
Givors F 117 B4
Givry B 79 B4
Givry F 104 C3
Givry-en-Argonne F 91 C4
Givskud DK 59 C2
Giźalki PL 76 B2
Gizeux F 102 B2
Giżycko PL 12 A4
Gizzeria I 175 C2
Gizzeria Lido I 175 C2
Gjedved DK 59 C2
Gjegjan AL 182 B2
Gjendesheim N 47 A5
Gjerde N 46 B3
Gjerlev DK 58 B3
Gjermundshamn N 46 B2
Gjerrild DK 58 B3
Gjerstad N 53 B5
Gjesås N 49 B4
Gjesvær N 193 A9
Gjirokastër AL 182 C2
Gjøfjell N 54 A1
Gjøl DK 58 A2
Gjøra N 198 C6
Gjøvik N 48 B2
Gladbeck D 80 A2
Gladenbach D 81 B4
Gladstad N 195 E2
Glamis GB 35 B4
Glamoč BIH 138 A2
Glamsbjerg DK 59 C3
Gland CH 105 C5
Glandorf D 71 B4
Glanegg A 110 C1
Glanshammar S 56 A1
Glarus CH 107 B4
Glasgow GB 35 C3
Glashütte, *Bayern* D 108 B2
Glashütte, *Sachsen* D 84 B1
Glastonbury GB 43 A4
Glatzau A 110 C2
Glauchau D 83 B4
Glava S 54 A3
Glavatičevo BIH 139 B4
Glavičice BIH 127 C1
Glein A 110 B1
Glein N 195 D3
Gleinstätten A 110 C2
Gleisdorf A 110 B2
Glenamoy IRL 26 B1
Glenarm GB 27 B5
Glenavy GB 27 B4
Glenbarr GB 34 C2
Glenbeigh IRL 29 B2
Glenbrittle GB 31 B2
Glencoe GB 34 B2
Glencolumbkille IRL 26 B2
Glendalough IRL 30 A2
Glenealy IRL 30 B2
Glenelg GB 31 B3
Glenfinnan GB 34 B2
Glengarriff IRL 29 C2
Glenluce GB 36 B2
Glennamaddy IRL 28 A3
Glenrothes GB 35 B4
Glenties IRL 26 B2
Glesborg DK 58 B3
Glesien D 83 A4
Gletsch CH 106 C3
Glewitz D 66 B1
Glifada GR 185 B4
Glimåkra S 63 B2
Glin IRL 29 B2
Glina HR 124 B2
Glinde D 72 A3
Glinojeck PL 77 B5
Glinsk IRL 28 A2
Gliwice PL 86 B2
Glödnitz A 109 C5
Gloggnitz A 110 B2
Głogoczów PL 99 B3
Glogonj SRB 127 C2
Glogovac SRB 127 C3
Głogów PL 85 A4
Głogówek PL 86 B1
Glomel F 100 A2
Glomfjord N 195 D4
Glommen S 60 C2
Glommersträsk S 196 D2
Glonn D 108 B2
Glorenza I 108 C1
Gloria P 154 B2
Glosa GR 183 D5
Glossop GB 40 B2
Gloucester GB 39 C4
Głowaczów PL 87 A5
Glówczyce PL 68 A2
Glöwen D 73 B5
Głowno PL 77 C4
Gložan SRB 126 B1
Głubczyce PL 86 B1
Głuchołazy PL 85 B5
Głuchów PL 87 A4
Głuchowo PL 75 B5
Glücksburg D 64 B2
Glückstadt D 64 C2
Glumina BIH 139 A5
Glumsø DK 65 A4
Glušci SRB 127 C1
Glusk BY 13 B8
Głuszyca PL 85 B4
Glyn Neath GB 39 C3
Glyngøre DK 58 B1
Gmünd, *Karnten* A 109 C4
Gmünd, *Nieder Östereich* A 96 C2
Gmund D 108 B2
Gmunden A 109 B4
Gnarp S 200 D3
Gnarrenburg D 72 A2
Gnesau A 109 C4
Gnesta S 56 A3
Gnięchowice PL 85 A4
Gniew PL 69 B3
Gniewkowo PL 76 B3
Gniezno PL 76 B2
Gnoien D 66 C1
Gnojnice BIH 139 B3
Gnojno PL 87 B4
Gnosall GB 40 C1
Gnosjö S 60 B3
Göbel TR 186 B3
Göçbeyli TR 186 C2
Goch D 80 A2
Gochsheim D 94 A2
Göd H 112 B3
Godalming GB 44 B3
Godby FIN 51 B6
Goddelsheim D 81 A4
Gódega di Sant'Urbano I 122 B1
Godegård S 56 B1
Godelheim D 81 A5
Goderville F 89 A4
Goðdalir IS 190 B6
Godiasco I 120 C2
Godič SLO 123 A3
Godkowo PL 69 A4
Godmanchester GB 44 A3
Gödöllö H 112 B3
Gödre H 125 A3
Godshill GB 44 C2
Godzikowice PL 85 B5
Godziszewo PL 69 A3
Goes NL 79 A3
Goetzenbrück F 93 C3
Góglio I 119 A5
Gogolin PL 86 B2
Göhren D 66 B2
Goirle NL 79 A5
Góis P 148 B1
Góito I 121 B3
Goizueta E 144 A2
Gojna Gora SRB 127 D2
Gójsk PL 77 B4
Gökçedağ TR 186 C3
Gökçen TR 188 A2
Gökçeören TR 188 A3
Gökçeyazı TR 186 C2
Göktepe TR 188 B3
Gol N 47 B5
Gola HR 124 A3
Gola N 48 A1
Gołańcz PL 76 B2
Gölbaşı TR 23 B7
Gölby FIN 51 B6
Gölcük, *Kocaeli* TR 187 B4
Gölcük, *Niğde* TR 23 B8
Golčův Jenikov CZ 97 B3
Gołczewo PL 67 C3
Goldach CH 107 B4
Goldbach D 93 A5
Goldbeck D 73 B4
Goldberg D 73 A5
Goldelund D 64 B2
Goldenstedt D 72 B1
Gołębiewo PL 69 A3
Golegã P 154 B2
Goleniów PL 75 A3
Golfo Aranci I 178 B3
Gölhisar TR 189 B4
Golina PL 76 B3
Gölle H 112 C2
Göllersdorf A 97 C4
Golling an der Salzach A 109 B4
Gölmarmara TR 186 D2
Golnice PL 84 A3
Golnik SLO 123 A3
Gölova TR 189 C5
Gölpazarı TR 187 B5
Gols A 111 B3
Golspie GB 32 D3
Golssen D 74 C2
Golub-Dobrzyń PL 77 A4
Golubinci SRB 127 C2
Goluchów PL 86 A1
Golymin-Ośrodek PL 77 B5
Golzow D 73 B5
Gomagoi I 108 C1
Gómara E 152 A1
Gomaringen D 93 C5
Gömbe TR 189 C4
Gömeç TR 186 C1
Gomel = Homyel BY 13 B9
Gomes Aires P 160 B1
Gómezserracin E 150 A3
Gommern D 73 B4
Gomulin PL 86 A3
Gonäs S 50 B2
Goncelin F 118 B2
Gończyce PL 87 A5
Gondomar E 140 B2
Gondomar P 148 A1
Gondrecourt-le-Château F 92 C1
Gondrin F 128 C3
Gönen, *Balıkesir* TR 186 B2
Gönen, *İsparta* TR 189 B5
Gonfaron F 132 B2
Goñi E 144 B2
Goni GR 182 D4
Goni I 179 C3
Gonnesa I 179 C2
Gonnosfanádiga I 179 C2
Gönyü H 111 B4
Gonzaga I 121 C3
Goodrich GB 39 C4
Goodwick GB 39 B1
Gooik B 79 B4
Goole GB 40 B3
Goor NL 71 B3
Göpfritz an der Wild A 97 C3
Goppenstein CH 119 A4
Göppingen D 94 C1
Gor E 164 B2
Góra, *Dolnośląskie* PL 85 A4
Góra, *Mazowieckie* PL 77 B5
Gorafe E 164 B1
Gorawino PL 67 C4
Goražde BIH 139 B4
Gőrbeháza H 113 B5
Gordaliza del Pino E 142 B1
Gördes TR 186 D3
Gørding DK 59 C1

Name	Country	Page	Grid
Górdola	CH	120	A1
Gordon	GB	35	C5
Gordoncillo	E	142	B1
Gorebridge	GB	35	C4
Gorenja Vas	SLO	123	A3
Gorenje Jelenje	HR	123	B3
Gorey	GB	88	A1
Gorey	IRL	30	B2
Gorgonzola	I	120	B2
Gorica	HR	137	A4
Gorican	HR	124	A2
Gorinchem	NL	79	A4
Goring	GB	44	B2
Goritsy	RUS	9	D10
Göritz	D	74	A2
Gorízia	I	122	B2
Górki	PL	77	B4
Gorleben	D	73	A4
Gorleston-on-sea	GB	41	C5
Gørlev	DK	61	D1
Görlitz	D	84	A4
Górliz	E	143	A4
Görmin	D	66	C2
Górna Grupa	PL	69	B3
Gorna Oryakhovitsa	BG	17	D6
Gornja Gorevnica	SRB	127	D2
Gornja Ploča	HR	137	A4
Gornja Radgona	SLO	110	C2
Gornja Sabanta	SRB	127	D3
Gornja Trešnjevica	SRB	127	C2
Gornja Tuzla	BIH	125	C4
Gornje Polje	MNE	139	C4
Gornje Ratkovo	HR	124	C2
Gornji Grad	SLO	123	A3
Gornji Humac	HR	138	B2
Gornji Jasenjani	BIH	139	B3
Gornji Kamengrad	BIH	124	C2
Gornji Kneginec	HR	124	A2
Gornji Kosinj	HR	123	C4
Gornji Milanovac	SRB	127	C2
Gornji Podgradci	BIH	124	B3
Gornji Ravno	BIH	138	B3
Gornji Sjenicak	HR	124	B1
Gornji Vakuf	BIH	138	B3
Górno	PL	87	B4
Görömböly	H	113	A4
Górowo Iławeckie	PL	69	A5
Gorran Haven	GB	42	B2
Gorredijk	NL	70	A3
Gorron	F	88	B3
Gorseinon	GB	39	C2
Gort	IRL	28	A3
Gortin	GB	27	B3
Görzke	D	73	B5
Gorzkowice	PL	86	A3
Górzno, *Kujawsko-Pomorskie*	PL	77	A4
Górzno, *Zachodnio-Pomorskie*	PL	75	A4
Gorzów Śląski	PL	86	A2
Gorzów Wielkopolski	PL	75	A4
Górzyca	PL	74	B3
Gorzyce	PL	98	B2
Górzyn, *Lubuskie*	PL	84	A2
Gorzyń, *Wielkopolskie*	PL	75	A4
Gorzyno	PL	68	A2
Gosaldo	I	121	A4
Gosau	A	109	B4
Gosberton	GB	41	C3
Gościcino	PL	68	A3
Gościęcin	PL	86	B2
Gościm	PL	75	A4
Gościno	PL	67	B4
Gosdorf	A	110	C2
Gosforth	GB	36	B3
Goslar	D	82	A2
Goslice	PL	77	B4
Gospič	HR	137	A4
Gosport	GB	44	C2
Goss Ilsede	D	72	B3
Gössäter	S	55	B4
Gossau	CH	107	B4
Gössnitz	D	83	B4
Gössweinstein	D	95	B3
Gostivar	MK	182	B2
Gostkow	PL	77	B4
Göstling an der Ybbs	A	110	B1
Gostomia	PL	75	A5
Gostycyn	PL	76	A2
Gostyń	PL	85	A3
Gostynin	PL	77	B4
Goszczyn	PL	87	A4
Göta	S	54	B3
Göteborg = Gothenburg	S	60	B1
Götene	S	55	B4
Gotha	D	82	B2
Gothem	S	57	C4
Gothenburg = Göteborg	S	60	B1
Gotse Delchev	BG	183	B5
Gottersdorf	D	95	C4
Göttingen	D	82	A1
Gottne	S	200	C4
Götzis	A	107	B4
Gouarec	F	100	A2
Gouda	NL	70	B1
Goudhurst	GB	45	B4
Goumenissa	GR	182	C4
Goura	GR	184	B3
Gourdon	F	129	B4
Gourgançon	F	91	C4
Gourin	F	100	A2
Gournay-en-Bray	F	90	B1
Gourock	GB	34	C3
Gouveia	P	148	B2
Gouvy	B	80	B1
Gouzeacourt	F	90	A3
Gouzon	F	116	A2
Govedari	HR	138	C3
Govérnolo	I	121	B3
Gowarczów	PL	87	A4
Gowerton	GB	39	C2
Gowidlino	PL	68	A2
Gowran	IRL	30	B1
Goyatz	D	74	B3
Göynük, *Antalya*	TR	189	C5
Göynük	TR	187	B5
Gozdnica	PL	84	A3
Gozdowo	PL	77	B4
Gozee	B	79	B4
Graal-Müritz	D	65	B5
Grabenstätt	D	109	B3
Grabhair	GB	31	A2
Gråbo	S	60	B2
Grabovac	HR	138	B2
Grabovac	SRB	127	C2
Grabovci	SRB	127	C1
Grabow	D	73	A4
Grabów	PL	77	B4
Grabów nad Pilicą	PL	87	A5
Grabów nad Prosną	PL	86	A2
Grabowno	PL	76	A2
Grabs	CH	107	B4
Gračac	HR	138	A1
Gračanica	BIH	125	C4
Graçay	F	103	B3
Grad	SLO	111	C3
Gradac	BIH	139	C4
Gradac	BIH	138	B3
Gradac	MNE	139	B5
Gradačac	BIH	125	C4
Gradec	HR	124	B2
Gradefes	E	142	B1
Grades	A	110	C1
Gradil	P	154	C1
Gradina	HR	124	B3
Gradina	MNE	139	B5
Gradisca d'Isonzo	I	122	B2
Gradište	HR	125	B4
Grado	I	141	A4
Grado	I	122	B2
Grærup Strand	DK	59	C1
Græsted	DK	61	C2
Grafenau	D	96	C1
Gräfenberg	D	95	B3
Gräfenhainichen	D	83	A4
Grafenschlag	A	97	C3
Grafenstein	A	110	C1
Gräfenthal	D	82	B3
Grafentonna	D	82	A2
Grafenwöhr	D	95	B3
Grafing	D	108	A2
Grafling	D	95	C4
Gräfsnäs	S	54	B3
Gragnano	I	170	C2
Grahovo	SLO	122	A2
Graiguenamanagh	IRL	30	B2
Grain	GB	45	B4
Grainau	D	108	B2
Graja de Iniesta	E	158	B2
Grajera	E	151	A4
Gram	DK	59	C2
Gramais	A	108	B1
Gramat	F	129	B4
Gramatneusiedl	A	111	A3
Grambow	D	74	A3
Grammichele	I	177	B3
Gramsh	AL	182	C2
Gramzow	D	74	A3
Gran	N	48	B2
Granada	E	163	A4
Granard	IRL	27	C3
Grañas	E	140	A3
Granátula de Calatrava	E	157	B4
Grancey-le-Château	F	105	B3
Grand-Champ	F	100	B3
Grand Couronne	F	89	A5
Grand-Fougeray	F	101	B4
Grandas de Salime	E	141	A4
Grandcamp-Maisy	F	88	A2
Grândola	P	160	A1
Grandpré	F	91	B4
Grandrieu	F	117	C3
Grandrieu	B	79	B4
Grandson	CH	106	C1
Grandvillars	F	106	B1
Grandvilliers	F	90	B1
Grañén	E	145	C3
Grängärde	S	50	B1
Grange-over-Sands	GB	36	B4
Grangemouth	GB	35	B4
Granges-de-Crouhens	F	145	B4
Granges-sur-Vologne	F	106	A1
Grängesberg	S	50	B1
Gräningen	D	73	B5
Granitola-Torretta	I	176	B1
Granja, *Évora*	P	155	C3
Granja, *Porto*	P	148	A1
Granja de Moreruela	E	142	C1
Granja de Torrehermosa	E	156	B2
Gränna	S	55	B5
Grannäs, *Västerbotten*	S	195	E7
Grannäs, *Västerbotten*	S	195	E8
Granö	S	200	B5
Granollers	E	147	C3
Granowiec	PL	85	A5
Granowo	PL	75	B5
Gransee	D	74	A2
Gransherad	N	53	A5
Grantham	GB	40	C3
Grantown-on-Spey	GB	32	D3
Grantshouse	GB	35	C5
Granville	F	88	B2
Granvin	N	46	B3
Gräsås	S	60	C2
Grasbakken	N	193	B12
Grasberg	D	72	A2
Grasmere	GB	36	B3
Gräsmyr	S	200	C5
Grasö	S	51	B5
Grassano	I	172	B2
Grassau	D	109	B3
Grasse	F	132	B2
Grassington	GB	40	A2
Gråsten	DK	64	B2
Grästorp	S	54	B3
Gratkorn	A	110	B2
Gråträsk	S	196	D2
Gratwein	A	110	B2
Graulhet	F	129	C4
Graus	E	145	B4
Grávalos	E	144	B2
Gravberget	N	49	B4
Grave	NL	80	A1
Gravedona	I	120	A2
Gravelines	F	78	A2
Gravellona Toce	I	119	B5
Gravendal	S	50	B1
's-Gravendeel	NL	79	A4
's-Gravenhage = The Hague	NL	70	B1
Gravens	DK	59	C2
's-Gravenzande	NL	79	A4
Gravesend	GB	45	B4
Graveson	F	131	B3
Gravina in Púglia	I	172	B2
Gray	F	105	B4
Grayrigg	GB	37	B4
Grays	GB	45	B4
Grayshott	GB	44	B3
Graz	A	110	B2
Grazalema	E	162	B2
Grążawy	PL	69	B4
Grazzano Visconti	I	120	C2
Greåker	N	54	A2
Great Dunmow	GB	45	B4
Great Malvern	GB	39	B4
Great Torrington	GB	42	B2
Great Waltham	GB	45	B4
Great Yarmouth	GB	41	C5
Grebbestad	S	54	B2
Grebenstein	D	81	A5
Grebocice	PL	85	A4
Grebocin	PL	76	A3
Greding	D	95	B3
Gredstedbro	DK	59	C1
Greenhead	GB	37	B4
Greenisland	GB	27	B5
Greenlaw	GB	35	C5
Greenock	GB	34	C3
Greenway	GB	39	C2
Greenwich	GB	45	B4
Grefrath	D	80	A2
Greifenburg	A	109	C4
Greiffenberg	D	74	A2
Greifswald	D	66	B2
Grein	A	110	A1
Greipstad	N	53	B3
Greiz	D	83	B4
Grenaa	DK	58	B3
Grenade	F	129	C4
Grenade-sur-l'Adour	F	128	C2
Grenchen	CH	106	B2
Grendi	N	53	B3
Grenivik	IS	191	B7
Grenoble	F	118	B2
Gréoux-les-Bains	F	132	B1
Gresenhorst	D	66	B1
Gressoney-la-Trinité	I	119	B4
Gressoney-St.-Jean	I	119	B4
Gressthal	D	82	B2
Gressvik	N	54	A1
Gresten	A	110	B2
Gretna	GB	36	B3
Greussen	D	82	A2
Greve in Chianti	I	135	B4
Greven, *Mecklenburg-Vorpommern*	D	73	A3
Greven, *Nordrhein-Westfalen*	D	71	B4
Grevena	GR	182	C3
Grevenbroich	D	80	A2
Grevenbrück	D	81	A4
Grevenmacher	L	92	B2
Grevesmühlen	D	65	C4
Grevestrand	DK	61	D2
Grevie	S	61	C2
Greystoke	GB	36	B4
Greystones	IRL	30	A2
Grez-Doiceau	B	79	B4
Grez-en-Bouère	F	102	B1
Grèzec	F	129	B4
Grezzana	I	121	B4
Grgar	SLO	122	B2
Grgurevci	SRB	127	B1
Gries	A	108	B2
Gries in Sellrain	A	108	B2
Griesbach	D	96	C1
Griesheim	D	93	B4
Grieskirchen	A	109	A4
Griffen	A	110	C1
Grignan	F	131	A3
Grignano	I	122	B2
Grigno	I	121	A4
Grignols	F	128	B2
Grignon	F	118	B3
Grijota	E	142	B2
Grijpskerk	NL	71	A3
Grillby	S	56	A3
Grimaud	F	132	B2
Grimbergen	B	79	B4
Grimma	D	83	A4
Grimmen	D	66	B2
Grimmialp	CH	106	C2
Grimsås	S	60	B3
Grimsby	GB	41	B3
Grímslöv	S	62	B2
Grímsstaðir	IS	191	B9
Grimstad	N	53	B4
Grimstorp	S	62	A2
Grindavík	IS	190	D3
Grindelwald	CH	106	C3
Grindheim	N	52	B3
Grindsted	DK	59	C1
Griñón	E	151	B4
Gripenberg	S	62	A2
Gripsholm	S	56	A3
Grisolles	F	129	C4
Grisslehamn	S	51	B5
Gritley	GB	33	C4
Grizebeck	GB	36	B3
Grndina	BIH	124	C2
Gröbming	A	109	B4
Gröbzig	D	83	A3
Grocka	SRB	127	C2
Gröditz	D	83	A5
Gródki	PL	77	A5
Grodków	PL	85	B5
Grodziec	PL	76	B3
Grodzisk Mazowiecki	PL	77	B5
Groenlo	NL	71	B3
Groesbeek	NL	80	A1
Grohote	HR	138	B2
Groitzsch	D	83	A4
Groix	F	100	B2
Grójec	PL	77	C5
Grom	PL	77	A5
Gromilica	BIH	139	B4
Grömitz	D	65	B3
Gromnik	PL	99	B4
Gromo	I	120	B2
Gronau, *Niedersachsen*	D	72	B2
Gronau, *Nordrhein-Westfalen*	D	71	B4
Grønbjerg	DK	59	B1
Grönenbach	D	107	B5
Grong	N	199	A9
Grönhögen	S	63	B4
Groningen	D	82	A3
Groningen	NL	71	A3
Grønnestrand	DK	58	A2
Grono	CH	120	A2
Grönskåra	S	62	A3
Grootegast	NL	71	A3
Gropello Cairoli	I	120	B1
Grorud	N	48	C2
Grósio	I	120	A3
Grošnica	SRB	127	D2
Gross Warnow	D	73	A4
Gross-Weikersdorf	A	97	C3
Gross-Welle	D	73	A5
Gross Wokern	D	65	C5
Grossalmerode	D	82	A1
Grossarl	A	109	B4
Grossbodungen	D	82	A2
Grossschönau	D	84	B2
Grossenbrode	D	65	B4
Grossenehrich	D	82	A2
Grossengottern	D	82	A2
Grossenhain	D	83	A5
Grossenkneten	D	71	B5
Grossenlüder	D	81	B5
Grossensee	D	72	A3
Grossenzersdorf	A	111	A3
Grosseto	I	135	C4
Grossgerungs	A	96	C2
Grossglobnitz	A	97	C3
Grosshabersdorf	D	94	B2
Grossharras	A	97	C4
Grosshöchstetten	CH	106	C2
Grosskrut	A	97	C4
Grosslohra	D	82	A2
Grossmehring	D	95	C3
Grossostheim	D	93	B5
Grosspertholz	A	96	C2
Grosspetersdorf	A	111	B3
Grosspostwitz	D	84	A2
Grossraming	A	110	B1
Grossräschen	D	84	A2
Grossrinderfeld	D	94	B1
Grossröhrsdorf	D	84	A2
Grossschirma	D	83	B5
Grossschweinbarth	A	97	C4
Grosssiegharts	A	97	C3
Grosssölk	A	109	B4
Grosswarasdorf	A	111	B3
Grosswilfersdorf	A	110	B2
Grostenquin	F	92	C2
Grosuplje	SLO	123	B3
Grotli	N	198	C4
Grötlingbo	S	57	C4
Grottáglie	I	173	B3
Grottaminarda	I	170	B3
Grottammare	I	136	C2
Grotte di Castro	I	168	A1
Grotteria	I	175	C2
Gróttole	I	172	B2
Grou	NL	70	A2
Grov	N	194	B8
Grova	N	53	A4
Grove	E	140	B2
Grua	N	48	B2
Grube	D	65	B4
Grubišno Polje	HR	124	B3
Grudovo	BG	17	D7
Grudusk	PL	77	A5
Grudziądz	PL	69	B3
Grue	N	49	B4
Gruissan	F	130	B2
Grullos	E	141	A4
Grumo Áppula	I	171	B4
Grums	S	55	B4
Grünau im Almtal	A	109	B4
Grünberg	D	81	B4
Grünburg	A	110	B1
Grundarfjörður	IS	190	C2
Gründau	D	81	B5
Gründelhardt	D	94	B1
Grundforsen	S	49	A5
Grundlsee	A	109	B4
Grundsund	S	54	B2
Grunewald	D	84	A1
Grungedal	N	53	A3
Grunow	D	74	B3
Grünstadt	D	93	B4
Gruvberget	S	50	A3
Gruyères	CH	106	C2
Gruža	SRB	127	D2
Grybów	PL	99	B4
Grycksbo	S	50	B2
Gryfice	PL	67	C4
Gryfino	PL	74	A3
Gryfów Śląski	PL	84	A3
Gryllefjord	N	194	A8
Grymyr	N	48	B2
Gryt	S	56	B2
Grytgöl	S	56	B1
Grythyttan	S	55	A5
Grytnäs	S	57	B3
Grzmiąca	PL	68	B1
Grzybno	PL	74	A3
Grzywna	PL	76	A3
Gschnitz	A	108	B2
Gstaad	CH	106	C2
Gsteig	CH	119	A4
Guagnano	I	173	B3
Guagno	F	180	A1
Guajar-Faragüit	E	163	B4
Gualchos	E	163	B4
Gualdo Tadino	I	136	B1
Gualtieri	I	121	C3
Guarcino	I	169	B3
Guarda	P	149	B2
Guardamar del Segura	E	165	A4
Guardão	P	148	B1
Guardavalle	I	175	C2
Guardea	I	168	A2
Guárdia	I	172	B1
Guárdia Sanframondi	I	170	B2
Guardiagrele	I	169	A4
Guardiarégia	I	170	B2
Guareña	E	156	B1
Guaro	E	162	B3
Guarromán	E	157	B4
Guasila	I	179	C3
Guastalla	I	121	C3
Gubbhögen	S	199	A12
Gúbbio	I	136	B1
Guben	D	74	C3
Gubin	PL	74	C3
Gudå	N	199	B8
Gudavac	BIH	124	C2
Guddal	N	46	A2
Güderup	DK	64	B2
Gudhem	S	55	B4
Gudhjem	DK	67	A3
Gudovac	HR	124	B2
Gudow	D	73	A3
Güdül	TR	187	B7
Gudvangen	N	46	B3
Guebwiller	F	106	B2
Guéjar-Sierra	E	163	A4
Guémené-Penfao	F	101	B4
Guémené-sur-Scorff	F	100	A2
Güeñes	E	143	A3
Guer	F	101	B3
Guérande	F	101	B3
Guéret	F	116	A1
Guérigny	F	104	B2
Guesa	E	144	B2
Gueugnon	F	104	C3
Gühlen Glienicke	D	74	A1
Guia	P	154	B2
Guichen	F	101	B4
Guidizzolo	I	121	B3
Guidónia-Montecélio	I	168	B2
Guiglia	I	135	A3
Guignes	F	90	C2
Guijo	E	156	B3
Guijo de Coria	E	149	B3
Guijo de Santa Bábera	E	150	B2
Guijuelo	E	150	B2
Guildford	GB	44	B3
Guillaumes	F	132	A2
Guillena	E	162	A1
Guillestre	F	118	C3
Guillos	F	128	B2
Guilsfield	GB	38	B3
Guilvinec	F	100	B1
Guimarães	P	148	A1
Guincho	P	154	C1
Guînes	F	78	B1
Guingamp	F	100	A2
Guipavas	F	100	A1
Guisborough	GB	37	B5
Guiscard	F	90	B3
Guiscriff	F	100	A2
Guise	F	91	B3
Guisona	E	147	C2
Guitiriz	E	140	A3
Guîtres	F	128	A2
Gujan-Mestras	F	128	B1
Gulbene	LV	8	D5
Gulçayır	TR	187	C5
Guldborg	DK	65	B4
Gullabo	S	63	B3
Gullane	GB	35	B5
Gullbrå	N	46	B3
Gullbrandstorp	S	61	C2
Gulleråsen	S	50	A2
Gullhaug	N	53	A6
Gullspång	S	55	B5
Gullstein	N	198	B5
Gülnar	TR	23	C7
Gülpınar	TR	186	C1
Gülşehir	TR	23	B8
Gulsvik	N	48	B1
Gumiel de Hizán	E	143	C3
Gummersbach	D	81	A3
Gümüldür	TR	188	A2
Gümüşhacıköy	TR	23	A8
Gümüşova	TR	187	B5
Gundelfingen	D	106	A2
Gundelsheim	D	93	B5
Gunderschoffen	F	93	C3
Gundertshausen	A	109	A3

Gundinci HR 125 B4
Gündoğmuş TR 189 C7
Güney, *Burdur* TR 189 B4
Güney, *Denizli* TR 188 A4
Gunja HR 125 C4
Günlüce TR 188 C3
Gunnarn S 195 E8
Gunnarsbyn S 196 C4
Gunnarskog S 49 C4
Gunnebo S 62 A4
Gunnislake GB 42 B2
Günselsdorf A 111 B3
Guntersblum D 93 B4
Guntersdorf A 97 C4
Guntin E 140 B3
Günyüzü TR 187 C6
Günzburg D 94 C2
Gunzenhausen D 94 B2
Güre, *Balıkesir* TR 186 C1
Güre, *Uşak* TR 186 D4
Gurk A 110 C1
Gurrea de Gállego E 144 B3
Gürsu TR 186 B4
Gušće HR 124 B2
Gusev RUS 12 A5
Gúspini I 179 C2
Gusselby S 56 A1
Güssing A 111 B3
Gusswerk A 110 B2
Gustav Adolf S 49 B5
Gustavsberg S 57 A4
Gustavsfors S 54 A3
Güstrow D 65 C5
Gusum S 56 B2
Gutcher GB 33 A5
Gutenstein A 110 B2
Gütersloh D 81 A4
Guttannen CH 106 C3
Guttaring A 110 C1
Guttau D 84 A2
Güttingen CH 107 B4
Gützkow D 66 C2
Guzów PL 77 B5
Gvardeysk RUS 12 A4
Gvarv N 53 A5
Gvozd MNE 139 C5
Gvozdansko HR 124 B2
Gwda Wielka PL 68 B1
Gwennap GB 42 B1
Gy F 105 B4
Gyál H 112 B3
Gyarmat H 111 B4
Gyé-sur-Seine F 104 A3
Gyékényes H 124 A3
Gyljen S 196 C5
Gylling DK 59 C3
Gyoma H 113 C4
Gyömöre H 111 B4
Gyömrö H 112 B3
Gyón H 112 B3
Gyöngyfa H 125 B3
Gyöngyös H 113 B3
Gyöngyöspata H 113 B3
Gyönk H 112 C2
Györ H 111 B4
Györszemere H 111 B4
Gypsera CH 106 C2
Gysinge S 51 B3
Gyttorp S 55 A5
Gyula H 113 C5
Gyulafirátót H 112 B1
Gyulaj H 112 C2

H

Haacht B 79 B4
Haag, *Nieder Östereich* A 110 A1
Haag, *Ober Östereich* A 109 A4
Haag D 108 A3
Haaksbergen NL 71 B3
Haamstede NL 79 A3
Haan D 80 A3
Haapajärvi FIN 3 E9
Haapsalu EST 8 C3
Haarlem NL 70 B1
Habas F 128 C2
Habay B 92 B1
Habo S 62 A2
Håbol S 54 B3
Habry CZ 97 B3
Habsheim F 106 B2
Hachenburg D 81 B3
Hacıbektaş TR 23 B8
Hacılar TR 23 B8
Hacinas E 143 C3
Hackås S 199 C11
Hacketstown IRL 30 B2
Hackthorpe GB 37 B4
Hadamar D 81 B4
Hädanberg S 200 C4
Haddington GB 35 C5
Hadersdorf am Kamp A 97 C3
Haderslev DK 59 C2
Haderup DK 59 B1
Hadım TR 23 C7
Hadleigh, *Essex* GB 45 B4
Hadleigh, *Suffolk* GB 45 A4
Hadlow GB 45 B4
Hadmersleben D 73 B4
Hadsten DK 59 B3
Hadsund DK 58 B3
Hadžići BIH 139 B4
Hægebostad N 52 B3
Hægeland N 53 B3
Hafnarfjörður IS 190 C4
Hafnir IS 190 D3
Hafslo N 47 A4
Haganj HR 124 B2
Hagby S 63 B4
Hage D 71 A4
Hagen, *Niedersachsen* D 72 A1
Hagen, *Nordrhein-Westfalen* D 80 A3
Hagenbach D 93 B4
Hagenow D 73 A4
Hagetmau F 128 C2
Hagfors S 49 B5
Häggenås S 199 B11
Hagondange F 92 B2
Hagsta S 51 B4
Haguenau F 93 C3
Hahnbach D 95 B3
Hahnslätten D 81 B4
Hahót H 111 C3
Haiger D 81 B4
Haigerloch D 93 C4
Hailsham GB 45 C4
Hainburg A 111 A3
Hainfeld A 110 A2
Hainichen D 83 B5
Hajdúböszörmény H 113 B5
Hajdučica SRB 126 B2
Hajdúdorogo H 113 B5
Hajdúnánás H 113 B5
Hajdúszoboszló H 113 B5
Hajnáčka SK 113 A3
Hajnówka PL 13 B5
Hajós H 112 C3
Håkafot S 199 A11
Hakkas S 196 C4
Håksberg S 50 B2
Halaszi H 111 B4
Halberstadt D 82 A3
Halberton GB 43 B3
Hald Ege DK 58 B2
Haldem D 71 B5
Halden N 54 A2
Haldensleben D 73 B4
Halenbeck D 73 A5
Halesowen GB 40 C1
Halesworth GB 45 A5
Halfing D 109 B3
Halhjem N 46 B2
Håliden S 49 B5
Halifax GB 40 B2
Häljelöt S 56 B2
Halkida GR 185 A4
Halkirk GB 32 C3
Hall S 57 C4
Hall in Tirol A 108 B2
Hälla S 200 C3
Hallabro S 63 B3
Hällabrottet S 56 A1
Halland GB 45 C4
Hällaryd, *Blekinge* S 63 B2
Hallaryd, *Kronoberg* S 61 C3
Hällberga S 56 A2
Hällbybrunn S 56 A2
Halle B 79 B4
Halle, *Nordrhein-Westfalen* D 72 B1
Halle, *Sachsen-Anhalt* D 83 A3
Hålleberga S 62 B3
Hällefors S 55 A5
Hälleforsnäs S 56 A2
Hallein A 109 B4
Hällekis S 55 B4
Hallen, *Jämtland* S 199 B11
Hållen, *Uppsala* S 51 B4
Hallenberg D 81 A4
Hällestad S 56 B1
Hällevadsholm S 54 B2
Hällevik S 63 B2
Hälleviksstrand S 54 B2
Hallingby N 48 B2
Hallingeberg S 62 A4
Hallingen N 47 B6
Hällnäs, *Norrbotten* S 195 D9
Hållnäs, *Uppsala* S 51 B4
Hällnäs, *Västerbotten* S 200 B5
Hallormsstaður IS 191 B11
Hallsberg S 56 A1
Hållsta S 56 A2
Hallstahammar S 56 A2
Hallstatt A 109 B4
Hallstavik S 51 B5
Halltorp S 63 B4
Halluin F 78 B3
Hallviken S 199 B12
Hallworthy GB 42 B2
Halmstad S 61 C2
Hals DK 58 A3
Halsa N 198 B5
Halstead GB 45 B4
Haltdalen N 199 C8
Haltern D 80 A3
Haltwhistle GB 37 B4
Halvarsgårdarna S 50 B2
Halver D 80 A3
Halvrimmen DK 58 A2
Ham F 90 B3
Hamar N 48 B3
Hamarhaug N 46 B2
Hamarøy N 194 B6
Hambach F 92 B3
Hambergen D 72 A1
Hambergsund S 54 B2
Hambledon GB 44 C2
Hambuhren D 72 B2
Hamburg D 72 A3
Hamdibey TR 186 C2
Hamdorf D 64 B2
Hämeenlinna FIN 8 B4
Hameln = Hamlin D 72 B2
Hamersleben D 73 B4
Hamidiye TR 187 C5
Hamilton GB 36 A2
Hamina FIN 8 B5
Hamlagrø N 46 B3
Hamlin = Hameln D 72 B2
Hamm D 81 A3
Hammar S 55 B5
Hammarland FIN 51 B6
Hammarö S 55 A4
Hammarstrand S 200 C2
Hamme B 79 A4
Hammel DK 59 B2
Hammelburg D 82 B1
Hammelspring D 74 A2
Hammenhög S 66 A3
Hammerdal S 199 B12
Hammerfest N 192 B7
Hammershøj DK 58 B2
Hammerum DK 59 B2
Hamminkeln D 80 A2
Hamnavoe GB 33 A5
Hamneda S 60 C3
Hamningberg N 193 B14
Hamoir B 80 B1
Hamont B 80 A1
Hámor H 113 A4
Hamra, *Gävleborg* S 199 D12
Hamra, *Gotland* S 57 D4
Hamrångefjärden S 51 B4
Hamstreet GB 45 B4
Hamsund N 194 B6
Han TR 187 C5
Han Knežica BIH 124 B2
Han Pijesak BIH 139 A4
Hanaskog S 61 C4
Hanau D 81 B4
Händelöp S 62 A4
Handlová SK 98 C2
Hanerau-Hademarschen D 64 B2
Hånger S 60 B3
Hanhimaa FIN 197 B8
Hanken S 55 B5
Hankensbüttel D 73 B3
Hanko FIN 8 C3
Hannover D 72 B2
Hannut B 79 B5
Hansnes N 192 C3
Hanstedt D 72 A3
Hanstholm DK 58 A1
Hantsavichy BY 13 B7
Hanušovice CZ 85 B4
Haparanda S 196 D7
Haradok BY 13 A8
Harads S 196 C4
Häradsbäck S 63 B2
Häradsbygden S 50 B2
Harbo S 51 B4
Harboør DK 58 B1
Harburg, *Bayern* D 94 C2
Harburg, *Hamburg* D 72 A2
Hårby DK 59 C3
Harc H 112 C2
Hardegarijp NL 70 A2
Hardegsen D 82 A1
Hardelot Plage F 78 B1
Hardenbeck D 74 A2
Hardenberg NL 71 B3
Harderwijk NL 70 B2
Hardheim D 94 B1
Hardt D 106 A3
Hareid N 198 C3
Haren D 71 B4
Haren NL 71 A3
Harestua N 48 B2
Harfleur F 89 A4
Harg S 51 B5
Hargicourt F 90 B3
Hargnies F 91 A4
Hargshamn S 51 B5
Härja S 55 B4
Harkány H 125 B4
Härkeberga S 56 A3
Harkebrügge D 71 A4
Harlech GB 38 B2
Harleston GB 45 A5
Hårlev DK 65 A5
Harlingen NL 70 A2
Harlösa S 61 D3
Harlow GB 45 B4
Harmancık TR 186 C4
Harmånger S 200 E3
Härnevi S 56 A3
Härnösand S 200 D3
Haro E 143 B4
Haroldswick GB 33 A6
Háromfa H 124 A3
Haroué F 92 C2
Harpenden GB 44 B3
Harplinge S 60 C2
Harpstedt D 72 B1
Harrogate GB 40 A2
Harrow GB 44 B3
Härryda S 60 B2
Harsefeld D 72 A2
Harsewinkel D 71 C5
Hârşova RO 17 C7
Harstad N 194 B7
Harsum D 72 B2
Harsvik N 199 A7
Harta H 112 C3
Hartberg A 110 B2
Hartburn GB 37 A5
Hartennes F 90 B3
Hartest GB 45 A4
Hartha D 83 A4
Hartland GB 42 B2
Hartlepool GB 37 B5
Hartmanice CZ 96 B1
Hartmannsdorf A 110 B2
Harvassdal N 195 E5
Harwell GB 44 B2
Harwich GB 45 B5
Harzgerode D 82 A3
Häselgehr A 108 B1
Haselünne D 71 B4
Hasköy TR 186 A1
Haslach D 106 A3
Haslach an der Mühl A 96 C2
Hasle DK 67 A3
Haslemere GB 44 B3
Haslev DK 65 A4
Hasloch D 94 B1
Hasparren F 144 A2
Hassela S 200 D2
Hasselfelde D 82 A2
Hasselfors S 55 A5
Hasselt B 79 B5
Hasselt NL 70 B3
Hassfurt D 94 A2
Hassleben D 74 A2
Hässleholm S 61 C3
Hasslö S 63 B3
Hassloch D 93 B4
Hästbo S 51 B4
Hastersboda FIN 51 B7
Hästholmen S 55 B5
Hastière-Lavaux B 79 B4
Hastigrow GB 32 C3
Hastings GB 45 C4
Hästveda S 61 C3
Hasvik N 192 B6
Hatfield, *Hertfordshire* GB 44 B3
Hatfield, *South Yorkshire* GB 40 B3
Hatherleigh GB 42 B2
Hathersage GB 40 B2
Hatlestrand N 46 B2
Hattem NL 70 B3
Hatten D 71 A5
Hatten F 93 C3
Hattfjelldal N 195 E4
Hatting DK 59 C2
Hattingen D 80 A3
Hattstadt F 106 A2
Hattstedt D 64 B2
Hatvan H 112 B3
Hatvik N 46 B2
Hau D 80 A2
Haudainville F 92 B1
Hauganes IS 191 B7
Haugastøl N 47 B4
Hauge N 52 B2
Haugesund N 52 A1
Haughom N 52 B2
Haugsdal N 46 B2
Haugsdorf A 97 C4
Haukedal N 46 A3
Haukeland N 46 B2
Haukeligrend N 52 A3
Haukeliseter N 52 A3
Haukipudas FIN 3 D9
Haulerwijk NL 71 A3
Haunersdorf D 95 C4
Haus N 46 B2
Hausach D 106 A3
Hausham D 108 B2
Hausmannstätten A 110 C2
Hausvik N 52 B2
Haut-Fays B 91 A5
Hautajärvi FIN 197 C12
Hautefort F 129 A4
Hauterives F 117 B5
Hauteville-Lompnès F 118 B2
Hautmont F 79 B3
Hautrage B 79 B3
Hauzenberg D 96 C1
Havant GB 44 C3
Havdhem S 57 C4
Havdrup DK 61 D2
Havelange B 79 B5
Havelberg D 73 B5
Havelte NL 70 B3
Haverfordwest GB 39 C2
Haverhill GB 45 A4
Havering GB 45 B4
Håverud S 54 B3
Havířov CZ 98 B2
Havixbeck D 71 C4
Havlíčkův Brod CZ 97 B3
Havndal DK 58 B3
Havneby DK 64 A1
Havnebyen DK 61 D1
Havnsø DK 61 D1
Havøysund N 193 A8
Havran TR 186 C2
Havrebjerg DK 61 D1
Havsa TR 186 A1
Havstenssund S 54 B2
Havza TR 23 A8
Hawes GB 37 B4
Hawick GB 35 C5
Hawkhurst GB 45 B4
Hawkinge GB 45 B5
Haxey GB 40 B3
Hay-on-Wye GB 39 B3
Hayange F 92 B2
Haydarlı TR 189 A5
Haydon Bridge GB 37 B4
Hayle GB 42 B1
Haymana TR 187 C7
Hayrabolu TR 186 A2
Haysyn UA 13 D8
Hayvoron UA 13 D8
Haywards Heath GB 44 C3
Hazebrouck F 78 B2
Hazlov CZ 83 B4
Heacham GB 41 C4
Headcorn GB 45 B4
Headford IRL 28 A2
Heanor GB 40 B2
Héas F 145 B4
Heathfield GB 45 C4
Hebden Bridge GB 40 B1
Heberg S 60 C2
Heby S 51 C3
Hechingen D 93 C4
Hechlingen D 94 C2
Hecho E 144 B3
Hechtel B 79 A5
Hechthausen D 72 A2
Heckelberg D 74 B2
Heckington GB 41 C3
Hecklingen D 82 A3
Hed S 56 A1
Hedalen N 48 B1
Hedared S 60 B2
Heddal N 53 A5
Hédé F 101 A4
Hede S 199 C10
Hedekas S 54 B2
Hedemora S 50 B2
Hedenäset S 196 C6
Hedensted DK 59 C2
Hedersleben D 82 A3
Hedesunda S 51 B4
Hedge End GB 44 C2
Hedon GB 41 B3
Heede D 71 B4
Heek D 71 B4
Heemstede NL 70 B1
Heerde NL 70 B3
Heerenveen NL 70 B2
Heerhugowaard NL 70 B1
Heerlen NL 80 B1
Heeze NL 80 A1
Heggenes N 47 A6
Hegra N 199 B8
Hegyeshalom H 111 B4
Hegyközség H 111 B3
Heia N 199 A9
Heide D 64 B2
Heidelberg D 93 B4
Heiden D 80 A2
Heidenau D 84 B1
Heidenheim D 94 C2
Heidenreichstein A 97 C3
Heikendorf D 64 B3
Heikkilä FIN 197 C12
Heilam GB 32 C2
Heiland N 53 B4
Heilbad Heiligenstadt D 82 A2
Heilbronn D 93 B5
Heiligenblut A 109 B3
Heiligendamn D 65 B4
Heiligendorf D 73 B3
Heiligengrabe D 73 A5
Heiligenhafen D 65 B3
Heiligenhaus D 80 A2
Heiligenkreuz A 111 C3
Heiligenstadt D 94 B3
Heiloo NL 70 B1
Heilsbronn D 94 B2
Heim N 198 B6
Heimburg D 82 A2
Heimdal N 199 B7
Heinerscheid L 92 A2
Heinersdorf D 74 B3
Heining D 96 C1
Heiningen D 94 C1
Heinola FIN 8 B5
Heinsberg D 80 A2
Heist-op-den-Berg B 79 A4
Hejde S 57 C4
Hejdeby S 57 C4
Hejls DK 59 C2
Hejnice CZ 84 B3
Hel PL 69 A3
Helchteren B 79 A5
Heldburg D 82 B2
Heldrungen D 82 A3
Helechosa E 156 A3
Helensburgh GB 34 B3
Helfenberg A 96 C2
Helgen N 53 A5
Helgeroa N 53 B5
Hella IS 190 D5
Hella N 46 A3
Helland N 194 B7
Hellas S 55 B3
Helle N 52 B2
Helleland N 52 B2
Hellendoorn NL 71 B3
Hellenthal D 80 B2
Hellesøy N 46 B1
Hellesylt N 198 C3
Hellevoetsluis NL 79 A4
Helligskogen N 192 C4
Hellín E 158 C2
Hellissandur IS 190 C2
Hellnar IS 190 C2
Hellum DK 58 A3
Hellvi S 57 C4
Hellvik N 52 B1
Helm-brechts D 83 B3
Helmond NL 80 A1
Helmsdale GB 32 C3
Helmsley GB 37 B5
Helmstedt D 73 B3
Hel'pa SK 99 C3
Helsa D 82 A1
Helsby GB 38 A4
Helsingborg S 61 C2
Helsinge DK 61 C2
Helsingør DK 61 C2
Helsinki FIN 8 B4
Helston GB 42 B1
Hemau D 95 B3
Hemavan S 195 E6
Hemel Hempstead GB 44 B3
Hemer D 81 A3
Héming F 92 C2
Hemmet DK 59 C1
Hemmingstedt D 64 B2
Hemmoor D 64 C2
Hemnes N 54 A2
Hemnesberget N 195 D4
Hemse S 57 C4
Hemsedal N 47 B5
Hemslingen D 72 A2
Hemsworth GB 40 B2
Hen N 48 B2
Henån S 54 B2
Hendaye F 144 A2
Hendek TR 187 B5
Hendungen D 82 B2
Henfield GB 44 C3
Hengelo, *Gelderland* NL 71 B3
Hengelo, *Overijssel* NL 71 B3
Hengersberg D 95 C5
Hengoed GB 39 C3
Hénin-Beaumont F 78 B2
Henley-on-Thames GB 44 B3
Hennan S 200 D1
Henne Strand DK 59 C1
Henneberg D 82 B2
Hennebont F 100 B2
Hennigsdorf D 74 B2
Hennset N 198 B5
Hennstedt, *Schleswig-Holstein* D 64 B2
Hennstedt, *Schleswig-Holstein* D 64 B2
Henrichemont F 103 B4
Henryków PL 85 B5
Henrykowo PL 69 A5
Hensås N 47 A5
Henstedt-Ulzburg D 64 C2
Heppenheim D 93 B4
Herad, *Buskerud* N 47 B6
Herad, *Vest-Agder* N 52 B2
Heradsbygd N 48 B3
Heraklion = Iraklio GR 185 D6
Herálec CZ 97 B4
Herand N 46 B3
Herbault F 103 B3
Herbern D 81 A3
Herbertstown IRL 29 B3
Herbeumont B 91 B5
Herbignac F 101 B3
Herbisse F 91 C4
Herbitzheim F 92 B3
Herbolzheim D 106 A2
Herborn D 81 B4
Herbrechtingen D 94 C2
Herby PL 86 B2
Herceg-Novi MNE 16 D3
Hercegovać HR 124 B3
Hercegszántó H 125 B4
Herchen D 80 B3
Heréd H 112 B3
Hereford GB 39 B4
Herefoss N 53 B4
Hereke TR 187 B4
Herencia E 157 A4
Herend H 111 B4
Herent B 79 B4
Herentals B 79 A4
Hérépian F 130 B2
Herfølge DK 61 D2
Herford D 72 B1
Herguijuela E 156 B2
Héric F 101 B4

Name		Page	Grid
Héricourt	F	106	B1
Héricourt-en-Caux	F	89	A4
Hérimoncourt	F	106	B1
Heringsdorf	D	65	B4
Herisau	CH	107	B3
Hérisson	F	103	C4
Herk-de-Stad	B	79	B5
Herlufmagle	DK	65	A4
Hermagor	A	109	C4
Hermannsburg	D	72	B3
Hermansverk	N	46	A3
Heřmanův Městec	CZ	97	B3
Herment	F	116	B2
Hermeskeil	D	92	B2
Hermisende	E	141	C4
Hermonville	F	91	B3
Hermsdorf	D	83	B3
Hernani	E	144	A2
Hernansancho	E	150	B3
Herne	D	80	A3
Herne Bay	GB	45	B5
Hernes	N	48	B3
Herning	DK	59	B1
Herøya	N	53	A5
Herramelluri	E	143	B3
Herräng	S	51	B5
Herre	N	53	A5
Herrenberg	D	93	C4
Herrera	E	162	A3
Herrera de Alcántara	E	155	B3
Herrera de los Navarros	E	152	A2
Herrera de Pisuerga	E	142	B2
Herrera del Duque	E	156	A2
Herrerias	E	161	B2
Herreros del Suso	E	150	B2
Herrestad	S	54	B2
Herrhamra	S	57	B3
Herritslev	DK	65	B4
Herrlisheim	F	93	C3
Herrljunga	S	55	B4
Herrnhut	D	84	A2
Herrsching	D	108	A2
Hersbruck	D	95	B3
Hersby	S	57	A4
Herscheid	D	81	A3
Herselt	B	79	A4
Herso	GR	182	B4
Herstal	B	80	B1
Herstmonceux	GB	45	C4
Herten	D	80	A3
Hertford	GB	44	B3
's-Hertogenbosch	NL	79	A5
Hervás	E	149	B4
Hervik	N	52	A1
Herxheim	D	93	B4
Herzberg, *Brandenburg*	D	83	A5
Herzberg, *Brandenburg*	D	74	B1
Herzberg, *Niedersachsen*	D	82	A2
Herzebrock	D	81	A4
Herzfelde	D	74	B2
Herzlake	D	71	B4
Herzogenaurach	D	94	B2
Herzogenbuchsee	CH	106	B2
Herzogenburg	A	110	A2
Herzsprung	D	73	A5
Hesby	N	52	A1
Hesdin	F	78	B2
Hesel	D	71	A4
Heskestad	N	52	B2
Hessdalen	N	199	C8
Hesselager	DK	65	A4
Hesseng	N	193	C13
Hessisch Lichtenau	D	82	A1
Hessisch-Oldendorf	D	72	B2
Hestra	S	60	B3
Heswall	GB	38	A3
Hetlevik	N	46	B2
Hettange-Grande	F	92	B2
Hetton-le-Hole	GB	37	B5
Hettstedt	D	82	A3
Heuchin	F	78	B2
Heudicourt-sous-les-Côtes	F	92	C1
Heunezel	F	105	A5
Heuqueville	F	89	A4
Heves	H	113	B4
Héviz	H	111	C4
Hexham	GB	37	B4
Heysham	GB	36	B4
Heytesbury	GB	43	A4
Hidas	H	125	A4
Hieflau	A	110	B1
Hiendelaencina	E	151	A5
Hiersac	F	115	C4
High Bentham	GB	37	B4
High Hesket	GB	37	B4
High Wycombe	GB	44	B3
Highclere	GB	44	B2
Highley	GB	39	B4
Higuera de Arjona	E	157	C4
Higuera de Calatrava	E	163	A3
Higuera de la Serena	E	156	B2
Higuera de la Sierra	E	161	B3
Higuera de Vargas	E	155	C4
Higuera la Real	E	161	A3
Higuers de Llerena	E	156	B1
Higueruela	E	158	C2
Híjar	E	153	C3
Hilchenbach	D	81	A4
Hildburghausen	D	82	B2
Hilden	D	80	A2
Hilders	D	82	B1
Hildesheim	D	72	B2
Hilgay	GB	41	C4
Hillared	S	60	B3
Hille	D	72	B1
Hillegom	NL	70	B1
Hillerød	DK	61	D2
Hillerstorp	S	60	B3
Hillesheim	D	80	B2
Hillestad	N	53	A6
Hillmersdorf	D	83	A5
Hillsborough	GB	27	B4
Hillswick	GB	33	A5
Hilpoltstein	D	95	B3
Hiltpoltstein	D	94	B3
Hilvarenbeek	NL	79	A5
Hilversum	NL	70	B2
Himarë	AL	182	C1
Himbergen	D	73	A3
Himesháza	H	125	A4
Himmelberg	A	109	C5
Himmelpforten	D	72	A2
Himod	H	111	B4
Hinckley	GB	40	C2
Hindås	S	60	B2
Hindelang	D	108	B1
Hindelbank	CH	106	B2
Hinderavåg	N	52	A1
Hindhead	GB	44	B3
Hinjosa del Valle	E	156	B1
Hinnerup	DK	59	B3
Hinneryd	S	61	C3
Hinojal	E	155	B4
Hinojales	E	161	B3
Hinojos	E	161	B3
Hinojosa del Duque	E	156	B2
Hinojosas de Calatrava	E	157	B3
Hinterhornbach	A	108	B1
Hinterriss	A	108	B2
Hintersee	A	109	B4
Hintersee	D	74	A3
Hinterstoder	A	110	B1
Hintertux	A	108	B2
Hinterweidenthal	D	93	B3
Hinwil	CH	107	B3
Hios	GR	185	A7
Hippolytushoef	NL	70	B1
Hirschaid	D	94	B2
Hirschau	D	95	B3
Hirschfeld	D	83	A5
Hirschhorn	D	93	B4
Hirsingue	F	106	B2
Hirson	F	91	B4
Hirtshals	DK	58	A2
Hirvaskoski	FIN	197	D10
Hirzenhain	D	81	B5
Hisarcik	TR	186	C4
Hishult	S	61	C3
Hissjön	S	200	C6
Hitchin	GB	44	B3
Hitra	N	198	B5
Hittarp	S	61	C2
Hittisau	A	107	B4
Hittun	N	46	A1
Hitzacker	D	73	A4
Hjallerup	DK	58	A3
Hjällstad	S	49	B5
Hjältevad	S	62	A3
Hjärnarp	S	61	C2
Hjartdal	N	53	A4
Hjellestad	N	46	B2
Hjelmeland	N	52	A2
Hjelset	N	198	C4
Hjerkinn	N	198	C6
Hjerm	DK	58	B1
Hjerpsted	DK	64	A1
Hjerting	DK	59	C1
Hjo	S	55	B5
Hjordkær	DK	64	A2
Hjørring	DK	58	A2
Hjorted	S	62	A4
Hjortkvarn	S	56	B1
Hjortnäs	S	50	B1
Hjortsberga	S	62	B2
Hjukse	N	53	A5
Hjuksebø	N	53	A5
Hjulsjö	S	55	A5
Hliník nad Hronom	SK	98	C2
Hlinsko	CZ	97	B3
Hlío	IS	191	A10
Hlohovec	SK	98	C1
Hluboká nad Vltavou	CZ	96	B2
Hlučín	CZ	98	B2
Hlyboka	UA	17	A6
Hlybokaye	BY	13	A7
Hniezdne	SK	99	B4
Hnilec	SK	99	C4
Hnúšťa	SK	99	C3
Hobol	H	125	A3
Hobro	DK	58	B2
Hobscheid	L	92	B1
Hocalar	TR	189	A4
Hochdonn	D	64	B2
Hochdorf	CH	106	B3
Hochfelden	F	93	C3
Hochspeyer	D	93	B3
Höchst im Odenwald	D	93	B5
Höchstadt, *Bayern*	D	94	B2
Höchstädt, *Bayern*	D	94	C2
Hochstenbach	D	81	B3
Höckendorf	D	83	B5
Hockenheim	D	93	B4
Hoddesdon	GB	44	B3
Hodejov	SK	99	C3
Hodenhagen	D	72	B2
Hodkovice	CZ	84	B3
Hódmezővásárhely	H	113	C4
Hodnet	GB	38	B4
Hodonín	CZ	98	C1
Hodslavice	CZ	98	B2
Hoedekenskerke	NL	79	A3
Hoegaarden	B	79	B4
Hoek van Holland	NL	79	A4
Hoenderlo	NL	70	B2
Hof	D	83	B3
Hof	N	53	A6
Hofbieber	D	82	B1
Hoff	GB	37	B4
Hofgeismar	D	81	A5
Hofheim, *Bayern*	D	82	B2
Hofheim, *Hessen*	D	93	A4
Hofkirchen im Mühlkreis	A	96	C1
Höfn	IS	191	C10
Hofors	S	50	B3
Hofsós	IS	190	B6
Hofstad	N	199	A7
Höganäs	S	61	C2
Högbo	S	51	B3
Hogdal	S	54	A2
Høgebru	N	46	A4
Høgfors	S	50	C2
Högklint	S	57	C4
Högsäter	S	54	B3
Högsby	S	62	A4
Högsjö	S	56	A1
Hogstad	S	55	B6
Högyész	H	112	C2
Hohen Neuendorf	D	74	B2
Hohenau	A	97	C4
Hohenberg	A	110	B2
Hohenbucko	D	83	A5
Hohenburg	D	95	B3
Hohendorf	D	66	B1
Hohenems	A	107	B4
Hohenhameln	D	72	B3
Hohenhausen	D	72	B1
Hohenkirchen	D	71	A4
Hohenlinden	D	108	A2
Hohenlockstedt	D	64	C2
Hohenmölsen	D	83	A4
Hohennauen	D	73	B5
Hohenseeden	D	73	B5
Hohentauern	A	110	B1
Hohentengen	D	106	B3
Hohenwepel	D	81	A5
Hohenwestedt	D	64	B2
Hohenwutzen	D	74	B3
Hohenzieritz	D	74	A2
Hohn	D	64	B2
Hohne	D	72	B3
Hohnstorf	D	73	A3
Højer	DK	64	B1
Højslev Stby	DK	58	B2
Hok	S	62	A2
Hökerum	S	60	B3
Hökhuvud	S	51	B5
Hokksund	N	53	A5
Hökön	S	63	B2
Hol	N	47	B5
Hólar	IS	190	B6
Holašovice	CZ	96	C2
Holbæk, *Aarhus Amt.*	DK	58	B3
Holbæk, *Vestsjællands Amt.*	DK	61	D1
Holbeach	GB	41	C4
Holdenstedt	D	73	B3
Holdhus	N	46	B2
Holdorf	D	71	B5
Holeby	DK	65	B4
Holešov	CZ	98	B1
Holguera	E	155	B4
Holíč	SK	98	C1
Holice	CZ	97	A3
Höljes	S	49	B4
Hollabrunn	A	97	C4
Hollandstoun	GB	33	B4
Høllen	N	53	B3
Hollfeld	D	95	B3
Hollókő	H	112	B3
Hollstadt	D	82	B2
Hollum	NL	70	A2
Höllviksnäs	S	66	A1
Holm	N	195	E3
Hólmavík	IS	190	B4
Holmbukt	N	192	B5
Holme-on-Spalding-Moor	GB	40	B3
Holmedal	S	54	A2
Holmegil	N	54	A2
Holmen	N	48	B2
Holmes Chapel	GB	38	A4
Holmestrand	N	54	A1
Holmfirth	GB	40	B2
Holmfoss	N	193	C14
Holmsbu	N	54	A1
Holmsjö	S	63	B3
Holmsund	S	200	C6
Holmsveden	S	50	A3
Holmudden	S	57	C5
Hölö	S	57	A3
Holøydal	N	199	C8
Holsbybrunn	S	62	A3
Holseter	N	48	A1
Holsljunga	S	60	B2
Holstebro	DK	59	B1
Holsted	DK	59	C1
Holsworthy	GB	42	B2
Holt	D	64	B2
Holt, *Norfolk*	GB	41	C5
Holt, *Wrexham*	GB	38	A4
Holt	IS	190	D6
Holt	N	53	B4
Holten	NL	71	B3
Holtwick	D	71	B4
Holum	N	52	B3
Holwerd	NL	70	A2
Holycross	IRL	29	B4
Holyhead	GB	38	A2
Holýšov	CZ	95	B5
Holywell	GB	38	A3
Holywood	GB	27	B5
Holzdorf	D	83	A5
Holzhausen	D	72	B1
Holzheim	D	94	C2
Holzkirchen	D	108	B2
Holzminden	D	81	A5
Holzthaleben	D	82	A2
Homberg, *Hessen*	D	81	A5
Homberg, *Hessen*	D	81	B5
Homburg	D	93	B3
Hommelstø	N	195	E3
Hommersåk	N	52	B1
Homokmegy	H	112	C3
Homokszentgyörgy	H	124	A3
Homyel = Gomel	BY	13	B9
Honaz	TR	188	B4
Hondarribia	E	144	A2
Hondón de los Frailes	E	165	A4
Hondschoote	F	78	B2
Hönebach	D	82	B1
Hønefoss	N	48	B2
Honfleur	F	89	A4
Høng	DK	61	D1
Honiton	GB	43	B3
Hönningen	D	80	B2
Honningsvåg	N	193	B9
Hönö	S	60	B1
Honrubia	E	158	B1
Hontalbilla	E	151	A3
Hontheim	D	92	A2
Hontianske-Nemce	SK	98	C2
Hontoria de la Cantera	E	143	B3
Hontoria de Valdearados	E	143	C3
Hontoria del Pinar	E	143	C3
Hoofddorp	NL	70	B1
Hoogerheide	NL	79	A4
Hoogeveen	NL	71	B3
Hoogezand-Sappemeer	NL	71	A3
Hoogkarspel	NL	70	B2
Hoogkerk	NL	71	A3
Hoogstede	D	71	B3
Hoogstraten	B	79	A4
Hook	GB	44	B3
Hooksiel	D	71	A5
Höör	S	61	D3
Hoorn	NL	70	B2
Hope	GB	38	A3
Hope under Dinmore	GB	39	B4
Hopen	N	194	C6
Hopfgarten	A	108	B3
Hopfgarten in Defereggen	A	109	C3
Hopseidet	N	193	B11
Hopsten	D	71	B4
Hoptrup	DK	59	C2
Hora Svaté Sebestiána	CZ	83	B5
Horažďovice	CZ	96	B1
Horb am Neckar	D	93	C4
Horbelev	DK	65	B5
Hørby	DK	58	A3
Hörby	S	61	D3
Horcajada de la Torre	E	158	A1
Horcajo de los Montes	E	156	A3
Horcajo de Santiago	E	151	C4
Horcajo-Medianero	E	150	B2
Horche	E	151	B4
Horda	S	62	A2
Hordabø	N	46	B1
Hordalia	N	52	A2
Hordvik	N	46	B2
Hořesedly	CZ	83	B5
Horezu	RO	17	C6
Horgen	CH	107	B3
Horgoš	SRB	126	A1
Horia	RO	126	A3
Hořice	CZ	84	B3
Horjul	SLO	123	A3
Horka	D	84	A2
Hörken	S	50	B1
Horki	BY	13	A9
Hörle	S	60	B3
Horn	A	97	C3
Horn	D	81	A4
Horn	N	48	B2
Horn	S	62	A3
Horna	E	158	C2
Horná Mariková	SK	98	B2
Horná Streda	SK	98	C1
Horná Štrubna	SK	98	C2
Horná Súča	SK	98	C1
Hornachuelos	E	162	A2
Hornanes	N	46	C2
Hornbæk, *Aarhus Amt.*	DK	58	B2
Hornbæk, *Frederiksværk*	DK	61	C2
Hornberg	D	106	A3
Hornburg	D	73	B3
Horncastle	GB	41	B3
Horndal	S	50	B3
Horndean	GB	44	C2
Horne, *Fyns Amt.*	DK	64	A3
Horne, *Ribe Amt.*	DK	59	C1
Hörnebo	S	55	B5
Horneburg	D	72	A2
Hörnefors	S	200	C5
Horní Bečva	CZ	98	B2
Horní Benešov	CZ	98	B1
Horni Cerekev	CZ	97	B3
Horní Jiřetín	CZ	83	B5
Horní Lomná	CZ	98	B2
Horní Maršov	CZ	85	B3
Horní Planá	CZ	96	C2
Horni Slavkov	CZ	83	B4
Horni Vltavice	CZ	96	C1
Hornindal	N	198	D3
Hørning	DK	59	B3
Hörningsholm	S	57	A3
Hornnes	N	53	B3
Horno	D	84	A2
Hornos	E	164	A2
Hornoy-le-Bourg	F	90	B1
Hornsea	GB	41	B3
Hornslet	DK	59	B3
Hornstein	A	111	B3
Hornum	DK	58	B2
Hornum	D	64	B1
Horný Tisovník	SK	99	C3
Horodenka	UA	13	D6
Horodnya	UA	13	C9
Horodok, *Khmelnytskyy*	UA	13	D7
Horodok, *Lviv*	UA	13	D5
Horokhiv	UA	13	C6
Horovice	CZ	96	B1
Horred	S	60	B2
Hörröd	S	61	D4
Hörsching	A	110	A1
Horsens	DK	59	C2
Horsham	GB	44	B3
Hørsholm	DK	61	D2
Horslunde	DK	65	B4
Horšovský Týn	CZ	95	B4
Horst	NL	80	A2
Horstel	D	71	B4
Horsten	D	71	A4
Horstmar	D	71	B4
Hort	H	113	B3
Horta	P	148	A2
Horten	N	54	A1
Hortezuela	E	151	A4
Hortiguela	E	143	B3
Hortobágy	H	113	B5
Hostomice	CZ	96	B2
Hostouň	CZ	95	B4
Hotagen	S	199	B11
Hoting	S	200	B2
Hotolisht	AL	182	B2
Hotton	B	79	B5
Houdain	F	78	B2
Houdan	F	90	C1
Houdelaincourt	F	92	C1
Houeillès	F	128	B3
Houffalize	B	92	A1
Houghton-le-Spring	GB	37	B5
Houlberg	DK	59	B2
Houlgate	F	89	A3
Hounslow	GB	44	B3
Hourtin	F	128	A1
Hourtin-Plage	F	128	A1
Houthalen	B	79	A5
Houyet	B	79	B4
Hov	DK	59	C3
Hov	N	48	B2
Hova	S	55	B5
Høvåg	N	53	B4
Hovborg	DK	59	C1
Hovda	N	47	B6
Hovden	N	52	A3
Hove	GB	44	C3
Hovedgård	DK	59	C2
Hovelhof	D	81	A4
Hoven	DK	59	C1
Hovet	N	47	B5
Hovingham	GB	40	A3
Hovmantorp	S	62	B3
Hovsta	S	56	A1
Howden	GB	40	B3
Howe	D	72	A3
Höxter	D	81	A5
Hoya	D	72	B2
Hoya de Santa Maria	E	161	B3
Hoya-Gonzalo	E	158	C2
Høyanger	N	46	A3
Hoyerswerda	D	84	A2
Høyjord	N	53	A6
Hoylake	GB	38	A3
Høylandet	N	199	A9
Hoym	D	82	A3
Høymyr	N	47	C6
Hoyo de Manzanares	E	151	B4
Hoyo de Pinares	E	150	B3
Hoyocasero	E	150	B3
Hoyos	E	149	B3
Hoyos del Espino	E	150	B2
Hrabušiče	SK	99	C4
Hradec Králové	CZ	85	B3
Hradec nad Moravicí	CZ	98	B1
Hrádek	CZ	97	C4
Hrádek nad Nisou	CZ	84	B2
Hradište	SK	98	C2
Hrafnagil	IS	191	B7
Hrafnseyri	IS	190	B2
Hranice, *Severomoravsky*	CZ	98	B1
Hranice, *Západočeský*	CZ	83	B4
Hranovnica	SK	99	C4
Hrasnica	BIH	139	B4
Hrastnik	SLO	123	A4
Hřensko	CZ	84	B2
Hriňová	SK	99	C3
Hrisoupoli	GR	183	C6
Hrochov	CZ	97	B4
Hrochův Tynec	CZ	97	B3
Hrodna	BY	13	B5
Hrodzyanka	BY	13	B8
Hronov	CZ	85	B4
Hronský Beňadik	SK	98	C2
Hrotovice	CZ	97	B4
Hrtkovci	SRB	127	C1
Hrun	IS	190	A5
Hrušov	SK	112	A3
Hrušovany nad Jevišovkou	CZ	97	C4
Hřuštin	SK	99	B3
Hrvaćani	BIH	124	C3
Hrvace	HR	138	B2
Hrymayliv	UA	13	D7
Huben	A	109	C3
Hückel-hoven	D	80	A2
Hückeswagen	D	80	A3
Hucknall	GB	40	B2
Hucqueliers	F	78	B1
Huddersfield	GB	40	B2
Huddinge	S	57	A3
Huddunge	S	51	B3
Hude	D	72	A1
Hudiksvall	S	200	E3
Huélago	E	163	A4
Huélamo	E	152	B2
Huelgoat	F	100	A2
Huelma	E	163	A4
Huelva	E	161	B3
Huércal de Almería	E	164	C2
Huércal-Overa	E	164	B3
Huerta de Abajo	E	143	B3
Huerta de Valdecarábanos	E	151	C4

Name	Country	Page	Grid
Huerta del Rey	E	143	C3
Huetahernando	E	152	B1
Huesa	E	164	B1
Huéscar	E	164	B2
Huesca	E	145	B3
Huete	E	151	B4
Huétor Tájar	E	163	A3
Hüfingen	D	106	B3
Hugh Town	GB	42	B1
Huglfing	D	108	B2
Huissen	NL	70	C2
Huittinen	FIN	8	B3
Huizen	NL	70	B2
Hulín	CZ	98	B1
Hüls	D	80	A2
Hulsig	DK	58	A3
Hulst	NL	79	A4
Hult	S	62	A3
Hulta	S	56	B2
Hulteby	S	55	A5
Hulterstad	S	63	B4
Hultsfred	S	62	A3
Humanes	E	151	B4
Humberston	GB	41	B3
Humble	DK	65	B3
Humenné	SK	12	D4
Humilladero	E	163	A3
Humlebæk	DK	61	D2
Humlum	DK	58	B1
Hummelsta	S	56	A3
Humpolec	CZ	97	B3
Humshaugh	GB	37	A4
Hundåla	N	195	E3
Hundested	DK	61	D1
Hundorp	N	48	A1
Hundvåg	N	52	A1
Hundvin	N	46	B2
Hunedoara	RO	17	C5
Hünfeld	D	82	B1
Hungen	D	81	B4
Hungerford	GB	44	B2
Hunndalen	N	48	B2
Hunnebostrand	S	54	B2
Hunstanton	GB	41	C4
Huntingdon	GB	44	A3
Huntley	GB	39	C4
Huntly	GB	33	D4
Hünxe	D	80	A2
Hurbanovo	SK	112	B2
Hürbel	D	107	A4
Hurdal	N	48	B3
Hurezani	RO	17	C5
Hurlford	GB	36	A2
Hurstbourne Tarrant	GB	44	B2
Hurstpierpoint	GB	44	C3
Hürth	D	80	B2
Hurum	N	47	A5
Hurup	DK	58	B1
Húsafell	IS	190	C5
Húsavík	IS	191	A8
Husbands Bosworth	GB	44	A2
Husby	D	64	B2
Husby	DK	59	B1
Husey	IS	191	B11
Huşi	RO	17	B8
Husina	BIH	139	A4
Husinec	CZ	96	B1
Husinish	GB	31	B1
Huskvarna	S	62	A2
Husnes	N	46	C2
Husøy	N	194	A8
Hustad	N	198	C4
Hüsten	D	81	A3
Hustopeče	CZ	97	C4
Hustopeče nad Bečvou	CZ	98	B1
Husum	D	64	B2
Husum	S	200	C5
Husvika	N	195	E3
Huta	PL	75	B5
Hutovo	BIH	139	C3
Hüttenberg	A	110	C1
Hüttlingen	D	94	C2
Huttoft	GB	41	B4
Hutton Cranswick	GB	40	B3
Hüttschlag	A	109	B4
Huttwil	CH	106	B2
Huy	B	79	B5
Hüyük	TR	189	B6
Hval	N	48	B2
Hvåle	N	47	B6
Hvaler	N	54	A2
Hvalpsund	DK	58	B2
Hvammstangi	IS	190	B5
Hvammur	IS	190	B6
Hvanneyri	IS	190	C4
Hvar	HR	138	B2
Hvarnes	N	53	A5
Hveragerði	IS	190	D4
Hvidbjerg	DK	58	B1
Hvide Sande	DK	59	C1
Hvittingfoss	N	53	A6
Hvolsvöllur	IS	190	D5
Hybe	SK	99	B3
Hycklinge	S	62	A3
Hydra	GR	185	B4
Hyen	N	198	D2
Hyères	F	132	B2
Hyères Plage	F	132	B2
Hylestad	N	52	A3
Hylke	DK	59	C2
Hyllestad	N	46	A2
Hyllstofta	S	61	C3
Hyltebruk	S	60	B3
Hynnekleiv	N	53	B4
Hythe, Hampshire	GB	44	C2
Hythe, Kent	GB	45	B5
Hyvinkää	FIN	8	B4
I			
Iam	RO	127	B3
Iaşi	RO	17	B7
Iasmos	GR	183	B7
Ibahernando	E	156	A2
Ibarranguelua	E	143	A4
Ibbenbüren	D	71	B4
Ibeas de Juarros	E	143	B3
Ibestad	N	194	B8
Ibi	E	159	C3
Ibiza = Eivissa	E	166	C1
Ibradı	TR	189	B6
Ibriktepe	TR	186	A1
Ibros	E	157	B4
Ibstock	GB	40	C2
İçel	TR	23	C8
Ichenhausen	D	94	C2
Ichtegem	B	78	A3
Ichtershausen	D	82	B2
Idanha-a-Novo	P	155	B3
Idar-Oberstein	D	93	B3
Idd	N	54	A2
Idiazábal	E	144	B1
Idivuoma	S	196	A4
Idkerberget	S	50	B2
Idre	S	199	D9
Idrija	SLO	123	A3
Idritsa	RUS	9	D6
Idstein	D	81	B4
Idvor	SRB	126	B2
Iecca Mare	RO	126	B2
Ielsi	I	170	B2
Ieper = Ypres	B	78	B2
Ierapetra	GR	185	D6
Ierissos	GR	183	C5
Ifjord	N	193	B11
Ig	SLO	123	B3
Igal	H	112	C1
Igea	E	144	B1
Igea Marina	I	136	A1
Igelfors	S	56	B1
Igersheim	D	94	B1
Iggesund	S	200	E3
Iglesias	E	143	B3
Iglésias	I	179	C2
Igls	A	108	B2
İğneada	TR	186	A2
Igny-Comblizy	F	91	B3
Igorre	E	143	A4
Igoumenitsa	GR	182	D2
Igries	E	145	B3
Igualada	E	147	C2
Igüeña	E	141	B4
Iguerande	F	117	A4
Iharosberény	H	124	A3
Ihl'any	SK	99	B4
Ihlienworth	D	64	C1
Ihringen	D	106	A2
Ihrlerstein	D	95	C3
Ihsaniye	TR	187	C5
Ii	FIN	197	D8
Iijärvi	FIN	193	C11
Iisalmi	FIN	3	E10
IJmuiden	NL	70	B1
IJsselmuiden	NL	70	B2
IJzendijke	NL	79	A3
Ikast	DK	59	B2
Ikervár	H	111	B3
il Castagno	I	135	B3
Ilandža	SRB	126	B2
Ilanz	CH	107	C4
Ilava	SK	98	C2
Iława	PL	69	B4
Ilche	E	145	C4
Ilchester	GB	43	B4
Ilfeld	D	82	A2
Ilfracombe	GB	42	A2
Ilgaz	TR	23	A7
Ilgın	TR	189	A6
Ilhavo	P	148	B1
Ilica	TR	186	C2
Ilidža	BIH	139	B4
Ilijaš	BIH	139	A4
Ilirska Bistrica	SLO	123	B3
Ilkeston	GB	40	C2
Ilkley	GB	40	B2
Illana	E	151	B5
Illano	E	141	A4
Illar	E	164	C2
Illas	E	141	A5
Ille-sur-Têt	F	146	B3
Illertissen	D	94	C2
Illescas	E	151	B3
Illfurth	F	106	B2
Illichivsk	UA	17	B9
Illiers-Combray	F	89	B5
Illkirch-Graffenstaden	F	93	C3
Illmersdorf	D	74	C2
Illmitz	A	111	B3
Illora	E	163	A4
Illueca	E	152	A2
Ilok	HR	126	B1
Ilomantsi	FIN	9	A7
Iłow	PL	77	B5
Iłowa	PL	84	A3
Iłowo-Osada	PL	77	A5
Ilsenburg	D	82	A2
Ilshofen	D	94	B1
Ilz	A	110	B2
Iłża	PL	87	A5
Imatra	FIN	9	B6
Imielin	PL	86	B3
Imingen	N	47	B5
Immeln	S	63	B2
Immenhausen	D	81	A5
Immenstadt	D	107	B5
Immingham	GB	41	B3
Imola	I	135	A4
Imon	E	151	A5
Imotski	HR	138	B3
Impéria	I	133	B4
Imphy	F	104	C2
Imroz	TR	183	C7
Imsland	N	52	A1
Imst	A	108	B1
Inagh	IRL	28	B2
Inari	FIN	193	D10
Inca	E	167	B2
Inchnadamph	GB	32	C2
Incinillas	E	143	B3
Indal	S	200	D3
Indija	SRB	127	B2
Indre Arna	N	46	B2
Indre Billefjord	N	193	B9
Indre Brenna	N	193	B9
Inebolu	TR	23	A7
İnecik	TR	186	B2
İnegöl	TR	187	B4
Inerthal	CH	107	B3
Infiesto	E	142	A1
Ingatorp	S	62	A3
Ingedal	S	54	A2
Ingelheim	D	93	B4
Ingelmunster	B	78	B3
Ingelstad	S	62	B2
Ingleton	GB	37	B4
Ingolfsland	N	47	C5
Ingolstadt	D	95	C3
Ingrandes, Maine-et-Loire	F	101	B5
Ingrandes, Vienne	F	102	C2
Ingwiller	F	93	C3
İnhisar	TR	187	B5
Iniesta	E	158	B2
Inishannon	IRL	29	C3
Inishcrone	IRL	26	B1
Inke	H	124	A3
Inndyr	N	195	C5
Innellan	GB	34	C3
Innerleithen	GB	35	C4
Innermessan	GB	36	B2
Innerkirchen	CH	106	C3
Innervillgraten	A	109	C3
Innsbruck	A	108	B2
Innset	N	194	B9
Innvik	N	198	D3
İnönü	TR	187	C5
Inowłódz	PL	87	A4
Inowrocław	PL	76	B3
Ins	CH	106	B2
Insch	GB	33	D4
Insjön	S	50	B2
Ińsko	PL	75	A4
Instow	GB	42	A2
İntepe	TR	186	B1
Interlaken	CH	106	C2
Intragna	CH	120	A1
Introbio	I	120	B2
Inveran	GB	32	D3
Inveran	IRL	28	A2
Inveraray	GB	34	B2
Inverbervie	GB	35	B5
Invergarry	GB	32	D2
Invergordon	GB	32	D2
Invergowrie	GB	35	B4
Inverkeilor	GB	35	B5
Inverkeithing	GB	35	B4
Invermoriston	GB	32	D2
Inverness	GB	32	D2
Inveruno	I	120	B1
Inverurie	GB	33	D4
Ioannina	GR	182	D2
Iolanda di Savoia	I	121	C4
Ion Corvin	RO	17	C7
Ióppolo	I	175	C1
Ios	GR	185	C6
Ipati	GR	182	E4
Ipsala	TR	186	B1
Ipswich	GB	45	A5
Iraklia	GR	183	B5
Iraklio = Heraklion	GR	185	D6
Irdning	A	110	B1
Iregszemcse	H	112	C2
Irgoli	I	178	B3
Irig	SRB	127	B1
Ironbridge	GB	39	B4
Irpin	UA	13	C9
Irrel	D	92	B2
Irsina	I	172	B2
Irsta	S	56	A2
Irthlingborough	GB	44	A3
Iruela	E	141	B4
Irún	E	144	A2
Irurita	E	144	A2
Irurzun	E	144	B2
Irvine	GB	36	A2
Irvinestown	GB	27	B3
Is-sur-Tille	F	105	B4
Isaba	E	144	B3
Isabela	E	157	B4
Ísafjörður	IS	190	A2
Isane	N	198	D2
Isaszeg	H	112	B3
Isbister	GB	33	A5
Íscar	E	150	A3
Iscehisar	TR	187	D5
Ischgl	A	107	B5
Ischia	I	170	C1
Ischia di Castro	I	168	A1
Ischitella	I	171	B3
Isdes	F	103	B4
Ise	N	54	A2
Iselle	I	119	A5
Iseltwald	CH	106	C2
Isen	D	108	A3
Isenbüttel	D	73	B3
Iseo	I	120	B3
Iserlohn	D	81	A3
Isérnia	I	170	B2
Isfjorden	N	198	C4
Ishëm	AL	182	B1
Isigny-sur-Mer	F	88	A2
Işıklı	TR	189	A4
Ísili	I	179	C3
Iskilip	TR	23	A8
Isla Canela	E	161	B2
Isla Cristina	E	161	B2
Íslares	E	143	A3
Isle Of Whithorn	GB	36	B2
Isleham	GB	45	A4
Ismaning	D	108	A2
Isna	P	154	B3
Isnestoften	N	192	B6
Isny	D	107	B5
Isoba	E	142	A1
Isokylä	FIN	197	C10
Isokylä	S	196	B5
Isola	F	132	A3
Ísola del Gran Sasso d'Itália	I	169	A3
Ísola del Liri	I	169	B3
Ísola della Scala	I	121	B4
Isola delle Fémmine	I	176	A2
Ísola di Capo Rizzuto	I	175	C3
Isona	E	147	B2
Ispagnac	F	130	A2
Isparta	TR	189	B5
İsperikh	BG	17	D7
Íspica	I	177	C3
Isselburg	D	80	A2
Issigeac	F	129	B3
Issogne	I	119	B4
Issoire	F	116	B3
Issoncourt	F	91	C5
Issoudun	F	103	C4
Issum	D	80	A2
Issy-l'Evêque	F	104	C2
Istán	E	162	B3
İstanbul	TR	186	A3
Istebna	PL	98	B2
Ístia d'Ombrone	I	135	C4
Istiea	GR	183	E5
Istres	F	131	B3
Istvándi	H	125	A3
Itea	GR	184	A3
Ithaki	GR	184	A1
Itoiz	E	144	B2
Ítrabo	E	163	B4
Itri	I	169	B3
Itireddu	I	178	B2
Íttiri	I	178	B2
Itzehoe	D	64	C2
Ivalo	FIN	193	D11
Iván	H	111	B3
Ivanava	BY	13	B6
Ivančice	CZ	97	B4
Ivančna Gorica	SLO	123	B3
Iváncsa	H	112	B2
Ivanec	HR	124	A2
Ivanić Grad	HR	124	B2
Ivanjska	BIH	124	C3
Ivanka	SK	98	C2
Ivankovo	HR	125	B4
Ivano-Frankivsk	UA	13	D6
Ivanovice na Hané	CZ	98	B1
Ivanska	HR	124	B2
Ivatsevichy	BY	13	B6
Ivaylovgrad	BG	183	B8
Iveland	N	53	B3
Ivoz Ramet	B	79	B5
Ivrea	I	119	B4
Ivrindi	TR	186	C2
Ivry-en-Montagne	F	104	B3
Ivry-la-Bataille	F	90	C1
Ivybridge	GB	42	B3
Iwaniska	PL	87	B5
Iwiny	PL	85	A3
Iwuy	F	78	B3
Ixworth	GB	45	A4
Izarra	E	143	B4
Izbica Kujawska	PL	76	B3
Izbište	SRB	127	B3
Izeda	P	149	A3
Izernore	F	118	A2
Izmayil	UA	17	C8
İzmir	TR	188	A2
İzmit = Kocaeli	TR	187	B4
Iznájar	E	163	A3
Iznalloz	E	163	A4
Iznatoraf	E	164	A1
İznik	TR	187	B4
Izola	SLO	122	B2
Izsák	H	112	C3
Izsófalva	H	99	C4
Izyaslav	UA	13	C7
J			
Jabalquinto	E	157	B4
Jablanac	HR	123	C3
Jablanica	BIH	139	B3
Jablonec nad Jizerou	CZ	84	B3
Jablonec nad Nisou	CZ	84	B3
Jablonica	SK	98	C1
Jablonka	PL	99	B3
Jabłonna	PL	77	B5
Jablonné nad Orlicí	CZ	97	A4
Jablonné Podještědi	CZ	84	B2
Jablonov nad Turňou	SK	99	C4
Jabłonowo Pomorskie	PL	69	B4
Jablůnka	CZ	98	B1
Jablunkov	CZ	98	B2
Jabučje	SRB	127	C2
Jabugo	E	161	B3
Jabuka	SRB	127	C2
Jabukovac	HR	124	B2
Jaca	E	145	B3
Jáchymov	CZ	83	B4
Jacobidrebber	D	72	B1
Jade	D	71	A5
Jäderfors	S	50	B3
Jädraås	S	50	B3
Jadraque	E	151	B5
Jægerspris	DK	61	D1
Jaén	E	163	A4
Jagare	BIH	124	C3
Jagel	D	64	B2
Jagenbach	A	96	C3
Jagodina	SRB	127	D3
Jagodnjak	HR	125	B4
Jagodzin	PL	84	A3
Jagstheim	D	94	B2
Jagstzell	D	94	B2
Jahodna	SK	111	A4
Jajce	BIH	138	A3
Ják	H	111	B3
Jakabszálbs	H	112	C3
Jäkkvik	S	195	D8
Jakobsnes	N	193	C14
Jakovlje	HR	124	B1
Jakšic	HR	125	B3
Jakubany	SK	99	B4
Jalance	E	159	B2
Jalasjärvi	FIN	8	A3
Jalhay	B	80	B1
Jaligny-sur-Besbre	F	117	A3
Jallais	F	102	B1
Jalón	E	159	C3
Jâlons	F	91	C4
Jamena	SRB	125	C5
Jamilena	E	163	A4
Jämjö	S	63	B3
Jamnička Kiselica	HR	124	B1
Jamno	PL	67	B5
Jamoigne	B	92	B1
Jämsä	FIN	8	B4
Jämshög	S	63	B2
Jamu Mare	RO	126	B3
Janakkala	FIN	8	B4
Jandelsbrunn	D	96	C1
Jänickendorf	D	74	B2
Janikowo	PL	76	B3
Janja	BIH	125	C5
Janjina	HR	138	C3
Janki, Łódzkie	PL	86	A3
Janki, Mazowieckie	PL	77	B5
Jankov	CZ	96	B2
Jankowo Dolne	PL	76	B2
Jánoshalma	H	126	A1
Jánosháza	H	111	B3
Jánossomorja	H	111	B4
Janovice nad Uhlavou	CZ	96	B1
Janów	PL	86	B3
Janowiec Wielkopolski	PL	76	B2
Janowo	PL	77	A5
Jänsmässholmen	S	199	B10
Janville	F	103	A3
Janzé	F	101	B4
Jarabá	SK	99	C3
Jaraczewo	PL	76	B2
Jarafuel	E	159	B2
Jaraicejo	E	156	A2
Jaraíz de la Vera	E	150	B2
Jarak	SRB	127	C1
Jarandilla de la Vera	E	150	B2
Jaray	E	152	A1
Järbo	S	50	B3
Jard-sur-Mer	F	114	B2
Jaren	N	48	B2
Jargeau	F	103	B4
Jarkovac	SRB	126	B2
Järlåsa	S	51	C4
Jarmen	D	66	C2
Järna	S	57	A3
Jarnac	F	115	C3
Järnäs	S	200	C5
Järnforsen	S	62	A3
Jarny	F	92	B1
Jarocin	PL	76	C2
Jaroměř	CZ	85	B3
Jaroměřice nad Rokytnou	CZ	97	B3
Jaroslav	CZ	97	A3
Jaroslavice	CZ	97	C4
Jarosław	PL	12	C5
Jarosławiec	PL	68	A1
Jarošov nad Nežárkou	CZ	96	B3
Järpås	S	55	B3
Järpen	S	199	B10
Jarrow	GB	37	B5
Järso	FIN	51	B6
Järvenpää	FIN	8	B4
Jarvorník	CZ	85	B4
Järvsö	S	200	E2
Jarzé	F	102	B1
Jaša Tomic	SRB	126	B2
Jasenak	HR	123	B4
Jasenica	BIH	124	C2
Jasenice	HR	137	A4
Jasenovac	HR	124	B2
Jasenovo	SRB	127	C3
Jasień	PL	84	A3
Jasienica	PL	84	A2
Jasło	PL	12	D4
Jásova	SK	112	B2
Jasseron	F	118	A2
Jastarnia	PL	69	A3
Jastrebarsko	HR	123	B4
Jastrowie	PL	68	B1
Jastrzębia-Góra	PL	68	A3
Jastrzębie Zdrój	PL	98	B2
Jászals-Lószentgyörgy	H	113	B4
Jászapáti	H	113	B4
Jászárokszállás	H	113	B3
Jászberény	H	113	B3
Jászdózsa	H	113	B4
Jászfényszaru	H	113	B3
Jászjakóhalma	H	113	B4
Jászkarajenő	H	113	B4
Jászkisér	H	113	B4
Jászladány	H	113	B4
Jászszentlászló	H	113	C3
Jásztelek	H	113	B4
Játar	E	163	B4
Jättendal	S	200	E3
Jatznick	D	74	A2
Jaun	CH	106	C2
Jausiers	F	132	A2
Jávea	E	159	C4
Jävenitz	D	73	B4
Javerlhac	F	115	C4
Javier	E	144	B2
Javorani	BIH	124	C3
Javorina	SK	99	B4
Javron	F	89	B3
Jawor	PL	85	A4
Jaworzno	PL	86	B3
Jaworzyna Śl.	PL	85	B4
Jayena	E	163	B4
Jażow	PL	84	A2
Jebel	RO	126	B3
Jebjerg	DK	58	B2
Jedburgh	GB	35	C5
Jedlinsk	PL	87	A5
Jednia	PL	87	A5
Jednia Letnisko	PL	87	A5
Jednorożec	PL	77	A6
Jedovnice	CZ	97	B4
Jędrychow	PL	69	B4
Jędrzejów	PL	87	B4
Jedwabno	PL	77	A5
Jeesio	FIN	197	B9
Jegłownik	PL	69	A4
Jegun	F	129	C3
Jēkabpils	LV	8	D4
Jektevik	N	46	C2
Jektvik	N	195	D4
Jelcz-Laskowice	PL	85	A5
Jelenec	SK	98	C2
Jelenia Góra	PL	85	B3
Jelgava	LV	8	D3
Jelka	SK	111	A4
Jelling	DK	59	C2
Jelsa	HR	138	B2
Jelsa	N	52	A2
Jelšava	SK	99	C4
Jemgum	D	71	A4
Jemnice	CZ	97	B3
Jena	D	82	B3
Jenaz	CH	107	C4
Jenbach	A	108	B2
Jenikow	PL	75	A4
Jennersdorf	A	111	C3
Jenny	S	62	A4
Jerchel	D	73	B4
Jeres del Marquesado	E	164	B1
Jerez de la Frontera	E	162	B1
Jerez de los Caballeros	E	155	C4
Jerica	E	159	B3
Jerichow	D	73	B5

Name			
Jerka	PL	75	B5
Jermenovci	SRB	126	B3
Jerslev	DK	58	A3
Jerte	E	150	B2
Jerup	DK	58	A3
Jerxheim	D	73	B4
Jerzmanowice	PL	87	B3
Jerzu	I	179	C3
Jerzwałd	PL	69	B4
Jesberg	D	81	B5
Jesenice, Středočeský	CZ	83	B5
Jesenice, Středočeský	CZ	96	B2
Jesenice	SLO	109	C5
Jeseník	CZ	85	B5
Jesenké	SK	99	C4
Jesi	I	136	B2
Jésolo	I	122	B1
Jessen	D	83	A4
Jessenitz	D	73	A4
Jessheim	N	48	B3
Jessnitz	D	83	A4
Jesteburg	D	72	A2
Jestebnice	CZ	96	B2
Jeumont	F	79	B4
Jeven-stedt	D	64	B2
Jever	D	71	A4
Jevičko	CZ	97	B4
Jevišovice	CZ	97	C3
Jevnaker	N	48	B2
Jezerane	HR	123	B4
Jezero	BIH	138	A3
Jezero	HR	123	B4
Jezów	PL	87	A3
Jičín	CZ	84	B3
Jičíněves	CZ	84	B3
Jihlava	CZ	97	B3
Jijona	E	159	C3
Jilemnice	CZ	84	A3
Jilové	CZ	84	B2
Jilové u Prahy	CZ	96	B2
Jimbolia	RO	126	B2
Jimena	E	163	A4
Jimena de la Frontera	E	162	B2
Jimera de Libar	E	162	B2
Jimramov	CZ	97	B4
Jince	CZ	96	B1
Jindřichovice	CZ	83	B4
Jindřichův Hradec	CZ	96	B3
Jirkov	CZ	83	B5
Jistebnice	CZ	96	B2
Joachimsthal	D	74	B2
João da Loura	P	154	C2
Jobbágyi	H	112	B3
Jochberg	A	109	B3
Jockfall	S	196	C5
Jódar	E	163	A4
Jodoigne	B	79	B4
Joensuu	FIN	9	A6
Joesjö	S	195	E5
Jœuf	F	92	B1
Jõgeva	EST	8	C5
Johann-georgen-stadt	D	83	B4
Johannishus	S	63	B3
Johanniskirchen	D	95	C4
Johansfors	S	63	B3
John o'Groats	GB	32	C3
Johnshaven	GB	35	B5
Johnstone	GB	34	C3
Johnstown	IRL	30	B1
Jõhvi	EST	8	C5
Joigny	F	104	B2
Joinville	F	91	C5
Jokkmokk	S	196	C2
Jöllenbeck	D	72	B1
Jomala	FIN	51	B6
Jönåker	S	56	B2
Jonava	LT	13	A6
Jonchery-sur-Vesle	F	91	B3
Jondal	N	46	B3
Jondalen	N	53	A5
Joniškis	LT	8	D3
Jönköping	S	62	A2
Jonkowo	PL	69	B5
Jønnbu	N	53	A5
Jonsberg	S	56	B2
Jonsered	S	60	B2
Jonstorp	S	61	C2
Jonzac	F	114	C3
Jorba	E	147	C2
Jordanów	PL	99	B3
Jordanów Śląski	PL	85	B4
Jordanowo	PL	75	B4
Jordbro	S	57	A4
Jordbrua	N	195	D5
Jördenstorf	D	66	C1
Jordet	N	49	A4
Jordøse	DK	59	C3
Jork	D	72	A2
Jörlanda	S	60	B1
Jormlien	S	199	A10
Jormvattnet	S	199	A11
Jörn	S	200	A6
Jørpeland	N	52	A2
Jorquera	E	158	C2
Jošan	HR	123	C4
Jošavka	BIH	124	C3
Josipdol	HR	123	B4
Josipovac	HR	125	B4
Jössefors	S	54	A3
Josselin	F	101	B3
Jøssund	N	199	A7
Jostedal	N	47	A4

Name			
Jósvafö	H	99	C4
Jou	P	148	A2
Jouarre	F	90	C3
Joué-lès-Tours	F	102	B2
Joué-sur-Erdre	F	101	B4
Joure	NL	70	B2
Joutseno	FIN	9	B6
Joutsijärvi	FIN	197	C10
Joux-la-Ville	F	104	B2
Jouy	F	90	C1
Jouy-le-Châtel	F	90	C3
Jouy-le-Potier	F	103	B3
Joyeuse	F	131	A3
Joze	F	116	B3
Juan-les-Pins	F	132	B3
Juankoski	FIN	8	A6
Jübek	D	64	B2
Jubrique	E	162	B2
Jüchsen	D	82	B2
Judaberg	N	52	A1
Judenburg	A	110	B1
Juelsminde	DK	59	C3
Jugon-les-Lacs	F	101	A3
Juillac	F	129	A4
Juillan	F	145	A4
Juist	D	71	A4
Jukkasjärvi	S	196	B3
Jule	N	199	A10
Julianadorp	NL	70	B1
Julianstown	IRL	30	A2
Jülich	D	80	B2
Jullouville	F	88	B2
Jumeaux	F	117	B3
Jumièges	F	89	A4
Jumilhac-le-Grand	F	115	C5
Jumilla	E	159	C2
Jumisko	FIN	197	C11
Juncosa	E	153	A4
Juneda	E	147	C1
Jung	S	55	B4
Jungingen	D	93	C5
Junglingster	L	92	B2
Juniville	F	91	B4
Junosuando	S	196	B5
Junqueira	P	149	A2
Junsele	S	200	C2
Juoksengi	S	196	C6
Juoksenki	FIN	196	C6
Juprelle	B	80	B1
Jurata	PL	69	A3
Jurbarkas	LT	12	A5
Jurjevo	HR	123	C3
Jūrmala	LV	8	D3
Jurmu	FIN	197	D10
Juromenha	P	155	C3
Jursla	S	56	B2
Jussac	F	116	C2
Jussey	F	105	B4
Jussy	F	90	B3
Juta	H	125	A3
Jüterbog	D	74	C2
Juuka	FIN	3	E11
Juuma	FIN	197	C12
Juvigny-le-Terte	F	88	B2
Juvigny-sous-Andaine	F	89	B3
Juzennecourt	F	105	A3
Jyderup	DK	61	D1
Jyrkänkoski	FIN	197	C12
Jyväskylä	FIN	8	A4

K

Name			
Kaamanen	FIN	193	C11
Kaamasmukka	FIN	193	C10
Kaaresuvanto	FIN	192	D6
Kaarssen	D	73	A4
Kaatscheuvel	NL	79	A5
Kaba	H	113	B5
Kåbdalis	S	196	C3
Kačarevo	SRB	127	C2
Kács	H	113	B4
Kadan	CZ	83	B5
Kadarkút	H	125	A3
Kadınhanı	TR	189	A7
Kaduy	RUS	9	C10
Käfalla	S	56	A1
Kåfjord	N	192	C7
Kåfjordbotn	N	192	C4
Kågeröd	S	61	D3
Kahl	D	93	A5
Kahla	D	82	B3
Kainach bei Voitsberg	A	110	B2
Kaindorf	A	110	B2
Kainulasjärvi	S	196	C5
Kairala	FIN	197	B10
Kaisepakte	S	192	D3
Kaisersesch	D	80	B3
Kaiserslautern	D	93	B3
Kajaani	FIN	3	D10
Kajárpéc	H	111	B4
Kajdacs	H	112	C2
Kakanj	BIH	139	A4
Kakasd	H	125	A4
Kakolewo	PL	85	A4
Kål	E	163	A4
Kalajoki	FIN	3	D8
Kalak	N	193	B11
Kalamata	GR	184	B3
Kalambaka	GR	182	D3
Kalamria	GR	182	C4

Name			
Kalandra	GR	183	D5
Kälarne	S	200	D2
Kalavrita	GR	184	A3
Kalbe	D	73	B4
Kalce	SLO	123	B3
Káld	H	111	B4
Kale, Antalya	TR	189	C4
Kale, Denizli	TR	188	B3
Kalecik	TR	23	A7
Kalefeld	D	82	A2
Kalesija	BIH	139	A4
Kalety	PL	86	B2
Kalevala	RUS	3	D12
Kalhovd	N	47	B5
Kalí	HR	137	A4
Kalimnos	GR	188	C2
Kalinkavichy	BY	13	B8
Kalinovac	HR	124	A3
Kalinovik	BIH	139	B4
Kalirachi	GR	183	C6
Kaliska, Pomorskie	PL	68	B3
Kaliska, Pomorskie	PL	68	A3
Kalisz	PL	86	A2
Kalisz Pomorski	PL	75	A4
Kaljord	N	194	B6
Kalkan	TR	189	C4
Kalkar	D	80	A2
Kalkim	TR	186	C2
Kall	D	80	B2
Kall	S	199	B10
Källby	S	55	B4
Kållered	S	60	B2
Kållerstad	S	60	B3
Kallinge	S	63	B3
Kallmünz	D	95	B3
Kallo	FIN	196	B7
Kallsedet	S	199	B9
Källvik	S	56	B3
Kalmar	S	63	B4
Kalmthout	B	79	A4
Kalná	SK	112	A2
Kalo Nero	GR	184	B2
Kalocsa	H	112	C2
Kalokhorio	CY	181	B2
Kaloni	GR	186	C1
Káloz	H	112	C2
Kals	A	109	B3
Kalsdorf	A	110	C2
Kaltbrunn	CH	107	B4
Kaltenbach	A	108	B2
Kaltenkirchen	D	64	C2
Kaltennordheim	D	82	B2
Kalundborg	DK	61	D1
Kalush	UA	13	D6
Kalv	S	60	B3
Kalvåg	N	198	D1
Kalvehave	DK	65	A5
Kalwaria-Zebrzydowska	PL	99	B3
Kalyazin	RUS	9	D10
Kam	H	111	B3
Kaman	TR	23	B7
Kamares	GR	185	C5
Kambos	CY	181	A1
Kamen	D	81	A3
Kamenice	CZ	97	B3
Kamenice nad Lipou	CZ	96	B3
Kameničná	SK	112	B2
Kamenný Most	SK	112	B2
Kamenný Ujezd	CZ	96	C2
Kamenska	HR	124	B3
Kamensko	HR	138	B2
Kamenz	D	84	A2
Kamičak	BIH	124	C2
Kamień	PL	87	A4
Kamień Krajeński	PL	76	A2
Kamień Pomorski	PL	67	C3
Kamienica Zabk.	PL	85	B4
Kamienka	SK	99	B4
Kamienna Góra	PL	85	B4
Kamieńsk	PL	86	A3
Kamiros Skala	GR	188	C2
Kamnik	SLO	123	A3
Kamp-Lintfort	D	80	A2
Kampen	NL	70	B2
Kampinos	PL	77	B5
Kampor	HR	123	C3
Kamyanets-Podil's'kyy	UA	13	D7
Kamyanka-Buz'ka	UA	13	C6
Kamýk nad Vltavou	CZ	96	B2
Kanal	SLO	122	A2
Kanalia	GR	182	D4
Kandalaksha	RUS	3	C13
Kandanos	GR	185	D4
Kandel	D	93	B4
Kandern	D	106	B2
Kandersteg	CH	106	C2
Kandila	GR	184	B3
Kandıra	TR	187	A5
Kandyty	PL	69	A5
Kanfanar	HR	122	B2
Kangasala	FIN	8	B4
Kangos	S	196	B5
Kangosjärvi	FIN	196	B6
Kaniów	PL	75	C3

Name			
Kanjiža	SRB	126	A2
Kankaanpää	FIN	8	B3
Kannus	FIN	3	E8
Kanturk	IRL	29	B3
Kapaklı	TR	186	A2
Kapellen	A	110	B2
Kapellen	B	79	A4
Kapellskär	S	57	A4
Kapfenberg	A	110	B2
Kapfenstein	A	110	C2
Kaplice	CZ	96	C2
Kapljuh	BIH	124	C2
Kápolna	H	113	B4
Kápolnásnyék	H	112	B2
Kaposfö	H	125	A3
Kaposfüred	H	125	A3
Kaposszekcsö	H	125	A3
Kaposvár	H	125	A3
Kapp	N	48	B2
Kappel	D	93	C3
Kappeln	D	64	B2
Kappelshamn	S	57	C4
Kappl	A	107	B5
Kappstad	S	55	A4
Kaprun	A	109	B3
Kaptol	HR	125	B3
Kapuvár	H	111	B4
Karaadilli	TR	189	A5
Karabiğa	TR	186	B2
Karabük	TR	187	A7
Karaburun	TR	186	D1
Karacabey	TR	186	B3
Karacaköy	TR	186	A3
Karacaören	TR	189	A5
Karacasu	TR	188	B3
Karácsond	H	113	B4
Karád	H	112	C1
Karahallı	TR	189	A4
Karaisali	TR	23	C8
Karaman, Balıkesir	TR	186	C3
Karaman, Karaman	TR	23	C7
Karamanlı	TR	189	B4
Karamürsel	TR	187	B4
Karan	SRB	127	D1
Karancslapujto	H	113	A3
Karaova	TR	188	B2
Karapınar	TR	23	C7
Karasjok	N	193	C9
Karasu	TR	187	A5
Karataş, Adana	TR	23	C8
Karataş, Manisa	TR	188	A3
Karatoprak	TR	188	B2
Karavostasi	CY	181	A1
Karbenning	S	50	B3
Kårberg	S	55	B5
Kårböle	S	199	D12
Karby	D	64	B2
Karby	DK	58	B1
Kårby, Kalmar	S	62	A4
Karby, Stockholm	S	57	A4
Karcag	H	113	B4
Karczew	PL	86	B1
Karczowiska	PL	85	A4
Kardamena	GR	188	C2
Kardamili	GR	184	A7
Kardašova Rečice	CZ	96	B2
Kardis	S	196	C6
Karditsa	GR	182	D3
Kärdla	EST	8	C3
Kardoskút	H	113	C4
Karesuando	S	192	D6
Kargı	TR	23	A8
Kargopol	RUS	9	B11
Kargowa	PL	75	B4
Karigasniemi	FIN	193	C9
Karise	DK	65	A5
Karistos	GR	185	A5
Karkkila	FIN	8	B4
Karlholmsbruk	S	51	B4
Karlino	PL	67	B4
Karlobag	HR	137	A4
Karlovac	HR	123	B4
Karlovasi	GR	188	B1
Karlovčic	SRB	127	C2
Karlovice	CZ	85	B5
Karlovo	BG	17	D6
Karłowice	PL	85	B5
Karlsborg	S	55	B5
Karlshamn	S	63	B2
Karlshöfen	D	72	A2
Karlshus	N	54	A1
Karlskoga	S	55	A5
Karlskrona	S	63	B3
Karlsrud	N	47	B5
Karlsruhe	D	93	B4
Karlstad	S	55	A4
Karlstadt	D	94	B1
Karlstift	A	96	C2
Karlstorp	S	62	A3
Karmacs	H	111	C4
Karmin	PL	85	A5
Kärna	S	60	B1
Karnobat	BG	17	D7
Karojba	HR	122	B2
Karow	D	73	B5
Karpacz	PL	85	B3
Karpathos	GR	188	D2
Karpenisi	GR	182	E3
Karpuzlu	TR	188	B2
Kärrbo	S	56	A2

Name			
Karrebaeksminde	DK	65	A4
Karshult	S	60	B3
Karsin	PL	68	B2
Kårsta	S	57	A4
Karstädt	D	73	A4
Kartal	TR	186	B4
Kartitsch	A	109	C3
Kartuzy	PL	68	A3
Karungi	S	196	C6
Karunki	FIN	196	C7
Karup	DK	59	B2
Karviná	CZ	98	B2
Kås	DK	58	A2
Kaş	TR	189	C4
Kasaba	TR	189	C4
Kašava	CZ	98	B1
Kåseberga	S	66	A3
Kasejovice	CZ	96	B1
Kasfjord	N	194	B7
Kashin	RUS	9	D10
Kašina	HR	124	B2
Kasina-Wielka	PL	99	B4
Kaskinen	FIN	8	A2
Kašperské Hory	CZ	96	B1
Kassandrino	GR	183	C5
Kassel	D	81	A5
Kassiopi	GR	182	D1
Kastamonu	TR	23	A7
Kastav	HR	123	B3
Kaštel-Stari	HR	138	B2
Kaštel Zegarski	HR	138	A1
Kasteli	GR	185	D4
Kastellaun	D	93	A3
Kasterlee	B	79	A4
Kastl	D	95	B3
Kastlösa	S	63	B4
Kastorf	D	65	C3
Kastoria	GR	182	C3
Kastorio	GR	184	B3
Kastraki	GR	185	C6
Kastrosikia	GR	182	D2
Kastsyukovichy	BY	13	B10
Kaszaper	H	113	C4
Katakolo	GR	184	B2
Katapola	GR	185	C6
Katastari	GR	184	B1
Katerbow	D	74	B1
Katerini	GR	182	C4
Kathikas	CY	181	B1
Kätkesuando	S	196	A6
Katlenburg-Lindau	D	82	A2
Kato Achaia	GR	184	A2
Káto Pyrgos	CY	181	A1
Katouna	GR	182	E3
Katovice	CZ	96	B1
Katowice	PL	86	B3
Katrineberg	S	50	A3
Katrineholm	S	56	B2
Kattarp	S	61	C2
Kattavia	GR	188	D2
Katthammarsvik	S	57	C4
Kattilstorp	S	55	B4
Katwijk	NL	70	B1
Katy Wrocławskie	PL	85	A4
Katymár	H	125	A5
Katzenelnbogen	D	81	B3
Katzhütte	D	82	B3
Kaub	D	93	A3
Kaufbeuren	D	108	B1
Kauhajoki	FIN	8	A3
Kauhava	FIN	8	A3
Kaukonen	FIN	196	B7
Kauliranta	FIN	196	C6
Kaulsdorf	D	82	B3
Kaunas	LT	13	A5
Kaunisvaara	S	196	B6
Kaupanger	N	47	A4
Kautokeino	N	192	C7
Kautzen	A	97	C3
Kavadarci	MK	182	B4
Kavajë	AL	182	B1
Kavakköy	TR	186	B1
Kavaklı	TR	186	A2
Kavaklıdere	TR	188	B3
Kavarna	BG	17	D8
Kävlinge	S	61	D3
Kawczyn	PL	77	B5
Kaxås	S	199	B10
Kaxholmen	S	62	A2
Käylä	FIN	197	C12
Kaymakçı	TR	188	A3
Kaymaz	TR	187	C6
Kaynarca	TR	187	A5
Käyrämö	FIN	197	C9
Kayseri	TR	23	B8
Kaysersberg	F	106	A2
Kazanlük	BG	17	D6
Kazimierza Wielka	PL	87	B4
Kazincbarcika	H	113	A4
Kaźmierz	PL	75	B5
Kcynia	PL	76	B2
Kdyně	CZ	95	B5
Kea	GR	185	B5
Keadew	IRL	26	B2
Keady	GB	27	B4
Kecel	H	112	C3
Keçiborlu	TR	189	B5
Kecskemét	H	113	C3
Kédainiai	LT	13	A5

Name			
Kędzierzyn-Koźle	PL	86	B2
Keel	IRL	28	A1
Keenagh	IRL	28	A3
Keerbergen	B	79	A4
Kefalos	GR	188	C1
Kefken	TR	187	A5
Keflavík	IS	190	C3
Kegworth	GB	40	C2
Kehl	D	93	C3
Kehrigk	D	74	B2
Keighley	GB	40	B2
Keila	EST	8	C4
Keillmore	GB	34	C2
Keiss	GB	32	C3
Keith	GB	33	D4
Kelankylä	FIN	197	D10
Kelberg	D	80	B2
Kelbra	D	82	A3
Kelč	CZ	98	B1
Kelchsau	A	108	B3
Kělcyrë	AL	182	C2
Keld	GB	37	B4
Kelebia	H	126	A1
Kelekçi	TR	188	B4
Kelemér	H	99	C4
Keles	TR	186	C4
Kelheim	D	95	C3
Kell	D	92	B2
Kellas	GB	32	D3
Kellinghusen	D	64	C2
Kelloselkä	FIN	197	C11
Kells	GB	27	B4
Kells	IRL	27	C4
Kelmis	B	80	B2
Kelokedhara	CY	181	B1
Kelottijärvi	FIN	192	D6
Kelsall	GB	38	A4
Kelso	GB	35	C5
Kelsterbach	D	93	A4
Keltneyburn	GB	35	B3
Kelujärvi	FIN	197	B10
Kemaliye	TR	188	A3
Kemalpaşa	TR	188	A2
Kematen	A	108	B2
Kemberg	D	83	A4
Kemer, Antalya	TR	189	C5
Kemer, Burdur	TR	189	B5
Kemer, Muğla	TR	189	C4
Kemerkaya	TR	187	D6
Kemeten	A	111	B3
Kemi	FIN	196	D7
Kemijärvi	FIN	197	C10
Keminmaa	FIN	196	D7
Kemnath	D	95	B3
Kemnay	GB	33	D4
Kemnitz, Brandenburg	D	74	B1
Kemnitz, Mecklenburg-Vorpommern	D	66	B2
Kempen	D	80	A2
Kempsey	GB	39	B4
Kempten	D	107	B5
Kemptthal	CH	107	B3
Kendal	GB	37	B4
Kenderes	H	113	B4
Kengyel	H	113	B4
Kenilworth	GB	44	A2
Kenmare	IRL	29	C2
Kenmore	GB	35	B4
Kennacraig	GB	34	C2
Kenyeri	H	111	B4
Kenzingen	D	106	A2
Kepez	TR	186	B1
Kępice	PL	68	A1
Kępno	PL	86	A2
Kepsut	TR	186	C3
Keramoti	GR	183	C6
Keräntöjärvi	S	196	B6
Keratea	GR	185	B4
Kerava	FIN	8	B4
Kerecsend	H	113	B4
Kerekegyhaza	H	112	C3
Kerepestarcsa	H	112	B3
Keri	GR	184	B1
Kérien	F	100	A2
Kerkafalva	H	111	C3
Kerken	D	80	A2
Kerkrade	NL	80	B2
Kerkyra	GR	182	D1
Kerlouan	F	100	A1
Kernascléden	F	100	A2
Kernhof	A	110	B2
Kerns	CH	106	C3
Kerpen	D	80	B2
Kerrysdale	GB	31	B3
Kerta	H	111	B4
Kerteminde	DK	59	C3
Kerzers	CH	106	C2
Keşan	TR	186	B1
Kesgrave	GB	45	A5
Kesh	GB	26	B3
Keswick	GB	36	B3
Keszthely	H	111	C4
Kéthely	H	111	C4
Kętrzyn	PL	12	A4
Kettering	GB	44	A3
Kettlewell	GB	40	A1
Kęty	PL	99	B3
Ketzin	D	74	B1
Keula	D	82	A2
Keuruu	FIN	8	A4

Kevelaer D 80 A2
Kevermes H 113 C5
Kevi SRB 126 B1
Keyingham GB 41 B3
Keynsham GB 43 A4
Kežmarok SK 99 B4
Kharmanli BG 183 B7
Khaskovo BG 183 B7
Khimki RUS 9 E10
Khisinev = Chişinău MD 17 B8
Khmelnik UA 13 D7
Khmelnytskyy UA 13 D7
Khodoriv UA 13 D6
Kholm RUS 9 D7
Khotyn UA 13 D7
Khoyniki BY 13 C8
Khust UA 17 A5
Khvoynaya RUS 9 C9
Kiato GR 184 A3
Kibæk DK 59 B1
Kiberg N 193 B14
Kicasalih TR 186 A1
Kičevo MK 182 B2
Kidderminster GB 39 B4
Kidlington GB 44 B2
Kidsgrove GB 40 B1
Kidwelly GB 39 C2
Kiefersfelden D 108 B3
Kiel D 64 B3
Kielce PL 87 B4
Kiełczygłów PL 86 A3
Kielder GB 37 A4
Kiełpino PL 68 A3
Kielpiny PL 77 A4
Kierinki FIN 197 B8
Kiernozia PL 77 B4
Kierspe D 81 A3
Kietrz PL 86 B2
Kietz D 74 B3
Kiev = Kyyiv UA 13 C9
Kiezmark PL 69 A3
Kiffisia GR 185 A4
Kifino Selo BIH 139 B4
Kihlanki FIN 196 B6
Kihlanki S 196 B6
Kiistala FIN 197 B8
Kije PL 87 B4
Kijevo HR 138 B2
Kikallen N 46 B2
Kikinda SRB 126 B2
Kil N 53 B5
Kil, *Örebro* S 55 A6
Kil, *Värmland* S 55 A4
Kila S 55 A3
Kilafors S 50 A3
Kilb Rabenstein A 110 A2
Kilbaha IRL 29 B2
Kilbeggan IRL 30 A1
Kilberry GB 34 C2
Kilbirnie GB 34 C3
Kilboghamn N 195 D4
Kilbotn N 194 B7
Kilchattan GB 34 C2
Kilchoan GB 34 B1
Kilcock IRL 30 A2
Kilconnell IRL 28 A3
Kilcormac IRL 28 A4
Kilcreggan GB 34 C3
Kilcullen IRL 30 A2
Kilcurry IRL 27 B4
Kildare IRL 30 A2
Kildinstroy RUS 3 B13
Kildonan GB 32 C3
Kildorrery IRL 29 B3
Kilegrend N 53 A4
Kilen N 53 A4
Kilgarvan IRL 29 C2
Kiliya UA 17 C8
Kilkee IRL 29 B2
Kilkeel GB 27 B4
Kilkelly IRL 26 C2
Kilkenny IRL 30 B1
Kilkieran IRL 28 A2
Kilkinlea IRL 29 B2
Kilkis GR 182 B4
Killadysert IRL 29 B2
Killala IRL 26 B1
Killaloe IRL 28 B3
Killarney IRL 29 B2
Killashandra IRL 27 B3
Killashee IRL 28 A4
Killearn GB 34 B3
Killeberg S 61 C4
Killeigh IRL 30 A1
Killenaule IRL 29 B4
Killimor IRL 28 A3
Killin GB 34 B3
Killinaboy IRL 28 B2
Killinge S 196 B3
Killinick IRL 30 B2
Killorglin IRL 29 B2
Killucan IRL 30 A1
Killybegs IRL 26 B2
Killyleagh GB 27 B5
Kilmacrenan IRL 26 A3
Kilmacthomas IRL 30 B1
Kilmaine IRL 28 A2
Kilmallock IRL 29 B3
Kilmarnock GB 36 A2
Kilmartin GB 34 B2
Kilmaurs GB 36 A2
Kilmeadan IRL 30 B1
Kilmeedy IRL 29 B3
Kilmelford GB 34 B2
Kilmore Quay IRL 30 B2
Kilmuir GB 32 D2
Kilnaleck IRL 27 C3
Kilninver GB 34 B2
Kilpisjärvi FIN 192 C4
Kilrea GB 27 B4
Kilrush IRL 29 B2
Kilsmo S 56 A1
Kilsyth GB 35 C3
Kiltoom IRL 28 A3
Kilwinning GB 36 A2
Kimasozero RUS 3 D12
Kimi GR 185 A5
Kimolos GR 185 C5
Kimovsk RUS 9 E10
Kimratshofen D 107 B5
Kimry RUS 9 D10
Kimstad S 56 B1
Kinbrace GB 32 C3
Kincardine GB 35 B4
Kincraig GB 32 D3
Kindberg A 110 B2
Kindelbruck D 82 A3
Kingarrow IRL 26 B2
Kingisepp RUS 9 C6
King's Lynn GB 41 C4
Kingsbridge GB 43 B3
Kingsclere GB 44 B2
Kingscourt IRL 27 C4
Kingsteignton GB 43 B3
Kingston, *Greater London* GB 44 B3
Kingston, *Moray* GB 32 D3
Kingston Bagpuize GB 44 B2
Kingston upon Hull GB 40 B3
Kingswear GB 43 B3
Kingswood GB 43 A4
Kington GB 39 B3
Kingussie GB 32 D2
Kınık, *Antalya* TR 188 C4
Kınık, *İzmır* TR 186 C2
Kinloch, *Highland* GB 31 B2
Kinloch, *Highland* GB 32 C2
Kinloch Rannoch GB 35 B3
Kinlochbervie GB 32 C1
Kinlochewe GB 32 D1
Kinlochleven GB 34 B3
Kinlochmoidart GB 34 B2
Kinloss GB 32 D3
Kinlough IRL 26 B2
Kinn N 48 B2
Kinna S 60 B2
Kinnared S 60 B3
Kinnarp S 55 B4
Kinne-Kleva S 55 B4
Kinnegad IRL 30 A1
Kinnitty IRL 28 A4
Kinrooi B 80 A1
Kinross GB 35 B4
Kinsale IRL 29 C3
Kinsarvik N 46 B3
Kintarvie GB 31 A2
Kintore GB 33 D4
Kinvarra IRL 28 A3
Kioni GR 184 A1
Kiparissia GR 184 B2
Kipfenburg D 95 C3
Kippen GB 35 B3
Kiraz TR 188 A3
Kirazlı TR 186 B1
Kirberg D 81 B4
Kirchbach in Steiermark A 110 C2
Kirchberg CH 106 B2
Kirchberg, *Baden-Württemberg* D 94 B1
Kirchberg, *Rheinland-Pfalz* D 93 B3
Kirchberg am Wechsel A 110 B2
Kirchberg an der Pielach A 110 A2
Kirchberg in Tirol A 109 B3
Kirchbichl A 108 B3
Kirchdorf, *Bayern* D 96 C1
Kirchdorf, *Mecklenburg-Vorpommern* D 65 C4
Kirchdorf, *Niedersachsen* D 72 B1
Kirchdorf an der Krems A 109 B5
Kirchdorf in Tirol A 109 B3
Kirchenlamitz D 83 B3
Kirchenthumbach D 95 B3
Kirchhain D 81 B4
Kirchheim, *Baden-Württemberg* D 94 C1
Kirchheim, *Bayern* D 108 A1
Kirchheim, *Hessen* D 81 B5
Kirchheim-bolanden D 93 B4
Kirchhundem D 81 A4
Kirchlintein D 72 B2
Kirchschlag A 111 B3
Kirchweidach D 109 A3
Kirchzarten D 106 B2
Kircubbin GB 27 B5
Kireç TR 186 C3
Kırıkkale TR 23 B7
Kirillov RUS 9 C11
Kirishi RUS 9 C8
Kirk Michael GB 36 B2
Kırka TR 187 C5
Kırkağaç TR 186 C2
Kirkbean GB 36 B3
Kirkbride GB 36 B3
Kirkby GB 38 A4
Kirkby Lonsdale GB 37 B4
Kirkby Malzeard GB 40 A2
Kirkby Stephen GB 37 B4
Kirkbymoorside GB 37 B6
Kirkcaldy GB 35 B4
Kirkcolm GB 36 B1
Kirkconnel GB 36 A2
Kirkcowan GB 36 B2
Kirkcudbright GB 36 B2
Kirke Hyllinge DK 61 D1
Kirkehamn N 52 B2
Kirkenær N 49 B4
Kirkenes N 193 C14
Kirkham GB 38 A4
Kirkintilloch GB 35 C3
Kirkjubæjarklaustur IS 191 D7
Kirkkonummi FIN 8 B4
Kırklareli TR 186 A2
Kirkmichael GB 35 B4
Kirkoswald GB 36 A2
Kirkpatrick Fleming GB 36 A3
Kirkton of Glenisla GB 35 B4
Kirkwall GB 33 C4
Kirkwhelpington GB 37 A5
Kirn D 93 B3
Kirovsk RUS 3 C13
Kirriemuir GB 35 B5
Kırşehir TR 23 B8
Kirton GB 41 C3
Kirton in Lindsey GB 40 B3
Kirtorf D 81 B5
Kiruna S 196 B3
Kisa S 62 A3
Kisač SRB 126 B1
Kisbér H 112 B2
Kiseljak BIH 139 B4
Kisielice PL 69 B4
Kisköre H 113 B4
Kiskőrös H 112 C3
Kiskunfélegyháza H 113 C3
Kiskunhalas H 112 C3
Kiskunlacháza H 112 B2
Kiskunmajsa H 113 C3
Kisláng H 112 C2
Kisslegg D 107 B4
Kissolt H 112 C3
Kissónerga CY 181 B1
Kist D 94 B1
Kistanje HR 138 B1
Kistelek H 113 C3
Kisterenye H 113 A3
Kisújszállás H 113 B4
Kisvárda H 16 A5
Kisvejke H 112 C2
Kiszkowo PL 76 B2
Kiszombor H 126 A2
Kitee FIN 9 A7
Kithnos GR 185 B5
Kiti CY 181 B2
Kitkiöjärvi S 196 B6
Kitkiöjoki S 196 B6
Kittelfjäll S 195 E6
Kittendorf D 74 A1
Kittilä FIN 196 B7
Kittlitz D 84 A2
Kittsee A 111 A4
Kitzbühel A 109 B3
Kitzingen D 94 B2
Kiuruvesi FIN 3 E10
Kivertsi UA 13 C6
Kividhes CY 181 B1
Kivik S 63 C2
Kivotos GR 182 C3
Kıyıköy TR 186 A3
Kızılcabölük TR 188 B4
Kızılcadağ TR 189 B4
Kızılcahamam TR 23 A7
Kızılırmak TR 23 A7
Kızılkaya TR 189 B5
Kızılkuyu TR 187 D6
Kızılören, *Afyon* TR 189 A5
Kızılören, *Konya* TR 189 B7
Kjeldebotn N 194 B7
Kjellerup DK 59 B2
Kjellmyra N 49 B4
Kjøllefjord N 193 B11
Kjopmannskjaer N 54 A1
Kjøpsvik N 194 B7
Kľačno SK 98 C2
Kladanj BIH 139 A4
Kläden D 73 B4
Klädesholmen S 60 B1
Kladnice HR 138 B2
Kladno CZ 84 B2
Kladruby CZ 95 B4
Klagenfurt A 110 C1
Klågerup S 61 D3
Klagstorp S 66 A2
Klaipėda LT 8 E2
Klaistow D 74 B1
Klaksvík FO 4 A3
Klana HR 123 B3
Klanac HR 123 C4
Klanjec HR 123 A4
Klardorf D 95 B4
Klarup DK 58 A3
Klašnice BIH 124 C3
Klässbol S 55 A3
Klášterec nad Ohří CZ 83 B5
Kláštor pod Znievom SK 98 C2
Klatovy CZ 96 B1
Klaus an der Pyhrnbahn A 110 B1
Klazienaveen NL 71 B3
Kłecko PL 76 B2
Kleczew PL 76 B3
Klein Plasten D 74 A1
Klein Sankt Paul A 110 C1
Kleinsölk A 109 B4
Kleinzell A 110 B2
Klejtrup DK 58 B2
Klek SRB 126 B2
Klemensker DK 67 A3
Klenak SRB 127 C1
Klenci pod Cerchovem CZ 95 B4
Klenica PL 75 C4
Klenje SRB 127 C1
Klenoec MK 182 B2
Klenovec SK 99 C3
Klenovica HR 123 B3
Klenovnik HR 124 A2
Kleppe N 52 B1
Kleppestø N 46 B2
Kleptow D 74 A2
Kleszewo PL 77 B6
Kleve D 80 A2
Klevshult S 60 B4
Klewki PL 77 A5
Kličevac SRB 127 C3
Kliening A 110 C1
Klietz D 73 B5
Klikuszowa PL 99 B3
Klimkovice CZ 98 B2
Klimontów PL 87 B5
Klimovichi BY 13 B9
Klimpfjäll S 195 E5
Klin RUS 9 D10
Klinča Sela HR 123 B4
Klingenbach A 111 B3
Klingenberg D 93 B5
Klingenmunster D 93 B4
Klingenthal D 83 B4
Klinken D 73 A4
Klintehamn S 57 C4
Kliny PL 87 A4
Kliplev DK 64 B2
Klippan S 61 C3
Klis HR 138 B2
Klitmøller DK 58 A1
Klitten S 49 A6
Klixbüll D 64 B1
Kljajićevo SRB 126 B1
Ključ BIH 138 A2
Klobouky CZ 97 C4
Kłobuck PL 86 B2
Klockestrand S 200 D3
Kłodawa, *Lubuskie* PL 75 B4
Kłodawa, *Wielkopolskie* PL 76 B3
Kłodzko PL 85 B4
Kløfta N 48 B3
Klokkarvik N 46 B2
Klokkerholm DK 58 A3
Klokočov SK 98 B2
Kłomnice PL 86 B3
Klonowa PL 86 A2
Kloosterzande NL 79 A4
Kłopot PL 74 B3
Klos AL 182 B2
Kloštar Ivanić HR 124 B2
Kloster D 66 B2
Kloster DK 59 B1
Klösterle A 107 B5
Klostermansfeld D 82 A3
Klosterneuburg A 97 C4
Klosters CH 107 C4
Kloten CH 107 B3
Klötze D 73 B4
Klöverträsk S 196 D4
Klövsjö S 199 C11
Kluczbork PL 86 B2
Kluczewo PL 75 A5
Kluisbergen B 79 B3
Klundert NL 79 A4
Klutz D 65 C4
Klwów PL 87 A4
Klyetsk BY 13 B7
Knaben N 52 B2
Knaften S 200 B4
Knapstad N 54 A2
Knäred S 61 C3
Knaresborough GB 40 A2
Knarvik N 46 B2
Knebel DK 59 B3
Knebworth GB 44 B3
Knesebeck D 73 B3
Knesselare B 78 A3
Knežak SLO 123 B3
Kneževi Vinogradi HR 125 B4
Kneževo HR 125 B4
Knić SRB 127 D2
Knighton GB 39 B3
Knin HR 138 A2
Knislinge S 61 C4
Knittelfeld A 110 B1
Knivsta S 57 A3
Knock IRL 28 A3
Knocktopher IRL 30 B1
Knokke-Heist B 78 A3
Knowle GB 44 A2
Knurów PL 86 B2
Knutby S 51 C5
Knutsford GB 38 A4
Kobarid SLO 122 A2
København = Copenhagen DK 61 D2
Kobenz A 110 B1
Kobersdorf A 111 B3
Kobiernice PL 99 B3
Kobierzyce PL 85 B4
Kobilje SLO 111 C3
Kobiór PL 86 B2
Koblenz CH 106 B3
Koblenz D 81 B3
Kobryn BY 13 B6
Kobylanka PL 75 A3
Kobylin PL 85 A5
Kobylniki PL 77 B5
Kocaali TR 187 A5
Kocaaliler TR 189 B5
Kocaeli = İzmit TR 187 B4
Kočani MK 182 B4
Koçarlı TR 188 B2
Koceljevo SRB 127 C1
Kočerin BIH 138 B3
Kočevje SLO 123 B3
Kočevska Reka SLO 123 B3
Kochel am see D 108 B2
Kocs H 112 B2
Kocsér H 113 B3
Kocsola H 112 C2
Koczala PL 68 B2
Kodal N 53 A6
Kode S 60 B1
Kodersdorf D 84 A2
Kodrab PL 86 A3
Koekelare B 78 A2
Kofçaz TR 186 A2
Köflach A 110 B2
Køge DK 61 D2
Kohlberg D 95 B4
Kohtla-Järve EST 8 C5
Köinge S 60 B2
Kojetín CZ 98 B1
Kökar FIN 51 C7
Kokava SK 99 C3
Kokkola FIN 3 E8
Kokori BIH 124 C3
Kokoski PL 69 A3
Koksijde B 78 A2
Kola BIH 124 C3
Kola RUS 3 B13
Köla S 54 A3
Kołacin PL 87 A3
Kolari FIN 196 B6
Kolárovo SK 112 B1
Kolašin MNE 16 D3
Kolbäck S 56 A2
Kolbacz PL 75 A3
Kolbeinsstaðir IS 190 C3
Kolbermoor D 108 B3
Kolbnitz A 109 C4
Kolbotn N 54 A1
Kolbu N 48 B2
Kolby Kås DK 59 C3
Kolczewo PL 67 C3
Kolczyglowy PL 68 A2
Kolding DK 59 C2
Kölesd H 112 C2
Kolgrov N 46 A1
Kolín CZ 97 A3
Kolind DK 59 B3
Kolinec CZ 96 B1
Koljane HR 138 B2
Kølkær DK 59 B2
Kölleda D 82 A3
Kollum NL 70 A3
Köln = Cologne D 80 B2
Koło PL 76 B3
Kołobrzeg PL 67 B4
Kolochau D 83 A5
Kolomyya UA 13 D6
Kolonowskie PL 86 B2
Koloveč CZ 95 B5
Kolpino RUS 9 C7
Kolrep D 73 A5
Kölsillre S 199 C12
Kolsko PL 75 C4
Kolsva S 56 A1
Kolta SK 112 A2
Kolunič BIH 138 A2
Koluszki PL 87 A3
Kolut SRB 125 B4
Kolvereid N 199 A8
Kølvrå DK 59 B2
Komadi H 113 B5
Komagvær N 193 B14
Komarica BIH 125 C3
Komárno SK 112 B2
Komárom H 112 B2
Komatou Yialou CY 181 A3
Komboti GR 182 D3
Komen SLO 122 B2
Komin HR 138 B3
Komiža HR 138 B2
Komjáti H 99 C4
Komjatice SK 112 A2
Komletinci HR 125 B4
Komló, *Baranya* H 125 A4
Kömlo, *Heves* H 113 B4
Komoča SK 112 B2
Komorniki PL 75 B5
Komorzno PL 86 A2
Komotini GR 183 B7
Konak SRB 126 B2
Konakovo RUS 9 D10
Konarzyny PL 68 B2
Kondias GR 183 D7
Kondopaga RUS 9 A9
Kondorfa H 111 C3
Kondoros H 113 C4
Konevo RUS 9 A11
Køng DK 65 A4
Konga S 63 B3
Köngäs FIN 196 B7
Kongerslev DK 58 B3
Kongsberg N 53 A5
Kongshamn N 53 B4
Kongsmark DK 64 A1
Kongsmoen N 199 A9
Kongsvik N 194 B7
Kongsvinger N 48 B3
Konice CZ 97 B4
Konie PL 77 C5
Koniecpol PL 86 B3
Königs Wusterhausen D 74 B2
Königsberg D 82 B2
Königsbronn D 94 C2
Königsbrück D 84 A1
Königsbrunn D 94 C2
Königsdorf D 108 B2
Königsee D 82 B3
Königshorst D 74 B1
Königslutter D 73 B3
Königssee D 109 B3
Königstein, *Hessen* D 81 B4
Königstein, *Sachsen* D 84 B2
Königstetten A 97 C4
Königswartha D 84 A2
Konigswiesen A 96 C2
Königswinter D 80 B3
Konin PL 76 B3
Konispol AL 182 D2
Konitsa GR 182 C2
Köniz CH 106 C2
Konjevići BIH 139 A5
Konjevrate HR 138 B2
Konjic BIH 139 B3
Konjščina HR 124 A2
Könnern D 83 A3
Konnerud N 53 A6
Konopiska PL 86 B2
Konotop PL 75 C4
Końskie PL 87 A4
Konsmo N 52 B3
Konstancin-Jeziorna PL 77 B6
Konstantynów Łódźki PL 86 A3
Konstanz D 107 B4
Kontich B 79 A4
Kontiolahti FIN 9 A6
Konya TR 189 B7
Konz D 92 B2
Kópasker IS 191 A9
Kópavogur IS 190 C4
Kopčany SK 98 C1
Koper SLO 122 B2
Kopervik N 52 A1
Kópháza H 111 B3
Kopice PL 85 B5
Kopidlno CZ 84 B3
Köping S 56 A1
Köpingebro S 66 A2
Köpingsvik S 62 B4
Köpmanholmen S 200 C4
Koppang N 48 A3
Koppangen N 192 C4
Kopparberg S 50 C1
Koppelo FIN 193 D11
Koppom S 54 A3
Koprivlen BG 183 B5
Koprivna BIH 125 C4
Koprivnica HR 124 A2
Kopřivnice CZ 98 B2
Köprübaşı TR 186 D3
Koprzywnica PL 87 B5
Kopstal L 92 B2
Kopychyntsi UA 13 D6
Kopytkowo PL 69 B3
Korbach D 81 A4
Körbecke D 81 A4
Korçë AL 182 C2
Korčula HR 138 C3
Korczyców PL 75 B3
Korenita SRB 127 C1
Korets UA 13 C7
Korfantów PL 85 B5
Körfez TR 187 B4
Korgen N 195 D4
Korinth DK 64 A3
Korinthos = Corinth GR 184 B3
Korita BIH 138 A2
Korita HR 139 C3
Korithi GR 184 B1
Korkuteli TR 189 B5
Körmend H 111 B3
Korne PL 68 A2
Korneuburg A 97 C4
Kornevo RUS 69 A5
Kórnik PL 76 B2
Kornsjø N 54 B2
Környe H 112 B2
Koromačno HR 123 C3

Name	Country	Page	Grid
Koroni	GR	184	C2
Koronos	GR	184	C2
Koronowo	PL	76	A2
Körösladány	H	113	C5
Köröstarcsa	H	113	C5
Korosten	UA	13	C8
Korostyshev	UA	13	C8
Korpikå	S	196	D6
Korpikylä	FIN	196	C6
Korpilombolo	S	196	C6
Korsberga, Jönköping	S	62	A3
Korsberga, Skaraborg	S	55	B5
Korshavn	N	54	A1
Korskrogen	S	200	E1
Korsnäs	S	50	B2
Korsør	DK	65	A4
Korsun Shevchenkovskiy	UA	13	D9
Korträsk	S	196	D3
Kortrijk	B	78	B3
Korucu	TR	186	C2
Koryčany	CZ	98	B1
Korzeńsko	PL	85	A4
Korzybie	PL	68	A1
Kos	GR	188	C2
Kosakowo	PL	69	A3
Kosanica	MNE	139	B5
Kösching	D	95	C3
Kościan	PL	75	B5
Kościelec	PL	76	B3
Kościerzyna	PL	68	A2
Koserow	D	66	B2
Košetice	CZ	97	B3
Košice	SK	12	D4
Kosjerić	SRB	127	D1
Koška	HR	125	B4
Koskullskulle	S	196	B3
Kosovska Mitrovica	KOS	16	D4
Kosta	S	62	B3
Kostajnica	HR	124	B2
Kostajnik	SRB	127	C1
Kostanjevica	SLO	123	B4
Kostelec na Hané	CZ	97	B5
Kostelec nad Černými Lesy	CZ	96	B2
Kostice	CZ	84	B1
Kostkowo	PL	68	A3
Kostojevići	SRB	127	C1
Kostolac	SRB	127	C3
Kostomłoty	PL	85	A4
Kostopil	UA	13	C7
Kostów	PL	86	A2
Kostrzyn, Lubuskie	PL	74	B3
Kostrzyn, Wielkopolskie	PL	76	B2
Koszalin	PL	67	B5
Koszęcin	PL	86	B2
Kőszeg	H	111	B3
Koszwaly	PL	69	A3
Koszyce	PL	87	B4
Kot	SLO	123	B4
Kotala	FIN	197	B11
Kötelek	H	113	B4
Köthen	D	83	A3
Kotka	FIN	8	B5
Kotomierz	PL	76	A3
Kotor	MNE	16	D3
Kotor Varoš	BIH	124	C3
Kotoriba	HR	124	A2
Kotorsko	BIH	125	C4
Kotovsk	UA	17	B8
Kotronas	GR	184	C3
Kötschach	A	109	C3
Kötzting	D	95	B4
Koudum	NL	70	B2
Kouřim	CZ	96	A2
Kout na Šumave	CZ	95	B5
Kouvola	FIN	8	B5
Kovačevac	SRB	127	C2
Kovačica	SRB	126	B2
Kovdor	RUS	197	B13
Kovel'	UA	13	C6
Kovilj	SRB	126	B2
Kovin	SRB	127	C2
Kowal	PL	77	B4
Kowalewo Pomorskie	PL	69	B3
Kowalów	PL	75	B3
Kowary	PL	85	B3
Köyceğiz	TR	188	C3
Kozani	GR	182	C3
Kozarac	BIH	124	C2
Kozarac	HR	124	B1
Kozárovce	SK	98	C2
Kozelets	UA	13	C9
Kozica	HR	138	B3
Koziegłowy	PL	86	B3
Kozienice	PL	87	A5
Kozina	SLO	122	B2
Kozje	SLO	123	A4
Kozlu	TR	187	B6
Kozluk	BIH	139	A5
Koźmin	PL	85	A5
Koźminek	PL	86	A2
Kozolupy	CZ	96	B1
Kožuchów	PL	85	A3
Kožuhe	BIH	125	C4
Kozyatyn	UA	13	D8
Kozyürük	TR	186	A1
Kräckelbräken	S	49	A6
Krackow	D	74	A3
Kraddsele	S	195	E7
Krag	PL	68	A1
Kragenæs	DK	65	B4
Kragerø	N	53	B5
Kragi	PL	68	B1
Kragujevac	SRB	127	C2
Krajenburg	D	109	A3
Krajenka	PL	68	B1
Krajišnik	SRB	126	B2
Krajková	CZ	83	B4
Krajné	SK	98	C1
Krajnik Dolny	PL	74	A3
Krakača	BIH	124	B1
Kräklingbo	S	57	C4
Kraków = Cracow	PL	99	A3
Krakow am See	D	73	A5
Králíky	CZ	85	B4
Kraljevica	HR	123	B3
Kraljevo	SRB	16	D4
Kral'ov Brod	SK	111	A4
Kral'ovany	SK	99	B3
Kralovice	CZ	96	B1
Kralupy nad Vltavou	CZ	84	B2
Králův Dvůr	CZ	96	B2
Kramfors	S	200	D3
Kramsach	A	108	B2
Kramsk	PL	76	B3
Kråmvik	N	53	A4
Kranenburg	D	80	A2
Kranichfeld	D	82	B3
Kranidi	GR	184	B3
Kranj	SLO	123	A3
Kranjska Gora	SLO	109	C4
Krapanj	HR	138	B1
Krapina	HR	124	A1
Krapje	HR	124	B2
Krapkowice	PL	86	B1
Kraselov	CZ	96	B1
Krašić	HR	123	B4
Kräslava	LV	8	E5
Kraslice	CZ	83	B4
Krasna	PL	87	A4
Krasna Lipa	CZ	84	B2
Krasne	PL	77	B5
Kraśnik	PL	12	C5
Krašnja	SLO	123	A3
Krásno	SK	98	B2
Krasno Polje	HR	123	C4
Krásnohorské Podhradie	SK	99	C4
Krasnozavodsk	RUS	9	D11
Krasnystaw	PL	13	C5
Krasnyy	RUS	13	A9
Krasnyy Kholm	RUS	9	C10
Krasocin	PL	87	B4
Kraszewice	PL	86	A2
Kraszkowice	PL	86	A2
Kratigos	GR	186	C1
Kratovo	MK	182	A4
Kraubath	A	110	B1
Krausnick	D	74	B2
Krautheim	D	94	B1
Kravaře, Severočeský	CZ	84	B2
Kraváre, Severomoravsky			
Kravarsko	HR	124	B2
Kraznějov	CZ	96	B1
Krčedin	SRB	126	B2
Krefeld	D	80	A2
Kregme	DK	61	D2
Krembz	D	73	A4
Kremenets	UA	13	C6
Kremmen	D	74	B2
Kremna	SRB	127	D1
Kremnica	SK	98	C2
Krempe	D	64	C2
Krems	A	97	C3
Kremsbrücke	A	109	C4
Kremsmünster	A	110	A1
Křemže	CZ	96	C2
Křenov	CZ	97	B4
Krepa	PL	76	C3
Krępa Krajeńska	PL	75	A5
Krepsko	PL	68	B1
Kréševo	BIH	139	B4
Kressbronn	D	107	B4
Krestena	GR	184	B2
Kretinga	LT	8	E2
Krettsy	RUS	9	C8
Kreuth	D	108	B2
Kreuzau	D	80	B2
Kreuzlingen	CH	107	B4
Kreuztal	D	81	B4
Krewelin	D	74	B2
Krezluk	BIH	138	A3
Krichem	BG	183	A6
Krieglach	A	110	B2
Kriegsfeld	D	93	B3
Kriens	CH	106	B3
Krimml	A	108	B3
Krimpen aan de IJssel	NL	79	A4
Křinec	CZ	84	B3
Kristdala	S	62	A4
Kristiansand	N	53	B4
Kristianstad	S	61	C4
Kristiansund	N	198	B4
Kristiinankaupunki	FIN	8	A2
Kristinefors	S	49	B4
Kristinehamn	S	55	A5
Kriva Palanka	MK	182	A4
Kriváň	SK	99	C3
Křivoklát	CZ	96	A1
Križ	HR	124	B2
Križanov	CZ	97	B4
Križevci	HR	124	A2
Krk	HR	123	B3
Krka	SLO	123	B3
Krnjača	SRB	127	C2
Krnjak	HR	123	B4
Krnjeuša	BIH	124	C2
Krnjevo	SRB	127	C3
Krnov	CZ	98	A1
Krobia	PL	85	A4
Kroczyce	PL	86	B3
Krøderen	N	48	B1
Krokees	GR	184	C3
Krokek	S	56	B2
Krokom	S	199	B11
Krokowa	PL	68	A3
Krokstad-elva	N	53	A5
Kroksund	N	54	A2
Kroměříž	CZ	98	B1
Krommenie	NL	70	B1
Krompachy	SK	99	C4
Kronach	D	82	B3
Kronshagen	D	64	B3
Kronshtadt	RUS	9	C6
Kröpelin	D	65	B4
Kropp	D	64	B2
Kroppenstedt	D	73	C4
Kropstädt	D	74	C1
Krościenko nad Dunajcem	PL	99	B4
Kröslin	D	66	B2
Krośnice	PL	85	A5
Krośniewice	PL	77	B4
Krosno	PL	12	D4
Krosno Odrzańskie	PL	75	B4
Krostitz	D	83	A4
Krotoszyn	PL	85	A5
Krottendorf	A	110	B2
Krouna	CZ	97	B4
Krowiarki	PL	86	B2
Krrabë	AL	182	B1
Kršan	HR	123	B3
Krško	SLO	123	B4
Krstac	MNE	139	B4
Krstur	SRB	126	A2
Křtiny	CZ	97	B4
Kruft	D	80	B3
Kruishoutem	B	79	B3
Krujë	AL	182	B1
Krulyewshchyna	BY	13	A7
Krumbach	A	111	B3
Krumbach	D	94	C2
Krumovgrad	BG	183	B7
Krün	D	108	B2
Krupá	CZ	84	B1
Krupa na Vrbasu	BIH	124	C3
Krupanj	SRB	127	C1
Krupina	SK	99	C3
Krupka	CZ	84	B1
Krupki	BY	13	A8
Kruså	DK	64	B2
Kruščica	BIH	139	A3
Kruševac	SRB	16	D4
Kruševo	MK	182	B3
Kruszwica	PL	76	B3
Kruszyn	PL	77	B4
Krychaw	BY	13	B9
Krynica	PL	99	B4
Krynica Morska	PL	69	A4
Krzęcin	PL	75	A4
Krzelów	PL	85	A4
Krzepice	PL	86	B2
Krzepielów	PL	85	A4
Krzeszowice	PL	86	B3
Krzeszyce	PL	75	B4
Krzynowlaga Mała	PL	77	A5
Krzywiń	PL	75	C5
Krzyż Wielkopolski	PL	75	B5
Krzyżanowice	PL	98	B2
Krzyżowa	PL	99	B3
Ksiaz Wielkopolski, Małopolskie	PL	87	B4
Książ Wielkopolski, Wielkopolskie	PL	76	B2
Ktębowiec	PL	75	A5
Kübekháza	H	126	B2
Küblis	CH	107	C4
Kuchary	PL	86	A1
Kuchl	A	109	B4
Kucice	PL	77	B5
Kuciste	HR	138	C3
Kuçovë	AL	182	B1
Küçükbahçe	TR	188	A1
Küçükköy	TR	186	C1
Küçükkuyu	TR	186	C1
Kucura	SRB	126	B1
Kuczbork-Osada	PL	77	A5
Kudowa-Zdrój	PL	85	B4
Kufstein	A	108	B3
Kuggeboda	S	63	B3
Kuggörana	S	200	E3
Kühbach	D	95	C3
Kuhmo	FIN	3	D11
Kuhmoinen	FIN	8	B4
Kuhnsdorf	A	110	C1
Kuhstedt	D	72	A1
Kuinre	NL	70	B2
Kuivaniemi	FIN	197	D8
Kuivastu	EST	8	C3
Kukës	AL	182	A2
Kuklin	PL	77	A5
Kukljica	HR	137	A4
Kukujevci	SRB	127	B1
Kula, Srbija	SRB	127	C3
Kula, Vojvodina	SRB	126	B1
Kula	TR	188	A3
Kuldīga	LV	8	D2
Kulen Vakuf	BIH	124	C2
Kulina	BIH	125	C4
Kullstedt	D	82	A2
Kulmain	D	95	B3
Kulmbach	D	82	B3
Kuloharju	FIN	197	D11
Kulu	TR	23	B7
Kumachevo	RUS	69	A5
Kumafşarı	TR	189	B4
Kumane	SRB	126	B2
Kumanovo	MK	182	A3
Kumbağ	TR	186	B2
Kumdanlı	TR	189	A5
Kumkale	TR	186	C1
Kumla	S	56	A1
Kumlakyrkby	S	50	C3
Kumlinge	FIN	51	B7
Kumluca	TR	189	C5
Kumrovec	HR	123	A4
Kunadacs	H	112	C3
Kunágota	H	113	C5
Kunbaja	H	126	A1
Kunda	EST	8	C5
Kundl	A	108	B2
Kunes	N	193	B10
Kunfehértó	H	126	A1
Kungälv	S	60	B1
Kungs-Husby	S	56	A3
Kungsängen	S	57	A3
Kungsäter	S	60	B2
Kungsbacka	S	60	B2
Kungsgården	S	50	B3
Kungshamn	S	54	B2
Kungsör	S	56	A2
Kunhegyes	H	113	B4
Kunmadaras	H	113	B4
Kunovice	CZ	98	B1
Kunów	PL	87	B5
Kunowo, Wielkopolskie	PL	76	C2
Kunowo, Zachodnio-Pomorskie	PL	74	A3
Kunštát	CZ	97	B4
Kunszállás	H	113	C3
Kunszentmárton	H	113	C4
Kunszentmiklós	H	112	B3
Kunžak	CZ	97	B3
Künzelsau	D	94	B1
Kuolayarvi	RUS	197	C12
Kuolio	FIN	197	D11
Kuopio	FIN	8	A5
Kuosku	FIN	197	B11
Kup	H	111	B4
Kup	PL	86	B1
Kupferzell	D	94	B1
Kupinec	HR	123	B4
Kupinečki Kraljevac	HR	124	B1
Kupinovo	SRB	127	C2
Kupirovo	HR	138	A2
Kupjak	HR	123	B3
Kuppenheim	D	93	C4
Kupres	BIH	138	B3
Küps	D	82	B3
Kurd	H	112	C2
Kürdzhali	BG	183	B7
Küre	TR	23	A7
Kuressaare	EST	8	C3
Kurikka	FIN	8	A3
Kuřim	CZ	97	B4
Kuřivody	CZ	84	B2
Kurki	PL	77	A5
Kurort Oberwiesenthal	D	83	B4
Kurort Schmalkalden	D	82	B2
Kurort Stolberg	D	82	A2
Kurort Wippra	D	82	A3
Kurów	PL	12	C5
Kurowice	PL	86	A3
Kurravaara	S	196	B3
Kuršėnai	LT	8	E2
Kurşunlu, Bursa	TR	187	B4
Kurşunlu, Çankırı	TR	23	A7
Kurtakko	FIN	196	B7
Kurten	D	80	A3
Kurucaşile	TR	187	A7
Kurvinen	FIN	197	D12
Kusadak	SRB	127	C2
Kuşadası	TR	188	B2
Kusel	D	93	B3
Küsnacht	CH	106	B3
Kütahya	TR	187	C4
Kutenholz	D	72	A2
Kutina	HR	124	B2
Kutjevo	HR	125	B3
Kutná Hora	CZ	97	B3
Kutno	PL	77	B4
Kuttara	FIN	193	D10
Küttingen	CH	106	B3
Kuvshinovo	RUS	9	D9
Kuyucak	TR	188	B3
Kuzmin	SRB	127	B1
Kuźnia Raciborska	PL	86	B2
Kuźnica Czarnkowska	PL	75	B5
Kuźnica Żelichowska	PL	75	B5
Kvænangsbotn	N	192	C6
Kværndrup	DK	59	C3
Kvaløysletta	N	192	C2
Kvalsund	N	192	B7
Kvam, Nord-Trøndelag	N	199	A8
Kvam, Oppland	N	198	D6
Kvamsøy	N	46	A3
Kvanndal	N	46	B3
Kvänum	S	55	B4
Kvås	N	52	B3
Kvasice	CZ	98	B1
Kvelde	N	53	A5
Kvenna	N	198	C5
Kvernaland	N	52	B1
Kvicksund	S	56	A2
Kvidinge	S	61	C3
Kvikkjokk	S	195	D8
Kvikne, Hedmark	N	199	C7
Kvikne, Oppland	N	47	A6
Kvilda	CZ	96	B1
Kville	S	54	B2
Kvillsfors	S	62	A3
Kvinesdal	N	52	B2
Kvinlog	N	52	B2
Kvinnherad	N	46	C3
Kvissel	DK	58	A3
Kvissleby	S	200	D3
Kviteseid	N	53	A4
Kvitsøy	N	52	A1
Kwakowo	PL	68	A2
Kwidzyn	PL	69	B3
Kwilcz	PL	75	B5
Kyjov	CZ	98	C1
Kyle of Lochalsh	GB	31	B3
Kyleakin	GB	31	B3
Kylerhea	GB	31	B3
Kylestrome	GB	32	C1
Kyllburg	D	92	A2
Kyllini	GR	184	B2
Kynšperk nad Ohří	CZ	83	B4
Kyperounda	CY	181	B1
Kyrenia	CY	181	A2
Kyritz	D	73	B5
Kyrkesund	S	60	A1
Kyrkhult	S	63	B2
Kyrksæterøra	N	198	B6
Kysucké Nové Mesto	SK	98	B2
Kythira	GR	184	C3
Kythréa	CY	181	A2
Kyustendil	BG	16	D5
Kyyiv = Kiev	UA	13	C9
Kyyjärvi	FIN	8	A4

L

La Adrada	E	150	B3
La Alameda	E	157	B4
La Alberca	E	149	B3
La Alberca de Záncara	E	158	B1
La Albergueria de Argañán	E	149	B3
La Albuera	E	155	C4
La Aldea del Portillo del Busto	E	143	B3
La Algaba	E	162	A1
La Aliseda de Tormes	E	150	B2
La Almarcha	E	158	B1
La Almolda	E	153	A3
La Almunia de Doña Godina	E	152	A2
La Antillas	E	161	B2
La Arena	E	141	A4
La Aulaga	E	161	B3
La Balme-de-Sillingy	F	118	B3
La Bañeza	E	141	B5
La Barca de la Florida	E	162	B2
La Barre-de-Monts	F	114	B1
La Barre-en-Ouche	F	89	B4
La Barrosa	E	162	B1
La Barthe-de-Neste	F	145	A4
La Bassée	F	78	B2
La Bastide-de-Sèrou	F	146	A2
La Bastide-des-Jourdans	F	132	B1
La Bathie	F	118	B3
La Bazoche-Gouet	F	102	A2
La Bégude-de-Mazenc	F	131	A3
La Bernerie-en-Retz	F	114	A1
La Bisbal d'Empordà	E	147	C4
La Boissière	F	89	A4
La Bourboule	F	116	B2
La Bóveda de Toro	E	150	A2
La Brède	F	128	B2
La Bresse	F	106	A1
La Bridoire	F	118	B2
La Brillanne	F	132	B1
La Bruffière	F	114	A2
La Bussière	F	103	B4
La Caillère	F	114	B3
La Caletta, Cágliari	I	179	C2
La Caletta, Núoro	I	178	B3
La Calmette	F	131	B3
La Calzada de Oropesa	E	150	C2
La Campana	E	162	A2
La Cañada	E	150	B3
La Canourgue	F	130	A2
La Capelle	F	91	B3
La Cardanchosa	E	156	B2
La Caridad	E	141	A4
La Carlota	E	162	A3
La Carolina	E	157	B4
La Cava	E	153	B4
La Cavalerie	F	130	A2
La Celle-en-Moravan	F	104	B3
La Celle-St.-Avant	F	102	B2
La Cerca	E	143	B3
La Chaise-Dieu	F	117	B3
La Chaize-Giraud	F	114	B2
La Chaize-le-Vicomte	F	114	B2
La Chambre	F	118	B3
La Chapelaude	F	116	A2
La Chapelle-d'Angillon	F	103	B4
La Chapelle-en-Aalgaudémar	F	118	C3
La Chapelle-en-Vercors	F	118	C2
La Chapelle-Glain	F	101	B4
La Chapelle-la-Reine	F	90	C2
La Chapelle-Laurent	F	116	B3
La Chapelle-St.-Luc	F	91	C4
La Chapelle-sur-Erdre	F	101	B4
La Chapelle-Vicomtesse	F	103	B3
La Charce	F	132	A1
La Charité-sur-Loire	F	104	B2
La Chartre-sur-le-Loir	F	102	B2
La Châtaigneraie	F	114	B3
La Châtre	F	103	C3
La Chaussée-sur-Marne	F	91	C4
La Chaux-de-Fonds	CH	106	B1
La Cheppe	F	91	B4
La Chèze	F	101	A3
La Ciotat	F	132	B1
La Clayette	F	117	A4
La Clusaz	F	118	B3
La Codosera	E	155	B3
La Concha	E	143	A3
La Condamine-Châtelard	F	132	A2
La Contienda	E	161	A3
La Coquille	F	115	C4
La Coronada	E	156	B2
La Côte-St.-André	F	118	B2
La Cotinière	F	114	C2
La Courtine	F	116	B2
La Crau	F	132	B2
La Crèche	F	115	B3
La Croix	F	102	B2
La Croix-Valmer	F	132	B2
La Cumbre	E	156	A2
La Douze	F	129	A3
La Espina	E	141	A4
La Estrella	E	156	A2
La Farga de Moles	E	146	B2
La Fatarella	E	153	A4
La Felipa	E	158	B2
La Fère	F	90	B3
La Ferrière, Indre-et-Loire	F	102	B2
La Ferrière, Vendée	F	114	B2
La Ferrière-en-Parthenay	F	115	B3
La Ferté-Alais	F	90	C2
La Ferté-Bernard	F	102	A2
La Ferté-Frênel	F	89	B4
La Ferté-Gaucher	F	90	C3
La Ferté-Imbault	F	103	B3
La Ferté-Macé	F	89	B3
La Ferté-Milon	F	90	B3

Name		Page	Grid
La Ferté-St. Aubin	F	103	B3
La Ferté-St.Cyr	F	103	B3
La Ferté-sous-Jouarre	F	90	C3
La Ferté-Vidame	F	89	B4
La Ferté Villeneuil	F	103	B3
La Feuillie	F	90	B1
La Flèche	F	102	B1
La Flotte	F	114	B2
La Font de la Figuera	F	159	C3
La Fouillade	F	130	A1
La Fregeneda	E	149	B3
La Fresneda	E	153	B4
La Fuencubierta	E	162	A3
La Fuente de San Esteban	E	149	B3
La Fulioala	E	147	C2
La Gacilly	F	101	B3
La Galera	E	153	B4
La Garde-Freinet	F	132	B2
La Garnache	F	114	B2
La Garriga	E	147	C3
La Garrovilla	E	155	C4
La Gaubretière	F	114	B2
La Gineta	E	158	B1
La Granadella, *Alicante*	E	159	C4
La Granadella, *Lleida*	E	153	A4
La Grand-Combe	F	131	A3
La Grande-Croix	F	117	B4
La Grande-Motte	F	131	B3
La Granja d'Escarp	E	153	A4
La Granjuela	E	156	B2
La Grave	F	118	B3
La Gravelle	F	101	A4
La Guardia	E	151	C4
La Guardia de Jaén	E	163	A4
La Guerche-de-Bretagne	F	101	B4
La Guerche-sur-l'Aubois	F	104	C1
La Guérinière	F	114	B1
La Haba	E	156	B2
La Haye-du-Puits	F	88	A2
La Haye-Pesnel	F	88	B2
La Herlière	F	78	B2
La Hermida	E	142	A2
La Herrera	E	158	C1
La Higuera	E	158	C1
La Hiniesta	E	149	A4
La Horcajada	E	150	B2
La Horra	E	143	C3
La Hulpe	B	79	B4
La Hutte	F	89	B4
La Iglesuela	E	150	B3
La Iglesuela del Cid	E	153	B3
La Iruela	E	164	B2
La Javie	F	132	A2
La Jonchère-St. Maurice	F	116	A1
La Jonquera	E	146	B3
La Lantejuela	E	162	A2
La Línea de la Concepción	E	162	B2
La Llacuna	E	147	C2
La Londe-les-Maures	F	132	B2
La Loupe	F	89	B5
La Louvière	B	79	B4
La Luisiana	E	162	A2
La Machine	F	104	C2
la Maddalena	I	178	A3
La Mailleraye-sur-Seine	F	89	A4
La Malène	F	130	A2
La Mamola	E	163	B4
La Manresana dels Prats	E	147	C2
La Masadera	E	145	C3
La Mata	E	150	C3
La Mata de Ledesma	E	149	A4
La Mata de Monteagudo	E	142	B1
La Meilleraye-de-Bretagne	F	101	B4
La Ménitré	F	102	B1
La Mojonera	E	164	C2
La Mole	F	132	B2
La Molina	E	147	B2
La Monnerie-le-Montel	F	117	B3
La Morera	E	155	C4
La Mothe-Achard	F	114	B2
La Mothe-St.Héray	F	115	B3
La Motte-Chalançon	F	131	A4
La Motte-du-Caire	F	132	A2
La Motte-Servolex	F	118	B2
La Mudarra	E	142	C2
La Muela	E	152	A2
La Mure	F	118	C2
La Nava	E	161	B3
La Nava de Ricomalillo	E	156	A3
La Nava de Santiago	E	155	B3
La Neuve-Lyre	F	89	B4
La Neuveville	CH	106	B2
La Nocle-Maulaix	F	104	C2
La Nuez de Arriba	E	143	B3
La Paca	E	164	B3
La Pacaudière	F	117	A3
La Palma d'Ebre	E	153	A4
La Palma del Condado	E	161	B3
La Palme	F	146	B4
La Palmyre	F	114	C2
La Parra	E	155	C4
La Pedraja de Portillo	E	150	A3
La Peraleja	E	152	B1
La Petit-Pierre	F	93	C3
La Pinilla	E	165	B3
La Plagne	F	118	B3
La Plaza	E	141	A4
La Pobla de Lillet	E	147	B3
La Pobla de Vallbona	E	159	B3
La Pobla Llarga	E	159	B3
La Pola de Gordón	E	142	B1
la Porta	F	180	A2
La Pouëze	F	102	B1
La Póveda de Soria	E	143	B4
La Preste	F	146	B3
La Primaube	F	130	A1
La Puebla de Almoradie	E	157	A4
La Puebla de Cazalla	E	162	A2
La Puebla de los Infantes	E	162	A2
La Puebla de Montalbán	E	150	C3
La Puebla de Roda	E	145	B4
La Puebla de Valdavia	E	142	B2
La Puebla de Valverde	E	152	B3
La Puebla del Río	E	162	A1
La Pueblanueva	E	150	C3
La Puerta de Segura	E	164	A2
La Punt	CH	107	C4
La Quintana	E	162	A3
La Quintera	E	162	A2
La Rábita, *Granada*	E	164	C1
La Rábita, *Jaén*	E	163	A4
La Rambla	E	163	A3
La Reale	I	178	A2
La Redondela	E	161	B2
La Réole	F	128	B2
La Riera	E	141	A4
La Riera de Gaià	E	147	C2
La Rinconada	E	162	A1
La Rivière-Thibouville	F	89	A4
La Robla	E	142	B1
La Roca de la Sierra	E	155	B4
La Roche	CH	106	C2
La Roche-Bernard	F	101	B3
La Roche-Canillac	F	116	B1
La Roche-Chalais	F	128	A3
La Roche-Derrien	F	100	A2
La Roche-des-Arnauds	F	132	A1
La Roche-en-Ardenne	B	80	B1
La Roche-en-Brénil	F	104	B3
La Roche-Guyon	F	90	B1
La Roche-Posay	F	115	B4
La Roche-sur-Foron	F	118	A3
La Roche-sur-Yon	F	114	B2
La Rochebeaucourt-et-Argentine	F	115	C4
La Rochefoucauld	F	115	C4
La Rochelle	F	114	B2
La Rochette	F	131	A4
La Roda, *Albacete*	E	158	B1
La Roda, *Oviedo*	E	141	A4
La Roda de Andalucía	E	162	A3
La Roque-Gageac	F	129	B4
La Roque-Ste.Marguerite	F	130	A2
La Roquebrussanne	F	132	B1
La Rubia	E	143	C4
La Sagrada	E	149	B3
La Salceda	E	151	A4
La Salle	F	118	C3
la Salute di Livenza	I	122	B1
La Salvetat-Peyralés	F	130	A1
La Salvetat-sur-Agout	F	130	B1
La Sarraz	CH	105	C5
La Seca	E	150	A3
La Selva del Camp	E	147	C2
La Senia	E	153	B4
La Serra	E	147	C2
La Seu d'Urgell	E	146	B2
La Seyne-sur-Mer	F	132	B1
La Solana	E	157	B4
La Souterraine	F	116	A1
La Spézia	I	134	A2
La Storta	I	168	B2
La Suze-sur-Sarthe	F	102	B2
La Teste	F	128	B1
La Thuile	I	119	B3
La Toba	E	152	B2
La Toledana	E	157	A3
La Torre de Cabdella	E	146	B1
La Torre de Esteban Hambrán	E	151	B3
La Torre del l'Espanyol	E	153	A4
La Torresaviñán	E	152	B1
La Tour d'Aigues	F	132	B1
La Tour de Peilz	CH	106	C1
La Tour-du-Pin	F	118	B2
La Tranche-sur-Mer	F	114	B2
La Tremblade	F	114	C2
La Trimouille	F	115	B5
La Trinité	F	100	B2
La Trinité-Porhoët	F	101	A3
La Turballe	F	101	B3
La Uña	E	142	A1
La Unión	E	165	B4
La Vall d'Uixó	E	159	B3
La Vecilla de Curueño	E	142	B1
La Vega, *Asturias*	E	142	A1
La Vega, *Asturias*	E	141	A5
La Vega, *Cantabria*	E	142	A2
La Velilla	E	151	A4
La Velles	E	150	A2
La Ventosa	E	152	B1
La Victoria	E	162	A3
La Vid	E	151	A4
La Vilavella	E	159	B3
La Vilella Baixa	E	147	C1
La Villa de Don Fadrique	E	157	A4
La Ville Dieu-du-Temple	F	129	B4
La Villedieu	F	115	B3
La Voulte-sur-Rhône	F	117	C4
La Wantzenau	F	93	C3
La Yesa	E	159	B3
La Zubia	E	163	A4
Laa an der Thaya	A	97	C4
Laage	D	65	C5
Laanila	FIN	193	D11
Laatzen	D	72	B2
Laban	IRL	28	A3
Labastide-Murat	F	129	B4
Labastide-Rouairoux	F	130	B1
Labastide-St.Pierre	F	129	C4
Lábatlan	H	112	B2
Labenne	F	128	C1
Labin	HR	123	B3
Łabiszyn	PL	76	B2
Lablachère	F	131	A3
Łábod	H	124	A3
Laboe	D	64	B3
Labouheyre	F	128	B2
Łabowa	PL	99	B4
Labrit	F	128	B2
Labros	E	152	A2
Labruguière	F	130	B1
Labrujo	P	148	A1
L'Absie	F	114	B3
Laç	AL	182	B1
Lacalahorra	E	164	B1
Lacanau	F	128	B1
Lacanau-Océan	F	128	B1
Lacanche	F	104	B3
Lacapelle-Marival	F	129	B4
Láčarak	SRB	127	B1
Lacaune	F	130	B1
Laceby	GB	41	B3
Lacedónia	I	172	A1
Láces	I	108	C1
Lachania	GR	188	D2
Lachen	CH	107	B3
Lachendorf	D	72	B3
Lachowice	PL	99	B3
Łąck	PL	77	B4
Läckeby	S	62	B4
Läckö	S	55	B4
Lacock	GB	43	A4
Láconi	I	179	C3
Lacq	F	145	A3
Lacroix-Barrez	F	116	C2
Lacroix-St. Ouen	F	90	B2
Lacroix-sur-Meuse	F	92	C1
Łącznik	PL	86	B1
Lad	H	125	A3
Ladbergen	D	71	B4
Lądek-Zdrój	PL	85	B4
Ladelund	D	64	B2
Ladendorf	A	97	C4
Ladignac-le-Long	F	115	C5
Ladíspoli	I	168	B2
Ladoeiro	P	155	B3
Ladon	F	103	B4
Ladushkin	RUS	69	A5
Ladybank	GB	35	B4
Laer	D	71	B4
Lærdalsøyri	N	47	A4
Læfkos	GR	183	D5
Lafnitz	A	111	B3
Lafrançaise	F	129	B4
Lagan	S	60	C3
Laganadi	I	175	C1
Lagarde	F	146	A2
Lagares, *Coimbra*	P	148	B2
Lagares, *Porto*	P	148	A1
Lagaro	I	135	A4
Lagartera	E	150	C2
Lage	D	72	C1
Lägerdorf	D	64	C2
Lagg	GB	34	C2
Laggan	GB	32	D2
Laggartorp	S	55	A5
Łagiewniki	PL	85	B4
Láglio	I	120	B2
Lagnieu	F	118	B2
Lagny-sur-Marne	F	90	C2
Lago, *Calabria*	I	175	B2
Lago, *Veneto*	I	121	B5
Lagonegro	I	174	A1
Lagos	GR	183	B7
Lagos	P	160	B1
Lagosanto	I	121	C5
Łagów, *Lubuskie*	PL	75	B4
Łagów, *Świętokrzyskie*	PL	87	B5
Lagrasse	F	146	A3
Laguardia	E	143	B4
Laguarres	E	145	B4
Laguenne	F	116	B1
Laguépie	F	129	B4
Laguiole	F	116	C2
Laguna de Duera	E	150	A3
Laguna de Negrillos	E	142	B1
Laguna del Marquesado	E	152	B2
Lagundo	I	108	C2
Lagunilla	E	149	B3
Laharie	F	128	B1
Lahden	D	71	B4
Laheycourt	F	91	C5
Lahnstein	D	81	B3
Laholm	S	61	C3
Lahr	D	93	C3
Lahti	FIN	8	B4
Laichingen	D	94	C1
L'Aigle	F	89	B4
Laignes	F	104	B3
Laiguéglia	I	133	B4
Laimbach am Ostrong	A	97	C3
Laina	E	152	A1
Lainio	S	196	B5
Lairg	GB	32	C2
Laissac	F	130	A1
Laisvall	S	195	D8
Láives	I	121	A4
Lajkovac	SRB	127	C2
Lajoskomárom	H	112	C2
Lajosmizse	H	112	B3
Lak	H	99	C4
Lakenheath	GB	45	A4
Lakitelek	H	113	C4
Lakki	GR	185	D4
Lakolk	DK	64	A1
Łąkorz	PL	69	B4
Lakšárska Nová Ves	SK	98	C1
Lakselv	N	193	B8
Laksfors	N	195	E4
Laktaši	BIH	124	B3
Lalapaşa	TR	186	A1
L'Albagès	E	153	A4
L'Alcudia	E	159	B3
L'Aldea	E	153	B4
Lalín	E	140	B2
Lalinde	F	129	B3
Lalizolle	F	116	A3
Lalley	F	118	C2
Lalling	D	95	C4
Lalm	N	198	D6
Laluque	F	128	C1
Lam	D	95	B4
Lama dei Peligni	I	169	A4
Lama Mocogno	I	135	A3
Lamadrid	E	142	A2
Lamagistère	F	129	B3
Lamarche	F	105	A4
Lamarche-sur-Saône	F	105	B4
Lamargelle	F	105	B3
Lamarosa	P	154	B2
Lamarque	F	128	A2
Lamas	P	148	B1
Lamas de Moaro	P	140	B2
Lamastre	F	117	C4
Lambach	A	109	A4
Lamballe	F	101	A3
Lamberhurst	GB	45	B4
Lambesc	F	131	B4
Lambia	GR	184	B2
Lambley	GB	37	B4
Lambourn	GB	44	B2
Lamego	P	148	A2
L'Ametlla de Mar	E	153	B4
Lamia	GR	182	E4
Lammhult	S	62	A2
Lamothe-Cassel	F	129	B4
Lamothe-Montravel	F	128	B3
Lamotte-Beuvron	F	103	B4
Lampertheim	D	93	B4
Lampeter	GB	39	B2
L'Ampolla	E	153	B4
Lamprechtshausen	A	109	B3
Lamsfeld	D	74	C3
Lamspringe	D	72	C3
Lamstedt	D	72	A2
Lamure-sur-Azergues	F	117	A4
Lana	I	108	C2
Lanaja	E	145	C3
Lanarce	F	117	C3
Lanark	GB	36	A3
Lancaster	GB	37	B4
Lanchester	GB	37	B5
Lanciano	I	169	A4
Lancing	GB	44	C3
Lançon-Provence	F	131	B4
Lancova Vas	SLO	124	A1
Landau, *Bayern*	D	95	C4
Landau, *Rheinland-Pfalz*	D	93	B4
Landeck	A	108	B1
Landen	B	79	B5
Landerneau	F	100	A1
Landeryd	S	60	B3
Landesbergen	D	72	B2
Landete	E	158	B2
Landévant	F	100	B2
Landévennec	F	100	A1
Landivisiau	F	100	A1
Landivy	F	88	B2
Landl	A	108	B3
Landön	S	199	B11
Landos	F	117	C3
Landouzy-le-Ville	F	91	B4
Landquart	CH	107	C4
Landrecies	F	91	A3
Landreville	F	104	A3
Landriano	I	120	B2
Lands-berg	D	83	A4
Landsberg	D	108	A1
Landsbro	S	62	A2
Landscheid	D	92	B2
Landshut	D	95	C4
Landskrona	S	61	D2
Landstuhl	D	93	B3
Lanesborough	IRL	28	A4
Lanester	F	100	B2
Lanestosa	E	143	A3
Langå	DK	59	B2
Langa de Duero	E	151	A4
Langada	GR	185	A7
Langadas	GR	183	C5
Langadia	GR	184	B3
Langangen	N	53	A5
Långared	S	60	A2
Långaröd	S	61	D3
Långaryd	S	60	B3
Långås	S	60	C2
Långasjö	S	63	B3
Langau	A	97	C3
Langeac	F	117	B3
Langeais	F	102	B2
Langedijk	NL	70	B1
Langeln	D	73	C3
Langelsheim	D	72	C3
Langemark-Poelkapelle	B	78	B2
Langen, *Hessen*	D	93	B4
Langen, *Niedersachsen*	D	72	A1
Langenau	D	94	C2
Langenberg	D	81	A4
Langenbruck	D	106	B2
Langenburg	D	94	B1
Längenfeld	A	108	B1
Langenfeld	D	80	A2
Langenhorn	D	64	B1
Langenlois	A	97	C3
Langenlonsheim	D	93	B3
Langennaudorf	D	83	A5
Langenneufnach	D	94	C2
Langenthal	CH	106	B2
Langenzenn	D	94	B2
Langeoog	D	71	A4
Langeskov	DK	59	C3
Langesund	N	53	A5
Langewiesen	D	82	B2
Långflon	S	49	A4
Långförden	D	71	B5
Langhagen	D	73	A5
Länghem	S	60	B3
Langhirano	I	120	C3
Langholm	GB	36	A4
Langholt	IS	191	D7
Långlöt	S	62	B4
Langnau	CH	106	C2
Langø	DK	65	B4
Langogne	F	117	C3
Langon	F	128	B2
Langquaid	D	95	C4
Långrådna	S	56	B2
Langreo	E	142	A1
Langres	F	105	B4
Långsele	S	200	C3
Långserud	S	54	A3
Langset	N	48	B3
Langstrand	N	192	B7
Långträsk	S	196	D3
Langueux	F	101	A3
Languidic	F	100	B2
Längvik	S	57	A4
Langwarden	D	71	A5
Langwathby	GB	37	B4
Langwedel	D	72	B2
Langweid	D	94	C2
Langwies	CH	107	C4
Lanheses	P	148	A1
Lanięta	PL	77	B4
Lanildut	F	100	A1
Lanjarón	E	163	B4
Lanmeur	F	100	A2
Lanna, *Jönköping*	S	60	B3
Lanna, *Örebro*	S	55	A5
Lännaholm	S	51	C4
Lannavaara	S	196	A4
Lannéanou	F	100	A2
Lannemezan	F	145	A4
Lanneuville-sur-Meuse	F	91	B5
Lannilis	F	100	A1
Lannion	F	100	A2
Lanouaille	F	115	C5
Lansjärv	S	196	C5
Lanškroun	CZ	97	B4
Lanslebourg-Mont-Cenis	F	119	B3
Lanta	F	129	C4
Lantadilla	E	142	B2
Lanton	F	128	B1
Lantosque	F	133	B3
Lanusei	I	179	C3
Lanúvio	I	168	B2
Lanvollon	F	100	A3
Lánycsók	H	125	A4
Lanz	D	73	A4
Lanza	E	140	A2
Lanzada	E	140	B2
Lanzahita	E	150	B3
Lanžhot	CZ	97	C4
Lanzo Torinese	I	119	B4
Laole	SRB	127	C3
Laon	F	91	B3
Laons	F	89	B5
Lapalisse	F	117	A3
Łapczyna Wola	PL	87	B3
Lapeyrade	F	128	B2
Lapeyrouse	F	116	A2
Lapford	GB	42	B3
Lapithos	CY	181	A2
Laplume	F	129	B3
Lapoutroie	F	106	A2
Lapovo	SRB	127	C3
Läppe	S	56	A1
Lappeenranta	FIN	8	B6
Lappoluobbal	N	192	C7
Lappträsk	S	196	C6
Lapseki	TR	186	B1
Lapua	FIN	8	A3
L'Áquila	I	169	A3
Laracha	E	140	A2
Laragh	IRL	30	A2
Laragne-Montéglin	F	132	A1
l'Arboç	E	147	C2
L'Arbresle	F	117	B4
Lärbro	S	57	C4
Larceveau	F	144	A2
Larche, *Alpes-de-Haute-Provence*	F	132	A2
Larche, *Corrèze*	F	129	A4
Lårdal	N	53	A4
Lardosa	P	155	B3
Laredo	E	143	A3
Largentière	F	131	A3
L'Argentière-la-Bessée	F	118	C3
Largs	GB	34	C3
Lari	I	134	B3
Lariño	E	140	B1
Larino	I	170	B2
Larisa	GR	182	D4
Larkhall	GB	35	C4
Larkollen	N	54	A1
Larmor-Plage	F	100	B2

Name		Page	Grid
Larnaca	CY	181	B2
Larne	GB	27	B5
Larochette	L	92	B2
Laroque d'Olmes	F	146	B2
Laroque-Timbaut	F	129	B3
Laroquebrou	F	116	C2
Larouco	E	141	B3
Larraga	E	144	B2
Larrau	F	144	A3
Larrazet	F	129	C4
Larsnes	N	198	C2
Laruns	F	145	A3
Larva	E	164	B1
Larvik	N	53	A6
Las Arenas	E	142	A2
Las Cabezadas	E	151	A4
Las Cabezas de San Juan	E	162	B2
Las Correderas	E	157	B4
Las Cuevas de Cañart	E	153	B3
Las Gabias	E	163	A4
Las Herencias	E	150	C3
Las Labores	E	157	A4
Las Mesas	E	158	B1
Las Minas	E	164	A3
Las Navas	E	163	A3
Las Navas de la Concepción	E	156	C2
Las Navas del Marqués	E	150	B3
Las Navillas	E	157	A3
Las Negras	E	164	C3
Las Pajanosas	E	161	B3
Las Pedroñas	E	158	B1
Las Planes d'Hostoles	E	147	B3
Las Rozas, *Cantabria*	E	142	B2
Las Rozas, *Madrid*	E	151	B4
Las Uces	E	149	A3
Las Veguillas	E	149	B4
Las Ventas con Peña Aguilera	E	157	A3
Las Ventas de San Julián	E	150	B2
Las Villes	E	153	B4
Lasalle	F	131	A2
Lasarte	E	144	A1
Låsby	DK	59	B2
Łasin	PL	69	B4
Lask	PL	86	A3
Laska	PL	68	B2
Łaskarzew	PL	87	A5
Laško	SLO	123	A4
Laskowice	PL	76	A3
Laspaules	E	145	B4
Laspuña	E	145	B4
Lassan	D	66	C2
Lassay-les-Châteaux	F	89	B3
Lasseube	F	145	A3
Lassigny	F	90	B2
Lastovo	HR	138	C2
Lastras de Cuéllar	E	151	A3
Lästringe	S	56	B3
Lastrup	D	71	B4
Latasa	E	144	B2
Látera	I	168	A1
Laterza	I	171	C4
Lathen	D	71	B4
Latheron	GB	32	C3
Latiano	I	173	B3
Latina	I	169	B2
Latisana	I	122	B2
Látky	SK	99	C3
Latrónico	I	174	A2
Latronquière	F	116	C2
Latterbach	CH	106	C2
Laubach	D	81	B4
Laubert	F	117	C3
Laucha	D	83	A3
Lauchhammer	D	84	A1
Lauchheim	D	94	C2
Lauda-Königshofen	D	94	B1
Laudal	N	52	B3
Lauder	GB	35	C5
Lauenau	D	72	B2
Lauenburg	D	73	A3
Lauf	D	95	B3
Laufach	D	94	B1
Laufen	CH	106	B2
Laufen	D	109	B3
Lauffen	D	93	B5
Laugar	IS	191	B8
Laugarás	IS	190	C5
Laugarbakki	IS	190	B5
Laugarvatn	IS	190	C5
Laugharne	GB	39	C2
Lauingen	D	94	C2
Laujar de Andarax	E	164	C2
Laukaa	FIN	8	A4
Lauker	S	196	D2
Laukvik	N	194	B5
Launceston	GB	42	B2
Launois-sur-Vence	F	91	B4
Laupheim	D	94	C1
Lauragh	IRL	29	C2
Laureana di Borrello	I	175	C2
Laurencekirk	GB	35	B5
Laurencetown	IRL	28	A3
Laurenzana	I	172	B1
Lauria	I	174	A1
Laurière	F	116	A1
Laurieston	GB	36	B2
Laurino	I	172	B1
Lausanne	CH	106	C1
Laussonne	F	117	C4
Lauta	D	84	A2
Lautenthal	D	82	A2
Lauterach	A	107	B4
Lauterbach	D	81	B5
Lauterbrunnen	CH	106	C2
Lauterecken	D	93	B3
Lauterhofen	D	95	B3
Lautrec	F	130	B1
Lauvsnes	N	199	A7
Lauvvlk	N	52	B2
Lauzerte	F	129	B4
Lauzès	F	129	B4
Lauzun	F	129	B3
Lavagna	I	134	A2
Laval	F	102	A1
Lavamünd	A	110	C1
Lavara	GR	186	A1
Lavardac	F	129	B3
Lavaris	P	148	B1
Lavarone	I	121	B4
Lavau	F	104	B1
Lavelanet	F	146	B2
Lavello	I	172	A1
Lavelsloh	D	72	B1
Lavenham	GB	45	A4
Laveno	I	120	B1
Lavezzola	I	135	A4
Laviano	I	172	B1
Lavik	N	46	A2
Lavilledieu	F	131	A3
Lavinio-Lido di Enea	I	168	B2
Lavis	I	121	A4
Lavit	F	129	C3
Lavoncourt	F	105	B4
Lavos	P	148	B1
Lavoûter-Chilhac	F	117	B3
Lavradio	P	154	C1
Lavre	P	154	C2
Lavrio	GR	185	B5
Lawers	GB	35	B3
Ławy	PL	75	B3
Laxå	S	55	B5
Laxamýri	IS	191	B8
Laxe	E	140	A2
Laxey	GB	36	B2
Laxford Bridge	GB	32	C1
Laxhall	S	55	B4
Laxsjö	S	199	B11
Laxtjarn	S	49	B6
Laxvik	S	61	C2
Laxviken	S	199	B11
Laza	E	141	B3
Lazarevac	SRB	127	C2
Lazarevo	SRB	126	B2
Lazise	I	121	B3
Łaziska Grn.	PL	86	B2
Lazkao	E	144	A1
Lázně Bělohrad	CZ	84	B3
Lázně Bohdaneč	CZ	97	A3
Lázně Kynžvart	CZ	95	A4
Lazonby	GB	37	B4
Łazy	PL	67	B5
Lazzaro	I	175	D1
Le Bar-sur-Loup	F	132	B2
Le Barp	F	128	B2
Le Béage	F	117	C4
Le Beausset	F	132	B1
Le Bessat	F	117	B4
Le Blanc	F	115	B5
Le Bleymard	F	130	A2
Le Boullay-Mivoye	F	89	B5
Le Boulou	F	146	B3
Le Bourg	F	129	B4
Le Bourg-d'Oisans	F	118	B3
Le Bourget-du-Lac	F	118	B2
Le Bourgneuf-la-Forêt	F	101	A5
Le Bousquet d'Orb	F	130	B2
Le Brassus	CH	105	C5
Le Breuil	F	117	A3
Le Breuil-en-Auge	F	89	A4
Le Brusquet	F	132	A2
Le Bry	CH	106	C2
Le Bugue	F	129	B3
Le Buisson	F	129	B3
Le Caloy	F	128	C2
Le Cap d'Agde	F	130	B2
Le Cateau Cambrésis	F	91	A3
Le Caylar	F	130	B2
Le Cayrol	F	116	C2
Le Chambon-Feugerolles	F	117	B4
Le Chambon-sur-Lignon	F	117	B4
Le Château d'Oléron	F	114	C2
Le Châtelard	F	118	B3
Le Châtelet	F	103	C4
Le Chatelet-en-Brie	F	90	C2
Le Chesne	F	91	B4
Le Cheylard	F	117	C4
Le Collet-de-Deze	F	131	A2
Le Conquet	F	100	A1
Le Creusot	F	104	C3
Le Croisic	F	101	B3
Le Crotoy	F	78	B1
Le Deschaux	F	105	C4
Le Donjon	F	117	A3
Le Dorat	F	115	B5
Le Faou	F	100	A1
Le Faoüet	F	100	A2
Le Folgoet	F	100	A1
Le Fossat	F	146	A2
Le Fousseret	F	146	A2
Le Fugeret	F	132	A2
Le Gault-Soigny	F	91	C3
Le Grand-Bornand	F	118	B3
Le-Grand-Bourg	F	116	A1
Le Grand-Lucé	F	102	B2
Le Grand-Pressigny	F	102	C2
Le Grand-Quevilly	F	89	A5
Le Grau-du-Roi	F	131	B3
Le Havre	F	89	A4
Le Hohwald	F	93	C3
Le Houga	F	128	C2
Le Lardin-St.-Lazare	F	129	A4
Le Lauzet-Ubaye	F	132	A2
Le Lavandou	F	132	B2
Le Lion-d'Angers	F	102	B1
Le Locle	CH	106	B1
Le Loroux-Bottereau	F	101	B4
Le Louroux-Béconnais	F	101	B5
Le Luc	F	132	B2
Le Lude	F	102	B2
Le Malzieu-Ville	F	116	C3
Le Mans	F	102	A2
Le Mas-d'Azil	F	146	A2
Le Massegros	F	130	A2
Le May-sur-Evre	F	101	B5
Le Mayet-de-Montagne	F	117	A3
Le Mêle-sur-Sarthe	F	89	B4
Le Ménil	F	105	A5
Le Merlerault	F	89	B4
Le Mesnil-sur-Oger	F	91	C4
Le Miroir	F	105	C4
Le Molay-Littry	F	88	A3
Le Monastier-sur-Gazeille	F	117	C3
Le Monêtier-les-Bains	F	118	C3
Le Mont-Dore	F	116	B2
Le Mont-St.-Michel	F	88	B2
Le Montet	F	116	A3
Le Muret	F	128	B2
Le Muy	F	132	B2
Le Neubourg	F	89	A4
Le Nouvion-en-Thiérache	F	91	A3
Le Palais	F	100	B2
Le Parcq	F	78	B2
Le Péage-de-Roussillon	F	117	B4
Le Pellerin	F	101	B4
Le Perthus	F	146	B3
Le Pertuis	F	117	B4
Le Petit-Bornand	F	118	B3
Le Poët	F	132	A1
Le Poirè-sur-Vie	F	114	B2
Le Pont-de-Montvert	F	130	A2
Le Porge	F	128	B1
Le Porge-Océan	F	128	B1
Le Portel	F	78	B1
Le Pouldu	F	100	B2
Le Pouliguen	F	101	B3
le Prese	I	120	A3
Le Puy-en-Velay	F	117	B3
Le Puy-Ste.-Réparade	F	131	B4
Le Quesnoy	F	79	B3
Le Rayol	F	132	B2
Le Rœulx	B	79	B4
Le Rouget	F	116	C2
Le Rozier	F	130	A2
Le Russey	F	106	B1
Le Sel-de-Bretagne	F	101	B4
Le Sentier	CH	105	C5
Le Souquet	F	128	C1
Le Teil	F	131	A3
Le Teilleul	F	88	B3
Le Temple-de-Bretagne	F	101	B4
Le Theil	F	89	B4
Le Thillot	F	106	B1
Le Touquet-Paris-Plage	F	78	B1
Le Touvet	F	118	B2
Le Translay	F	90	B1
Le Tréport	F	90	A1
Le Val	F	132	B2
Le Val-André	F	101	A3
Le Val-d'Ajol	F	105	B5
Le Verdon-sur-Mer	F	114	C2
Le Vernet	F	132	A2
Le Vigan	F	130	B2
le Ville	I	135	B2
Le Vivier-sur-Mer	F	88	B2
Lea	GB	40	B3
Leadburn	GB	35	C4
Leadhills	GB	36	A3
Leap	IRL	29	C2
Leatherhead	GB	44	B3
Łeba	PL	68	A2
Lebach	D	92	B2
Lebekke	B	79	A4
Lébény	H	111	B4
Leberoiro	E	140	B3
Lębork	PL	68	A2
Lebrija	E	162	B1
Lebring	A	110	C2
Lebus	D	74	B3
Lebusa	D	83	A5
Leca da Palmeira	P	148	A1
Lecce	I	173	B4
Lecco	I	120	B2
Lécera	E	153	A3
Lećevica	HR	138	B2
Lech	A	107	B5
Lechbruck	D	108	B1
Lechena	GR	184	B2
Lechlade	GB	44	B2
Lechovice	CZ	97	C4
Leciñena	E	145	C3
Leck	D	64	B1
Lectoure	F	129	C3
Łęczyca, *Łódzkie*	PL	77	B4
Łęczyca, *Zachodnio-Pomorskie*	PL	75	A4
Ledaña	E	158	B2
Ledbury	GB	39	B4
Lede	B	79	B3
Ledeč nad Sazavou	CZ	97	B3
Ledenice	CZ	96	C2
Ledesma	E	149	A3
Lédignan	F	131	B3
Lédigos	E	142	B2
Ledmore	GB	32	C2
Lednice	CZ	97	C4
Lednicke-Rovné	SK	98	B2
Lędyczek	PL	68	B1
Lędziny	PL	86	B3
Leeds	GB	40	B2
Leek	GB	40	B1
Leek	NL	71	A3
Leenaun	IRL	28	A2
Leens	NL	71	A3
Leer	D	71	A4
Leerdam	NL	79	A5
Leerhafe	D	71	A4
Leese	D	72	B2
Leeuwarden	NL	70	A2
Leezen	D	64	C3
Lefka	CY	181	A1
Lefkada	GR	182	E2
Lefkimis	GR	182	D2
Lefkoniko	CY	181	A2
Leganés	E	151	B4
Legau	D	107	B5
Legbąd	PL	68	B2
Legé	F	114	B2
Lège-Cap-Ferret	F	128	B1
Legionowo	PL	77	B5
Léglise	B	92	B1
Legnago	I	121	B4
Legnano	I	120	B1
Legnaro	I	121	B4
Legnica	PL	85	A4
Łęgowo	PL	69	A3
Legrad	HR	124	B2
Léguevin	F	129	C4
Legutiano	E	143	B4
Lehesten	D	82	B3
Lehnice	SK	111	A4
Lehnin	D	74	B1
Lehrberg	D	94	B2
Lehre	D	73	B3
Lehrte	D	72	B2
Lehsen	D	73	A3
Leibnitz	A	110	C2
Leicester	GB	40	C2
Leiden	NL	70	B1
Leidschendam	NL	70	B1
Leigh	GB	38	A4
Leighlinbridge	IRL	30	B2
Leighton Buzzard	GB	44	B3
Leignon	B	79	B5
Leikanger	N	198	C2
Leimen	D	93	B4
Leinefelde	D	82	A2
Leinesfjord	N	194	C6
Leintwardine	GB	39	B4
Leipojärvi	S	196	B4
Leipzig	D	83	A4
Leira, *Nordland*	N	195	D4
Leira, *Oppland*	N	47	B6
Leiråmoen	N	195	D5
Leiria	P	154	B2
Leirvassbu	N	47	A5
Leirvik, *Hordaland*	N	52	A1
Leirvik, *Sogn og Fjordane*	N	46	A2
Leisach	A	109	C3
Leisnig	D	83	A4
Leiston	GB	45	A5
Leitholm	GB	35	C5
Leitrim	IRL	26	C2
Leitza	E	144	A2
Leitzkau	D	73	B4
Lejkowo	PL	68	A1
Lekani	GR	183	B6
Łękawa	PL	86	A3
Łękawica	PL	99	B3
Lekeitio	E	143	A4
Lekenik	HR	124	B2
Lekeryd	S	62	A2
Leknes	N	194	B5
Leknica	PL	84	A2
Leksand	S	50	B1
Leksvik	N	199	B7
Lekunberri	E	144	A2
Lekvattnet	S	49	B4
Lelkowo	PL	69	A5
Lelów	PL	86	B3
Lelystad	NL	70	B2
Lem, *Ringkøbing*	DK	59	B1
Lem, *Viborg Amt.*	DK	58	B1
Lembach	F	93	B3
Lemberg	F	93	B3
Lembèye	F	145	A3
Lemelerveld	NL	71	B3
Lemförde	D	71	B5
Lemgo	D	72	B1
Lemland	FIN	51	B7
Lemmer	NL	70	B2
Lempdes	F	116	B3
Lemvig	DK	58	B1
Lemwerder	D	72	A1
Lena	N	48	B2
Lenart	SLO	110	C2
Lenartovce	SK	99	C4
Lenauheim	RO	126	B2
Lencloître	F	102	C2
Lend	A	109	B4
Lendalfoot	GB	36	A2
Lendava	SLO	111	C3
Lendery	RUS	3	E12
Lendinara	I	121	B4
Lendorf	A	109	C4
Lendum	DK	58	A3
Lengefeld	D	83	B5
Lengerich, *Niedersachsen*	D	71	B4
Lengerich, *Nordrhein-Westfalen*	D	71	B4
Lenggries	D	108	B2
Lengyeltóti	H	111	C4
Lenhovda	S	62	B3
Lenk	CH	106	C2
Lennartsfors	S	54	A2
Lennestadt	D	81	A4
Lennoxtown	GB	35	C3
Leno	I	120	B3
Lénola	I	169	B3
Lens	B	79	B3
Lens	F	78	B2
Lens Lestang	F	117	B5
Lensahn	D	65	B3
Lensvik	N	198	B6
Lentellais	F	141	B3
Lentföhrden	D	64	C2
Lenti	H	111	C3
Lentini	I	177	B3
Lenungshammar	S	54	A3
Lenzburg	CH	106	B3
Lenzen	D	73	A4
Lenzerheide	CH	107	C4
Leoben	A	110	B2
Leogang	A	109	B3
Leominster	GB	39	B4
León	E	142	B1
Léon	F	128	C1
Leonberg	D	93	C5
Léoncel	F	118	C2
Leonding	A	96	C2
Leonessa	I	169	A2
Leonforte	I	177	B3
Leonidio	GR	184	B3
Leopoldsburg	B	79	A5
Leopoldsdorf im Marchfeld	A	111	A3
Leopoldshagen	D	74	A2
Lepe	E	161	B2
Lepenou	GR	182	E3
Lephin	GB	31	B2
L'Epine	F	132	A1
Lepoglava	HR	124	A2
Leppäjärvi	FIN	192	D7
Leppävirta	FIN	8	A5
Lercara Friddi	I	176	B2
Lerdal	S	54	B2
Leré	F	103	B4
Lerici	I	134	A2
Lerin	E	144	B2
Lerma	E	143	B3
Lerm-et-Musset	F	128	B2
Lermoos	A	108	B1
Lérouville	F	92	C1
Lerum	S	60	B2
Lervik	N	54	A1
Lerwick	GB	33	A5
Lés	E	145	B4
Les Abrets	F	118	B2
Les Aix-d'Angillon	F	103	B4
Les Ancizes-Comps	F	116	B2
Les Andelys	F	90	B1
Les Arcs, *Savoie*	F	119	B3
Les Arcs, *Var*	F	132	B2
Les-Aubiers	F	102	C1
Les Baux-de-Provence	F	131	B3
Les Bézards	F	103	B4
Les Bois	CH	106	B1
Les Bordes	F	103	B4
Les Borges Blanques	E	147	C1
Les Borges del Camp	E	147	C2
Les Brunettes	F	104	C2
Les Cabannes	F	146	B2
Les Contamines-Montjoie	F	118	B3
les Coves de Vinroma	E	153	B4
Les Déserts	F	118	B2
Les Deux-Alpes	F	118	C3
Les Diablerets	CH	119	A4
Les Echelles	F	118	B2
Les Escaldes	AND	146	B2
Les Essarts	F	114	B2
Les Estables	F	117	C4
Les Eyzies-de-Tayac	F	129	B4
Les Gets	F	118	A3
Les Grandes-Ventes	F	89	A5
Les Haudères	CH	119	A4
Les Herbiers	F	114	B2
Les Hôpitaux-Neufs	F	105	C5
Les Lucs-sur-Boulogne	F	114	B2
Les Mages	F	131	A3
Les Mazures	F	91	B4
Les Mées	F	132	A1
Les Mureaux	F	90	C1
Les Omergues	F	132	A1
Les Ormes-sur-Voulzie	F	90	C3
Les Orres	F	132	A2
Les Pieux	F	88	A2
Les Ponts-de-Cé	F	102	B1
Les Ponts-de-Martel	CH	106	C1
Les Riceys	F	104	B3
Les Roches	F	117	B4
Les Rosaires	F	101	A3
Les Rosiers	F	102	B1
Les Rousses	F	105	C5
Les Sables-d'Olonne	F	114	B2
Les Settons	F	104	B3
Les Ternes	F	116	B2
Les Thilliers en-Vexin	F	90	B1
Les Touches	F	101	B4
Les Trois Moûtiers	F	102	B2
Les Vans	F	131	A3
Les Verrières	CH	105	C5
Les Vignes	F	130	A2
Lesaka	E	144	A2
L'Escala	E	147	B4
Lescar	F	145	A3
L'Escarène	F	133	B3
Lesce	SLO	123	A3
Lescheraines	F	118	B3
Lesconil	F	100	B1
Lesdins	F	90	B3
Lesično	SLO	123	A4
Lésina	I	171	B3
Lesjaskog	N	198	C5
Lesjöfors	S	49	C6
Leskova Dolina	SLO	123	B3
Leskovac	SRB	16	D4
Leskovec	CZ	98	B1
Leskovec	SLO	123	B1
Leskovice	CZ	97	B3
Leskovik	AL	182	C2
Leslie	GB	35	B4
Lesmahagow	GB	36	A3
Lesmont	F	91	C4
Leśna	PL	84	A3
Lesneven	F	100	A1
Leśnica	PL	86	B2
Lešnica	SRB	127	C1
Leśniów Wielkopolski	PL	75	C4
Lesnoye	RUS	9	C9
Lesparre-Médoc	F	128	A2
l'Espérance	F	91	B3
l'Esperou	F	130	A2
Lesponne	F	145	A4
L'Espunyola	E	147	B2
Lessach	A	109	B4
Lessay	F	88	A2
Lessebo	S	62	B3
Lessines	B	79	B3
L'Estany	E	147	C3
Lesterps	F	115	B4
Leswalt	GB	36	B1
Leszno, *Mazowieckie*	PL	77	B5
Leszno, *Wielkopolskie*	PL	85	A4
Leszno Górne	PL	84	A3

252

Place	Country	Page	Grid
Letchworth	GB	44	B3
Letenye	H	111	C3
Letino	I	170	B2
Letohrad	CZ	97	A4
Letovice	CZ	97	B4
Letschin	D	74	B3
Letterfrack	IRL	28	A2
Letterkenny	IRL	26	A3
Lettermacaward	IRL	26	A3
Lettoch	GB	32	D3
Letur	E	164	A3
Letux	E	153	A3
Letzlingen	D	73	B3
Leucate	F	146	B3
Leuchars	GB	35	B5
Leuglay	F	105	B3
Leuk	CH	119	A4
Leukerbad	CH	119	A4
Leumrabhagh	GB	31	A2
Leuna	D	83	A4
Leusden	NL	70	B2
Leutenberg	D	82	B2
Leuterschach	D	108	B1
Leutershausen	D	94	B2
Leutkirch	D	107	B5
Leuven	B	79	B4
Leuze-en-Hainaut	B	79	B3
Levan	AL	182	C1
Levanger	N	199	B8
Levanjska Varoš	HR	125	B4
Lévanto	I	134	A2
Levaré	F	88	B3
Levata	I	120	B3
Leveld	N	47	B5
Leven, *East Yorkshire*	GB	41	B3
Leven, *Fife*	GB	35	B5
Leverano	I	173	B3
Leverkusen	D	80	A2
Levern	D	72	B1
Levet	F	103	C4
Levice	SK	112	A2
Lévico Terme	I	121	A4
Levie	F	180	B2
Levier	F	105	C5
Lévignen	F	90	B2
Levinovac	HR	124	B3
Levoča	SK	99	B4
Levroux	F	103	C3
Lewes	GB	45	C4
Lewin Brzeski	PL	85	B5
Lewisham	GB	44	B3
Leyburn	GB	37	B5
Leyland	GB	38	A4
Leysdown-on-Sea	GB	45	B4
Leysin	CH	119	A4
Lezajsk	PL	12	C5
Lézardrieux	F	100	A2
Lézat-sur-Léze	F	146	A2
Lezay	F	115	B3
Lezhë	AL	182	B1
Lézignan-Corbières	F	130	B1
Lezignan-la-Cèbe	F	130	B2
Ležimir	SRB	126	B1
Lézinnes	F	104	B3
Lezoux	F	117	B3
Lezuza	E	158	C1
Lhenice	CZ	96	C2
Lherm	F	146	A2
Lhommaizé	F	115	B4
L'Hospitalet	F	146	B2
L'Hospitalet de l'Infant	E	147	D1
L'Hospitalet de Llobregat	E	147	C3
L'Hospitalet-du-Larzac	F	130	B2
Lhuître	F	91	C4
Liancourt	F	90	B2
Liart	F	91	B4
Liatorp	S	63	B2
Liatrie	GB	32	D2
Libán	CZ	84	B3
Libceves	CZ	84	B1
Liběchov	CZ	84	B2
Liber	E	141	B3
Liberec	CZ	84	B3
Libiąż	PL	86	B3
Libina	CZ	98	B1
Libochovice	CZ	84	B1
Libohovë	AL	182	C2
Libourne	F	128	B2
Libramont	B	92	B1
Librazhd	AL	182	B2
Librilla	E	165	B3
Libros	E	152	B2
Licata	I	176	B2
Licciana Nardi	I	134	A3
Licenza	I	169	A2
Liceros	E	151	A4
Lich	D	81	B4
Lichères-près-Aigremont	F	104	B2
Lichfield	GB	40	C2
Lichtenau	A	97	C3
Lichtenau	D	81	A4
Lichtenberg	D	83	B3
Lichtenfels	D	82	B3
Lichtensteig	CH	107	B4
Lichtenstein	D	83	B4
Lichtenvoorde	NL	71	C3
Lichtervelde	B	78	A3
Lička Jesenica	HR	123	B4
Lickershamn	S	57	C4
LičOsik	HR	123	C4
Ličko Lešce	HR	123	C4
Licodía Eubéa	I	177	B3
Licques	F	78	B1
Lida	BY	13	B6
Lidar	N	47	A6
Lidečko	CZ	98	B1
Liden	S	200	D2
Lidhult	S	60	C3
Lidköping	S	55	B4
Lido	I	122	B1
Lido Azzurro	I	173	B3
Lido degli Estensi	I	122	C1
Lido degli Scacchi	I	122	C1
Lido della Nazioni	I	122	C1
Lido di Camaiore	I	134	B3
Lido di Casalbordino	I	169	A4
Lido di Castél Fusano	I	168	B2
Lido di Cincinnato	I	168	B2
Lido di Classe	I	135	A5
Lido di Fermo	I	136	B2
Lido di Fondi	I	169	B3
Lido di Jésolo	I	122	B1
Lido di Lícola	I	170	C2
Lido di Metaponto	I	174	A2
Lido di Óstia	I	168	B2
Lido di Policoro	I	174	A2
Lido di Pomposa	I	122	C1
Lido di Savio	I	135	A5
Lido di Scanzano	I	174	A2
Lido di Siponto	I	171	B3
Lido di Squillace	I	175	C2
Lido di Volano	I	122	C1
Lido Riccio	I	169	A4
Lido Silvana	I	173	B3
Lidoriki	GR	184	A3
Lidsjöberg	S	199	A12
Lidzbark	PL	77	A4
Lidzbark Warmiński	PL	69	A5
Liebenau	A	96	C2
Liebenau	D	72	B2
Liebenwalde	D	74	B2
Lieberose	D	74	C3
Liebling	RO	126	B3
Lieboch	A	110	C2
Liège	B	80	B1
Lieksa	FIN	3	E12
Lienen	D	71	B4
Lienz	A	109	C3
Liepāja	LV	8	D2
Lier	B	79	A4
Lierbyen	N	54	A1
Liernais	F	104	B3
Liesing	A	109	C3
Liestal	CH	106	B2
Liétor	E	158	C2
Lieurac	F	146	B2
Lieurey	F	89	A4
Liévin	F	78	B2
Liezen	A	110	B1
Liffol-le-Grand	F	92	C1
Lifford	IRL	27	B3
Liffré	F	101	A4
Ligardes	F	129	B3
Lignano Sabbiadoro	I	122	B2
Ligne	F	101	B4
Lignières	F	103	C4
Ligny-en-Barrois	F	92	C1
Ligny-le-Châtel	F	104	B2
Ligoła Polska	PL	85	A5
Ligourio	GR	184	B4
Ligowo	PL	77	B4
Ligueil	F	102	B2
Likavka	SK	99	B3
Likenäs	S	49	B5
Likhoslavl	RUS	9	D9
Lild Strand	DK	58	A1
L'Île-Bouchard	F	102	B2
L'Île-Rousse	F	180	A1
Lilienfeld	D	110	A2
Lilienthal	D	72	A1
Lilla Edet	S	54	B3
Lilla Tjärby	S	61	C3
Lille	F	78	B3
Lille	B	79	A4
Lillebonne	F	89	A4
Lillehammer	N	48	A2
Lillerød	DK	61	D2
Lillers	F	78	B2
Lillesand	N	53	B4
Lillestrøm	N	48	C3
Lillhärdal	S	199	D11
Lillkyrka	S	56	A3
Lillo	E	157	A4
Lillögda	S	200	B3
Lillpite	S	196	D4
Lima	S	49	B5
Limanowa	PL	99	B4
Limassol	CY	181	B2
Limbach-Oberfrohna	D	83	B4
Limbaži	LV	8	D4
Limburg	D	81	B4
Limburg	B	80	B1
Lime	DK	58	B3
Limedsforsen	S	49	B5
Limenária	GR	183	C6
Limenas Chersonisou	GR	185	D6
Limerick	IRL	29	B3
Limes	I	121	B3
Limésy	F	89	A4
Limmared	S	60	B3
Limni	GR	183	E5
Limoges	F	115	C5
Limogne-en-Quercy	F	129	B4
Limoise	F	104	C2
Limone Piemonte	I	133	A3
Limone sul Garda	I	121	B3
Limons	F	117	B3
Limours	F	90	C2
Limoux	F	146	A3
Linares	E	157	B4
Linares de Mora	E	153	B3
Linares de Riofrio	E	149	B4
Linária	GR	183	E6
Linas de Broto	E	145	B3
Lincoln	GB	40	B3
Lind	DK	59	B1
Lindås	N	46	B2
Lindau	D	107	B4
Lindberget	N	48	A3
Lindelse	DK	65	B3
Lindenberg	D	74	B3
Lindenberg im Allgäu	D	107	B4
Lindern	D	71	B4
Linderöd	S	61	D3
Lindesberg	S	56	A1
Lindesnäs	S	50	B1
Lindesnes	N	52	C3
Lindholmen	S	57	A4
Lindknud	DK	59	C2
Lindlar	D	80	A3
Lindö	S	56	B2
Lindome	S	60	B2
Lindos	GR	188	C3
Lindoso	P	148	A1
Lindow	D	74	B1
Lindsdal	S	62	B4
Lindshammar	S	62	A3
Lindstedt	D	73	B4
Lindved	DK	59	C2
Líně	CZ	96	B1
Lingbo	S	50	A3
Lingen	D	71	B4
Linghed	S	50	B2
Linghem	S	56	B1
Linguaglossa	I	177	B4
Linia	PL	68	A2
Linie	PL	74	A3
Liniewo	PL	68	A3
Linkenheim	D	93	B4
Linköping	S	56	B1
Linksness	GB	33	C3
Linlithgow	GB	35	C4
Linneryd	S	63	B3
Linnes Hammarby	S	51	C4
Linnich	D	80	B2
Linsell	S	199	C10
Linslade	GB	44	B3
Linthal	CH	107	C4
Linyola	E	147	C1
Linz	A	96	C2
Linz	D	80	B3
Liomseter	N	47	A6
Lion-sur-Mer	F	89	A3
Lionárisso	CY	181	A3
Lioni	I	172	B1
Lipany	SK	99	B4
Lipar	SRB	126	B1
Lípari	I	177	A3
Lipcani	MD	17	A7
Liperi	FIN	9	A6
Liphook	GB	44	B3
Lipiany	PL	75	A3
Lipik	HR	124	B3
Lipka	PL	68	B2
Lipki Wielkie	PL	75	B4
Lipnica	PL	68	B2
Lipnica Murowana	PL	99	B4
Lipnik	PL	87	B5
Lipník nad Bečvou	CZ	98	B1
Lipno, *Kujawsko-Pomorskie*	PL	77	B4
Lipno, *Łódzkie*	PL	86	A2
Liposthey	F	128	B2
Lipovac	HR	125	B5
Lipovets	UA	13	D8
Lipovljani	HR	124	B3
Lipowiec	PL	77	A6
Lipowina	PL	69	A4
Lippborg	D	81	A4
Lippó	H	125	B4
Lippoldsberg	D	81	A5
Lippstadt	D	81	A4
Lipsko	PL	87	A5
Liptál	CZ	98	B1
Liptovská-Lúžna	SK	99	C3
Liptovská Osada	SK	99	C3
Liptovská-Teplička	SK	99	C4
Liptovský Hrádok	SK	99	B3
Liptovský Milkuláš	SK	99	B3
Lipusz	PL	68	A2
Lipůvka	CZ	97	B4
Liré	F	101	B4
Lisac	BIH	139	A3
Lisbellaw	GB	27	B3
Lisboa = Lisbon	P	154	C1
Lisbon = Lisboa	P	154	C1
Lisburn	GB	27	B4
Liscannor	IRL	28	B2
Lisdoonvarna	IRL	28	A2
Lisewo	PL	69	B3
Lisięcice	PL	86	B1
Lisieux	F	89	A4
Lisjö	S	56	A2
Liskeard	GB	42	B2
L'Isle	CH	105	C5
L'Isle-Adam	F	90	B2
L'Isle-de-Noé	F	129	C3
L'Isle-en-Dodon	F	145	A4
L'Isle-Jourdain, *Gers*	F	129	C4
L'Isle-Jourdain, *Vienne*	F	115	B4
L'Isle-sur-la-Sorgue	F	131	B4
L'Isle-sur-le-Doubs	F	105	B5
L'Isle-sur-Serein	F	104	B3
Lisle-sur-Tarn	F	129	C4
Lismore	IRL	29	B4
Lisnaskea	GB	27	B3
Lišov	CZ	96	B2
Lisów, *Lubuskie*	PL	74	B3
Lisów, *Śląskie*	PL	86	B2
Lisse	NL	70	B1
Lissycasey	IRL	28	B2
List	D	64	A1
Listerby	S	63	B3
Listowel	IRL	29	B2
Listrac-Médoc	F	128	A2
Liszki	PL	99	A3
Liszkowo	PL	76	A2
Lit	S	199	B11
Lit-et-Mixe	F	128	B1
Litava	SK	99	C3
Litcham	GB	41	C4
Litija	SLO	123	A3
Litke	H	112	A3
Litlabø	N	52	A1
Litochoro	GR	182	C4
Litoměřice	CZ	84	B2
Litomyšl	CZ	97	B4
Litovel	CZ	98	B1
Litschau	A	96	C3
Little Walsingham	GB	41	C4
Littlehampton	GB	44	C3
Littleport	GB	45	A4
Littleton	IRL	29	B4
Litvínov	CZ	83	B5
Livadero	GR	182	C3
Livadhia	CY	181	B2
Livadi	GR	182	C4
Livadia	GR	184	A3
Livarot	F	89	B4
Liveras	CY	181	A1
Livernon	F	129	B4
Liverovici	MNE	139	C5
Liverpool	GB	38	A4
Livigno	I	107	C5
Livingston	GB	35	C4
Livno	BIH	138	B2
Livo	FIN	197	D9
Livold	SLO	123	B3
Livorno	I	134	B3
Livorno Ferraris	I	119	B5
Livron-sur-Drôme	F	117	C4
Livry-Louvercy	F	91	B4
Lixheim	F	92	C3
Lixouri	GR	184	A1
Lizard	GB	42	C1
Lizy-sur-Ourcq	F	90	B3
Lizzano	I	173	B3
Lizzano in Belvedere	I	135	A3
Ljig	SRB	127	C2
Ljørdalen	N	49	A4
Ljosland	N	52	B3
Ljubija	BIH	124	C2
Ljubinje	BIH	139	C4
Ljubljana	SLO	123	A3
Ljubno ob Savinji	SLO	123	A3
Ljubovija	SRB	127	C1
Ljubuški	BIH	138	B3
Ljugarn	S	57	C4
Ljung	S	60	B3
Ljungaverk	S	200	D2
Ljungby	S	60	C3
Ljungbyhed	S	61	C3
Ljungbyholm	S	63	B4
Ljungdalen	S	199	C9
Ljungsarp	S	60	B3
Ljungsbro	S	56	B1
Ljungskile	S	54	B2
Ljusdal	S	200	E2
Ljusfallshammar	S	56	B1
Ljusne	S	51	A4
Ljusterö	S	57	A4
Ljutomer	SLO	111	C3
Lladurs	E	147	B2
Llafranc	E	147	C4
Llagostera	E	147	C3
Llanaelhaiarn	GB	38	B2
Llanarth	GB	39	B2
Llanbedr	GB	38	B2
Llanbedrog	GB	38	B2
Llanberis	GB	38	A2
Llanbister	GB	39	B3
Llanbrynmair	GB	39	B3
Llançà	E	146	B4
Llandeilo	GB	39	C3
Llandissilio	GB	39	C2
Llandovery	GB	39	C3
Llandrillo	GB	38	B3
Llandrindod Wells	GB	39	B3
Llandudec	F	100	A1
Llandudno	GB	38	A3
Llandysul	GB	39	B2
Llanelli	GB	39	C2
Llanerchymedd	GB	38	A2
Llanes	E	142	A2
Llanfair Caereinion	GB	38	B3
Llanfairfechan	GB	38	A3
Llanfyllin	GB	38	B3
Llangadog	GB	39	C3
Llangefni	GB	38	A2
Llangollen	GB	38	B3
Llangranog	GB	39	B2
Llangurig	GB	39	B3
Llanidloes	GB	39	B3
Llanilar	GB	39	B2
Llanrhystud	GB	39	B2
Llanrwst	GB	38	A3
Llansannan	GB	38	A3
Llansawel	GB	39	B2
Llanstephan	GB	39	C2
Llanteno	E	143	A3
Llanthony	GB	39	C3
Llantrisant	GB	39	C3
Llantwit-Major	GB	39	C3
Llanuwchllyn	GB	38	B3
Llanwddyn	GB	38	B3
Llanwrda	GB	39	C3
Llanwrtyd Wells	GB	39	B3
Llanybydder	GB	39	B2
Llanymynech	GB	38	B3
Llavorsi	E	146	B2
Lleida	E	153	A4
Llera	E	156	B1
Llerena	E	156	B1
Lles	E	146	B2
Llessui	E	146	B2
Llinars	E	147	B3
Lliria	E	159	B3
Llívia	E	146	B2
Llodio	E	143	A4
Lloret de Mar	E	147	C3
Llosa de Ranes	E	159	B3
Lloseta	E	167	B2
Llucena del Cid	E	153	B3
Llucmajor	E	167	B2
Llutxent	E	159	C3
Llwyngwril	GB	38	B2
Llyswen	GB	39	B3
Lnáře	CZ	96	B1
Lniano	PL	76	A3
Lo Pagán	E	165	B4
Loanhead	GB	35	C4
Loano	I	133	A4
Loarre	E	145	B3
Löbau	D	84	A2
Löbejün	D	83	A3
Löberöd	S	61	D3
Łobez	PL	75	A4
Löbnitz	D	66	B1
Lobón	E	155	C4
Loburg	D	73	B5
Locana	I	119	B4
Locarno	CH	120	A1
Loccum	D	72	B2
Loče	SLO	123	A4
Loch Baghasdail	GB	31	B1
Loch nam Madadh	GB	31	B1
Lochailort	GB	34	B2
Lochaline	GB	34	B2
Lochans	GB	36	B1
Locharbriggs	GB	36	A3
Lochau	A	107	B4
Lochcarron	GB	31	B3
Lochearnhead	GB	34	B3
Lochem	NL	71	B3
Loches	F	102	B2
Lochgelly	GB	35	B4
Lochgilphead	GB	34	B2
Lochgoilhead	GB	34	B3
Lochinver	GB	32	C1
Lochranza	GB	34	C2
Ločika	SRB	127	D3
Lockenhaus	A	111	B3
Lockerbie	GB	36	A4
Löcknitz	D	74	A3
Locmaria	F	100	B2
Locmariaquer	F	100	B2
Locminé	F	100	B3
Locorotondo	I	173	B3
Locquirec	F	100	A2
Locri	I	175	C2
Locronan	F	100	A1
Loctudy	F	100	B1
Lodares de Osma	E	151	A5
Lodé	I	178	B3
Lodeinoye Pole	RUS	9	B8
Lodève	F	130	B2
Lodi	I	120	B2
Løding	N	194	C5
Lødingen	N	194	B6
Lodosa	E	144	B1
Lödöse	S	54	B3
Łódź	PL	86	A3
Loeches	E	151	B4
Löfallstrand	N	46	B3
Lofer	A	109	B3
Lofsdalen	S	199	C10
Loftahammar	S	62	A4
Lofthus	N	46	B3
Loftus	GB	37	B6
Loga	N	52	B2
Logatec	SLO	123	B3
Lögdeå	S	200	C5
Lograto	I	120	B3
Logroño	E	143	B4
Logrosán	E	156	A2
Løgstør	DK	58	B2
Løgumgårde	DK	64	A1
Løgumkloster	DK	64	A1
Lohals	DK	65	A3
Lohiniva	FIN	197	B8
Lohja	FIN	8	B4
Löhlbach	D	81	A4
Lohmen, *Mecklenburg-Vorpommern*	D	65	C5
Lohmen, *Sachsen*	D	84	B2
Löhnberg	D	81	B4
Lohne, *Niedersachsen*	D	71	B5
Löhne, *Nordrhein-Westfalen*	D	72	B1
Lohr	D	94	B1
Lohra	D	81	B4
Lohsa	D	84	A2
Loiano	I	135	A4
Loimaa	FIN	8	B3
Lóiri	I	178	B3
Loitz	D	66	C2
Loivos	P	148	A2
Loivos do Monte	P	148	A2
Loja	E	163	A3
Lojanice	SRB	127	C1
Lojsta	S	57	C4
Løjt Kirkeby	DK	64	A2
Lok	SK	112	A2
Lokca	SK	99	B3
Løken	N	54	A2
Lokeren	B	79	A3
Loket	CZ	83	B4
Lokka	FIN	197	B10
Løkken	DK	58	A2
Løkken	N	198	B6
Loknya	RUS	9	D7
Lökösháza	H	113	C5
Lokve	SRB	126	B3
Lollar	D	81	B4
Lolling-Graben	A	110	C1
L'Olleria	E	159	C3
Lom	BG	17	D5
Lom	N	198	D5
Lom	SK	99	C3
Lombez	F	146	A1
Lomello	I	120	B1
Łomianki	PL	77	B5
Lomma	S	61	D3
Lommaryd	S	62	A2
Lommatzsch	D	83	A5
Lommel	B	79	A5
Lommersum	D	80	B2
Lomnice	CZ	97	B4
Lomnice nad Lužnici	CZ	96	B2
Lomnice-nad Popelkou	CZ	84	B3
Lompolo	FIN	196	A7
Łomza	PL	12	B5
Lönashult	S	63	B2
Lønborg	DK	59	C1
Londerzeel	B	79	A4
Londinières	F	89	A5
London	GB	44	B3
Lonevåg	N	46	B2
Long Bennington	GB	40	C3
Long Eaton	GB	40	C2
Long Melford	GB	45	A4
Long Preston	GB	40	A1
Long Sutton	GB	41	C4
Longa	GR	184	C2
Longare	I	121	B4
Longares	E	152	A2
Longarone	I	122	A1
Longastrino	I	135	A5
Longbenton	GB	37	A5
Longchamp-sur-Aujon	F	105	A3
Longchaumois	F	118	A2
Longeau	F	105	B4
Longecourt-en-Plaine	F	105	B4
Longeville-les-St. Avold	F	92	B2
Longeville-sur-Mer	F	114	B2
Longford	IRL	28	A4
Longframlington	GB	37	A5
Longhope	GB	33	C3
Longhorsley	GB	37	A5
Longhoughton	GB	37	A5
Longi	I	177	A3

Longny-au-Perche	F	89	B4
Longobucco	I	174	B2
Longré	F	115	B3
Longridge	GB	38	A4
Longroiva	P	149	B2
Longtown, *Cumbria*	GB	36	A4
Longtown, *Herefordshire*	GB	39	C4
Longué-Jumelles	F	102	B1
Longueau	F	90	B2
Longuyon	F	92	B1
Longvic	F	105	B4
Longvilly	B	92	A1
Longwy	F	92	B1
Lonigo	I	121	B4
Löningen	D	71	B4
Lonja	HR	124	B2
Lönneberga	S	62	A3
Lons-le-Saunier	F	105	C4
Lönsboda	S	63	B2
Lønset	N	198	C6
Lønstrup	DK	58	A2
Looe	GB	42	B2
Loon op Zand	NL	79	A5
Loone-Plage	F	78	A2
Loosdorf	A	110	A2
Lopar	HR	123	C3
Lopare	BIH	125	C4
Lopera	E	157	C3
Lopigna	F	180	A1
Loppersum	NL	71	A3
Łopuszna	PL	99	B4
Łopuszno	PL	87	B4
Lor	F	91	B4
Lora	N	198	C5
Lora de Estepa	E	162	A3
Lora del Río	E	162	A2
Loranca del Campo	E	151	B5
Lörby	S	63	B2
Lorca	E	164	B3
Lorch	D	93	A3
Lørenfallet	N	48	B3
Lørenskog	N	48	C2
Loreo	I	122	B1
Loreto	I	136	B2
Lorgues	F	132	B2
Lorica	I	174	B2
Lorient	F	100	B2
Lorignac	F	114	C3
Lörinci	H	112	B3
Loriol-sur-Drôme	F	117	C4
Lormes	F	104	B2
Loro Ciuffenna	I	135	B4
Lorqui	E	165	A3
Lörrach	D	106	B2
Lorrez-le-Bocage	F	103	A4
Lorris	F	103	B4
Lorup	D	71	B4
Łoś	PL	77	C5
Los	S	199	D12
Los Alcázares	E	165	B4
Los Arcos	E	144	B1
Los Barios de Luna	E	141	B5
Los Barrios	E	162	B2
Los Caños de Meca	E	162	B1
Los Cerricos	E	164	B2
Los Corrales	E	162	A3
Los Corrales de Buelna	E	142	A2
Los Dolores	E	165	B3
Los Gallardos	E	164	B3
Los Hinojosos	E	158	B1
Los Isidros	E	159	B2
Los Molinos	E	151	B3
Los Morales	E	162	A2
Los Navalmorales	E	156	A3
Los Navalucillos	E	156	A3
Los Nietos	E	165	B4
Los Palacios y Villafranca	E	162	A2
Los Pozuelos de Calatrava	E	157	B3
Los Rábanos	E	143	C4
Los Santos	E	149	B4
Los Santos de la Humosa	E	151	B4
Los Santos de Maimona	E	155	C4
Los Tijos	E	142	A2
Los Villares	E	163	A4
Los Yébenes	E	157	A4
Losacino	E	149	A3
Losar de la Vera	E	150	B2
Losenstein	A	110	B1
Losheim, *Nordrhein-Westfalen*	D	80	B2
Losheim, *Saarland*	D	92	B2
Losne	F	105	B4
Løsning	DK	59	C2
Lossburg	D	93	C4
Losse	F	128	B2
Losser	NL	71	B4
Lossiemouth	GB	32	D3
Lössnitz	D	83	B4
Loštice	CZ	97	B4
Lostwithiel	GB	42	B2
Løten	N	48	B3
Lotorp	S	56	B1
Lottefors	S	50	A3
Löttorp	S	62	A5
Lotyń	PL	68	B1
Lotzorai	I	179	C3
Louargat	F	100	A2
Loudéac	F	101	A3
Loudun	F	102	B2
Loué	F	102	B1
Loughborough	GB	40	C2
Loughbrickland	GB	27	B4
Loughrea	IRL	28	A3
Louhans	F	105	C4
Louisburgh	IRL	28	A2
Loukhi	RUS	3	C13
Loulay	F	114	B3
Loulé	P	160	B1
Louny	CZ	84	B1
Lourdes	F	145	A3
Lourenzá	E	141	A3
Loures	P	154	C1
Loures-Barousse	F	145	A4
Louriçal	P	154	A2
Lourinhã	P	154	B1
Lourmarin	F	131	B4
Loury	F	103	B4
Lousa, *Bragança*	P	149	A2
Lousa, *Castelo Branco*	P	155	B3
Lousã, *Coimbra*	P	148	B1
Lousa, *Lisboa*	P	154	C1
Lousada	E	140	B3
Lousada	P	148	A1
Louth	GB	41	B3
Loutra Edipsou	GR	183	E5
Loutraki	GR	184	B3
Loutropoli Thermis	GR	186	C1
Louverné	F	102	A1
Louvie-Juzon	F	145	A3
Louviers	F	89	A5
Louvigné-du-Désert	F	88	B2
Louvois	F	91	B4
Lova	I	121	B5
Lovasberény	H	112	B2
Lövåsen	S	49	C5
Lovászpatona	H	111	B4
Lövberga	S	200	C1
Lovech	BG	17	D6
Lövenich	D	80	A2
Lóvere	I	120	B3
Lövestad	S	61	D3
Loviisa	FIN	8	B5
Lovikka	S	196	B5
Lovinobaňa	SK	99	C3
Loviste	HR	138	B3
Lovke	HR	123	B3
Lovnäs	S	49	A5
Lövö	H	111	B3
Lovosice	CZ	84	B2
Lovozero	RUS	3	C14
Lovran	HR	123	B3
Lovreć	HR	138	B2
Lovrenc na Pohorju	SLO	110	C2
Lovrin	RO	126	B2
Lövstabruk	S	51	B4
Löwenberg	D	74	B2
Löwenstein	D	94	B1
Lowestoft	GB	41	C5
Lowick	GB	37	A5
Łowicz	PL	77	B4
Loxstedt	D	72	A1
Loyew	BY	13	C9
Lož	SLO	123	B3
Loza	CZ	96	B1
Łozina	PL	85	A5
Loznica	SRB	127	C1
Lozničko Polje	SRB	127	C1
Lozorno	SK	111	A4
Lozovik	SRB	127	C3
Lozoya	E	151	B4
Lozoyuela	E	151	B4
Lozzo di Cadore	I	109	C3
Luanco	E	141	A5
Luarca	E	141	A4
Lubaczów	PL	13	C5
Lubań	PL	84	A3
Lubanie	PL	76	B3
Lubanów	PL	86	A3
Lubars	D	73	B5
Lubasz	PL	75	B5
Lubawa	PL	69	B4
Lubawka	PL	85	B4
Lübbecke	D	72	B1
Lübben	D	74	C2
Lübbenau	D	84	A1
Lubczyna	PL	74	A3
Lübeck	D	65	C3
Lubenec	CZ	83	B5
Lubersac	F	115	C5
Lübesse	D	73	A4
Lubia	E	152	A1
Lubian	E	141	B4
Lubiatowo	PL	75	A4
Lubichowo	PL	69	B3
Lubicz Dolny	PL	76	A3
Lubień	PL	99	B3
Lubień Kujawski	PL	77	B4
Lubienia	PL	87	A5
Lubieszewo	PL	75	A4
Lubin, *Dolnośląskie*	PL	85	A4
Lubin, *Zachodnio-Pomorskie*	PL	67	C3
Lublin	PL	12	C5
Lubliniec	PL	86	B2
Lubmin	D	66	B2
Lubniewice	PL	75	B4
Lubochnia	PL	87	A4
Lubomierz, *Dolnośląskie*	PL	84	A3
Lubomierz, *Małopolskie*	PL	99	B4
Lubomino	PL	69	A5
Luboń	PL	76	B1
L'ubotín	SK	99	B4
Lubowidz	PL	77	A4
Łubowo, *Wielkopolskie*	PL	76	B2
Łubowo, *Zachodnio-Pomorskie*	PL	68	B1
Lubraniec	PL	76	B3
Lubrin	E	164	B2
Lubrza	PL	85	B5
Lubsko	PL	84	A2
Lübtheen	D	73	A4
Lubuczewo	PL	68	A2
Luby	CZ	83	B4
Lübz	D	73	A5
Luc	F	117	C3
Luc-en-Diois	F	118	C2
Luc-sur-Mer	F	89	A3
Lucainena de las Torres	E	164	B2
Lucan	IRL	30	A2
Lučani	SRB	127	D2
Lúcar	E	164	B2
Luçay-le-Mâle	F	103	B3
Lucca	I	134	B3
Lucciana	F	180	A2
Lucé	F	90	C1
Luče	SLO	123	A3
Lucena, *Córdoba*	E	163	A3
Lucena, *Huelva*	E	161	B3
Lucenay-les-Aix	F	104	C2
Lucenay-l'Evéque	F	104	B3
Lučenec	SK	99	C3
Luceni	E	144	C2
Lucens	CH	106	C1
Lucera	I	171	B3
Luceram	F	133	B3
Lüchow	D	73	B4
Luciana	E	157	B3
Lucignano	I	135	B4
Lucija	SLO	122	B2
Lucka	D	83	A4
Luckau	D	84	A1
Luckenwalde	D	74	B2
Lückstedt	D	73	B4
Luco dei Marsi	I	169	B3
Luçon	F	114	B2
Ludanice	SK	98	C2
Ludbreg	HR	124	A2
Lüdenscheid	D	81	A3
Lüderitz	D	73	B4
Lüdersdorf	D	65	C3
Ludgershall	GB	44	B2
Ludgo	S	56	B3
Lüdinghausen	D	80	A3
Ludlow	GB	39	B4
Ludomy	PL	75	B5
Ludvika	S	50	B2
Ludweiler Warndt	D	92	B2
Ludwigsburg	D	94	C1
Ludwigsfelde	D	74	B2
Ludwigshafen	D	93	B4
Ludwigslust	D	73	A4
Ludwigsstadt	D	82	B3
Ludza	LV	8	D5
Luesia	E	144	B2
Luftkurort Arendsee	D	73	B4
Lug	BIH	139	C4
Lug	HR	125	B4
Luga	RUS	9	C6
Lugagnano Val d'Arda	I	120	C2
Lugano	CH	120	A1
Lugau	D	83	B4
Lugnas	S	55	B4
Lúgnola	I	168	A2
Lugny	F	105	C3
Lugo	E	140	A3
Lugo	I	135	A4
Lugoj	RO	16	C4
Lugones	E	141	A5
Lugros	E	163	A4
Luhačovice	CZ	98	B1
Luhe	D	95	B4
Luino	I	120	B1
Luintra	E	140	B3
Lújar	E	163	B4
Luka nad Jihlavou	CZ	97	B3
Lukavac	BIH	125	C4
Lukavika	BIH	125	C4
Lüki	BG	183	B6
Lukovë	AL	182	D1
Lukovica	SLO	123	A3
Lukovit	BG	17	D6
Lukovo	HR	123	C3
Lukovo Šugorje	HR	137	A4
Łuków	PL	12	C5
Łukowice Brzeskie	PL	85	B5
Luksefjell	N	53	A5
Łukta	PL	69	B5
Lula	I	178	B3
Luleå	S	196	D5
Lüleburgaz	TR	186	A2
Lumbarda	HR	138	C3
Lumbier	E	144	B2
Lumbrales	E	149	B3
Lumbreras	E	143	B4
Lumbres	F	78	B2
Lummelunda	S	57	C4
Lummen	B	79	B5
Lumparland	FIN	51	B7
Lumpiaque	E	152	A2
Lumsås	DK	61	D1
Lumsden	GB	33	D4
Lumsheden	S	50	B3
Lun	HR	123	C3
Luna	E	144	B3
Lunamatrona	I	179	C2
Lunano	I	136	B1
Lunas	F	130	B2
Lund	N	199	A8
Lund, *Skåne*	S	61	D3
Lund, *Västra Götaland*	S	54	A3
Lundamo	N	199	B7
Lunde	DK	59	C1
Lunde, *Sogn og Fjordane*	N	46	A3
Lunde, *Sogn og Fjordane*	N	46	A3
Lunde, *Telemark*	N	53	A5
Lunde	S	200	D3
Lundebyvollen	N	49	B4
Lunden	D	64	B2
Lunderseter	N	49	B4
Lunderskov	DK	59	C2
Lundsberg	S	55	A5
Lüneburg	D	72	A3
Lunel	F	131	B3
Lünen	D	81	A3
Lunéville	F	92	C2
Lungern	CH	106	C3
Lungro	I	174	B2
Luninyets	BY	13	B7
Lünne	D	71	B4
Lunner	N	48	B2
Lunteren	NL	70	B2
Lunz am See	A	110	B2
Luogosanto	I	178	A3
Łupawa	PL	68	A2
Lupión	E	157	B4
Lupoglav	HR	123	B3
Luppa	D	83	A4
Luque	E	163	A3
Lurago d'Erba	I	120	B2
Lúras	I	178	B3
Lurcy-Lévis	F	104	C1
Lure	F	105	B5
Lurgan	GB	27	B4
Luri	F	180	A2
Lury-sur-Arnon	F	103	B4
Lušci Palanka	BIH	124	C2
Lusévera	I	122	A2
Lushnjë	AL	182	C1
Lusignan	F	115	B4
Lusigny-sur-Barse	F	104	A3
Lusnić	BIH	138	B2
Luso	P	148	B1
Lusówko	PL	75	B5
Luspebryggan	S	196	B2
Luss	GB	34	B3
Lussac	F	128	B2
Lussac-les-Châteaux	F	115	B4
Lussac-les-Eglises	F	115	B5
Lussan	F	131	A3
Lüssow	D	65	C5
Lustenau	A	107	B4
Luštěnice	CZ	84	B2
Luster	N	47	A4
Lutago	I	108	C2
Lutherstadt Wittenberg	D	83	A4
Lütjenburg	D	65	B3
Lutnes	N	49	A4
Lutocin	PL	77	B4
Lutomiersk	PL	86	A3
Luton	GB	44	B3
Lutry	CH	106	C1
Lutsk	UA	13	C6
Lutter am Barenberge	D	72	C3
Lutterworth	GB	40	C2
Lututów	PL	86	A2
Lützen	D	83	A4
Lutzow	D	73	A4
Luusua	FIN	197	C10
Luvos	S	196	C1
Luxembourg	L	92	B2
Luxeuil-les-Bains	F	105	B5
Luxey	F	128	B2
Luz, *Évora*	P	155	C3
Luz, *Faro*	P	160	B2
Luz, *Faro*	P	160	B1
Luz-St. Sauveur	F	145	B3
Luzarches	F	90	B2
Luže	CZ	97	B4
Luzech	F	129	B4
Luzern	CH	106	B3
Luzino	PL	68	A3
Luzy	F	104	C2
Luzzi	I	174	B2
L'viv	UA	13	D6
Lwówek	PL	75	B5
Lwówek Śląski	PL	84	A3
Lyakhavichy	BY	13	B7
Lybster	GB	32	C3
Lychen	D	74	A2
Lychkova	RUS	9	D8
Lyckeby	S	63	B3
Lycksele	S	200	B4
Lydd	GB	45	C4
Lydford	GB	42	B2
Lydney	GB	39	C4
Lyepyel	BY	13	A8
Lygna	N	48	B2
Lykkja	N	47	B5
Lykling	N	52	A1
Lyme Regis	GB	43	B4
Lymington	GB	44	C2
Lympne	GB	45	B5
Lyndhurst	GB	44	C2
Lyneham	GB	43	A5
Lyness	GB	33	C3
Lyngdal, *Buskerud*	N	47	C6
Lyngdal, *Vest-Agder*	N	52	B3
Lyngør	N	53	B5
Lyngsa	DK	58	A3
Lyngseidet	N	192	C4
Lyngsnes	N	199	A8
Lynmouth	GB	42	A3
Lynton	GB	42	A3
Lyntupy	BY	13	A7
Lyon	F	117	B4
Lyons-la-Forêt	F	90	B1
Lyozna	BY	13	A9
Lyrestad	S	55	B5
Lysá nad Labem	CZ	84	B2
Lysá pod Makytou	SK	98	B2
Lysebotn	N	52	A2
Lysekil	S	54	B2
Lysice	CZ	97	B4
Lysomice	PL	76	A3
Lysøysund	N	198	B6
Lyss	CH	106	B2
Lystrup	DK	59	B3
Lysvik	S	49	B5
Łyszkowice	PL	77	C4
Lytham St. Anne's	GB	38	A3
Lyuban	RUS	9	C7
Lyubertsy	RUS	9	E10
Lyubimets	BG	183	B8
Lyuboml'	UA	13	C6
Lyubytino	RUS	9	C8

M

Maaninkavaara	FIN	197	C11
Maarheeze	NL	80	A1
Maaseik	B	80	A1
Maastricht	NL	80	B1
Mablethorpe	GB	41	B4
Mably	F	117	A4
Macael	E	164	B2
Maçanet de Cabrenys	E	146	B3
Mação	P	154	B2
Macau	F	128	A2
Maccagno-Agra	I	120	A1
Maccarese	I	168	B2
Macchiagódena	I	170	B2
Macclesfield	GB	40	B1
Macduff	GB	33	D4
Maceda	E	140	B3
Macedo de Cavaleiros	P	149	A3
Maceira, *Guarda*	P	148	B2
Maceira, *Leiria*	P	154	B2
Macelj	HR	124	A1
Macerata	I	136	B2
Macerata Féltria	I	136	B1
Machault	F	91	B4
Machecoul	F	114	B2
Machrihanish	GB	34	C2
Machynlleth	GB	39	B3
Macieira	P	148	A1
Maciejowice	PL	87	A5
Macinaggio	F	180	A2
Mackenrode	D	82	A2
Mačkovci	SLO	111	C3
Macomer	I	178	B2
Macon	B	91	A4
Mâcon	F	117	A4
Macotera	E	150	B2
Macroom	IRL	29	C3
Macugnaga	I	119	B4
Madan	BG	183	B6
Madängsholm	S	55	B4
Madaras	H	126	A1
Maddaloni	I	170	B2
Made	NL	79	A4
Madeley	GB	38	B4
Maderuelo	E	151	A4
Madetkoski	FIN	197	B9
Madley	GB	39	B4
Madocsa	H	112	C2
Madona	LV	8	D5
Madonna di Campíglio	I	121	A3
Madrid	E	151	B4
Madridejos	E	157	A4
Madrigal de la Vera	E	150	B2
Madrigal de las Altas Torres	E	150	A2
Madrigalejo	E	156	A2
Madrigalejo de Monte	E	143	B3
Madriguera	E	151	A4
Madrigueras	E	158	B2
Madroñera	E	156	A2
Maël-Carhaix	F	100	A2
Maella	E	153	A4
Maello	E	150	B3
Maesteg	GB	39	C3
Mafra	P	154	C1
Magacela	E	156	B2
Magallon	E	144	C2
Magaluf	E	166	B2
Magán	E	151	C4
Magaña	E	144	C1
Magasa	I	121	B3
Magaz	E	142	C2
Magdeburg	D	73	B4
Magenta	I	120	B1
Magescq	F	128	C1
Maghera	GB	27	B4
Magherafelt	GB	27	B4
Maghull	GB	38	A4
Magione	I	135	B5
Maglaj	BIH	125	C4
Maglehem	S	63	C2
Magliano de'Marsi	I	169	A3
Magliano in Toscana	I	168	A1
Magliano Sabina	I	168	A2
Maglić	SRB	126	B1
Máglie	I	173	B4
Maglód	H	112	B3
Magnac-Bourg	F	115	C5
Magnac-Laval	F	115	B5
Magnieres	F	92	C2
Magnor	N	49	C4
Magnuszew	PL	87	A5
Magny-Cours	F	104	C2
Magny-en-Vexin	F	90	B1
Mágocs	H	125	A4
Magoute	P	154	C1
Maguilla	E	156	B2
Maguiresbridge	GB	27	B3
Magyarbóly	H	125	B4
Magyarkeszi	H	112	C2
Magyarszék	H	125	A4
Mahide	E	141	C4
Mahilyow	BY	13	B9
Mahmudiye	TR	187	C5
Mahora	E	158	B2
Mahovo	HR	124	B2
Mähring	D	95	B4
Maia	E	144	A2
Maia	P	148	A1
Maiaelrayo	E	151	A4
Maials	E	153	A4
Maîche	F	106	B1
Máida	I	175	C2
Maiden Bradley	GB	43	A4
Maiden Newton	GB	43	B4
Maidenhead	GB	44	B3
Maidstone	GB	45	B4
Maienfeld	CH	107	B4
Maignelay Montigny	F	90	B2
Maijanen	FIN	197	B8
Maillezais	F	114	B3
Mailly-le-Camp	F	91	C4
Mailly-le-Château	F	104	B2
Mainar	E	152	A2
Mainbernheim	D	94	B2
Mainburg	D	95	C3
Mainhardt	D	94	B1
Maintal	D	81	B4
Maintenon	F	90	C1
Mainvilliers	F	90	C1
Mainz	D	93	A4
Maiorca	P	148	B1
Mairena de Aljarafe	E	162	A1
Mairena del Alcor	E	162	A2
Maisach	D	108	A2
Maishofen	A	109	B3
Maison-Rouge	F	90	C3
Maissau	A	97	C3
Maisse	F	90	C2
Maizières-lès-Vic	F	92	C2
Maja	HR	124	B2
Majadahonda	E	151	B4
Majadas	E	150	C2
Majavatn	N	195	E4
Majs	H	125	B4
Majšperk	SLO	123	A4
Makarska	HR	138	B3
Makkum	NL	70	A2
Maklár	H	113	B4
Makó	H	126	A2
Makoszyce	PL	85	B5
Makov	SK	98	B2
Maków Mazowiecki	PL	77	B6
Maków Podhalański	PL	99	B3
Mąkowarsko	PL	76	A2
Makrakomi	GR	182	E4
Maksniemi	FIN	196	D7
Malå	S	195	E9
Mala Bosna	SRB	126	A1
Mala Kladuša	BIH	124	B1
Mala Krsna	SRB	127	C3
Malá Lehota	SK	98	C2
Mala Pijace	SRB	126	A1
Mala Subotica	HR	124	A2

Name	Country	Page	Grid
Malacky	SK	97	C5
Maladzyechna	BY	13	A7
Málaga	E	163	B3
Malagón	E	157	A4
Malaguilla	E	151	B4
Malahide	IRL	30	A2
Malalbergo	I	121	C4
Malanów	PL	76	C3
Malaucène	F	131	A4
Malaunay	F	89	A5
Malaya Vishera	RUS	9	C8
Malborghetto	I	109	C4
Malbork	PL	69	A4
Malborn	D	92	B2
Malbuisson	F	105	C5
Malcésine	I	121	B3
Malchin	D	74	A1
Malching	D	96	C1
Malchow	D	73	A5
Malcocinado	E	156	B2
Malczyce	PL	85	A4
Maldegem	B	79	A3
Maldon	GB	45	B4
Małdyty	PL	69	B4
Malè	I	121	B4
Malemort	F	129	A4
Malente	D	65	B3
Målerås	S	62	B3
Males	GR	185	D6
Malesherbes	F	90	C2
Malesina	GR	183	E5
Malestroit	F	101	B3
Maletto	I	177	B3
Malexander	S	56	B1
Malgrat de Mar	E	147	C3
Malhadas	P	149	A3
Mali Lošinj	HR	137	A3
Malia	CY	181	B1
Malia	GR	185	D6
Malicorne-sur-Sarthe	F	102	B1
Malijai	F	132	A2
Malildjoš	SRB	126	B1
Målilla	S	62	A3
Malin	IRL	27	A3
Málinec	SK	99	C3
Malingsbo	S	50	C2
Maliniec	PL	76	B3
Malinska	HR	123	B3
Maliq	AL	182	C2
Maljevac	HR	123	B4
Malkara	TR	186	B1
Małki	PL	69	B4
Malko Tŭrnovo	BG	17	D7
Mallaig	GB	34	B2
Mallaranny	IRL	28	A2
Mallemort	F	131	B4
Mallén	E	144	C2
Malléon	F	146	A2
Mallersdorf-Pfaffenberg	D	95	C4
Málles Venosta	I	108	C1
Malling	DK	59	B3
Mallnitz	A	109	C4
Mallow	IRL	29	B3
Mallwyd	GB	38	B3
Malm	N	199	A8
Malmbäck	S	62	A2
Malmberget	S	196	C3
Malmby	S	56	A3
Malmédy	B	80	B2
Malmesbury	GB	43	A4
Malmköping	S	56	A2
Malmö	S	61	D3
Malmon	S	54	B2
Malmslätt	S	56	B1
Malnate	I	120	B1
Malo	I	121	B4
Małogoszcz	PL	87	B4
Maloja	CH	120	A3
Małomice	PL	84	A3
Måløy	N	198	D2
Malpartida	E	155	B4
Malpartida de la Serena	E	156	B2
Malpartida de Plasencia	E	150	C1
Malpas	GB	38	A4
Malpas	P	155	B3
Malpica	P	155	B3
Malpica de Bergantiños	E	140	A2
Malpica de Tajo	E	150	C3
Malsch	D	93	C4
Malšice	CZ	96	B2
Malta	A	109	C4
Maltat	F	104	C2
Maltby	GB	40	B2
Malung	S	49	B5
Malungsfors	S	49	B5
Maluszów	PL	75	B4
Maluszyn	PL	87	B3
Malva	E	142	C1
Malvaglia	CH	120	A1
Malveira	P	154	C1
Malvik	N	199	B7
Malyn	UA	13	C8
Mamarrosa	P	148	B1
Mamer	L	92	B2
Mamers	F	89	B4
Mamirolle	F	105	B5
Mammendorf	D	108	A2
Mámmola	I	175	C2
Mamonovo	RUS	69	A4
Mamuras	AL	182	B1
Maña	SK	112	A2
Manacor	E	167	B3
Manavgat	TR	189	C6
Mancera de Abajo	E	150	B2
Mancha Real	E	163	A4
Manchester	GB	40	B1
Manching	D	95	C3
Manchita	E	156	B1
Manciano	I	168	A1
Manciet	F	128	C3
Mandal	N	52	B3
Mandanici	I	177	A4
Mándas	I	179	C3
Mandatoríccio	I	174	B2
Mandayona	E	151	B5
Mandelieu-la-Napoule	F	132	B2
Mandello del Lário	I	120	B2
Mandelsloh	D	72	B2
Manderfeld	B	80	B2
Manderscheid	D	80	B2
Mandino Selo	BIH	138	B3
Mandoudi	GR	183	E5
Mandra	GR	185	A4
Mandraki	GR	188	C2
Mandúria	I	173	B3
Mane, Alpes-de-Haute-Provence	F	132	B1
Mane, Haute-Garonne	F	145	A4
Manérbio	I	120	B3
Mañeru	E	144	B2
Manetin	CZ	96	B1
Manfredónia	I	171	B3
Mangalia	RO	17	D8
Manganeses de la Lampreana	E	149	A4
Manganeses de la Polvorosa	E	141	B5
Mangen	N	48	C3
Manger	N	46	B2
Mangiennes	F	92	B1
Mangotsfield	GB	43	A4
Mångsbodarna	S	49	A5
Mangualde	P	148	B2
Maniago	I	122	A1
Manilva	E	162	B2
Manisa	TR	186	D2
Mank	A	110	A2
Månkarbo	S	51	B4
Manlleu	E	147	C3
Manna	DK	58	A2
Männedorf	CH	107	B3
Mannersdorf am Leithagebirge	A	111	B3
Mannheim	D	93	B4
Manningtree	GB	45	B5
Manoppello	I	169	A4
Manorbier	GB	39	C2
Manorhamilton	IRL	26	B2
Manosque	F	132	B1
Manowo	PL	67	B5
Manresa	E	147	C2
Manschnow	D	74	B3
Mansfeld	D	82	A3
Mansfield	GB	40	B2
Mansilla de Burgos	E	143	B3
Mansilla de las Mulas	E	142	B1
Manskog	S	55	A3
Mansle	F	115	C4
Manso	F	180	A1
Manteigas	P	148	B2
Mantel	D	95	B4
Mantes-la-Jolie	F	90	C1
Mantes-la-Ville	F	90	C1
Manthelan	F	102	B2
Mantorp	S	56	B1
Mántova	I	121	B3
Mänttä	FIN	8	A4
Mäntyjärvi	FIN	197	C10
Manuel	E	159	B3
Manzanal de Arriba	E	141	B4
Manzanares	E	157	A4
Manzanares el Real	E	151	B4
Manzaneda, León	E	141	B4
Manzaneda, Orense	E	141	B3
Manzanedo	E	143	B3
Manzaneque	E	157	A4
Manzanilla	E	161	B3
Manzat	F	116	B2
Manziana	I	168	A2
Manziat	F	117	A4
Maó	E	167	B4
Maoča	BIH	125	C4
Maqueda	E	150	B3
Mara	E	152	A2
Maramaraereğlisi	TR	186	B3
Maraña	E	142	A1
Maranchón	E	152	A1
Maranello	I	135	A3
Marano	I	170	C2
Marano Lagunare	I	122	B2
Marans	F	114	B2
Maratea	I	174	B1
Marateca	P	154	C2
Marathokambos	GR	188	B1
Marathonas	GR	185	A4
Marathóvouno	CY	181	A2
Marazion	GB	42	B1
Marbach, Baden-Württemberg	D	94	C1
Marbach, Hessen	D	82	B1
Marbach	F	92	C2
Marbäck	S	60	B3
Mårbacka	S	55	A4
Marbella	E	162	B3
Marboz	F	118	A2
Marburg	H	81	B4
Marcali	H	111	C4
Marčana	HR	122	C2
Marcaria	I	121	B3
Marcelová	SK	112	B2
Marcenat	F	116	B2
March	GB	41	C4
Marchamalo	E	151	B4
Marchaux	F	105	B5
Marche-en-Famenne	B	79	B5
Marchegg	A	111	A3
Marchena	E	162	A2
Marchenoir	F	103	B3
Marcheprime	F	128	B2
Marciac	F	128	C3
Marciana Marina	I	134	C3
Marcianise	I	170	B2
Marcigny	F	117	A4
Marcilla	E	144	B2
Marcillac-la-Croisille	F	116	B2
Marcillac-Vallon	F	130	A1
Marcillat-en-Combraille	F	116	A2
Marcille-sur-Seine	F	91	C3
Marcilloles	F	118	B2
Marcilly-le-Hayer	F	91	C3
Marcinkowice	PL	75	A5
Marciszów	PL	85	B4
Marck	F	78	B1
Marckolsheim	F	106	A2
Marco de Canevezes	P	148	A1
Mårdsele	S	200	B5
Mårdsjö	S	200	C1
Mareham le Fen	GB	41	B3
Marek	S	62	A3
Marennes	F	114	C2
Maresquel	F	78	B1
Mareuil	F	115	C4
Mareuil-en-Brie	F	91	C3
Mareuil-sur-Arnon	F	103	C4
Mareuil-sur-Lay	F	114	B2
Mareuil-sur-Ourcq	F	90	B3
Margam	GB	39	C3
Margariti	GR	182	D2
Margate	GB	45	B5
Margaux	F	128	A2
Margerie-Hancourt	F	91	C4
Margès	F	117	B5
Margherita di Savóia	I	171	B4
Margita	SRB	126	B3
Margone	I	119	B4
Margonin	PL	76	B2
Marguerittes	F	131	B3
Margut	F	91	B5
Maria	E	164	B2
Maria Neustift	A	110	B1
Maria Saal	A	110	C1
Mariager	DK	58	B2
Mariana	E	152	B1
Mariannelund	S	62	A3
Marianópoli	I	176	B2
Mariánské Lázně	CZ	95	B4
Mariapfarr	A	109	B4
Mariazell	A	110	B2
Maribo	DK	65	B4
Maribor	SLO	110	C2
Marieberg	S	56	A1
Mariefred	S	56	A3
Mariehamn	FIN	51	B6
Marieholm	S	61	D3
Mariembourg	B	91	A4
Marienbaum	D	80	A2
Marienberg	D	83	B5
Marienheide	D	81	A3
Mariental	D	73	B3
Mariestad	S	55	B4
Marieux	F	90	A2
Marigliano	I	170	C2
Marignane	F	131	B4
Marigny, Jura	F	105	C4
Marigny, Manche	F	88	A2
Marigny-le-Châtel	F	91	C3
Marija Bistrica	HR	124	A2
Marijampolė	LT	13	A5
Marín	E	140	B2
Marina	HR	138	B2
Marina del Cantone	I	170	C2
Marina di Acquappesa	I	174	B1
Marina di Alberese	I	168	A1
Marina di Amendolara	I	174	B2
Marina di Árbus	I	179	C2
Marina di Campo	I	134	C3
Marina di Carrara	I	134	A3
Marina di Castagneto-Donorático	I	134	B3
Marina di Cécina	I	134	B3
Marina di Gáiro	I	179	C3
Marina di Ginosa	I	173	B2
Marina di Gioiosa Iónica	I	175	C2
Marina di Grosseto	I	135	C3
Marina di Léuca	I	173	C4
Marina di Massa	I	134	A3
Marina di Nováglie	I	173	C4
Marina di Pisa	I	134	B3
Marina di Ragusa	I	177	C3
Marina di Ravenna	I	135	A5
Marina di Torre Grande	I	179	C2
Marina Romea	I	135	A5
Marinaleda	E	162	A3
Marine de Sisco	F	180	A2
Marinella	I	176	B1
Marinella di Sarzana	I	134	A3
Marineo	I	176	B2
Marines	F	90	B1
Maringues	F	116	B3
Marinha das Ondas	P	154	A2
Marinha Grande	P	154	B2
Marinhas	P	148	A1
Marino	I	168	B2
Marjaliza	E	157	A4
Markabygd	N	199	B8
Markaryd	S	61	C3
Markdorf	D	107	B4
Markelo	NL	71	B3
Market Deeping	GB	40	C3
Market Drayton	GB	38	B4
Market Harborough	GB	40	C3
Market Rasen	GB	40	B3
Market Warsop	GB	40	B2
Market Weighton	GB	40	B3
Markethill	GB	27	B4
Markgröningen	D	93	C5
Markhausen	D	71	B4
Marki	PL	77	B6
Markina-Xemein	E	143	A4
Markinch	GB	35	B4
Märkische Buchholz	D	74	B2
Markitta	S	196	B4
Markkleeberg	D	83	A4
Marklohe	D	72	B2
Marknesse	NL	70	B2
Markneukirchen	D	83	B4
Markopoulo	GR	185	B4
Markovac, Srbija	SRB	127	C3
Markovac, Vojvodina	SRB	126	B3
Markowice	PL	86	B2
Markranstädt	D	83	A4
Marksuhl	D	82	B2
Markt Allhau	A	111	B3
Markt Bibart	D	94	B2
Markt Erlbach	D	94	B2
Markt-heidenfeld	D	94	B1
Markt Indersdorf	D	95	C3
Markt Rettenbach	D	108	B1
Markt Schwaben	D	108	A2
Markt-Übelbach	A	110	B2
Marktbreit	D	94	B2
Marktl	D	95	C4
Marktleuthen	D	83	B3
Marktoberdorf	D	108	B1
Marktredwitz	D	95	A4
Markusica	HR	125	B4
Markušovce	SK	99	C4
Marl	D	80	A3
Marlborough, Devon	GB	42	B3
Marlborough, Wiltshire	GB	44	B2
Marle	F	91	B3
Marlieux	F	117	A4
Marlow	D	66	B1
Marlow	GB	44	B3
Marma	S	51	B4
Marmagne	F	104	C3
Marmande	F	128	B3
Marmara	TR	186	B2
Marmaris	TR	188	C3
Marmelete	P	160	B1
Marmolejo	E	157	B3
Marmoutier	F	93	C3
Marnay	F	105	B4
Marne	D	64	C2
Marnheim	D	93	B4
Marnitz	D	73	A4
Maroldsweisach	D	82	B2
Marolles-les-Braults	F	89	B4
Maromme	F	89	A5
Marone	I	120	B3
Maronia	GR	183	C7
Maroslele	H	126	A2
Maróstica	I	121	B4
Marotta	I	136	B2
Marpisa	GR	185	B6
Marquion	F	78	B3
Marquise	F	78	B1
Marradi	I	135	A4
Marrasjärvi	FIN	197	C8
Marraskoski	FIN	197	C8
Marratxi	E	166	B2
Marrúbiu	I	179	C2
Marrum	NL	70	A2
Marrupe	E	150	B3
Mars-la-Tours	F	92	B1
Marsac	F	129	C5
Marsac-en-Livradois	F	117	B3
Marságlia	I	120	C2
Marsala	I	176	B1
Marsberg	D	81	A4
Marsciano	I	135	C5
Marseillan	F	130	B2
Marseille = Marseilles	F	131	B4
Marseille en Beauvaisis	F	90	B1
Marseilles = Marseille	F	131	B4
Marske-by-the-Sea	GB	37	B5
Marsliden	S	195	E6
Marson	F	91	C4
Märsta	S	57	A3
Marstal	DK	65	B3
Marstrand	S	60	B1
Marta	I	168	A1
Martano	I	173	B4
Martel	F	129	B4
Martelange	B	92	B1
Martfeld	D	72	B2
Martfű	H	113	B4
Martham	GB	41	C5
Marthon	F	115	C4
Martiago	E	149	B3
Martigné-Briand	F	102	B1
Martigné-Ferchaud	F	101	B4
Martigne-sur-Mayenne	F	102	A1
Martigny	CH	119	A3
Martigny-les-Bains	F	105	A4
Martigues	F	131	B4
Martim-Longo	P	160	B2
Martin	SK	98	B2
Martin de la Jara	E	162	A3
Martin Muñoz de las Posadas	E	150	A3
Martina	CH	108	C1
Martina Franca	I	173	B3
Martinamor	E	150	B2
Martinengo	I	120	B2
Martinsberg	A	97	C3
Martinšćica	HR	123	C3
Martinšhöhe	D	93	B3
Martinsicuro	I	136	C2
Martinszell	D	107	B5
Mártis	I	178	B2
Martofte	DK	59	C3
Martonvásár	H	112	B2
Martorell	E	147	C2
Martos	E	163	A4
Martres Tolosane	F	146	A1
Martti	FIN	197	B11
Marugán	E	150	B3
Marúggio	I	173	B3
Marvão	P	155	B3
Marvejols	F	130	A2
Marville	F	92	B1
Marwałd	PL	77	A4
Marykirk	GB	35	B5
Marypark	GB	32	D3
Maryport	GB	36	B3
Marytavy	GB	42	B2
Marzabotto	I	135	A4
Marzahna	D	74	B1
Marzahne	D	73	B5
Marzamemi	I	177	C4
Marzocca	I	136	B2
Mas-Cabardès	F	146	A3
Mas de Barberáns	E	153	B4
Mas de las Matas	E	153	B3
Masa	E	143	B3
Mascali	I	177	B4
Mascaraque	E	157	A4
Mascarenhas	P	149	A2
Masegoso	E	158	C1
Masegoso de Tajuña	E	151	B5
Masera	I	119	A5
Masevaux	F	106	B1
Masfjorden	N	46	B2
Masham	GB	37	B5
Masi	N	192	C7
Maside	E	140	B2
Maslacq	F	144	A3
Maslinica	HR	138	B2
Masloc	RO	126	B3
Maslovare	BIH	138	A3
Masone	I	133	A4
Massa	I	134	A3
Massa Fiscáglia	I	121	C5
Massa Lombarda	I	135	A4
Massa Lubrense	I	170	C2
Massa Maríttima	I	135	B3
Massa Martana	I	136	C1
Massafra	I	173	B3
Massamagrell	E	159	B3
Massanassa	E	159	B3
Massarosa	I	134	B3
Massat	F	146	B2
Massay	F	103	B3
Massbach	D	82	B2
Masseret	F	116	B1
Masseube	F	145	A4
Massiac	F	116	B3
Massignac	F	115	C4
Massing	D	95	C4
Massmechelen	B	80	B1
Masterud	N	49	B4
Mästocka	S	61	C3
Masty	BY	13	B6
Masúa	I	179	C2
Masueco	E	149	A3
Masugnsbyn	S	196	B5
Mašun	SLO	123	B3
Maszewo, Lubuskie	PL	75	B3
Maszewo, Zachodnio-Pomorskie	PL	75	A4
Mata de Alcántara	E	155	B4
Matalebreras	E	144	C1
Matallana de Torio	E	142	B1
Matamala	E	151	A5
Mataporquera	E	142	B2
Matapozuelos	E	150	A3
Mataró	E	147	C3
Matarocco	I	176	B1
Matélica	I	136	B2
Matera	I	172	B2
Mátészalka	H	16	B5
Matet	E	159	B3
Matfors	S	200	D3
Matha	F	115	C3
Mathay	F	106	B1
Matignon	F	101	A3
Matilla de los Caños del Rio	E	149	B4
Matlock	GB	40	B2
Matosinhos	P	148	A1
Matour	F	117	A4
Mátrafüred	H	113	B3
Mátraterenye	H	113	A3
Matre, Hordaland	N	46	B2
Matre, Hordaland	N	52	A1
Matrei am Brenner	A	108	B2
Matrei in Osttirol	A	109	B3
Matrice	I	170	B2
Matsdal	S	195	E6
Mattersburg	A	111	B3
Mattighofen	A	109	A4
Mattinata	I	171	B4
Mattos	P	154	B2
Mattsee	A	109	B4
Mattsmyra	S	50	A2
Måttsund	S	196	D5
Matulji	HR	123	B3
Maubert-Fontaine	F	91	B4
Maubeuge	F	79	B3
Maubourguet	F	145	A4
Mauchline	GB	36	A2
Mauguio	F	131	B3
Maulbronn	D	93	C4
Mauléon	F	114	B3
Mauléon-Barousse	F	145	B4
Mauléon-Licharre	F	144	A3
Maulévrier	F	114	A3
Maum	IRL	28	A2
Maurach	A	108	B2
Maure-de-Bretagne	F	101	B4
Maureilhan	F	130	B2
Măureni	RO	126	B3
Mauriac	F	116	B2
Mauron	F	101	A3
Maurs	F	116	C2
Maury	F	146	B3
Maussane-les-Alpilles	F	131	B3
Mautern	A	97	C3
Mautern im Steiermark	A	110	B1
Mauterndorf	A	109	B4
Mauthausen	A	110	A1
Mauthen	A	109	C3
Mauvezin	F	129	C3
Mauzé-sur-le-Mignon	F	114	B3
Maxent	F	101	B3
Maxey-sur-Vaise	F	92	C1
Maxial	P	154	B1

Maxieira P 154 B2
Maxwellheugh GB 35 C5
Mayalde E 149 A4
Maybole GB 36 A2
Mayen D 80 B3
Mayenne F 88 B3
Mayet F 102 B2
Maylough IRL 28 A3
Mayorga E 142 B1
Mayres F 117 C4
Mayrhofen A 108 B2
Mazagón E 161 B3
Mazaleón E 153 A4
Mazamet F 130 B1
Mazan F 131 A4
Mazara del Vallo I 176 B1
Mazarambroz E 157 A3
Mazarete E 152 B1
Mazaricos E 140 B2
Mazarrón E 165 B3
Mažeikiai LT 8 D3
Mazères F 146 A2
Mazères-sur-Salat F 145 A4
Mazières-en-Gâtine F 115 B3
Mazin HR 138 A1
Mazuelo E 143 B3
Mazyr BY 13 B8
Mazzarino I 177 B3
Mazzarrà Sant'Andrea I 177 A4
Mazzo di Valtellina I 120 A3
Mchowo PL 77 A5
Mdzewo PL 77 B5
Mealabost GB 31 A2
Mealhada P 148 B1
Méan B 79 B5
Meana Sardo I 179 C3
Meaulne F 103 C4
Meaux F 90 C2
Mebonden N 199 B8
Mecerreyes E 143 B3
Mechelen B 79 A4
Mechernich D 80 B2
Mechnica PL 86 B2
Mechowo PL 67 C4
Mechterstädt D 82 B2
Mecidiye TR 186 B1
Mecikal PL 68 B2
Mecina-Bombarón E 164 C1
Mecitözü TR 23 A8
Meckenbeuren D 107 B4
Meckenheim, *Rheinland-Pfalz* D 80 B3
Meckenheim, *Rheinland-Pfalz* D 93 B4
Meckesheim D 93 B4
Mecseknádasd H 125 A4
Meda I 120 B2
Meda P 149 B2
Medak HR 137 A4
Mede I 120 B1
Medebach D 81 A4
Medelim P 155 A3
Medemblik NL 70 B2
Medena Selista BIH 138 A2
Medesano I 120 C3
Medevi S 55 B5
Medgidia RO 17 C8
Medgyesháza H 113 C5
Medhamn S 55 A4
Mediaş RO 17 B6
Medicina I 135 A4
Medina de las Torres E 155 C4
Medina de Pomar E 143 B3
Medina de Rioseco E 142 C1
Medina del Campo E 150 A3
Medina Sidonia E 162 B2
Medinaceli E 152 A1
Medinilla E 150 B2
Medja SRB 126 B2
Medjedja BIH 139 B5
Medulin HR 122 C2
Meduno I 122 A1
Medveda SRB 127 C3
Medvedov SK 111 B4
Medvezhyegorsk RUS 9 A9
Medvide HR 137 A4
Medvode SLO 123 A3
Medzev SK 99 C4
Medžitlija MK 182 C3
Meerane D 83 B4
Meerle B 79 A4
Meersburg D 107 B4
Meeuwen B 79 A5
Megalo Horio GR 188 C2
Megalopoli GR 184 B3
Megara GR 185 A4
Megève F 118 B3
Meggenhofen A 109 A4
Megra RUS 9 B10
Megyaszó H 113 A5
Mehamn N 193 A11
Mehedeby S 51 B4
Méhkerék H 113 C5
Mehun-sur-Yèvre F 103 B4
Meigle GB 35 B4
Meijel NL 80 A1
Meilen CH 107 B3
Meilhan F 128 C2
Meimôa P 149 B2
Meina I 119 B5
Meine D 73 B3
Meinersen D 72 B3
Meinerzhagen D 81 A3
Meiningen D 82 B2
Meira E 141 A3
Meiringen CH 106 C3
Meisenheim D 93 B3
Meissen D 83 A5
Meitingen D 94 C2
Meix-devant-Virton B 92 B1
Męka PL 86 A2
Meka Gruda BIH 139 B4
Mel I 121 A5
Melbu N 194 B5
Melč CZ 98 B1
Meldal N 198 B6
Méldola I 135 A5
Meldorf D 64 B2
Melegnano I 120 B2
Melenci SRB 126 B2
Melendugno I 173 B4
Melfi I 172 B1
Melfjordbotn N 195 D4
Melgaço P 140 B2
Melgar de Arriba E 142 B1
Melgar de Fernamental E 142 B2
Melgar de Yuso E 142 B2
Melhus N 199 B7
Meliana E 159 B3
Melide CH 120 B1
Melide E 140 B2
Melides P 160 A1
Meligales GR 184 B2
Melilli I 177 B4
Melinovac HR 124 C1
Melisenda I 179 C3
Melisey F 105 B5
Mélito di Porto Salvo I 175 D1
Melk A 110 A2
Melksham GB 43 A4
Mellakoski FIN 196 C7
Mellanström S 195 E9
Mellbystrand S 61 C2
Melle B 79 A3
Melle D 71 B5
Melle F 115 B3
Mellendorf D 72 B2
Mellerud S 54 B3
Mellieha M 175 C3
Mellösa S 56 A2
Mellrichstadt D 82 B2
Mělnické Vtelno CZ 84 B2
Mělník CZ 84 B2
Melón E 140 B2
Melrose GB 35 C5
Mels CH 107 B4
Melsungen D 82 A1
Meltaus FIN 197 C8
Meltham GB 40 B2
Melton Mowbray GB 40 C3
Meltosjärvi FIN 196 C7
Melun F 90 C2
Melvaig GB 31 B3
Melvich GB 32 C3
Mélykút H 126 A1
Melzo I 120 B2
Memaliaj AL 182 C1
Membrilla E 157 B4
Membrio E 155 B3
Memer F 129 B4
Memmelsdorf D 94 B2
Memmingen D 107 B5
Memoria P 154 B2
Menággio I 120 A2
Menai Bridge GB 38 A2
Menasalbas E 157 A3
Menat F 116 A2
Mendavia E 144 B1
Mendaza E 144 B1
Mende F 130 A2
Menden D 81 A3
Menderes TR 188 A2
Mendig D 80 B3
Mendiga P 154 B2
Mendrisio CH 120 B1
Ménéac F 101 A3
Menemen TR 188 A2
Menen B 78 B3
Menesjärvi FIN 193 D10
Menetou-Salon F 103 B4
Menfi I 176 B1
Ménfőcsanak H 111 B4
Mengamuñoz E 150 B3
Mengen D 107 A4
Mengen TR 187 B7
Mengeš SLO 123 A3
Mengíbar E 157 C4
Mengkofen D 95 C4
Menou F 104 B2
Mens F 118 C2
Menslage D 71 B4
Mensträsk S 200 A5
Mentana I 168 A2
Menton F 133 B3
Méntrida E 151 B3
Méobecq F 115 B5
Méounes-les-Montrieux F 132 B1
Meppel NL 70 B3
Meppen D 71 B4
Mequinenza E 153 A4
Mer F 103 B3
Mera, *Coruña* E 140 A2
Mera, *Coruña* E 140 A3
Meråker N 199 B8
Merano I 108 C2
Merate I 120 B2
Mercadillo E 143 A3
Mercatale I 135 B5
Mercatino Conca I 136 B1
Mercato San Severino I 170 C2
Mercato Saraceno I 135 B5
Merching D 108 A1
Merchtem B 79 B4
Merdrignac F 101 A3
Merdžanići BIH 139 B3
Meré E 142 A2
Mere GB 43 A4
Meréville F 90 C2
Merfeld D 80 A3
Méribel F 118 B3
Méribel Motraret F 118 B3
Meriç TR 186 A1
Mérida E 155 C4
Mérignac F 128 B2
Měřín CZ 97 B3
Mering D 94 C2
Merkendorf D 94 B2
Merklin CZ 96 B1
Merksplas B 79 A4
Merlånna S 56 A2
Merlimont Plage F 78 B1
Mern DK 65 A5
Mernye H 111 C4
Mers-les-Bains F 90 A1
Mersch L 92 B2
Merseburg D 83 A3
Merthyr Tydfil GB 39 C3
Mertingen D 94 C2
Mértola P 160 B2
Méru F 90 B2
Merufe P 140 B2
Mervans F 105 C4
Merville F 78 B2
Méry-sur-Seine F 91 C3
Merzen D 71 B4
Merzifon TR 23 A8
Merzig D 92 B2
Mesagne I 173 B3
Mesão Frio P 148 A2
Mesas de Ibor E 156 A2
Meschede D 81 A4
Meschers-sur-Gironde F 114 C3
Meslay-du-Maine F 102 B1
Mesna N 48 A2
Mesnalien N 48 A2
Mesocco CH 120 A2
Mésola I 122 C1
Mesologi GR 184 A2
Mesopotamo GR 182 D2
Mesoraca I 175 B2
Messac F 101 B4
Messancy B 92 B1
Messdorf D 73 B4
Messei F 88 B3
Messejana P 160 B1
Messelt N 48 A3
Messina I 177 A4
Messingen D 71 B4
Messini GR 184 B3
Messkirch D 107 B4
Messlingen S 199 C9
Messtetten D 107 A3
Mesta GR 185 A6
Mestanza E 157 B3
Městec Králové CZ 84 B3
Mestlin D 73 A4
Město Albrechtice CZ 85 B5
Město Libavá CZ 98 B1
Město Touškov CZ 96 B1
Mestre I 122 B1
Mesvres F 104 C3
Mesztegnyő H 111 C4
Meta I 170 C2
Metajna HR 137 A4
Metelen D 71 B4
Methana GR 185 B4
Methlick GB 33 D4
Methven GB 35 B4
Methwold GB 41 C4
Metković HR 139 B3
Metlika SLO 123 B4
Metnitz A 110 C1
Metsäkylä FIN 197 D11
Metslawier NL 70 A3
Metsovo GR 182 D3
Metten D 95 C4
Mettendorf D 92 B2
Mettet B 79 B4
Mettingen D 71 B4
Mettlach D 92 B2
Mettlen CH 106 C2
Mettmann D 80 A2
Metz F 92 B2
Metzervisse F 92 B2
Metzingen D 94 C1
Meulan F 90 B1
Meung-sur-Loire F 103 B3
Meuselwitz D 83 A4
Meuzac F 115 C5
Mevagissey GB 42 B2
Mexborough GB 40 B2
Meximieux F 118 B2
Mey GB 32 C3
Meyenburg D 73 A5
Meyerhöfen D 71 B5
Meylan F 118 B2
Meymac F 116 B2
Meyrargues F 132 B1
Meyrueis F 130 A2
Meyssac F 129 A4
Meysse F 117 C4
Meyzieu F 117 B4
Mèze F 130 B2
Mézériat F 117 A5
Mežica SLO 110 C1
Mézidon-Canon F 89 A3
Mézières-en-Brenne F 115 B5
Mézières-sur-Issoire F 115 B4
Mézilhac F 117 C4
Mézilles F 104 B2
Mézin F 128 B3
Mezőberény H 113 C5
Mezőcsát H 113 B4
Mezőfalva H 112 C2
Mezőhegyes H 126 A2
Mezőkeresztes H 113 B4
Mezőkomárom H 112 C2
Mezőkövácsháza H 113 C4
Mezőkövesd H 113 B4
Mezőörs H 111 B4
Mézos F 128 B1
Mezőszilas H 112 C2
Mezőtúr H 113 B4
Mezquita de Jarque E 153 B3
Mezzano, *Emilia Romagna* I 135 A5
Mezzano, *Trentino Alto Adige* I 121 A4
Mezzojuso I 176 B2
Mezzoldo I 120 A2
Mezzolombardo I 121 A4
Mgarr M 175 C3
Miajadas E 156 A2
Miały PL 75 B5
Mianowice PL 68 A2
Miasteczko Krajeńskie PL 76 A2
Miasteczko Śl. PL 86 B2
Miastko PL 68 A1
Michalovce SK 12 D4
Michałowice PL 87 B3
Michelau D 94 B2
Michelbach D 94 B2
Micheldorf A 110 B1
Michelhausen A 110 A2
Michelsneukirchen D 95 B4
Michelstadt D 93 B5
Michendorf D 74 B2
Michurin BG 17 D7
Mickleover GB 40 C2
Mid Yell GB 33 A5
Midbea GB 33 B4
Middelburg NL 79 A3
Middelfart DK 59 C2
Middelharnis NL 79 A4
Middelkerke B 78 A2
Middelstum NL 71 A3
Middlesbrough GB 37 B5
Middleton Cheney GB 44 A2
Middleton-in-Teesdale GB 37 B4
Middletown GB 27 B4
Middlewich GB 38 A4
Middlezoy GB 43 A4
Midhurst GB 44 C3
Midleton IRL 29 C3
Midlum D 64 C1
Midsomer Norton GB 43 A4
Midtgulen N 198 D2
Midtskogberget N 49 A4
Midwolda NL 71 A4
Miechów PL 87 B4
Miedes de Aragón E 152 A2
Miedes de Atienza E 151 A4
Międzybodzie Bielskie PL 99 B3
Międzybórz PL 85 A5
Międzychód PL 75 B4
Międzylesie PL 85 B4
Międzyrzec Podlaski PL 12 C5
Międzyrzecz PL 75 B4
Międzywodzie PL 67 B3
Międzyzdroje PL 67 C3
Miejska Górka PL 85 A4
Miélan F 145 A4
Mielec PL 87 B5
Mielęcin PL 75 A3
Mielno, *Warmińsko-Mazurskie* PL 77 A5
Mielno, *Zachodnio-Pomorskie* PL 67 B5
Miengo E 143 A3
Mieraslompolo FIN 193 C11
Miercurea Ciuc RO 17 B6
Mieres, *Asturias* E 141 A5
Mieres, *Girona* E 147 B3
Mieroszów PL 85 B4
Mierzyn PL 86 A3
Miesau D 93 B3
Miesbach D 108 B2
Mieścisko PL 76 B2
Mieste D 73 B4
Miesterhorst D 73 B4
Mieszków PL 76 B2
Mieszkowice PL 74 B3
Mietków PL 85 B4
Migennes F 104 B2
Miggiano I 173 C4
Migliánico I 169 A4
Migliarino I 121 C4
Migliónico I 172 B2
Mignano Monte Lungo I 169 B3
Migné F 115 B5
Miguel Esteban E 157 A4
Miguelturra E 157 B4
Mihajlovac SRB 127 C2
Miháld H 111 C4
Mihalgazi TR 187 B5
Mihaliççık TR 187 C6
Mihályi H 111 B4
Mihla D 82 A2
Mihohnić HR 123 B3
Miholjsko HR 123 B4
Mihovljan HR 124 A1
Mijares E 150 B3
Mijas E 163 B3
Mike H 124 A3
Mikines GR 184 B3
Mikkeli FIN 8 B5
Mikkelvik N 192 B3
Mikleuš HR 125 B3
Mikołajki Pomorskie PL 69 B4
Mikołów PL 86 B2
Mikonos GR 185 B6
Mikorzyn PL 86 A2
Mikro Derio GR 183 B8
Mikstat PL 86 A1
Mikulášovice CZ 84 B2
Mikulov CZ 97 C4
Mikulovice CZ 85 B5
Milagro E 144 B2
Miłakowo PL 69 A5
Milan = Milano I 120 B2
Miland N 47 C5
Milano = Milan I 120 B2
Milano Marittima I 135 A5
Milas TR 188 B2
Milazzo I 177 A4
Mildenhall GB 45 A4
Milejewo PL 69 A4
Milelín CZ 85 B3
Miletić SRB 125 B5
Miletićevo SRB 126 B3
Mileto I 175 C2
Milevsko CZ 96 B2
Milford IRL 26 A3
Milford Haven GB 39 C1
Milford on Sea GB 44 C2
Milhão P 149 A3
Milići BIH 139 A5
Miličin CZ 96 B2
Milicz PL 85 A5
Milín CZ 96 B2
Militello in Val di Catánia I 177 B3
Miljevina BIH 139 B4
Milkowice PL 85 A4
Millançay F 103 B3
Millares E 159 B3
Millas F 146 B3
Millau F 130 A2
Millesimo I 133 A4
Millevaches F 116 B2
Millom GB 36 B3
Millport GB 34 C3
Millstatt A 109 C4
Millstreet, *Cork* IRL 29 B2
Millstreet, *Waterford* IRL 29 B4
Milltown, *Galway* IRL 28 A3
Milltown, *Kerry* IRL 29 B1
Milltown Malbay IRL 28 B2
Milly-la-Forêt F 90 C2
Milmarcos E 152 A2
Milmersdorf D 74 A2
Milna HR 138 B2
Milnthorpe GB 37 B4
Milogórze PL 69 A5
Miłomłyn PL 69 B4
Milos GR 185 C5
Miloševo SRB 127 C3
Miłosław PL 76 B2
Milot AL 182 B1
Milówka PL 99 B3
Miltach D 95 B4
Miltenberg D 94 B1
Milton Keynes GB 44 A3
Miltzow D 66 B2
Milverton GB 43 A3
Milzyn PL 76 B3
Mimice HR 138 B2
Mimizan F 128 B1
Mimizan-Plage F 128 B1
Mimoň CZ 84 B2
Mina de Juliana P 160 B1
Mina de São Domingos P 160 B2
Minas de Riotinto E 161 B3
Minateda E 158 C2
Minaya E 158 B1
Minde P 154 B2
Mindelheim D 108 A1
Mindelstetten D 95 C3
Minden D 72 B1
Mindszent H 113 C4
Minehead GB 43 A3
Mineo I 177 B3
Minerbe I 121 B4
Minérbio I 121 C4
Minervino Murge I 171 B4
Minglanilla E 158 B2
Mingorria E 150 B3
Minnesund N 48 B3
Miño E 140 A2
Miño de San Esteban E 151 A4
Minsen D 71 A4
Minsk BY 13 B7
Mińsk Mazowiecki PL 12 B4
Minsterley GB 39 B4
Mintlaw GB 33 D4
Minturno I 169 B3
Mionica BIH 125 C4
Mionica SRB 127 C2
Mios F 128 B2
Mira E 158 B2
Mira I 121 B5
Mira P 148 B1
Mirabel E 155 B4
Mirabel-aux-Baronnies F 131 A4
Mirabella Eclano I 170 B3
Mirabella Imbáccari I 177 B3
Mirabello I 121 C4
Miradoux F 129 B3
Miraflores de la Sierra E 151 B4
Miralrio E 151 B5
Miramar P 148 A1
Miramare I 136 A1
Miramas F 131 B3
Mirambeau F 114 C3
Miramont-de-Guyenne F 129 B3
Miranda de Arga E 144 B2
Miranda de Ebro E 143 B4
Miranda do Corvo P 148 B1
Miranda do Douro P 149 A3
Mirande F 129 C3
Mirandela P 149 A2
Mirandilla E 155 C4
Mirándola I 121 C4
Miranje HR 137 A4
Mirano I 121 B5
Miras AL 182 C2
Miravet E 153 A4
Miré F 102 B1
Mirebeau F 102 C2
Mirebeau-sur-Bèze F 105 B4
Mirecourt F 105 A5
Mirepoix F 146 A2
Mires GR 185 D5
Miribel F 117 B4
Miričina BIH 125 C4
Mirina GR 183 D7
Mirna SLO 123 B4
Miroslav CZ 97 C4
Mirosławice PL 85 B4
Mirosławiec PL 75 A5
Mirošov CZ 96 B1
Mirotice CZ 96 B2
Mirovice CZ 96 B2
Mirow D 74 A1
Mirsk PL 84 B3
Mirzec PL 87 A5
Misi FIN 197 C9
Misilmeri I 176 A2
Miske H 112 C3
Miskolc H 113 A4
Mislinja SLO 110 C2
Missanello I 174 A2
Missillac F 101 B3
Mistelbach A 97 C4
Mistelbach D 95 B3
Misten N 194 C5
Misterbianco I 177 B4
Misterhult S 62 A4
Mistretta I 177 B3
Misurina I 109 C3
Mitchelstown IRL 29 B3
Mithimna GR 186 C1
Mithoni GR 184 C2
Mitilini GR 186 C1
Mitilinii GR 188 B1
Mittelberg, *Tirol* A 108 C1
Mittelberg, *Vorarlberg* A 107 B5
Mittenwald D 108 B2
Mittenwalde D 74 B2
Mitter-Kleinarl A 109 B4
Mitterback A 110 B2
Mitterdorf im Mürztal A 110 B2
Mittersheim F 92 C2
Mittersill A 109 B3
Mitterskirchen D 95 C4
Mitterteich D 95 B4
Mitton F 128 B2

Name		Page	Grid
Mittweida	D	83	B4
Mitwitz	D	82	B3
Mizhhir'ya	UA	13	D5
Mjällby	S	63	B2
Mjåvatn	N	53	B2
Mjöbäck	S	60	B2
Mjölby	S	56	B1
Mjølfjell	N	46	B1
Mjøndalen	N	53	A6
Mjørlund	N	48	B2
Mladá Boleslav	CZ	84	B4
Mladá Vožice	CZ	96	B2
Mladé Buky	CZ	85	B3
Mladenovac	SRB	127	C2
Mladenovo	SRB	126	B1
Mladikovine	BIH	139	A3
Mława	PL	77	A5
Mlinište	BIH	138	A2
Młodzieszyn	PL	77	B5
Młogoszyn	PL	77	B4
Młynary	PL	69	A4
Mnichóvice	CZ	96	B2
Mnichovo Hradiště	CZ	84	B2
Mniów	PL	87	A4
Mnisek nad Hnilcom	SK	99	C4
Mníšek pod Brdy	CZ	96	B2
Mniszek	PL	87	A4
Mniszków	PL	87	A4
Mo, *Hedmark*	N	48	B3
Mo, *Hordaland*	N	46	B2
Mo, *Møre og Romsdal*	N	198	C5
Mo, *Telemark*	N	53	A3
Mo, *Gävleborg*	S	51	A3
Mo, *Västra Götaland*	S	54	B2
Mo i Rana	N	195	D5
Moaña	E	140	B2
Moate	IRL	28	A4
Mocejón	E	151	C4
Močenok	SK	111	A4
Mochales	E	152	A1
Mochowo	PL	77	B4
Mochy	PL	75	B5
Mockern	D	73	B4
Mockfjärd	S	50	B1
Möckmühl	D	94	B1
Mockrehna	D	83	A4
Moclin	E	163	A4
Mocsa	H	112	B2
Möcsény	H	125	A4
Modane	F	118	B3
Modbury	GB	42	B3
Módena	I	121	C3
Möðrudalur	IS	191	B10
Módica	I	177	C3
Modigliana	I	135	A4
Modlin	PL	77	B5
Mödling	A	111	A3
Modliszewice	PL	87	A4
Modliszewko	PL	76	B2
Modogno	I	171	B4
Modra	SK	98	C1
Modran	BIH	125	C3
Modriča	BIH	125	C4
Modrý Kameň	SK	99	C3
Moëlan-sur-Mer	F	100	B2
Moelfre	GB	38	A2
Moelv	N	48	B2
Moen	I	194	A9
Moena	I	121	A4
Moerbeke	B	79	A3
Moers	D	80	A2
Móes	P	148	B2
Moffat	GB	36	A3
Mogadouro	P	149	A3
Mogata	S	56	B2
Móggio Udinese	I	122	A2
Mogielnica	PL	87	A4
Mogilany	PL	99	B3
Mogilno	PL	76	B2
Mogliano	I	136	B2
Mogliano Véneto	I	122	B1
Mogor	E	140	B2
Mógoro	I	179	C2
Moguer	E	161	B3
Mohács	H	125	B4
Moheda	S	62	A2
Mohedas	E	149	B3
Mohedas de la Jara	E	156	A2
Mohelnice	CZ	97	B4
Mohill	IRL	26	C3
Möhlin	CH	106	B2
Moholm	S	55	B5
Mohorn	D	83	A5
Mohyliv-Podil's'kyy	UA	13	D7
Moi	N	52	B2
Moià	E	147	C3
Móie	I	136	B2
Moimenta da Beira	P	148	B2
Moirans	F	118	B2
Moirans-en-Montagne	F	118	A2
Moisaküla	EST	8	C4
Moisdon-la-Rivière	F	101	B4
Moissac	F	129	B4
Moita, *Coimbra*	P	148	B1
Moita, *Guarda*	P	149	B2
Moita, *Santarém*	P	154	B2
Moita, *Setúbal*	P	154	C1
Moita dos Ferreiros	P	154	B1
Moixent	E	159	C3
Mojacar	E	164	B3
Mojados	E	150	A3
Mojmírovce	SK	112	A2
Mojtin	SK	98	C2
Möklinta	S	50	B3
Mokošica	HR	139	C4
Mokro Polje	HR	138	A2
Mokronog	SLO	123	B4
Mokrzyska	PL	99	A4
Møkster	N	46	B1
Mol	B	79	A5
Mol	SRB	126	B2
Mola di Bari	I	173	A3
Molai	GR	184	C3
Molare	I	133	A4
Molaretto	I	119	B4
Molas	F	145	A4
Molassano	I	134	A1
Molberger	D	71	B4
Mold	GB	38	A3
Molde	N	198	C4
Moldrup	DK	58	B2
Moledo do Minho	P	148	A1
Molfetta	I	171	B4
Molfsee	D	64	B3
Moliden	S	200	C4
Molières	F	129	B4
Molina de Aragón	E	152	B2
Molina de Segura	E	165	A3
Molinar	E	143	A3
Molinaseca	E	141	B4
Molinella	I	121	C4
Molinet	F	104	C2
Molini di Tures	I	108	C2
Molinicos	E	158	C1
Molinos de Duero	E	143	C4
Molins de Rei	E	147	C3
Moliterno	I	174	A1
Molkom	S	55	A4
Möllbrücke	A	109	C4
Mölle	S	61	C2
Molledo	E	142	A2
Möllenbeck	D	74	A2
Mollerussa	E	147	C1
Mollet de Perelada	E	146	B3
Mollina	E	163	A3
Mölln	D	73	A3
Mollö	S	54	B2
Mölltorp	S	55	B5
Mölnbo	S	56	A3
Mölndal	S	60	B2
Mölnlycke	S	60	B2
Molompize	F	116	B3
Moloy	F	105	B3
Molsheim	F	93	C3
Moltzow	D	73	A5
Molve	HR	124	A3
Molveno	I	121	A3
Molvizar	E	163	B4
Molzbichl	A	109	C4
Mombaróccio	I	136	B1
Mombeltrán	E	150	B2
Mombris	D	93	A5
Mombuey	E	141	B4
Momchilgrad	BG	183	B7
Mommark	DK	64	B3
Momo	I	119	B5
Monaghan	IRL	27	B4
Monar Lodge	GB	32	D2
Monasterace Marina	I	175	C2
Monasterevin	IRL	30	A1
Monasterio de Rodilla	E	143	B3
Monastir	I	179	C3
Monbahus	F	129	B3
Monbazillac	F	129	B3
Moncada	E	159	B3
Moncalieri	I	119	B4
Moncalvo	I	119	B5
Monção	P	140	B2
Moncarapacho	P	160	B2
Moncel-sur-Seille	F	92	C2
Monchegorsk	RUS	3	C13
Mönchen-gladbach = Munchen-Gladbach	D	80	A2
Mónchio della Corti	I	134	A3
Monchique	P	160	B1
Monclar-de-Quercy	F	129	C4
Moncofa	E	159	B3
Moncontour	F	101	A3
Moncoutant	F	114	B3
Monda	E	162	B3
Mondariz	E	140	B2
Mondavio	I	136	B1
Mondéjar	E	151	B4
Mondello	I	176	A2
Mondim de Basto	P	148	A2
Mondolfo	I	136	B2
Mondoñedo	E	141	A3
Mondorf-les-Bains	L	92	B2
Mondoubleau	F	102	B2
Mondovì	I	133	A3
Mondragon	F	131	A3
Mondragone	I	170	B1
Mondsee	A	109	B4
Monéglia	I	134	A2
Monegrillo	E	153	A3
Monein	F	145	A3
Monemvasia	GR	184	C4
Mónesi	I	133	A3
Monesiglio	I	133	A4
Monesterio	E	161	A3
Monestier-de-Clermont	F	118	C2
Monestiés	F	130	A1
Monéteau	F	104	B2
Moneygall	IRL	28	B4
Moneymore	GB	27	B4
Monfalcone	I	122	B2
Monfero	E	140	A2
Monflanquin	F	129	B3
Monflorite	E	145	B3
Monforte	P	155	B3
Monforte da Beira	E	155	B3
Monforte da Beira	P	155	B3
Monforte d'Alba	I	133	A3
Monforte de Lemos	E	140	B3
Monforte de Moyuela	E	152	A2
Monforte del Cid	E	165	A4
Monghidoro	I	135	A4
Mongiana	I	175	C2
Monguelfo	I	108	C3
Monheim	D	94	C2
Moniaive	GB	36	A3
Monifieth	GB	35	B5
Monikie	GB	35	B5
Monistrol-d'Allier	F	117	C3
Monistrol de Montserrat	E	147	C2
Monistrol-sur-Loire	F	117	B4
Mönkebude	D	74	A2
Monkton	GB	36	A2
Monmouth	GB	39	C4
Monnaie	F	102	B2
Monnerville	F	90	C2
Monnickendam	NL	70	B2
Monolithos	GR	188	C2
Monópoli	I	173	B3
Monor	H	112	B3
Monóvar	E	159	C3
Monpazier	F	129	B3
Monreal	D	80	B3
Monreal	E	144	B2
Monreal del Campo	E	152	B2
Monreale	I	176	A2
Monroy	E	155	B4
Monroyo	E	153	B3
Mons	B	79	B3
Monsaraz	P	155	C3
Monschau	D	80	B2
Monségur	F	128	B3
Monsélice	I	121	B4
Mønshaug	N	46	B3
Monster	NL	70	B1
Mönsterås	S	62	A4
Monsummano Terme	I	135	B3
Mont-de-Marsan	F	128	C2
Mont-Louis	F	146	B3
Mont-roig del Camp	E	147	C1
Mont-St. Aignan	F	89	A5
Mont-St. Vincent	F	104	C3
Mont-sous-Vaudrey	F	105	C4
Montabaur	D	81	B3
Montafia	I	119	C5
Montagnac	F	130	B2
Montagnana	I	121	B4
Montaigu	F	114	B2
Montaigu-de-Quercy	F	129	B4
Montaiguët-en-Forez	F	117	A3
Montaigut	F	116	A2
Montaigut-sur-Save	F	129	C4
Montainville	F	90	C1
Montalbán	E	153	B3
Montalbán de Córdoba	E	163	A3
Montalbano Elicona	I	177	A4
Montalbano Iónico	I	174	A2
Montalbo	E	158	B1
Montalcino	I	135	B4
Montaldo di Cósola	I	120	C2
Montalegre	P	148	A2
Montalieu-Vercieu	F	118	B2
Montalivet-les-Bains	F	114	C2
Montallegro	I	176	B2
Montalto delle Marche	I	136	C2
Montalto di Castro	I	168	A1
Montalto Pavese	I	120	C2
Montalto Uffugo	I	174	B2
Montalvão	P	155	B3
Montamarta	E	149	A4
Montana	BG	17	D5
Montana-Vermala	CH	119	A4
Montánchez	E	156	A1
Montanejos	E	153	B3
Montano Antília	I	172	B1
Montans	F	129	C4
Montargil	P	154	B2
Montargis	F	103	B4
Montastruc-la-Conseillère	F	129	C4
Montauban	F	129	B4
Montauban-de-Bretagne	F	101	A3
Montbard	F	104	B3
Montbarrey	F	105	B4
Montbazens	F	130	A1
Montbazon	F	102	B2
Montbéliard	F	106	B1
Montbenoit	F	105	C5
Montbeugny	F	104	C2
Montblanc	E	147	C2
Montbozon	F	105	B5
Montbron	F	115	C4
Montbrun-les-Bains	F	131	A4
Montceau-les-Mines	F	104	C3
Montcenis	F	104	C3
Montchanin	F	104	C3
Montcornet	F	91	B4
Montcuq	F	129	B4
Montdardier	F	130	B2
Montdidier	F	90	B2
Monte-Carlo	MC	133	B3
Monte Clara	P	155	B3
Monte Clérigo	P	160	B1
Monte da Pedra	P	155	B3
Monte de Goula	P	155	B3
Monte do Trigo	P	155	C3
Monte Gordo	P	160	B2
Monte Juntos	P	155	C3
Monte Porzio	I	136	B2
Monte Real	P	154	B2
Monte Redondo	P	154	B2
Monte Romano	I	168	A1
Monte San Giovanni Campano	I	169	B3
Monte San Savino	I	135	B4
Monte Sant'Ángelo	I	171	B3
Monte Vilar	P	154	B1
Monteagudo	E	165	A3
Monteagudo de las Vicarias	E	152	A1
Montealegre	E	142	C2
Montealegre del Castillo	E	159	C2
Montebello Iónico	I	175	D1
Montebello Vicentino	I	121	B4
Montebelluna	I	121	B5
Montebourg	F	88	A2
Montebruno	I	134	A2
Montecarotto	I	136	B2
Montecassiano	I	136	B2
Montecastrilli	I	168	A2
Montecatini Terme	I	135	B3
Montécchio	I	136	B1
Montécchio Emilia	I	121	C3
Montécchio Maggiore	I	121	B4
Montech	F	129	C4
Montechiaro d'Asti	I	119	B5
Montecórice	I	170	C2
Montecorvino Rovella	I	170	C2
Montederramo	E	141	B3
Montedoro	I	176	B2
Montefalco	I	136	C1
Montefalcone di Val Fortore	I	170	B3
Montefalcone nel Sánnio	I	170	B2
Montefano	E	136	B2
Montefiascone	I	168	A2
Montefiorino	I	134	A3
Montefortino	I	136	C2
Montefranco	I	168	A2
Montefrío	E	163	A4
Montegiordano Marina	I	174	A2
Montegiórgio	I	136	B2
Montegranaro	I	136	B2
Montehermoso	E	149	B3
Montejicar	E	163	A4
Montejo de la Sierra	E	151	A4
Montejo de Tiermes	E	151	A4
Montel-de-Gelat	F	116	B2
Monteleone di Púglia	I	171	B3
Monteleone di Spoleto	I	169	A2
Monteleone d'Orvieto	I	135	C5
Montelepre	I	176	A2
Montelibretti	I	168	A2
Montelier	F	117	C5
Montélimar	F	131	A3
Montella	I	146	B2
Montellano	I	170	C3
Montellano	E	162	A2
Montelupo Fiorentino	I	135	B4
Montemaggiore Belsito	I	176	B2
Montemagno	I	119	C5
Montemayor	E	163	A3
Montemayor de Pinilla	E	150	A3
Montemésola	I	173	B3
Montemilleto	I	170	B2
Montemilone	I	172	A1
Montemolin	E	161	A3
Montemónaco	I	136	C2
Montemor-o-Novo	P	154	C2
Montemor-o-Velho	P	148	B1
Montemurro	I	174	A1
Montendre	F	128	A2
Montenegro de Cameros	E	143	B4
Montenero di Bisáccia	I	170	B2
Montenero	I	101	B3
Monteparano	I	173	B3
Montepescali	I	135	C4
Montepiano	I	135	A4
Montepulciano	I	135	B4
Montereale	I	169	A3
Montereale Valcellina	I	122	A1
Montereau-Faut-Yonne	F	90	C2
Monterénzio	I	135	A4
Monteroni d'Arbia	I	135	B4
Monteroni di Lecce	I	173	B4
Monterosso al Mare	I	134	A2
Monterosso Almo	I	177	B3
Monterosso Grana	I	133	A3
Monterotondo	I	168	A2
Monterotondo Maríttimo	I	135	B4
Monterrey	E	141	C3
Monterroso	E	140	B3
Monterrubio de la Serena	E	156	B2
Monterubbiano	I	136	B2
Montes Velhos	P	160	B1
Montesa	E	159	C3
Montesalgueiro	E	140	A2
Montesano sulla Marcellana	I	174	A1
Montesárchio	I	170	B2
Montescaglioso	I	171	C4
Montesclaros	E	150	B3
Montesilvano	I	169	A4
Montespértoli	I	135	B4
Montesquieu-Volvestre	F	146	A2
Montesquiou	F	129	C3
Montestruc-sur-Gers	F	129	C3
Montevarchi	I	135	B4
Montevéglio	I	135	A4
Montfaucon	F	101	B4
Montfaucon-d'Argonne	F	91	B5
Montfaucon-en-Velay	F	117	B4
Montferrat, *Isère*	F	118	B2
Montferrat, *Var*	F	132	B2
Montfort-en-Chalosse	F	128	C2
Montfort-l'Amaury	F	90	C1
Montfort-le-Gesnois	F	102	A2
Montfort-sur-Meu	F	101	A4
Montfort-sur-Risle	F	89	A4
Montgai	E	147	C1
Montgaillard	F	145	A4
Montgenèvre	F	118	C3
Montgiscard	F	146	A2
Montgomery	GB	39	B3
Montguyon	F	128	A2
Monthermé	F	91	B4
Monthey	CH	119	A3
Monthois	F	91	B4
Monthureux-sur-Saône	F	105	A4
Monti	I	178	B3
Monticelli d'Ongina	I	120	B2
Montichiari	I	120	B3
Monticiano	I	135	B4
Montiel	E	158	C1
Montier-en-Der	F	91	C4
Montieri	I	135	B4
Montiglio	I	119	B5
Montignac	F	129	A4
Montigny-le-Roi	F	105	B4
Montigny-lès-Metz	F	92	B2
Montigny-sur-Aube	F	105	B3
Montijo	E	155	C4
Montijo	P	154	C2
Montilla	E	163	A3
Montillana	E	163	A4
Montilly	F	104	C2
Montivilliers	F	89	A4
Montjaux	F	130	A1
Montjean-sur-Loire	F	102	B1
Montlhéry	F	90	C2
Montlieu-la-Gard	F	128	A2
Montlouis-sur-Loire	F	102	B2
Montluçon	F	116	A2
Montluel	F	117	B5
Montmarault	F	116	A2
Montmartin-sur-Mer	F	88	B2
Montmédy	F	92	B1
Montmélian	F	118	B3
Montmeyan	F	132	B2
Montmeyran	F	117	C4
Montmirail, *Marne*	F	91	C3
Montmirail, *Sarthe*	F	102	A2
Montmiral	F	118	B2
Montmirat	F	131	B3
Montmirey-le-Château	F	105	B4
Montmoreau-St. Cybard	F	115	C4
Montmorency	F	90	C2
Montmorillon	F	115	B4
Montmoir-Lucy	F	91	C3
Montoir-de-Bretagne	F	101	B3
Montoire-sur-le-Loir	F	102	B2
Montoito	P	155	C3
Montolieu	F	146	A3
Montório al Vomano	I	169	A3
Montoro	E	157	B3
Montpellier	F	131	B2
Montpezat-de-Quercy	F	129	B4
Montpezat-sous-Bouzon	F	117	C4
Montpon-Ménestérol	F	128	A3
Montpont-en-Bresse	F	105	C4
Montréal, *Aude*	F	146	A3
Montréal, *Gers*	F	128	C3
Montredon-Labessonnié	F	130	B1
Montréjeau	F	145	A4
Montrésor	F	103	B3
Montresta	I	178	B2
Montret	F	105	C4
Montreuil, *Pas de Calais*	F	78	B1
Montreuil, *Seine St. Denis*	F	90	C2
Montreuil-aux-Lions	F	90	B3
Montreuil-Bellay	F	102	B1
Montreux	CH	106	C1
Montrevault	F	101	B4
Montrevel-en-Bresse	F	118	A2
Montrichard	F	103	B3
Montricoux	F	129	B4
Montrond-les-Bains	F	117	B4
Montrose	GB	35	B5
Montroy	E	159	B3
Monts-sur-Guesnes	F	102	C2
Montsalvy	F	116	C2
Montsauche-les-Settons	F	104	B3
Montseny	E	147	C3
Montsoreau	F	102	B2
Montsûrs	F	102	A1
Montuenga	E	150	A3
Montuïri	E	167	B3
Monturque	E	163	A3
Monza	I	120	B2
Monzón	E	145	C4
Monzón de Campos	E	142	B2
Moorbad Lobenstein	D	83	B3
Moordorf	D	71	A4
Moorslede	B	78	B3
Moos	D	107	B3
Moosburg	S	95	C3
Moosburg im Kärnten	A	110	C1
Mór	H	112	B2
Mora	E	157	A4
Móra	E	154	C2
Mora	S	50	A1
Mora de Rubielos	E	153	B3
Móra d'Ebre	E	153	A4
Móra la Nova	E	153	A4
Moraby	S	50	B2
Moradillo de Roa	E	151	A4
Morąg	PL	69	B4
Mórahalom	H	126	A1
Moraime	E	140	A1
Morais	P	149	A3

Name		Page	Grid
Moral de Calatrava	E	157	B4
Moraleda de Zafayona	E	163	A4
Moraleja	E	149	B3
Moraleja del Vino	E	150	A2
Morales de Toro	E	150	A2
Morales de Valverde	E	141	C5
Morales del Vino	E	150	A2
Moralina	E	149	A3
Morano Cálabro	I	174	B2
Mörarp	S	61	C2
Morasverdes	E	149	B3
Morata de Jalón	E	152	A2
Morata de Jiloca	E	152	A2
Morata de Tajuña	E	151	B4
Moratalla	E	164	A3
Moravče	SLO	123	A3
Moravec	CZ	97	B4
Moraviţa	RO	126	B3
Morávka	CZ	98	B2
Moravská Třebová	CZ	97	B4
Moravské Budějovice	CZ	97	B3
Moravské Lieskové	SK	98	C1
Moravske Toplice	SLO	111	C3
Moravský-Beroun	CZ	98	B1
Moravský Krumlov	CZ	97	B4
Moravský Svätý Ján	SK	98	C1
Morawica	PL	87	B4
Morawin	PL	86	A2
Morbach	D	92	B3
Morbegno	I	120	A2
Morbier	F	105	C5
Mörbisch am See	A	111	B3
Mörbylånga	S	63	B4
Morcenx	F	128	B2
Morciano di Romagna	I	136	B1
Morcone	I	170	B2
Morcuera	E	151	A4
Mordelles	F	101	A4
Mordoğan	TR	188	A1
Moréac	F	100	B3
Morebattle	GB	35	C5
Morecambe	GB	36	B4
Moreda, *Granada*	E	163	A4
Moreda, *Oviedo*	E	142	A1
Morée	F	103	B3
Moreles de Rey	E	141	B5
Morella	E	153	B3
Moreruela de los Infanzones	E	149	A4
Morés	E	152	A2
Móres	I	178	B2
Morestel	F	118	B2
Moret-sur-Loing	F	90	C2
Moreton-in-Marsh	GB	44	B2
Moretonhampstead	GB	43	B3
Moretta	I	119	C4
Moreuil	F	90	B2
Morez	F	105	C5
Mörfelden	D	93	B4
Morgat	F	100	A1
Morges	CH	105	C5
Morgex	I	119	B4
Morgongåva	S	51	C3
Morhange	F	92	C2
Morhet	B	92	B1
Mori	I	121	B3
Morialmé	B	79	B4
Morianes	I	160	B2
Moriani Plage	F	180	A2
Mórichida	H	111	B4
Moriles	E	163	A3
Morille	E	150	B2
Moringen	D	82	A1
Morjärv	S	196	C5
Morkarla	S	51	B4
Mørke	DK	59	B3
Mørkøv	DK	61	D1
Morkovice-Slížany	CZ	98	B1
Morlaàs	F	145	A3
Morlaix	F	100	A2
Morley	F	91	C5
Mörlunda	S	62	A3
Mormanno	I	174	B1
Mormant	F	90	C2
Mornant	F	117	B4
Mornay-Berry	F	103	B4
Morón de Almazán	E	152	A1
Morón de la Frontera	E	162	A2
Morović	SRB	125	B5
Morozzo	I	133	A4
Morpeth	GB	37	A5
Morphou	CY	181	A1
Mörrum	S	63	B2
Morsbach	D	81	B3
Mörsch	D	93	C4
Mörsil	S	199	B10
Morsum	D	64	B1
Mørsvikbotn	N	194	C6
Mortagne-au-Perche	F	89	B4
Mortagne-sur-Gironde	F	114	C3
Mortagne-sur-Sèvre	F	114	B3
Mortágua	P	148	B1
Mortain	F	88	B3
Mortara	I	120	B1
Morteau	F	105	B5
Mortegliano	I	122	B2
Mortelle	I	177	A4
Mortemart	F	115	B4
Mortimer's Cross	GB	39	B4
Mortrée	F	89	B4
Mörtschach	A	109	C3
Mortsel	B	79	A4
Morud	DK	59	C3
Morwenstow	GB	42	B2
Moryń	PL	74	B3
Morzeszczyn	PL	69	B3
Morzewo	PL	69	B4
Morzine	F	118	A3
Mosbach	D	93	B5
Mosbjerg	DK	58	A3
Mosby	N	53	B3
Mosca	P	149	A3
Moscavide	P	154	C1
Mošćenica	HR	124	B2
Mošćenice	HR	123	B3
Moščenicka Draga	HR	123	B3
Mosciano Sant'Ángelo	I	136	C2
Mościsko	PL	85	B4
Moscow = Moskva	RUS	9	E10
Mosina	PL	75	B5
Mosjøen	N	195	E4
Moskog	N	46	A3
Moskorzew	PL	87	B3
Moskosel	S	196	D2
Moskuvarra	FIN	197	B9
Moskva = Moscow	RUS	9	E10
Moslavina Podravska	HR	125	B3
Moşniţa Nouă	RO	126	B3
Moso in Passiria	I	108	C2
Mosonmagyaróvár	H	111	B4
Mošorin	SRB	126	B2
Mošovce	SK	98	C2
Mosqueruela	E	153	B3
Moss	N	54	A1
Mossfellsbær	IS	190	C4
Mössingen	D	93	C5
Møsstrand	N	47	C5
Most	CZ	83	B5
Most na Soči	SLO	122	A2
Mosta	M	175	C3
Mostar	BIH	139	B3
Mosterhamn	N	52	A1
Mostki	PL	75	B4
Móstoles	E	151	B4
Mostová	SK	111	A4
Mostowo	PL	68	A1
Mosty	PL	75	A3
Mostys'ka	UA	13	D5
Mosvik	N	199	B7
Mota del Cuervo	E	158	B1
Mota del Marqués	E	150	A2
Motala	S	55	B6
Motherwell	GB	35	C4
Möthlow	D	74	B1
Motilla del Palancar	E	158	B2
Motnik	SLO	123	A3
Motovun	HR	122	B2
Motril	E	163	B4
Motta	I	121	B4
Motta di Livenza	I	122	B1
Motta Montecorvino	I	170	B3
Motta Visconti	I	120	B1
Mottisfont	GB	44	B2
Móttola	I	173	B3
Mou	DK	58	B3
Mouchard	F	105	C4
Moudon	CH	106	C1
Moudros	GR	183	D7
Mougins	F	132	B2
Mouilleron en-Pareds	F	114	B3
Mouliherne	F	102	B2
Moulinet	F	133	B3
Moulins	F	104	C2
Moulins-Engilbert	F	104	C2
Moulins-la-Marche	F	89	B4
Moulismes	F	115	B4
Moult	F	89	A3
Mount Bellew Bridge	IRL	28	A3
Mountain Ash	GB	39	C3
Mountfield	GB	27	B3
Mountmellick	IRL	30	A1
Mountrath	IRL	30	A1
Mountsorrel	GB	40	C2
Moura	P	160	A2
Mourão	P	155	C3
Mourenx	F	145	A3
Mouriés	F	131	B3
Mourmelon-le-Grand	F	91	B4
Mouronho	P	148	B1
Mourujärvi	FIN	197	C11
Mouscron	B	78	B3
Mousehole	GB	42	B1
Moussac	F	131	B3
Moussey	F	92	C2
Mousteru	F	100	A2
Moustey	F	128	B2
Moustiers-Ste. Marie	F	132	B2
Mouthe	F	105	C5
Mouthier-Haute-Pierre	F	105	B5
Mouthoumet	F	146	B3
Moutier	CH	106	B2
Moûtiers	F	118	B3
Moutiers-les-Mauxfaits	F	114	B2
Mouy	F	90	B2
Mouzaki	GR	182	D3
Mouzon	F	91	B5
Møvik	N	46	B1
Moville	IRL	27	A3
Moy, *Highland*	GB	32	D2
Moy, *Tyrone*	GB	27	B4
Moycullen	IRL	28	A2
Moyenmoutier	F	92	C2
Moyenvic	F	92	C2
Mózar	E	141	A4
Mozhaysk	RUS	9	E10
Mozirje	SLO	123	A3
Mözs	H	112	C2
Mozzanica	I	120	B2
Mramorak	SRB	127	C2
Mrčajevci	SRB	127	D2
Mrkonjić Grad	BIH	138	A3
Mrkopalj	HR	123	B3
Mrocza	PL	76	A2
Mroczeń	PL	86	A1
Mroczno	PL	69	B4
Mrzezyno	PL	67	B4
Mšec	CZ	84	B1
Mšeno	CZ	84	B2
Mstów	PL	86	B3
Mstsislaw	BY	13	A9
Mszana Dolna	PL	99	B4
Mszczonów	PL	77	C5
Muć	HR	138	B2
Múccia	I	136	B2
Much	D	80	B3
Much Marcle	GB	39	C4
Much Wenlock	GB	39	B4
Mücheln	D	83	A3
Muchów	PL	85	A4
Mucientes	E	142	C2
Muckross	IRL	29	B2
Mucur	TR	23	B8
Muda	P	160	B1
Mudanya	TR	186	B3
Mudau	D	93	B5
Müden	D	72	B3
Mudersbach	D	81	B3
Mudurnu	TR	187	B6
Muel	E	152	A2
Muelas del Pan	E	149	A4
Muess	D	73	A4
Muff	IRL	27	A3
Mugardos	E	140	A2
Muge	P	154	B2
Mügeln, *Sachsen-Anhalt*	D	83	A5
Mügeln, *Sachsen*	D	83	A5
Múggia	I	122	B2
Muğla	TR	188	B3
Mugnano	I	135	B5
Mugron	F	128	C2
Mugueimes	E	140	C3
Muhi	H	113	B4
Mühlacker	D	93	C4
Mühlbach am Hochkönig	A	109	B4
Mühlberg, *Brandenburg*	D	83	A5
Mühlberg, *Thüringen*	D	82	B2
Mühldorf	D	109	C4
Mühldorf	D	95	C4
Muhleberg	CH	106	C2
Mühleim	D	107	A3
Muhlen-Eichsen	D	65	C4
Mühlhausen, *Bayern*	D	94	B2
Mühlhausen, *Thüringen*	D	82	A2
Mühltroff	D	83	B3
Muhos	FIN	3	D10
Muhr	A	109	B4
Muine Bheag	IRL	30	B2
Muir of Ord	GB	32	D2
Muirkirk	GB	36	A2
Muirteira	P	154	B1
Mukacheve	UA	13	D5
Muker	GB	37	B4
Mula	E	165	A3
Mulben	GB	32	D3
Mulegns	CH	107	C4
Mules	I	108	C2
Mülheim	D	80	A2
Mulhouse	F	106	B2
Muljava	SLO	123	B3
Mullanys Cross	IRL	26	B1
Müllheim	D	106	B2
Mullhyttan	S	55	A5
Mullinavat	IRL	30	B1
Mullingar	IRL	30	A1
Mullion	GB	42	B1
Müllrose	D	74	B3
Mullsjö	S	60	B3
Mulseryd	S	60	B3
Munaðarnes	IS	190	A4
Munana	E	150	B2
Muñás	E	141	A4
Münchberg	D	83	B3
Müncheberg	D	74	B3
München = Munich	D	108	A2
Munchen-Gladbach = Mönchen-gladbach	D	80	A2
Münchhausen	D	81	B4
Mundaka	E	143	A4
Münden	D	82	A1
Munderfing	A	109	A4
Munderkingen	D	107	A4
Mundesley	GB	41	C5
Munera	E	158	B1
Mungia	E	143	A4
Munich = München	D	108	A2
Muñico	E	150	B2
Muniesa	E	153	A3
Munka-Ljungby	S	61	C2
Munkebo	DK	59	C3
Munkedal	S	54	B2
Munkflohögen	S	199	B11
Munkfors	S	49	C5
Munktorp	S	56	A2
Münnerstadt	D	82	B2
Muñopepe	E	150	B3
Muñotello	E	150	B2
Münsingen	CH	106	C2
Münsingen	D	94	C1
Munsö	S	57	A3
Münster	CH	106	C3
Munster, *Niedersachsen*	D	72	B3
Münster, *Hessen*	D	93	B4
Münster, *Nordrhein-Westfalen*	D	71	C4
Munster	F	106	A2
Muntibar	E	143	A4
Münzkirchen	A	96	C1
Muodoslompolo	S	196	B6
Muonio	FIN	196	B6
Muotathal	CH	107	C3
Mur-de-Barrez	F	116	C2
Mur-de-Bretagne	F	100	A2
Mur-de-Sologne	F	103	B3
Muradiye	TR	186	D2
Murakeresztúr	H	124	A2
Murán	SK	99	C4
Murano	I	122	B1
Muras	E	140	A3
Murat	F	116	B2
Murat-sur-Vèbre	F	130	B1
Muratlı	TR	186	A2
Murato	F	180	A2
Murau	A	109	B5
Muravera	I	179	C3
Murazzano	I	133	A4
Murça	P	148	A2
Murchante	E	144	B2
Murchin	D	66	C2
Murcia	E	165	B3
Murczyn	PL	76	B2
Mureck	A	110	C2
Mürefte	TR	186	B2
Muret	F	146	A2
Murg	CH	107	B4
Murguia	E	143	B4
Muri	CH	106	B3
Murias de Paredes	E	141	B4
Muriedas	E	143	A3
Muriel Viejo	E	143	C4
Murillo de Rio Leza	E	143	B4
Murillo el Fruto	E	144	B2
Murjek	S	196	C3
Murlaggan	GB	34	B2
Murmansk	RUS	3	B13
Murmashi	RUS	3	B13
Murnau	D	108	B2
Muro	F	180	A1
Muro	E	167	B3
Muro de Alcoy	E	159	C3
Muro Lucano	I	172	B1
Muron	F	114	B3
Muros	E	140	B1
Muros de Nalón	E	141	A4
Murowana Goślina	PL	76	B1
Mürren	CH	106	C2
Murrhardt	D	94	C1
Murska Sobota	SLO	111	C3
Mursko Središče	HR	111	C3
Murtas	E	164	C1
Murten	CH	106	C2
Murter	HR	137	B4
Murtiçi	TR	189	C6
Murtosa	P	148	B1
Murtovaara	FIN	197	D12
Murvica	HR	137	A4
Murviel-lès-Béziers	F	130	B2
Mürzsteg	A	110	B2
Murzynowo	PL	75	B4
Mürzzuschlag	A	110	B2
Musculdy	F	144	A3
Muskö	S	57	A4
Mušov	CZ	97	C4
Musselburgh	GB	35	C4
Musselkanaal	NL	71	B4
Mussidan	F	129	A3
Mussomeli	I	176	B2
Musson	B	92	B1
Mussy-sur-Seine	F	104	B3
Mustafakemalpaşa	TR	186	B3
Muszaki	PL	77	A5
Muszyna	PL	99	B4
Mut	TR	23	C7
Muta	SLO	110	C2
Muthill	GB	35	B4
Mutné	SK	99	B3
Mutriku	E	143	A4
Muttalip	TR	187	C5
Mutterbergalm	A	108	B2
Muurola	FIN	197	C8
Muxía	E	140	A1
Muxilka-Ugarte	E	143	A4
Muzillac	F	101	B3
Mužla	SK	112	B2
Muzzano del Turgnano	I	122	B2
Mybster	GB	32	C3
Myckelgensjö	S	200	C3
Myennes	F	104	B1
Myjava	SK	98	C1
Myking	N	46	B2
Mykland	N	53	B4
Myra	N	53	B5
Myrdal	N	46	B4
Myre, *Nordland*	N	194	B6
Myre, *Nordland*	N	194	A6
Myresjö	S	62	A2
Mýri	IS	191	B8
Myrtou	CY	181	A2
Mysen	N	54	A2
Mysłakowice	PL	85	B3
Myślenice	PL	99	B3
Myślibórz	PL	75	B3
Mysłowice	PL	86	B3
Myszków	PL	86	B3
Mytishchi	RUS	9	E10
Mýtna	SK	99	C3
Mýtne Ludany	SK	112	A2
Mýto	CZ	96	B1

N

Name		Page	Grid
N Unnaryd	S	60	B3
Nå	N	46	B3
Naaldwijk	NL	79	A4
Naantali	FIN	8	B2
Naas	IRL	30	A2
Nabais	P	148	B2
Nabbelund	S	62	A5
Nabburg	D	95	B4
Náchod	CZ	85	B4
Nacław	PL	68	A1
Nadarzyce	PL	75	A5
Nadarzyn	PL	77	B5
Nádasd	H	111	C3
Nádlac	RO	126	A2
Nádudvar	H	113	B5
Nadvirna	UA	13	D6
Nærbø	N	52	B1
Næsbjerg	DK	59	C1
Næstved	DK	65	A4
Näfels	CH	107	B4
Nafpaktos	GR	184	A2
Nafplio	GR	184	B3
Nagel	D	95	B3
Nagele	NL	70	B2
Naggen	S	200	D2
Nagłowice	PL	87	B4
Nagold	D	93	C4
Nagore	E	144	B2
Nagyatád	H	124	A3
Nagybajom	H	124	A3
Nagybaracska	H	125	A4
Nagybátony	H	113	B3
Nagyberény	H	112	C2
Nagybörzsöny	H	112	B2
Nagycenk	H	111	B3
Nagycserkesz	H	113	B5
Nagydorog	H	112	C2
Nagyfüged	H	113	B4
Nagyhersány	H	125	B4
Nagyigmánd	H	112	B2
Nagyiván	H	113	B4
Nagykanizsa	H	111	C3
Nagykáta	H	113	B3
Nagykonyi	H	112	C2
Nagykörös	H	113	B3
Nagylóc	H	112	A3
Nagymágocs	H	113	C4
Nagymányok	H	125	A4
Nagymaros	H	112	B2
Nagyoroszi	H	112	A3
Nagyréde	H	113	B3
Nagyszénás	H	113	C4
Nagyszokoly	H	112	C2
Nagytőke	H	113	C4
Nagyvázsony	H	111	C4
Nagyvenyim	H	112	C2
Naharros	E	152	B1
Nahe	D	64	C3
Naila	D	83	B3
Nailloux	F	146	A2
Nailsworth	GB	43	A4
Naintré	F	115	B4
Nairn	GB	32	D3
Najac	F	129	B4
Nájera	E	143	B4
Nak	H	112	C2
Nakksjø	N	53	A5
Nakło nad Notecią	PL	76	A2
Nakskov	DK	65	B4
Nalda	E	143	B4
Nälden	S	199	B11
Nálepkovo	SK	99	C4
Nalliers	F	114	B2
Nallıhan	TR	187	B6
Nalzen	F	146	B2
Nalžouské Hory	CZ	96	B1
Namdalseid	N	199	A8
Náměšt'nad Oslavou	CZ	97	B3
Námestovo	SK	99	B3
Namna	N	49	B4
Namsos	N	199	A8
Namsskogan	N	199	A10
Namur	B	79	B4
Namysłów	PL	86	A2
Nançay	F	103	B4
Nanclares de la Oca	E	143	B4
Nancy	F	92	C2
Nangis	F	90	C3
Nannestad	N	48	B3
Nant	F	130	A2
Nanterre	F	90	C2
Nantes	F	101	B4
Nanteuil-le-Haudouin	F	90	B2
Nantiat	F	115	B5
Nantua	F	118	A2
Nantwich	GB	38	A4
Naoussa, *Imathia*	GR	182	C4
Naoussa, *Cyclades*	GR	185	B6
Napajedla	CZ	98	B1
Napiwoda	PL	77	A5
Naples = Nápoli	I	170	C2
Nápoli = Naples	I	170	C2
Nar	S	57	C4
Nara	N	46	A1
Naraval	E	141	A4
Narberth	GB	39	C2
Narbonne	F	130	B1
Narbonne-Plage	F	130	B2
Narbuvollen	N	199	C8
Narcao	I	179	C2
Nardò	I	173	B4
Narkaus	FIN	197	C9
Narken	S	196	C5
Narmo	N	48	B3
Narni	I	168	A2
Naro	I	176	B2
Naro Fominsk	RUS	9	E10
Narón	E	140	A2
Narros del Castillo	E	150	B2
Narta	HR	124	B2
Naruszewo	PL	77	B5
Narva	EST	8	C6
Narvik	N	194	B8
Narzole	I	133	A4
Näs	FIN	51	B7
Nås, *Dalarnas*	S	50	B1
Näs, *Gotland*	S	57	C4
Näsåker	S	200	C2
Năsăud	RO	17	B6
Nasavrky	CZ	97	B3
Nasbinals	F	116	C3
Näshull	S	62	A3
Našice	HR	125	B4
Nasielsk	PL	77	B5
Naso	I	177	A3
Nassau	D	81	B3
Nassenfels	D	95	C3
Nassenheide	D	74	B2
Nassereith	A	108	B1
Nässjö	S	62	A2
Nastätten	D	81	B3
Näsum	S	63	B2
Näsviken	S	199	B12
Natalinci	SRB	127	C2
Nater-Stetten	D	108	A2
Naters	CH	119	C3
Nattavaara	S	196	C3
Natters	A	108	B2
Nättraby	S	63	B3
Naturno	I	108	C1
Naucelle	F	130	A1
Nauders	A	108	C1
Nauen	D	74	B1
Naul	IRL	30	A2
Naumburg	D	83	A3
Naundorf	D	83	B5
Naunhof	D	83	A4
Naustdal	N	46	A2
Nautijaur	S	196	C2
Nautsi	RUS	193	D13
Nava	E	142	A1
Nava de Arévalo	E	150	B3
Nava de la Asunción	E	150	A3

Nava del Rey E 150 A2
Navacerrada E 151 B3
Navaconcejo E 149 B4
Navafriá E 151 A4
Navahermosa E 157 A3
Navahrudak BY 13 B6
Naval E 145 B4
Navalacruz E 150 B3
Navalcán E 150 B2
Navalcarnero E 151 B3
Navaleno E 143 C3
Navalmanzano E 151 A3
Navalmoral E 150 B3
Navalmoral de la Mata E 150 C2
Naválón E 159 C3
Navalonguilla E 150 B2
Navalperal de Pinares E 150 B3
Navalpino E 157 A3
Navaltalgordo E 150 B3
Navaltoril E 156 A3
Navaluenga E 150 B3
Navalvillar de Pela E 156 A2
Navan IRL 30 A2
Navaperal de Tormes E 150 B2
Navapolatsk BY 13 A8
Navarclés E 147 C2
Navarredonda de Gredos E 150 B2
Navarrenx F 144 A3
Navarrés E 159 B3
Navarrete E 143 B4
Navarrevisca E 150 B3
Navás E 147 C2
Navas de Oro E 150 A3
Navas de San Juan E 157 B4
Navas del Madroño E 155 B4
Navas del Rey E 151 B3
Navas del Sepillar E 163 A3
Navascués E 144 B2
Navasfrias E 149 B3
Nave I 120 B3
Nave de Haver P 149 B3
Nävekvarn S 56 B2
Navelli I 169 A3
Navenby GB 40 B3
Näverkärret S 56 A1
Naverstad S 54 B2
Navés E 147 C2
Navezuelas E 156 A2
Navia E 141 A4
Navia de Suarna E 141 B4
Navilly F 105 C4
Năvodari RO 17 C8
Naxos GR 185 B6
Nay F 145 A3
Nazaré P 154 B1
Nazarje SLO 123 A3
Nazilli TR 188 B3
Nazza D 82 A2
Nea Anchialos GR 182 D4
Nea Epidavros GR 184 B4
Nea Flippias GR 182 D2
Nea Kalikratia GR 183 C5
Nea Makri GR 185 A4
Nea Moudania GR 183 C5
Nea Peramos GR 183 C6
Nea Stira GR 185 A5
Nea Visa GR 186 A1
Nea Zichni GR 183 B5
Neap GB 33 A5
Neapoli, *Kozani* GR 182 C3
Neapoli, *Kriti* GR 185 D6
Neapoli, *Lakonia* GR 184 C4
Neath GB 39 C3
Nebljusi HR 124 C1
Neblo SLO 122 A2
Nebolchy RUS 9 C8
Nebra D 82 A3
Nebreda E 143 C3
Nechanice CZ 84 B3
Neckargemünd D 93 B4
Neckarsulm D 94 B1
Neda E 140 A2
Neded SK 112 A1
Nedelišće HR 124 A2
Nederweert NL 80 A1
Nedre Gärdsjö S 50 B2
Nedre Soppero S 196 A4
Nedreberg N 48 B3
Nedstrand N 52 A1
Nedvědice CZ 97 B4
Nędza PL 86 B2
Neede NL 71 B3
Needham Market GB 45 A5
Needingworth GB 44 A3
Neermoor D 71 A4
Neeroeteren B 80 A1
Neerpelt B 79 A5
Neesen D 72 B1
Neetze D 73 A3
Nefyn GB 38 B2
Negotin SRB 16 C5
Negotino MK 182 B4
Negrar I 121 B3
Negredo E 151 A5
Negreira E 140 B2
Nègrepelisse F 129 B4
Negru Vodă RO 17 D8
Negueira de Muñiz E 141 A4
Neheim D 81 A3
Neila E 143 B4
Néive I 119 C5
Nejdek CZ 83 B4
Nekla PL 76 B2
Neksø DK 67 A4
Nelas P 148 B2
Nelaug N 53 B4
Nelidovo RUS 9 D8
Nelim FIN 193 D12
Nellingen D 94 C1
Nelson GB 40 B1
Neman RUS 12 A5
Nemea GR 184 B3
Nemesgörzsöny H 111 B4
Nemeskér H 111 B3
Nemesnádudvar H 125 A5
Nemesszalók H 111 B4
Németkér H 112 C2
Nemours F 103 A4
Nemška Loka SLO 123 B4
Nemšová SK 98 C2
Nenagh IRL 28 B3
Nenince SK 112 A3
Nenita GR 185 A7
Nenzing A 107 B4
Neo Chori GR 184 A2
Neochori GR 182 D3
Neon Petritsi GR 183 B5
Nepi I 168 A2
Nepomuk CZ 96 B1
Nérac F 129 B3
Neratovice CZ 84 B2
Nerchau D 83 A4
Néré F 115 C3
Neresheim D 94 C2
Nereto I 136 C2
Nerezine HR 123 C3
Nerežišća HR 138 B2
Neringa LT 12 A4
Néris-les Bains F 116 A2
Nerito I 169 A3
Nerja E 163 B4
Néronde F 117 B4
Nérondes F 103 C4
Nerpio E 164 A2
Nersingen D 94 C2
Nerva E 161 B3
Nervesa della Battáglia I 121 B5
Nervi I 134 A2
Nes, *Buskerud* N 48 B1
Nes, *Hedmark* N 48 B2
Nes, *Sogn og Fjordane* N 46 A3
Nes, *Sør-Trøndelag* N 198 B6
Nes NL 70 A2
Nesbyen N 47 B6
Neset N 199 D7
Nesflaten N 52 A2
Nesjahverfi IS 191 C10
Neskaupstaður IS 191 B12
Nesland N 53 A3
Neslandsvatn N 53 B5
Nesle F 90 B2
Nesna N 195 D4
Nesoddtangen N 48 C2
Nesovice CZ 98 B1
Nesselwang D 108 B1
Nesslau CH 107 B4
Nessmersiel D 71 A4
Nesso I 120 B2
Nesterov UA 13 C5
Nestorio GR 182 C3
Nesttun N 46 B2
Nesvady SK 112 B2
Nesvatnstemmen N 53 B4
Nether Stowey GB 43 A3
Netland N 52 B2
Netolice CZ 96 B2
Netphen D 81 B4
Netstal CH 107 B4
Nettancourt F 91 C4
Nettetal D 80 A2
Nettlingen D 72 B3
Nettuno I 168 B2
Neu Darchau D 73 A3
Neu-Isenburg D 93 A4
Neu Kaliss D 73 A4
Neu Lübbenau D 74 B2
Neu-Ulm D 94 C2
Neualbenreuth D 95 B4
Neubeckum D 81 A4
Neubrandenburg D 74 A2
Neubruchhausen D 72 B1
Neubukow D 65 B4
Neuburg D 94 C3
Neuchâtel CH 106 C1
Neudau A 111 B3
Neudietendorf D 82 B2
Neudorf D 93 B4
Neuenbürg, *Baden-Württemberg* D 93 C4
Neuenburg, *Niedersachsen* D 71 A4
Neuendorf D 66 B2
Neuenhagen D 74 B2
Neuenhaus D 71 B3
Neuenkirchen, *Niedersachsen* D 71 B5
Neuenkirchen, *Niedersachsen* D 72 A2
Neuenkirchen, *Nordrhein-Westfalen* D 71 B4
Neuenkirchen, *Nordrhein-Westfalen* D 81 B3
Neuenrade D 81 A3
Neuenwalde D 64 C1
Neuerburg D 92 A2
Neuf-Brisach F 106 A2
Neufahrn, *Bayern* D 95 C3
Neufahrn, *Bayern* D 95 C4
Neufchâteau B 92 B1
Neufchâteau F 92 C1
Neufchâtel-en-Bray F 90 B1
Neufchâtel-sur-Aisne F 91 B4
Neuflize F 91 B4
Neugersdorf D 84 B2
Neuhardenberg D 74 B3
Neuharlingersiel D 71 A4
Neuhaus, *Bayern* D 95 B3
Neuhaus, *Bayern* D 96 C1
Neuhaus, *Niedersachsen* D 73 A3
Neuhaus, *Niedersachsen* D 81 A5
Neuhaus, *Niedersachsen* D 64 C2
Neuhaus a Rennweg D 82 B3
Neuhausen CH 107 B3
Neuhausen ob Eck D 107 B3
Neuhof, *Bayern* D 94 B2
Neuhof, *Hessen* D 82 B1
Neuhofen an der Krems A 110 A1
Neuillé-Pont-Pierre F 102 B2
Neuilly-en-Thelle F 90 B2
Neuilly-le-Réal F 104 C2
Neuilly-l'Évêque F 105 B4
Neuilly-St. Front F 90 B3
Neukalen D 66 C1
Neukirch D 84 A2
Neukirchen A 109 A4
Neukirchen, *Hessen* D 81 B5
Neukirchen, *Schleswig-Holstein* D 64 B1
Neukirchen am Grossvenediger A 109 B3
Neukirchen bei Heiligen Blut D 95 B4
Neukloster D 65 C4
Neulengbach A 110 A2
Neulise F 117 B4
Neum BIH 139 C3
Neumagen D 92 B2
Neumarkt D 95 B3
Neumarkt am Wallersee A 109 B4
Neumarkt im Hausruckkreis A 109 A4
Neumarkt im Mühlkreis A 96 C2
Neumarkt im Steiermark A 110 B1
Neumarkt Sankt Veit D 95 C4
Neumünster D 64 B2
Neunburg vorm Wald D 95 B4
Neung-sur-Beuvron F 103 B3
Neunkirch, *Luzern* CH 106 B3
Neunkirch, *Schaffhausen* CH 107 B3
Neunkirchen A 111 B3
Neunkirchen, *Nordrhein-Westfalen* D 80 B3
Neunkirchen, *Saarland* D 92 B3
Neunkirchen am Brand D 94 B3
Neuötting D 95 C4
Neupetershain D 84 A2
Neuravensburg D 107 B4
Neureut D 93 B4
Neuruppin D 74 B1
Neusäss D 94 C2
Neusiedl A 111 B3
Neuss D 80 A2
Neussargues-Moissac F 116 B2
Neustadt, *Bayern* D 94 B2
Neustadt, *Bayern* D 95 C3
Neustadt, *Bayern* D 95 B4
Neustadt, *Brandenburg* D 73 B5
Neustadt, *Hessen* D 81 B5
Neustadt, *Niedersachsen* D 72 B2
Neustadt, *Rheinland-Pfalz* D 93 B4
Neustadt, *Sachsen* D 84 A2
Neustadt, *Schleswig-Holstein* D 65 B3
Neustadt, *Thüringen* D 82 B3
Neustadt, *Thüringen* D 83 B3
Neustadt-Glewe D 73 A4
Neustift im Stubaital A 108 B2
Neustrelitz D 74 A2
Neutal A 111 B3
Neutrebbin D 74 B3
Neuves-Maisons F 92 C2
Neuvic, *Corrèze* F 116 B2
Neuvic, *Dordogne* F 129 A3
Neuville-aux-Bois F 103 A4
Neuville-de-Poitou F 115 B4
Neuville-les-Dames F 117 A5
Neuville-sur-Saône F 117 B4
Neuvy-le-Roi F 102 B2
Neuvy-St. Sépulchre F 103 C3
Neuvy-Santour F 104 A2
Neuvy-sur-Barangeon F 103 B4
Neuwied D 80 B3
Neuzelle D 74 B3
Névache F 118 B3
Neveklov CZ 96 B2
Nevel RUS 9 D6
Neverfjord N 192 B7
Nevers F 104 C2
Nevesinje BIH 139 B4
Névez F 100 B2
Nevlunghavn N 53 B5
Nevşehir TR 23 B8
New Abbey GB 36 B3
New Aberdour GB 33 D4
New Alresford GB 44 B2
New Costessey GB 41 C5
New Cumnock GB 36 A2
New Galloway GB 36 A2
New Mills GB 40 B2
New Milton GB 44 C2
New Pitsligo GB 33 D4
New Quay GB 39 B2
New Radnor GB 39 B3
New Romney GB 45 C4
New Ross IRL 30 B2
New Scone GB 35 B4
Newark-on-Trent GB 40 B3
Newbiggin-by-the-Sea GB 37 A5
Newbliss IRL 27 B3
Newborough GB 38 A2
Newbridge IRL 30 A2
Newbridge on Wye GB 39 B3
Newburgh, *Aberdeenshire* GB 33 D4
Newburgh, *Fife* GB 35 B4
Newbury GB 44 B2
Newby Bridge GB 36 B4
Newcastle GB 27 B5
Newcastle Emlyn GB 39 B2
Newcastle-under-Lyme GB 40 B1
Newcastle-Upon-Tyne GB 37 B5
Newcastle West IRL 29 B2
Newcastleton GB 37 A4
Newchurch GB 39 B3
Newent GB 39 C4
Newham GB 45 B4
Newhaven GB 45 C4
Newington GB 45 B5
Newinn IRL 29 B4
Newlyn GB 42 B1
Newmachar GB 33 D4
Newmarket, *Suffolk* GB 45 A4
Newmarket, *Western Isles* GB 31 A2
Newmarket IRL 29 B3
Newmarket-on-Fergus IRL 28 B3
Newport, *Isle of Wight* GB 44 C2
Newport, *Newport* GB 39 C4
Newport, *Pembrokeshire* GB 39 B2
Newport, *Telford & Wrekin* GB 38 B4
Newport, *Mayo* IRL 28 A2
Newport, *Tipperary* IRL 29 B3
Newport-on-Tay GB 35 B5
Newport Pagnell GB 44 A3
Newquay GB 42 B1
Newry GB 27 B4
Newton Abbot GB 43 B3
Newton Arlosh GB 36 B3
Newton Aycliffe GB 37 B5
Newton Ferrers GB 42 B2
Newton Stewart GB 36 B2
Newtonhill GB 33 D4
Newtonmore GB 32 D2
Newtown, *Herefordshire* GB 39 B4
Newtown, *Powys* GB 39 B3
Newtown Cunningham IRL 27 B3
Newtown Hamilton GB 27 B4
Newtown St. Boswells GB 35 C5
Newtown Sands IRL 29 B2
Newtownabbey GB 27 B5
Newtownards GB 27 B5
Newtownbutler GB 27 B3
Newtownmountkennedy IRL 30 A2
Newtownstewart GB 27 B3
Nexon F 115 C5
Neyland GB 39 C2
Nibbiano I 120 C2
Nibe DK 58 B2
Nicastro I 175 C2
Niccone I 135 B5
Nice F 133 B3
Nickelsdorf A 111 B4
Nicolosi I 177 B4
Nicosia CY 181 A2
Nicosia I 177 B3
Nicótera I 175 C1
Nidda D 81 B5
Nidzica PL 77 A5
Niebla E 161 B3
Nieborów PL 77 B5
Niebüll D 64 B1
Niechanowo PL 76 B2
Niechorze PL 67 B4
Niedalino PL 67 B5
Nieder-Olm D 93 B4
Niederaula D 82 B1
Niederbipp CH 106 B2
Niederbronn-les-Bains F 93 C3
Niederfischbach D 81 B3
Niedergörsdorf D 74 C1
Niederkrüchten D 80 A2
Niederndorf A 108 B3
Niedersachswerfen D 82 A2
Niederstetten D 94 B1
Niederurnen CH 107 B4
Niederwölz A 110 B1
Niedoradz PL 85 A3
Niedzica PL 99 B4
Niegosławice PL 85 A3
Nieheim D 81 A5
Niemcza PL 85 B4
Niemegk D 74 B1
Niemisel S 196 C5
Niemodlin PL 85 B5
Nienburg, *Niedersachsen* D 72 B2
Nienburg, *Sachsen-Anhalt* D 83 A3
Niepołomice PL 99 A4
Nierstein D 93 B4
Niesky D 84 A2
Niestronno PL 76 B2
Nieświń PL 87 A4
Nieszawa PL 76 B3
Nieul-le-Dolent F 114 B2
Nieul-sur-Mer F 114 B2
Nieuw-Amsterdam NL 71 B3
Nieuw-Buinen NL 71 B3
Nieuw-Weerdinge NL 71 B3
Nieuwe Niedorp NL 70 B1
Nieuwe-Pekela NL 71 A3
Nieuwe-schans NL 71 A4
Nieuwegein NL 70 B2
Nieuwerkerken B 79 B5
Nieuwolda NL 71 A3
Nieuwpoort B 78 A2
Niğde TR 23 C8
Nigrita GR 183 C5
Nigüelas E 163 B4
Níjar E 164 C2
Nijemci HR 125 B5
Nijkerk NL 70 B2
Nijlen B 79 A4
Nijmegen NL 80 A1
Nijverdal NL 71 B3
Nikel RUS 193 C14
Nikinci SRB 127 C1
Nikiti GR 183 C5
Nikitsch A 111 B3
Nikkaluokta S 196 B2
Nikla H 111 C4
Niklasdorf A 110 B2
Nikšić MNE 139 C4
Nilivaara S 196 B4
Nîmes F 131 B3
Nimis I 122 A2
Nimtofte DK 58 B3
Nin HR 137 A4
Nindorf D 64 B2
Ninemilehouse IRL 30 B1
Ninove B 79 B4
Niort F 114 B3
Niš SRB 16 D4
Nisa P 155 B3
Niscemi I 177 B3
Niskala FIN 197 D10
Nissafors S 60 B3
Nissan-lez-Ensérune F 130 B2
Nissedal N 53 A4
Nissumby DK 58 B1
Nisterud N 53 A5
Niton GB 44 C2
Nitra SK 98 C2
Nitrianske-Pravno SK 98 C2
Nitrianske Rudno SK 98 C2
Nitry F 104 B2
Nittedal N 48 B2
Nittenau D 95 B4
Nittendorf D 95 B3
Nivala FIN 3 E9
Nivelles B 79 B4
Nivnice CZ 98 C1
Nižná SK 99 B3
Nižná Boca SK 99 C3
Nižne Repaše SK 99 B4
Nizza Monferrato I 119 C5
Njarðvík IS 190 D3
Njegůsevo SRB 126 B1
Njivice HR 123 B3
Njurundabommen S 200 D3
Njutånger S 200 E3
Noailles F 90 B2
Noain E 144 B2
Noale I 121 B5
Noalejo E 163 A4
Noblejas E 151 C4
Noceda E 141 B4
Nocera Inferiore I 170 C2
Nocera Terinese I 175 B2
Nocera Umbra I 136 B1
Noceto I 120 C3
Noci I 173 B3
Nociglia I 173 B4
Nodeland N 53 B3
Nödinge S 60 B2
Nods F 105 B5
Noé F 146 A2
Noépoli I 174 A2
Noeux-les-Mines F 78 B2
Noez E 157 A3
Nogales E 155 C4
Nogara I 121 B4
Nogarejas E 141 B4
Nogaro F 128 C2
Nogent F 105 A4
Nogent l'Artaud F 90 C3
Nogent-le-Roi F 90 C1
Nogent-le-Rotrou F 89 B4
Nogent-sur-Seine F 91 C3
Nogent-sur-Vernisson F 103 B4
Nogersund S 63 B2
Noguera E 152 B2
Noguerones E 163 A3
Nohfelden D 92 B3
Nohn D 80 B2
Noia E 140 B2
Noicáttaro I 173 A2
Noirétable F 117 B3
Noirmoutier-en-l'Île F 114 A1
Noja E 143 A3
Nojewo PL 75 B5
Nokia FIN 8 B3
Nol S 60 B2
Nola I 170 C2
Nolay F 104 C3
Noli I 133 A4
Nolnyra S 51 B4
Nombela E 150 B3
Nomeny F 92 C2
Nomexy F 92 C2
Nonancourt F 89 B5
Nonant-le-Pin F 89 B4
Nonántola I 121 C4
Nonaspe E 153 A4
None I 119 C4
Nontron F 115 C4
Nonza F 180 A2
Noordhorn NL 71 A3
Noordwijk NL 70 B1
Noordwijkerhout NL 70 B1
Noordwolde NL 70 B2
Noppikoski S 50 A1
Nora S 55 A6
Nørager DK 58 B2
Norberg S 50 B2
Norboda S 51 B5
Nórcia I 136 C2
Nord-Odal N 48 B3
Nordagutu N 53 A5
Nordanås S 200 B4
Nordausques F 78 B2
Nordborg DK 64 A2
Nordby, *Aarhus Amt.* DK 59 C3
Nordby, *Ribe Amt.* DK 59 C1
Norddeich D 71 A4
Norddorf D 64 B1
Norden D 71 A4
Nordenham D 72 A1
Norderhov N 48 B2
Norderney D 71 A4
Norderstapel D 64 B2
Norderstedt D 64 C3
Nordfjord N 193 B14

Nordfjordeid N 198 D3
Nordfold N 194 C6
Nordhalben D 82 B3
Nordhausen D 82 A2
Nordheim vor der Rhön D 82 B2
Nordholz D 64 C1
Nordhorn D 71 B4
Nordingrå S 200 D4
Nordkjosbotn N 192 C3
Nordli N 199 A10
Nördlingen D 94 C2
Nordmaling S 200 C5
Nordmark S 49 C6
Nordmela N 194 A6
Nordre Osen N 48 A3
Nordsinni N 48 B1
Nørdstedalsseter N 198 D4
Nordstemmen D 72 B2
Nordvågen N 193 B10
Nordwalde D 71 B4
Noreña E 142 A1
Noresund N 48 B1
Norg NL 71 A3
Norheimsund N 46 B3
Norie S 63 B2
Norma I 169 B2
Nornäs S 49 A5
Norra Vi S 62 A3
Norrahammar S 62 A2
Norråker S 200 B1
Norrala S 51 A3
Nørre Aaby DK 59 C2
Nørre Alslev DK 65 B4
Nørre Lyndelse DK 59 C3
Nørre Nebel DK 59 C1
Nørre Snede DK 59 C2
Nørre Vorupør DK 58 B1
Norrent-Fontes F 78 B2
Nørresundby DK 58 A2
Norrfjärden S 196 D4
Norrhed S 196 C3
Norrhult Klavreström S 62 A3
Norrköping S 56 B2
Norrskedika S 51 B5
Norrsundet S 51 B4
Norrtälje S 57 A4
Nors DK 58 A1
Norsbron S 55 A4
Norsholm S 56 B1
Norsjö S 200 B5
Nort-sur-Erdre F 101 B4
Nörten-Hardenberg D 82 A1
North Berwick GB 35 B5
North Charlton GB 37 A5
North Frodingham GB 40 B3
North Kessock GB 32 D2
North Molton GB 42 A3
North Petherton GB 43 A3
North Somercotes GB 41 B4
North Tawton GB 42 B3
North Thoresby GB 41 B3
North Walsham GB 41 C5
Northallerton GB 37 B5
Northampton GB 44 A3
Northeim D 82 A1
Northfleet GB 45 B4
Northleach GB 44 B2
Northpunds GB 33 B5
Northwich GB 38 A4
Norton GB 40 A3
Nortorf D 64 B2
Nörvenich D 80 B2
Norwich GB 41 C5
Norwick GB 33 A6
Nøsen N 47 B5
Nossa Senhora do Cabo P 154 C1
Nossebro S 55 B3
Nössemark S 54 A2
Nossen D 83 A5
Notaresco I 169 A3
Noto I 177 C4
Notodden N 53 A5
Nottingham GB 40 C2
Nottuln D 71 C4
Nouan-le-Fuzelier F 103 B4
Nouans-les-Fontaines F 103 B3
Nougaroulet F 129 C3
Nouvion F 78 B1
Nouzonville F 91 B4
Nova H 111 C3
Nová Baňa SK 98 C2
Nová Bystrica SK 99 B3
Nová Bystřice CZ 97 B3
Nova Crnja SRB 126 B2
Nova Gorica SLO 122 B2
Nova Gradiška HR 124 B3
Nova Levante I 108 C2
Nová Paka CZ 84 B3
Nova Pazova SRB 127 C2
Nová Pec CZ 96 C1
Nova Siri I 174 A2
Nova Topola BIH 124 B3
Nova Zagora BG 17 D6
Novaféltria I 135 B5
Nováky SK 98 C2
Novalaise F 118 B2
Novales E 145 B3
Novalja HR 137 A3
Novara I 120 B1
Novara di Sicilia I 177 A4
Novate Mezzola I 120 A2
Novaya Ladoga RUS 9 B8
Nové Hrady CZ 96 C2
Nové Město SK 98 C1
Nové Město na Moravě CZ 97 B4
Nové Město nad Metují CZ 85 B4
Nové Město pod Smrkem CZ 84 B3
Nové Mitrovice CZ 96 B1
Nové Sady SK 98 C1
Nové Strašeci CZ 84 B1
Nové Zámky SK 112 B2
Novelda E 165 A4
Novellara I 121 C3
Noventa di Piave I 122 B1
Noventa Vicentina I 121 B4
Novés E 151 B3
Noves F 131 B3
Novés de Segre E 147 B2
Novgorod RUS 9 C7
Novi Bečej SRB 126 B2
Novi di Módena I 121 C3
Novi Kneževac SRB 126 A2
Novi Lígure I 120 C1
Novi Marof HR 124 A2
Novi Pazar BG 17 D7
Novi Pazar SRB 16 D4
Novi Sad SRB 126 B1
Novi Slankamen SRB 126 B2
Novi Travnik BIH 139 A3
Novi Vinodolski HR 123 B3
Novigrad, *Istarska* HR 122 B2
Novigrad, *Zadarsko-Kninska* HR 137 A4
Novigrad Podravski HR 124 A2
Noville B 92 A1
Novion-Porcien F 91 B4
Novo Mesto SLO 123 B4
Novo Miloševo SRB 126 B2
Novo Selo BIH 125 B3
Novohrad-Volynskyy UA 13 C7
Novorzhev RUS 9 D6
Novoselytsya UA 17 A7
Novosokolniki RUS 9 D6
Novoveská Huta SK 99 C4
Novovolynsk UA 13 C6
Novska HR 124 B2
Nový Bor CZ 84 B2
Nový Bydžov CZ 84 B3
Novy-Chevrières F 91 B4
Novy Dwór Mazowiecki PL 77 B5
Nový-Hrozenkov CZ 98 B2
Nový Jičín CZ 98 B2
Novy Knin CZ 96 B2
Nowa Cerekwia PL 86 B1
Nowa Dęba PL 87 B5
Nowa Karczma PL 68 A3
Nowa Kościoł PL 85 A3
Nowa Ruda PL 85 B4
Nowa Słupia PL 87 B5
Nowa Sól PL 85 A3
Nowa Wieś PL 69 B4
Nowa-Wieś Wielka PL 76 B3
Nowe PL 69 B3
Nowe Brzesko PL 87 B4
Nowe Grudze PL 77 B4
Nowe Kiejkuty PL 77 A6
Nowe Miasteczko PL 85 A3
Nowe Miasto, *Mazowieckie* PL 87 A4
Nowe Miasto, *Mazowieckie* PL 77 B5
Nowe Miasto Lubawskie PL 69 B4
Nowe Miasto nad Wartą PL 76 B2
Nowe Skalmierzyce PL 86 A2
Nowe Warpno PL 74 A3
Nowica PL 69 A4
Nowogard PL 75 A4
Nowogród Bobrzanski PL 84 A3
Nowogrodziec PL 84 A3
Nowosolna PL 86 A3
Nowy Dwór Gdański PL 69 A4
Nowy Korczyn PL 87 B4
Nowy Sącz PL 99 B4
Nowy Staw PL 69 A4
Nowy Targ PL 99 B4
Nowy Tomyśl PL 75 B5
Nowy Wiśnicz PL 99 B4
Noyal-Pontivy F 100 A3
Noyalo F 101 B3
Noyant F 102 B2
Noyelles-sur-Mer F 78 B1
Noyen-sur-Sarthe F 102 B1
Noyers F 104 B2
Noyers-sur-Cher F 103 B3
Noyers-sur-Jabron F 132 A1
Noyon F 90 B2
Nozay F 101 B4
Nuaillé F 102 B1
Nuaillé-d'Aunis F 114 B3
Nuars F 104 B2
Nubledo E 141 A5
Nuéno E 145 B3
Nuestra Señora Sa Verge des Pilar E 166 C1
Nueva E 142 A2
Nueva Carteya E 163 A3
Nuevalos E 152 A2
Nuits F 104 B3
Nuits-St. Georges F 105 B3
Nule I 178 B3
Nules E 159 B3
Nulvi I 178 B2
Numana I 136 B2
Numansdorp NL 79 A4
Nümbrecht D 81 B3
Nunchritz D 83 A5
Nuneaton GB 40 C2
Nunnanen FIN 196 A7
Nuñomoral E 149 B3
Nunspeet NL 70 B2
Nuorgam FIN 193 B11
Núoro I 178 B3
Nurallao I 179 C3
Nuremberg = Nürnberg D 94 B3
Nurmes FIN 3 E11
Nürnberg = Nuremberg D 94 B3
Nurri I 179 C3
Nürtingen D 94 C1
Nus I 119 B4
Nusnäs S 50 B1
Nusplingen D 107 A3
Nuštar HR 125 B4
Nuupas FIN 197 C9
Nyåker S 200 C5
Nyáregyháza H 112 B3
Nyarlörinc H 113 C3
Nyasvizh BY 13 B7
Nybble S 55 A5
Nybergsund N 49 A4
Nybøl DK 64 B2
Nyborg DK 59 C3
Nyborg S 196 D6
Nybro S 62 B3
Nybster GB 32 C3
Nyby DK 65 B5
Nye S 62 A3
Nyékládháza H 113 B4
Nyergesujfalu H 112 B2
Nyhammar S 50 B1
Nyhyttan S 55 A5
Nyirád H 111 B4
Nyirbátor H 16 B5
Nyíregyháza H 16 B4
Nyker DK 67 A3
Nykil S 56 B1
Nykirke N 48 B2
Nykøbing, *Falster* DK 65 B4
Nykøbing, *Vestsjællands Amt.* DK 61 D1
Nykøbing M DK 58 B1
Nyköping S 56 B3
Nykroppa S 55 A5
Nykvarn S 56 A3
Nykyrke S 55 B5
Nyland S 200 C3
Nylars DK 67 A3
Nymburk CZ 84 B3
Nynäshamn S 57 B3
Nyon CH 118 A3
Nyons F 131 A4
Nýřany CZ 96 B1
Nýrsko CZ 95 B5
Nyrud N 193 C13
Nysa PL 85 B5
Nysäter S 55 A3
Nyseter N 198 C5
Nyskoga S 49 B4
Nysted DK 65 B4
Nystrand N 53 A5
Nyúl H 111 B4
Nyvoll N 192 B7

O

O Barco E 141 B4
O Bolo E 141 B3
O Carballiño E 140 B2
O Corgo E 141 B3
Ö Lagnö S 57 A4
Ö Näsberg S 49 B5
O Páramo E 140 B3
O Pedrouzo E 140 B2
O Pino E 140 B2
O Porriño E 140 B2
O Rosal E 140 C2
Oadby GB 40 C2
Oakengates GB 38 B4
Oakham GB 40 C3
Oanes N 52 B2
Obalj BIH 139 B4
Oban GB 34 B2
Obbola S 200 C6
Obdach A 110 B1
Obejo E 156 B3
Ober Grafendorf A 110 A2
Ober-Morlen D 81 B4
Oberammergau D 108 B2
Oberasbach D 94 B2
Oberau D 108 B2
Oberaudorf D 108 B3
Oberbruck F 106 B1
Oberdiessbach CH 106 C2
Oberdorf CH 106 B2
Oberdrauburg A 109 C3
Obere Stanz A 110 B2
Oberelsbach D 82 B2
Obergünzburg D 108 B1
Obergurgl A 108 C2
Oberhausen D 80 A2
Oberhof D 82 B2
Oberkirch D 93 C4
Oberkirchen D 81 A4
Oberkochen D 94 C2
Obermassfeld-Grimmenthal D 82 B2
Obermünchen D 95 C3
Obernai F 93 C3
Obernberg A 96 C1
Obernburg D 93 B5
Oberndorf D 93 C4
Oberndorf bei Salzburg A 109 B3
Obernkirchen D 72 B2
Oberort A 110 B2
Oberpullendorf A 111 B3
Oberriet CH 107 B4
Oberröblingen D 82 A3
Oberrot D 94 B1
Oberstaufen D 107 B5
Oberstdorf D 107 B5
Obertauern A 109 B4
Obertilliach A 109 C3
Obertraubling D 95 C4
Obertraun A 109 B4
Obertrubach D 95 B3
Obertrum A 109 B4
Oberursel D 81 B4
Obervellach A 109 C4
Oberviechtach D 95 B4
Oberwart A 111 B3
Oberwesel D 93 A3
Oberwinter D 80 B3
Oberwölzstadt A 110 B1
Oberzell D 96 C1
Obice PL 87 B4
Óbidos P 154 B1
Obing D 109 B3
Objat F 129 A4
Objazda PL 68 A2
Öblarn A 109 B5
Obninsk RUS 9 E10
Oborniki PL 75 B5
Oborniki Śląskie PL 85 A4
Obornjača SRB 126 B1
Obrenovac SRB 127 C2
Obrež SRB 127 C1
Obrigheim D 93 B5
Obrov SLO 123 B3
Obrovac HR 137 A4
Obrovac SRB 126 B1
Obrovac Sinjski HR 138 B2
Obruk TR 23 B7
Obrzycko PL 75 B5
Obudovac BIH 125 C4
Ocaña E 151 C4
Occhiobello I 121 C4
Occimiano I 119 B5
Očevlja BIH 139 A4
Ochagavía E 144 B2
Ochiltree GB 36 A2
Ochla PL 84 A3
Ochotnica-Dolna PL 99 B4
Ochotnica-Górna PL 99 B4
Ochsenfurt D 94 B2
Ochsenhausen D 107 A4
Ochtendung D 80 B3
Ochtrup D 71 B4
Ocieka PL 87 B5
Ockelbo S 50 B3
Öckerö S 60 B1
Ocniţa MD 17 A7
Očová SK 99 C3
Ócsa H 112 B3
Öcseny H 125 A4
Öcsöd H 113 C4
Octeville F 88 A2
Ocypel PL 69 B3
Ödåkra S 61 C2
Odby DK 58 B1
Odda N 46 B3
Odder DK 59 C3
Ödeborg S 54 B2
Odeceixe P 160 B1
Odechów PL 87 A5
Odeleite P 160 B2
Odemira P 160 B1
Ödemiş TR 188 A2
Odensbacken S 56 A1
Odense DK 59 C3
Odensjö, *Jönköping* S 62 A2
Odensjö, *Kronoberg* S 60 C3
Oderberg D 74 B3
Oderzo I 122 B1
Odesa = Odessa UA 17 B9
Ödeshög S 55 B5
Odessa = Odesa UA 17 B9
Odiáxere P 160 B1
Odie GB 33 B4
Odiham GB 44 B3
Odintsovo RUS 9 E10
Odivelas P 160 A1
Odolanów PL 85 A5
Odón E 152 B2
Odorheiu Secuiesc RO 17 B6
Odrowaz PL 87 A4
Odry CZ 98 B1
Odrzywół PL 87 A4
Ødsted DK 59 C2
Odžaci SRB 126 B1
Odžak BIH 125 B4
Oebisfelde D 73 B3
Oederan D 83 B5
Oeding D 71 C3
Oegstgeest NL 70 B1
Oelde D 81 A4
Oelsnitz D 83 B4
Oer-Erkenschwick D 80 A3
Oerlinghausen D 72 C1
Oettingen D 94 C2
Oetz A 108 B1
Oeventrop D 81 A4
Offanengo I 120 B2
Offenbach D 81 B4
Offenburg D 93 C3
Offida I 136 C2
Offingen D 94 C2
Offranville F 89 A5
Ofir P 148 A1
Ofte N 53 A4
Ofterschwang D 107 B5
Oggiono I 120 B2
Ogihares E 163 A4
Ogliastro Cilento I 170 C3
Ogliastro Marina I 170 C2
Ogmore-by-Sea GB 39 C3
Ogna N 52 B1
Ogre LV 8 D4
Ogrodzieniec PL 86 B3
Ogulin HR 123 B4
Ögur IS 190 A3
Ohanes E 164 B2
Ohey B 79 B5
Ohlstadt D 108 B2
Ohrdorf D 73 B3
Ohrdruf D 82 B2
Ohrid MK 182 B2
Öhringen D 94 B1
Oia E 140 B2
Oiã P 148 B1
Oiartzun E 144 A2
Oijärvi FIN 197 D8
Oilgate IRL 30 B2
Oimbra E 148 A2
Oiselay-et-Grachoux F 105 B4
Oisemont F 90 B1
Oisterwijk NL 79 A5
Öja S 57 C4
Öje S 49 B5
Ojén E 162 B3
Ojrzeń PL 77 B5
Ojuelos Altos E 156 B2
Okalewo PL 77 A4
Okány H 113 C5
Okehampton GB 42 B2
Oklaj HR 138 B2
Økneshamn N 194 B6
Okoč SK 111 B4
Okoličné SK 99 B3
Okonek PL 68 B1
Okonin PL 69 B3
Okřisky CZ 97 B3
Oksa PL 87 B4
Oksbøl DK 59 C1
Oksby DK 59 C1
Øksfjord N 192 B6
Øksna N 48 B3
Okučani HR 124 B3
Okulovka RUS 9 C8
Ólafsfjörður IS 191 A7
Ólafsvík IS 190 C2
Olagüe E 144 B2
Oland N 53 B4
Olargues F 130 B1
Oława PL 85 B5
Olazagutia E 144 B1
Olbernhau D 83 B5
Ólbia I 178 B3
Olching D 108 A2
Old Deer GB 33 D4
Oldbury GB 43 A4
Oldcastle IRL 27 C3
Oldeberkoop NL 70 B3
Oldeboorn NL 70 A2
Olden N 198 D3
Oldenbrok D 71 A5
Oldenburg, *Niedersachsen* D 71 A5
Oldenburg, *Schleswig-Holstein* D 65 B3
Oldenzaal NL 71 B3
Olderdalen N 192 C4
Olderfjord N 193 B9
Oldersum D 71 A4
Oldervik N 192 C2
Oldham GB 40 B1
Oldisleben D 82 A3
Oldmeldrum GB 33 D4
Olea E 142 B2
Oleby S 49 B5
Olechów PL 87 A5
Oledo P 155 B3
Oléggio I 120 B1
Oleiros, *Coruña* E 140 A2
Oleiros, *Coruña* E 140 B1
Oleiros P 154 B3
Oleksandriya UA 13 C7
Olen B 79 A4
Ølen N 52 A1
Olenegorsk RUS 3 B13
Olenino RUS 9 D8
Olesa de Montserrat E 147 C2
Oleśnica PL 85 A5
Olešnice CZ 97 B4
Olesno PL 86 B2
Oletta F 180 A2
Olette F 146 B3
Olevsk UA 13 C7
Olfen D 80 A3
Olgiate Comasco I 120 B1
Olginate I 120 B2
Ølgod DK 59 C1
Olgrinmore GB 32 C3
Olhão P 160 B2
Olhava FIN 197 D8
Olhavo P 154 B1
Oliana E 147 B2
Olias del Rey E 151 C4
Oliena I 178 B3
Oliete E 153 B3
Olimbos GR 188 D2
Olite E 144 B2
Oliva E 159 C3
Oliva de la Frontera E 155 C4
Oliva de Mérida E 156 B1
Oliva de Plasencia E 149 B3
Olivadi I 175 C2
Olival P 154 B2
Olivar E 163 B4
Olivares E 161 B3
Olivares de Duero E 142 C2
Olivares de Júcar E 158 B1
Oliveira de Azeméis P 148 B1
Oliveira de Frades P 148 B1
Oliveira do Conde P 148 B2
Oliveira do Douro P 148 A1
Oliveira do Hospital P 148 B2
Olivenza E 155 C3
Olivet F 103 B3
Olivone CH 107 C3
Öljehult S 63 B3
Olkusz PL 86 B3
Ollerton GB 40 B2
Ollerup DK 65 A3
Olliergues F 117 B3
Ölmbrotorp S 56 A1
Ölme S 55 A4
Olmedilla de Alarcón E 158 B1
Olmedillo de Roa E 143 C3
Olmedo E 150 A3
Olmedo I 178 B2
Olmeto F 180 B1
Olmillos de Castro E 149 A3
Olmos de Ojeda E 142 B2
Olney GB 44 A3
Ołobok PL 86 A2
Olocau del Rey E 153 B3
Olofström S 63 B2
Olomouc CZ 98 B1
Olonets RUS 9 B8
Olonne-sur-Mer F 114 B2
Olonzac F 130 B1
Oloron-Ste. Marie F 145 A3
Olost E 147 C3
Olot E 147 B3
Olovo BIH 139 A4
Olpe D 81 A3
Olsberg D 81 A4
Olsene B 79 B3
Olserud S 55 A4
Olshammar S 55 B5
Olshanka UA 13 D9
Olszanica PL 85 A3
Olsztyn, *Śląskie* PL 86 B3
Olsztyn, *Warmińsko-Mazurskie* PL 69 B5
Olsztynek PL 77 A5
Olszyna PL 84 A3
Olszyny PL 77 A6
Oltedal N 52 B2
Olten CH 106 B2
Olteniţa RO 17 C7
Olula del Rio E 164 B2
Ølve N 46 B2
Olvega E 144 C2
Olvera E 162 B2
Olympia GR 184 B2
Olzai I 178 B3
Omagh GB 27 B3
Omalos GR 185 D4
Omegna I 119 B5
Omiš HR 138 B2
Omišalj HR 123 B3
Ommen NL 71 B3
Omodhos CY 181 B1
Omoljica SRB 127 C2

On	B	79	B5	Orchamps-Vennes	F	105	B5	Ortakent	TR	188	B2	Øster Jølby	DK	58	B1
Oña	E	143	B3	Orches	F	102	C2	Ortaklar	TR	188	B2	Øster-marie	DK	67	A4
Onano	I	168	A1	Orchete	E	159	C3	Ortaköy	TR	23	B8	Øster Torslev	DK	58	B3
Oñati	E	143	A4	Orchies	F	78	B3	Orte	I	168	A2	Øster Vrå	DK	58	A3
Onda	E	159	B3	Orchowo	PL	76	B3	Ortenburg	D	96	C1	Osterburg	D	73	B4
Ondara	E	159	C4	Orcières	F	118	C3	Orth	A	111	A3	Osterburken	D	94	B1
Ondarroa	E	143	A4	Ordes	E	140	A2	Orthez	F	128	C2	Österbybruk	S	51	B4
Onesse-et-Laharie	F	128	B1	Ordhead	GB	33	D4	Ortigueira	E	140	A3	Österbymo	S	62	A3
Oneşti	RO	17	B7	Ordino	AND	146	B2	Ortilla	E	145	B3	Ostercappeln	D	71	B5
Onhaye	B	79	B4	Ordizia	E	144	A1	Ortisei	I	108	C2	Österfärnebo	S	51	B3
Onich	GB	34	B2	Orduña	E	143	B4	Orţişoara	RO	126	B3	Osterfeld	D	83	A3
Onil	E	159	C3	Ore	S	50	A2	Ortnevik	N	46	A3	Österforse	S	200	C3
Onis	E	142	A2	Orea	E	152	B2	Orton	GB	37	B4	Osterhever	D	64	B1
Önnestad	S	61	C4	Orebić	HR	138	C3	Ortona	I	169	A4	Osterhofen	D	95	C5
Onsala	S	60	B2	Örebro	S	56	A1	Ortrand	D	84	A1	Osterholz-Scharmbeck	D	72	A1
Ontinyent	E	159	C3	Öregcsertö	H	112	C3	Orubica	HR	124	B3	Østerild	DK	58	A1
Ontur	E	158	C2	Öregrund	S	51	B5	Ørum	DK	58	B2	Österlövsta	S	51	B4
Onzain	F	103	B3	Ørehoved	DK	65	B4	Orune	I	178	B3	Ostermiething	A	109	A3
Onzonilla	E	142	B1	Orellana	E	156	A2	Orusco	E	151	B4	Osterode am Harz	D	82	A2
Oost-Vlieland	NL	70	A2	Orellana de la Sierra	E	156	A2	Orvalho	P	155	A3	Ostersiel	D	64	B1
Oostburg	NL	79	A3	Ören	TR	188	B2	Orvault	F	101	B4	Östersund	S	199	B11
Oostende	B	78	A2	Örencik	TR	186	A1	Ørvella	N	53	A5	Östervåla	S	51	B4
Oosterend	NL	70	A2	Orestiada	GR	186	A1	Orvieto	I	168	A2	Östervallskog	S	54	A2
Oosterhout	NL	79	A4	Organyà	E	147	B2	Orvínio	I	169	A2	Osterwieck	D	73	C3
Oosterwolde	NL	71	B3	Orgaz	E	157	A4	Oryakhovo	BG	17	D5	Osterzell	D	108	B1
Oosterzele	B	79	B3	Orgelet	F	105	C4	Orzesze	PL	86	B2	Ostffyasszonyfa	H	111	B4
Oosthuizen	NL	70	B2	Ørgenvika	N	48	B1	Orzinuovi	I	120	B2	Östfora	S	51	C4
Oostkamp	B	78	A3	Orgères-en-Beauce	F	103	A3	Orziveechi	I	120	B2	Osthammar	S	51	B5
Oostmalle	B	79	A4	Orgibet	F	145	B4	Orzyny	PL	77	A6	Ostheim	F	106	A2
Oostvoorne	NL	79	A4	Orgnac-l'Aven	F	131	A3	Os, *Hedmark*	N	199	C8	Ostheim vor der Rhön	D	82	B2
Ootmarsum	NL	71	B3	Orgon	F	131	B3	Os, *Hedmark*	N	48	B3	Osthofen	D	93	B4
Opalenica	PL	75	B5	Orgósolo	I	178	B3	Os Peares	E	140	B3	Ostiano	I	120	B3
Opařany	CZ	96	B2	Orhaneli	TR	186	B3	Osann-Monzel	D	92	B2	Ostíglia	I	121	B4
Opatija	HR	123	B3	Orhangazi	TR	187	B4	Osbruk	S	62	A2	Ostiz	E	144	B2
Opatów, *Śląskie*	PL	86	B2	Orhei	MD	17	B8	Øsby	DK	59	C2	Östmark	S	49	B4
Opatów, *Świętokrzyskie*	PL	87	B5	Orhomenos	GR	184	A3	Osby	S	61	C3	Östnor	S	50	A1
Opatów, *Wielkopolskie*	PL	86	A2	Oria	E	164	B2	Oščadnica	SK	98	B2	Ostojićevo	SRB	126	B2
Opatówek	PL	86	A2	Oria	I	173	B3	Oschatz	D	83	A5	Ostra	I	136	B2
Opatowiec	PL	87	B4	Origny-Ste.-Benoite	F	91	B3	Oschersleben	D	73	B4	Östra Amtervik	S	55	A4
Opava	CZ	98	B1	Orihuela	E	165	A4	Óschiri	I	178	B3	Östra Husby	S	56	B2
Opeinde	NL	70	A3	Orihuela del Tremedal	E	152	B2	Oscilowo	PL	77	B5	Östra Ljungby	S	61	C3
Oper Thalkirchdorf	D	107	B5	Orikum	AL	182	C1	Osdorf	D	64	B3	Östra Ryd	S	56	B2
Opglabbeek	B	80	A1	Oriola	P	154	C3	Osečina	SRB	127	C1	Östraby	S	61	D3
Opicina	I	122	B2	Oriolo	I	174	A2	Osečná	CZ	84	B2	Ostrach	D	107	B4
Oplotnica	SLO	123	A4	Oriovac	HR	125	B3	Oseja de Sajambre	E	142	A1	Ostrau	D	83	A5
Opmeer	NL	70	B1	Orissaare	EST	8	C3	Osek	CZ	84	B1	Ostrava	CZ	98	B2
Opochka	RUS	9	D6	Oristano	I	179	C2	Osen	N	199	A7	Østre Halsen	N	53	A6
Opočno	CZ	85	B4	Öriszentpéter	H	111	C3	Osera de Ebro	E	153	A3	Østrhauderfehn	D	71	A4
Opoczno	PL	87	A4	Ørje	N	54	A2	Osidda	I	178	B3	Ostritz	D	84	A2
Opole	PL	86	B1	Orjiva	E	163	B4	Osie	PL	69	B3	Ostróda	PL	69	B4
Oporów	PL	77	B4	Orkanger	N	198	B6	Osieczna, *Pomorskie*	PL	68	B3	Ostroh	UA	13	C7
Opovo	SRB	127	B2	Ørkelljunga	S	61	C3	Osieczna, *Wielkopolskie*	PL	75	C5	Ostrołęka	PL	12	B4
Oppach	D	84	A2	Örkény	H	112	B3	Osieczno	PL	75	A4	Ostropole	PL	68	B1
Oppdal	N	198	C6	Orlamünde	D	82	B3	Osiek, *Kujawsko-Pomorskie*	PL	77	A4	Ostroróg	PL	75	B5
Oppeby, *Östergötland*	S	56	B1	Orléans	F	103	B3	Osiek, *Kujawsko-Pomorskie*	PL	76	B3	Ostrošovac	BIH	124	C1
Oppeby, *Södermanland*	S	56	B2	Orlová	CZ	98	B2	Osiek, *Pomorskie*	PL	69	B3	Ostrov	CZ	83	B4
Oppedal	N	46	A2	Orlovat	SRB	126	B2	Osiek, *Świętokrzyskie*	PL	87	B5	Ostrov	RUS	8	D6
Oppegård	N	54	A1	Ormea	I	133	A3	Osiek nad Notecią	PL	76	A2	Ostrov nad Oslavou	CZ	97	B3
Oppenau	D	93	C4	Ormelet	N	54	A1	Osielsko	PL	76	A3	Ostrów Mazowiecka	PL	12	B4
Oppenberg	A	110	B1	Ormemyr	N	53	A5	Osijek	HR	125	B4	Ostrów Wielkopolski	PL	86	A1
Oppenheim	D	93	B4	Ormília	GR	183	C5	Osilnica	SLO	123	B3	Ostrówek	PL	86	A2
Óppido Lucano	I	172	B1	Ormos	GR	185	B5	Ósilo	I	178	B2	Ostrowiec	PL	68	A1
Óppido Mamertina	I	175	C1	Ormož	SLO	124	A2	Ósimo	I	136	B2	Ostrowiec-Świętokrzyski	PL	87	B5
Opponitz	A	110	B1	Ormskirk	GB	38	A4	Osinja	BIH	125	C3	Ostrowite	PL	77	A4
Oppstad	N	48	B3	Ornans	F	105	B5	Osintorf	BY	13	A9	Ostrowo	PL	76	B3
Oprtalj	HR	122	B2	Orneta	PL	69	A5	Osipaonica	SRB	127	C3	Ostrožac	BIH	139	B3
Opsaheden	S	49	B5	Ørnhøj	DK	59	B1	Osjaków	PL	86	A2	Ostrzeszów	PL	86	A1
Opusztaszer	H	113	C4	Ørnö	N	57	A4	Oskamull	GB	34	B1	Ostseebad Kühlungsborn	D	65	B4
Opuzen	HR	138	B3	Örnsköldsvik	S	200	C4	Oskarshamn	S	62	A4	Ostuni	I	173	B3
Ora	CY	181	B2	Orolik	HR	125	B4	Oskarström	S	60	C2	Osuna	E	162	A2
Ora	I	121	A4	Orom	SRB	126	B1	Oslany	SK	98	C2	Oswestry	GB	38	B3
Orada	P	155	C3	Oron-la-Ville	CH	106	C1	Oslavany	CZ	97	B4	Oświęcim	PL	86	B3
Oradea	RO	16	B4	Oronsko	PL	87	A4	Ošlje	HR	139	C3	Osztopán	H	111	C4
Oradour-sur-Glane	F	115	C5	Oropa	I	119	B4	Oslo	N	48	C2	Oteiza	E	144	B2
Oradour-sur-Vayres	F	115	C4	Oropesa, *Castellón de la Plana*	E	153	B4	Øslös	DK	58	A1	Otelec	RO	126	B2
Oragonja	SLO	122	B2	Oropesa, *Toledo*	E	150	C2	Osmancık	TR	23	A8	Oteo	E	143	A3
Orah	BIH	139	C4	Orosei	I	178	B3	Osmaneli	TR	187	B4	Oterbekk	N	54	A1
Orahova	BIH	138	A3	Orosháza	H	113	C4	Ósmo	S	57	B3	Otero de Herreros	E	151	B3
Orahovica	HR	125	B3	Oroslavje	HR	124	B1	Osmolin	PL	77	B4	Otero de O Bodas	E	141	C4
Orahovo	BIH	124	B3	Oroszlány	H	112	B2	Osnabrück	D	71	B5	Othem	S	57	C4
Oraison	F	132	B1	Oroszlo	H	125	A4	Ośno Lubuskie	PL	75	B3	Otilia	GB	40	B2
Orajärvi	FIN	196	C7	Orotelli	I	178	B3	Osoblaha	CZ	85	B5	Otmuchów	PL	85	B5
Orange	F	131	A3	Orozko	E	143	A4	Osor	E	147	C3	Otočac	HR	123	C4
Orani	I	178	B3	Orphir	GB	33	C3	Osor	HR	123	C3	Otok, *Splitsko-Dalmatinska*	HR	138	B2
Oranienbaum	D	83	A4	Orpington	GB	45	B4	Osorno	E	142	B2	Otok, *Vukovarsko-Srijemska*	HR	125	B4
Oranienburg	D	74	B2	Orreaga-Roncesvalles	F	144	A2	Øsoyra	N	46	A2	Otoka	BIH	124	C2
Oranmore	IRL	28	A3	Orrefors	S	62	B3	Óspakseyri	IS	190	B4	Otranto	I	173	B4
Orašac	SRB	127	C2	Orrviken	S	199	B11	Ospedaletti	I	133	B3	Otrić	HR	138	A2
Orašje	BIH	125	B4	Orsa	S	50	A1	Ospitaletto	I	120	B3	Otríčoki	I	168	A3
Oravská Lesná	SK	99	B3	Orsara di Púglia	I	171	B3	Oss	NL	80	A1	Otrokovice	CZ	98	B1
Oravská Polhora	SK	99	B3	Orsay	F	90	C2	Ossa de Montiel	E	158	C1	Otta	N	198	D6
Oravské Veselé	SK	99	B3	Orscholz	D	92	B2	Ossi	I	178	B2	Ottana	I	178	B3
Oravsky-Podzámok	SK	99	B3	Orsennes	F	103	C3	Ossjøen	N	47	B5	Ottaviano	I	170	C2
Orba	E	159	C3	Orsières	CH	119	A4	Ostanå	S	61	C4	Ottenby	S	63	B4
Orbacém	P	148	A1	Örsjö	S	63	B3	Ostanvik	S	50	A2	Ottendorf-Okrilla	D	84	A1
Ørbæk	DK	59	C3	Ørslev	DK	65	A4	Ostashkov	RUS	9	D8	Ottenhöfen	D	93	C4
Orbais	F	91	C3	Örslösa	S	55	B3	Östavall	S	200	D1	Ottenschlag	A	97	C3
Orbassano	I	119	B4	Orsogna	I	169	A4	Ostbevern	D	71	B4	Ottensheim	A	96	C2
Orbe	CH	105	C5	Orsomarso	I	174	B1	Østby	N	49	A4	Otter Ferry	GB	34	B2
Orbetello	I	168	A1	Orşova	RO	16	C5	Osted	DK	61	D1	Otterbach	D	93	B3
Orbetello Scalo	I	168	A1	Ørsta	N	198	C3	Ostenfeld	D	64	B2	Otterbäcken	S	55	B5
Orbigny	F	103	B3	Ørsted	DK	58	B3	Oster	UA	13	C9	Otterberg	D	93	B3
Ørby	DK	59	B3	Örsundsbro	S	56	A3	Øster Assels	DK	58	B1	Otter Ferry	GB	34	B2
Ørbyhus	S	51	B4	Orta Nova	I	171	B3	Øster Hornum	DK	58	B2	Otterbach	D	93	B3
Orce	E	164	B2	Ortaca	TR	188	C3	Øster Hurup	DK	58	B3	Otterberg	D	93	B3
Orcera	E	164	A2												

Otterburn	GB	37	A4	Øyuvsbu	N	52	A3
Otterndorf	D	64	C1	Ozaeta	E	143	B4
Ottersburg	D	72	A2	Ozalj	HR	123	B4
Ottersweier	D	93	C4	Ożarów	PL	87	B5
Otterup	DK	59	C3	Ożarów Maz	PL	77	B5
Ottery St. Mary	GB	43	B3	Ožbalt	SLO	110	C2
Ottignies	B	79	B4	Ózd	H	113	A4
Ottmarsheim	F	106	B2	Ož'dany	SK	99	C3
Ottobeuren	D	107	B5	Ozieri	I	178	B3
Öttömös	H	126	A1	Ozimek	PL	86	B2
Ottone	I	120	C2	Ozimica	BIH	139	A4
Ottsjö	S	199	B10	Ozora	H	112	C2
Ottweiler	D	92	B3	Ozorków	PL	77	C4
Otveşti	RO	126	B3	Ozzano Monferrato	I	119	B5
Ötvöskónyi	H	124	A3				
Otwock	PL	12	B4	**P**			
Ouanne	F	104	B2				
Ouarville	F	90	C1	Paakkola	FIN	196	D7
Oucques	F	103	B3	Paal	B	79	A5
Oud-Beijerland	NL	79	A4	Pabianice	PL	86	A3
Oud Gastel	NL	79	A4	Pacanów	PL	87	B5
Ouddorp	NL	79	A3	Paceco	I	176	B1
Oude-Pekela	NL	71	A4	Pachino	I	177	C4
Oude-Tonge	NL	79	A4	Pačir	SRB	126	B1
Oudemirdum	NL	70	B2	Pack	A	110	B2
Oudenaarde	B	79	B3	Paços de Ferreira	P	148	A1
Oudenbosch	NL	79	A4	Pacov	CZ	96	B3
Oudenburg	B	78	A3	Pacsa	H	111	C4
Oudewater	NL	70	B1	Pacy-sur-Eure	F	89	A5
Oudon	F	101	B4	Paczków	PL	85	B5
Oughterard	IRL	28	A2	Padany	RUS	3	E13
Ouguela	P	155	B3	Padborg	DK	64	B2
Ouistreham	F	89	A3	Padej	SRB	126	B2
Oulainen	FIN	3	D9	Padene	HR	138	A2
Oulchy-le-Château	F	91	B3	Paderborn	D	81	A4
Oullins	F	117	B4	Paderne	P	160	B1
Oulmes	F	114	B3	Padiham	GB	40	B1
Oulton	GB	41	C5	Padina	SRB	126	B2
Oulton Broad	GB	41	C5	Padinska Skela	SRB	127	C2
Oulu	FIN	3	D9	Padornelo	P	148	A1
Oulx	I	119	B3	Pádova	I	121	B4
Oundle	GB	40	C3	Padragkút	H	111	B4
Ouranopoli	GR	183	C6	Padria	I	178	B2
Ourém	P	154	B2	Padrón	E	140	B2
Ourense	E	140	B3	Padru	I	178	B3
Ourique	P	160	B1	Padstow	GB	42	B2
Ourol	E	140	A3	Padul	E	163	A4
Ouroux-en-Morvan	F	104	B2	Padula	I	172	B1
Ousdale	GB	32	C3	Paduli	I	170	B2
Oust	F	145	B4	Paesana	I	119	C4
Outakoski	FIN	193	C10	Paese	I	121	B5
Outeiro	P	148	B1	Pag	HR	137	A4
Outeiro de Rei	E	140	A3	Pagani	I	170	C2
Outes	E	140	B2	Pagánica	I	169	A3
Outokumpu	FIN	9	A6	Paglieta	I	169	A4
Outreau	F	78	B1	Pagny-sur-Moselle	F	92	C2
Outwell	GB	41	C4	Páhi	H	112	C3
Ouzouer-le-Marché	F	103	B3	Pahkakumpu	FIN	197	C11
Ouzouer-sur-Loire	F	103	B4	Pahl	D	108	B2
Ovada	I	133	A4	Paide	EST	8	C4
Ovar	P	148	B1	Paignton	GB	43	B3
Ove	DK	58	B2	Pailhès	F	146	A2
Ovelgönne	D	72	A1	Paimboeuf	F	101	B3
Over-jerstal	DK	59	C2	Paimpol	F	100	A2
Overath	D	80	B3	Paimpont	F	101	A3
Overbister	GB	33	B4	Painswick	GB	43	A4
Øverbygd	N	192	D3	Painten	D	95	C3
Overdinkel	NL	71	B4	Paisley	GB	34	C3
Overenhörna	S	56	A3	Pajala	S	196	B6
Overhalla	N	199	A8	Pajares de los Oteros	E	142	B1
Overijse	B	79	B4	Pajęczno	PL	86	A2
Overlade	DK	58	B2	Páka	H	111	C3
Överlida	S	60	B2	Pakość	PL	76	B3
Överö	FIN	51	B7	Pakosławice	PL	85	B5
Overpelt	B	79	A5	Pakoštane	HR	137	B4
Overton	GB	38	B4	Pakrac	HR	124	B3
Övertorneå	S	196	C6	Paks	H	112	C2
Överum	S	62	A4	Palacios de la Sierra	E	143	C3
Ovidiopol	UA	17	B9	Palaciòs de la Valduerna	E	141	B5
Oviedo	E	141	A5	Palacios del Sil	E	141	B4
Óviglio	I	119	C5	Palaciosrubios	E	150	A2
Ovindoli	I	169	A3	Palafrugell	E	147	C4
Ovodda	I	178	B3	Palagiano	I	173	B3
Øvre Ärdal	N	47	A4	Palagonía	I	177	B3
Øvre Rendal	N	199	D8	Paláia	I	135	B3
Øvre Sirdal	N	52	B2	Palaiokastritsa	GR	182	D1
Øvre Soppero	S	196	A4	Palaiseau	F	90	C2
Øvre Ullerud	S	55	A4	Palamas	GR	182	D4
Øvrebygd	N	52	B2	Palamòs	E	147	C4
Ovruch	UA	13	C8	Påläng	S	196	D5
Ovtrup	DK	59	C1	Palanga	LT	8	E2
Owińska	PL	76	B1	Palanzano	I	134	A3
Oxaback	S	60	B2	Palárikovo	SK	112	A2
Oxberg	S	49	A6	Palas de Rei	E	140	B3
Oxelösund	S	56	B3	Palata	I	170	B2
Oxenholme	GB	37	B4	Palau	I	178	A3
Oxford	GB	44	B2	Palavas-les-Flots	F	131	B2
Oxie	S	61	D3	Palazuelos de la Sierra	E	143	B3
Oxilithos	GR	185	A5	Palazzo Adriano	I	176	B2
Oxted	GB	45	B4	Palazzo del Pero	I	135	B4
Oyaca	TR	187	C7	Palazzo San Gervásio	I	172	B1
Øye	N	47	A5	Palazzolo Acréide	I	177	B3
Øyenkilen	N	54	A1				
Øyer	N	48	A2				
Øyeren	N	49	B4				
Oyfiell	N	53	A4				
Øygärdslia	N	53	B4				
Oykel Bridge	GB	32	D2				
Øymark	N	54	A2				
Oyonnax	F	118	A2				
Øysang	N	53	B5				
Øyslebø	N	52	B3				
Øystese	N	46	B3				
Oyten	D	72	A2				

Name	Country	Page	Grid
Palazzolo sull Oglio	I	120	B2
Palazzuolo sul Senio	I	135	A4
Paldiski	EST	8	C4
Pale	BIH	139	B4
Palekastro	GR	185	D7
Palena	I	169	B4
Palencia	E	142	A4
Palenciana	E	163	A3
Paleochora	GR	185	D4
Paleometokho	CY	181	A2
Palermo	I	176	A2
Paleros	GR	182	E2
Palestrina	I	169	B2
Pálfa	H	112	C2
Palfau	A	110	B1
Palhaça	P	148	B1
Palheiros da Tocha	P	148	B1
Palheiros de Quiaios	P	148	B1
Paliaopoli	GR	185	B5
Palić	SRB	126	A1
Palidoro	I	168	B2
Palinuro	I	172	B1
Paliouri	GR	183	D5
Paliseul	B	91	B5
Pallanza	I	119	B5
Pallares	E	161	A3
Pallaruelo de Monegros	E	153	A3
Pallas Green	IRL	29	B3
Pallerols	E	146	B2
Palling	D	109	A3
Palluau	F	114	B2
Palma	P	154	C2
Palma Campánia	I	170	C2
Palma de Mallorca	E	166	B2
Palma del Río	E	162	A2
Palma di Montechiaro	I	176	B2
Palma Nova	E	166	B2
Palmádula	I	178	B2
Palmanova	I	122	B2
Palmela	P	154	C2
Palmerola	E	147	B3
Palmi	I	175	C1
Pälmonostora	H	113	C3
Palo del Colle	I	171	B4
Palojärvi	FIN	192	D7
Palojoensuu	FIN	196	A6
Palomares	E	164	B3
Palomares del Campo	E	158	B1
Palomas	E	156	B1
Palombara Sabina	I	168	A2
Palos de la Frontera	E	161	B2
Palotaboszok	H	125	A4
Palotás	H	112	B3
Pals	E	147	C4
Pålsboda	S	56	A1
Paluzza	I	109	C4
Pamhagen	A	111	B3
Pamiers	F	146	A2
Pamiętowo	PL	76	A2
Pampaneira	E	163	B4
Pamparato	I	133	A3
Pampilhosa, Aveiro	P	148	B1
Pampilhosa, Coimbra	P	148	B2
Pampliega	E	143	B3
Pamplona	E	144	B2
Pampow	D	73	A4
Pamukçu	TR	186	C2
Pamukkale	TR	188	B4
Pamukova	TR	187	B5
Panagyurishte	BG	17	D6
Pancalieri	I	119	C4
Pančevo	SRB	127	C2
Pancey	F	91	C5
Pancorvo	E	143	B3
Pancrudo	E	152	B2
Pandino	I	120	B2
Pandrup	DK	58	A2
Panenský-Týnec	CZ	84	B1
Panes	E	142	A2
Panevėžys	LT	8	E4
Pangbourne	GB	44	B2
Panissières	F	117	B4
Panki	PL	86	B2
Pannes	F	103	A4
Panningen	NL	80	A1
Pannonhalma	H	111	B4
Pano Lefkara	CY	181	B2
Pano Panayia	CY	181	B1
Panormos	GR	185	B6
Panschwitz-Kuckau	D	84	A2
Pansdorf	D	65	C3
Pantano de Cijara	E	156	A3
Panticosa	E	145	B3
Pantín	E	140	A2
Pantoja	E	151	B4
Pantón	E	140	B3
Panxon	E	140	B2
Páola	I	174	B2
Paola	M	175	C3
Pápa	H	111	B4
Papasídero	I	174	B1
Pápateszér	H	111	B4
Papenburg	D	71	A4
Paphos	CY	181	B1
Pappenheim	D	94	C2
Paprotnia	PL	77	B5
Parábita	I	173	B4
Paracín	SRB	127	D3
Parád	H	113	B4
Parada, Bragança	P	149	A3
Parada, Viseu	P	148	B1
Paradas	E	162	A2
Paradela	E	140	B3
Parades de Rubiales	E	150	A2
Paradinas de San Juan	E	150	B2
Paradiso di Cevadale	I	108	C1
Paradyż	PL	87	A4
Parainen	FIN	8	B3
Parakhino Paddubye	RUS	9	C8
Parakka	S	196	B4
Paralimni	CY	181	A2
Parallo Astros	GR	184	B3
Paramé	F	88	B2
Paramithia	GR	182	D2
Páramo	E	141	A4
Páramo del Sil	E	141	B4
Parandaça	P	148	A2
Paravadella	E	141	A3
Paray-le-Monial	F	104	C3
Parceiros	P	154	B2
Parcey	F	105	B4
Parchim	D	73	A4
Parciaki	PL	77	A6
Parcice	PL	86	A2
Pardubice	CZ	97	A3
Pardilla	E	151	A4
Paredes	E	151	B5
Paredes	P	148	A1
Paredes de Coura	P	140	C2
Paredes de Nava	E	142	B2
Paredes de Siguenza	E	151	A5
Pareja	E	151	B5
Parennes	F	102	A1
Parentis-en-Born	F	128	B1
Parey	D	73	B4
Parfino	RUS	9	D7
Parga	GR	182	D2
Pargny-sur-Saulx	F	91	C4
Pari-Gagné	F	117	A4
Parigné-l'Évêque	F	102	B2
Parikkala	FIN	9	B6
Paris	F	90	C2
Parisot	F	129	B4
Parkalompolo	S	196	B5
Parkano	FIN	8	A3
Parknasilla	IRL	29	C2
Parlavá	E	147	B4
Parma	I	120	C3
Parndorf	A	111	B3
Párnica	SK	99	B3
Parnu	EST	8	C4
Parolis	E	164	A2
Paros	GR	185	B6
Parrillas	E	150	B2
Parsberg	D	95	B3
Parstein	D	74	B3
Partakko	FIN	193	C11
Partanna	I	176	B1
Parthenay	F	102	C1
Partinico	I	176	A2
Partizani	SRB	127	C2
Partizánske	SK	98	C2
Partney	GB	41	B4
Påryd	S	63	B3
Parzymiechy	PL	86	A2
Paşcani	RO	17	B7
Pasewalk	D	74	A2
Pašina Voda	MNE	139	B5
Påskallavik	S	62	A4
Pasłęk	PL	69	A4
Pašman	HR	137	B4
Passage East	IRL	30	B2
Passail	A	110	B2
Passais	F	88	B3
Passau	D	96	C1
Passegueiro	P	148	B1
Passignano sul Trasimeno	I	135	B5
Passo di Tréia	I	136	B2
Passopisciaro	I	177	B4
Passow	D	74	A3
Passy	F	118	B3
Pastavy	BY	13	A7
Pástena	I	170	B2
Pastrana	E	151	B5
Pastrengo	I	121	B3
Pasym	PL	77	A5
Pásztó	H	113	B3
Pata	SK	98	C1
Patay	F	103	A3
Pateley Bridge	GB	40	A2
Paterek	PL	76	A2
Paterna	E	159	B3
Paterna de Rivera	E	162	B2
Paterna del Campo	E	161	B3
Paterna del Madera	E	158	C1
Paternion	A	109	C4
Paternò	I	177	B3
Paternópoli	I	170	C3
Patersdorf	D	95	B4
Paterswolde	NL	71	A3
Patitiri	GR	183	D5
Patmos	GR	188	B1
Patna	GB	36	A2
Pątnow	PL	76	B3
Patoniva	FIN	193	C11
Patopirtti	FIN	197	D12
Patos	AL	182	C1
Patra = Patras	GR	184	A2
Patras = Patra	GR	184	A2
Patreksfjörður	IS	190	B2
Patrickswell	IRL	29	B3
Patrimonio	F	180	A2
Patrington	GB	41	B3
Pattada	I	178	B3
Pattensen, Niedersachsen	D	72	A3
Pattensen, Niedersachsen	D	72	B2
Patterdale	GB	36	B4
Patti	I	177	A3
Páty	H	112	B2
Pau	F	145	A3
Pauillac	F	128	A2
Paularo	I	109	C4
Paulhaguet	F	117	B3
Paulhan	F	130	B2
Paulilátino	I	178	B2
Pauliström	S	62	A3
Paullo	I	120	B2
Paulstown	IRL	30	B1
Pausa	D	83	B3
Pauträsk	S	200	B3
Pavia	I	120	B2
Pavia	E	154	C2
Pavias	E	159	B3
Pavilly	F	89	A4
Pãvilosta	LV	8	D2
Pavullo nel Frignano	I	135	A3
Pawłowice, Opolskie	PL	86	A1
Pawłowice, Śląskie	PL	98	B2
Paxi	GR	182	D2
Payallar	TR	189	C6
Payerne	CH	106	C1
Paymogo	E	161	B2
Payrac	F	129	B4
Pazardzhik	BG	183	A6
Pazaryeri	TR	187	B4
Pazin	HR	122	B2
Paziols	F	146	B3
Pčelić	HR	124	B3
Peal de Becerro	E	164	B1
Peasmarsh	GB	45	C4
Peć	KOS	16	D4
Péccioli	I	135	B3
Pécel	H	112	B3
Pechao	P	160	B2
Pechenga	RUS	3	B12
Pechenizhyn	UA	13	D6
Pecica	RO	126	A3
Pećinci	SRB	127	C1
Pecka	SRB	127	C1
Peckelsheim	D	81	A5
Pečory	RUS	8	D5
Pécs	H	125	A4
Pécsvárad	H	125	A4
Peczniew	PL	86	A2
Pedaso	I	136	B2
Pedavena	I	121	A4
Pedérobba	I	121	B4
Pedersker	DK	67	A3
Pedescala	I	121	B4
Pedrafita	E	141	B3
Pedrajas de San Esteban	E	150	A3
Pedralba	E	159	B3
Pedralba de la Praderia	E	141	B4
Pedraza	E	151	A4
Pedreguer	E	159	C4
Pedrera	E	162	A3
Pedro Abad	E	157	C3
Pedro Bernardo	E	150	B3
Pedro-Martinez	E	164	B1
Pedro Muñoz	E	158	B1
Pedroche	E	156	B3
Pedrógao, Beja	P	160	A2
Pedrogao, Castelo Branco	P	149	B2
Pedrógão, Leiria	P	154	B2
Pedrógão Grande	P	154	B2
Pedrola	E	144	C2
Pedrosa de Tobalina	E	143	B3
Pedrosa del Rey	E	150	A2
Pedrosa del Rio Urbel	E	143	B3
Pedrosillo de los Aires	E	150	B2
Pedrosillo el Ralo	E	150	A2
Pędzewo	PL	76	A3
Peebles	GB	35	C4
Peel	GB	36	B2
Peenemünde	D	66	B2
Peer	B	79	A5
Pega	P	149	B2
Pegalajar	E	163	A4
Pegau	D	83	A4
Peggau	A	110	B2
Pegli	I	133	A4
Pegnitz	D	95	B3
Pego	E	159	C3
Pegões-Estação	P	154	C2
Pegões Velhos	P	154	C2
Pegów	PL	85	A4
Pegswood	GB	37	A5
Peguera	E	166	B2
Pehlivanköy	TR	186	A1
Peine	D	72	B3
Peisey-Nancroix	F	118	B3
Peissenberg	D	108	B2
Peiting	D	108	B1
Peitz	D	84	A2
Péjo	I	121	A3
Pelagićevo	BIH	125	C4
Pelahustán	E	150	B3
Pełczyce	PL	75	A4
Pelhřimov	CZ	97	B3
Pélissanne	F	131	B4
Pelkosenniemi	FIN	197	B10
Pellegrino Parmense	I	120	C2
Pellegrue	F	128	B3
Pellérd	H	125	A4
Pellestrina	I	122	B1
Pellevoisin	F	103	C3
Pellizzano	I	121	A3
Pello	FIN	196	C7
Pello	S	196	C6
Peloche	E	156	A2
Pelplin	PL	69	B3
Pelussin	F	117	B4
Pély	H	113	B4
Pembroke	GB	39	C2
Pembroke Dock	GB	39	C2
Peña de Cabra	E	149	B4
Peñacerrada	E	143	B4
Penacova	P	148	B1
Peñafiel	E	151	A3
Penafiel	P	148	A1
Peñaflor	E	162	A2
Peñalba de Santiago	E	141	B4
Peñalsordo	E	156	B2
Penalva do Castelo	P	148	B2
Penamacôr	P	149	B2
Peñaparda	E	149	B3
Peñaranda de Bracamonte	E	150	B2
Peñaranda de Duero	E	143	C3
Peñarroya de Tastavins	E	153	B4
Peñarroya-Pueblonuevo	E	156	B2
Peñarrubia	E	141	B3
Penarth	GB	39	C3
Peñas de San Pedro	E	158	C2
Peñascosa	E	158	C1
Peñausende	E	149	A4
Penc	H	112	B3
Pencoed	GB	39	C3
Pendalofos	GR	182	C3
Pendeen	GB	42	B1
Pendine	GB	39	C2
Pendueles	E	142	A2
Penedono	P	148	B2
Penela	P	154	A2
Penhas Juntas	P	149	A2
Peniche	P	154	B1
Penicuik	GB	35	C4
Penig	D	83	B4
Penilhos	P	160	B2
Peñíscola	E	153	B4
Penistone	GB	40	B2
Penkridge	GB	40	C1
Penkun	D	74	A3
Penmarch	F	100	A1
Pennabilli	I	135	B5
Penne	I	169	A3
Penne-d'Agenais	F	129	B3
Pennes	F	108	C2
Pennyghael	GB	34	B1
Peno	RUS	9	D8
Penpont	GB	36	A3
Penrhyndeudraeth	GB	38	B3
Penrith	GB	37	B4
Penryn	GB	42	B1
Pentraeth	GB	38	A2
Penybontfawr	GB	38	B3
Penygroes, Carmarthenshire	GB	39	C2
Penygroes, Gwynedd	GB	38	A2
Penzance	GB	42	B1
Penzberg	D	108	B2
Penzlin	D	74	A2
Pepinster	B	80	B1
Peqin	AL	182	B1
Pér	H	111	B4
Pera Boa	P	148	B2
Perachora	GR	184	A3
Perafita	P	148	A1
Peraleda de la Mata	E	150	C2
Peraleda de San Román	E	156	A2
Peraleda del Zaucejo	E	156	B2
Perales de Alfambra	E	152	B2
Perales de Tajuña	E	151	B4
Perales del Puerto	E	149	B3
Peralta	E	144	B2
Peralta de la Sal	E	145	C4
Peralva	P	160	B2
Peralveche	E	152	B1
Perama	GR	185	D5
Peranka	FIN	197	D12
Perbál	H	112	B2
Perchtoldsdorf	A	111	A3
Percy	F	88	B2
Perdasdefogu	I	179	C3
Perdiguera	E	145	C3
Peredo	P	149	A3
Peregu Mare	RO	126	A2
Pereiro, Faro	P	160	B2
Pereiro, Guarda	P	149	B2
Pereiro, Santarém	P	154	B2
Pereiro de Aguiar	E	140	B3
Perelada	E	147	B4
Perelejos de las Truchas	E	152	B2
Pereña	E	149	A3
Pereruela	E	149	A4
Pérfugas	I	178	B2
Perg	A	110	A1
Pérgine Valsugana	I	121	A4
Pérgola	I	136	B1
Pergusa	I	177	B3
Periam	RO	126	A2
Periana	E	163	B3
Périers	F	88	A2
Périgueux	F	129	A3
Perino	I	120	C2
Perjasica	HR	123	B4
Perkáta	H	112	B2
Perković	HR	138	B2
Perleberg	D	73	A4
Perlez	SRB	126	B2
Përmet	AL	182	C2
Pernarec	CZ	95	B5
Pernek	SK	98	C1
Pernes	P	154	B2
Pernes-les-Fontaines	F	131	A4
Pernik	BG	17	D5
Pernink	CZ	83	B4
Pernitz	A	110	B2
Pernu	FIN	197	C10
Pero Pinheiro	P	154	C1
Peroguarda	P	160	A1
Peróls	F	131	B2
Péronne	F	90	B2
Péronnes	B	79	B4
Perorrubio	E	151	A4
Perosa Argentina	I	119	C4
Perozinho	P	148	A1
Perpignan	F	146	B3
Perranporth	GB	42	B1
Perranzabuloe	GB	42	B1
Perrecy-les-Forges	F	104	C3
Perrero	I	119	C4
Perrignier	F	118	A3
Perros-Guirec	F	100	A2
Persan	F	90	B2
Persberg	S	55	A5
Persenbeug	A	110	A2
Pershore	GB	44	A1
Persön	S	196	D5
Perstorp	S	61	C3
Perth	GB	35	B4
Pertisau	A	108	B2
Pertoča	SLO	111	C3
Pertuis	F	131	B4
Perućac	SRB	127	D1
Perúgia	I	136	B1
Perušić	HR	123	C4
Peruwelz	B	79	B3
Pervomaysk	UA	13	D9
Perwez	B	79	B4
Pesadas de Burgos	E	143	B3
Pesaguero	E	142	A2
Pésaro	I	136	B1
Pescantina	I	121	B3
Pescara	I	169	A4
Pescasséroli	I	169	B3
Peschici	I	171	B4
Peschiera del Garda	I	121	B3
Péscia	I	135	B3
Pescina	I	169	A3
Pesco Sannita	I	170	B2
Pescocostanzo	I	169	B4
Pescopagano	I	172	B1
Pescueza	E	149	B4
Peshkopi	AL	182	B2
Peshtera	BG	183	A6
Pesmes	F	105	B4
Pesnica	SLO	110	C2
Peso da Régua	P	148	A2
Pesquera de Duero	E	142	C2
Pessac	F	128	B2
Pestovo	RUS	9	C9
Petäjäskoski	FIN	197	C8
Petalidi	GR	184	C2
Pétange	L	92	B1
Petas	GR	182	D3
Peteranec	HR	124	A2
Peterborough	GB	41	C3
Peterculter	GB	33	D4
Peterhead	GB	33	D5
Peterlee	GB	37	B5
Petersfield	GB	44	B3
Petershagen, Brandenburg	D	74	B2
Petershagen, Brandenburg	D	74	B3
Petershagen, Nordrhein-Westfalen	D	72	B1
Petershausen	D	95	C3
Peterswell	IRL	28	A3
Pétervására	H	113	A4
Petilia Policastro	I	175	B2
Petín	E	141	B3
Pětipsy	CZ	83	B5
Petkus	D	74	C2
Petlovac	HR	125	B4
Petlovača	SRB	127	C1
Petöfiszallás	H	113	C3
Petra	E	167	B3
Petralia Sottana	I	177	B3
Petrčane	HR	137	A4
Petrella Tifernina	I	170	B2
Petrer	E	159	C3
Petreto-Bicchisano	F	180	B1
Petrich	BG	183	B5
Petrijevci	HR	125	B4
Petrinja	HR	124	B2
Petrodvorets	RUS	9	C6
Pétrola	E	158	C2
Petronà	I	175	B2
Petronell	A	111	A3
Petroşani	RO	17	C5
Petrovac	SRB	127	C3
Petrovaradin	SRB	126	B1
Petrovice	BIH	139	A4
Petrovice	CZ	84	B1
Petrovo	RUS	69	A5
Petrozavodsk	RUS	9	B9
Pettigo	IRL	26	B3
Petworth	GB	44	C3
Peuerbach	A	96	C1
Peuntenansa	E	142	A2
Peurasuvanto	FIN	197	B9
Pevensey Bay	GB	45	C4
Peveragno	I	133	A3
Pewsey	GB	44	B2
Pewsum	D	71	A4
Peyrat-le-Château	F	116	B1
Peyrehorade	F	128	C1
Peyriac-Minervois	F	146	A3
Peyrins	F	117	B5
Peyrissac	F	116	B1
Peyrolles-en-Provence	F	132	B1
Peyruis	F	132	A1
Pézarches	F	90	C2
Pézenas	F	130	B2
Pezinok	SK	111	A4
Pezuls	F	129	B3
Pfaffenhausen	D	108	A1
Pfaffenhofen, Bayern	D	95	C3
Pfaffenhofen, Bayern	D	94	C2
Pfaffenhoffen	F	93	C3
Pfäffikon	CH	107	B3
Pfarrkirchen	D	95	C4
Pfeffenhausen	D	95	C3
Pfetterhouse	F	106	B2
Pforzheim	D	93	C4
Pfreimd	D	95	B4
Pfronten	D	108	B1
Pfullendorf	D	107	B4
Pfullingen	D	94	C1
Pfunds	A	108	C1
Pfungstadt	D	93	B4
Pfyn	CH	107	B3
Phalsbourg	F	92	C3
Philippeville	B	79	B4
Philippsreut	D	96	C1
Philippsthal	D	82	B1
Piacenza	I	120	B2
Piacenza d'Adige	I	121	B4
Piádena	I	120	B3
Piana	F	180	A1
Piana Crixia	I	133	A4
Piana degli Albanesi	I	176	B2
Piana di Monte Verna	I	170	B2
Piancastagnáio	I	135	C4
Piandelagotti	I	134	A3
Pianella, Abruzzi	I	169	A4
Pianella, Toscana	I	135	B4
Pianello Val Tidone	I	120	C2
Piano	I	119	C5
Pianoro	I	135	A4
Pians	A	108	B1
Pías	E	141	B4
Pias	P	160	A2
Piaseczno	PL	77	B6
Piasek	PL	74	B3
Piaski	PL	69	A4
Piastów	PL	77	B5
Piaszczyna	PL	68	A2
Piątek	PL	77	B4
Piatra Neamţ	RO	17	B7

Name	Country	Page	Grid
Piazza al Sérchio	I	134	A3
Piazza Armerina	I	177	B3
Piazza Brembana	I	120	B2
Piazze	I	135	C4
Piazzola sul Brenta	I	121	B4
Picassent	E	159	A4
Piccione	I	136	B1
Picerno	I	172	B1
Picher	D	73	A4
Pickering	GB	40	A3
Pico	I	169	B3
Picón	E	157	A3
Picquigny	F	90	B2
Piechowice	PL	84	B3
Piecnik	PL	75	A5
Piedicavallo	I	119	B4
Piedicroce	F	180	A2
Piedimonte Etneo	I	177	B4
Piedimonte Matese	I	170	B2
Piedimulera	I	119	A5
Piedipaterno	I	136	C1
Piedrabuena	E	157	A3
Piedraescrita	E	156	A3
Piedrafita	E	142	A1
Piedrahita	E	150	B2
Piedralaves	E	150	B3
Piedras Albas	E	155	B4
Piedras Blancas	E	141	A5
Piegaro	I	135	C5
Piekary Śl.	PL	86	B2
Piekoszów	PL	87	B4
Pieksämäki	FIN	8	A4
Pielenhofen	D	95	B3
Pielgrzymka	PL	85	A3
Pieniężno	PL	69	A5
Pieńsk	PL	84	A3
Pienza	I	135	B4
Piera	E	147	C2
Pieranie	PL	76	B3
Pierowall	GB	33	A4
Pierre-Buffière	F	115	C5
Pierre-de-Bresse	F	105	C4
Pierrecourt	F	105	B4
Pierrefeu-du-Var	F	132	B2
Pierrefitte-Nestalas	F	145	B3
Pierrefitte-sur-Aire	F	92	C1
Pierrefonds	F	90	B2
Pierrefontaine-les-Varans	F	105	B5
Pierrefort	F	116	C2
Pierrelatte	F	131	A3
Pierrepont, *Aisne*	F	91	B4
Pierrepont, *Meurthe-et-Moselle*	F	92	B1
Piesendorf	A	109	B3
Pieštany	SK	98	C1
Pieszkowo	PL	69	A5
Pieszyce	PL	85	B4
Pietarsaari	FIN	3	E8
Pietra Ligure	I	133	A4
Pietragalla	I	172	B1
Pietralunga	I	136	B1
Pietramelara	I	170	B2
Pietraperzía	I	177	B3
Pietrasanta	I	134	B3
Pietravairano	I	170	B2
Pieve del Cáiro	I	120	B1
Pieve di Bono	I	121	B3
Pieve di Cadore	I	122	A1
Pieve di Cento	I	121	C4
Pieve di Soligo	I	121	B5
Pieve di Teco	I	133	A3
Pieve Santo Stefano	I	135	B5
Pieve Torina	I	136	B2
Pievepélago	I	134	A3
Piges	GR	182	D3
Píglio	I	169	B3
Pigna	I	133	B3
Pignan	F	130	B2
Pignataro Maggiore	I	170	B2
Piittisjärvi	FIN	197	C9
Pijnacker	NL	70	B1
Pikalevo	RUS	9	C9
Piła	PL	75	A5
Pilar de la Horadada	E	165	B4
Pilas	E	161	B3
Pilastri	I	121	C4
Piława Górna	PL	85	B4
Piławki	PL	69	B4
Pilchowice	PL	86	B2
Pilea	GR	183	C5
Pilgrimstad	S	199	C12
Pili, *Dodekanisa*	GR	188	C2
Pili, *Trikala*	GR	182	D3
Pilica	PL	86	B3
Pilis	H	112	B3
Piliscaba	H	112	B2
Pilisszántó	H	112	B2
Pilisvörösvár	H	112	B2
Pilos	GR	184	C2
Pilsting	D	95	C4
Pilszcz	PL	98	A1
Pilterud	N	48	C2
Pilu	RO	113	C5
Pina de Ebro	E	153	A3
Piñar	E	163	A4
Pınarbaşı	TR	186	C1
Pınarhisar	TR	186	A2
Pinas	F	145	A4
Pincehely	H	112	C2
Pinchbeck	GB	41	C3
Pińczów	PL	87	B4
Pineda de la Sierra	E	143	B3
Pineda de Mar	E	147	C3
Pinerella	I	135	A5
Pinerolo	I	119	C4
Pineta Grande	I	170	C1
Pineto	I	169	A4
Piney	F	91	C4
Pinggau	A	111	B3
Pinhal Novo	P	154	C2
Pinhão	P	148	A2
Pinheiro, *Aveiro*	P	148	B1
Pinheiro, *Aveiro*	P	148	A1
Pinheiro Grande	P	154	B2
Pinhel	P	149	B2
Pinhoe	GB	43	B3
Pinilla	E	158	C2
Pinilla de Toro	E	150	A2
Pinkafeld	A	111	B3
Pinneberg	D	72	A2
Pinnow	D	74	A3
Pino	I	180	A2
Pino de Val	E	140	B2
Pino del Rio	E	142	B2
Pinofranqueado	E	149	B3
Pinols	F	117	B3
Piñor	E	140	B2
Pinos del Valle	E	163	B4
Pinos Puente	E	163	A4
Pinoso	E	159	C2
Pinsk	BY	13	B7
Pintamo	FIN	197	D10
Pinto	E	151	B4
Pinzano al Tagliamento	I	122	A1
Pinzio	P	149	B2
Pinzolo	I	121	A3
Pióbbico	I	136	B1
Piombino	I	134	C3
Pionki	PL	87	A5
Pionsat	F	116	A2
Pióraco	I	136	B1
Piornal	E	150	B2
Piotrków-Kujawski	PL	76	B3
Piotrków Trybunalski	PL	86	A3
Piotrkowice	PL	87	B4
Piotrowo	PL	75	B5
Piove di Sacco	I	121	B5
Piovene	I	121	B4
Piperskärr	S	62	A4
Pipriac	F	101	B4
Piraeus = Pireas	GR	185	B4
Piran	SLO	122	B2
Piré-sur-Seiche	F	101	A4
Pireas = Piraeus	GR	185	B4
Pirgi	GR	185	A6
Pirgos, *Ilia*	GR	184	B2
Pirgos, *Kriti*	GR	185	D6
Piriac-sur-Mer	F	101	B3
Piringsdorf	A	111	B3
Pirmasens	D	93	B3
Pirna	D	84	B1
Pirnmill	GB	34	C2
Pirot	SRB	16	D5
Pirovac	HR	137	B4
Pirttivuopio	S	196	B2
Pisa	I	134	B3
Pisany	F	114	C3
Pisarovina	HR	124	B1
Pischelsdorf in der Steiermark	A	110	B2
Pischia	RO	126	B3
Pisciotta	I	172	B1
Písek	CZ	96	B2
Pisogne	I	120	B3
Pissos	F	128	B2
Pissouri	CY	181	B1
Pisticci	I	174	A2
Pistóia	I	135	B4
Piteå	S	196	D4
Piteşti	RO	17	C6
Pithiviers	F	103	A4
Pitigliano	I	168	A1
Pitkyaranta	RUS	9	B11
Pitlochry	GB	35	B4
Pitomača	HR	124	B3
Pitres	E	163	B4
Pittentrail	GB	32	D2
Pitvaros	H	126	A2
Pivka	SLO	123	B3
Pivnice	SRB	126	B1
Piwniczna	PL	99	B4
Pizarra	E	163	B3
Pizzano	I	121	A3
Pizzighettone	I	120	B2
Pizzo	I	175	C2
Pizzoli	I	169	A3
Pizzolungo	I	176	A1
Pjätteryd	S	61	C4
Plabennec	F	100	A1
Placencia	E	143	A4
Plaffeien	CH	106	C2
Plaisance, *Gers*	F	128	C3
Plaisance, *Haute-Garonne*	F	129	C4
Plaisance, *Tarn*	F	130	B1
Plaka	GR	183	D7
Plan	F	145	B4
Plan-de-Baix	F	118	C2
Plan-d'Orgon	F	131	B3
Planá	CZ	95	B4
Planá nad Lužnici	CZ	96	B2
Plaňany	CZ	96	A2
Planchez	F	104	B3
Plancoët	F	101	A3
Plancy-l'Abbaye	F	91	C3
Plandište	SRB	126	B3
Plánice	CZ	96	B1
Planina	SLO	123	B3
Planina	SLO	123	A4
Plankenfels	D	95	B3
Plasencia	E	149	B3
Plasenzuela	E	156	A1
Plaški	HR	123	B4
Plassen, *Buskerud*	N	47	B4
Plassen, *Hedmark*	N	49	A4
Plášt'ovce	SK	112	A3
Plasy	CZ	96	B1
Platamona Lido	I	178	B2
Platania	I	175	B2
Platanos	GR	185	D4
Platí	I	175	C2
Platičevo	SRB	127	C1
Platja d'Aro	E	147	C4
Plattling	D	95	C4
Plau	D	73	A5
Plaue, *Brandenburg*	D	73	B5
Plaue, *Thüringen*	D	82	B2
Plauen	D	83	B4
Plavecký Mikuláš	SK	98	C1
Plavinas	LV	8	D4
Plavna	SRB	125	B5
Plavnica	SK	99	B4
Plavno	HR	138	A2
Playben	F	100	A2
Pléaux	F	116	B2
Pleine-Fourgères	F	88	B2
Pleinfeld	D	94	B2
Pleinting	D	95	C5
Plélan-le-Grand	F	101	B3
Plémet	F	101	A3
Pléneuf-Val-André	F	101	A3
Plentzia	E	143	A4
Plérin	F	101	A3
Plešivec	SK	99	C4
Plessa	D	83	A5
Plessé	F	101	B4
Plestin-les-Grèves	F	100	A2
Pleszew	PL	76	C2
Pleternica	HR	125	B3
Plettenberg	D	81	A3
Pleubian	F	100	A2
Pleumartin	F	115	B4
Pleumeur-Bodou	F	100	A2
Pleurs	F	91	C3
Pleven	BG	17	D6
Plevnik-Drienové	SK	98	B2
Pleyber-Christ	F	100	A2
Pliego	E	165	B3
Pliešovce	SK	99	C3
Plitvička Jezera	HR	123	C4
Plitvički Ljeskovac	HR	123	C4
Ploaghe	I	178	B2
Ploče	HR	138	B3
Plochingen	D	94	C1
Płock	PL	77	B4
Ploemeur	F	100	B2
Ploërmel	F	101	B3
Plœuc-sur-Lie	F	101	A3
Plogastel St. Germain	F	100	B1
Plogoff	F	100	A1
Ploieşti	RO	17	C7
Plomari	GR	186	D1
Plombières-les-Bains	F	105	B5
Plomin	HR	123	B3
Plön	D	65	B3
Plonéour-Lanvern	F	100	B1
Płonia	PL	74	A3
Płoniawy	PL	77	B6
Płońsk	PL	77	B5
Płoskinia	PL	69	A4
Plössberg	D	95	B4
Płoty	PL	67	C4
Plouagat	F	100	A2
Plouaret	F	100	A2
Plouarzel	F	100	A1
Plouay	F	100	B2
Ploubalay	F	101	A3
Ploubazlanec	F	100	A2
Ploudalmézeau	F	100	A1
Ploudiry	F	100	A1
Plouescat	F	100	A1
Plouézec	F	100	A2
Plougasnou	F	100	A2
Plougastel-Daoulas	F	100	A1
Plougonven	F	100	A2
Plougonver	F	100	A2
Plougrescant	F	100	A2
Plouguenast	F	101	A3
Plouha	F	100	A2
Plouhinec	F	100	A1
Plouigneau	F	100	A2
Ploumanach	F	100	A2
Plounévez-Quintin	F	100	A2
Plouray	F	100	A2
Plouzévédé	F	100	A1
Plovdiv	BG	183	A6
Plozévet	F	100	B1
Plumbridge	GB	27	B3
Pluméliau	F	100	B3
Plumlov	CZ	97	B5
Plungė	LT	8	E2
Pluty	PL	69	A5
Pluvigner	F	100	B3
Plužine	BIH	139	B4
Plužine	MNE	139	B4
Płuznica	PL	69	B3
Plymouth	GB	42	B2
Plymstock	GB	42	B2
Płytnica	PL	68	B1
Plyusa	RUS	9	C6
Plzeň	CZ	96	B1
Pniewy	PL	75	B5
Pobes	E	143	B4
Pobeżovice	CZ	95	B4
Pobiedziska	PL	76	B2
Pobierowo	PL	67	B4
Pobla de Segur	E	145	B4
Pobla-Tornesa	E	153	B4
Pobladura del Valle	E	142	B1
Pobra de Trives	E	141	B3
Pobra do Brollón	E	141	B3
Pobra do Caramiñal	E	140	B2
Pobudje	BIH	139	A5
Počátky	CZ	97	B3
Poceirão	P	154	C2
Pöchlarn	A	110	A2
Pociecha	PL	87	A4
Pockau	D	83	B5
Pocking	D	96	C1
Pocklington	GB	40	B3
Poćkun	LT	13	A6
Poco	E	142	B2
Podbořany	CZ	83	B5
Podbrezová	SK	99	C3
Podčetrtek	SLO	123	A4
Poděbrady	CZ	84	B3
Podence	P	149	A3
Podensac	F	128	B2
Podenzano	I	120	C2
Podersdorf am See	A	111	B3
Podgaje	PL	68	B1
Podgora	HR	138	B3
Podgóra	PL	87	A5
Podgorač	HR	125	B4
Podgorica	MNE	16	D3
Podgorie	AL	182	C2
Podgrad	SLO	123	B3
Podhájska	SK	112	A2
Podkova	BG	183	B7
Podlapača	HR	123	C4
Podlejki	PL	69	B5
Podlugżany	SK	98	C2
Podnovlje	BIH	125	C4
Podolie	SK	98	C1
Podolínec	SK	99	B4
Podolsk	RUS	9	E10
Podporozhy	RUS	9	B9
Podromanija	BIH	139	B4
Podturen	HR	111	C3
Podvín	CZ	97	C4
Podwilk	PL	99	B3
Poetto	I	179	C3
Poggendorf	D	66	B2
Poggiardo	I	173	B4
Poggibonsi	I	135	B4
Póggio a Caiano	I	135	B4
Poggio Imperiale	I	171	B3
Póggio Mirteto	I	168	A2
Póggio Moiano	I	169	A2
Poggio Renatico	I	121	C4
Póggio Rusco	I	121	C4
Pöggstall	A	97	C3
Pogny	F	91	C4
Pogorzela	PL	85	A5
Pogorzelice	PL	68	A2
Pogradec	AL	182	C2
Pogrodzie	PL	69	A4
Pohořelice	CZ	97	C2
Pohorská	SK	99	C3
Pohronská Polhora	SK	99	C3
Poiares	P	148	B1
Poio	E	140	B2
Poirino	I	119	C4
Poisson	F	117	A4
Poissons	F	91	C5
Poissy	F	90	C2
Poitiers	F	115	B4
Poix-de-Picardie	F	90	B1
Poix-Terron	F	91	B4
Pokka	FIN	197	A8
Pokój	PL	86	B1
Pokupsko	HR	124	B1
Pol	E	141	A3
Pol a Charra	GB	31	B1
Pola	RUS	9	D7
Pola de Allande	E	141	A4
Pola de Laviana	E	142	A1
Pola de Lena	E	141	A5
Pola de Siero	E	142	A1
Pola de Somiedo	E	141	A4
Polaincourt-et-Clairefontaine	F	105	B5
Polán	E	151	C3
Polanica-Zdrój	PL	85	B4
Połaniec	PL	87	B5
Polanów	PL	68	A1
Polatı	TR	187	C7
Polatsk	BY	13	A8
Polch	D	80	B3
Polcirkeln	S	196	C4
Półczno	PL	68	A2
Połczyn-Zdrój	PL	67	C5
Polegate	GB	45	C4
Poleñino	E	145	C3
Polesella	I	121	C4
Polessk	RUS	12	A5
Polgár	H	113	B5
Polgárdi	H	112	B2
Polhov Gradec	SLO	123	A3
Police	PL	74	A3
Police nad Metují	CZ	85	B4
Polichnitos	GR	186	C1
Polička	CZ	97	B4
Poličnik	HR	137	A4
Policoro	I	174	A2
Policzna	PL	87	A5
Poligiros	GR	183	C5
Polignano a Mare	I	173	B3
Poligny	F	105	C4
Polis	CY	181	A1
Polístena	I	175	C2
Polizzi Generosa	I	176	B3
Poljana	SRB	127	C3
Poljanák	HR	123	C4
Poljčane	SLO	123	A4
Polje	BIH	125	C3
Poljice	BIH	139	A4
Poljice	BIH	138	A2
Polkowice	PL	85	A4
Polla	I	172	B1
Pollau	A	110	B2
Polleben	D	82	A3
Pollença	E	167	B3
Pollenfeld	D	95	C3
Pollfoss	N	198	D4
Póllica	I	170	C3
Pollina	I	176	B3
Polminhac	F	116	C2
Polná	CZ	97	B3
Polna	RUS	9	C6
Polne	PL	75	A5
Polomka	SK	99	C3
Polonne	UA	13	C7
Polperro	GB	42	B2
Polruan	GB	42	B2
Pöls	A	110	B1
Polska Cerekiew	PL	86	B2
Poltár	SK	99	C3
Põltsamaa	EST	8	C4
Polyarny	RUS	3	B13
Polyarnyye Zori	RUS	3	C13
Polzela	SLO	123	A4
Pomarance	I	135	B3
Pomarez	F	128	C2
Pomárico	I	172	B2
Pomáz	H	112	B3
Pombal	P	154	B2
Pomeroy	GB	27	B4
Pomézia	I	168	B2
Pommard	F	105	B3
Pommelsbrunn	D	95	B3
Pomonte	I	134	C3
Pomorie	BG	17	D7
Pomos	CY	181	A1
Pompei	I	170	C2
Pompey	F	92	C2
Pomposa	I	122	C1
Poncin	F	118	A2
Pondorf	D	95	C3
Ponferrada	E	141	B4
Poniec	PL	85	A4
Ponikva	SLO	123	A4
Poniky	SK	99	C3
Pons	F	114	C3
Ponsacco	I	134	B3
Pont	I	119	B4
Pont-a-Celles	B	79	B4
Pont-a-Marcq	F	78	B3
Pont-à-Mousson	F	92	C2
Pont-Audemer	F	89	A4
Pont-Aven	F	100	B2
Pont Canavese	I	119	B4
Pont-Croix	F	100	A1
Pont-d'Ain	F	118	A2
Pont de-Beauvoisin	F	118	B2
Pont-de-Buis-lès-Quimerch	F	100	A1
Pont-de-Chéruy	F	118	B2
Pont-de-Dore	F	117	B3
Pont-de-Labeaume	F	117	C4
Pont de Molins	E	147	B3
Pont-de-Roide	F	106	B1
Pont-de-Salars	F	130	A1
Pont de Suert	E	145	B4
Pont-de-Vaux	F	117	A4
Pont-de-Veyle	F	117	A4
Pont-d'Espagne	F	145	B3
Pont-d'Ouilly	F	89	B3
Pont-du-Château	F	116	B3
Pont-du-Navoy	F	105	C4
Pont-en-Royans	F	118	B2
Pont Farcy	F	88	B2
Pont-l'Abbé	F	100	B1
Pont-l'Évêque	F	89	A4
Pont-Remy	F	90	A1
Pont-St. Esprit	F	131	A3
Pont-St. Mamet	F	129	B3
Pont-St. Martin	F	101	B4
Pont-St. Martin	I	119	B4
Pont-St. Vincent	F	92	C2
Pont-Ste. Maxence	F	90	B2
Pont Scorff	F	100	B2
Pont-sur-Yonne	F	104	A2
Pontacq	F	145	A3
Pontailler-sur-Saône	F	105	B4
Pontão	P	154	B2
Pontardawe	GB	39	C3
Pontarddulais	GB	39	C2
Pontarion	F	116	B1
Pontarlier	F	105	C5
Pontassieve	I	135	B4
Pontaubault	F	88	B2
Pontaumur	F	116	B2
Pontcharra-sur-Turdine	F	117	B4
Pontchâteau	F	101	B3
Ponte a Moriano	I	134	B3
Ponte Arche	I	121	A3
Ponte-Caldelas	E	140	B2
Ponte da Barca	P	148	A1
Ponte de Lima	P	148	A1
Ponte de Sor	P	154	B2
Ponte dell'Ólio	I	120	C2
Ponte di Barbarano	I	121	B4
Ponte di Legno	I	121	A3
Ponte di Nava	I	133	A3
Ponte di Piave	I	122	B1
Ponte Felcino	I	136	B1
Ponte Gardena	I	108	C2
Ponte-Leccia	F	180	A2
Ponte nelle Alpi	I	122	A1
Ponte San Giovanni	I	136	B1
Ponte San Pietro	I	120	B2
Ponteareas	E	140	B2
Pontebba	I	109	C4
Pontecagnano	I	170	C2
Ponteceso	E	140	A2
Pontecesures	E	140	B2
Pontecorvo	I	169	B3
Pontedécimo	I	133	A4
Pontedera	I	134	B3
Pontedeume	E	140	A2
Pontefract	GB	40	B2
Ponteginori	I	135	B3
Pontegradella	I	121	C4
Ponteland	GB	37	A5
Pontelandolfo	I	170	B2
Pontelongo	I	121	B5
Pontenure	I	120	C2
Pontenx-les-Forges	F	128	B1
Ponterwyd	GB	39	B3
Pontevedra	E	140	B2
Pontevico	I	120	B3
Pontfaverger-Moronvillers	F	91	B4
Pontgibaud	F	116	B2
Ponticino	I	135	B4
Pontigny	F	104	B2
Pontijou	F	103	B3
Pontinvrea	I	133	A4
Pontivy	F	100	A3
Pontlevoy	F	103	B3
Pontoise	F	90	B2
Pontones	E	164	A2
Pontonx-sur-l'Abour	F	128	C2
Pontoon	IRL	26	C1
Pontorson	F	88	B2
Pontrémoli	I	134	A2
Pontresina	CH	107	C4
Pontrhydfendigaid	GB	39	B3
Pontrieux	F	100	A2
Ponts	E	147	C2
Ponts-aux-Dames	F	90	C2
Pöntsö	FIN	196	B7
Pontvallain	F	102	B2
Pontypool	GB	39	C3
Pontypridd	GB	39	C3
Ponza	I	169	C2
Poo	E	142	A2
Poole	GB	43	B5
Poolewe	GB	31	B3
Poperinge	B	78	B2
Pópoli	I	169	A3
Popovac	SRB	127	D3
Popovača	HR	124	B2
Popow	PL	77	B4
Poppel	B	79	A5
Poppenhausen, *Bayern*	D	82	B2
Poppenhausen, *Hessen*	D	82	B1
Poppi	I	135	B4
Poprad	SK	99	B4
Popučke	SRB	127	C1
Pópulo	P	148	A2
Populónia	I	134	C3
Pörböly	H	125	A4
Porcuna	E	163	A3
Pordenone	I	122	B1

Name		Page	Grid
Pordic	F	100	A3
Poręba	PL	86	B3
Poreč	HR	122	B2
Pori	FIN	8	B2
Porjus	S	196	C2
Porkhov	RUS	9	D6
Porlezza	I	120	A2
Porlock	GB	43	A3
Pörnbach	D	95	C3
Pornic	F	101	B3
Pornichet	F	101	B3
Porodin	SRB	127	C3
Poronin	PL	99	B3
Poros, *Attiki*	GR	185	B4
Poros, *Kefalonia*	GR	184	A1
Poroszló	H	113	B4
Porozina	HR	123	B3
Porquerolles	F	132	C2
Porrentruy	CH	106	B2
Porreres	E	167	B3
Porretta Terme	I	135	A4
Porsgrunn	N	53	A5
Porspoder	F	100	A1
Port-a-Binson	F	91	B3
Port Askaig	GB	34	C1
Port Bannatyne	GB	34	C2
Port-Barcarès	F	146	B4
Port-Camargue	F	131	B3
Port Charlotte	GB	34	C1
Port d'Andratx	E	166	B2
Port-de-Bouc	F	131	B3
Port-de-Lanne	F	128	C1
Port de Pollença	E	167	B3
Port de Sóller	E	166	B2
Port-des-Barques	F	114	C2
Port Ellen	GB	34	C1
Port-en-Bessin	F	88	A3
Port Erin	GB	36	B2
Port Eynon	GB	39	C2
Port Glasgow	GB	34	C3
Port Henderson	GB	31	B3
Port Isaac	GB	42	B2
Port-Joinville	F	114	B1
Port-la-Nouvelle	F	130	B2
Port Logan	GB	36	B2
Port Louis	F	100	B2
Port Manech	F	100	B2
Port Nan Giuran	GB	31	A2
Port-Navalo	F	100	B3
Port Nis	GB	31	A2
Port-St.-Louis-du-Rhône	F	131	B3
Port St. Mary	GB	36	B2
Port-Ste. Marie	F	129	B3
Port-sur-Saône	F	105	B5
Port Talbot	GB	39	C3
Port-Vendres	F	146	B4
Port William	GB	36	B2
Portacloy	IRL	26	B1
Portadown	GB	27	B4
Portaferry	GB	27	B5
Portaje	E	155	B4
Portalegre	P	155	B3
Portarlington	IRL	30	A1
Portavadie	GB	34	C2
Portavogie	GB	27	B5
Portbail	F	88	A2
Portbou	E	146	B4
Portegrandi	I	122	B1
Portel	P	155	C3
Portela	P	148	B1
Portelo	P	141	C4
Portemouro	P	140	B2
Port'Ercole	I	168	A1
Portes-lès-Valence	F	117	C4
Portets	F	128	B2
Portezuelo	E	155	B4
Portglenone	GB	27	B4
Porthcawl	GB	39	C3
Porthleven	GB	42	B1
Porthmadog	GB	38	B2
Porticcio	F	180	B1
Portici	I	170	C2
Portico di Romagna	I	135	A4
Portilla de la Reina	E	142	A2
Portillo	E	150	A3
Portimao	P	160	B1
Portinatx	E	166	B1
Portinho da Arrabida	P	154	C1
Portishead	GB	43	A4
Portknockie	GB	33	D4
Portlaoise	IRL	30	A1
Portlethen	GB	33	D4
Portmagne	IRL	29	C1
Portmahomack	GB	32	D3
Portman	E	165	B4
Portnacroish	GB	34	B2
Portnahaven	GB	34	C1
Porto	F	180	A1
Porto	P	148	A1
Porto-Alto	P	154	C2
Porto Azzurro	I	134	C3
Porto Cerésio	I	120	B1
Porto Cervo	I	178	A3
Porto Cesáreo	I	173	B3
Porto Colom	E	167	B3
Porto Covo	P	160	B1
Porto Cristo	E	167	B3
Porto d'Áscoli	I	136	C2
Porto de Lagos	P	160	B1
Porto de Mos	P	154	B2
Porto de Rei	P	154	C2
Porto do Son	E	140	B2
Porto Empédocle	I	176	B2
Porto Garibaldi	I	122	C1
Porto Petro	I	167	B3
Porto Pino	I	179	D2
Porto Potenza Picena	I	136	B2
Porto Recanati	I	136	B2
Porto San Giórgio	I	136	B2
Porto Santo Stéfano	I	168	A1
Porto Tolle	I	122	C1
Porto Tórres	I	178	B2
Porto-Vecchio	F	180	B2
Portocannone	I	170	B3
Portoferráio	I	134	C3
Portofino	I	134	A2
Portogruaro	I	122	B1
Portokhelion	GR	184	B4
Portomaggiore	I	121	C4
Portomarin	E	140	B3
Porton	GB	44	B2
Portonovo	E	140	B2
Portopalo di Capo Passero	I	177	C4
Portör	N	53	B5
Portoscuso	I	179	C2
Portovénere	I	134	A2
Portpatrick	GB	36	B1
Portreath	GB	42	B1
Portree	GB	31	B2
Portroe	IRL	28	B3
Portrush	GB	27	A4
Portsall	F	100	A1
Portsmouth	GB	44	C2
Portsoy	GB	33	D4
Portstewart	GB	27	A4
Portumna	IRL	28	A3
Porvoo	FIN	8	B4
Porzuna	E	157	A3
Posada, *Oviedo*	E	142	A2
Posada, *Oviedo*	E	141	A5
Posada	I	178	B3
Posada de Valdeón	E	142	A2
Posadas	E	162	A2
Poschiavo	CH	120	A3
Posedarje	HR	137	A4
Posio	FIN	197	C11
Positano	I	170	C2
Possagno	I	121	B4
Posseck	D	83	B4
Possesse	F	91	C4
Pössneck	D	83	B3
Posta	I	169	A3
Posta Piana	I	172	A1
Postal	I	108	C2
Postbauer-Heng	D	95	B3
Posterholt	NL	80	A2
Postioma	I	121	B5
Postira	HR	138	B2
Postojna	SLO	123	B3
Postoloprty	CZ	84	B1
Postomino	PL	68	A1
Posušje	BIH	138	B3
Potamos, *Attiki*	GR	184	D4
Potamos, *Attiki*	GR	184	C3
Potegowo	PL	68	A2
Potenza	I	172	B1
Potenza Picena	I	136	B2
Potes	E	142	A2
Potigny	F	89	B3
Potočari	BIH	127	C1
Potoci,	BIH	139	B3
Potoci,	BIH	138	A2
Potony	H	125	B3
Potries	E	159	C3
Potsdam	D	74	B2
Potštát	CZ	98	B1
Pottenbrunn	A	110	A2
Pottendorf	A	111	B3
Pottenstein	A	111	B3
Pottenstein	D	95	B3
Potters Bar	GB	44	B3
Pöttmes	D	94	C3
Potworów	PL	87	A4
Pouan	F	101	B4
Pougues-les-Eaux	F	104	B2
Pouillon	F	128	C2
Pouilly-en-Auxois	F	104	B3
Pouilly-sous-Charlieu	F	117	A4
Pouilly-sur-Loire	F	104	B1
Poujol-sur-Orb	F	130	B2
Poullaouen	F	100	A2
Poulton-le-Fylde	GB	38	A4
Poundstock	GB	42	B2
Pourcy	F	91	B3
Pourrain	F	104	B2
Poussu	FIN	197	D12
Pouy-de-Touges	F	146	A2
Pouyastruc	F	145	A4
Pouzauges	F	114	B3
Pova de Santa Iria	P	154	C1
Považská Bystrica	SK	98	B2
Povedilla	E	158	C1
Povenets	RUS	9	A9
Povlja	HR	138	B2
Povljana	HR	137	A4
Póvoa, *Beja*	P	161	A2
Póvoa, *Santarém*	P	154	B2
Póvoa de Lanhoso	P	148	A1
Póvoa de Varzim	P	148	A1
Póvoa e Meadas	P	155	B3
Powidz	PL	76	B2
Poyales del Hoyo	E	150	B2
Poynton	GB	40	B1
Poyntz Pass	GB	27	B4
Poysdorf	A	97	C4
Poza de la Sal	E	143	B3
Pozaldez	E	150	A3
Pozán de Vero	E	145	B4
Pozanti	TR	23	C8
Požarevac	SRB	127	C3
Požega	HR	125	B3
Požega	SRB	127	D2
Poznań	PL	76	B1
Pozo Alcón	E	164	B2
Pozo Cañada	E	158	C2
Pozo de Guadalajara	E	151	B4
Pozo de la Serna	E	157	B4
Pozoantiguo	E	150	A2
Pozoblanco	E	156	B3
Pozohondo	E	158	C2
Pozondón	E	152	B2
Pozrzadło Wielkie	PL	75	A4
Pozuel del Campo	E	152	B2
Pozuelo de Alarcón	E	151	B4
Pozuelo de Calatrava	E	157	B4
Pozuelo de Zarzón	E	149	B3
Pozuelo del Páramo	E	142	B1
Pozzallo	I	177	C3
Pozzo San Nicola	I	178	B2
Pozzomaggiore	I	178	B2
Pozzuoli	I	170	C2
Pozzuolo	I	135	B4
Prabuty	PL	69	B4
Prača	BIH	139	B4
Prachatice	CZ	96	B1
Prada	E	141	B3
Pradelle	F	118	C2
Pradelles	F	117	C3
Prades	F	147	C1
Prades	F	146	B3
Pradła	PL	86	B3
Prado	F	142	A1
Prado	E	148	A1
Prado del Rey	E	162	B2
Pradoluengo	E	143	B3
Præstø	DK	65	A5
Pragelato	I	119	B3
Pragersko	SLO	123	A4
Prägraten	A	109	B3
Prague = Praha	CZ	84	B2
Praha = Prague	CZ	84	B2
Prahecq	F	115	B3
Praia	P	154	B1
Práia a Mare	I	174	B1
Praia da Rocha	P	160	B1
Praia da Viera	P	154	B2
Praia de Mira	P	148	B1
Praiano	I	170	C2
Pralboino	I	120	B3
Pralognan-la-Vanoise	F	118	B3
Pramanda	GR	182	D3
Pranjani	SRB	127	C2
Prapatnica	HR	138	B2
Praszka	PL	86	A2
Prat	F	135	B3
Prat de Compte	E	153	B3
Prata	I	135	B3
Prata di Pordenone	I	122	B1
Pratau	D	83	A4
Pratdip	E	147	C1
Pratella	I	170	B2
Prato	I	135	B4
Prátola Peligna	I	169	A3
Pratola Serra	I	170	C2
Prats-de-Mollo-la-Preste	F	146	B3
Prauthoy	F	105	B4
Pravia	E	141	A4
Praxmar	A	108	B2
Prayssac	F	129	B4
Prazzo	I	132	A2
Pré-en-Pail	F	89	B3
Prebold	SLO	123	A4
Préchac	F	128	B2
Précy-sur-Thil	F	104	B3
Predáppio	I	135	A4
Predazzo	I	121	A4
Předin	CZ	97	B3
Preding	A	110	C2
Predjame	SLO	123	B3
Predlitz	A	109	B4
Predmeja	SLO	122	B2
Predoi	I	108	B3
Prees	GB	38	B4
Preetz	D	64	B3
Préfailles	F	101	B3
Pregarten	A	96	C2
Pregrada	HR	123	A4
Preignan	F	129	C3
Preiļi	LV	8	D5
Preitenegg	A	110	C1
Prekaja	BIH	138	A2
Preko	HR	137	A4
Preljina	SRB	127	C2
Prelog	HR	124	A2
Preložca	HR	124	B2
Přelouč	CZ	97	A3
Prem	SLO	123	B3
Premantura	HR	122	C2
Prémery	F	104	B2
Prémia	I	119	A5
Premià de Mar	E	147	C3
Premnitz	D	73	B5
Prémont	F	91	A3
Prenzlau	D	74	A2
Preodac	BIH	138	A2
Přerov	CZ	98	B1
Prerow	D	66	B1
Presencio	E	143	B3
Presicce	I	173	C4
Presly	F	103	B4
Prešov	SK	12	D4
Pressac	F	115	B4
Pressath	D	95	B3
Pressbaum	A	111	A3
Prestatyn	GB	38	A3
Prestebakke	N	54	B2
Presteigne	GB	39	B3
Přeštice	CZ	96	B1
Preston, *Lancashire*	GB	38	A4
Preston, *Scottish Borders*	GB	35	C5
Prestonpans	GB	35	C5
Prestwick	GB	36	A2
Prettin	D	83	A4
Preturo	I	169	A3
Pretzchendorf	D	83	B5
Pretzier	D	73	B4
Pretzsch	D	83	A4
Preuilly-sur-Claise	F	115	B4
Prevalje	SLO	110	C1
Prevenchères	F	131	A2
Préveranges	F	116	A2
Preveza	GR	182	E2
Prevršac	HR	124	B2
Prezid	HR	123	B3
Priaranda del Bierzo	E	141	B4
Priay	F	118	A2
Pribeta	SK	112	B2
Priboj	BIH	125	C4
Priboj	SRB	16	D3
Příbor	CZ	98	B2
Příbram	CZ	96	B2
Pribylina	SK	99	B3
Přibyslav	CZ	97	B3
Pričević	SRB	127	C1
Pridjel	BIH	125	C4
Priego	E	152	B1
Priego de Córdoba	E	163	A3
Priekule	LV	8	D2
Priekule	LT	13	A5
Prien	D	109	B3
Prienai	LT	13	A5
Prievidza	SK	98	C2
Prigradica	HR	138	C2
Prigrevica	SRB	125	B5
Prijeboj	HR	123	C4
Prijedor	BIH	124	C2
Prijepolje	SRB	16	D3
Prilep	MK	182	B3
Priluka	BIH	138	B2
Primda	CZ	95	B4
Primel-Trégastel	F	100	A2
Primišje	HR	123	B4
Primorsk, *Kaliningrad*	RUS	69	A5
Primorsk, *Severo-Zapadnyy*	RUS	9	B6
Primošten	HR	138	B1
Primstal	D	92	B2
Princes Risborough	GB	44	B3
Princetown	GB	42	B2
Principina a Mare	I	135	C4
Priolo Gargallo	I	177	B4
Prioro	E	142	B2
Priozersk	RUS	9	B7
Prirechnyy	RUS	193	C14
Prisoje	BIH	138	B3
Priština	KOS	16	D4
Pritzerbe	D	73	B5
Pritzier	D	73	A4
Pritzwalk	D	73	A5
Privas	F	117	C4
Priverno	I	169	B3
Privlaka, *Vukovarsko-Srijemska*	HR	125	B4
Privlaka, *Zadarska*	HR	137	A4
Prizna	HR	123	C3
Prizren	KOS	16	D4
Prizzi	I	176	B2
Prnjavor	BIH	125	C3
Prnjavor	SRB	127	C1
Proaza	E	141	A4
Probstzella	D	82	B3
Probus	GB	42	B2
Próchcio	I	134	C3
Prochowice	PL	85	A4
Prócida	I	170	C2
Prodhromos	CY	181	B1
Prodo	I	135	C5
Proença-a-Nova	P	154	B3
Proença-a-Velha	P	155	A3
Profondeville	B	79	B4
Propriano	F	180	B1
Prosec	CZ	97	B3
Prösen	D	83	A5
Prosenjakovci	SLO	111	C3
Prosotsani	GR	183	B5
Prostějov	CZ	98	B1
Prószków	PL	86	B1
Proszowice	PL	87	B4
Protić	BIH	138	A2
Protivanov	CZ	97	B4
Protivín	CZ	96	B2
Prötzel	D	74	B2
Provins	F	90	C3
Prrenjas	AL	182	B2
Prudhoe	GB	37	B5
Prudnik	PL	85	B5
Pruggern	A	109	B4
Prügy	H	113	A5
Prüm	D	80	B2
Pruna	E	162	B2
Prunelli-di-Fiumorbo	F	180	A2
Prunetta	I	135	A3
Pruniers	F	103	C4
Prusice	PL	85	A4
Pruské	SK	98	B2
Pruszce	PL	76	A3
Pruszcz Gdański	PL	69	A3
Pruszków	PL	77	B5
Prutz	A	108	B1
Prüzen	D	65	C5
Pružany	BY	13	B6
Pružina	SK	98	B2
Pryłęg	PL	75	B4
Przasnysz	PL	77	A5
Przechlewo	PL	68	B2
Przecław	PL	87	B5
Przedbórz	PL	87	A3
Przedecz	PL	76	B3
Przejęslav	PL	84	A3
Przemków	PL	85	A3
Przemocze	PL	75	A3
Przemyśl	PL	12	D5
Przerąb	PL	87	A3
Przewodnik	PL	69	B3
Przewodowo Parcele	PL	77	B5
Przewóz	PL	84	A2
Przezmark	PL	69	B4
Przodkowo	PL	68	A3
Przybiernów	PL	75	A3
Przyborowice	PL	77	B5
Przybyszew	PL	87	A4
Przybyszów	PL	86	A3
Przylęg	PL	75	B4
Przysucha	PL	87	A4
Przytoczna	PL	75	B4
Przytyk	PL	87	A4
Przywidz	PL	68	A3
Psachna	GR	185	A4
Psara	GR	185	A6
Psary	PL	76	C3
Pskov	RUS	8	D6
Pszczew	PL	75	B4
Pszczółki	PL	69	A3
Pszczyna	PL	98	B2
Pszów	PL	86	B2
Pteleos	GR	182	C4
Ptolemaida	GR	182	C3
Ptuj	SLO	124	A1
Ptusza	PL	68	B1
Puch	A	109	B4
Puchberg am Schneeberg	A	110	B2
Puchevillers	F	90	A2
Puchheim	D	108	A2
Púchov	SK	98	B2
Pučišća	HR	138	B2
Puck	PL	69	A3
Puçol	E	159	B3
Puconci	SLO	111	C3
Pudasjärvi	FIN	197	D10
Puderbach	D	81	B3
Pudozh	RUS	9	B10
Puebla de Albortón	E	153	A3
Puebla de Alcocer	E	156	B2
Puebla de Beleña	E	151	B4
Puebla de Don Fadrique	E	164	B2
Puebla de Don Rodrigo	E	156	A3
Puebla de Guzmán	E	161	B2
Puebla de la Calzada	E	155	C4
Puebla de la Reina	E	156	B1
Puebla de Lillo	E	142	B1
Puebla de Obando	E	155	B4
Puebla de Sanabria	E	141	B4
Puebla de Sancho Pérez	E	155	C4
Puebla del Maestre	E	161	A3
Puebla del Principe	E	158	C1
Puente Almuhey	E	142	B2
Puente de Domingo Flórez	E	141	B4
Puente de Génave	E	164	A2
Puente de Montañana	E	145	B4
Puente del Congosto	E	150	B2
Puente Duero	E	150	A3
Puente-Genil	E	162	A3
Puente la Reina	E	144	B2
Puente la Reina de Jaca	E	144	B3
Puente Mayorga	E	162	B2
Puente Viesgo	E	143	A3
Puentelarra	E	143	B3
Puertas, *Asturias*	E	142	A2
Puertas, *Salamanca*	E	149	A3
Puerto de Mazarrón	E	165	B3
Puerto de San Vicente	E	156	A2
Puerto de Santa Cruz	E	156	A2
Puerto-Lápice	E	157	A4
Puerto Lumbreras	E	164	B3
Puerto Moral	E	161	B3
Puerto Real	E	162	B1
Puerto Rey	E	156	A2
Puerto Seguro	E	149	B3
Puerto Serrano	E	162	B2
Puertollano	E	157	B3
Puget-sur-Argens	F	132	B2
Puget-Théniers	F	132	B2
Puget-ville	F	132	B2
Pugnochiuso	I	171	B4
Puig Reig	E	147	C2
Puigcerdà	E	146	B2
Puigpunyent	E	166	B2
Puillon	F	128	C2
Puimichel	F	132	B2
Puimoisson	F	132	B2
Puiseaux	F	103	A4
Puisieux	F	90	A2
Puisserguier	F	130	B2
Puivert	F	146	B3
Pujols	F	128	B2
Pukanec	SK	98	C2
Pukavik	S	63	B2
Pukë	AL	182	A1
Pula	HR	122	C2
Pula	I	179	C2
Puławy	PL	12	C4
Pulborough	GB	44	C3
Pulfero	I	122	A2
Pulgar	E	157	A3
Pulheim	D	80	A2
Pulkau	A	97	C3
Pulpí	E	164	B3
Pulsano	I	173	B3
Pulsnitz	D	84	A2
Pułtusk	PL	77	B6
Pumpsaint	GB	39	B3
Punat	HR	123	B3
Punta Marina	I	135	A5
Punta Prima	E	167	B4
Punta Sabbioni	I	122	B1
Punta Umbria	E	161	B3
Puntas de Calnegre	E	165	B3
Puolanka	FIN	3	D10
Puoltikasvaara	S	196	B4
Puoltsa	S	196	B4
Puračić	BIH	125	C4
Purbach am Neusiedler See	A	111	B3
Purchena	E	164	B2
Purfleet	GB	45	B4
Purgstall	A	110	A2
Purkersdorf	A	111	A3
Purmerend	NL	70	B1
Purullena	E	164	B1
Púrvomay	BG	183	A7
Pushkin	RUS	9	C7
Pushkino	RUS	9	D10
Püspökládány	H	113	B5
Pusté Ulany	SK	111	A4
Pustoshka	RUS	9	D6
Puszcza Mariańska	PL	77	C5
Puszczykowo	PL	76	B1
Pusztamagyaród	H	111	C3
Pusztamonostor	H	113	B3
Pusztaszabolcs	H	112	B2
Pusztavám	H	112	B2
Putanges-Pont-Ecrepin	F	89	B3
Putbus	D	66	B2
Putignano	I	173	B3
Putlitz	D	73	A5
Putnok	H	99	C4
Putte	B	79	A4
Puttelange-aux-Lacs	F	92	B2
Putten	NL	70	B2
Puttgarden	D	65	B4
Püttlingen	D	92	B2
Putzu Idu	I	179	B2
Puy-Guillaume	F	117	B3
Puy-l'Évêque	F	129	B4

Puylaroque F 129 B4
Puylaurens F 146 A3
Puymirol F 129 B3
Puyôo F 128 C2
Puyrolland F 114 B3
Pwllheli GB 38 B2
Pyetrikaw BY 13 B8
Pyhäjärvi FIN 3 E9
Pyhäkylä FIN 197 D11
Pyla CY 181 A2
Pyla-sur-Mer F 128 B1
Pyrzyce PL 75 A3
Pysely CZ 96 B2
Pyskowice PL 86 B2
Pytalovo RUS 8 D5
Pyzdry PL 76 B2

Q

Quakenbrück D 71 B4
Quargnento I 119 C5
Quarré-les-Tombes F 104 B2
Quarteira P 160 B1
Quartu Sant'Élena I 179 C3
Quatre-Champs F 91 B4
Quedlinburg D 82 A3
Queensferry, *Edinburgh* GB 35 C4
Queensferry, *Flintshire* GB 38 A3
Queige F 118 B3
Queipo E 161 B3
Queixans E 146 B2
Quel E 144 B1
Quelaines-St-Gault F 102 B1
Queljada P 148 A1
Quemada E 143 C3
Queralbs E 147 B3
Quercianella I 134 B3
Querfurt D 82 A3
Quérigut F 146 B3
Quero E 157 A4
Quero I 121 B4
Querqueville F 88 A2
Quesada E 164 B1
Questembert F 101 B3
Quettehou F 88 A2
Quevauvillers F 90 B2
Quevy B 79 B4
Quiaois P 148 B1
Quiberon F 100 B2
Quiberville F 89 A4
Quickborn D 64 C2
Quiévrain B 79 B3
Quillan F 146 B3
Quillebeuf F 89 A4
Quimper F 100 A1
Quimperlé F 100 B2
Quincampoix F 89 A5
Quincoces de Yuso E 143 B3
Quincy F 103 B4
Quinéville F 88 A2
Quingey F 105 B4
Quinson F 132 B2
Quinssaines F 116 A2
Quinta-Grande P 154 C2
Quintana de la Serena E 156 B2
Quintana del Castillo E 141 B4
Quintana del Marco E 141 B5
Quintana del Puenta E 142 B2
Quintana-Martin Galindez E 143 B3
Quintanaortuño E 143 B3
Quintanapalla E 143 B3
Quintanar de la Orden E 157 A4
Quintanar de la Sierra E 143 C3
Quintanar del Rey E 158 B2
Quintanilla de la Mata E 143 C3
Quintanilla de Onésimo E 150 A3
Quintanilla de Somoza E 141 B4
Quintanilla del Coco E 143 C3
Quintas de Valdelucio E 142 B2
Quintela P 148 B2
Quintin F 100 A3
Quinto E 153 A3
Quinzano d'Oglio I 120 B3
Quiroga E 141 B3
Quismondo E 150 B3
Quissac F 131 B2
Quistello I 121 B3

R

Raab A 96 C1
Raabs an der Thaya A 97 C3
Raahe FIN 3 D9
Raajärvi FIN 197 C9
Raalte NL 71 B3
Raamsdonksveer NL 79 A4
Raanujarvi FIN 196 C7
Raattama FIN 196 A7
Rab HR 123 C3
Rabac HR 123 B3
Rábade E 140 A3
Rábafüzes H 111 C3
Rábahidvég H 111 B3
Rabanales E 149 A3
Rábapatona H 111 B4
Rabapordány H 111 B4
Rabastens F 129 C4
Rabastens-de-Bigorre F 145 A4
Rabat = Victoria, *Gozo* M 175 C3
Rabat, *Malta* M 175 C3
Rabča SK 99 B3
Rabe SRB 126 A2
Rabi CZ 96 B1
Rabino PL 67 C4
Rabka PL 99 B3
Rabrovo SRB 127 C3
Rača SRB 127 C3
Rácale I 173 C4
Rácalmás H 112 B2
Racalmuto I 176 B2
Racconigi I 119 C4
Rače SLO 123 A4
Rachecourt-sur-Marne F 91 C5
Raciąż PL 77 B5
Racibórz PL 86 B2
Račinovci HR 125 C4
Ráckeve H 112 B2
Racławice PL 87 B4
Racławice Śląskie PL 86 B1
Racot PL 75 B5
Råda, *Skaraborg* S 55 B4
Råda, *Värmland* S 49 B5
Radalj SRB 127 C1
Rădăuţi RO 17 B6
Radda in Chianti I 135 B4
Raddusa I 177 B3
Radeberg D 84 A1
Radebeul D 84 A1
Radeburg D 84 A1
Radeče SLO 123 A4
Radekhiv UA 13 C6
Radenci SLO 111 C3
Radenthein A 109 C4
Radevormwald D 80 A3
Radicófani I 135 C4
Radicóndoli I 135 B4
Radišići BIH 138 B3
Radizel SLO 110 C2
Radków PL 85 B4
Radlje ob Dravi SLO 110 C2
Radlów PL 87 B4
Radmer an der Stube A 110 B1
Radnejaur S 195 E9
Radnice CZ 96 B1
Radohova BIH 138 A3
Radojevo SRB 126 B2
Radolfzell D 107 B3
Radom PL 87 A5
Radomice PL 77 B4
Radomin PL 77 A4
Radomsko PL 86 A3
Radomyshl UA 13 C8
Radomyśl Wielki PL 87 B5
Radošina SK 98 C1
Radošovce SK 98 C1
Radoszewice PL 86 A2
Radoszyce PL 87 A4
Radotin CZ 96 B2
Radovets BG 186 A1
Radoviš MK 182 B4
Radovljica SLO 123 A3
Radowo Wielkie PL 75 A4
Radstadt A 109 B4
Radstock GB 43 A4
Raduc HR 137 A4
Raduša MK 182 A3
Radviliškis LT 8 E3
Radzanów, *Mazowieckie* PL 77 B5
Radzanów, *Mazowieckie* PL 87 A4
Radziejów PL 76 B3
Radziejowice PL 77 B5
Radzovce SK 113 A3
Radzyń Chełmiński PL 69 B3
Raeren B 80 B2
Raesfeld D 80 A2
Raffadali I 176 B2
Rafina GR 185 A4
Rafsbotn N 192 B7
Ragachow BY 13 B9
Ragály H 99 C4
Rågeleje DK 61 C2
Raglan GB 39 C4
Ragnitz A 110 C2
Ragusa I 177 C3
Rahden D 72 B1
Råholt N 48 B3
Raiano I 169 A3
Raigada E 141 B3
Rain D 94 C2
Rainbach im Mühlkreis A 96 C2
Rainham GB 45 B4
Rairiz de Veiga E 140 B3
Raisdorf D 64 B3
Raisio FIN 8 B3
Raiskio FIN 197 D9
Raiva, *Aveiro* P 148 A1
Raiva, *Coimbra* P 148 B1
Raja-Jooseppi FIN 193 D12
Rajala FIN 197 B9
Rajcza PL 99 B3
Rajec SK 98 B2
Rájec-Jestřebi CZ 97 B4
Rajecké Teplice SK 98 B2
Rajevo Selo HR 125 C4
Rajhrad CZ 97 B4
Rajić HR 124 B3
Rajka H 111 B4
Rakaca H 99 C4
Rakamaz H 113 A5
Rakek SLO 123 B3
Rakhiv UA 17 A6
Rakitna SLO 123 B3
Rakitovo BG 183 B6
Rakkestad N 54 A2
Rákóczifalva H 113 B4
Rakoniewice PL 75 B5
Rakoszyce PL 85 A4
Raková SK 98 B2
Rakovac BIH 125 B3
Rakovica HR 123 C4
Rakovník CZ 96 A1
Rakow D 66 B2
Raków PL 87 B5
Rakvere EST 8 C5
Ralja SRB 127 C2
Rälla S 62 B4
Ramacastañas E 150 B2
Ramacca I 177 B3
Ramales de la Victoria E 143 A3
Ramberg N 194 B4
Rambervillers F 92 C2
Rambouillet F 90 C1
Rambucourt F 92 C1
Ramdala S 63 B3
Ramerupt F 91 C4
Ramingstein A 109 B4
Ramirás E 140 B2
Ramiswil CH 106 B2
Ramkvilla S 62 A2
Ramme DK 58 B1
Rämmen S 49 B6
Ramnäs S 56 A2
Ramnes N 54 A1
Râmnicu Vâlcea RO 17 C6
Ramonville-St. Agne F 129 C4
Rampside GB 36 B3
Ramsau D 109 B3
Ramsbeck D 81 A4
Ramsberg S 56 A1
Ramsele S 200 C2
Ramsey, *Cambridgeshire* GB 44 A3
Ramsey, *Isle of Man* GB 36 B2
Ramseycleuch GB 36 A3
Ramsgate GB 45 B5
Ramsjö S 200 D1
Ramstein-Meisenbach D 93 B3
Ramsund N 194 B7
Ramundberget S 199 C9
Ramvik S 200 D3
Ranalt A 108 B2
Rånäs S 51 C5
Rånåsfoss N 48 B3
Rance B 91 A4
Ránchio I 135 B5
Randaberg N 52 A1
Randalstown GB 27 B4
Randan F 117 A3
Randazzo I 177 B3
Rånddalen S 199 C10
Randegg A 110 A1
Randers DK 58 B3
Randijaur S 196 C2
Randin E 140 C3
Randsverk N 198 D6
Råneå S 196 D5
Rånes F 89 B3
Rångedala S 60 B3
Ranis D 82 B3
Rankweil A 107 B4
Rånnaväg S 60 B3
Ränneslöv S 61 C3
Rannoch Station GB 34 B3
Ranovac SRB 127 C3
Ransäter S 55 A4
Ransbach-Baumbach D 81 B3
Ransta S 56 A2
Ranttila FIN 193 C9
Ranua FIN 197 D9
Ranum DK 58 B2
Ranvalhal P 154 B1
Raon-l'Étape F 92 C2
Ráossi I 121 B4
Rapallo I 134 A2
Rapla EST 8 C4
Rapness GB 33 B4
Rapolano Terme I 135 B4
Rapolla I 172 B1
Raposa P 154 B2
Rapperswil CH 107 B3
Raša HR 123 B3
Rasal E 145 B3
Rascafria E 151 B4
Rasdorf D 82 B1
Raseiniai LT 13 A5
Rašica SLO 123 B3
Rasines E 143 A3
Rasquera E 153 A4
Rássina I 135 B4
Rastatt D 93 C4
Rastede D 71 A5
Rastenberg D 82 A3
Rastošnica BIH 125 C4
Rastovac MNE 139 C4
Rasueros E 150 A2
Rasy PL 86 A3
Raszków PL 86 A1
Rätan S 199 C11
Rateče SLO 109 C4
Ratekau D 65 C3
Ratež SLO 123 B4
Rathangan IRL 30 A2
Rathcoole IRL 30 A2
Rathcormack IRL 29 B3
Rathdrum IRL 30 B2
Rathebur D 74 A2
Rathenow D 73 B5
Rathfriland GB 27 B4
Rathkeale IRL 29 B3
Rathmelton IRL 27 A3
Rathmolyon IRL 30 A2
Rathmore IRL 29 B2
Rathmullan IRL 27 A3
Rathnew IRL 30 B2
Rathvilly IRL 30 B2
Ratibořské Hory CZ 96 B2
Ratingen D 80 A2
Ratková SK 99 C4
Ratkovo SRB 126 B1
Ratne UA 13 C6
Rattelsdorf D 94 A2
Ratten A 110 B2
Rattosjärvi FIN 196 C7
Rattray GB 35 B4
Rättvik S 50 B2
Ratvika N 199 B7
Ratzeburg D 65 C3
Rätzlingen D 73 B4
Raucourt-et-Flaba F 91 B4
Raudeberg N 198 D2
Raufarhöfn IS 191 A10
Raufoss N 48 B2
Rauhala FIN 196 B7
Rauland N 53 A4
Raulhac F 116 C2
Raulia N 195 E5
Rauma FIN 8 B2
Raundal N 46 B3
Raunds GB 44 A3
Rauris A 109 B4
Rautas S 196 B2
Rautavaara FIN 3 E11
Rauville-la-Bigot F 88 A2
Rauzan F 128 B2
Rava-Rus'ka UA 13 C5
Ravanusa I 176 B2
Ravča HR 138 B3
Ravels B 79 A4
Rävemåla S 63 B3
Ravenglass GB 36 B3
Ravenna I 135 A5
Ravensburg D 107 B4
Rävlanda S 60 B2
Ravna Gora HR 123 B3
Ravne na Koroškem SLO 110 C1
Ravnje SRB 127 C1
Ravno BIH 139 C3
Ravno Selo SRB 126 B1
Rawa Mazowiecka PL 87 A4
Rawicz PL 85 A4
Rawtenstall GB 40 B1
Rayleigh GB 45 B4
Ražana SRB 127 C1
Ražanac HR 137 A4
Razboj BIH 124 B3
Razes F 115 B5
Razgrad BG 17 D7
Razkrižie SLO 111 C3
Razlog BG 183 B5
Razo E 140 A2
Reading GB 44 B3
Réalmont F 130 B1
Rebais F 90 C3
Reboly RUS 3 E12
Rebordelo P 149 A2
Recanati I 136 B2
Recas E 151 B4
Recaş RO 126 B3
Recco I 134 A2
Recess IRL 28 A2
Recey-sur-Ource F 105 B3
Recezinhos P 148 A1
Rechnitz A 111 B3
Rechytsa BY 13 B9
Recke D 71 B4
Recklinghausen D 80 A3
Recoaro Terme I 121 B4
Recogne B 92 B1
Recoules-Prévinquières F 130 A1
Recsk H 113 B4
Recz PL 75 A4
Red Point GB 31 B3
Reda PL 69 A3
Redalen N 48 B2
Redange L 92 B1
Redcar GB 37 B5
Redditch GB 44 A2
Redefin D 73 A4
Redhill GB 44 B3
Redics H 111 C3
Redkino RUS 9 D10
Redland GB 33 B3
Redlin D 73 A5
Redon F 101 B3
Redondela E 140 B2
Redondo P 155 C3
Redruth GB 42 B1
Redzikowo PL 68 A2
Reepham GB 41 C5
Rees D 80 A2
Reeth GB 37 B5
Reetz D 73 A4
Reftele S 60 B3
Regalbuto I 177 B3
Regen D 95 C5
Regensburg D 95 B4
Regenstauf D 95 B4
Reggello I 135 B4
Réggio di Calábria I 175 C1
Réggio nell'Emília I 121 C3
Reggiolo I 121 C3
Reghin RO 17 B6
Régil E 144 A1
Regna S 56 B1
Regniéville F 92 C1
Regny F 117 B4
Rego da Leirosa P 154 A2
Regöly H 112 C2
Regueiro E 140 B2
Reguengo, *Portalegre* P 155 B3
Reguengo, *Santarém* P 154 B2
Reguengos de Monsaraz P 155 C3
Rehau D 83 B4
Rehburg D 72 B2
Rehden D 72 B1
Rehna D 65 C4
Reichelsheim D 93 B4
Reichelshofen D 94 B2
Reichenau A 110 B2
Reichenbach, *Sachsen* D 83 B4
Reichenbach, *Sachsen* D 84 A2
Reichenfels A 110 B1
Reichensachsen D 82 A2
Reichertshofen D 95 C3
Reichshoffen F 93 C3
Reiden CH 106 B2
Reigada E 141 A4
Reigada P 149 B3
Reigate GB 44 B3
Reillanne F 132 B1
Reillo E 158 B2
Reims F 91 B4
Reinach CH 106 B3
Reinbek D 72 A3
Reinberg D 66 B2
Reine N 194 C4
Reinfeld D 65 C3
Reinheim D 93 B4
Reinli N 47 B6
Reinosa E 142 A2
Reinstorf D 65 C4
Reinsvoll N 48 B2
Reisach A 109 C4
Reiss GB 32 C3
Reit im Winkl D 109 B3
Reitan N 199 C8
Rejmyre S 56 B1
Rekavice BIH 124 C3
Rekovac SRB 127 D3
Relleu E 159 C3
Rém H 125 A5
Remagen D 80 B3
Rémalard F 89 B4
Rembercourt-aux-Pots F 91 C5
Remedios P 154 B1
Remels D 71 A4
Remetea Mare RO 126 B3
Remich L 92 B2
Rémilly F 92 B2
Remiremont F 105 A5
Remolinos E 144 C2
Remoulins F 131 B3
Remscheid D 80 A3
Rémuzat F 131 A4
Rena N 48 A3
Renaison F 117 A3
Renazé F 101 B4
Renchen D 93 C4
Rencurel F 118 B2
Rende I 174 B2
Rendina GR 182 D3
Rendsburg D 64 B2
Renedo E 150 A3
Renens CH 105 C5
Renfrew GB 34 C3
Rengsjö S 50 A3
Reni UA 17 C8
Rennebu N 198 C6
Rennerod D 81 B4
Rennertshofen D 94 C3
Rennes F 101 A4
Rennes-les-Bains F 146 B3
Rennweg A 109 B4
Rens DK 64 B2
Rensjön S 196 A2
Rentería E 144 A2
Rentjärn S 200 A4
Répcelak H 111 B4
Repojoki FIN 193 D9
Repvåg N 193 B9
Requena E 159 B2
Réquista F 130 A1
Rerik D 65 B4
Resana I 121 B4
Resarö S 57 A4
Reschen = Résia I 108 C1
Resen MK 182 B3
Resende P 148 A2
Résia = Reschen I 108 C1
Reşiţa RO 16 C4
Resko PL 67 C4
Resnik SRB 127 C2
Ressons-sur-Matz F 90 B2
Restábal E 163 B4
Resuttano I 177 B3
Retamal E 155 C4
Retford GB 40 B3
Rethel F 91 B4
Rethem D 72 B2
Rethimno GR 185 D5
Retie B 79 A5
Retiers F 101 B4
Retortillo E 149 B3
Retortillo de Soria E 151 A4
Retournac F 117 B4
Rétság H 112 B3
Rettenegg A 110 B2
Retuerta del Bullaque E 157 A3
Retz A 97 C3
Retzbach D 94 B1
Reuden D 73 B5
Reuilly F 103 B4
Reus E 147 C2
Reusel NL 79 A5
Reuterstadt Stavenhagen D 74 A1
Reuth D 95 B4
Reutlingen D 94 C1
Reutte A 108 B1
Reuver NL 80 A2
Revel F 146 A2
Revello I 119 C4
Revenga E 151 B3
Revest-du-Bion F 132 A1
Révfülöp H 111 C4
Revigny-sur-Ornain F 91 C4
Revin F 91 B4
Řevnice CZ 96 B2
Řevničov CZ 84 B1
Revo I 121 A4
Revsnes N 47 A4
Revúca SK 99 C4
Rewa PL 69 A3
Rewal PL 67 B4
Rexbo S 50 B2
Reyðarfjörður IS 191 B11
Reyero E 142 B1
Reykhólar IS 190 B3
Reykholt, *Árnessýsla* IS 190 C5
Reykholt, *Borgarfjarðarsýsla* IS 190 C4
Reykjahlið IS 191 B9
Reykjavík IS 190 C4
Rezé F 101 B4
Rēzekne LV 8 D5
Rezovo BG 17 E8
Rezzato I 120 B3
Rezzoáglio I 134 A2
Rhade D 72 A2
Rhaunen D 93 B3
Rhayader GB 39 B3
Rheda-Wiedenbrück D 81 A4
Rhede, *Niedersachsen* D 71 A4
Rhede, *Nordrhein-Westfalen* D 80 A2
Rheinau D 93 C3
Rheinbach D 80 B2
Rheinberg D 80 A2
Rheine D 71 B4
Rheinfelden D 106 B2
Rheinsberg D 74 A1
Rhêmes-Notre-Dame I 119 B4
Rhenen NL 70 C2
Rhens D 81 B3
Rheydt D 80 A2
Rhiconich GB 32 C2
Rhinow D 73 B5
Rhiw GB 38 B2
Rho I 120 B2
Rhoden D 81 A5
Rhodes GR 188 C3
Rhondda GB 39 C3
Rhosllanerchrugog GB 38 A3
Rhosneigr GB 38 A2
Rhossili GB 39 C2
Rhubodach GB 34 C2
Rhuddlan GB 38 A3
Rhyl GB 38 A3
Rhynie GB 33 D4

Name	Country	Page	Grid
Riala	S	57	A4
Riallé	F	101	B4
Riaño	E	142	A3
Riano	I	168	A2
Rians	F	132	B1
Rianxo	E	140	A1
Riaza	E	151	A4
Riba	E	143	A3
Riba de Saelices	E	152	B1
Riba-Roja de Turia	E	159	B3
Riba-roja d'Ebre	E	153	A4
Ribadavia	E	140	B2
Ribadeo	E	141	A3
Ribadesella	E	142	A1
Ribaflecha	E	143	B4
Ribaforada	E	144	C2
Ribare	SRB	127	C3
Ribe	DK	59	C1
Ribeauvillé	F	106	A2
Ribécourt-Dreslincourt	F	90	B2
Ribeira da Pena	P	148	A2
Ribeira de Piquín	E	141	A3
Ribemont	F	91	B3
Ribera	I	176	B2
Ribera de Cardós	E	146	B2
Ribera del Fresno	E	156	B1
Ribérac	F	129	A3
Ribes de Freser	E	147	B3
Ribesalbes	E	159	A3
Ribiers	F	132	A1
Ribnica	BIH	139	A4
Ribnica	SLO	123	B3
Ribnica na Potorju	SLO	110	C2
Ribnik	HR	123	B4
Rîbnița	MD	17	B8
Ribnitz-Damgarten	D	66	B1
Ribolla	I	135	C4
Říčany, *Jihomoravský*	CZ	97	B4
Říčany, *Středočeský*	CZ	96	B2
Ríccia	I	170	B2
Riccione	I	136	A1
Ricco Del Golfo	I	134	A2
Richebourg	F	105	A4
Richelieu	F	102	B2
Richisau	CH	107	B3
Richmond, *Greater London*	GB	44	B3
Richmond, *North Yorkshire*	GB	37	B5
Richtenberg	D	66	B1
Richterswil	CH	107	B3
Rickling	D	64	B3
Rickmansworth	GB	44	B3
Ricla	E	152	A2
Riddarhyttan	S	50	C2
Ridderkerk	NL	79	A4
Riddes	CH	119	A4
Ridjica	SRB	125	B5
Riec-sur-Bélon	F	100	B2
Ried	A	109	A4
Ried im Oberinntal	A	108	B1
Riedenburg	D	95	C3
Riedlingen	D	107	A4
Riedstadt	D	93	B4
Riegersburg	A	110	C2
Riego de la Vega	E	141	B5
Riego del Camino	E	149	A4
Riello	E	141	B5
Riemst	B	80	B1
Rienne	B	91	B4
Riénsena	E	142	A2
Riesa	D	83	A5
Riese Pio X	I	121	B4
Riesi	I	177	B3
Riestedt	D	82	A3
Rietberg	D	81	A4
Rieti	I	169	A2
Rietschen	D	84	A2
Rieumes	F	146	A2
Rieupeyroux	F	130	A1
Rieux	F	146	A2
Riez	F	132	B2
Rīga	LV	8	D4
Riggisberg	CH	106	C2
Rignac	F	130	A1
Rignano Gargánico	I	171	B3
Rigolato	I	109	C3
Rigside	GB	36	A3
Rigutino	I	135	B4
Riihimäki	FIN	8	B15
Rijeka	HR	123	B3
Rijen	NL	79	A4
Rijkevorsel	B	79	A4
Rijssen	NL	71	B3
Rila	BG	183	A5
Rilić	BIH	138	B3
Rilievo	I	176	B1
Rillé	F	102	B2
Rillo de Gallo	E	152	B2
Rimavská Baňa	SK	99	C3
Rimavská Seč	SK	99	C4
Rimavská Sobota	SK	99	C4
Rimbo	S	57	A4
Rimforsa	S	56	B1
Rímini	I	136	A1
Rîmnicu Sărat	RO	17	C7
Rimogne	F	91	B4
Rimpar	D	94	B1
Rimske Toplice	SLO	123	A4
Rincón de la Victoria	E	163	B3
Rincón de Soto	E	144	B2
Rindal	N	198	B6
Rinde	N	46	A3
Ringarum	S	56	B2
Ringaskiddy	IRL	29	C3
Ringe	DK	59	C3
Ringebu	N	48	A2
Ringkøbing	DK	59	B1
Ringsaker	N	48	B2
Ringsted	DK	61	D1
Ringwood	GB	44	C2
Rinkaby	S	63	C2
Rinkabyholm	S	63	B4
Rinlo	E	141	A3
Rinn	A	108	B2
Rinteln	D	72	B2
Rio do Coures	P	154	B2
Rio Douro	P	148	A2
Rio Frio	P	154	C2
Rio frio de Riaza	E	151	A4
Rio Maior	P	154	B2
Rio Marina	I	134	C3
Riobo	E	140	B2
Riodeva	E	152	B2
Riofrio	E	150	B3
Riofrio de Aliste	E	149	A3
Riogordo	E	163	B3
Rioja	E	164	C2
Riola	I	135	A4
Riola Sardo	I	179	C2
Riolobos	E	155	B4
Riom	F	116	B3
Riom-ès-Montagnes	F	116	B2
Riomaggiore	I	134	A2
Rion-des-Landes	F	128	C2
Rionegro del Puente	E	141	B4
Rionero in Vúlture	I	172	B1
Riopar	E	158	C1
Ríos	E	141	C3
Rioseco	E	142	A1
Rioseco de Tapia	E	141	B5
Riotord	F	117	B4
Riotorto	E	141	A3
Rioz	F	105	B5
Ripač	BIH	124	C1
Ripacándida	I	172	B1
Ripanj	SRB	127	C2
Ripatransone	I	136	C2
Ripley	GB	40	B2
Ripoll	E	147	B3
Ripon	GB	40	A2
Riposto	I	177	B4
Ripsa	S	56	B2
Risan	MNE	16	D3
Risbäck	S	200	B1
Risca	GB	39	C3
Rischenau	D	81	A5
Riscle	F	128	C2
Risebo	S	56	B2
Risnes	N	46	A2
Rišňovce	SK	98	C1
Risør	N	53	B5
Risøyhamn	N	194	B6
Rissna	S	199	B12
Ritsem	S	194	C8
Ritterhude	D	72	A1
Riutula	FIN	193	D10
Riva del Garda	I	121	B3
Riva Lígure	I	133	B3
Rivanazzano	I	120	C2
Rivarolo Canavese	I	119	B4
Rivarolo Mantovano	I	121	B3
Rive-de-Gier	F	117	B4
Rivedoux-Plage	F	114	B2
Rivello	I	174	A1
Rivergaro	I	120	C2
Rives	F	118	B2
Rivesaltes	F	146	B3
Rivignano	I	122	B2
Rivne	UA	13	C7
Rívoli	I	119	B4
Rivolta d'Adda	I	120	B2
Rixheim	F	106	B2
Rixo	S	54	B2
Riza	GR	183	C5
Rizokarpaso	CY	181	A3
Rjukan	N	47	C5
Rø	DK	67	A3
Rö	S	57	A4
Roa	E	143	C3
Roa	N	48	B2
Roade	GB	44	A3
Roager	DK	59	C1
Roaldkvam	N	52	A2
Roanne	F	117	A4
Röbäck	S	200	C6
Robakowo	PL	69	B3
Róbbio	I	120	B1
Röbel	D	73	A5
Roberton	GB	35	C5
Robertsfors	S	200	B6
Robertville	B	80	B2
Robin Hood's Bay	GB	37	B6
Robleda	E	149	B3
Robledillo de Trujillo	E	156	A2
Robledo, *Albacete*	E	158	C1
Robledo, *Orense*	E	141	B4
Robledo de Chavela	E	151	B3
Robledo del Buey	E	156	A3
Robledo del Mazo	E	156	A3
Robledollano	E	156	A2
Robles de la Valcueva	E	142	B1
Robliza de Cojos	E	149	B4
Robres	E	145	C3
Robres del Castillo	E	144	B1
Rocafort de Queralt	E	147	C2
Rocamadour	F	129	B4
Rocca di Mezzo	I	169	A3
Rocca di Papa	I	168	B2
Rocca Imperiale	I	174	A2
Rocca Priora	I	136	B2
Rocca San Casciano	I	135	A4
Rocca Sinibalda	I	169	A2
Roccabernarda	I	175	B2
Roccabianca	I	120	B3
Roccadáspide	I	172	B1
Roccagorga	I	169	B3
Roccalbegna	I	135	C4
Roccalumera	I	177	B4
Roccamena	I	176	B2
Roccamonfina	I	170	B1
Roccanova	I	174	A2
Roccapalumba	I	176	B2
Roccapassa	I	169	A3
Roccaraso	I	169	B4
Roccasecca	I	169	B3
Roccastrada	I	135	B4
Roccatederighi	I	135	B4
Roccella Iónica	I	175	C2
Rocchetta Sant'António	I	172	A1
Rocester	GB	40	C2
Rochdale	GB	40	B1
Roche-lez-Beaupré	F	105	B5
Rochechouart	F	115	C4
Rochefort	B	79	B5
Rochefort	F	114	C3
Rochefort-en-Terre	F	101	B3
Rochefort-Montagne	F	116	B2
Rochefort-sur-Nenon	F	105	B4
Rochemaure	F	131	A3
Rocheservière	F	114	B2
Rochester, *Medway*	GB	45	B4
Rochester, *Northumberland*	GB	37	A4
Rochlitz	D	83	A4
Rociana del Condado	E	161	B3
Rockenhausen	D	93	B3
Rockhammar	S	56	A1
Rockneby	S	62	B4
Ročko Polje	HR	123	B3
Ročov	CZ	84	B1
Rocroi	F	91	B4
Roda de Bara	E	147	C2
Roda de Ter	E	147	C3
Rodach	D	82	B2
Rodalben	D	93	B3
Rødberg	N	47	B5
Rødby	DK	65	B4
Rødbyhavn	DK	65	B4
Rødding, *Sønderjyllands Amt.*	DK	59	C2
Rødding, *Viborg Amt.*	DK	58	B1
Rödeby	S	63	B3
Rodeiro	E	140	B3
Rødekro	DK	64	A2
Roden	NL	71	A3
Ródenas	E	152	B2
Rodenkirchen	D	72	A1
Rödental	D	82	B3
Rödermark	D	93	B4
Rodewisch	D	83	B4
Rodez	F	130	A1
Rodi Gargánico	I	171	B3
Roding	D	95	B4
Rødjebro	S	51	B4
Rødkærsbro	DK	59	B2
Rodolivos	GR	183	C5
Rodoña	E	147	C2
Rødvig	DK	65	A5
Roermond	NL	80	A1
Roesbrugge	B	78	B2
Roeschwoog	F	93	C4
Roeselare	B	78	B3
Roetgen	D	80	B2
Roffiac	F	116	B2
Röfors	S	55	B5
Rofrano	I	172	B1
Rogač	HR	138	B2
Rogačica	SRB	127	C1
Rogalinek	PL	76	B1
Rogaška Slatina	SLO	123	A4
Rogatec	SLO	123	A4
Rogatica	BIH	139	B5
Rogatyn	UA	13	D6
Rogätz	D	73	B4
Roggendorf	D	65	C4
Roggiano Gravina	I	174	B2
Roghadal	GB	31	B1
Rogliano	F	180	A2
Rogliano	I	175	B2
Rognan	N	195	C6
Rogne	N	47	A6
Rognes	F	131	B4
Rogny-les-7-Ecluses	F	103	B4
Rogowo	PL	76	B2
Rogoznica	HR	138	B1
Rogoźnica	PL	85	A4
Rogoźno	PL	76	B2
Rohan	F	101	A3
Röhlingen	D	94	C2
Rohožník	SK	98	C1
Rohr	D	82	B2
Rohr im Gebirge	A	110	B2
Rohrbach	A	96	C1
Rohrbach-lès-Bitche	F	92	B3
Rohrberg	D	73	B4
Röhrnbach	D	96	C1
Roisel	F	90	B3
Roja	LV	8	D3
Rojales	E	165	A4
Röjeråsen	S	50	B1
Rojewo	PL	76	B2
Rokiciny	PL	87	A3
Rokietnica	PL	75	B5
Rokiškis	LT	8	E4
Rokitki	PL	85	A3
Rokycany	CZ	96	B1
Rolampont	F	105	B4
Rold	DK	58	B2
Røldal	N	52	A2
Rolde	NL	71	B3
Rolfs	S	196	D6
Rollag	N	47	B6
Rollán	E	149	B4
Rolle	CH	105	C5
Roma = Rome	I	168	B2
Roma	S	57	C4
Romagnano Sésia	I	119	B5
Romagné	F	88	B2
Romakloster	S	57	C4
Roman	RO	17	B7
Romana	I	178	B2
Romanèche-Thorins	F	117	A4
Romano di Lombardia	I	120	B2
Romans-sur-Isère	F	118	B2
Romanshorn	CH	107	B4
Rombas	F	92	B2
Rome = Roma	I	168	B2
Romeán	E	141	B3
Romenay	F	105	C4
Romeral	E	157	A4
Römerstein	D	94	C1
Rometta	I	177	A4
Romford	GB	45	B4
Romhány	H	112	B3
Römhild	D	82	B2
Romilly-sur-Seine	F	91	C3
Romont	CH	106	C1
Romorantin-Lanthenay	F	103	B3
Romrod	D	81	B5
Romsey	GB	44	C2
Rømskog	N	54	A2
Rønbjerg	DK	58	B1
Roncal	E	144	B3
Ronce-les-Bains	F	114	C2
Ronchamp	F	106	B1
Ronchi dei Legionari	I	122	B2
Ronciglione	I	168	A2
Ronco Canavese	I	119	B4
Ronco Scrivia	I	120	C1
Ronda	E	162	B2
Rønde	DK	59	B3
Rone	S	57	C4
Ronehamn	S	57	C4
Rong	N	46	B1
Rönnäng	S	60	B1
Ronneburg	D	83	B4
Ronneby	S	63	B3
Rønnede	DK	65	A5
Ronnenberg	D	72	B2
Rønninge	DK	59	C3
Rönninge	S	57	A3
Rönnöfors	S	199	B10
Rönö	S	56	B2
Ronov nad Doubravou	CZ	97	B3
Ronse	B	79	B3
Roosendaal	NL	79	A4
Roosky	IRL	26	C3
Ropczyce	PL	87	B5
Ropeid	N	52	A2
Ropinsalmi	FIN	192	D5
Ropuerelos del Páramo	E	141	B5
Roquebilière	F	133	A3
Roquebrun	F	130	B2
Roquecourbe	F	130	B1
Roquefort	F	128	B2
Roquemaure	F	131	A3
Roquesteron	F	132	B3
Roquetas de Mar	E	164	C2
Roquetes	E	153	B4
Roquevaire	F	132	B1
Røra	N	199	B8
Rörbäcksnäs	S	49	A4
Rørbæk	DK	58	B2
Rore	BIH	138	A2
Røros	N	199	C8
Rørvig	DK	61	D1
Rørvik	N	199	A8
Rörvik	S	62	A2
Rosà	I	121	B4
Rosa Marina	I	173	B3
Rosal de la Frontera	E	161	B2
Rosalina Mare	I	122	B1
Rosans	F	132	A1
Rosário	P	160	B1
Rosarno	I	175	C1
Rosbach	D	81	B3
Rosche	D	73	B3
Rościszewo	PL	77	B4
Roscoff	F	100	A2
Roscommon	IRL	28	A3
Roscrea	IRL	28	B4
Rosdorf	D	82	A1
Rose	I	174	B2
Rosegg	A	109	C5
Rosehall	GB	32	D2
Rosehearty	GB	33	D4
Rosel	GB	88	A1
Rosell	E	153	B4
Roselló	E	153	A4
Rosenfeld	D	93	C4
Rosenfors	S	62	A3
Rosenheim	D	108	B3
Rosenow	D	74	A2
Rosersberg	S	57	A3
Roses	E	147	B4
Roseto degli Abruzzi	I	169	A4
Roseto Valfortore	I	170	B3
Rosheim	F	93	C3
Rosia	I	135	B4
Rosice	CZ	97	B4
Rosières-en-Santerre	F	90	B2
Rosignano Maríttimo	I	134	B3
Rosignano Solvay	I	134	B3
Roşiori-de-Vede	RO	17	C6
Roskhill	GB	31	B2
Roskilde	DK	61	D2
Roskovec	AL	182	C1
Röslau	D	83	B3
Roslev	DK	58	B1
Rosmaninhal	P	155	B3
Rosnowo	PL	67	B5
Rosolini	I	177	C3
Rosova	MNE	139	B5
Rosoy	F	104	A2
Rosporden	F	100	B2
Rosquete	P	154	B2
Rosrath	D	80	B3
Ross-on-Wye	GB	39	C4
Rossa	CH	120	A2
Rossano	I	174	B2
Rossas, *Aveiro*	P	148	B1
Rossas, *Braga*	P	148	A1
Rossdorf	D	82	B2
Rossett	GB	38	A4
Rosshaupten	D	108	B1
Rossiglione	I	133	A4
Rossignol	B	92	B1
Rossla	D	82	A3
Rosslare	IRL	30	B2
Rosslare Harbour	IRL	30	B2
Rosslau	D	83	A4
Rosslea	GB	27	B3
Rossleben	D	82	A3
Rossön	S	200	C2
Rossoszyca	PL	86	A2
Rosswein	D	83	A5
Röstånga	S	61	C3
Roštár	SK	99	C4
Rostock	D	65	B5
Rostrenen	F	100	A2
Røsvik	N	194	C6
Rosvik	S	196	D5
Rosyth	GB	35	B4
Röszke	H	126	A2
Rot am See	D	94	B2
Rota	E	161	C3
Rota Greca	I	174	B2
Rotberget	N	49	B4
Rotella	I	136	C2
Rotenburg, *Hessen*	D	82	B1
Rotenburg, *Niedersachsen*	D	72	A2
Roth, *Bayern*	D	94	B3
Roth, *Rheinland-Pfalz*	D	81	B3
Rothbury	GB	37	A5
Rothemühl	D	74	A2
Rothen-kempenow	D	74	A3
Röthenbach	D	95	B3
Rothenburg	D	84	A2
Rothenburg ob der Tauber	D	94	B2
Rothéneuf	F	88	B2
Rothenstein	D	94	C3
Rotherham	GB	40	B2
Rothes	GB	32	D3
Rothesay	GB	34	C2
Rothwell	GB	44	A3
Rotnes	N	48	B2
Rotonda	I	174	B2
Rotondella	I	174	A2
Rotova	E	159	C3
Rott, *Bayern*	D	108	B3
Rott, *Bayern*	D	108	B3
Rottach-Egern	D	108	B2
Röttenbach	D	94	B3
Rottenbuch	D	108	B1
Rottenburg, *Baden-Württemberg*	D	93	C4
Rottenburg, *Bayern*	D	95	C4
Rottenmann	A	110	B1
Rotterdam	NL	79	A4
Rotthalmünster	D	96	C1
Rottingdean	GB	44	C3
Röttingen	D	94	B1
Rottleberode	D	82	A2
Rottne	S	62	A2
Rottneros	S	55	A4
Rottofreno	I	120	B2
Rottweil	D	107	A3
Rötz	D	95	B4
Roubaix	F	78	B3
Roudnice nad Labem	CZ	84	B2
Roudouallec	F	100	A2
Rouen	F	89	A4
Rouffach	F	106	B2
Rougé	F	101	B4
Rougemont	F	105	B5
Rougemont le-Château	F	106	B1
Rouillac	F	115	C3
Rouillé	F	115	B4
Roujan	F	130	B2
Roulans	F	105	B5
Roundwood	IRL	30	A2
Rousínov	CZ	97	B4
Roussac	F	115	B5
Roussennac	F	130	A1
Roussillon	F	117	B4
Rouvroy-sur-Audry	F	91	B4
Rouy	F	104	B2
Rovanieman maalaiskunta	FIN	197	C9
Rovaniemi	FIN	197	C8
Rovato	I	120	B2
Rovensko pod Troskami	CZ	84	B3
Roverbella	I	121	B3
Rovereto	I	121	B4
Rövershagen	D	65	B5
Roverud	N	49	B4
Rovigo	I	121	B4
Rovinj	HR	122	B2
Rovišće	HR	124	B2
Rów	PL	74	B3
Rowy	PL	68	A2
Royal Leamington Spa	GB	44	A2
Royal Tunbridge Wells	GB	45	B4
Royan	F	114	C2
Royat	F	116	B3
Roybon	F	118	B2
Roybridge	GB	34	B3
Roye	F	90	B2
Royère-de-Vassivière	F	116	B1
Røykenvik	N	48	B2
Royos	E	164	B2
Røyrvik	N	199	A10
Royston	GB	44	A3
Rozadas	E	141	A4
Rozalén del Monte	E	151	C5
Różańsko	PL	75	B3
Rozay-en-Brie	F	90	C2
Roždalovice	CZ	84	B3
Rozdilna	UA	17	B9
Rozental	PL	69	B4
Rozhyshche	UA	13	C6
Rožmitál pod Třemšínem	CZ	96	B1
Rožňava	SK	99	C4
Rožnov pod Radhoštěm	CZ	98	B2
Rozoy-sur-Serre	F	91	B4
Rozprza	PL	86	A3
Roztoky	CZ	84	B2
Rozvadov	CZ	95	B4
Rozzano	I	120	B2
Rrëshen	AL	182	B1
Rrogozhinë	AL	182	B1
Ruanes	E	156	A2
Rubbestadneset	N	46	C2
Rubi	E	147	C3

Rubiá E 141 B4
Rubiacedo de Abajo E 143 B3
Rubielos Bajos E 158 B1
Rubielos de Mora E 153 B3
Rubiera I 121 C3
Rubik AL 182 B1
Rucandio E 143 B3
Rud, *Akershus* N 48 B3
Rud, *Buskerud* N 48 B2
Ruda PL 86 A2
Ruda S 62 A4
Ruda Maleniecka PL 87 A4
Ruda Pilczycka PL 87 A4
Ruda Śl. PL 86 B2
Rudabánya H 99 C4
Ruddervorde B 78 A3
Ruden A 110 C1
Rudersberg D 94 C1
Rudersdorf A 111 B3
Rüdersdorf D 74 B2
Ruderting D 96 C1
Rüdesheim D 93 B3
Rudkøbing DK 65 B3
Rudmanns A 97 C3
Rudna CZ 96 A2
Rudna PL 85 A4
Rudnik SRB 127 C2
Rudniki, *Opolskie* PL 86 A2
Rudniki, *Śląskie* PL 86 B3
Rudno, *Dolnośląskie* PL 85 A4
Rudno, *Pomorskie* PL 69 B3
Rudnya RUS 13 A9
Rudolstadt D 82 B3
Rudowica PL 84 A3
Rudozem BG 183 B6
Ruds Vedby DK 61 D1
Rudskoga S 55 A5
Rudston GB 40 A3
Rudy PL 86 B2
Rue F 78 B1
Rueda E 150 A3
Rueda de Jalón E 152 A2
Ruelle-sur-Touvre F 115 C4
Ruerrero E 143 B3
Ruffano I 173 C4
Ruffec F 115 B4
Rufina I 135 B4
Rugby GB 44 A2
Rugeley GB 40 C2
Ruggstrop S 62 B4
Rugles F 89 B4
Rugozero RUS 3 D13
Rühen D 73 B3
Ruhla D 82 B2
Ruhland D 84 A1
Ruhle D 71 B4
Ruhpolding D 109 B3
Ruhstorf D 96 C1
Ruidera E 158 C1
Ruillé-sur-le-Loir F 102 B2
Ruinen NL 71 B3
Ruiselede B 78 A3
Ruka FIN 197 C12
Rulles B 92 B1
Rülzheim D 93 B4
Rum H 111 B3
Ruma SRB 127 B1
Rumboci BIH 138 B3
Rumburk CZ 84 B2
Rumenka SRB 126 B1
Rumia PL 69 A3
Rumigny F 91 B4
Rumilly F 118 B2
Rumma S 56 B2
Rumney GB 39 C3
Rumont F 91 C5
Runa P 154 B1
Runcorn GB 38 A4
Rundmoen N 195 D5
Rungsted DK 61 D2
Runhällen S 51 B3
Runowo PL 69 A5
Ruokojärvi FIN 196 B7
Ruokolahti FIN 9 B6
Ruokto S 196 B2
Ruoms F 131 A3
Ruoti I 172 B1
Rupa HR 123 B3
Ruppichteroth D 80 B3
Rupt-sur-Moselle F 106 B1
Rus E 157 B4
Ruse BG 17 D7
Ruše SLO 110 C2
Rusele S 200 B4
Ruševo HR 125 B4
Rush IRL 30 A2
Rushden GB 44 A3
Rusiec PL 86 A2
Rusinowo, *Zachodnio-Pomorskie* PL 75 A5
Rusinowo, *Zachodnio-Pomorskie* PL 67 C4
Ruskele S 200 B4
Ruski Krstur SRB 126 B1
Ruskington GB 40 B3
Rusovce SK 111 A4
Rüsselsheim D 93 B4
Russelv N 192 C4
Russi I 135 A5
Rust A 111 B3
Rustefjelbma N 193 B12
Rustrel F 131 B4
Ruszki PL 77 B5
Ruszów PL 84 A3
Rute E 163 A3
Rüthen D 81 A4
Rutherglen GB 35 C3
Ruthin GB 38 A3
Ruthven GB 32 D2
Ruthwell GB 36 B3
Rüti CH 107 B3
Rutigliano I 173 A3
Rutledal N 46 A2
Rutuna S 56 B3
Rutvik S 196 D5
Ruurlo NL 71 B3
Ruuvaoja FIN 197 B11
Ruvo del Monte I 172 B1
Ruvo di Púglia I 171 B4
Ruynes-en-Margeride F 116 C3
Ružic HR 138 B2
Ružomberok SK 99 B3
Ruzsa H 126 A1
Ry DK 59 B2
Rybany SK 98 C2
Rybina PL 69 A4
Rybnik PL 86 B2
Rychliki PL 69 B4
Rychlocice PL 86 A2
Rychnov nad Kněžnou CZ 85 B4
Rychnowo PL 77 A5
Rychtal PL 86 A1
Rychwał PL 76 B3
Ryczywół, *Mazowieckie* PL 87 A5
Ryczywół, *Wielkopolskie* PL 75 B5
Ryd S 63 B2
Rydaholm S 62 B2
Rydal S 60 B2
Rydbo S 57 A4
Rydboholm S 60 B2
Ryde GB 44 C2
Rydöbruk S 60 C3
Rydsgård S 66 A2
Rydsnäs S 62 A3
Rydultowy PL 86 B2
Rydzyna PL 85 A4
Rye GB 45 C4
Rygge N 54 A1
Ryjewo PL 69 B3
Rykene N 53 B4
Rymań PL 67 C4
Rýmařov CZ 98 B1
Rynarzewo PL 76 A2
Ryomgård DK 59 B3
Rypefjord N 192 B7
Rypin PL 77 A4
Rysjedalsvika N 46 A2
Ryssby S 60 C4
Rytel PL 68 B2
Rytinki FIN 197 D10
Rytro PL 99 B4
Rywociny PL 77 A5
Rzeczenica PL 68 B2
Rzeczniów PL 87 A5
Rzeczyca PL 87 A4
Rzęgnowo PL 77 A5
Rzejowice PL 87 A3
Rzemień PL 87 B5
Rzepin PL 75 B3
Rzesznikowo PL 67 C4
Rzeszów PL 12 C4
Rzgów PL 86 A3
Rzhev RUS 9 D9

S

Sa Pobla E 167 B3
Sa Savina E 166 C1
Saal, *Bayern* D 95 C3
Saal, *Bayern* D 82 B2
Saalbach A 109 B3
Saalburg D 83 B3
Saales F 92 C3
Saalfeld D 82 B3
Saalfelden am Steinernen Meer A 109 B3
Saanen CH 106 C2
Saarbrücken D 92 B2
Saarburg D 92 B2
Saari-Kämä FIN 197 C9
Saarijärvi FIN 8 A4
Saarlouis D 92 B2
Saas-Fee CH 119 A4
Šabac SRB 127 C1
Sabadell E 147 C3
Sabáudia I 169 B3
Sabbioneta I 121 C3
Sabero E 142 B1
Sabiñánigo E 145 B3
Sabiote E 157 B4
Sablé-sur-Sarthe F 102 B1
Sables-d'Or-les-Pins F 101 A3
Sabóia P 160 B1
Saborsko HR 123 B4
Sabres F 128 B2
Sabrosa P 148 A2
Sabugal P 149 B2
Sabuncu TR 187 C5
Săcălaz RO 126 B3
Sacecorbo E 152 B1
Saceda del Rio E 151 B5
Sacedón E 151 B5
Săcele RO 17 C6
Saceruela E 156 B3
Sachsenburg A 109 C4
Sachsenhagen D 72 B2
Sacile I 122 B1
Sacramenia E 151 A4
Sada E 140 A2
Sádaba E 144 B2
Saddell GB 34 C2
Sadernes E 147 B3
Sadki PL 76 A2
Sadkowice PL 87 A4
Sadlinki PL 69 B3
Sadów PL 75 B3
Sadská CZ 84 B2
Sæbøvik N 52 A1
Sæby DK 58 A3
Saelices E 151 C5
Saelices de Mayorga E 142 B1
Saerbeck D 71 B4
Særslev DK 59 C3
Sætre N 54 A1
Saeul L 92 B1
Sævareid N 46 B2
Sævråsvåg N 46 B2
Safaalan TR 186 A3
Safara P 161 A2
Säffle S 55 A3
Saffron Walden GB 45 A4
Safranbolu TR 187 A7
Säfsnäs S 50 B1
Şag RO 126 B3
Sagard D 66 B2
S'Agaro E 147 C4
Sågmyra S 50 B2
Sagone F 180 A1
Sagres P 160 C1
Ságújfalu H 113 A3
Sagunt E 159 B3
Sagvåg N 52 A1
Ságvár H 112 C2
Sagy F 105 C4
Sahagún E 142 B1
Šahy SK 112 A2
Saignelégier CH 106 B1
Saignes F 116 B2
Saija FIN 197 B11
Saillagouse F 146 B3
Saillans F 118 C2
Sains F 91 B3
St. Abb's GB 35 C5
St. Affrique F 130 B1
St. Agnan F 104 C2
St. Agnant F 114 C3
St. Agnes GB 42 B1
St. Agrève F 117 B4
St. Aignan F 103 B3
St. Aignan-sur-Roë F 101 B4
St. Alban-sur-Limagnole F 117 C3
St. Albans GB 44 B3
St. Amand-en-Puisaye F 104 B2
St. Amand-les-Eaux F 79 B3
St. Amand-Longpré F 103 B3
St. Amand-Montrond F 103 C4
St. Amans F 117 C3
St. Amans-Soult F 130 B1
St. Amant-Roche-Savine F 117 B3
St. Amarin F 106 B1
St. Ambroix F 131 A3
St. Amé F 106 A1
St. Amour F 118 A2
St. André-de-Corcy F 117 B4
St. André-de-Cubzac F 128 B2
St. André-de-l'Eure F 89 B5
St. André-de-Roquepertuis F 131 A3
St. André-de-Sangonis F 130 B2
St. André-de-Valborgne F 130 A2
St. André-les-Alpes F 132 B2
St. Andrews GB 35 B5
St. Angel F 116 B2
St. Anthème F 117 B3
St. Antoine F 180 A2
St. Antoine-de-Ficalba F 129 B3
St. Antönien CH 107 C4
St. Antonin-Noble-Val F 129 B4
St. Août F 103 C3
St. Armant-Tallende F 116 B3
St. Arnoult F 90 C1
St. Asaph GB 38 A3
St. Astier F 129 A3
St. Athan GB 39 C3
St. Auban F 132 B2
St. Aubin CH 106 C1
St. Aubin F 105 B4
St. Aubin GB 88 A1
St. Aubin-d'Aubigné F 101 A4
St. Aubin-du-Cormier F 101 A4
St. Aubin-sur-Aire F 92 C1
St. Aubin-sur-Mer F 89 A3
St. Aulaye F 128 A3
St. Austell GB 42 B2
St. Avit F 116 B2
St. Avold F 92 B2
St. Aygulf F 132 B2
St. Bauzille-de-Putois F 130 B2
St. Béat F 145 B4
St. Beauzély F 130 A1
St. Bees GB 36 B3
St. Benim-d'Azy F 104 C2
St. Benoît-du-Sault F 115 B5
St. Benoit-en-Woëvre F 92 C1
St. Berthevin F 102 A1
St. Blaise-la-Roche F 92 C3
St. Blazey GB 42 B2
St. Blin F 105 A4
St. Bonnet F 118 C3
St. Bonnet Briance F 115 C5
St. Bonnet-de-Joux F 104 C3
St. Bonnet-le-Château F 117 B4
St. Bonnet-le-Froid F 117 B4
St. Brévin-les-Pins F 101 B3
St. Briac-sur-Mer F 101 A3
St. Brice-en-Coglès F 88 B2
St. Brieuc F 101 A3
St. Bris-le-Vineux F 104 B2
St. Broladre F 88 B2
St. Calais F 102 B2
St. Cannat F 131 B4
St. Cast-le-Guildo F 101 A3
St. Céré F 129 B4
St. Cergue CH 118 A3
St. Cergues F 118 A3
St. Cernin F 116 B2
St. Chamant F 116 B1
St. Chamas F 131 B4
St. Chamond F 117 B4
St. Chély-d'Apcher F 116 C3
St. Chély-d'Aubrac F 116 C2
St. Chinian F 130 B1
St. Christol F 131 A4
St. Christol-lès-Alès F 131 A3
St. Christoly-Médoc F 114 C3
St. Christophe-du-Ligneron F 114 B2
St. Christophe-en-Brionnais F 117 A4
St. Ciers-sur-Gironde F 128 A2
St. Clair-sur-Epte F 90 B1
St. Clar F 129 C3
St. Claud F 115 C4
St. Claude F 118 A2
St. Clears GB 39 C2
St. Columb Major GB 42 B2
St. Come-d'Olt F 130 A1
St. Cosme-en-Vairais F 89 B4
St. Cyprien, *Dordogne* F 129 B4
St. Cyprien, *Pyrénées-Orientales* F 146 B4
St. Cyr-sur-Loire F 102 B2
St. Cyr-sur-Mer F 132 B1
St. Cyr-sur-Methon F 117 A4
St. David's GB 39 C1
St. Denis F 90 C2
St. Denis-d'Oléron F 114 B2
St. Denis-d'Orques F 102 A1
St. Didier F 117 A4
St. Didier-en-Velay F 117 B4
St. Dié F 92 C2
St. Dier-d'Auvergne F 117 B3
St. Dizier F 91 C4
St. Dizier-Leyrenne F 116 A1
St. Dogmaels GB 39 B2
St. Efflam F 100 A2
St. Égrève F 118 B2
St. Eloy-les-Mines F 116 A2
St. Emiland F 104 C3
St. Émilion F 128 B2
St. Enoder GB 42 B2
St. Esteben F 144 A2
St. Estèphe F 128 A2
St. Étienne F 117 B4
St. Etienne-de-Baigorry F 144 A2
St. Étienne-de-Cuines F 118 B3
St. Etienne-de-Fursac F 116 A1
St. Etienne-de-Montluc F 101 B4
St. Etienne-de-St. Geoirs F 118 B2
St. Étienne-de-Tinée F 132 A2
St. Étienne-du-Bois F 118 A2
St. Étienne-du-Rouvray F 89 A5
St. Etienne-les-Orgues F 132 A1
St. Fargeau F 104 B2
St. Félicien F 117 B4
St. Felix-de-Sorgues F 130 B1
St. Félix-Lauragais F 146 A2
St. Fillans GB 35 B3
St. Firmin F 118 C3
St. Florent F 180 A2
St. Florent-le-Vieil F 101 B4
St. Florent-sur-Cher F 103 C4
St. Florentin F 104 B2
St. Flour F 116 B3
St. Flovier F 103 C3
St. Fort-sur-le-Né F 115 C3
St. Fulgent F 114 B2
St. Galmier F 117 B4
St. Gaudens F 145 A4
St. Gaultier F 115 B5
St. Gély-du-Fesc F 130 B2
St. Genest-Malifaux F 117 B4
St. Gengoux-le-National F 104 C3
St. Geniez F 132 A2
St. Geniez-d'Olt F 130 A1
St. Genis-de-Saintonge F 114 C3
St. Genis-Pouilly F 118 A3
St. Genix-sur-Guiers F 118 B2
St. Georges Buttavent F 88 B3
St. Georges-d'Aurac F 117 B3
St. Georges-de-Commiers F 118 B2
St. Georges-de-Didonne F 114 C3
St. Georges-de-Luzençon F 130 A1
St. Georges-de Mons F 116 B2
St. Georges-de-Reneins F 117 A4
St. Georges d'Oléron F 114 C2
St. Georges-en-Couzan F 117 B3
St. Georges-lès-Baillargeaux F 115 B4
St. Georges-sur-Loire F 102 B1
St. Georges-sur-Meuse B 79 B5
St. Geours-de-Maremne F 128 C1
St. Gérand-de-Vaux F 117 A3
St. Gérand-le-Puy F 117 A3
St. Germain F 105 B5
St. Germain-Chassenay F 104 C2
St. Germain-de-Calberte F 130 A2
St. Germain-de-Confolens F 115 B4
St. Germain-de-Joux F 118 A2
St. Germain-des-Fossés F 117 A3
St. Germain-du-Bois F 105 C4
St. Germain-du-Plain F 105 C3
St. Germain-du Puy F 103 B4
St. Germain-en-Laye F 90 C2
St. Germain-Laval F 117 B4
St. Germain-Lembron F 116 B3
St. Germain-les-Belles F 116 B1
St. Germain-Lespinasse F 117 A3
St. Germain-l'Herm F 117 B3
St. Gervais-d'Auvergne F 116 A2
St. Gervais-les-Bains F 118 B3
St. Gervais-sur-Mare F 130 B2
St. Gildas-de-Rhuys F 100 B3
St. Gildas-des-Bois F 101 B3
St. Gilles, *Gard* F 131 B3
St. Gilles, *Ille-et-Vilaine* F 101 A4
St. Gilles-Croix-de-Vie F 114 B2
St. Gingolph F 119 A3
St. Girons, *Ariège* F 146 B2
St. Girons, *Landes* F 128 C1
St. Girons-Plage F 128 C1
St. Gobain F 91 B3
St. Gorgon-Main F 105 B5
St. Guénolé F 100 B1
St. Harmon GB 39 B3
St. Helens GB 38 A4
St. Helier GB 88 A1
St. Herblain F 101 B4
St. Hilaire, *Allier* F 104 C2
St. Hilaire, *Aude* F 146 A3
St. Hilaire-de-Riez F 114 B2
St. Hilaire-de-Villefranche F 114 C3
St. Hilaire-des-Loges F 114 B3
St. Hilaire-du-Harcouët F 88 B2
St. Hilaire-du-Rosier F 118 B2
St. Hippolyte, *Aveyron* F 116 C2
St. Hippolyte, *Doubs* F 106 B1
St. Hippolyte-du-Fort F 130 B2
St. Honoré-les-Bains F 104 C2
St. Hubert B 92 A1
St. Imier CH 106 B2
St. Issey GB 42 B2
St. Ives, *Cambridgeshire* GB 44 A3
St. Ives, *Cornwall* GB 42 B1
St. Izaire F 130 B1
St. Jacques-de-la-Lande F 101 A4
St. Jacut-de-la-Mer F 101 A3
St. James F 88 B2
St. Jaume d'Enveja E 153 B4
St. Jean-Brévelay F 101 B3
St. Jean-d'Angély F 114 C3
St. Jean-de-Belleville F 118 B3
St. Jean-de-Bournay F 118 B2
St. Jean-de-Braye F 103 B3
St. Jean-de-Côle F 115 C4
St. Jean-de-Daye F 88 A2
St. Jean de Losne F 105 B4
St. Jean-de-Luz F 144 A2
St. Jean-de-Maurienne F 118 B3
St. Jean-de-Monts F 114 B1
St. Jean-d'Illac F 128 B2
St. Jean-du-Bruel F 130 A2
St. Jean-du-Gard F 131 A2
St. Jean-en-Royans F 118 B2
St. Jean-la-Riviere F 133 B3
St. Jean-Pied-de-Port F 144 A2
St. Jean-Poutge F 129 C3
St. Jeoire F 118 A3
St. Joachim F 101 B3
St. Johnstown IRL 27 B3
St. Jorioz F 118 B3
St. Joris Winge B 79 B4
St. Jouin-de-Marnes F 102 C1
St. Juéry F 130 B1
St. Julien F 118 A2
St. Julien-Chapteuil F 117 B4
St. Julien-de-Vouvantes F 101 B4
St. Julien-du-Sault F 104 A2
St. Julien-du-Verdon F 132 B2
St. Julien-en-Born F 128 B1
St. Julien-en-Genevois F 118 A3
St. Julien la-Vêtre F 117 B3

St. Julien-l'Ars F 115 B4
St. Julien-Mont-Denis F 118 B3
St. Julien-sur-Reyssouze F 118 A2
St. Junien F 115 C4
St. Just F 131 A3
St. Just GB 42 B1
St. Just-en-Chaussée F 90 B2
St. Just-en-Chevalet F 117 B3
St. Just-St.-Rambert F 117 B4
St. Justin F 128 C2
St. Keverne GB 42 B1
St. Lary-Soulan F 145 B4
St. Laurent-d'Aigouze F 131 B3
St. Laurent-de-Chamousset F 117 B4
St. Laurent-de-Condel F 89 A3
St. Laurent-de-la-Cabrerisse F 146 A3
St. Laurent-de-la-Salanque F 146 B3
St. Laurent-des-Autels F 101 B4
St. Laurent-du-Pont F 118 B2
St. Laurent-en-Caux F 89 A4
St. Laurent-en-Grandvaux F 105 C4
St. Laurent-Médoc F 128 A2
St. Laurent-sur-Gorre F 115 C4
St. Laurent-sur-Mer F 88 A3
St. Laurent-sur-Sèvre F 114 B3
St. Leger B 92 B1
St. Léger-de-Vignes F 104 C2
St. Léger-sous-Beuvray F 104 C3
St. Léger-sur-Dheune F 104 C3
St. Léonard-de-Noblat F 116 B1
St. Leonards GB 45 C4
St. Lô F 88 A2
St. Lon-les-Mines F 128 C1
St. Louis F 106 B2
St. Loup F 117 A3
St. Loup-de-la-Salle F 105 C3
St. Loup-sur-Semouse F 105 B5
St. Lunaire F 101 A3
St. Lupicin F 118 A2
St. Lyphard F 101 B3
St. Lys F 146 A2
St. Macaire F 128 B2
St. Maclou F 89 A4
St. Maixent-l'École F 115 B3
St. Malo F 88 B1
St. Mamet-la-Salvetat F 116 C2
St. Mandrier-sur-Mer F 132 B1
St. Marcel, Drôme F 117 C4
St. Marcel, Saône-et-Loire F 105 C3
St. Marcellin F 118 B2
St. Marcellin sur Loire F 117 B4
St. Marcet F 145 A4
St. Mards-en-Othe F 104 A2
St. Margaret's-at-Cliffe GB 45 B5
St. Margaret's Hope GB 33 B4
St. Mars-la-Jaille F 101 B4
St. Martin-d'Ablois F 91 C3
St. Martin-d'Auxigny F 103 B4
St. Martin-de-Belleville F 118 B3
St. Martin-de-Bossenay F 91 C3
St. Martin-de-Crau F 131 B3
St. Martin-de-Londres F 130 B2
St. Martin-de-Queyrières F 118 C3
St. Martin-de-Ré F 114 B2
St. Martin-de-Valamas F 117 C4
St. Martin-d'Entraunes F 132 A2
St. Martin des Besaces F 88 A3
St. Martin-d'Estreaux F 117 A3
St. Martin-d'Hères F 118 B2

St. Martin-du-Frêne F 118 A2
St. Martin-en-Bresse F 105 C4
St. Martin-en-Haut F 117 B4
St. Martin-la-Méanne F 116 B1
St. Martin-sur-Ouanne F 104 B2
St. Martin-Valmeroux F 116 B2
St. Martin-Vésubie F 133 A3
St. Martory F 145 A4
St. Mary's GB 33 C4
St. Mathieu F 115 C4
St. Mathurin-de-Tréviers F 131 B2
St. Maurice CH 119 A3
St. Maurice-Navacelles F 130 B2
St. Maurice-sur-Moselle F 106 B1
St. Mawes GB 42 B1
St. Maximin-la-Ste. Baume F 132 B1
St. Méard-de-Gurçon F 128 B3
St. Médard-de-Guizières F 128 A2
St. Médard-en-Jalles F 128 B2
St. Méen-le-Grand F 101 A3
St. Menges F 91 B4
St. Merløse DK 61 D1
St. Město CZ 85 B4
St. M'Hervé F 101 A4
St. Michel, Aisne F 91 B4
St. Michel, Gers F 145 A4
St. Michel-Chef-Chef F 101 B3
St. Michel-de-Castelnau F 128 B2
St. Michel-de-Maurienne F 118 B3
St. Michel-en-Grève F 100 A2
St. Michel-en-l'Herm F 114 B2
St. Michel-Mont-Mercure F 114 B3
St. Mihiel F 92 C1
St. Monance GB 35 B5
St. Montant F 131 A3
St. Moritz CH 107 C4
St. Nazaire F 101 B3
St. Nazaire-en-Royans F 118 B2
St. Nazaire-le-Désert F 131 A4
St. Nectaire F 116 B2
St. Neots GB 44 A3
St. Nicolas-de-Port F 92 C2
St. Nicolas-de-Redon F 101 B3
St. Nicolas-du-Pélem F 100 A2
St. Niklaas B 79 A4
St. Omer F 78 B2
St. Pair-sur-Mer F 88 B2
St. Palais F 144 A2
St. Palais-sur-Mer F 114 C2
St. Pardoux-la-Rivière F 115 C4
St. Paul-Cap-de-Joux F 129 C4
St. Paul-de-Fenouillet F 146 B3
St. Paul-de-Varax F 118 A2
St. Paul-le-Jeune F 131 A3
St. Paul-lès-Dax F 128 C1
St. Paul-Trois-Châteaux F 131 A3
St. Paulien F 117 B3
St. Pé-de-Bigorre F 145 A3
St. Pée-sur-Nivelle F 144 A2
St. Péravy-la-Colombe F 103 B3
St. Péray F 117 C4
St. Père-en-Retz F 101 B3
St. Peter Port GB 88 A1
St. Petersburg = Sankt-Peterburg RUS 9 C7
St. Philbert-de-Grand-Lieu F 114 A2
St. Pierre F 130 B1
St. Pierre-d'Albigny F 118 B3
St. Pierre-d'Allevard F 118 B3
St. Pierre-de-Chartreuse F 118 B2
St. Pierre-de-Chignac F 129 A3
St. Pierre-de-la-Fage F 130 B2
St. Pierre-d'Entremont F 118 B2

St. Pierre-d'Oléron F 114 C2
St. Pierre-Eglise F 88 A2
St. Pierre-en-Port F 89 A4
St. Pierre-le-Moûtier F 104 C2
St. Pierre Montlimart F 101 B4
St. Pierre-Quiberon F 100 B2
St. Pierre-sur-Dives F 89 A3
St. Pierreville F 117 C4
St. Plancard F 145 A4
St. Poix F 101 B4
St. Pol-de-Léon F 100 A2
St. Pol-sur-Ternoise F 78 B2
St. Polgues F 117 B3
St. Pons-de-Thomières F 130 B1
St. Porchaire F 114 C3
St. Pourçain-sur-Sioule F 116 A3
St. Priest F 117 B4
St. Privat F 116 B2
St. Quay-Portrieux F 100 A3
St. Quentin F 90 B3
St. Quentin-la-Poterie F 131 A3
St. Quentin-les-Anges F 102 B1
St. Rambert-d'Albon F 117 B4
St. Rambert-en-Bugey F 118 B2
St. Raphaël F 132 B2
St. Rémy-de-Provence F 131 B3
St. Rémy-du-Val F 89 B4
St. Remy-en-Bouzemont F 91 C4
St. Renan F 100 A1
St. Révérien F 104 B2
St. Riquier F 90 A1
St. Romain-de-Colbosc F 89 A4
St. Rome-de-Cernon F 130 A1
St. Rome-de-Tarn F 130 A1
St. Sadurní d'Anoia F 147 C2
St. Saëns F 89 A5
St. Sampson GB 88 A1
St. Samson-la-Poterie F 90 B1
St. Saturnin-de-Lenne F 130 A2
St. Saturnin-lès-Apt F 131 B4
St. Sauflieu F 90 B2
St. Saulge F 104 B2
St. Sauveur, Finistère F 100 A2
St. Sauveur, Haute-Saône F 105 B5
St. Sauveur-de-Montagut F 117 C4
St. Sauveur-en-Puisaye F 104 B2
St. Sauveur-en-Rue F 117 B4
St. Sauveur-le-Vicomte F 88 A2
St. Sauveur-Lendelin F 88 A2
St. Sauveur-sur-Tinée F 132 A3
St. Savin, Gironde F 128 A2
St. Savin, Vienne F 115 B4
St. Savinien F 114 C3
St. Savournin F 131 B4
St. Seine-l'Abbaye F 105 B3
St. Sernin-sur-Rance F 130 B1
St. Sevan-sur-Mer F 88 B1
St. Sever F 128 C2
St. Sever-Calvados F 88 B2
St. Sorlin-d'Arves F 118 B3
St. Soupplets F 90 B2
St. Sulpice F 129 C4
St. Sulpice-Laurière F 116 A1
St. Sulpice-les-Feuilles F 115 B5
St. Symphorien F 128 B2
St. Symphorien-de-Lay F 117 B4
St. Symphorien-d'Ozon F 117 B4
St. Symphorien-sur-Coise F 117 B4
St. Teath GB 42 B2
St. Thégonnec F 100 A2
St. Thiébault F 105 A4
St. Trivier-de-Courtes F 118 A2

St. Trivier sur-Moignans F 117 A4
St. Trojan-les-Bains F 114 C2
St. Tropez F 132 B2
St. Truiden B 79 B5
St. Vaast-la-Hougue F 88 A2
St. Valérien F 104 A2
St. Valery-en-Caux F 89 A4
St. Valéry-sur-Somme F 78 B1
St. Vallier, Drôme F 117 B4
St. Vallier, Saône-et-Loire F 104 C3
St. Vallier-de-Thiey F 132 B2
St. Varent F 102 C1
St. Vaury F 116 A1
St. Venant F 78 B2
St. Véran F 119 C3
St. Vincent I 119 B4
St. Vincent-de-Tyrosse F 128 C1
St. Vit F 105 B4
St. Vith B 80 B2
St. Vivien-de-Médoc F 114 C2
St. Yan F 117 A4
St. Ybars F 146 A2
St. Yorre F 117 A3
St. Yrieix-la-Perche F 115 C5
Ste. Adresse F 89 A4
Ste. Anne F 89 B4
Ste. Anne-d'Auray F 100 B2
Ste. Croix CH 105 C5
Ste. Croix-Volvestre F 146 A2
Ste. Engrâce F 144 A3
Ste. Enimie F 130 A2
Ste. Foy-Peyrolières F 146 A2
Ste. Foy-la-Grande F 128 B3
Ste. Foy l'Argentiere F 117 B4
Ste. Gauburge-Ste. Colombe F 89 B4
Ste. Gemme la Plaine F 114 B2
Ste. Geneviève F 90 B2
Ste. Hélène F 128 B2
Ste. Hélène-sur-Isère F 118 B3
Ste. Hermine F 114 B2
Ste. Jalle F 131 A4
Ste. Livrade-sur-Lot F 129 B3
Ste. Marie-aux-Mines F 106 A2
Ste. Marie-du-Mont F 88 A2
Ste. Maure-de-Touraine F 102 B2
Ste. Maxime F 132 B2
Ste. Ménéhould F 91 B4
Ste. Mère-Église F 88 A2
Ste. Ode B 92 A1
Ste. Savine F 91 C4
Ste. Sévère-sur-Indre F 103 C4
Ste. Sigolène F 117 B4
Ste. Suzanne F 102 A1
Ste. Tulle F 132 B1
Sainteny F 88 A2
Saintes F 114 C3
Stes. Maries-de-la-Mer F 131 B3
Saintfield GB 27 B5
Saissac F 146 A3
Saja E 142 A2
Sajan SRB 126 B2
Sajkaš SRB 126 B2
Sajókaza H 99 C4
Sajószentpéter H 113 A4
Sajóvámos H 113 A4
Sakarya TR 187 B5
Šakiai LT 13 A5
Sakskøbing DK 65 B4
Sakule SRB 126 B2
Sala S 50 C3
Šal'a SK 111 A4
Sala Baganza I 120 C3
Sala Consilina I 172 B1
Salakovac SRB 127 C3
Salamanca E 150 B2
Salamina GR 185 A4
Salandra I 172 B2
Salaparuta I 176 B1
Salar E 163 A3
Salardú E 145 B4
Salas E 141 A4
Salas de los Infantes E 143 B3
Salau F 146 B2
Salavaux CH 106 C2
Salbertrand I 119 B3
Salbohed S 50 C3
Salbris F 103 B4
Salbu N 46 A2
Salce E 141 B4
Salching D 95 C4

Salcombe GB 43 B3
Saldaña E 142 B2
Saldus LV 8 D3
Sale I 120 C1
Saleby S 55 B4
Salem D 107 B4
Salemi I 176 B1
Salen, Argyll & Bute GB 34 B2
Salen, Highland GB 34 B2
Salen N 199 A8
Sälen S 49 A5
Salernes F 132 B2
Salerno I 170 C2
Salers F 116 B2
Salford GB 40 B1
Salgótarján H 113 A3
Salgueiro P 155 B3
Salhus N 46 B2
Sali HR 137 B4
Sálice Salentino I 173 B3
Salientes E 141 B4
Salies-de-Béarn F 144 A3
Salies-du-Salat F 145 A4
Salignac-Eyvigues F 129 B4
Saligney-sur-Roudon F 104 C2
Salihli TR 188 A3
Salihorsk BY 13 B7
Salinas, Alicante E 159 C3
Salinas, Huesca E 145 B4
Salinas de Medinaceli E 152 A1
Salinas de Pisuerga E 142 B2
Salindres F 131 A3
Saline di Volterra I 135 B3
Salins-les-Bains F 105 C4
Salir P 160 B1
Salisbury GB 44 B2
Salla A 110 B1
Salla FIN 197 C11
Sallachy GB 32 C2
Sallanches F 118 B3
Sallent E 147 C3
Sallent de Gállego E 145 B3
Salles F 128 B2
Salles-Curan F 130 A1
Salles-sur-l'Hers F 146 A2
Sallins IRL 30 A2
Sällsjö S 199 B10
Salmerón E 152 B1
Salmiech F 130 A1
Salmivaara FIN 197 C11
Salmoral E 150 B2
Salo FIN 8 B3
Salò I 121 B3
Salobreña E 163 B4
Salon-de-Provence F 131 B4
Salonica = Thessaloniki GR 182 C4
Salonta RO 16 B4
Salorino E 155 B3
Salornay-sur-Guye F 104 C3
Salorno I 121 A4
Salou E 147 C2
Šalovci SLO 111 C3
Salsbruket N 199 A8
Salses-le-Chateau F 146 B3
Salsomaggiore Terme I 120 C2
Salt E 147 C3
Saltaire GB 40 B2
Saltara I 136 B1
Saltash GB 42 B2
Saltburn-by-the-Sea GB 37 B6
Saltcoats GB 34 C3
Saltfleet GB 41 B4
Salto P 148 A2
Saltrød N 53 B4
Saltsjöbaden S 57 A4
Saltvik FIN 51 B7
Saltvik S 62 A4
Saludécio I 136 B1
Salussola I 119 B5
Saluzzo I 119 C4
Salvacañete E 152 B2
Salvada P 160 B2
Salvagnac F 129 C4
Salvaleon E 155 C4
Salvaterra de Magos P 154 B2
Salvaterra do Extremo P 155 B4
Salvatierra, Avila E 143 B4
Salvatierra, Badajoz E 155 C4
Salviac F 129 B4
Salz-hemmendorf D 72 B2
Salzburg A 109 B4
Salzgitter D 72 B3
Salzgitter Bad D 72 B3
Salzhausen D 72 A3
Salzkotten D 81 A4
Salzmünde D 83 A3
Salzwedel D 73 B4

Samassi I 179 C2
Samatan F 146 A1
Sambiase I 175 C2
Sambir UA 13 D5
Samborowo PL 69 B4
Sambuca di Sicília I 176 B2
Samedan CH 107 C4
Samer F 78 B1
Sami GR 184 A1
Şamlı TR 186 C2
Sammichele di Bari I 173 B2
Samnaun CH 107 C5
Samobor HR 123 B4
Samoëns F 118 A3
Samogneux F 92 B1
Samora Correia P 154 C2
Šamorín SK 111 A4
Samos E 141 B3
Samos GR 188 B1
Samoš SRB 126 B2
Samothraki GR 183 C7
Samper de Calanda E 153 A3
Sampéyre I 133 A3
Sampieri I 177 C3
Sampigny F 92 C1
Samplawa PL 69 B4
Samproniano I 168 A1
Samtens D 66 B2
Samugheo I 179 C2
San Adrián E 144 B2
San Agustín E 164 C2
San Agustin de Guadalix E 151 B4
San Alberto I 135 A5
San Amaro E 140 B2
San Andrês del Rabanedo E 142 B1
San Antanio di Santadi I 179 C2
San Antolín de Ibias E 141 A4
San Arcángelo I 174 A2
San Asensio E 143 B4
San Bartolomé de la Torre E 161 B2
San Bartolomé de las Abiertas E 150 C3
San Bartolomé de Pinares E 150 B3
San Bartolomeo in Galdo I 170 B3
San Benedetto del Tronto I 136 C2
San Benedetto in Alpe I 135 B4
San Benedetto Po I 121 B3
San Benito E 156 B3
San Benito de la Contienda E 155 C3
San Biágio Plátani I 176 B2
San Biágio Saracinisco I 169 B3
San Bonifacio I 121 B4
San Calixto E 156 C2
San Cándido I 109 C3
San Carlo CH 119 A5
San Carlo I 176 B2
San Carlos del Valle E 157 B4
San Casciano dei Bagni I 135 C4
San Casciano in Val di Pesa I 135 B4
San Cataldo, Puglia I 173 B4
San Cataldo, Sicilia I 176 B2
San Cebrián de Castro E 149 A4
San Cesário di Lecce I 173 B4
San Chírico Raparo I 174 A2
San Cibrao das Viñas E 140 B3
San Cipirello I 176 B2
San Ciprián E 141 A3
San Clemente E 158 B1
San Clodio E 141 B3
San Colombano al Lambro I 120 B2
San Costanzo I 136 B2
San Crisóbal de Entreviñas E 142 B1
San Cristóbal de la Polantera E 141 B5
San Cristóbal de la Vega E 150 A3
San Cristovo E 141 C3
San Damiano d'Asti I 119 C5
San Damiano Macra I 133 A3
San Daniele del Friuli I 122 A2
San Demétrio Corone I 174 B2
San Demétrio né Vestini I 169 A3
San Donà di Piave I 122 B1

Place	Country	Page	Grid
San Dónaci	I	173	B3
San Donato Val di Comino	I	169	B3
San Enrique	E	141	B5
San Esteban	E	141	A4
San Esteban de Gormaz	E	151	A4
San Esteban de la Sierra	E	149	B4
San Esteban de Litera	E	145	C4
San Esteban de Valdueza	E	141	B4
San Esteban del Molar	E	142	C1
San Esteban del Valle	E	150	B3
San Fele	I	172	B1
San Felice Circeo	I	169	B3
San Felice sul Panaro	I	121	C4
San Felices	E	143	B3
San Felices de los Gallégos	E	149	B3
San Ferdinando di Púglia	I	171	B4
San Fernando	E	162	B1
San Fernando de Henares	E	151	B4
San Fili	I	174	B2
San Foca	I	173	B4
San Fratello	I	177	B3
San Gavino Monreale	I	179	C2
San Gémini Fonte	I	168	A2
San Germano Vercellese	I	119	B5
San Giácomo, *Trentino Alto Adige*	I	108	C2
San Giácomo, *Umbria*	I	136	C1
San Gimignano	I	135	B4
San Ginésio	I	136	B2
San Giórgio a Liri	I	169	B3
San Giórgio del Sánnio	I	170	B2
San Giorgio della Richinvelda	I	122	A1
San Giórgio di Lomellina	I	120	B1
San Giórgio di Nogaro	I	122	B2
San Giorgio di Piano	I	121	C4
San Giorgio Iónico	I	173	B3
San Giovanni a Piro	I	172	B1
San Giovanni Bianco	I	120	B2
San Giovanni di Sinis	I	179	C2
San Giovanni in Croce	I	120	B3
San Giovanni in Fiore	I	174	B2
San Giovanni in Persiceto	I	121	C4
San Giovanni Reatino	I	169	A2
San Giovanni Rotondo	I	171	B3
San Giovanni Suérgiu	I	179	C2
San Giovanni Valdarno	I	135	B4
San Giuliano Terme	I	134	B3
San Giustino	I	135	B5
San Godenzo	I	135	B4
San Gregorio Magno	I	172	B1
San Giuseppe Jato	I	176	B2
San Javier	E	165	B4
San Jorge	P	154	B2
San José	E	164	C2
San Juan	E	143	B3
San Juan de Alicante	E	165	A4
San Juan de la Nava	E	150	B3
San Justo de la Vega	E	141	B4
San Lazzaro di Sávena	I	135	A4
San Leo	I	135	B5
San Leonardo de Yagüe	E	143	C3
San Leonardo in Passiria	I	108	C2
San Lorenzo a Merse	I	135	B4
San Lorenzo al Mare	I	133	B3
San Lorenzo Bellizzi	I	174	B2
San Lorenzo de Calatrava	E	157	A4
San Lorenzo de El Escorial	E	151	B3
San Lorenzo de la Parrilla	E	158	B1
San Lorenzo di Sebato	I	108	C2
San Lorenzo in Campo	I	136	B1
San Lorenzo Nuovo	I	168	A1
San Lourenco	P	160	A1
San Luca	I	175	C2
San Lúcido	I	174	B2
San Marcello	I	136	B2
San Marcello Pistoiese	I	135	A3
San Marcial	E	149	A4
San Marco	I	170	C2
San Marco Argentano	I	174	B2
San Marco dei Cavoti	I	170	B2
San Marco in Lámis	I	171	B3
San Marino	RSM	136	B1
San Martin de Castañeda	E	141	B4
San Martín de la Vega	E	151	B3
San Martin de la Vega del Alberche	E	150	B2
San Martin de Luiña	E	141	A4
San Martin de Montalbán	E	157	A3
San Martin de Oscos	E	141	A4
San Martin de Pusa	E	150	C3
San Martin de Unx	E	144	B2
San Martín de Valdeiglesias	E	150	B3
San Martín del Tesorillo	E	162	B2
San Martino di Campagna	I	122	A1
San Martino di Castrozza	I	121	A4
San-Martino-di-Lota	F	180	A2
San Martino in Pénsilis	I	170	B3
San Mateo de Gallego	E	144	C3
San Máuro Forte	I	172	B2
San Michele all'Adige	I	121	A4
San Michele di Ganzaria	I	177	B3
San Michele Mondovì	I	133	A3
San Miguel de Aguayo	E	142	A2
San Miguel de Bernuy	E	151	A4
San Miguel de Salinas	E	165	B4
San Miguel del Arroyo	E	150	A3
San Millán de la Cogolla	E	143	B4
San Miniato	I	135	B3
San Muñoz	E	149	B3
San Nicola del'Alto	I	174	B2
San Nicolás del Puerto	E	156	C2
San Nicolò	I	121	C4
San Nicolò Gerrei	I	179	C2
San Pablo de los Montes	E	157	A3
San Pancrázio Salentino	I	173	B3
San Pantaleo	I	178	A3
San Páolo di Civitate	I	171	B3
San Pawl il-Bahar	M	175	C3
San Pedro, *Albacete*	E	158	C1
San Pedro, *Oviedo*	E	141	A4
San Pedro de Alcántara	E	162	B3
San Pedro de Cadeira	P	154	B1
San Pedro de Ceque	E	141	B4
San Pedro de Latarce	E	142	C1
San Pedro de Merida	E	156	B1
San Pedro de Valderaduey	E	142	B2
San Pedro del Arroyo	E	150	B3
San Pedro del Pinatar	E	165	B4
San Pedro del Romeral	E	143	A3
San Pedro Manrique	E	144	B1
San Pellegrino Terme	I	120	B2
San Piero a Sieve	I	135	B4
San Piero in Bagno	I	135	B4
San Piero Patti	I	177	A3
San Pietro	I	177	B3
San Pietro in Casale	I	121	C4
San Pietro in Gu	I	121	B4
San Pietro in Palazzi	I	134	B3
San Pietro in Volta	I	122	B1
San Pietro Vara	I	134	A2
San Pietro Vernótico	I	173	B3
San Polo d'Enza	I	121	C3
San Quírico d'Órcia	I	135	B4
San Rafael del Rio	E	153	B4
San Remo	I	133	B3
San Román de Cameros	E	143	B4
San Roman de Hernija	E	150	A2
San Román de la Cuba	E	142	B2
San Roman de los Montes	E	150	B3
San Romao	P	155	C3
San Roque	E	162	B2
San Roque de Riomera	E	143	A3
San Rufo	I	172	B1
San Sabastián de los Ballesteros	E	162	A3
San Salvador de Cantamuda	E	142	B2
San Salvo	I	170	A2
San Salvo Marina	I	170	A2
San Sebastián de los Reyes	E	151	B4
San Sebastiano Curone	I	120	C2
San Secondo Parmense	I	120	C3
San Serverino Marche	I	136	B2
San Severino Lucano	I	174	A2
San Severo	I	171	B3
San Silvestre de Guzmán	E	161	B2
San Sosti	I	174	B2
San Stéfano di Cadore	I	109	C3
San Stino di Livenza	I	122	B1
San Telmo	E	161	B3
San Tirso de Abres	I	141	A3
San Valentino alla Muta	I	108	C1
San Venanzo	I	135	C5
San Vicente de Alcántara	E	155	B3
San Vicente de Arana	E	144	B1
San Vicente de la Barquera	E	142	A2
San Vicente de la Sonsierra	E	143	B4
San Vicente de Toranzo	E	143	A3
San Vietro	E	149	A3
San Vigilio	I	108	C2
San Vincente del Raspeig	E	165	A4
San Vincenzo	I	134	B3
San Vito	I	179	C3
San Vito al Tagliamento	I	122	B1
San Vito Chietino	I	169	A4
San Vito dei Normanni	I	173	B3
San Vito di Cadore	I	108	C3
San Vito lo Capo	I	176	A1
San Vito Romano	I	169	B2
Sanaigmore	GB	34	C1
Sânandrei	RO	126	B3
Sanary-sur-Mer	F	132	B1
Sancergues	F	104	B1
Sancerre	F	103	B4
Sancey-le-Long	F	105	B5
Sanchiorian	E	150	B3
Sanchonuño	E	151	A3
Sancoins	F	104	C1
Sancti-Petri	E	162	B1
Sancti-Spiritus	E	149	B3
Sand, *Hedmark*	N	48	B3
Sand, *Rogaland*	N	52	A2
Sanda	S	57	C4
Sandane	N	198	D3
Sandanski	BG	183	B5
Sandared	S	60	B2
Sandarne	S	51	A4
Sandau	D	73	B5
Sandbach	I	96	C1
Sandbach	GB	38	A4
Sandbank	GB	34	C3
Sandbanks	GB	43	B5
Sandbukt	N	192	C5
Sandby	DK	65	B4
Sande	D	71	A5
Sande, *Sogn og Fjordane*	N	46	A2
Sande, *Vestfold*	N	54	A1
Sandefjord	N	54	A1
Sandeid	N	52	A1
Sandersleben	D	82	A3
Sanderstølen	N	47	B6
Sandes	N	53	B3
Sandesneben	D	65	C3
Sandhead	GB	36	B2
Sandhem	S	60	B3
Sandhorst	D	71	A4
Sandhurst	GB	44	B3
Sandikli	TR	189	A5
Sandillon	F	103	B4
Sandl	A	96	C2
Sandnes	N	52	B1
Sandness	GB	33	A5
Sandnessjøen	N	195	D3
Sando	E	149	B3
Sandomierz	PL	87	B5
Sándorfalva	H	126	A3
Sandown	GB	44	C2
Sandøysund	N	54	A1
Sandrigo	I	121	B4
Sandsele	S	195	E8
Sandset	N	194	B5
Sandsjöfors	S	62	A2
Sandstad	N	198	B6
Sandvatn	N	52	B2
Sandvig-Allinge	DK	67	A3
Sandvika, *Akershus*	N	48	C2
Sandvika, *Hedmark*	N	48	B3
Sandvika, *Nord-Trøndelag*	N	199	B9
Sandviken	S	51	B3
Sandvikvåg	N	46	C2
Sandwich	GB	45	B5
Sandy	GB	44	A3
Sangatte	F	78	B1
Sangerhausen	D	82	A3
Sangineto Lido	I	174	B1
Sangis	S	196	D6
Sangonera la Verde	E	165	B3
Sangüesa	E	144	B2
Sanguinet	F	128	B1
Sanica	BIH	124	C2
Sanitz	D	65	B5
Sankt Aegyd am Neuwalde	A	110	B2
Sankt Andrä	A	110	C1
Sankt Andreasberg	D	82	A2
Sankt Anna	S	56	B2
Sankt Anna am Aigen	A	110	C2
Sankt Anton am Arlberg	A	107	B5
Sankt Anton an der Jessnitz	A	110	B2
Sankt Augustin	D	80	B3
Sankt Blasien	D	106	B3
Sankt Englmar	D	95	B4
Sankt Gallen	A	110	B1
Sankt Gallen	CH	107	B4
Sankt Gallenkirch	A	107	B4
Sankt Georgen	A	96	C2
Sankt Georgen	D	106	A3
Sankt Georgen am Reith	A	110	B1
Sankt Georgen ob Judenburg	A	110	B1
Sankt Georgen ob Murau	A	109	B5
Sankt Gilgen	A	109	B4
Sankt Goar	D	81	B3
Sankt Goarshausen	D	81	B3
Sankt Ingbert	D	92	B3
Sankt Jacob	A	109	C5
Sankt Jakob in Defereggen	A	109	C3
Sankt Johann am Tauern	A	110	B1
Sankt Johann am Wesen	A	109	A4
Sankt Johann im Pongau	A	109	B4
Sankt Johann in Tirol	A	109	B3
Sankt Katharein an der Laming	A	110	B2
Sankt Kathrein am Hauenstein	A	110	B2
Sankt Lambrecht	A	110	B1
Sankt Leonhard	A	110	B2
Sankt Leonhard im Pitztal	A	108	B1
Sankt Lorenzen	A	109	C3
Sankt Marein, *Steiermark*	A	110	B2
Sankt Marein, *Steiermark*	A	110	B2
Sankt Margarethen im Lavanttal	A	110	C1
Sankt Margrethen	CH	107	B4
Sankt Michael	A	110	B2
Sankt Michael im Burgenland	A	111	B3
Sankt Michael im Lungau	A	109	B4
Sankt Michaelisdonn	D	64	C2
Sankt Niklaus	CH	119	A4
Sankt Nikolai im Sölktal	A	109	B5
Sankt Olof	S	63	C2
Sankt Oswald	A	96	C1
Sankt Paul	A	110	C1
Sankt Paul	F	132	A2
Sankt Peter	A	106	A3
Sankt Peter am Kammersberg	A	110	B1
Sankt Peter-Ording	D	64	B1
Sankt-Peterburg = St. Petersburg	RUS	9	C7
Sankt Pölten	A	110	A2
Sankt Radegund	A	110	B2
Sankt Ruprecht an der Raab	A	110	B2
Sankt Salvator	A	110	C1
Sankt Stefan	A	110	C1
Sankt Stefan an der Gail	A	109	C4
Sankt Stefan im Rosental	A	110	C2
Sankt Valentin	A	110	A1
Sankt Veit an der Glan	A	110	C1
Sankt Veit an der Gölsen	A	110	A2
Sankt Veit in Defereggen	A	109	C3
Sankt Wendel	D	92	B3
Sankt Wolfgang	A	109	B4
Sankt Wolfgang	D	108	A3
Sanlúcar de Barrameda	E	161	C3
Sanlúcar de Guadiana	E	160	B2
Sanlúcar la Mayor	E	161	B3
Sanluri	I	179	C2
Sânmihaiu Roman	RO	126	B3
Sänna	S	55	B5
Sannazzaro de'Burgondi	I	120	B1
Sanne	D	73	B4
Sannicandro di Bari	I	171	B4
Sannicandro Gargánico	I	171	B3
Sânnicolau Mare	RO	126	A2
Sannidal	N	53	B5
Sanniki	PL	77	B4
Sanok	PL	12	D5
Sanquhar	GB	36	A3
Sansepolcro	I	135	B5
Sanski Most	BIH	124	C2
Sant Agustí de Lluçanès	E	147	B3
Sant Antoni Abat	E	166	C1
Sant Antoni de Calonge	E	147	C4
Sant Boi de Llobregat	E	147	C3
Sant Carles de la Ràpita	E	153	B4
Sant Carlos	E	166	B1
Sant Celoni	E	147	C3
Sant Climent	E	167	B4
Sant Feliu	E	147	C3
Sant Feliu de Codines	E	147	C3
Sant Feliu de Guíxols	E	147	C4
Sant Feliu Sasserra	E	147	C3
Sant Ferran	E	166	C1
Sant Francesc de Formentera	E	166	C1
Sant Francesc de ses Salines	E	166	C1
Sant Hilari Sacalm	E	147	C3
Sant Hipòlit de Voltregà	E	147	B3
Sant Jaume dels Domenys	E	147	C2
Sant Joan Baptista	E	166	B1
Sant Joan de les Abadesses	E	147	B3
Sant Jordi	E	153	B4
Sant Josep	E	166	C1
Sant Julià de Loria	AND	146	B2
Sant Llorenç de Morunys	E	147	B2
Sant Llorenç des Carctassar	E	167	B3
Sant Llorenç Savall	E	147	C3
Sant Luis	E	167	B4
Sant Martí de Llemaná	E	147	B3
Sant Martí de Maldá	E	147	C2
Sant Marti Sarroca	E	147	C2
Sant Mateu	E	153	B4
Sant Miquel	E	166	B1
Sant Pau de Seguries	E	147	B3
Sant Pere de Riudebitles	E	147	C2
Sant Pere Pescador	E	147	B4
Sant Pere Sallavinera	E	147	C2
Sant Quirze de Besora	E	147	B3
Sant Rafel	E	166	C1
Sant Ramon	E	147	C2
Sant Vincenç de Castellet	E	147	C2
Santa Agnès	E	166	B1
Santa Amalia	E	156	A1
Santa Ana, *Cáceres*	E	156	A2
Santa Ana, *Jaén*	E	163	A4
Santa Ana de Pusa	E	150	C3
Santa Barbara	E	153	B4
Santa Bárbara	P	160	B2
Santa Barbara de Casa	E	161	B2
Santa Bárbara de Padrões	P	160	B2
Santa Caterina di Pittinuri	I	178	B2
Santa Caterina Villarmosa	I	177	B3
Santa Cesárea Terme	I	173	B4
Santa Clara-a-Nova	P	160	B1
Santa Clara-a-Velha	P	160	B1
Santa Clara de Louredo	P	160	B2
Santa Coloma de Farners	E	147	C3
Santa Coloma de Gramenet	E	147	C3
Santa Coloma de Queralt	E	147	C2
Santa Colomba de Curueño	E	142	B1
Santa Colomba de Somoza	E	141	B4
Santa Comba	E	140	A2
Santa Comba Dáo	P	148	B1
Santa Comba de Rossas	P	149	A3
Santa Cristina	I	120	B2
Santa Cristina de la Polvorosa	E	141	B5
Santa Croce Camerina	I	177	C3
Santa Croce di Magliano	I	170	B2
Santa Cruz	E	140	A2
Santa Cruz	P	154	B1
Santa Cruz de Alhama	E	163	A4
Santa Cruz de Campezo	E	143	B4
Santa Cruz de Grio	E	152	A2
Santa Cruz de la Salceda	E	151	A4
Santa Cruz de la Sierra	E	156	A2
Santa Cruz de la Zarza	E	151	C4
Santa Cruz de Moya	E	159	B2
Santa Cruz de Mudela	E	157	B4
Santa Cruz de Paniagua	E	149	B3
Santa Cruz del Retamar	E	151	B3
Santa Cruz del Valle	E	150	B2
Santa Doménica Talao	I	174	B1
Santa Doménica Vittória	I	177	B3
Santa Elena	E	157	B4
Santa Elena de Jamuz	E	141	B5
Santa Eufemia	E	156	B3
Santa Eufémia d'Aspromonte	I	175	C1
Santa Eulalia	E	152	B2
Santa Eulália	P	155	C3
Santa Eulalia de Oscos	E	141	A3
Santa Eulália des Riu	E	166	C1
Santa Fe	E	163	A4
Santa Fiora	I	135	C4
Santa Gertrude	I	108	C1
Santa Giustina	I	121	A5
Santa Iria	P	160	B2
Santa Leocadia	P	148	A1
Santa Lucia-de-Porto-Vecchio	F	180	B2
Santa Lucia del Mela	I	177	A4
Santa Luzia	P	160	B1

Name		Page	Grid
Santa Maddalena Vallalta	I	108	C3
Santa Magdalena de Polpis	E	153	B4
Santa Margalida	E	167	B3
Santa Margarida	P	154	B2
Santa Margarida do Sado	P	160	A1
Santa Margaridao de Montbui	E	147	C2
Santa Margherita	I	179	D2
Santa Margherita di Belice	I	176	B2
Santa Margherita Ligure	I	134	A2
Santa Maria	CH	108	C1
Santa Maria	E	144	B3
Santa Maria al Bagno	I	173	B3
Santa Maria Cápua Vétere	I	170	B2
Santa Maria da Feira	P	148	B1
Santa Maria de Cayón	E	143	A3
Santa Maria de Corco	E	147	B3
Santa Maria de Huerta	E	152	A1
Santa Maria de la Alameda	E	151	B3
Santa Maria de las Hoyas	E	143	C3
Santa Maria de Mercadillo	E	143	C3
Santa Maria de Nieva	E	164	B3
Santa Maria de Trassierra	E	156	C3
Santa Maria del Camí	E	167	B2
Santa Maria del Campo	E	143	B3
Santa Maria del Campo Rus	E	158	B1
Santa Maria del Páramo	E	142	B1
Santa Maria del Taro	I	134	A2
Santa Maria della Versa	I	120	C2
Santa Maria di Licodia	I	177	B3
Santa Maria-di-Rispéscia	I	168	A1
Santa Maria la Palma	I	178	B2
Santa María la Real de Nieva	E	150	A3
Santa Maria Maggiore	I	119	A5
Santa Maria Ribarredonda	E	143	B3
Santa Marina del Rey	E	141	B5
Santa Marinella	I	168	A1
Santa Marta, Albacete	E	158	B1
Santa Marta, Badajoz	E	155	C4
Santa Marta de Magasca	E	156	A1
Santa Marta de Penaguião	P	148	A2
Santa Marta de Tormes	E	150	B2
Santa Ninfa	I	176	B1
Santa Olalla, Huelva	E	161	B3
Santa Olalla, Toledo	E	150	B3
Santa Pau	E	147	B3
Santa Pola	E	165	A4
Santa Ponça	E	166	B2
Santa Severa	I	180	A2
Santa Severa	F	168	A1
Santa Severina	I	175	B2
Santa Sofia	I	135	B4
Santa Suzana, Évora	P	155	C3
Santa Suzana, Setúbal	P	154	C2
Santa Teresa di Riva	I	177	B4
Santa Teresa Gallura	I	178	A3
Santa Uxía	E	140	B2
Santa Valburga	I	108	C1
Santa Vittória in Matenano	I	136	B2
Santacara	E	144	B2
Santadi	I	179	C3
Santaella	E	162	A3
Sant'Ágata dei Goti	I	170	B2
Sant'Ágata di Ésaro	I	174	B1
Sant'Ágata di Puglia	I	171	B3
Sant'Ágata Feltria	I	135	B5
Sant'Ágata Militello	I	177	A3
Santana, Évora	P	154	C2
Santana, Setúbal	P	154	C1
Sântana	RO	126	A3
Santana da Serra	P	160	B1
Sant'Ana de Cambas	P	160	B2
Santana do Mato	P	154	C2
Sant'Anastasia	I	170	C2
Santander	E	143	A3
Sant'Andrea Fríus	I	179	C3
Sant'Ángelo dei Lombardi	I	172	B1
Sant'Angelo in Vado	I	136	B1
Sant'Angelo Lodigiano	I	120	B2
Sant'Antíoco	I	179	C2
Sant'Antonio-di-Gallura	I	178	B3
Santanyí	E	167	B3
Santarcángelo di Romagna	I	136	A1
Santarém	P	154	B2
Santas Martas	E	142	B1
Sant'Caterina	I	135	C4
Santed	E	152	A2
Sant'Egídio alla Vibrata	I	136	C2
Sant'Elia a Pianisi	I	170	B2
Sant'Elia Fiumerapido	I	169	B3
Santelices	E	143	A3
Sant'Elpídio a Mare	I	136	B2
Santéramo in Colle	I	171	C4
Santervas de la Vega	E	142	B2
Santhià	I	119	B5
Santiago de Alcántara	E	155	B3
Santiago de Calatrava	E	163	A3
Santiago de Compostela	E	140	B2
Santiago de la Espade	E	164	A2
Santiago de la Puebla	E	150	B2
Santiago de la Ribera	E	165	B4
Santiago de Litem	P	154	B2
Santiago del Campo	E	155	B4
Santiago do Cacém	P	160	B1
Santiago do Escoural	P	154	C2
Santiago Maior	P	155	C3
Santibáñez de Béjar	E	150	B2
Santibáñez de la Peña	E	142	B2
Santibáñez de Murias	E	142	A1
Santibáñez de Vidriales	E	141	B4
Santibáñez el Alto	E	149	B3
Santibáñez el Bajo	E	149	B3
Santillana	E	142	A2
Santiponce	E	162	A1
Santisteban del Puerto	E	157	B4
Santiuste de San Juan Bautiste	E	150	A3
Santiz	E	149	A4
Sant'llario d'Enza	I	121	C3
Santo Aleixo	P	161	A3
Santo Amado	P	161	A2
Santo Amaro	P	155	C3
Santo André	P	160	A1
Santo Domingo	E	155	C3
Santo Domingo de la Calzada	E	143	B4
Santo Domingo de Silos	E	143	C3
Santo Estêvão, Faro	P	160	B2
Santo Estêvão, Santarém	P	154	C2
Santo-Pietro-di-Tenda	F	180	A2
Santo Spirito	I	171	B4
Santo Stefano d'Aveto	I	134	A2
Santo Stéfano di Camastra	I	177	A3
Santo Stefano di Magra	I	134	A2
Santo Stéfano Quisquina	I	176	B2
Santo Tirso	P	148	A1
Santo Tomé	E	164	A1
Santok	PL	75	B4
Santomera	E	165	A3
Santoña	E	143	A3
Sant'Oreste	I	168	A2
Santotis	E	142	A2
Santovenia, Burgos	E	143	B3
Santovenia, Zamora	E	142	C1
Santpedor	E	147	C2
Santu Lussurgiu	I	178	B2
Santutzi	E	143	A3
Sanxenxo	E	140	B2
Sanza	I	172	B1
São Aleixo	P	155	C3
São Barnabé	P	160	B1
São Bartolomé da Serra	P	160	A1
São Bartolomeu de Messines	P	160	B1
São Bento	P	140	C2
São Brás	P	160	B2
São Brás de Alportel	P .	160	B2
São Braz do Reguedoura	P	154	C2
São Cristóvão	P	154	C2
São Domingos	P	160	B1
São Geraldo	P	154	C2
São Jacinto	P	148	B1
São João da Madeira	P	148	B1
São João da Pesqueira	P	148	A2
São João da Ribeira	P	154	B2
São João da Serra	P	148	B1
São João da Venda	P	160	B2
São João dos Caldeireiros	P	160	B2
São Julião	P	155	B3
São Leonardo	P	155	C3
São Luis	P	160	B1
São Manços	P	155	C3
São Marcos da Ataboeira	P	160	B2
Saõ Marcos da Serra	P	160	B1
São Marcos de Campo	P	155	C3
São Martinho da Cortiça	P	148	B1
São Martinho das Amoreiras	P	160	B1
São Martinho do Porto	P	154	B1
São Matias, Beja	P	160	A2
São Matias, Évora	P	154	C2
São Miguel d'Acha	P	155	A3
São Miguel de Machede	P	155	C3
São Pedro da Torre	P	140	C2
São Pedro de Muel	P	154	B1
São Pedro de Solis	P	160	B2
São Pedro do Sul	P	148	B1
São Romão	P	154	C2
São Sebastião dos Carros	P	160	B2
São Teotónio	P	160	B1
São Torcato	P	148	A1
Saorge	F	133	B3
Sapataria	P	154	C1
Sapes	GR	183	B7
Sapiãos	P	148	A2
Sappada	I	109	C3
Sappen	N	192	C5
Sapri	I	174	A1
Sarajärvi	FIN	197	D10
Sarajevo	BIH	139	B4
Saramon	F	129	C3
Sarandë	AL	182	D2
Saranovo	SRB	127	C3
Saraorci	SRB	127	C3
Saray	TR	186	A2
Saraycık	TR	187	C4
Sarayköy	TR	188	B3
Saraylar	TR	186	B2
Sarayönü	TR	189	A7
Sarbia	PL	75	B5
Sarbinowo, Zachodnio-Pomorskie	PL	67	B4
Sarbinowo, Zachodnio-Pomorskie	PL	74	B3
Sárbogárd	H	112	C2
Sarcelles	F	90	B2
Sarche	I	121	A3
Sardara	I	179	C2
Sardón de Duero	E	150	A3
Sare	F	144	A2
S'Arenal	E	166	B2
Šarengrad	HR	125	B5
Sarentino	I	108	C2
Sarezzo	I	120	B3
Sargans	CH	107	B4
Sári	H	112	B3
Sari-d'Orcino	F	180	A1
Saribeyler	TR	186	C2
Sarıcakaya	TR	187	B5
Sarıgöl	TR	188	A3
Sarıkaya	TR	23	B8
Sarıköy	TR	186	B2
Sarilhos Grandes	P	154	C2
Sariñena	E	145	C3
Sárioba	TR	187	C7
Sárisáp	H	112	B2
Sariyer	TR	186	A4
Sarkad	H	113	C5
Sárkeresztes	H	112	B2
Sárkeresztúr	H	112	B2
Sarkijärvi	FIN	196	B6
Şarkikaraağaç	TR	189	A6
Şarköy	TR	186	B2
Sarlat-la-Canéda	F	129	B4
Sarliac-sur-l'Isle	F	129	A3
Sármellék	H	111	C4
Särna	S	199	D10
Sarnadas	P	155	B3
Sarnano	I	136	B2
Sarnen	CH	106	C3
Sarnesfield	GB	39	B4
Sárnico	I	120	B2
Sarno	I	170	C2
Sarnonico	I	121	A4
Sarnow	D	74	A2
Sarny	UA	13	C7
Särö	S	60	B1
Saronno	I	120	B2
Sárosd	H	112	B2
Šarovce	SK	112	A2
Sarpoil	F	117	B3
Sarpsborg	N	54	A2
Sarracín	E	143	B3
Sarral	E	147	C2
Sarralbe	F	92	B3
Sarrancolin	F	145	B4
Sarras	F	117	B4
Sarre	F	119	B4
Sarre-Union	F	92	C3
Sarreaus	E	140	B3
Sarrebourg	F	92	C3
Sarreguemines	F	92	B3
Sárrétudvari	H	113	B5
Sarria	E	141	B3
Sarrià de Ter	E	147	B3
Sarrión	E	153	B3
Sarroca de Lleida	E	153	A4
Sarroch	I	179	C3
Sarron	F	128	C2
Sársina	I	135	B5
Sarstedt	D	72	B2
Sárszentlörinc	H	112	C2
Sárszentmihaly	H	112	B2
Sárszentmiklós	H	112	C2
Sarteano	I	135	C4
Sartène	F	180	B1
Sartilly	F	88	B2
Sartirana Lomellina	I	120	B1
Saruhanlı	TR	186	D2
Sárvár	H	111	B3
Sarvisvaara	S	196	C4
Sarzana	I	134	A2
Sarzeau	F	101	B3
Sarzedas	P	155	B3
Sas van Gent	NL	79	A3
Sasalli	TR	188	A1
Sasamón	E	142	B2
Sásd	H	125	A4
Sasino	PL	68	A2
Sássari	I	178	B2
Sassello	I	133	A4
Sassenberg	D	71	C5
Sassetta	I	134	B3
Sassnitz	D	66	B2
Sasso d'Ombrone	I	135	C4
Sasso Marconi	I	135	A4
Sassocorvaro	I	136	B1
Sassoferrato	I	136	B1
Sassoleone	I	135	A4
Sassuolo	I	135	A3
Sástago	E	153	A3
Šaštinske Stráže	SK	98	C1
Sátåhaugen	N	199	C7
Satão	P	148	B2
Såtenäs	S	55	B3
Säter	S	50	B2
Sätila	S	60	B2
Satillieu	F	117	B4
Satnica Đakovačka	HR	125	B4
Sátoraljaújhely	H	16	A4
Satow	D	65	C4
Sätra-brunn	S	50	C3
Satrup	D	64	B2
Satteins	A	107	B4
Satu Mare	RO	17	B5
Saturnia	I	168	A1
Saucelle	E	149	A3
Sauda	N	52	A2
Saudasjøen	N	52	A2
Sauðárkrókur	IS	190	B6
Sauerlach	D	108	B2
Saugues	F	117	C3
Sauherad	N	53	A5
Saujon	F	114	C3
Sauland	N	53	A4
Saulces Monclin	F	91	B4
Saulgau	D	107	A4
Saulgrub	D	108	B2
Saulieu	F	104	B3
Saulnot	F	106	B1
Sault	F	131	A4
Sault-Brénaz	F	118	B2
Sault-de-Navailles	F	128	C2
Saulx	F	105	B5
Saulxures-sur-Moselotte	F	106	B1
Saulzais-le-Potier	F	103	C4
Saumos	F	128	B1
Saumur	F	102	B1
Saunavaara	FIN	197	B10
Saundersfoot	GB	39	C2
Saurat	F	146	B2
Saurbær, Borgarfjarðarsýsla	IS	190	C4
Saurbær, Dalasýsla	IS	190	B4
Saurbær, Eyjafjarðarsýsla	IS	191	B7
Sáuris	I	109	C3
Sausset-les-Pins	F	131	B4
Sauteyrargues	F	131	B2
Sauvagnat	F	116	B2
Sauve	F	131	B2
Sauveterre-de-Béarn	F	144	A3
Sauveterre-de-Guyenne	F	128	B2
Sauviat-sur-Vige	F	116	B1
Sauxillanges	F	117	B3
Sauzé-Vaussais	F	115	B4
Sauzet, Drôme	F	117	C4
Sauzet, Lot	F	129	B4
Sauzon	F	100	B2
Sava	I	173	B3
Sävar	S	200	C6
Savarsin	RO	16	B5
Sävast	S	196	D4
Savaştepe	TR	186	C2
Savci	SLO	111	C3
Säve	S	60	B1
Savelletri	I	173	B3
Savelli	I	174	B2
Savenay	F	101	B4
Saverdun	F.	146	A2
Saverne	F	93	C3
Saviñán	E	152	A2
Savières	F	91	C3
Savigliano	I	119	C4
Savignac-les-Eglises	F	129	A3
Savignano Irpino	I	171	B3
Savignano sul Rubicone	I	136	A1
Savigny-sur-Braye	F	102	B2
Savines-le-lac	F	132	A2
Savino Selo	SRB	126	B1
Savio	I	135	A5
Savognin	CH	107	C4
Savona	I	133	A4
Savonlinna	FIN	9	B6
Savournon	F	132	A1
Sävsjö	S	62	A2
Savsjön	S	50	C1
Sävsjöström	S	62	A3
Savudrija	HR	122	B2
Savukoski	FIN	197	B11
Sawbridgeworth	GB	45	B4
Sawtry	GB	44	A3
Sax	E	159	C3
Saxdalen	S	50	B1
Saxilby	GB	40	B3
Saxmundham	GB	45	A5
Saxnäs	S	195	F6
Saxthorpe	GB	41	C5
Sayalonga	E	163	B3
Sayatón	E	151	B5
Sayda	D	83	B5
Schalkau	D	82	B3
Schangnau	CH	106	C2
Schapbach	D	93	C4
Scharbeutz	D	65	B3
Schärding	A	96	C1
Scharnitz	A	108	B2
Scharrel	D	71	A4
Schattendorf	A	111	B3
Scheemda	NL	71	A3
Scheessel	D	72	A2
Schéggia	I	136	B1
Scheibbs	A	110	A2
Scheibenberg	D	83	B4
Scheidegg	D	107	B4
Scheifling	A	110	B1
Scheinfeld	D	94	B2
Schelklingen	D	94	C1
Schenefeld, Schleswig-Holstein	D	64	B2
Schenefeld, Schleswig-Holstein	D	72	A2
Schenklengsfeld	D	82	B1
Scherfede	D	81	A5
Schermbeck	D	80	A2
Scherpenzeel	NL	70	B2
Schesslitz	D	94	B3
Scheveningen	NL	70	B1
Schiedam	NL	79	A4
Schieder-Schwalenberg	D	72	C2
Schierling	D	95	C4
Schiers	CH	107	C4
Schildau	D	83	A4
Schillingen	D	92	B2
Schillingsfürst	D	94	B2
Schilpário	I	120	A3
Schiltach	D	93	C4
Schiltigheim	F	93	C3
Schio	I	121	B4
Schirmeck	F	92	C3
Schirnding	D	83	B4
Schkeuditz	D	83	A4
Schkölen	D	83	A3
Schladen	D	73	B3
Schladming	A	109	B4
Schlangen	D	81	A4
Schleiden	D	80	B2
Schleiz	D	83	B3
Schleswig	D	64	B2
Schleusingen	D	82	B2
Schlieben	D	83	A5
Schliengen	D	106	B2
Schliersee	D	108	B2
Schlitz	D	81	B5
Schloss Neuhans	D	81	A4
Schlossvippach	D	82	A3
Schlotheim	D	82	A2
Schluchsee	D	106	B3
Schlüchtern	D	81	B5
Schmallenberg	D	81	A4
Schmelz	D	92	B2
Schmidmühlen	D	95	B3
Schmiedeberg	D	84	B1
Schmiedefeld	D	82	B2
Schmirn	A	108	B2
Schmölln, Brandenburg	D	74	A3
Schmölln, Sachsen	D	83	B4
Schnaittach	D	95	B3
Schneeberg	D	83	B4
Schneizlreuth	D	109	B3
Schneverdingen	D	72	A2
Schöder	A	109	B5
Schoenburg	D	80	B2
Schollene	D	73	B5
Schöllkrippen	D	81	B5
Schomberg	D	107	A3
Schönach	D	95	C4
Schönau, Baden-Württemberg	D	106	B2
Schönau, Bayern	D	95	C4
Schönbeck	D	74	A2
Schönberg, Bayern	D	96	C1
Schönberg, Mecklenburg-Vorpommern	D	65	C3
Schönberg, Schleswig-Holstein	D	65	B3
Schönebeck	D	73	B4
Schöneck	D	83	B4
Schönecken-	D	80	B2
Schönermark	D	74	A2
Schönewalde	D	83	A5
Schongau	D	108	B1
Schöngrabern	A	97	C4
Schönhagen	D	81	A5
Schönhausen	D	73	B5
Schöningen	D	73	B3
Schönkirchen	D	64	B3
Schönsee	D	95	B4
Schöntal	D	94	B1
Schönthal	D	95	B4
Schönwalde	D	65	B3
Schoondijke	NL	79	A3
Schoonebeek	NL	71	B3
Schoonhoven	NL	79	A4
Schopfheim	D	106	B2
Schöppenstedt	D	73	B3

Name		Page	Grid
Schörfling	A	109	B4
Schorndorf	D	94	C1
Schortens	D	71	A4
Schotten	D	81	B5
Schramberg	D	106	A3
Schraplau	D	83	A3
Schrattenberg	A	97	C4
Schrecksbach	D	81	B5
Schrems	A	96	C3
Schrobenhausen	D	95	C3
Schröcken	A	107	B5
Schrozberg	D	94	B1
Schruns	A	107	B4
Schüpfheim	CH	106	C3
Schüttorf	D	71	B4
Schwaan	D	65	C5
Schwabach	D	94	B3
Schwäbisch Gmünd	D	94	C1
Schwäbisch Hall	D	94	B1
Schwabmünchen	D	108	A1
Schwadorf	A	111	A3
Schwagstorf	D	71	B4
Schwaigern	D	93	B5
Schwalmstadt	D	81	B5
Schwanberg	A	110	C2
Schwanden	CH	107	C4
Schwandorf	D	95	B4
Schwanebeck	D	73	C4
Schwanenstadt	A	109	A4
Schwanewede	D	72	A1
Schwanfeld	D	94	B2
Schwangau	D	108	B1
Schwarmstedt	D	72	B2
Schwarz-heide	D	84	A1
Schwarza	D	82	B2
Schwarzach im Pongau	A	109	B4
Schwarzau im Gebirge	A	110	B2
Schwarzenau	A	97	C3
Schwarzenbach	D	83	B3
Schwarzenbach am Wald	D	83	B3
Schwarzenberg	D	83	B4
Schwarzenburg	CH	106	C2
Schwarzenfeld	D	95	B4
Schwaz	A	108	B2
Schwechat	A	111	A3
Schwedt	D	74	A3
Schwei	D	71	A5
Schweich	D	92	B2
Schweighausen	D	106	A2
Schweinfurt	D	94	A2
Schweinitz	D	83	A5
Schweinrich	D	74	A1
Schwelm	D	80	A3
Schwemsal	D	83	A4
Schwendt	A	109	B3
Schwenningen	D	107	A3
Schwepnitz	D	84	A1
Schwerin	D	73	A4
Schwerte	D	81	A3
Schweskau	D	73	B4
Schwetzingen	D	93	B4
Schwyz	CH	107	B3
Sciacca	I	176	B2
Scicli	I	177	C3
Ściechów	PL	75	B3
Scigliano	I	175	B2
Scilla	I	175	C1
Ścinawa	PL	85	A4
Scionzier	F	118	A3
Scoglitti	I	177	C3
Scole	GB	45	A5
Sconser	GB	31	B2
Scopello, *Piemonte*	I	119	B5
Scopello, *Sicilia*	I	176	A1
Scordia	I	177	B3
Scorzè	I	121	B5
Scotch Corner	GB	37	B5
Scotter	GB	40	B3
Scourie	GB	32	C1
Scousburgh	GB	33	B5
Scrabster	GB	32	C3
Screeb	IRL	28	A2
Scremerston	GB	37	A5
Scritto	I	136	B1
Scunthorpe	GB	40	B3
Scuol	CH	107	C5
Scúrcola Marsicana	I	169	A3
Seaford	GB	45	C4
Seaham	GB	37	B5
Seahouses	GB	37	A5
Seascale	GB	36	B3
Seaton	GB	43	B4
Sebazac-Concourès	F	130	A1
Seben	TR	187	B6
Sebersdorf	A	110	B2
Sebezh	RUS	8	D6
Sebnitz	D	84	B2
Seborga	I	133	B3
Seby	S	63	B4
Seč, *Východočeský*	CZ	97	B3
Seč, *Západočeský*	CZ	96	B1
Sečanj	SRB	126	B2
Secemin	PL	87	B3
Séchault	F	91	B4
Seckau	A	110	B1
Seclin	F	78	B3
Secondigny	F	114	B3
Seda	P	155	B3
Sedan	F	91	B4
Sedano	E	143	B3
Sedbergh	GB	37	B4
Sedella	E	163	B3
Séderon	F	131	A4
Sedgefield	GB	37	B5
Sedico	I	121	A5
Sédilo	I	178	B2
Sédini	I	178	B2
Sedlarica	HR	124	B3
Sedlčany	CZ	96	B2
Sedlec-Prčice	CZ	96	B2
Sedlice	CZ	96	B1
Sędziejowice	PL	86	A3
Sędziszów	PL	87	B4
Sędziszów Małopolski	PL	87	B5
Seebach	F	93	C3
Seeboden	A	109	C4
Seefeld, *Brandenburg*	D	74	B2
Seefeld, *Niedersachsen*	D	71	A5
Seefeld in Tirol	A	108	B2
Seeg	D	108	B1
Seehausen, *Sachsen-Anhalt*	D	73	B4
Seehausen, *Sachsen-Anhalt*	D	73	B4
Seeheim-Jugenheim	D	93	B4
Seelbach	D	93	C3
Seelow	D	74	B3
Seelze	D	72	B2
Seerhausen	D	83	A5
Sées	F	89	B4
Seesen	D	82	A2
Seeshaupt	D	108	B2
Seewalchen	A	109	B4
Seferihisar	TR	188	A1
Sefkerin	SRB	127	B2
Segård	N	48	B2
Segerstad	S	55	A4
Seglinge	FIN	51	B7
Segmon	S	55	A4
Segonzac	F	115	C3
Segorbe	E	159	B3
Segovia	E	151	B3
Segré	F	101	B5
Ségur-les-Villas	F	116	B2
Segura	E	144	B1
Segura	E	155	B3
Segura de León	E	161	A3
Segura de los Baños	E	152	B3
Segurrilla	E	150	B3
Sehnde	D	72	B2
Seia	P	148	B2
Seiches-sur-le-Loir	F	102	B1
Seifhennersdorf	D	84	B2
Seignelay	F	104	B2
Seijo	E	140	C2
Seilhac	F	116	B1
Seilles	B	79	B5
Seim	N	46	B2
Seinäjoki	FIN	8	A3
Seissan	F	145	A4
Seitenstetten Markt	A	110	A1
Seixal	P	154	C1
Seiz	A	110	B1
Seizthal	A	110	B1
Sejerslev	DK	58	B1
Seksna	RUS	9	C11
Selárdalur	IS	190	A1
Selárgius	I	179	C3
Selb	D	83	B4
Selby	GB	40	B2
Selca	HR	138	B2
Selce	HR	123	B3
Selçuk	TR	188	B2
Selde	DK	58	B2
Selenča	SRB	126	B1
Selendi, *Manisa*	TR	186	D3
Selendi, *Manisa*	TR	186	D2
Selenicë	AL	182	C1
Sélestat	F	106	A2
Seleuš	SRB	126	B2
Selevac	SRB	127	C2
Selfoss	IS	190	D5
Selgua	E	145	B4
Selice	SK	112	A1
Seligenstadt	D	93	A4
Seligenthal	D	82	B2
Selimiye	TR	188	B2
Selizharovo	RUS	9	D8
Selja	N	198	D3
Seljelvnes	N	192	C3
Seljord	N	53	A4
Selkirk	GB	35	C5
Sellano	I	136	C1
Selles-St. Denis	F	103	B3
Selles-sur-Cher	F	103	B3
Sellières	F	105	C4
Sellin	D	66	B2
Sellye	H	125	B3
Selm	D	80	A3
Selnica ob Dravi	SLO	110	C2
Selongey	F	105	B4
Selonnet	F	132	A2
Selow	D	65	C4
Selsey	GB	44	C3
Selsingen	D	72	A2
Selters	D	81	B3
Seltz	F	93	C4
Selva	E	167	B3
Selva di Cadore	I	108	C3
Selva di Val Gardena	I	108	C2
Selvik, *Sogn og Fjordane*	N	46	A2
Selvik, *Vestfold*	N	54	A1
Selvino	I	120	B2
Selyatyn	UA	17	B6
Sem	N	54	A1
Semeljci	HR	125	B4
Semič	SLO	123	B4
Semide	F	91	B4
Semide	P	148	B1
Semily	CZ	84	B3
Seminara	I	175	C1
Semlac	RO	126	A2
Semlacu Mare	RO	126	B3
Semmen-stedt	D	73	B3
Šempeter	SLO	123	A4
Semriach	A	110	B2
Semur-en-Auxois	F	104	B3
Sena	E	145	C3
Sena de Luna	E	141	B5
Senarpont	F	90	B1
Sénas	F	131	B4
Senćanski Trešnjevac	SRB	126	B1
Sencelles	E	167	B3
Senčur	SLO	123	A3
Senden, *Bayern*	D	94	C2
Senden, *Nordrhein-Westfalen*	D	80	A3
Sendenhorst	D	81	A3
Sendim	P	149	A3
Senec	SK	111	A4
Seneffe	B	79	B4
Séneghe	I	178	B2
Senés	E	164	B2
Senez	F	132	B2
Senftenberg	D	84	A1
Sengouagnet	F	145	B4
Sengwarden	D	71	A5
Senica	SK	98	C1
Senice na Hané	CZ	98	B1
Senigállia	I	136	B2
Senirkent	TR	189	A5
Sénis	I	179	C2
Senise	I	174	A2
Senj	HR	123	C3
Senje	SRB	127	D3
Senjehopen	N	194	A8
Senjski Rudnik	SRB	127	D3
Senlis	F	90	B2
Sennan	S	60	C2
Sennecey-le-Grand	F	105	C3
Sennen	GB	42	B1
Senno	BY	13	A8
Sénnori	I	178	B2
Sennwald	CH	107	B4
Sennybridge	GB	39	C3
Senohrad	SK	99	C3
Senonches	F	89	B5
Senones	F	92	C2
Senorbì	I	179	C3
Senovo	SLO	123	A4
Senožeče	SLO	123	B3
Senožeti	SLO	123	A3
Sens	F	104	A2
Sens-de-Bretagne	F	101	A4
Senta	SRB	126	B2
Senterada	E	145	B4
Šentilj	SLO	110	C2
Šentjernej	SLO	123	B4
Šentjur	SLO	123	A4
Senumstad	N	53	B4
Seoane	E	141	B3
Seon	CH	106	B3
Sépeaux	F	104	B2
Sépey	CH	119	A4
Sepino	I	170	B2
Sępólno Krajeńskie	PL	76	A2
Seppenrade	D	80	A3
Seppois	F	106	B2
Septemvri	BG	183	A6
Septeuil	F	90	C1
Sepúlveda	E	151	A4
Sequals	I	122	A1
Sequeros	E	149	B3
Seraincourt	F	91	B4
Seraing	B	80	B1
Seravezza	I	134	B3
Sered'	SK	98	C1
Sereda	RUS	9	C6
Şereflikoçhisar	TR	23	B7
Seregélyes	H	112	B2
Seregno	I	120	B2
Sérent	F	101	B3
Serfaus	A	108	B1
Sergiyev Posad	RUS	9	D11
Seriate	I	120	B2
Sérifontaine	F	90	B1
Sérifos	GR	185	B5
Sérignan	F	130	B2
Serik	TR	189	C6
Serina	I	120	B2
Serinhisar	TR	188	B4
Sermaises	F	90	C2
Sermaize-les-Bains	F	91	C4
Sérmide	I	121	C4
Sermoneta	I	169	B2
Sernache de Bonjardim	P	154	B2
Sernancelhe	P	148	B2
Serock	PL	77	B6
Serón	E	164	B2
Serón de Najima	E	152	A1
Serooskerke	NL	79	A3
Seròs	E	153	A4
Serpa	P	160	B2
Serra de Outes	E	140	B2
Serra San Bruno	I	175	C2
Serra San Quírico	I	136	B2
Serracapriola	I	171	B3
Serrada	I	150	A3
Serradifalco	I	176	B2
Serradilla	E	155	B4
Serradilla del Arroyo	E	149	B3
Serradilla del Llano	E	149	B3
Serramanna	I	179	C2
Serramazzoni	I	135	A3
Serranillos	E	150	B3
Serrapetrona	I	136	B2
Serrastretta	I	175	B2
Serravalle, *Piemonte*	I	119	B5
Serravalle, *Umbria*	I	136	C2
Serravalle di Chienti	I	136	B1
Serravalle Scrívia	I	120	C1
Serre	I	172	B1
Serrejón	E	150	C2
Serres	F	132	A1
Serres	GR	183	B5
Serrières	F	117	B4
Serrières-de-Briord	F	118	B2
Sersale	I	175	B2
Sertã	P	154	B2
Sertig Dörfli	CH	107	C4
Servance	F	106	B1
Serverette	F	117	C3
Servia	GR	182	C4
Servian	F	130	B2
Serviers	F	131	A3
Servigliano	I	136	B2
Ses Salines	E	167	B3
Seseña Nuevo	E	151	B4
Sesimbra	P	154	C1
Seskarö	S	196	D6
Seskinore	GB	27	B3
Sesma	E	144	B1
Sessa Aurunca	I	170	B1
Sesta Godano	I	134	A2
Šestanovac	HR	138	B2
Sestao	E	143	A4
Sestino	I	135	B5
Sesto	I	109	C3
Sesto Calende	I	120	B1
Sesto Fiorentino	I	135	B4
Sesto San Giovanni	I	120	B2
Séstola	I	135	A3
Sestri Levante	I	134	A2
Sestriere	I	119	C3
Sestroretsk	RUS	9	B7
Sestu	I	179	C3
Sesvete	HR	124	B2
Setcases	E	146	B3
Sète	F	130	B2
Setenil	E	162	B2
Setermoen	N	194	B9
Šetonje	SRB	127	C3
Setskog	N	54	A2
Séttimo Torinese	I	119	B4
Settimo Vittone	I	119	B4
Settle	GB	40	A1
Setúbal	P	154	C2
Seubersdorf	D	95	B3
Seúi	I	179	C3
Seúlo	I	179	C3
Seurre	F	105	C4
Sevel	DK	58	B1
Sevenoaks	GB	45	B4
Sever do Vouga	P	148	B1
Sévérac-le-Château	F	130	A2
Severin	HR	123	B4
Severomorsk	RUS	3	B13
Séveso	I	120	B2
Sevětín	CZ	96	B2
Sevettijärvi	FIN	193	C12
Sévigny	F	91	B4
Sevilla = Seville	E	162	A2
Sevilla la Nueva	E	151	B3
Seville = Sevilla	E	162	A2
Sevilleja de la Jara	E	156	A3
Sevlievo	BG	17	D6
Sevnica	SLO	123	A4
Sevojno	SRB	127	D1
Sevrier	F	118	B2
Sexdrega	S	60	B3
Seyches	F	129	B3
Seyda	D	83	A4
Seyðisfjörður	IS	191	B12
Seydişehir	TR	189	B6
Seyitgazi	TR	187	C5
Seyitömer	TR	187	C4
Seymen	TR	186	A2
Seyne	F	132	A2
Seynes	F	131	A3
Seyssel	F	118	B2
Sežana	SLO	122	B2
Sézanne	F	91	C3
Sezulfe	P	149	A2
Sezze	I	169	B3
Sfântu Gheorghe	RO	17	C6
Sforzacosta	I	136	B2
Sgarasta Mhor	GB	31	B1
Shaftesbury	GB	43	A4
Shaldon	GB	43	B3
Shalskiy	RUS	9	B9
Shanagolden	IRL	29	B2
Shanklin	GB	44	C2
Shap	GB	37	B4
Sharpness	GB	43	A4
Shawbury	GB	38	B4
'sHeerenberg	NL	80	A2
Sheerness	GB	45	B4
Sheffield	GB	40	B2
Shefford	GB	44	A3
Shëmri	AL	182	A2
Shenfield	GB	45	B4
Shëngjergj	AL	182	B2
Shepetivka	UA	13	C7
Shepshed	GB	40	C2
Shepton Mallet	GB	43	A4
Sherborne	GB	43	B4
Shercock	IRL	27	C4
Sheringham	GB	41	C5
Shiel Bridge	GB	32	D1
Shieldaig	GB	31	B3
Shijak	AL	182	B1
Shillelagh	IRL	30	B2
Shimsk	RUS	9	C7
Shipston-on-Stour	GB	44	A2
Shklow	BY	13	A9
Shkodër	AL	182	A1
Shoeburyness	GB	45	B4
Shoreham-by-Sea	GB	44	C3
Shotley Gate	GB	45	B5
Shrewsbury	GB	38	B4
Shugozero	RUS	9	C9
Shumen	BG	17	D7
Siabost	GB	31	A2
Siamanna	I	179	C2
Sianów	PL	67	B5
Siatista	GR	182	C3
Siauges-St. Romain	F	117	B3
Šiauliai	LT	8	E3
Sibari	I	174	B2
Sibbhult	S	63	B2
Šibenik	HR	138	B1
Sibinj	HR	125	B3
Sibiu	RO	17	C6
Sibnica	SRB	127	C2
Sibsey	GB	41	B4
Siculiana	I	176	B2
Šid	SRB	125	B5
Sidari	GR	182	D1
Siddeburen	NL	71	A3
Sidensjö	S	200	C4
Siderno	I	175	C2
Sidirokastro	GR	183	B5
Sidmouth	GB	43	B3
Sidzina	PL	99	B3
Siebenlehn	D	83	A5
Siedlce	PL	12	B5
Siedlice	PL	75	A4
Siedlinghausen	D	81	A4
Siedlisko	PL	75	B5
Siegburg	D	80	B3
Siegen	D	81	B4
Siegenburg	D	95	C3
Sieghartskirchen	A	111	A3
Siegsdorf	D	109	B3
Siekierki	PL	74	B3
Sielpia	PL	87	A4
Siemiany	PL	69	B4
Siena	I	135	B4
Sieniawka	PL	84	B2
Sienno	PL	87	A5
Sieppijärvi	FIN	196	B7
Sieradz	PL	86	A2
Sieraków, *Śląskie*	PL	86	B2
Sieraków, *Wielkopolskie*	PL	75	B5
Sierakowice	PL	68	A2
Sierck-les-Bains	F	92	B2
Sierentz	D	106	B2
Sierning	A	110	A1
Sierpc	PL	77	B4
Sierra de Fuentes	E	155	A4
Sierra de Luna	E	144	A3
Sierra de Yeguas	E	162	A3
Sierre	CH	119	A4
Siestrzeń	PL	77	B5
Sietamo	E	145	B3
Siewierz	PL	86	B3
Sigdal	N	48	B1
Sigean	F	130	B1
Sigerfjord	N	194	B6
Sighetu-Marmatiei	RO	17	B5
Sighişoara	RO	17	B6
Sigillo	I	136	B1
Siglufjörður	IS	191	A7
Sigmaringen	D	107	A4
Signa	I	135	B4
Signes	F	132	B1
Signy-l'Abbaye	F	91	B4
Signy-le-Petit	F	91	B4
Sigogne	F	115	C3
Sigri	GR	183	D7
Sigtuna	S	57	A3
Sigueiro	E	140	B2
Sigüenza	E	151	A5
Sigües	E	144	B2
Sigulda	LV	8	D4
Siilinjärvi	FIN	8	A5
Sikenica	SK	112	A2
Sikfors	S	196	D4
Sikia	GR	183	C5
Sikinos	GR	185	C6
Sikkilsdalseter	N	47	A6
Siklós	H	125	B4
Sikórz	PL	77	B4
Sikselet	S	195	D8
Silandro	I	108	C1
Silánus	I	178	B2
Silbaš	SRB	126	B1
Silberstedt	D	64	B2
Şile	TR	187	A4
Siles	E	164	A2
Silgueiros	P	148	B2
Silifke	TR	23	C7
Síligo	I	178	B2
Silistra	BG	17	C7
Silivri	TR	186	A3
Siljan	N	53	A5
Siljansnäs	S	50	B1
Silkeborg	DK	59	B2
Silla	E	159	B3
Sillamäe	EST	8	C5
Sillé-le-Guillaume	F	102	A1
Silleda	E	140	B2
Sillenstede	D	71	A4
Sillerud	S	54	A3
Sillian	A	109	C3
Silloth	GB	36	B3
Silno	PL	68	B2
Silnowo	PL	68	B1
Silo	HR	123	B3
Sils	E	147	C3
Silsand	N	194	A8
Silte	S	57	C4
Šilute	LT	12	A4
Silvalen	N	195	E3
Silvaplana	CH	107	C4
Silvares	P	148	B2
Silverdalen	S	62	A3
Silvermines	IRL	28	B3
Silverstone	GB	44	A2
Silverton	GB	43	B3
Silves	P	160	B1
Silvi Marina	I	169	A4
Simandre	F	105	C3
Šimanovci	SRB	127	C2
Simard	F	105	C4
Simat de Valldigna	E	159	B3
Simav	TR	186	C3
Simbach, *Bayern*	D	95	C5
Simbach, *Bayern*	D	95	C4
Simbário	I	175	C2
Simeonovgrad	BG	183	A7
Simeria	RO	17	C5
Simi	GR	188	C2
Simićevo	SRB	127	C3
Simitli	BG	183	B5
Simlångsdalen	S	60	C3
Simmerath	D	80	B2
Simmerberg	D	107	B4
Simmern	D	93	B3
Simo	FIN	197	D8
Šimonovce	SK	99	C4
Simonsbath	GB	43	A3
Simonstorp	S	56	B2
Simontornya	H	112	C2
Simplon	CH	119	A5
Simrishamn	S	63	C2
Sinaia	RO	17	C6
Sinalunga	I	135	B4
Sinarcas	E	159	B2
Sincan	TR	187	C7
Sincanlı	TR	187	D5
Sindal	DK	58	A3
Sindelfingen	D	93	C5
Sindia	I	178	B2
Sındırgı	TR	186	C3
Sinekli	TR	186	A3
Sines	P	160	B1
Sinetta	FIN	197	C8
Sineu	E	167	B3
Singen	D	107	B3
Singleton	GB	44	C3
Singsås	N	199	C7
Siniscóla	I	178	B2
Sinj	HR	138	B2
Sinlabajos	E	150	A3
Sinn	D	81	B4
Sínnai	I	179	C3
Sinnes	N	52	B2
Sinop	TR	23	A8
Sins	CH	106	B3
Sinsheim	D	93	B4
Sint Annaland	NL	79	A4
Sint Annaparochie	NL	70	A2
Sint Athonis	NL	80	A1
Sint Nicolaasga	NL	70	B2
Sint Oedenrode	NL	79	A5

Name	Country	Page	Grid
Sintra	P	154	C1
Sinzheim	D	93	C4
Sinzig	D	80	B3
Siófok	H	112	C2
Sion	CH	119	A4
Sion Mills	GB	27	B3
Siorac-en-Périgord	F	129	B3
Šipanska Luka	HR	139	C3
Šipovo	BIH	138	A3
Sira	N	52	B2
Siracusa	I	177	B4
Siret	RO	17	B7
Sirevåg	N	52	B1
Sirig	SRB	126	B1
Sirkka	FIN	196	B2
Sirmione	I	121	B3
Sirniö	FIN	197	D11
Sirok	H	113	B4
Široké	SK	99	C4
Široki Brijeg	BIH	139	B3
Sirolo	I	136	B2
Siruela	E	156	B2
Sisak	HR	124	B2
Sisante	E	158	B1
Šišljavić	HR	123	B4
Sissach	CH	106	B2
Sissonne	F	91	B3
Sistelo	P	140	C2
Sisteron	F	132	A1
Sistiana	I	122	B2
Sistranda	N	198	B5
Sitasjaurestugorna	S	194	C8
Sitges	E	147	C2
Sitia	GR	185	D7
Sittard	NL	80	A1
Sittensen	D	72	A2
Sittingbourne	GB	45	B4
Sitzenroda	D	83	A4
Sivac	SRB	126	B1
Sivaslı	TR	189	A4
Siverić	HR	138	B2
Sivrihisar	TR	187	C6
Sixt-Fer-á-Cheval	F	119	A3
Siziano	I	120	B2
Sizun	F	100	A1
Sjenica	SRB	16	D3
Sjoa	N	198	D6
Sjøåsen	N	199	A8
Sjöbo	S	61	D3
Sjøenden, Hedmark	N	48	A3
Sjøenden, Hedmark	N	48	B3
Sjøholt	N	198	C3
Sjøli	N	48	A3
Sjølstad	N	199	A9
Sjölunda	S	56	A1
Sjømarken	S	60	B2
Sjørring	DK	58	B1
Sjötofta	S	60	B3
Sjötorp	S	55	B4
Sjoutnäset	S	199	A11
Sjøvegan	N	194	B8
Sjuntorp	S	54	B3
Skåbu	N	47	A6
Skælskør	DK	65	A4
Skærbæk	DK	64	A1
Skafså	N	53	A4
Skaftafell	IS	191	D9
Skagaströnd	IS	190	B5
Skagen	DK	58	A3
Skagersvik	S	55	B5
Skaiå	N	53	B3
Skaidi	RO	193	B8
Skala	GR	184	A1
Skała	PL	87	B3
Skala Oropou	GR	185	A4
Skala-Podilska	UA	13	D7
Skaland	N	194	A8
Skalat	UA	13	D6
Skalbmierz	PL	87	B4
Skålevik	N	53	B4
Skalica	SK	98	C1
Skalité	SK	98	B2
Skällinge	S	60	B2
Skalná	CZ	83	B4
Skals	DK	58	B2
Skalstugan	S	199	B9
Skanderborg	DK	59	B2
Skåne-Tranås	S	61	D3
Skånes-Fagerhult	S	61	C3
Skånevik	N	52	A1
Skänninge	S	55	B6
Skanör med Falsterbo	S	66	A1
Skåpafors	S	54	A3
Skąpe	PL	75	B4
Skara	S	55	B4
Skarberget	N	194	B7
Skärblacka	S	56	B1
Skarda	S	200	B4
Skarð	IS	190	B3
Skare	N	46	C3
Skåre	S	55	A4
Skärhamn	S	60	B1
Skarnes	N	48	B3
Skarp Salling	DK	58	B2
Skärplinge	S	51	B4
Skarpnåtö	FIN	51	B6
Skarrild	DK	59	C1
Skarstad	N	194	B7
Skärstad	S	62	A2
Skarsvåg	N	193	A9
Skarszewy	PL	69	A3
Skårup	DK	65	A3
Skärvången	S	199	B11
Skarvsjöby	S	195	F8
Skaryszew	PL	87	A5
Skarżysko-Kamienna	PL	87	A4
Skarzysko Ksiazece	PL	87	A4
Skatøy	N	53	B5
Skattkärr	S	55	A4
Skattungbyn	S	50	A1
Skatval	N	199	B7
Skaulo	S	196	B4
Skave	DK	59	B1
Skawina	PL	99	B3
Skebobruk	S	51	C5
Skebokvarn	S	56	A2
Skedala	S	61	C2
Skedevi	S	56	B1
Skedsmokorset	N	48	B3
Skee	S	54	B2
Skegness	GB	41	B4
Skei	N	46	A3
Skela	SRB	127	C2
Skelani	BIH	127	D1
Skellefteå	S	2	D7
Skelleftehamn	S	2	D7
Skelmersdale	GB	38	A4
Skelmorlie	GB	34	C2
Skelund	DK	58	B3
Skender Vakuf	BIH	138	A3
Skene	S	60	B2
Skępe	PL	77	B4
Skepplanda	S	60	B2
Skeppshult	S	60	B3
Skerries	IRL	30	A2
Ski	N	54	A1
Skiathos	GR	183	D5
Skibbereen	IRL	29	C2
Skibotn	N	192	C4
Skidra	GR	182	C4
Skien	N	53	A5
Skierniewice	PL	77	C5
Skillingaryd	S	60	B4
Skillinge	S	63	C2
Skillingmark	S	49	C4
Skilloura	CY	181	A2
Skinnardai	S	57	A4
Skinnskatteberg	S	50	C2
Skipmannvik	N	195	C6
Skipness	GB	34	C2
Skipsea	GB	41	B3
Skipton	GB	40	B1
Skiptvet	N	54	A2
Skiros	GR	183	E6
Skivarp	S	66	A2
Skive	DK	58	B2
Skjærhalden	N	54	A2
Skjånes	N	193	B12
Skjeberg	N	54	A2
Skjeggedal	N	46	B3
Skjeljanger	N	46	B1
Skjeljavik	N	46	C2
Skjern	DK	59	C1
Skjervøy	N	192	B4
Skjold, Rogaland	N	52	A1
Skjold, Troms	N	192	C3
Skjoldastraumen	N	52	A1
Skjolden	N	47	A4
Skjønhaug	N	54	A2
Skjøtningberg	N	193	A11
Škocjan	SLO	123	B4
Skoczów	PL	98	B2
Skodborg	DK	59	C2
Škofja Loka	SLO	123	A3
Škofljica	SLO	123	B3
Skog	S	51	A3
Skoganvarre	N	193	C9
Skogen	S	54	A3
Skogfoss	N	193	C13
Skoghall	S	55	A4
Skogly	N	193	C13
Skogn	N	199	B8
Skognes	N	192	C3
Skogstorp, Halland	S	60	C2
Skogstorp, Södermanland	S	56	A2
Skoki	PL	76	B2
Skokloster	S	57	A3
Sköldinge	S	56	A2
Skole	UA	13	D5
Skollenborg	N	53	A5
Sköllersta	S	56	A1
Skomlin	PL	86	A2
Skonseng	N	195	D5
Skopelos	GR	183	D5
Skopje	MK	182	A3
Skoppum	N	54	A1
Skórcz	PL	69	B3
Skorogoszcz	PL	86	B1
Skoroszów	PL	85	A5
Skorovatn	N	199	A10
Skorped	S	200	C3
Skørping	DK	58	B2
Skotfoss	N	53	A5
Skotniki	PL	87	A3
Skotselv	N	48	C1
Skotterud	N	49	C4
Skottorp	S	61	C2
Skovby	DK	64	B2
Skövde	S	55	B4
Skovsgård	DK	58	A2
Skrad	HR	123	B3
Skradin	HR	138	B1
Skradnik	HR	123	B4
Skråmestø	N	46	B1
Škrdlovice	CZ	97	B3
Skrea	S	60	C2
Skreia	N	48	B2
Skrolsvik	N	194	A7
Skruv	S	63	B3
Skrwilno	PL	77	A4
Skrydstrup	DK	59	C2
Skucani	BIH	138	B2
Skudeneshavn	N	52	A1
Skui	N	48	C2
Skulsk	PL	76	B3
Skultorp	S	55	B4
Skultuna	S	56	A2
Skuodas	LT	8	D2
Skurup	S	66	A2
Skute	N	48	B2
Skuteč	CZ	97	B3
Skutskär	S	51	B4
Skutvik	N	194	B6
Skvyra	UA	13	D8
Skwierzyna	PL	75	B4
Skýcov	SK	98	C2
Skyllberg	S	55	B5
Skyttmon	S	200	C1
Skyttorp	S	51	B4
Sládkovičovo	SK	111	A4
Slagelse	DK	61	D1
Slagharen	NL	71	B3
Slagnäs	S	195	E9
Slaidburn	GB	40	B1
Slane	IRL	30	A2
Slangerup	DK	61	D2
Slano	HR	139	C3
Slantsy	RUS	8	C6
Slaný	CZ	84	B2
Slap	SLO	122	A2
Šlapanice	CZ	97	B4
Slåstad	N	48	B3
Slatina	BIH	139	B3
Slatina	HR	125	B3
Slatina	RO	17	C6
Slatiňany	CZ	97	B3
Slatinice	CZ	98	B1
Slättberg	S	50	A1
Slattum	N	48	C2
Slavičin	CZ	98	B1
Slavkov	CZ	98	C1
Slavkov u Brna	CZ	97	B4
Slavkovica	SRB	127	C2
Slavonice	CZ	97	C3
Slavonski Brod	HR	125	B4
Slavonski Kobas	HR	125	B3
Slavošovce	SK	99	C4
Slavskoye	RUS	69	A5
Slavuta	UA	13	C7
Sława, Lubuskie	PL	85	A4
Sława, Zachodnio-Pomorskie	PL	67	C4
Slawharad	BY	13	B9
Sławków	PL	86	B3
Sławno, Wielkopolskie	PL	76	B2
Sławno, Zachodnio-Pomorskie	PL	68	A1
Sławoborze	PL	67	C4
Sl'ažany	SK	98	C2
Sleaford	GB	40	C3
Sleðbrjótur	IS	191	B11
Sledmere	GB	40	A3
Sleights	GB	37	B6
Slemmestad	N	54	A1
Ślesin	PL	76	B3
Sliač	SK	99	C3
Sliema	M	175	C3
Sligo	IRL	26	B2
Slite	S	57	C4
Slitu	N	54	A2
Sliven	BG	17	D7
Śliwice	PL	68	B3
Slobozia	RO	17	C7
Slochteren	NL	71	A3
Slöinge	S	60	C2
Słomniki	PL	87	B4
Slonim	BY	13	B6
Słońsk	PL	75	B3
Slootdorp	NL	70	B1
Slottsbron	S	55	A4
Slough	GB	44	B3
Slövag	N	46	B2
Slovenj Gradec	SLO	110	C2
Slovenska Bistrica	SLO	123	A4
Slovenska L'upča	SK	99	C3
Slovenské-Ves	SK	99	B4
Slovenské Darmoty	SK	112	A3
Slovenske Konjice	SLO	123	A4
Słubice	PL	74	B3
Sluderno	I	108	C1
Sluis	NL	78	A4
Šluknov	CZ	84	A2
Słupca	PL	76	B2
Słupia	PL	87	A3
Słupiec	PL	85	B4
Słupsk	PL	68	A2
Slutsk	BY	13	B7
Smålandsstenar	S	60	B3
Smalåsen	N	195	E4
Smardzewo	PL	75	B4
Smarhon	BY	13	A7
Smarje	SLO	123	A4
Šmarjeta	SLO	123	B4
Šmartno	SLO	123	A3
Smečno	CZ	84	B2
Smedby	S	63	B4
Smedjebacken	S	50	B2
Smęgorzów	PL	87	B5
Smeland	N	53	B4
Smidary	CZ	84	B3
Śmigiel	PL	75	B5
Smilde	NL	71	B3
Smiřice	CZ	85	B3
Smithfield	GB	36	B4
Smitowo	PL	75	A5
Smögen	S	54	B2
Smogulec	PL	76	A2
Smołdzino	PL	68	A2
Smolenice	SK	98	C1
Smolensk	RUS	13	A10
Smolník	SK	99	C4
Smolyan	BG	183	B6
Smuka	SLO	123	B3
Smygehamn	S	66	A2
Smykow	PL	87	A4
Snainton	GB	40	A3
Snaith	GB	40	B2
Snaptun	DK	59	C3
Snarby	N	192	C3
Snarum	N	48	B1
Snåsa	N	199	A9
Snedsted	DK	58	B1
Sneek	NL	70	A2
Sneem	IRL	29	C2
Snejbjerg	DK	59	B1
Snillfjord	N	198	B6
Snøde	DK	65	B3
Snøfjord	N	193	B8
Snogebaek	DK	67	A4
Snyatyn	UA	13	D6
Soave	I	121	B4
Sober	E	140	B3
Sobernheim	D	93	B3
Soběslav	CZ	96	B2
Sobota, Dolnośląskie	PL	85	A3
Sobota, Łódzkie	PL	77	B4
Sobotište	SK	98	C1
Sobotka	CZ	84	B3
Sobótka, Dolnośląskie	PL	85	B4
Sobótka, Wielkopolskie	PL	86	A1
Sobra	HR	139	C3
Sobrado, Coruña	E	140	A2
Sobrado, Lugo	E	141	B3
Sobral da Adica	P	161	A2
Sobral de Monte Argraço	P	154	C1
Sobreira Formosa	P	154	B3
Søby	DK	64	B3
Soca	SLO	122	A2
Sochaczew	PL	77	B5
Sochos	GR	183	C5
Socodor	RO	113	C5
Socol	RO	127	C3
Socovos	E	164	A3
Socuéllamos	E	158	B1
Sodankylä	FIN	197	B9
Soderåkra	S	63	B4
Söderala	S	51	A3
Söderås	S	50	B2
Söderbärke	S	50	B2
Söderby-Karl	S	51	C5
Söderfors	S	51	B4
Söderhamn	S	51	A4
Söderköping	S	56	B1
Söderön	N	54	A2
Södertälje	S	57	A3
Södingberg	A	110	B2
Södra Finnö	S	56	B2
Södra Ny	S	55	A4
Södra Råda	S	55	A5
Södra Sandby	S	61	D3
Södra Vi	S	62	A3
Sodražica	SLO	123	B3
Sodupe	E	143	A3
Soengas	P	148	A1
Soest	D	81	A4
Soest	NL	70	B2
Sofades	GR	182	D4
Sofia = Sofiya	BG	17	D5
Sofikon	GR	184	B3
Sofiya = Sofia	BG	17	D5
Şofronea	RO	126	A3
Sögel	D	71	B4
Sogliano al Rubicone	I	135	A5
Sogndalsfjøra	N	46	A4
Sögüt, Bilecik	TR	187	B5
Sögüt, Burdur	TR	189	B4
Söğütköy	TR	188	C3
Soham	GB	45	A4
Sohland	D	84	A2
Sohren	D	93	B3
Soignies	B	79	B4
Soini	FIN	8	A4
Soissons	F	90	B3
Sokal'	UA	13	C6
Söke	TR	188	B2
Sokna	N	48	B1
Sokndal	N	52	B2
Soknedal	N	199	C7
Soko	BIH	125	C4
Sokolac	BIH	139	B4
Sokółka	PL	13	B5
Sokolov	CZ	83	B4
Sokołowo Podlaski	PL	12	B5
Sokołowo	PL	76	B3
Sola	N	52	B1
Solana de los Barros	E	155	C4
Solana del Pino	E	157	B3
Solánas	I	179	C3
Solares	E	143	A3
Solarino	I	177	B4
Solarussa	I	179	C2
Solas	GB	31	B1
Solber-gelva	N	53	A6
Solberg	S	200	C3
Solberga	S	62	A2
Solbjørg	N	46	B2
Solčany	SK	98	C2
Solčava	SLO	123	A3
Solda	I	108	C1
Solden	A	108	C2
Solec Kujawski	PL	76	A3
Soleils	F	132	B2
Solenzara	F	180	B2
Solera	E	163	A4
Solesmes	F	79	B3
Soleto	I	173	B4
Solgne	F	92	C2
Solheim	N	46	B2
Solheimsvik	N	52	A2
Solignac	F	115	C5
Solihull	GB	44	A2
Solin	HR	138	B2
Solingen	D	80	A3
Solivella	E	147	C2
Solkan	SLO	122	B2
Söll	A	108	B3
Sollana	E	159	B3
Sollebrunn	S	54	B3
Sollefteå	S	200	C3
Sollen-tuna	S	57	A3
Sollenau	A	111	B3
Sóller	E	166	B2
Sollerön	S	50	B1
Søllested	DK	65	B4
Solliès-Pont	F	132	B2
Sollihøgda	N	48	C2
Solnechnogorsk	RUS	9	D10
Solnice	CZ	85	B4
Solofra	I	170	C2
Solomiac	F	129	C3
Solopaca	I	170	B2
Solórzano	E	143	A3
Solothurn	CH	106	B2
Solre-le-Château	F	79	B4
Solsona	E	147	C2
Solsvik	N	46	B1
Solt	H	112	C3
Soltau	D	72	B2
Soltsy	RUS	9	C7
Soltszentimre	H	112	C3
Soltvadkert	H	112	C3
Solumsmoen	N	48	C1
Solund	N	46	A1
Solva	GB	39	C1
Sölvesborg	S	63	B2
Solymár	H	112	B2
Soma	TR	186	C2
Somain	F	78	B3
Somberek	H	125	A4
Sombernon	F	104	B3
Sombor	SRB	125	B5
Sombreffe	B	79	B4
Someren	NL	80	A1
Somero	FIN	8	B3
Somersham	GB	44	A3
Somerton	GB	43	A4
Sominy	PL	68	A2
Somma Lombardo	I	120	B1
Sommariva del Bosco	I	119	C4
Sommarøy	N	192	C2
Sommarset	N	194	C6
Sommatino	I	176	B2
Somme-Tourbe	F	91	B4
Sommeilles	F	91	C4
Sommen	S	55	B5
Sommepy-Tahure	F	91	B4
Sömmerda	D	82	A3
Sommerfeld	D	74	B2
Sommersted	DK	59	C2
Sommesous	F	91	C4
Sommières	F	131	B3
Sommières-du-Clain	F	115	B4
Somo	E	143	A3
Somogyfajsz	H	111	C4
Somogyjád	H	111	C4
Somogysámson	H	111	C4
Somogyszil	H	125	A4
Somogyszob	H	124	A3
Somogyvár	H	111	C4
Somontin	E	164	B2
Somosierra	E	151	A4
Somoskőújfalu	H	113	A3
Sompolno	PL	76	B3
Sompuis	F	91	C4
Son	NL	80	A1
Son Bou	E	167	B4
Son en Breugel	NL	80	A1
Son Servera	E	167	B3
Sonceboz	CH	106	B2
Soncillo	E	143	B3
Soncino	I	120	B2
Sóndalo	I	120	A3
Søndeled	N	53	B5
Sønder Bjert	DK	59	C2
Sønder Felding	DK	59	C1
Sønder Hygum	DK	59	C1
Sønder Omme	DK	59	C1
Sønderborg	DK	64	B2
Sønderby	DK	64	B2
Sønderho	DK	59	C1
Sondershausen	D	82	A2
Søndersø	DK	59	C3
Søndervig	DK	59	B1
Søndre Enningdal Kappel	N	54	B2
Sóndrio	I	120	A2
Soneja	E	159	B3
Songe	N	53	B5
Songeons	F	90	B1
Sonkamuotka	FIN	196	A6
Sonkovo	RUS	9	D10
Sönnarslöv	S	61	D4
Sonneberg	D	82	B3
Sonnefeld	D	82	B3
Sonnewalde	D	84	A1
Sonnino	I	169	B3
Sonogno	CH	120	A1
Sonsbeck	D	80	A2
Sonseca	E	157	A4
Sønsterud	S	49	B4
Sonstorp	S	56	B1
Sonta	SRB	125	B5
Sontheim	D	94	C2
Sonthofen	D	107	B5
Sontra	D	82	A1
Sopelana	E	143	A4
Sopje	HR	125	B3
Šoporňa	SK	111	A4
Sopot	PL	69	A3
Sopot	SRB	127	C2
Sopotnica	MK	182	B3
Sopron	H	111	B3
Šor	SRB	127	C1
Sora	I	169	B3
Soragna	I	120	C3
Söråker	S	200	D3
Sorano	I	168	A1
Sorbara	I	121	C4
Sorbas	E	164	B2
Sórbolo	I	121	C3
Sörbygden	S	200	D2
Sordal	N	52	B3
Sordale	GB	32	C3
Sore	F	128	B2
Sörenberg	CH	106	C3
Soresina	I	120	B2
Sörezê	F	146	A3
Sörforsa	S	200	E3
Sorges	F	115	C4
Sorgues	F	131	B3
Sorgun	TR	23	B8
Soria	E	143	C4
Soriano Cálabro	I	175	C2
Soriano nel Cimino	I	168	A2
Sorihuela del Guadalimar	E	164	A1
Sorisdale	GB	34	B1
Sørkjosen	N	192	C4
Sørli	N	199	A10
Sormás	H	111	C3
Sörmjöle	S	200	C6
Sørmo	N	194	B9
Sornac	F	116	B2
Sorø	DK	61	D1
Soroca	MD	17	A8
Sørreisa	N	194	A9
Sorrento	I	170	C2
Sorsele	S	195	E8
Sörsjön	S	49	A5
Sorso	I	178	B2
Sort	E	146	B2
Sortavala	RUS	9	B7
Sortino	I	177	B4
Sortland	N	194	B6
Sørum	N	48	B2
Sørumsand	N	48	C3
Sorunda	S	57	A3
Sörup	D	64	B2
Sørvær	N	192	B6
Sørvågen	N	194	C3
Sorvik	S	50	B2
Sørvika	N	199	C8
Sos	F	128	B3
Sos del Rey Católico	E	144	B2
Sösdala	S	61	C3
Sošice	HR	123	B4
Sośnica	PL	75	A5
Sośnicowice	PL	86	B2
Sosno	PL	76	A2
Sosnovyy Bor	RUS	9	C6
Sosnowiec	PL	86	B3
Sospel	F	133	B3
Šoštanj	SLO	123	A4
Sotaseter	N	198	D4
Sotillo de Adrada	E	150	B3
Sotillo de la Ribera	E	143	C3
Sotin	HR	125	B5

Name	Country	Page	Grid
Sotkamo	FIN	3	D11
Soto de la Marina	E	143	A3
Soto de los Infantes	E	141	A4
Soto de Real	E	151	B4
Soto de Ribera	E	141	A5
Soto del Barco	E	141	B5
Sotobañado y Priorato	E	142	B2
Sotoserrano	E	149	B3
Sotresgudo	E	142	B2
Sotrondio	E	142	A1
Sotta	F	180	B2
Sottomarina	I	122	B4
Sottrum	D	72	A2
Sottunga	FIN	51	B7
Souain	F	91	B4
Soual	F	146	A3
Soucy	F	104	A2
Souda	GR	185	D5
Soudron	F	91	C4
Souesmes	F	103	B4
Souffelweyersheim	F	93	C3
Soufli	GR	186	A1
Souillac	F	129	B4
Souilly	F	91	B5
Soulac-sur-Mer	F	114	C2
Soulaines-Dhuys	F	91	C4
Soulatgé	F	146	B3
Soultz-Haut-Rhin	F	106	B2
Soultz-sous-Forêts	F	93	C3
Soumagne	B	80	B1
Soumoulou	F	145	A3
Souppes-sur-Loing	F	103	A4
Souprosse	F	128	C2
Sourdeval	F	88	B3
Soure	P	154	A2
Sournia	F	146	B3
Souro Pires	P	149	B2
Sourpi	GR	182	D4
Sours	F	90	C1
Sousceyrac	F	116	C2
Sousel	P	155	C3
Soustons	F	128	C1
Soutelo de Montes	E	140	B2
South Brent	GB	42	B3
South Cave	GB	40	B3
South Hayling	GB	44	C3
South Molton	GB	42	A3
South Ockendon	GB	45	B4
South Petherton	GB	43	B4
South Shields	GB	37	B5
South Tawton	GB	42	B3
South Woodham Ferrers	GB	45	B4
Southam	GB	44	A2
Southampton	GB	44	C2
Southborough	GB	45	B4
Southend	GB	34	C2
Southend-on-Sea	GB	45	B4
Southport	GB	38	A3
Southwell	GB	40	B3
Southwold	GB	45	A5
Souto	P	148	B2
Souto da Carpalhosa	P	154	B2
Soutochao	E	141	C3
Souvigny	F	104	C2
Souzay-Champigny	F	102	B1
Soverato	I	175	C2
Soveria Mannelli	I	175	B2
Sövestad	S	66	A2
Sovetsk	RUS	12	A4
Sovići	BIH	138	B3
Sovicille	I	135	B4
Søvik	N	198	C3
Sowerby	GB	37	B5
Soyaux	F	115	C4
Søyland	N	52	B1
Spa	B	80	B1
Spadafora	I	177	A4
Spaichingen	D	107	A3
Spakenburg	NL	70	B2
Spalding	GB	41	C3
Spálené Poříčí	CZ	96	B1
Spalt	D	94	B2
Spangenberg	D	82	A1
Spangereid	N	52	B3
Spantekow	D	74	A2
Sparanise	I	170	B2
Sparbu	N	199	B8
Sparkær	DK	58	B2
Sparkford	GB	43	A4
Sparreholm	S	56	A2
Sparta = Sparti	GR	184	B3
Spartà	I	177	A4
Sparti = Sparta	GR	184	B3
Spean Bridge	GB	34	B3
Speicher	D	92	B2
Speichersdorf	D	95	B3
Speke	GB	38	A4
Spello	I	136	C1
Spenge	D	72	B1
Spennymoor	GB	37	B5
Spentrup	DK	58	B3
Sperenberg	D	74	B2
Sperlinga	I	177	B3
Sperlonga	I	169	B3
Spetalen	N	54	A1
Spetses	GR	184	B4
Speyer	D	93	B4
Spézet	F	100	A2
Spezzano Albanese	I	174	B2
Spezzano della Sila	I	174	B2
Spiddle	IRL	28	A2
Spiegelau	D	96	C1
Spiekeroog	D	71	A4
Spiez	CH	106	C2
Spigno Monferrato	I	133	A4
Spijk	NL	71	A3
Spijkenisse	NL	79	A4
Spilamberto	I	135	A4
Spili	GR	185	D5
Spilimbergo	I	122	A1
Spilsby	GB	41	B4
Spinazzola	I	172	B2
Spincourt	F	92	B1
Spind	N	52	B2
Spindleruv-Mlyn	CZ	84	B3
Spinoso	I	174	A2
Špišić Bukovica	HR	124	B3
Spišská Belá	SK	99	B4
Spišská Nová Ves	SK	99	C4
Spisská Stará Ves	SK	99	C4
Spišské-Hanušovce	SK	99	B4
Spišské Podhradie	SK	99	C4
Spišské Vlachy	SK	99	C4
Spišský-Štvrtok	SK	99	C4
Spital	A	110	B1
Spital am Semmering	A	110	B2
Spittal an der Drau	A	109	C4
Spittle of Glenshee	GB	35	B4
Spitz	A	97	C3
Spjærøy	N	54	A1
Spjald	DK	59	B1
Spjelkavik	N	198	C3
Spjutsbygd	S	63	B3
Split	HR	138	B2
Splügen	CH	107	C4
Spodsbjerg	DK	65	B3
Spofforth	GB	40	B2
Spohle	D	71	A5
Spoleto	I	136	C1
Spoltore	I	169	A4
Spondigna	I	108	C1
Sponvika	N	54	A1
Spornitz	D	73	A4
Spotorno	I	133	A4
Spraitbach	D	94	C1
Sprakensehl	D	72	B3
Sprakovo	PL	69	B5
Spremberg	D	84	A2
Spresiano	I	122	B1
Sprimont	B	80	B1
Springe	D	72	B2
Sproatley	GB	41	B3
Spydeberg	N	54	A2
Spytkowice	PL	99	B3
Squillace	I	175	C2
Squinzano	I	173	B4
Sračinec	HR	124	A2
Srbac	BIH	124	B3
Srbobran	SRB	126	B1
Srebrenica	BIH	127	C1
Srebrenik	BIH	125	C4
Središče	SLO	124	A2
Srem	PL	76	B2
Sremska Mitrovica	SRB	127	C1
Sremski Karlovci	SRB	126	B1
Srní	CZ	96	B3
Srnice Gornje	BIH	125	C4
Srock	PL	86	A3
Środa Śląska	PL	85	A4
Środa Wielkopolski	PL	76	B2
Srpska Crnja	SRB	126	B2
Srpski Itebej	SRB	126	B2
Srpski Miletić	SRB	125	B5
Staatz	A	97	C4
Stabbursnes	N	193	B8
Staberdorf	D	65	B4
Stabroek	B	79	A4
Stachy	CZ	96	B1
Stade	D	72	A2
Staden	B	78	B3
Staðarfell	IS	190	B4
Stadl an der Mur	A	109	B4
Stadskanaal	NL	71	B4
Stadtallendorf	D	81	B5
Stadthagen	D	72	B2
Stadtilm	D	82	B3
Stadtkyll	D	80	B2
Stadtlauringen	D	82	B2
Stadtlengsfeld	D	82	B2
Stadtlohn	D	71	C3
Stadtoldendorf	D	82	A1
Stadtroda	D	83	B3
Stadtsteinach	D	82	B3
Stäfa	CH	107	B3
Staffanstorp	S	61	D3
Staffelstein	D	82	B2
Staffin	GB	31	B2
Stafford	GB	40	C1
Stainach	A	110	B1
Staindrop	GB	37	B5
Staines	GB	44	B3
Stainville	F	91	C5
Stainz	A	110	C2
Staithes	GB	37	B6
Staíti	I	175	D2
Stäket	S	57	A3
Stakroge	DK	59	C1
Štalcerji	SLO	123	B3
Stalden	CH	119	A4
Stalham	GB	41	C5
Stallarholmen	S	56	A3
Ställberg	S	50	C1
Ställdalen	S	50	C1
Stallhofen	A	110	B2
Stalon	S	195	F6
Stalowa Wola	PL	12	C5
Stamford	GB	40	C3
Stamford Bridge	GB	40	B3
Stamnes	N	46	B2
Stams	A	108	B1
Stamsried	D	95	B4
Stamsund	N	194	B4
Stanford le Hope	GB	45	B4
Stånga	S	57	C4
Stange	N	48	B3
Stanghella	I	121	B4
Stanhope	GB	37	B4
Staniši	SRB	125	B5
Staňkov	CZ	95	B5
Stankovci	HR	137	B4
Stanley	GB	37	B5
Stans	CH	106	C3
Stansted Mountfitchet	GB	45	B4
Stanzach	A	108	B1
Stapar	SRB	125	B5
Staphorst	NL	70	B3
Staplehurst	GB	45	B4
Stąporków	PL	87	A4
Stara Baška	HR	123	C3
Stara Fužina	SLO	122	A2
Stara Kamienica	PL	84	B3
Stara Kiszewa	PL	68	B3
Stará Ľubovňa	SK	99	B4
Stara Moravica	HR	126	B1
Stara Novalja	HR	137	A3
Stara Pazova	SRB	127	C2
Stará Turá	SK	98	C1
Stara Zagora	BG	17	D7
Starachowice	PL	87	A5
Staraya Russa	RUS	9	D7
Stärbsnäs	S	51	C6
Starčevo	SRB	127	C2
Stare Dłutowo	PL	77	A4
Staré Hamry	CZ	98	B2
Stare Jablonki	PL	69	B5
Staré Město	CZ	98	B1
Stare Pole	PL	69	A4
Stare Sedlo	CZ	96	B2
Stare Strącze	PL	85	A4
Stargard Szczeciński	PL	75	A4
Stårheim	N	198	D2
Stari Banovci	SRB	127	C2
Stari Gradac	HR	124	B3
Stari Jankovci	HR	125	B4
Stari Majdan	BIH	124	C2
Stari-Mikanovci	HR	125	B4
Starigrad, Ličko-Senjska	HR	123	C3
Starigrad, Splitsko-Dalmatinska	HR	138	B2
Starigrad-Paklenica	HR	137	A4
Staritsa	RUS	9	D9
Starkenbach	D	81	B1
Starnberg	D	108	B2
Staro Petrovo Selo	HR	124	B3
Staro Selo	HR	124	B3
Staro Selo	SRB	127	C3
Starogard	PL	75	A4
Starogard Gdański	PL	69	B3
Starokonstyantyniv	UA	13	D7
Stary Brzozów	PL	77	B5
Stary Dzierzgoń	PL	69	B4
Stary Hrozenkov	CZ	98	C1
Stary Jaroslaw	PL	68	A1
Stary Plzenec	CZ	96	B1
Stary Sącz	PL	99	B4
Starý Smokovec	SK	99	B4
Staryy Chartoriysk	UA	13	C6
Staškov	SK	98	B2
Stassfurt	D	82	A3
Staszów	PL	87	B5
Stathelle	N	53	A5
Staufen	D	106	B2
Staunton	GB	39	C4
Stavang	N	46	A2
Stavanger	N	52	B1
Stavåsnäs	S	49	B4
Stavby	S	51	B5
Staveley	GB	40	B2
Stavelot	B	80	B1
Stavenisse	NL	79	A4
Stavern	N	53	B6
Stavoren	NL	70	B2
Stavros	CY	181	A1
Stavros	GR	183	C5
Stavroupoli	GR	183	B6
Stavseng	N	47	A6
Stavsjø	N	48	B3
Stavsnäs	S	57	A4
Stawiszyn	PL	76	C3
Steane	N	53	A4
Steblevë	AL	182	B2
Stechelberg	CH	106	C2
Štechovice	CZ	96	B2
Stechow	D	73	B5
Steckborn	CH	107	B3
Stede Broek	NL	70	B2
Steeg	A	107	B5
Steenbergen	NL	79	A4
Steenvoorde	F	78	B2
Steenwijk	NL	70	B3
Štefanje	HR	124	B2
Steffisburg	CH	106	C2
Stegaurach	D	94	B2
Stege	DK	65	B5
Stegelitz	D	74	A2
Stegersbach	A	111	B3
Stegna	PL	69	A4
Steimbke	D	72	B2
Stein an Rhein	CH	107	B3
Steinach	A	108	B2
Steinach, Baden-Württemberg	D	106	A3
Steinach, Bayern	D	82	B2
Steinach, Thüringen	D	82	B3
Steinau, Bayern	D	81	B5
Steinau, Niedersachsen	D	64	C1
Steinbeck	D	74	B2
Steinberg am Rofan	A	108	B2
Steindorf	A	109	C5
Steine	N	46	B2
Steinen	D	106	B2
Steinfeld	A	109	C4
Steinfeld	D	71	B5
Steinfurt	D	71	B4
Steingaden	D	108	B1
Steinhagen	D	72	B1
Steinheid	D	82	B3
Steinheim, Bayern	D	107	A5
Steinheim, Nordrhein-Westfalen	D	81	A5
Steinhöfel	D	74	B3
Steinhorst	D	72	B3
Steinigtwolmsdorf	D	84	A2
Steinkjer	N	199	A8
Steinsholt	N	53	A5
Stekene	B	79	A4
Stelle	D	72	A3
Stellendam	NL	79	A4
Stenåsa	S	63	B4
Stenay	F	91	B5
Stenberga	S	62	A3
Stendal	D	73	B4
Stenhammar	S	55	B4
Stenhamra	S	57	A3
Stenhousemuir	GB	35	B4
Stenlose	DK	61	D2
Stensätra	S	50	B3
Stenstorp	S	55	B4
Stenstrup	DK	65	A3
Stenudden	S	195	D8
Stenungsund	S	54	B2
Štěpánov	CZ	98	B1
Stephanskirchen	D	108	B3
Stepnica	PL	74	A3
Stepojevac	SRB	127	C2
Stepping	DK	59	C2
Sterbfritz	D	82	B1
Sternberg	D	65	C4
Šternberk	CZ	98	B1
Sterup	D	64	B2
Stęszew	PL	75	B5
Štěti	CZ	84	B2
Stevenage	GB	44	B3
Stewarton	GB	36	A2
Steyerburg	D	72	B2
Steyning	GB	44	C3
Steyr	A	110	A1
Stężyca	PL	68	A3
Stezzano	I	120	B2
Stia	I	135	B4
Stibb Cross	GB	42	B2
Sticciano Scalo	I	135	C4
Stidsvig	S	61	C3
Stiens	NL	70	A2
Stige	DK	59	C3
Stigen	S	54	B3
Stigliano	I	174	A2
Stigtomta	S	56	B2
Stilida	GR	182	E4
Stilla	N	192	C7
Stillington	GB	40	A2
Stilo	I	175	C2
Stintino	I	178	B2
Stio	I	172	B1
Štip	MK	182	B4
Stira	GR	185	A5
Stirling	GB	35	B4
Štítnik	SK	99	C4
Štíty	CZ	97	B4
Stjärnhov	S	56	A3
Stjärnsund	S	50	B3
Stjørdalshalsen	N	199	B8
Stobno	PL	75	A5
Stobreč	HR	138	B2
Stochov	CZ	84	B1
Stockach	D	107	B4
Stöckalp	CH	106	C3
Stockaryd	S	62	A2
Stockbridge	GB	44	B2
Stockerau	A	97	C4
Stockheim	D	82	B3
Stockholm	S	57	A4
Stockport	GB	40	B1
Stocksbridge	GB	40	B2
Stockton-on-Tees	GB	37	B5
Stod	CZ	96	B1
Stöde	S	200	D2
Stöðvarfjörður	IS	191	C12
Stødi	N	195	D6
Stoer	GB	32	C1
Stoholm	DK	58	B2
Stoke Ferry	GB	41	C4
Stoke Fleming	GB	43	B3
Stoke Mandeville	GB	44	B3
Stoke-on-Trent	GB	40	B1
Stokesley	GB	37	B5
Stokke	N	54	A1
Stokkemarke	DK	65	B4
Stokken	N	53	B4
Stokkseyri	IS	190	D4
Stokkvågen	N	195	D4
Stoky	CZ	97	B3
Stolac	BIH	139	B3
Stolberg	D	80	B2
Stolin	BY	13	C7
Stollberg	D	83	B4
Stöllet	S	49	B5
Stollhamm	D	71	A5
Stolno	PL	76	A3
Stolpen	D	84	A2
Stolzenau	D	72	B2
Stompetoren	NL	70	B1
Ston	HR	139	C3
Stonařov	CZ	97	B3
Stone	GB	40	C1
Stonehaven	GB	33	E4
Stonehouse	GB	36	A3
Stongfjorden	N	46	A2
Stonndalen	N	47	B5
Stony Stratford	GB	44	A3
Stopnica	PL	87	B4
Storå	S	56	A1
Storås	N	198	B6
Storby	FIN	51	B6
Stordal, Møre og Romsdal	N	198	C4
Stordal, Nord-Trøndelag	N	199	B8
Store	GB	33	B4
Store Damme	DK	65	B5
Store Heddinge	DK	65	A5
Store Herrestad	S	66	A2
Store Levene	S	55	B3
Store Molvik	N	193	B12
Store Skedvi	S	50	B2
Store Vika	S	57	B3
Storebø	N	46	B2
Storebro	S	62	A3
Storelv	N	192	B6
Støren	N	199	B7
Storfjellseter	N	199	D7
Storfjord	N	192	C3
Storfors	S	55	A5
Storforshei	N	195	D5
Storhøliseter	N	47	A6
Storjord	N	195	D6
Storkow, Brandenburg	D	74	B2
Storkow, Mecklenburg-Vorpommern	D	74	A3
Storli	N	198	C6
Storlien	S	199	B9
Stornara	I	171	B3
Stornoway	GB	31	A2
Storo	I	121	B3
Storozhynets	UA	17	A6
Storrington	GB	44	C3
Storseleby	S	200	B3
Storsjön	S	50	A3
Storslett	N	192	C5
Storsteinnes	N	192	C3
Storsund	S	196	D3
Storuman	S	195	E8
Störvattnet	S	199	C9
Storvik	N	195	D4
Storvik	S	50	B3
Storvorde	DK	58	B3
Storvreta	S	51	C4
Štos	SK	99	C4
Stössen	D	83	A3
Stötten	D	108	B1
Stotternheim	D	82	A3
Stouby	DK	59	C2
Stourbridge	GB	40	C1
Stourport-on-Severn	GB	39	B4
Støvring	DK	58	B2
Stow	GB	35	C5
Stow-on-the-Wold	GB	44	B2
Stowbtsy	BY	13	B7
Stowmarket	GB	45	A5
Straach	D	73	C5
Strabane	GB	27	B3
Strachan	GB	33	D4
Strachur	GB	34	B2
Stracin	MK	182	A4
Strackholt	D	71	A4
Stradbally	IRL	29	B1
Stradella	I	120	B2
Straelen	D	80	A2
Stragari	SRB	127	C2
Strakonice	CZ	96	B1
Stralsnäs	S	55	B6
Stralsund	D	66	B2
Strand	N	48	A3
Stranda	N	198	C3
Strandby	DK	58	A3
Strandebarm	N	46	B3
Strandhill	IRL	26	B2
Strandlykkja	N	48	B3
Strandvik	N	46	B2
Strangford	GB	27	B5
Strängnäs	S	56	A3
Strångsjö	S	56	B2
Stráni	CZ	98	C1
Stranice	SLO	123	A4
Stranorlar	IRL	26	B3
Stranraer	GB	36	B1
Strasatti	I	176	B1
Strasbourg	F	93	C3
Strasburg	D	74	A2
Strašice	CZ	96	B1
Strass im Steiermark	A	110	C2
Strassen	A	109	C3
Strasshof	A	97	C4
Strasswalchen	A	109	B4
Stratford-upon-Avon	GB	44	A2
Strathaven	GB	36	A2
Strathdon	GB	32	D3
Strathkanaird	GB	32	D1
Strathpeffer	GB	32	D2
Strathy	GB	32	C3
Strathyre	GB	34	B3
Stratinska	BIH	124	C2
Stratton	GB	42	B2
Straubing	D	95	C4
Straulas	I	178	B3
Straume	N	53	A5
Straumen, Nord-Trøndelag	N	199	B8
Straumen, Nordland	N	194	C6
Straumsjøen	N	194	B5
Straumsnes	N	194	C6
Straupitz	D	74	C3
Strausberg	D	74	B2
Straussfurt	D	82	A3
Strawczyn	PL	87	B4
Straž nad Nezárkou	CZ	96	B2
Stráž Pod Ralskem	CZ	84	B2
Straža	SLO	123	B4
Straža	SRB	127	C3
Strážnice	CZ	98	C1
Strážný	CZ	96	C1
Štrbské Pleso	SK	99	B4
Strečno	SK	98	B2
Street	GB	43	A4
Strehla	D	83	A5
Strekov	SK	112	B2
Strem	A	111	B3
Stremska-Rača	SRB	127	C1
Strengberg	A	110	A1
Strengelvåg	N	194	B6
Stresa	I	119	B5
Streufdorf	D	82	B2
Strib	DK	59	C2
Striberg	S	55	A5
Stříbro	CZ	95	B4
Strichen	GB	33	D4
Strigno	I	121	A4
Štrigova	HR	111	C3
Strijen	NL	79	A4
Strizivojna	HR	125	B4
Strmica	HR	138	A2
Strmilov	CZ	97	B3
Ströhen	D	72	B1
Strokestown	IRL	28	A3
Stromberg, Nordrhein-Westfalen	D	81	A4
Stromberg, Rheinland-Pfalz	D	93	B3
Stromeferry	GB	31	B3
Strömnäs	S	200	B2
Stromness	GB	33	C3
Strömsberg	S	51	B4
Strömsbruk	S	200	E3
Strömsfors	S	56	B2
Strömsnäsbruk	S	61	C3
Strömstad	S	54	B2
Strömsund, Jämtland	S	199	B12
Strömsund, Västerbotten	S	195	E7
Stronachlachar	GB	34	B3
Stróngoli	I	174	B3
Stronie Śląskie	PL	85	B4
Strontian	GB	34	B2
Stroppiana	I	119	B5
Stroud	GB	43	A4
Stroumbi	CY	181	B1
Stróża	PL	99	B3
Strücklingen	D	71	A4
Struer	DK	58	B1

Name	Country	Page	Grid
Struga	MK	182	B2
Strugi Krasnyye	RUS	9	C6
Strumica	MK	182	B2
Strumien	PL	98	B2
Struy	GB	32	D2
Stružec	HR	124	B2
Stryków	PL	77	C4
Stryn	N	198	D3
Stryy	UA	13	D5
Strzałkowo	PL	76	B2
Strzegocin	PL	77	A5
Strzegom	PL	85	B4
Strzegowo	PL	77	B5
Strzelce	PL	77	B5
Strzelce Krajeńskie	PL	75	B4
Strzelce Kurowo	PL	75	B4
Strzelce Opolskie	PL	86	B2
Strzelin	PL	85	B5
Strzelno	PL	76	B3
Strzepcz	PL	68	A3
Strzybnica	PL	86	B2
Strzygi	PL	77	A4
Stubbekøbing	DK	65	B5
Stuben	A	107	B5
Stubenberg	A	110	B2
Stubline	SRB	127	C2
Studená	CZ	97	B3
Studenci	HR	138	B3
Studenka	CZ	98	B2
Studenzen	A	110	B2
Studienka	SK	98	C1
Studland	GB	43	B5
Studley	GB	44	A2
Studzienice	PL	68	A2
Stuer	D	73	A5
Stugudal	N	199	C8
Stugun	S	200	C1
Stuhr	D	72	A1
Stukenbrock	D	81	A4
Stülpe	D	74	B2
Stupava	SK	111	A4
Stupnik	HR	124	B1
Stupsk	PL	77	A5
Sturkö	S	63	B3
Sturminster Newton	GB	43	B4
Štúrovo	SK	112	B2
Sturton	GB	40	B3
Stuttgart	D	94	C1
Stvolny	CZ	96	A1
Stykkishólmur	IS	190	B3
Styri	N	48	B3
Stysö	S	60	B1
Suances	E	142	A2
Subbiano	I	135	B4
Subiaco	I	169	B3
Subotica	SRB	126	A1
Subotište	SRB	127	C1
Sučany	SK	98	B2
Suceava	RO	17	B7
Sucha-Beskidzka	PL	99	B3
Suchacz	PL	69	A4
Suchań	PL	75	A4
Suchdol nad Lužnice	CZ	96	C2
Suchedniów	PL	87	A4
Suchorze	PL	68	A2
Suchteln	D	80	A2
Sucina	E	165	B4
Suckow	D	73	A4
Sućuraj	HR	138	B3
Sudbury	GB	45	A4
Suddesjaur	S	195	E10
Suden	D	64	B1
Süderbrarup	D	64	B2
Süderlügum	D	64	B1
Suðavík	IS	190	A2
Suðureyri	IS	190	A2
Sudoměřice u Bechyně	CZ	96	B2
Sudovec	HR	124	A2
Sueca	E	159	B3
Suelli	I	179	C3
Sugenheim	D	94	B2
Sugères	F	117	B3
Sugny	B	91	B4
Suhl	D	82	B2
Suhlendorf	D	73	B3
Suho Polje	BIH	125	C5
Suhopolje	HR	124	B3
Şuhut	TR	189	A5
Šuica	BIH	138	B3
Suippes	F	91	B4
Sukošan	HR	137	A4
Sükösd	H	125	A4
Suków	PL	87	B4
Šuľa	SK	99	C3
Suldalsosen	N	52	A2
Suldrup	DK	58	B2
Sulechów	PL	75	B4
Sulęcin	PL	75	B4
Sulęczyno	PL	68	A2
Sulejów	PL	87	A3
Süleymanlı	TR	186	D2
Sulgen	CH	107	B4
Sulibórz	PL	75	A4
Sulina	RO	17	C8
Sulingen	D	72	B1
Suliszewo	PL	75	A4
Sulitjelma	N	195	C7
Sułkowice	PL	99	B3
Süller	TR	189	A4
Sully-sur-Loire	F	103	B4
Sulmierzyce, Łódzkie	PL	86	A3
Sulmierzyce, Wielkopolskie	PL	85	A5
Sulmona	I	169	A3
Süloğlu	TR	186	A1
Suloszowa	PL	87	B3
Sulów	PL	85	A5
Sulsdorf	D	65	B4
Sultandağı	TR	189	A6
Sülüklü	TR	187	D7
Suluova	TR	23	A8
Sulvik	S	54	A3
Sülysáp	H	112	B3
Sülz	D	93	C4
Sulzbach, Baden-Württemberg	D	94	C1
Sulzbach, Baden-Württemberg	D	94	B1
Sulzbach, Bayern	D	93	B5
Sulzbach, Saarland	D	92	B3
Sulzbach-Rosenberg	D	95	B3
Sülze	D	72	B3
Sulzfeld	D	82	B2
Sumartin	HR	138	B2
Sumburgh	GB	33	B5
Sümeg	H	111	C4
Sumiswald	CH	106	B2
Šumná	CZ	97	C3
Šumperk	CZ	97	B4
Šumvald	CZ	98	B1
Sunbilla	E	144	A2
Sünching	D	95	C4
Sund	FIN	51	B7
Sund	S	54	A2
Sundborn	S	50	B2
Sundby	DK	58	B1
Sunde	N	46	C2
Sunde bru	N	53	B5
Sunderland	GB	37	B5
Sundern	D	81	A4
Sundhultsbrunn	S	62	A2
Sundnäs	S	195	D8
Sundom	S	196	D5
Sunds	DK	59	B2
Sundsfjord	N	195	D5
Sundsvall	S	200	D3
Sungurlu	TR	23	A8
Suni	I	178	B2
Sunja	HR	124	B2
Sunnansjö	S	50	B1
Sunnaryd	S	60	B3
Sunndalsøra	N	198	C5
Sunne	S	49	C5
Sunnemo	S	49	C5
Sunnersberg	S	55	B4
Suolovuopmio	N	192	C7
Suomussalmi	FIN	3	D11
Suoyarvi	RUS	9	A8
Super Sauze	F	132	A2
Supetar	HR	138	B2
Supetarska Draga	HR	123	C3
Supino	I	169	B3
Šuplja Stijena	MNE	139	B5
Surahammar	S	56	A2
Şurany	SK	112	A2
Surazh	BY	13	A9
Surbo	I	173	B4
Surčin	SRB	127	C2
Surgères	F	114	B3
Surhuisterveen	NL	70	A3
Sùria	E	147	C2
Surin	F	115	B4
Surka	N	48	B2
Surnadalsøra	N	198	C5
Sursee	CH	106	B3
Surte	S	60	B2
Surwold	D	71	B4
Sury-le-Comtal	F	117	B4
Susa	I	119	B4
Šušara	SRB	127	C3
Susch	CH	107	C4
Susegana	I	122	B1
Süsel	D	65	B3
Sušice	CZ	96	B1
Šušnjevica	HR	123	B3
Sussen	D	94	C1
Susurluk	TR	186	C3
Susz	PL	69	B4
Sütçüler	TR	189	B5
Sutivan	HR	138	B2
Sutjeska	SRB	126	B2
Sutri	I	168	A2
Sutton	GB	44	B4
Sutton Coldfield	GB	40	C2
Sutton-in-Ashfield	GB	40	B2
Sutton-on-Sea	GB	41	B4
Sutton-on-Trent	GB	40	B2
Sutton Scotney	GB	44	B2
Sutton Valence	GB	45	B4
Suvaja	BIH	124	B2
Suvereto	I	135	B3
Suwałki	PL	12	A5
Suze-la-Rousse	F	131	A3
Suzzara	I	121	C3
Svabensverk	S	50	A2
Svalbard	IS	191	A10
Svalöv	S	61	D3
Svanabyn	S	200	B3
Svanberga	S	51	C5
Svaneke	DK	67	A4
Svanesund	S	54	B2
Svängsta	S	63	B2
Svannäs	S	195	D9
Svanskog	S	54	A3
Svanstein	S	196	C6
Svappavaara	S	196	B4
Svärdsjö	S	50	B2
Svarstad	N	53	A5
Svartå, Örebro	S	55	A5
Svärta, Södermanland	S	56	B3
Svartå, Värmland	S	55	A4
Svartbyn	S	196	C5
Svärtinge	S	56	B2
Svartlå	S	196	D4
Svartnäs	S	50	B3
Svartnes	N	195	C5
Svarttjärn	S	195	E7
Svatsum	N	48	A1
Svätý Jur	SK	111	A4
Svätý Peter	SK	112	B2
Svedala	S	61	D3
Sveg	S	199	C11
Sveindal	N	52	B3
Sveio	N	52	A1
Svejbæk	DK	59	B2
Svelgen	N	198	D2
Svelvik	N	54	A1
Svendborg	DK	65	A3
Svene	N	53	A5
Svenljunga	S	60	B3
Svennevad	S	56	A1
Svenstavik	S	199	C11
Svenstrup	DK	58	B2
Švermov	CZ	84	B2
Sveti Ivan Zabno	HR	124	B2
Sveti Ivan Zelina	HR	124	B2
Sveti Nikole	MK	182	B3
Sveti Rok	HR	137	A4
Světlá nad Sázavou	CZ	97	B3
Svetlyy	RUS	69	A5
Svetvinčenat	HR	122	B2
Švica	HR	123	C4
Svidník	SK	12	D4
Švihov	CZ	96	B1
Svilajnac	SRB	127	C3
Svilengrad	BG	183	B8
Svindal	N	54	A2
Svinhult	S	62	A3
Svinna	SK	98	C2
Svinninge	DK	61	D1
Svinninge	S	57	A4
Sviritsa	RUS	9	B8
Svishtov	BG	17	D6
Svislach	BY	13	B6
Svit	SK	99	B4
Svitavy	CZ	97	B4
Svodin	SK	112	B2
Svolvær	N	194	B5
Svortemyr	N	46	A2
Svortland	N	52	A1
Svratka	CZ	97	B3
Svrčinovec	SK	98	B2
Svullrya	N	49	B4
Svyetlahorsk	BY	13	B8
Swadlincote	GB	40	C2
Swaffham	GB	41	C4
Swanage	GB	43	B5
Swanley	GB	45	B4
Swanlinbar	IRL	26	B3
Swansea	GB	39	C3
Swarzędz	PL	76	B2
Swatragh	GB	27	B4
Świątki	PL	69	B5
Świdnica, Dolnośląskie	PL	85	B4
Świdnica, Lubuskie	PL	84	A3
Świdnik	PL	12	C5
Świdwin	PL	67	C4
Świebodzice	PL	85	B4
Świebodzin	PL	75	B4
Świecie	PL	76	A3
Świedziebnia	PL	77	A4
Świeradów Zdrój	PL	84	B3
Świerki	PL	85	B4
Świerzawa	PL	85	A3
Świerzno	PL	67	C3
Swięta	PL	74	A3
Swieta Anna	PL	86	B3
Świętno	PL	75	B4
Swifterbant	NL	70	B2
Swindon	GB	44	B2
Swineshead	GB	41	C3
Swinford	IRL	26	C2
Świnoujście	PL	66	C3
Swinton	GB	35	C5
Swobnica	PL	74	A3
Swords	IRL	30	A2
Swornegacie	PL	68	B2
Sya	S	56	B1
Syasstroy	RUS	9	B8
Sycewice	PL	68	A1
Sychevka	RUS	9	E9
Syców	PL	86	A1
Sycowice	PL	75	B4
Sydnes	N	52	A1
Syfteland	N	46	B2
Syke	N	72	B1
Sykkylven	N	198	C3
Sylling	N	48	C2
Sylte	N	198	C4
Symbister	GB	33	A5
Symington	GB	36	A3
Symonds Yat	GB	39	C4
Sypniewo, Kujawsko-Pomorskie	PL	76	A2
Sypniewo, Wielkopolskie	PL	68	B1
Syserum	S	62	A4
Sysslebäck	S	49	B4
Syväjärvi	FIN	197	C9
Szabadbattyán	H	112	B2
Szabadegyháza	H	112	B2
Szabadszállás	H	112	C3
Szadek	PL	86	A2
Szajol	H	113	B4
Szakály	H	112	C2
Szakcs	H	112	C2
Szakmár	H	112	C3
Szałas	H	87	A4
Szalkszentmárton	H	112	C3
Szalonna	H	99	C4
Szamocin	PL	76	A2
Szamotuły	PL	75	B5
Szany	H	111	B4
Szarvas	H	113	C4
Szarvaskö	H	113	B4
Szászvár	H	125	A4
Százhalombatta	H	112	B2
Szczawa	PL	99	B4
Szczawnica	PL	99	B4
Szczecin	PL	74	A3
Szczecinek	PL	68	B1
Szczekociny	PL	87	B3
Szczerców	PL	86	A3
Szczucin	PL	87	B5
Szczuczarz	PL	75	A5
Szczuki	PL	77	B5
Szczurowa	PL	87	B4
Szczyrk	PL	99	B3
Szczytna	PL	85	B4
Szczytno	PL	77	A5
Szczyty	PL	86	A2
Szécsény	H	112	A3
Szederkény	H	125	B4
Szedres	H	112	C2
Szeged	H	126	A2
Szeghalom	H	113	B5
Szegvár	H	113	C4
Székesfehérvár	H	112	B2
Székkutas	H	113	C4
Szekszárd	H	125	A4
Szemplino Czarne	PL	77	A5
Szemud	PL	68	A3
Szendehely	H	112	B3
Szendrő	H	99	C4
Szentendre	H	112	B3
Szentes	H	113	C4
Szentgotthárd	H	111	C3
Szentlászló	H	125	A3
Szentlörinc	H	125	A3
Szentmártonkáta	H	113	B3
Szenyér	H	111	C4
Szeremle	H	125	A4
Szerencs	H	113	A5
Szerep	H	113	B5
Szigetszentmiklós	H	112	B3
Szigetvár	H	125	A3
Szikáncs	H	126	A2
Szikszó	H	113	A4
Szil	H	111	B4
Szilvásvárad	H	113	A4
Szklarska Poręba	PL	84	B3
Szlichtyngowa	PL	85	A4
Szob	H	112	B2
Szolnok	H	113	B4
Szombathely	H	111	B3
Szorosad	H	112	C2
Szpetal Graniczny	PL	77	B4
Szprotawa	PL	84	A3
Szreńsk	PL	77	A5
Sztum	PL	69	B4
Sztutowo	PL	69	A4
Szubin	PL	76	A2
Szücsi	H	113	B3
Szulmierz	PL	77	B5
Szulok	H	124	A3
Szumanie	PL	77	B4
Szwecja	PL	75	A5
Szydłów, Łódzkie	PL	86	A3
Szydłów, Świętokrzyskie	PL	87	B5
Szydłowiec	PL	87	A4
Szydlowo, Mazowieckie	PL	77	A5
Szydlowo, Wielkopolskie	PL	75	A5
Szymanów	PL	77	B5
Szynkielów	PL	86	A2

T

Taastrup	DK	61	D2
Tab	H	112	C2
Tabanera la Luenga	E	151	A3
Tabaqueros	E	158	B2
Tábara	E	149	A4
Tabenera de Cerrato	E	142	B2
Tabernas	E	164	B2
Tabiano Bagni	I	120	C3
Taboada	E	140	B3
Taboadela	E	140	B3
Tábor	CZ	96	B2
Táborfalva	H	112	B3
Taborište	HR	124	B2
Tábua	P	148	B1
Tabuaco	P	148	A2
Tabuenca	E	152	A2
Tabuyo del Monte	E	141	B4
Täby	S	57	A4
Tác	H	112	B2
Tachov	CZ	95	B4
Tadcaster	GB	40	B2
Tadley	GB	44	B2
Tafalla	E	144	B2
Tafjord	N	198	C4
Taganheira	P	160	B1
Tågarp	S	61	D2
Tàggia	I	133	B3
Tagliacozzo	I	169	A3
Táglio di Po	I	121	C5
Tagnon	F	91	B4
Tahal	E	164	B2
Tahitótfalu	H	112	B3
Tahtaköprü	TR	187	C4
Tailfingen	D	107	A4
Taillis	F	101	A4
Tain	GB	32	D2
Tain-l'Hermitage	F	117	B4
Taipadas	P	154	C2
Taivalkoski	FIN	197	D11
Taivassalo	FIN	8	B2
Takovo	SRB	127	C2
Taksony	H	112	B3
Tal	H	140	B2
Tal-Y-Llyn	GB	38	B3
Talachyn	BY	13	A8
Talamello	I	135	B5
Talamone	I	168	A1
Talant	F	105	B3
Talarrubias	E	156	A2
Talaván	E	155	B4
Talavera de la Reina	E	150	C3
Talavera la Real	E	155	C4
Talayuela	E	150	C2
Talayuelas	E	159	B2
Talgarth	GB	39	C3
Talgje	N	52	A1
Talhadas	P	148	B1
Táliga	E	155	C3
Talizat	F	116	B3
Tålknafjörður	IS	190	B2
Talla	I	135	B4
Talladale	GB	31	B3
Tallaght	IRL	30	A2
Tallard	F	132	A2
Tällberg, Dalarnas	S	50	B1
Tallberg, Norrbotten	S	196	C5
Tallinn	EST	8	C4
Talloires	F	118	B3
Tallow	IRL	29	B3
Tallsjö	S	200	B4
Tallvik	S	196	C5
Talmay	F	105	B4
Talmont-St. Hilaire	F	114	B2
Talmont-sur-Gironde	F	114	C3
Talne	UA	13	D9
Talsano	I	173	B3
Talsi	LV	8	D3
Talvik	N	192	B6
Talybont	GB	39	B3
Tamajón	E	151	B4
Tamame	E	149	A4
Tamames	E	149	B3
Tamarit de Mar	E	147	C2
Tamarite de Litera	E	145	C4
Tamariu	E	147	C4
Tamási	H	112	C2
Tambach-Dietharz	D	82	B2
Tameza	E	141	A4
Tammisaari	FIN	8	B3
Tampere	FIN	8	B3
Tamsweg	A	109	B4
Tamurejo	E	156	B3
Tana bru	N	193	B12
Tanakajd	H	111	B3
Tananger	N	52	B1
Tanaunella	I	178	B3
Tancarville	F	89	A4
Tandsjöborg	S	199	D11
Tånga	S	61	C2
Tangelic	H	112	C2
Tangen	N	48	B3
Tangerhütte	D	73	B4
Tangermünde	D	73	B4
Tanhua	FIN	197	B10
Taninges	F	118	A3
Tankavaara	FIN	197	A10
Tann	D	82	B2
Tanna	D	83	B3
Tannåker	S	60	C3
Tännäs	S	199	C9
Tannay, Ardennes	F	91	B4
Tannay, Nièvre	F	104	B2
Tannenbergsthal	D	83	B4
Tännesberg	D	95	B4
Tannheim	A	108	B1
Tannila	FIN	197	D8
Tanowo	PL	74	A3
Tanum	S	54	B2
Tanumshede	S	54	B2
Tanus	F	130	A1
Tanvald	CZ	84	B3
Taormina	I	177	B4
Tapa	EST	8	C4
Tapfheim	D	94	C2
Tapia de Casariego	E	141	A4
Tapio	F	146	A2
Tápióbicske	H	112	B3
Tápiógyörgye	H	113	B3
Tápióság	H	112	B3
Tápiószecsö	H	112	B3
Tápiószele	H	113	B3
Tápiószentmárton	H	113	B3
Tapolca	H	111	C4
Tapolcafö	H	111	B4
Tar	HR	122	B2
Tarabo	S	60	B2
Taradell	E	147	C3
Taraklı	TR	187	B5
Taramundi	E	141	A3
Tarancón	E	151	B4
Táranto	I	173	B3
Tarare	F	117	B4
Tarascon	F	131	B3
Tarascon-sur-Ariège	F	146	B2
Tarashcha	UA	13	D9
Tarazona	F	144	C2
Tarazona de la Mancha	E	158	B2
Tarbena	E	159	C3
Tarbert	GB	34	C2
Tarbert	IRL	29	B2
Tarbes	F	145	A4
Tarbet	GB	34	B3
Tarbolton	GB	36	A2
Tarcento	I	122	A2
Tarčin	BIH	139	B4
Tarczyn	PL	77	C5
Tardajos	E	143	B3
Tardelcuende	E	151	A5
Tardets-Sorholus	F	144	A3
Tardienta	E	145	C3
Tärendö	S	196	B5
Targon	F	128	B2
Târgovişte	RO	17	C6
Târgu-Jiu	RO	17	C5
Târgu Mureş	RO	17	B6
Târgu Ocna	RO	17	B7
Târgu Secuiesc	RO	17	C7
Tarifa	E	162	B2
Tariquejas	E	161	B2
Tarján	H	112	B2
Tárkany	H	112	B2
Tarland	GB	33	D4
Tarłów	PL	87	A5
Tarm	DK	59	C1
Tarmstedt	D	72	A2
Tärnaby	S	195	E6
Tarnalelesz	H	113	A4
Tarnaörs	H	113	B3
Târnăveni	RO	17	B6
Târnet	N	193	C14
Tarnobrzeg	PL	87	B5
Tarnos	F	128	C1
Tarnów, Lubuskie	PL	75	B3
Tarnów, Małopolskie	PL	87	B4
Tarnowo Podgórne	PL	75	B5
Tarnowskie Góry	PL	86	B2
Tärnsjö	S	51	B3
Tårnvik	S	194	C6
Tarouca	P	148	B2
Tarp	D	64	B2
Tarquínia	I	168	A1
Tarquínia Lido	I	168	A1
Tarragona	E	147	C2
Tàrrajaur	S	196	C2
Tàrrega	E	147	C2
Tårs, Nordjyllands	DK	58	A3
Tårs, Storstrøms	DK	65	B4
Tarsia	I	174	B2
Tarsus	TR	23	C8
Tartas	F	128	C2
Tartu	EST	8	C5
Tarves	GB	33	D4
Tarvísio	I	109	C4
Taşağıl	TR	189	C6
Täsch	CH	119	A4
Taşköprü	TR	23	A8
Tasov	CZ	97	B4
Tasovčići	BIH	139	B3
Taşucuo	TR	23	C7
Tát	H	112	B2
Tata	H	112	B2
Tatabánya	H	112	B2
Tataháza	H	126	A1
Tatarbunary	UA	17	C8
Tatárszentgyörgy	H	112	B3
Tatranská-Lomnica	SK	99	B4
Tau	N	52	A1

Name	Country	Page	Grid
Tauber-bischofsheim	D	94	B1
Taucha	D	83	A4
Taufkirchen	D	95	C4
Taufkirchen an der Pram	A	96	C1
Taulé	F	100	A2
Taulignan	F	131	A3
Taulov	DK	59	C2
Taunton	GB	43	A4
Taunusstein	D	81	B4
Tauragé	LT	12	A4
Taurianova	I	175	C2
Taurisano	I	173	C4
Tauste	E	144	C2
Tauves	F	116	B2
Tavankut	SRB	126	A1
Tavannes	CH	106	B2
Tavarnelle val di Pesa	I	135	B4
Tavas	TR	188	B4
Tavaux	F	105	B4
Tävelsås	S	62	B2
Taverna	I	175	B2
Taverne	CH	120	A1
Tavernelle	I	135	B5
Tavernes de la Valldigna	E	159	B3
Tavernola Bergamasca	I	120	B2
Taverny	F	90	B2
Tavescan	E	146	B2
Taviano	I	173	C4
Tavira	P	160	B2
Tavistock	GB	42	B2
Tavşanlı	TR	187	C4
Tayinloan	GB	34	C2
Taynuilt	GB	34	B2
Tayport	GB	35	B5
Tázlár	H	112	C3
Tazones	E	142	A1
Tczew	PL	69	A3
Tczów	PL	87	A5
Teangue	GB	31	B3
Teano	I	170	B2
Teba	E	162	B3
Tebay	GB	37	B4
Techendorf	A	109	C4
Tecklenburg	D	71	B4
Tecko-matorp	S	61	D3
Tecuci	RO	17	C7
Tefenni	TR	189	B4
Tegelsmora	S	51	B4
Tegernsee	D	108	B2
Teggiano	I	172	B1
Tegoleto	I	135	B4
Teichel	D	82	B3
Teignmouth	GB	43	B3
Teillay	F	101	B4
Teillet	F	130	B1
Teisendorf	D	109	B3
Teistungen	D	82	A2
Teixeiro	E	140	A2
Tejada de Tiétar	E	150	B2
Tejado	E	152	A1
Tejares	E	150	B2
Tejn	DK	67	A3
Teke	TR	187	A4
Tekirdağ	TR	186	B2
Tekovské-Lužany	SK	112	A2
Telavåg	N	46	B1
Telč	CZ	97	B3
Telese Terme	I	170	B2
Telford	GB	38	B4
Telfs	A	108	B2
Telgárt	SK	99	C4
Telgte	D	71	C4
Tellingstedt	D	64	B2
Telšiai	LT	8	E3
Telti	I	178	B3
Teltow	D	74	B2
Tembleque	E	157	A4
Temelin	CZ	96	B2
Temerin	SRB	126	B1
Temiño	E	143	B3
Témpio Pausánia	I	178	B3
Temple Sowerby	GB	37	B4
Templederry	IRL	28	B3
Templemore	IRL	28	B4
Templin	D	74	A2
Temse	B	79	A4
Ten Boer	NL	71	A3
Tenay	F	118	B2
Tenbury Wells	GB	39	B4
Tenby	GB	39	C2
Tence	F	117	B4
Tende	F	133	A3
Tenhult	S	62	A2
Tenja	HR	125	B4
Tenneville	B	92	A1
Tennevoll	N	194	B8
Tensta	S	51	B4
Tenterden	GB	45	B4
Teo	E	140	B2
Teora	I	172	B1
Tepasto	FIN	196	B7
Tepelenë	AL	182	C2
Teplá	CZ	95	B4
Teplice	CZ	84	B1
Teplička nad Váhom	SK	98	B2
Tepsa	FIN	197	B8
Ter Apel	NL	71	B4
Tera	E	143	C4
Téramo	I	169	A3
Terborg	NL	71	C3
Terchová	SK	99	B3
Terebovlya	UA	13	D6
Teremia Mare	RO	126	B2
Terena	P	155	C3
Teresa de Cofrentes	E	159	B2
Terešov	CZ	96	B1
Terezín	CZ	84	B2
Terezino Polje	HR	124	B3
Tergnier	F	90	B3
Teriberka	RUS	3	B14
Terlizzi	I	171	B4
Termas de Monfortinho	P	155	A4
Terme di Súio	I	169	B3
Terme di Valdieri	I	133	A3
Termens	E	145	C4
Termes	F	116	C3
Términi Imerese	I	176	B2
Terminillo	I	169	A2
Térmoli	I	170	B3
Termonfeckin	IRL	27	C4
Ternberg	A	110	B1
Terndrup	DK	58	B3
Terneuzen	NL	79	A3
Terni	I	168	A2
Ternitz	A	111	B3
Ternopil	UA	13	D6
Terpni	GR	183	C5
Terracina	I	169	B3
Terråk	N	195	E3
Terralba	I	179	C2
Terranova di Pollino	I	174	B2
Terranova di Sibari	I	174	B2
Terras do Bouro	P	148	A1
Terrasini	I	176	A2
Terrassa	E	147	C3
Terrasson-la-Villedieu	F	129	A4
Terrazos	E	143	B3
Terriente	E	152	B2
Terrugem	P	155	C3
Terténia	I	179	C3
Teruel	E	152	B2
Tervola	FIN	196	C7
Tervuren	B	79	B4
Terzaga	E	152	B2
Tešanj	BIH	125	C3
Tesáske-Mlyňany	SK	98	C2
Teslić	BIH	125	C3
Tessin	D	66	B1
Tessy-sur-Vire	F	88	B2
Tét	H	111	B4
Tetbury	GB	43	A4
Teterchen	F	92	B2
Teterow	D	65	C5
Teteven	BG	17	D6
Tetiyev	UA	13	D8
Tetovo	MK	182	A2
Tettau	D	82	B3
Tettnang	D	107	B4
Teublitz	D	95	B4
Teuchern	D	83	A4
Teulada	E	159	C4
Teulada	I	179	D2
Teupitz	D	74	B2
Teurajärvi	S	196	C5
Teutschenthal	D	83	A3
Tevel	H	112	C2
Teviothead	GB	36	A4
Tewkesbury	GB	39	C4
Thale	D	82	A3
Thalfang	D	92	B2
Thalgau	A	109	B4
Thalkirch	CH	107	C4
Thalmässing	D	95	B3
Thalwil	CH	107	B3
Thame	GB	44	B3
Thann	F	106	B2
Thannhausen	D	94	C2
Thaon-les-Vosges	F	105	A5
Tharandt	D	83	B5
Tharsis	E	161	B2
Thasos	GR	183	C6
Thatcham	GB	44	B2
Thaxted	GB	45	B4
Thaynigen	CH	107	B3
The Barony	GB	33	B3
The Hague = 's-Gravenhage	NL	70	B1
The Mumbles	GB	39	C3
Theale	GB	44	B2
Thebes = Thiva	GR	185	A4
Theding-hausen	D	72	B2
Theessen	D	73	B5
Themar	D	82	B2
Thénezay	F	102	C1
Thenon	F	129	A4
Therouanne	F	78	B2
Thessaloniki = Salonica	GR	182	C4
Thetford	GB	45	A4
Theux	B	80	B1
Thézar-les-Corbières	F	146	A3
Thèze	F	145	A3
Thiberville	F	89	A4
Thibie	F	91	C4
Thiendorf	D	84	A1
Thiene	I	121	B4
Thierrens	CH	106	C1
Thiers	F	117	B3
Thiesi	I	178	B2
Thiessow	D	66	B2
Thiezac	F	116	B2
Þingeyri	IS	190	B2
Þingvellir	IS	190	C4
Thionville	F	92	B2
Thira	GR	185	C6
Thiron-Gardais	F	89	B4
Thirsk	GB	37	B5
Thisted	DK	58	B1
Thiva = Thebes	GR	185	A4
Thivars	F	90	C1
Thiviers	F	115	C4
Thizy	F	117	A4
Tholen	NL	79	A4
Tholey	D	92	B3
Thomas Street	IRL	28	A3
Thomastown	IRL	30	B1
Thônes	F	118	B3
Thonnance-les-Joinville	F	91	C5
Thonon-les-Bains	F	118	A3
Thorame-Basse	F	132	A2
Thorame-Haute	F	132	A2
Thorens-Glières	F	118	A3
Thorigny-sur-Oreuse	F	91	C3
Thörl	A	110	B2
Þorlákshöfn	IS	190	D4
Thornaby on Tees	GB	37	B5
Thornbury	GB	43	A4
Thorne	GB	40	B3
Thornhill, Dumfries & Galloway	GB	36	A3
Thornhill, Stirling	GB	35	B3
Thornthwaite	GB	36	B3
Thornton-le-Dale	GB	40	A3
Þórshöfn	IS	191	A10
Thouarcé	F	102	B1
Thouars	F	102	C1
Thrapston	GB	44	A3
Threlkeld	GB	36	B3
Thrumster	GB	32	C3
Thueyts	F	117	C4
Thuin	B	79	B4
Thuir	F	146	B3
Thumau	D	95	A3
Thun	CH	106	C2
Thuret	F	116	B3
Thurey	F	105	C4
Thüringen	A	107	B4
Thurins	F	117	B4
Thürkow	D	65	C5
Thurles	IRL	29	B4
Thurmaston	GB	40	C2
Thurø By	DK	65	A3
Thursby	GB	36	B3
Thurso	GB	32	C3
Thury-Harcourt	F	89	B3
Thusis	CH	107	C4
Thyborøn	DK	58	B1
Þykkvibær	IS	190	D5
Thyregod	DK	59	C2
Tibi	E	159	C3
Tibro	S	55	B5
Tidaholm	S	55	B4
Tidan	S	55	B5
Tidersrum	S	62	A3
Tiedra	E	150	A2
Tiefenbach	D	95	B4
Tiefencastel	CH	107	C4
Tiefenort	D	82	B2
Tiefensee	D	74	B2
Tiel	NL	79	A5
Tielmes	E	151	B4
Tielt	B	78	A3
Tienen	B	79	B4
Tiengen	D	106	B3
Tiercé	F	102	B1
Tierga	E	152	A2
Tiermas	E	144	B2
Tierp	S	51	B4
Tierrantona	E	145	B4
Tighina	MD	17	B8
Tighnabruaich	GB	34	C2
Tignes	F	119	B3
Tigy	F	103	B4
Tihany	H	112	C1
Tijnje	NL	70	A2
Tijola	E	164	B2
Tikhvin	RUS	9	C8
Til Châtel	F	105	B4
Tilh	F	128	C2
Tillac	F	145	A4
Tillberga	S	56	A2
Tille	F	90	B2
Tillicoultry	GB	35	B4
Tilloy Bellay	F	91	B4
Tilly	F	115	B5
Tilly-sur-Seulles	F	88	A3
Tim	DK	59	B1
Timau	I	109	C4
Timbaki	GR	185	D5
Timi	CY	181	B1
Timişoara	RO	126	B3
Timmele	S	60	B3
Timmendorfer Strand	D	65	C3
Timmernabben	S	62	B4
Timmersdala	S	55	B4
Timoleague	IRL	29	C3
Timolin	IRL	30	B2
Timrå	S	200	D3
Timsfors	S	61	C3
Timsgearraidh	GB	31	A1
Tinajas	E	152	B1
Tinalhas	P	155	B3
Tinchebray	F	88	B3
Tincques	F	78	B2
Tineo	E	141	A4
Tinglev	DK	64	B2
Tingsryd	S	63	B2
Tingstäde	S	57	C4
Tingvoll	N	198	C5
Tinlot	B	79	B5
Tinnoset	N	53	A5
Tinos	GR	185	B6
Tintagel	GB	42	B2
Tinténiac	F	101	A4
Tintern	GB	39	C4
Tintigny	B	92	B1
Tione di Trento	I	121	A3
Tipperary	IRL	29	B3
Tiptree	GB	45	B4
Tirana = Tiranë	AL	182	B1
Tiranë = Tirana	AL	182	B1
Tirano	I	120	A3
Tiraspol	MD	17	B8
Tire	TR	188	A2
Tires	I	108	C2
Tiriez	E	158	C1
Tirig	E	153	B4
Tiriolo	I	175	C2
Tirnavos	GR	182	D4
Tirrénia	I	134	B3
Tirschenreuth	D	95	B4
Tirstrup	DK	59	B3
Tirteafuera	E	157	B3
Tisno	HR	137	B4
Tišnov	CZ	97	B4
Tisovec	SK	99	C3
Tisselskog	S	54	B3
Tistedal	N	54	A2
Tistrup	DK	59	C1
Tisvildeleje	DK	61	C2
Tiszaalpár	H	113	C3
Tiszabő	H	113	B4
Tiszacsége	H	113	B5
Tiszadorogma	H	113	B4
Tiszaföldvár	H	113	C4
Tiszafüred	H	113	B4
Tiszajenő	H	113	B4
Tiszakécske	H	113	C4
Tiszakeszi	H	113	B4
Tiszakürt	H	113	C4
Tiszalök	H	113	A5
Tiszalúc	H	113	A5
Tiszanána	H	113	B4
Tiszaörs	H	113	B4
Tiszaroff	H	113	B4
Tiszasüly	H	113	B4
Tiszasziget	H	126	A2
Tiszaszőlős	H	113	B4
Tiszaújváros	H	113	B5
Tiszavasvári	H	113	B5
Titaguas	E	159	B2
Titel	SRB	126	B2
Titisee-Neustadt	D	106	B3
Titova Korenica	HR	123	C4
Titran	N	198	B5
Tittling	D	96	C1
Tittmoning	D	109	A3
Titz	D	80	A2
Tiurajärvi	FIN	196	B7
Tived	S	55	B5
Tiverton	GB	43	B3
Tivisa	E	153	A4
Tivoli	I	168	B2
Tjæreborg	DK	59	C1
Tjällmo	S	56	B1
Tjåmotis	S	195	D9
Tjautjas	S	196	B3
Tjøme	N	54	A1
Tjong	N	195	D4
Tjonnefoss	N	53	B4
Tjøtta	N	195	E3
Tjörn	S	61	D5
Tjörnarp	S	61	D3
Tjötta	N	195	E3
Tkon	HR	137	B4
Tleń	PL	68	B3
Tlmače	SK	98	C2
Tłuchowo	PL	77	B4
Tlumačov	CZ	98	B1
Tóalmas	H	112	B3
Toano	I	134	A3
Toba	D	82	A2
Tobarra	E	158	C2
Tobercurry	IRL	26	B2
Tobermore	GB	27	B4
Tobermory	GB	34	B1
Toberonochy	GB	34	B2
Tobha Mor	GB	31	B1
Tocane-St. Apre	F	129	A3
Tocha	P	148	B1
Tocina	E	162	A2
Töcksfors	S	54	A2
Tocón	E	163	A4
Todal	N	198	C5
Todi	I	136	C1
Todmorden	GB	40	B1
Todorici	BIH	138	A3
Todtmoos	D	106	B3
Todtnau	D	106	B2
Toén	E	140	B3
Tofta, Gotland	S	57	C4
Tofta, Skaraborg	S	55	B4
Toftbyn	S	50	B2
Tofte	N	54	A1
Töftedal	S	54	B2
Tofterup	DK	59	C1
Toftlund	DK	59	C2
Tófü	H	125	A4
Tohmo	FIN	197	C10
Tokaj	H	113	A5
Tokarnia	PL	87	B4
Tokary	PL	76	C3
Tokod	H	112	B2
Toköl	H	112	B2
Tolastadh bho Thuath	GB	31	A2
Tolbańos	E	150	B3
Toledo	E	151	C3
Tolentino	I	136	B2
Tolfa	I	168	A1
Tolg	S	62	A2
Tolga	N	199	C8
Tolkmicko	PL	69	A4
Tollarp	S	61	D3
Tollered	S	60	B2
Tolløse	DK	61	D1
Tolmachevo	RUS	9	C6
Tolmezzo	I	122	A2
Tolmin	SLO	122	A2
Tolna	H	112	C2
Tolnanémedi	H	112	C2
Tolob	GB	33	B5
Tolosa	E	144	A1
Tolosa	P	155	B3
Tolox	E	162	B3
Tolpuddle	GB	43	B4
Tolva	E	145	B4
Tolva	FIN	197	C11
Tolve	I	172	B2
Tomar	P	154	B2
Tomaševac	SRB	126	B2
Tomašica	BIH	124	C2
Tomášikovo	SK	111	A4
Tomašouka	BY	13	C5
Tomášovce	SK	99	C3
Tomaszów Mazowiecki	PL	87	A4
Tomatin	GB	32	D3
Tombeboeuf	F	129	B3
Tomdoun	GB	32	D1
Tomelilla	S	66	A2
Tomelloso	E	151	B5
Tomelloso	I	157	A4
Tomiño	E	140	C2
Tomintoul	GB	32	D3
Tomislavgrad	BIH	138	B3
Tomisław	PL	84	A3
Tomisławice	PL	76	B3
Tomnavoulin	GB	32	D3
Tompa	H	126	A1
Tompaládony	H	111	B3
Tomra	N	198	C3
Tomter	N	54	A1
Tona	E	147	C3
Tonara	I	179	B3
Tonbridge	GB	45	B4
Tondela	P	148	B1
Tønder	DK	64	B1
Tongeren	B	79	B5
Tongue	GB	32	C2
Tönisvorst	D	80	A2
Tønjum	N	47	A4
Tonkopuro	FIN	197	C11
Tonnay-Boutonne	F	114	C3
Tonnay-Charente	F	114	C3
Tonneins	F	129	B3
Tonnerre	F	104	B3
Tonnes	N	195	D4
Tönning	D	64	B1
Tonsåsen	N	47	B6
Tønsberg	N	54	A1
Tonstad	N	52	B2
Toomyvara	IRL	28	B3
Toormore	IRL	29	C2
Topares	E	164	B2
Topas	E	150	A2
Topliţa	RO	17	B6
Topla	SLO	110	C2
Topola	SRB	127	C2
Topolčani	MK	182	B3
Topol'čany	SK	98	C2
Topol'čianky	SK	98	C2
Topolje	HR	124	B2
Topólka	PL	76	B3
Topol'niky	SK	111	B4
Topolovăţu Mare	RO	126	B3
Toponár	H	125	A3
Toporów	PL	75	B4
Topsham	GB	43	B3
Topusko	HR	124	B1
Torà	E	147	C2
Toral de los Guzmanes	E	142	B1
Toral de los Vados	E	141	B4
Torballa	TR	188	A2
Torbjörntorp	S	55	B4
Torbole	I	121	B3
Torchiarolo	I	173	B4
Torcross	GB	43	C3
Torcy-le-Petit	F	89	A5
Torda	SRB	126	B2
Tørdal	N	53	A4
Tordehumos	E	142	C1
Tordera	E	147	C3
Tordesillas	E	150	A2
Tordesilos	E	152	B2
Töre	S	196	D5
Töreboda	S	55	B5
Toreby	DK	65	B4
Torekov	S	61	C2
Torella dei Lombardi	I	170	C3
Torellò	I	147	B3
Toreno	E	141	B4
Torfou	F	114	A2
Torgau	D	83	A5
Torgelow	D	74	A3
Torgueda	P	148	A2
Torhamn	S	63	B3
Torhop	N	193	B11
Torhout	B	78	A3
Torigni-sur-Vire	F	88	A3
Torija	E	151	B4
Toril	E	152	B2
Torino = Turin	I	119	B4
Toritto	I	171	C4
Torkovichi	RUS	9	C7
Torla	E	145	B3
Tormac	RO	126	B3
Törmänen	FIN	193	D11
Tormestorp	S	61	C3
Tórmini	I	121	B3
Tornada	P	154	B1
Tornal'a	SK	99	C4
Tornavacas	E	150	B2
Tornby	DK	58	A2
Tornesch	D	72	A2
Torness	GB	32	D2
Torniella	I	135	B4
Tornimparte	I	169	A3
Torning	DK	59	B2
Tornio	FIN	196	D7
Tornjoš	SRB	126	B1
Tornos	E	152	B2
Toro	E	150	A2
Törökszentmiklós	H	113	B4
Toropets	RUS	9	D7
Torpa	S	61	C3
Torpè	I	178	B3
Torphins	GB	33	D4
Torpo	N	47	B5
Torpoint	GB	42	B2
Torpsbruk	S	62	A2
Torquay	GB	43	B3
Torquemada	E	142	B2
Torralba de Burgo	E	151	A5
Torralba de Calatrava	E	157	A4
Torrão	P	154	C2
Torre Annunziata	I	170	C2
Torre Canne	I	173	B3
Torre Cardela	E	163	A4
Torre das Vargens	P	154	B3
Torre de Coelheiros	P	154	C3
Torre de Dom Chama	P	149	A2
Torre de Juan Abad	E	157	B4
Torre de la Higuera	E	161	B3
Torre de Miguel Sesmero	E	155	C4
Torre de Moncorvo	P	149	A2
Torre de Santa Maria	E	156	A1
Torre del Bierzo	E	141	B4
Torre del Burgo	E	151	B4
Torre del Campo	E	163	A4
Torre del Greco	I	170	C2
Torre del Lago Puccini	I	134	B3
Torre del Mar	E	163	B3
Torre dell'Orso	I	173	B4
Torre do Terranho	P	148	B2
Torre Faro	I	177	A4
Torre la Ribera	E	145	B4
Torre los Negros	E	152	B2
Torre Orsária	I	172	B1
Torre-Pacheco	E	165	B4
Torre Péllice	I	119	C4
Torre Santa Susanna	I	173	B3
Toreblacos	E	143	C4
Torreblanca	E	153	B4
Torreblascopedro	E	157	B4
Torrecaballeros	E	151	A3
Torrecampo	E	156	B3
Torrecilla	E	152	B1
Torrecilla de la Jara	E	156	A3
Torrecilla de la Orden	E	150	A2
Torrecilla del Pinar	E	151	A3
Torrecilla en Cameros	E	143	B4
Torrecillas de la Tiesa	E	156	A2
Torredembarra	E	147	C2
Torredonjimeno	E	163	A4
Torregamones	E	149	A3
Torregrosa	E	147	C1
Torreira	P	148	B1
Torrejón de Ardoz	E	151	B4

Name	Country	Page	Grid
Torrejón de la Calzada	E	151	B4
Torrejón del Rey	E	151	B4
Torrejon el Rubio	E	156	A1
Torrejoncillo	E	155	B4
Torrelaguna	E	151	B4
Torrelapaja	E	152	A2
Torrelavega	E	142	A2
Torrelobatón	E	150	A2
Torrelodones	E	151	B4
Torremaggiore	I	171	B3
Torremanzanas	E	159	C3
Torremayor	E	155	C4
Torremezzo di Falconara	I	174	B2
Torremocha	E	156	A1
Torremolinos	E	163	B3
Torrenieri	I	135	B4
Torrenostra	E	153	B4
Torrenova	I	168	B2
Torrent	E	159	B3
Torrente de Cinca	E	153	A4
Torrenueva, *Ciudad Real*	E	157	B4
Torrenueva, *Granada*	E	163	B4
Torreorgaz	E	155	B4
Torreperogil	E	157	B4
Torres	E	163	A4
Torres-Cabrera	E	163	A3
Torres de la Alameda	E	151	B4
Torres Novas	P	154	B2
Torres Vedras	P	154	B1
Torresandino	E	143	C3
Torrevieja	E	165	B4
Torri del Benaco	I	121	B3
Torricella	I	173	B3
Torridon	GB	31	B3
Torriglia	I	134	A2
Torrijos	E	151	C3
Tørring	DK	59	C2
Torrita di Siena	I	135	B4
Torroal	P	154	C2
Torroella de Montgri	E	147	B4
Torrox	E	163	B4
Torrskog	S	54	A3
Torsåker	S	50	B3
Torsang	S	50	B2
Torsås	S	63	B4
Torsby	S	49	B4
Torsetra	N	48	B2
Torshälla	S	56	A2
Tórshavn	FO	4	A3
Torslanda	S	60	B1
Torsminde	DK	59	B1
Törtel	H	113	B3
Tórtoles	E	150	B2
Tórtoles de Esgueva	E	142	C2
Tortoli	I	179	C3
Tortona	I	120	C1
Tórtora	I	174	B1
Tortoreto Lido	I	136	C2
Tortorici	I	177	A3
Tortosa	E	153	B4
Tortosendo	P	148	B2
Tortuera	E	152	B2
Tortuero	E	151	B4
Toruń	PL	76	A3
Torup	S	60	C3
Torver	GB	36	B3
Tørvikbygde	N	46	B3
Torviscón	E	163	B4
Torzhok	RUS	9	D9
Torzym	PL	75	B4
Tosbotn	N	195	E3
Toscolano-Maderno	I	121	B3
Tosno	RUS	9	C7
Tossa de Mar	E	147	C3
Tossåsen	S	199	C10
Tosse	F	128	C1
Tösse	S	54	B3
Tossicía	I	169	A3
Tostedt	D	72	A2
Tosya	TR	23	A8
Tószeg	H	113	B4
Toszek	PL	86	B2
Totana	E	165	B3
Totebo	S	62	A4
Tôtes	F	89	A5
Totland	N	198	D2
Tøtlandsvik	N	52	A2
Totnes	GB	43	B3
Tótszerdahely	H	124	A2
Tøttdal	N	199	A8
Totton	GB	44	C2
Touça	P	149	A2
Toucy	F	104	B2
Toul	F	92	C1
Toulon	F	132	B1
Toulon-sur-Allier	F	104	C2
Toulon-sur-Arroux	F	104	C3
Toulouse	F	129	C4
Tour de la Parata	F	180	B1
Tourcoing	F	78	B3
Tourlaville	F	88	A2
Tournai	B	78	B3
Tournan-en-Brie	F	90	C2
Tournay	F	145	A4
Tournon-d'Agenais	F	129	B3
Tournon-St. Martin	F	115	B4
Tournon-sur-Rhône	F	117	B4
Tournus	F	105	C3
Touro	E	140	B2
Touro	P	148	B2
Tourouvre	F	89	B4
Tourriers	F	115	C4
Tours	F	102	B2
Tourteron	F	91	B4
Tourves	F	132	B1
Toury	F	103	A3
Touvedo	P	148	A1
Touvois	F	114	B2
Tovačov	CZ	98	B1
Tovariševo	SRB	126	B1
Tovarnik	HR	125	B5
Tovdal	N	53	B4
Towcester	GB	44	A3
Town Yetholm	GB	35	C5
Tråastølen	N	47	B4
Trabada	E	141	A3
Trabadelo	E	141	B4
Trabanca	E	149	A3
Trabazos	E	149	A3
Traben-Trarbach	D	92	B3
Trabia	I	176	B2
Tradate	I	120	B1
Trädet	S	60	B3
Trafaria	P	154	C1
Tragacete	E	152	B2
Tragwein	A	96	C2
Traiguera	E	153	B4
Trainel	F	91	C3
Traisen	A	110	A2
Traismauer	A	97	C3
Traitsching	D	95	B4
Trákhonas	CY	181	A2
Tralee	IRL	29	B2
Tramacastilla de Tena	E	145	B3
Tramagal	P	154	B2
Tramariglio	I	178	B2
Tramatza	I	179	B2
Tramelan	CH	106	B2
Tramonti di Sopra	I	122	A1
Tramore	IRL	30	B1
Trampot	F	92	C1
Trana	I	119	B4
Tranås	S	55	B5
Tranbjerg	DK	59	B3
Tranby	N	54	A1
Trancoso	P	148	B2
Tranebjerg	DK	59	C3
Tranekær	DK	65	B3
Tranemo	S	60	B3
Tranent	GB	35	C5
Tranevåg	N	52	B2
Trängslet	S	49	A5
Tranhult	S	60	B3
Trani	I	171	B4
Trans-en-Provence	F	132	B2
Transtrand	S	49	A5
Tranum	DK	58	A2
Tranvik	S	57	A4
Trápani	I	176	A1
Trappes	F	90	C2
Traryd	S	61	C3
Trasacco	I	169	B3
Trasierra	E	156	B1
Träslövsläge	S	60	B2
Trasmiras	E	140	B3
Traspinedo	E	150	A3
Trate	SLO	110	C2
Trauchgau	D	108	B1
Traun	A	110	A1
Traunreut	D	109	B3
Traunstein	D	109	B3
Traunwalchen	D	109	B3
Tråvad	S	55	B4
Travemünde	D	65	C3
Traversétolo	I	120	C3
Travnik	BIH	139	A3
Travnik	SLO	123	B3
Travo	F	180	B2
Travo	I	120	C2
Trawsfynydd	GB	38	B3
Trbovlje	SLO	123	A4
Trbušani	SRB	127	D2
Treban	F	116	B1
Třebařov	CZ	97	B4
Trebatsch	D	74	B3
Trebbin	D	74	B2
Třebechovice pod Orebem	CZ	85	B3
Trebel	D	73	B4
Třebenice	CZ	84	B1
Trébeurden	F	100	A2
Třebíč	CZ	97	B3
Trebisacce	I	174	B2
Trebitz	D	83	A4
Trebnje	SLO	123	B4
Třeboň	CZ	96	B2
Třebovice	CZ	97	B4
Trebsen	D	83	A4
Trebujena	E	161	C3
Trecastagni	I	177	B4
Trecate	I	120	B1
Trecenta	I	121	B4
Tredegar	GB	39	C3
Tredózio	I	135	A4
Treffen	A	109	C4
Treffort	F	118	A2
Treffurt	D	82	A2
Trefnant	GB	38	A3
Tregaron	GB	39	B3
Trégastel-Plage	F	100	A2
Tregnago	I	121	B4
Tregony	GB	42	B2
Tréguier	F	100	A2
Trégunc	F	100	B2
Treharris	GB	39	C3
Trehörningsjö	S	200	C4
Tréia	I	136	B2
Treignac	F	116	B1
Treignat	F	116	A2
Treignes	B	91	A4
Treis-Karden	D	80	B3
Trekanten	S	63	B4
Trélazé	F	102	B1
Trelech	GB	39	C2
Trélissac	F	129	A3
Trelleborg	S	66	A2
Trélon	F	91	A4
Trélou-sur-Marne	F	91	B3
Tremblay-le-Vicomte	F	89	B5
Tremés	P	154	B2
Tremezzo	I	120	B2
Třemošná	CZ	96	B1
Tremp	E	145	B4
Trenčianska Stankovce	SK	98	C1
Trenčianske Turná	SK	98	C2
Trenčianske Teplá	SK	98	C2
Trenčianske Teplice	SK	98	C2
Trenčín	SK	98	C2
Trendelburg	D	81	A5
Trengereid	N	46	B2
Trensacq	F	128	B2
Trent	D	66	B2
Trento	I	121	A4
Treorchy	GB	39	C3
Trept	F	118	B2
Trepuzzi	I	173	B4
Trescore Balneário	I	120	B2
Tresenda	I	120	A3
Tresfjord	N	198	C4
Tresigallo	I	121	C4
Trešnjevica	SRB	127	D3
Tresnurághes	I	178	B2
Trespaderne	E	143	B3
Třešt	CZ	97	B3
Trestina	I	135	B5
Tretower	GB	39	C3
Trets	F	132	B1
Tretten	N	48	A2
Treuchtlingen	D	94	C2
Treuen	D	83	B4
Treuenbrietzen	D	74	B1
Treungen	N	53	A4
Trevelez	E	163	B4
Trevi	I	136	C1
Trevi nel Lázio	I	169	B3
Treviana	E	143	B3
Treviglio	I	120	B2
Trevignano Romano	I	168	A2
Treviso	I	122	B1
Trévoux	F	117	B4
Trézelles	F	117	A3
Trezzo sull'Adda	I	120	B2
Trhová Kamenice	CZ	97	B3
Trhové Sviny	CZ	96	C2
Triacastela	E	141	B3
Triaize	F	114	B2
Trianda	GR	188	C3
Triaucourt-en-Argonne	F	91	C5
Tribanj Kruščica	HR	137	A4
Triberg	D	106	A3
Tribsees	D	66	B1
Tribuče	SLO	123	B4
Tricárico	I	172	B2
Tricase	I	173	C4
Tricésimo	I	122	A2
Trie-sur-Baïse	F	145	A4
Trieben	A	110	B1
Triebes	D	83	B4
Triepkendorf	D	74	A2
Trieste	I	122	B2
Triggiano	I	173	A2
Triglitz	D	73	B5
Trignac	F	101	B3
Trigueros	E	161	B3
Trigueros del Valle	E	142	C2
Trikala	GR	182	D3
Trikeri	GR	183	D5
Trikomo	CY	181	A2
Trilj	HR	138	B2
Trillo	E	152	B1
Trilport	F	90	C2
Trim	IRL	30	A2
Trimdon	GB	37	B5
Trindade, *Beja*	P	160	B2
Trindade, *Bragança*	P	149	A2
Třinec	CZ	98	B2
Tring	GB	44	B3
Trinità d'Agultu	I	178	B2
Trinitápoli	I	171	B4
Trino	I	119	B5
Trinta	P	148	B2
Triora	I	133	B3
Tripoli	GR	184	B3
Triponzo	I	136	C1
Triptis	D	83	B3
Triste	E	144	B3
Trittau	D	72	A3
Trivero	I	119	B5
Trivigno	I	172	B1
Trn	BIH	124	C3
Trnava	HR	125	B4
Trnava	SK	98	C1
Trnovec	BIH	139	B4
Trnovo	BIH	139	B4
Trnovska vas	SLO	110	C2
Troarn	F	89	A3
Trochtelfingen	D	94	C1
Trödje	S	51	B4
Trœnse	DK	65	A3
Trofa	P	148	A1
Trofaiach	A	110	B2
Trofors	N	195	E4
Trøgstad	N	54	A2
Tróia	I	171	B3
Troina	I	177	B3
Trois-Ponts	B	80	B1
Troisdorf	D	80	B3
Troisvierges	L	92	A2
Trojane	SLO	123	A3
Troldhede	DK	59	C1
Trollhättan	S	54	B3
Trolog	BIH	138	B2
Tromello	I	120	B1
Tromøy	N	53	B4
Tromsø	N	192	C3
Trondheim	N	199	B7
Tronget	F	116	A3
Trönninge	S	61	C2
Trönningeby	S	60	B2
Trönö	S	51	A3
Tronzano-Vercellese	I	119	B5
Trôo	F	102	B2
Troon	GB	36	A2
Tropea	I	175	C1
Tropy Sztumskie	PL	69	B4
Trosa	S	57	B3
Trösken	S	50	B3
Trosly-Breuil	F	90	B3
Trossingen	D	107	A3
Trostberg	D	109	A3
Trouville-sur-Mer	F	89	A4
Trowbridge	GB	43	A4
Troyes	F	104	A3
Trpanj	HR	138	B3
Trpinja	HR	125	B4
Tršće	HR	123	B3
Tršice	CZ	98	B1
Trstená	SK	99	B3
Trstenci	BIH	125	B3
Trsteno	HR	139	C3
Trstice	SK	111	A4
Trstin	SK	98	C1
Trubia	E	141	A5
Trubjela	MNE	139	C4
Truchas	E	141	B4
Trujillanos	E	155	C4
Trujillo	E	156	A2
Trumieje	PL	69	B4
Trun	CH	107	C3
Trun	F	89	B4
Truro	GB	42	B1
Trusetal	D	82	B2
Truskavets'	UA	13	D5
Trustrup	DK	59	B3
Trutnov	CZ	85	B3
Tryserum	S	56	B2
Trysil	N	49	A4
Tryszczyn	PL	76	A2
Trzcianka	PL	75	A5
Trzciel	PL	75	B4
Trzcińsko Zdrój	PL	74	B3
Trzebiatów	PL	67	B4
Trzebiel	PL	84	A2
Trzebielino	PL	68	A2
Trzebień	PL	84	A3
Trzebiez	PL	74	A3
Trzebinia	PL	86	B3
Trzebnica	PL	85	A5
Trzebnice	PL	85	A4
Trzeciewiec	PL	76	A3
Trzemeszno	PL	76	B2
Trzemeszno-Lubuskie	PL	75	B4
Trzetrzewina	PL	99	B4
Tržič	SLO	123	A3
Tsamandas	GR	182	D2
Tschagguns	A	107	B4
Tschernitz	D	84	A2
Tsebrykove	UA	17	B9
Tsyelyakhany	BY	13	B6
Tua	P	148	A2
Tubbergen	NL	71	B3
Tubilla del Lago	E	143	C3
Tübingen	D	93	C5
Tubize	B	79	B4
Tučapy	CZ	96	B2
Tučepi	HR	138	B3
Tuchan	F	146	B3
Tüchen	D	73	A5
Tuchola	PL	76	A2
Tuchomie	PL	68	A2
Tuchów	PL	99	B5
Tuczno	PL	75	A5
Tuddal	N	53	A4
Tudela	E	144	B2
Tudela de Duero	E	150	A3
Tudweiliog	GB	38	B2
Tuejar	E	159	B2
Tuffé	F	102	A2
Tufsingdalen	N	199	C8
Tuhaň	CZ	84	B2
Tui	E	140	B2
Tukhkala	RUS	197	D13
Tukums	LV	8	D3
Tula	I	178	B2
Tulcea	RO	17	C8
Tul'chyn	UA	13	D8
Tulette	F	131	A3
Tuliszków	PL	76	B3
Tulla	IRL	28	B3
Tullamore	IRL	30	A1
Tulle	F	116	B1
Tullins	F	118	B2
Tullow	IRL	30	B2
Tułowice	PL	85	B5
Tulppio	FIN	197	B12
Tulsk	IRL	28	A3
Tumba	S	57	A3
Tummel Bridge	GB	35	B3
Tun	S	55	B3
Tuna, *Kalmar*	S	62	A4
Tuna, *Uppsala*	S	51	B5
Tuna Hästberg	S	50	B2
Tunçbilek	TR	187	C4
Tunes	P	160	B1
Tungelsta	S	57	A4
Tunnerstad	S	55	B5
Tunnhovd	N	47	B5
Tunstall	GB	45	A5
Tuohikotti	FIN	8	B5
Tuoro sul Trasimeno	I	135	B5
Tupadły	PL	76	B3
Tupanari	BIH	139	A4
Tupik	RUS	9	E8
Tuplice	PL	84	A2
Tura	H	112	B3
Turanj	HR	137	B4
Turany	SK	99	B3
Turbe	BIH	139	A3
Turbenthal	CH	107	B3
Turcia	E	141	B5
Turčianske Teplice	SK	98	C2
Turcifal	P	154	B1
Turckheim	F	106	A2
Turda	RO	17	B5
Turégano	E	151	A4
Turek	PL	76	B3
Türgovishte	BG	17	D7
Turgutlu	TR	188	A2
Turi	I	173	B3
Turin = Torino	I	119	B4
Turis	E	159	B3
Türje	H	111	C4
Turka	UA	12	D5
Túrkeve	H	113	B4
Türkheim	D	108	A1
Türkmenli	TR	186	C1
Turku	FIN	8	B3
Turleque	E	157	A4
Turňa nad Bodvou	SK	99	C4
Turnberry	GB	36	A2
Turnhout	B	79	A4
Türnitz	A	110	B2
Turnov	CZ	84	B3
Turnu Măgurele	RO	17	D6
Turón	E	164	C1
Turoszów	PL	84	B2
Turowo	PL	77	A5
Turquel	P	154	B1
Turri	I	179	C2
Turries	F	132	A2
Turriff	GB	33	D4
Tursi	I	174	A2
Turtmann	CH	119	A4
Turtola	FIN	196	C6
Turze	PL	86	A1
Turzovka	SK	98	B2
Tusa	I	177	B3
Tuscánia	I	168	A1
Tuse	DK	61	D1
Tušilovic	HR	123	B4
Tuszyn	PL	86	A3
Tutow	D	66	C2
Tutrakan	BG	17	C7
Tuttlingen	D	107	B3
Tutzing	D	108	B2
Tuzla	BIH	125	C4
Tuzla	TR	23	C8
Tuzlukçu	TR	189	A6
Tvåaker	S	60	B2
Tväralund	S	200	B5
Tvärskog	S	63	B4
Tvedestrand	N	53	B4
Tveit, *Hordaland*	N	47	B4
Tveit, *Rogaland*	N	52	A2
Tver	RUS	9	D9
Tverrelvmo	N	192	D3
Tversted	DK	58	A3
Tving	S	63	B3
Tvrdošín	SK	99	B3
Tvrdošovce	SK	112	A2
Twardogóra	PL	85	A5
Twatt	GB	33	B3
Twello	NL	70	B3
Twimberg	A	110	C1
Twist	D	71	B4
Twistringen	D	72	B1
Tworóg	PL	86	B2
Twyford, *Hampshire*	GB	44	B2
Twyford, *Wokingham*	GB	44	B3
Tyachiv	UA	17	A5
Tychówka	PL	67	C5
Tychowo	PL	67	C5
Tychy	PL	86	B2
Týec nad Labem	CZ	97	B3
Tyfors	S	49	B6
Tygelsjö	S	61	D2
Tylldal	N	199	C7
Tylstrup	DK	58	A2
Tymbark	PL	99	B4
Tymowa	PL	99	B4
Týn nad Vltavou	CZ	96	B2
Tyndrum	GB	34	B3
Týnec nad Sázavou	CZ	96	B2
Tynemouth	GB	37	A5
Tyngsjö	S	49	B5
Týniště nad Orlicí	CZ	85	B4
Tynset	N	199	C7
Tyresö	S	57	A4
Tyringe	S	61	C3
Tyrislöt	S	56	B2
Tyristrand	N	48	B2
Tyrrellspass	IRL	30	A1
Tysnes	N	46	B2
Tysse	N	46	B2
Tyssebotn	N	46	B2
Tyssedal	N	46	B3
Tystberga	S	56	B3
Tysvær	N	52	A1
Tywyn	GB	39	B2
Tzermiado	GR	185	D6
Tzummarum	NL	70	A2

U

Name	Country	Page	Grid
Ub	SRB	127	C2
Ubby	DK	61	D1
Úbeda	E	157	B4
Überlingen	D	107	B4
Ubidea	E	143	A4
Ubli	HR	138	C2
Ubrique	E	162	B2
Ucero	E	143	C3
Uchaud	F	131	B3
Uchte	D	72	B1
Uckerath	D	80	B3
Uckfield	GB	45	C4
Ucklum	S	54	B2
Uclés	E	151	C5
Ucria	I	177	A3
Udbina	HR	137	A4
Uddebo	S	60	B3
Uddeholm	S	49	B5
Uddevalla	S	54	B2
Uddheden	S	49	C4
Uden	NL	80	A1
Uder	D	82	A2
Udiča	SK	98	B2
Údine	I	122	A2
Udvar	H	125	B4
Ueckermünde	D	74	A3
Uelsen	D	71	B3
Uelzen	D	73	B3
Uetendorf	CH	106	C2
Uetersen	D	72	A2
Uetze	D	72	B3
Uffculme	GB	43	B3
Uffenheim	D	94	B2
Ugarana	E	143	A4
Ugento	I	173	C4
Ugerløse	DK	61	D1
Uggerby	DK	58	A3
Uggerslev	DK	59	C3
Uggiano la Chiesa	I	173	B4
Ugíjar	E	164	C1
Ugine	F	118	B3
Uglejevik	BIH	125	C5
Uglenes	N	46	B2
Uglich	RUS	9	D11
Ugljane	HR	138	B2
Ugod	H	111	B4
Uherské Hradiště	CZ	98	B1
Uherský Brod	CZ	98	B1
Uherský Ostroh	CZ	98	C1
Uhingen	D	94	C1
Uhlířské-Janovice	CZ	96	B2
Uhřiněves	CZ	96	A2
Uhyst	D	84	A2
Uig	GB	31	B2
Uitgeest	NL	70	B1
Uithoorn	NL	70	B1
Uithuizen	NL	71	A3
Uithuizermeeden	NL	71	A3
Uivar	RO	126	B2
Ujazd, *Łódzkie*	PL	87	A3
Ujazd, *Opolskie*	PL	86	B2
Ujezd u Brna	CZ	97	B4
Újhartyán	H	112	B3
Újkigyós	H	113	C5
Ujpetre	H	125	B4

Place		Pg	Grid
Ujście	PL	75	A5
Ujsolt	H	112	C3
Újszász	H	113	B4
Újszentmargita	H	113	B5
Ujué	E	144	B2
Ukanc	SLO	122	A2
Ukmergé	LT	13	A6
Ukna	S	56	B3
Ula	TR	188	B3
Ul'anka	SK	99	C3
Ulaş	TR	186	A2
Ulássai	I	179	C3
Ulbjerg	DK	58	B2
Ulbster	GB	32	C3
Ulceby	GB	40	B3
Ulcinj	MNE	16	E3
Uldum	DK	59	C2
Ulefoss	N	53	A5
Uleila del Campo	E	164	B2
Ulëz	AL	182	B3
Ulfborg	DK	59	B1
Uljma	SRB	127	B3
Ullånger	S	200	C4
Ullapool	GB	32	D1
Ullared	S	60	B2
Ullatti	S	196	B4
Ullatun	N	52	A2
Ulldecona	E	153	B4
Ulldemolins	E	147	C1
Ullerslev	DK	59	C3
Ullervad	S	55	B4
Üllés	H	126	A1
Üllő	H	112	B3
Ulm	D	94	C1
Ulme	D	154	B2
Ulmen	D	80	B2
Ulnes	N	47	B6
Ulog	BIH	139	B4
Ulricehamn	S	60	B3
Ulrichstein	D	81	B5
Ulrika	S	56	B1
Ulriksfors	S	200	C1
Ulrum	NL	71	A3
Ulsberg	N	198	C6
Ulsta	GB	33	A5
Ulsted	DK	58	A3
Ulsteinvik	N	198	C2
Ulstrup, Vestsjællands Amt.	DK	59	C3
Ulstrup, Viborg Amt.	DK	59	B2
Ulsvåg	N	194	B6
Ulubey	TR	188	A4
Uluborlu	TR	189	A5
Ulukışla	TR	23	C8
Ulverston	GB	36	B4
Ulvik	N	46	B3
Umag	HR	122	B2
Uman	UA	13	D9
Umba	RUS	3	C14
Umbértide	I	135	B5
Umbriático	I	174	B2
Umčari	SRB	127	C2
Umeå	S	200	C6
Umgransele	S	200	B4
Umhausen	A	108	B1
Umka	SRB	127	C2
Umljanovic	HR	138	B2
Umnäs	S	195	E7
Umurbey	TR	186	B1
Unaðsdalur	IS	190	A3
Unapool	GB	32	C1
Unari	FIN	197	B8
Unbyn	S	196	D4
Uncastillo	E	144	B2
Undenäs	S	55	B5
Undersaker	S	199	B10
Undredal	N	46	B4
Unešić	HR	138	B2
Úněšov	CZ	96	B1
Ungheni	MD	17	B7
Unhais da Serra	P	148	B2
Unhošt	CZ	84	B2
Unichov	PL	68	A2
Uničov	CZ	98	B1
Uniejów	PL	76	C3
Unisław	PL	76	A3
Unkel	D	80	B3
Unken	A	109	B3
Unna	D	81	A3
Unnaryd	S	60	C3
Unquera	E	142	A2
Unter Langkampfen	A	108	B3
Unter-steinbach	D	94	B2
Unterach	A	109	B4
Unterägeri	CH	107	B3
Unterammergau	D	108	B2
Unterhaching	D	108	A2
Unteriberg	CH	107	B3
Unterkochen	D	94	C2
Unterlaussa	A	110	B1
Unterlüss	D	72	B3
Untermünkheim	D	94	B1
Unterschächen	CH	107	C3
Unterschleissheim	D	95	C3
Unterschwaningen	D	94	B2
Untersiemau	D	82	B2
Unterweissenbach	A	96	C2
Unterzell	D	95	B4
Upavon	GB	44	B2
Úpice	CZ	85	B4
Upiłka	PL	68	B2
Upphärad	S	54	B3
Uppingham	GB	40	C3
Upplands-Väsby	S	57	A3
Uppsala	S	51	C4
Uppsjøhytta	N	48	A1
Upton-upon-Severn	GB	39	B4
Ur	F	146	B2
Uras	I	179	C2
Uraz	PL	85	A4
Urbánia	I	136	B1
Urbino	I	136	B1
Urçay	F	103	C4
Urda	E	157	A4
Urdax	E	144	A2
Urdilde	E	140	B2
Urdos	F	145	B3
Urk	NL	70	B2
Úrkút	H	111	B4
Urla	TR	188	A1
Urlingford	IRL	30	B1
Urnäsch	CH	107	B4
Urnes	N	47	A4
Uroševac	KOS	16	D4
Urracal	E	164	B2
Urries	E	144	B2
Urroz	E	144	B2
Ursensollen	D	95	B3
Urshult	S	63	B2
Uršna Sela	SLO	123	B4
Urszulewo	PL	77	B4
Ury	F	90	C2
Urziceni	RO	17	C7
Urzulei	I	178	B3
Usagre	E	156	B1
Uşak	TR	187	D4
Usedom	D	66	C2
Useldange	L	92	B1
Uséllus	I	179	C2
Ushakovo	RUS	69	A5
Usingen	D	81	B4
Usini	I	178	B2
Usk	GB	39	C4
Uskedal	N	46	C2
Üsküdar	TR	186	A4
Uslar	D	82	A1
Úsov	CZ	97	B5
Usquert	NL	71	A3
Ussássai	I	179	C3
Ussé	F	102	B2
Usséglio	I	119	B4
Ussel, Cantal	F	116	B2
Ussel, Corrèze	F	116	B2
Usson-du-Poitou	F	115	B4
Usson-en-Forez	F	117	B3
Usson-les-Bains	F	146	B3
Ust Luga	RUS	8	C6
Ustaoset	N	47	B5
Ustaritz	F	144	A2
Uštěk	CZ	84	B2
Uster	CH	107	B3
Ústí	CZ	98	B1
Ústí nad Labem	CZ	84	B2
Ústí nad Orlicí	CZ	97	B4
Ustikolina	BIH	139	B4
Ustipračà	BIH	139	B5
Ustka	PL	68	A1
Ustroń	PL	98	B2
Ustronie Morskie	PL	67	B4
Ustyuzhna	RUS	9	C10
Uszód	H	112	C2
Utåker	N	52	A1
Utansjö	S	200	D3
Utebo	E	152	A3
Utena	LT	13	A6
Utery	CZ	95	B5
Uthaug	N	198	B6
Utiel	E	159	B2
Utne	N	46	B3
Utö	S	57	B4
Utrecht	NL	70	B2
Utrera	E	162	A2
Utrillas	E	153	B3
Utsjoki	FIN	193	C11
Utstein kloster	N	52	A1
Uttendorf	A	109	B3
Uttenweiler	D	107	A4
Utterslev	DK	65	B4
Uttoxeter	GB	40	C2
Utvälinge	S	61	C2
Utvorda	N	199	A7
Uusikaarlepyy	FIN	3	E8
Uusikaupunki	FIN	8	B2
Uvaly	CZ	96	A2
Uvdal	N	47	B5
Uza	F	128	B1
Uzdin	SRB	126	B2
Uzdowo	PL	77	B5
Uzein	F	145	A3
Uzel	F	100	A3
Uzerche	F	116	B1
Uzès	F	131	A3
Uzhhorod	UA	12	D5
Uzhok	UA	12	D5
Uznach	CH	107	B3
Üzümlü, Konya	TR	189	B6
Üzümlü, Muğla	TR	188	C4
Uzunköprü	TR	186	A1

V

Place		Pg	Grid
Vaalajärvi	FIN	197	B9
Vaas	F	102	B2
Vaasa	FIN	8	A2
Vaasen	NL	70	B2
Vabre	F	130	B1
Vác	H	112	B3
Vacha	D	82	B2
Váchartyán	H	112	B3
Väckelsång	S	63	B2
Vacqueyras	F	131	A3
Vad	S	50	B2
Vada	I	134	B3
Väddö	S	51	C5
Väderstad	S	55	B5
Vadheim	N	46	A2
Vadillo de la Sierra	E	150	B2
Vadillos	E	152	B1
Vadla	N	52	A2
Vado	I	135	A4
Vado Lígure	I	133	A4
Vadsø	N	193	B13
Vadstena	S	55	B5
Vadum	DK	58	A2
Vaduz	FL	107	B4
Væggerløse	DK	65	B4
Vafos	N	53	B5
Våg	H	111	B4
Vågåmo	N	198	D6
Vaggeryd	S	62	A2
Vaghia	GR	184	A4
Vaglia	I	135	B4
Váglio Basilicata	I	172	B1
Vagney	F	106	A1
Vagnhärad	S	57	B3
Vagnsunda	S	57	A4
Vagos	P	148	B1
Vai	GR	185	D7
Vaiano	I	135	A4
Vaiges	F	102	A1
Vaihingen	D	93	C4
Vaillant	F	105	B4
Vailly-sur-Aisne	F	91	B3
Vailly-sur-Sauldre	F	103	B4
Vairano Scalo	I	170	B2
Vaison-la-Romaine	F	131	A4
Vaite	F	105	B4
Väjern	S	54	B2
Vajszló	H	125	B3
Vaksdal	N	46	B2
Vál	H	112	B2
Val de San Lorenzo	E	141	B4
Val de Santo Domingo	E	150	B3
Val d'Esquières	F	132	B2
Val-d'Isère	F	119	B3
Val-Suzon	F	105	B3
Val Thorens	F	118	B3
Valaam	RUS	9	B7
Valada	P	154	B2
Vålådalen	S	199	B10
Valadares	P	148	A1
Valado	P	154	B1
Valandovo	MK	182	B4
Valaská	SK	99	C3
Valaská Belá	SK	98	C2
Valaská Dubová	SK	99	B3
Valašská Polanka	CZ	98	B1
Valašské Klobouky	CZ	98	B2
Valašské Meziříčí	CZ	98	B1
Valberg	F	132	A2
Vålberg	S	55	A4
Valbo	S	51	B4
Valbom	P	148	A1
Valbondione	I	120	A3
Valbonnais	F	118	C2
Valbuena de Duero	E	142	C2
Välcani	RO	126	B2
Valdagno	I	121	B4
Valdahon	F	105	B5
Valdaracete	E	151	B4
Valday	RUS	9	D8
Valdealgorfa	E	153	B3
Valdecaballeros	E	156	A2
Valdecabras	E	152	B1
Valdecarros	E	150	B2
Valdeconcha	E	151	B5
Valdeflores	E	161	B3
Valdefresno	E	142	B1
Valdeganga	E	158	B2
Valdelacasa	E	150	B2
Valdelacasa de Tajo	E	156	A2
Valdelarco	E	161	B3
Valdelosa	E	149	A4
Valdeltormo	E	153	B4
Valdelugeros	E	142	B1
Valdemanco de Esteras	E	156	A3
Valdemarsvik	S	56	B2
Valdemorillo	E	151	B3
Valdemoro	E	151	B4
Valdemoro Sierra	E	152	B2
Valdenoceda	E	143	B3
Valdeobispo	E	149	B3
Valdeolivas	E	152	B1
Valdepeñas	E	157	B4
Valdepeñas de Jaén	E	163	A4
Valdepiélago	E	142	B1
Valdepolo	E	142	B1
Valderas	E	142	B1
Valdérice	I	176	A1
Valderrobres	E	153	B4
Valderrueda	E	142	B2
Valdestillas	E	150	A3
Valdetorres	E	156	B1
Valdetorres de Jarama	E	151	B4
Valdeverdeja	E	150	C2
Valdevimbre	E	142	B1
Valdieri	I	133	A3
Valdilecha	E	151	B4
Valdobbiádene	I	121	B4
Valdocondes	E	143	C3
Valdoviño	E	140	A2
Vale de Açor, Beja	P	160	B2
Vale de Açor, Portalegre	P	154	B3
Vale de Agua	P	160	B1
Vale de Cambra	P	148	B1
Vale de Lobo	P	160	B1
Vale de Prazeres	P	148	B2
Vale de Reis	P	154	C2
Vale de Rosa	P	160	B2
Vale de Santarém	P	154	B2
Vale de Vargo	P	160	B2
Vale do Peso	P	155	B3
Valea lui Mihai	RO	16	B5
Valega	P	148	B1
Valéggio sul Mincio	I	121	B3
Valeiro	P	154	C2
Valença	P	140	B2
Valençay	F	103	B3
Valence, Charente	F	115	C4
Valence, Drôme	F	117	C4
Valence d'Agen	F	129	B3
Valence-d'Albigeois	F	130	A1
Valence-sur-Baise	F	129	C3
Valencia	E	159	B3
Valencia de Alcántara	E	155	B3
Valencia de Don Juan	E	142	B1
Valencia de las Torres	E	156	B1
Valencia de Mombuey	E	161	A2
Valencia del Ventoso	E	161	A3
Valenciennes	F	79	B3
Valensole	F	132	B1
Valentano	I	168	A1
Valentigney	F	106	B1
Valentine	F	145	A4
Valenza	I	120	B1
Valenzuela	E	163	A3
Valenzuela de Calatrava	E	157	B4
Våler, Hedmark	N	48	B3
Våler, Østfold	N	54	A1
Valera de Abajo	E	158	B1
Valeria	E	158	B1
Valestrand	N	52	A1
Valestrandsfossen	N	46	B2
Valevåg	N	52	A1
Valfabbrica	I	136	B1
Valflaunes	F	131	B2
Valga	EST	8	D5
Valgorge	F	131	A3
Valgrisenche	I	119	B4
Valguarnera Caropepe	I	177	B3
Valhelhas	P	148	B2
Valjevo	SRB	127	C1
Valka	LV	8	D4
Valkeakoski	FIN	8	B4
Valkenburg	NL	80	B1
Valkenswaard	NL	79	A5
Valkó	H	112	B3
Vall d'Alba	E	153	B3
Valla	S	56	A2
Vallada	E	159	C3
Vallado	E	141	A4
Valladolid	E	150	A3
Vallåkra	S	61	D2
Vallata	I	172	A1
Vallberga	S	61	C3
Valldemossa	E	166	B2
Valle	N	52	A3
Valle Castellana	I	136	C2
Valle de Abdalajís	E	163	B3
Valle de Cabuérniga	E	142	A2
Valle de la Serena	E	156	B2
Valle de Matamoros	E	155	C4
Valle de Santa Ana	E	155	C4
Valle Mosso	I	119	B5
Valledolmo	I	176	B2
Valledoria	I	178	B2
Vallelado	E	150	A3
Vallelunga Pratameno	I	176	B2
Vallendar	D	81	B3
Vallentuna	S	57	A4
Vallerås	S	49	B5
Valleraugue	F	130	A2
Vallermosa	I	179	C2
Vallet	F	101	B4
Valletta	M	175	C3
Valley	GB	38	A2
Vallfogona de Riucorb	E	147	C2
Valli del Pasúbio	I	121	B4
Vallo della Lucánia	I	172	B1
Valloire	F	118	B3
Vallombrosa	I	135	B4
Vallon-Pont-d'Arc	F	131	A3
Vallorbe	CH	105	C5
Vallouise	F	118	C3
Valls	E	147	C2
Vallset	N	48	B3
Vallsta	S	50	A3
Vallstena	S	57	C4
Valmadrid	E	153	A3
Valmiera	LV	8	D4
Valmojado	E	151	B3
Valmont	F	89	A4
Valmontone	I	169	B2
Valö	S	51	B5
Valognes	F	88	A2
Valonga	P	148	B1
Valongo	P	148	A1
Válor	E	164	C1
Valøy	N	199	A7
Valozhyn	BY	13	A7
Valpaços	P	148	A2
Valpelline	I	119	B4
Valpiana	I	135	B3
Valpovo	HR	125	B4
Valras-Plage	F	130	B2
Valréas	F	131	A3
Vals	CH	107	C4
Vals-les-Bains	F	117	C4
Valsavarenche	I	119	B4
Vålse	DK	65	B4
Valsequillo	E	156	B2
Valsjöbyn	S	199	A11
Valsonne	F	117	B4
Valstagna	I	121	B4
Valtablado del Rio	E	152	B1
Valþjofsstaður	IS	191	B11
Valtice	CZ	97	C4
Valtiendas	E	151	A4
Valtierra	E	144	B2
Valtopina	I	136	B1
Valtorta	I	120	B2
Valtournenche	I	119	B4
Valverde	E	144	C2
Valverde de Burguillos	E	155	C4
Valverde de Júcar	E	158	B1
Valverde de la Vera	E	150	B2
Valverde de la Virgen	E	142	B1
Valverde de Llerena	E	156	B2
Valverde de Mérida	E	156	B1
Valverde del Camino	E	161	B3
Valverde del Fresno	E	149	B3
Valvträsk	S	196	C4
Vamberk	CZ	85	B4
Vamdrup	DK	59	C2
Våmhus	S	50	A1
Vamlingbo	S	57	D4
Vammala	FIN	8	B3
Vamos	GR	185	D5
Vámosmikola	H	112	B2
Vámosszabadi	H	111	B4
Vanault-les-Dames	F	91	C4
Vandel	DK	59	C2
Vandenesse	F	104	C2
Vandenesse-en-Auxois	F	104	B3
Vandóies	I	108	C2
Väne-Ås aka	S	54	B3
Vänersborg	S	54	B3
Vänersnäs	S	54	B3
Vang	N	47	A5
Vänge	S	51	C4
Vangsnes	N	46	A3
Vänjaurbäck	S	200	B4
Vännacka	S	54	A3
Vannareid	N	192	B3
Vännäs	S	200	C5
Vannes	F	101	B3
Vannsätter	S	51	A3
Vannvåg	N	192	B3
Vansbro	S	49	B6
Vanse	N	52	B2
Vantaa	FIN	8	B4
Vanttauskoski	FIN	197	C9
Vanviken	N	199	B7
Vanyarc	H	112	B3
Vaour	F	129	B4
Vapnyarka	UA	13	D8
Vaprio d'Adda	I	120	B2
Vara	S	55	B3
Varacieux	F	118	B2
Varades	F	101	B4
Varages	F	132	B1
Varaldsøy	N	46	B2
Varallo	I	119	B5
Varaždinske Toplice	HR	124	A2
Varazze	I	133	A4
Varberg	S	60	B2
Vardal	N	48	B2
Varde	DK	59	C1
Vårdö	FIN	51	B7
Vardø	N	193	B15
Vardomb	H	125	A4
Varejoki	FIN	196	C7
Varel	D	71	A5
Váréna	LT	13	A6
Vares	BIH	139	A4
Varese	I	120	B1
Varese Ligure	I	134	A2
Vårfurile	RO	16	B5
Vårgårda	S	60	A2
Vargas	E	143	A3
Vargas	P	154	B2
Vargön	S	54	B3
Variaş	RO	126	A2
Variaşu Mic	RO	126	A3
Varilhes	F	146	A2
Varin	SK	98	B2
Väring	S	55	B4
Váriz	P	149	A3
Varkaus	FIN	8	A5
Varmahlíð	IS	190	B6
Varmaland	IS	190	C4
Värmlands Bro	S	55	A4
Värmskog	S	55	A3
Varna	BG	17	D7
Varna	SRB	127	C1
Värnamo	S	60	B4
Varnhem	S	55	B4
Varnsdorf	CZ	84	B2
Varoška Rijeka	BIH	124	B2
Városlöd	H	111	B4
Várpalota	H	112	B2
Varreddes	F	90	C2
Vars	F	118	C3
Varsi	I	120	C2
Varssseveld	NL	71	C3
Vårsta	S	57	A3
Vartdal	N	198	C3
Vartofta	S	55	B4
Vårvik	S	54	A3
Várvölgy	H	111	C4
Varzi	I	120	C2
Varzjelas	P	148	B1
Varzo	I	119	A5
Varzy	F	104	B2
Vasad	H	112	B3
Väse	S	55	A4
Vašica	SRB	125	B5
Vasilevichi	BY	13	B8
Väskinde	S	57	C4
Vaskút	H	125	A4
Vaslui	RO	17	B7
Vassbotn	N	53	B4
Vassenden	N	47	A6
Vassieux-en-Vercors	F	118	C2
Vassmolösa	S	63	B4
Vassy	F	88	B3
Västanvik	S	50	B1
Västerås	S	56	A2
Västerby	S	50	B2
Västerfärnebo	S	50	C3
Västergarn	S	57	C4
Västerhaninge	S	57	A4
Västervik	S	62	A4
Vasto	I	170	A2
Västra Ämtervik	S	55	A4
Västra-Bodarne	S	60	B2
Västra Karup	S	61	C2
Vasvár	H	111	B3
Vasylkiv	UA	13	C9
Vát	H	111	B3
Vatan	F	103	B3
Vatican City = Cittá del Vaticano	I	168	B2
Vatili	CY	181	A2
Vatin	SRB	126	B3
Vatland	N	52	B3
Vatne	N	53	B3
Vatnestrøm	N	53	B4
Vätö	S	51	C5
Vatra-Dornei	RO	17	B6
Vatry	F	91	C4
Vattholma	S	51	B4
Vättis	CH	107	C4
Vauchamps	F	91	C3
Vauchassis	F	104	A2
Vaucouleurs	F	92	C1

Name	Country	Page	Grid
Vaudoy-en-Brie	F	90	C3
Vaulen	N	52	B1
Vaulruz	CH	106	C1
Vaulx Vraucourt	F	90	A2
Vaumas	F	104	C2
Vausseroux	F	115	B3
Vauvenargues	F	132	B1
Vauvert	F	131	B4
Vauvillers	F	105	B5
Vaux-sur-Sure	B	92	B1
Vawkavysk	BY	13	B6
Vaxholm	S	57	A4
Växjö	S	62	B2
Våxtorp	S	61	C3
Vayrac	F	129	B4
Važec	SK	99	B3
Veberöd	S	61	D3
Vechelde	D	72	B3
Vechta	D	71	B5
Vecinos	E	149	B4
Vecsés	H	112	B3
Vedavågen	N	52	A1
Veddige	S	60	B2
Vedersø	DK	59	B1
Vedeseta	I	120	B2
Vedevåg	S	56	A1
Vedra	E	140	B2
Vedum	S	55	B3
Veendam	NL	71	A3
Veenendaal	NL	70	B2
Vega, Asturias	E	142	A1
Vega, Asturias	E	142	A1
Vega de Espinareda	E	141	B4
Vega de Infanzones	E	142	B1
Vega de Pas	E	143	A3
Vega de Valcarce	E	141	B4
Vega de Valdetronco	E	150	A2
Vegadeo	E	141	A3
Vegårshei	N	53	B4
Vegas de Coria	E	149	B3
Vegas del Condado	E	142	B1
Vegby	S	60	B3
Vegger	DK	58	B2
Veggli	N	47	B6
Veghel	NL	80	A1
Veglast	D	66	B1
Véglie	I	173	B3
Veguillas	E	151	B4
Vegusdal	N	53	B4
Veidholmen	N	198	B4
Veidnes	N	193	B10
Veikåker	N	48	B1
Veinge	S	61	C3
Vejbystrand	S	61	C2
Vejen	DK	59	C2
Vejer de la Frontera	E	162	B2
Vejle	DK	59	C2
Vejprty	CZ	83	B5
Vela Luka	HR	138	C2
Velada	E	150	B3
Velayos	E	150	B3
Velbert	D	80	A3
Velburg	D	95	B3
Velde	N	199	A8
Velden, Bayern	D	95	B3
Velden, Bayern	D	95	C4
Velden am Worther See	A	109	C5
Velefique	E	164	B2
Velen	D	80	A2
Velenje	SLO	123	A4
Veles	MK	182	B3
Velesevec	HR	124	B2
Velešin	CZ	96	C2
Velestino	GR	182	D4
Velez Blanco	E	164	B2
Vélez de Benaudalla	E	163	B4
Vélez-Málaga	E	163	B3
Vélez Rubio	E	164	B2
Veli Lošinj	HR	137	A3
Veliki Radinci	SRB	127	B1
Velika	HR	125	B3
Velika Gorica	HR	124	B2
Velika Grdevac	HR	124	B3
Velika Greda	SRB	126	B3
Velika Ilova	BIH	125	C3
Velika Kladuša	BIH	124	B1
Velika Kopanica	HR	125	B4
Velika Krsna	SRB	127	C2
Velika Obarska	BIH	125	C5
Velika Pisanica	HR	124	B3
Velika Plana	SRB	127	C3
Velika Zdenci	HR	124	B3
Velike Lašče	SLO	123	B3
Velike Središte	SRB	126	B3
Veliki Gaj	SRB	126	B3
Veliki Popović	SRB	127	C3
Velikiye Luki	RUS	9	D7
Veliko Gradište	SRB	127	C3
Veliko Orašje	SRB	127	C3
Veliko Selo	SRB	127	C3
Veliko Tŭrnovo	BG	17	D6
Velilla de San Antonio	E	151	B4
Velilla del Río Carrió	E	142	B2
Velingrad	BG	183	A5
Velizh	RUS	9	E7
Veljun	HR	123	B4
Velká Bíteš	CZ	97	B4
Velka Hled'scbe	CZ	95	B4
Velká Lomnica	SK	99	B4
Velká nad Veličkou	CZ	98	C1
Velké Bystřice	CZ	98	B1
Velké Heraltice	CZ	98	B1
Velké Karlovice	CZ	98	B2
Vel'ké Leváre	SK	97	C5
Velké Losiny	CZ	98	A1
Velké Meziříčí	CZ	97	B4
Vel'ké Pavlovice	CZ	97	C4
Vel'ké Rovné	SK	98	B2
Velké Uherce	SK	98	C2
Vel'ké Zálužie	SK	98	C1
Vel'ke'Kostol'any	SK	98	C1
Vel'ký Blahovo	SK	99	C4
Velky Bor	CZ	96	B1
Vel'ký Cetin	SK	112	A2
Vel'ký Krtíš	SK	112	A3
Vel'ký Meder	SK	111	B4
Velky Ujezd	CZ	98	B1
Vellahn	D	73	A3
Vellberg	D	94	B1
Velles	F	103	C3
Velletri	I	168	B2
Vellinge	S	66	A2
Vellisca	E	151	B5
Velliza	E	150	A3
Vellmar	D	81	A5
Velp	NL	70	B2
Velten	D	74	B2
Velvary	CZ	84	B2
Velvendos	GR	182	C4
Vemb	DK	59	B1
Vemdalen	S	199	C10
Veme	N	48	B2
Véménd	H	125	A4
Vemmedrup	DK	61	D2
Vena	S	62	A3
Venaco	F	180	A2
Venafro	I	169	B4
Venarey-les-Laumes	F	104	B3
Venaría	I	119	B4
Venasca	I	133	A3
Vençane	SRB	127	C2
Vence	F	132	B3
Venda Nova, Coimbra	P	154	A2
Venda Nova, Leiria	P	154	B2
Vendas Novas	P	154	C2
Vendays-Montalivet	F	114	C2
Vendel	S	51	B4
Vendelso	S	57	A4
Vendeuil	F	91	B3
Vendeuvre-sur-Barse	F	104	A3
Vendœuvres	F	115	B5
Vendôme	F	103	B3
Venelles	F	131	B4
Veness	GB	33	B4
Venézia = Venice	I	122	B1
Venialbo	E	150	A2
Venice = Venézia	I	122	B1
Vénissieux	F	117	B4
Venjan	S	49	B5
Venlo	NL	80	A2
Venn Green	GB	42	B2
Vennesla	N	53	B3
Vennesund	N	195	E3
Vennezey	F	92	C2
Venosa	I	172	B1
Venray	NL	80	A1
Vent	A	108	C1
Venta de Baños	E	142	C2
Venta de los Santos	E	157	B4
Venta del Moro	E	158	B2
Venta las Ranas	E	142	A1
Ventanueva	E	141	A4
Ventas de Huelma	E	163	A4
Ventas de Zafarraya	E	163	B3
Ventavon	F	132	A1
Ventimiglia	I	133	B3
Ventnor	GB	44	C2
Ventosa de la Sierra	E	143	C4
Ventosilla	E	143	C4
Ventspils	LV	8	D2
Venturina	I	134	B3
Venzolasca	F	180	A2
Venzone	I	122	A2
Vép	H	111	B3
Vera	E	164	B3
Vera	N	199	B9
Vera Cruz	P	160	A2
Vera de Bidasoa	E	144	A2
Vera de Moncayo	E	144	C2
Verbánia	I	119	B5
Verberie	F	90	B2
Verbicaro	I	174	B1
Verbier	CH	119	A4
Vercel-Villedieu-le-Camp	F	105	B5
Vercelli	I	119	B5
Verchen	D	66	C1
Vercheny	F	118	C2
Verclause	F	131	A4
Verdalsøra	N	199	B8
Verden	D	72	B2
Verdens Ende	N	54	A1
Verdikoussa	GR	182	D3
Verdille	F	115	C3
Verdú	E	147	C2
Verdun	F	92	B1
Verdun-sur-Garonne	F	129	C4
Verdun-sur-le-Doubs	F	105	C4
Veresegyház	H	112	B3
Verfeil	F	129	C4
Vergato	I	135	A4
Vergel	E	159	C4
Vergeletto	CH	120	A1
Verges	E	147	B4
Vergiate	I	120	B1
Vergt	F	129	A3
Veria	GR	182	C4
Verín	E	141	C3
Veringenstadt	D	107	A4
Verl	D	81	A4
Verma	N	198	C5
Vermand	F	90	B3
Vermelha	P	154	B1
Vermenton	F	104	B2
Vern-d'Anjou	F	102	B1
Vernago	I	108	C1
Vernante	F	133	A3
Vernantes	F	102	B2
Vernár	SK	99	C4
Vernasca	I	120	C2
Vernayaz	CH	119	A4
Vernazza	I	134	A2
Verneřice	CZ	84	B2
Vernet	F	146	A2
Vernet-les-Bains	F	146	B3
Verneuil	F	91	B3
Verneuil-sur-Avre	F	89	B4
Vernier	CH	118	A3
Vérnio	I	135	A4
Vérnole	I	173	B4
Vernon	F	90	B1
Vernoux-en-Vivarais	F	117	C4
Veróce	H	112	B3
Verolanuova	I	120	B3
Véroli	I	169	B3
Verona	I	121	B4
Verpelét	H	113	B4
Verrabotn	N	199	B7
Verrès	I	119	B4
Verrey-sous-Salmaise	F	104	B3
Verrières	F	115	B4
Versailles	F	90	C2
Versam	CH	107	C4
Verseg	H	112	B3
Versmold	D	71	B5
Versoix	CH	118	A3
Verteillac	F	115	C4
Vértesacsa	H	112	B2
Vertou	F	101	B4
Vertus	F	91	C3
Verviers	B	80	B1
Vervins	F	91	B3
Verwood	GB	43	B5
Veryan	GB	42	B2
Veržej	SLO	111	C3
Verzuolo	I	133	A3
Verzy	F	91	B4
Vescovato	F	180	A2
Vése	H	124	A3
Veselí nad Lužnicí	CZ	96	B2
Veselí nad Moravou	CZ	98	C1
Veseliy	BG	17	D7
Vésime	I	119	C5
Veskoniemi	FIN	193	D11
Vesoul	F	105	B5
Vespolate	I	120	B1
Vessigebro	S	60	C2
Vestbygd	N	52	B2
Vestenanova	I	121	B4
Vester Husby	S	56	B2
Vester Nebel	DK	59	C2
Vester Torup	DK	58	A2
Vester Vedsted	DK	59	C1
Vesterøhavn	DK	58	A3
Vestervig	DK	58	B1
Vestfossen	N	53	A5
Vestmannaeyjar	IS	190	D5
Vestmarka	N	48	C3
Vestnes	N	198	C4
Vestone	I	120	B3
Vestre Gausdal	N	48	A2
Vestre Jakobselv	N	193	B13
Vestre Slidre	N	47	A5
Vesyegonsk	RUS	9	C10
Veszprém	H	112	B1
Veszprémvarsány	H	112	B1
Vésztö	H	113	C5
Vetlanda	S	62	A3
Vetovo	HR	125	B3
Vetralla	I	168	A2
Vetschau	D	84	A2
Větrný Jeníkov	CZ	97	B3
Větroz	CH	119	A4
Vetschau	D	84	A2
Vettasjärvi	S	196	B4
Vetto	I	134	A3
Vetulónia	I	135	C3
Veules-les-Roses	F	89	A4
Veulettes-sur-Mer	F	89	A4
Veum	N	53	A4
Veurne	B	78	A2
Veverská Bítýška	CZ	97	B4
Vevey	CH	106	C1
Vevi	GR	182	C3
Vevring	N	46	A2
Vex	CH	119	A4
Veynes	F	132	A1
Veyre-Monton	F	116	B3
Veyrier	F	118	B3
Vézelay	F	104	B2
Vézelise	F	92	C2
Vézenobres	F	131	A3
Vezins	F	102	B1
Vézins-de-Lévézou	F	130	A1
Vezirhan	TR	187	B5
Vezirköprü	TR	23	A8
Vezza di Óglio	I	120	A3
Vezzani	F	180	A2
Vezzano	I	121	A4
Vezzano sul Cróstolo	I	121	C3
Vi	S	200	D3
Via Gloria	P	160	B2
Viadana	I	121	C3
Viana do Alentejo	P	154	C2
Viana do Bolo	E	141	B3
Viana do Castelo	P	148	A1
Vianden	L	92	B2
Viannos	GR	185	D6
Viaréggio	I	134	B3
Viator	E	164	C2
Vibble	S	57	C4
Vibo Valéntia	I	175	C2
Viborg	DK	58	B2
Vibraye	F	102	A2
Vic	E	147	C3
Vic-en-Bigorre	F	145	A4
Vic-Fézensac	F	129	C3
Vic-le-Comte	F	116	B3
Vic-sur-Aisne	F	90	B3
Vic-sur-Cère	F	116	C2
Vícar	E	164	C2
Vicarello	I	134	B3
Vicari	I	176	B2
Vicchio	I	135	B4
Vicdessos	F	146	B2
Vicenza	I	121	B4
Vichy	F	117	A3
Vickan	S	60	B2
Vickerstown	GB	36	B3
Vico	F	180	A1
Vico del Gargano	I	171	B3
Vico Equense	I	170	C2
Vicopisano	I	134	B3
Vicosoprano	CH	120	A2
Vicovaro	I	169	A2
Victoria = Rabat	M	175	C3
Vidago	P	148	A2
Vidauban	F	132	B2
Vide	P	148	B2
Videbæk	DK	59	B1
Videm	SLO	123	B3
Videseter	N	198	D4
Vidigueira	P	160	A2
Vidin	BG	16	D5
Vidlin	GB	33	A5
Vidsel	S	196	D3
Vidzy	BY	13	A7
Viechtach	D	95	B4
Vieille-Brioude	F	117	B3
Vieira	P	154	B2
Vieira do Minho	P	148	A1
Vieiros	P	155	C3
Vielha	E	145	B4
Vielle-Aure	F	145	B4
Viellespesse	F	116	B3
Viellevigne	F	114	B2
Vielmur-sur-Agout	F	130	B1
Viels Maison	F	91	C3
Vielsalm	B	80	B1
Vienenburg	D	73	C3
Vienna = Wien	A	111	A3
Vienne	F	117	B4
Vieritz	D	73	B5
Viernheim	D	93	B4
Vierraden	D	74	A3
Viersen	D	80	A2
Vierville-sur-Mer	F	88	A3
Vierzon	F	103	B4
Vieselbach	D	82	B3
Vieste	I	171	B4
Vietas	S	194	C9
Vietri di Potenza	I	172	B1
Vietri sul Mare	I	170	C2
Vieux-Boucau-les-Bains	F	128	C1
Vif	F	118	B2
Vigásio	I	121	B3
Vigaun	A	109	B4
Vigeland	N	52	B3
Vigeois	F	116	B1
Vigévano	I	120	B1
Viggianello	I	174	B2
Viggiano	I	174	A1
Vigliano	I	169	A3
Vigmostad	N	52	B3
Vignale	I	119	B5
Vignanello	I	168	A2
Vigneulles-lès-Hattonchâtel	F	92	C1
Vignevieille	F	146	B3
Vignola	I	135	A4
Vignory	F	105	A4
Vignoux-sur-Barangeon	F	103	B4
Vigo	E	140	B2
Vigo di Fassa	I	121	A4
Vigone	I	119	C4
Vigrestad	N	52	B1
Viitasaari	FIN	8	A4
Vík	IS	190	D6
Vik, Nordland	N	195	E3
Vik, Rogaland	N	52	B1
Vik, Sogn og Fjordane	N	46	A3
Vik	S	63	C2
Vika	S	50	B2
Vikajärvi	FIN	197	C9
Vikane	N	54	A1
Vikarbyn	S	50	B2
Vike	N	46	B2
Vikedal	N	52	A1
Vikeland	N	53	B3
Viken, Jämtland	S	199	A10
Viken, Skåne	S	61	C2
Viker	N	48	B2
Vikersund	N	48	C1
Vikeså	N	52	B2
Vikevåg	N	52	A1
Vikingstad	S	56	B1
Vikmanshyttan	S	50	B2
Vikna	N	199	A7
Vikøy	N	46	B3
Vikran, Troms	N	192	C2
Vikran, Troms	N	194	B7
Viksjö	S	200	D3
Viksøyri	N	46	A3
Viksta	S	51	B4
Vila Boim	P	155	C3
Vila Chã de Ourique	P	154	B2
Vila de Cruces	E	140	B2
Vila de Rei	P	154	B2
Vila do Bispo	P	160	B1
Vila do Conde	P	148	A1
Vila Flor	P	149	A2
Vila Franca das Navas	P	149	B2
Vila Franca de Xira	P	154	C1
Vila Fresca	P	154	C1
Vila Nogueira	P	154	C1
Vila Nova da Baronia	P	154	C2
Vila Nova de Cerveira	P	140	C2
Vila Nova de Famalicão	P	148	A1
Vila Nova de Foz Côa	P	149	A2
Vila Nova de Gaia	P	148	A1
Vila Nova de Milfontes	P	160	B1
Vila Nova de Paiva	P	148	B2
Vila Nova de São Bento	P	161	B2
Vila Pouca de Aguiar	P	148	A2
Vila Praia de Ancora	P	148	A1
Vila Real	P	148	A2
Vila-real de los Infantes	E	159	B3
Vila Real de Santo António	P	160	B2
Vila-Rodona	E	147	C2
Vila Ruiva	P	160	A2
Vila Seca	P	148	B1
Vila Velha de Ródão	P	155	B3
Vila Verde, Braga	P	148	A1
Vila Verde, Lisboa	P	154	B1
Vila Viçosa	P	155	C3
Viladamat	E	147	B4
Viladrau	E	147	C3
Vilafranca del Maestrat	E	153	B3
Vilafranca del Penedès	E	147	C2
Vilagarcía de Arousa	E	140	B2
Vilajuiga	E	147	B4
Vilamarin	E	140	B3
Vilamartín de Valdeorras	E	141	B3
Vilanova de Castelló	E	159	B3
Vilanova de Sau	E	147	C3
Vilanova i la Geltrú	E	147	C2
Vilar de Santos	E	140	B3
Vilar Formoso	P	149	B2
Vilarandelo	P	148	A2
Vilardevós	E	141	C3
Vilasantar	E	140	A2
Vilaseca	E	147	C2
Vilassar de Mar	E	147	C3
Vilasund	S	195	D5
Vilches	E	157	B4
Vildbjerg	DK	59	B1
Vilémov	CZ	97	B3
Vileyka	BY	13	A7
Vilhelmina	S	200	B2
Vilia	GR	184	A4
Viljandi	EST	8	C4
Villa Castelli	I	173	B3
Villa Cova de Lixa	P	148	A1
Villa de Peralonso	E	149	A3
Villa del Prado	E	150	B3
Villa del Rio	E	157	C3
Villa di Chiavenna	I	120	A2
Villa Minozzo	I	134	A3
Villa San Giovanni	I	175	C1
Villa Santa Maria	I	169	B4
Villa Santina	I	122	A1
Villabáñez	E	150	A3
Villablanca	E	161	B2
Villablino	E	141	B4
Villabona	E	144	A1
Villabragima	E	142	C1
Villabuena del Puente	E	150	A2
Villacadima	E	151	A4
Villacañas	E	157	A4
Villacarriedo	E	143	A3
Villacarrillo	E	164	A1
Villacastín	E	150	B3
Villach	A	109	C4
Villacidro	I	179	C2
Villaconejos	E	151	B4
Villaconejos de Trabaque	E	152	B1
Villada	E	142	B2
Villadangos del Páramo	E	141	B5
Villadecanes	E	141	B4
Villadepera	E	149	A3
Villadiego	E	142	B2
Villadompardo	E	163	A3
Villadóssola	I	119	A5
Villaeles de Valdavia	E	142	B2
Villaescusa de Haro	E	158	B1
Villafáfila	E	142	C1
Villafeliche	E	152	A2
Villaflores	E	150	A2
Villafrades de Campos	E	142	B2
Villafranca, Avila	E	150	B2
Villafranca, Navarra	E	144	B2
Villafranca de Córdoba	E	157	C3
Villafranca de los Barros	E	155	C4
Villafranca de los Caballeros	E	157	A4
Villafranca del Bierzo	E	141	B4
Villafranca di Verona	I	121	B3
Villafranca in Lunigiana	I	134	A2
Villafranca-Montes de Oca	E	143	B3
Villafranca Tirrena	I	177	A4
Villafranco del Campo	E	152	B2
Villafranco del Guadalquivir	E	161	B3
Villafrati	I	176	B2
Villafrechós	E	142	C1
Villafruela	E	143	C3
Villagarcía de las Torres	E	156	B1
Villaggio Mancuso	I	175	B2
Villagonzalo	E	156	B1
Villagotón	E	141	B4
Villagrains	F	128	B2
Villaharta	E	156	B3
Villahermosa	E	158	C1
Villaherreros	E	142	B2
Villahoz	E	143	B3
Villaines-la-Juhel	F	89	B3
Villajoyosa	E	159	C3
Villalago	I	169	B3
Villalba	I	176	B2
Villalba de Calatrava	E	157	B4
Villalba de Guardo	E	142	B2
Villalba de la Sierra	E	152	B1
Villalba de los Alcores	E	142	C2
Villalba de los Barros	E	155	C4
Villalba del Alcor	E	161	B3
Villalba del Rey	E	151	B5
Villalcampo	E	149	A3
Villalcázar de Sirga	E	142	B2
Villalengua	E	152	A2
Villalgordo del Júcar	E	158	B1
Villalgordo del Marquesado	E	158	B1
Villalmóndar	E	143	B3

Name		Page	Grid
Villalón de Campos	E	142	B1
Villalonga	E	159	C3
Villalonso	E	150	A2
Villalpando	E	142	C1
Villaluenga	E	151	B4
Villalmbroso	E	142	B2
Villálvaro	E	143	C3
Villamalea	E	158	B2
Villamanán	E	142	B1
Villamanín	E	142	B1
Villamanrique	E	157	B5
Villamanrique de la Condesa	E	161	B3
Villamanta	E	151	B3
Villamantilla	E	151	B3
Villamar	I	179	C2
Villamartín	E	162	B2
Villamartín de Campos	E	142	B2
Villamartín de Don Sancho	E	142	B1
Villamassárgia	I	179	C2
Villamayor	E	142	A1
Villamayor de Calatrava	E	157	B3
Villamayor de Campos	E	142	C1
Villamayor de Santiago	E	157	A5
Villamblard	F	129	A3
Villamejil	E	141	B4
Villamesias	E	156	A2
Villaminaya	E	157	A4
Villamor de los Escuderos	E	150	A2
Villamoronta	E	142	B2
Villamuelas	E	151	C4
Villamuriel de Cerrato	E	142	C2
Villandraut	F	128	B2
Villante	I	120	B2
Villanubla	E	142	C2
Villanova	I	173	B3
Villanova d'Asti	I	119	C4
Villanova del Battista	I	171	B3
Villanova Mondovì	I	133	A3
Villanova Monteleone	I	178	B2
Villante	E	143	B3
Villantério	I	120	B2
Villanubla	E	142	C2
Villanueva de Alcardete	E	157	A4
Villanueva de Alcorón	E	152	B1
Villanueva de Algaidas	E	163	A3
Villanueva de Argaña	E	143	B3
Villanueva de Bogas	E	157	A4
Villanueva de Córdoba	E	156	B3
Villanueva de Gállego	E	144	C3
Villanueva de la Concepcion	E	163	B3
Villanueva de la Fuente	E	158	C1
Villanueva de la Jara	E	158	B2
Villanueva de la Reina	E	157	B4
Villanueva de la Serena	E	156	B2
Villanueva de la Sierra	E	149	B3
Villanueva de la Vera	E	150	B2
Villanueva de las Manzanas	E	142	B1
Villanueva de las Peras	E	141	C5
Villanueva de las Torres	E	164	B1
Villanueva de los Castillejos	E	161	B2
Villanueva de los Infantes	E	157	B5
Villanueva de Mesia	E	163	A4
Villanueva de Nía	E	142	B2
Villanueva de Oscos	E	141	A4
Villanueva de San Carlos	E	157	B4
Villanueva de San Juan	E	162	A2
Villanueva de Tapia	E	163	A3
Villanueva de Valdegovia	E	143	B3
Villanueva del Aceral	E	150	A3
Villanueva del Arzobispo	E	164	A2
Villanueva del Campo	E	142	C1
Villanueva del Duque	E	156	B3
Villanueva del Fresno	E	155	C3
Villanueva del Huerva	E	152	A2
Villanueva del Rey	E	156	B2
Villanueva del Rio	E	162	A2
Villanueva del Río y Minas	E	162	A2
Villanueva del Rosario	E	163	B3
Villanueva del Trabuco	E	163	A3
Villány	H	125	B4
Villaputzu	I	179	C3
Villaquejida	E	142	B1
Villaquilambre	E	142	B1
Villaquiran de los Infantes	E	142	B2
Villar de Barrio	E	140	B3
Villar de Cañas	E	158	B1
Villar de Chinchilla	E	158	C2
Villar de Ciervo	E	149	B3
Villar de Domingo Garcia	E	152	B1
Villar de los Navarros	E	152	A2
Villar de Rena	E	156	A2
Villar del Arzobispo	E	159	B3
Villar del Buey	E	149	A3
Villar del Cobo	E	152	B2
Villar del Humo	E	158	B2
Villar del Pedroso	E	156	A2
Villar del Rey	E	155	B4
Villar del Rio	E	143	B4
Villar del Saz de Navalón	E	152	B1
Villar Perosa	I	119	C4
Villaralto	E	156	B3
Villarcayo	E	143	B3
Villard-de-Lans	F	118	B2
Villardeciervos	E	141	C4
Villardefrades	E	142	C1
Villarejo	E	151	A4
Villarejo de Fuentes	E	158	B1
Villarejo de Orbigo	E	141	B5
Villarejo de Salvanes	E	151	B4
Villarejo-Periesteban	E	158	B1
Villares del Saz	E	158	B1
Villaretto	I	119	B4
Villargordo del Cabriel	E	158	B2
Villarino	E	149	A3
Villarino de Conso	E	141	B3
Villarluengo	E	153	B3
Villarobe	E	143	B3
Villarosa	I	177	B3
Villarramiel	E	142	B2
Villarrasa	E	161	B3
Villarreal de San Carlos	E	150	C1
Villarrin de Campos	E	142	C1
Villarrobledo	E	158	B1
Villarroya de la Sierra	E	152	A2
Villarroya de los Pinares	E	153	B3
Villarrubia de los Ojos	E	157	A4
Villarrubia de Santiago	E	151	C4
Villarrubio	E	151	C5
Villars-les-Dombes	F	117	A5
Villarta	E	158	B2
Villarta de los Montes	E	156	A3
Villarta de San Juan	E	157	A4
Villasana de Mena	E	143	A3
Villasandino	E	142	B2
Villasante	E	143	A3
Villasarracino	E	142	B2
Villasayas	E	151	A5
Villasdardo	E	149	A3
Villaseca de Henares	E	151	B5
Villaseca de la Sagra	E	151	C4
Villaseca de Laciana	E	141	B4
Villaseco de los Gamitos	E	149	A3
Villaseco de los Reyes	E	149	A3
Villasequilla de Yepes	E	151	C4
Villasimíus	I	179	C3
Villasmundo	I	177	B4
Villasor	I	179	C2
Villastar	E	152	B2
Villastellone	I	119	C4
Villatobas	E	151	C4
Villatoya	E	158	B2
Villavaliente	E	158	B2
Villavelayo	E	143	B4
Villaver de de Guadalimar	E	158	C1
Villaverde del Rio	E	162	A2
Villaviciosa	E	142	A1
Villaviciosa de Córdoba	E	156	B3
Villaviciosa de Odón	E	151	B4
Villavieja de Yeltes	E	149	B3
Villayón	E	141	A4
Villé	F	93	C3
Ville-di-Pietrabugno	F	180	A2
Ville-sous-la-Ferté	F	105	A3
Ville-sur-Illon	F	105	A5
Ville-sur-Tourbe	F	91	B4
Villebois-Lavalette	F	115	C4
Villecerf	F	90	C2
Villecomtal	F	130	A1
Villedieu-les-Poêles	F	88	B2
Villedieu-sur-Indre	F	103	C3
Villedômain	F	103	B3
Villefagnan	F	115	B4
Villefontaine	F	118	B2
Villefort	F	131	A2
Villefranche-d'Albigeois	F	130	B1
Villefranche-d'Allier	F	116	A2
Villefranche-de-Lauragais	F	146	A2
Villefranche-de-Lonchat	F	128	B3
Villefranche-de-Panat	F	130	A1
Villefranche-de-Rouergue	F	130	A1
Villefranche-du-Périgord	F	129	B4
Villefranche-sur-Cher	F	103	B3
Villefranche-sur-Mer	F	133	B3
Villefranche-sur-Saône	F	117	A4
Villegenon	F	103	B4
Villel	E	152	B2
Villemaur-sur-Vanne	F	104	A2
Villemur-sur-Tarn	F	129	C4
Villena	E	159	C3
Villenauxe-la-Grande	F	91	C3
Villeneuve-d'Ornon	F	128	B2
Villeneuve	CH	119	A3
Villeneuve	F	129	B5
Villeneuve-d'Ascq	F	78	B3
Villeneuve-de-Berg	F	131	A3
Villeneuve-de-Marsan	F	128	C2
Villeneuve-de-Rivière	F	145	A4
Villeneuve-la-Guyard	F	90	C3
Villeneuve-l'Archevêque	F	104	A2
Villeneuve-le-Comte	F	90	C2
Villeneuve-lès-Avignon	F	131	B3
Villeneuve-lès-Corbières	F	146	B3
Villeneuve-St. Georges	F	90	C2
Villeneuve-sur-Allier	F	104	C2
Villeneuve-sur-Lot	F	129	B3
Villeneuve-sur-Yonne	F	104	A2
Villeréal	F	129	B3
Villerias	E	142	C2
Villeromain	F	103	B3
Villers-Bocage, *Calvados*	F	88	A3
Villers-Bocage, *Somme*	F	90	B2
Villers-Bretonneux	F	90	B2
Villers-Carbonnel	F	90	B2
Villers-Cotterêts	F	90	B3
Villers-Farlay	F	105	C4
Villers-le-Gambon	B	79	B4
Villers-le-Lac	F	106	B1
Villers-sur-Mer	F	89	A3
Villersexel	F	105	B5
Villerupt	F	92	B1
Villerville	F	89	A4
Villeseneux	F	91	C4
Villetrun	F	103	B3
Villetta Barrea	I	169	B3
Villeurbanne	F	117	B4
Villevocance	F	117	B4
Villiers-St. Benoit	F	104	B2
Villiers-St. Georges	F	91	C3
Villingen	D	106	A3
Villmar	D	81	B4
Villoldo	E	142	B2
Villon	F	104	B3
Villoria	E	150	B2
Vilnes	N	46	A1
Vilnius	LT	13	A6
Vils	A	108	B1
Vils	DK	58	B1
Vilsbiburg	D	95	C4
Vilseck	D	95	B3
Vilshofen	D	96	C1
Vilshult	S	63	B2
Vilusi	MNE	139	C4
Vilvestre	E	149	A3
Vilvoorde	B	79	B4
Vimeiro	P	154	B1
Vimercate	I	120	B2
Vimianzo	E	140	A1
Vimieiro	P	154	C3
Vimioso	P	149	A3
Vimmerby	S	62	A3
Vimoutiers	F	89	B1
Vimperk	CZ	96	B1
Vimy	F	78	B2
Vinadi	CH	108	C1
Vinadio	I	133	A3
Vinaixa	E	147	C1
Vinarós	E	153	B4
Vinäs	S	50	B1
Vinay	F	118	B2
Vinberg	S	60	C2
Vinca	F	146	B3
Vinča	SRB	127	C2
Vinchiaturo	I	170	B2
Vinci	I	135	B3
Vindeby	DK	65	A3
Vindelgransele	S	195	E9
Vindeln	S	200	B5
Vinderup	DK	58	B1
Vindsvik	N	52	A2
Vinets	F	91	C4
Vineuil	F	103	B3
Vinga	RO	126	A3
Vingåker	S	56	A1
Vingnes	N	48	A2
Vingrau	F	146	B3
Vingrom	N	48	A2
Vinhais	P	149	A3
Vinica	HR	124	A2
Vinica	MK	182	B4
Vinica	SK	112	A3
Vinica	SLO	123	B4
Viniegra de Arriba	E	143	B4
Vinje, *Hordaland*	N	46	B3
Vinje, *Sør-Trøndelag*	N	198	B6
Vinje, *Telemark*	N	53	A4
Vinkovci	HR	125	B4
Vinliden	S	200	B3
Vinninga	S	55	B4
Vinnytsya	UA	13	D8
Vinon	F	103	B4
Vinon-sur-Verdon	F	132	B1
Vinslöv	S	61	C3
Vinstra	N	48	A1
Vintrosa	S	55	A5
Viñuela	E	163	B3
Viñuela de Sayago	E	149	A4
Viñuelas	E	151	B4
Vinuesa	E	143	C4
Vinzelberg	D	73	B4
Viöl	D	64	B2
Viola	I	133	A3
Violay	F	117	B4
Vipava	SLO	122	B2
Vipiteno	I	108	C2
Vipperow	D	74	A1
Vir	BIH	138	B3
Vir	HR	137	A4
Vira	CH	120	A1
Vire	F	88	B3
Vireda	S	62	A2
Vireux	F	91	A4
Virgen	A	109	B3
Virgen de la Cabeza	E	157	B3
Virginia	IRL	27	C3
Virieu	F	118	B2
Virieu-le-Grand	F	118	B2
Virje	HR	124	A2
Virkkunen	FIN	197	D10
Virklund	DK	59	B2
Virovitica	HR	124	B3
Virsbo	S	50	C3
Virserum	S	62	A3
Virtaniemi	FIN	193	D12
Virton	B	92	B1
Virtsu	EST	8	C3
Viry	F	118	A3
Vis	HR	138	B2
Visbek	D	71	B5
Visby	DK	64	A1
Visby	S	57	C4
Visé	B	80	B1
Višegrad	BIH	139	B5
Viserba	I	136	A1
Viseu	P	148	B2
Visiedo	E	152	B2
Visignano	HR	122	B2
Visingsö	S	55	B5
Viskafors	S	60	B2
Visland	N	52	B2
Visnes	N	52	A1
Višnja Gora	SLO	123	B3
Višnjan	HR	122	B2
Višnové	CZ	97	C2
Visnums-Kil	S	55	A5
Viso del Marqués	E	157	B4
Visoko	BIH	139	B4
Visoko	SLO	123	A3
Visone	I	119	C5
Visp	CH	119	A4
Vissefjärda	S	63	B3
Visselhövede	D	72	B2
Vissenbjerg	DK	59	C3
Visso	I	136	C2
Vistabella del Maestrat	E	153	B3
Vistheden	S	196	D3
Vita	I	176	B1
Vitanje	SLO	123	A4
Vitebsk = Vitsyebsk	BY	13	A9
Viterbo	I	168	A2
Vitez	BIH	139	A3
Vithkuq	AL	182	C2
Vitigudino	E	149	A3
Vitina	BIH	138	B3
Vitina	GR	184	B3
Vitis	A	97	C3
Vitoria-Gasteiz	E	143	B4
Vitré	F	101	A4
Vitrey-sur-Mance	F	105	B4
Vitry-en-Artois	F	78	B2
Vitry-le-François	F	91	C4
Vitry-sur-Seine	F	90	C2
Vitsand	S	49	B4
Vitsyebsk = Vitebsk	BY	13	A9
Vittangi	S	196	B4
Vittaryd	S	60	C3
Vitteaux	F	104	B3
Vittel	F	105	A4
Vittinge	S	51	C4
Vittória	I	177	C3
Vittório Véneto	I	122	B1
Vittsjö	S	61	C3
Viù	I	119	B4
Vivario	F	180	A2
Viveiro	E	140	A3
Vivel del Rio Martin	E	152	B3
Viver	E	159	B3
Viverols	F	117	B3
Viveros	E	158	C1
Viviers	F	131	A3
Vivonne	F	115	B4
Vivy	F	102	B1
Vize	TR	186	A2
Vizille	F	118	B2
Viziňada	HR	122	B2
Viziru	RO	17	C7
Vizovice	CZ	98	B1
Vizvár	H	124	A3
Vizzavona	F	180	A2
Vizzini	I	177	B3
Vlachiotis	GR	184	C3
Vlachovice	CZ	98	B1
Vlachovo	SK	99	C4
Vlachovo Březi	CZ	96	B1
Vladimirci	SRB	127	C1
Vladimirovac	SRB	127	B2
Vladislav	CZ	97	B3
Vlagtwedde	NL	71	A4
Vlajkovac	SRB	127	B3
Vlasenica	BIH	139	A4
Vlašim	CZ	96	B2
Vlatković	BIH	138	A3
Vledder	NL	70	B3
Vlissingen	NL	79	A3
Vlkolínec	SK	99	B3
Vloře	AL	182	C1
Vlotho	D	72	B1
Vnanje Gorice	SLO	123	B3
Vobarno	I	121	B3
Voćin	HR	124	B3
Vöcklabruck	A	109	A4
Vöcklamarkt	A	109	B3
Vodanj	SRB	127	C2
Voderady	SK	98	C1
Vodice, *Istarska*	HR	123	B3
Vodice, *Šibenska*	HR	137	B4
Vodice	SLO	123	A3
Vodňany	CZ	96	B2
Vodnjan	HR	122	C2
Vodskov	DK	58	A3
Voe	GB	33	A5
Voerså	DK	58	A3
Voghera	I	120	C2
Vogogna	I	119	A5
Vogošća	BIH	139	B4
Vogué	F	131	A3
Vohburg	D	95	C3
Vohenstrauss	D	95	B4
Vöhl	D	81	A4
Vöhrenbach	D	106	A3
Vöhringen	D	94	C2
Void-Vacon	F	92	C1
Voiron	F	118	B2
Voise	F	90	C1
Voisey	F	105	B4
Voiteg	RO	126	B3
Voiteur	F	105	C4
Voitsberg	A	110	B2
Vojakkala	FIN	196	D7
Vojens	DK	59	C2
Vojka	SRB	127	C2
Vojlovica	SRB	127	C2
Vojnić	HR	123	B4
Vojnic	SK	112	B2
Vojnik	SLO	123	A4
Vojvoda Stepa	SRB	126	B2
Volada	GR	188	D2
Volargne	I	121	B3
Volary	CZ	96	C1
Volče	SLO	122	A2
Volda	N	198	C3
Volendam	NL	70	B2
Volga	RUS	9	C11
Volimes	GR	184	B1
Volissos	GR	185	A6
Volkach	D	94	B2
Völkermarkt	A	110	C1
Völklingen	D	92	B2
Volkmarsen	D	81	A5
Voll	N	198	C4
Vollenhove	NL	70	B2
Vollore-Montagne	F	117	B3
Volodymyr-Volyns'kyy	UA	13	C6
Volokolamsk	RUS	9	D9
Volos	GR	182	D4
Volosovo	RUS	9	C6
Volovets	UA	13	D5
Volta Mantovana	I	121	B3
Voltággio	I	120	C1
Volterra	I	135	B4
Voltri	I	133	A4
Volturara Áppula	I	170	B3
Volturara Irpina	I	170	C2
Volvic	F	116	B3
Volx	F	132	B1
Volyně	CZ	96	B1
Vonitsa	GR	182	E2
Vönöck	H	111	B4
Vonsild	DK	59	C2
Voorschoten	NL	70	B1
Vopnafjörður	IS	191	B11
Vorau	A	110	B2
Vorbasse	DK	59	C2
Vorchdorf	A	109	B4
Vorden	D	71	B5
Vorden	NL	71	B3
Vordernberg	A	110	B1
Vordingborg	DK	65	A4
Vorë	AL	182	B1
Voreppe	F	118	B2
Vorey	F	117	B3
Vorgod	DK	59	B1
Vormsund	N	48	B3
Voskopojë	AL	182	C2
Voss	N	46	B3
Votice	CZ	96	B2
Vouillé	F	115	B4
Voulx	F	90	C2
Voussac	F	116	A3
Vouvray	F	102	B2
Vouvry	CH	119	A3
Vouzela	P	148	B1
Vouziers	F	91	B4
Voves	F	103	A3
Voxna	S	50	A2
Voynitsa	RUS	3	D12
Voznesenye	RUS	9	B9
Vrå	DK	58	A2
Vrå	S	60	C3
Vráble	SK	98	C2
Vračenovići	MNE	139	C4
Vračev Gaj	SRB	127	C3
Vraćevsnica	SRB	127	C2
Vrådal	N	53	A4
Vrakneika	GR	184	A2
Vrana	HR	123	C3
Vranduk	BIH	139	A3
Vrångö	S	60	B1
Vrani	RO	127	B3
Vranić	SRB	127	C2
Vranja	BIH	139	B4
Vranja	HR	123	B3
Vranjak	BIH	125	C4
Vranje	SRB	16	D4
Vranov nad Dyje	CZ	97	C3
Vranovice	CZ	97	C4
Vransko	SLO	123	A3
Vrapčići	BIH	139	B3
Vratimov	CZ	98	B2
Vratsa	BG	17	D5
Vrbanja	HR	125	C4
Vrbanjci	BIH	124	C3
Vrbas	SRB	126	B1
Vrbaška	BIH	124	B3
Vrbnik, *Primorsko-Goranska*	HR	123	B3
Vrbnik, *Zadarsko-Kninska*	HR	138	A2
Vrbno pod Pradědem	CZ	85	B5
Vrboska	HR	138	B2
Vrbov	SK	99	B4
Vrbovce	SK	98	C1
Vrbové	SK	98	C1
Vrbovec	HR	124	B2
Vrbovski	SRB	127	C2
Vrchlabí	CZ	84	B3
Vrčin	SRB	127	C2

Vrdy CZ 97 B3
Vrebac HR 137 A4
Vreden D 71 B3
Vreoci SRB 127 C2
Vretstorp S 55 A5
Vrginmost HR 124 B1
Vrgorac HR 138 B3
Vrhnika SLO 123 B3
Vrhovine HR 123 C4
Vrhpolie SRB 127 C1
Vriezenveen NL 71 B3
Vrigne-aux-Bois F 91 B4
Vrigstad S 62 A2
Vrlika HR 138 B2
Vrnograč BIH 124 B1
Vron F 78 B1
Vroomshoop NL 71 B3
Vroutek CZ 83 B5
Vrpolje HR 125 B4
Vršac SRB 126 B3
Vrsar HR 122 B2
Vrsi HR 137 A4
Vrtoče BIH 124 C2
Vrútky SK 98 B2
Všeruby CZ 95 B4
Všestary CZ 85 B3
Vsetín CZ 98 B1
Vučkovica SRB 127 D2
Vught NL 79 A5
Vuillafans F 105 B5
Vukovar HR 125 B5
Vuku N 199 B8
Vulcan RO 17 C5
Vulcaneşti MD 17 C8
Vuoggatjålme S 195 D7
Vuojärvi FIN 197 B9
Vuolijoki FIN 3 D10
Vuollerim S 196 C3
Vuotso FIN 197 A10
Vuzenica SLO 110 C2
Vy-lès Lure F 105 B5
Vyartsilya RUS 9 A7
Vyborg RUS 9 B6
Výčapy CZ 97 B3
Výčapy-Opatovce SK 98 C2
Východna SK 99 B3
Vydrany SK 111 A4
Vyerkhnyadzvinsk BY 13 A7
Vyhne SK 98 C2
Vylkove UA 17 C8
Vynohradiv UA 17 A5
Vyshniy Volochek RUS 9 D9
Vyškov CZ 97 B5
Vysoká nad Kysucou SK 98 B2
Vysoké Mýto CZ 97 B4
Vysokovsk RUS 9 D10
Vyšší Brod CZ 96 C2
Vytegra RUS 9 B10

W

Waabs D 64 B2
Waalwijk NL 79 A5
Waarschoot B 79 A3
Wabern D 81 A5
Wąbrzeźno PL 69 B3
Wąchock PL 87 A5
Wachow D 74 B1
Wachów PL 86 B2
Wächtersbach D 81 B5
Wackersdorf D 95 B4
Waddington GB 40 B3
Wadebridge GB 42 B2
Wadelsdorf D 84 A2
Wädenswil CH 107 B3
Wadern D 92 B2
Wadersloh D 81 A4
Wadlew PL 86 A3
Wadowice PL 99 B3
Wagenfeld D 72 B1
Wageningen NL 70 C2
Waghäusel D 93 B4
Waging D 109 B3
Wagrain A 109 B4
Wągrowiec PL 76 B2
Wahlsdorf D 74 C2
Wahlstedt D 64 C3
Wahrenholz D 73 B3
Waiblingen D 94 C1
Waidhaus D 95 B4
Waidhofen an der Thaya A 97 C3
Waidhofen an der Ybbs A 110 B1
Waimes B 80 B2
Wainfleet All Saints GB 41 B4
Waizenkirchen A 96 C1
Wakefield GB 40 B2
Wałbrzych PL 85 B4
Walchensee D 108 B2
Walchsee A 109 B3
Wałcz PL 75 A5
Wald CH 107 B3
Wald-Michelbach D 93 B4
Waldaschaff D 94 B1
Waldbach A 110 B2
Waldböckelheim D 93 B3
Waldbröl D 81 B3
Waldeck D 81 A5
Waldenburg D 83 B4
Waldfischbach-Burgalben D 93 B3
Waldheim D 83 A5
Waldkappel D 82 A1
Waldkirch D 106 A2
Waldkirchen D 96 C1
Waldkirchen am Wesen A 96 C1
Waldkraiburg D 109 A3
Waldmohr D 93 B3
Waldmünchen D 95 B4
Waldring A 109 B3
Waldsassen D 95 A4
Waldshut D 106 B3
Waldstatt CH 107 B4
Waldwisse F 92 B2
Walenstadt CH 107 B4
Walentynów PL 87 A5
Walichnowy PL 86 A2
Walincourt F 90 A3
Walkenried D 82 A2
Walkeringham GB 40 B3
Wallasey GB 38 A3
Walldürn D 94 B1
Wallenfells D 82 B3
Wallenhorst D 71 B5
Wallers F 78 B3
Wallersdorf D 95 C4
Wallerstein D 94 C2
Wallingford GB 44 B2
Wallitz D 74 A1
Walls GB 33 A5
Wallsbüll D 64 B2
Walmer GB 45 B5
Walsall GB 40 C2
Walshoutem B 79 B5
Walsrode D 72 B2
Waltenhofen D 107 B5
Waltershausen D 82 B2
Waltham Abbey GB 45 B4
Waltham on the Wolds GB 40 C3
Walton-on-Thames GB 44 B3
Walton-on-the-Naze GB 45 B5
Wamba E 142 C2
Wanderup D 64 B2
Wandlitz D 74 B2
Wanfried D 82 A2
Wangen im Allgäu D 107 B4
Wangerooge D 71 A4
Wangersen D 72 A2
Wängi CH 107 B3
Wanna D 64 C1
Wansford GB 40 C3
Wantage GB 44 B2
Wanzleben D 73 B4
Waplewo PL 77 A5
Wapnica PL 75 A4
Wapno PL 76 B2
Warburg D 81 A5
Wardenburg D 71 A5
Ware GB 44 B3
Waregem B 79 B3
Wareham GB 43 B4
Waremme B 79 B5
Waren D 74 A1
Warendorf D 71 C4
Warga NL 70 A2
Warin D 65 C4
Wark GB 37 A4
Warka PL 87 A5
Warkworth GB 37 A5
Warlubie PL 69 B3
Warminster GB 43 A4
Warnemünde D 65 B5
Warnow D 65 C4
Warnsveld NL 70 B3
Warrenpoint GB 27 B4
Warrington GB 38 A4
Warsaw = Warszawa PL 77 B6
Warsingsfehn D 71 A4
Warsow D 73 A4
Warstein D 81 A4
Warszawa = Warsaw PL 77 B6
Warta PL 86 A2
Wartberg A 110 B1
Warth A 107 B5
Warwick GB 44 A2
Warza D 82 B2
Wasbister GB 33 B3
Washington GB 37 B5
Wąsosz PL 85 A4
Wasselonne F 93 C3
Wassen CH 107 C3
Wassenaar NL 70 B1
Wasserauen CH 107 B4
Wasserburg D 108 A3
Wassertrüdingen D 94 B2
Wassy F 91 C4
Wasungen D 82 B2
Watchet GB 43 A3
Waterford IRL 30 B1
Watergrasshill IRL 29 B3
Waterloo B 79 B4
Waterville IRL 29 C1
Watford GB 44 B3
Wathlingen D 72 B3
Watten F 78 B2
Watten GB 32 C3
Wattens A 108 B2
Watton GB 41 C4
Wattwil CH 107 B4
Waunfawr GB 38 A2
Wavignies F 90 B2
Wavre B 79 B4
Wearhead GB 37 B4
Węchadlow PL 87 B4
Wedel D 72 A2
Wedemark D 72 B2
Weedon Bec GB 44 A2
Weener D 71 A4
Weert NL 80 A1
Weesp NL 70 B2
Weeze D 80 A2
Weferlingen D 73 B4
Wegeleben D 82 A3
Weggis CH 106 B3
Węgierska-Górka PL 99 B3
Wegliniec PL 84 A3
Węgorzyno PL 75 A4
Węgrzynice PL 75 B4
Wegscheid D 96 C1
Wehdel D 72 A1
Wehr D 106 B2
Weibersbrunn D 94 B1
Weichering D 95 C3
Weida D 83 B4
Weiden D 95 B4
Weidenberg D 95 B3
Weidenhain D 83 A4
Weidenstetten D 94 C1
Weierbach D 93 B3
Weikersheim D 94 B1
Weil D 108 A1
Weil am Rhein D 106 B2
Weil der Stadt D 93 C4
Weilburg D 81 B4
Weilerswist D 80 B2
Weilheim, *Baden-Württemberg* D 94 C1
Weilheim, *Bayern* D 108 B2
Weilmünster D 81 B4
Weiltensfeld A 110 C1
Weimar D 82 B3
Weinberg D 94 B2
Weinfelden CH 107 B4
Weingarten, *Baden-Württemberg* D 93 B4
Weingarten, *Baden-Württemberg* D 107 B4
Weinheim D 93 B4
Weinstadt D 94 C1
Weismain D 82 B3
Weissbriach A 109 C4
Weissenbach A 108 B1
Weissenberg D 84 A2
Weissenbrunn D 82 B3
Weissenburg D 94 B2
Weissenfels D 83 A3
Weissenhorn D 94 C2
Weissenkirchen A 97 C3
Weissensee D 82 A3
Weissenstadt D 83 B3
Weisskirchen im Steiermark A 110 B1
Weisstannen CH 107 C4
Weisswasser D 84 A2
Weitendorf D 65 C5
Weitersfeld A 97 C3
Weitersfelden A 96 C2
Weitnau D 107 B5
Wéitra A 96 C2
Weiz A 110 B2
Wejherowo PL 68 A3
Welkenraedt B 80 B1
Wellaune D 83 A4
Wellin B 91 A5
Wellingborough GB 44 A3
Wellington, *Somerset* GB 43 B3
Wellington, *Telford & Wrekin* GB 38 B4
Wellingtonbridge IRL 30 B2
Wells GB 43 A4
Wells-next-the-Sea GB 41 C4
Wels A 109 A5
Welschenrohr CH 106 B2
Welshpool GB 38 B3
Welver D 81 A3
Welwyn Garden City GB 44 B3
Welzheim D 94 C1
Welzow D 84 A2
Wem GB 38 B4
Wembury GB 42 B2
Wemding D 94 C2
Wenden D 81 B3
Wendisch Rietz D 74 B3
Wendlingen D 94 C1
Weng A 109 A4
Weng bei Admont A 110 B1
Wengen CH 106 C2
Wenigzell A 110 B2
Wennigsen D 72 B2
Wenns A 108 B1
Wenzenbach D 95 B4
Weppersdorf A 111 B3
Werben D 73 B4
Werbig D 74 C2
Werdau D 83 B4
Werder D 74 B1
Werdohl D 81 A3
Werfen A 109 B4
Werkendam NL 79 A4
Werl D 81 A3
Werlte D 71 B4
Wermelskirchen D 80 A3
Wermsdorf D 83 A4
Wernberg Köblitz D 95 B4
Werne D 81 A3
Werneck D 94 B2
Werneuchen D 74 B2
Wernigerode D 82 A2
Wertach D 108 B1
Wertheim D 94 B1
Wertingen D 94 C2
Weseke D 80 A2
Wesel D 80 A2
Wesenberg D 74 A1
Wesendorf D 73 B3
Wesołowo PL 77 A5
Wesselburen D 64 B1
Wesseling D 80 B2
West Bridgford GB 40 C2
West Bromwich GB 40 C2
West Haddon GB 44 A2
West Kilbride GB 34 C3
West Linton GB 35 C4
West Lulworth GB 43 B4
West Mersea GB 45 B4
West-Terschelling NL 70 A2
West Woodburn GB 37 A4
Westbury, *Shropshire* GB 38 B4
Westbury, *Wiltshire* GB 43 A4
Westbury-on-Severn GB 39 C4
Westendorf A 108 B3
Westensee D 64 B2
Westerbork NL 71 B3
Westerburg D 81 B3
Westerhaar NL 71 B3
Westerholt D 71 A4
Westerkappeln D 71 B4
Westerland D 64 B1
Westerlo B 79 A4
Westerstede D 71 A4
Westheim D 94 B2
Westhill GB 33 D4
Westkapelle B 78 A3
Westkapelle NL 79 A3
Westminster GB 44 B3
Weston GB 40 C1
Weston-super-Mare GB 43 A4
Westport IRL 28 A2
Westruther GB 35 C5
Westward Ho! GB 42 A2
Wetheral GB 37 B4
Wetherby GB 40 B2
Wetter, *Hessen* D 81 B4
Wetter, *Nordrhein-Westfalen* D 80 A3
Wetteren B 79 A3
Wettin D 83 A3
Wettringen D 71 B4
Wetzikon CH 107 B3
Wetzlar D 81 B4
Wewelsfleth D 64 C2
Wexford IRL 30 B2
Weybridge GB 44 B3
Weyer Markt A 110 B1
Weyerbusch D 81 B3
Weyersheim F 93 C3
Weyhe D 72 B1
Weyhill GB 44 B2
Weymouth GB 43 B4
Weyregg A 109 B4
Węzyska PL 75 B3
Whalton GB 37 A5
Whauphill GB 36 B2
Wheatley GB 44 B2
Whickham GB 37 B5
Whipsnade GB 44 B3
Whitburn GB 35 C4
Whitby GB 37 B6
Whitchurch, *Hampshire* GB 44 B2
Whitchurch, *Herefordshire* GB 39 C4
Whitchurch, *Shropshire* GB 38 B4
White Bridge GB 32 D2
Whitegate IRL 29 C3
Whitehaven GB 36 B3
Whitehead GB 27 B5
Whithorn GB 36 B2
Whitley Bay GB 37 A5
Whitstable GB 45 B5
Whittington GB 38 B4
Whittlesey GB 41 C3
Wiązów PL 85 B5
Wick GB 32 C3
Wickede D 81 A3
Wickford GB 45 B4
Wickham GB 44 C2
Wickham Market GB 45 A5
Wicklow IRL 30 B2
Wicko PL 68 A2
Widawa PL 86 A2
Widdrington GB 37 A5
Widecombe in the Moor GB 42 B3
Widemouth GB 42 B2
Widnes GB 38 A4
Widuchowo PL 74 A3
Więcbork PL 76 A2
Wiefelstede D 71 A5
Wiehe D 82 A3
Wiehl D 81 B3
Wiek D 66 B2
Większyce PL 86 B1
Wielbark PL 77 A5
Wiele PL 68 B2
Wieleń PL 75 B5
Wielgie, *Kujawsko-Pomorskie* PL 77 B4
Wielgie, *Łódzkie* PL 86 A2
Wielgie, *Mazowieckie* PL 87 A5
Wielgomłyny PL 87 A3
Wielichowo PL 75 B5
Wieliczka PL 99 B4
Wielka Łąka PL 76 A3
Wielowies PL 86 B2
Wieluń PL 86 A2
Wien = Vienna A 111 A3
Wiener Neustadt A 111 B3
Wiepke D 73 B4
Wierden NL 71 B3
Wieren D 73 B3
Wieruszów PL 86 A2
Wierzbica, *Mazowieckie* PL 77 B6
Wierzbica, *Mazowieckie* PL 87 A5
Wierzbie PL 86 A2
Wierzbięcin PL 75 A4
Wierzchowo PL 75 A5
Wierzchucino PL 68 A3
Wierzchy PL 86 A2
Wies A 110 C2
Wiesau D 95 B4
Wiesbaden D 93 A4
Wieselburg A 110 A2
Wiesen CH 107 C4
Wiesenburg D 73 B5
Wiesenfelden D 95 B4
Wiesensteig D 94 C1
Wiesentheid D 94 B2
Wiesloch D 93 B4
Wiesmath A 111 B3
Wiesmoor D 71 A4
Wietmarschen D 71 B4
Wietze D 72 B2
Wigan GB 38 A4
Wiggen CH 106 C2
Wigston GB 40 C2
Wigton GB 36 B3
Wigtown GB 36 B2
Wijchen NL 80 A1
Wijhe NL 70 B3
Wijk bij Duurstede NL 70 C2
Wil CH 107 B4
Wilamowice PL 99 B3
Wilczęta PL 69 A4
Wilczkowice PL 77 B4
Wilczna PL 76 B3
Wilczyn PL 76 B3
Wildalpen A 110 B1
Wildbad D 93 C4
Wildberg, *Baden-Württemberg* D 93 C4
Wildberg, *Brandenburg* D 74 B1
Wildegg CH 106 B3
Wildendürnbach A 97 C4
Wildeshausen D 72 B1
Wildon A 110 C2
Wilfersdorf A 97 C4
Wilhelmsburg A 110 A2
Wilhelmsburg D 74 A2
Wilhelmsdorf D 107 B4
Wilhelmshaven D 71 A5
Wilków PL 77 B5
Willebadessen D 81 A5
Willebroek B 79 A4
Willgottheim F 93 C3
Willhermsdorf D 94 B2
Willich D 80 A2
Willingen D 81 A4
Willington GB 37 B5
Willisau CH 106 B3
Wilmslow GB 40 B1
Wilsdruff D 83 A5
Wilster D 64 C2
Wilsum D 71 B3
Wilton GB 44 B2
Wiltz L 92 B1
Wimborne Minster GB 43 B5
Wimereux F 78 B1
Wimmenau F 93 C3
Wimmis CH 106 C2
Wincanton GB 43 A4
Winchcombe GB 44 B2
Winchelsea GB 45 C4
Winchester GB 44 B2
Windermere GB 36 B4
Windisch-eschenbach D 95 B4
Windischgarsten A 110 B1
Windorf D 96 C1
Windsbach D 94 B2
Windsor GB 44 B3
Wingene B 78 A3
Wingham GB 45 B5
Winkleigh GB 42 B3
Winklern A 109 C3
Winnenden D 94 C1
Winnica PL 77 B5
Winnigstedt D 73 B3
Winnweiler D 93 B3
Winschoten NL 71 A4
Winsen, *Niedersachsen* D 72 A3
Winsen, *Niedersachsen* D 72 B2
Winsford GB 38 A4
Wińsko PL 85 A4
Winslow GB 44 B3
Winsum, *Friesland* NL 70 A2
Winsum, *Groningen* NL 71 A3
Winterberg D 81 A4
Winterfeld D 73 B4
Winterswijk NL 71 C3
Winterthur CH 107 B3
Wintzenheim F 106 A2
Winzer D 95 C5
Wipperdorf D 82 A2
Wipperfürth D 80 A3
Wirksworth GB 40 B2
Wisbech GB 41 C4
Wischhafen D 64 C2
Wishaw GB 35 C4
Wisła PL 98 B2
Wisła Wielka PL 98 B2
Wislica PL 87 B4
Wismar D 65 C4
Wisniewo PL 77 A5
Wiśniowa PL 99 B4
Wissant F 78 B1
Wissembourg F 93 B3
Wissen D 81 B3
Witanowice PL 99 B3
Witham GB 45 B4
Withern GB 41 B4
Withernsea GB 41 B4
Witkowo PL 76 B2
Witmarsum NL 70 A2
Witney GB 44 B2
Witnica PL 75 B3
Witonia PL 77 B4
Witry-les-Reims F 91 B4
Wittdün D 64 B1
Wittelsheim F 106 B2
Witten D 80 A3
Wittenberge D 73 A4
Wittenburg D 73 A4
Wittenheim F 106 B2
Wittichenau D 84 A2
Wittighausen D 94 B1
Wittingen D 73 B3
Wittislingen D 94 C2
Wittlich D 92 B2
Wittmannsdorf A 110 C2
Wittmund D 71 A4
Wittorf D 72 A2
Wittstock D 73 A5
Witzenhausen D 82 A1
Wiveliscombe GB 43 A3
Wivenhoe GB 45 B4
Władysławowo PL 69 A3
Wleń PL 84 A3
Włocławek PL 77 B4
Włodawa PL 13 C5
Włodzimierzów PL 87 A3
Włosień PL 84 A3
Włostow PL 87 B5
Włoszakowice PL 75 C5
Włoszczowa PL 87 B3
Wöbbelin D 73 A4
Woburn GB 44 B3
Wodzisław PL 87 B4
Wodzisław Śląski PL 98 B2
Woerden NL 70 B1
Wœrth F 93 C3
Wohlen CH 106 B3
Woippy F 92 B2
Wojcieszow PL 85 B3
Wojkowice Kościelne PL 86 B3
Wojnicz PL 99 B4
Woking GB 44 B3
Wokingham GB 44 B3
Wola Jachowa PL 87 B4
Wola Niechcicka PL 86 A3
Wolbórz PL 87 A3
Wolbrom PL 87 B3
Wołczyn PL 86 A2
Woldegk D 74 A2
Wolfach D 93 C4
Wolfegg D 107 B4
Wolfen D 83 A4
Wolfenbüttel D 73 B3
Wolfersheim D 81 B4
Wolfhagen D 81 A5
Wolfratshausen D 108 B2
Wolf's Castle GB 39 C2
Wolfsberg A 110 C1
Wolfsburg D 73 B3
Wolfshagen D 74 A2
Wolfstein D 93 B3
Wolfurt A 107 B4
Wolgast D 66 B2
Wolhusen CH 106 B3
Wolin PL 67 C3
Wolka PL 87 A4
Wolkenstein D 83 B5
Wolkersdorf A 97 C4
Wöllersdorf A 111 B3
Wollin D 73 B5
Wöllstadt D 81 B4
Wolmirstedt D 73 B4
Wolnzach D 95 C3
Wołów PL 85 A4

Name	Country	Page	Grid
Wolsztyn	PL	75	B5
Wolvega	NL	70	B2
Wolverhampton	GB	40	C1
Wolverton	GB	44	A3
Wombwell	GB	40	B2
Woodbridge	GB	45	A5
Woodhall Spa	GB	41	B3
Woodstock	GB	44	B2
Wookey Hole	GB	43	A4
Wool	GB	43	B4
Woolacombe	GB	42	A2
Wooler	GB	37	A4
Woolwich	GB	45	B4
Wooperton	GB	37	A5
Worb	CH	106	C2
Worbis	D	82	A2
Worcester	GB	39	B4
Wördern	A	97	C4
Wörgl	A	108	B3
Workington	GB	36	B3
Worksop	GB	40	B2
Workum	NL	70	B2
Wörlitz	D	83	A4
Wormer	NL	70	B1
Wormhout	F	78	B2
Wormit	GB	35	B5
Worms	D	93	B4
Worpswede	D	72	A1
Wörrstadt	D	93	B4
Wörschach	A	110	B1
Worsley	GB	38	A4
Wörth, *Bayern*	D	95	B4
Wörth, *Bayern*	D	93	B5
Wörth, *Bayern*	D	95	C4
Wörth, *Rheinland-Pfalz*	D	93	B4
Worthing	GB	44	C3
Woudsend	NL	70	B2
Woumen	B	78	A2
Woźniki	PL	86	B3
Wragby	GB	41	B3
Wrangle	GB	41	B4
Wręczyca Wlk.	PL	86	B2
Wredenhagen	D	73	A5
Wremen	D	72	A1
Wrentham	GB	45	A5
Wrexham	GB	38	A3
Wriedel	D	72	A3
Wriezen	D	74	B3
Wrist	D	64	C2
Wróblewo, *Mazowieckie*	PL	77	B5
Wróblewo, *Wielkopolskie*	PL	75	B5
Wrocki	PL	69	B4
Wrocław	PL	85	A5
Wronki	PL	75	B5
Wroxham	GB	41	C5
Września	PL	76	B2
Wrzosowo	PL	67	B4
Wschowa	PL	85	A4
Wulfen, *Nordrhein-Westfalen*	D	80	A3
Wülfen, *Sachsen-Anhalt*	D	83	A3
Wulkau	D	73	B5
Wünnenberg	D	81	A4
Wünsdorf	D	74	B2
Wunsiedel	D	95	A4
Wunstorf	D	72	B2
Wuppertal	D	80	A3
Wurmannsquick	D	95	C4
Würselen	D	80	B2
Wurzbach	D	82	B3
Würzburg	D	94	B1
Wurzen	D	83	A4
Wust	D	74	B1
Wusterhausen	D	73	B5
Wusterwitz	D	73	B5
Wustrau-Altfriesack	D	74	B1
Wustrow	D	66	B1
Wuustwezel	B	79	A4
Wye	GB	45	B4
Wyględów	PL	87	A5
Wyk	D	64	B1
Wykroty	PL	84	A3
Wylye	GB	43	A5
Wymiarki	PL	84	A3
Wymondham	GB	41	C5
Wyrzysk	PL	76	A2
Wyśmierzyce	PL	87	A4
Wysoka, *Dolnośląskie*	PL	85	A3
Wysoka, *Wielkopolskie*	PL	76	A2
Wyszków	PL	86	A2
Wyszogród	PL	77	B5

X

Name	Country	Page	Grid
Xanten	D	80	A2
Xanthi	GR	183	B6
Xarrë	AL	182	D2
Xátiva	E	159	C3
Xeraco	E	159	B3
Xert	E	153	B4
Xerta	E	153	B4
Xertigny	F	105	A5
Xilagani	GR	183	C7
Xilokastro	GR	184	A3
Xinzo de Limia	E	140	B3
Xixón = Gijón	E	142	A1
Xove	E	140	A3
Xubia	E	140	A2
Xunqueira de Ambia	E	140	B3
Xunqueira de Espadañedo	E	140	B3
Xylophagou	CY	181	B2

Y

Name	Country	Page	Grid
Y Felinheli	GB	38	A2
Yablanitsa	BG	17	D6
Yağcilar	TR	186	C3
Yahyalı	TR	23	B8
Yakoruda	BG	183	A5
Yalova	TR	187	B4
Yalvaç	TR	189	A6
Yambol	BG	17	D7
Yampil	UA	13	D8
Yaniskoski	RUS	193	D12
Yantarnyy	RUS	69	A4
Yarbasan	TR	186	D3
Yarcombe	GB	43	B3
Yaremcha	UA	13	D6
Yarm	GB	37	B5
Yarmouth	GB	44	C2
Yarrow	GB	35	C4
Yasinya	UA	17	A6
Yatağan	TR	188	B3
Yate	GB	43	A4
Yatton	GB	43	A4
Yavoriv	UA	13	D5
Yaxley	GB	41	C3
Yazıca	TR	187	B6
Yazıköy	TR	188	C2
Ybbs	A	110	A2
Ybbsitz	A	110	B1
Ydby	DK	58	B1
Yddal	N	46	B2
Yealmpton	GB	42	B3
Yebra de Basa	E	145	B3
Yecla	E	159	C2
Yecla de Yeltes	E	149	B3
Yelsk	BY	13	C8
Yelverton	GB	42	B2
Yena	RUS	197	B14
Yenice, *Ankara*	TR	23	B7
Yenice, *Aydın*	TR	188	B3
Yenice, *Çanakkale*	TR	186	C2
Yenice, *Edirne*	TR	183	C8
Yenifoça	TR	186	D1
Yenihisar	TR	186	D4
Yeniköy	TR	186	D4
Yeniköy Plaji	TR	186	B3
Yenipazar	TR	188	B3
Yenişarbademli	TR	189	B6
Yenişehir	TR	187	B4
Yenne	F	118	B2
Yeovil	GB	43	B4
Yepes	E	151	C4
Yerköy	TR	23	B8
Yerólakkos	CY	181	A2
Yeroskipos	CY	181	B1
Yerseke	NL	79	A4
Yerville	F	89	A4
Yeşildağ	TR	189	B6
Yeşilhisar	TR	23	B8
Yeşilköy	TR	186	B3
Yeşilova	TR	189	B4
Yeşilyurt	TR	188	A3
Yeste	E	164	A2
Yezerishche	BY	9	E6
Ygos-St. Saturnin	F	128	C2
Ygrande	F	104	C1
Yialousa	CY	181	A3
Yığılca	TR	187	B6
Yli-Ii	FIN	197	D8
Yli-Kärppä	FIN	197	D8
Yli-Muonia	FIN	196	A6
Ylitornio	FIN	196	C6
Ylivieska	FIN	3	D9
Ylläsjärvi	FIN	196	B7
Ymonville	F	103	A3
Yngsjö	S	63	C2
Yoğuntaş	TR	186	A2
York	GB	40	B2
Youghal	IRL	29	C4
Yozgat	TR	23	B8
Yport	F	89	A4
Ypres = Ieper	B	78	B2
Yssingeaux	F	117	B4
Ystad	S	66	A2
Ystalyfera	GB	39	C3
Ystebrod	N	52	B1
Ystradgynlais	GB	39	C3
Ytre Arna	N	46	B2
Ytre Enebakk	N	54	A2
Ytre Rendal	N	199	D8
Ytteran	S	199	B11
Ytterhogdal	S	199	C11
Yttermalung	S	49	B5
Yunak	TR	187	D6
Yuncos	E	151	B4
Yunquera	E	162	B3
Yunquera de Henares	E	151	B4
Yushkozero	RUS	3	D13
Yverdon-les-Bains	CH	106	C1
Yvetot	F	89	A4
Yvignac	F	101	A3
Yvonand	CH	106	C1
Yvoir	B	79	B4
Yzeure	F	104	C2

Z

Name	Country	Page	Grid
Zaamslag	NL	79	A3
Zaanstad	NL	70	B1
Žabalj	SRB	126	B2
Zabar	H	113	A4
Žabari	SRB	127	C3
Zabiče	SLO	123	B3
Zabierzów	PL	87	B3
Ząbki	PL	77	B6
Ząbkowice Śląskie	PL	85	B4
Zablaće	HR	138	B1
Žabljak	MNE	139	B5
Żabno	PL	87	B4
Zabok	HR	124	A2
Zabokreky	SK	98	C2
Zabor	PL	75	C4
Żabowo	PL	75	A4
Zabrdje	BIH	125	C4
Zábřeh	CZ	97	B4
Zabrežje	SRB	127	C2
Ząbrowo	PL	67	C4
Zabrze	PL	86	B2
Zabrzeź	PL	99	B4
Zacharo	GR	184	B2
Zadar	HR	137	A4
Zadzim	PL	86	A2
Zafarraya	E	163	B3
Zafferana Etnea	I	177	B4
Zafra	E	155	C4
Žaga	SLO	122	A2
Zagajica	SRB	127	C3
Zagań	PL	84	A3
Zaglav	HR	137	B4
Zaglavak	SRB	127	D1
Zagnańsk	PL	87	B4
Zagora	GR	183	D5
Zagorc	SLO	110	C2
Zagorićani	BIH	138	B3
Zagorje	SLO	123	A4
Zagórów	PL	76	B2
Zagradje	SRB	127	C2
Zagreb	HR	124	B1
Zagrilla	E	163	A3
Zagvozd	HR	138	B3
Zagwiździe	PL	86	B1
Zagyvarekas	H	113	B4
Zagyvaróna	H	113	A3
Zahara	E	162	B2
Zahara de los Atunes	E	162	B2
Zahinos	E	155	C4
Zahna	D	83	A4
Zahořy	CZ	96	B2
Zahrádka	CZ	97	B3
Zahrensdorf	D	73	A3
Zaidin	E	153	A4
Zaječar	SRB	16	D5
Zákamenné	SK	99	B3
Zákány	H	124	A2
Zákányszék	H	126	A1
Zakliczyn	PL	99	B4
Zakopane	PL	99	B3
Zakroczym	PL	77	B5
Zakrzew	PL	87	A5
Zakrzewo	PL	76	B3
Zakupy	CZ	84	B2
Zakynthos	GR	184	B1
Zalaapáti	H	111	C4
Zalabaksa	H	111	C3
Zalaegerszeg	H	111	C3
Zalakomár	H	111	C4
Zalakoppány	H	111	C4
Zalalövö	H	111	C3
Zalamea de la Serena	E	156	B2
Zalamea la Real	E	161	B3
Zalaszentgrót	H	111	C4
Zalaszentiván	H	111	C3
Zalău	RO	17	B5
Zalcsie	PL	86	A3
Zaldibar	E	143	A4
Žalec	SLO	123	A4
Zalesie	PL	77	A5
Zalewo	PL	69	B4
Zalishchyky	UA	13	D6
Zalla	E	143	A3
Zaltbommel	NL	79	A5
Zamárdi	H	112	C1
Zamarte	PL	68	B2
Žamberk	CZ	85	B4
Zambra	E	163	A3
Zambugueira do Mar	P	160	B1
Zámoly	H	112	B2
Zamora	E	149	A4
Zamość	PL	13	C6
Zamoście	PL	86	A3
Zams	A	108	B1
Zandhoven	B	79	A4
Žandov	CZ	84	B2
Zandvoort	NL	70	B1
Zangliveri	GR	183	C5
Zánka	H	111	C4
Zaorejas	E	152	B1
Zaovine	SRB	127	D1
Zapadnaya Dvina	RUS	9	D8
Zapfend	D	94	A2
Zapole	PL	86	A2
Zapolyarnyy	RUS	193	C14
Zapponeta	I	171	B3
Zaprešić	HR	124	B1
Zaragoza	E	153	A3
Zarasai	LT	13	A7
Zarautz	E	144	A1
Zarcilla de Ramos	E	164	B3
Zaręby	PL	77	A6
Żarki	PL	86	B3
Żarko	GR	182	D4
Žarnovica	SK	98	C2
Zarnow	PL	87	A4
Zarnowiec	PL	68	A3
Zárošice	CZ	97	B4
Żarów	PL	85	B4
Zarren	B	78	A2
Zarrentin	D	73	A3
Żary	PL	84	A3
Zarza Capilla	E	156	B2
Zarza de Alange	E	156	B1
Zarza de Granadilla	E	149	B3
Zarza de Tajo	E	151	B4
Zarza la Mayor	E	155	B4
Zarzadilla de Totana	E	164	B3
Zarzuela del Monte	E	150	B3
Zarzuela del Pinar	E	151	A3
Zas	E	140	A2
Zasavica	SRB	127	C1
Zasieki	PL	84	A2
Zásmuky	CZ	96	B3
Żatec	CZ	83	B5
Zaton	HR	139	C4
Zatonie	PL	84	A3
Zator	PL	99	A3
Zauchwitz	D	74	B2
Zavala	BIH	139	C3
Zavalje	BIH	124	C1
Zavattarello	I	120	C2
Zavidovići	BIH	139	A4
Zavlaka	SRB	127	C1
Zawady	PL	77	C5
Zawadzkie	PL	86	B2
Zawdy	PL	86	A2
Zawidów	PL	84	A3
Zawidz	PL	77	B4
Zawiercie	PL	86	B3
Zawoja	PL	99	B3
Zawonia	PL	85	A5
Žažina	HR	124	B2
Zázrivá	SK	99	B3
Zbarazh	UA	13	D6
Zbąszyń	PL	75	B4
Zbąszynek	PL	75	B4
Zbehy	SK	98	C2
Zbiersk	PL	76	C3
Zbiroh	CZ	96	B1
Zblewo	PL	69	B3
Zbójno	PL	77	A4
Zbrachlin	PL	76	A3
Zbraslav	CZ	96	B2
Zbraslavice	CZ	97	B3
Ždala	HR	124	A3
Ždánice	CZ	98	B1
Ždár nad Sázavou	CZ	97	B3
Zdbice	PL	75	A5
Zdenci	HR	125	B3
Ždiar	SK	99	B4
Zdice	CZ	96	B1
Zdirec nad Doubravou	CZ	97	B3
Zdolbuniv	UA	13	C7
Zdounky	CZ	98	B1
Ždrelo	SRB	127	C3
Zduńska Wola	PL	86	A2
Zduny, *Łódzkie*	PL	77	B4
Zduny, *Wielkopolskie*	PL	85	A5
Żdżary	PL	87	A5
Zdziechowice, *Opolskie*	PL	86	A2
Zdziechowice, *Wielkopolskie*	PL	76	B2
Zdziszowice	PL	86	B2
Zeberio	E	143	A4
Žebrák	CZ	96	B1
Zebreira	P	155	B3
Zebrzydowa	PL	84	A3
Zechlin	D	74	A1
Zechlinerhütte	D	74	A1
Zederhaus	A	109	B4
Žednik	SRB	126	B1
Zeebrugge	B	78	A3
Zegrze	PL	77	B6
Zehdenick	D	74	B2
Zehren	D	83	A5
Zeil	D	94	A2
Zeilarn	D	95	C4
Zeist	NL	70	B2
Zeithain	D	83	A5
Zeitz	D	83	A4
Želatava	CZ	97	B3
Żelazno, *Dolnośląskie*	PL	85	B4
Żelazno, *Pomorskie*	PL	68	A2
Zele	B	79	A4
Zelenoborskiy	RUS	3	C13
Zelenogorsk	RUS	9	B6
Zelenograd	RUS	9	D10
Zelenogradsk	RUS	12	A4
Železná Ruda	CZ	96	B1
Železnice	CZ	84	B3
Železnik	SRB	127	C2
Železny Brod	CZ	84	B3
Zelhem	NL	71	B3
Želiezovce	SK	112	A2
Zelkowo	PL	68	A2
Zell	CH	106	B2
Zell, *Baden-Württemberg*	D	106	B2
Zell, *Baden-Württemberg*	D	93	C4
Zell, *Rheinland-Pfalz*	D	92	A3
Zell am See	A	109	B3
Zell am Ziller	A	108	B2
Zell an der Pram	A	96	C1
Zell bei Zellhof	A	96	C2
Zella-Mehlis	D	82	B2
Zellerndorf	A	97	C3
Zellingen	D	94	B1
Želovce	SK	112	A3
Zelów	PL	86	A3
Zeltweg	A	110	B1
Zelzate	B	79	A3
Zemberovce	SK	98	C2
Zembrzyce	PL	99	B3
Zemianske-Kostol'any	SK	98	C2
Zemitz	D	66	C2
Zemné	SK	112	B1
Zemun	SRB	127	C2
Zemunik Donji	HR	137	A4
Zenica	BIH	139	A3
Zennor	GB	42	B1
Žepa	BIH	139	B5
Žepče	BIH	139	A4
Zepponami	I	168	A2
Zerbst	D	73	C5
Zerf	D	92	B2
Zerind	RO	113	C5
Żerków	PL	76	B2
Zermatt	CH	119	A4
Zernez	CH	107	C5
Zerpenschleuse	D	74	B2
Zestoa	E	144	A1
Zetel	D	71	A4
Zeulenroda	D	83	B3
Zeven	D	72	A2
Zevenaar	NL	70	C3
Zevenbergen	NL	79	A4
Zévio	I	121	B4
Zeytinbaği	TR	186	B3
Zeytindağ	TR	186	D2
Zgierz	PL	86	A3
Zgorzelec	PL	84	A2
Zgošča	BIH	139	A4
Zhabinka	BY	13	B6
Zharkovskiy	RUS	9	E8
Zhashkiv	UA	13	D9
Zhlobin	BY	13	B9
Zhmerynka	UA	13	D8
Zhodzina	BY	13	A8
Zhytomyr	UA	13	C8
Žiar nad Hronom	SK	98	C2
Zicavo	F	180	B2
Zickhusen	D	65	C4
Zidani Most	SLO	123	A4
Ziddorf	D	73	A5
Židlochovice	CZ	97	B4
Ziębice	PL	85	B5
Ziegendorf	D	73	A4
Ziegenrück	D	83	B3
Zieleniec, *Dolnośląskie*	PL	85	B4
Zieleniec, *Warmińsko-Mazurskie*	PL	77	A6
Zielona	PL	77	A4
Zielona Góra	PL	75	C4
Zieluń-Osada	PL	77	A4
Ziemetshausen	D	94	C2
Zierenberg	D	81	A5
Zierikzee	NL	79	A3
Ziersdorf	A	97	C3
Zierzow	D	73	A4
Ziesar	D	73	B5
Ziesendorf	D	65	C5
Ziethen	D	74	B2
Žihle	CZ	96	A1
Žilina	SK	98	B2
Ziltendorf	D	74	B3
Zimandu Nou	RO	126	A3
Zimna Woda	PL	77	A5
Zimnicea	RO	17	D6
Zinal	CH	119	A4
Zinasco	I	120	B2
Zingst	D	66	B1
Zinkgruvan	S	55	B6
Žinkovy	CZ	96	B1
Zinnowitz	D	66	B2
Zirc	H	112	B1
Žiri	SLO	123	A3
Zirl	A	108	B2
Zirovnica	SRB	127	C3
Žirovnice	CZ	97	B3
Zisterdorf	A	97	C4
Žitište	SRB	126	B2
Zitsa	GR	182	D2
Zittau	D	84	B2
Živaja	HR	124	B2
Živinice	BIH	139	A4
Zlatar	HR	124	A2
Zlatar Bistrica	HR	124	A2
Zlate Hory	CZ	85	B5
Zlaté Klasy	SK	111	A4
Zlaté Moravce	SK	98	C2
Zlatná na Ostrove	SK	112	B1
Zlatniky	SK	98	C2
Zlatograd	BG	183	B7
Žlebič	SLO	123	B3
Zlín	CZ	98	B1
Złocieniec	PL	75	A5
Złoczew	PL	86	A2
Zlonice	CZ	84	B2
Złotniki Kujawskie	PL	76	B3
Złotoryja	PL	85	A3
Złotów	PL	68	B2
Złoty Stok	PL	85	B4
Zlutice	CZ	83	B5
Zmajevac	BIH	124	C2
Zmajevo	SRB	126	B1
Żmigród	PL	85	A4
Žmijavci	HR	138	B3
Žminj	HR	122	B2
Žnin	PL	76	B2
Znojmo	CZ	97	C4
Zöblitz	D	83	B5
Zocca	I	135	A3
Zoetermeer	NL	70	B1
Zofingen	CH	106	B2
Zogno	I	120	B2
Zohor	SK	111	A3
Zolling	D	95	C3
Zolochiv	UA	13	D6
Zomba	H	112	C2
Zomergem	B	79	A3
Zoñán	E	141	A3
Zonguldak	TR	187	A6
Zonhoven	B	79	B5
Zonza	F	180	B2
Zörbig	D	83	A4
Zorita	E	156	A2
Żory	PL	98	A2
Zossen	D	74	B2
Zottegem	B	79	B3
Zoutkamp	NL	71	A3
Zovi Do	BIH	139	B4
Zreče	SLO	123	A4
Zrenjanin	SRB	126	B2
Zrnovica	HR	138	B2
Zruč nad Sazavou	CZ	97	B3
Zsámbék	H	112	B2
Zsámbok	H	112	B3
Zsana	H	126	A1
Zschopau	D	83	B5
Zuberec	SK	99	B3
Zubieta	E	144	A2
Zubiri	E	144	A2
Zubtsov	RUS	9	D9
Zucaina	E	153	B3
Zudar	D	66	B2
Zufre	E	161	B3
Zug	CH	107	B3
Zuheros	E	163	A3
Zuidhorn	NL	71	A3
Zuidlaren	NL	71	A3
Zuidwolde	NL	71	B3
Zújar	E	164	B2
Żukowo	PL	69	A3
Žuljana	HR	138	C3
Žulová	CZ	85	B5
Zülpich	D	80	B2
Zumaia	E	144	A1
Zumárraga	E	143	A4
Zundert	NL	79	A4
Županja	HR	125	B4
Zurgena	E	164	B2
Zürich	CH	107	B3
Żuromin	PL	77	A4
Zurzach	CH	106	B3
Zusmarshausen	D	94	C2
Zusow	D	65	C4
Züssow	D	66	C2
Žuta Lovka	HR	123	C4
Zutphen	NL	70	B3
Žužemberk	SLO	123	B3
Zvenyhorodka	UA	13	D9
Zvikovské Podhradi	CZ	96	B2
Zvolen	SK	99	C3
Zvolenská Slatina	SK	99	C3
Zvornik	BIH	139	A5
Zwartsluis	NL	70	B3
Zweibrücken	D	93	B3
Zweisimmen	CH	106	C2
Zwettl	A	97	C3
Zwettl an der Rodl	A	96	C2
Zwickau	D	83	B4
Zwiefalten	D	107	A4
Zwierzno	PL	69	A4
Zwiesel	D	96	B1
Zwieselstein	A	108	C2
Zwoleń	PL	87	A5
Zwolle	NL	70	B3
Zwönitz	D	83	B4
Zychlin	PL	77	B4
Zydowo, *Wielkopolskie*	PL	76	B2
Zydowo, *Zachodnio-Pomorskie*	PL	68	A1
Żyrardów	PL	77	B5
Żytno	PL	86	B3
Żywiec	PL	99	B3
Zyyi	CY	181	B2